ROUTLEDGE LIBRARY E
GERMAN LITERATU̲ᴿᴸ

Volume 4

THE RECEPTION OF CLASSICAL GERMAN LITERATURE IN ENGLAND, 1760–1860, VOLUME 3

THE RECEPTION OF CLASSICAL GERMAN LITERATURE IN ENGLAND, 1760–1860, VOLUME 3

A Documentary History from Contemporary Periodicals

Edited by
JOHN BOENING

Routledge
Taylor & Francis Group

LONDON AND NEW YORK

First published in 1977 by Garland Publishing Inc.

This edition first published in 2020
by Routledge
2 Park Square, Milton Park, Abingdon, Oxon OX14 4RN

and by Routledge
52 Vanderbilt Avenue, New York, NY 10017

Routledge is an imprint of the Taylor & Francis Group, an informa business

British Library Cataloguing in Publication Data
A catalogue record for this book is available from the British Library

ISBN: 978-0-367-41588-4 (Set)
ISBN: 978-1-00-301460-7 (Set) (ebk)
ISBN: 978-0-367-81756-5 (Volume 4) (hbk)
ISBN: 978-1-00-301053-1 (Volume 4) (ebk)

Publisher's Note
The publisher has gone to great lengths to ensure the quality of this reprint but points out that some imperfections in the original copies may be apparent.

Disclaimer
The publisher has made every effort to trace copyright holders and would welcome correspondence from those they have been unable to trace.

The Reception of
Classical German Literature
in England, 1760-1860

*A Documentary History
from Contemporary Periodicals*

Edited by John Boening

Volume 3

Garland Publishing, Inc. · New York and London

1977

Library of Congress Cataloging in Publication Data

Main entry under title:

The Reception of classical German literature in England,
   1760-1860.

   A facsimile collection of reviews of German literature that appeared in contemporary English periodicals.
   Includes index.
   1. German literature—18th century—Book reviews.
2. German literature—19th century—Book reviews.
3. German literature—18th century—History and criticism. 4. English literature—18th century—History and
criticism. 5. Classicism. I. Boening, John.
PT312.R4 1977   830'.9'006   77-24149
ISBN 0-8240-0992-4

Printed in the United States of America

In Memory of My Father
John Georg Boening
1898 - 1962

Contents of Series

PART I

General reviews of German literature; includes reviews of two or more authors, notices of anthologies, and appreciations devoted to an entire genre.

PART II

Reviews of individual authors, excluding Goethe and Schiller, with volumes arranged chronologically by date of author's birth.

PART III

Reviews of Goethe and Schiller.

Contents

Abbreviations Used in the Headnotes

Carré   Jean-Marie Carré, *Bibliographie critique et analytique de "Goethe en Angle-terre."* Paris: Librairie Plon, 1920.

M/H   Bayard Quincy Morgan and A. R. Hohlfeld, comps., *German Literature in British Magazines, 1750-1860.* Madison: University of Wisconsin Press, 1949.

WIVP   *Wellesley Index to Victorian Periodicals,* ed. Walter Houghton, *et. al.* Toronto and London: University of Toronto Press, 1966 *et seq.* [two volumes have appeared to date].

General Comment and Criticism: 1836-1860

Germany in 1831. By John Strang. 2 vols. Macrone.

Notes of a Ramble through France, Italy, Germany, &c. By a Lover of the Picturesque. Hamilton & Co.

WE shall dispose of the latter of these works first, and that briefly. Its history appears to be this: "time and circumstances agreeing," the writer started, as his countrymen are accustomed to do, on a summer trip to Italy, going by way of France, and returning by the Rhine. As he moved on from scene to scene, he kept such notes, "the rapid transcript of impressions made on the mind, as the eye glanced over the surface of things," as might revive the recollection of what he saw and heard in his travels. So far well: but unfortunately on his return he stumbled on a passage in Goldsmith, where it is observed, that "to a philosopher, no circumstance however trifling is too minute; he finds instruction and entertainment in circumstances which are passed over by the rest of mankind;" and hence, we presume, he jumped to the conclusion, that he was bound to publish his notes for the benefit of philosophers. To their especial use we are content to leave them. In truth, all that we said respecting Mr. Twining and his travels in Norway, might with equal propriety have introduced the Lover of the Picturesque, and his Ramble, to the reader. He is equally unacquainted with the history, the literature, and we suspect even the languages, beyond perhaps a conversational facility, of the countries he visited; and taking into consideration that he travelled over the most beaten track in Europe, we leave the reader to set his own conjectural value on "the *rapid* transcript of impressions made on the mind, as the eye *glanced* over the *surface* of things."

Mr. Strang however is "another gait" kind of man—one well prepared to benefit by what he saw and heard; and we ought perhaps to apologize for putting so ill-matched a pair in harness together. But we have lately gone somewhat minutely over his whole route, and must therefore be brief in our introductory remarks: indeed, we mean to confine ourselves principally to extracts, relating to the state of literature and literary men in Germany, a rich harvest field hitherto comparatively untouched, but in which Mr. Strang has laboured zealously and well. We must not however restrict our commendation in like manner, for the work is a valuable one, and interesting throughout. Our first extract will be a sketch of the literary history of Hamburgh:—

"Hamburgh being, more than any other place in the world, a purely mercantile city, it is scarcely to be expected that her sons have either time on their own hands to follow literary or scientific pursuits, or inclination to encourage these in others. The fact is, literary distinction here is nearly about as valueless as stars or ribbons; and hence there are but few who have really done anything for the literature or science of Germany, who have made choice of this town as a permanent residence. Klopstock, no doubt, occupied for nearly thirty years a house in the Königstrasse—on the front of which is emblazoned the well-known sentiment of the poet, 'Die unsterblichkeit ist ein grosser gedanke'—'Immortality is a mighty thought,'—and there wrote his Messiah. Hagedorn wandered about Harvestehude, and wove his fancies into verse. Gerstenberg when in Altona penned the majority of his dramas, and improved his famous war-songs. Büsch, when living in the vicinity of St. John's Church, pursued his mathematical and historical labours, and there prepared for the press his several important works on commerce and banking. Ebeling, when a professor in the Gymnasium, wrote and superintended the publication of his masterly work on North America; while Bode laid the foundation of his astronomical fame amid the noise of this busy mart. But with these, and a few more of whom it is unnecessary to speak, we may be said to have summed up the past catalogue of Hamburgh's most celebrated literary and scientific men.

"Of the few litterateurs who at present reside here, who have justly acquired literary distinction in Germany, I know of none who better deserves to be introduced to you, than my kind friend Dr. Wurm, the editor of the 'Kritische Blätter der Börsenhalle,' a publication similar to our Literary Gazette or Athenæum. * * The Doctor is in the prime of life, and although he has been a hard student, his countenance does not exhibit any tokens of suffering from the use of the midnight oil. He is acute, quick, and lively; while his conversation, although teeming with information, is altogether free from pedantry or egotism. As a foreigner he is decidedly the best English scholar I ever met with. He, in fact, speaks our language like a native; and in addition to this, he possesses what very few of our own countrymen possess—a most intimate acquaintanceship with English literature, particularly in its most palmy days. * *

"Through the pages of the periodical which Dr. Wurm at present conducts with so much credit to himself, he has lately sent forth much valuable and just criticism on the modern literature of our country—criticism that might well shame the misnamed Reviews of England. In Germany there is as yet happily very little pandering to authors and booksellers as in England: and none of that shameless systematic puffing and critical quackery which has of late so strikingly characterised the Zoili of your newspaper and magazine press. Happily for Hamburgh, the editor's pen is placed in the hands of men whose critical acumen is only equalled by their critical candour. What a contrast do the opinions of such men hold out to those of

> Your crawling critics—underlings of sense,
> Who damn for spite and eulogise for pence!"

We rejoice to hear so good a report of the state of critical literature in Germany, and believe that it is well deserved. But does Mr. Strang suppose, that the best way to raise the character of our own, is to condemn it after this wholesale fashion? He must know that the moral and literary standard can only be raised by individual exertion and personal integrity, at enormous sacrifices in the first instance, and with very doubtful results: and pretty encouragement is held out, if a man like Mr. Strang, of ability as we know, and of integrity as we are willing to believe, feels himself at liberty to characterize all literary periodicals, and those who conduct them, as "pandering to authors and booksellers," as guilty of "shameless systematic puffing and critical quackery," as "damning for spite and eulogizing for pence"! Now, so far as the *Athenæum* is concerned, we demand proof of this; and we at once release Mr. Strang from all legal consequences, if, as an honest man, he believes that he can justify what he has so daringly asserted, and will undertake to justify it.—We now proceed with our extracts.

"The newspapers printed here, amounting to three or four, are little better than mere compilations from the journals of other countries. The editors of Hamburgh rarely indulge in penning what with you is technically denominated a 'leader;' and although they did so, it would be of little value to the public, seeing that the press, in the free Hanse Towns, is subjected to the controul of a constant, prying censorship. The fact is, that the political opinions of a Hamburgh newspaper, like the majority of those poured forth in other quarters of Germany, are nothing but an echo of the wishes and sentiments of the German Diet, whose spirit animates every censor. The valuable information collected for the 'Börsenhalle List,' however, is the beau ideal of what a mercantile newspaper should be.

"Hamburgh produces three monthly magazines and three or four weekly publications on literature and science, with at least a dozen other smaller popular periodicals. The circulation of these is not confined to the City and its immediate neighbourhood, but extends over a great part of the north-west of Germany. In this country, like our own, I find a growing love for cheap and light periodical literature; the majority of mankind finding it more convenient to take a short digest of a copious or bulky work from some editorial bookworm, than be at the trouble of reading the book itself.

"My friend Dr. Julius, whom you may remember having met in Scotland, I find has left this City, and taken up his abode in Berlin. The Doctor, you are perhaps not aware, commenced life as a Jew, but of late years has become a convert to Christianity, and is now a most strenuous supporter and champion of the Roman Catholic faith! In addition to his antiquarian pursuits, and his love for the Minnesingers, he has been of late labouring most worthily for the improvement of prison discipline, and has just sent a book full of valuable facts connected with that most interesting subject. * *

"Among the living literary men, besides those above mentioned, connected with Hamburgh, there is not perhaps one who has made himself more conspicuous, or is better known over Germany, than *Henrich Heine*, the friend and follower of the ultra-liberal journalist, *Ludwig Börne*, of Frankfort. These two individuals are of Jewish extraction, and, so far as I know, have not, like Dr. Julius, departed from the faith of their fathers. The work by which Heine has made himself most notorious, is what he calls his *Reisebilder*, or 'Travelling Sketches,' which, besides having the peculiarity of alternating from prose to verse, is written in a very clever, original, and outré style. Two new volumes of these sketches have just now made their appearance, and are exciting no little sensation, from the energy, freedom, and boldness with which their author expresses his religious and political opinions—opinions certainly at perfect antipodes to the doctrines and practices of the abettors of the Holy Alliance.

"As a key to the character of the writings of Heine and Börne, and to the school which they would attempt to institute, I may mention, that both writers regard France and the French as the beau ideal of the social system, and consider that country far superior even to Great Britain in substantial freedom;—our countrymen, in their eyes, being by far too aristocratic and exclusive, and too fondly addicted to isolated and family life. * *

"Börne, in particular, represents Paris as an *Eldorado*, and counsels all German students to quit their antiquated universities, and to flee to France, where, if they will only live one twelvemonth, they will acquire more knowledge of law, government, and philosophy, than is to be gathered from all the libraries and lecture-rooms of Germany in a lifetime. The only thing French which Börne does not admire, is the language, the poverty and unpoetical nature of which admit neither of originality nor variety of expression. He thinks, too, that it has become the conversational medium of the higher classes in all countries, because it is best suited for the mediocrity of intellect by which the upper ranks of all European society are characterised and held together. * *

"Heine, although by no means politically extravagant in his early writings, fairly out-herods Börne in his last volumes. In the use of scurrilous invective against all acknowledged and established opinions, he shows himself a master, while he seems to consider it as his most glorious privilege to sit in the chair of the scorner.

"Against the German nobility, tribunals, courts, and manners, both Börne and Heine have pointed the most poisoned shafts of their ridicule, and have consequently incurred the displeasure of every *Graf* and *Fräulein* in the land. The force and originality of expression, for which both writers are so celebrated, arise from the free use which they make of the cant vocabulary of the *Burschen*, especially of that strange *lingo* which is to be found in the pages of a work published some ten years ago, under the title of 'Göttingen Student.' * *

"I have only another living literary man connected with Hamburgh, to introduce to your notice; and he is one, who, as a romance writer, is certainly one of the most original in Germany;—the individual I mean, is Dr. Kruse, first known in England through Mr. R. P. Gillies's translation of the 'Crystal Dagger.' As a living novelist, there are few who rival this writer in the intricacies and developement of a plot; I know of none who can so well conceal the result of history, who so successfully sustains the curiosity of his readers, and so happily brings out the denouement. Among the late works of Kruse, the most remarkable is his tales of criminals, or stories founded upon the more striking individuals who figure in the Newgate Calendar of Germany. * * With a spirit nearly akin to that of *Schiller*, he dives into the secret springs of human action, and presents to the mind of his reader an idea of the hidden workings of human feelings and human passions. Dr. Kruse generally contrives to make us acquainted with his hero, before we observe him acting. We see him actually *will* the action before he performs it; and it cannot be denied, that, in a hero's thoughts and imaginings, there lies infinitely more for observation and study than in his actions, and still more in the sources of his thoughts than in the consequences of those actions. The author of Wallenstein, I remember, asks, 'If the soil of Vesuvius has been examined, to discover the cause of its burning, why should we bestow less attention on a moral than on a physical phenomenon? Why do we not attach an equal degree of importance to the nature of the circumstances in which a particular individual was placed ere the collected fuel is burned into a flame within?' Kruse occasionally seeks and shows the course of action, in the unchangeable structure of the human soul, and in the varying circumstances which modified it from without; and hence, his reader is but little surprised to find thriving in the same plot of earth, the poisonous hemlock and the most wholesome herbs; no astonishment to meet with wisdom and folly, virtue and vice, in the self-same cradle."

According to our intention of confining ourselves to the state of literature and literary men, we hurry on to Berlin. We submit to the critics, that here is another case of 'Pencillings':—

"There is no city in Germany where literature and science are more valued and patronized than in Berlin, and nowhere else do we meet, in general society, with a greater number of literary and scientific men. * *

"The first living literary character to whom I shall now introduce you, is *A. F. E. Langbein*, perhaps one of the most voluminous writers of his time. To this venerable but hale litterateur, I had a letter of introduction. On consulting the Directory, for the purpose of paying my respects to him, I found that his address was *Unter den Linden*. But when I reached his domicile, I discovered by the number of stairs I had to climb, that, like most authors, instead of living under the *lime trees*, he dwelt far above them. On ringing the bell, an old wizened-faced female opened a small pannel of the door, which was grated, and eyeing me with something like suspicion, inquired what I wanted. I explained, as well as I could, the object of my visit, and soon obtained admission. * *

"The best picture I can give you of Langbein, is to say, that he is the very impersonation of one of his own *Schwänke* or Jokes. In stature, he forms the most exact antithesis to one's idea of the great Frederick's grenadiers, being scarcely five feet in height, while his slender corpus is the very counterpart of the round, plump, paunchy figure of his own *Her Von Pampel!* He is upwards of seventy years of age; but his eye, in spite of its long familiarity with the lamp, seems to have lost but little of its lambent sharpness. There is an archness about his mouth, which at once proclaims his love of Momus, and you discover occasionally no little leer that bespeaks the salacious spirit of a Casti. Our conversation naturally turned upon his own works, at least upon those with which I was acquainted; and he seemed highly pleased to learn that certain of them were not unknown in England. I told him I had translated

two or three of his *Schwänke*, but hinted, at the same time, that I was prevented continuing the task, from these Jokes being combined with too much of the indelicate gallantry of his prototype Boccaccio. He smiled at this proof of English prudery, and asked with a sarcastic smile, if Smollett and Sterne were now forgotten in Britain. * *

"Having thus described the oldest living literary man of Berlin, I shall introduce to your notice one of the youngest. The personage I mean, is *Mr. Philip Kaufmann*. * * I have already hinted to you, that in Germany the beauties and mysteries of Shakspeare are perhaps more generally appreciated and more fondly prized than they are in the land of his nativity. This is, however, not to be wondered at, when it is recollected, not only that the beings of his creative fancy are at this hour actually dividing the possession of the German stage, with the heroes of all the other dramatists of the world; but that his plays form, as it were, a perpetual text-book for the ablest critics, Göthe, Tieck, Schlegel, and Börne having successively made them the themes of acute critical analysis. The literature of this country boasts of several translations of the 'Bard of Avon;' of which those by Schlegel and Tieck are the most celebrated. But another translator, and one, too, who seems destined to share with his gifted predecessors the fame which they have so justly acquired in this particular walk, has appeared in the person of my friend Mr. Kaufmann, whose knowledge of the English language is only surpassed by his acquaintance-ship with our best poets."

We have now the pleasure to introduce to our readers, a man as well known in England as in Germany:—

"Of the many literary men who reside in Berlin, and of the few justly entitled to a European reputation, I cannot resist mentioning with respect, the learned and able historian of the 'Family of the Hohenstauffen,' *Frederick Von Raumer*. * * The unwearied industry and indefatigable perseverance which Von Raumer bestowed in collecting materials, and in examining documents to enable him to write this truly Ghibeline history, have won for him the highest esteem and applause from all who can value such pursuits; and they afford another proof, among the many, of the peculiarly characteristic qualities of the German mind for the investigation and elucidation of truth. Von Raumer is about forty-five years of age, of short stature, with a countenance which bespeaks thoughtfulness rather than genius. There is a soberness of demeanour about him, indicating a philosophical rather than an imaginative disposition, though his clear gray eye at once marks the sharp and inquisitive turn of his intellect. The acute, industrious qualities of Von Raumer's mind, having early attracted the attention of Von Hardenberg, he was employed by that well-known Prussian minister, in his own private cabinet, and had the honour of assisting the reforming statesman in working out the details of some of his most important and ameliorating measures. There, he became acquainted with the practical working of courts, a circumstance which no doubt proved most useful to him in his after historical researches. Von Raumer ultimately left Berlin, but has again returned to it, and is now one of the Board of Censors, a situation which, from his liberal opinions, and from the present unpopular nature of the office, I should think can be no great pleasure to him. It is in fact slyly hinted, that he himself is secretly opposed to the censorship, and though strictly a conservatist, is not blind to the folly of first training a people by education for free discussion, and poisoning or damming back the sources from which they are to derive the materials of thought and study. * *

"While on the subject of historians, I must not omit to mention, that when I was the other day in the *Börsenhalle*—where certainly one meets with abundance of foreign liberal papers—I was introduced to the celebrated liberal *Professor Gans*, whose lectures in the University, on Modern History, have produced no little sensation among all classes of the community, not even excepting the Government, whose jealousy is seldom roused by such means. To find, in such a city as Berlin, twelve or fifteen hundred students, many of them belonging to the garrison, anxiously listening to lectures on the best prin-

ciples of government, and those principles of a democratic quality,—is a striking feature of the times, and shows a spirit of liberality on the part of the authorities, singularly at variance with the present heavy restrictions on the press. It can only be accounted for, on the German principle of supporting academic freedom of discussion.

"Among the letters of introduction which my friend Wurm of Hamburgh has given me, I found one for *Ludolph Chamisso*, the great Naturalist, but better known by his strange and original literary work entitled 'Peter Schlemihl.' I must confess I felt some curiosity to see the author of the 'Man who had lost his Shadow,' and whose fame, from this little philosophical novel, has become almost European. I regret, however, that I have not yet been able to get a glimpse of him *in propria persona*, although the lithographed *shadow* of his fine head and flowing hair, forms a common ornament to many of the print-shop windows of this city. This portrait certainly gives one an idea of his dreamy mind, but it cannot at all be said to indicate anything of that determined character, which one would conceive should so necessarily belong to a man who has braved the dangers of a three years' voyage in search of a north-west passage. Chamisso is a French emigrant, but may now be said to be a naturalized German. He came, with other members of his family, to Berlin, at the first breaking out of the French Revolution; and although he has once or twice re-visited France for some time, he seems now to have chosen for life his adopted country. He is attached to the Botanical Garden, where he pursues his natural history inquiries with all the enthusiasm which belongs to his nature. He is now about fifty years of age."

Here we conclude for the present.

Germany in 1831. By John Strang.
[Second Notice.]

We cannot better introduce our further extracts from this work than by an account of that great literary mart, Leipsic.

"In the commerce of Leipsic, there is nothing so extraordinary as its trade in books. The fact is, this city is the grand and sole emporium of the literature of Germany. At one period, Frankfort could boast of possessing some portion of the book trade; but it may now be justly said, that Leipsic has got the entire monopoly of it. At the two great fairs, the booksellers congregate from every quarter of Germany, each bringing along with him the books he proposes to publish to the world. Here the publications of one publisher are exchanged or bartered for those of another; and at the close of every fair, each returns to his own particular town or city, with a selected stock of all that is new throughout the empire.

"To give you some idea of the extent of this trade, I may mention, that, besides music and maps, there are rarely fewer than three thousand new works brought out at each fair. The waggons of printed paper, which enter and leave this mart of the brain, exceed in number an Indian caravan. Only think of the statement by Dr. Menzel, that there are at least ten millions of new volumes printed annually in Germany! Of the extent of authorship in this country, you may also form some notion, when I tell you, that each half-year's Leipsic catalogue, numbers at least a thousand new writers; hence it may fairly be inferred, that at the present moment there cannot be fewer than fifty thousand persons living in Germany who have written a book! If authorship goes on in a similarly progressive ratio to that which it has lately done, it may be fairly assumed, that in a few years the names of German authors will exceed the number of living German readers.‡ The mass of books, which increases every day, already baffles all calculation; and when we think of its extent, we are lost in astonishment, at this new wonder of the world, which has been conjured into existence by the pen and the printing-press. The German booksellers, when they do not repair to the two fairs themselves, invariably transmit their works for subscription through their agents in this city. The books thus sent for sale, remain here a twelvemonth and a day, after which the *remainders*, which means the unsold, are sent back to their respective publishers."

We shall now pay a visit to Dresden :—

"Yesterday afternoon, I took an opportunity of calling on the Hofrath, *Ludwig Tieck*, who, next to Goethe, is the most renowned litterateur in Germany. Having learned that he lived in the *Neumarkt*, I proceeded thither; and on ascending the stair of one of the corner houses of the square, soon found myself within the poet's habitation. I had taken the precaution of sending my card of introduction, an hour or two before claiming an audience; and when I again presented it to the domestic, I was at once ushered into a handsome apartment, adorned with several very good engravings, among which was a portrait of Tieck himself. His daughter, a young lady of rather pleasing demeanour, received me very politely, and told me that her father would be occupied for a few moments, but that I should see him almost immediately. Whether or not this was the fair personage whom the splenetic Müllner so grossly attacked, I know not; but if so, and should it be allowable in such a case to judge physiognomically, her appearance certainly affords presumptive evidence of the little fellow's utter want of conscientiousness.

"A pair of stiff-starched fräulein, the very *beauideal* of stale aristocratical virginity, occupied a sofa on one side of the room; while I seated myself opposite to them, on the other. The conversation, which, on the part of the ladies, was conducted in terms of the coldest politeness, was fortunately soon cut short, by the appearance of the poet himself, who, on entering the apartment, saluted me kindly, and took a seat by my side.

"Tieck, if I may judge from appearances, must be on the wrong side of fifty. In face as well as person he exhibits all the usual indications of that stage of life, and he does not seem to be at all in good health. His countenance is open, and his large forehead bespeaks a mind fraught with thought and intelligence. There is an unaffected nobleness in his speech and demeanour, which is as impressive as it is pleasing; while the style of his conversation, at every turn, indicates the poet-mind, rich in imaginative conceptions, and 'soaring from earthly to ethereal things.' My remarks upon his works naturally led him to inquire how they were appreciated in England; a question which, I confess, I could not well answer. I told him, however, that I had seen translations of several of his romances, and also of his *Märchen*; and by way of fillip to his self-love as an author, I hinted that his two tales, entitled 'The Betrothed' and 'The Pictures,' had won him some celebrity among English novel-readers. He put many questions to me respecting Sir Walter Scott and his works, with all of which he appeared to be peculiarly conversant; and it struck me, that he entertained the pleasing conviction, that his own fame, like Sir Walter's, rested much on the acquaintanceship, displayed in his writings, with the manners and feelings of the past. * *

"On Tieck's alluding to Shakspeare, I took occasion to thank him for the pleasure I had received from the perusal of his able preface to the works of the unfortunate Lenz, which he published about three years ago. Poor Lenz, you know, was the first in Germany who advocated the poetical and dramatic character of Shakspeare, in opposition to that of

‡ The great increase in the publication of works in Germany, may be best illustrated from the catalogue of the successive Leipsic fairs.
Previous to the year 1814, the annual amount of works published in Germany, according to the Leipsic catalogue, was about 2 000.

In 1814 there were	2,529	In 1831 there were	5,598
1816	3,197	1832	6,122
1822	4,288	1833	5 653
1827	5,108	1834	6,074
1830	5,920		

Racine; and may justly be said to have fallen a victim to the enthusiastic attempt which he made to reform the drama of his native land.

"During my interview with Tieck, the ladies seemed to listen to him as an oracle; and it was not without reason. His conversation is even superior to his writings. I could not help being gratified with the manner in which he spoke of his literary contemporaries, and even of those who were his declared foes. Aware of his being one of that celebrated critical clique, of which Schlegel and Novalis were confederates, and whose admiration of Catholic mysticism Tieck had abetted and advocated, I took care to avoid the dangerous whirlpool of polemics. His religious prejudices, like those of Dr. Johnson, are incurable. They are displayed in an obvious hostility to the spirit of Protestantism, and may be said to be constitutional. This is, perhaps, the only blot in his character.

"Among other particulars, I learned from Tieck that there are five periodicals at present published in the Saxon capital, viz. the *Merkur*, published six times a week, being a selection of short literary papers, consisting of tales, poetry, anecdotes, &c.; 2d, *Der Sachsische Stadtverordnete und Communalgardist*, another literary paper, published weekly; 3d, *Anzeiger Dresdener*, an advertising paper, published daily; 4th, *Tageblatt von Arnold*, another collection of tales, criticisms, &c.; and, 5th, *Denkwürdigkeiten für Sachsen*, which appears four times a week, and gives an account of passing events, extracted chiefly from foreign prints, together with original papers. The whole of these publications, however, are rather of a tea-table sort, and, according to Tieck's account, have very few pretensions either to learning or philosophy."

The censorship in Austria is so rigorous and oppressive, that we can only wonder that literature exists at all.

"I am told, (says Mr. Strang,) that no work whatever can be put to press, until it has actually undergone the revision of three distinct officers. For example, the manuscript is sent first to the office of Police, where there are censors appointed for every department of art, science, literature, politics, and religion. One of the censors, of course, immediately sits in judgment on the various passages of the work. This functionary having made his remarks upon the margin, it is next submitted to another officer to consider these remarks. If the work be political, it is then sent to the Chancery-office; and if religious, to the Consistorial-office. On being sent back from either, it is then returned to the office of Police, where it is again revised, and the passages that are permitted to be printed, and those to be condemned, are finally fixed upon; when, to crown the whole ordeal, it is necessary that either the Graff Von Sedlnitzky or the Hofrath Von Ohms, the two individuals at the head of the censorship, append their permissive seal of *imprimatur*."

In defiance of these deadening influences, literature still struggles on. Von Hammer's name is known throughout Europe, but Mr. Strang does not appear to have been introduced to him. Of Grillparzer he observes—

"Yesterday, when passing through St. Stephen's Platz, he was pointed out to me, and you cannot imagine how happy I was at the circumstance. I assure you I had all the wish in the world to run up and salute him, and to tell him how much I had been pleased with the representation of his 'Ahnfrau,' in the Prussian capital; but just as I was about to follow and accost him, a friend stepped forward, and hurried him through a large gateway. I had time enough allowed, however, 'to take a slight map' of him, as a friend of mine used jocularly to say; and here it is :—Imagine, then, a pale, attenuated countenance encircled with dark hair; the features strongly marked; particularly the eye, which, in spite of a pair of spectacles, seems to sparkle with intelligence; and a finely formed mouth, which, whether it were reality or imagination, I fancied bespoke the romantic sensibility that characterizes the fine feeling of his own creation—Bertha. Next, suppose this head placed on a pair of high shoulders, surmounting a tall spare figure, and you will be able to form some notion of the full-length portraiture of Franz Grillparzer. The author of the 'Ahnfrau' is, I am told, about forty-one years of age, and his appearance does not belie it. As I gazed upon him, I could not help regretting, that the fine sarcastic spirit which breathes in every line of the poetical diatribe that he wrote amid the ruins of Rome, should have been repressed or extinguished by the various deadening influences which must have encompassed him since his return from the Eternal to the Imperial City."

There are some minor stars at Vienna, but not of sufficient importance to deserve notice here. At Augsburg Mr. Strang paid a visit to the editor of the *Allgemeine Zeitung*.

" Having got the regular sights over, I hurried to pay my respects to *Mr. Stegmann*, the editor of the well-known journal, entitled the *Allgemeine Zeitung*, one of the ablest and most judicious political organs in Europe. This newspaper was originally printed in Ulm, but was removed from that town to Augsburg in 1810. When I entered the editorial sanctum, Mr. Stegmann was busy writing; but on stating the object of my visit—which I said was to satisfy a wish I had long entertained, to meet an individual whose extensive views and varied knowledge had raised the newspaper he conducted, to the rank of the leading journal of Germany—he immediately laid aside his pen, and was all attention. He is a man, I should suppose, about sixty; but still hale and active. His countenance is a good index to his character, as illustrated in the management of his paper. It bespeaks shrewdness and caution, as well as quick perception and decision, which, you will allow, are, of all other qualifications, the most important for a political writer. Mr. Stegmann is the son of a most respectable, but unfortunate man, and was at a very early age left to shift for himself. After many vicissitudes, and passing through various situations, he became editor of the *Allgemeine Zeitung*, as far back as the year 1804; and since that period, he has laboured most industriously to sustain its high character. You are perhaps aware that this is the only political journal of Germany, which is allowed freely to circulate in Austria and its dependencies; but the reason for so gracious a toleration, which I am about to explain, will no doubt be new to you. Since my arrival here, I have heard it repeatedly asserted, that the edition for Germany is often very different from that which is circulated in Austria; in other words, that while in the former there are frequently articles of the most liberal description admitted, it universally happens, that from the latter these are carefully excluded, and their place supplied by a quantity of *Balaam*. I threw out some hints on this subject to Mr. Stegmann, but he had too much tact and prudence to make any confession. * * It may be said to be the mirror of the policy of the great Northern Powers, and it is well understood to be the medium through which Prince Metternich not unfrequently pours forth his political sophistry, to charm the conservatives of the Continent. In the editorial chamber, there were four persons busily employed in translating the English and French newspapers. Of the English journals, the 'Times' and the ' Courier' were those that seemed to be most patronised and esteemed by the editor. The Allgemeine Zeitung, as you may well suppose, has a very extensive circulation. It is published daily, and is printed by a steam-press. The establishment, altogether, is on a large scale, and I believe it is generally considered one of the first in Germany."

At Stuttgart we are introduced to the editor of the *Litteratur-Blatt*.

" On reaching the house, I was at once ushered into his study, where I found the Doctor busily engaged with his books and papers. He received me in the kindest and most affable manner; and after a few minutes conversation, I found myself as much at ease as if I had been at home.

" Among the many living literary men of Germany, there are few that can be compared with Wolfgang Menzel; he excels in many branches of literature; but in criticism, he is accounted supereminent. Among German critics, the Doctor has been fairly placed next to Lessing; and that, you will allow, is saying a great deal. If Menzel had lived in the first half of the last century, I am persuaded he would have figured still more conspicu-

ously in the literary arena. But he was born so late as 1798; and when qualified to enter the lists, he found almost every department pre-occupied. * * Since the time of Lessing, classical literature, and the history of literary criticism, has been partly cultivated with much more taste, and partly set aside as a subordinate pursuit, when put in contrast with the stirring questions of the day; and Menzel has not even endeavoured to withstand the claims of the moment, which called him away from that species of recondite research. He is peculiarly conversant with the chroniclers and poets of the middle ages; but instead of making them the object of distinct treatises or elaborate investigation, he has been content to receive the general impression which their works leave on the mind, and to range over the rich and variegated picture of men and manners, formed by their rude, but animated descriptions; from which he can draw the most characteristic traits, as occasion may require, either in conversation or in his writings. His ' German History' is a succession of what the French designate, *Tableaux Vivans*—a series of living portraits rather than a connected and regular narrative of facts. * *

" In 1824, at the first festival held in Stuttgart, in honour of Schiller, Menzel wrote an eloquent speech in praise of that accomplished author, which was delivered by a friend, as he maintained that, being a stranger and unaccustomed to public speaking, the impression would be injured were he to speak it himself. At this meeting, where thousands congregated to celebrate the memory of their great countryman, the well known Baron Cotta, Schiller's publisher, and warm personal friend, was among the listeners to the oration. Cotta inquired about its author, immediately made his acquaintance, and in a few days it was settled that Menzel should undertake the editorship of the ' *Litteratur-Blatt*.' It was a bold step, you must admit, for the publisher of Goethe's works thus to engage his literary foe. Menzel set to work with his accustomed zeal, and with all the vigour and determination of one who was fully conscious that he had been called to the task of sweeping the Augean stable. He wielded his critical tomahawk with merciless skill and dexterity; and I have no doubt, that in many instances he was exceedingly unjust. But his rigour sprung from principle, and I believe that his motives were pure. His standing at this moment is very high. As a critic he is dreaded, but not more dreaded than respected. The Doctor, who is a member of the Lower House of Wirtemberg, is, I am told, an excellent speaker. He has made a motion ' on the repression of literary piracy,' which attracted a good deal of attention at the time. In politics, his votes are on the *liberal side*, and his parliamentary career has been spotless.

" The appearance of Dr. Menzel, on a first look, reminded me much of our old acquaintance, Hazlitt, particularly in the form and expression of the face. He has the same broad brow—the same shape of the nose—and the same lambent eye that our English critic so strikingly possessed; but in person, the superiority is on the side of the German critic, since he is considerably taller, and far more orderly in his gait and habiliments. His complexion has, however, much of the same bilious hue that characterized the author of ' Table Talk'—the natural result of a sedentary and studious life."

Having so lately accompanied other travellers over Germany, we have chosen, on this occasion, to confine ourselves to notices of literature and literary men. It must, however, be understood, that Mr. Strang's work is more varied in its character, and is one which we can, and do, recommend to the public.

3. BLACKWOOD'S MAGAZINE, 39 (1836), 699-716. M/H No. 3303. By George Moir.

SHAKSPEARE IN GERMANY.

PART IV.

THE HISTORICAL PLAYS.—THE TWO PARTS OF HENRY IV.

WITH what success the genius of Shakspeare, unassisted by learning, could reanimate the dry bones of classical antiquity, clothe them with body and colour, and impart to them a true spiritual life, the plays of Coriolanus, Julius Cæsar, and Antony and Cleopatra, sufficiently show. In the outward garb and mere form of antiquity; in all that is accidental, local, and variable; in the painting of manners and customs, particularly among the lower classes of society, we grant the inferiority of his sketches, in point of mere correctness of outline, to those which "learned Jonson" drew. The English doublet and hose of the sixteenth century sometimes protrude beneath the toga. The mobs which throng the forum to witness the triumph of Cæsar, or lift up their most sweet voices in the Capitol for Coriolanus, have a marvellous resemblance to those who cry shame on Richard, or throw up their stinking caps for Gloucester at St Paul's. The language of his Roman cobblers might pass for that of an English artisan of the days of Elizabeth, and the activity and dexterity with which they manage their staves and clubs, were probably suggested by some similar exhibitions on the part of the 'prentices of Eastcheap, in which our dramatist had doubtless played his part. So far it is true these plays have less of the antique Roman about them than some of Shakspeare's enthusiastic German admirers are disposed to admit. Shakspeare indeed saw that the populace in all countries and in all ages are pretty much the same, nor was it in the least essential to his purpose to discriminate those smaller traits of character and manners which separate a Roman mob from an English one; and accordingly he has dashed them in with a careless hand, and with the nearest materials which presented themselves. But in the essential spirit of the classic times, and in the felicitous combination of the universal with the particular, in his pictures of the more elevated, intellectual, and marked personages of ancient history, we have already said that they leave all other attempts of the same nature at an immeasurable distance. The Roman Actor of Massinger — Valentinian and Caractacus of Beaumont and Fletcher—the Catiline and Sejanus of Jonson — appear either stilted or out of keeping when placed beside those speaking and moving portraits with which every scene of Julius Cæsar abounds. In reading these Roman pages, the sun seems to go back for ages on the dial of Time: the two thousand years that lie between us and them disappear; and the lost scenes of existence are re-enacted before our eyes anew.

Turn we now from Italy to England: to that brilliant cyclus of Dramas from English history, which forms one of the most peculiar features and brightest ornaments of British literature; a monument to the glory of England, reared not less by patriotism than by poetry; and which, more perhaps than his most imaginative and wonderful creations, has rendered Shakspeare pre-eminently the popular, the national dramatist of his country. Here the poet brings himself fairly within our own circle. He stoops from that aerial elevation into which none but a kindred genius could follow him; he no longer places us in enchanted isles, still vext by tempests, haunted by spirits, or beings whose primeval innocence associates them more with a spiritual than an earthly nature; he leaves behind him the moonlight woods of Athens, with their tiny fairy train, that sweetest of midsummer dreams; he shrouds himself no longer in the obscurity of remote classic antiquity, with Timon, Brutus, and Antony; or of the fabulous mythic period of the British annals with Cymbeline and Lear; he seeks not even, as in the Merchant of Venice, and As You Like it, to invest his subject with an Arcadian clothing, or steep it in the rosy hues of romance and melody; he ventures fairly and boldly into the clear daylight of English history—into the sad and often prosaic realities of his own century, or that which preceded it; he attempts a task, where all men believe themselves to be, and all are to a certain extent, judges: for it is wonderful how far, in the most uneducated and least intellectual of beings, the perception of conformity or disconformity to nature is visible. However little calculated to appreciate the *finesses* of Molière's plays, the delicacy of their satire, the point and beauty of their language, we doubt not that, so far as regarded their great outlines, and the question how far he had presented a true epitome of nature, he might have found worse critics at the Académie Française than his old woman. Such was the test to which Shakspeare submitted himself in these dramas. And how has he succeeded? It is not long since one of our legislators confessed that his acquaintance with English history was chiefly derived from Shakspeare; and this gentleman's case, if the truth were told, we believe to be by no means singular. At least, for our own part, we feel an uneasy consciousness that we are much better acquainted with that portion of our history which extends from Richard II. to Henry VIII. than with those which precede or follow it. It seems to us like an explored spot in the midst of a terra incognita. And while, guided by our recollections of Shakspeare, we feel a certain degree of modest assurance in regard to facts, dates, and other puzzling occurrences within that sphere, we are always remarkably nervous about venturing beyond its confine. But without presuming to conjecture how many "candid readers" are indebted to Shakspeare for their facts, we will venture to say, that in as far as regards the spirit of the English history of the period—the grand outlines of the social and political movement which is obvious between the fourteenth century and the sixteenth —the feelings, habits, amusements, and conversational tone of our ancestors —as well as the personal character, motives, and objects of the leading actors in these tumultuous scenes;—these historical plays are actually more instructive than all the chronicles of the time. Every age of a nation's history has a moral meaning, which, though written in hieroglyphics unintelligible to the uninitiated, or obscured by the trivial and unimportant matter with which, as in some of the Palempsests of the Vatican, the original characters are written over—is yet discernible by the eye of genius. To decipher this meaning, to express it in an abstract form, is the study of the philosophic historian; to seize and to embody it in living and popular symbols, is the far higher aim of the poet. And in this spirit is our English history studied and dramatized by Shakspeare. It is not the character or the fortunes of a King John, a Bolingbroke, or a Henry VI. that he seeks to lay before us, for the history of an individual monarch could afford no proper materials for tragic composition; what he aims at is the exhibition of the age and body of the time. Each drama in this historical cyclus is a picture gallery in which the nominal hero is at best "the centre of the glittering ring,"—one of a varied and extensive group, in which each individual is drawn with the same care, and many with even greater prominence. To this assembly the virtues and vices of the age, its passions, tastes, and opinions, its piety and superstitions, its rudeness or refinement, its joys and sorrows, send their representatives, selected by the hand of genius: the substance of a hundred chronicles is here found combined, purified, and concentrated; and in this combination we see epitomized human nature as it appeared in England in those days of struggling and imperfect civilisation. Let it not, however, be supposed that Shakspeare has limited himself to a mere picture of the spirit of the time, however accurate and true. Not so; for these would have but imperfectly fulfilled the highest duty and aim of poetry. In these sections of English life, there is a spell beyond the mere representation of the actual; in all of them their poetical relation to a higher ideal and to the general destinies of mankind is indicated. The idea of an overruling Providence guiding by its secret springs this restless movement to its glorious ends, and at times striking like a finger from the clouds, into the calculated machinery of human affairs, is perpetually suggested. This indeed is the secret of the peculiar charm with which, apart from the mere liveliness and truth of the portraiture, or the rapid interest of the plot, the historical plays of Shakspeare are invested, and which distinguishes them so remarkably from the dramatized chronicles of a Dumas, a Merimee, or a Vitet. In the latter, the ideas of a providence or a future state, of the terrors of conscience, the punishment of evil even on this earth, and the consolations which religion imparts under the heaviest weight of suffering, are never for an instant hinted at. Chance seems to preside over a weltering chaos of blood and crime. The lots of good and evil appear to be drawn indiscriminately by virtue and vice, and the personages pass from this world to the next like Scott's dying desperado cavalier, hoping nothing, believing nothing, and fearing nothing. In Shakspeare, on the contrary, though his morality is never formal or abstruse, the thought of this higher agency is ever and anon brought before us; a spirit of calm celestial reflection steals in like a still small voice, amidst the most troubled and harrowing scenes of human passions, selfishness and crime; in the barest and most blighting aspects of existence which are presented to our view, we are mysteriously reminded of another, and the shadow of the Infinite and the Eternal is seen brooding above the finite and the quickly fading, even as this earth is over-canopied by the boundless azure of the sky.

"Shakspeare's historical plays from English history," says Schlegel, "are as it were an historical heroic poem in the dramatic form, of which the separate plays constitute the rhapsodies. The principal features of the events represented are exhibited with such fidelity,—their causes, and even their secret springs, are placed in such a clear light, that we may attain from them a knowledge of history in all its truth, while the living picture makes an impression

on the imagination which can never be effaced. But this series of dramas is intended as the vehicle of much higher and more general instruction. It affords examples of the political course of the world applicable to all times. This mirror of kings should be the manual of young princes; they may learn from it the inward dignity of their hereditary vocation, but they will also learn the difficulties of their situation, the dangers of usurpation, the inevitable fall of tyranny, which buries itself under its attempts to obtain a firmer foundation; lastly, the ruinous consequences of the weaknesses, errors, and crimes of kings for whole nations and many coming generations. Eight of these plays, from Richard II. to Richard III., are linked together in an uninterrupted succession, and embrace a most eventful period of nearly a century of English history. The events portrayed in them not only follow each other, but they are linked together in the closest and most exact manner: the circle of revolts, factions, civil and foreign wars which began with the deposition of Richard II., first ends with the accession of Henry VII. to the throne. The negligent government of the first of these monarchs, and his ir licious conduct towards his own relations, drew upon him the rebellion of Bolingbroke. His dethronement was, however, altogether unjust, and in no case could Bolingbroke be considered the true heir of the crown. This shrewd founder of the House of Lancaster never enjoyed, as Henry IV., the fruits of his usurpation in peace; his turbulent barons, the same who aided him in ascending the throne, never afterwards allowed him a moment's repose. On the other hand, he was jealous of the brilliant qualities of his son, and this distrust, more than any real inclination, induced Prince to give himself up to dissolute society, that he might avoid every appearance of ambition. These two circumstances form the subject of the two divisions of Henry IV.; the enterprises of the discontented in the serious, and the wild youthful frolics of the heir apparent in the comic scenes. When this warlike Prince ascended the throne, under the name of Henry V., he was

determined to assert his ambiguous title; he considered foreign conquest as the best means of guarding against internal disturbances, and this gave rise to the glorious but ruinous war with France, which Shakspeare has celebrated in Henry V. The early death of this king, the long minority of Henry VI., and his continual minority in the art of government, brought the greatest misfortunes on England. The dissensions among the regents, and the wretched administration which was the consequence, occasioned the loss of the French crown; this brought forward a bold candidate for the crown, whose title was indisputable, if the prescription of three governments is not to be assumed as conferring validity on an usurpation. Such was the origin of the wars between the Houses of York and Lancaster, which desolated the kingdom for a number of years, and ended with the triumph of the House of York. All this Shakspeare has represented in the three parts of Henry VI. Edward IV. shortened his life by excesses, and did not long enjoy the throne purchased at the expense of so many cruelties. His brother Richard, who had a great share in the elevation of the House of York, was not contented with the regency, and his ambition paved a way for him to the throne by treachery and violence, but his gloomy tyranny made him the object of the people's hatred, and at length drew upon him the destruction which he merited. He was conquered by a descendant of the Royal House, who was unstained by the civil wars; and what seemed defective in his title was atoned for by the merit of freeing his country from a monster. With the accession of Henry VII. to the throne, a new epoch of English history begins; the curse seems at length to be at an end, and the scenes of usurpations, revolts, and civil wars, all occasioned by the levity with which Richard II. sported away the crown, to be brought to a termination."

"The two other historical plays, taken from the English history, are chronologically separated from this series. King John reigned nearly two centuries before Richard II.; and between Richard III. and

Henry VIII. comes the long reign of Henry VII., which Shakspeare justly passed over as susceptible of no dramatic interest. However, these two plays may in some measure be considered as the prologue and the epilogue to the other eight. In King John all the political and national motions which play so great a part in the following pieces, are already indicated; wars and treaties with France, a usurpation, and the tyrannical actions which it draws after it; the influence of the clergy, the factions of the nobles. Henry VIII. again shows us the transition to another age; the policy of modern Europe, a refined court life under a voluptuous monarch, the dangerous situation of favourites, who are themselves precipitated after they have assisted in effecting the fall of others; in a word, despotism under milder forms, but not less unjust and cruel. By the prophecies on the birth of Elizabeth, Shakspeare has in some degree brought his great poem on the English history down to his own time, at least as far as such recent events could be yet handled with security. With this view, probably, he composed the two plays of King John and Henry VIII. at a later period, as an addition to the others."

The first of the series of dramas, the connexion of which is thus traced by Schlegel, is King John. It is difficult at first sight to see by what interest Shakspeare was attracted to this period of English history, or what dramatic idea he could hope to evolve from the mass of confused, indecisive, and often degrading events which occur in the reign of John. We are at first inclined to wonder, with all the romantic interest which now attaches to the Crusades, that the more brilliant and spirit-stirring days and reckless gallantry of Cœur de Lion, should not rather have attracted his attention. But the reign of Richard and his personal character probably appeared to him to have exercised too little influence on the destinies of England to form a fit introduction to his dramatic chronicles. Richard had passed away with the rapidity of a meteor; his short career, chiefly spent on the plains of Palestine or in the dungeons of Austria, seemed but like an episode in English history; he had left no traces of his existence in the policy of England. But the reign of John was marked by traits of a more striking and distinct, though painful character. Outward pomp combined with inward meanness; magnificent pretensions with paltry performance; high-sounding phrases of virtue and disinterestedness used as the cloak to utter hollow-hearted selfishness in conduct—these had been the distinguishing features of the policy of the time; the chief materials of the "state comedy" of the thirteenth century. And of these qualities, the weak, mean, treacherous, and gloomy John was a most striking and impressive representative. He is the pattern of his age in its worst form. Whatever vices of selfishness, or cruelty, or meanness stain the characters of the Philips, Pandulfs, and Austrias, by whom he is surrounded, appear in him in deeper and darker shade. Shakspeare represents him as a coward at heart, amidst all his affectation of courage and warlike dignity: insolent and overbearing in prosperity—in adversity, grovelling and abject; restrained by no principle, on the one hand—but, on the other, guided by no judgment; so that while he plunges into crime he reaps not the fruit of his villany, and is at once an object of dislike and contempt. Conscious of his doubtful claims to the throne, he is not supported by the inward consciousness of native majesty. He feels that on the love and loyalty of his subjects he can have no claim—that crime, artifice, or mean submission, alone can preserve him on that elevation which he has attained. He is ready to stoop to any equivocation which will serve his turn. He would lay England at the feet of Innocent, could he but borrow the thunders of the Vatican to aid him against his own turbulent and high-spirited nobles. He would sacrifice his helpless nephew—he would extinguish his young and innocent life—deliberately, without passion—simply because he is the object of his fears. The very thought that he has secured the consent of his creature to the murder, rejoices his gloomy heart. "Enough! I could be *merry now*;

Hubert, I love thee." He breaks his fearful purpose in hints and glances only—he has not the courage to speak out the crime he meditates—he speaks in monosyllables, as if shuddering at the sounds he uttered—

" *King J.* Death.
Hubert.   My Lord?
King J.   A grave.
Hubert.   He shall not live."

Remorse is a feeling to which, while all goes on well with him, his bosom is a stranger; but he can " repent" the instant he finds that Arthur's death has roused the indignation of Salisbury and Pembroke, and begins to deal in moral reflections on the instability of power based in blood. How admirably are the cause and the effect associated by Shakspeare in these lines—

" *They burn in indignation. I repent;*
There is no sure foundation set in blood—
No certain life achieved by others' death!"

With his characteristic meanness, he endeavours to justify himself even to his associate, by the apology that he had not in express terms required the murder: and with this miserable self-delusion of guilt, he consoles himself with the thought, that had Hubert " but shook his head, or made a pause, or turned an eye of doubt upon his face," the bloody deed would have been undone. Every one must feel that the catastrophe, which Shakspeare has borrowed from the old play, and which represented John's death as occasioned by poison administered by a fanatical friar, is almost the only fit tragic termination for the career of this cold-hearted and cruel tyrant. A Macbeth or Richard may fall in honourable battle; for their courage, or intellectual power, redeem them from contempt—the memory of their early virtues, or great qualities, survives amidst their career of crime—and we willingly see their last appearance on the stage of existence undisturbed by the debasing effect of physical pain, and even gilded by a ray of dignity and resolution. But the death of a John could be redeemed by no such admixture of elevating feeling. He must die as he had lived—meanly, miserably; with his intellectual energies sunk and prostrated under the tortures of his body—

" There is so hot a summer in my bosom,
That all my bowels crumble up to dust;
I am a scribbled form, drawn with a pen
Upon a parchment—and against this fire
Do I shrink up."

When Romeo drinks the poison, death follows, as if he dropt asleep ere we have time to think of its effects—

      " O true apothecary,
Thy drugs are quick—thus with a kiss
I die."

When Hamlet is wounded by the poisoned rapier there is no display of his bodily sufferings.

" The potent poison quite o'ercrows his spirit; "

but he dies seemingly without pain, administering consolation and reproof to Horatio,— occupied with the thoughts of his country, giving his dying voice for Fortinbras; " and flights of angels sing him to his rest." It is reserved for John, in the agony of his fever, to call on the winter to come " and thrust his icy fingers in his maw," or his kingdom's rivers " to take their course through his burnt bosom," to feel a " hell within him," where the poison

" Is as a fiend confin'd to tyrannize
On unreprievable condemned blood."

A ghastly picture, and yet with that art and moderation which is so conspicuous in the scenes of Shakspeare, and so seldom to be found in those of Beaumont and Fletcher, Webster, or Ford, the horrors of the scene are relieved by a multitude of little touches and images which mitigate the physical horrors of the scene. The death of the King takes place in the open air, in the sheltered orchard of Swinstead Abbey. We seem to feel that " the breeze of heaven fresh blowing" must " comfort him with cold." We are reminded by Prince Henry, that " death having preyed upon the outward parts, leaves them insensible; " that his siege is now chiefly against the mind. Ere the dying monarch is brought in, Pembroke observes, " He is more patient—even now he sung! "

" *Prince Henry.*   'Tis strange that death should sing.—

I am the cygnet to this pale faint swan,
Who chants a doleful hymn to his own death;

And, from the organ-pipe of frailty, sings
His soul and body to their lasting rest."

Other things also are introduced, obviously with the view of leaving on the mind that degree of tragic consolation which Shakspeare never loses sight of.

Tidings of peace for England have been breathed into the ear of the dying King. The Dauphin and his power are about to return for France, and we are left at the close to share the hope of Salisbury, that the reign of Henry is to repair the evils of that of John, and set a form of order and tranquillity on that constitution which his father had left " so indigest and rude."

To bring out with all the force of contrast the hollowness, duplicity, and selfishness of John's character, Shakspeare has—in this instance alone—prominently brought forward a boy as one of the chief personages of the drama; for, by the innocence, artlessness, and affection of Arthur, all the opposite qualities of his gloomy uncle, and of the policy of the time, are presented in more remarkable relief. Indeed, the character of Arthur is not only unique in Shakspeare, but, we may venture to add, in dramatic literature. Nothing is indeed more common—not in Shakspeare certainly—but in some of his contemporaries, and not a few of his successors in more modern times, than the introduction upon the stage of ingenious youths and maidens; children in years, but men and women in sentiment and expression, who alternately astonish us with precocious displays of resolution, generosity, and resignation, or seek to captivate our feelings by an affectation of more than childish simplicity. The charm of Arthur's character lies in his perfectly unconscious childishness; he fascinates us from his very entrance upon the scene, but it is by his helplessness—his inability to comprehend the motives and the conduct of the personages by whom he is surrounded—by the shrinking and retiring part which he takes—so long as there are others on whom he feels that he can rely. He appears like a tender flower, which might have expanded into bloom and beauty under the fostering care of a fostering hand; but which, torn from its place of shelter, and exposed to the storms of life, must soon droop, and wither, and die. We see how willingly he would be back in the haunts of his childhood in Bretagne, with his boyish companions, his sports, his exercises, his studies—how wearily all the stir and tumult around him, and the sight of those kings, queens, legates, and warriors, who quarrel and draw the sword for or against him, press upon his spirit. Above all, he shrinks from witnessing the angry features and inflamed language of the mother whom he loves so tenderly, and whom, till now, he has seen only in moods as gentle as his own. He is so unused to these scenes of passion and vehemence, particularly from her, that he looks upon the whole with a feeling of instinctive terror. What are the secret objects and views of the contending parties he understands but imperfectly; but he sees that a long, and probably a bloody war, on his account, is in preparation—he feels at this moment a weary of the world, even on its threshold —and the wish to be at rest, and removed from all the sorrows which he sees in sad perspective, is visible even in the first words he speaks—

" Good my mother peace !
I would that I were laid low in my grave—
I am not worth this coil that's made about me."

But sadness is not natural to childhood. This is but a momentary cloud of sorrow—the elasticity of his spirit revives again ; even in the prison of Northampton it has not forsaken him—" were he but out of prison, and kept sheep, he would be merry as the day is long." There is no sullenness or selfishness in his sorrow—in his hours of imprisonment he has found time to confer many an act of kindness upon his stern gaoler ; he has nursed him in his sickness—the poor boy has been lavishing on others that sympathy and tenderness which he so much required for himself. The scene with Hubert, where he pleads to have his eyes preserved, and vanquishes the resolve of the stern warrior, notwithstanding his oath, by the pathos and childish innocence of his appeals, is, as all the world have felt, superlatively masterly. Nothing, indeed, but the magical beauty and tenderness of the speeches of Arthur

could render tolerable the horrors of the situation—which, in the somewhat similar case of Glo'ster, in King Lear, is felt to overpass the legitimate boundaries of tragic emotion ; but while we listen to his gentle pleadings, Hubert and his fierce attendants, the cord and the hideous irons, disappear—we feel an inward persuasion that the cruel deed will not — cannot be done. What human bosom, indeed, could resist an appeal such as this ?—

" Have you the heart ? When your head did but ache,
I knit my handkerchief about your brows—
(The best I had, a princess wrought it me,)
And I did never ask it you again :
And with my hand at midnight held your head ;
And, like the watchful minutes to the hour,
Still and anon cheered up the heavy time,
Saying, What lack you ? and, Where lies your grief ?
Or, What good love may I perform for you ?
Many a poor man's son would have lain still,
And ne'er have spoke a loving word to you ;
But you at your sick service had a prince.
Nay, you may think, my love was crafty love,
And call it cunning : Do, and if you will :
If Heaven be pleased that you must use me ill,
Why, then you must. — Will you put out mine eyes ?
The eyes, that never did, nor never shall,
So much as frown on you ?"

While we listen to these heartbreaking words, we feel assured that Hubert—sworn as he is to do the deed—must relent. We see that with every fresh appeal his purpose is more and more shaken ; that he is vainly endeavouring to varnish over his feelings with an appearance of harshness, and long before he utters the words, we anticipate the confession,

" I will not touch thine eyes
For all the treasure that thine uncle owes."

The peculiar design of Shakspeare in the play of King John, to illustrate and expose the hollowness, pretension, hypocrisy, and conventional dignity of the time, appears most distinctly in the singular character of Falconbridge, on which much care has been bestowed, and which was obviously a favourite with the author. Falconbridge, himself an adventurer, whose principles sat most loosely about him, and who is perfectly ready to catch and imitate

the tone and spirit of those with whom he mingles, has yet the fullest perception of the ridiculous ; he cannot disguise from himself—nor occasionally from others—the comic, the contemptible impression which this mock heroic pageant makes upon his mind. He plays the part of a chorus in the piece ; he delights to strip those " illustrious personages" of their diadems and royal mantles, and to hang a calf's-skin on their recreant limbs. He translates their pompous and high-sounding phrases into the vulgar tongue—into their true, selfish, and ignoble meaning. He laughs in his heart at the whole scene; he despises the actors in it ; he can even be moved to strong feeling and energy by such an event as the death of Arthur; but he sees no reason, on the whole, why he should not imitate others, and belong rather to the class of the deceivers than the deceived. If the world around him be out of joint, he feels no inward call to set it right.

" And why rail I on this commodity,
But for because he hath not wooed me yet :
Not that I have the power to clutch my hand,
When his fair angels would salute my palm :
But for my hand, as unattempted yet,
Like a poor beggar, raileth on the rich.
Well,—whiles I am a beggar I will rail,
And say there is no sin but to be rich—
And being rich, my virtue then shall be,
To say,—there is no vice but beggary :
Since kings break faith upon commodity,
Gain, be my lord !—for I will worship thee !"

The striking and masterly character of Constance is dismissed by Schlegel with the single remark, that " her maternal despair on the imprisonment of her son is of the highest beauty." So it is ; but the character deserved a more detailed and discriminating analysis, and it should not have wanted it, if we could have hoped to add any thing to the remarks which have already been made upon the subject by Mrs Jameson.

The play of Richard II. stands like a porch before the more magnificent edifice of the Two Parts of Henry IV. Its perusal is absolutely necessary to enable the reader to comprehend the position of events at the opening of the latter, and to give the key to the character of Bolingbroke. " In Richard the Second,"

says Schlegel, " Shakspeare exhibits to us a noble kingly nature, at first obscured by levity and the errors of an unbridled youth, and afterwards purified by misfortune, and rendered more highly and splendidly illustrious. When he has lost the love and reverence of his subjects, and is on the point of losing also his throne, he then feels with painful inspiration the elevated vocation of the kingly dignity and its prerogatives over personal merit and changeable institutions. When the earthly crown has fallen from off his head, he first appears as a king whose innate nobility no humiliation can annihilate. This is felt by a poor groom. He is shocked that his master's favourite horse should have carried the proud Bolingbroke at his coronation—he visits the captive king in his prison, and shames the desertion of the great. The political history of the deposition is represented with extraordinary knowledge of the world;—the ebb of fortune on the one hand, and the swelling tide on the other, which carries every thing along with it. While Bolingbroke acts as a king, and his attendants behave towards him as if he really were so, he still continues to give out that he comes with an armed band merely to demand the restoration of his birthright and the removal of abuses. The usurpation has been long completed before the word is pronounced, and the thing publicly avowed." Nothing can be more just than Schlegel's remark on the skill and knowledge of the world displayed in depicting the march of the political events in this play, but in his estimate of Richard's character it is impossible to concur. Of the noble kingly nature which he supposes Richard to have possessed, which is only obscured by levity and the disorders of youth, and which reappears in its former lustre when his character has been purified by misfortune, this play affords no traces, though Shakspeare, by commencing his play within two years of Richard's deposition, and sinking twenty of violence, rapacity, and tyranny, has given his hero every advantage which he could dramatically possess. We see in him, in the outset, a mixture of levity and cold

9

selfishness — boundless vanity and presumption in success, with instant and total despondency in misfortune. His is one of those natures on which no feelings can be lasting; all impressions glide off from him as from a hard and polished surface. He might be described in the lines which Wallenstein addresses to Illo when he learns the flight of Isolani:

" In swiftly fading characters are writ
The forms of life upon the glassy brow ;
Nought sinks into the bosom's silent depth ;
And though a giddy spirit wake the blood,
No soul exists to warm the frame within."

He is the companion of low flatterers, like Bushy, Bagot, Green, and the treacherous Aumerle. We see him cold and unmoved by the noble appeal of Norfolk at the tournament, and, careless as to the investigation of truth and right, arbitrarily banishing both him and his antagonist Bolingbroke. We listen to his heartless speech when York communicates to him the death of his uncle, " Old John of Gaunt, time-honoured Lancaster "—a noble model of chivalrous truth standing there, as Schlegel says, like a pillar of the olden time which he has outlived.

" The ripest fruit first falls, and so doth he :
His time is spent, our pilgrimage must be :
So much for that."

How strongly are the weaknesses of his character brought out in the scene on the coast of Wales, when he learns from successive messengers the progress of Bolingbroke's rebellion ! his overweening confidence in himself and in the influence of his royal name in the outset, and his pusillanimity the instant he learns from Salisbury that the Welsh had fled to his rival ! He, who but the moment before had been comparing himself with the sun, " darting his light through every guilty hole," and making the traitor Bolingbroke tremble at himself, is in the next plunged into the deepest despair, and ready to resign his crown when he hears that some thousands of his liegemen had fallen off. But his subsequent resignation has no true and consistent dignity. He is no martyr purified by suffering ; for we feel at least doubtful whether, had fortune eventually favoured him, he would not have been as thought-

less, heartless, and presumptuous as before. He is ever relapsing into passionate bursts, regrets, and expostulations, and sarcasms — most true to nature, we grant, but certainly by no means consistent with that " innate nobility" for which Schlegel gives him credit in misfortune.

The whole interest in the play centres in Richard himself and his rival, for the other characters are but slightly traced—even Gaunt, though a fine outline, is but a sketch. In this respect the play presents a remarkable contrast to those to which it forms the introduction; for the two Parts of Henry IV. contain the most complete and varied picture-gallery of character which is to be found in Shakspeare : Henry himself, the Prince, his rival Hotspur, Glendower, Falstaff, Bardolph, Pistol, Poins, Shallow, Silence, Mrs Quickly—each laboured with as much care, and marked with as distinctive traits, as if the chief interest of the piece had been dependent on that individual alone.

The outlines of Bolingbroke's character had been indicated in Richard II. He is the personification of worldly prudence ; bold where it is necessary, but never beyond what is necessary ; sagacious, cold-hearted, cautious, and moderate, with little in him to love—much to respect—something to fear—nothing absolutely to hate. Though the death of Richard has removed the immediate object of his fears, he feels that the very principle on which his authority rests may be turned against him. He has himself violated the sanctity of right. What security can he have that others will regard it ? Already he begins to feel how uneasy lies the head that wears a crown, when force alone has placed it on his brow, or can preserve it there. Already, in the thoughtless and dissolute conduct of his son, he begins to feel the punishment of his own political delinquency, and that Heaven, " out of his blood hath bred revengement and a scourge for him." A monarch, confident in his title, might have tried the influence of mildness, frankness, simplicity of demeanour, but Henry sees that his security lies only in maintaining, in all their

extent, the reserve, the pomp, and the severity of royalty. Nothing in the conduct of his son grieves or alarms him more than the levity with which he throws aside the conventional dignity of his rank. This is the main topic on which he insists, in the masterly interview with his son in the presence chamber. He feels that, in his own case, his rise has been mainly owing to the very opposite line of conduct ; and his admonitions to his son are founded, not on general topics of morality, but on considerations drawn from his own successful example, the downfall of Bolingbroke, and the similar fate which he anticipates for his reckless heir.

" Had I so lavish of my presence been,
So common-hackney'd in the eyes of men,
So stale and cheap to vulgar company ;
Opinion, that did help me to the crown,
Had still kept loyal to possession ;
And left me in reputeless banishment.
By being seldom seen, I could not stir,
But, like a comet, I was wondered at :
That men would tell their children, this is he ;
Others would say, Where—where is Bolingbroke ?
And then I stole all courtesy from heaven,
And dressed myself in such humility,
That I did pluck allegiance from men's hearts,
Loud shouts and salutations from their mouths,
Even in the presence of the crowned king.
Thus did I keep my person fresh, and new ;
My presence, like a robe pontifical,
Ne'er seen, but wondered at ; and so my state,
Seldom, but sumptuous, showed like a feast,
And won, by rareness, such solemnity.
The skipping king, he ambled up and down
With shallow jesters, and rash bavin wits,
Soon kindled, and soon burnt : carded his state ;
Mingled his royalty with capering fools ;
Had his great name profaned with their scorns ;
Grew a companion to the common streets ;
Enfeoff'd himself to popularity :
So, when he had occasion to be seen,
He was but as the cuckoo is in June,
Heard, not regarded * * * *
And in that very line, Harry, stand'st thou ;
For thou hast lost thy princely privilege,
With vile participation ; not an eye
But is a-weary of thy common sight,
Save mine, which hath desired to see thee more ;

Which now doth—that I would not have it do—
Make blind itself with foolish tenderness."

Henry had attained greatness by acting a part, and by the same arts he feels he must maintain it. Restless, disappointed, and apprehensive of the future, he seems anxious to bring matters to a point. He rather urges on than seeks to check in the outset the rebellion of Northumberland ; for he knows the characters with whom he has to deal, and his own superiority ; he is assured that, from such antagonists, so rash, so wayward, and so divided, he has no serious danger to fear—and he looks upon their insurrection as a storm by which the atmosphere is to be cleared, and after which he can breathe more freely. The dramatic idea which the whole serious part of the play embodies, is that of the contrast between the outward prosperity of Henry's life, as he stands before the world, placed, apparently, on the summit of his ambition—a powerful monarch, the founder of a new race of kings, triumphant over his enemies—and the deep, secret, internal suffering and restlessness under which he truly labours. To the world his position appears an enviable one, and he would wish it to appear so. But within all is vanity and vexation of spirit.

It is our perception of this secret grief—this drop which embitters the whole cup of prosperity, which, notwithstanding the coldness and distrust with which we at first regard his character, softens our hearts towards Henry, and enlists at last our sympathies on his side. Usurper as he is, he is also a father ; and in this, the nicest point, the one where he is most accessible to feeling, he has been made to feel deeply. We perceive at once with what contempt and dislike he would have regarded a character like that of the prince, had he been any other than his son. He finds him apparently, in all points, the antipodes to himself ; rash and unthinking, when he himself was cautious ; dissolute and riotous, when he had been temperate and calm ; courting the very society which he had most carefully avoided ; degrading the name and

3. continued

rank which it had been his constant study to surround with all associations of grandeur and awe. He sees the edifice of state policy which he had himself built up with such labour, and which he had hoped to see cemented and strengthened by the hand of his son, threatening to crumble again into the dust, if not to be more speedily dashed asunder by him who should have been its prop and bulwark.

" Therefore his grief
Stretches itself beyond the hour of death.
The blood weeps from his heart when he
    doth shape
In forms imaginary the unguided days
And rotten times England should look upon,
When he is sleeping with his ancestors."

These gloomy reflections are deepened by the comparison which is forced upon him, between the wild excesses of his own " unthrifty son " and the youthful promise of the heir of Northumberland —that Percy who, but eight years before, had been " the man nearest his soul," but who is now leagued against him with Douglas and Glendower, and labouring to push him from that throne to which he had helped to raise him.

" O that it could be proved
That some night-tripping fairy had exchanged,
In cradle-clothes, our children where they
    lay,
And called mine Percy, his Plantagenet ;—
Then would I have his Harry and he
    mine ! "

This is the consideration which, more than any other, rankles in his heart. The high character, the warlike accomplishments, and universal popularity of young Percy, are the themes by which, in the interview in the third act, after pointing out and illustrating, by the contrast of Richard and himself, the dangers of the course which the Prince was pursuing, he chiefly seeks to rouse his own seemingly degenerate heir to a sense of his degradation and his duty. For all these traits, which so finely humanize the character of Henry IV., and redeem it from its more political hardness, Shakspeare obtained scarcely a hint from

Hollingshed, or from the old play, entitled, " The Famous Victories of Henry V.," which is known to have furnished him with the outline, and with some few lines of the two parts of Henry IV. Any one who wishes to see with what inimitable superiority a mind like that of Shakspeare can treat an incident which he adopts from the chronicle, and from his anonymous predecessor, has only to compare the admirable interview in the third act of the first part of Henry IV.,* between the King and his son, with the corresponding passages in Hollingshed and the old play. The King's part in the dialogue, in particular, is inimitably sustained ; his gradual transition from the censure of his son's conduct, to a contrast of it with his own when young, and of the policy by which he had raised himself and the house of Plantagenet to greatness; his contempt for the conduct of Richard, as owing his ruin to the very same thoughtless abasement of the royal dignity in which Prince Henry indulges ; the eulogy on Percy, by which, if by any thing, he hopes to awaken the dormant seeds of shame and good feeling in the heart of his son, and to rouse him to the necessity of manly and honourable exertion, and that burst of natural tears in which it ends, are given with equal grace, pathos, propriety, and characteristic truth.

We pass, however, from the father to the son—a character which Shakspeare has obviously portrayed in the spirit of love, and has graced, amidst all its wild extravagances, with a thousand amiable and redeeming features. Whence arose this obvious leaning towards this " rascalliest sweet young prince"— this evident fellow-feeling with him, who plays off practical mystifications upon waiters, and " robs me his father's exchequer upon Gad's Hill ?" Might not all this have some connexion with his own youthful peccadilloes—his moonlight deerstealing excursions at Charlecote— and all those mad frolics by which, long ere he had thought of inditing dramas, he had made Warwickshire

too hot to hold him ? In painting this wild early career of Prince Hal, afterwards matured into so brilliant and glorious a manhood, was not the poet, in some sense, pleading his own apology, and proving, by a parallel instance, how often in the seemingly dissolute and careless youth might lie dormant the seeds of the great and accomplished man ?

Be that as it may, it is certain that no character has been arrayed by Shakspeare in more attractive, and almost dangerously fascinating, colours. He has endowed him, amidst his errors, with every attractive and amiable quality—with wit, intelligence, generosity, modesty, and courage. He has been anxious, from the first, to make the reader distinctly aware of the great qualities which lie hid under the garb of levity, and to prepare us for their ultimate developement ; for, even in the second scene of the first act of the First Part, no sooner have Falstaff and his companion Poins disappeared—after an encounter of tongues, in which the wit is nearly equalled by the profanity, and after the project of stripping Falstaff and his companions of their ill-gotten gains, has been adjusted between the Prince and Poins— than he vindicates his present association in the well-known and beautiful lines—

" I know you all, and will a while uphold
The unyoked humours of your idleness :
Yet herein will I imitate the sun,
Who doth permit the base contagious clouds
To smother up his beauty from the world,
That. when he please again to be himself,
Being wanted he may be more wondered at,
By breaking through the foul and ugly mists
Of vapours, that did seem to strangle him."

The Prince was indeed entitled to say that he knew his companions well—for no one more thoroughly appreciated their real worthlessness —including that of their masterspirit Falstaff himself. But the confession would have been more true and complete if he had added that he upheld " the unyoked humours of their idleness " from the real gratification which their society afforded. His heart, indeed, has not been contaminated, nor his high feeling of honour impaired (though the falsehood to which he

resorts in the scene with the Sheriff appears somewhat suspicious), but he has a natural turn for dissipation, provided only it be redeemed and elevated by wit and humour. He turns with real pleasure from the stiffness and formality of his father's court, where men are measured by the artificial and extrinsic advantages of wealth and rank, to the freedom of the Boar's-head, where they are estimated at their true value. He willingly leaves his place at the council-board to his brother of Lancaster, for there he can play but a secondary part while his father lives, with that supremacy to which his wit not less than his rank entitle him, in the revels of Eastcheap. He loves to study men in all situations, high and low ; and, in truth, is rather inclined to the belief that man is a more agreeable object of study in the latter situation than the former. It is his pride to be master " of all humours that have shown themselves humours since the old days of goodman Adam." And in this investigation he is, for the time, sufficiently engrossed to forget all matters of higher moment. It is sufficiently obvious, from the spirit with which he not only enters into those scenes of low life, but occasionally organizes them, that whatever higher capacities he may feel within him, he cares not how long they lie dormant while Falstaff's exhaustless wit is there to grace these follies with an intellectual character. Nay, so easily is he disposed to be pleased, that even Bardolph, Poins, or Francis, will serve his turn : Bardolph's nose had evidently been so long a mine of wit both to Falstaff and the Prince, that the Prince might have a pride in showing that the vein was even yet not wrought out; and that in the hands of a man of talent, it might still be turned to some account. But the delight which he receives from the dilemma in which he places the foolish Francis, with his single parrot note of " anon, anon, sir ! " and the account of his sworn brotherhood with the Drawers, in which he truly says, that he sounded the very base string of humility, evince a still less critical taste. Laughter, no matter how caused, seems to him to be the end of life.

---

* Scene ii. Act 3.

"But the scene with his father," says Horn, "plainly evinces how little the better feelings of his heart had suffered by this unworthy association. That scene, we must recollect, had been already parodied by anticipation by Falstaff; and how natural, how pardonable would it have been, if a smile at the recollection of the lecture of the night had mingled with the morning's audience. Must he not have perceived, as clearly as we, the hollowness and inconsequence of two thirds of his father's reproaches? As a stranger he might, but not as a son. The object of the reproof is in truth more in the right than he who administers it: but it is a father who does so, and against him the son can avail himself of no other weapons but patience and love. He admits the justice of the reproach—he asks only forgiveness.

' I shall hereafter, my most gracious Lord,
Be more myself.'

"With what a noble fire of enthusiasm does he appear inflamed, when the opportunity of great deeds in behalf of his king and country is presented to him! how generous is his voluntary eulogium on the bravery and knightly worth of Percy!—an eulogium which flows from that sympathy which he feels for all excellence, and which pauses not to consider whether the object on which it is bestowed be friend or foe.

"But does this interview with his father effect a change in Henry's character? Has he really determined in future to change his course, and to avoid this wild and discreditable society? 'Not a whit.' His better understanding with his father only seems to raise his spirits, and the first place to which he adjourns from the palace is the tavern. He who is so soon to wield so nobly the general's truncheon, must begin by playing upon it like a fife.* He allows himself ample t' to listen to the delightful squabbles of Falstaff and the Hostess. When, at last, notwithstanding the brilliancy and full-

ness of his own wit, he feels himself fairly overcome by the irresistible flood of Falstaff's humour, he contrives, like a true humorist, to furnish himself with the materials of laughter for a month, by assigning to the poor fat knight 'a charge of *foot*.' Here the humour almost amounts to cruelty, were it not that his knowledge of Falstaff's resources assures him that he will not really be the sufferer on this occasion any more than on those that have preceded it."

The character of his rival Percy is a simple one: the name of Hotspur describes it at once; he is a being of fire from head to heel. He has many of the great qualities that should adorn knighthood, high honour, boundless courage, respect to engagements, generosity; but he wants its great ornament, the spirit of love—and its greatest safeguard, reflective prudence. In love his character is altogether deficient: he treats his wife with no tenderness; he intrusts her with no confidence; she is to him but a housekeeper, an indispensable, but on the whole irksome, appendage to his state. Even for friendship he seems to have little inclination: his attachments take their rise in a spirit of opposition; the best passport to his friendship and protection is that the individual shall have been injured or rejected by others. In prudence he is, if possible, still more deficient. Incapable of reflection, he can form no due estimate of himself and others; impelled by the fire within him, he thinks that every thing must yield to it as he has done himself. His courage is more animal than intellectual; he is far too wordy and too self-laudatory to be a great leader. But out of this very propensity, however, Shakspeare has drawn one of his simple and pathetic touches. "Would to heaven," exclaims Percy but the instant before he falls beneath the sword of the victorious Prince, "thy name in arms were now as great as mine!" Self-confident, secure of conquest, Hotspur only wishes that his victim

were adorned with higher renown, that he might offer him a worthier sacrifice on the altar of his vanity; he never contemplates the alternation, that he himself should so soon stoop his crest to him whom he almost despises as unknown in arms. Such a character as Hotspur would, in ordinary hands, have been an extremely unpleasing one; but Shakspeare has softened its rugged outlines, and given it a peculiar and even pleasing individuality, by the rough humour with which he has invested it, which in this instance is not merely ornamental, but is truly the cementing quality—the spirit of life by which the whole character is moulded into an animated and natural whole.

Shakspeare has given us but a few glimpses of the conspirators, but these few are sufficient to illustrate their characters, and to set us at ease as to the danger of Henry from such a rebellion. The single scene in which they are discovered parcelling out their respective shares of England upon the map;—dividing the bear's skin before they have killed him;—their already apparent dissensions, the contempt which Hotspur openly expresses for Glendower's magical pretensions, the firm belief which the Welsh chief entertains in them; his boast of having thrice sent Bolingbroke

" Bootless home, and weather-beaten back,"

and Hotspur's coolly sarcastic rejoinder,

" Home without boots, and in foul weather too !
How 'scapes he agues, in the devil's name?"

All these admirably prepare us for the jealousies, the divided councils, and rashness which led to the encounter of the rebels with the royal army during the absence of Glendower, and to the defeat and suppression of the rebellion at Shrewsbury. They make us feel how poignantly Northumberland must have afterwards felt the pathetic reproach of Lady Percy—on his failure to bring up his troops to the assistance of his son.

" Let them alone :
The marshal, and the archbishop, are strong :
Had my sweet Harry had but half their numbers,
To-day might I, hanging on Hotspur's neck,
Have talked of Monmouth's grave."

The part of the Prince is the connecting link between the tragic and the comic portions of Henry IV. The conqueror of Percy is also the companion of Falstaff and his group. "But Falstaff, unimitated, inimitable Falstaff, how shall I describe thee?" So asked Dr Johnson, breaking out into an unwonted fit of enthusiasm; —for, strange to say, the grave and moral Doctor seems to have been more deeply struck with Shakspeare's powers in this comic conception of character than in any of his tragic and dignified creations. Most certainly the effort required for the production of such a character as Falstaff was not less than that by which a Lear, a Caliban, a Macbeth, an Imogen, or a Miranda was called into being. All were equally drawn purely from the regions of imagination; for Falstaff, though represented by Shakspeare as walking, or rather "larding" this earth, and frequenting some of those haunts with which the poet himself was familiar, was as little the mere result of actual observation, and as purely an ideal conception, as the airiest or most supernatural of his characters. No such being, we may be assured, ever figured at the Globe or graced the festivities of the Mitre or the Mermaid. Gross and earthly as he seems —he has yet come to us from the same region from which those more spiritual visitants had preceded him; from that world of imagination with which Shakspeare was as familiar while he stood a culprit before Sir Thomas Lucy, as when in after life he walked the streets of London, or sat an honoured guest in the hospitable halls of Lord Southampton.

The substance of our English criticism on the subject of Falstaff (except the ingenious but paradoxical attempt of Mr Morgan to prove that Falstaff was neither cowardly nor selfish) is pretty well embodied in the following remarks of Cumberland.*

* Horn has not here evinced his usual accuracy. It is Falstaff, not the Prince, who converts his truncheon to these "base uses."

* The Observer. No. 86.

" To fill up the drawing of this personage, Shakspeare conceived a voluptuary in whose figure and character there should be an assemblage of comic qualities; in his person he should be bloated and blown up to the size of a Silenus, lazy, luxurious; in sensuality a Satyr, in intemperance a Bacchanalian. As he was to stand in the post of a ringleader among thieves and cutpurses, he made him a notorious liar, a swaggering coward, vainglorious, arbitrary, knavish, crafty, voracious of plunder, lavish of his gains, without credit, honour, or honesty, and in debt to every body about him. As he was to be the chief seducer and misleader of the heir-apparent to the crown, it was incumbent on the poet to qualify him for that part—in such a manner as should give probability and even a plea to the temptation; this was only to be done by the strongest touches and the happiest colourings of a master; by hitting off a humour so happy, so facetious, and of so alluring a cast as should tempt even royalty to forget itself, and virtue to turn reveller in his company. His lies, his vanity, and his cowardice, too gross to deceive, were to be so ingenious as to give delight; his cunning evasions, his witty resources, his mock solemnity, his vapouring self-consequence, serve to furnish a continual feast of laughter to his royal companion. He was not only to be witty himself, but the cause of wit in others; a whetstone for raillery, a buffoon, whose very person was a jest. Compounded of these humours, Shakspeare produced the character of Sir John Falstaff, a character which neither ancient nor modern comedy has ever equalled, which was so much the favourite of the author as to be introduced in three several plays, and which is likely to be the idol of the English stage as long as it shall speak the language of Shakspeare."

No very substantial addition is made to these observations by the criticism of Schlegel: and, indeed, the features of Falstaff's character are so broad and palpable, that they could hardly be mistaken by those who first attempted to delineate them. The best remark in Schlegel's critique is, that Falstaff employs the activity of his understanding as the means of obtaining the pleasing repose of sensuality for his body. Situated as Falstaff is—he feels this to be the price which he must pay in order to take his ease in his inn; —and he pays it (the only debt he does pay) honestly, and to the last farthing.

" Falstaff," says Schlegel, " is the summit of Shakspeare's comic invention. He has continued this character through three plays, and exhibited him in every variety of situation, without exhausting himself: the figure is drawn so definitely and individually, that, to the mere reader, it affords the complete impression of a personal acquaintance. Falstaff is the most agreeable and entertaining knave that ever was portrayed. His contemptible qualities are not disguised: he is old, lecherous, and dissolute; corpulent beyond measure, and always attentive to cherish his body by eating, drinking, and sleeping; constantly in debt, and any thing but conscientious in the choice of the means by which money is to be procured; a cowardly soldier and a lying braggart, a flatterer to the face, and a satirist behind the backs of his friends, and yet we are never disgusted with him. We see that his tender care of himself is without any mixture of malice towards others; he would only not be disturbed in the pleasing repose of his sensuality, and this he attains through the activity of his understanding. Always on the alert, and good-humoured, ever ready to crack jokes on others, and to listen to those of which he is himself the subject—so that he justly boasts that he is not only witty himself, but the cause of wit in others—he is an admirable companion for youthful idleness and levity. Under a helpless exterior, he conceals an extremely acute mind; he has always some dexterous turn at command whenever any of his free jokes begin to give displeasure; he is shrewd in his distinctions between those from whom he has favours to solicit and those over whom he may assume a familiar ascendency. He is so convinced that the part he plays can only pass under the cloak of wit, that even when alone he is never altogether serious, but gives the drollest colouring to his love intrigues, his relations with others, and his sensual philosophy—witness his inimitable soliloquies on honour, on the influence of wine upon bravery, and his description of the beggarly vagabonds whom he had enlisted."

Perhaps the cowardice of Falstaff is too much insisted on, both by the English and the German critic. In Falstaff, cowardice is not so much a weakness as a principle,—less an innate quality than the dictate of wisdom and reflection. He has the sense of danger, but not the discomposure of fear. He retains his sagacity, quick-wittedness, and presence of mind—and invariably contrives to extricate himself from his dangers or embarrassments. With such a body as he is obliged to drag about him, what could courage avail him? He sees that military prowess would, on his part, be a ridiculous and hopeless affectation; the better part of valour, whatever it may be in other cases, he most potently believes in his own case must be discretion. Falstaff's cowardice is only proportionate to the danger, and so would every wise man's be, did not other feelings make him valiant. To such feelings—the dread of disgrace, the sense of honour, and the love of fame, he makes no pretension. It is the very characteristic of his nature to be totally insensible to them. He looks only to self preservation, and that he finds can be much more effectually secured by wit than weapons.

On the wit of Falstaff we find little in our German friends that is new or deserves quotation. We prefer extracting the following pleasing and discriminating passage from one of the essays of Mackenzie.*
" The imagination of Falstaff is wonderfully quick and creative, in the pictures of humour and the associations of wit. But the 'pregnancy of his wit,' according to his own phrase, ' is made a tapster;' and his fancy, how vivid soever, still subjects itself to the grossness of those sensual conceptions which are familiar to his mind. We are astonished at that art by which Shakspeare leads the powers of genius, imagination, and wisdom in captivity to this son of earth; it is as if, transported into the enchanted island in the Tempest, we saw the rebellion of Caliban successful, and the airy spirits of Prospero ministering to the brutality of his slave.

" Hence, perhaps, may be derived great part of that infinite amusement which succeeding audiences have always found from the representation of Falstaff. We have not only the enjoyment of those combinations and that contrast to which philosophers have ascribed the pleasure we derive from wit in general; but we have that singular combination and contrast which the gross, the sensual, and the brutish mind of Falstaff exhibits, when joined and compared with that admirable power of invention, of wit, and of humour, which his conversation perpetually displays.

" In the immortal work of Cervantes, we find a character with a remarkable mixture of wisdom and absurdity, which in one page excites our highest ridicule, and in the next is entitled to our highest respect. Don Quixote, like Falstaff, is endowed with excellent discernment, sagacity, and genius; but his good sense holds fief of his diseased imagination, of his overruling madness for the achievements of knight-errantry, for heroic valour, and heroic love. The ridicule in the character of Don Quixote consists in raising low and vulgar incidents, through the medium of his disordered fancy, to a rank of importance, dignity, and solemnity, to which in their nature they are the most opposite that can be imagined. With Falstaff it is nearly the reverse; the ridicule is produced by subjecting wisdom, honour, and other the most grave and dignified principles, to the control of grossness, buffoonery, and folly. It is like the pastime of a family masquerade, where the laughter is equally excited by dressing clowns as gentlemen, or gentlemen as clowns."

Almost all critics have concurred in condemning the needless harshness of Falstaff's treatment by the new king. Falstaff, agreeably surprised by the intelligence of the death of Henry IV., while engaged in a most serious carousal at Justice Shallow's, posts up to London, in the full persuasion of the truth of Pistol's assu-

---

* Lounger, No. 69.

rance. "Sweet Knight, thou art now one of the greatest men in the realm." He has even begun to lavish dignities upon his friends on the strength of his own immediate promotion; and to threaten his enemies with his vengeance. "Master Robert Shallow, choose what office thou wilt in the land — 'Tis thine."—"Let us take any man's horses,—the laws of England are at our commandment. Happy are they which have been my friends,—and woe to my Lord Chief Justice!" Such is the magic which the wit and *bonhommie* of Falstaff exercise over our minds, that we feel it like a personal stroke of injustice and cruelty, when in return for the enthusiastic and hearty, "God save thee, my sweet boy," with which he greets his old associate in the coronation procession, he receives the freezing answer,—not even addressed to himself,—" My Lord Chief Justice, speak to that vain man." And this at last is followed by a sermon on his vices, and a sentence of banishment for ten miles from the royal person. At first he cannot believe his misfortune real; "'tis but a colour." "I shall be sent for in private to him;" he endeavours, though obviously with some sinkings of heart, to persuade Shallow that his thousand pounds are safe : till the entrance of the Chief Justice, and his committal to the Fleet Prison—a committal for which there is no warrant in the speech of the King—banish the last remains of his delusion. It is singular, that Shakspeare should have introduced this needless and unmeaning piece of cruelty; for the real conduct of Henry, as described by Stowe, would have afforded materials for a noble scene, in which justice might have been done to the cause of morality without any injury to feeling. "After his coronation, King Henry called unto him all those young lords and gentlemen who were the followers of his young acts, *to every one of whom he gave rich gifts,* and then commanded that as many as would change their manners, as he intended to do, *should abide with him in his court; and to all that would persevere in their former like conversation,* he gave express commandment, upon

* Part 2. act ii, scene 4.

pain of their heads, never after that day to come into his presence."

In the First Part of Henry IV. Falstaff is the Atlas upon whose shoulders the support of almost the whole comic portion of the plot is laid ; for Bardolph is but the recipient and the butt of the wit of other men. He has no wit save in his "malmsey nose;" deprived of that feature, he would be less than nothing and vanity. Shakspeare himself, however, appears to have felt the demands on his humorous invention in the character of Falstaff to be too great and incessant; for, in the second part of the play, he divides the duties of the comic among several auxiliaries —Pistol, the Hostess, Shallow, and Silence—and the comic is more of the passive than the active kind. Pistol is a character of a more temporary and local cast than is usual with Shakspeare; a braggadocio, whose language is a patchwork of passages from plays in which the poet had been occasionally a performer. This language, originally adopted to aid his swaggering manner, has, in the end, become natural to him; he thinks, as well as he speaks, in fustian. It is in vain that Falstaff entreats him, when he brings the news of Henry's death, to "deliver them like a man of this world." The only answer he receives is,

" A foutra for the world and worldlings base ! I speak of Africa, and golden joys."

To many he appears, by dint of his " Ercles' vein," an absolute hero ; but Falstaff, with his usual sagacity, has detected his thorough cowardice, has long set him down as "a *tame cheater*," and actually dares (!) to draw his sword upon the boaster,* and drive him out of the Boar's Head with contempt. The Hostess is a still more carefully finished character, and more interesting, because less connected with the mere manners of the time. Hers is one of which the prototype can never entirely disappear. To her imagination, the knight whom she has known " these nine-and-twenty years, come peascod time," appears a very pattern of honour and a mirror of knighthood. It is evident she could never have mustered up courage to have him arrested, had her bill

amounted to two hundred nobles instead of one, but for his breach of promise of marriage, after that engagement of his on "Wednesday in Whitsun-week, upon the parcel-gilt goblet, sitting in the Dolphin chamber, the day the Prince broke his head for likening his father to a singing man of Windsor." And how instantaneously does the old respect and attachment revive when Falstaff reappears ! He has but to whisper in her ear, " As I am a gentleman," —a phrase which she has too good reason to say she has heard from him before,—and the demand for the hundred nobles is converted into a loan of ten pounds more, though "she pawn her gown for it."

There is something peculiarly delightful in the country scenes at Justice Shallow's. Every one, indeed, must have felt the pleasing effect produced in a novel or play, by carrying the hero out of the turbulence and bustle of the city into the calm and retirement of the country. Don Quixote never appears more delightful than when lecturing the goatherds on the golden age in the Sierra Morena, or assisting in the festivities of the marriage of Camacho; Gil Blas is never so great a favourite with us than when we see him with Scipio, in the pavilion at Lirias, sitting down to the first olla podrida which had been produced under the auspices of Master Joachim ; and Falstaff no where appears more imposing or agreeable than when accepting the hospitalities of the Justice's seat, and eating pippins and carraways in the orchard, in Gloucestershire. With what a consciousness of the favour he is conferring does he yield to the importunities of the Justice to stay and taste his short-legged hens, his joint of mutton, and "tiny little kickshaws." He accepts the homage which is paid him by Shallow and his cousin with the same lordly air with which he receives the sword of his captive, Sir John Colville of the Dale.

Shallow and Silence—what a pair ! We should hesitate at first to admit the possibility of a lower depth of commonplace imbecility than is exhibited in Shallow, till we see him fairly placed beside his cousin Silence; but in *his* company he absolutely appears sprightly or philosophical. Well might Falstaff observe of him, "I do see the bottom of Justice Shallow." He is the very pattern of self-conceited, characterless inanity. He even seems to think it necessary to translate his ideas so as to render them level to the capacity of others, for he generally repeats his observations three or four times over, varying the phrase in all ways. "I will not excuse you—you shall not be excused—excuses shall not be admitted—there is no excuse shall serve—you shall not be excused." With what senile triumph does he recal to the recollection of Silence the days when he was called mad Shallow, lusty Shallow, when, in company with Falstaff, little John Dort, and others, he had known the haunts of the *bona robas,* the swash-bucklers of the inns of court, and fought "with one Sampson Stockfish, a fruiterer, behind Gray's Inn !" Then his inimitable transitions from moralizing on death to the price of fat cattle—

" O, the mad days I have spent ! and to see how many of mine old acquaintances are dead !

" *Silence.* We shall all follow, cousin.

" *Shallow.* Certain—'tis certain : very sure, very sure ; death, as the Psalmist says, is certain to all—all shall die.—How a good yoke of bullocks at Stamford fair ?

" *Silence.* Truly, cousin, I was not there.

" *Shallow.* Death is certain.—Is old Double of your town living yet ? "

Silence, though an absolute *caput mortuum* when sober, has an undercurrent of gaiety in him too—when drunk. Wine seems to make little impression on Shallow, or rather, on the whole, he is more reasonable in his cups than otherwise. But Silence loses the only safeguard he had when sober, namely, the consciousness of his own utter imbecility : he becomes a roysterer, insists on inflicting on the company a variety of new songs, then subsides, like an expiring candle, into second childishness and mere oblivion, till Falstaff, who, amidst all the excitement which the news of Henry's death and his own prospects produces, has kept an eye on his new pupil in the art of toping, consigns him to that Euthanasia for which he was most fitted—" Carry Master Silence to bed."

4. BLACKWOOD'S MAGAZINE, 40 (1836), 139-148, 427-436. M/H No. 3305. By George Moir.

SHAKSPEARE IN GERMANY.

PART V.

SHAKSPEARE'S COMEDIES.—MIDSUMMER NIGHT'S DREAM.

A MIDSUMMER NIGHT'S DREAM! Had Shakspeare pondered for a lifetime to discover the most appropriate title for this enchanting play, he could have found none which so accurately and expressively embodies its poetical essence. The Winter's Tale is a happy title for the strange, gossip-like, and slenderly connected drama which paints the insane and meaningless jealousy of Leontes, the patient sufferings of Hermione, the loss and recognition of Perdita—her growth from infancy to womanhood in the course of the piece. It is such a "sad tale," fit for winter, as might be supposed to be told "by the dead and drowsy fire," to the accompaniment of a November wind without, and the deep bass of the neighbouring sea; a tale of changes and chances, in which stormy passions and wild incidents rage through the first three acts; quiet affections, and pastoral stillness reign over the fourth, when Time, in his swift passage, has slid o'er sixteen years; and the pathetic and soothing close of which, bearing upon it the impress of still wonder, "sends the hearers weeping to their beds," but with no unpleasing tears. But still more poetically and truly is the spirit of Midsummer Night's Dream expressed in its title. This is truly the shadow of a dream; such a dream as might be supposed to pass before the eye of a poet, in the glimmering twilight of a summer evening, when he abandoned himself passively to the wonder working influences of nature, when the most familiar objects of nature are seen changing their shapes to gigantic and mysterious forms, and in the dim perspective fairy beings sailing, "with the slow motion of a summer cloud," through an atmosphere steeped in moonlight and dew. Calderon's "Life a Dream" is the Tragedy of Dreams; a work of great imagination and power, but it is characterised by those depths of wayward gloom and painful gleams of wizard splendour, those uneasy bewildering transitions, that constant feeling of insecurity and anxiety, and restraint, which accompany the dreams of suffering and pain. We follow the changing fortunes of Sigismund from the desert to the dungeon—from the dungeon to the throne—from the throne again to the dungeon—as under the influence of a spell which we would fain shake off, but cannot. All is presented to us in sad or terrible colours. "What is life," asks the sceptical and unfortunate prince, and the answer is given in these profoundly pathetic and affecting lines :*

" What is life ? 'Tis but a madness.
What is life ? A wild illusion,
Fleeting shadow, fond delusion ;
Short-lived joy that ends in sadness,
Whose most steadfast substance seems
But the dream of other dreams."

Calderon's is like the dream of disease; in Shakspeare—"after life's fitful fever we sleep well," and enjoy the sweet and soothing dreams of youth and health. Here we meet but with the comedy of life, at most its griefs and anxieties so softened and shaded away by the lightness of the touch with which they are painted, the airy accompaniments by which they are surrounded, and the gentle irony which plays through and penetrates the whole, that they cease to affect us with any feeling of suffering. The whole passes before us like a vision in which a thousand feelings, some pleasant, some painful, have succeeded each other with such intricate variety of combination, that as a mixture of all colours produces white, so these emotions in their restless rotation produce only a gentle and pleasureable sensation, and we rise from them as awaking to the freshness of morning, with the confused but pleasing remembrances of sleep.

" If we shadows have offended,
Think but this and all is mended,
That you have but slumbered here
While these visions did appear ;
And this weak and idle theme
No more yielding than a dream.
Gentles, do us reprehend ;
If you pardon we will mend."

So says Puck in the Epilogue, and in these lines lies the secret by which the strange elements of this drama have been harmonized into a whole, of which the charm is felt to some extent by all, though in its full potency only by the imaginative. It is a poetic dream, and to be judged of by the laws of dreams. The strong painting of individual character we are not to expect in it; for it professes not to connect itself, save by the slenderest threads, with the world of reality; the beings who figure in it are shadows and symbols rather than real existences; and for the wildest intermixture of the actual with the supernatural; of the mythology of the classic times with the creations of romance—of the loves, griefs, mistakes, and jealousies of high born nobles and dames with the rudest mummeries of Athenian artisans, "hard handed men who never laboured in their minds till now;" for all this we must be prepared. A Warburton may object to this introduction of the Fairy mythology of Modern Europe among the fabulous events and superstitions of Ancient Greece; but Shakspeare sees no inconsistency or hostility between them, forming, as they do, mere decorations in a wondrous arabesque, which acknowledges not the laws of this waking and working world. He sees not why on this neutral territory or limbo of Dream, Diana may not, jointly with Titania, head the morrice-dancers of Elves upon the yellow moonlit sands; why Oberon may not hold divided empire in these Athenian woods with antique Pan; and piping Satyrs, with cleft heel, live in kindly fellowship with Robin Goodfellow, Monsieur Mustard-seed, and Cavalero Cobweb. As little can he perceive that the broadest farce, the most "palpable gross play" of rude mechanics, may not be made to blend with and cross the tangled web of love intrigue among the more tragic personages of the play, or that the fairy train may not mingle in and embroil the affairs of both. Nay, he scruples not to connect the mythology of the classic times with the most direct allusions to the court of the Maiden Queen, in the well-known passage in which Oberon describes the flower once milk white, now purple, since the bolt of Cupid had lighted on it, which had been harmlessly aimed against the bosom of the Fair Vestal throned by the West. In that region of pure imagination in which this piece hovers, he feels that there is room enough for them all; he throws himself with confidence on the sympathies of congenial imaginations, and not in vain.

But fully to apprehend its charm, the reader must be endowed with a deep sensibility to the magic of nature, particularly to the sweet and fragrant twilight of a summer evening, when

" All around to rest draws nigh,
Where the grain its ears is stooping,
The o'erwearied roses drooping
In the hush of night their eye.
And the restless cypress-trees
Slumber moveless in the breeze."

It is when the moonlight sleeps upon the bank, or glitters on the dew-sprinkled leaves and flowers—when the recollections of childhood coming thronging back into our memories—and all those fancies awake, which in this dim twilight find their cradle and home—when sounds as if of fairy harps and still small voices make themselves heard, which, in the noise and bustle of the garish day, have been unheard or unheeded—when all objects around, magnified by the haze of the balmy eve, begin to flit and waver, and change into fantastic and mysterious forms—when a gentle

---

* Que es la vida ? Un frenesi ;
Que es la vida ? Una ilusion
Una sombra una ficcion
Y el mayor bien es pequeno.
Que toda la vida es sueno
Y los suenos sueno son.
La Vida es Sueno Jorn. II.

weariness steals over our senses, and we find ourselves as it were between sleeping and waking, with dreams beginning already to wave before the half shut eye;—then it is alone that we can enter into the full spirit of this piece—then it is that we purpose in earnest with Theseus and Hippolyto to dream away the time, for a fortnight, "in nightly revels and new jollity"—then only do we fairly take a side in the quarrels of Oberon and Titania—we dance our ringlets with their fairy elves upon the beached margent of the sea—we follow the lovers in their mazy goblin-guided rambles through the wood where Hermia and Helena so oft "upon *faint* primrose beds were wont to lie"—we smile at the simple duty of the honest "rude mechanicals who work for bread upon Athenian stalls," and here with their hard hands, have so boldly made their first assay piece in the new and delicate craft of poetry—we even sympathise with the fate of the ill-starred but eloquent Pyramus, and his truly tragic and dignified companion Thisbe; nay, if stage-manager Quince should apply to us, would be ready to take a part in the piece ourselves, at the shortest notice, though it were nothing more important than that of Wall, or the Man in the Moon!

Every thing in this beautiful aerial drama indicates one of the early offspring of the poet's fancy. It was, in fact, so far as can be ascertained, one of his juvenile productions, being supposed by Malone (apparently on very satisfactory grounds) to have been produced so early as 1594; and immediately after, the comparatively immature productions of the Two Gentlemen of Verona (1591), The Comedy of Errors (1592), and Love's Labour Lost (also in 1594.) In the two former, indeed, little of Shakspeare's peculiar turn of mind is at all visible. The Two Gentlemen of Verona, borrowed in all its main outlines from Montemayor's Diana, a fashionable pastoral romance of the day, with which Shakspeare had apparently become acquainted through the early English translation of Thomas Wilson, is,

with the exception of the single comic character of Launce, a mere sketch, in which, no doubt, the germ of future poetical conceptions may be faintly traced, but from which assuredly no one, with any confidence, could have predicted the future high vocation of its author. Though containing some sweet and graceful poetry, and more distinguished than most of his later works by attention to the strict rules of versification (such as Valentine's description of his friend,* and his reflections on a solitary life †), it is undistinguished by much depth of passion or power of imagination, and, except in the comic outline to which we have alluded, by any detailed or discriminating portraiture of character. In the whole play, in truth, we perceive the hesitating and still imperfect artist, who has laid his hand somewhat bewildered upon the strings of the human heart, is afraid to press them with energy, and recoils with apprehension even from the sounds himself has made. No great advance is perceptible in the Comedy of Errors. By what means Shakspeare became acquainted with the Menæchmi of Plautus, from which, with slender variations, the Comedy of Errors is undoubtedly taken, is still a question which, as Sir Thomas Brown says of the "Song the Siren's Sung, might admit of a wide solution," since the only English translation which is known to have existed of the play, bearing on the titlepage the initials W. W., seems to have appeared in 1595, three years subsequent to the time at which Malone supposes the comedy of Errors to have been first represented. But, from whatever quarter the plot came to him, it cannot be said to have improved in his hands. The improbabilities of the plot are increased beyond endurance, and certainly with no corresponding increase of comic effect, by the multiplication of resemblances, which arises from furnishing the twin-brothers with servants who are also twin-brothers, and thus over complicating a plot already sufficiently complex and difficult to follow. In fact, the taste of Shakspeare, in this rudi-

mental period of his dramatic apprenticeship, seems decidedly to have been a false one. He appears to have aimed at producing effect, not by that simplicity of means which is the result of consummate knowledge and command of our resources, and which he afterwards attained in such rare perfection, but by the multiplication of incidents, the accumulation of comic embarrassments, and a taste closely analogous to the principles of the Spanish school of his great contemporary, Lope de Vega.* A tinge of this remaining fondness for intricacy of plot, and for the dramatic suspense which is so easily excited and so cheaply maintained by that mazy intermixture or cross-fire of affections which is so frequent on the Spanish stage, is still perhaps sufficiently perceptible even in the Midsummer Night's Dream; but no one can fail to see that here an immense advance has been made; that a gulf lies between it and its predecessors, which only the agency of genius, working, as it always does, secretly and invisibly, could bridge over; that here for the first time the true poet comes before us in no questionable shape; and that while his youthful mind still delights to dwell rather in regions of pure fancy than to grapple with and to elevate into poetry the conditions of this our actual existence, it no longer submits to be the imitator of others, but gives room and verge for its creative powers in an airy series of pictures hanging in a half-ideal atmosphere, yet warm with all the purple light of love, and bright with the hues of innocence and the romance of youth.

It must be admitted, that, as a specimen of this drama of intrigue, where the whole plot is first artificially complicated, and then naturally and gracefully unwound, nothing, even in the best dramas of Calderon, surpasses that portion of the plot of our own Shakspeare's Midsummer Night's Dream, which depicts the labyrinthine loves of Lysander, Demetrius, Hermia, and Helena. It has all the apparent confusion, yet real and artful arrangement of a dance, in which the parties

are constantly changing partners, but always according to certain laws, by means of which we are assured that each will in the end be restored to the point from which they set out. They only "dance the hayes" for a time through the mazes of love, where the ballroom is a moonlight forest, and Puck acts as master of the ceremonies, to fall back again with a grace into the first position. We feel assured, however puzzling the imbroglio at first may seem, that, in the end, as Puck rather unceremoniously expresses it, "The man shall have his mare again, and all shall go well." Let us glance then at the successive figures of the dance.

Two Athenian maidens—Helena, tall and fair—Hermia, little, and a brunette, who have grown together,

" Like to a double cherry seeming parted,
But yet a union in partition,
Two lovely berries moulded on one stem,
So with two seeming bodies, but one heart,"

have yielded to the power of love. Helena loves Demetrius—Hermia Lysander, and they are beloved in turn. This is the picture which the parties present at the outset—two pairs, two reciprocal attachments. But Demetrius is fickle; he becomes untrue to the fair Helena; his heart has suddenly become entangled by the duskier charms of Hermia, and his wooing is favoured by her father. Thus the two reciprocal attachments are suddenly converted into two onesided, and one reciprocal. Helena loves Demetrius as before—Demetrius loves Hermia; Hermia loves Lysander, who loves her again, but to whose love the father is opposed. This is the second movement of the ballet. Hermia and Lysander, in order to evade "the sharp Athenian law," resolve to fly the capital. Helena betrays their intended flight to Demetrius, in hopes by this means to win back his favour; he follows them into "the wood a league beyond the town," and thither he in turn is followed by Helena. This wood has been selected by Oberon as the place of punishment of Titania for her refusal to deliver

---

* Act ii. sc. 4.　　† Act v. sc. 4.　　　　　　* Lope was born in 1562; Shakspeare within two years after, in 1564.

up her Indian boy to be his hench-man; he witnesses the coldness and cruelty with which Demetrius, intent only on the pursuit of Hermia, re-pulses the attachment of Helena; and in pity he resolves to call in the aid of " Love in idleness " to restore him to his former state of feeling.

" That herb, whose juice on sleeping eye-
lids laid,
Will make or man or woman madly doat
Upon the next live creature that it sees."

He directs Puck to anoint the eyes of the disdainful Demetrius with this balsam, that so, on awakening, Helena, who lies wearied and travel-worn by his side in the haunted fo-rest, may be the first object that presents itself to his eyes. Puck stumbling first upon Lysander and Hermia, and thinking he has found the man, "by the Athenian garments he hath on," drops the charm upon his eyes instead of those of De-metrius. Unfortunately the first glances of Lysander on awakening, fall on Helena, who, in the pursuit of Demetrius, has wandered to the spot where Lysander and Hermia had taken shelter; and now the two original reciprocal attachments are suddenly converted in the third stage into four unrequited ones; Helena loves Demetrius, Deme-trius Hermia — Hermia Lysander, Lysander Helena. Oberon chides Puck for his carelessness, and by an application of the charm to the eyes of Demetrius, for whom it was first intended, restores him to his first attachment to Helena. Thus then we have again two unrequited and one reciprocal attachment, yet with a difference from the second figure of this mazy dance; for now Hermia loves Lysander, Lysander Helena, and Helena Demetrius, by whom she is again beloved. As in a former figure of the dance, both the gentlemen were by the side of Hermia, while Helena stood alone; so now both stand by the side of Helena, and Hermia is forsaken. The application of a counter charm, through the medium of Puck, to the eyes of the enchanted Lysander, an herb

" That takes from thence all error with
his might,
And makes his eyeballs roll with wonted
sight,"

restores every thing with the most graceful and easy *dénouement* to its former state—the dance of life, not of death, is completed; and, again, as at the outset—Helena loves De-metrius, Hermia Lysander, and each is beloved in turn.

The movements of this eccentric love-dance take place round a more stationary group of buffo perform-ers of the most singular descrip-tion. Five common Athenian arti-sans, who have determined to dis-tinguish themselves by an exhibi-tion of private theatricals in honour of the wedding-day of Theseus with the Amazon queen, have chosen for their place of rehearsal the shades of the same wood, through the mazes of which these enamoured couples are thus pursuing each other at cross-purposes, and where the fairy monarch and his queen have so lately met and parted in anger. The elves now begin to take a part in the performance. Puck damns the piece, and disperses the players, by sud-denly investing the chief actor with an ass's head. The first glances of Titania, as she awakes under the in-fluence of the charm of Oberon's purple flower, fall upon the dis-guised Bottom, and he becomes the object of an insane adoration. With what consummate grace is the picture here disposed! In the centre sits Titania, sticking musk roses in the sleek smooth head and kissing the large ears of Bottom; Cobweb, Peas-blossom, Moth, Mustard-seed, nodding to him and doing him cour-tesies; and round this central fairy masque, flitting in alternate succes-sion, the comic quadrille of Quince, Snug, Snout, and Starveling seeking their lost companion through the wood; or the grave quadrille of the enamoured lovers, now seeking, now shunning each other, in most artifi-cial, most admired disorder. When these scattered and tangled threads of intrigue are all drawn to a point on the festival of Theseus' nuptials, the piece concludes with a triple marriage and with the broadest and boldest scenes of buffoonery—scenes in which the poet seems to have pa-rodied, by anticipation, some of the most touching and tragic situations in his own Romeo and Juliet, a play which appeared shortly afterwards, and the germ of which probably had

already begun to be developed in his mind. It is worthy of observa-tion, that Shakspeare does not allow the impression of broad parody to be the last feeling which he leaves upon the mind. He returns again for a moment into the key of the supernatural. When the iron tongue of midnight has told twelve, and sleep has descended equally upon the cottage of the artisan and the palace of the Duke, Oberon with his fairy train comes once more stealing in, now reconciled to Titania, to bless the bride-bed of the lovers—

" That the issue, there create,
Ever may be fortunate,
So shall all the couples three
Ever true and loving be :
And the blots of Nature's hand
Shall not in their issue stand ;
Never mole, hare-lip, nor scar,
Nor mark prodigious, such as are
Despised in nativity,
Shall upon their children be.—
With this field-dew consecrate,
Every fairy take his gate ;
And each several chamber bless,
Through this palace with sweet peace :
E'er shall it in safety rest,
And the owner of it blest.
   Trip away ;
   Make no stay ;
Meet me all by break of day."

Thus the whole fades and flies away like a lovely dream with the ap-proach of morning—a dream so airy, so ethereal in its more elevated pa-geants—so cheerful, so sunny in its humorous features, that, on waking from it, we almost "cry to sleep again."

It is no uncommon fault, even of distinguished poets, that having cre-ated some one striking conception of character, or exhibited some poe-tical aspect of life with success, they are led to repeat the same idea over and over, with merely some slight difference of external form and or-nament. Were it necessary to re-fer to examples in support of this remark, the literature of our own day would furnish us with instances in abundance. Shakspeare alone, such is the extent of his poetical re-sources, and his prodigality in their use, can never be said to have re-peated himself in any one of his con-

ceptions of character, or of the rela-tions of life. Thus we have but one Hamlet, one Lear, one Brutus, one Othello, one Desdemona, one Imo-gen, one Cordelia; they come but for a moment, perform their part, and disappear for ever to make way for new forms of character placed amidst other scenes, and illustrating some new truth in our complicated and mysterious nature. This obser-vation is not less applicable to this fairy melodrame. Calderon, not content with once painting the dream of life in lurid colours in his *Vida es Sueno*, repeats the same theme in his *Todo es verdad y todo Mentira* * in a weaker and more cloudy shape. Who can doubt that Shakspeare might with ease have furnished us with many visions as enchanting as this Midsummer Night's Dream? But beautiful as its texture was, Shak-speare felt that in this world we had too much to do with realities to bestow an undue portion of atten-tion upon airy visions. He has left us as a legacy one glimpse into the world of dreams which yet remains without its fellow; but the cloud-land in which the youth dwelt is no home for the matured man,—" He twitches his mantle blue," and with the morrow seeks " fresh fields and pastures new."

Turning from the intrigue of the piece to the characters, we have al-ready said, that strong or minute de-velopement of character would have been altogether inconsistent with the light and gossamer texture of the play. To have attempted to in-corporate the strong play of passion, or the peculiar individuality of cha-racter or humour, with a fable so wild, and lying so totally beyond the confines of the visible diurnal sphere, would have been like building an edifice of marble on the unsubstan-tial basis of an evening cloud. All the more serious characters, there-fore, are but sketches. Between Lysander and Demetrius scarcely any distinction is to be traced. In Theseus we see nothing but an im-posing outside, a love for hunting, and a taste for puns and quibbles, for which the dramatic representation of the Athenian operatives affords

---

* The source from which Corneille borrowed his Heraclius.

17

ample scope. Somewhat more of discrimination is shown in the characters of Hermia and Helena; the mildness of the tall beauty, the vivacity and somewhat shrewish temper of the little brunette, qualities of which her rival does not fail to remind her in their encounter in the wood,* are brought out with a few touches of a light pencil, but so as quite sufficiently to paint to the mind's eye the difference of their possessors. Though no strong feeling of anxiety or suffering is created by the crosses to which the lovers are subjected; though we follow their footsteps with a secret assurance, that all these misconceptions and mislikings, these instances of fickleness, these words of reproach, these acts of ungentleness, are but the perplexing dream of a night, and to disappear with the to-morrow, there is yet a gentle air of softened earnestness and qualified reality spread over them sufficient to create a mild interest in their fate. All the pensive and desponding thoughts, for instance, which cloud and overshadow young and loving hearts, when they first begin to encounter difficulties, and to awake to the conviction that love, so far from being omnipotent, is in this life checked or overborne by a thousand contingencies and calamities, are summed up with the most pensive and pathetic beauty in those lines of Lysander's, which who that has read them can forget?

" Ah me ! for aught that ever I could
    read,
Could ever hear by tale or history,
The course of true love never did run
    smooth.
But either it was different in blood,
Or else misgrafed in respect of years,
Or else it stood upon the choice of friends;
Or, if there were a sympathy in choice,
War, death, or sickness did lay siege to it,
Making it momentary as a sound,
Swift as a shadow, short as any dream ;
Brief as the lightning in the collied night,
That, in a spleen, unfolds both heaven and
    earth,
And ere a man hath power to say—behold !
The jaws of darkness do devour it up :
So quick bright things come to confusion ! "

" So fares it with the lovely in this world," says Schiller ; borrowing the thought, and almost the words of our own Shakspeare, and placing them in the mouth of the bereaved daughter of Wallenstein, when she learns the vanishing of all her dreams of hope ; and that the youthful hero, who, on the threshold of life,

" Had hailed her like an angel newly
    lighted,
When first she crossed it with a maiden
    fear,"

has been trampled to death under the hard hoofs of horses in the skirmish at Neustadt, and now lies a cold and lifeless heap in his laurel covered coffin in the cloister of St Catherine.

And now to glance at the supernatural beings of the piece, whose tiny passions and jealousies are made to mingle with the love passages of mortals. Horn's remarks on this subject are, on the whole, so good, that, though the passage is a long one, and in some parts a little fantastic (as in the best he is), we hope it will be found no unpleasant reading.

" The lovers," says he,† " have to contend not only with the severe father Ægeus, with the warlike Duke Theseus, and with the charm of love itself, but even the world of spirits mingles in the fray—no *ghostly* world of spirits, but a gay, fluttering race of beings, clothed with tenderest flesh and bone, which, compassionating the sufferings of love, would fain help the sufferers, but who with all good intentions act, in a manner, half blindly, so that for a time their interference only makes the evil worse. For this, indeed, Oberon the Elfin monarch is himself in a great measure answerable, since he ought never to have intrusted the management of these tender love affairs to the joyous and recklesss spirit Puck. No better agent could be found, where the task is but to clap an ass's head upon Bottom ; but his talent fails him when he is called on to distinguish a loving from an unloving Athenian youth. This may no doubt be said for Oberon, that he is at that moment too much occupied with his own concerns to be able to do more than to send assistance, and every one knows what comes of it, when the servant does the master's business.

" These private concerns of the Elfin King, are not, it is true, very important. He has had a quarrel with his wife, the fair Titania, because she will not surrender to him the son of a deceased Indian princess, her friend, to be his henchman. For the boy himself he cares not much, for he calls him 'a little *changeling* boy,' but he has commanded, and he has been disobeyed : and the very thought that Titania can refuse obedience in any thing, is enough to occasion him annoyance. Through this misunderstanding between the royal pair, blight and distemperature have fallen on wood and plain, on ploughman and ox.

————'The green corn
Hath rotted ere his youth attained a beard,
The fold stands empty in the drowned field,
The crows are fatted with the murrain
    flock.'

" The very seasons seem to have altered.

—— ——'Hoary-headed frosts
Fall in the fresh lap of the crimson rose,
And on old Hyem's chin and icy crown,
An odorous chaplet of sweet summer
    buds
Is as in mockery set. The spring, the
    summer,
The childing autumn, angry winter
    change
Their wonted liveries, and the mazed
    world,
By their increase, now knows not which
    is which.
And this same progeny of evils comes
From their debate, from their dissension.'

To all this Titania could put an end : she has but to surrender her Indian *protegé* ; but that point cannot be so easily yielded ; and, in truth, if the boy resembles his mother, of whose wild gambols the Queen presents so picturesque a sketch,* it must be admitted it must have gone hard with her to part with so interesting a page. In any view the object of the strife seems not altogether unworthy of the importance attached to him, and the strife itself is so steeped in all the colours of poetry, that we look on as witnesses with delight.

"But is not the punishment to which the poor Elfin Queen is subjected for her denial something too harsh ? Is it not too bad to be condemned to fall in love with an unlicked cub, who, to make the matter worse, believes himself to be witty ? So it may appear, and yet it is not so. Her attachment to him is but an evil dream, —the source of infinite delight to us—the strangest, in fact, which is dreamt in all this visionary drama ; and to such dreams as a punishment the fairest and the most amiable, so soon as they abandon their sex's best ornament, 'loving obedience,' are exposed. Fortunately they are momentary ; and after the feeling of annoyance that one should ever have had such a dream, follows the perception of its comic features, and the ridicule of one's self.

" In order, however, fully to enjoy this Oberon and Titania, this Puck, Mustard-seed, Pease-blossom, Cobweb, and so forth, some things must first be put upon their right footing. It would seem that an overweening fondness for 'the gods of Greece,' which for a time was regarded as an indispensable poetical accompaniment, had somewhat impaired our knowledge and our love of our own modern and domestic mythology. We leave these Grecian deities and demi-gods in all their beauty and attraction, in all their majesty of action and repose—we leave them, we say, in all honour ; but we ask whether they have not found fit substitutes among ourselves, and we answer our own question in the affirmative. Learn only to know those Elves and Erles, those Undines and Gnomes—those spirits of fire and air—those nut-brown maidens, who, concealed in thickets, lure on the hunter—those alps and goblins, those nixies and wood-nymphs, which appear in so many of our early heroic or later popular songs, and you will be disposed to moderate your lamentations over the vanished Eldorado of Grecian fable. All of us have indeed heard of these, but most with but half an ear, for this laboriously learned mythology of Greece had anticipated them, and had left too

---

* Your hands than mine are quicker for a fray—
My legs are longer though to run away.—*Act* iii. *Scene* 2.
† Vol. iv. p. 202.

* In the passage in act ii. scene 2 :

" His mother was a vot'ress of my order,
And in the spiced Indian air by night
Full often hath she gossipped by my side," &c.

little room for them in the memory and the imagination. And yet it needed only such poems as the Erlking and the Fisher,* to open to us at once a prospect into the treasures of this rich and romantic world.

" It happens, therefore, often enough that we form a false conception as to the true poetic character of many of these beings, airy and fantastic indeed, but marked by a sufficiently clear and palpable individuality. We Germans in particular are apt to be led astray by that craving for 'the elevated,' which we everywhere aim at, and with which we find it so difficult to dispense. And even if we do dispense with this supposed requisite, we either draw the outlines of their characters too close and narrow, or leave them misty and undefined. Thus, for example, our conception of the fairies has long been that of mere ethereal beings leading the moonlight dance, and to whom nothing is permitted beyond the most delicate raillery, and the sweetest and most refined language. We forget that a sphere so narrow as this to which we attempt to confine them, must soon become monotonous and wearisome both to them and to ourselves. Their real sphere must be a wider one; they dance indeed, they teaze mortals with their tiny and playful tricks, but their power extends farther; their realm is the whole world of dreams, and in particular, that wide world of dreams inspired by passion and sense, which acknowledges no other laws but that of fancy, and to which Oberon himself, not less than his subaltern spirits, owes allegiance."

The confidence of Shakspeare in the inherent and indestructibly poetical character of this melodrama (for such in the higher and better sense of the term it is), is shown by the introduction of what is commonly considered an interlude, but which in truth is quite as much an essential part of the piece as the fairy scenes or the cross purposes of the lovers, namely, the low comedy of the burlesque drama represented by the Athenian artisans. Poetry and theatricals being in this piping time of marriages and festivity the order of the day, the taste has spread like a fancy for reform, vote by ballot,

or any other popular epidemic, to the lowest classes; and moved by love of fame and the hope of " sixpence a-day for life"—(for Flute protests that the Duke would have deserved hanging if he had paid Pyramus with less)—they have boldly ventured into the tragic field : *In properties* they feel they are rather scanty : for, their scenery, they candidly confess, they must borrow from the great storehouse of mother Nature—to present Moonshine, they " must leave a casement of the great chamber window where they play open;" but to balance this, they have boundless confidence in themselves and in the indulgence of the audience. A man with some roughcast about him shall present Wall, even the difficult problem of depicting the Man in the Moon is in their eyes (for we have no doubt they thoroughly despised, if they heard them, the hypercritical objections of Theseus and Demetrius) most satisfactory solved. Most honest painstaking creatures they seem to be; they set about this as about any other bespoken piece of work wherein the credit of their craft was concerned, less indeed from pure love than from example, but with a magnanimous feeling, as some of our own cross-legged *artists* observed in a late crisis, when a collision took place with their journeymen, that the eyes of the whole world were upon them. It is this honest downright simplicity in all their proceedings which makes us annoyed, in the course of the final representation, by the sneers and sarcasms of Demetrius, who, lolling at his ease in his cushioned chair, smiles superior at what had cost those hard-working artists the hardest of all labour—that of the brain. It is thus that we feel almost mortified by the dry observation of Hippolyta—" This is the silliest stuff that ever I heard;" and recomforted by the answer of Theseus—" The best in this kind are but shadows; and the worst are no worse if imagination mend them." How beautifully, how unobtrusively does Shakspeare turn the homeliest circumstance of this sort into the subject of some true and touching reflection. Theseus judges of this caricature tragedy not by the result, but by the

intention ; he seems to feel by anticipation the truth of Dr Johnson's observation, that no one who tenders his all, be it ever so insignificant, likes to have it rejected, and so he accepts with courtly kindness the burlesque offering of the poor operatives in the complimentary sense in which it was intended. He pays no heed to the protestations of Philostrate, that " the play is nothing—nothing in the world ! " but with the good feeling of a man acknowledging the kindness of his fellow-men, answers :—

" I will hear that play :
For never any thing can be amiss,
When simpleness and duty tender it.
And what poor duty cannot do,
Noble respect takes it in might, not merit—
Love, therefore, and tongue-tied simplicity,
In least speak most to my capacity."

Of the comic characters who are introduced into this wild masque, Bottom is the one who is sketched (for, after all, it is but a sketch) with the most careful outline. He has all the swagger of an accomplished prentice—is obviously a knowing fellow in the shops and streets of Athens—if he has not heard the chimes at midnight, he has seen the sun rise often enough upon his potations—is a favourite with the Hetairæ of the Piræus, as Shallow was with the bona-robas of the Strand; and, presuming upon his admitted superiority as a wit and a man about town, is desirous to engross, if possible, all the available parts of the drama at once. Not content with *leading* in the part of Pyramus, he would fain have the lion's *share* also. He insists on doubling it, even with that part, to the great discomfiture of poor Snug, to whom, as a sort of outcast, which no other person was likely to wish for or even accept, the part of the lion had been assigned; and who, with a commendable distrust of his own powers, had at first moved the previous question, whether the lion's part were written, as he was slow of study, and who, having received the satisfactory answer that it might be performed *extempore*, as it was " nothing but roaring," has at last, " pressed by hunger and

desire of friends," been on the point of accepting the part. Bottom evidently throughout considers himself as the star of the company. He sets at nought the authority of Quince, who, in the first instance, had taken upon himself, we know not on what qualification, the important duties of stage-manager, but who is soon taught, like every other manager, the thousand natural ills that flesh is heir to in the person of him who legislates for others, and the impossibility of adjusting the role of the " premier amoureux " to his own satisfaction, where he has to deal with an amateur performer. This easy self-confidence and perfect self-satisfaction is still more strikingly visible after his metamorphosis. Poor Quince, Snout, Flute, or Starveling would have given way entirely under the unexpected circumstance of becoming all at once the favoured minion of the Fairy Queen. Not so Bottom : never did weaver more gracefully or naturally reconcile himself to his fate. With as much ease as Don Quixote persuaded himself that he was the cynosure of the eyes, not only of Altisidora, but of some twenty others beside, does the gracious Bottom seriously incline to accept the homage of Titania and her attendant spirits. He accepts with the most easy indifference the caresses of the Elfin Queen—assigns to Peas-blossom the high office of scratching his head—grants to Cobweb letters of marque against the red-hipped humble-bees —then despatches Monsieur Cobweb to assist Peas-blossom in his difficult commission—and concludes by expressing the strongest desire towards a bottle of good hay— " Sweet hay, that hath no fellow." The moral of all which appears to be this, that a mixture of sheer stupidity and vanity will carry the possessor comfortably through all failures and difficulties.

A genuine " Bully Bottom," who has been " translated," as Quince has it, cares not for such rubs ; he simply turns upon his side, and goes to sleep, exclaiming,—" Let none of your people stir me ; I have an exposition of sleep come upon me."

---

* Two beautiful and well-known ballads of Goethe.

4. continued

SHAKSPEARE IN GERMANY.—PART THE LAST.

SHAKSPEARE'S COMEDIES.—THE MERCHANT OF VENICE.

SHAKSPEARE was the first who gave to comedy its most elevated and (strange as the expression may appear) its most serious character. What was the conception of comedy before his time, as it appears in Aristophanes, in Menander, and Terence, or in the few rude works of his predecessors on the English stage—in Gammer Gurton's Needle, for instance, where the whole plot relates merely to the loss of a needle with which an old woman was mending an ignorant countryman's nether raiment, and which is afterwards detected in most inconvenient approximation to the seat of honour of the proprietor of the apparel? or in the farcical extravagances of Ralph Royster Doyster?* It appears simply as a *parody* of tragedy; the antipodes of every thing earnest, exalted, or agitating; a gallery of human absurdities, vanities, and misconceptions; of desires and passions seemingly born of nothing, and ending in nothing; an accumulation, in short, of every thing which could display the perfect meanness and nothingness of existence, and the momentary and delusive character of "all this world is proud of." A painful picture—and neither morally nor poetically a true one. As the ideal of tragedy does not consist in a collection of all the virtuous and lofty emotions, so neither does that of comedy consist in an exclusive and one-sided exhibition of the vices and animal propensities of our nature. The elements are so mixed in us, that he who represents man truly, cannot admit this total separation of the earthly and the divine. There can be no pure and unmixed tragedy or comedy, if by tragedy be exclusively understood an ideal of seriousness and loftiness, and by comedy an ideal of the ludicrous and the low. Yet it may be convenient for purposes of art to use these terms, as indicating the preponderance of the one ele-

ment or the other in the picture, and showing the point of view in which the poet has chosen for the time to place himself, and according to which the one or the other class of emotions are brought most prominently forward. In this sense only does Shakspeare seem to understand these terms. With his deepest tragedies, comedy mingles; and through almost all his comedies, a vein of earnestness, more or less perceptible according to the nature of the play and the object in view, may be seen to run like a deep stream among flowers.

The comedies of Shakspeare differ not, then, from his tragedies in the exclusion of tragic matter; but in the manner in which that matter is handled. While in his tragedies the depth, earnestness, and apparent steadfastness and permanency of the passions represented, the high hopes which are awakened, the concentration of means upon an end, and the ultimate failure of human labours and struggles, excite, during the progress of the piece, a lofty feeling of the energy of human nature, and a profound but not painful sympathy with the catastrophe which sends the hearers weeping to their beds;—in the comedies, on the contrary, these passions are represented as transitory and evanescent, liable to be turned aside or converted into their opposites by a thousand trifles; chance and caprice are seen guiding the current of affairs rather than counsel; the fool detects the plot which escaped the notice of the wise man; the sagest resolves of wisdom and philosophy are seen to vanish at the dictates of desire and opportunity; the points of resemblance which connect all men are dwelt upon, as in tragedy the points of distinction which elevate uncommon over common natures; and the result is a feeling of quiet irony, which vents itself not

in loud Aristophanic laughter, but in still smiles not unallied to tears.

The tendency of the youthful poet is towards the complete separation of the tragic from the comic. He is unwilling to sully the grandeur of solemn tragedy by any intermixture of less noble elements. He loves to look upon human resolutions and passions, as stamped with an impression of eternity on the mind; on love, friendship, devotion, duty, as pure and unmingled with any stain of selfishness, and as triumphant over circumstances. Or if in a different mood, and under the influence of disappointed experience, he casts his eye over human life, he is likely to run into the opposite extreme; to regard this whole existence as a troubled dream, and to place his whole philosophy in extracting matter for mirth out of its absurd or unexpected combinations.

This is sufficiently visible in the plays of Shakspeare. In the earliest of his tragedies, Romeo and Juliet, how little of a comic character is allowed to delay the rapid and tragic movement of the scene. Less even than is admitted beside the melancholy of Hamlet, the madness of Lear, or the remorse of Macbeth. This play is the true reflection of the poet's spirit in its first prime, when it feels as if by its own strength it could make or unmake a world, or shape the conditions of the world, that is, according to its longings. So, in the same way, in Shakspeare's earliest comedies, human nature is viewed in a purely ludicrous light, and life as a mere pageant, diversified by droll rencontres, absurd misconceptions, and bewildering enigmas, without any stay of noble or durable feeling. To this period belong the perplexities of the Comedy of Errors, where the characters seem the puppets of accident, sent into the world apparently for no other purpose than to confound and to be confounded; the gay capriccio of Love's Labour Lost, with its epigrammatic points and cutting satire against the wise saws and goodly resolutions of scholars, and the mock dignity of melancholy and gentlemanlike cavaliers; the airy masque of Midsummer Night's Dream, in which this world, with all which it inherit, appears avowedly but as a vision; the levity of the

Two Gentlemen of Verona, where love and friendship seem to come and go, and return like summer clouds at the breath of accident, leaving on the mind scarcely any impression of reality; and the broad coarse satire of The Taming of the Shrew, written as if to disenchant love of all its graces and courtesies, and to instal force in the seat of affection.

But juster and more comprehensive views of the true field and scope of comedy soon appear to have replaced these earlier, and, we cannot help thinking, defective notions of its character. In As You Like It, Much Ado about Nothing, Twelfth Night, and The Merchant of Venice, though the whole result is truly comic, awakening not the feeling of sorrow, but of that chastened irony to which we have alluded; there is no want of an intermixture of higher principle to leaven and support the mass of meaner motives and desires, nor of steadiness of feeling amidst the shifting accidents of life. The fresh breath of youthful love and ancient fidelity in As You Like It; the suddenness, the all confiding influence of passion in Twelfth Night; the offended dignity of maiden innocence in Much Ado about Nothing; the strength of friendship unto death in the Merchant of Venice;—these are the fixed centres of earnest emotion, round which the shifting comic panorama of human life revolves in so many smiling and smile-exciting aspects — these give meaning, importance, and dignity to what were otherwise unsubstantial or farcical. Yet they form, it will be observed, the background only to the piece; they do not obtrude themselves; they appear rather as sentiments than as passions. Compare the love of Orlando with that of Romeo. The former is a still delight, a feeling which brightens existence to him, but interferes not with his plans. He could enjoy the woodland freedom of the forest of Ardennes with the Duke and old Adam, though " heavenly Rosalind" had still adorned the court of the usurper Frederick. He has no " lean cheek," as Rosalind tells him, —no " blue eye and sunken "—he is still " rather *point de vice* in his accoutrements, as being himself more

---

* Though Gammer Gurton's Needle has generally been considered as the earliest regular English comedy which has come down to us, it would rather appear from Mr Collier's enquiries, that Ralph Royster Doyster, supposed to have been written by Nicholas Rudall about 1550, is entitled to that distinction.

4. continued

than seeming the lover of any other."
His attachment is serious, but the
seriousness rises out of, and sinks
again gracefully back into, the comic.
It is presented only in bas relief.
The fiery passion of a Romeo, to
whom

" There is no world beyond Verona's
walls
But Purgatory—torture—hell itself "—

could have found no place beside
the calmly contemplative spirit and
pastoral melancholy of this enchanting comedy. It would have been a
harsh discord among the soft echoes
of those woods. So in the same
way love forms the tragic basis of
Twelfth Night; but a love quite as
much of the fancy as the heart, or
springing up so unaccountably, that
we regard it more as the result of
the influence of a magic charm than
as a feeling naturally awakened.
Much as the melancholy Duke
speaks of his love, we believe he
loves the music, which was its food,
better; and we feel from the first
but little surprise that this visionary
attachment is so lightly diverted at
last to another object—while the
suddenness with which the dignified
and mourning Olivia yields to her
passion, with the impossibility of its
requital, divest her love, fervid as
it is represented, of any too tragic
character, and give to it that fantastic
and semi-comic character which
brings it into harmony with the frolics of Sir Toby, and the follies of
an Aguecheek or a Malvolio.

Of all the plays of Shakspeare,
however, that in which he has most
happily and harmoniously combined
all the elements of the higher comedy,
is the Merchant of Venice. The
main incident, the fate of the royal
merchant Antonio, and the bargain
for the pound of flesh, is in itself
completely tragical, but it is so surrounded with other accessaries, and
our confidence in a happy solution
of the difficulty so skilfully excited
and maintained, that it loses its tragic and agitating character, and
merely gives interest and elevation
to the more familiar incidents of the
piece. Dryden used to boast of the
dramatic tact with which he had
managed to combine the two plots
of his Spanish Friar. But here three
plots are combined far more skilfully

and naturally; and without this union
the comic character of the play could
hardly have been preserved. The
relation of Antonio to Shylock, as
we have said, borders on the tragical;
and in fact, in the judgment-scene,
did we not feel certain that the invention of Portia will triumph over
the malignity of the Jew, the situation would be far too agitating for
comedy. As it is, we feel at once
that some gradations are necessary
to let us down naturally to the level
of the comic, and to bear on the
mind that feeling of quiet cheerfulness which it is the aim of comedy
to produce.

The first of these gradations is afforded by the love of Portia and
Bassanio. Here we are withdrawn
from the fierce and tragic reality
of the bond into the region of romance. Every thing in this portion
of the piece is, particularly in
the commencement, airy, fantastic,
magical. Belmont is like a fairy
palace, tenanted by some spell-
bound princess, whom thronging
adventurers flock to liberate. The
strange condition attached to the
hand of the heiress by the solution of a riddle; the locked caskets with their quaint inscriptions;
the foreign Princes of Morocco and
Arragon, who come to try the adventure, powerfully excite the imagination, while they give repose to
the feelings. Even when the two
lovers stand trembling on the
brink of that choice which is to
unite or separate them for ever,
the soft music which precedes his
choice, the wild fairy-like chant,
" Tell me where is fancy bred," give
a dream-like character to the scene,
and restrain our interest and suspense within the boundaries of the
pleasing. From the higher elevation
of the attachment of Bassanio and
Portia, and the half-magic machinery by which their fates are united,
we descend a step lower, to the level
of common life in the third plot of
Lorenzo and Jessica. Here common beings are united by common
means. A sudden attachment of a
young and good-natured Venetian,
to a pretty, laughter-loving, thoughtless Jewess; a love in which levity
and accident mingle much more
than strong feeling or imagination;
a marriage effected by the simple

medium of an elopement; the practical jokes of a roguish servant
against his poor high gravel-blind
father; all these bring us back to ordinary life and to the levity and familiarity of the comic, so that, as
Bassanio says—
" Every something being blent together,
Turns to a wild of nothing, save of joy."

Of the art with which these different plots, all necessary to the production of the final result, have been
blended, the most ordinary reader
need not be reminded. It is indeed,
as Schlegel justly remarks, a play
" popular to an extraordinary degree, and calculated to produce the
most wonderful effect on the stage;
and at the same time, a wonder of
ingenuity and art for the reflecting
critic." The preparations for Bassanio's courtship are the cause of
Antonio's subscribing the dangerous
bond; and Portia again, by means of
the advice of her uncle, a celebrated
lawyer, effects the safety of her
husband's friend. In short, the personages who have awakened our interest and love in the retirement of
Belmont, are inseparably connected
with the more agitating scenes on
the Rialto and in the court at Venice; Portia is not less indispensable
to the tragic portion of the play than
Shylock himself. The portion of
the play which relates to Lorenzo
and Jessica is no doubt more of an
under-plot, but still sufficiently connected with the main plot to take
from it all appearance of being a
needless excrescence. Not only has
Shakspeare, as Schlegel observes,
" contrived to throw a veil of
sweetness over the natural features
in the fugitive daughter of the Jew,"
but this elopement leads to two of
the most characteristic scenes in the
play—that where Shylock, baited by
Salanio and Salarino, unveils to us,
in the agony of his heart, the whole
depths of his fierce and implacable
soul, with a fervid eloquence which
for a moment takes the reason prisoner, and makes us feel as if his
great revenge were justice; and
that other, where he is alternately
tortured by the cruel Tubal's news

of his daughter's extravagance in
Genoa, and consoled by the account
of the losses which are bearing the
royal merchant down.

But did this underplot hang more
loosely on the piece than it does,
what reader would look upon that
as an intrusion which leads to the
charming moonlight dialogue in the
gardens of Belmont in the fifth act,
and to the scenes that follow? This
fifth act is like a musical afterpiece,
tranquillizing the feeling which the
deep suspense of the judgment-scene
had awakened. Antonio has been
saved; we have no longer to tremble
for the forfeiture of the bond. Shylock, defeated, trampled upon, insulted by such nothings as Gratiano, has retired to his desolate
home, with a composure which almost awakes our pity; but to have
finished the piece with the fourth
act, would have left upon the mind
a gloomy and perturbed, rather than
a tranquil and cheerful impression.
Hence Shakspeare has introduced
a succession of scenes in which nothing is placed before or around us
but the tranquillity and verdure of the
country, moonshine, illumination,
music, the conversations of newly
united lovers, the playful contest of
badinage, a series of mirthful surprises, and the gay solution, in
smiles and laughter, of all the enigmas and embarrassments of life.
The very spirit of still beauty sits
upon these scenes at Belmont. It is
impossible to read them without
feeling the mind calmed, the spirits
sobered, and attuned to cheerful
harmony. The noises and tempests
of the world seem to recede into
the background. From the spot
" where the moonlight sleeps upon
the bank," and the little candle burning in the hall, throws its beams far
into the night, " like a good deed
in a naughty world,"—" its murmuring waves are heard, but scarcely
heard to flow." Our thoughts are
raised, like Lorenzo's (on whose
somewhat commonplace mind the
scene produces an unexpected impression), to the contemplation of a
better existence.

" Sit, Jessica. Look how the floor of heaven
Is thick inlaid with patines of bright gold;
There's not the smallest orb which thou behold'st,
But in his motion like an angel sings,

21

Still quiring to the young-eyed cherubins :
Such harmony is in immortal souls ;
But, whilst this muddy vesture of decay
Doth grossly close it in, we cannot hear it."

We must confess, with all defer-ence, however, that it has always appeared to us that the plot of the Merchant of Venice, ingenious and deeply interesting as it is, is in one point deficient in probability, and this is the more to be regretted, be-cause the slightest change would have removed the defect. We do not speak of the improbability of the condition in the bond receiving effect from any court—though, to our notions, the matter would pro-bably have been very shortly set-tled in most courts on the plea of illegal contract. But it does seem to us improbable that Shylock should have proposed an arrangement, by which he is to have " no doit of usance" for his money, merely on the chance that the bond might be forfeited, and the pound of flesh exacted. Had he been represented as aware at the time, from some secret source, that Antonio's argo-sies had been lost, which might very easily have been supposed, his con-duct would have been characteris-tic ; but when Antonio solicits the loan,

" His ventures are not in one bottom
trusted,
Nor to one place, nor is his whole estate
Upon the fortune of the present year."

He is rich apparently, and sur-rounded by rich and faithful friends ; so that the contingency of the for-feiture of the bond appears the re-motest possible ; far too remote to make it probable that Shylock would in that hope abate the usances.

Pre-eminent, of course, among the characters of the piece is the great conception of Shylock, of which Schlegel thus justly speaks :—

" Shylock the Jew is one of the inconceivable masterpieces of cha-racterisation of which Shakspeare alone furnishes us with examples.

It is easy for the poet and the player to exhibit a caricature of national sentiments, modes of speaking, and gestures. Shylock, however, is any thing but a common Jew; he pos-sesses a very determinate and ori-ginal individuality, and yet we per-ceive a light touch of Judaism in every thing which he says or does.* We imagine we hear a sprinkling of the Jewish pronunciation in the mere written words. In tranquil situations, what is foreign to the European blood and Christian sen-timents is less perceptible, but in passion the national stamp appears more strongly marked. All these inimitable niceties the finished art of a great actor alone can properly express. Shylock is a man of infor-mation, even a philosopher in his own way ; he has only not discover-ed the region where human feelings dwell ; his ethical system is founded on disbelief in goodness and magna-nimity. The desire of revenging the oppressions and humiliations suffered by his nation is, after avarice, his principal spring of action. His hate is naturally directed chiefly against those Christians who possess truly Christian sentiments; the ex-ample of disinterested love of our neighbour seems to him the most unrelenting persecution of the Jews. The letter of the law is his idol. He refuses to lend an ear to the voice of mercy, which speaks to him from the mouth of Portia with heavenly eloquence; he insists on severe and inflexible justice, and it at last recoils on his own head. Here he becomes a symbol of the general history of his unfortunate nation."

These views have been expanded by Horn, though perhaps with no very substantial addition to the ideas they contain.

" Shylock," he observes, " is a Jew

in the loftiest style. He is proud of being so ;- he seems to himself to move like a prince among his people. The highest pride of no-bility among us is thrown into shade by his. With this feeling he sees himself the object of hate, nay, of contempt, to Christians, and these Christians are the rulers of Europe, and, as he thinks, the oppressors of his people. Against them, there-fore, he holds all things lawful ; and as fortune has favoured his endea-vours to amass wealth, he lacks not opportunity to still the fever of his heart, glowing with the thirst of ven-geance, not for his own sake only, but for that of his people. He knows and will hear of nothing beside his Jewish law, which he can interpret to suit his purposes : but faith, love, hope, and the doctrine of grace, are to him mere fantasies, and as such hateful and intolerable. Thus he has become such as we see him, a mixture of the serpent and the tiger ; but to maintain this position, the character requires a constant caustic *humour*, which, strangely enough, so far as I know, has not yet been adverted to.

" The poet knew well that with-out this vein of humour the cha-racter would want tone and harmony of colouring, and accordingly he has richly invested him with this quality. The whole part indeed is full of it; but we may here notice the allusion to the land-rats and water-rats, the habitation which the Nazarene pro-phet conjured the devil into ; the humorous application of the story of Jacob's thrift—the biting wit of the reply, in which all his rankling recollections of former injuries and insults are enumerated, ' Hath a *dog* money ? Is it possible a *cur* can lend three thousand ducats?' The irony of the assurance that 'a pound of man's flesh taken from a man,

' Is not so estimable, profitable, neither
As flesh of muttons, beefs, or goats; '

his unbounded insolence, even in presence of the Doge, when he goes on enumerating, with studied coarse-ness, all kinds of strange idiosyn-crasies in defence of his own appe-tite for blood—

' Some men there are love not a gaping
pig,' &c.

" But why is Antonio the chief object of his hatred ? Not merely be-cause he is the most distinguished merchant in Venice, nor because he has received most of his ill-treatment at his hands, nor (although he does allude to this) because Antonio takes no interest, and by this excess of beneficence, has brought him into evil repute as a pitiless usurer; all these, no doubt, might afford cause enough, but the chief cause lies deeper—Antonio appears to him as the purest representative of Chris-tian virtue; which is to him inex-pressibly odious; for it appears to him but as a fantastic sadness—a poetic dream—ever found in con-nexion with harshness towards his own nation, which he looks upon as the elect of God."

What alone, however, redeems the character of Shylock, is the strength of his intellectual resources. There is a grandeur and firmness of purpose about him, a power of argu-ment, a readiness of reply, which make it impossible for us not to sympathize with him to some ex-tent. All that he says or does is the emanation of a bold and masculine understanding. He sees his end from the first, he keeps it steadily in view, he adapts himself with con-summate art to the characters of those with whom he has to deal, and whom he would persuade. Observe with what art he negotiates his bond, his seeming coolness, his plausible exaggeration of the dangers to which Antonio's property is subjected, his mixture of bitter sarcasms and in-sulting gibes in the outset, with his affected candour and desire of re-conciliation at the close; hear the rapid and unanswerable burst, " Hath not a Jew eyes; hath not a Jew hands," &c. Follow him to the tribunal, where he stands alone against a hostile court. Behold him maintaining his superiority in argu-ment, unmoved by insult, unawed by power, till the suddenness and completeness of the ruin that falls on him strike him dumb—and we are made to feel that there is a spell, in intellectual vigour, a species of gloomy fascination which the display of mind must always exercise over mind, and which even its combina-tion with cruelty and malignity can-not entirely impair.

* How true and fine is this remark ! In how many little traits does the Judaism of Shylock manifest itself ! How appositely does he bring the Old Testament narra-tive in aid of his " defence of usury." How natural the oath, " By Jacob's staff I swear, I have no mind of feasting forth to-night;" and the reply to Tubal, when he learns that the turquoise he had of Leah when a bachelor had been given in exchange for a monkey, " I would not have given it for a *wilderness* of monkeys." So, in the same way, his occasional neologisms, " Flesh of muttons, beefs, or goats."

4. continued

In strong contrast with the relentless Jew stands the noble merchant Antonio, a character on which Shakspeare has bestowed much care, and to which he has succeeded in imparting a scarcely less marked individuality than he has given to Shylock. There is a calm dignity about all his conduct, an unobtrusive magnanimity, such as appears suitable to the character of a royal merchant. We see in him a kindred spirit to the Medici, the Merchant Princes of Florence, scattering his treasures around him with a truer liberality than kings. The shade of melancholy which is represented as hanging about him from the first—innate it would seem, for he can ascribe it to no outward cause,* gives a softening and pathetic interest to his character. When he repels with a "fye, fye," the conjecture of Salanio as to the cause of his melancholy : " Why then you are in love," as if the very possibility of such a feeling were in

" I am as like to call thee so again,
To spit on thee again, to spurn thee too.
If thou wilt lend this money, lend it not
As to thy friends ; (for when did friendship take
A breed for barren metal of his friend ?)
But lend it rather to thine enemy,
Who, if he break, thou may'st with better face
Exact the penalty."

One is tempted to wish that Bassanio had stood out a little more firmly against his generous friend's

" You shall not seal to such a bond for me,
I'll rather dwell in my necessity,"

seems rather a weak resistance to a proposal which even to him appeared to carry with it an evil intent. " I like not fair terms, and a villain's mind." But Bassanio has been the child of fortune and good luck; every thing has hitherto gone well with him; sanguine and confident, he cannot believe there is any serious danger for Antonio ; he neither fears for himself nor for him, for at this moment his natural reliance on his good fortune is increased by the intoxication of passion—and so

* In sooth I know not why I am so sad ;
It wearies me ; you say it wearies you ;
But how I caught it, found it, or came by it,
What stuff 'tis made of, whereof it is born,
I am to learn. *Act I. Scene I.*
† Fye, Fye, Gratiano ! where are all the rest ? &c. *Act II. Scene VI.*

his case hopeless, we are led to regard with the more admiration, that warm sympathy with which he enters into the love of others, and which leads him to peril his own life to procure for his friend a happiness which he knows but by name. His stern deportment towards Shylock when he looks down upon the Jew, in all the Christian might of the middle ages, is not less characteristic than his lavish generosity and tenderness to his friend. For that friend's sake he has condescended to solicit what he never would have asked for himself; but he will not descend to obtain it by disguising one jot of the just indignation with which he regards the merciless usurer ; he will not retract, but rather repeats, the harsh expressions of which the Jew complains ; in the language of cool contempt, he makes him fairly and fully aware on what footing alone the money is to be given and received.

committing himself to the miser's stipulation of the pound of flesh. The mere protest—not repeated—

he passively allows the fatal bond to be prepared. Melancholy as Antonio naturally is, he throws aside every such feeling when his friend's interests are at stake, and urges on his future preparations with a warmth and energy which throw all Bassanio's other friends into the shade.† The lines in which Salarino describes the parting of Bassanio and Antonio are at once strikingly characteristic of the gentle-spirited, self-sacrificing noble merchant ; and, as Malone observes, afford in the close the outline of a

beautiful picture. " Many passages of his works," says he, " might furnish hints to painters. It is, indeed,

" Bassanio told him, he would make some speed
Of his return : he answered,—Do not so,
Slubber not business for my sake, Bassanio,
But stay the very riping of the time ;
And for the Jew's bond, which he hath of me,
Let it not enter in your mind of love :
Be merry ; and employ your chiefest thoughts
To courtship, and such fair ostents of love
As shall conveniently become you there :
*And even there, his eye being big with tears,
Turning his face, he put his hand behind him,*
And with affection wondrous sensible
He wrung Bassanio's hand, and so they parted.
Salanio. I think, he only loves the world for him."

" Of his letter to Bassanio," says Horn, " which the latter receives in the sunshine of his good fortune, we shall say nothing, because we perceive that no one can mistake that divinity in the human breast which here speaks with such still but deep meaning. That Shakspeare is the richest of all poets we all know; but that he is also simple, child-like, and gentle, many do not know ; and to these we would especially recommend this scene, that they may learn to know it.
" Antonio's bearing during the universally admired trial scene, is truly classic. From Shylock he has never expected any thing else. The latter, who knows nothing but The LAW, expects to triumph through it. Antonio willingly concedes to him this triumph: for he, a pure Christian requiring not such, lives in grace, and through that alone is blessed. His hatred of the Jew is over ; for in the feeling of the higher happiness which is approaching, there remains in his spirit nothing but a dignified pity. He has once more found his friend ; all his fellow-citizens regard him with esteem and sympathy ; the Doge himself pleads in his favour; and thus from all sides a halo of noble renown surrounds him, which might lighten death even to one less worthy."
Portia's character has, on the whole, received little justice at the hands of the German critics. Schlegel, who has so well seized the features of Shylock's character, dismisses that of Portia in three words; and Horn's remarks, though somewhat more expanded, seem quite un-

surprising that they do not study his plays with this view."

satisfactory, vague, and unworthy of the character. Yet Mrs Jamieson is right in saying that " Shylock is not a finer or more finished character in his way than Portia is in hers. These two splendid figures are worthy of each other, worthy of being placed together within the same rich framework of enchanting poetry and glorious and graceful forms. She hangs beside the terrible inexorable Jew, the brilliant lights of her character set off by the shadowy power of his, like a magnificent beauty-breathing Titian by the side of a gorgeous Rembrandt."
" Portia," says Horn, " the supporter of the whole piece, expresses her noble individuality so decisively, that she may be comprehended at the first glance. It is with this character as with sky, it is at once clear and yet of unfathomable depth. Her father has been a strange and mysterious personage who has left her boundless wealth ; but a fettered will in the all-important choice of her life. In this, perhaps, her untiring and full-streaming wit has its origin ; a superabundance of wit which would make us apprehensive of a defect of heart, did not her deep and generous love for Bassanio, and her active sympathy for Antonio, satisfy us on this point. Thus she stands before us almost perfection, yet without mere generality, but, on the contrary, firmly defined and bounded."
Of the elements which make up the perfection and peculiarity of Portia's character certainly no one, from these vague expresions of Horn, could form the least idea. Let

23

us see how much more acutely and eloquently these features have been seized by our English critic.*

"Portia is endued with her own share of those delightful qualities which Shakspeare has lavished on many of his female characters; but besides the dignity, the sweetness and tenderness which should distinguish her sex generally, she is individualized by qualities peculiar to herself, by her high mental powers, her enthusiasm of temperament, her decision of purpose, and her buoyancy of spirit. These are innate. She has other distinguishing qualities more external, and which are the result of the circumstances in which she is placed. Thus she is the heiress of a princely name and countless wealth; a train of obedient pleasures have ever waited round her, and from infancy she has breathed an atmosphere redolent of perfume and blandishment. Accordingly, there is a commanding grace, a high-bred airy elegance, a spirit of magnificence in all that she does or says, as one to whom splendour had been familiar from her very birth. She treads as though her footsteps had been among marble palaces, beneath roofs of fretted gold, over cedar floors and pavements of jasper and porphyry, and gardens full of statues, and flowers, and fountains, and haunting music. She is

' But he may win;
And what is music, then? Then music is
Even as the flourish, when true subjects bow
To a new-crowned monarch : such it is,
As are those dulcet sounds in break of day,
That creep into the dreaming bridegroom's ear,
And summon him to marriage. Now he goes,
With no less presence, but with much more love,
Than young Alcides, when he did redeem
The virgin tribute paid by howling Troy
To the sea monster : I stand for sacrifice.'

" Here not only the feeling itself, born of the elastic and sanguine spirit which had never been touched with grief, but the images in which it comes arrayed to her fancy—the bridegroom waked by music on his wedding-morn—the newly crowned monarch, the comparison of Bassanio to the young Alcides, and of herself to the daughter of Laomedon, are all precisely what would have suggested themselves to the fine poeti-

full of penetration, wisdom, and genuine tenderness, and lively wit; but as she has never known want, or grief, or fear, or disappointment, her wisdom is without a touch of the sombre or the sad; her affections are all mixed up with faith, hope, and joy, and her wit has not a particle of malevolence or causticity.

"A disposition to doubt, to suspect, and to despond in the young, argues in general some inherent weakness, moral or physical, or some miserable and radical error of education; in the old, it is one of the first symptoms of age; it speaks of the influence of sorrow and experience, and foreshows the decay of the stronger and more generous powers of the soul. Portia's strength of intellect takes a natural tinge from the flush and bloom of her young and prosperous existence, and from her fervent imagination. In the casket scene, she fears indeed the issue of the trial on which more than her life is hazarded; but while she trembles, her hope is stronger than her fear. While Bassanio is contemplating the caskets, she suffers herself to dwell one moment on the possibility of disappointment and misery; then immediately follows that revulsion of feeling so beautifully characteristic of the hopeful, trusting, mounting spirit of this noble creature.

cal imagination of Portia in such a moment.

"Her subsequent surrender of herself in heart and soul, of her maiden freedom and her vast possessions, can never be read without deep emotion; for not only all the tenderness and delicacy of a devoted woman are here blended with the dignity which becomes the princely heiress of Belmont, but the serious measured self-possession of her ad-

dress to her lover, when all suspense is over, and all concealment superfluous, is most beautifully consistent with the character. It is in truth an awful moment, that in which a gifted woman first discovers, that besides talents and powers, she has also passions and affections,—when she first begins to suspect their vast importance in the sum of her existence,—when she first confesses that her happiness is no longer in her own keeping, but is surrendered for ever into the dominion of another! The possession of uncommon powers of mind is so far from affording relief or resource in the first intoxicating surprise, I had almost said terror, of such a revolution, that they render it more intense. The sources of thought multiply beyond calculation the sources of feeling, and mingled, they rush together a torrent deep as strong. Because Portia is endowed with that enlarged comprehension which looks before and after, she does not feel the less, but the more; because, from the height of her commanding intellect, she can contemplate the force, the tendency, the consequences of her own sentiments,—because she is fully sensible of her own situation, and the value of all she concedes, the concession is not made with less entireness and devotion of heart, less confidence in the truth and worth of her lover, than when Juliet, in a similar moment, but without any such intrusive reflections, any check but the instinctive delicacy of her sex, flings herself and her fortunes at the feet of her lover. In Portia's confession, which is not breathed from a moon-lit balcony, but spoken openly in the presence of her attendants and vassals, there is nothing of the passionate self-abandonment of Juliet, nor of the artless simplicity of Miranda, but a consciousness and tender seriousness approaching to solemnity, which are not less touching."

* * * *

It is observable that something of the intellectual brilliance of Portia is reflected on the other female characters of the Merchant of Venice, so as to preserve in the midst of contrast a certain harmony and keeping. Thus Jessica, though properly kept subordinate, is certainly " a most beautiful Jew." She cannot be called a sketch; or if a sketch, she is like one of those dashed off in glaring colours from the rainbow palette of a Rubens; she has a rich tinge of orientalism shed on her worthy of her Eastern origin. In any other play, and in any other companionship than that of the matchless Portia, Jessica would make a very beautiful heroine of herself. Nothing can be more poetical, more classically fanciful and elegant than the scenes between her and Lorenzo; the celebrated moonlight dialogue, for instance, which we have all by heart. Every sentiment she utters interests us for her; more particularly her bashful self-reproach when flying in the disguise of a page.

* * * *

We should not, however, easily pardon her for cheating her father with so much indifference, but for the perception that Shylock values his daughter far beneath his wealth. " I would my daughter were dead at my foot, and the jewels in her ear ! —Would she were hearsed at my foot, and the ducats in her coffin."

Nerissa is a good specimen of a common genus of characters; she is a clever, confidential waiting-woman who has caught a little of her lady's elegance and romance; she affects to be lively and sententious, falls in love, and makes her favour conditional on the fortune of the caskets, and, in short, mimics her mistress with good emphasis and discretion. Nerissa and the gay, talkative Gratiano are as well matched as the incomparable Portia and her magnificent and captivating lover.

* Mrs Jamieson's Characteristics, vol. i. p. 71, *et seq.*

LITERATURE.

Sketches of Germany and the Germans.
2 vols.

We observed last week of Mr Barrow's interesting work that its author deserves to travel. Of the author of the present volumes, by an "Englishman resident in Germany," we may observe that their author deserves to stay at home—by which we simply mean that he merits the most cordial wishes from all; he describes so well, and is so exceedingly companionable, that he ought to be a resident in England. However, if he feels himself at home in sketching the characters of other countries so that we can all enjoy them, the effect is much the same. We could fill half a number of the C. J. with amusing extracts from these volumes. Even then we should not be satisfied, unless we could extract the pretty coloured frontispieces, or some of the elegant outline vignettes, illustrative of costume and character, which add beauty to the handsomely-printed pages. The period during which our author's pen is employed extends from the spring of 1834 to the present time, and his observation and experience take a sufficient range to qualify him in pronouncing upon the merits of the various scenes he has surveyed, and the character of the extraordinary people amongst whom he has resided. He has done justice to Germany without being borne away into the obscure regions of her philosophy, and has sketched the German people with an eye to truth and picturesque effect, without surveying them through clouds of smoke. We recommend all who can venture upon a tour in Germany, to try the experiment of a perusal—it will set before them an excellent pen-and-ink panorama of a land abounding in various points of interest—and if many of them have often been pictured before, and some of them are dull or trifling compared with others, yet taking the whole range of the excursion, it will be owned to be a most pleasant and profitable trip. Of the author's somewhat copious but easy style of description, we shall at once give the reader a few amusing specimens. We shall begin with

A miracle :—

Ratzeburg, with its small territory, was formerly an independent bishopric. In the thirteenth century two of its bishops, ancestors of Prince Blucher, performed miracles of such magnitude as to create a fame as great as the military renown of their brave descendant. For the edification of my readers I have translated two of them.—It appears that in the year 1256 a dreadful famine reduced the starving inhabitants to utter despair; when, in consequence of the intercession of the holy bishop Ulrich, the empty granaries were filled in one night with a sufficient quantity of corn to supply not alone his own subjects, but the inhabitants of the surrounding country. His successor and nephew, Weipert, was more selfish in the exercise of his miraculous power; for his Holiness the Pope having refused to confirm him in the vacant see, on account of his extreme youth,—behold, the auburn locks of the young saint suddenly changed to a venerable gray! The Pope acknowledged the miracle, and not only confirmed him in the see, but canonized him.

A legend :—

I next proceeded to view all that remains of the outer wall, so memorable as the scene of the cruelty of the proud and beautiful Kunigunde. This fair lady was the sole heiress of the castle and its domains; and as her charms and wealth were celebrated throughout the country, she had many suitors; but unfortunately for their success, though she was partial to bows and arrows, they were not those of Cupid, but Diana, and she preferred slaying on the field to killing with her eyes; indeed, to such a length did she carry her frigid disdain for the lords of the creation, that she caused it

to be promulgated, she had made a vow never to bestow her hand except upon the knight who should make the circuit of the castle on the outer wall, and this not with the cautious step of a pedestrian, but on the back of a prancing courser; now, the promenade selected for this neck-breaking exploit is so narrow, as to render even a walk dangerous; it also overhangs the most frightful precipices, one of which we have already described as bearing the name of the bottomless pit. This declaration had the desired effect; the ardent among her lovers became lukewarm, and the lukewarm cold, and the majority voted, *nem con.*, to leave this lordly flower to wither within the castle walls. In process of time some few were found who had the temerity to make the rash attempt; but whether they were bankrupts in all that this world contains of good, and thus wished to play one more stake for happiness, or felt assured that both themselves and steeds were secure against giddiness, history has not recorded,—she has only told, that they all miserably perished. Fate had, however, willed their revenge; for at length a young and handsome knight requested an interview with the mountain beauty, who, the moment she saw him, felt that he held the fate of her happiness in his hands: gladly would she now have given castle, domains, all, to have accompanied him as his bride, even to a cottage, for his courteous manners and noble bearing rivetted her chains still faster;—but then her oath! Add to which, the knight was fixedly resolved to make the attempt: he, however, took care to receive, in the presence of her confessor, a confirmation of her vow to become his bride in the event of success, and then went forth, leaving the weeping Kunigunde to weary the saints with prayers. In a short time, the multitude assembled in the court yard, on the castle, and the mountains opposite, rent the air with their shouts, announcing that the miraculous deed was accomplished. The lady sprung from her knees, and rushed forward to throw herself in his arms; but he coldly and repulsively stood aloof. " No, proud woman!" said the noble knight; " never could I take to my heart one who has blood upon her hands: you are mine, but I spurn you with abhorrence and contempt. I have risked my life not to win your hand, but to humble your pride, by repaying cruelty with scorn; moreover, know that I am Albert, Landgrave of Thuringia, and wedded to a woman not only your superior in beauty, but nature, in forming her, did not forget to give a heart." Thus saying, the triumphant knight sprang into his saddle and galloped forth, leaving the despairing Kunigunde a prey to the worm of disappointment, who, having for some months wandered a maniac through her castle, sunk into her grave, and may still be seen (says the legend) hunting with her bow and arrows in the adjoining forests.

Royal residents at Prague :—

One wing of this immense edifice (which is more remarkable for extent than beauty) is occupied by the ex-king Charles X. and his suite; the remainder is appropriated to the service of the different departments of the government. The illustrious exile lives in the most unostentatious manner, and is still the same hospitable, good natured man that he has ever been in public and private life, and quite as popular with the good people of Prague as he was at Edinburgh. He was looking extremely well for his age, and if we might judge from the tranquil smile that played around his mouth, is perfectly happy in his retirement. The Duke of Bordeaux has grown up a handsome boy, but rather short for his age, and his form, which is robust, exhibits more of strength than gracefulness; his complexion is ruddy, with light eyes, Grecian nose, and a very expressive mouth. He is said to possess an extraordinary capacity for learning, and altogether promises to be a most accomplished Prince; for which he is much indebted to the tuition of the Duke de Blacas, who is acknowledged, even by his opponents in politics, to be one of the most intellectual men of his day. There is hardly any restraint imposed upon the young Prince, who is seen, every other day, riding on his little pony, or sauntering through the shops or public places in Prague, and is not only the idol of the court, but of the citizens, who are loud in his praise. His sister Mademoiselle is equally popular; her countenance is interesting and expressive, but she appears very delicate; I scarcely observed any alteration in the appearance of the Duc d'Angouleme, but in that of the Duchess grief has anticipated age, and she appears to exist merely for the sake of her youthful relatives. However, in none of the royal party are the ravages of time and adversity more distinctly perceptible than in the Duchess de Berri; her restless, ambitious mind has not adapted itself to the severe reverses her fortunes have sustained. At the time I visited Prague, she occupied a small villa a few leagues distant from the town.

Carlsbad Inns :—

Before I reached the town, I was met by a band of hotel and lodging house agents, who showered into my carriage their cards of address; many of them baptized with names sufficiently bizarre to excite the risibility of the traveller. Therefore I had to choose whether I should repose in the " Eye of God," the " Lap of the Virgin," the " Nest of the Seven Wise Swallows," or in the " Arms of the beautiful Mermaid;" and, if this

did not please me, who could refuse the tempting invitation, " This night shalt thou sleep in paradise."

German literature :—

The numerical account of the books annually published is perfectly astonishing; this may be inferred from the fact that it is computed there are twelve thousand authors. A friend assured me, that the last Leipsick annual catalogue contained more books than imperial Russia had produced from the foundation of her greatness to the present time.

In civil and natural history, mathematics, and theology, the Germans are equal if not superior to those of other nations; and in metaphysics Kant, Wolf, Leibnitz, Fichte, and Schelling have filled Europe with their works and the mad houses with patients! It is well known that Kant's philosophy alone has had this effect upon thousands in Germany.

Newspapers are little better than waste paper; for they only promulgate such facts and opinions as the censor permits, but several of the annuals and periodical publications hold a high rank; the embellishments of the former are as inferior to our own, as the text is superior. Works of fiction, in which metaphysics, sentiment, and the marvellous predominate, are the most popular; however, I do not know of any contemporary German author whose works are so widely spread as those of our own Sir Walter Scott, for they are to be found in almost every village throughout the Empire.

The second volume is at least as interesting, and both derive variety and value from the glance which is accorded to us of Poland, Hungary, and Switzerland. We must not omit to mention, as a hint to other intelligent but less considerate travellers, that the author has " studiously refrained from invading the recesses of private life," and has neither divulged names, nor published secrets that can subject anybody to inconvenience. Others have done this to such an extent, that he tells us, " an English gentleman is now too frequently regarded by foreigners in the character of a domestic spy."

6. EDINBURGH REVIEW, 63 (1836), 442-469. M/H No. 3323. *Cf.* Carré, p. 122. By George Moir.

ART. VII.—*Die Deutsche Literatur.* Von WOLFANG MENZEL, Zweite vermehrte Auflage. Stuttgart: 1836.

THE name of Menzel, though familiar to English admirers of German literature as that of a pleasing poet and eminent critic, is as yet scarcely known to the English public; while the work of Heine, on German literature, a publication written in the most despicable spirit of personal hostility to individuals, affording the most distorted pictures of many of the most eminent men of Germany, and inculcating views and principles equally at variance with truth, good taste, and morality, has been abundantly read, criticised, and even lauded by our English Reviewers, the corresponding work of Menzel, which has now reached a second (and very enlarged) edition, has been, so far as we are aware, but once noticed. This seems the more singular, that the work is not only one of high talent, originality, and comprehensiveness of view, but one which, from its manner of treating the subject, and its freedom from many of those defects which deform even the best specimens of German criticism, was peculiarly likely to have found in England fit audience, and that not few. Menzel has in fact steered clear of the two rocks on which so many of his critical predecessors have foundered, mysticism of views, and tediousness in their developement. In the compass of two volumes, of no great bulk, we are presented with a full, and even minute view of the peculiarities of the German literary character, the rise of German literature, the points of distinction by which it is differenced from those of other nations, the changes impressed upon its spirit from time to time by political or social changes within, or the influence of foreign nations from without, the reaction in favour of a national taste, its causes and gradual developement; and lastly, a very eloquent, masterly, and discriminating view of the present direction of literature, its connexion with the character of the time, its beauties and defects, the circumstances which are likely to purify and elevate its tendencies, and those which are at work to corrupt and debase it. It is almost needless to remark, that the literary historian who accomplishes this task effectually, without wandering beyond the confines of two volumes, cannot be a tedious writer. Dr Menzel has in fact the somewhat rare merit, particularly in Germany, of ' coming to the point.' He does not insist on laboriously evolving his conclusions by strict demonstration, through every step of his proposition. He ventures to rely a little on the intelligence and previous reading of those whom he addresses; he communicates, by hints and allusions, many things which others would have made the subject of a formal discussion or explanation; and is generally content to leave his opinions, when stated, to operate by their own weight and force, without supporting them by a formal array of arguments or citations. Thus only could a characteristic of the literature of Germany be brought within the compass to which it is here reduced. As a consequence, however, it will be at once understood the book is by no means adapted to an elementary student. It is not, in truth, so much a history, as a bold and philosophical sketch; a map of the literature of Germany, from the survey of an adventurous, yet experienced navigator. It presupposes, indeed, a pretty extensive though not profound acquaintance with German literature, and aims chiefly at furnishing the student, somewhat bewildered in the tangled mazes ' of that wild wood,' with a clue which may lead him safely through its intricacies. In perusing it, we feel as if we were conducted out of the crowded and confused streets of a city, where we had long been tolerably familiar with every object taken by itself in detail, but could form no clear idea of their positions and proportions, and were suddenly placed on some commanding eminence, from which the lines of the streets, the relative heights of the domes and steeples, the breadth and mass of the buildings, the whole lights and shadows of the scene, were first made distinct and palpable to the eye. To the student, however, who already possesses this general and desultory knowledge of German literature (and this, we believe, is the situation in which most English scholars stand), the work of Menzel will be found a valuable assistant. For, in the next place, Menzel is, of all German critics with whom we are acquainted, the one who can least justly be accused of these vague, indefinite, or fanciful views, which (for want of a better term) we are accustomed to designate by the general name of mysticism. Without the mocking spirit and persiflage of a Heine—without his indifference to all enthusiasm and nobleness of view—(for, on the contrary, no one kindles into a warmer admiration of genius and greatness, devoting themselves to the cause of goodness, than Menzel);—his strong and vigorous understanding—never separating theory from practice, never permitting itself to deviate into the regions of abstract speculation, but sticking close to the highway of actual life, and of nature as he finds it, always clearly perceiving its object, and aiming at it by the most direct means—has entirely banished from his works that indistinctness of speculation, which sometimes so painfully interferes with the pleasure arising from the wide reading and acute views of Tieck and the Schlegels. Whether we agree with the opinions of Menzel, or dissent from them, we always know clearly with what propositions we are dealing; into the more theoretical and abstract questions of taste indeed he seldom enters; nor can we pretend to say with what success the attempt would have been made, for Menzel by no means appears to be the man to plunge 'extra flammantia mœnia mundi' into the region of the metaphysics of taste; but in the sphere to which he confines himself, he sees clearly, thinks vigorously, and writes with singular force, precision, and vivacity.

We believe Menzel to be a man of warm feelings, which have in some instances left their traces in his work, and not in the most favourable form. He has long lived in an element of strife, having at an early period of life drawn down upon himself the hostility and abuse of Voss and his partisans, by his work entitled ' Voss und die Symbolik;' * and by undertaking, after the retirement of Adolph Mullner, the directorship of the Morgenblatt, one of the most able of the literary journals of Germany—a task which he has performed, so far as we can judge (by an experience of some years standing), in a fearless, honest, and impartial spirit, but of course with the usual consequence of making more enemies than friends. He was the first man of real ability who, undeterred by the literary despotism exercised by Goethe, ventured to question the grounds of his supremacy, and to reduce to their real meaning the high but somewhat hollow-sounding panegyrics of his admirers. Nothing can present a stronger contrast, or better illustrate the different characters of the two minds, than the way in which Heine and Menzel have dealt with the literary character and pretensions of Goethe. Both have done their best to dispel the *prestige* which attached to that great name,—

' And put to proof his strong supremacy,
Whether obtained by strength or chance of fate;'

but the latter employs the honourable weapons of fair argument— the former contents himself with the discreditable missiles of ribald wit, and personal abuse. Menzel, while he refuses to bow the knee in undiscriminating adoration with the common worshippers of Goethe, gives honour where he really thinks honour is due; nay, tenders warmly and willingly the tribute of respect and even admiration to which he conceives him in some respects to be justly indebted. He does not, like Heine, endeavour to disparage his unquestionable powers by mere sarcasm, any more than he condescends

---

* Stuttgart, 1835.

to imitate the vulgar insolence of Börne, who boldly denounces Goethe as ' the cancer of the German body,' ' a very pattern of ' baseness,' ' the first of despots,' and so forth. But he assails with the weapons both of wit and reasoning, and with the generous warmth of one who feels the evil consequences in literature of a spirit of moral indifference—the spirit and tendency of Goethe's works; and though here, as in one or two other instances, his former polemics on the subject have led him too far, and tempted him to maintain positions which had been at first rashly taken up, we must admit, that in the main his view of the moral worthlessness of Goethe's poetry, and of his evil influence upon the age with whose vices and weaknesses he deals so gently, if indeed he does not beautify them over by his genius, is painfully true. We should doubt whether even the most thoroughgoing idolator of Goethe could peruse the articles of impeachment against him as drawn up by Menzel without being led into some uneasy doubts of his divinity; and sure we are that those who are not idolators will be abundantly satisfied that this marvel of the nineteenth century is but a man—a great man, doubtless—and, in the ordinary relations of life, a good one; but whose genius, exercised indifferently on all subjects, never warming into enthusiasm for excellence, never revolted by the exhibition of vice, polishing with the same careful and finished elegance his pictures of both, and taking refuge in an ideal world of art from the labours, and duties, and sufferings which it is our proper task in life to bear and overcome, however much it may have done to refine the taste of the German public, and to improve the poetical form, has done but little towards elevating or bettering the substance.

In the case of Voss, against whom another of his attacks is directed, the justice of his remarks is far more doubtful. Indeed, we believe the feeling has universally been, that they are overcharged in the highest degree. The recollection of the treatment he had himself experienced at the hands of Voss and his partisans, has obviously guided the pen of Menzel in his criticism upon the author of Louise, which, by its very extravagance, and over-anxiety to present the object in a ludicrous light, produces an opposite result, and merely satisfies the reader, not that Voss was, in all he wrote or translated, a miserable pedant, but that Dr Wolfgang Menzel is not, in this instance, an honest critic; and that, forsaking that principle of impartiality by which he is in general guided, he has here written, not for the world or for futurity, but for the present gratification of personal hostility. He does not, indeed, like Heine in his criticism on the Schlegels, carry his attacks into the domestic relations of life; but he scruples not to present his person *in caricatura*, ' walking to-' wards eternity in a damask dressing-gown, and white-washed ' night-cap.' He is accused of the most pitiable vanity; of flattering princes and nobles, at the same time that he pretended to be a friend of the people; of converting the idea of ' patriotism' into the life of a narrow family circle, and that of religion into a ' rancorous old Protestant polemic;' of preaching to the Catho-lics that tolerance which he was never disposed to exercise to-wards them. In the same temper, and with the same justice, is his literary character treated. ' His Idylls, his celebrated ' Louise, and his Letters,' only deserve to be immortal, because they are the records of the whole *Philisteici*,* and family cocker-ings (familien hätschelei) of the last century. He is accused of dislocating every limb of the German language, in a vain at-tempt to approximate it to the measures and construction of the Greek; of labouring for half a century at the Sisyphus task of rolling up the rough old Runenstein of the German tongue to the summit of the Greek Parnassus, from which, however, it speedily comes thundering down again upon the head and shoul-ders of the philologist. His translations, it is said, are so slavishly true to the words and false to the spirit, that they only become intelligible by a reference to the original. ' Whether he trans-' late from Hesiod, Homer, Theocritus, Virgil, Ovid, Horace, ' Shakspeare, or an old love song, we still hear nothing but the ' stiff tramp of his own prose. Even the mighty genius of ' Shakspeare cannot lead him out of his regular monotony. ' The worthy poets of old are plunged into his witch-caldron ' fresh and healthy, and they come out again miserable change-' lings—all converted into little Vosses, all marching in buck-' ram uniforms.' This is ' pleasant but wrong,' containing some truth, but mixed with monstrous exaggeration. If Voss did not penetrate so deeply as some others into the spirit of the classic literatures—if he did at times attach too great an importance to the mere form, and in the pursuit of verbal strictness of translation, suffered the fire and spirit, the ethe-real essence, of the original to escape him, such at least is not the case with his works in general. His Louise, notwithstand-ing the sneer at its homely pictures and trifling details of a

village life, will always, from the real truth and simple beauty of those scenes, have a charm for the lover of nature; and so Goethe appears to have felt, when he so obviously framed his 'Civic-epic' of Hermann and Dorothea on this model. Voss's Homer remains at this moment the best translation of that poet into any European tongue; and he must have a jaundiced eye indeed, who cannot, in Voss's translations, distinguish the peculiar manner of Theocritus from that of Homer, or of Hesiod from Virgil. His Horace we grant is less successful. The *curiosa felicitas* of the Roman lyrist was of a nature too subtle and too delicate to be caught and reflected in his somewhat un-bending strains. In like manner, his translation of Shakspeare, though in point of mere verbal rendering of the text it far surpasses even that of Schlegel, cannot be compared with it as a poetical version of the original. It is true, that had Schlegel not proved how far it was possible to combine even close accuracy with the graces of the most poetical expression, and the most harmonious and natural arrangement of works, we should probably have been well contented with the translation of Voss. But we fairly admit, that in Voss's Shakspeare there is a want of the spirit of poetry—of the power of seizing and giving back the very impression produced by the changing tone of the original; while in Schlegel's we are surrounded by the very in-fluences which are awakened by the perusal of Shakspeare himself —by the southern glow and purple light of love in Romeo and Juliet; the glimmering haze in which elves hover, and through which bewildered lovers wander in Midsummer Night's Dream; the sentiment of wayward gloom in Hamlet—a reflection as it were from the lowering and changing skies of the north; the feeling of dew-besprinkled woodland freshness ' and pastoral melancholy' in As You Like it; the magic atmosphere of virgin solitude and purity that envelopes the Tempest; the elements of music and moonlight in which Twelfth Night and the Merchant of Venice appear to float; and the broad flood of gaiety and wild humour which is poured over the Merry Wives of Windsor and the two parts of King Henry IV. But with the exception of Voss's Horace and his Shakspeare, his translations are excellent—his Homer, in many respects, truly admirable; and Dr Menzel may rest assured, that his prejudiced and petulant observations in regard to Voss are far more likely to be injurious to his own reputation than to that of the distinguished philologist.

Another person, against whom his censure appears to be of a one-sided and unmeasured nature, is Kotzebue. Not even Menzel can feel more strongly than we do, that the vast reputation which Kotzebue once enjoyed was a hollow and unfounded one; that

---

* *Philistinism.* This word is untranslateable by any single English word. But it may be said to mean every thing old fashioned, pedantic, absurd, and common-place.

his influence upon the literature of his time was most unfortunate; that the tendency of his works was to introduce a sophistry of the heart—a mixture of frivolity with a sentimentalism, in which all our conceptions of virtue and vice are confounded; that his innocent adulteresses, generous footpads, forgiving husbands, unsophisticated innocents, who throw themselves into the arms of every man they meet; virgins of the sun, so pure and unconscious of evil, that they know not that they have lost all claims to the title:—that these, with many other favourite characters in his dramatic gallery, are conceptions equally revolting to good taste, good sense, and decent feeling. We assuredly do not go the same length in regard to Kotzebue, with his enthusiastic admirer Mr Taylor of Norwich, who, in his history (!) of German Poetry, has the courage to make the following astounding avowal: ' According to my judgment, Kotzebue is the greatest ' dramatic genius that Europe has evolved since Shakspeare.' ' His power over space already transcends that of Shakspeare; ' it remains to be seen whether his power over time will also ' stand the test of centuries.' With all deference it does not remain to be seen; the fame of Kotzebue, once of European extent, has diminished, is diminishing, and, so far as concerns his claims as a *great dramatist* or *true poet*, will probably at no distant period be extinct. But granting all this, we think there is much needless vituperation wasted upon the unlucky dramatist, as if because the tendency of his works was to introduce a kind of moral chaos, such had also been his constant object and design. The truth is, Kotzebue lived in a corrupted period; he possessed within himself no very elevated standard of moral excellence, and none such presented itself in the world with which he was familiar; but this seems the extent of his offending, that he was neither better nor worse than his age; that he adopted its weaknesses, vices, and follies as he found them, and imparted to his dramatic world no higher principles of action than those which he found to operate in a state of society, which irreligion and the vicious influence of foreign example had thoroughly demoralized. That he made the most of his materials, and executed the task he had prescribed to himself with consummate cleverness and address, it were mere folly to deny. Indifferent as his tragedies may be, and even to these a considerable degree of dramatic effect must be conceded, his comedies are unquestionably marked by a rich fund of humour, and frequently by extremely novel and happy conceptions and oppositions of character. Nor is there any justice in the view which the work of Menzel would lead a reader to adopt, that *all* the works of Kotzebue are tainted with the moral stain to which we have alluded; or that he had in view

any systematic attack on the bulwarks of social order, or the principles of morality. Menzel says of him, with more coarseness than either wit or truth, ' He made Parnassus a bagnio, and ' secured the post of go-between for himself. No one so well ' understood how to operate on the weaknesses and evil inclina- ' tions of the educated, and to flatter the vanity of the uneducated ' public. It was only in the attempt to catch the tone of high ' refinement that Kotzebue failed. His nature was too common ' to enable him to discover that tenderness of expression behind ' which vice conceals itself in more delicate natures.' Menzel is no doubt consistent with himself, for he does not exempt Goëthe from the censure which he thus bestows upon Kotzebue; he merely awards to the former the palm of success in attaining that refinement which Kotzebue failed to seize; but the singularity is to find that many of those who are loudest and most indignant against the immoral pictures and vices of Kotzebue, are the very same who can see nothing but the most instructive moral lessons in the licentious frivolities of a Wilhelm Meister's Apprenticeship, and perfect purity, both in aim and execution, in that work, to which Menzel ascribes the ' bad eminence' of being the archtype of the class of ' adultery romances'—a very numerous one in Germany;—we mean the Affinities of Choice.

Leaving, however, these instances, in which the feelings or prejudices of Menzel have carried him beyond the fair bounds of impartial criticism, let us see how he deals with his subject, when no such influences distort his views, or impart an undue rancour to his strictures. We have, within the last few years, so fully stated our views in regard to German literature, that any formal disquisition on the subject as a whole would be out of place. We shall confine ourselves, on the present occasion, to a few extracts from the more striking portion of Menzel's work, merely connecting them by such remarks as may render their relation to his general views intelligible. We shall take the liberty, therefore, of passing over parts first and second of the work, in which he discusses, ' The ' Mass of Literature, The Nationality of the Germans, The Influ- ' ence of School Learning, of Foreign Literature; The Trade of ' Literature; Religion; Philosophy; History; Education.' They abound with striking and valuable remarks; they are written, in many parts, with a glowing enthusiasm, and in a spirit of the utmost liberality and toleration; but they refer to matters which would require a good deal of preliminary discussion, and would seduce us, in more points than one, into controversial questions which we would at present avoid. Our extracts shall therefore be made from that portion of the work which is devoted to the progress and present prospects of belles lettres in Germany.

A dreary period of inaction, and, as it may be called, poetical death, followed in Germany the bright, but brief flash of the Minne-Singer Poetry (from 1138 to 1268), and the vast revolution in society effected by the Reformation. Favourable as that great change may have ultimately proved, even to the interests of literature, its first effects were undoubtedly far otherwise. It seemed as if that spirit of polemical discussion, of critical enquiry, of aversion to all those arts which were supposed to ' make the ' reason prisoner,' were fatal to all pursuits connected with the imagination. Reason had done so much in that great struggle, that men began to imagine she could do all; and, absorbed in the investigation of the truths which the understanding could detect, they had no ears for the equally certain, and often profounder truths (as regards man and his destiny), which genius calls forth from the recesses of the imagination. The objects which had most attracted their veneration and love during the early period of wonder and belief, suddenly lost their charms, nay, were viewed with disgust, as links in the chain by which reason had been fettered. From idolators they became iconoclasts. Churches and cloisters were destroyed; the ministers and cathedrals, which were shooting up their aspiring domes into the air, remained unfinished; painting was denounced as a monkish device leading only to the violation of the second commandment; the music of the pealing organ ceased with the fall of those ' studious cloisters ' pale,' through which it had echoed; for popular belief, came general doubt; for the steadfastness of former days, a constant looking for of change; science flourished; learning increased with the rise of universities; but manners, morals, poetry, decayed. In two strongholds only indeed did literature attempt to maintain a struggle against the rationalizing spirit of the time, in the spiritual lyrics of Luther and his successors, and in the popular songs, plays, and farces of Hans Sachs. Luther's whole adventurous career, like Sidney's, might be said to be poetry put in action; but he has peculiarly impressed the stamp of his poetical sensibilities upon his devotional songs, which, glowing with the fervor of piety and enthusiastic feeling, had an irresistible fascination for the people.

The plays of the honest old Shoemaker, again—in number nearly equalling those of Lope de Vega,* and treating, in a style of a broad, coarse humour, the Catholic legends of the middle ages, harmonized with the mocking spirit of the time,

---

* The list of his productions, as given by himself, contains 4200 songs, 208 comedies and tragedies, 1700 farces, fables, and other poems, besides 73 spiritual lyrics. Of this vast collection, however, only a small part has been printed.

and supplied the popular taste with the only imaginative nutriment which in this period of poetical inanition it seemed capable of digesting. Then followed, after a troubled and louring period of suspense and preparation, the Thirty Years' War, crushing the rising progress of learning and civilisation, and trampling under foot the monuments of art and the institutions of science. The peace of Westphalia left Germany both in a state of intellectual and political exhaustion. From this period to the death of Louis XIV., the aspect which Germany presents, in a literary point of view, is deplorable. From Dan to Beersheba all is barrenness. Scarcely do some feeble, farthing-candle lights, such as Opitz, the dramatist Gryphius, and Hoffmannswaldau, glimmer through the gloom. Literature, so far as it existed in a vernacular form, had sunk into a lifeless imitation of the ancients; borrowing the form, but incapable of apprehending the spirit of the classics; reproducing, but only with less success, the ideas of the French: profuse of mythology, penurious of feeling, destitute of nationality. ' Apollo,' says Menzel, with liveliness and truth, 'sat on the Ger' man Parnassus in a full-bottomed peruke, and with fiddle in ' hand led the concert of the well-powdered Muses.'

The first great name which greets us on the threshold of the reviving German literature, is that of Klopstock, whose merits and defects, as well as his influence on his age, are characterised by Menzel with great acuteness and truth. After alluding to the Horatian imitations of Ramler, the anacreontics of Gleim, and the Idylls of the Swiss Theocritus, Gessner—with their French coquetry of sentiment, and sheepish modesty, he proceeds:—

' Far before these German Horaces, Anacreons, Pindars, ' Theocrituses, and Æsops, stands the German Homer, Klop' stock. It was he who, by the strong influence of his Messias ' and his Odes, established the supremacy of the antique taste, ' not, however, to the prejudice of German and Christian asso' ciations, but rather to their advantage. Religion and patriot' ism were with him the highest of conceptions; but in reference ' to the form, he considered that of ancient Greece to be the ' most perfect, and hoped to unite the greatest beauty of sub' stance with the greatest beauty of form, by attiring Christian' ity and Germanism in the garb of Greece; a singular error, ' yet not unnaturally arising out of the singular character of the ' social developement of his time. . . . Klopstock, though in ' the form of his works a Greek, was still in their spirit a true ' German, and he it was who introduced that inspiration of patriot' ism, and that adoration of Germanism, which amidst all changes ' of taste has never disappeared, or rather, has often, in its oppo-

'sition to all things foreign, deviated into injustice and extrava-
'gance. Strangely as it sounds at first to hear *him*, the offspring
'of the French peruke-period (perücken-zeit), styling himself a
'*bard* in his Alcaic verses, and mingling three heterogeneous
'periods, the modern, the antique, and the old German together,
'yet here we trace the commencement of that manly confidence,
'which enabled German poetry to cast aside its foreign fetters,
'and to drop the humiliating attitude which it had maintained
'since the peace of Westphalia. It was, indeed, time that one
'should come, who could strike his hand upon his breast, and
'say, " I am a German." His poetry, like his patriotism, was
'deeply rooted in that lofty, moral, and religious belief, which
'sheds such lustre over his Messias, and it was he who, next to
'Gellert, imparted to modern German poetry that dignified, ear-
'nest, and pious character, which amidst all the excesses of fancy
'and wit, has never entirely deserted it, and which foreign na-
'tions have always continued to contemplate in us with admira-
'tion or awe. When we recollect the influence of the frivolous
'old French philosophy, and of the ridicule of Voltaire, we are
'first made sensible, how strong a bulwark was opposed by Klop-
'stock to those foreign influences upon the taste of Germany.

' His patriotism and his exalted religious feeling have contri-
'buted more to the high position which he will always occupy,
'than his improvements on the language. It is true he loses
'every thing when we examine him too near and in detail. He
'must be viewed in the mass, and at a certain distance. When
'we read him, he often appears pedantic and tedious; when we
'have read him, when we think of him in recollection, he appears
'great and majestic. Then his two dominant ideas of patriotism
'and religion shine forth in all their simplicity, and leave on our
'minds an impression of majesty. We seem to look on some
'gigantic spirit of Ossian, stretching forth a monstrous harp into
'the clouds. If we approach him nearer, he dissolves into a broad
'mass of unsubstantial vapour. Still the first impression remains,
'and attunes our minds to elevated and elevating feeling. Al-
'though too cold and metaphysical, he has taught us two great
'lessons: the one, that our un-germanized poetry, long a stranger
'to its natural home, must again strike its roots into that soil, if
'it would grow into a healthy and majestic tree; and next, that
'all poetry, as it has its source, must also find its " being's end
'and aim " in religion.'

This just appreciation of Klopstock is immediately followed
by the extravagant and prejudiced attack upon Voss, to which
we alluded in the outset. With one observation, however, of
Menzel as applicable both to Klopstock and Voss we concur;

namely, that neither of them penetrated beyond the form and
into the spirit of antiquity. The first impulse in that direction
was given in the arts by the well-known and imaginative work of
Winckelmann. In poetry, it first appears distinctly in the graceful strains of Wieland. We rejoice to think that this true poet
and amiable man, whom it has of late been too much the fashion
to decry as a mere German Voltaire, dedicating his talents to
the advocacy of a French taste, and corrupting the literature of
Germany by a licentious pruriency of description, has found in
Menzel an eloquent, and as we think successful, defender.

' It was Wieland,' he observes, 'who transported into our German
'woods and Gothic cities, the light spirit of Athens, though not
'without an admixture of the still greater levity and playfulness
'of French genius. Wieland united in his character the Gallo-
'mania with the Greco-mania. He was born in the first faith,
'he passed at a later age into the latter; but he perceived at once
'the deviations of Klopstock and Voss from the true path, and led
'back the German poetry from its pompous stiffness to the free
'and natural graces of France and of Greece. The German muse,
'moving with cheerful freedom in the days of the Minnezeit
'(Lovetime), attired in starched linen by the Meister Sängers,*
'disguised in a periwig and hoop petticoats after the Thirty Years'
'War, knew not how to dispose of her hands, and continued to
'play lackadaisically with her fan. To assign to grace its due
'place and importance, a genial spirit was required, in whom
'this tendency should be exclusively developed. Wieland ap-
'peared, the cheerful, amiable, refined Wieland, a genius exhaust-
'less in grace and lightness, in wit and jest. We must first be
'acquainted with the stiff, disjointed, mannered, and puling period
'which preceded him ere we can appreciate the free movement of
'his genius. Wieland first restored to German poetry the free
'and fearless glance of a child of the world; a natural grace; a
'taste for cheerful merriment, and the power of affording it. Bold,
'humorsome, imposing, he cut off relentlessly the pigtails of the
'Philistines, stripped the blushing muse of her hoop petticoat, and
'taught the honest Germans of his day not to spend their time in
'playing with lambs in an ideal Idyllic world, like their predeces-
'sors the pastoral poets, but, by banishing the unnatural, to dis-
'cover nature in the world as it is, and to let the limbs restored
'to liberty move easily, firmly, and in harmony.

' The genius of Wieland was most strongly attracted towards

---

* The period of the Minnesingers, or Swabian period of German
literature.

'Greece. There he found the ideal of his graces; there he im-
'bibed the clear stream of life and nature. Few minds have
'domesticated themselves in that home of the beautiful—and each
'after his own fashion. An existence like that of Greek society
'is too great to be comprehended by a single mind. Only a life
'commenced and continued under such a form of existence could
'fully prepare us for the task. But we stand at a distance from
'that world; to few pilgrims is it vouchsafed to visit it, and even
'to these as to passing strangers. Wieland made the harmony
'and grace by which the whole life of Greece was interpenetrated
'his own. What Winckelmann did for the plastic arts, Wieland
'achieved for poetry. He taught us, by the example of the
'Greeks, to reacknowledge and to reproduce the beauty of nature.
'But while it is undeniable that he had successfully seized one of
'the prominent sides of Grecian existence, it is impossible to
'maintain that he has entirely penetrated either the spirit of
'Greek genius, or fathomed the profundity of the romantic.
'The plastic beauty of Greek architecture and statuary, the
'gaiety and harmony of the Grecian enjoyment of life; and the
'mirror-like smoothness, mingled with depth, of the Greek philo-
'sophy; all these seemed to stretch their rich and flowery
'blossoms to him partially as it were over the wall of Time,
'but nothing more. His Greek romances connect themselves
'only in a certain limited sense with the genius of Greece; in
'other respects, they are completely the productions of Wieland
'and the offspring of his time; in the creation of which also the
'French taste was by no means without its influence.

'His taste had turned towards the French in that original
'period of need which Frederick the Great and others of his time
'had felt so strongly. In knowledge of the world; in a taste for the
'clear treatment of the subject, and of all its relations, the French
'had then far surpassed the Germans. Since Voltaire, however,
'these writers had followed in so imitative a routine track, that be-
'tween them and the wittiest author of later antiquity, Lucian,
'there was actually but little difference. When we find then that
'Wieland, in his romantic poems, takes for his models not only
'Ariosto, but also Voltaire and Parny: in his romances, not only
'Lucian and Cervantes, but also Crebillon, Diderot, and Cazotte,
'we cannot but admire the address with which, in the midst of all
'his levity, he lays aside the filthiness, the moral poison of these
'talented but depraved Frenchmen, and places beside the grace of
'antiquity and the grace of France, a younger German grace, fair,
'naïve, coquettish, but innocent with all her coquetry. The skill
'with which Wieland moderated the French frivolity does more
'honour to his taste than his adoption of it does discredit to him.

'He has been often censured, often denounced as the destroyer of
'the moral purity of our nation, and in particular, our modern old
'German Nazarenes and Whiners (Seufzerer) have long made him
'the mark for their special condemnation. When I first ventured to
'vindicate and to praise him, the world was astonished, as the nu-
'merous and absurd reviews of the first edition sufficiently proved.
'Our wise generation really thought themselves entitled to look
'down on Wieland. That gentle spirit, nature's confident, through
'whose sun-illumined existence a smiling genius seemed to move,
'and touching with Oberon's lily sceptre the every-day realities of
'life, converted them into beauteous wonders: him whose clear
'calm-thinking spirit found in wisdom the measure of happiness,
'and moved towards the temple of Venus only through that of
'Urania; him, the graceful Apollo among the shepherds, a very
'present deity beside our German coteries, with skulls of more than
'Bœotian thickness; him did these prudish and malicious back-
'biters, with hanging mouth, blinking eyes, and folded hands,
'attempt to slander and defame. No! so long as the world
'knows what it is to smile and kiss, immortal Wieland, it
'will defend thee against these apes of the middle ages; and
'if ever a grace walked or shall walk on earth, in Wieland
'will she recognise her favoured son. It is not this natural
'and harmless merriment, but hypocritical sentimental unchas-
'tity, that we should condemn. Far from being the seducer
'of a nation from its purity, Wieland has rather brought back a
'people, already corrupted by the Gallomania, to decency and
'moderation, to cheerful and intellectual social enjoyment; it was
'the later sentimental and romantic writers, who, under cover of
'lofty and irresistible sensibilities, circulated that poison of morbid
'voluptuousness which was entirely foreign to the sound-hearted
'Wieland. It is not smiling pleasure we have to fear, but volup-
'tuousness—earnest, brooding, weeping and praying—voluptuous-
'ness such as we find it in Goëthe's, Heinsé's, Frederick Schle-
'gel's, and similar writings.'

What Wieland did for poetry, Lessing performed for German
prose. He gave it ease and strength, combining pellucid clearness of expression with profundity of thought. He has the clearness of Leibnitz, with a variety and consummate finish of style
which his predecessor wanted. He works out his thoughts with
the precision and polish of sculptured marble. Yet the labour is
not visible, for he leaves on them no mark of the chisel. Menzel
assigns him an almost equally high rank as a poet and as a critic,
a view in which we cannot concur. Lessing himself fairly confessed that to poetry he had no claim; that he did not feel
within himself ' the living spring working its way out by its

'own strength, and shooting forth in pure fresh and glowing 'streams. Every thing must be pressed out by dint of springs 'and wheel-work.' The true bent of his mind was not towards the creative art, but towards the investigation of its laws, and in this department he is a giant. It is true, that even in his criticism something of the same coldness is perceptible which we feel in his poetry. He does not readily warm into enthusiasm; he is too rigidly demonstrative, too anxious to be the Euclid of criticism.

Perhaps, however, this rigid and polemical style of criticism was a necessary consequence of the existing state of the public taste. Lessing seemed formed by nature for the task of clearing the ground for the reception of the good seed, by eradicating without mercy the noxious weeds which then encumbered the soil. To awaken the slumbering imagination of his country, and to give it a proper direction, it was first necessary to reform the intellect itself, and to teach men to think and reason rightly ere they gave the reins to their fancy: otherwise the probable transition would have been from the extreme of rigour to that of extravagance; from the cant of classical propriety and correctness, to the cant of romantic license and offensive sentimentalism. Hence the criticism of Lessing is naturally more of a destructive than of a constructive character; it is a continual crusade against the literary Philistines of his time. Single as he stood in the contest, he bore up with Atlantean shoulders against all opponents: wherever he turned in the conflict of opinions he made a wide and fearful opening in the ranks: in the struggle he neither gave nor took quarter. He bore down all opposition before him, and during the latter part of his life bestrode the world of criticism like a colossus in unquestioned supremacy.

His poetry, however, as we have already said, appears a less spontaneous product of his mind—a work of logical skill rather than of imagination. Emilia Galotti, for instance, is worthy of all praise, so far as regards the compactness of the plan; it has wit, eloquence, an appearance of symmetry and strong reasoning, but no one can be deceived into a belief that it is otherwise than prosaic. 'We start, for soul is wanting there.' Nathan the Wise appears to have more of the character of a great work of art. It flowed more naturally from the heart of Lessing, for it was the poetical developement of certain ideas of religious toleration which lay at the bottom of all his philosophy; in painting Nathan he painted himself or his friend Moses Mendelsohn, from whom many of his philosophical opinions took their rise. There is a certain pure Idyllic tone of serene wisdom, a Bramin-like character about it, which will always render it pleasing—but we find it

impossible to regard it with the same admiration with which it seems to be viewed in Germany. Menzel speaks with peculiar admiration of Lessing's management of the Iambic verse in this play. Goëthe, he says, thought only of melody and outward glitter, Schiller of impetuous force, and both deviated much from the natural and unpretending simplicity with which the Iambic had been treated by Lessing. 'The dramatic Iambic of 'modern plays has become too lyrical; with Lessing it ap-'proaches more nearly to prose, and is more dramatic.'

Passing over the interesting and well-written characteristic of Herder, we come to that portion of Menzel's work which has excited most attention and opposition in his own country—we mean his view of the genius and influence of Goëthe on German literature. The passage is too long to admit of being extracted as a whole, but the substance of his criticism we shall endeavour to exhibit in an English dress, before making any remarks of our own on his opinions.

'In Goëthe we perceive the exact contrast to Lessing. As 'Lessing emancipated the German mind from foreign influence, 'so Goëthe subjected it to this influence anew; as Lessing, with 'the whole powers and graces of his mind, combated sentiment-'alism, so Goëthe did homage to this womanish weakness of his 'time, and recommended it by his sweet strains, to all hearts . . . 'The only good connected with this tendency, and by means of 'which he attained his influence, was his mastery of *form;* the 'talent of language, of representation, of adornment. When we 'penetrate beneath this variegated cloud of form, we perceive the 'internal essence of his poetry, as of his whole life, to be egotism, 'not, however, the egotism of heroes and heaven-defying Titans, 'but that of Sybarites and players, the egotism of love of enjoy-'ment, and of the vanity of an artist. Goëthe made himself the 'central point of creation, excluded all his neighbourhood whom 'he could not render serviceable to him; and, in truth, exercised, 'by means of his talents, a magical influence over weak minds; 'but he availed himself of his powers and of his lofty position, 'not to elevate, to improve, or to emancipate mankind; not to 'reveal or to advocate a great idea; not in the conflicts in which he 'was a contemporary, but not an actor, to combat for right, free-'dom, honour, or patriotism . . . . If he found applause, he 'cared not for the sufferings of his country; he even vented ve-'nom against the free and manly movements of the time, the 'moment they began to disturb his tranquillity . . . . Adora-'tion of himself forms the substance of all his poems; his ideal 'was himself, the weak-hearted, voluptuous, vain child of for-'tune. In all his works, with the exception of some which are

---

'mere imitations, this miserable ideal appears prominent, and is
'flattered and dandled with a truly apish affection. Werther,
'Clavigo, Weisslingen, Fernando, Egmont, Tasso, the Man of
'Forty Years, Edward in the Wahl-verwandschaften, and Faust,
'all these are reflections of his ideal. At first he seems to have
'been somewhat ashamed of it; and if he paints Werther,
'Clavigo, and Weisslingen with evident partiality, as highly ami-
'able and interesting, he represents them as punished for their
'weaknesses; for he thought that the public, to whom he appealed,
'still consisted of *men*, before whom he must blush, and to whom
'he felt it necessary, at least at the conclusion, to sacrifice his
'heroes. At a later period, when he perceived the growing in-
'fluence of women and womanish men, and that the few true
'men who remained were driven into the background, he no
'longer gave himself that trouble; he no longer punished or
'made sacrifices of his heroes, but represented them with all their
'weaknesses and vanities as triumphant, particularly in his two
'great works, in which he has painted his own peculiarities, Wil-
'helm Meister and Faust. . . . . .
  'Lessing was a man in a womanish time: Goëthe remained a
'woman in a manly one. How otherwise can we explain the
'position which he maintained in regard to his age? Had he not
'been so completely immersed in his vanity, love of comfort, and
'desire of enjoyment, he must have taken a part in the great inte-
'rests of his country during the storms by which it was agitated.
  'Every word of his had the weight of an oracle, but he has
'never uttered one to incite his countrymen to honour, to animate
'them to noble thought or deed. He saw the world's history pass
'before him with indifference, or only fretted a little when his
'hours of ease were broken in upon by the alarum of war. Till
'the French Revolution Germany had slumbered: by this event
'it was fearfully awakened. What feelings did it awaken in the
'heart of our poet? Should we not expect that he would either,
'like Schiller have been excited to enthusiastic sympathy with the
'new order of things, or, like Görres, glowing with shame for the
'treachery and deep misery to which Germany was subjected, have
'striven to rouse his country to the recollections of its ancient honour
'and greatness? Yet what did Goëthe? He wrote some trifling
'comedies, the *Bürger General*, and the *Aufgeregten*, the weakest
'assaults which Germany has made against the French Revolution,
'the most worthless which in that hour of divine indignation could
'have been conceived by human brain. Then came Napoleon—
'What did the first of German poets think and say of him?
'Surely either, like Arndt and Körner, he must have invoked
'curses on the destroyer of his country, and placed himself at

'the head of the Tugendbund; * or if, in German fashion,
'he was more a cosmopolitan than a patriot, we might at least
'expect him, like Lord Byron, to seize and embody the deep
'tragic meaning of the hero and his fortunes. But what did
'Goëthe? He waited till Napoleon bestowed on him a few
'flattering expressions, and then he indited for him a spiritless
'epithalamium. Napoleon fell: and Germany shook with the
'roar of battles, in which the people were the combatants; since
'the conquest of the world by Attila, nothing so vast, so over-
'powering, had been witnessed by man; since the destruction of
'the legions of Varus, the German breast had never been heaved
'so high by the awful inspiration of freedom. What was then the
'employment of the first of German poets? What did Goëthe? He
'shut himself up: he studied Chinese, as he himself complacently
'relates, and first found it convenient, after peace was concluded,
'and after solicitation from high quarters, to compose something
'patriotic, viz. the Waking of Epimenides, a miserable patch-
'work, a piece of constrained and simulated sympathy. To con-
'clude, he was intrusted with the duty of composing an inscrip-
'tion for the monument of Blucher, and the first of German
'poets wrote a few paltry verses, which would have done no cre-
'dit to the last of German poets. . . . .
'That Goëthe never entered the lists for the honour of
'Germany was of less injurious consequence than that the re-
'sources of his rich mind should have been lavished in favouring
'the progress of its debasement. He was the creator of that
'widely diffused modern poetry, which, under the pretext of
'abiding by and exhibiting the fair side of reality, had for its
'true object the embellishment and defence of all its weaknesses,
'vanities, follies, and sins. Goëthe has not laboured to ennoble
'the present by any poetical idealization; he has not even adhered
'to that Homeric simplicity and openness of delineation which
'adheres truly and closely to nature as it is, but his prevailing
'tendency is to take under his protection, on the one hand, the
'sentimental absurdities, the womanish weakness of character,
'which made us ripe plants for the giant scythe of Napoleon: and
'on the other, the aristocratic privileges of frivolity, the polite
'exceptions from moral rules, the poetical licenses to which the
'Don-Juan nature is entitled. The one necessarily required the
'other. His aristocratic libertinism could only have been tole-
'rated by the side of this civic sentimentality. So Goëthe

---

* A well-known patriotic association of the time.

34

'found his public: for his egotism whatever was was right; and
'so he wished it to remain. . . . .

'He was the most perfect mirror of modern life—in his life as
'in his poetry. He had but to paint himself, to depict the modern
'world—its views, its inclinations, its worth, and worthlessness.
'The same *talent* which he shows in his works he rendered avail-
'able in life. And who can deny that his example has become the
'life-maxim of the modern world? The talent of social existence,
'the knowledge of the comfortable, the light, the refined; the
'connoisseurship of enjoyment was his talisman in reality, and
'seemed to him also the worthiest subject for poetry. To this he
'owed a popularity which no ancient or romantic poet, with the
'exception of Schiller, ever attained. The noble, the humane,
'gave their voices for Schiller—the reigning opinion, the fashion
'of the moment, was in favour of Goëthe. Schiller writes for the
'noble of all time; Goëthe was the idol of his own, and he was,
'and could be so only by opening his mind with the same pas-
'siveness and indifference to its weaknesses and its unnatural
'character, as to that remnant of nobleness which it still retained.
'The tone of modern society he represents to the life. The
'external decency, the politeness, the mask of cheerfulness in
'social intercourse, the insinuation, the *delicatesse*, the thinly
'disguised malice, the *aqua toffana*, which circulates like cold
'blood through the veins of educated and polished society—these
'magic arts of talent we may find developed by Goëthe with con-
'summate mastery. His works form a school of polite culture,
'from which manners may be refined, and round him flocks an
'innumerable army of young men—the disciples and apostles of
'this gospel of politeness, the indefatigable opponents of the
'ancient rudeness, the *jeunesse dorée* of Germany. Under this
'smooth and smiling mask is concealed a refined epicurism, a
'sensuality and appetite for enjoyment, which, refine it as we
'may, still remains thoroughly mean and unworthy, which jests
'at every thing earnest and sacred, and allures its lightly seduced
'votaries into an earthly paradise—into that Venusberg, from
'which there is no issue to the light of day. . . . .

'Goëthe has always trod in beaten paths. His first work, the
'Sorrows of Werther, is nothing but a clever imitation of Rous-
'seau's new Heloise. This visionary sentimentalism proceeded
'not from Goëthe but from Rousseau; and Goëthe wreathed
'his brows with a laurel, which of right belonged to him of
'Geneva. With all this, Werther is inferior to the Heloise,
'however attractive some of its pictures may be.

'In his slighter comedies, such as the Accomplices, Goëthe
'copied Molière and Beaumarchais, without equalling them. In
'his earliest prosaic-tragedies, he took Lessing, and partly Shak-
'speare, for his models. Clavigo is a weak copy of Emilia Ga-
'lotti. Goetz of Berlichingen, and Egmont, betray a mixture
'of the styles of Lessing and Shakspeare. The beauties of
'Goetz are chiefly owing to the well-known and true-hearted
'autobiography of the knight; yet in these prose tragedies there
'is nothing which can entitle them to take their place beside
'those of Shakspeare and Lessing—they are deformed by co-
'quetry and affectation.

'In his lyric poems, Goëthe copied the ancient popular songs,
'and scrupled not, while he adopted these, occasionally to claim
'for himself the merit of their invention. In this department he
'was influenced by Herder, as in those already alluded to by
'Rousseau and Lessing. In Hermann and Dorothea he copied
'old Voss.

'Goëthe is truly original only in Faust and Wilhelm Meis-
'ter, because here, as already mentioned, he copied—himself.'

That there is much in this estimate of Goëthe's character,
moral, intellectual, and poetical, which is of questionable truth,
and some things which are unquestionably not true, we believe;
but, on the other hand, there is much in it to which the warmest
and ablest of his admirers have never yet made a satisfactory
answer. It matters not much whether we give him credit only
with Menzel for the perfection of mere talent, or whether we, with
more justice, admit his claim to a large portion of poetical *genius*.
In either case, we cannot ascribe to him the highest and purest
quality of genius, that which regards poetry as a divine gift, a talent intrusted to human hands to be put to account, and to be
employed only on the noblest subjects, to be expended only in
forwarding, elevating, and purifying the heart, and the great
destinies of men. There is an unholy admixture of egotism and
selfishness in that mind, which, instead of interesting itself in the
great interests of the time, shuts itself up forever in a passive
tranquillity; there is a want of that diviner spirit which shines
conspicuous in Milton and Schiller in him, whose source of inspiration is but a refined materialism, and from whose writings
no other principle of conduct is to be derived, but that of con-
forming ourselves to the world, and making its weaknesses and
worthlessness tributary to our enjoyment. A Milton and a
Schiller would have disdained to influence their age by ministering indifferently to its virtues or its follies, gilding over its hollowness, and placing the chief aim of existence in the cultivation of
the beautiful, and the substitution of a fanciful system of refined
Epicurism, an atheism of art, as Novalis happily styles it, for the

solid bulwarks of religion, and the active duties which Providence has prescribed to us in this ' weary working world.'

So far, then, as regards the spirit and tendency of Goëthe's works, we concur with every thing which Menzel has said. He was assuredly not one of those, ' whose soul was as a star, and dwelt apart.' He was content to lend himself to the influence of the spirit of his age, that he might, within his own favourite, but by no means elevated sphere of operation, influence it in turn. He has been its organ, but when has he been its legislator, its reformer, or its guide? A mind of the very highest order would not, from the mere pride of showing its plastic powers on all subjects, have betrayed in its pictures of life that indifference to the moral qualities of actions, and to the moral effect of the situations represented, which Goëthe manifests in all his novels, where the malice, the selfishness, the secret vices, the grovelling motives of society, are portrayed with the same indulgence, the same complacency, the same graceful finish of pencil—(which led Novalis to call Goëthe the Wedgewood of German literature)—as its traits of generosity, and kindliness, or redeeming feeling; all being seemingly regarded as matters in which there lies no essential beauty or deformity, but which are to receive their character from the artist-like skill with which they are handled. Nay, sometimes, as if by a peculiar degree of moral perverseness, he seems purposely to have selected (as in some of the scenes of the Wahlverwandschaften, which we are glad to see, for the credit of the public taste, has *not* yet found a translator) that class of delineations which he knew that the common feelings of right-minded men would have proscribed, merely to exhibit a literary *tour de force*, and to make the skill of the artist more apparent, by contrast with the almost revolting groundwork on which it was to be exercised. Goëthe certainly gained by this means the immediate popularity and patronage of that part of society whose vices he touched, with all the delicacy of one who never mentions hell to ears polite, and around whose better qualities he had thrown the charm of an inimitable style, and of the utmost subtlety and refinement of delineation. They hastened to return the obligation, by elevating their apologist at once to the high-priesthood of poetry, well aware that they had little to dread from the strictness with which the law was likely to be enforced at his hands. But to all who feel the close, the inseparable connexion which should subsist between the aim of literature and the cultivation of the heart, there is something in these novels of Goëthe which is chilling and deadening in a high degree. Amidst all the polished beauty and marble grace of their execution, we regard them with cold admiration, not with sympathy; we feel that they

contain nothing by which we can be made wiser and better; and we turn in disappointment from the man who, when we ask for bread, coldly presents us with a stone.

But while we thus subscribe to the truth of most of Menzel's opinions in regard to the moral defects of Goëthe's works, and the injurious effect on literature which is likely to have been produced by that supremacy over the German mind which he has enjoyed without a rival since the death of Schiller, we cannot but feel the injustice and prejudice which is apparent in the concluding observations of Menzel on the want of originality, or even merit in a purely literary point of view, in most of his productions. To say that Werther is a mere echo of the Heloise, that the inspiration which gave birth to that remarkable production was entirely derived from Rousseau, is almost ludicrously unjust. Rousseau's Heloise embodied only the passionate longings of a single morbid and most peculiarly constituted mind: Werther was the organ through which the complaints, the restlessness, the hopelessness; in short, the whole spirit and essence of a most remarkable era in the progress of human existence was vented in burning words, and with all the sincerity of one to whom (though at the moment of its composition he had outlived that morbid state of mind, in which it had its rise) the moral and political chaos which ushered in the close of the eighteenth century was still, in its stern and awe-inspiring reflections, painfully present and familiar. Werther is no copy from a French original; it is a portrait, painted as *we*, no doubt, are apt to think, in startling outlines, in theatrical colours, of what Goëthe himself, in the first flush of youth, had been,—of what half the youth of Germany had been during those days of reckless enquiry and self-satisfied illumination; the image of youthful presumption, full of gigantic projects for the reform of a degenerate world, which, however, result in no action, but evaporate in a puling and washy sentimentalism; aspiring to rule over others, yet incapable of controlling a single passion, vice, or propensity of its own; dashing itself with a vain effort against the barriers of society, yet without the manliness to endure the wounds and bruises which are the necessary result. A painful picture, no doubt, and to us—as we have said, far removed from the scene of action, or rather of confused babble, ending in no action whatever,—dashed, as it now seems, with a tinge of fierceness and extravagance. But the immediate and universal sensation which it produced on all who had been spectators or actors in this troubled scene, is a sufficient proof that the picture was one of strong resemblance and of deep interest and significance; and one for which Goëthe was indebted, not to Rousseau, but to his own accurate and acute poetic vision, which enabled him to discern with instinctive and prophetic eye the brooding and convulsive spirit of the age, as it floated before him; and with a gloomy but fascinating eloquence to give to its dim and uncertain lineaments colour and form.

In the observations on Goëthe's comedies, there is more justice. To Molière's, indeed, they have little resemblance; but a likeness to those of Beaumarchais is not unfrequently perceptible. In any view they are not entitled to a high rank. Of the *vis comica*, Goëthe had extremely little. He was always too intent on preserving his dignity, to abandon himself with sufficient nature and unreserve to the comic capabilities of his subject. 'Even ' his commonest thoughts,' says Menzel, not without truth, ' he ' used to dress up in silk stockings, and made them a low bow ' at parting.' But from the observations on Clavigo, Egmont, and Goetz of Berlichingen we entirely dissent. We believe Menzel monopolizes the opinion that Clavigo is either a weak copy, or indeed has any one point of connexion with Emilia Galotti. Egmont, if it be inspired by the spirits of Shakspeare and Lessing, has at least a decided and substantive individuality, and, with all deference, appears to us to be much superior to any drama which Lessing has ever attempted. It is still more prejudiced and ridiculous to ascribe the merits of Goetz of Berlichingen to the old autobiography of Goetz himself. The chronicle might, indeed, suggest a hint; but where, in the autobiography, were to be found the materials for this brilliant, comprehensive, and moving picture of the sixteenth century, with its contending religious creeds; the one defended with all the constancy of determination, founded on time-honoured faith, the other advocated with the equally conscientious zeal of newly-awakened Protestantism;—of the sixteenth century, with its struggles between feudal power and imperial despotism, the spirit of chivalry and the spirit of commerce;—the sixteenth century, with its iron-handed yet gentle-hearted warriors, like him of the iron hand himself; its noble matrons; its pure and simple-minded maidens, who, where they have once placed their hearts, with such bewitching and trusting openness bestow their hands; with its luxurious abbots; its weak and wavering court minions; its sweet and natural transitions from the battle and the banquet, to the stillness and household seclusion of ancestral castles, overhanging the silver-blue Maine or the winding Rhine; a pageant which first awakened the powers of Scott, and which Scott himself, in his brightest creations, has scarcely surpassed?

Of his lyrics we shall only say that while they may have owed something to the popular ballads, which Goëthe thoroughly studied, and the spirit of which he has caught with peculiar tact and beauty, their beauties, their peculiar charm, is in a great measure their own. We find, however, that our own opinion, in regard to Goëthe's lyrical pieces, has been so well expressed by the most eloquent of his English critics, that we beg to substitute his estimate of them for our own. ' Goëthe is no where more entirely ' original, more fascinating, more indescribable, than in his smaller ' poems. One quality which very generally marks them, particu-' larly those of a later date, is their peculiar expressiveness, their ' fulness of meaning. A single thing is said, and a thousand ' things are indicated. They are spells which cleave to our me-' mory, and by which we summon beautiful spirits from the vasty ' deep of thought. Often at the first aspect they appear com-' monplace or altogether destitute of significance; we look at the ' lines on the canvas, and they seem careless dashes, mere random ' strokes representing nothing save the caprices of their author; ' we change our places, we shift and shift, till we find the right ' point of view, and all at once a fair figure starts into being, en-' circled with graces and light charms, and by its witcheries at-' tracting heart and mind. In his songs he recalls to us those of ' Shakspeare; they are not speeches, but musical tones; the sen-' timent is not stated in logical sequence, but poured forth in fitful ' and fantastic suggestions; they are the wild wood-notes of the ' nightingale. They are to be *sung* not *said*.'

We feel the necessity, however, of breaking off somewhat abruptly from the subject of Goëthe, in order to spare room for a portion of Menzel's remarks on Schiller, who is his poetical ideal, and whom he delights to exhibit in favourable contrast with his great, but, as he thinks, over-estimated rival. We confess, in this respect, we most cordially and warmly second his views. The fame of Schiller is now placed on the sure basis of experience; and it may be safely said it has not declined since the close of his earthly career. We shall be much mistaken if that of Goëthe, great as it will always justly remain, be not shorn of many of its beams within an equal period. No two writers or men could be more decidedly contrasted in the character of their minds, or the principles of their composition. What Goëthe's views in these matters were, we have already seen; Schiller, on the contrary, though the experience of manhood modified the vehemence of youth, never ceased to his latest hour to regard literature, not as the object of his plastic dexterity, not as a mere airy allegoric dream, but in its most earnest and exalted aspect; he turns with disgust from the mean, the commonplace, the transitory; he invests all he looked upon with grandeur even the barest realities of life come forth from his hand with an ideal colouring of beauty and love; he clothes, like his own Wallenstein,

> 'The palpable and the familiar
> With golden exhalations of the dawn.'

What Goëthe wants, he possesses in perfection; he cannot be indifferent to the subject of which he treats; he seems to have thought it impossible to bestow the name of poetry on that which, while it imitated, did not also exalt and idealize humanity. His earnestness of character, the depth and sincerity of his convictions, rendered it impossible for him to descend to an æsthetic coquetry with the great interests of literature and of mankind. He resembles Goëthe only in this, that as Goëthe in his ideal creations draws from himself as his own 'great original,' so Schiller lends his own nobleness of soul, his own simplicity, purity, and unstudied dignity to all the creations of his genius. All of them resemble each other, for all of them resemble him. They may be compared to the spectres of the Brocken, for they are all shadows of himself, magnified upon a sun-gilt medium of cloud.

This is the source of the deep charm of Schiller's writings; their wonderful blending of passion with purity; of the liveliest, the most enthusiastic sympathies, with a philosophic breadth and comprehensiveness of view. But all we could say on this subject has been said so truly and so much better by Menzel, that we shall conclude this desultory article by extracting the conclusion of his noble panegyric on Schiller, with every word of which we concur.

'The heroes of Schiller are distinguished by a nobleness of 'nature which acts on us like the pure and perfect beauty of a 'picture of Raphael; by something regal which awakens in us a 'holy awe. This beam of higher light, cast into the dark shadows 'of earthly ruin, only shows the clearer; under the mask of hell 'the angelic countenance shines forth the more resplendent and 'lovely.

'The first secret of this loveliness lies in the angelic innocence 'which always forms the deep basis of the noblest natures. This 'nobility of innocence reappears under the features of a pure youth- 'ful angel in all Schiller's creations. In sun-like transfiguration, 'in the form of pure childhood, wholly unarmed, and yet invul- 'nerable, it manifests itself in Fridolin, like the king's son in 'the story, smiling and playing with the wild beasts of the forest, 'and yet uninjured by them.

'The moment they become conscious of their own bliss, that 'moment the envy of destiny is awakened against them. In this 'new and pathetic aspect, we contemplate them as Hero and 'Leander. Adorned with the warlike helmet, their cheeks flush- 'ing with the glow of noble passion, youthful innocence advances 'confident against all the dark powers of hell. Thus has Schiller 'represented them in the Diver and the Surety—in the unfortu- 'nate lovers Charles de Moor and Amelia—in Ferdinand and 'Louisa—above all in Max Piccolomini and Thekla. Above 'these touching forms, floats a magic of poetry which has never 'yet been equalled; it is the note of a flute amidst a peal of wild 'and dissonant music—a glimpse of blue sky amidst a storm—a 'paradise upon the edge of a crater.

'If Shakspeare's female creations appear to possess more of 'the charm of a lily-like purity, the virgins of Schiller possess 'more of that soul of the lily, its powerful and lively perfume, 'and approach nearer to the creations of Sophocles. They are 'not weaklings, like the saints of Carlo Dolce or Correggio; they 'have in them a sacred fire of strength, like the Madonnas of 'Raphael; they do not merely touch, but inspire us.

'The purity of the virgin appears most prominent at the mo- 'ment when she stands forth as the champion of God. It is the 'deep mystery of Christianity and of Christian poetry that the 'salvation of the world proceeds from a woman—the highest 'power from the purest innocence. In this sense has Schiller 'composed his Maid of Orleans; and she is the most perfect 'embodiment of that warlike angel who wears the helm and bears 'the banner of heaven.

'Schiller has succeeded also in portraying this virgin inno- 'cence in union with the noblest developement of genuine man- 'hood. Among these, three holy and heroic forms stand out pre- 'eminent; the warrior youth, Max Piccolomini, pure, unspotted 'by all the vices of the camp and of his home; the Marquis Posa, 'whose soul, though adorned by all intellectual culture, has yet 'remained the unsullied temple of innocence; and lastly, that 'strong and simple-hearted son of the mountain, William Tell, 'fit companion to the Maid of Orleans.

'If in them innocence shines forth in its purest glory, Schiller 'knew also how to represent the conflict between this original 'innocence and the guilty stain induced by strong passions; and 'he has called up before our souls the representation of this con- 'test with the same love and the same perfection of art. How 'deeply does the Magdalen-like character of Mary Stuart sink 'into our hearts! What can be more touching than Karl 'Moor's conquest over himself! How incomparably talented, 'true, and agitating is the mental conflict which shakes the great 'souls of Fiesco and Wallenstein!

'We turn now to the second secret of beauty in Schiller's ideal

6. continued

' characters; this is their nobility, their honourable nature. His
' heroes and heroines never belie that pride and dignity which are
' the appanages of noble natures; every thing that emanates from
' them bears the stamp of magnanimity and inborn nobleness.
' They are the antipodes to all that is common, and to all the
' conventional rules by which common natures are led and fet-
' tered. Powerful, free, self-relying, original, following only the
' impulse of a noble nature, Schiller's heroes tear in sunder the
' nets in which common men drag along their everyday exist-
' ence. It is highly characteristic of Schiller's poetry, that his
' heroes bear along with them that stamp of genius, that imposing
' majesty of deportment, which in actual life distinguishes the no-
' bility of nature. The seal of Jove is impressed upon all their
' brows. In his first poems, no doubt, this freedom and boldness of
' bearing displays itself in a somewhat rugged and uncouth form;
' and in the elegant Weimar the poet himself was afterwards in-
' duced to attempt the task of bestowing some tincture of refinement
' upon his Robbers. But who could fail through the rough crust to
' discern the pure diamond of the noble nature that lay beneath?
' Whatever weaknesses we may point out in Moor, in Cabal and
' Love, and in Fiesco, I can look upon them only as those of the old
' German hero Perceval, who, even as an untutored boy, and in
' childish garb, manifested his noble and heroic heart, to the con-
' fusion of all scoffers; nay, the power of moral beauty in a noble
' nature can never be more touching, more fascinating, than when
' it so unconsciously exposes itself to a one-sided ridicule.

' The third and highest secret of the beauty of Schiller's crea-
' tions is the fire of noble passions. This is the fire which ani-
' mates every noble heart; it is the fire of the ascending sacrifice
' to the powers of heaven—the vestal flame guarded by consecrated
' hands in the temple of God—the Promethean spark brought
' down from heaven to infuse a godlike spirit into mankind—the
' Pentecost fire of inspiration in which souls are baptized—the
' phœnix flame in which our race renews its youth for ever. With-
' out the glow of noble passions, there can be nothing great either
' in life or poetry. Genius ever bears within it this celestial
' fire, and all its creations are interpenetrated by it. Schiller's ideal
' creations are the legitimate offspring of his own noble heart;
' parted beams from his own central fire. The honour of pos-
' sessing at once the purest and the strongest passion belongs to
' Schiller above all other poets. None with so pure a heart ever
' possessed so much fire; none with so much fire possessed such
' purity. Thus we see the purest of earthly substances, the
' diamond, when once inflamed, burn with a splendour and a
' glow, beside which all other fire seems dim and troubled.

' Where, we ask, is love to be found more chaste, more sacred,
' than that which Schiller felt and breathed into the souls of his
' lovers? And where, on the other hand, do we find it so glow-
' ing and powerful—invincible against a world in arms—awaken-
' ing the deepest energies of the soul—patiently enduring the
' most trying of sacrifices? From its earliest and softest charm
' —from the first meeting of the eyes—from the first light beat-
' ing of the heart to the most convulsive tempest of feeling—
' from the overpowering deed of virgin valour to the sublime
' sacrifice of two loving souls,—love here unfolds before us the
' incalculable riches of its beauty—like a sacred music rising from
' the softest note into the fullest storm of pealing chords.'

With this eloquent tribute to our favourite Schiller we take
our leave of Dr Menzel. The quotations we have made will, we
admit, give little or no idea of the views which he entertains of
German literature at the present day, or his hopes and fears in
regard to its future prospects; but we hope we have quoted
enough to satisfy our readers that his views on these subjects are
not likely to be commonplace in conception, deficient in comprehensiveness, or feeble in expression, and to induce them to satisfy
themselves on these points by a perusal of his volumes.

39

7. FOREIGN QUARTERLY REVIEW, 16 (1836), 1-26. M/H No. 3246. *Cf.* Carré, p. 124. By J. S. Blackie.

THE

FOREIGN

QUARTERLY REVIEW

ART. I.—1. *Die Deutsche Litteratur*, von Wolfgang Menzel. Stuttgart. 1828.
2. *Menzel's Geschichte der Deutschen*, in einem Bande. Stuttgart und Tübingen. 1834. 7te Lieferung. 21stes Buch. Die moderne Bildung.
3. *Conversations Lexicon der neuesten Zeit und Litteratur.* Leipzig. 1833. Voce, Menzel.

WOLFGANG MENZEL is a writer who deserves to be better known than he is in this country. He is a man of more than ordinary calibre. He has *stuff* in him. The German authors in general may be divided into five classes: *Fantastics, Mystics, System-builders, Poetical-idealists*, or men of fancy and feeling, *Eruditi*, ὅπλιται, or men of learning and science. Hoffman, Chamisso, Fouqué, are well known as heads of the fantastic school; devils, gnomes, sylphs, Undines, *Doppelgänger*, and animal magnetists, are the commodities in which they deal; a pair of seven-league boots, or a bottle of devil's elixir, is the magic wand of their enchantments. Tauler and Jacob Böhmen, Novalis, Friedrich Schlegel, Steffens, Jung Stilling, Görres, &c. are the no less celebrated heads of the mystic school. They rise a degree above the fantastics, and, amid much of the childish, contain a great deal of the essentially sublime. Their ideas, though not apt to be over clear, are never shallow, often profound, and not seldom grand; if they sit not on the throne of Jove, they float upon the clouds wherewith it is encompassed. The System-builders, again, are men of enterprize and of grasp. If they are mad—as to a British perception they sometimes appear—their madness has "method" in it. Their mysticism—when mystics they are—is not a floating dream, a creation of clouds, but a pervading principle, an organizing power, a vivifying emanation. Schelling may be considered as the king of this higher class of mystics: and it may well be doubted whether the human mind is ever exhibited in a more august and commanding form than in their brotherly amalgamation of science, religion, and poetry.

Applied more closely to nature, this systematic mysticism produces such men as Oken and Schubert; whose comprehensive minds seem, in studying to recreate nature, to give us an anticipation, if not a knowledge, of her secret workings and wondrous developments. But the System-builders are not all mystics; Kant and Hegel are not less wonderful examples of the power and compass of the German mind than Schelling—the clear acuteness of the one, and the abstract logicality of the other, belong equally to the wide domain of German intellect. Our fourth class is that of the Poetical-idealists. Schiller is a larger and Körner a minor star in the constellation. Jean Paul's weeping heroes are scarcely less celebrated than Werther and Siegwart. There is a deep fountain of feeling in the German mind, often opened into tears, with which the robuster Briton cannot always sympathize; but, if tearful eyes are sometimes a sign of babyhood, tearless eyes are often the index of selfishness. Next follow the men of mere talent, to whom frugal Nature hath denied the *divini ignis particula*—these men are more numerous every where than the men of genius; but in Germany they are particularly abundant and of a higher order. There are few trifling, few superficial minds in Germany—what an honest *Deutscher* does, he does with all his might, and leaves no corner of the earth unransacked, where stones of fit size and beauty may be found, with which to fabricate his erudite mosaics. Therefore it is that we have designated the learned of Germany ὅπλιται; they are heavy-armed soldiers, panoplied with the lore of all tongues and of all ages; their works are sometimes splendid temples of science, often proud-towering rubbish-heaps of useless learning. The perseverance of a German is proverbial—"*cui nationi, inter animi dotes*"—says Leibnitz, though a German himself—*sola laboriositas concessa esse videtur.*" A hard saying: but in some respects true. If German literature is useful for nothing else, it is useful, yea indispensable, as an index to the literature of the whole world.

Sed quorsum hæc? Our end is to show what Wolfgang Menzel is, by first setting forth, comprehensively, what he is not. He is neither a fantastic, nor a mystic, nor a system-builder, nor a poetical-idealist, nor a mere heavy-armed man of erudition. In so far as by *Germanism* we understand *nonsense*, whether it be ignorant nonsense or learned nonsense, nonsense puerile, or nonsense senile—whether it be clever nonsense or silly nonsense, nonsense religious, philosophical, poetical, musical, artistical, political—thus far, we can assure such of our readers as are, not without reason, apprehensive of being infected with the epidemic disease of *Teutomania*—that Wolfgang Menzel is no German. "*Er schreibt wie ein Britte*"—said one of his countrymen, in giving his opinion of Menzel's style. " He writes like an Eng-lishman!" certainly a very strange, and to us, a very compli-mentary manner for a German to express his admiration of one of his native authors.

To pass from negatives to positives, we would say—Menzel is a man of a sound mind, of a strong mind, of an acute mind, and of a comprehensive mind. He is essentially of the Doric order. He has more power than beauty, and his beauty is always of a masculine cast, seldom if ever softened down into feminine sweet-ness. To illustrate the unknown by the known, he has more affi-nity with Lessing than with any other German author familiar to the British student. He has also some of the fire and some of the sarcasm of Martin Luther; and when we have compared him with two such great names in the history of German litera-ture—always, of course, *deductis deducendis*—we have said enough to indicate that we have to do with a mind of no ordinary calibre. Menzel is decidedly a practical man and a sound-headed man; with him there is no vague dreaming, no inter-minable groping, no high-sounding but empty palaver—he fixes his eyes upon that which human eyes can see at one glance, and pursues his cue with indefatigable endeavour and certain success. He never prefers a circuitous route to a straight one, when the straight is equally convenient—he never loses sight of the end in the means—and, from all his speculations, which, as being those of a German, are many, both wide and deep, returns to the all-important question—how, under present circumstances, the civil and religious condition of his country may most surely and most speedily be ameliorated? With Pfitzer, Schott, and a few other high-minded patriots in south-western Germany, Menzel has done a great deal to draw the minds of his countrymen away from those splendid but profitless dreameries in which they have too long indulged, and taught them to apply their hands to the more solid though less dazzling architecture of practical life. With this tendency, Menzel's literary existence could not do otherwise than assume a polemical character; and, to sustain this character, Nature seems to have armed her chosen champion with the choicest weapons, both offensive and defensive, for intellectual warfare. Strong and able-bodied from his youth, he endeavoured, though unsuccessfully, to realize in practice those gymnastics of the Greeks on which the erudition of consumptive pedants had so long fruitlessly commented; to recal his transcendental coun-trymen from the learning of the dead to the wisdom of the living, has been, and is, his unremitting endeavour. To attain these ends, unflinching rebukes and unsparing satires could not be applied with too much resolution; and in the fearlessness of the

one, Menzel has no equal but in Fichte, as in the severity of the other he has no rival but in Richter. Heine and Börne be-spatter their countrymen with the merciless mud of vulgar abuse, and hold their political sloth up to the scorn of Europe, amid the squibs and crackers of Parisian wit. Not so Menzel. He sees the weakness of his country, but he also knows its strength; his lash, when called for, is speedy and unsparing, but not inflicted with a willing hand, or with an air of malignant triumph. He may warn, he may rebuke, but he will not curse the mother that bore him. Like the author of the *Reisebilder*, Wolfgang Menzel is a ringleader of that bold sect which has ventured to call in question the title of Göthe to the kingly seat on the German Parnassus—but he is too dignified to indulge in literary Billings-gate, and no protrusive egotism leads us to question the purity of those motives by which his opposition is animated. He is a preacher of new doctrines, but not as a babbler; a caster-down of images, but not as a fanatic.

Our author is a poet, a critic, an historian, a politician—and, as all German authors are, a philosopher. It is only in his critical capacity that we have at present any concern with him—but no man can read a page of his " German Literature" without per-ceiving that the acuteness of the critic is here merely an instru-ment in the hand of the profound philosopher, the brilliant poet, the patriotic politician.

The work to which we propose more particularly to direct our attention—the " Deutsche Litteratur"—has been long known and valued in Germany as the most profound and most original work on its native literature that has yet appeared in that country. Franz Horn's works are brisk and lively, and at the same time most comprehensive and exhaustive in their erudition—but he is too thoroughly German in his feelings to be relished by those who have not studied at Berlin or at Munich—his veneration, too, for a certain Christian simplicity and quietistical calmness of character often borders closely on mawkishness and puerility. Menzel again, is, as we have said, a man of nerve—nothing femi-nine, weak, or dreamy, nothing empty or childish, can he tolerate; *manly* is the image and superscription of his being. We have little doubt, therefore, that, if ever introduced, this author will become a favourite with the British public—at least such of them who, amid the bustle of ephemeral politics, still retain an eye for the beauty of art and the dignity of intellect.

The work on German literature is not a history but a charac-teristic—not a geographical tracing of the stream from its foun-tain-head to its æstuary, but a panoramic view of the landscape, its present state, and future prospects. It is divided into two parts,

41

7. continued

that stand to one another in the relation of spirit to body, of principle to practice. The one is the physiology, the other the classification, of literary botany. The first part contains the following titles: " The Mass of Literature—Nationality—Influence of School-learning—Influence of Foreign Literature—The Trade of Literature—Religion—Philosophy—History—State-Education." The second part is well digested under three heads: " Nature—Art—Criticism." The style of Menzel is so solid and so well squared, that there is little or no room for the lopping or epitomizing work of the reviewer. He himself gives us only the essence and extract of long digested and closely compacted thoughts. There remains for us, therefore, little or nothing to do but to select and give prominence to some of those paragraphs that, either from their own nature or from British associations, are likely to be read with peculiar interest.

The literature of a nation is but the reflex, or rather we should say it is the offspring, of its character—and he who would know the son must know the father. What then is the national character of the Germans? Some people tell us that they have no national character at all; or, if they have any, it consists in a sort of " wise passiveness" (not exactly in Wordsworth's sense) whereby they receive into themselves and appropriate the characters of all nations that are or have been on the stage of the world. " We are bears," says Menzel, " in the eyes of many, and can do nothing without a foreign dancing-master." And, truly, if we consider the successive Gallomania, Anglomania, and Græcomania, that gave a name to the most important eras of German literature, we shall see some causes to fear that this accusation is not altogether groundless. No person can say that Shakspeare or Milton imitated any man or nation of men: they are as thoroughly original, as much *sui generis*, as Homer and Æschylus; but Wieland, it is said, was a Frenchman, Klopstock an Englishman (a caricature of Milton), and Göthe was a Greek. Certain it is that in no country is foreign literature so universally studied as in Germany. To see the ardour with which they throw themselves on our Shakspeares and our Scotts, and even our Bulwers and our Wilsons,* one should imagine that the idolatry which is paid to Göthe and Schiller consists more in a sort of national pride, than in a real admiration of any thing substantially excellent in these authors. Surely a nation that imports so

* We have on our table a work entitled " Tom Cringle's Schiff 's Tagebuch, oder Abentheuer eines Offiziers der Englischen Marine, von Wilson: aus dem Englischen übersetzt von August Schaefer." We congratulate the learned professor on this unexpected accession to his continental fame!

much foreign corn must be wofully barren of native aliment. Such are the arguments of those who decry the literature of Germany without knowing it; forgetting too, that, even if the Germans were so devoid of originality as they represent them, this very lack of national character, this very merging of the character of *German* in that of *man*, is capable of an explanation which redounds most highly to the honour of the Teutonic race. Menzel sees the evil and acknowledges it as freely as any of our dogmatical criticasters may; but he knows also that there is no evil that has not also its concomitant good; and, of this universality, and manysidedness, as it is called, this imitative instinct and appropriating power of the German mind, he gives the following account.

" The deepest fount of this inclination for things foreign (says he, p. 44) is the *humanity* of the German character. We are thorough cosmopolitans. Our nationality is to have no nationality at all, but to substitute what belongs to man in general for the particular peculiarities that distinguish other nations. We appropriate the culture of all nations, and would regenerate in ourselves the blossoms of the human mind in every age. Other nations strive to make themselves a normal nation for the whole world; but this they do not by self-annihilation, but by imprinting their own image on all mankind. We have the same ambition to make our race a normal race for the whole world; but we strive after a different fashion; we strive to realize the ideal of a philosophical archetype. Other nations reverence what is foreign, but they do not therefore think it necessary to undervalue themselves. Nevertheless, this self-denial has its good side, and its foundation in nature. There can be no true love without self-denial. Egotism and national vanity are the greatest enemies of culture. *The noblest nations have always been the most tolerant, and the basest always the most conceited.*

" Our love for what is foreign thus arises from our philosophical and cosmopolitan character; but it has also another root, and that is our poetical and romantic disposition. A poetical illusion floats with a beautifying power around all that is foreign, and takes our imagination captive. We possess this magic art of mystifying ourselves; we metamorphose ourselves into dramatic personages and give ourselves over to a foreign illusion. Many of our learned men have thought themselves so into Greeks, many of our romanticists so into the middle ages, many of our politicians so into France and French, many of our theologians so into the Bible, that they know no more of what is going on around them than a somnambulist. This state of mind is very closely allied to madness, and in madness it too often ends."

This is severity following upon apology, and almost neutralizing its kindly influence. But it is in this species of unsparing attack, this unqualified slash of the scimitar, that Menzel's strength lies. He has too great a love for beauty to soften down distortion, even in the features of his German mother.

But we recur to the question and ask, what is the distinguishing feature of the German character? That they have no character at all, as the French Abbé supposed they had no genius, is a proposition too absurd to be maintained in the present era of European development. Sterne may be a weak imitator of Cervantes and Rabelais; but to call Jean Paul Richter a weak imitator of Sterne would betray an ignorance and a presumption equal only to that of Voltaire, when he proclaimed himself the rival of Æschylus and the judge of Shakspeare. They who deny originality, wit, and humour, to every other German author, must surely concede them all, and much more than all, to Richter. This man's name is of itself sufficient to answer all the unworthy jibes and jeers that have been idly thrown in the face of the German muse. When we find united in one mind all the humour of Rabelais, without its nastiness—all the feeling of Sterne, without its affectation—all the intellect of Kant, without its systematic stiffness—all the beauty of Göthe, without its coldness—shall we say that the nation which possesses such a mind is destitute of originality and invention? To the man who knows and sympathises with German literature the very thought is treason, and the broaching of the question only shows that it deserves no answer.

Madame de Staël long ago drew the proper line of designation, when she said that "Germany is the native country of thought." The Germans are a sort of "intellectual miners," and spiritual moles—and this is one among the many reasons why their merits are so often concealed from superficial eyes. As the Hindoo philosophers convert every thing into religion, and every thing in nature is with them a mere modification of Brahma, Vishnu, and Siva, these sacred three themselves being mere modifications of the one eternal Brahm—so the Germans can do nothing without metaphysics. They must have a principle and a soul in every thing, and the whole of external nature and life is valuable to them only in so far as it is a revelation of the internal Divinity, in whom we live and move and have our being. Jean Paul said ironically that God had given them the air for their domain, as he had the land to the French and the sea to the English. He might have said with more truth, though with less humour, that the Germans are masters of the soul, while other nations control the body—the one are lords of the world within, the other lords of the world without. Menzel has given a prominent place to this distinctive character under the head of nationality—and, as usual, he shows us both the light and the dark side of this picture, and begins, after his fashion, with the most unsparing severity.

" From the oldest times have we Germans been a fantastical nation. In the middle ages we were mystical, and now we can live only in the cold region of intellect. In all ages we have manifested an exuberant power and fulness of soul, that, welling forth impetuously within, pays but little regard to the world without. Ever have we been awkward and helpless in practical life, but so much more at home in the inner world, and all our national virtues and vices can be deduced from this one source—this meditative, brooding propensity of our inward man. It is this that makes us, κατ' ἐξοχήν, a literary nation, and it is this that gives our literature its distinctive character. The writings of other nations are more practical, because their life is more practical; our writings have a cast of *overnaturality* or *unnaturality*, something savouring of ghosts and kobolds, which is always at war with the actual state of the world, and that because we never have our eyes on any thing but the strange world of our inner man. We are more fantastical than other nations, not only because our fancy takes more monstrous flights into the regions of the ideal, but also because we believe our dreams to be true. Our feelings follow our imaginations, and now sink as low into the mawkishness of domestic sentiment as they at other times rise high into the exuberance of pietistical reveries.* Our intellect takes even larger flights than our fancy—we launch out into the infinite blue of empty space, and, as speculatists and system-builders, we are followed by a *fama clamosa*, a hue and cry, from every corner of the globe. Our splendid theories, however, we can realize nowhere but in our literature, and thus we give an undue preponderance to the world of words, above the life, of which words are but the sign—and foreign nations are not far wrong, when they despise us as book-worms and as pedants.

" But this is only the dark side of the picture, as to which, however, we are unwilling to practise any self-deception. Opposed to this, we can boast a light side of our national literature, to which strangers much less frequently do justice. We aim at a universal cultivation of mind, and not in vain do we offer, to attain this important end, all our energies and all our national ambition. The knowledge which we acquire might well be more beneficial to our race than many loudly-trumpeted deeds of glory; and there may be more true honour in learning from a foreign nation than in achieving a victory over it. There is in our national character something peculiarly fitted to elevate and humanize the race. In every possible direction, we put forth our strength in the great work of extending our knowledge. Nature has given us a sympathy with all her doings; and our intellect collects from all quarters the objects that its capacious grasp desires, and penetrates into the inmost depths of all the mysteries of nature, life,

---

* It is worth while to remark how exactly this criticism of Menzel's tallies with what Mr. Bulwer puts into the mouth of his German student in the Pilgrims of the Rhine. " With our most imaginative works we mix a homeliness that we fancy touching, but which in reality is ludicrous. We eternally step from the sublime to the ridiculous—we want taste."

and the soul. There is no nation so multifarious in its intellectual development as the German; and what the individual wants is made complete in the varied whole. It is only by a wise distribution of the different organs of knowledge among individuals that an accumulation of science in the mass can be realized.

We appeal to any person in the least acquainted with German literature—we appeal to every unprejudiced observer of national character—whether this be not a most impartial and a most just self-anatomizing of the German mind. Could any judge sum up more impartially the opposite evidence on both sides of a case? Our critics in this country either condemn the Germans wholesale, or run into a sort of wild idolatry, which perhaps does more harm than indiscriminate censure,—but a masterly portrait of the thing as it is—a just estimate of its good and its bad—it is strange, passing strange, that we should have first received from a German!

One evil, and not a small one, which flows from this contemplative habit of the Germans, is what they in their language very impressively designate by one word, *Vielschreiberei*, but which we are forced to make intelligible to ourselves by two Latin words, *cacoëthes scribendi*. A man cannot think and feel much, without having a desire to express what he thinks and feels. A woman cannot be always in labour—she must bring forth;—even so a man cannot be always a thinker—he must write a book. And thus is generated that chaos of mis-born imps, that tumble and reel annually, to the amount of millions,* in the literary mud and slime of the Leipsic fair. On this great evil our author is peculiarly severe. He gives vent to his bile in the very first page;—yea, in the very first sentence of his work. The following is certainly a very abrupt, and, to German ears, not a little startling (we fear to many an ungrateful), proëmium of a work on literary history.

" We Germans do little, but write so much the more. When one of our descendants, in future centuries, shall look back upon the present epoch of German history, he will be apt to find more books than men in our nation. He may march back through past years, as through so many repositories. He will say, that we have been sleeping, and that books are our dreams. We have made ourselves a nation of scribblers, and might fitly exchange the double eagle of our heraldry for a goose. The pen governs and serves, works and rewards, fights and feeds, blesses and curses for us. We leave the Italians their sky, the Spaniards their saints, the French their deeds, the English

their bags of money, and sit contentedly at our books. The meditative German nation, devoted to thinking and feeling, has time for nothing but writing. It invented the art of printing, and thinks it a duty to work indefatigably at the great machine. School erudition, affectation of things foreign, fashion, and bibliopolism have done the rest: and thus is piled up the immeasurable mass of books that waxes with every day. And we stand astounded at this *monstrum horrendum*, this new wonder of the world, the Cyclopean walls, which the mind has raised, not the hands."

We assent to every word of this powerful writing, except one. Are not the *deeds* of the British as glorious as those of the French?—and is the reproach of *la nation boutiquière* to stick to us for ever? We sincerely hope that this reproach is altogether unfounded.

Under the heads " Religion"—" Philosophy"—"State-Education"—which explain themselves, there is much that could not fail to interest the British reader; but we are compelled to pass by them, with scarcely a hasty glance at their contents. Though writing professedly on literature, Menzel has thought it necessary to dedicate full eighty pages to a searching examination of the present state of religion in his native country; convinced probably, as we are, that religion is the mother of poetry, and that a literature, which has no devotion to animate it, must always remain in a great measure shallow and unsatisfactory. He complains, not without reason, of the indifference to religion at present so common in Germany, especially amongst the Protestants; and notes it, as at once an evidence and an effect of this universal apathy, that Catholicism and Pietism† are every where on the increase. To this latter, indeed, our author seems to attribute a degree of importance which, from a man of his strong understanding, we could scarcely have expected; but we are to bear in mind that Menzel is no mere anatomizer—no mere " reasoning self-sufficient thing"—no " intellectual all in all:" he has a heart as well as a head, and the proud temple of science is to him little better than a death-vault, when not animated by the genial life-glow of poesy. Himself a poet, it is no wonder that he should prefer the deep earnestness of the Pietists and the Mystics to the cold calculation of the self-styled Rationalists. There is one class of men in particular, whom Menzel, influenced by this feeling, has, though himself a stanch Protestant, taken under his peculiar protection. We mean the much-undervalued

---

* " According to a moderate calculation, ten millions of volumes are printed every year in Germany."—*Menzel*.

† *Pietism* in Germany is pretty much the same as *Methodism* with us; the worthy Spener, we believe, was the father of the sect to which this appellation was originally applied.

7. continued

poetical Catholics, with Tieck, Friedrich Schlegel, and Novalis at their head, whom Göthe used to sit in his chair with so much self-complacency, and laugh at. The "master-mind," however great he might be, in his own element of the beautiful in art, seems to have been a perfect child in devotion—a good easy David Hume of poesy, who, enjoying the present, allowed the religionists to fight to their hearts' content about the future—and looked on and smiled. Menzel is not a man to trifle with any thing, much less with religion; and he is not ashamed to profess his preference of a warm glowing Catholicism of the heart to a cold self-contained Protestantism of the understanding. On this principle is based his defence of Görres, Steffens, and other fraternal spirits, whom the narrow and exclusive criticism of the Kantians has condemned, wholesale, as enthusiasts and "whirl-heads."

"A whole band of slavish souls" says he, "has united to banish such a man as Görres from the literary hemisphere of Germany—a man of the most original genius, and whose works are a triumph of the most complete spiritual freedom. The view taken by these ostracists is the most narrow and slavish that can be conceived. To the mere outward form of faith they ascribe an omnipotent influence over the mind of man—whereas it is the mind that exercises dominion over his faith. These men vainly conceive that, as the seal of Protestantism, wherewith they are stamped, has metamorphosed them at once into free and cultivated men, so the seal of Catholicism, wherewith their adversaries are stamped, has necessarily rendered them barbarians and slaves: and they have no perception of this most simple truth, that, as Catholicism, in a great and pure mind, may assume a most worthy and venerable shape, so Protestantism, in such narrow minds as theirs, may sink down into a most unworthy caricature."

Thus far of religion and Catholicism. We only remark, by way of practical inference, that there is not a little here from which we moral church-going English might take a useful hint. If there were as much piety as there is church-going in our land, as much true Protestantism as there is a superstitious cry of "No Popery," we should be an exemplary nation indeed!

It is with much reluctance that we make no extracts from the interesting chapters on philosophy, politics, and education. The narrow exclusiveness of Kant, the notional despotism of Hegel, in philosophy; the shameful passiveness of the German people, the insinuating circumvention of the Prussian *bureaucratic*, in politics; the bigotry of the classical monopolists, the mania of the utilitarian *pandidactics*, in education—all these, most fitting subjects as they are for the application of Menzel's lash, we are compelled to pass over, in our haste to arrive at the proper literary department of the work.

Our readers have already seen enough of the manly grasp which our author takes of his subject, to form a pretty accurate anticipation of the manner in which Menzel walks over the proper literary division of his extensive domain. He takes a broad and expanded view of the mighty field of action that lies before him, and is too anxious for important results to dwell upon those ephemeral phenomena, that, however beautiful, flit before the eyes but for a minute, and then disappear, leaving no trace of their working behind. Hence it is that he sometimes seems to make too sweeping conclusions, and, with an unqualified reprobation, to condemn that in the gross, which in the detail unquestionably presents many singular and attractive beauties. But, in a work which aims to give not the history but the spirit of literature, this is the only practicable, the only rational, procedure. It is not with pretty poems, but with great poets, that in such a case we have to do. It is not on mere verses, much less on rhymes, that we are to descant, but it is on the soul, the animating spirit, that breathes in the literature as in the life of a people. It is a trite saying, that the noblest poetry is often written in prose; and it is a saying which we must peculiarly bear in mind, when attempting to form to ourselves an intelligible outline of the great body of German literature. There is a poetical element in every member of that mighty leviathan. We must expect to find poetry in its metaphysics, poetry in its theology, and poetry in its philosophy of nature. Schelling, Oken, and Görres, are no less poets than Göthe, Wieland, and Schiller.

With this understanding, we shall not be surprised at the summary manner in which Menzel dismisses not a few names of might from his literary review. Are they men of strong intellect, of pure heart, and of elevated principles? what have they done, either by word or deed, to assist in the great work of the advancement and amelioration of human nature? These are the questions to which every candidate for a place on Menzel's Parnassus of the Germans must give a ready and an explicit answer; and, if the answer is unsatisfactory or suspicious, the petitioners are immediately elbowed out, as mere cumberers of the ground and impeders of necessary business. The mere man of amusement, the mere poetical mountebank, the mere carver and gilder, the mere rareeshow-man of literature, however much he may have been estimated in his day, if he has done nothing else, meets with no more attention from our stern Aristippus than if he were a dancing bear. Amusement is all very well for

7. continued

a recreation, but to make a business of amusement, even though it be amusement of the highest kind, as in developing the formation of the bones, or watching the metamorphosis of plants, if it have no reference to the moral amelioration and advancement of our race, is with Menzel an unpardonable sin: and, on this score, as we shall see, even the universal and autocratic Göthe is treated with a nonchalance, and dismissed with an unceremoniousness, which might almost make a weak mind tremble for the stability of the universe itself.

With some qualifications, however, which the tenor of these remarks will easily suggest to the reader, Menzel is a most just and impartial critic. No man could possibly be more catholic. He delights to search out and acknowledge every thing that is noble and great in the intellectual world, under whatever form it may appear. Having once set himself forth as the advocate of Schiller and the antagonist of Göthe, he has naturally been led to maintain his original polemical character, and preserve the same attitude of war through all the successive scenes of his literary activity. With regard to these men, therefore, his *dictum* must always be received *cum grano salis*. But, when there is no reason to suspect any bias, his judgment is always deserving of the very highest respect. If we except Göthe, to whom he seems to cherish a declared and unmitigated hostility, there is no great German author, none of the *Dii majorum gentium*, to whom he has not done merited justice. Lessing, Herder, Schiller, Tieck, Richter, and even Wieland, all receive from him the full meed of ready and discriminating praise. Still the polemical Brougham-like activity of his nature never sleeps long: and the unintelligent herd of imitators, that turn every thing great into caricature, seldom escape unchastised from his hand. He has also a most savage enmity against Voss, which, to the degree Menzel carries it, we find it very difficult to excuse or even to palliate; for surely the man who wrote "Luise," though he might be a weak and a narrow, certainly was a good and an amiable, man. We give a hint here *in transitu*, which we hope may come to Menzel's ear, that in moderation and tolerance of criticism that arch-heretic Göthe might give him some most useful lessons. Most pitiless in particular, though certainly in many respects not undeserved, is the censure with which he endeavours to annihilate that whole class of "destiny or fatalistic tragedies," which, since the precedent shown by Müllner, has been inundating the German stage. The thing may be overdone, certainly, and if it is a good thing, the overdoing of it will only make it so much the worse: but what is there in the "Guilt" more than there is in "Hamlet," or many other plays

that we could mention, to authorize the indiscriminate charge of fatalism, upon which the destiny-tragedies have been so often condemned wholesale? It rather appears to us, that in Müllner's play there is a satisfactory reason assigned in the very name, for the apparently indiscriminate game which Fate plays among her victims. "The iniquities of the fathers are visited upon the children even unto the third and fourth generations." But in Hamlet all is chance, all is blind, inexplicable, contradictory fate; man is made the football of fortune; and a capricious God seems to take delight in defeating the best concerted plans of the wise, and thrusting unmerited advancement upon the foolish. Menzel, however, who has had better opportunities of seeing the destiny-system in full operation than could possibly have fallen to our lot, admits of no such favourable comparisons. He distinguishes philosophically between the Fate of the ancient Greek tragedians and the Destiny of the modern fatalistic playwrights. As Mr. Gillies some years ago laboured, we hope not altogether unsuccessfully, to introduce Müllner, Grillparzer, and the other destiny-tragedians to the British public, perhaps a sample of Menzel's criticism on this theme may not be altogether unwelcome.

"Müllner," says he, "treading in Werner's steps, drew the destiny-tragedy out into that frightful caricature in which it now walks abroad, ghost-like, on every German stage. Werner's ' February,' gave the first impulse, and Müllner's ' Guilt' was the culminating point, and this strange mannerism straightway spread abroad on all sides like a pestilence. The new phasis was not essentially different from the old; but its Fate is always a hostile, destructive, revengeful power. With the ancient Greek tragedy it agrees only in name. We must be allowed, however, to draw a little more accurately the line of distinction.

" In the ancient tragedy, Fate was an iron, inexorable, truly sublime power, horrible and yet beautiful, worthy of the idea that we have of an all-ruling destiny. It stood as eternal necessity opposed to heaven-storming liberty, and the measure of its sublimity lay in the power and dignity of the hero. The more free, the more exalted, the more divine the hero, so much the mightier, deeper, holier, was the power that set bounds to his striving. This pervading idea of the Greek drama is in the conflict of the hero against Destiny; and this Destiny, though in itself invincible and unchanging, receives, nevertheless, a relative greatness from the strength of the resistance that is made to it, and the worth of the victim that is sacrificed to it, which relative greatness alone gives Fate a right to assume a poetical significancy. In the free will, the power, and the inward worth of the hero, the criterion of tragedy lay. By how much greater and worthier the hero, by so much more powerful was Fate, so much nobler was the conflict, so much more sublime the poetical fiction. The resistance of the hero was the measure of the whole poem. Such is also the tragedy of Schiller,

46

and such tragedy alone did he make a favourite with the Germans. But now what has become of all his promising blossom, when moral impotence and a sickly striving after originality presumptuously seek to lair themselves upon his laurels?

" The heroes of our modern destiny-tragedies are without volition, without worth, without dignity. From their birth upward they are in the hand of a dark mysterious power.* They commit their monstrous crimes, not as free agents but as predestined. A curse, inherited from an ancestress, or inflicted by a malignant Sycorax, drives them on to their fate; and their sin, like its punishment, is indissolubly connected with one unavoidable fatal hour of their existence. The poor sinner must sin because this happens to be the 24th or 29th of February, and no other day. Not from any incitement of passion, not from any determination of will, does his sin proceed; if there is any motive in him, it is not his own, but inherited as a judicial punishment, transmitted as a curse. Yea even the Devil himself needs take no trouble to seduce him; he must sin when the clock strikes twelve, and the dagger is the hour-hand, and the heart which he transfixes is the mysterious number—the hand advances, and the deed of terror is done. The witch-trials are profound and intellectual, when compared with this meaningless fatalism. In them, man, however beset with devils, has yet a free choice left, and the powers of darkness must work for their prey before they are sure of it. But in these Destiny-plays there is no need of a compact between Faust and Mephistopheles. The hero has neither choice nor enjoyment; and the powers of darkness themselves have not the pleasure of combating the yielding strength of man, and leaving the field of battle with a solemn ovation. It is an unmeaning game with puppets. It is impossible that even the Devil himself can feel any thing but *ennui* at a sport, where he has no strength to baffle, no will to overreach, no holiness to corrupt, no angel to seduce,—no office to perform but that of a common executioner on subjects, which are delivered ready for decapitation to his hand."

So much for Müllner and Grillparzer. It is time, however, that we leave this skirmishing with lesser heroes, and advance into the very heat and throng of the battle. We must endeavour to grapple with the grand *quæstio vexata* of German literature—the *articulus stantis aut cadentis ecclesiæ*. We are called upon to decide the great question, whether Göthe or Schiller be the king of the German Parnassus—and the divided worshippers of the literary world wait with suspense upon our decision, whether Göthe be a divine Shekinah, or a golden calf of the idolaters.

We perceive Menzel, like a sturdy old Gaul, advance fearlessly up to the chief-consul of literary senators, and, regardless of his

calm, dignified, godlike demeanour, impiously pluck his beard. Heaven and earth are in awe-struck expectation, what punishment shall follow such unheard-of audacity.

The truth of the matter is, that the great Göthe—for great he certainly was, by the admission of all parties—has been so much bepraised and bewondered, and the admiration justly due to his genius, has run wild, as well in this country as in Germany, into such a rankness of besotted idolatry, that there was an imperative necessity that some one should arise to revindicate to the literary mind its lost independence, and dispel from the eye-sight of men that mist which an overheated enthusiasm had raised. The Minerva who was destined to perform this kind office is Menzel; and none could have been chosen better fitted for such an honourable enterprize. Schlegel (A. W. we mean) has once again, by a few miserable squibs and lampoons,* attempted to darken that halo of glory which shines round the consecrated head of Schiller; but, we believe, the blasts of his penny trumpet never produced any effect, but to throw back ridicule on him who blew them: and the name of Schiller still stands resplendent in its own unsullied purity. Not so ineffective, we fear, have been the shafts, or rather the blows, which Wolfgang Menzel has from time to time directed against the Olympian head of Germany's poetical Jove. Menzel was not a man to strike, without knowing what he was striking at; the words that he wrote are as well-aimed strokes of a hammer—they are sure to *tell*. We must not, therefore, expect to find Göthe coming entirely unscathed out of this doughty warfare—though the crown may still remain on his head, yet, to Menzel-illumined eyes, it shines no more with a divine, but with a human, lustre. Göthe still remains a great man, a splendid piece of humanity; but he is no more the only great man that Germany or Europe contains. He is a man, according to Menzel's view, and merely a man; no demi-god, much less a god, the last and greatest incarnation of the poetic Brahma.

Our space, as well as our tactics, on this occasion, lead us to plunge straightway *in medias res*. We have no inclination to dash off our critical arabesques upon the Doric portico of Menzel's well-compacted edifice. We extract the following quintessence of our author's *Anti-Götheism* from the " History of the Germans."—p. 776.

" Göthe had all the delicate tact of Lessing, with a much richer

---

* We beg pardon for this interruption, but we must be permitted to ask Dr. Menzel whether this observation does not apply to Œdipus Tyrannus as well as to the heroes of " *Die Schuld*" and of " *Die Ahnfrau?*"

* As that,

> " So lang es Schwaben gibt, in Schwaben
> Wird Schiller stets Bewunderer haben."

imagination, but without his manliness; all the tenderness and sensibility of Herder, but without his faith. So far as the mere handling of his subject was concerned, he was, doubtless, the greatest of our poets; but he had no enthusiasm for any thing but himself, and his works are merely flattering portraitures of his own individuality. As, in his study at Weimar, he was wont so to dispose himself in reference to the light, that he might appear to strangers who came to visit him under the most pictorial distribution of light and shade, so were all his works mere artificial means of throwing a favourable light upon himself. He had no sympathy with the world, but in so far as it served him for this end. For the affairs of his country he had no eye—he positively hated them. He sung the praise of Napoleon, because Napoleon flattered him, and during the great liberation war (in 1813) he shut himself up in his study, occupied with Chinese trifles, and disgusted with an age that acknowledged something greater than himself. This man, however, to his cotemporaries appeared to be the greatest man alive; and that, because he could not flatter himself, without at the same time flattering a countless number of souls as base as his own, and because his talent threw a poetical beauty over the inclinations of an aristocracy, that, boasting of a high degree of refinement, submitted willingly to the lowest grade of national degradation. Lessing had frightened the weaklings of the age—they were contented to admire him, but felt his sting not the less severely. Göthe was their favourite, because he convinced them that their weakness was beauty."

This certainly is no spare measure of rebuke; but the reader must remember that it is Menzel who is attacking, and Göthe who is attacked. "In the wars of the giants," as Jeffray said, in speaking of Lord Brougham, "great blows must be given and received." The admirers of Göthe were too numerous and too loud to be affected by what might appear to them to be the mere "whisper of a faction." A declared and open war was necessary to make head against the long-established monarchy of Götheism; and none but a bold and dauntless leader could change the presumptive name of rebel into that of hero and of patriot.

Not to go too far into a vague and loose declamation, the charges brought against Göthe by Menzel and his friends may be reduced to the following:—
1. That he was no politician.
2. That he was no patriot.
3. That he was selfish and egotistical.
4. That he had no enthusiasm.
5. That he had no religion.
6. That he had no morality.
7. That he affected an air of state and majesty, and thought himself entitled to the veneration of the whole world.

The charges in this indictment are clearly and distinctly stated, and we shall endeavour to answer them with as great brevity as possible, pleading either guilty or not guilty, with or without such modifications as shall appear necessary or advisable.

Article 1. Admitted. "Göthe wanted to *observe*, his age wanted to *act*."--FALK. . . Every man cannot be a politician, even though a Universal Suffrage Bill should attempt to make him so by force. At the same time, we cannot help observing, that that lack of interest in things political, which Göthe himself again and again admits, squares but ill with the "universality and manysidedness" of which we have of late heard so much. Göthe himself allows (in his Morphologie), "Wir sind an's Leben, nicht an die Betrachtung angewiesen,—Man is an active, not a contemplative, being;" and yet his own life is a continual practical denial of his own maxim. A man of action must take an interest in politics. Göthe was no man of action, therefore he was no politician. What dreaming, passive, substanceless, creatures are his heroes! What is Werther? a die-away. What is Faust? a dreamer, and one who cannot even dream himself, but lets the Devil dream for him. What is Meister? a milksop, a nincompoop, the football of circumstance.

Article 2. Admitted as a corollary from article one; but under the qualification, *Non omnia possumus omnes*. Horace was a great poet, but a bad soldier. Cicero was a great orator, but a bad poet. Bacon was a great philosopher, but he could not withstand a bribe. It was not in Göthe's nature to be fired with the enthusiasm of a Körner or an Arndt, because he had no eye for things political. Whether Homer was as valiant in the fight as that Achilles whose valour he celebrates, we cannot tell; but we know that to do great deeds is one faculty, and to sing of great deeds is another faculty. It would be absurd to demand of an artist to *be* all that which it is his vocation only to *describe*.

Article 3. Denied *in toto*. A kindlier man than Göthe, except perhaps Jean Paul, never existed. Of this the manner in which he has spoken of Herder, Voss, and Schiller—men in many respects the antipodes of himself—is a sufficient proof. Göthe loved nature and loved art, with a fondness and a constancy never equalled. And the man who does so cannot be selfish, cannot be egotistical.

Article 4. Denied—Göthe had an enthusiasm, but a calm and clear, not a noisy and troubled enthusiasm. His enthusiasm, however, was not, like that of many men of the present age, vented entirely in chasing political, theological, and pedagogical bubbles. He had an enthusiasm for the beautiful in nature, and for the beautiful in art, as imitative thereof. With the grand, the sublime, the powerful, the terrible, he had no sympathy—his strength is the strength of rest, and his sublime is the sublime of composure. There is no objection that is brought against Göthe, under this head, that cannot at the same time be brought against Wordsworth, Coleridge, and a host of other most elect sons of the Muse. Nay, this lack of enthusiasm may, with equal force, be urged against the whole art and ideal of the Greeks. The Jupiter Capitolinus shakes his ambrosian locks in quiet dignity, and the Apollo aims his certain shaft without perturbation. It is only in the low regions of earth that the storms rage and the winds contend; above, all is serene, all is divine.

Article 5. This article is denied, when stated in the unqualified terms in which it appears in the indictment. It is admitted, however, that religion was not the element in which Göthe's muse delighted to dwell.

Here, again, the trumpeters of the " manysided master-mind of Germany" find themselves at a discount. We never could discover that strong development of the bump of veneration on Göthe's cranium, of which Carlyle and some of our German *illuminati* so mysteriously discourse. Franz Horn, who sets out with that intolerant rule of criticism, that none but a true Christian can be a true poet, has great difficulty in discovering where Göthe's Christianity lies. At the same time, as the " *dear dear man*" whom he reveres as the first of poets after Shakspeare, must be brought within the orthodox fold by some contrivance or other, he sees the secret sun of Göthe's Christian piety glowing in that beautiful little Indian legend—" The God and the Bayadere." The critic of Shakspeare is right, if, from this poem he draws the conclusion that Göthe had one of those chords in his heart which might, if properly touched, have learned to vibrate to the music of the Christian scheme. But if he attempts to go further, and thinks to tie down this poetical Proteus to the definite and exact shape of the Gospel of Christ, he will find himself egregiously deceived. The smiling angel will straightway metamorphose itself into a lascivious faun, and the woman, so beautiful above, prove a filthy sea-monster below.

Article 6. This article is in one sense true, and in another sense false. Göthe was not a moralist, but he was not therefore an immoral man. None of his works are written with a view of inculcating any moral precept, but they do not, therefore, inculcate immorality. To him, the *good* (τὸ ἀγαθὸν) appeared only under the avatar of the *beautiful* (τὸ καλὸν), and that which is *right* appeared only under the phasis of the *natural*. The words *duty*, and *ought*, were not in his dictionary, but for these

he substituted *beauty* and *is*. He could not oppose *man* to *nature*, as Schiller, Tiedge, and the Kantian poets did—" *vivere convenienter naturæ*" was his watch-word, and he conceived that all the distortions, excesses, and monstrosities, with which the moral world was defaced, arose from not observing and imitating Nature. At the same time, it cannot be denied that there is a sort of tendency to Epicureanism in some of his works, against which the youth of Germany and of Europe ought to be warned. It is absurd and ridiculous to torture the mind into moral systems, as Hindoo yogees do their bodies into devotional distortions—but it is irrational and unmanly to be sensual.

Article 7. To this article it is shortly answered, that Göthe would have been more than a man, had he remained altogether unaffected by the profound homage that was paid to his genius, not only by Germany but by universal Europe. We remark further, that Göthe was, in all his doings, animated by a love of order, which sometimes bordered very closely upon formality.

With these few remarks we must leave Göthe. That Menzel underrates him we hold to be quite certain; that Carlyle overrates him is equally certain; but what the true measure of his stature is may long remain a problem. We may, perhaps, have acted injudiciously in putting the question into a systematic shape, and arguing the point *pro* and *con*, in our own person; but it appeared to us the most brief and comprehensive, as well as the most impartial, mode of stating the substance of Menzel's philippic. To have calmly translated the whole oration, without one word of explanation or reply, would have gone beyond the compass of our endurance, if not contrary to our most conscientious principles. We shall, however, make amends by allowing Menzel to plead the cause of Schiller in his own words, and we know that many a warm heart will glow, and many a bright eye beam with sympathy, as the eulogy of that purest of poets flows in ready translation from our pen.

" The greatest of the poetical idealists was Schiller. He brought back the abstract ideal to the fullness of nature, as Göthe also did—but he did further, what Göthe did not do—he elevated nature up to the ideal. His heroes were, in romantic poetry, what the gods of the Greek sculpture were to the Greeks—divine men, human gods.

" Schiller has concentrated his whole poetical energies in the representation of man, and that not vulgar man, but the ideal of all grandeur and beauty of soul, the highest and most mysterious of all wonders. The external world served him only as a foil to set off, a comparison to illustrate, man. To the blind powers of nature he opposes the moral energy of man, that he may thus exhibit human nature in its highest nobility, or wrestling in triumphant strength, as in ' The Diver,' and in the ' Surety ;' or, again, he introduces human sympathies with nature, and gives a moral significancy to her blind powers, as in 'The Lament of Ceres,' 'Hero and Leander,' the 'Cranes of Ibicus,' the 'Bell,' &c. Even in his historical works, it is not his aim to set forth the epic progress of the whole, subject as that is to the necessary laws of nature; he delights in painting character, and bringing out in *alto relievo* the powerful heroes of the drama, who oppose human freedom to changeless necessity.

"The soul of all Schiller's creations is his ideal characters. He paints nothing but man, and man in his highest moral beauty and sublimity. He seems to have thought it impossible to give the name of poetry to that, which, while it imitated, did not, at the same time, idealize humanity. We do not, indeed, go so far as to assert that mere moral dignity can ever constitute true poetry. On the contrary, our earlier poets, who were all great moralists, were at the same time the greatest sinners against true poetry; and it is as difficult a thing to paint as to possess a noble soul, though nothing is more easy than the assumption of both. When ideals of moral beauty are to be represented in poetry, it is indispensable that the nature of the characters be not made to suffer under their morality. It is as erroneous to defend bad poetry by the allegation of good morality, as it is to make good poetry a veil of grace thrown over the deformities of bad morality. Most of our moral poets, however, are like the vulgar painters of the images of saints; they claim veneration for the vilest daubing, merely because the daub represents, or is intended to represent, a saint. Few of them are like Raphael, whose saints are real saints, and whose art is as holy as the subject of it. Among these few, Schiller is a chief. Even in his youthful productions, which are so often and so severely criticized as unnatural, this inward truth to nature is triumphant over all extravagance—which extravagance accordingly disappears altogether in his later works. We have some great poets, who have painted beauties, but not moral beauties; and these poets, perhaps, possessed the tact of the artist in greater perfection than Schiller, but we have no poet who so well knew how to unite poetry and virtue into one beautiful whole. We have no representation of virtue which is more poetical, no poetry which is more virtuous.

"In Schiller's ideals we find no dead mechanical law, no theory, no dry system of morality, but a living organic nature, an active life of acting men. This idealized nature is the creation of true genius, and of that alone. It is the vocation of genius to develop from its own internal depth the noblest humanity. It is genius alone that brings to full glowing bloom what in the minds of common men slumbers deep beneath the earthly covering of the soul. The true poet re-creates, as it were, the world to us by the new light which his genius sheds over it, by the new view which he enables us to take of it, by bringing that which is old to a higher development, awaking the sleeping germ to life, unfolding to us inclinations, capacities, virtues, talents, which we knew not of before—enriching, ennobling, and elevating us—in one word, by spreading the magic light of god-given thoughts upon all nature, internal and external, in us and about us, and thus raising us, and

the world along with us, to a purer and a nobler existence. A poetic nature creates by necessity its own poetical world, and the only wonder is that these poetical worlds are at once so manifold and so peculiar. Greater than the world itself are the worlds that genius creates in it. Nature, which is but one, blows out into a thousand natures, and each metamorphosis is richer, more wonderful, and more lovely, than that which went before. This regeneration is the work of genius. Every great genius is a rare species of flower, of which only one single plant exists, peculiar in its habit in its colour, in its fragrance. The inner, spiritual and vital power of such a plant is a mystery—self-created, to be perfectly comprehended by none. Who has ever accounted for the colour and the fragrance of flowers, or been able to give a reason why it is so in one and so in another? Who has ever explained the mystery that draws us on to admire a picture of Raphael's, and who the spiritual atmosphere, the paradisaic charm, that dwells in the characters of Schiller? Here no mere definition of the understanding can avail: comparison alone may help us more closely to define the inexplicable feeling.

"Raphael's name has forced itself upon me, and it is an undeniable conclusion that, as Raphael's pictures are remarkable for the most perfect *natural* beauty, so are Schiller's poetical creations for the most perfect *moral* beauty. Moral beauty has its origin and its waxing in the history of man, and action and conflict are the conditions of its existence; the beauty of nature and of sense is, like nature itself, calm, great, unchangeable.

"According to this distinction, the ideal characters of Schiller must manifest themselves in conflict, those of Raphael in calm and sublime repose. Michael, the warlike angel, was a fit symbol of Schiller's genius; Raphael was most fitly characterized by the mild angel whose name he bore. But the same original, inexplicable charm, the same heavenly magic, the same reflex of a higher world, that lie in the countenances of Raphael, lie also in the characters of Schiller. No painter has painted the human countenance, no poet has exhibited the human soul, in equal grace and majesty of beauty. And as Raphael's genius is always like to itself, and the same mild, peace-bringing angel, in many-named apparition, still meets our eyes in the same divine beatitude and glory; so is Schiller's genius always like to itself, and we see the same warlike angel in Karl Moor, in Amelia, Ferdinand, Louisa, Marquis Posa, Max Piccolomini, Thecla, Mary Stuart, Mortimer, Joanna, and William Tell. The one rests in the consciousness of a peace that nothing can destroy, of a glory not borrowed from another; the other turns its beautiful, angelic countenance, threatening, and yet sad, against the monsters of the deep.

"The first mystery in Schiller's characters is that ANGELIC PURITY, which is ever found in the noblest natures. This nobility of innocence re-appears in all the creations of Schiller, under the same features of a pure youthful angel. In sun-belit glorification, as pure childhood, unarmed and yet invulnerable, it appears in Fridolin—like that king's child in the ancient fairy tale, who played with lions in the forest and yet was scathless.

" When the blessed creatures of Schiller's fancy become conscious of their own bliss, then the Nemesis of the heavenly powers is aroused against them. This is the circumstance that confers an additional charm on his ' Hero and Leander.' Adorned with the helmet of war, and with the fire of noble passion reddening upon its blooming cheek, the youthful innocence of his heroes marches dauntless against the darkest powers of Hell. In ' The Diver' and in ' The Surety,' in Charles Moor, in Amelia, and in Max Piccolomini, this interesting spectacle is presented. Over these moving figures floats a magic of poesy that has never been equalled. It is the tone of a heavenly flute amid wild discordant music, the blue of ether amid a storm, a Paradise on the edge of a crater.

" This purity and innocence is equally compatible with the male as with the female characters. The Virgin of Orleans is then most a virgin when she stands forth as the consecrated amazon of God. It is the deep mystery of the Christian religion and of Christian poetry, that the salvation of the world goes forth from a woman, the highest power from the purest innocence. Joanna of Arc is the most perfect impersonation of that angel who bears the helm and waves the banner of heaven. So in Schiller's male characters. Among these, three heroes stand in holy pre-eminence; Max Piccolomini, the warrior-youth, pure and uncorrupted amid all the vices of his general's tent, and of his father's home; Marquis Posa, whose soul, though decked out with all the intellectual culture that this world can afford, is yet a pure temple of innocence; and lastly, that stalworth son of the mountain, William Tell, a finished companion, in its way, to the Virgin of Orleans.

" A second mystery of beauty in Schiller's ideal characters is their DIGNITY, their NOBILITY. His heroes and heroines never belie that pride and that lofty bearing which are the indication of a higher nature; and all their expressions bear the stamp of magnanimity and innate nobility. Every thing low is their antipodes. Powerful, free, independent, original, following only the impulse of a noble nature, Schiller's heroes tear in pieces the webs in which common men drag along their prosaic existence. It is none of the least remarkable characteristics of Schiller's poetry, that the stamp of genius which they bear, the imposing attitude which they assume, is the very same that in actual life is wont to distinguish the noble mind from the mean. The stamp of Jove is impressed upon the brow of all his heroes. In his first poems indeed this free, bold demeanour appears in a somewhat uncouth and uncivilized exterior; and, in the elegant Weimar, the poet himself was seduced to attempt to civilize his Robbers a little from their original fierceness. But what man that has eyes can fail to perceive the diamond heart of a noble nature, even through the rough crust of a Karl Moor and a Fiesco? This power of moral beauty is only made so much the stronger by the contrast.

" The third and highest secret of the beauty of Schiller's characters is the FIRE OF NOBLE PASSION. This is the fire that animates every noble heart: it is the altar-flame which ascends heavenward,—the vestal flame fed by consecrated hands in the temple of God,—the Promethean spark brought down from heaven,—the Pentecost fire of enthusiasm, in which the souls of men are baptized : it is the phœnix fire, in which our race renews its youth eternally. Without the glow of noble passion there can be nothing great either in life or in poetry. Every man of genius bears within him this holy fire, and all the creations of genius are penetrated by it. Schiller's poetry is as strong and fiery wines. All his words are flames of the noblest feeling. Those ideals whom he has created are the genuine children of his own glowing heart, parted beams of his own fire. The honour of at once the purest and the strongest passion belongs undoubtedly to Schiller before all other poets. None with such a pure heart ever possessed so much fire ; none with so much fire ever retained such purity. Thus we see the diamond, which is the purest of earthly substances, when it is inflamed, burn with a glow and a splendour in comparison of which all other fire is weak and cloudy.

" Does there exist—can we conceive, a more chaste, a more holy love, than that which Schiller has breathed into the souls of his lovers ? And where again do we find a love so fiery and so powerful, invincible before a world of foes, at once stirring up the highest strength of soul, and patiently enduring the most unheard-of sacrifices ? From its softest charm, from the first meeting of the eyes, from the first gentle beat of the heart, to the storm of feeling that shakes the whole being, to the awe-striking deed of virgin valour, to the sublime sacrifice of two loving souls—love here unfolds the unmeasured riches of its beauty, like a sacred music, that from the tenderest tone rises to the fullest storm of sound, but always in the purest accords.

" The glow of an enthusiastic heart in Schiller communicates its influences to all that is dear to humanity; and here his genius arms itself with the flaming sword of heaven: here begins the contest of that warlike angel with the spirits of the abyss.

" Schiller's pure soul could suffer no unrighteousness : and he steps forth, panoplied, into the lists where RIGHT is the watchword of the battle. Like an inspired prophet, he proclaims the holy love of that blessing which dwells in right, and of that curse which follows unavoidably on all injustice. And never does the glow of his feeling, or the glitter of his ornate speeches, throw a dazzling indistinctness over the truth of his piercing judgment : they only bring it forward in more striking and brilliant relief.

" FREEDOM, which is inseparable from Right, was the dearest jewel of his heart. But that lawless freedom which proceeds from, as it ends in, injustice, belongs to the order of the demoniac powers, against which he wages an unmitigated war.

" We possess no poet who has exhibited Right and Liberty with such fiery enthusiasm and with such lovely adornment of poesy ; and none who has at the same time known so well how to temper his enthusiasm with moderation, and march onward in the triumphal path of truth and integrity.

" His genius belongs to mankind. Never were the rights of man advocated from a higher point of view than by his Marquis Posa. For the rights of the people, his Virgin of Orleans enters the lists: the rights of individuals are maintained by Tell. And not only in these instances, but in all his other heroes, do we find Right and Liberty in combat with tyranny and arbitrary will; and Schiller is manifestly as much the poet of Liberty as he is of Love."

With this splendid eulogy of Schiller, we hope that we have done justice both to Menzel and to German literature. The bard of Wallenstein is evidently the *magnus Apollo* of our author; and his unqualified veneration of Schiller will, no doubt, seem to many over-critical minds as uncalled-for as his unqualified reprobation of Göthe. As to the latter, we have already spoken our sentiments; but we pity the narrow self-containedness of that man's mind who measures, by degrees of the understanding, the admiration due to such a genius as that of Schiller. We pity the icy coldness of that man's heart who can apply the thermometer of a calculating criticism to measure the glow of poetical enthusiasm.

On that mysterious question, the character of Göthe, our minds, we confess honestly, are not yet entirely made up. But on the merits of Menzel, as a literary and philosophical writer, and that of a high order, we think there can be but one opinion. We deem, too, that we have, on the present occasion, spoken a word in season, by making audible to English ears the Anti-Göthian philippics of Wolfgang Menzel. Certain it is that to the *Kotzebue-mania*, so prevalent at the end of the last century, a *Göthe-mania* has, after an interval of forty years, succeeded; the German epidemic has appeared under a new form; and though the calf that we now worship may be a *golden*, whereas the object of our former veneration was merely a *gilded*, calf,— still, if there is any truth in Menzel's views, we are worshipping an idol, and the sooner the mystical nimbus is removed from the brow of this pseudo-divinity the better. We are not, however, apprehensive that the fame of Göthe is based upon a foundation that can be shaken even by the strong arm of such a man as Menzel. We only protest against the unlimited idolatry paid to a foreign genius, whom even his most ardent admirers confess to be in many views not altogether intelligible. We fear that the *omne ignotum pro magnifico* applies here, and that there is a great deal of childish mystification and sheer fudge written and spoken about Johann Wolfgang von Göthe. However this be, the study of Menzel's writings can do no harm to our German students: if he is a hollow pretender, he will soon be exposed; if he speaks truth, he ought to be listened to. We advise the translation of some of his works, as an edifying *passer le temps*

for some of our young scholars. The "History of the Germans" were well worthy of such an honour; and surely the translator of such a work, though he might attempt less, would achieve more, than many of the monomaniacs of the age, who work as if they thought it necessary for their salvation to translate Göthe's Faust. It is time that this travestie and caricature manufactory of English Fausts should be put down as a public nuisance. We may touch upon this subject some other day: in the mean time—

> " Est modus in rebus, sunt certi denique fines,
> Quos ultra citraque nequit consistere notum."

8. FOREIGN QUARTERLY REVIEW, 17 (1836), 391-417 (pagination differs). M/H No. 3329. By Elizabeth Eastlake.

ART. VI.—*Briefe an Johann Heinrich Merck, von Göthe, Herder, Wieland, und andern bedeutenden Zeitgenossen. Mit Merck's biographischer Skizze.* Herausgegeben von Dr. Karl Wagner, Lehrer am Gross-Herzoglichen Gymnasium zu Darmstadt. (Letters to John Henry Merck, from Göthe, Herder, Wieland, and other eminent Cotemporaries. With a Biographical Sketch of Merck's Life. Edited by Dr. Charles Wagner, Teacher at the Grand Ducal Gymnasium, Darmstadt.) 8vo. 1835.

THIS work is not only full of attraction for the man of letters, and the lover of modern German literature in general, but it equally invites the attention of the poet and philosopher, of the artist, naturalist, and geologist; comprising, as it does, a series of letters from most of the eminent men (between the years 1770 and 1790) who belong to those classes. For more than half a century have these interesting documents of the most interesting period of German and perhaps of general literature been kept back from the world. The person to whom they were addressed, Johann Heinrich Merck, was a gentleman of ample fortune, resident at Darmstadt, whose varied talents and enlightened appreciation of merit have linked his name with the first geniuses of that prolific period. Of him Göthe declares—" This singular man has, of all others, exercised the greatest influence over my life." Herder exclaims—" Good man! Heaven grant me always a friend like you!" And Wieland, in the fulness of his warm heart, says—" Should it ever happen that I could love nothing more, I should still love Göthe and Merck;" and, on another occasion, " Excellent friend! before I desert you, I shall have poisoned my wife and strangled my seven children!" Göthe, in his own early biography, gives an account of Merck, which we here insert rather as illustrative of part, than as a complete picture, of his character.

" Of his early education I know but little. After completing his studies, he accompanied a gentleman to Switzerland, where he remained some time, and returned married. When I first knew him, he was paymaster of the forces at Darmstadt. Endowed with the highest intellect and understanding, he had made himself extensively acquainted more especially with modern literature, and particularly studied the history of mankind and of the world in all ages and places. He was peculiarly gifted with the power of judging accurately and acutely. As a man of business also, and a ready accountant, he was much distinguished. By all, save those in whom his biting sarcasms had excited personal dread, was he hailed as a welcome acquisition to society. His visage was long and thin, with a pointed prominent nose, and light blue eyes, approaching to grey, which seemed eagerly to observe all around him, and gave his expression something tiger-like. Lavater's Physiognomy has pre-

served his profile. A strange incongruity characterized his mind. By nature noble, trustworthy, and upright, he had become so embittered against the world, and had so yielded to this morbid feeling of irritation, that an almost irresistible inclination for mischief, and even for knavery, seemed at times to overpower him."

Here it must be remembered that Göthe was not sitting as a moral judge, but rather reviewing the picture of human life in a poetic sense; and that " rogue" and " knave" bore very different meanings in his vocabulary from what they did in Lavater's. Göthe adds:—" But as we willingly seek the excitement of that danger from which we believe ourselves secure, so was I the more anxious for the enjoyment of his good qualities, feeling convinced that he would not turn his evil side towards me." He continues in the same strain to expatiate on his peculiar and seemingly contradictory qualities, and the subsequent correspondence amply fills up the measure of his character; which we here see reflected in that of others over whom he exercised a never flagging sway, and whom he was constantly urging, by seasonable encouragement or undisguised sarcasm, to the fulfilment of that contract which great talents tacitly make with the public. No lack of energy, or falling off of power, escaped his eagle eye; the friend who had once obtained his interest felt that he must labour to retain it; and even the name of Göthe did not screen him from Merck's criticising lash;—of which an instance occurs in the short preliminary biography from which these particulars are extracted. When that great poet sent him his Clavigo to peruse, Merck reminded him of his higher powers, adding, " You must not write such stuff again—anybody could do as much."

With regard to himself, fortune had made him too independent, and nature too versatile, to acquire great individual celebrity. To enumerate the various subjects on which he tried his powers will suffice to prove why he did not attain any European fame. To few is it given to be great in more than one line. Merck excelled alike in poetry, descriptive prose, tales, satire, and epigrams. A few of his smaller satirical poems are annexed to this work, and remind us of the humour of Swift. As a critic he stood the first of his day; all the cotemporary writers were reviewed by him, and in him the candidate for fame either hailed or feared the stern examiner, whose opinion would make or mar his fortune with the public. His criticisms on the works of the day formed one of the great supports of the *Teutscher Merkur* (German Mercury); and Wieland, the editor of that periodical, emphatically says, " Your reviews give life or death to the Mercury:" and again— " Really and truly, dear friend, you ought to write more; all you have hitherto thrown on paper is pure gold." There is every reason also to assert that his pen was always employed on the side of truth, and for the maintenance of a severity and purity of taste, which had a most salutary effect upon the numerous candidates for fame at that period. In all subjects connected with art he displayed the same powers of judgment. His own house was a museum of collections. In him rising talent of every kind found a ready patron, and several of the distinguished German artists of that time owe their outset in life, and their support on the road to improvement, to his judicious advice and liberality; while the letters from the Grand Duke and Duchess of Weimar, and from Göthe, evidence his high repute as a connoisseur. Notwithstanding all these occupations, and the regular attendance which his official situation required, he found time for deep research into natural history, geology, and physiology; and prosecuted these sciences with an ardour which attracted the notice of the first professors, and procured him the correspondence of a Blumenbach, a Camper, and a Sir Joseph Banks.

With all long-established prejudices of society—with all fallacies of system, or mannerisms of style—Merck waged unceasing war. No moral imposture, or quackery in literature or science, eluded his scrutiny; and, no matter how exalted the individual, or how triumphant the party, the darts of his sarcastic spirit were always hurled at them. On all occasions he was clear, severe, and practical; with sufficient shrewdness and knowledge of the world to know where harshness and ridicule would be good, and with kindness and poetry enough in his nature to feel where tenderness and encouragement would be better. For his own peace of mind, his ideal of perfection was placed too high. He knew too well what was excellent, to be satisfied with what he himself did. His was indeed " the quick bosom to which quiet is a hell;" and, in change and multiplicity of avocations, he sought that satisfaction which one alone would not afford. " Whenever," as Göthe says, " he began to curse his own abilities, and was disgusted at not finding his powers of production come up to the standard which he had fixed, he would throw aside the politer arts, and transfer all his energies to some public speculation or mercantile enterprise, which, while it yielded pecuniary profit, also afforded food for a while to his restless mind." Such was the man who held in his hands all the ends of that graceful knot of Weimar *beaux esprits*, and was either the open friend, or confidential arbiter, of its poets and princes—of its literature and politics.

On reviewing his character and life, we are struck with a congeniality in many respects between Merck and the late William Roscoe. In thirst for knowledge, in versatility of talent, and in philanthropic efforts for the dissemination of science and the promotion of intellectual pursuits, there is a striking coincidence between them. Happy were the task of the biographer had the resemblance extended throughout life, and the same serene sky marked the setting of each bright luminary. Suffice it here to say, that, disappointed in spirit, and exhausted with a painful disease, Merck put an end to his life with his own hand, on the 27th of June, 1791, at the age of fifty. Let us deal gently with his memory, and leave judgment to Him who alone could know the force of the temptation, or the severity of the conflict.

Of the variety of subjects discussed in the letters composing this work, some conception may be formed from the following list of correspondents:—

Herder.	G. Forster.
Sophie de la Roche.	K. Hess.
Boie.	Voigt.
G. Schlosser.	von Schmerfeld.
Nicolai.	von Sömmering.
Göthe.	Lichtenberg.
Wieland.	G. M. de la Roche.
Grand Duchess of Weimar.	Göthe's mother.
Grand Duke of Weimar.	Knigge.
H. Fuseli.	P. Camper.
Caroline Herder.	Baron Hohenfeld.
Ursinus.	Blumenbach.
F. Jacobi.	Sir Joseph Banks.
Baron von Beroldingen.	Faujas de St. Fond.
Louisa von Gochhausen.	Hemsterhuis.
Dalberg, Prince Primate of Frankfort.	Prince Gallitzin.
	A. Camper.
Bode.	Count Frederick Stolberg
Wille.	Baron de Luc.
W. Tischbein.	Schneider.
Zentner.	Eberhard.
Count von Veltheim.	Wyttenbach.
Bertuch.	Sarasin.

Such a list of names as the above seems almost to supersede the necessity of any further remark. Fortunate should we esteem our countrymen, had any of those bright cycles of talent, which at various periods have illumined, and still illumine our progress to civilization, bequeathed to us so rich a legacy of biographical characteristics as is here presented. For although we have no lack of posthumous correspondence of the good, the great, the witty, and the notorious of our own country, yet we know of no English work which can compare in aggregate value with the one before us. Dating from the most prosperous period of German literature, it includes the chief actors on the theatre of letters, and more especially that brilliant constellation of genius which encircled the ducal coronet of Weimar during the latter half of the last century, and from thence shed its light over the whole cultivated world. To those, therefore, who are at all conversant in the writings and biography of this poetical groupe, we would earnestly recommend this correspondence as an indispensable supplement—as a test by which they may prove the conclusions to which that study has advanced them. Here they will find the hopes, the fears, and the ambitions of the poet's heart; the varieties of character under which the same productive principle displays itself—by turns the careless thought, or profound reflection—the spontaneous opinion, or mature criticism. Here they may trace the first conception, the opening childhood, and the gradual ripening of those works which we now behold only in their full-grown form; and compare, as it were, the private cipher of the man with the public autograph of the author; while, in the numerous letters from the grand duchess, and her enlightened son, Charles Augustus, we recognise the intelligent and philanthropic patronage which at once inspired the talents, and secured the welfare of their illustrious literary dependents.

To the English reader, also, who has only a common share of patriotism, the high rank awarded to our literature, in the course of these Letters, cannot be a subject of indifference. We remark, with undisguised pride, the veneration of these writers for their English predecessors in the beginning of the eighteenth century; while the excellencies of Shakspeare, whose genius has become European property, are gladly claimed by them as current coin for the acquirement of human knowledge, and the interchange of poetical feeling. Our remarks must chiefly be confined to the Weimar circle, and we shall be gratified if, by a few translated specimens, we can induce those possessing the language-key, to unlock and partake of the feast before them; and still more so, should some spirited individual be thereby encouraged to present the collective work to the public in an English dress.

Herder's letters we find first in order, commencing in 1770; between the age of twenty-six and twenty-eight, and, as such, too early to exhibit more than that ardent thirst for knowledge and deep-seated affection for mankind and truth, which afterwards overflowed in his maturer works. He commences this correspondence while travelling with the unfortunate Prince of Holstein, immediately on quitting Darmstadt. There he had first made the acquaintance of Merck, and, under his auspices, been introduced to Caroline Flachsland, the lady who subsequently became his wife. His stay there lasted a fortnight, and he left the place betrothed in heart and hand. This was an attachment which formed the main staff of his domestic happiness throughout

life, and upon which he could always rest his weary mind, amidst the disappointments and vexations which always attend the promoter of any good, or the opponent of any corrupt public system, and which finally and prematurely brought Herder to the grave. These letters, therefore, occurring at this eventful time, are marked with all those alternations of hope and despair, sunshine and gloom, which the excitement of loving and being loved, first awakened in such a mind, could not fail to exhibit. Merck was the confidant of his affection, and the bearer of his letters to its object, whom he recommends urgently to his kindness. " Countless times during these last two days," he writes in his first letter after their separation, " have I been with you all in Darmstadt. How can I help it, if you are of such material natures as not to feel my presence?"—and in a postscript he adds:—

" The enclosed I beg you to deliver; but, of course, only into the hands and before the eyes of her for whom it is intended. The contents, upon my priestly conscience, are only such as will make you no go-between, although, like the left hand in Scripture, ' you know not what your right hand doeth.' "

In these letters we find frequent outbursts of that admiration for Ossian and Shakspeare which first suggested his collection of different National Songs, (" Volks Lieder,") by which he has unfolded a page of popular tradition, as valuable to the historian as to the poet. His enthusiasm on this subject is best told in his own words.

" In rummaging my papers a day or two ago I found some translations which I had made some time back from the finest English ballads, and especially from Shakspeare. Concluding that you have not given up Shakspeare, I enclose a few of these scraps. In the original English, with their own metre, old-fashioned rhymes and peculiar fable style, each is excellent in its kind, and in the places where they are introduced of most astonishing effect. But precisely for this reason are they entirely untranslatable. On this account has Wieland* omitted, or at best most unmercifully mutilated them. This last is especially the case with Ariel's song, and indeed with both the songs in ' The Tempest;' the one so solemnly mystical, the other so etherially sylph-like joyous; both which, as far as I can remember from a couple of lines, are miserably travestied by Wieland. The latter song, ' Where the bee sucks,' &c. has been also attempted by Moses, and by the translator of the ' Essay on the Genius of Pope;' but neither of them to my fancy. Just see now whether my version satisfies you better; but, for the life of you, attend only to tones, not to words—you must only sing, not read. The Cuckoo song has been charmingly set to music by Handel; in German, however, the play upon words is not so striking, at least not to the perception of

---

* Wieland translated 22 of Shakspeare's plays between the years 1762 and 1766.

every blockhead. Besides this, I cannot help thinking that I have discovered some faint traces of this cuckoo prophecy, and of the owl's song, (the latter, however, in the character of a death-watch,) amongst the provincial traditions of my own father-land; which induces me to deviate entirely from the English version. The ballad 'Come away, come away Death,' has a wonderful effect where it is introduced, and Shakspeare has done well in making the duke, before whom it is sung, so loud in its praise. This is an old romance, much older than Shakspeare; as also 'Take, oh take those lips away.' These old songs have that effect upon me, that I am firmly resolved, should I ever set foot on British ground, merely to skim through London, just peep at the theatre and Garrick, pay my respects to Hume, and then fly off to Wales, Scotland, and the Western Isles; on one of which, like the youngest son of Ossian, Macpherson sits enthroned. There shall I hear the Celtic national songs wildly chanted in the real language and tone of the country—those songs which, in their present metamorphosis into hexameters and Greek metre, I can only liken to a painted perfumed paper flower, instead of that living and fair-blooming daughter of the earth, who exhales her fragrance on the wild mountain side. But to return to Shakspeare; help me to bewail a loss, at which certainly every other honest man would only laugh. During my frenzy for Shakspeare, I had particularly studied those scenes wherein he opens to us his world of ghosts and fairies—those parts which the English prize as his finest, and in which I took the more delight having dreamed away my childhood among such fables. I had, for instance, translated the fairy 'divertissement' in the Midsummer Night's Dream, (which Wieland has, I believe, entirely omitted,) and the witch scene in Macbeth, where the witches are boiling, conjuring, muttering, and bubbling through a whole discant of ghostly tones—but my translations have disappeared, and I can find nothing, nothing but a few soliloquies from King Lear, Hamlet, Macbeth, &c. This is enough to make me tear my eyes out. In short I find every thing but my conjurations, and these must have been swept away, or burnt, when the witches last cleaned out my rooms at Riga. To my own private gratification such a loss is irreparable;—but I continue prating about Shakspeare; whom I never can leave, when once I get upon him."

Herder sojourned some months at Strasburg, whence the greater part of these letters are dated, and where he parted from the Prince of Holstein. This city had a double claim upon his recollections, having led to his first acquaintance with Göthe, whom he characteristically describes, (as Göthe does him in his Life,) and also as having been the scene of a series of painful operations for a fistula lachrymalis under which he laboured, and which he describes with stoical detail. His disgust of Strasburg on first entering it is expressed with a true lover's whimsicality. "Strasburg," he says, "is the most miserable, the most barren, and the most disagreeable place, that, speaking with all due consideration, I have yet seen in my life. Here is not even a wood, or a spot, where one can repose with one's book and one's genius in the shade—and then that it should lie so near Darmstadt, and yet not be Darmstadt, is certainly great part of the annoyance, but I assure you not all." In short, in these letters he runs down every note of the gamut, from the highest glee of mirth to the deepest gloom of despondency. For the latter, he had, however, besides the circumstance of being in love, some rational grounds, having been assailed in the most sensitive part by the officiousness of some individuals, who, as Herder's wife, alluding subsequently to this period in her "Erinnerungen," says, "interfered in our engagement, and wanted to model it to their own way of thinking." Writing on this to Merck, Herder says, "Let me embrace you, dear friend, for all the affection, patience, and kindness you have shown to me, and my, or rather, your friend, (for in many respects she belongs more to you than to me,) in her present uncomfortable situation—a situation at which I am as much annoyed as astonished. Really between four or five people such an entangled skein of love, friendship, jealousy, hatred and humbug has been drawn, as would hardly be credited to exist in so eventless a little circle; and, as all the ends seem to lead towards you, I can only call to you, 'Hold tight, dear Merck, till time shall in pity have unravelled some of the shreds.'"

Göthe and Merck were at this time engaged in the "Frankfurt Journal," to which Herder evidently largely contributed; reviewing, among others, several English works; and it is not a little interesting to notice the different effusions, now an original ode or versified translation, of which the post between Strasburg and Darmstadt (and doubtless a slow one) was the bearer. In his fits of lightheartedness, which were here and there spiced with a little irony, (for Herder rather piqued himself on resembling our English Swift, and was on that account nicknamed "the Dean" by his friends,) he seems to have struck rather harder than he intended. Merck's peculiar temperament disliked perhaps to be encountered with its own weapons, and in his last letters Herder labours to remove some unfriendly impression with all the earnestness and generosity which man as man could exert, or as friend require. We could almost forgive Merck his ill-temper for having brought to light so beautiful a side of Herder's character; but, with these letters before us, we cannot exculpate the man who could read them to misinterpret, or, what is worse, to pervert. And this it seems was the case; for the acquaintance apparently ceases with these letters, and some after-passages bespeak no kindly feeling on Merck's part towards his former friend.

We continue to catch glimpses of Herder's career through the letters from the Weimar circle, which he joined in 1776. One

56

passage in Wieland's correspondence is too superb in itself, and too flattering to the excellent Herder, to be omitted. In mentioning the birth of an heir to the house of Weimar, he says, " *Herder spoke at the Baptism of the Prince like a God.* His discourse shall be sent to you when printed. There are only five sheets of it, but I know nothing more pure, more sublime, more simple, more touching, more finely conceived, or more exquisitely delivered, either in the German or any other tongue. I doubt whether a nobler or more impressive baptism was ever conferred on any German prince. Welcome be therefore Charles Frederick, Dei Gratia, and may it be well with our grandchildren, by, with or under him—*over* him will come none ' *ex nostris.*' "*

It were much to be desired that we possessed some complete biography of this delightful poet, sound divine, and amiable man. Those published in Germany, although severally of great merit, do not even collectively do justice either to the extent of his usefulness, or to the spirit which dictated his writings. His only daughter, a lady of the highest worth and talent, resident at Weimar, is in possession of most interesting documents; and especially of her father's correspondence with a certain princess, which, in point of epistolary style and beauty of moral and poetical sentiment, stands unrivalled.

The short sketch of his life and works, in the late William Taylor's Survey of German Poetry, offers, as far as it goes, a comprehensive view of Herder's character.

Sophie de la Roche's letters follow next. She is celebrated as having written a novel called " Fräulein von Sternheim," " Rosalie's Letters," and other light, but interesting works ; as having been the first love of Wieland, and the grandmother of Bettina von Arnim, whose correspondence with Göthe was reviewed in Number XXXII. of our Journal. Madame de la Roche's letters are interesting, as showing the place awarded to female talent in Germany, and the union of the domestic wife and mother with the now exploded character of " blue stocking" at an earlier period even than with us. She writes with much elegance and lively anecdote, but seems thoroughly afraid of Merck's satirical vein, although not too much to tell him so in the plainest terms.

Next follow six letters from Boie, which are highly interesting, as belonging to that period when he, and his circle of young associates, Burger, Gotter, Voss, Hölty, the two counts Stolberg, Miller, Leisewitz, &c. of whom Boie was the eldest, formed by a study of the Grecian poets, and especially of Homer, by a perfect familiarity with Shakspeare, and by a new acquaintance with

---

* This baptismal Sermon is printed among Herder's collective works.

" Percy's Reliques of Ancient English Poetry," which unlocked to them the beauties of the real ballad style, kept the muses in full employment at Göttingen, and poured forth upon the world a stream of lyrical poetry through the much frequented channels of the " Musen Almanach," and the " Deutsches Museum." Boie was co-editor with Gotter of the Almanach, and announces in these letters his cession of it to Voss (the celebrated translator of Homer), who married his sister, and his having engaged with Dohm in the " Deutsches Museum," which he subsequently carried on for years alone. His assiduity in collecting contributions for these periodicals is most entertaining. (Herder not inaptly calls him the Muses' Accoucheur.) Merck was evidently a contributor of no little importance, but always in a strict incognito. This correspondence also shows that, with all the boisterous wit and joviality of the Göttingen party, and their resolution to enjoy life, cost what it might, Boie was not happy. Towards the close we find him satiated with dissipation and sighing for quieter joys. " Pity me," he says; " I have a heart, and am banished to a university, where I cannot use it. My situation, it is true, has much of real good; but I am lonely in heart and desponding." Of Herder he speaks delightfully. " I am tired," he writes, " of the students, and of being the learned man, and still more so, since I have known Herder—the only sage in whom I have found the *man* as I wished to find him. The friendship he has granted to me is one of the purest joys of my life."

G. Schlosser, brother-in-law of Göthe, known by several small didactic pieces, has three letters here, as distinct in character as they are separate in time. In a strain of sentimental philosophy, he analyzes the difference between the understanding and the heart; the independence of the one, the miserable dependence of the other. Evidently unprovided with the rudder of religion, he longs for the haven of peace which he cannot find, and touchingly laments that mental darkness in which his thoughts run foul of one another. From various natural arguments he adduces the fact of another world, and appeals to Merck to confirm his trembling opinions. " I have, and you know it, always hoped and believed in a future state ; now I hope and believe, because I need it more than ever. Without it the creation would be an imperfect work, and I would rather be a stock or a stone—any thing but a man." The other letters are more cheerful ; time and a wife having effected much, his style becomes matrimonial and contented.

Nicolai's letters next appear. He was known as a great bookseller at Berlin; as the author of the " Joys of Werther "—of a novel called " Sebaldus Nothanker "—as editor of the " Allgemeine Deutsche Bibliothek," &c. He was cotemporary, friend and follower of Lessing, and one in whom the nervous opposition of that great genius to the prejudices of the age, and the trammels of an over-formal orthodoxy, had degenerated into a jeering rationalism, and a denial of the higher aspirations of our nature. From his editorial chair, which was a conspicuous object in the intellectual arena, he waged continual war with the ranks of authorship. In this correspondence Göthe appears as head culprit, and his spleen against this arch-innovator is the burden of every letter. They exhibit, however, a striking picture of the times, and of Nicolai's restless activity of mind, which afterwards induced that extraordinary state of nervous optical delusion, so interestingly recorded by Whiter; a portion of his biography best known in England.

Göthe now stands before us. His letters, twenty-six in number, commence at the age of twenty-five, and, carrying us to the very meridian of his powers, progressively show us the grand bases on which his wide-extended popularity was founded. The prevailing character of this correspondence, and especially of the earlier part, consists in that independent energy of mind, that animation of conscious power, which propelled him forward in the race he ran, with an impetus above the comprehension of timid minds; and which, subduing alike the passions of mankind and the difficulties of science to his will, would have rendered Göthe a great man, in whatever circumstances he might have been placed.

No mind has perhaps yet appeared before the public more difficult to decipher, more impossible to square with our usual sympathies, than Göthe's. In attempting, therefore, this analysis, we presume not to pronounce a decisive judgment, but only to present those impressions to which a knowledge of Germany, of Göthe's works, and more especially the private disclosures of this correspondence, have given rise. From the letters of the other Weimar literati, who seemingly acknowledged their allegiance to this monarch of intellect as willingly as he could have required it, these observations are equally gleaned as from his own. With regard, however, to the real motives and innate workings of his superior mind, which, in an intercourse of this intimate nature, might be expected to exhibit themselves, we are still left rather to guess than to decide. His character, on the other hand, appears as clear as day-light; but that character consisted precisely in never exposing his mind. He generally writes, also, in a hurry, giving biographical data rather than private feelings. Calm and dispassionate observation appears to be his great object in life; and though he occasionally utters a maxim, he never expresses a sentiment.

As this correspondence included no less a period than eleven years, it necessarily involved the most momentous transactions of his life, and must have exposed Göthe, like other men, to the average vicissitudes of fortune; yet we find him invariably erect and collected, appealing to no sympathy, indulging in no affection, expressing neither hope nor fear; so that, with this total absence of all the usual topics of friendship, his attachment for the cynical but useful Merck seems rather to be the pretext than the object of this intercourse, and, although offering an indispensable aspect of his character, this work is adapted rather for the votary of science than of fancy. Poetry, it is true, peeps through every subject, forming at all times a graceful background, but seldom obtruding as a prominent object; and on this account we can indulge in but slender extracts for an article of this kind. The following letter, however, strikingly exemplifies the man, and shows when and where were laid the foundations upon which the mighty fabric of his Faust was erected:

"Weimar, August 5th, 1778.

"I must now tell you something about my journeyings. Last winter a tour through the Hartz gave me much pleasure: for you know that much as I hate to see Nature tortured into Romance, so much do I delight in finding Romance consistent with Nature. I started alone; about the last day of November—on horseback, with a knapsack—rode through hail, frost, and mud to Nordhausen, entered the Hartz by the Baumann's Höble, and so by Wernigerode and Goslar into the Upper Hartz, (the details I will give you another time,) overcame all difficulties, and stood, I think, on the 8th of December, at noon, on the summit of the Brocken. A cheerful genial sun above—snow an ell and half thick on the ground, and the cloud-bedecked panorama of Germany beneath me; so that the forester, whom, having lived for years at the foot, and always deemed the ascent impossible, I had with difficulty persuaded to accompany me, was quite beside himself with admiration. Here I spent a fortnight alone—no human being knowing where I was: of the thousand thoughts in this solitude, the enclosure will give you some idea.

"In the spring I was in Berlin—quite a different spectacle. We spent a few days there, and I only peeped in, as a child into a penny show. But you know that I exist in contemplation, and a thousand new lights broke upon me. I saw much of old Fritz*,—of his gold, silver, marble, monkeys, parrots, and torn curtains;—and overheard his own minions snarl at the great man. A large portion of Prince Henry's army which we passed—the various manœuvres we witnessed, and the persons of the generals who sat opposite to me by half dozens at dinner, have made me much more familiar with the present war. Otherwise, I had no intercourse with mankind, and did not utter a word in the Prussian dominions which they might not have printed; for which I was exclaimed against as proud, &c.

* Frederick the Great.

" The Raphaels which the duchess has brought with her are a great enjoyment to me. Now I am in search of all kinds of drawings. I have also just re-opened an old quarry, which probably had been in disuse for centuries. The porch at the old castle was built of this stone, which can be worked to the greatest pitch of delicacy. It is very hard, but can be shaved or rasped with ease; has no cracks, imbibes no moisture, and is of that beautiful grey colour so much in request and so seldom found. French snuff-boxes are of the same hue—neither blue nor yellow. It is a woodstone—the middle sort between common and marble. Adieu, old man. Now you have heard again from me, tell me something in return, and don't forget me. Should there be no war, I will some day visit you."

In appreciating the vantage-ground which the collected mind obtains over the being of impulse and passion, Göthe seems to have aimed and arrived at that stoical atmosphere of self-possession, whence he could leisurely survey the vast mass of human nature (lying like the " cloud-bedecked panorama of Germany") beneath him; and deliberately choose and appropriate those portions best adapted for his use. To accomplish this, he necessarily sacrificed the indulgence of those affections by which the independence of other minds is compromised. To Nature he gave his heart, and felt it securely invested; to Mankind his understanding, and nothing more, and though, by the immense range and ardent cultivation of his versatile genius, for which no subject was so intricate that it did not seek to explore it, no fact so simple that it disdained to appropriate it, he indirectly included the direct benefit of his fellow-creatures, (he was, for instance, the original inventor and first projector of the excellent system of national schools in Germany,) yet we may safely question whether he was influenced so much by an expanded philanthropy as by a refined selfishness. At the same time, by the same process by which he controlled the elements of his own passions, was he enabled to agitate them in the bosom of others. No one could kindle stronger and more lasting attachments; no heart remain more fire-proof than his own. He despised not the sweets of love or friendship, and no author has more vividly described them, but he culled them only so far as was consistent with his prescribed law of independence. After his first boyish fancies, it may be doubted whether he ever loved; but as the fresh breath of youth is supposed to invigorate the failing energies of old age, so did Göthe refresh the powers of his imagination at the fountain of an overflowing heart, and catch the very tone of truth from the impassioned effusions of his votaries.*

* Those who may be startled at these opinions, we must refer to " Göthe's Briefwechsel mit einem Kinde," already mentioned.

To disarm affliction of its weapons by voluntarily withdrawing from the objects within its reach, is the specious reasoning of many a cold-blooded Epicurean in happiness. Of this principle Göthe seems to have partaken. Like every system of human presumption, however, this involves its own punishment. " The man," as Bacon says, " who has wife and children, has taken hostages of fortune;" and he who has nothing to lose is more pitiable than he who mourns the lost. Göthe lived a worshipped but loveless life ; his marriage was formed comparatively late in life by conventional decorum ; his son proved no blessing ; and, if selfishness were not the cause, it was at all events the result of such a policy.

This systematic coldness and reserve, which apparently date from his first elevation in the political world, naturally engendered discontent, as well in those who penetrated, as in those who misunderstood, its motives. Vanity it was called by some ; pride, more correctly, by others. Even Wieland, the kind and sincere friend, laments the ill-will borne towards him; but even Wieland admits the change that had come over Göthe. Alluding to Göthe's employment in the state, he says, " His imagination seems quenched;' instead of the all-enlivening warmth which used to emanate from him, he seems to be enveloped in an atmosphere of political frost. He is always gentle and harmless, but is friends with no one, and nothing can be done with him." The sincerity of this avowal may be confirmed by the following sentence. Speaking of a report of Göthe's being ill, which had reached Merck, Wieland adds, "About Göthe don't be uneasy, dear brother; he is well, and the gossip of certain good people about the decline of his health reminds me of the fable of the two wolves, who, hearing that the stag was ill, thus addressed the fawn : ' How is your father?' ' Better than you gentlemen could wish,' answered the fawn; and 'fiat applicatio' as far and as much as you please."

In this correspondence we find a lively picture of the esteem in which Göthe was held by the reigning family and court of Weimar. His presence formed an indispensable portion of their public pageantry and private comfort; and we see his active and intelligent influence extending over every part of the state. Nowhere can the relation of prince and subject appear to such advantage as between the enlightened Duke of Weimar and his illustrious minister. Each seems to have found in the other the friend best fitted to develop the energies of his nature ; and, whether in the public plans of agricultural improvement or state economy, of which these letters treat largely, or in the social tour and amusing search for works of art, where no professed picture-dealer could drive a bargain with more *gusto* than the duke and his premier, we find them acting with one mind, and without a single interruption to their friendship. Here again, however, we must forbear to pry too deeply, or we may fancy we discern Göthe using Charles Augustus rather as the most valuable of his tools than as the most liberal of his friends. " I am now," he said, " mixed up in all court and political subjects, and shall probably not extricate myself again. My situation, however, is favourable enough, and the dukedom of Weimar and Eisenach a theatre sufficient to practise the *rôle* of the world."

On all subjects connected with science, this correspondence assumes a high biographical value, and for England, where Göthe is recognized as a great poet, and but little more, it is peculiarly adapted to fill up the measure of his character. Here we see him by turns the artist, geologist, anatomist, physiologist, and politician,—alike indefatigable in all pursuits, and passing from one subject to another with a rapidity in which we hardly know whether most to admire the depth of his research or the versatility of his powers.

In poetry, although he has bequeathed so much to posterity, he seems, like our Pope, to display rather a systematic versification of prose, than a spontaneous effusion of verse. He had neither the poet's timidity nor the poet's flights. Mankind he took as he found them, neither seeking nor caring to make them better. He fixed no ideal standard, therefore experienced no disappointment. He was highly receptive, but rarely sensitive— imaginative without an ideal—poetical without fiction : and the good old age to which he attained may be attributed less to his robust physical constitution than to the absence of all mental irritation. The enthusiastic reader, therefore, who may expect to find the flowers of fancy or the sweets of sentiment scattered in these leaves, must quit Göthe, and pass on to that poet of the graces, Wieland—whose sixty letters to Merck form the most attractive essence of this work. Considered either as a poet or as a man, the analysis of Wieland's character imposes both an easy and an agreeable task ; and, among the rich harvest of ideas which these letters offer, the only difficulty is that of selection. High as the fame of Wieland already stands in the scale of public genius and private excellence, these letters were still wanting to pay the full tribute to his praise; and although we rejoice to be able to offer some of these epistolary specimens of his delightful mind, yet for the enjoyment of all their beauties not a letter ought to be retrenched. The " Teutscher Merkur," a monthly work, of which he was editor from the year 1773 to 1795, which formed not the least important of Wieland's pretensions to fame,

and mainly contributed to procure for Weimar the title of the German Athens, is the ostensible object of this intercourse. Merck largely contributed, especially in the way of reviews; and the correspondence opens by Wieland's formally making over to him the critical department. In this glance behind the scenes, we find him apprising Merck that Berlin and Vienna were the two cities that he would wish to have handled softly and *prudenter*. " All universities," he says, " I surrender to your mercy." Prussia, indeed, under Frederick the Great, seems to have inspired awe in all classes. Speaking of an historical novel which had attracted some notice, Wieland says, " Be as bold upon it as you please, only not *too biting;* for the author is a Prussian officer, and has a crowd of friends in blue coats (the Prussian uniform) whom I would not wish to offend." In this periodical most of Wieland's poetical works appeared piecemeal—a kind of rehearsal, before printing them separately, which both felt the pulse of public opinion, and contributed to that delicacy of polish which distinguishes his style.

From the length of time which this correspondence includes, and the perfect openness with which it is conducted, we are enabled to trace the progress of many of his popular works, and more especially of that master-piece of his genius, Oberon. The manner in which he details the beginning of this immortal poem, of which he gives no hint till he is fairly launched into its adventures, and the glimpses he affords of the progress of his constant couple through their various assailments, is no little acquisition to the lover of poetry. Seldom are we thus allowed to peep into the poet's work-shop. Indeed Wieland had not that confidence in his own powers which could induce him to expose the growth of this darling work even to the eye of a friend ; on the contrary he mentions it with all the timidity and anxiety as to result which ever accompany true genius, and reminds Merck never to forget that, in the strictest sense of the word, he is " the only man on God's earth to whom he either would, could, or might, thus expose the inmost secrets of his mind, heart, and whole being." In many instances he complains of want of leisure and of the necessary repose of mind, and of the absence of all inspiration in the persons and things around him, (yet, if he found this not in Weimar, we know not where he would have sought it,) and makes it a powerful plea with Merck, in his reiterated requests for more contributory help to the Mercury, which at this time seems to weigh heavily upon him, and to call him from the dewy meads of imagination, which were his peculiar province, to the mere dusty highroad of business.

Speaking of his progress, he says, " My fifth and sixth cantos are I think, *entre nous,* so good, so *omnibus numeris* good, that I am only provoked that I cannot defer their publication until after my death." " Day and night," he adds, " Oberon is all my thought;" and again, " Oberon is my resource against a crowd of *desagrémens.* To those who maintain rapidity of composition to be a necessary test of genius the following quotation from Wieland's pen may prove either encouragement or reproof.

" Of the time and labour I devote to this work, no poet, great or small, of the Holy Roman empire can well form an idea. Those gentry, with few exceptions, seek how they may best make the task of verse-making easy. I, on the contrary, give myself all possible trouble. The difficulties which lie in the mechanism of my eight-lined stanzas, in the nature of the iambics, and in the comparatively limited range of our rhyming words; the fatigue of manipulating the stubborn clay into the exact image which I require, and of giving it that roundness and *fini,* without which I have no pleasure in the performance, are unspeakable. I vow to you, I have in this last week spent not less than three days and a half upon one stanza—the whole machinery being at a stand-still for one single word, which I wanted and could not supply."

He then proceeds to explain his pecuniary views with regard to Oberon, which, he says, are very " miserable," and describes the slender profits likely to arise. " But, says the German public," he continues, " why is this good gentleman such a fool as to devote so much time and labour to a work which no one will thank him for? and to this I have nothing to answer."

" With the *gloriola* of the thing," he adds, " it will be much the same as with the *utile.* Nine-tenths of the reading world are the last people to repay a poor fellow even in that coin. The remaining tenth, with the exception of about a dozen, are hard and fast determined beforehand not to give me any credit, but to pretend that they would weave such stuff as that any day *à la douzaine;* and for the dozen remaining honest folk, they will doubtless find real enjoyment in the work, but quite *in private;* and, should a parcel of saucy boys take it into their heads to pelt me the next day in the open market-place, no living soul would take my part—if even they did not join the assailants. On the other hand, I shall have full liberty to sit down and feast myself, *ad nauseam usque,* on the name and fame which awaits me in the twentieth century. These, dear brother, are my views, but again, I repeat, I complain not; my lot is of my own casting. Certainly, had I spent one-hundredth part of the time I have bestowed on my Idrises and Oberons in a well-turned panegyric on Maria Theresa, or Catherine the Great, my coffers would wear a different aspect; but such wisdom I never had, nor shall have. All that remains is to be resigned to my fate—to do what I can —to bear what I must—and to expect from mankind nothing I do not earn. And so much for Oberon."

In spite of these half-sad, half-playful prognostics, Wieland

was destined to reap much of that glory which Oberon has now permanently established.

In another letter we find an interesting account of Göthe's first introduction to the king of elves and sprites.

" Last week I had a delightful day with Göthe. He and I were obliged to make up our minds to sit to May, who, *ex voto* of the Duchess of Wirtemberg, was to paint us for her highness. Göthe sat both fore and afternoon, and begged me, *serenissimus** being *absens,* to bear him company, and read Oberon aloud. Fortunately for me, this generally capricious man was in one of his best and most receptive moods, and as *amusable* as a girl of sixteen. Never did I see a man so delighted with the production of another, as he was with my Oberon; especially with the fifth canto, where Huon acquits himself *verbo tenus* of the emperor's commands. It was a true *jouissance,* as you may guess, to me. A day or two afterwards, he owned to me that it might perhaps be three years before this degree of susceptibility and openness of every sense of enjoyment for a work *hujus furfuris et farinæ* would again come over him."

Wieland's modesty, it would seem, was one of the causes which conspired to spoil " this generally capricious man," who, with his vaunted coolness and self-possession, must, we fancy, have rather belied himself in owning that only once in three years could he command his own powers to the enjoyment of such a work as Oberon.

To all those acquainted with Wieland's works, the skill with which he identifies himself with the age and country in which he introduces his poetic personages, and the perfectly harmonious keeping of his rich and varied accessories with the principal subject of his piece, have been a matter of surprise and admiration; and, although accounted for, it is not diminished, when we observe how completely he concentrated all his powers on one object, and bent the whole energy of his mind to its attainment. The letters, at this time, are pregnant with fairy imagery, and, whether plaintive or jocund, Oberon is ever the burden of his song. Apologising for want of punctuality in correspondence, and trusting in Merck's friendship to excuse it, he adds:—

" And if it were not so, Heaven knows how impossible it would be for me to think, or attempt to think, or write, of any thing else but Oberon; and woe to me if it were otherwise ! For I am only in the ninth canto, with three more before me, and must exert myself to the utmost, lest this immense *amphora* should turn out a mere *urceus* at last."

And on a previous occasion, with the reaction of spirits succeeding a difficulty overcome, he thus concludes:—

" Oberon sends you his compliments—I am now in the midst of the seventh canto; and my enamoured pair, hero and heroine, have just,

---

* The grand duke.

during a dreadful storm, been thrown overboard, without the incensed Oberon's deigning to take the slightest notice of them. Heaven help them out of this watery ordeal, and me to a happy conclusion! Amen."

Lastly, he announces the appearance of this master-piece, " which," he says, " is born just time enough to escape the effects of a miserable influenza, in which my soul is sticking like an oyster in the mud;" and adds, " the shares of my credit with the duke, Göthe, and the Weimar public, have risen one hundred per cent. in consequence of this little production. May it only fare the same in the larger world without."

We do not apologize to our readers for attracting their attention to those portions of this correspondence which treat of Oberon, feeling convinced that those, who know its full-grown beauties, cannot be indifferent to these early annals of its progress. That a work of this kind should completely engross the mind of its author, during the period of its composition, is not surprising; but Wieland's appears at times to have been kept at that extreme tension of productive excitement, which, though the surest earnest of his success, it is almost painful to trace, and which makes us wonder at the healthy longevity of mind and body to which he attained. He himself, in a letter to some one, expresses his surprise at this extension of power, having been, to borrow the late Mr. Taylor's translation, " a hot-house plant; reared within doors; too much nursed by women, and too much confined by study." The secret of this, however, seems to consist in the wholesome atmosphere in which his affections were ever maintained. Wieland's private character required no veiling: the poetical license which his charity inclined him to grant to the domestic failings of his genial friends, he never claimed for himself. And while his imagination wandered to the fertile shores of Greece, or the luxurious halls of the East, his heart and good sense, uncloyed by the voluptuous and sensual imagery which had been passing before his mental vision, were ever found stationary, and occupied with the little circle of his home-joys in Weimar.

Although peculiarly fitted, by the gentleness of his nature and the purity of his taste, to move in the politest circles, and called thither by the general recognition of his talents, Wieland never deviated from that simplicity which was his great charm. A poet without caprice, a courtier without intrigue, he pursued the even tenor of his way; and, though in the enlightened court of Weimar the distinctions of genius seemed to be substituted for those of rank, he never forgot where the friend left off, or the sovereign began, or ought to begin. Returning from a visit at Ettersburg (one of the ducal residences), he jocularly observes, " I have put it down as a *regula sanitatis et prudentiæ*, in my *liber memorialis*,

that none of my sort should stay longer than three days with a prince."

Nowhere, however, has the noble ducal family been more worthily panegyrised than in this correspondence, which teems with expressions of gratitude and respect, untainted by the semblance of adulation or ambition. Ambition, indeed, in the meaner sense of the word, was as foreign to Wieland's character as bombast to his muse; and, at the time when the court of Mannheim intimated a desire, and held out a lure, to attach him to its service, we find him thus answering Merck :—

" You remind me that I ought to profit by the favourable gale which seems to blow me towards the Neckar, and to turn my back on this land where no wine grows, where the water is good for nothing, and where Eurus and Boreas, during eight months of the year, make themselves as troublesome as possible. Yes, my dear sir, all well and good, if, *pro primo*, it were as easy as moving from one street to another; if, *pro secundo*, the cloven foot were not every where to be found (" wenn der Teufel nicht überall im Nest wäre); and if, *pro tertio*, it were not a hundred to one that, by so doing, I should jump out of the frying-pan into the fire (aus dem Regen in die Traufe). Then, although Hompesch,[*] I believe, would do all in his power, I am by no means certain how far this good-will in Mannheim extends. Granting, however, that they really desire my company, under what class and *quo titulo* could I appear? And what worldly advantages could compensate for all the leisure, peace, liberty, independence, esteem, and affection which I here enjoy? True it is that I *signify* (*bedeute*) but little here, and am, *in sensu politico*, seven times less than I signify. *But I neither wish to be, nor signify anything;* and in this precisely consists one-third of my comfort. The ruling personages here are perhaps the best in the whole world. They regard me favourably, do not oppress me, would do every thing for my comfort, and require so little at my hands that I am almost ashamed to eat their bread. Their serene highnesses in Gotha are almost as kindly disposed, so that, even should the greatest of misfortunes befal Weimar, I see nothing in a wordly sense to fear. I sit, therefore, peaceably beneath the shade of my own trees; and would it not be hard, if, from all the 110 beautiful apple, pear, and cherry trees which I planted last year, I were to have no fruit? Would it not be a folly in me to exchange the safety of my present obscurity (*qui bene latuit*, &c.), and plunge myself into the *mare infidum* of Mannheim, where, the moment one pair of eyes is sealed, I risk much more than here—even in case of the dreaded event of the extinction of the present line? Should I be wise to barter my delightful independence, my *sacrosanto far niente*, and the golden privilege of saying to all and anybody, ' What's that to me?' for the slavery, the grievous bondage of Mannheim vanity? Add to this a wife and five children, with a sixth upon the road, and an aged mother, all of whom concur to form a whole, which, in mutual love, harmony and joy, is one of the happiest in the world."

---

[*] Count Hompesch, minister to the court of the Palatinate.

He continues in this strain, and then adds :—

" *Au contraire*, I am fairly in the way for a lasting breach with the Palatinate. Guess why ? Are there not sins which a poet, neither in this nor in the next world, can forgive ? Only imagine ; these Mannheim people have been teasing and baiting me to compose an opera for them, and, now it is all ready, it comes out that they have given their best actress, an angel of beauty and voice, *leave of absence for a year* ; for a pilgrimage to London and Paris, to dance in the planets, or God knows where ; and my little piece, which, with the assistance of the lovely nymph Danzy, might, must, and ought to have had the most splendid success, now, for want of an actress who can either look or sing like Rosamond, may be thrown to the dogs. Is not this enough to drive a man mad ?—and are these the people I am to have any thing more to do with ? So, fare ye well, ye banks of my paternal Neckar !"

In these sixty letters we have ample proof of Wieland's peculiar talent for and love of letter-writing. With a happy vivacity he details the minutiæ of the world of letters, of business, and of intrigue around him ; and while he introduces us to the personages, habits, literature, and gossip of the day, leads us on with all the interest of an historico-biographic novel. His style, abounding in native wit and classic allusion, forbids the slightest approach to garrulity ; and, whether considered as a picture of the times, or as a model of epistolary elegance, this correspondence is equally valuable.

To his wife, a being of simple nature and unaspiring manners, whom he often mentions, he was tenderly attached. She brought him fourteen children ; nine of whom survived him, and every now and then he announces an accession to his family or to his works, with equal complacency. This called forth the following remark from the Grand Duchess to Merck :—

" ' Danishmend (for so she complimentarily called him in allusion to his history of Danishmend the wise) has again been christening. *Je crains qu'à la fin il se ressente un peu*' at the indefatigable accouchements of his wife and of the Mercury. He appears, however, well pleased with both ; so we must let him have his own way—*chacun à sa folie.*' "

Wieland was indeed just what a poet ought to be. Dwelling in a dream of beauty and home of love, no views of aggrandisement, or visions of perfection, disturbed the one or embittered the other. Health, peace, and competence, were all he sought for his muse, his family, or himself. Poetry he loved for poetry's sake, and, quoting from a former work of his own, he thus addresses his muse :—

" Thou art, oh, Muse ! the blessing of my life,
And if the world be deaf, then sing to me alone."

Pure and lively in diction, fanciful and elegant in sentiment, he neither provokes to mirth, nor depresses to melancholy. In the same relation as flowers and birds in the scale of animated nature, is Wieland's verse in the ranks of modern literature. He aspired not to form one of the seven pillars of the temple of wisdom, but his were the roses which clustered to the very pinnacle. And, to conclude in the words of the late Mr. Taylor—" If not the greatest genius among the poets, he was the greatest poet among the geniuses of Germany."

The letters from the Grand Duchess Amalie, and her illustrious son, Charles Augustus, though last in order here, are almost first in interest. Relating individually to Merck, they prove the high esteem in which he was held at the court of Weimar, and, generally, the liberal tone of politics and literature which these enlightened personages so mainly contributed to maintain at that period in Germany. Of the grand duchess, Wieland says :—

" The longer I live with her, the more am I convinced that she, *telle qu'elle est*, is one of the most amiable and glorious compounds of human nature, female nature, and princely nature, (Menschlichkeit, Weiblichkeit und Fürstlichkeit,) that ever appeared on this globe."

And in another place :—

" This lady is really one of the best on God's earth. I doubt whether there is one of her rank whose head and heart are superior, or who could live on more dignified and delightful terms with people of our caste. For my part, I should be the most ungrateful creature between heaven and earth, did I ever forget how much she has contributed to the happiness of my life. I assure you I cannot even contemplate the idea of losing her, should it be my lot to outlive this affliction before I am seventy years of age."

This was the tone of all who knew this excellent princess, who, without interfering in the government, exactly stood in that gap of the state which is best filled by, and seems intended for, a feminine mind. After resigning the regency, and viewing the fulfilment of all her hopes and cares in the person of her son, her's became the province of gracious remembrance, little kindnesses, and beneficent patronage, which, like their kindred, the gentle courtesies of speech, though small in cost are rich in produce.

Her highness's acquaintance with Merck originated in a tour among the Rhine scenery, where he accidentally met with her, and was induced to join her suite, and where, by the refinement and cultivation of his tastes, he greatly enhanced her enjoyment of the beauties both of art and nature. He was subsequently much at the court of Weimar, and on one occasion spent more than half a year in its delightful circle. From that period till shortly before his death, the grand duchess maintained a friendly correspondence with him, which exhibits that interval, probably the happiest of her life, when, reposing from the anxieties of government, she enjoyed, without restraint, the literary society that she had been the first to summon around the court, and, little foreseeing the cloud which was to darken her latter days, spent her time in the dignified cultivation of her taste and talents. Writing to Merck she says:

"The good old Oeser* has been here, and has brought with him some splendid specimens of art and a Mengs of indescribable beauty. My love for drawing continues as strong as ever. I have a camera obscura, in which I sketch, and which I find most serviceable in facilitating an acquaintance with the proportions of Nature. For me, it is of great service, as I commenced my devotion to drawing rather late in life. This year I have also purchased an electrifying machine, which is good and powerful, and affords me much occupation. In the mean time the theatrical world is also flourishing, to which friend Wolf † is a faithful ally. You will shortly receive, through Frau Aja,‡ a new dramatic piece, which has just issued from the prolific pen of the privy councillor (Göthe). Thus pass our days quietly and cheerfully; and did not the lean cherries and unripe strawberries of our desserts remind us, we should almost forget that *Madre Natura* has visited us with a cold, nasty, summer."

Again, when Merck's fit of anatomy was at its height, she writes:

"Your elephant bone affairs appear to sever you from all human intercourse. We see nothing of you, and hear of nothing but bones and skeletons. Notwithstanding this, I pluck up heart to address you, having a request to make somewhat in character with your present studies. A short time ago, I was reading Camper's Lecture to the Academy of Painting, and was much struck by the truth and profundity of his remarks. I now wish, if possible, to procure some of Camper's drawings of the human head. You must know, dear Merck, that I have for some time past applied myself to portrait painting, and they flatter me by saying I am rather happy in my likenesses. In order, therefore, to perfect myself further in this line, I should much like to see some of those drawings where Camper has divided the head into compartments; and, having heard that you anticipate the pleasure of seeing him this spring, I beg you will employ this opportunity of facilitating my request; without, however, mentioning my name. As for the rest, dear Merck,

---

* A painter and engraver of some eminence, and a friend of Winckelmann's.
† An abbreviation of Wolfgang, Göthe's christian name.
‡ Göthe's mother, resident in Frankfurt; so named by the Counts Stolberg, from one of the popular traditions of the middle ages, where Frau Aja, a princess by birth, and mother of several brave sons, plays a conspicuous part. These old documents, which teem with poetic beauty and historic character, were much in vogue with the Weimar set; and, Madame Göthe's character partaking somewhat of the heroism and tenderness of her ancient namesake, she was generally known by this appellation among her son's acquaintances.

I should much enjoy seeing you here again. If bones are your only attraction, we can oblige you with a whole crop of them. Farewell, and keep me in good remembrance. Your friend,

AMALIE."

Without doubting the sincerity of Merck's devotion to the amiable duchess, he was evidently courtier enough to know how peculiarly he was adapted to serve her; and we find him at all times pouring into the ducal palace a succession of works of art, which, while they gratified her taste, renewed her remembrance of the sender. Her highness, in return, freely availed herself of his services, and frequently consulted him on little acts of patronage and benevolence, which she probably found to be better entrusted to the distant than to the nearer friend. But we must here leave the examination of her various excellencies, and proceed to the character of her son, in whom they were completely reflected.

The letters from the grand duke are twenty-three in number, and, both in elegance of style and moral excellence, exhibit that enlightened prince of modern days, who, although his reign has justly been compared to the Augustan age of literature, and to the later lustre of the Italian States, has left no obsequious flatteries to sully his fame. In this correspondence, conjointly with that of his illustrious mother, we find a delightful picture of sovereignty on a small scale—that happy degree which its owners may wear lightly and cheerfully, without compromising their dignity or denying themselves the indulgence of the social affections, and which, though circumscribed in public power, may be widely diffusive of private good.

The earliest date of these letters is at twenty-three years of age, and we find the young duke already familiar with the details of government, with the affections of a husband, and the hopes of a father. His young duchess, a princess of the House of Darmstadt, who, however, rather tried her husband's and people's patience in the hopes of an heir, is often mentioned by him with the most domestic complacency; and, in her firm but gentle character, seems to afford an earnest of the heroic matron who was one of the few at once to awe and win the heart of Napoleon during his insolent career of conquest.

His highness, as if determined to make his little principality the very essence of all the sweets of art and literature, here appears ardently engaged in forming a collection of pictures, prints, and drawings, by old masters; and from the number of his agents stationed in different parts of Germany, and the discrimination of taste evident in this correspondence, Sir Thomas Lawrence himself would not have despised the walls and folios of the Weimar palaces. The salutary influence of Merck's judgment,

8. continued

and the respect shown to his talents, are conspicuous in every letter. Dating from Weimar, August 26th, 1780, his highness begins,

" Dear Merck : My letter has no object beyond that which the commonest flint in the world would effect with a genuine Darmstadt steel—namely, that of eliciting a spark. I am in the most miserable of letter-writing humours, and am so spoiled by your frequent and delightful epistles, that I can hardly live without them."

And again,

" This is only an avant-courier of the acknowledgment of all your kindnesses ; among which I may class the *Everding*, which is exquisitely beautiful, and which, in spite of the wretched state of obtusity in which a succession of coughs, colds, and formal visits have imprisoned my senses, has given me the greatest pleasure. As soon as I am free from all three, I will write to you properly."

Evidently recognizing in Merck one of that rare species of the human kind who carry a practical good sense into all they undertake, his highness largely employed his talents in the advancement of his political plans ; and, while sentiment was hardly to be expected from a friend and disciple of Göthe's, its place is occupied by that strong moral sense and practical philanthropy which are infinitely preferable in the head of a state. From the situation occupied by Merck in the Darmstadt government, he was the more adapted to promote the latter virtue, and it appears that a comparison between the economy of both states was frequently made with mutual advantage. The establishment of different manufactures in his territories seems here to be a favourite object with the grand duke ; and, though he has been accused of being the man of letters rather than the man of business, this correspondence fully acquits him of any undue predominance. In the first letter, after a long list of commissions regarding works of art, we find his highness thus adding :

" And now for *politica*. In the first place I wish to procure some written account of the advantages attending the present disposal of the crown estates ; with a calculation made from some individual instance of the same, in your country, in order that I may see how the old revenues are continued to be produced from them.

" Secondly, I want to see a description of the madder manufacture, as far as it concerns the agriculturist, and how the land is prepared for its cultivation ; and I must beg you, dear M. Merck, to inquire, in a private way, among the Swiss, if they would not be inclined to establish a similar manufacture in other countries.

" Thirdly, Would you have the goodness to look out for a few *Anabaptists*, who would be induced to undertake a journey next summer to Eisenach, at my cost, in order to inspect an estate which I should be glad to let to them. You may promise them the following terms in my name :

" The expenses of the journey thither and back ; whatever the result ;

" Free exercise of their religion, as they enjoy it in other places ;

" As long a lease as they can desire ;

" Exemption from all surety and affidavits upon oath.

" If you can meet with a few people of this description to make the trial on these terms, they may apply next summer forthwith to the President von Herd, at Eisenach, inspect the estate, and enter as tenants the following autumn.

" My list of commissions is now at length finished ; but your kindness in undertaking all requests spoils a person so much that one hardly knows where to set proper limits."

The reason for the duke's preference of Anabaptists as tenants for his estate does not appear. They seem, however, to have differed little in principle of conduct from their brethren of the present day, giving him much trouble by their extortion, discontent, and laziness ; and they were at last ejected from the estate.

With these varied attractions in and around the sovereign, it will not appear surprising that so many travellers should have turned their faces towards Weimar. The Duke himself says,

" I have been living for the last three weeks in such a round of dissipation, that I have had time neither to think nor write. During this time we have had more strangers here at once, than the course of many years had previously brought to Weimar. This evening we also expect a fresh arrival, and one of a most interesting kind—Prince Augustus of Gotha, with the celebrated Abbé Raynal. I hear wonderful things of his powers of conversation, and all here, from the chief to the heyduke, are on the tiptoe of expectation."

We regret to be obliged to cut short our extracts, but the reader will probably be interested in pursuing the biography of a prince who so much promoted the advance of European intellect, and who, whether in art, science, or agriculture, would have created a Holkham out of a wilderness. Nor is the attraction of this correspondence confined to the character and pursuits of his highness. The events detailed, of course, assume a value proportionate to the station of the writer, and are adapted to supply many an authentic anecdote for future history. From the frequent and characteristic mention of Frederick the Great, who was great-uncle to the duke, a comprehensive sketch may be obtained, and though in some instances the foibles as well as the virtues of that monarch may be here exhibited, yet these are also valuable as illustrative of the spirit of the times.

Our limits forbid our proceeding further, and we must leave his highness's correspondence, together with the rest of the work,

8. continued

to proclaim their own value to the mind of the reader. The list at the commencement of this article will show how small a portion we have noticed, and the large remnant yet untouched. Of this the correspondence of the artists, and that of the men of science, afford the two most distinct kinds of interest—to the general reader, the former especially, containing, as it does, many delightful letters from Wille, the celebrated engraver, and from Tischbein, the no-less-famed German artist. The latter, among other anecdotes connected with painting, details his intimacy with the Chevalier Hamilton (Sir William Hamilton) at Naples, and his admiration of a girl in the chevalier's suite, whom he describes as an angel of grace and beauty, and in whom we immediately recognize that modern Venus, both in morals and person, the lovely Lady Hamilton. A letter also from Fuseli to Lavater is here introduced, and we quite approve of its introduction, for Fuseli is here seen to the life, and all who at all remember the witty, clever, madcap president, will recognize him as distinctly in every line as in all the wild legacies of his pencil. But here we must stay our remarks, and conclude with expressing a hope that this comprehensive biographic correspondence may meet with the attention that it deserves.

GERMAN POPULAR POETRY.

In the West and South of Germany, both the country and the people present a very poetical aspect. But before we lead the reader to the flourishing regions of Austria and Suabia, and the hilly vinevards of the Rhine, let him cast a look on the Eastern frontier, Silesia and her majestic mountains. The Silesian peasantry do not sing much; but the Giant Mountains harbour a whole host of fairy tales; the principal actor in which is the mischievous and fanciful goblin *Rübezahl*, whose name has been happily translated into English by *Number Nip*. There is, however, one corner in the South-eastern part of Silesia, the valley of the Oder, between Silesia, Moravia, and Hungary, called the *Kuländchen*, which may be considered in respect to our subject as one of the most remarkable spots in all the world. The German language spoken here, is exceedingly impure and corrupt; but although surrounded by a Slavic population, we discover in it traces of only a slight Slavic influence. In this valley, comprising not more than about sixteen square miles, containing two cities and twenty-three villages, with not much more than thirty thousand souls, a friend of popular poetry succeeded in collecting nearly one hundred and fifty songs and ballads; all of them banished, alas! from the dwellings of the educated and the genteel, and permitted to be heard only in the dust of spinning halls, amidst the noise of inns, or accompanied by the bells of the flocks. They are mostly sung by the women, "with more voice than feeling," the collector observes, in old-fashioned dancing tunes; often they hardly themselves understand what they are singing. There are, moreover, even in this small territory, whole villages, where these songs are already unknown; and to write them down seemed indeed to snatch them from oblivion. These songs did not all originate among this people; whom the above-mentioned collector describes as " friends of song,'dancing, and drinking, curious, talkative, sensual in their love; manifesting, however, in their choice of a mistress, a partiality for their country, and adhering to it with a certain degree of fidelity." We meet here with many songs which were once sung in different dialects in other provinces of Germany. The ballad called the " Lay of the young Count," is also sung here, and indeed in a much finer version than the more common ones; although perhaps in the most uncouth and corrupt jargon of all Germany. The ancient ballads, the " Castle in Austria," and the " King's Daughter," resound here still in living accents; both, however, with many variations. We give here the first of these, in its more ancient form, omitting the additions of modern times. The ballad which follows it will, in its simplicity, remind the reader of Sweet William's Ghost, and serve to confirm our remarks in respect to the coincidence of popular ballads among different nations.

" THE CASTLE IN AUSTRIA.

" There lies a castle in Austria,
    Right goodly to behold,
Wall'd up with marble stones so fair,
    With silver and red gold.

Therein lies captive a young boy,
    For life and death he lies bound;
Full forty fathoms under the earth,
    'Midst vipers and snakes around.

His father came from Rosenberg,
    Before the tower he went:
My son, my dearest son, how hard
    Is thy imprisonment!

O father, dearest father mine,
    So hardly I am bound;
Full forty fathoms under the earth,
    'Midst vipers and snakes around.

His father went before the lord;
    Let loose thy captive to me!
I have at home three casks of gold,
    And these for the boy I'll gi'e.

Three casks of gold, they help you not,
    That boy, and he must die!
He wears round his neck a golden chain;
    Therein doth his ruin lie.

And if he wear thus a golden chain,
    He hath not stolen it; nay!
A maiden good gave it to him;
    For true love, did she say,

They led the boy forth from the tower,
    And the sacrament took he:
Help thou, rich Christ, from heaven high.
    It's come to an end with me.

They led him to the scaffold place,
    Up the ladder he must go;
O headsman, dearest headsman, do
    But a short respite allow.

A short respite I must not grant;
  Thou would'st escape and fly;
Reach me a silken handkerchief
  Around his eyes to tie.

O do not, do not blind mine eyes!
  I must look on the world so fine;
I see it to-day, then never more,
  With these weeping eyes of mine.

His father near the scaffold stood,
  And his heart, it almost rends;
O son, O thou my dearest son,
  Thy death I will avenge.

O father, dearest father mine,
  My death thou shalt not avenge,
'Twould bring to my soul but heavy pains;
  Let me die in innocence.

It is not for this life of mine,
  Nor for my body proud;
'Tis but for my dear mother's sake,
  At home she weeps aloud.

Not yet three days had pass'd away,
  When an angel from heaven came down:
Take ye the boy from the scaffold away!
  Else the city shall sink under ground.

And not six months had pass'd away,
  Ere his death was avenged amain,
And upwards of three hundred men
  For the boy's life were slain.

Who is it that hath made this lay,
  Hath sung it, and so on?
That, in Vienna in Austria,
  Three maidens fair have done. '

"THE DEAD BRIDEGROOM.

"There went a boy so stilly,
  To the window small went he;
Art thou within, my fair sweet-heart?
  Rise up, and open to me.

We well may speak together,
  But I may not open to thee:
For I have plighted my faith to one'
  And want no other but he.

The one to whom thou'rt plighted,
  Fair sweet-heart, I am he;
Reach me thy snow-white little hand,
  And then perhaps thou'lt see.

But nay! thou smellest of the earth:
  And thou art Death, I ween!
Why should I not smell of the earth,
  When I have lain therein?

Wake up thy father and mother,
  Wake up thy friends so dear;
The chaplet green shalt thou ever wear,
  Till thou in heaven appear."

Besides these ancient ballads, which probably were common to all Germany, the inhabitants of the southern valley of the Oder sing Christmas carols and roughly versified Scripture tales, which are still more or less current in all the Catholic provinces of Germany. There is, however, one species of ballads, which in Germany is peculiar to this district. These are such as we would call Slavic ballads, i. e. in which the Slavic influence is manifest; since the Slavic influence, although described as slight in respect to the language, is not inconsiderable in respect to the spirit of their poetry. The German village-bards, surrounded by a Slavic population which finds in music and song its best recreation, are prone to imitate them; as on the other hand, the Bohemian and Moravian rustic singers borrow from their German neighbours.

The happy and childlike disposition of the inhabitants of Austria, together with the blessings of a blooming and pictu-resque country, a productive soil, and a paternal government—for the Austrian government is severe and tyrannical only to-wards its foreign provinces—makes life to them a succes-sion of holidays; and every moment generates a new song. Max Schottky has collected the songs and ballads current in Lower Austria, for the most part the vicinity of the ca-pital. Those of Upper Austria have another and more sen-timental character, but, so far as we know, have never been collected. Whether as much of ancient poetry is preserved in any other part, as in the Kuhländchen, we are not aware; but the whole country, as it is, breathes of poetry and music.

The disposition of the Bavarians is heavier; the climate is rough, the soil less fertile; and the celebrated Bavarian beer has not the inspiring power enjoyed by the population of the neighbouring wine-countries. The regions of the Rhine and the Neckar have ever been the true home of German popular poetry, and are so still. No province of Germany has contri-buted more to the glory of their common country, than Saubia.

9. continued

Here dwells a race naturally of a serious disposition; but happily influenced by a mild climate, a soil easily yielding to reasonable industry, but not rich enough to indulge indolence, and a scenery which unites the grand and the lovely. The following pretty song, which exists in different versions, may serve as a specimen of the peculiar *naïveté* of a Suabian peasant lad. The melody is sweet and pensive.

"THE FAREWELL LETTER.

" Now I go to the fountain,
  But I drink not;
There I seek my heart's dearie,
  But find her not.

Then I send my eyes round
  Hither and thither;
There I see my heart's dearie,
  Stand by another.

See her stand by another,
  O that hurts sore!
God keep thee, my heart's dearie,
  I see thee never more!

Now I buy me a pen,
  And buy ink and paper,
And write to my heart's dearie
  A farewell letter.

Write a farewell letter,
  O that hurts sore!
God keep thee my heart's dearie,
  I see thee never more!

Now on the moss and hay
  I lay me down;
And there into my lap
  Three roses are thrown.

And lo! these three roses,
  They are all blood-red!
I knew not if my heart's dearie
  Be living or dead!

Now I go to the chapel,
  And pray for her bliss;
And when I come out again,
  She gives me a kiss!"

That among the peasantry of Alsace, the French portion of Germany, more ancient poetry is still current than in other provinces, can easily be accounted for. The education of the higher classes is French. German books, although of course understood by the lower ranks, are comparatively rare; and French ones hardly intelligible, and mostly disliked by them. Thus the old ballads, transmitted down from the time when the national ties of the Alsatian people were not yet broken, seem to have been the only means of satisfying their fondness for poetry and song.

(*To be continued*).

69

GERMAN POPULAR POETRY.
(*Concluded from page* 103.)

CENTRAL GERMANY, i. e. Saxony, the electorate of Hesse, and Franconia, presents, in many respects, a very different aspect from the other more southern parts. The people are decidedly musical; they sing a great deal; but they sing opera-airs, disseminated even among the peasantry by students travelling during their vacations, and by the wandering journeymen—and popular songs alternately. Books are frequent; but a Saxon peasant-woman goes seldom to market without bringing home a broad sheet of poetry. The maid-servants in the cities sing many old ballads to the children; but whatever is preserved, is preserved only accidentally. There is no real love for the relics of former days; and the romances of Schiller and Bürger are mingled pell-mell with disfigured ballads from the fifteenth century. The following beautiful ballad, which was first taken down by Herder, is called by this great writer, " a little lyric picture, while Othello is a powerful fresco painting —unchecked action in all its boldness and terror." " The tune," he says, " has the clear solemn sound of an evening hymn, chanted in star-light."

LAY OF THE JEALOUS LAD.

" Three stars are in the heavens
    Beaming with love on high;
God keep thee, gentle maiden,
    My horse where shall I tie?

Thy horse take by the bridle,
    And tie to the fig tree;
Sit down awhile by me here,
    And make some sport for me.

I cannot now be seated,
    I may not merry be;
My heart is sorely troubled,
    Sweet love, it is for thee!

What draws he from his pocket?
    A knife both sharp and long!
He stabb'd his love to the heart with it,
    The red blood on him sprung.

And as he draws it out again,
    With blood it was all red;
O thou, great God in heaven,
    How bitter is my death!

What draws he from her finger?
    A little bright gold ring;
He throws it in the river,
    There lies the shining thing.

Swim on, swim on, thou little ring,
    Away to the deep, deep sea;
For dead is now my sweet love,
    No sweet love lives for me!

And thus it never doth end well,
    With a maid that would love two;
And thus we both have learned now,
    What a false love can do!"

The valleys of Switzerland and Tyrol are rich in poetic echoes; and their songs are to the ear what the clear, silvery, transparent cascades, which gush numberless from their mountains, are to the eye; the impression of one supplants that of the preceding, and the traveller gets so accustomed to the cheering, refreshing aspect and sound, that he learns to consider them as necessary ingredients of the landscape. The peculiar *naïveté* of these mountain dialects makes their songs utterly untranslateable into any other language. They lose entirely their character and charm; and if Goethe's saying, " Nature has neither core nor peel," holds good as to all popular poetry, it is especially applicable to these purely *idiomatic* lays and ditties. Of the two following specimens we give the originals, and subjoin a verbal translation, only in order to make them more intelligible to the foreign reader of German, without pretending to give their spirit. Both are sung by peasant-girls, and the tunes correspond well with the words.

I.

" Mein Herzel is zu,
    'S kann 's keiner aufthu';
Ein einziger Bu'
    Hat den Schlüssel dazu!"

" My heart is shut to,
    None can it undo;
Only one laddie true
    Has the key thereto!"

II.

" Uf'm Bergli hab i sässe,
    Hab den Vögli zugeschaut;
      Hänt gesunge,
      Hänt gesprunge,
Hänt 's Nestli gebaut.

In à Garte bin i g'stande,
    Ha' de Imbli zugeschaut,
      Hänt gesummet,
      Hänt gebrummet,
Hänt's Zelli gebaut.

Uf de Wiese bin i gange
    Lug de Sommervögli an,
      Hänt gefloge,
      Hänt gesoge,
Gar zu'schön hänt 's g'than.

Und da kummt nu der Liebste,
Und da zeig i em froh,

Wie se 's mache,
Und mer lache,
Und mer mache's au' so."

" I sat upon the mountain,
And saw the little birds;
How they sung,
How they sprung,
How they built their little nests.

I stood in the garden,
And saw the little bees;
How they humm'd,
How they drumm'd,
How they built their little cells.

I walked in the meadow,
And saw the butterflies;
How they skipp'd,
How they sipp'd,
And how prettily they woo'd.

And just then comes my dearie,
And him I laughing show,
How they play,
And we're gay,
And we do even so."

We conclude our subject with one lay more; which, displaying as it does a good deal of imagination, seems to us happily calculated to characterize German popular poetry in its relation to that of the other Teutonic nations. From the verse, " Flög' ich zu dir, mein Schatz, *ins Reich*," which we have rendered, " I'd fly far far away to thee," we must conclude that Northern Germany is its home; since the common people used this expression to designate the South, with the exception of Austria.

LOVE'S WISHES.

" In the world I have no pleasure,
Far away's my heart's own treasure!
Could I but speak to him, oh then
My heart were whole and well again.

Lady Nightingale, Lady Nightingale,
To greet my treasure never fail;
Greet him kindly, right prettily,
And bid him ever mine to be.

Then to the goldsmith's house I go,
The goldsmith looks from his window:

Ah goldsmith, ah, dear goldsmith mine,
Make me a ring quite small and fine.

Not too large, not too small, let it
A pretty little finger fit;
And let my name be written there,
My heart's own dear the ring shall wear.

Had I of purest gold a key,
My heart I would unlock to thee;
A picture fair would there be shown,
My treasure, it must be thy own!

If I a little wood-bird were,
I'd sit upon the tall green tree;
And when I'd sung enough, from there
I'd fly far far away to thee.

Had I two wings as has the dove,
Then would I fly o'er hill and dell;
O'er all the world I'd soar away,
To where my dearest one does dwell.

And when I was at last by thee,
Ah! shouldst thou then not speak to me,
Then must I turn in grief to dwell
Away from thee—my love, farewell!"

71

GERMAN LITERATURE.

TIECK.

Yesterday afternoon, I took an opportunity of calling on the Hofrath, *Ludwig Tieck*, who, next to Goethe, is the most renowned littérateur in Germany. Having learned that he lived in the *Neumarkt*, I proceeded thither; and on ascending the stair of one of the corner houses of the square, soon found myself within the poet's habitation. I had taken the precaution of sending my card of introduction, an hour or two before claiming an audience; and when I again presented it to the domestic, I was at once ushered into a handsome apartment, adorned with several very good engravings, among which was a portrait of Tieck himself. His daughter, a young lady of rather pleasing demeanour, received me very politely, and told me that her father would be occupied for a few moments, but that I should see him almost immediately. Whether or not this was the fair personage whom the splenetic Müllner so grossly attacked, I know not; but if so, and should it be allowable in such a case to judge physiognomically, her appearance certainly affords presumptive evidence of the little fellow's utter want of conscientiousness.

A pair of stiff-starched fräulein, the very *beau ideal* of stale aristocratical virginity, occupied a sofa on one side of the room; while I seated myself opposite to them, on the other. The conversation, which, on the part of the ladies, was conducted in terms of the coldest politeness, was fortunately soon cut short by the appearance of the poet himself, who, on entering the apartment, saluted me kindly, and took a seat by my side.

Tieck, if I may judge from appearances, must be on the wrong side of fifty. In face as well as person he exhibits all the usual indications of that stage of life, and he does not seem to be at all in good health. His countenance is open, and his large forehead bespeaks a mind fraught with thought and intelligence. There is an unaffected nobleness in his speech and demeanour, which is as impressive as it is pleasing ; while the style of his conversation, at every turn, indicates the poet-mind, rich in imaginative conceptions, and 'soaring from earthly to ethereal things.' My remarks upon his works naturally led him to inquire how they were appreciated in England ; a question which, I confess, I could not well answer. I told him, however, that I had seen translations of several of his romances, and also of his *Marchen ;* and by way of fillip to his self-love as an author, I hinted that his two tales, entitled 'The Betrothed' and 'The Pictures,' had won him some celebrity among English novel-readers. He put many questions to me respecting Sir Walter Scott and his works, with all of which he appeared to be peculiarly conversant ; and it struck me, that he entertained the pleasing conviction, that his own fame, like Sir Walter's, rested much on the acquaintanceship, displayed in his writings, with the manners and feelings of the past. *   *

On Tieck's alluding to Shakspeare, I took occasion to thank him for the pleasure I had received from the perusal of his able preface to the works of the unfortunate Lenz, which he published about three years ago. Poor Lenz, you know, was the first in Germany who advocated the poetical and dramatic character of Shakspeare, in opposition to that of Racine ; and may justly be said to have fallen a victim to the enthusiastic attempt which he made to reform the drama of his native land.

During my interview with Tieck, the ladies seemed to listen to him as an oracle ; and it was not without reason. His conversation is even superior to his writings. I could not help being gratified with the manner in which he spoke of his literary contemporaries, and even of those who were his declared foes. Aware of his being one of that celebrated critical clique, of which Schlegel and Novalis were confederates, and whose admiration of Catholic mysticism Tieck had abetted and advocated, I took care to avoid the dangerous whirlpool of polemics. His religious prejudices, like those of Dr. Johnson, are incurable. They are displayed in an obvious hostility to the spirit of Protestantism, and may be said to be constitutional. This is, perhaps, the only blot in his character.

Among other particulars, I learned from Tieck that there are five periodicals at present published in the Saxon capital, viz., the *Merkur,* published six times a week, being a selection of short literary papers, consisting of tales, poetry, anecdotes, &c. ; 2d, *Der Sachsiche Stadtverordnete und Communalgardist,* another literary paper, published weekly ; 3d, *Anzeiger Dresdener,* an advertising paper, published daily ; 4th, *Tageblatt von Arnold,* another collection of tales, criticisms, &c. ; and, 5th, *Denkwurdigkeiten fur Sachsen,* which appears four times a week, and gives an account of passing events, extracted chiefly from foreign prints, together with original papers. The whole of these publications, however, are rather of a tea-table sort, and, according to Tieck's account, have very few pretensions either to learning or philosophy.

CENSORSHIP IN AUSTRIA.

I am told (says Mr. Strang) that no work whatever can be put to press, until it has actually undergone the revision of three distinct officers. For example, the manuscript is sent first to the office of Police, where there are censors appointed for every department of art, science, literature, politics, and religion. One of the censors, of course, immediately sits in judgment on the various passages of the work. This functionary having made his remarks upon the margin, it is next submitted to another officer to consider these remarks. If the work be political, it is then sent to the Chancery-office ; and if religious, to the Consistorial-office. On being sent back from either, it is then returned to the office of Police, where it is again revised, and the passages that are permitted to be printed, and those to be condemned, are finally fixed upon ; when, to crown the whole ordeal, it is necessary that either the Graff Von Sedlmitzky or the Hofrath Von Ohms, the two individuals at the head of the censorship, append their permissive seal of *imprimatur.*

GRILLPARZER.

Yesterday, when passing through St. Stephen's Platz, he was pointed out to me, and you cannot imagine how happy I was at the circumstance. I assure you I had all the wish in the world to run up and salute him, and to tell him how much I had been pleased with the representation of his "Ahnfrau," in the Prussian capital ; but just as I was about to follow and accost him, a friend stepped forward, and hurried him through a large gateway. I had time enough allowed, however, 'to take a slight map' of him, as a friend of mine used jocularly to say ; and here it is :—Imagine, then, a pale, attenuated countenance encircled with dark hair ; the features strongly marked ; particularly the eye, which, in spite of a pair of spectacles, seems to sparkle with intelligence ; and a finely formed mouth, which, whether it were reality or imagination, I fancied bespoke the romantic sensibility that characterizes the fine feeling of his own creation—Bertha. Next, suppose this head placed on a pair of high shoulders, surmounting a tall spare figure, and you will be able to form some notion of the full-length portraiture of Franz Grillparzer. The author of the 'Ahnfrau' is, I am told, about forty-one years of age, and his appearance does not belie it. As I gazed upon him, I could not help regretting, that the fine sarcastic spirit which breathes in every line of the poetical diatribe that he wrote amid the ruins of Rome, should have been repressed or extinguished by the various deadening influences which must have encompassed him since his return from the Eternal to the Imperial City.

11. QUARTERLY REVIEW, 58 (1837), 297-333. Not listed in M/H. *Cf.* Carré, p. 125. By Abraham Hayward.

ART. I.—1. *Germany in* 1831. By John Strang, author of 'Tales of Humour and Romance, from the German of Hoffmann, Langbein, Lafontaine, &c.' 'Necropolis Glasguensis,' &c. 2 vols. 8vo. London, 1836.

2. *Sketches of Germany and the Germans; with a Glance at Poland, Hungary, and Switzerland in* 1834, 1835, *and* 1836. By an Englishman resident in Germany. 2 vols. 8vo. London, 1836.

IN reviewing, two or three years ago, Heine's 'History of recent German Literature,' we took occasion to refer the ignorance of the English public regarding the subject-matter of his book, to a habit of looking to Madame de Staël as the grand authority on German belles-lettres and philosophy, in entire forgetfulness of the changes effected since she wrote. With equal justice might the ignorance of the self-same public, regarding the social and political condition of Germany, be referred to the habit of relying on Mr. Russell's Tour, which concludes with the year 1822—since which society and government have made prodigious advances, though it may well be made a question whether these advances have been towards evil or towards good. There is thus a chasm of fourteen years, in stirring and eventful times, to be filled up; and had either of the authors before us succeeded in correcting Mr. Russell's errors, supplying his deficiencies, and finishing off an accurate picture of Germany as it is, he might have reckoned confidently on soon dividing the honours of his predecessor, and eventually superseding him. But neither of them can be complimented on having succeeded to this extent; not even Mr. Strang, who, for fullness of information and general accuracy of remark, deserves to rank far before his more immediate competitor. He is evidently well skilled in the language, and thoroughly conversant with what, for the sake of distinction, may be termed the *classical* literature of Germany. The translations mentioned in his title-page were also the means of procuring him introductions to many of the principal living writers. But he did not stay long enough to avail himself of these advantages to the full, and many of his impressions appear to have been hastily caught up; whilst the ultra-liberal turn of his political opinions affords strong additional ground for questioning the justice of his reflections on

subjects directly or indirectly connected with government. Moreover, Mr. Strang's book was written six years ago, and much of it relates to matters belonging more to the last century than to this. It is obvious that he has, in many places, recently re-touched his letters,—as the chapters are called, though there is nothing of the epistolary style or form about them,—but the effect has been rather to destroy their authenticity as actual impressions of what he saw in 1831, than to make them a faithful representation of what was to be seen in 1836.

The other gentleman is so extremely superficial that we have frequently been led to doubt the applicability of the designation which it is his pleasure to substitute for a name. At least, we should be glad to know the precise number of months, weeks, or days which, in his opinion, constitute *residence* in a place—for his book (excepting the chapters on Vienna) contains little beyond what an ordinary traveller might collect from valets-de-place, guide-books, newspapers, and tables-d'hôte, with the occasional assistance of a stationary acquaintance or two. His observations on so much of manners as may be seen in passing, are good, and some of his descriptions of scenery are striking, but whenever he attempts to penetrate an inch below the surface he is wrong. His literary taste and information may be estimated from the fact that he speaks of Rotteck (a radical rhetorician of Carlsruhe) as 'placed, by the united suffrages of his countrymen, at the head of German cotemporary literature'—which is about as correct as to term Lord John Russell the first English poet and historian of his age. We also think it a duty to reprobate, in the strongest terms, the tone adopted by this gentleman in alluding to English travellers on the continent, for matters are coming to a fine pass indeed if every man who has acquired a smattering of foreign habits is to set up for a Horace Walpole, and exclaim,—'I should like my *country* well enough, if it were not for my *countrymen.*' At page 3, for example, describing the company on board the steam-boat, he says,—'One family of my dear wandering countrymen, evidently better acquainted with pounds, shillings, and pence than Germany, had hired a French servant in London, who persuaded them that through Hamburgh was the most convenient route to the mineral baths of Nassau.' Matthews used to personate a Londoner starting on his first expedition to Margate with Cook's Voyages in his carpet-bag, and if our 'dear wandering countrymen' be characterized by one thing more than another, it is the eagerness with which they cram themselves for a trip to foreign parts by a preparatory course of maps, guide-books, and itineraries. Yet in the teeth of this known peculiarity, the author risks his credit at the commencement on such a story as the above.

We have briefly characterized these books, to which we shall have frequent occasion to refer, by way of showing what degree of reliance is to be placed in them.

Mr. Russell did not visit Hamburgh, and only passingly alludes to it. Hamburgh, however, is undeniably one of the best starting points for a tour, and both of the travellers now under review commence with it; the Resident giving us a short, dashing sketch, —Mr. Strang a long, elaborate account, occupying a full half of his first volume. Still, though this seems a most disproportioned space to be allotted to a town, we should rather say that too little labour has been expended on Berlin, Dresden, Vienna, and Munich, than too much on this northern Venice; so rich are the author's materials, and so valuable the observations he has blended with them. The times are gone when a colony or corporation of traders, possessing only a few square miles of territory, could contend with monarchs for the prize of empire; and the glories of Hamburgh and Lubeck, Venice and Genoa, are departed never to return. But Hamburgh still retains a highly respectable position as the grand mercantile emporium of the north, sufficient, without referring to history, to justify us in noting down a few particulars relating to it.

One singular anomaly in its legislation is the facility which seems to be afforded to insolvency. ' I am told,' says Mr. Strang, ' that an individual in Hamburgh makes a regular business and a very comfortable livelihood from manufacturing sets of false books for unprincipled debtors.' A privilege enjoyed by the wives of traders is said to add not a little to this facility—

'The law holds that, for five years after marriage, the dowry of a wife is a preferable debt to all others upon the estate; and hence, should the husband see fit to become bankrupt, before the lapse of five years subsequent to his marriage, the fortune brought by his wife, from being preferable to all other debts, forms, as it were, a new capital to recommence with. The consequence of this peculiarly favourable law towards married men is, that of all eras in a mercantile man's history, the most important to creditors is the period when the debtor is called upon to decide with himself whether he shall or shall not take advantage of this privilege by declaring himself bankrupt; and let me tell you it is a privilege of which not a few are constantly found to avail themselves. There is a shrewd suspicion entertained that the early matrons of Hamburgh have had some hand in making this law, as holding out an encouragement to matrimony!'—Strang, vol. i. pp. 104, 105.

An important part of the population consist of the English residents and the Jews. The Jews are about six thousand in number, and, as usual, amongst the wealthiest of the inhabitants; yet they are still persecuted with a degree of rancour for which nothing but the bitter spirit of commercial jealousy can account.

In August, 1835, an attempt was made to expel some young men of the Jewish persuasion from one of the places of public resort; the Jews resisted, but were overpowered by numbers and turned out. Three days afterwards the chief police magistrate caused an intimation to be conveyed to the elders of the synagogue, that they had better warn their young friends to abstain from visiting public places for some time, as he could not answer for the consequences. The position of the English residents is thus described by Mr. Strang:—

' The English merchants residing here herd together in the same way that they do everywhere else, and retain as usual their national manners, prejudices, and mode of living. They are a jovial, happy set of fellows, whose industry is only surpassed by their hospitality, and whose love of good eating makes them prefer their own national dishes to the more varied and greasy cookery of Germany. The English residents mix but little with the natives, and seldom take any interest in matters connected with this country, save its commerce, to the changes of which they are obliged to be as much alive as are their most indefatigable opponents in trade—the Jews. Beyond acquiring a perfect knowledge of their business, the generality of the English in Hamburgh may be put in the same category with a noble emigrant who once resided in this city, of whom it was said, that he had lived five-and-twenty years abroad, and had forgotten nothing, but at the same time had learned nothing!'

Mr. Strang is here applying, probably unconsciously, to his countrymen, what was originally said of the French emigrants who returned with the Bourbons in 1814. In hospitality it is impossible for the English to excel the Hamburghians. But we are far from agreeing with Mr. Strang that Hamburgh is the residence which a gourmand of discrimination would select, unless he brought his own cook along with him; for gastronomy, considered as one of the fine arts, has been cultivated with little better success than painting and architecture by the citizens. The eel-soup which he so joyously commemorates, struck us to be about upon a par with the conger-pie in which our Land's-Endians exult; and it would require the stomach of a Cornish miner or a Hanseatic burgomaster to digest either the one or the other of these delicacies.

Mr. Strang opens the topic of Hamburgh literature with the remark, that ' literary distinction here is about as valueless as stars or ribbons, and hence there are but few who have really done anything for the literature or science of Germany, who have made choice of this town as a permanent residence.' It is amusing to contrast this estimate with Mr. William Taylor's, founded on probably nearly the same statement of facts. In a section of his ' Historic Survey of German Poetry,' entitled *Hamburgh Poets*, he says—' Early provided with respectable schools of learning, this city has asserted literary rank from the times of Lambreius and Gronovius to the present. It vied with Zurich and Leipzig in the early cultivation of German vernacular literature, and continues to be a patroness of instruction and an emporium of literature.' Mr. Taylor's list of Hamburgh poets comprises Hagedorn, J. E. Schlegel, Ebert, Kramer, and Klopstock; to which may be added Voss, who passed the latter part of his life at Wansdeck, a village in the vicinity. Coleridge relates, that on hearing Klopstock termed the German Milton, he contented himself with drily observing, 'a *very German* Milton indeed.' There are passages, however, both in the ' Messiah ' and in the ' Odes,' which go far towards justifying the comparison; and it is impossible to deny Klopstock the praise of being the first to awaken—or rather to re-awaken—the national genius of his countrymen, to show them of what their language was capable, and teach them to found a new literature of their own. Hamburgh, therefore, may well feel proud of having numbered such a man amongst her sons—i. e. her adopted sons, for Klopstock did not come to live at Hamburgh till he was past thirty, and the charms which lured him thither were not those of the climate, the situation, the libraries, or the eel-soup, but the charms of a Miss Molly Moller, for whom he deserted his former love, Fanny (immortalized in one of the finest of his odes), on the alleged grounds of indifference to his attentions when with her, and a decided tendency to promiscuous flirtation when he was away.

Amongst living literary characters connected with Hamburgh the most conspicuous are Heinrich Heine, whose peculiar political opinions are attributable, as we formerly intimated, to his having been born a member of the oppressed Jewish community in this place; Dr. Julius, a modest and amiable scholar, author of a valuable work on prison discipline; Dr. Lappenberg, known, among other things, for some good antiquarian essays, and one of the most accomplished gentlemen we ever met in any country; and Dr. Wurm, the editor of the *Kritische Blätter*—a sort of Literary Gazette or Athenæum, conducted with considerable spirit and ability.

'Through the pages,' says Mr. Strang, 'of the periodical [work?] which Dr. Wurm at present conducts with so much credit to himself, he has lately sent forth much valuable and just criticism on the modern literature of our country—criticism that might well shame the misnamed Reviews of England. In Germany there is as yet happily very little pandering to authors and booksellers as in England; and none of that shameless systematic puffing and critical quackery which has of late so strikingly characterized the Zoili of your newspaper and magazine press. Happily for Hamburgh, the editor's pen is placed in the hands of men whose critical acumen is only equalled by their critical candour. What a contrast do the opinions of such men hold out to those of

" Your crawling critics—underlings of sense,
Who damn for spite and eulogize for pence !"

The exceeding acrimony of this passage induces us to suspect that Mr. Strang is not quite satisfied with the reception which he himself has received from the *pressgang*, as Mrs. Butler politely denominates these Zoili. Still, we have no objection to admit to him that the periodical press of Germany is, on the whole, characterized by a better spirit of impartiality and good faith; but, on the other hand, he must allow to us,—what indeed is too glaring to admit of dispute,—that it is far inferior in talent and extent of influence to our own. The principal cause is obvious enough. In Germany the general rule is for each contributor to subscribe his name to his contribution—a rule which may act beneficially by keeping the writer on his guard both against unfounded eulogy and intemperate censure; but which certainly acts injuriously by cramping the freedom of the criticism, and excluding a large and valuable class of contributors altogether; for many of our best reviews are chiefly composed by persons who would as soon think of engaging in personal conflict with a mad bull as with an angry author; or who, from temper, rank, or connexion, would decidedly object to appearing before the public at all in this manner. ' Besides,' says Sir Walter Scott, ' there will always be a greater authority ascribed by the generality of readers to the oracular opinion issued from the cloudy sanctuary of an invisible body than to the mere dictum of a man with a christian name and sirname, which may not sound much better than those of the author over whom he predominates.' * Sir Walter might well have said, ' which may sound much worse.' Who, for instance, would even look at a pamphlet by *John Thompson* on Mr. Hallam's Literary History or any other new work by an author of established reputation?

As to the influence of the periodical press on literature, the evil is slight in comparison with the good. We ourselves may have had the misfortune to kill off a cockney poet or two in our time—

' Oh, that the soul, that very fiery particle,
Should let itself be snuffed out by an article !'

and Lord Brougham is accused, on pretty strong evidence, of having broken the heart of a philosopher by similar means.†

But

* ' Life of Cumberland'—in allusion to the ' London Review,' which was started on the continental principle and failed; and see Byron's Works, vol. ix. p. 62, note.
† Dr. Young's theory of light was treated with the most sovereign contempt by Lord Brougham in the earlier numbers of the Edinburgh Review, and Dr. Young died without reaping the honour of it. The theory is now recognised as true; and

But these are accidents; and on the whole Dr. Johnson was quite right in saying that no man was ever written down except by himself. Puffing, again, is, in the long run, as powerless to elevate as undue severity to depress, of which no stronger proof can be afforded than some facts cited by us a few years ago, illustrative of the fate of the dandy school of novel writers. It thence appeared that books published at half-a-guinea a volume, and puffed at the rate of thousands a year, were regularly advertised as on sale for exportation at the average rate of ninepence a-piece.

The Hamburgh theatre enjoys a high reputation, thanks to Schroeder, who filled the post of director for upwards of thirty years, and successfully made head against the French (misnamed classical) drama, which was in its zenith at the commencement of his management. Shakspeare is now the fashion; and the English company who embarked with Mr. Barham Livius for Germany in 1834, were enthusiastically received by all classes; but their career was rudely cut short by the refusal of the Hamburgh manager to allow the use of his theatre for less than three-fourths of the profits per night, and by the prospect of having similar difficulties to encounter in Dresden and Berlin.

The journey from Hamburgh to Berlin affords to Mr. Strang an opportunity of introducing an animated account of the military poet Theodore Körner, who was killed upon the road—and to the Resident, an opportunity of making two singular statements regarding Mecklenburg; the one as to the nobility, the other as to the geese.

'During my progress through the country, I met with a Herr Baron, who exercised the profession of relieving men's chins of what in Christendom is considered an incumbrance; and at one of the inns I found a Herr Graf [i. e. Count] for a landlord, a Frau Gräfin for a landlady, the young Herren Grafen filled the places of ostler, waiter, and boots, while the fair young Fräulein Gräfinnen were the cooks and chambermaids. I was informed, that in one village, of which I now forget the name, the whole of the inhabitants were noble except four, and these were married to Geborne Fräuleins! [born lady-countesses.] During one of my lake excursions, I had for my companion a retired merchant from a southern state in Germany, who, ignorant of this prepossession in favour of noble rank, purchased an estate on the banks of one of its beautiful lakes. He had wealth, talents, intelligence, and gentlemanly manners, but he had no quarterings! How, then, was it possible for

the high-blood natives, who perhaps traced their descent from the Vandal deities, to visit him! At length, finding that the humid air and lakes of Mecklenburg were no equivalent for absolute solitude, he was preparing to remove to some country less aristocratical in its social institutions.'—*Sketches*, vol. i. pp. 44, 45.

At one time it was not uncommon in English farces to tickle our national pride by turning Italian counts into valets and French marquesses into barbers and cooks. The above strikes us to be neither more nor less than a clumsy revival of the joke. Mecklenburg undoubtedly abounds in families privileged to prefix *von* to their names, and the pride of birth will there, as in other places, be often found in connexion with poverty; but the story of the retired merchant is a palpable absurdity. Far from its being a point of etiquette in Mecklenburg for the noble to keep aloof from the plebeian, the Grand Duke may frequently be seen dining at the table-d'hôte of his capital, and familiarly conversing with the guests; nor are his subjects in the habit of considering such acts of condescension as derogating from the dignity of their sovereign. We undertake to say that there are counties in England where a retired merchant would find much more difficulty in establishing himself among the landed gentry than in any district of Northern Germany. After reading such injurious insinuations we are by no means astonished to find that this gentleman's progress through the country was impeded, with a sort of patriotic instinct, by another class of denizens, whom, to the best of our recollection, he has equally calumniated.

'In every part of Mecklenburg herds of swine and flocks of geese abound; the former wander nearly wild through the extensive forests, supported by acorns and roots, while the latter literally cover the banks of the lakes and rivers with their white plumage, resembling at a distance flakes of moving snow. In my rambles through the country, it was my fate to become more than once the object of their most violent animosity, particularly in passing through narrow lanes; here I repeatedly encountered flocks of some hundreds, who, with outstretched necks and extended wings, were hissing and gabbling, evidently determined to dispute my further progress. Pray don't laugh, reader, for I assure you that blows from my cane only infuriated them still more; for as fast as I beat off one score of my assailants, another came boldly to the attack; but perseverance will conquer geese of every description, and this weapon at length subdued my hostile gabblers in Mecklenburg.'—*ibid.*, vol. i. pp. 45, 46.

In our opinion, the world would not have lost much if the geese had proved victorious in the fray.

The approach to Berlin is certainly very fine, though the flatness of the country somewhat diminishes the effect; and we quite agree with Mr. Strang that the drive from Charlottenburg is infi-

M. Arago has formally vindicated Dr. Young from the noble critic's animadversions, in a discourse delivered at the Institute. Lord Byron, by-the-bye, believed to his dying day that Lord Brougham was the reviewer of the Hours of Idleness—witness some well-known lines in one of the later cantos of Don Juan; but this, we believe, was quite a mistake.

nitely superior to the boasted opening into Paris from the west. It has been remarked as a curious trait of national character, that the modest Prussians call the entrance to their capital a *Thiergarten* (zoological garden), and the conceited Frenchmen the entrance to theirs *Les Champ Elysées*, which is about as applicable as the term *belle* to France itself,—one of the ugliest and most uninteresting countries in the world to travel through. Berlin is generally and justly esteemed one of the handsomest cities in Europe, for it abounds in broad streets and fine squares, and boasts a great variety of public buildings extremely well situated for effect Entering by the Brandenburg gate, crossing the *Pariser Platz*, driving up the whole extent of the Linden street, and stopping at the Hotel de Russie near the bridge, the traveller must be very fastidious, or very sleepy, who is not lost in admiration and astonishment. But the first view of Berlin is everything, and the impression rapidly wears off. Being almost as much the creation of Frederick the Great, as Petersburg was the creation of *the* Czar, it presents hardly any building of historic interest—no Westminster Abbey or Notre Dame—for the imagination to rest upon: so that, as regards association, one might fancy one's self in Liverpool or New York. Then the architecture is exceedingly monotonous, and there is a staring, glaring look about the houses which on a bright day is absolutely intolerable. Yet far from presenting a gay and exhilarating appearance, Berlin presents exactly the reverse; for in consequence of the great extent of the city compared with the population (more than twelve miles of circumference for less than 230,000 inhabitants), there is a total absence of life and bustle in the streets—except in the Linden Street at the particular hours when it is the fashion to promenade there. This effect may be traced to the founder's vanity, who wished to possess a capital bearing the same rank amongst capitals which he himself had succeeded in acquiring amongst kings. When the city was considerably advanced, he exclaimed exultingly to the French ambassador,—'Well, we are getting on —Berlin is nearly as large as Paris.' 'Certainly,' replied the ambassador, 'only we don't grow corn in Paris.' The river, again, is a dull, heavy, slow, melancholy-looking stream, rather impairing than improving the salubrity of the place. 'Its sluggish course,' says the Resident, 'is so tedious in conveying away the pollutions it receives, that during the heat of summer the public health is seriously affected; and it was a fact, announced by the authorities, that during the summer of 1834 the deaths exceeded the births by forty-four weekly.' But he should not have forgotten to add, that during the summer of 1834 Berlin was suffering severely from the cholera.

Architecture has made greater advances in Germany since the commencement of the present century than in any other country that could be named, and some of the public buildings recently erected in Berlin are peculiarly deserving of the attention of the connoisseur. Amongst the most remarkable is the Royal Museum, after a design by Schinkel, the Prussian Palladio, an edifice by the side of which our National Gallery would look supremely ridiculous. The arrangement of the pictures is also well worthy of imitation, when a collection is large enough to warrant it; the several schools being arranged chronologically, so that the gradual progress of each may be traced with facility. The *Sing-Academie* by Ottimer, the court-architect of Brunswick, is a Grecian building of great beauty, and having been erected at the expense of a private society as a concert-hall and school for the study of sacred music, bears equal testimony to the musical and architectural taste of Berlin. The arsenal, the guard-house, the opera-house, the royal palace, the library, the university, with some fine specimens of sculpture by Rauch, an artist of first-rate genius, &c. &c. are sufficiently described by Russell and other travellers. Leaving, therefore, the external condition of the capital, we proceed to make a few remarks on the constitution, the social state, the internal administration, and the political prospects of the monarchy.

The Prussian government is, to all intents and purposes, an autocracy, so far as the total absence of constitutional checks can make it one. There is no chamber, no parliament, no privileged class or representative body of any kind empowered to lay a *veto* on the will of the sovereign, in whatever direction he may think proper to exercise it, nor is he even subjected to the salutary admonitions of a press; yet there is not a country in the world where enlightened public opinion exercises a more immediate influence on the conduct of affairs, or where sterling merit is more sure of its reward. 'Why, Sir, (said Johnson) in such a government as ours, no man is appointed to an office because he is the fittest for it, nor hardly in any other government, because there are so many connexions and dependencies to be studied. A despotic prince may choose a man to an office merely because he is the fittest for it: *the King of Prussia may do it.*'* A glance at what he is now doing will amply verify the justice of this remark. In England, under the dynasty of *Reform*, public opinion means brute clamour—the best qualification for official employment is incapacity—and almost the only parliamentary candidates of literary or scientific notoriety who stand the slightest chance of gaining the sweet voices of the populace, are persons who have contrived to acquire a factitious and fugitive reputation by quackery. In

* Boswell's Johnson, vol. iii. p. 186, Edit. 1835.

America, where the people are all in all, matters are still worse: the bare notion of promoting a man who was not a partisan of the President, would be scouted as an absurdity, and few and far between are the instances in which a distinguished name has proved a passport to the Chamber of Representatives.* In France, conflicting factions divide the attention of the people, and views of personal aggrandizement exclusively occupy the King's—who has this excuse, however, that there seems no mode of saving the nation from a renewal of the horrors of the first revolution but despotism.

It follows, that to find a practical example of the blessings which are commonly supposed the necessary results of liberty, we are obliged to turn from countries rife with it to a country where it is nominally extinct. In Prussia, the King is actually doing what Johnson stated he might do: talent is not merely appreciated when known, but sedulously sought out and courted into the public service, so that each department is filled by persons occupying the first rank in the science, art, pursuit, or study, a knowledge of which may be necessary or useful for the due discharge of the duties of their post; and no sooner is a measure called for by the deliberate opinions of those best qualified to form an opinion on it, than it is done. Every branch of the internal administration bears evidence to the truth of these observations; but we will content ourselves with referring to the now well-known educational system,† and the progress made in commerce and manufactures since the peace.

'No reform (says Mr. Strang) is ever permitted to emanate from the people themselves. Every change that takes place, whether civil, ecclesiastical, or political, is the result of government concoction; and be the object what it may, nothing is tolerated unless previously decreed and regulated at head-quarters.'

---

* 'When (says M. de Tocqueville) you enter the Chamber of Representatives at Washington, you feel struck by the vulgar aspect of this great assembly. The eye often looks round in vain for a man of celebrity within its bosom. Almost all the members are obscure personages whose names present no image to the thought. They are for the most part village lawyers, traders, or even men belonging to the lowest classes. In a country where education is almost universally diffused, it is said that the representatives of the people do not always know how to write correctly. —Two paces off is the entrance of the Senate, whose narrow precincts contain a large proportion of the celebrities of America. Hardly a man is to be seen in it who does not recall the idea of a recent illustration. These are eloquent advocates, distinguished generals, able magistrates, or tried statesmen. Every word that escapes from this assembly would do honour to the greatest parliamentary debates of Europe.'
The obvious cause is that the representatives are elected directly by the people, the senators are not.
† See Cousin's Report, translated by Mrs. Austin, and the admirable preface prefixed by that lady to the work.

Mr. Strang should tell us how any change—civil, ecclesiastical, or political—could take place otherwise in a country where the whole legislative authority is vested in the King; but we are not to infer that public opinion goes for nothing on that account. Some eight or ten years ago, for example, it was in contemplation to extend the Prussian code to the Rhenish provinces, which retained, and still retain, the French. A strong feeling of dissatisfaction was manifested on the part of the provinces in question, and the project, though a pet one of the King and ministry, was laid aside. The victory was celebrated, in true John Bull style, by a grand dinner at Bonn, where speeches were made which would have done honour to an English county meeting for freedom of expression. Still the privilege of being heard is subject to one important restriction: *ne sutor ultra crepidam* is the word, and no one is listened to about matters not affecting himself—so that if useful discussion be occasionally suppressed, the people are rescued, on the other hand, from the baneful influence of demagogues, and left free to pursue the noiseless tenor of their ordinary occupations undisturbed, instead of being periodically inflated with the restless spirit of self-conceit, as in England, where agitation (to borrow an expression of Burke's) is rapidly becoming the daily bread of the constitution—where every idle mechanic or bankrupt shopkeeper thinks himself capable of deciding summarily on questions which have perplexed the best and wisest for centuries —where convicted swindlers are respectfully listened to on questions of the greatest moral and religious, as well as political importance—and the majesty of the Monarch is obliged to submit to be bearded in St. James's by *honourable* members of Parliament, who in no preceding reign could have found access to the drawing-room of the humblest gentleman in the land. Since the days of Trajan, therefore, perhaps there never was a country to which Pope's celebrated couplet was more applicable than to Prussia under the King now upon the throne—

'For forms of government let fools contest,
Whatever's best administered is best.'

But then comes the grand question—what guarantee have the Prussians for the continuance of good government, and are the really enlightened amongst them satisfied with a state of things so palpably dependent upon accident?* Both Mr. Strang and the Resident assure us that they are not, and concur in stating that a free press and a free constitution are generally demanded by the thinking classes of society; but we believe we

---

* We on a former occasion quoted the reply made by Alexander of Russia to Madame de Staël, when she was expatiating on the prosperity of his empire under his rule.—'Madam, I am but a happy accident.'

have enjoyed as ample opportunities of becoming acquainted with the opinions of the thinking classes as either of them, and our impression is, that the removal of the censorship and the grant of a representative assembly (which are what is meant by a free press and constitution) are regarded as measures of doubtful expediency, whilst the army, the municipal assemblies, and the poverty of the nobles, are confidently relied on as safeguards against any undue exercise of the prerogative. This may require a few words of explanation; first, as to the army.

On the trial of the poor ex-ministers of Charles X., M. Arago (the celebrated mathematician) deposed that Prince de Polignac, on being informed that the troops were going over to the people, exclaimed,—'Well, then, the troops also must be fired upon!' This is just the sort of order which a Prussian minister would have to issue in the case of a popular movement emanating from a strong national feeling of oppression; for the Prussian army is neither more nor less than a large standing militia, in which every male, on attaining twenty years of age, takes his period of service—so that each citizen is a soldier, each soldier a citizen, and the feelings and interests of the two orders are the same. Nor has the crown so much as left itself the means of conciliating the attachment of the officers. An indispensable preliminary to the obtaining of a commission is service during a given period in the ranks; whilst money and favour are equally unavailing to advance promotion a step. Blücher's son is a subaltern of many years standing, which (considering the enthusiastic admiration with which the memory of Marshal Forwards, as they call him, is cherished) affords the most decisive exemplification of the rule.

Another check, of a yet more formidable description, is presented by the municipalities. The administration of the affairs of each town, city, or municipal district throughout Prussia, is vested in representatives chosen by the inhabitants, and magistrates chosen by the representatives. The only control over their choice retained by the crown, is the privilege of selecting the burgomaster out of three candidates named on the part of the town. The qualification for voting is rather higher than that created by the new corporation bill in England, but sufficiently low (under 25l. a year) to give a decided democratic tendency to the institution; and there can be little doubt, that should any serious attempt be made to convert the government practically into what it already is theoretically—a despotism—these corporate bodies would not be deterred from venturing beyond the recognised limits of their jurisdiction, but meet, pass resolutions, present addresses, and take any other steps that might be deemed necessary for the protection of their liberties.

A third ground of security is afforded by the non-existence of any privileged class interested in making common cause with the king. This anomaly is principally attributed to the celebrated law of 1810. Till within a few years previously to the passing of this law, the greater part of the landed property of Prussia consisted of *estates noble*—that is, estates which could only be held by persons of noble birth—and was, moreover, subjected to a variety of feudal restrictions which materially impeded the progress of agricultural improvement. The tenant was ordinarily restricted to a particular mode of cultivation, and the landlord to a particular family or class of tenantry, being in no case permitted to turn farmer or employ his own capital on the land. Stein, who was appointed minister soon after the battle of Jena at the express dictation of Napoleon, removed some of the most invidious of these restrictions, and Hardenberg, who succeeded him, swept the whole of them away by the edict above mentioned, which provided that the actual possessors for the time being under leases (renewable or otherwise) should be free hereditary proprietors of the land on giving up a certain portion to the lord, one-third when the lease was renewable, and one-half when the holding was for life or a fixed number of years. The justice of this measure is ably discussed by Mr. Russell. The 'Resident,' who seems to have a very loose and vague notion of it, asserts that Hardenberg refused all indemnification to the proprietors for the loss of the services of their boors. This was not the fact: the right to indemnification was distinctly admitted, and the mode of awarding it defined, although, as may be collected from Prince Pückler Muskau's last work, neither party was eventually a gainer by the good intentions of the government in this respect. We shall quote the passage, because it throws light on a kind of jobbing which the Whig party are doing their utmost to bring into general reception in this country.

'If it had been carried into effect without any unnecessary vexatious interference, and at the least possible expense; if proper attention had been paid to the various local circumstances which presented themselves in the different provinces; if it had been carried on with energy and the difficulties determinately surmounted, there would be little cause to complain. But instead of this, the inhabitants have been exposed to a tedious and harassing process, in furtherance of which multitudes of new appointments have been created under the name of general commissioners, for the purpose of separating and dissolving the connexion of the serf with the lord of the soil.

'A whole army of economy commissioners have been enlisted, principally consisting of bankrupt proprietors, ruined farmers, discharged civil officers, bonneteurs, and engineers, the whole brood let loose upon the already impoverished and miserable inhabitants, who have been,

79

through their instrumentality, betrayed into innumerable disputes, and subjected to various and expensive pecuniary charges.

'We have witnessed the commissaries enriching themselves at the rate of more than two thousand rix dollars annually; many of the overseers have become small capitalists, while the valuable crumbs which fall from the table of the principal commissioners have dropped into the pockets of their clerks and underlings.

' Notwithstanding all this expense, the regulation remained, in most cases, defective and undetermined; and in many instances it has been well attested that the charges attending the fulfilment of this law, even before it was completed, exceeded the whole worth of the indemnification to the proprietor, so that he not only lost the services of the peasants, but was absolutely obliged to pay for being deprived of their services.

' Thus the proprietors of landed estates and the peasants are naturally becoming poorer and poorer during the wearisome, protracted, and expensive proceedings, and behold, with a state of mind bordering on despair, an evil averted for the sake of carrying into effect a theory which will be productive of advantage to none *except a mass of civil officers, whom the government has created without necessity, and when the business is terminated, will be turned adrift upon society, thereby producing a still greater necessity;* and to accomplish this the interests of one generation are sacrificed! This sounds harsh, but it is too true.'—*Tutti Frutti*, vol. i. p. 150.

We should be glad to know what is to be done with the host of commissioners whom our Whig government has created without necessity, and will, some time or other, we presume, be obliged to turn adrift. The more respectable members of the legal profession are already complaining loudly of the deteriorating effects of this kind of patronage on the bar.

To return to Prussia:—the nobility lost much in property, and more in influence, by the direct operation of this measure; but it was its indirect operation that has destroyed them as a class. ' The law (says Mr. Russell, vol. ii. p. 88,) appeared at a moment when the greater part of their estates were burdened with debts, and the proprietors were now deprived of their rentals. They indeed had land thrown back upon their hands, but this only multiplied their embarrassments. In the hands of the boors the soil had been productive to them; now that it was in their own, they had neither skill nor capital to carry on its profitable cultivation, and new loans only added to the interest which already threatened to consume its probable fruits. The consequence of all this was, that besides the portion of land secured in free property to the peasantry, much of the remainder came into the market, and the purchasers were generally persons who had acquired wealth by trade or manufactures.' As a landed

aristocracy, therefore, the Prussian nobility can hardly be said to exist; and the *prestige* of birth avails them next to nothing with the people and little with the crown. With the exception of a few places about the court, honours and offices are distributed with exclusive reference to the personal merits of the candidate.

It is obvious that a king, without the aid of a nobility or an army personally dependent upon him, would stand little chance in a struggle against a people so far advanced in civilization as the Prussians, and with such ample means of combination within their reach. The most enlightened amongst them are well aware of the strength of their position, and are far from anxious to see the quiet of the country disturbed by election contests, and their domestic privacy invaded by the press. Indeed, we once heard a distinguished jurist contend, with the apparent approbation of a mixed company at Berlin, that the evil of what are termed free institutions more than counterbalanced the good; for ' would not a stranger,' he added, ' from the tone of your newspapers, and the speeches of the leading members of your reforming ministry, infer that the sole objects of human life were the making and altering of laws, and the modelling and remodelling of constitutions?'—In Prussia, moreover, it would be hardly possible to form a chamber of deputies duly representing the feelings of the nation, on account of the various and conflicting interests that must clash in it; for the Prussian monarchy is principally made up of territories acquired by cession or conquest within a comparatively recent period, and held together by the strong arm of compulsion, so that on the first show of a popular movement they would probably fall asunder of themselves. In such an event, the Rhenish provinces would be appropriated by France, the Silesian by Austria, the Polish by Russia, and little would remain to profit by the liberality of the sovereign beyond the original dominions of his electorate. A catastrophe of the kind is thought by sagacious observers to be even now impending over the United States of America; but they, fortunately for them, have no powerful neighbours to take instant advantage of a false step. It must be admitted, however, that at the time Mr. Strang's book was written, the call for a free constitution was much more general than now, because considerable apprehensions were entertained regarding the conduct and character of the Crown Prince. As many heirs apparent have done before him, the heir apparent of the Prussian crown was wont in early youth to amuse himself by quizzing his father's confidential servants, and many good stories are related of the jokes which he was in the habit of playing off at Hardenberg's expense. ' Can you divine, Hardenberg, what is the first thing I shall do when I am king?' said he once to the chancellor. ' I am

11. continued

'confident,' replied the premier, ' it will be something equally
honourable to your royal highness and beneficial to the public.'
Right for once, chancellor, for it will be to send you to Spandau!'*
But he is grown older and wiser since he is reported to have talked
in this manner ; and he would now (unless public report speaks
false) be more inclined to say, like Henry V. to the Chief Justice
who had committed him,—

> ' There is my hand ;
> You shall be as a father to my youth—
> My voice shall sound as you do prompt mine ear,
> And I will stoop and humble my intents
> To your well-practised wise directions.'

The Prince is understood to lean at present to the *liberal* side,
which would have the effect of bringing the administration into still
closer harmony with the national feeling ; so far, at all events, as
its foreign policy is concerned—for some jealousy undoubtedly
prevails of the influence of Russian counsels at court. On this
subject the Resident remarks—

' Whether it be owing to this influence that the government manifests
such a decided hostility to England and her interests, I know not ; but,
certainly, in her exhibitions of this enmity she has been most industrious,
both in her commercial tariff, to which she has had the adroitness to gain
over the minor states in Germany, and also in the language of the public
press, which is, we know, here the organ of government. Let us take
up any of her *say-nothing*, stupid, political journals, and we shall probably
find some bitter censure'—[is this saying nothing?]—' upon England
and her inhabitants. But, for our consolation, we know that they do not
speak the sentiments of the people, but those of the government ; for the
Germans have just as much of a free press as coincides with the will of
the Dictator, the Imperial Nicholas :—whose puppet, with what truth I
know not, the Prussians assert M. Ancillon to be. However, we must
admire the sagacity of the writers ; for, whether manufactured in Frankfurt, Augsburg, or Berlin, the pills given to the British lion are very
carefully sugared over. Still, if an English statesman breaks the sweet
incrustation, he will make several notable discoveries ; for instance, that
our commerce is rapidly declining ! our trade with Germany at an end !
and our feeble, tottering, Whig administration scarcely able to restrain
a people on the verge of anarchy ! and, above all, burdened with a debt
that cripples all our energies !'—*Sketches*, vol i., pp. 90, 91.

The contemptuous feeling with which our 'feeble, tottering,
Whig administration' is generally regarded on the Continent has
certainly extended to the Prussians, and our national character is
proportionably degraded in their esteem—but we have searched in
vain for proofs of decided hostility ; and we are convinced that

* A fortress in which convicts and other prisoners are detained. Some other
anecdotes to the same purport are related by Mr. Russell.

the return of the Duke of Wellington or Sir Robert Peel to
office would instantly re-establish us on our ancient footing with
our allies. The same writer subsequently states the common
opinion in Berlin to be that the commercial league has originated
in the refusal of England to receive Prussian corn and timber
unless burdened with duties which almost amount to a prohibition ;
' but the fact is,' he adds, ' that Prussia's real object was the extension of her political influence.' That this was one of her
objects we have no reason to disbelieve ; yet where is the necessity for speculating about the sinister motives of a measure which
carries so ample a justification on the face of it ? The vexatious
manner in which the custom-house duties were levied throughout
Germany was the subject of universal complaint—it being necessary for the traveller or merchant to stop and submit to be
searched anew at the frontiers of each petty state through which
his goods or his person had to pass. Some notion may be formed
of the extent of this inconvenience by the simple inspection of
one of the larger sort of coloured maps. The professed object
of the commercial league was to remedy this inconvenience, by
subjecting the whole of the north of Germany to one general
tariff of duties, to be collected on one grand frontier, and equitably
divided amongst the several states comprehended within the line.
So long as the average amount of duty remains the same, and no
particular country is favoured at our expense, it is obvious that we
have no just ground of complaint ; and the only mode in which
England can be expected to suffer from this arrangement is by
the indirect facilities afforded to France and Switzerland—who
have several of the petty states to cross on their way to furnish
the north of Germany with commodities which England supplies
direct through Hamburg.

The manufactures of Prussia herself are flourishing, and her
exports in woollen stuffs and wrought iron, branches of trade in
which she comes into direct competition with England, are increasing yearly. For beauty and finish, the articles manufactured
at the Prussian iron-foundries confessedly excel those manufactured at Sheffield or Birmingham—a superiority (according to
Mr. Strang) entirely owing to the peculiar fineness of the sand.
' The cotton manufactures,' says the Resident, ' established by
Frederick the Great, have not kept pace with some of the other
branches of national industry ; and it is only by imposing a pro-
hibitory duty on English manufactures, that the public can be
compelled to wear them.' We are not aware of the precise amount
of duty ; but as English cottons are in very general use amongst
the ladies of Berlin, the duty can hardly be described as a pro-
hibitory one. Indeed we do not hesitate to say that the principles

81

of free trade are better understood in Prussia than in any other country of the Continent, not excepting France, where, with all her pretension to liberality, the most injurious prejudices on these subjects are in full activity, and the most absurd jealousies of their commercial rivals prevail amongst the merchants and manufacturers.

The principal remaining topics are jurisprudence, literature, the drama, and society.

Both the writers before us agree in lauding the administration of the law in Prussia; but their opinions are evidently taken up at second-hand from Prussians comparing their own system with that of the neighbouring states; for in this point, and in this only, is it commendable. The procedure in a suit is made up of a succession of allegations and counter-allegations, strongly resembling our bills and answers in chancery. There is no oral pleading, and the duty of the advocate is limited to the preparation of the voluminous papers in the cause. The judgment is also delivered in writing, with the reasons at length. In all cases of the slightest moment it is a matter of course to carry the cause through each of the allowed stages of appeal, ending with the law faculty of a university; and, as these are numerous, it is a matter of rare occurrence to find a suit involving a debatable question definitively decided in less than three or four years. In criminal cases, the duty ordinarily undertaken by the private prosecutor in England devolves on the district magistrate or judge, who, when he has collected all the evidence, documentary or otherwise, calculated in his opinion to throw light upon the case, transmits the whole in the shape of a report, with the documents appended, to a superior tribunal, which directs additional inquiries to be instituted, or forthwith proceeds to the acquittal or condemnation of the prisoner. There is nothing wearing the semblance of a public trial; and the accused is subjected to a series of personal examinations in order to induce a confession. The judges, generally speaking, are men of talent and integrity; but no talent or integrity can cure the defects of a system so radically wrong. Jurisprudence, considered as a branch of public study, is nowhere better taught than in Prussia, and in Professor von Savigny the university of Berlin may pride herself on the possession of the first of living civilians. Professor Gans is another Berlin jurist of celebrity; but his enthusiasm in favour of what he terms liberal principles has led him into indiscretions ill becoming his situation as an instructor of youth. Four or five years ago he delivered a series of lectures on modern history, which set the university in a flame, and led to much disorderly conduct on the part of the most hot-headed of his auditory; yet he was allowed to lecture on, and still retains his professorship, though entirely dependent on the crown.

German literature at the present moment is much in the same condition as our own; most of the celebrated authors by whom the close of the eighteenth and the commencement of the nineteenth century have been illustrated are dead, or have ceased to write: as for rising poets of distinction, there are none: criticism is principally occupied in settling the respective claims of the past or passing generation (particularly of Goethe and Schiller) upon posterity; and the public interest is frittered away on novelists, manifesting little merit beyond the slender one of cleverness. Menzel* enumerates several classes of prose fictions now or recently popular in Germany, as the amatory, the physiological, the philosophical, the historical, &c.; the last, he tells us, from the time Sir Walter Scott first set the fashion, have been produced in such numbers that no critic can possibly keep pace with them, and they are forgotten as speedily as read. Yet not content with the home-manufacture, the Germans import largely and very indiscriminately from England; for every tawdry production of the silver-fork school, as well as every feeble drivelling imitation of Scott, that can obtain by puffing the slightest show of notoriety, is sure to be translated without delay. On inspection of the Leipsic catalogues for 1835, it will be seen that German translations of *fifty-eight* foreign novels appeared within the year —a number which puts selection out of the question. Foreign circulation, we observe, is commonly cited as an unerring test of genius, an unequivocal pledge of immortality; but it really proves nothing more than that the tastes and habits of the idle classes are nearly alike in all countries that have arrived at nearly the same point of cultivation, and that there exists a large class in each to whom the excitement of fictitious narrative has become as much a necessary of life as opium to the opium-eater. When the thoughts, sentiments, images, and characters of a poet or novelist have so thoroughly worked themselves into the minds of a foreign people, as to influence their modes of thinking and form part of their ordinary speech, he may well term such homage decisive of his claims; but such homage has not yet been paid in Germany to any English authors of the present age except Scott and Byron; and such assuredly never will be paid anywhere to the fifty-eight *facile principes* of the puffing paragraphs and the shop-windows.

The Resident is silent as to the literary and scientific characters of Berlin. Mr. Strang contents himself with giving short accounts of the personal appearance and pretensions of the following:— Langbein (since dead), a sort of would-be Boccaccio, two or three of whose tales of humour have been translated by Mr. Strang;

---

* Die Deutsche Literature, vol. iv., last edition.

Philip Kaufman, a clever translator of Shakspeare and Burns; Raupach, the principal dramatic writer of Berlin; the antiquarian collector Raumer, with whose name the English public are already familiar; Gans, the law-professor above mentioned; Chamisso, the author of Peter Schlemil;* Mitscherlik, the celebrated chemist; and Alexander von Humboldt, the traveller. His estimate of these gentlemen's claims to distinction is impartially and accurately drawn up; with the exception of Raupach, who is described as a tragic writer exclusively, though his comic writings are amongst the most remarkable of his works. His favourite character, *Till*, is one of the most humorous and original that exist in any language. Mr. Strang appears to have limited his observation to those with whom he had opportunities of forming a personal acquaintance: yet it is surprising that the translator of Shakspeare did not call his attention to (after Tieck and Schlegel) the ablest of the German commentators on Shakspeare, Franz Horn—that Gans did not suggest von Savigny—and that the names of Varnhagen von Ense, Boeckh, and Becker, are omitted in the list. There are several others which might well have found a place there, but it would require readier means of information than exist elsewhere than on the spot to qualify us for supplying the deficiency; and we shall, therefore, close this topic with a remark on the social position of the literary and scientific men of Germany, who have often been held up as objects of envy to their English contemporaries.

Now, it is a matter beyond dispute that many of the solid advantages, and the most catching of the factitious advantages, are with them. Hardly a man amongst them of the slightest merit is to be found without a riband at his button-hole or a collar round his neck; and a large majority of those who have attracted general attention by their works hold places at court, employments under the government, or, at the least, professorships in the universities. Thus, Goethe was a sort of prime minister at Weimar; the Humboldts, Frederick Schlegel, and Niebuhr were ambassadors; Tieck is a court-counsellor; A. W. Schlegel, Heeren, Müller, Boeckh, the Grimms, Gans, Blumenbach, Hugo, Savigny, Mittermaief, &c., &c., are professors. The prizes, however, are few in proportion to the number of those who play for them, it being computed that there are not less

* Dr. Bowring, the translator of Peter Schlemil, states it to be the work of the Baron de la Motte Fouqué; why, it is for the Doctor to explain, as there was never the slightest doubt upon the point. This tale constitutes the least of von Chamisso's titles to distinction. The Baron de la Motte Fouqué resides at Halle. His first wife, who rivalled her husband in literary celebrity, died many years ago. His present wife, one of the most beautiful and accomplished women in Germany, has never yet appeared in print, but she is constantly confounded by travellers with the authoress.

than fourteen or fifteen (Mr. Strang says fifty) thousand living authors in Germany; and an author who relies on the public will find it very difficult to eke out more than a scanty subsistence by his pen. The periodical works pay next to nothing, the best articles being ordinarily supplied gratis by the leading members of the universities; and original books have hitherto afforded a very inadequate return. Science may thrive best under the existing state of things; but we incline to think that measures recently adopted for giving authors an exclusive copyright throughout the whole of the Confederation (a privilege accorded by special favour to Goethe) will do more for literature than all the state patronage that has ever yet been lavished on it.*

With regard to the reception of the learned in society, it is no easy matter to estimate it. In such university towns as Halle and Bonn, they, of course, take the lead, and in the capital they stand high, though perhaps rather by reason of the limited influence of the aristocratical circle than as part of it; a distinction which we will here endeavour to explain.

It has been said that the grand essentials to success in English society are three: rank, wealth, and celebrity or notoriety of some sort—it little matters how gotten, or for what—

—————' the few
Or many (for the number's sometimes such),
Whom a good mien, especially if new,
Or fame or name for wit, war, sense, or nonsense,
Permits whate'er they please, or did not long since.'

We rather think that most countries of Europe will be found, on a close inspection, to resemble England, more or less, in this respect. But in a metropolis like London, wealth abounds in such prodigious masses, it is so frequently found united with rank, and there are so many paths to celebrity, that literature has unavoidably a harder battle to fight, and, single-handed, has certainly a sorry chance against the field. There are, first, our rich nobles and commoners, constituting the landed aristocracy; then our bankers and merchants, rivalling or outdoing the class just mentioned in munificence; then the professions, particularly the law, which has the singular advantage of conferring wealth, rank, and celebrity, at a blow; then the parliamentary adventurers, like Tierney, or Sheridan—who, according to his biographer, was indebted for his brilliant position in society to his politics.

* The question was brought before the Congress at Vienna, by Cotta, the celebrated publisher. An attempt is at present making, under the auspices of Miss Martineau and certain leading members of Congress, to secure some kind of copyright for English authors in America; and Mr. Serjeant Talfourd has given notice of a motion for extending the very limited period during which literary property is protected by our English Copyright Acts. To each of these schemes we wish all possible success.

11. continued

'By him (says Mr. Moore) who has not been born among the great, this (equality) can only be achieved by politics. In that arena which they look upon as their own, the legislature of the land, let a man of genius, like Sheridan, but assert his supremacy—at once all these barriers of reserve and pride give way, and he takes by right a station at their side which a Shakspeare or a Newton would but have enjoyed by courtesy.'

Mr. Moore, however, errs in supposing that this equalizing tendency is peculiar to politics. Any common pursuit or interest which brings men much together will cause the barriers in question to be thrown down or forgotten for the time,—not excepting literature when followed *con amore* by the great; and it may well be doubted whether Sheridan felt more upon a level with his company at Devonshire House, than Swift at Harley's levee, or Pope in Bolingbroke's hay-field.

The same causes are in operation at Paris, though controlled or rendered less obvious by the weakness of the aristocracy, and the disorder into which the established rules of social intercourse have been thrown by a series of revolutionary changes, almost daily opening some new land of promise to the adventurer. But we are not to suppose that the relative positions of rank, wealth, and fame, have been reversed, because a journalist (like Bertin de Vaux) is occasionally raised to a life-peerage (a very different thing from an English peerage, by the way), or because a flashy historian (like Thiers) actually managed to become premier for a time—since even he found it expedient to strengthen his position by marrying a rich wife and setting up a handsome establishment. In a word, literary distinction in an educated community will always raise a man in the estimation of his own immediate circle or class, including the highest; but the utmost it can ever do for one who, without birth or connection, aspires to mingle with the aristocracy (landed, monied, or political) of a large metropolis, is to give him an introduction. If his manners suit those of his new associates, and his means are sufficient to enable him to fall in with their habits and modes of living without restraint—if, above all, he shows no consciousness of inferiority, and invariably respects himself—he will gradually come to be considered a regular member of their society.—If not, he must be content, at the end of his first season, to fall back upon the circle from which he started, and console himself by railing at the ignorance, prejudice, superciliousness, and narrow-mindedness of the higher classes, who refuse to place a fashionable novelist or a dandy poetaster on precisely the same footing with a duke, or a *millionaire*, whose banquets and balls are the envy of the town.

Mr. Allan Cunningham, a sensible and manly writer in general, thus peevishly remarks on Burns's reception in Edinburgh:—'A man with ten thousand a-year will always be considered by the world around superior to a man whose wealth lies in his genius; the dullest can estimate what landed property is worth, but who can say what is the annual value of an estate which lies in the imagination? In fame, there was no rivalry; and in station, what hope had a poet, with the earth of his last-turned furrow still red on his shoes, to rival the Montgomerys, the Hamiltons, and the Gordons, with counties for estates, and the traditionary *éclat* of a thousand years accompanying them?' —Burns may have been hardly used by his noble friends, and we cordially agree with Mr. Allan Cunningham that something better than an exciseman's place should have been got for him; but all accounts of Burns's manners and habits tend to show that he was radically unfit for, and took no real pleasure in, the polished circles of a metropolis; and with regard to the complaint expressed in the above passage, we challenge our good friend Mr. Cunningham to consult his own thoughts and feelings, and declare whether he himself does not fully participate in the very prejudice (allowing it to be one) which he condemns. Johnson has probed it to the bottom in his usual sturdy, downright way:—'I said (says Boswell), I consider distinction of rank to be of so much importance in civilized society, that if I were asked on the same day to dine with the first duke in England, and with the first man in Britain for genius, I should hesitate which to prefer. *Johnson*.—To be sure, Sir, if you were to dine only once, and it were never to be known where you dined, you would choose rather to dine with the first man for genius; but to gain most respect you should dine with the first duke in England. For nine people in ten that you meet with would have a higher opinion of you for having dined with a duke: *and the great genius himself would receive you better because you had been with the great duke.*'—Whether it be that the fancy of men of genius delights to revel in the images associated with rank—that their taste is more refined, or their vanity more excitable—it does appear to us, after studying a good many of such characters, that they partake even more largely than other people of this tendency. Johnson complains in another place of the little attention paid him by the nobility—(which in truth was very little)—and accounts for it by saying that great lords and ladies did not like to have their mouths stopped—as if great lords and ladies were singular in this respect. Congreve, when Voltaire called on him as a dramatic writer, said he wished to be called on as a gentleman; which elicited from his visiter the sarcastic retort—that if Congreve had been only a gentleman he should never have called on him at all. Byron had the same weakness—so has Manzoni; and many English writers of far inferior stamp have carried it to an extent that made them general objects of ridicule ; forgetting that the best proof of the extent of their literary fame was to be found in this very circumstance,—that their other claims to social distinction were merged in it.

In Germany there prevailed, till very lately, an undue eagerness to obtain the privilege of prefixing the mystic *von*, the symbol of nobility, to the name, as *von* Goethe and *von* Schlegel, neither of whom had any title to it by birth. But this, which is rapidly diminishing, constitutes almost the only weakness that can be adduced against them. Whether titled or untitled, they are thoroughly in earnest in their pursuits ; with them, intellectual distinction is the end, not the means : they take a just pride in their literary or scientific character, and are rarely smitten with the ambition of shining amongst the *beaumonde*; being probably actuated by a lurking consciousness that, whilst woman is woman, the *savant* must rest satisfied with much that sort of reception in the boudoir which Beauty accords to Reason in the song ; and that there is, or ought to be, a heavy respectability about a professor or man of science which must inspire a *belle* in the full flush of *coquetterie* with a feeling near akin to that which one of Mrs. Siddons's admirers avowed when accused of flirting with her—' Flirt with a stiff, stately, grave person like that—I should as soon think of flirting with the Archbishop of Canterbury.'

In applying these remarks to living characters, the reader will hardly fail to observe how large a number of our most distinguished writers derive incomes and influence from other sources than literature—from birth, connexions, hereditary or acquired property, or professional success. This is a sign of good augury and cannot fail to add to their consideration in the world ; for when born nobles, estated gentlemen, wealthy bankers, bishops, deans, canons, and eminent lawyers, make up the best part of the corporation of authors, authorship must soon cease to be employed as a synonym for poverty, and it will be absurd to sneer at poets as denizens of Grub-street, when they are notoriously giving the best possible dinners in St. James's Place. But the best sign of all is the increasing appetite for reading—in other words, the increasing demand for the commodity which the author has to sell. So widely spread is this demand already, and so rapidly is it increasing, that literary labour will soon become as sure a source of profit as any other kind of intellectual labour that can be named. Nay, pass but a perpetual copyright act, (a measure against which it would be difficult to discover any valid argument,) and we may see as many powerful families founded by the pen, as by

the gown, the mitre, or the sword. Why should not Wordsworth's poetry constitute a *majorat* as well as Blenheim or Strathfield-saye ? In the mean time it is evidently the duty of the government to follow the example of Prussia in giving the intellectual classes a share of the employments which their habits and acquirements peculiarly qualify them to fill, whilst honours and titles might be distributed occasionally. However, we lay little stress on ribands and decorations, particularly such a riband as the Guelph, which appears to have been conferred in entire forgetfulness of the rule that, at the commencement at all events, the man should decorate the order, not simply the order the man. If Lord Brougham—with whom we believe the plan originated—really wished it to succeed, he should first have conferred the order (as he conferred an increase of retiring pension) on himself, and have got some of the most distinguished of the Whig circle—Mr. Moore, Mr. Rogers, Lord Jeffrey, Mr. Hallam, and the Rev. Sydney Smith—as prelate, or dean, or at least as acting chaplain with a sufficient salary—to strut about with him similarly adorned.*

We have heard it asked whether it would not greatly strengthen the English universities, as well as afford an additional provision for the class whose interests we are now discussing, if laymen were more generally eligible to the professorships and the headships of the colleges. At present, no doubt, England offers, in this respect, a striking contrast to Germany, where most of the living, acting, influential science and literature emanates directly from the universities, which are proportionally elevated in public esteem. The fact is, that *our* academical foundations date mostly from the time when all our lawyers, physicians, &c., were usually in holy orders. But however we may regret some consequences of this fact, we had rather see things remain as they are, than encourage rash tampering, on any, however plausible pretexts, with English charters.

The drama constitutes the chief amusement of Berlin ; the three theatres—the opera-house, the theatre royal, and a minor theatre devoted to comic pieces—being regularly attended by all classes. Mr. Strang attributes their success to the early hour of dinner, seldom later than three, and the shortness of the representation, occupying not more than three hours, usually from six to nine. Both these causes exercise a certain degree of influence, though not quite so much as Mr. Strang attributes to them ; and it would be taking a very superficial view of a curious and important question to account for the decline of the drama in England by the lateness of fashionable hours and the unconscionable

---

* Those who wish to pursue this subject further may consult *Babbage on the Decline of Science*, and *D'Israeli on the Literary Character*, vol. ii. ch. 24.

length of the performances. The theatre never was, perhaps never will be, the strictly national amusement of this country; it never formed part of the regular arrangements of the day with either of the grand divisions of society, though there have frequently been influential knots of wits and people of fashion who for a period made a practice of frequenting it. The mass of English playgoers are persons who take this mode of enjoying a holiday or giving their families a treat; whilst in most of the continental capitals a large portion of the middle class are as much *habitués* of the theatre as the highest class in England of the Italian Opera. Whatever the cause of our inferiority—it undoubtedly exists, and will probably go on increasing now that the last of the most distinguished family that ever adorned any stage has retired, whilst Germany still retains her Schroeders and Devrients.

Music is another of the national tastes of Germany; and we believe there are more genuine amateurs in Berlin than in London, though the population of London is more than five times as numerous. Nothing can well exceed the enthusiasm with which a performer of genius is received. It is said that on Sontag's first appearance in Berlin, a party of her military admirers bribed her maid to give them one of her cast-off slippers, and toasted her in it nightly till it was worn out. To the best of our recollection the same compliment was paid to Ninon in France. There is another anecdote to the effect that a party of students forced their way into her hotel whilst her carriage was driving from the door, and made prey of a wineglass containing about a spoonful of wine, which, it was conjectured, her pretty lips had touched; this they forthwith put up to auction, and seventeen dollars were bid and paid down by one of the party to obtain possession of the prize.

Mr. Strang was only in Berlin during the summer months, when the principal inhabitants are away, and frankly owns that he knows little of the best society but what was told him; but he has, notwithstanding, discovered a custom which we certainly never witnessed, and never even remember to have heard of before :—

' On rising from the board [at a banker's dinner] I was somewhat struck with the kindliness of the custom which preceded the retiring movements to the ante-room. The host saluted his wife and the other ladies with a kiss, which was instantly followed by the other male guests. I may merely add that with all the admiration which my companion and myself felt for the beauty of several of the fair guests, we could not so far get over our national *mauvaise-honte* as to enable us to do the *amiable* [query *aimable?*] with grace by thus kissing in public.'

Mr. Strang's good fortune, of which he showed himself so utterly undeserving, is remarkable—not simply in his being the first foreigner to light upon so pleasing a custom, but in his meeting with so much beauty in Berlin, where the women in general are more than ordinarily plain. The Resident has evidently borrowed the little he says about society from Prince Pückler Muskau's letter from Berlin, published in his *Tutti Frutti*. According to this weighty authority the court circle is the best, but it is strictly exclusive. Even foreigners of rank are rarely admitted, with the exception of the Russians, who have hitherto been highly favoured; though it seems not improbable that the unfriendly feeling recently manifested by the Emperor Nicholas towards his German visiters at Petersburgh, may produce corresponding dispositions towards his own subjects in Berlin. The *corps diplomatique* form no exception to the rule: little intercourse beyond what is strictly official being kept up between them and the court—nor do they visit much in any circle but their own. ' Berlin,' adds the Prince, ' is, generally speaking, destitute of any decided tone: fashion exercises but a feeble sway; and there is no individual subject of paramount importance to impart a determined character to society. There is neither political nor indeed any other description of party feeling, which it is well known always animates conversation.'

The Resident, without anywhere referring to the Prince, copies the last remark almost verbatim; but we shall, notwithstanding, take the liberty of challenging both its truth and application. In the first place, the animation imparted by political or party feeling to conversation, is utterly destructive of its agreeability, and generally ends by putting knowledge and ignorance, vivacity and dulness, on a par; since every fool can bandy fustian phrases, got by rote from the newspapers, with an antagonist. In the second place, there is no want of this ingredient at Berlin. Never, for instance, was party question discussed with greater heat than the Polish revolution there, and in no town of Europe was the conduct of the Russian autocrat more vehemently condemned. This is a fact about which no doubt can be entertained; but to verify our own impression of the general tone of political discussion, we have consulted many who have enjoyed the best means of information, and the result has been that it is free and uncompromising in the extreme. Most of our Prussian friends refer us to a recent novel by Immerman, called *Die Epigonen*, (composed much after the plan of Wilhelm Meister,) as conveying a faithful picture of the manners and conversation of the time. We have referred to it accordingly; and if the author, who holds a high judicial situation in Prussia, has not greatly overcharged his picture, the coteries of Berlin fully equal the coteries of Paris and London in liberalism.

We have made Prussia our principal object in this article, because her institutions are very imperfectly understood, whilst the problem presented by them—a country theoretically enslaved and practically free—is peculiarly calculated to excite the curiosity of the investigator. We shall be comparatively brief in our notice of the other grand divisions of Germany, whose characters, social and political, are broadly and palpably defined.

Saxony has lamentably declined in strength and influence since she headed the Protestant interest in Germany. She has been growing weaker and weaker from the period of the reigning family's adoption of the Romish faith: but the fatal blow was given by the allied monarchs at the final settlement of Europe after the overthrow of Napoleon, to whom the king of Saxony remained faithful to the last. A partial dismemberment of territory in favour of Prussia was enforced amongst other measures of humiliation, and at present the whole population is said not to exceed twelve hundred thousand. Saxony enjoys what is called a constitution, i.e., a chamber of representatives; but this avails her nothing against the Diet, which, directly or indirectly, controls the policy of every minor state within its reach. Despite of Austrian and Prussian dieting, however, the Saxon censorship is tolerant enough to admit of Leipzic becoming the focus of most of the political literature of Germany. The number of pamphlets forthcoming at each of the great book-fairs is immense, and the tone of some of them is free enough in all conscience. Whatever, too, the Saxons lose by restrictions on the liberty of the press, they manage (like the Prussians) to make up by the most unrestricted liberty of speech—and altogether they seem to suffer little from any undue pressure of authority. Indeed, their apparent happiness gives Mr. Strang occasion for one of those outbursts of common-place radicalism which contrast so strangely with the general good reasoning and good feeling of his book. An example is subjoined to justify the distrust we have felt it our duty to express.

'Saxony, to be sure, can boast of none of the hot-bed splendour of Britain, but then she is utterly exempt from the moral and political corruption that distinguishes our oligarchy, and which is the cause, not only of many a withering blight in the fair garden of industry, but of that wide-spreading wretchedness which may be said emphatically to be the foul manure which supports the glaring flowers, &c. &c. . . . My gorge always rises, however, when I think of the system under which our vast debt accumulated to so hopeless an amount. The annals of the world do not afford another instance of so long and prosperous a career of insolent political peculation, fraud and villany. In Venice the same system was carried to perfection; but in point of extent it was, in comparison to ours, as a farthing candle to the sun,' &c. &c.

There is good deal more of the same sort of trash—but we have quoted quite enough for a specimen. The chief literary importance of Dresden at present is derived from its being the residence of Tieck, the most distinguished living writer of Germany. He receives company every evening from six to ten, and is peculiarly kind to Englishmen. Mr. Strang has given a description of him, but we prefer borrowing a passage from Mrs. Jameson's, which is much the more graphic of the two.

'While he spoke I could not help looking at his head, which is wonderfully fine; the noble breadth and amplitude of his brow, and his quiet but penetrating eye, with an expression of latent humour hovering round his lips, formed altogether a striking physiognomy. The numerous prints and portraits of Tieck which are scattered over Germany are very defective as resemblances: they have a heavy look; they give the weight and power of his head, but nothing of the *finesse* which lurks in the lower part of his face. His manner is courteous, and his voice particularly sweet and winning. He is apparently fond of the society of women, or the women are fond of his society, for in the evening his room is generally crowded with fair worshippers. Yet Tieck, like Goethe, is accused of entertaining some unworthy sentiments with regard to the sex, and is also said, like Goethe, not to have upheld us in his writings as the true philosopher, to say nothing of the true poet, ought to have done.'[*]

It strikes us that Mrs. Jameson is unnecessarily sensitive in the concluding remark. We remember nothing in Tieck that can fairly be called an unworthy sentiment regarding women; and though Goethe may have been betrayed into a few passing expressions of a depreciating tone or tendency, such characters as Mignon and Clara should at least exempt him from the imputation of any leaning to Mahommedanism in this particular—

> 'Oh, who young Leila's glance could read,
> And keep that portion of his creed
> Which says that woman is but dust,
> A soulless toy for tyrants' lust!'

The ordinary amusement at Tieck's *soirées* is a dramatic reading by himself—usually scenes from his own and Schlegel's admirable translation of Shakspeare. We had the good fortune to be present at one of his readings, and agree with Mrs. Jameson, that, with the exception of Mrs. Siddons, there has been nothing of the kind within living memory to be compared with them. This lady's description of the Dresden Gallery is also much the best we are acquainted with; but this has been described so very often, that we probably should only weary our readers by dwelling on it, and the guide-books are sufficiently eloquent about the Green

---

* Visits and Sketches at Home and Abroad, vol. ii. p. 97.—This work, in addition to its many other merits, contains copious and varied information relating to the history and progress of the fine arts in Germany, particularly in Dresden and Munich.

Vault and the other curiosities, to save future travellers the trouble of enumerating them.* We cannot quit Dresden without alluding to Retzsch, whose portrait has been sketched by the same graphic pencil to which we are indebted for Tieck's.

'His figure is rather larger and more portly than I expected, but I admired his fine Titanic head, so large and so sublime in its expression; his light-blue eye, wild and wide, which seemed to drink in meaning and flash out light; his hair profuse, grizzled, and flowing in masses round his head, and his expanded forehead full of poetry and power. In his deportment he is a mere child of nature,—simple, careless, saying just what he feels and thinks at the moment, without regard to forms, yet pleasing from the benevolent earnestness of his manner, and intuitively polite without being polished.'

Mr. Strang enters Austria by the way of Prague, which gives him an opportunity of collecting much valuable information regarding Bohemia. The Resident prefers descending the Danube, and treats us to two or three lively descriptions of the most striking scenes upon his track. This writer, indeed, improves amazingly on entering Austria, and in the little we have to say about Vienna we shall have more than once occasion to refer to him. The Austrian empire, however, is little altered since Mr. Russell wrote. Its policy is still directed by the one same mastermind, Metternich's; whilst the inhabitants are the same gay, lively, good-humoured; thoughtless, and contented race of mortals that they were fifteen years ago, and, for aught we see to the contrary, are likely to remain for fifteen or fifty years to come. 'Eat, drink, and be merry, for to-morrow we die,' is the motto the Viennese should place upon their gates, whilst the Epicurean is the only system of philosophy which would have the slightest chance of finding ardent votaries within their walls. How comes this? Here is a mighty nation, without a constitution, without a house of commons, without a free press, without trial by jury, without, in short, any one of the elements which go to make up what is termed liberty,—yet travellers of all persuasions agree in terming it the happiest nation in the world! Leaving others to account for the anomaly, it shall be our business to put the facts beyond dispute :—

'There is no city, I am persuaded,' says the honest *radical* Mr. Strang, 'where a foreigner sooner finds himself at home than in Vienna;—and nowhere is a stranger sooner taught to forget all the preconceived political grudges which he may have acquired against the Austrian government. Here he finds the people all comfortably housed, and all well dressed; all living well, and all in the best possible temper, both with themselves

* The fullest account of all matters of the kind, in addition to the ordinary information, will be found in *A Hand-book for Travellers on the Continent,* &c , published in the summer of 1836.

and others. The thousands who frequent the beer-houses and winecellars, are either singing or laughing; and if, by accident, they allude to anything connected with politics, which is very seldom, you never fail to find, amid the inuendos which may be thrown out respecting the conduct of certain inferior officers of the state, or among the passing jokes levelled against the misgovernment of Metternich, and his not over-popular coadjutor, Mittrovsky, the whole assembly are ever ready to join in one chorus of loyalty towards each member of the royal family, and particularly their good "*Koaser Franzerl,*" as the emperor is here emphatically designated. In the public walks and public gardens, every one seems more merry than another; and the individual who can mingle with the crowds of pretty faces that smile upon him in the Esplanade, or can gaze upon the fairy forms that flit through the brightly illuminated Volks-garten, in such evenings as the present, and who does not catch the spirit of universal happiness which prevails, must be a stoic indeed. And then, in the social circle, although the foreigner, no doubt, if he mixes with the people, must be prepared to take a hard hit now and then, adroitly levelled against the habits, manners, or feelings of his native country, yet the sarcasm is poured forth with so much good nature, and with such a kindly air, that one cannot help joining in the laugh, although raised at the expense of one's country. England affords the Vienna joker endless materials for his wit, which, to my cost, I have frequently experienced since I came here. For instance, the burning of stacks of grain to better the condition of the people—the impressment of seamen to defend liberty—our religious enthusiasm, and our devotion to the spirit-bottle—our vaunted morals, and our thousands of criminals—and a hundred other things, were ready to be thrown in my teeth whenever I began to hint about the Austrian censorship of the press, the severity and prying secrecy of the police, or the insecurity of the post-office. So you see, our glorious constitution in church and state is not as yet altogether the envy of the world and the admiration of surrounding nations!'—*Strang*, vol. ii. pp. 284-286.

The tinkering our constitution has undergone at the hands of Whig-Radical ministers has certainly not tended to elevate it in the estimation of foreigners, and Lord Palmerston's foreign policy bids fair to bring the English flag into downright contempt from one end of Europe to the other. For the present, therefore, it seems most prudent not to institute comparisons, and submit with the best possible grace to the sneer. Our other traveller is equally decisive in his testimony :—

'Happy people! Badinage apart, in good truth, it would be difficult to find, at this moment, a more good-humoured, more contented, or a happier population. Enjoyment is with them the great business of existence, from the noble to the peasant. A fine fat capon from the fertile valleys of Styria, and a flask of genuine Hungarian wine, are more acceptable than the most liberal constitution; and a Bohemian pheasant, garnished with sauerkraut and salami di Milano, more palatable than the production of the most able pen. But notwithstanding this devotion to sensual enjoyments, yet, on trying occasions, the Viennese have ever proved themselves zealous lovers of their country; and the trait in their character, which shines out in most beautiful relief to their epicurism, is unshaken fidelity to their rulers; for surely no part of Germany suffered more during the late war; and yet, when their armies were beaten, the emperor in retreat, Vienna sacked by the invader, and the country bankrupt, they never raised a murmur against the government, but threw the whole blame of their disasters upon the traitor princes of Germany, who had shamefully deserted their emperor. No native of Austria figured in the ranks of the Corsican; no artist immortalized the triumph of the enemy of his country; no pen eulogized his victories; no vivats welcomed the triumphal entry of Napoleon the Great into Vienna, as we find was the case in the Prussian metropolis. On the contrary, the nobles and citizens emulated each other in sacrificing their property to support the war, and in volunteering to fill the ranks of the army. It is well known, that the volunteer corps, composed of the citizens of Vienna, were among the bravest soldiers in the Austrian army.'— *Sketches*, vol. ii. pp. 156, 157.

We shall be told, perhaps, that these enviable effects are produced by a Machiavelian refinement in policy—by plunging the people in bigotry, or keeping them in blind ignorance of everything that might lure them from sensual indulgence, and rouse the true energies of intellect. Quite the contrary. Though the Romish is the dominant faith, its persecuting spirit is kept down—most other modes of belief are freely tolerated—and, in 1821, a college was founded by the Government expressly for the education of Protestants. Education, again, is widely, almost universally, diffused through the instrumentality of schools established by imperial authority. Mr. Strang states, that one normal school (in the Johannesgasse at Vienna) sends out annually from 1600 to 1700 persons capable of teaching. No one, after this, can well venture to deny that the schoolmaster is abroad in Austria, or assert that Metternich has shown much anxiety to block up all approaches to the point from which our political Archimedeses assume to move the world.

Literature has made less progress in Austria than in the north of Germany—partly in consequence of the self-indulgent character of the people, and partly, we do not doubt, in consequence of the strictness of the censorship. Yet Vienna boasts some names of celebrity: as the orientalist of orientalists, Joseph von Hammer—(now—we beg pardon—Baron Hammer-Pürgstall—he having inherited the Schloss-Hainfeld immortalized by Captain Basil Hall)—Grillparzer, the Collins, Deinhardstein, Mailath, Zedlitz, Bauernfeld, Castelli, Caroline Pickler, &c. &c.; and it is remarkable that some of the most distinguished have shone in

a walk—the drama—which is more peculiarly liable to suffer from restraint. The higher classes of the capital are eminently remarkable for cultivation and accomplishment: French, Italian, and English, are currently spoken in the best circles, and an enlightened patronage is extended to the fine arts by the nobility—the wealthiest nobility in Europe, with, perhaps, the exception of our own.

The criminal code of Austria is characterized by mildness, and the civil code is not deemed inferior to the Prussian or the French. Supplemental codes are at present under the consideration of the Government—unless, indeed, they have already received the force of laws; and a law-commission, composed of enlightened jurists, is constantly at work to correct the errors and supply the deficiencies of the whole. A despotic prince is necessarily invested with power to supersede the ordinary administration of justice, but complaints of the oppressive exercise of this privilege are rarely heard in the hereditary dominions of the emperor; though it is far otherwise, we fear, in the Italian provinces, where the Austrian rule appears to be animated by the same spirit of oppression which is almost invariably manifested by democratic states towards their colonies.

Admitting, therefore, the full force of the ordinary objections against autocracies—the present state of Austria, equally with that of Prussia, must be allowed to throw some plausibility, at least, around Coleridge's favourite doctrine, that the best form of government is one in which the people, whilst they exercise a certain degree of control over their rulers from without, take no active or initiative part whatever in the administration;—for even the Austrians have given popular demonstrations enough to show that no positive encroachment on their actual means of enjoyment would be tolerated, although they may be culpably careless in not providing against contingencies which may happen once or twice in a century, and stupidly insensible to fears, which, like the sword over the head of Damocles, are utterly destructive of present peace and comfort in almost every country pretending to be free.

The chief objects of interest at Munich, are painting, sculpture, architecture, and beer. The King is the chief patron of the last: unless much belied, he is personally acquainted with the interior of every beer-shop in his capital; and he reigns over subjects well worthy of their prince, for, according to Mr. Strang, when you see a Bavarian peasant not working, you are sure to find him with a can in his hand. Beer, indeed, must be to him what it was to Boniface—meat, drink, sleep, and clothing; since despite of a failing which seldom fails of bringing an Englishman to want, no signs of poverty are discernible from one end of his Bavarian majesty's dominions to the other. ' Let the thunders of the pulpit' (said Burke) ' descend on drunkenness—I for one stand up for gin.' Had he lived at Munich, it would have been simply necessary for him to change the last word of his peroration. The old maxim, however, that those who drink beer will think beer, is inapplicable ; for the king, with all his eccentricities, is perhaps the most accomplished monarch of his day ; and the fine arts, under his auspices, have been cultivated to a point which, considering the limited resources of the nation, is astonishing. We allude not merely to the patronage lavished on painters and sculptors, but to the national galleries, built after designs by Klenze. The opera-house, too, opened about ten or twelve years since, is one of the finest theatres of Germany. With the exception of Schelling, to whom neither of our travellers alludes, there is no writer of European celebrity at Munich, and the literature of the place is certainly below the level of its intellect. ' How can it be otherwise,' exclaims the Resident, ' restricted as it is by the surveillance of the censorship ?' How *is* it otherwise in Prussia and Austria, where the censorship is incomparably more strict ? Yet such is ever the shallow flippant philosophy of radicalism. Bavaria, in truth, enjoys more liberty in the widest sense than any of the other members of the confederation, for she has an upper house and a lower house, in the last of which all state-matters are publicly discussed, as well as several political journals, in which the debates are reported and freely commented upon. The criminal code of Bavaria was the *chef d'œuvre* of the celebrated Feuerbach, but it is far from giving satisfaction ; his favourite principle, that punishments are efficacious in proportion to their severity, being pushed to an impolitic excess.

Society at Munich is pleasant but wrong, there being a good deal of amusement combined with a good deal of quiet immorality. ' *Se passioner, se battre, se ruiner, enlever, epouser, et divorcer,* is given by Mrs. Jameson, on a Polish count's authority, as the rise, progress, and catastrophe of a Polish amour ; thus making a six-act piece. An amour at Munich may be generally included in two : *se passioner, s'ennuyer—s'ennuyer, se passioner.—*

'Like the waves of the summer, as one dies away, Another as sweet and as shining comes on.'

In this sentimental gallantry the lives of half the women in Munich pass away ; love with them being rather a breeze just ruffling the surface than a tempest wasting the recesses of the heart. Clubs and associations which, in other places, are said (we believe untruly) to be detrimental to society, here confes-

sedly enliven it, as they are constantly giving balls and parties ; a practice which it might be as well for English establishments of the sort to adopt occasionally. A ball or two per annum, at least at the really aristocratic clubs,* would go further towards removing the ladies' objections to them than the most logical series of reflections that could be adduced in their vindication. A *fête* was given a few years since at Munich, which may afford the managers a hint. Each lady's ticket specified the name of a cavalier, who was to present her with a bouquet on entering the ball-room and attend upon her during the day. There were nearly three thousand present, yet such tact was shown in the arrangement, and so well had the respective inclinations of the company been guessed, that, we are credibly informed, only fifty-four ladies were dissatisfied, and only twenty-three reputations deteriorated, of which nineteen belonged to Englishwomen. Most of the fair Bavarians, probably, had little of the sort susceptible of deterioration, or, from long practice, they were more upon their guard against imprudencies, which must be very glaring to injure them in the opinion of their compatriots. Sir James Mackintosh has an entry in his Paris Diary which would exactly suit a Munich one :—' I am told Madame de—— is excluded from society. I really should like to know what *her* offence can be.'

From Munich we pass through Stuttgardt and Augsburg towards Carlsruhe, the capital of the Grand Duchy of Baden ; and it is to be regretted that we have no time to stop upon the way, for at Augsburg is published the celebrated *Allgemeine Zeitung,* supposed to have the largest circulation of any paper in the world, though much inferior to the English *Times* in extent of influence ; and at Stuttgardt reside Menzel, one of the most remarkable writers of modern times, and Dannecker, the Canova or Chantrey of Germany, unless the title be contested by Rauch—not that we mean to say that the styles of these great sculptors are the same, but simply that nearly the same relative rank is held by each amongst his countrymen. Uhland, also, the lyrical poet, is living in the immediate neighbourhood of Stuttgardt, and, to the best of our information, is a member of the Chamber of Deputies at Würtemberg. But we are compelled to pass over his Majesty of Würtemberg's dominions, with the remark, that his subjects enjoy as much liberty as the Diet thinks good for them, and that the women of his capital are amongst the prettiest in Germany.

* We limit our remark, because many of our most flourishing clubs are so composed that, though the members have no objection to reading the papers and eating their chops in the same dining-room, the congregation of their respective woman-kind in a drawing room would not be at all desirable.

And this reminds us of a circumstance illustrative of the King of Bavaria's gallantry, which well deserves to be commemorated. In his chivalrous zeal for the honour of Bavarian beauty, he has founded a gallery for portraits of all the handsome women of all ranks his painters can get to sit to them, and we are assured that numbers have already yielded to the wishes of royalty thus flatteringly expressed, although apprehensions are entertained that their reputations will not fare the better with posterity. They probably encounter the risk in much the same spirit of philosophy in which a beautiful Englishwoman of rank answered the objection of a prudish friend, who begged her not to sit to Sir Thomas Lawrence, because he was apt to paint women with a certain impropriety of expression, a kind of *Sir Peter Lely* look about the eyes. 'And if he does, my dear, what can *that* signify, so long as he makes one look *so* handsome?' Pauline's retort on the subject of her sitting to Canova for her statue is well known. When a lady asked her how she could bear to sit to him in the requisite state of nudity? she replied, ' Oh, I did'nt feel at all cold: there was always a fire in the room.'

Of all the minor states of Germany in which a constitution has been conferred, Baden has shown herself most worthy of one, by the talent displayed in her House of Commons, and the number of useful reforms that have been set on foot. The debates in the *second chamber* (as it is termed) are conducted with a high degree of order and ability, and we have heard extempore speeches there which would do no discredit to a Stanley or a Peel.

The Grand Duke's fiddling, the chief point of attraction at Darmstadt, has ceased; the Brunnen of Nassau have been completely dried up by Sir Francis Head; the fame of Westphalia still rests upon her hams, which cut a much better figure on a table than in a book: Hesse Cassel is too near Prussia to be worth considering apart—and Weimar, since Goethe's death, has dropped into insignificance, and lives only in recollections of the past. Hanover, as our readers are aware, has been undertaken by Mr. Theodore Hook, who promises a complete history of the reigning family, with ample and accurate accounts of the constitution, revenue, agriculture, commerce, manufactures, institutions, manners, customs, habits, &c. &c. of the electorate. In such hands we are quite satisfied to leave it ;—and here for the present the subject of Germany and the Germans may be dropped.

ANSTER'S XENIOLA.*

WE chanced to recollect, as we sat down the other day with this little volume before us, that Mr. Locke's idea of writing an essay on the understanding was suggested by his suspecting that most human mistakes arose from the want of having a fixed and definite meaning attached to words. Now, as we are disposed fully to concur with the learned Mr. Locke on this point, we resolved to institute a strict scrutiny into our own vocabulary; and, accordingly set to work upon our first sentence, intending to go through all to the end; but the very *first word* led us into such a labyrinth of thought, and suggested such a multitude of doubts, reflections and speculations, that we soon found that the inquiry would stretch beyond the limits of our capacity —perhaps of our life. WE; how do we define *we?*—what do we mean when we use this pregnant monosyllable every moment? Alas, we do not understand *ourselves!*—we, who assume so much over others—who convince so many that we understand them better than they do themselves, when we come to look within, are puzzled— confounded. We do not even comprehend the elements of our own constitution, much less our authority, duties, immunities, privileges, and sphere of action. Are *we* the aggregate of many intellects, or the many-sided wholeness of one? Do we come before the public as a criticizing multitude, rendered formidable by our numbers? or, do we derive our title from a delegation of literary authority, and claim for Dignity the respect and the appellation due to numerical force?

Us is an accusative used only by divinity, royalty, and the press. We pass by the first case; but halt at the second. Why is his majesty of England *we?* Why should he be more of a *pluralist* than any one of his subjects? Does "we" mean himself and his privy councillors, himself and his ministers, or does it simply imply that the king himself, in his own proper person, represents a variety of offices, authorities and dignities, sufficient to multiply him out of the reach of the singular number? We incline to the latter interpretation. In fact, the first might occasionally be productive of awkward consequences. How would the Howards, Hamiltons, Percys and Cavendishes, for instance, relish the royal address of "*our* trusty and well-beloved *cousin,*" if *Messrs. Wolfe and Co.* were to step forward and claim relationship on the highest authority? Would it not be at least embarrassing if, in his majesty's endearments towards his royal consort, his ministers were supposed to be sharers? and would not the awkwardness amount to something alarming, if the epithet "*our rightful heir*" were held to imply a *participation of paternity?* No: we cannot take this singular plural as extending itself an inch beyond the royal person, which we look upon as a *corporation-sole,* the collected majesty of Great Britain, the first estate of the realm, the generallissimo of our armies, the fountain of honour, the defender of the faith, that comprehensive ONE, in short, too great to be squeezed into the singular number, too vast to be circumscribed by that laconic particle, *I.*

In like manner *we,* the editor, are *one.* We repudiate contributors—we thrust them all from under our wing— we respect their talents, it is true, and accept their favours with gratitude— we gladly receive them to our pages— to our confidence—but peremptorily exclude them from *ourselves.* We cannot take them within the veil of the unapproachable *we.* They are near, but not of, *us.* We stand alone in the majesty of intellect, receiving the homage of public approbation, without allowing deduction, and ready to stand by the words we have spoken, for good or for evil, without shrinking for a moment behind the vagueness of our *i*-or rather, *we*-dentity.

Let it not be supposed that these observations savour of vanity. While we repel partnership on the one hand, we speak not of ourselves, merely as ourselves, on the other; and herein an editor differs from a king. The metaphysical plural *we,* consists of an editor and a thing edited—a workman and his work—body and spirit—steam-engine and boiler. Apart from our magazine we are simply I—nothing, in short. With it, we are everything. We are twin-born, co-equal and co-eval with it. We are the *Chang* to our literary *Eng;* or, more classically, our importance and authority stand in the same relation to our publication that the Hamadryad does to its oak. The blow that fells the one, dismisses the attendant spirit to the winds.

Having thus examined the first word we had written, and satisfied the shade of Mr. Locke, we think our readers will dispense with the continuance of a scrutiny, which, at the rate hitherto pursued, would carry us but slowly to Dr. Anster. Indeed, some of them may perhaps be inclined to ask what we mean by talking so much about ourselves at all; forgetting that it is always better to leave these matters to the judgment of the writer, who will seldom, as we hope, be found to want just motives for whatever he says. In the first place, *to begin with a digression* has all the charm of novelty; and this alone ought to recommend it to a large portion of the public. But besides, it gives importance to what is to follow, thus to execute an *ad libitum* passage by way of prelude, and usher the reader into the presence of the subject with as many flourishes, &c. as in a marriage settlement he has to struggle through to get at the mysterious blackletter of "𝔗𝔥𝔦𝔰 𝔍𝔫𝔡𝔢𝔫𝔱𝔲𝔯𝔢."

But, after all, there may be a few captious persons who are still dissatisfied with us, and unreasonable enough to long for Xeniola. Now, what if we were to shew that we have all this time *had a design* in our egotism? Yet even so it is. We set, in the *first* instance, about throwing our arms clear of that coil of contributors and others, who cling to our name as close as the snake to Laocoon, in order that, among the rest, we might cast off the *author of Xeniola himself,* and leave ourselves at liberty to praise him as he deserves, without his being considered directly or indirectly to praise himself. Dr. Anster, as our readers very well know, is connected with our pages by frequent communications; and for the commendations which admiration and justice unite in obliging us to lavish on him, we hastened to say, in the very beginning, that he is by no means responsible; and, indeed, even as it is, we feel the necessity of putting our pen under restraint, lest we should be suspected, *by him,* of flattering when we only criticise, and of bestowing that meed of praise as a gift, which is only due in the strictest justice to his literary merits.

We confess we looked with nervousness at the little volume before us, ere we opened it. We feared to have those illusions dispelled which had been thrown around the name of Anster by that most successful effort of industry and imagination, Faustus: we dreaded it as we should dread breaking the seal of a will in which we expected a legacy. However, a few hasty glances were sufficient to reassure us; and we formed almost at once that favourable judgment which a more attentive perusal has only authorised us to confirm. We shall produce passages which rise to sublimity, and melt into the truest pathos; and, although there is some unevenness in the compositions, we have met with nothing certainly below mediocrity; and this is more than can be said for most volumes of miscellaneous poetry published in this or any other country.

As we strung this additional gem on the carcanet of our memory, we could not help reflecting what a choice collection could be made, culled from among the *minor poems* of our countrymen. Casting all the flowers of their care and culture aside, how sweet— how fragrant a garland might be woven out of the mere wild and spontaneous growth of their untasked genius!— Goldsmith, Sheridan, Moore, Wolfe, Maturin, Anster, immediately occur to us, who could each contribute many a wild flower.

But we think it high time to present to our readers the gratification our title promised them, and accordingly we open the volume before us, which takes its name, we suppose, from its comprising productions which have been from time to time offered at the shrine of hospitality or friendship.* The dates subjoined to these would tell—even if the preface did not— that they have been most of them lying by the author for many years; and *two* of them have already ap-

* Xeniola. Poems, including Translations from Schiller and De La Motte Fouqué, by John Anster, L.L.D. Barrister at Law, author of "Faustus, a Dramatic Mystery," from Goethe. Dublin: Milliken and Son. 1837.

* Since this passage was written, we have found a note to Anster's Faustus, (p. 300), in which the meaning and application of the words *Xenia* and *Xeniola* are given. By it we learn that they were used pretty much in the sense our book-makers now affix to the terms "Gifts," and "Presents."

peared in the pages of this Magazine ; but the principal pieces, both as regards length and power of composition, the " Elegy," the " Ode to Fancy," " Reverie." and the translation from De La Motte Fouqué's " Pilgrimage," are new to us, and to these particularly we would direct the attention of our readers.

The first of them is too continuous a stream of melody and sadness to be broken by mutilation—surely the heart that *so young,* (it was written in 1817,) could even then (like Kirke White, at a yet earlier age,) have *looked back* to happiness as the shadow of a substance gone ; and turned forwards sorrowfully to a world from whence had for ever fled the

> " lingering hope,
> That flitted fearfully, like parent bird,
> Fast fluttering o'er its desolated nest —"

surely that heart must have had the soul of Poetry breathed into it with its first organization, and only have been speaking its natural language, when in boyhood it thus poured forth from its lonely height such a torrent of song upon the valley of the shadow of death !—But we leave this touching poem to speak for itself :—

ELEGY.

Oh breathe not—breathe not—sure 'twas something holy—
Earth hath no sounds like these—again it passes
With a wild, low voice, that slowly rolls away,
Leaving a silence not unmusical !—
And now again the wind-harp's frame hath felt
The spirit—like the organ's richest peal—
Rolls the long murmur—and again it comes,
That wild, low, wailing voice.—

These sounds to me
Bear record of strange feelings. It was evening.—
In my bowered window lay this talisman,
That the sighing breezes there might visit it ;—
And I was wont to leave my lonely heart,
Like this soft harp, the play-thing of each impulse,
The sport of every breath. I sate alone
Listening for many minutes— the sounds ceased,
Or, tho' unnoted by the idle ear,
Were mingling with my thoughts—I thought of one,
And she was of the dead—She stood before me,
With sweet sad smile, like the wan moon at midnight,
Smiling in silence on a world at rest.

I rushed away—I mingled with the mirth
Of the noisy many—it is strange, that night,
With a light heart, with light and lively words,
I sported hours away, and yet there came
At times wild feelings—words will not express them—
But it seemed, that a chill eye gazed upon my heart,
That a wan cheek, with sad smile, upbraided me,
I felt that mirth was but a mockery,
Yet I was mirthful.

I lay down to sleep—
I did not sleep—I could not choose but listen,
For o'er the wind-harp's strings the spirit came
With that same sweet low voice. Yes! thou mayest smile,
But I must think, my friend, as then I thought,
That the voice was her's, whose early death I mourned,
That she it was, who breathed those solemn notes,
Which like a spell possessed the soul.—

I lay
Wakeful, the prey of many feverish feelings,
My thoughts were of the dead !—at length I slept,
If it indeed were sleep.—She stood before me
In beauty—the wan smile had passed away—
Her eye was bright—I could not bear its brightness.

" Till now I knew not Death was terrible,
For seldom did I dwell upon the thought,
And if, in some wild moment, fancy shaped
A world of the departed, 'twas a scene
Most calm and cloudless, or, if clouds at times
Stained the blue quiet of the still soft sky,
They did not dim its charm, but suited well
The stillness of the scene, like thoughts that move
Silently o'er the soul, or linger there
Shedding a tender twilight pensiveness !

" This is an idle song !—I cannot tell
What charms were her's who died—I cannot tell
What grief is their's whose spirits weep for her !—
Oh, many were the agonies of prayer,
And many were the mockeries of hope ;
And many a heart, that loved the weak delusion,
Looked forward for the rosy smiles of health,
And many a rosy smile passed o'er that cheek,
Which will not smile again ;—and the soft tinge,
That often flushed across that fading face,
And made the stranger sigh, with friends would wake
A momentary hope ;—even the calm tone,
With which she spoke of death, gave birth to thought
Weak, trembling thoughts, that the lip uttered not.
And when she spoke with those, whom most she mourn'd
To leave, and when thro' clear calm tears the eye
Shone with unwonted light, oh, was there not
In its rich sparkle something, that forbade
The fear of death?—and when, in life's last days,
The same gay spirit, that in happier hours
Had charactered her countenance, still gleamed
On the sunk features—when such playful words,
As once could scatter gladness on all hearts,
Still trembled from the lip, and o'er the souls
Of those who listened shed a deeper gloom—
In hours of such most mournful gaiety,
Oh, was there not even then a lingering hope,
That flitted fearfully, like parent birds,
Fast fluttering o'er their desolated nest ?

" Mourn not for her who died !—she lived as saints
Might pray to live—she died as Christians die ;—
There was no earthward struggle of the heart,
No shuddering terror—no reluctant sigh.
They, who beheld her dying, fear not Death !
Silently—silently the spoiler came,
As sleep steals o'er the senses, unperceived,
And the last thoughts, that soothed the waking soul,
Mingle with our sweet dreams.—Mourn not for her !

" Oh, who art thou, that, with weak words of comfort,
Would'st bid the mourner not to weep ?—would'st win
The cheek of sorrow to a languid smile?
Thou dost not know with what a pious love
Grief dwells upon the dead !—thou dost not know
With what a holy zeal Grief treasures up
All that recalls the past !—when the dim eye
Rolls objectless around, thou dost not know
What forms are floating o'er the mourner's soul !—
Thou dost not know with what a soothing art
Grief, that rejects man's idle consolations,
Makes to itself companionable friends
Of all, that charmed the dead ! her robin still
Seeks at the wonted pane his morning crumbs,
And, surely, not less dear for the low sigh,

93

His visit wakes!—and the tame bird who loved
To follow with gay wing her every step,
Who oft, in playful fits of mimicry,
Echoed her song, is dearer for her sake!—
The wind, that from the hawthorn's dewy blossoms
Brings fragrance, breathes of her!—the moral lay,
That last she loved to hear, with deeper charm
Speaks to the spirit now!—even these low notes,
Breathed o'er her grave, will sink into the soul,
A pensive song that Memory will love
In pensive moments.

        " Mourners, is there not
An angel, that illumes the house of mourning?
The Spirit of the Dead—a holy image,
Shrined in the soul—for ever beautiful,
Undimmed with earth—its tears—its weaknesses—
And changeless, as within the exile's heart
The picture of his country ;—*there* no clouds
Darken the hills—no tempest sweeps the vale,—
And the loved forms, he never more must meet,
Are with him in the vision, fair, as when,
Long years ago, they clasped his hands at parting !

This poem is a fair specimen of Dr. Anster's powers, and of the character of the volume ; and yet we confess we think he is even more happy in his descriptive poetry ; and two or three passages we have met with, will probably remind the reader of some of Milton's exquisite descriptions of nature in his minor poems. Take the following specimens :—

" —At Spring's return the earth is glad.
    And yet to me, at this lone hour,
The wood-dove's note from yonder natural bower,
    Though winning sweet is sad ;—
Calmly the cool wind heaves
    The elm's broad boughs, whose shadows seem
    Like some deep vault below the stream .
—The melancholy beech still grieves,
    As in the scattering gale are shed
Her red and wrinkled leaves :—
And, from the yew, by yon forgotten grave,
Hark ! the lone robin mourning o'er the dead."—pp. 69, 70.

" —See where. most mild, most sad,
    The Goddess, on her mountain throne
Of rocks, with many-coloured lichens clad,
    Is soothed by gurgling waters near,
    Or song of sky-lark wild and clear,
    Or music's mellow tone :
The scarce-heard hum of distant strife
    Breaks not the consecrated rest,
    The sabbath quiet of that breast,
Unruffled by the woes, above the mirth of life :
    Awful thoughts for ever roll,
    Shadowing the silent soul,
    Like the twilight tall rocks throw
    Far into the vale below :—
Here Genius, in fantastic trance,
    Enjoys his wildest reverie,
    Or pores with serious eye
Upon some old romance,
    Till all the pomp of chivalry,
    The vizor quaint of armed knight,
    And stately dame, and tournay bright,
Are present to his glance."—pp. 70, 71.

And the following

SONNET.

" If I might choose, where my tired limbs shall lie
    When my task here is done, the Oak's green crest
    Shall rise above my grave—a little mound
Raised in some cheerful village cemetery—
And I could wish, that, with unceasing sound
    A lonely mountain rill was murmuring by—
    In music—through the long soft twilight hours ;—
And let the hand of her whom I love best,
Plant round the bright green grave those fragrant flowers,
    In whose deep bells the wild-bee loves to rest—
And should the robin, from some neighbouring tree,
    Pour his enchanted song—oh, softly tread,
    For sure, if aught of earth can soothe the dead,
He still must love that pensive melody !"

But the resemblance to Milton is still more striking in a passage which we extract from the " Ode to Fancy :" a poem, which, with a little more of vigour, would bid fair to rival the best lyrics in our language. It is remarkable for its originality of thought, and musical flow :—

" But chiefly on the Poet's mind
    Thine influence is shed,
His eye expatiates unconfined
Upon thy vast expanse,
He views with kindling glance
    Thy peopled scenes before him spread !
Then, Fancy, bid my page to gleam
With some faint colouring from thy beam;
To thee the Poet's hopes belong,
Bid then thy light illume my song!
I call thee by thy Collins' rage,
By thy Warton's Gothic page,
By thy Spenser's faerie slumbers,
By thy Shakspeare's witching numbers;—
Or, Spirit, if with partial ear,
A later name thou lovest to hear,
Then be the spell thy Southey's lay ;—
Shed, Fancy, shed thy solemn ray !
Oh, move me far from Mirth's vain folly,
To the haunts of Melancholy,

Where echoes, at the close of day,
Oft talk of empires passed away ;—
Come, like the maid that loves to weep
On lone Parnassus' misty steep,
When, in the silent time of night,
She hovers o'er the Poet's sleep,
And mingles with his slumbers deep
    Dreams of indefinite delight,
    That float with morning's gale along,
    Or live but in the breath of song !
—Then shall I view the air around,
    Haunted by many a spectral form,
Shall hear the boding Spirit sound,
    Amid the howlings of the storm :
Shall tremble at the night-bird's cry,
Dear prophetess of destiny ;
And, as the meteor's beams appal,
Behold the coming funeral,
Or view the ancient chieftain's lance
With momentary lustre glance,
As sitting in his cloudy car
He thinks upon his days of war !"
             —pp. 66, 67.

The Allegory, " Mirth and Grief," we give entire :—

MIRTH AND GRIEF.

AN ALLEGORY.

" In vain—ah me !—in vain, with murmured charm
Of love-inwoven sounds, would I recall
The long-forgotten art—in vain implore
At noon the colouring of the morning heavens !—
Glad WORDS, that once as with a robe of light
Would meet the coming FANCIES, where are they ?
And where, oh where are they, the angel guests ?
Why have they gone, or wherefore did they come ?
And yet, methinks, they are not far remote,
But that mine eye is dim and sees them not ,—
But that mine heart is dead and does not feel ;—
Where is the music of the spirit gone ?
Where now the heart that never knew a care—

That saw, in all things round, Love, only Love?
—Gone with the hues of morning—with the hopes
Of boyhood—with the glories of the spring;—
Gone with the dead—the unreturning dead!

" In vain—in vain—the Spirit will not come!
Yet I have watched each stirring of the heart,
Till Sorrow, self-amused, smiles playfully,
Till Fancies vague seem gifted with strange life,
Surprise the ear with voices of their own,
And shine distinct, and fair, and shadowless,
Self-radiant, on a self-illumined stage,
Pure Forms, whose Being is the magic light
In which they move—all beauty! How it hangs
Enamoured round them! In what tender folds
The thin veil, flowing with the sportive breeze
Of dallying thought, returns, and fondly stirs
The amber ringlets o'er each little brow,
Fans softly the blue veins—and lingering lies
Trembling and happy on the kindred cheek!

" In vain—in vain! They are not what they were!
The lights are dim,—the pageant fades away,
Lost on the disenchanted heart and eye;
Cold, icy cold, they glimmer—idle play
With languid feelings—feeble are the hues,
And faint the failing hand, that fears to trace
Forms seldom seen—seen only in still hours,
When dreams are passing into dream-like thought,
And, for a little moment, sleep the cares
That vex with pain, and each day grieve and wound
The God within, disquieting man's heart!

" Lady, forgive these broken images,—
Forgive the wiles of Grief, that fain would smile,
And so she plays with her dead brother's toys,
The cheerful boy who died in infancy;
Or wilt thou smile with me, and gaze with me
— As in the peaceful twilight of a dream
That mingles death and life,—on Mirth and Grief?

" One happy human bosom was their home,
And Mirth, with rosy lips and bold bright eyes,
That rolled, and laughed, and knew not where to rest,
Kissed off the tears from his pale sister's face;
'Twas sweet to see her smiling playfully,
While he, a masquer blythe, in tragic weeds
Robed his light limbs, and hid his laughing face,
And moved with pensive mien and solemn pomp
Of measured gesture;—'twas a part played well,
Yet half betrayed by the capricious voice,
That could not long uphold the lofty tone;
And by the glances of the conscious eye,
Where tell-tale smiles would slily still peep out;
While, half deluded by his own quaint humour,
And vain withal, no doubt, the lively elf
Looked round for praise;—but then he felt the tear
Come sudden to disturb the quivering eye,
And fall in fire upon the burning cheek!
*   *   *   *   *
Lady, forgive these broken images—
That, like the dew-drops from a shaken flower,
Fall cold, and shine, and are for ever lost,
Seen only in the breeze that scatters them."

We now approach the principal piece
in the collection, a poem in four parts,
entitled " Reverie." The name will
sufficiently shew the reader that he cannot expect to meet with such a plan or
argument, as would enable us to give an
outline, however faint, of its contents.
There is, however, sufficient connexion
to cause a great loss of effect in extracting passages for the purposes of
our review.

The year 1815 stirred the soul of
every one who was blessed—or *cursed*—
with an ardent and enthu-ia-tic temperament. It teemed with great events.
The age of chivalry seemed to rise
again from the mists of the middle
ages, realizing deeds of heroism before
considered fabulous, and begetting that
romantic sympathy, which such deeds
alone can call forth in the human
breast. It was at such a time that we
might have expected POETRY to have
sprung spontaneously from the most
barren soil, and to have shot up to gigantic growth in that of genius. But
how little can we calculate on such
things! The deeds of that year, if
they were to derive their immortality
from verse alone, might share the fate
of the heroes who lived before Agamemnon. Not a strain rose from the
hundred harps set in vibration, which
we would wish the most distant echo
to restore from oblivion for a moment,
if we except, perhaps, the few stanzas
in Childe Harold, relating to Water-
loo, which make, however, but a short
episode in that great poem, and are
quite eclipsed behind the glory of the
next cantos.

Here, however, more than twenty
years after, we have, turned up to our
view by the ploughshare of circumstances, the strong and vigorous imaginings of a young man of genius,
worked upon by those stirring events
as they struck their rays, keen and direct, into his soul at the time. There
is the freshness of the moment evident
upon them. No after-thought could
have kindled the strong and clear descriptions we meet with. " It is difficult," says Paley, "to resuscitate surprise, when familiarity has once laid
the feeling asleep." We think it is
impossible, as far, at least, as poetry is
concerned. The Iris in the skies is
only bright after *one* reflection.

The *spirit of the Poet's dream*—an
"angelic voice and vision"—after beck-
oning him along through a few pages
of sweet poetry, at last conducts him

" To that fatal field,
Where moonlight gleams on many a broken helm,
On many a shieldless warrior, o'er whose limbs
The trembling hand of love had linked the mail,
Alas in vain?—the supple limbs of youth,
And manhood's sinewy strength, and rigid age,
Together lie:—the boy, whose hands with blood
Where never stained before, upon whose lip
The mother's kiss was ominously pressed;—
The man, alive to every tenderest thought,
Who cherished every fire-side charity;—
And he, who, bending with the weight of years,
Felt the sword heavy in his training hand,
Who had outlived the social sympathies
That link us to our kind—here, side by side,
Sleep silent; he, who shrunk at every sound,
Who throbbed in terror for a worthless life,
Lies like a brother with the hopeless man,
Who desperately dared in scorn of death:—
He, who has wont to calculate each chance,
To measure out each probability,
Behold him now extended on the earth,
Near that robuster frame, whose tenant soul
Flashed rapid in the energetic eye,
Whose thoughts were scarce imagined, ere they sprang
Forth-shaped in instant action:—here lies one,
Whose soul was vexed by Passion's every gust,
And like the light leaf trembled:—gaze again,
Look on the mutilated hand, that still
Clings to the sword unconscious;—milder man
Than he, whose mutilated hand lies there,
Breathes not;—each passion that rebelled was hushed;
So placid was his brow, so mild his eye,
It seemed no power could break the quiet there," &c.—p. 82.

Here is a power of contrast displayed, such as we rarely meet with in these days of blending and mellowing. The picture is as like our usual modern attempts, as one of Rembrandt's *trowelled effects* is to the wishy-washy weaknesses of the water-colour exhibition. It is in such passages as these that Dr. Anster gives promise of great things. We venture to recommend his giving up the phantom of that "*ideal*" which has led Lytton Bulwer so many a weary chase, as clowns pursue a jack-o'-lanthorn, or children a butterfly, and sticking to such real, tangible, vivid *nature* as here thrills us into wholesome and healthy admiration. Themes such as these, and the beautiful modifications of character brought before us in the dialogue, "Matilda," form fitting subjects for the labours of the poet. The Germans go beyond this, and, we think, in so doing exceed their province and powers. We know not how far Dr. Anster may have been infected with this German influenza, which, now that "the Rovers" has become obsolete, has become again so prevalent in these islands; but we would willingly warn him, if we could do so without offending him, of the danger of allowing the success of his Faustus, translated as it is from professedly the most German production of a German author, to tinge his *home style*, or influence his *home feelings*. We, the English, deal more in the tangible,

the intelligible, the *real*. The German, on the contrary, delights in prancing his Pegasus up and down the line of light and darkness, sometimes wholly lost in metaphysics, and then again emerging for a moment at this side of common sense and reason. We have not yet learned that in poetic painting any of the shadows should be perfectly opake. We still continue to follow Titian in his maxim, that we ought to be able to see through even the darkest parts of the picture; and the "*nuvola che passa*" should always transmit some portion at least of the sun's rays.

We do not wish these observations to be considered as any thing more than a friendly caution to Dr. Anster, called forth by our admiration of the *startling reality* of the scene described in our extract.

From the "Reverie" we must give another remarkable passage, in which the idea is carried throughout in a masterly manner, and of which the *versification* is also peculiarly strong and harmonious; and this is a branch of composition for attention to which the poet seldom gets credit in these days, although many of the classical authors, Pope and Roscommon among the number, prided themselves almost as much upon their success in the structure of their verse as in the happiness of their thoughts and expressions.

" Time was—in dateless years—when spectral eve
Sent shadowy accusers from dark realms;
And at calm dead of night, tyrants, appalled,
Started and shrieked, lashed by avenging dreams;
And when the sunlight came, the joyous sun
Was, to the sickly and distracted sense,
The haunt of demons, and his living light
Seemed the hot blazes of the penal fire;
'Twas said that Furies o'er the bed of sleep
Watched with red eye, and, from the throbbing brow
Drank with delight the dew that agony
Forced forth;—but this, it seems, is fable all!—
Hath not Philosophy disproved a God?
Ere yet the chymist called the bolt from heaven,
We spoke of Spirits governing its beam,—
Ere yet he learned to part and analyse,
The rock, we deemed some more than human power
Had planted it in ocean,—till he stirred
The muscles of the dead with mimic breath,
And called the cold convulsion life, we deemed
That Heaven alone could bid the dry bones shake!
—But joy to Man! progressive centuries
Have erred, and Wisdom now at length appears—
And, lo! the Goddess! not with brow austere,
Features that tell of silent toil, and locks
Laurelled, as erst in the Athenian Schools;—
Nor yet with garment symbolled o'er with stars,

And signs, and talismans, as in the halls
Of parent Egypt; not with pensive eye,
And dim, as though 't were wearied from its watch
Through the long night, what time, to shepherd-tribes
Of fair Chaldæa, she had imaged forth
The host of Heaven, and mapped their mazy march," &c.—pp. 96, 97.

These are good lines. The versification, too, is easily perceived, even by the unpractised ear, to be vigorous and correct; and its harmony is brought out in still more striking relief from its contrast with the false *masonry*, as Shenstone would call it, of the six following lines, each of which begins with *three short syllables*.

" While the bright dew on her tiara'd brow,
And the cold moonlight on her pallid face,
And the loose wandering of her heavy hair,
As the breeze lifted the restraining bands,
And the slow motion of the graceful stole,
When with her jewelled wand she traced the line," &c.—p. 97.

As we advance in the fourth part of the "Reverie," we approach the climax of what is excellent in Xeniola. The poet rises above himself; and at last bursts into an apostrophe to the soul of his inspiration so noble, so dignified, so sublime, that we know of no modern effort which breathes so wholly the divine *afflatus*, if we except, perhaps, that glorious address to Ocean in Childe Harold—"the mirror,"

" ——Where the Almighty's form
Glasses itself in tempests."

We beg the attention of our readers to the lines we have marked in italics, and challenge the living poets of our country to match them if they are able,

" Spirit of Heaven, undying Poetry,
Effluence divine! for by too high a name
I cannot call thee,—ere the ocean rolled
Round earth, *ere yet the dewy light serene
Streamed from the silent fountains of the East,
To fill the urns of morning*, thou didst breathe,
And, musing near the secret seat of God,
Wert throned o'er Angels! thou alone could'st look
On the Eternal Glory; till thy voice
Was heard amid the halls of heaven, no breath
Disturbed the awful silence! Cherubim
Gazed on thy winning looks, and hung in trance
Of wonder, when thy lonely warblings came,
Sweet as all instruments, that after-art
Of angel or of man hath fashioned forth.
—Spirit of Heaven, didst thou not company
The great Creator?—thou didst see the sun
Rise like a giant from the chambering wave,
And, when he sank behind the new-formed hills,
Shrined in a purple cloud, wert thou not there,
Smiling in gladness from some shadowy knoll
Of larch, or graceful cedar, and at times
Viewing the stream that wound below in light,
And shewed upon its breast the imaged heaven,
And all those shades, which men in after-days
Liken to trees, and barks, and battlements,
And all seemed good to thee?—wert thou not near,
When first the starting sod awoke to life,
And Man arose in grandeur?—Thou didst weep
His fall from Eden, and in saddest hour
Thou wert not absent."
  *   *   *   *
" Spirit of Heaven, thy first best song on earth
Was Gratitude! Thy first best gift to man
The Charities—Love, in whose full eye gleams
The April-tear;—all dear Domestic Joys,
That sweetly smile in the secluded bowers

Of Innocence ! Thy presence hath illumed
The Temple ! With the Prophets Thou hast walked,
Iuspiring !—oh ! how seldom hast thou found
A worthy residence !—the world receives
Thy holiest emanations with cold heart ;
The bosom, where, as in a sanctuary,
Thy altar shines, with its own grossness dims
The blaze, or, faint with the ' excess of light,'
Thy votary sinks, and in a long repose
Would rest the wearied soul," &c.

―――――

" I may not venture on such theme : I feel
My many weaknesses ! a little while
Repose, my Harp, in silence ! We have waked
Numbers too lofty. Rest we here awhile !"—pp. 103-105.

We would gladly conclude our notice of this interesting volume here, where our approbation has warmed into praise, in proportion as our author's style has towered into sublimity ; but we feel it our duty as reviewers to point the reader's attention to some translations which appear in the volume. They are from German authors ; and in some we are given no clue to the original, so that criticism must be silent. The stanzas of S. E. Wilhelmina Von Sassen, are too different from those by Matthisson with the same refrain, to please us.

" Ich denke dein,
Wenn durch den Hain

Die Nachtigallen
Accorde Schallen,
Wenn denkst du mein !" &c.

The translation from De la Motte Fouqué is, as a piece of English poetry, even and good. We have had no opportunity of examining its merits as a translation ; however, we will take Faust as a pledge for the author's general faithfulness to his original. Few poems have ever been so literal as his Faustus.

Desultory poetic taste is so happily adumbrated in the following lines, extracted from a scene in Fouqué's drama, that we step out of our province as reviewers of the translation to quote the passage for the moral it conveys :—

" I know the land of the evening sun—
Of the giant oak—of the cloud and storm—
Whose lakes are roofed with ice.
Where the morning rises chill.
And the night, from dreary wing,
Showers hoar-frost on the shrinking flowers ;
And warriors, clad in arms, are there
Loud-sounding, splendid, heavy arms of steel ;
Swords in their hands, unlike the scimitar ;
The blade unbent, and double-edged, cuts straight
Into the faces of the enemy ;
From the heavy-visored helm
A cloud of many-coloured plumes
Streams in the playful breeze.
And my friends wished that I should be a soldier,
Already had I learned to bend
The war-horse to by will ;
Already with an active arm,
Could sway the warrior's sword ;
But, as I rested after my first battle.
There came, with friendly words, a gray old man.
He sate beside me. From his lips streamed forth
A wondrous tale. Unceasingly it streamed ;
Holding enchanted my surrendered soul,
'Till the sweet stars came gemming the blue sky.
And then he rose, but still the tale continued ;
And on we wandered, and the narrative
Was still unfinished, and we reached the shore ;
I following him, unable to resist
The magic of his voice !
Rapidly, rapidly he went,
Rapidly, rapidly I followed him ;
I threw away the shield that burthened me,
I threw away from me the encumbering sword,
And we embarked, and still the tale continued,
All day ! all night ! The moon did wax and wane,

I cannot tell how many times, while he
Was busy with his story ; while my soul
Lived on its magic ; and I felt no want
Of food, or drink, or sleep. At last we came
Here to Hormisdas, the magician's garden :
And when we reached this silver rivulet,
The tale was ended—the old man was vanished.
And now, for iron arms I wear
The soft silk, light and delicate,
And feel no wounds but those of Love !"—pp. 161-163.

⁕   ⁕   ⁕   ⁕

We almost regret that Dr. Anster allowed the poem " On the death of the Princess Charlotte," to form a part of the present collection. It is a prize poem in blank verse. Prize-poems are seldom highly prized beyond the walls where they have been read ; besides, the subject is one which, in our opinion, would be best treated in a more compressed and condensed form ; nevertheless there are, as the reader will observe, passages of considerable power scattered throughout the composition. We cannot help regretting that the loss of the child is not brought forward more prominently. What admirable use has Milton made of the infant, where in a nearly similar case, he elegizes the Marchioness of Winchester !

" So have I seen some tender slip,
Sav'd with care from winter's nip,
The pride of her carnation train,
Pluck'd up by some unheedy swain,
Who only thought to crop the flower,
New shot up from vernal shower."

" The Five Oaks of Dallwitz" is translated with freedom and grace, and partakes, even in its transfusion, of the characteristic bold romance of Körner's muse. We are not quite satisfied, however, with the expression—

" Bright records of a better day,"

as applied to the oaks ; nor is there any authority for the epithet in the original line—

" Alte Zeiten alte treue Zeugen."

Bright is an adjective properly applicable neither to oaks nor records, as its substantive. We fancy that in using this word the author intended to convey the clearness of the testimony ; but it is done awkwardly, at least, if not incorrectly.

As we are in a carping mood, we would here give expression to our wish that the book before us had been shorter by two pages. We could gladly have continued to recline under the peaceful shade of the " Five Oaks," without having our reverie interrupted by the howling and hooting of the animals let loose upon us in the " Nursery Rhymes," which immediately follow. We much fear that whatever custom may have sanctioned in the land of Goethe and Retsch, as applicable to the education or amusement of the wunder-kinder of the fatherland, our " march of intellect" nurseries would repel with phrenologic horror such primitive monstrosities as these. They teem with horrors such as

would be refused admittance into any of those duodecimos, in which, under the name of " libraries," are comprised all legitimate knowledge for youth ; and as they would be thus legally excluded from the region of governesses and go-carts above, so they would scarcely gain a welcome in the more adult and less castigated collection below. Seriously, the lines are unfit for children, and thus lose their principal claim upon our notice.

With such objections, which, slight as they are, are all we can make, we take our leave of Dr. Anster's volume. We thought it our duty both to him and to the public, to speak sincerely, both in praise and blame. Our commendations are heart-felt, and our criticism, even where it appears condemnatory, is kindly meant, the author may be assured. We hail with gratitude the gift of a little work like this to our studies and boudoirs, filled as they generally are with the outpourings of the London press. In the language we have already used, (see our last number,) we are beginning "to collect our scattered forces," and to concentrate here a literature and a communicating medium of our own. Could we but ensure such contributions as these, we might look to vying with the " modern Athens" at no very distant period. It should be the object of the thinking portion of the public, the gentry, the aristocracy, the talent of the land, to confirm and strengthen what has begun under such happy auspices. Let them be assured, that the domestication of intellect will tend more than they are aware to unite us to our fellow-countrymen at the other side of the channel, and to render those fellow-countrymen desirous of more intimate union with us. It will tend in no small degree, we are confident, to smooth the turbulence of faction, thus to cast taste and refinement like oil upon the waters. We have a natural jealousy of receiving our intellectual aliment from hands not native. We seize with avidity and pride what we know to be indigenous. Let us hope that the patriotic example of Dr. Anster will be followed by all Irish aspirants to literary fame ; and that Xeniola will but be one of the earliest of a series of popular productions, emanating from the head and heart of our countrymen, and given publicity through the Irish press.

13. ECLECTIC REVIEW, 3rd ser. 65 (1837), 396-409. M/H No. 3401.

No. I.

Art. VII. *Menzel on German Literature. Die deutsche Literatur. Von Wolfgang Menzel. 1836. Stuttgart.*

IN the following series of articles, we propose to give a more
copious and connected view of German literature than any
which, so far as we are aware, has yet been laid before the English
reader. In accomplishing this object we propose, simply, to give
an extensive analysis (accompanied with very copious citations*
of the work of an eminent German writer. This, we apprehend,
will be far better than indulging in any lucubrations of our own;
since the views of a native must necessarily be far more accurate
and profound than those of a foreigner. It is true, indeed, that
a writer is apt to form an exaggerated estimate of the merits of
his own national literature; still his errors are not so serious, or so
difficult of correction, as those of one to whom that literature
is foreign. In the one case, we have only prejudice to contend
against; in the other, we have prejudice and ignorance too; not
to mention those early associations and habits of mind which
render it absolutely impossible to do full justice to modes of
thought and forms of literature to which we are unaccustomed. Witness the recent work of Chateaubriand on English
Literature, in which, by the bye, the author candidly admits
the truth of what we have just said. An English writer of any
thing like the same talents could by no possibility have fallen into
such errors, or delivered such absurd judgments as those which
disfigure this work.

Happily the subject of German literature has been treated by
Wolfgang Menzel in a manner which leaves little to be desired. The
work cannot fail to be more acceptable to the English public, when
we state that its author is almost entirely exempt from the prevailing
faults of many celebrated writers of his nation. With the best
and highest qualities of the German mind, he possesses none of
its defects. First, he is entirely free from diffuseness and prolixity;
his work is of moderate compass, compressing into two volumes
about as much as many German writers would have got into fifty.
Secondly, he is no mystic; whatever he says is intelligible; and
even where you dissent from his opinions, you cannot at least pretend that you do not understand him. Thirdly, he is by no means
given to useless and transcendental speculations; on the contrary,
he is thoroughly practical. He has seen much of life, and has
turned his knowledge to account. Indeed one great object of his
work is to recal the Germans from the exclusive study of *books*, to
a healthful contemplation of nature, and to infuse into their
literature more of the spirit of real life.—So much do these
qualities distinguish him from the generality of his contemporaries,
that they say of him (whether in the way of praise or censure we
cannot pretend to say), " er schreibt wie ein Britte," " he writes
like an Englishman."

While characterised throughout by a spirit of most extensive
research, the work is any thing but a mass of undigested compilation, or a tissue of petty details. Menzel is no mere collector of
materials; his materials have evidently been subjected to the examination of a mind of great compass and power; the whole work,
indeed, is imbued with a philosophical spirit which renders the
driest details interesting, and enables the author to gather up the
multifarious parts of his most extensive and otherwise intractable
subject under a few well-arranged and thoroughly digested heads.
To the above excellent qualities we must add a very active and
beautiful imagination, great wit and powers of sarcasm, and a style
in which all these splendid endowments of intellect need not be
ashamed to embody their conceptions. In the singular conjunction
Menzel's mind exhibits, of many of the highest qualities of the philosophical and poetic genius;—in the power of seizing the principal
points of a subject; of engrafting profound and original reflections on apparently unimportant facts, and of animating the dullest
and most uninteresting details with beautiful illustrations, our author
often strongly reminds us of our own BURKE. And what higher
praise could we bestow upon him?

Before proceeding to give any further account of his work on
" German Literature," we shall extract some few particulars of
his history from the short account given of him in the supplement
to the Conversation's Lexicon.*

---

* These citations we are enabled to give from a MS. translation of the
whole work, which is now in course of preparation for the press, and will
appear after the completion of this series of articles.—EDITOR.

* By the way, nothing can better exemplify the literary activity of the
German people, and the spirit of boundless and insatiable research which
animates them, than the supplement to this work. It contains an account
of living authors, not only of Germany, but of all other nations; nay, lives
of all living men, who have in any way rendered themselves notorious. Thus
in the number from which we extract this brief account of Menzel, we
have biographical articles on the following, some of whom have died
since this part was published (1830); on M'Adam, of " road-making" celebrity; M'Culloch, Mackenzie (Sir Alexander, and Sir George), Sir John
Malcolm, Malthus, Lord Melbourne (then Home Secretary), Lord Melville,
James Montgomery, Robert Montgomery, Lord Mulgrave, Sir George Murray,
Murray the bookseller, and Henry Neele. There is also a long article on
Missions, in which Mr. Ellis, his labours and his writings, receive frequent and
honorable mention.

Considering the difficulties under which this portion of the 'Conversation's Lexicon' must have been conducted, especially of obtaining authentic
information, it might naturally be expected that some ludicrous errors would
here and there present themselves. And such we accordingly find. Thus

"Wolfgang Menzel was born at Waldenburgh, in Silesia, J... 21st, 1798. He lost his father (who was a surgeon) when very young; lived with his mother upon a country estate; was sent in 1814, to Elizabeth School, Breslau, where he devoted himself zealously to the studies of the Gymnasium. From 1818, to 1820, he studied philosophy at Jena and Boun. In 1820, he went to Switzerland, and became first master in the public school at Aarau. His first production was his " Streckverse,"* which contained many original views of life and art, and was full of poetry and good sense. This work excited general attention, and acquired for Menzel the warm friendship (amongst others) of Jean Paul In the following year he published his " Europaischen Blatter,"† in which he commenced his relentless war of extermination upon the vain fashion which prevailed in our poetry, as well as upon the much-lauded *nullities* in our literature generally; at the same time, however, by his attack upon Göthe, and especially upon the *School* of Göthe, he placed himself in direct hostility, not merely with the thorough-going, but even with the more moderate admirers of that poet. Under his banner were gathered the exclusive admirers of Schiller; hitherto scattered. At all times superior in South Germany in point of numbers, but hitherto repressed by the Schlegel School, they had been for the most part silent; they now hailed with joy this unexpected reaction in their favour. About the same time appeared at Zurich, the first volume of Menzel's history of the Germans. It was completed in 1827, in three volumes, and on its completion, Menzel went to Heidelburg .... On occasion of the controversies between Voss and Creuzer, he wrote a little piece, entitled " Voss und die Symbolik,"‡ by which he drew down upon himself the deadly hatred of that scholar and his partizans, without having committed himself to the opposite party. In 1825, Menzel removed to Stuttgart, where he soon after settled as a citizen: connected himself with Cotta, and married a lady of Wurtemburg, of the family of the celebrated philosopher, George Bernhard Bilfinger. He now undertook the " Litteraturblatt," from the superintendence of which Muller had retired; at first, however, not under his own name, in order that he might make himself thoroughly acquainted with so difficult a business. His work on German literature, first published in two volumes at Stuttgart, in 1828, affords a

_____

for example, Mr. *Robert* Montgomery (of whom by the way we are told what we certainly never knew before, that he is in genius at least as Mr. James Montgomery, " ein geistesverwandter von James Montgomery," is represented as the editor of Tyerman and Bennett's Missionary Travels)

* Heidellburg, 1823.
† Zurich.
‡ Stuttgart, 1825.

brilliant demonstration of the original and universal spirit of the author. ... The book was received by the German public with the greatest attention, and laid the foundation of Menzel's celebrity in foreign countries, especially in France. The polemical part of it, in which he further developed the views to which he had already given utterance, called forth vehement attacks from many quarters. Meanwhile Menzel perseveringly pursued his course, and by a systematic re-construction of the ' Litteraturblatt' (of which, from January 1829, he became the avowed editor) obtained a position from which he could disseminate his views, and began regularly to take the field as A LITERARY POWER. Conflict is his element, and he prosecutes it without respect to the fame or number of his adversaries, or of endlessly multiplying hostilities; and of this mortal enemy of the whole literary aristocracy, might be said what Livy says of the champion of the political democracy of Rome, the elder Cato,—' Simultates nimio plures et exercuerunt eum, et ipse exercuit eas. Nec facile dixeris, utrum magis presserit eum nobilitas, an ille agitaverit nobilitatem.' At the same time, he has also acquired many and warm friends; and with Tieck especially,—to whose great poetic fame in all its compass, he has done ample honor—he has formed a near and most cordial intimacy." The account then proceeds to mention two or three other publications of which Menzel is the author. Speaking of his ' Travels in Austria,' the writer declares that it is admitted by Austrians themselves to furnish the truest and most striking account of their national character and literature.

The whole work is divided into four parts; the first treats of the Mass of Literature, German Nationality, the Influence of School Learning, the Influence of Foreign Literature, the Trade of Literature; Religion and Philosophy. Some of these topics will require but scanty notice. The introductory chapter, however, entitled the Mass of Literature, is so important as giving a general view of the whole subject, that we shall devote the present article entirely to it.

The following is the introduction. It is a most vivid and impressive account of the literary activity of the Germans—the only species of activity, according to Menzel, which they possess.

"The Germans do little; but they write so much the more. When a citizen of some future age looks back upon the present epoch of German history, he will meet with more books than men. He may travel on through successive years as through so many repositories. He will say, we have slept, and our dreams were books. We have become a nation of writers, and for the double eagle in our armorial bearings might substitute a goose. With us the quill is both governor and servant, workman and paymaster, fighter and feeder, blessing and curse. We leave their sky to the Italians, their saints to the Spaniards, their ex-

99

ploits to the French, their money-bags to the English, and sit ourselves down to our books. Our meditative Germans love to cogitate and muse; and for writing, can always find time. They invented the art of printing: and they now work at the great machine without ceasing. The learning of the schools, the hankering after everything foreign, the power of fashion, and finally, the profits of the book-trade, have done all the rest: and thus is reared that immeasurable pile of books which is still increasing every day, until we stand astonished at this portentous phenomenon,—this new wonder of the world,—the Cyclopean walls whose builder is the mind.

"On a moderate computation there are ten millions of volumes published every year in Germany.* As each half-yearly catalogue of Leipzig fair enumerates upwards of a thousand German authors, we may assume that there are living in Germany at this present moment about fifty thousand men who have written one book or more. Should their numbers increase according to the present ratio of progression, a catalogue of all the ancient and modern authors of Germany might one day be prepared, outnumbering in names a catalogue of all the readers then alive.

"The effects of this literary activity perpetually obtrude themselves, as it were, upon us. Wherever we turn we catch a glimpse of books and readers. The smallest town has its reading-room; the poorest honoratior his little library. Whatever we may hold in one hand, a book is always sure to be in the other. From the government of a country down to the rocking of a cradle, everything has become a science, and must be studied. Literature is the universal dispensary for the nation; and though the whole empire is continually growing worse the more physic it takes, yet the physic, instead of diminishing, on that very account only increases. Books are the universal remedy. Whatever one is at a loss for, it is supplied in a book. The physician copies his prescription, the judge his sentence, the clergyman his sermon, the teacher (like the learner) his lesson, out of books. Our dear young folks, especially, would be quite ruined without books. A child and a book are things which always appear to us together.

"The *cacoëthes scribendi* is the universal distemper of the Germans, which extends its sway even beyond the bounds of literature, and in the business of public offices chains down a considerable part of the population to the writing-desk. Writers, wherever one looks! and yet these writers merely contribute by what they cost the public, to impoverish the land,—that the paper-mills may suffer no deficiency in the article of rags. But let us consider the sedentary mode of life, to which so many thousands

be sacrificed. Had it not become a subject of public observation long before Tissot * dedicated to it his humane compassion and medical counsel. Does not the noble Gellert, (destroyed by his pen,) offer us, upon the horse which Frederic in irony allotted him, an imperishable image of those poor galley-slaves, chained down to the desk ?—an image which in truth is much less agreeable than that of a Greek philosopher, who, under the shade of palms and laurels, was more occupied in thinking and speaking, than in writing.

"There is nothing of any sort of interest which is not made in Germany the subject of a book. Whatever happens, the most important consequence of it is that some one writes about it; nay, many things seem to happen for the sole purpose of being written about. For the most part, however, things in Germany are *written*, and not *acted*. Our activity is indeed, *par excellence*, to write. This is no infelicity, where the sage in writing a volume effects as much and often more than the general who wins a victory. But when ten thousand blockheads choose also to write books, that is just as bad as if every common soldier chose to be a general.

"We imbibe all our early education for the sole purpose of instantly re-consigning it to paper. We pay for the books which we read by those which we write. There are hundreds of thousands who learn only for the sake of teaching again; whose whole existence is modelled upon one or two books; who pass from the scholar's form to the professor's chair without one glance upon the green earth around them. With that by which they have themselves been tortured they torture others in their turn: priests of corruption in the midst of dried-up mummies, they transmit the old poison as the vestals did the sacred fire.

"Every young genius seems to have been born only to betake himself forthwith to paper. We have hardly more country people than writers. The path of fame, which has in Germany become somewhat tedious to warriors and statesmen, and to the artist is entirely beset with thorns, stands alluringly open only to the author. In Germany your man of talent becomes an author as commonly as in England and France he becomes a statesman. If he be unfit for business, at least he can write. . . . ."

This is a subject to which Menzel often returns; and the reason is obvious. As was stated in the introduction to this article, it is one of our author's main objects to recall his countrymen from the exclusive study of books, and to imbue literature with more of the spirit of real life.— Here follow some admirable

---

* Counting, of course, all the volumes of every impression.—Translator.

* See his "Avis aux Gens des Lettres et aux Personnes sedentaires sur leur Santé."—(Translator.)

observations on the extent to which the practical and the contemplative, the literary and the active life have been pursued to the exclusion of each other.

"From the remotest times, two different ages have alternated with one another. Either the arts and sciences have suffered under the oppression of barbarism, or public life has languished amidst the soft delights of the Muses. The heroic age and the literary stand in opposite relations to one another. When the great storms of the Reformation had passed away, we exchanged the sword for the pen, and, during a long interval of peace, devoted ourselves to the arts of peace. But this from the first was a peace of enervation; and those arts served, in their measure, only to increase this enervation. A happy equipoise between the practical and the speculative energy was so far from being maintained, that on the contrary, metaphysical subtlety, *book-dreamery*, self-indulged phantasy, and unsubstantial idealism were as exclusively predominant, as, under the external barbarism of former times, they had been disproportionately depressed. If at any time an idea from the field of theological, political, or moral speculation, wandered into the region of practical life, it was speedily driven back with spear and stave, into the *dream-world* of the author; and our external as well as our internal politics took care that we should continue dreamers. We had always our " Circenses,"* if not always " panem ;" and perhaps *reality* would have made a stronger impression upon us, but that we should have been obliged to wake up from our world of books; for the prison which we had painted so beautifully for ourselves— we loved.

"Whether it be that some malignant power keeps guard upon our eyelids, and chains us down in iron slumbers, like Prometheus, to punish us for having fashioned men, and that prophetic dreamings are (like his) our last repose from activity, of which not even that power can rob us;—or whether we ourselves, from native inclination, from an impulse such as that which nature has implanted in the chrysalis, weave around us the dim covering where in the mysterious darkness of creation, the beautiful Psyche-wings of the soul are to be unfolded ;—whether we are compelled, for want of realities, to console ourselves with dreams, or whether an indwelling Spirit hurries us beyond the bounds of the most beautiful realities into the higher regions of imagination; we must ever attribute to this luxuriance of literature, this paper-world of enterprise, a most important influence upon the character of the nation and the age."

Our author then proceeds, in a strain of uncommon eloquence, to point out the evils which must flow from the exclusive study

* Juvenal, Sat. x., v. 18.

of books; the true value of literature; its relation to real life; and the spirit in which it should be cultivated. This leads him to give a distinct exposition of the *point of view* from which he designs to contemplate the whole subject.

"Where national fame is that of *books* alone to the exclusion of *deeds,* where faith is sophisticated, the will unstrung, all energy relaxed, inaction palliated, and the age oppressed to death through "making many books;" where the great reminiscences and aspirations of mankind, instead of living hearts find only lifeless paper, there are we compelled to recognize the dark side of literature. Where literature checks the fresh energies of life, and forcibly contracts itself within its own domain, it becomes only negative and pernicious.

"Yet are there *words* which of themselves are *deeds.* The various recollections and imaginings of actual life connect themselves with that second world of knowledge and contemplation which becomes purer and brighter in proportion as action is generated from the mind. And in this world the Germans are especially at home. Nature has given us a preponderating profundity of thought, a ruling inclination to descend into the depths of our own bosoms, and unlock the boundless treasures they contain. So long as we resign ourselves to this national propensity, we exhibit the true greatness of our idiosyncrasy, and fulfil the law of our nature, the destiny to which we are called above every other people. Literature, however, which is the express image of this intellectual life, will on that very account, here show its bright side in all its lustre. Here its operation is positive, creative, and fraught with blessings. The light of the ideas which have gone forth from Germany will illuminate the world.

"At the same time we must guard against the error of esteeming the outward shape which the mind puts on in order to manifest itself, the words which are the receptacle of mind (but also the sepulchre of its imprisonment) more highly than the perennial, salient fountain of the mind itself. Words, lifeless and unvarying in their nature, are merely the outward tegument of the mind, thrown off upon a sunny day; as it were, the many-coloured skin which the world, aged, yet ever renewing its youth, leaves behind it, like the snake, at each successive metamorphosis. Yet men but too frequently prefer dead words to the quickening spirit. Nothing is more common than the error of valuing words (especially printed words) more highly than independent thought, and books more highly than men. In such a case the living spring is choked by the very mass of waters rolled back upon it. The mind is enervated amidst the books which owe their very being to its power alone. Men learn their words by rote, and feel themselves excused from the trouble of thinking. Nothing is so injurious to the spirit of independent exertion as the facility of living on the gains of another; and nothing gives so much support to the indolence and conceit of men as books. But in forfeiting its strength the mind forfeits its freedom also. There is no readier way of turning free-men into sheep than by teaching them merely to read.

" With reason have practical men been incapable of tolerating books, when they seduce the mind away from the fresh activities of life to an unessential world of phantoms. But really thinking men who know the heart, have always on deeper grounds distinguished between book-learning and the vital power of thought and feeling; and have placed mere literature, the world of words, not only beneath the world of action, but also beneath the still and inner world of the soul.

" When once they have been separated from it, words stand opposed to life in ten thousand ways. They are life in its torpor: they are its corpse, its shadow. Words are unvarying and inflexible. 'Not one iota,' says the poet, 'can be taken from a word: it is fixed among the everlasting stars,' and the mind from which it was produced has no further portion in it. Words are durable, life ever changing; words are ready made to our hands; life moulds itself.

" Hence a life dedicated to books has always in it something dead; something which reminds you of mummies or Troglodytes. Woe to the mind which sells itself for a book, and swears by words; the very spring of life in it is dried up. But in this " death-in-life" there lies hidden a demoniac power: it is the very head of Medusa, and turns every thing to stone. Its effects are unmeasured throughout the history of the world. A word has often petrified centuries into marble; and it has been late before the new Prometheus came, and reanimated the torpid generation with his living fire.

" In life, however, when it apprehends itself, there lies a spell too mighty for mere words. If it do not guard itself, it falls under the dominion of words. But when it relies upon itself, it has gained the talisman with which it overpowers the demoniac spirit of words. And this, which will avail every man whenever he takes *one* book in his hand, shall avail for us, while we contemplate our modern literature in its widest compass. We will go forth from real life so as continually to fall back upon it; and with this Ariadne's clue we trust to thread our way through the labyrinth of literature. While we journey with all the fresh feeling of life, through the dead region of literature, all mystery will unfold itself before us, instead of lulling us into an enchanted slumber. None but the living can like Dante travel through the world of shadows. We shall find many a German professor there, who, in sad-coloured cloak, with neck turned round, looks back upon the "sunny greenery" of life, yet never extricates himself from dark-hued theories; we shall see Sisyphus rolling the philo-sopher's stone up the hill, and Tantalus hungering for the apples of the tree of knowledge; we shall encounter all who seek from words what life only can supply.

"From this unobstructed point of view we shall first contemplate literature in its reciprocal relations with active life, and then as a work of art. It is one of the productions of life, and it re-acts on its original. It is a mirror which reflects the image of its Maker. Whether medicine or poison, it is derived from real life, which life it either heals or destroys. . . . .

" Certainly literature images the form of life, not only more comprehensively, but more clearly than perhaps any other instrument of thought; since no other medium of representation equals the compass and the depth of language. Yet language has its limits, while life alone has none. No book as yet has fathomed the immeasurable depths of life. They are only individual chords which vibrate within you, when you read a book; the infinite harmonies which slumber within you, as within living things, no book has ever fully comprehended. Then never hope to find in any music-book the key to all the tones of life; do not so much immure yourself within the school-room; rather, willingly and often suffer the Æolian harp within you to vibrate freely and naturally, softly or wildly, to the fresh airs of life.

"Let literature ever be only one of the resources of life, never the object to which life itself shall be sacrificed. Undoubtedly it is a noble thing to image and fashion our present life upon the recollection of the past; to act through words upon the present age, and to leave to futurity a memorial of our life, if it merit a memorial; yet let no man give up his mind a prisoner to books.

"Our ancestors were as yet unacquainted with the immense importance of literature; too deeply devoted to the enjoyment or the action of the moment, they rather lost themselves in the realities of the world than busied themselves about its image. The present age has well nigh gone into the opposite extreme: and men steal away from outward objects to transport themselves into a new-found world, and stun themselves with the wonders which their own curiosity has collected around them. The men of those days had more of life; the men of these know more *about* life. Literature has attracted an interest and extended an efficacy which was unknown to former ages. The invention of printing has given it a substantial basis, from which it has been able to extend its operations widely. It has since become one of the powers of Europe, and at times has served, at times commanded all. It has gained possession of the mind through the ministry of words, it has governed life through the form of life; yet at the same time it has proved an obsequious instrument in each successive struggle of the times. In its golden book has every man entered his suffrage. It has been a shield of rectitude and virtue, a temple of wisdom, a paradise of innocence, the lover's cup of bliss, the poet's ascent to heaven; but it has also been a cruel weapon of party-strife, a plaything of levity, a provocative to luxury, a couch for indolence, an incentive to babbling, a fashion for inanity, and an article of merchandise; and it has served as a handmaid to all the interests of the age, the great and the small, the pernicious and the useful, the noble and the vulgar."

Our author then proceeds to give a summary view of the present state of German literature in its several departments. 'Vielschreiberei,' however, is the bane of every one of them. He says,

"It is one of the greatest evils of our literature *that parties are so little concentrated*. While in Paris or London some ten distinguished authors struggle for the attainment of a determinate object by mutual agreement and by a skilful distribution of matter; in Germany the same thing would be attempted by some hundred authors, of proportionably less talent and without any agreement at all; without even taking any notice of one another. While in Paris or London, it is very easy to overlook the field of battle; in Germany it is almost impossible. A thousand theological publications appear annually. Who can read them all? Their very authors cannot tell all their opponents or fellow-combatants. They fight, in a manner, in the dark. The poor country parson has before him a dozen books and some half-dozen of college manuscripts, and thus he writes a new book; without at all troubling himself whether fifty of his fellow-students may not be at the same time writing just such another miserable book. On the occasion of the cholera there appeared in Germany several hundred publications, of which very few indicated lofty or comprehensive views on the part of the author. Again; since the last political movement, a prodigious number of works have been written on 'Constitution,' and 'Administration,' of which the greater part have related only to local circumstances and transient interests; to survey them for the purpose of extracting from them beneficial *general* results, is in the highest degree difficult. The Germans have begun to attain sound notions in all branches of politics; but the *sum* of our political knowledge is as it were scattered about in the smallest kinds of coin; we cannot melt it down into one great mass. Even the Belles Lettres form no exception to these observations; since even the most zealous reader of romance will never have done with that which each book-fair offers him for a fresh perusal.

"The passion for scribbling has in Germany become such a mania, that just in proportion as a new book finds it difficult to make its way through the prodigious mass of those which are already in existence, are our good people determined to see *every* book in print, even the most insignificant. Hence in our day the literature of *scraps and sweepings;* the collections of letters and occasional pieces of every man who is but remotely known to fame. Scarce was a polite note or washing-bill of the happy Matthison suffered to remain unprinted; of Jean Paul, we know to what date he preserved his first worked *braces;* of Voss, what he spent at each inn on his little excursions; of Schiller, in what equipage he drove with Göthe; and with such matter as this many hundred biographies and volumes of letters of this kind are crammed. And it is Protestants and Rationalists who are most zealous for this modern *relique-worship;* men who despise a far nobler form of the same superstition in the Catholics.

"I have often been solicited by learned Frenchmen to give them a sort of clue into the labyrinth of German literature. I represent to myself the Brahmin, who was recently in England, entering the immeasurable world of German books, and asking me, 'Is there not some *book of books* in which one may find all this knowledge comprised in a nutshell?' 'No,' I must reply; 'since the beasts lived together in the ark of Noah, they have multiplied so countlessly that now the Linnæuses, the Buffons, the Blumenbachs, the Cuviers find it no longer an easy task to discover amongst these individuals only the *species*." . . . . .

Of the present state of political literature, he says,

"Our political literature has improved; yet even were it admitted that all that is written on politics throughout Germany contained wisdom, we should still have to complain that we have not ears enough for such a many-tongued wisdom. . . . . .

"It has often been lamented that the German troubles himself so little about state affairs; but when he beholds before him a capacious table full of newspapers, and four long walls full of books, all which he must read for the mere purpose of setting himself right in the first instance,—surely one cannot blame him for thinking this extremely irksome."

Of the multitudinous works lately put forth on the subject of *education* in Germany, he speaks thus:

"The zeal which men have recently directed to the improvement of education, is certainly very desirable; but I would fain know the pedagogue who had read everything which has already been written on this point in Germany, and which is still being written, to the amount of some hundreds of new volumes yearly. Where is the new teacher who, instead of reading the old books, would not much rather write a new one? It has almost become a custom that each teacher should start a new method, or at least write a new manual for his immediate sphere of action. Hence the frightful number of 'manuals,' of which we can no longer take a survey, and from which we can in no way make a selection. . . . Then we have got a literature for children, which

13. continued

does not come much behind the literature for the adult. My son might have a library of 15,000 works which have been written and printed in Germany for those who are under sixteen years of age! Now, good father, sit you down, read over these fifteen thousand works, and then choose for your son the best of them!"

Poetry and polite literature it appears are in the same predicament. "Since 1814," says he, "there have been fabricated not less than from five to six thousand new romances. Even if they were all good, they would still be too many, since one could not read them all; if they are bad, they should not have been written at all. They are really for the most part *bad;* perhaps there is not one hundred of them which a reasonable man can lay down without being ashamed of the people which produces such romances. There will then still remain more than five thousand romances, which, within so short a time, have not only dissipated a vast capital, both of money and time on the part of authors, publishers, printers, and readers, but which have been essentially injurious to the nation in their influence; an influence which, when not demoralizing, has still been enervating. . . . .

"He who can exult in such a literature must be mad; for in truth none but a madman would collect a library, the books of which for the most part contain nothing behind the title; or which are crammed with chips and cobwebs. A reasonable man does not estimate the spirit of a nation principally by its books, nor even the worth of its books by their number. Instead of pluming ourselves upon our riches, we should only be meditating the means of compressing into a narrow compass the results of our *book-knowledge*, that we may still retain at least some portion of it. Without this process, we shall still, for a long time to come, see empty blockheads rambling about in the very midst of our book-crowded Germany.

"It is the last few years which form the most difficult portion of our survey; not merely because they have produced a far greater number of books than any former period, but also because these works, pressing so closely upon one another, cannot be registered with equal rapidity in the literary *guides.* A comparison of the catalogues of Leipsic fair, since the Restoration, gives the following results. In the year 1816, there appeared in the German trade for the first time, above three thousand books. In the year 1822, for the first time, above four thousand. In the year 1827, for the first time, above five thousand. In 1832, for the first time, above six thousand. Thus the number has increased every five years above a thousand. Since the peace of 1814 to the close of the year 1835 there have been printed in Germany not far short of one hundred thousand works!"

This chapter closes with an account of the various authors in Germany, who had already attempted the history of literature, whether as a whole or in some particular department; with a further exposition of the principles on which he designs to conduct his work.

14. ECLECTIC REVIEW, 3rd ser. 65 (1837), 503-516. M/H No. 3401.

No. II.

Art. VII. *Menzel on German Literature. Die deutsche Litera-tur. Von Wolfgang Menzel.* 1836. *Stuttgart.*

MENZEL'S Second Chapter is on 'The German Na-tionality.' After a few introductory observations, our author proceeds to give an account of the principal character-istics of the German mind, (considered in itself, and apart from those foreign or extrinsic influences to which he afterwards adverts), at once profound, eloquent, and honest. While he claims for his countrymen that high meditative and imaginative character, which all who are tolerably acquainted with their lite-rature will accord to them, he does not deny the excesses and ab-surdities to which it has often led, both in their philosophy and poetry;—in the former, to speculations of the most transcendental and *unpractical* character; in the latter, to all that is monstrous, incongruous, and remote from real life in fiction. But let our readers judge for themselves. There are few who are at all versed in German literature, but will at once recognize the truth and fidelity of the portrait.

'From the remotest times were the Germans a fantastical nation. In the middle ages they were mystical;—they now exist only in intellect. In all ages have they manifested an exuberant strength and fulness of mind, which has gushed forth from within, but has paid little attention to the *external*. In practical life, the Ger-mans have ever been more helpless than any other nation, but more at home in the world of the soul: and all their national virtues and vices may be traced back to this *inwardness*,—this musing and contemplative disposition. This it is which has made us *par excellence* a literary people, and which has at the same time stamped our literature with a peculiar character. The writings of other nations are more practical, because their life is more practical; those of our own have a tincture of the *super-natural*, or the *unnatural*—something ghostly and strange, which will never happen in the actual world;—and this because we have ever before our eyes only the extravagant world within. We are more fanciful than other nations, not merely because our fancy trans-ports us from reality into a region of prodigies, but because we take our dreams to be *true*. . . . . But it is our intellect which takes the farthest flights into the ideal azure; and we are consequently everywhere exclaimed against as speculatists and system-makers. Meantime, however, we can *realize* our theories nowhere but in our literature. Thus we give to the world of words a disproportionate ascendancy over the world of real life; and are with justice called book-worms and pedants.

'Meanwhile, this is only the dark side;—with respect to which, however, we would by no means deceive ourselves. Opposed to it, this thoughtful, literary spirit has its light side, which is less frequently estimated by foreigners. We strive after a universal cultivation of intellect, and sacrifice to this desire (not in vain) our energies, and our national pride. The knowledge we obtain, may well be considered more beneficial to the human race than certain great achievements, falsely so called: and the desire of *learning* from foreigners, may be allowed to do us more honour than a *victory* over them.'

While contending, however, that the prime and characteristic elements of the German intellect are such as he here represents them, he also contends that there is more variety in the combina-tions of those elements,—more *individuality*, among the writers of Germany, than among the writers of any other nation. What-ever may be thought of this opinion, the eloquence and force with which he advocates it will not be denied. He says,

'This *thoughtfulness* of the German character has always been conjoined with a great *variety* in the forms and products of intel-lect; our mental opulence seems capable of disclosing itself only in proportion as it is bound by no *law*. In our nation, more than in any other, has nature exhibited an exhaustless variety of distinctive intellects; in no nation are there so many different systems, tastes, tendencies, and talents, or such varieties of manner and of style, of thinking and composing, of speaking and writing. Men see at once that these intellects have never been subjected to one law or mode of culture. They have grown up wild,—here and there—varied only by nature and education; and their confluence in literature gives it a strange and heterogeneous appearance. Our authors speak one language as they live under one sky; but each man brings a peculiar accent with him. *Nature* pre-vails, however strongly the discipline of particular schools would fain root out the (so-called) barbarism. The German possesses little social flexibility, yet so much the stronger is his indivi-duality, and to that he will give free expression, even to wilful-ness and caricature. Genius bursts through every barrier that would oppose it; and even amongst the vulgar, the mother-wit breaks out. When one contemplates the literature of other nations, one observes more or less of *normality*—a sort of French art of gardening; it is the German alone which is forest-like—a field overrun with wild growth. Each intellect is a flower, distinct in form, colour, perfume.'

After this he proceeds to pass a magnificent but deserved eulo-gium on the German language; which, he justly contends, is an instrument of thought in exact harmony with the character of the German mind. In its compass, flexibility, and variety; in its power of combination,—of readily accommodating itself to the wants of every writer, and of furnishing each with a diction most precisely adapted to his style of intellect, he represents it as the impress and reflection of the principal qualities of the national mind. That mind has stamped itself on the language.—We must find room for one paragraph, and heartily wish we could find room for more.

' The German language is the perfect expression of the Ger'man character; it has followed the German intellect in all 'its depths and in its widest range. It corresponds exactly 'to the variety of intellectual character; and has granted to 'each writer a peculiar *tone*, which more clearly distinguishes 'him, than could be the case in any other language. The lan'guage gains by these manifold modes of using it. Its various 'and multiform character is peculiar to it, and constitutes its 'beauty. A field of flowers is nobler than a plain field of grass; 'and it is precisely the fairest countries which have the richest 'change of climate and temperature. All attempts to impose upon 'German authors a *normal* usage in language have signally failed, 'and that because they have contradicted nature. Each author 'writes as he may; each can say of himself with Göthe, "I sing 'as sings the bird which lives upon the boughs."'

The *third* chapter is entitled 'Schulgelehrsamkeit.' The meaning generally given to this word, in ordinary German and English dictionaries, would convey but a very erroneous or at best inadequate notion of our author's meaning. In the above-mentioned works, the reader would find the word explained as 'classical learning,' 'school learning;' and either of those words would convey to the reader's mind the idea of a particular *species* of literature; the former embracing the learned languages, the latter the scholastic sciences and philosophy of the middle ages. But Menzel does not mean his observations to apply to *any* particular kind of literature, but to illustrate the influence which the *school spirit* exerts on every branch. The chapter might therefore have been entitled 'The Spirit of the Schools,' or 'The Influence of the *School Spirit*, as exerted upon Literature.' While fully admitting the advantages of this same *school-system* in all ages, but especially in dark and barbarous ones, he fully and fairly points out the evils with which it is inevitably connected. He does this in a most masterly and philosophical style. His observations on this subject do not apply to Germany alone; they convey truth equally important to all nations; and, if read in the right spirit, might be read with great *profit*, by all the professors and students of Oxford and Cambridge.

' If we proceed to investigate the *historical* conditions of the 'present development of our literature, we must at once be 'struck by the fact, that all literary culture was originally con'nected with the church. Indeed, even at the present day, 'literature has not entirely escaped from its influence. The 'clerical *caste* gave literature the form of *a learned guild*; and 'all that school-restraint, which is visible in our writings, is de'rived from this source. Corporate interests, and the discipline 'of the schools, have perpetually stamped on each succeeding 'century an impression of the *past*; although, it is true, that im'pression has in each become fainter and fainter. Its conse'quences are, the exclusiveness which is so characteristic of *caste*; 'an aristocratic spirit in literature; intolerance; pedantic attach'ment to ancient customs; the learning of the recluse; and 'oblivion of nature. Yet has the system its fair and estimable 'aspects too. So long as all literary life emanated from a certain '*caste* (once that of ecclesiastics, more lately that of scholars), it 'took upon itself all the virtues and all the vices of the spirit 'corporate. Even now the interest of an exclusive order obtrudes 'itself, in a hard ossified form, on literature; even now theology 'is controlled by priests, and the secular sciences managed by 'the Faculties in a purely corporate spirit. The free genius, 'the vigorous nature of the Germans has, it is true, incessantly 'struggled against the spirit of *caste*, ever since the revival of let'ters; and we may observe a continued warfare on the part of original 'genius against the schools—a perpetual renewal of that most 'ancient feud between the priests and the prophets. . . . . The 'element, however, which has been cast away by one party has 'always been cherished and cultivated by another, and by means 'of this almost all have acquired their rights. Meanwhile, as in 'politics so in literature, the spirit of the old-accustomed 'dominion, after being vanquished, has always proceeded to work 'upon the conquerors themselves. The *negative* has immediately 'shifted round to the *positive*. The prophets have once more be'come priests; have taken upon themselves the principle of 'authority and legitimacy; under new forms of faith, have laid 'claim to the old monopoly, and sought to re-establish it against 'all innovation. What was yesterday heterodox, is to-day ortho'dox; what yesterday constituted the *individuality* of one great 'man, is to-day the despotic *manner* of a school. The reason of 'this phenomenon, however, must be sought, not only in the 'continued influence of the middle ages, but also in the character 'of the people. The German burns for the knowledge of truth, 'and he really believes that he knows it. It is the very same en'thusiasm which impels him both to *persist* and to *reform*.

' Much good is unquestionably connected with the corporate 'spirit. The fidelity with which the treasures of tradition 'are preserved; the dignity with which authority is invested; 'the enthusiasm and the piety with which we honour what is '*sacred*, what is *proved*, or what is *believed*; all those virtues, in 'short, which usually accompany the love of antiquity, must be 'acknowledged in all their worth as contrasted with the fickle-

'ness of many innovators, who so often set aside all moral autho-
'rity and historical tradition, and reject, together with the
'ancient school, its lessons of ancient experience also. The dis-
'ease, however, of that corporate spirit is, the principle of *non-*
'*progression*—the disposition to stand still where there should be
'perpetual progress; the narrow-mindedness which imposes limits
'where there are none. Hence necessarily results, on the one
'hand, a hierarchical system, the restraints of *caste*, party spirit,
'proselytism, the persecution of heretics, and nepotism; on the
'other, a cramped, circumscribed knowledge, clothed in forms
'monstrously prolix, which eternally return to the same point,
'and eternally iterate the same thing. In opposition to these
'vices of the antiquated corporate spirit, enters, in full dignity,
'the quickening power of innovators, who liberate knowledge from
'the narrow limits of the school, character itself from the uniform
'restraints of *caste*, and for this purpose strip off all those stiff
'forms, which only oppress vigorous, self-inspiring nature; but then
'it must be admitted, that as soon as their triumph is achieved,
'they themselves fall back into the ancient errors.

'The relations which all the sciences bore to religion, intro-
'duced a sort of priestly, *canting* tone into scholarship, which is
'still retained in the Faculties, and even taints every other de-
'partment of learning. Our authors are but too apt to play the
'oracle, to endeavour to spread around them a sort of ' nimbus,'
'and to mystify their readers, as the clergy do the laity or the
'school-master his scholars.

'In England and France an author finds himself much in the
'same situation as an orator on the tribune, and gives his vote as
'in a company of men who are his equals, and as well educated
'as himself. In Germany he is given to *preach*, and play the
'*school-master*.

The following is a most humorous description of a thorough
German student:—

'The secluded, monkish life of scholars, has undoubtedly pro-
'moted a propensity for profound meditation, learned subtleties,
'and extravagant fantasies; and the result has been a deficiency
'*in practical sense*, and an incapacity of enjoying life. Even now
'the majority of scholars and authors live in their *book-dens*, like
'Troglodytes, and lose, together with the *sight* of nature, all taste
'for it and all power of enjoying it. Life is to them a dream,
'and *their* life is but a dream. Whether a slater has fallen from
'a roof, or Napoleon from his throne, they alike exclaim, ' So,
'so; aye, aye;' and again bury themselves in their books.*

.. * 'Stecken die Nase wieder in die Bucher.' Literally, 'Thrust their noses
into their books.'

'But fruits which have been kept in a damp cellar soon become
'mouldy; and in like manner are the fruits of intellect affected by
'the learned atmosphere of the study. The parent communicates to
'his intellectual offspring, not only his mental, but also his physi-
'cal diseases. We may trace in books not merely the insensibility,
'the heartlessness, the hypochondriasis, but even the gout, the
'jaundice, nay, more, the deformity of their author.'

Nor are the remarks which are made on the *results* of such a
pursuit of literature, less worthy of notice.

'The scholastic spirit has introduced *learned pedantry*. Imme-
'diate, healthful contemplation has given place to hypochondriacal
'musings. Instead of borrowing from nature, we compile books
'out of books. We no longer exhibit things in their simplicity,
'but must display, together with them, the treasures of our *know-*
'*ledge*. We forget the original aim of science, and substi-
'tute what is merely the means for the end. In our learned
'*apparatus*, we forget the *results*. We seldom see a theologian
'or a jurist; we see only theological and juridical *philologists*.
'All historical knowledge is rendered unprofitable by philologico-
'critical learning. We inquire not about the *contents*, but merely
'about the *shell*. We do not measure the *weight*, but the *accuracy*
'of a citation. We exhibit a sort of childish exultation if we have
'diplomatically proved that this or that decision has been actually
'delivered, without troubling ourselves to inquire whether it is in
'conformity with *truth*, or, generally, whether it is of any conse-
'quence. With unspeakable industry we amass information, from
'which it requires just as much trouble to extract the little which
'is worth remembering. We waste the toil of a year in finding
'out the true reading of some old poet, who in many cases had
'better have been silent altogether. Even our modern poetry is
'crushed under the load of erudition. The language of natural
'feeling and of living thought, is but too often repressed by
'learned reflections, allusions, and citations; and there is no branch
'of literature on which *closet-learning* has not exerted a preju-
'cial influence.

'In school-learning, strictly so called (I mean in what are de-
'signated the ' Brod-Collegia'), a certain mechanical system pre-
'vails, vulgo 'Schlendrian,' which moves on in the old tracks, ab-
'solutely without life or soul. Universities are become the manu-
'factories of books and authors. We never depart from certain
'formulæ of the schools, and each succeeding generation implicitly
'follows them. Original truth, however, is darkened by the im-
'measurable commentary. The very point on which properly the
'whole depends, vanishes at last under the load of citations which
'should prove it. Life escapes under the knife of the anatomist.
'The weightiest subject becomes tedious; the worthiest, trivial.
'The mind will not suffer itself to be tied down to a mere skeleton,

'and nature resistlessly forces its way through the paragraphs 'which venture to imprison it.

'Polemics are the instrument for stirring up this mouldering 'bog of learning, while mephitic vapours spread themselves 'around. Nowhere is the *unnaturalness* of recluse scholars 'shown more surprisingly than in their polemical writings. Here 'that good old proverb is verified, 'The more learned, the more 'in the wrong.' Now, they are so superabundantly wise, that a 'healthy understanding finds it difficult to follow the labyrinthine 'windings of their logic; and now, so ignorant in the most ordi-'nary matters, that a peasant might instruct them. Now, they 'are so nice with their attic jokes and learned allusions, (which 'would redound to the honour of an Alexandrian librarian,) that 'an honest German is stultified with them;—now, they resort to 'the most arrant tricks or the grossest invectives—such as even 'the vulgar would be ashamed of.

'Even the corruptions of the German language are in a great 'part to be attributed to the scholastics. That with foreign con-'ceptions they should adopt a foreign terminology, was natural; 'but in their passion for learned distinction, they affected a sort 'of *sacred unintelligibility* for the purpose of making themselves 'more venerable in the eyes of the laity, or else because they 'were too lazy or too little necessitated to sacrifice any thing for 'popularity. The *Faculty-men* can express themselves in a man-'ner so exquisitely German, that no uninitiated person can under-'stand them; nay, in many cases, even philosophers cannot under-'stand themselves.'

After some exceedingly eloquent observations on the advantages secured by the schools during the dark ages, as centres of light, and receptacles of such knowledge and science as still remained in the world, he breaks out into the following noble reflections:

'This may be considered the luminous side of the school 'learning; but then did the light ever *emanate* from the schools? 'rather, did it not shine into them from *without*? Were not free-'born spirits perpetually obliged to purify the schools afresh, and to 'purge them from thick darkness, from accumulated filth? Were 'the great men who gave the impulse to their age, who originated 'a new order of things, or created new modes of thought,—were 'Abelard, Huss, Luther, Thomasius, Lessing, originally men of 'the schools? rather did they not wrestle *against* the schools? 'Has it not always been an evil adherent to the schools that it has 'sacrificed the spirit to the letter, exchanged freedom for bondage, 'light for darkness, till some new teachers from *without*,—from 'the *people*,—endowed with great natural gifts, put an end to 'this confusion for a short time, and laid the foundation of new 'schools, which were themselves destined to degenerate in the 'same manner?

'And is not this tendency to degenerate necessarily involved in 'the very essence of the school-system? The love of scholars for 'their master is sure to be carried to excess; we swear by the '*verba magistri*. The word which in the master's mouth was 'still flexible, becomes fixed and immoveable in the mouth of the 'scholar. The spirit which was free in the master, is circum-'scribed in the scholar. The zeal which was noble in the master, 'in the scholar degenerates into dogmatism and the spirit of 'persecution.'

The actual influence of the *school spirit* in the present Univer-sity-system of Germany is thus described, and alas! there is but too much truth in the representations it gives of the servile and ignominious dependence of literature on political power. The universities are the creatures and minions of the state.

'Where a school once exists, it forms to itself an *external* in-'terest,—its secular advantage,—or it serves a foreign one. Thus 'the ancient scholasticism served popes, and the modern serves 'kings. Each school is servile in the proportion in which its ad-'herents are called to worldly advantages and honours. The dex-'terous become time-servers; their sophistry disguises truth; and 'when once power is on their side, no one can contradict them. 'The band is made up of blockheads and scholarly under-strap-'pers, who conjoin with their support of falsehood a sort of en-'thusiasm, inasmuch as they are really inspired—for that which 'brings them both honour and bread.

'This is repeated in all ages under different forms; formerly 'the school learning was a department of the church, and the 'professors had *spiritual titles*; now it is a department of the 'state, and the professors have *court titles*. On that account it 'might even be prophesied that our *politically* servile school-'learning will advance, step by step, to a still deeper and 'deeper degeneracy, just as formerly the *hierarchically* servile 'scholasticism descended by the same swift path.—Such is the con-'sequence whenever power succeeds in enslaving intellect.'

The fourth chapter is entitled, 'The Influence of Foreign Litera-ture,' and is one of the most interesting in the whole work. The extravagant lengths to which the Germans carry their admiration of every species of foreign literature, and the extent to which they translate and imitate it, are hardly conceivable to those who have never paid attention to the subject. For example, the pro-ductions of almost every English poet and novelist who has the slightest pretensions to reputation, have been translated into Ger-man, while those of our most celebrated writers have been trans-lated several times over. This honour has even been extended to some of the occasional papers in our magazines. Menzel begins this chapter by the following remarks on this strong propensity for imitation:

'The well-known propensity for imitation, by which the Ger-
' mans are characterized, especially prevails in their literature. To
' stutter and hobble after foreigners is at once their delight and
' shame. For more than a thousand years have men disputed
' about this peculiarity of our national character, just as they
' would about some propensity of the heart which morality appears
' to forbid. Even in the earliest times there were in Germany
' two parties, the Imitators and the Purists. Despicable indeed
' are the apes who are in perpetual chase of foreign gew-gaws;
' despicable, indeed, the degenerate men who are ashamed that
' they are Germans. The prejudice that the German character is so
' bearish and rustic, as absolutely to require a foreign dancing-
' master, could be originated or maintained only by those who
' were themselves of a true plebeian stamp. Equally ridiculous,
' however, are the fools who would clear the *true* German character
' from all foreign tincture; who would enclose Germany by a
' sort of moral *preventive system;* nay, command the sun itself to
' shine—only upon Germany.

' Mental culture is like the light, restricted to no particular
' people; its beneficent influence is spread in all directions over
' the earth's surface, whatever the modifications of climate. No-
' where are there limits which it cannot pass. Commerce binds
' together all countries, and diffuses the peculiar products of each;
' literature should, in like manner, spread abroad the intellectual
' treasures of nations. Each land should receive from every other
' what is agreeable to its nature, and promotes its prosperity; and,
' in the same manner, may there be *transplanted* into the spirit of
' a nation what harmonizes with its character and more nobly deve-
' lopes it.

' If there are many things which only *one* nation can possess,
' and from which it receives its peculiar character, there are many
' blessings of a higher order that exclusively belong to none, but
' are the property of the whole human race. The phenomenon of
' Christianity alone rebukes the zeal of the Purists. In order ef-
' fectually to purify ourselves from all foreign influence, we must
' reverse all history; since our whole modern culture rests on the
' romantic basis of the middle ages. If we would disrobe our-
' selves of every thing which we have received from foreigners,
' we must run naked in the woods again. Apart, however,
' from the necessary interchange of knowledge between nation and
' nation, which is founded in nature, and is as ancient as history,
' we Germans are *especially* distinguished by an extraordinary
' predilection for what is foreign and a rare aptitude for imitation;
' and we are, in consequence, often led into extravagancies
' and an unnatural forgetfulness of our own worth.'

The following is his mode of accounting for this propensity.
' The deepest fountain of this inclination for what is foreign is the
' *humanity* of German character; we are thorough Cosmopoli-
' tans; our nationality consists in our wishing to have none, but
' to stamp upon ourselves, in opposition to all national peculiari-
' ties, a certain form of humanity which shall be universally cur-
' rent. We feel a perpetual desire to realize the *ideal* of a philo-
' sophical *normal-people.* We would appropriate to ourselves the
' culture of all nations, and all the flowers of the human intellect.
' This bias of our nature is stronger than our national pride; so
' much so, indeed, that we do not even seek our national pride *in it.*
' Other nations would fain be a normal-people too; and, indeed,
' without this persuasion, there would be no national pride; but then
' they would by no means renounce *themselves:* they seek only to
' impress their own image upon other nations. Other people as
' well as ourselves prize what is foreign; but they do not throw
' themselves away in exchange for it.—Yet this self-renunciation
' has its good aspect, and its natural foundation. True love always
' implies a strong principle of self-denial. To a passion for what
' is foreign, to that passion in which all cultivation originates,
' nothing is more hostile than egotism; to true culture nothing
' more friendly than national vanity. A certain self-surrender is
' necessary, if we would be fully susceptible of foreign impressions.
' If we investigate the obstacles which have arrested the progress
' of improvement among so many nations, we shall find that it is to
' be attributed less to their barbarism, than to their self-com-
' placency, and to the prejudices of their national pride. The
' noblest nations have been always the most tolerant; and the
' basest, the most vain.

' Meantime, it is not merely the philosophical complexion of
' our character, our plasticity, our thirst for knowledge, our
' instinct for development, and our striving after the *ideal* which
' make us love what is foreign, but the poetic complexion of our
' character,—*a romantic bias.* A poetical illusion, embellishing all
' that it touches, hovers over every thing foreign, and takes our
' fancy captive. What is foreign, merely *as such,* awakens a ro-
' mantic voice within us, even when it is inferior to what we have
' long possessed ourselves. It is thus that we take from foreign-
' ers so much that in no way promotes our further advancement:
' the imagination corrupts a propensity, which the understanding
' must approve so long as it duly moderates it. When once the
' imagination carries this propensity to excess, we fall into two
' errors at the same time; a blind surrender to every foreign influ-
' ence, and an equally blind denial of our own worth. We pos-
' sess the poetical faculty of self-mystification, of metamorphosing
' ourselves, as it were, into dramatic personages, and abandoning
' ourselves to a foreign illusion. Many of our scholars think them-
' selves so completely into Greeks, many of our romanticists are
' so deeply imbued with the spirit of the middle ages, many of our

'politicians are so exclusively occupied with France, and many of 'our theologians with the Bible, that they appear to know nothing 'of what is passing around them. This state of mind has some 'resemblance to madness, and to madness it often leads. Those 'who are thus possessed, are aided by the singular plasticity of 'German thought and language. They know excellently well how 'to counterfeit the peculiarities of a foreign language, and thus 'drive out the true spirit of the German tongue for the purpose of 'introducing foreign idols. They jeer at all who will not imitate 'their example, and are angry if now and then nature will not 'comply with art.—Similar extremes, however, obliterate the 'traces of one another. If there were only *one* nation in the world 'beside ourselves, we should probably so *study* ourselves into 'their character, that there would be nothing of ourselves left; 'but as there are *many*, and we *imitate* them all in turn, and as, 'moreover, these nations are *opposed* to one another, the equili-'brium is constantly restored. . . . . .

' Like foolish children, however, we break the play-thing, or 'throw the lesson-book into the corner, when we are no longer 'pleased with, or no longer want them. None are so sla-'vishly devoted, and none so ungrateful as ourselves. None 'know how to renounce their own worth so thoroughly, and 'none so wantonly impute to their neighbours the faults which 'are their own. Fifty years ago, we regarded the French 'as a sort of demi-gods; twenty years ago, we thought them 'demi-devils. We were brutal enough to cringe to them, and 'subsequently still more brutal, to despise them. In place of the 'blockheads, who provided French nurses for their sucking babes; 'nay, French lodgings for the mothers, appeared another kind of 'blockheads, who, with barbarian violence trampled under foot 'the noble flowers of the French *social* character. German poli-'ticians put on an edifying air, and preached against the Gallic 'Anti-Christ, while one or another simple historian endeavoured 'to deceive themselves and others into the belief that the French 'were descended from an ignoble Asiatic stock, and did not de-'serve the honour of being called Europeans. With like bar-'barity each of our parties reproached the rest with their idolatry. 'The Classical school inveighed against the Oriental and that of 'the Middle Ages; while the disciple of the latter still devoutly '*crossed* himself sometimes for fear of the—old heathen !'

Now comes his account of the extent to which the system of translation is carried.

' It was natural that our predilection for foreign literature 'should next exhibit itself in *translations*. It is well known that 'in Germany the quantity of this species of literature is prodigious; 'it is thrown off, as it were, by machinery. Where foreigners con-'tent themselves with a slovenly translation of *one* out of some

' thirty works of any distinguished German author, we translate the 'whole writings of every English or French author, who possesses 'any considerable reputation, *two or three times over*. Nay, we do 'them the honour of permitting our own manufactures to go to press 'under their name, as for example, in the case of Walter 'Scott !* Unquestionably the fame and the advantage are both on 'our side. If we want many of the virtues of foreigners, we at least 'do not participate in that aristocratic narrow-mindedness which 'shrugs its shoulders in contented ignorance at every thing fo-'reign. It does us honour to be acquainted with illustrious Bri-'tons; it can do *them* no honour to know nothing of illustrious 'Germans.'

The following observations, on the mode in which alone foreign excellence can be successfully imitated,—that is, with *a reference* to the national peculiarities and character of the people who at-tempt to transplant it,—are exceedingly just and beautiful.

' *Imitations* are the inevitable consequence of a perception of 'foreign excellence. Why should we not imitate what is useful, 'or beautiful, or noble?—But then we generally commit the error 'of imitating *forms* instead of *things*. We should endeavour to 'attain as harmonious and universal a culture as did the Greeks, 'but then it should be in the spirit of our age and after our own 'manner, as theirs was in the spirit of *their* own age and in *their* 'own manner. We make ourselves merely ridiculous when we 'counterfeit the Grecian *forms*, without the *life* and *spirit* which 'produced them.—We should endeavour to cultivate the same 'social refinement as the French; but then, as is the case with 'them, it should be with reference to our own peculiarities. We 'are but apes when we clumsily affect French *congées* and 'flourishes. We should aspire to freedom, manliness of thought 'and action, like the English and Americans, but not expect 'prosperity by aping their outward forms. We should renew in 'ourselves the ability and earnest spirit of the middle ages, but 'not cumbersomely affect ancient dress and phraseology.

' *Formal* imitations resemble fashions, and have the same fate. 'For a short time they prevail exclusively, and he who does not 'comply with them is called an odd-fellow. A little after, and they 'appear altogether ridiculous. A taste for what was Grecian 'was once all the vogue, even in Rome; but who would hesitate 'to prize infinitely higher the strength and seriousness of the 'Roman character, as exemplified in their own intellectual pro-'ductions, than the affectation of Attic refinement in their Greek

---

* A humorous allusion to the tale called 'Walladmor,' produced by the ready wit and pen of some German author, as another new novel of Walter Scott's. It was at a time when one of the Waverley Series was impatiently expected at Leipsic.

imitations? The French tragedies on the classical model, have long since appeared to us truly *comic*, and yet, however we may pride ourselves on a greater aptitude for imitation, the copies of Voss, which are acknowledged to be masterly, are not a whit less ridiculous.

'The experience we have had of so many fluctuating fashions, 'which perpetually contradict and destroy one another, appears 'not unattended by some good consequences. We have been 'under the dominion of so many parties that we are beginning to 'attempt an adjustment. After having studied all civilized nations, 'one after another, after having admired and imitated Romans, 'Greeks, French, English, Italians, Spanish, we have now, for a 'moment, returned home again, and are *bethinking ourselves.* We 'observe, that from our first acquaintance with a foreign nation, 'we have always rashly passed on to an excessive admiration and an 'absolutely slavish imitation of them; that we have then soon be-'come weary of this extreme; upon which a fresh interval of 'quiet thought has exhibited to our view and enabled us to ap-'propriate *that* in such foreign nations which is *worthy* of imita-'tion, and which we are *capable* of imitating. We gradually dis-'tinguish between the glorious power of transporting ourselves 'into the spirit of other ages and nations—the poetical faculty of 'subjecting ourselves to a foreign illusion- -and practically *aping* 'what is foreign. In the one, all incongruities are harmonized; 'in the other, they are all opposed. Fancy may one moment 'transport us to Greece, in another to London, and yet we our-'selves remain all the while in Germany.'

But it is time to stop for the present. We must, however, find room for the following paragraph, and our readers will agree with us that it is most felicitously characteristic of the writer.

'German literature is like a mad-house, in which some hun-'dred fools are aping the costume and manners, the language and 'the modes of thought, of a hundred different nations, ancient and 'modern. There are Gallo-maniacs, Anglo-maniacs, Italo-'maniacs, Hispano-maniacs, Normanno-maniacs, Græco-maniacs, 'Turco-maniacs, Perso-maniacs, Indo-maniacs, Chineso-maniacs, 'Irokeso-maniacs. In harmonious discord, these honest German 'simpletons sit down together and enact the world's history. 'The madness consists in their being all *in earnest* at it. If it 'were merely a masquerade, it would be the merriest of carnivals; 'but the fools make a serious business of the matter.'

111

15. FOREIGN QUARTERLY REVIEW, 20 (1837), 121-136 (pagination differs). M/H No. 3410. By Edmund Williams?

ART. VII.—*Histoire de la Littérature Allemande depuis les tems les plus reculés jusqu'à nos jours, précédée d'un parallèle entre la France et l'Allemagne.* Par A. Peschier, 2 vol. 8vo. Paris and Geneva. 1836.

This work is intended to fill up a void in modern philology, by giving, in a moderate compass, a comprehensive history of German literature, from the first rude specimens of the language to its present high state of cultivation. The literature of Germany is now one of the richest, and certainly the most prolific, in Europe; it is the literature of a country reckoning some forty and odd millions of people—a country which holds, together with France, the balance of the Continent. It is well to look to this latter fact, namely, that Germany, with its two great monarchies and its other kingdoms and principalities, is now more than ever the great focus of continental diplomacy. Russia itself, the great scarecrow of newspaper politics, could not attempt any thing serious, at least in western Europe, but as an auxiliary of one or both of the two great German powers. On the other side, if we look to the rational progress in modern society and to the spreading of liberal institutions, we find nearly one half of Germany under representative governments, which, although they may not have attained the expected perfection which some people attribute to the Spanish constitution of 1812, are still, it must be acknowledged, many steps in advance of the real absolutism of the late Ferdinand VII. In short, Germany, notwithstanding the grumblers both native and foreign, is a tolerably happy, thriving, moral, well-informed and contented country, at least as much so as France, and perhaps England too. Surely such a country and its people, their manners, opinions and language, and their literature, which is a reflection of all the rest, ought to be attentively studied by the philosopher, the statesman, the politician, the philologist—by every one, in short, who feels an interest about the general concerns of mankind. And yet the language and the literature of Germany are known both in France and England only to a chosen few. It is astonishing to see the ignorance and the indifference that have prevailed, especially in France, until very recently, concerning a nation which cannot even be said to be separated from it by the Rhine, for both banks of that river in Alsace and Lorraine, which are provinces of France, are inhabited by people of German stock, and speaking German as their vernacular tongue.

Madame de Stael was the first who broke through the wall which prejudice had raised between France and Germany. Her work, "L'Allemagne," although consisting of separate sketches, and not forming a connected history, yet eloquently and powerfully written, appeared at a time when a wilful man wished to fashion all human mind to a mould of his own. Official reproof and exile were the rewards of her truly fearless attempt; for at that time there were real grounds for fear from the displeasure of Napoleon. Savary's coarse and vulgar sneer remains an imperishable memorial of the system by which the mind was fettered in those times, through the will of one who has been styled the son and champion of the revolution, and who is still looked upon by some credulous people as a favourer of liberty. Peace came, and it was no longer treasonable to study and admire the productions of the German or the English muse. Since then Herder, Schiller, Göthe, Niebuhr, John Paul Richter, Hoffman and others, have been translated into French. The Revue Germanique and Revue des Etats du Nord have made known the contemporary progress of German literature. But still how little is known of the great majority of German writers, of the learned lucubrations of so many professors of the hundred German universities and colleges—the profound civilians, the abstruse metaphysicians, the accomplished scholars, the indefatigable geographers and historians, who toil and labour for the benefit of future generations? Savigny, Thibaut, Ritter, Heeren, Boeckh, Neander, Schlosser, Böttiger, O. Muller, Hammer, and many more, to how few are they known out of the limits of their own country? A work was wanted to class by order of dates and of departments of literature the best among the innumerable writers that Germany has produced, in order to impart some idea of what they have accomplished in their respective walks. This is what the book before us has in some degree performed. The author, M. Peschier, was happily situated for such a task. He is a native of Western or French, as it is commonly styled, or, more properly speaking, Romande Switzerland; a land of transition between Germany and France, which, without being either French or German, yet partakes of the moral temperament and intellectual character of both countries. That south-west corner of Switzerland, the Vaud, Geneva, and Neuchatel, the country of the ancient Burgundians, is like a stepping-stone between France and German Helvetia, which latter is itself one of the out-posts of real Germany. With much of the sound judgment, sincerity, and *bonhommie* of the German character, the natives of Romande Switzerland unite the liveliness of imagination, the quickness of repartee, and the social refinement of the French. They can therefore appreciate what is valuable in both, and as they belong to a neutral country and have no national prejudices against either, they are likely to be more impartial than either in their judgments. But besides this, our author has qualified himself for his undertaking by a residence of some years in Germany, by having visited its principal cities, by having mixed freely in German society, by having formed connexions in that country, and becoming, in fact, almost naturalized in it. His work bears in its dedication the name of a distinguished and highly estimable German writer, Baron La Motte Fouqué, which is of itself a recommendation. The first volume begins with an introduction of sixty pages, with the title " Germany and France." It is an original sketch of the disparities between the two countries, and is not the least interesting part of the work. We will quote a few passages, which will give the reader an idea of the author's turn of mind and of his style.

" ' Man is the same every where;' such has been one of the wise saws of certain critics, who, looking at the mere surface of the human mind, have observed some general tendencies which are common to almost all nations. It may be true that on the threshold of life men resemble each other; the cradle is the common starting point of all; but the resemblance stops there. Climate, manners, habits, religion, education, all tend to break the uniform mould into which nature seems to have cast us. As men proceed along the road of life, the individuals, one after another, separate themselves from the mass, and each attains a distinct physiognomy of his own. These characteristic features which constitute originality in man, form also the elements of the individuality of nations, which is one of the profoundest mysteries of creation. It were a most interesting subject for study, to seek out the causes which stamp each people with a peculiar character; but this is too vast a field of inquiry for our present work, and we must content ourselves with stating here some matter-of-fact observations. Two great principles exist simultaneously in Europe; on one side the spirit of order, stability, and unity; on the other the love of progressive ideas, of variety, and movement. These two principles exist together, but in very different proportions in each of two neighbouring countries which are divided by the course of the Rhine. In Germany, outward calmness and repose prevail, but in the moral and intellectual world within, there is a continual stimulus for progress and change. This moral activity, this constant desire of extending the sphere of the human mind, have earned for Germany the name of the country of thought. In France the principle of stability, of fixity, prevails internally; but externally every thing is under the influence of movement and variety. Germany has become long since the land of intellectual progress, while France is the centre of the political and social movement. . . . . The Germans look upon ideas as the source of all our impressions, whilst the French, placed at the other extremity of the moral scale, believe in the sovereign empire of sensations over the development of the intellect. This dangerous dogma is one of the articles of faith of Condillac's philosophy, and we all know the influence of that metaphysician and his disciples upon the philosophers of

the eighteenth century, who did not scruple at last to strip man of his soul, and the universe of its Creator. Thus, while the head is perhaps too busily at work in Germany, and the mind, by dint of soaring higher and higher, loses itself at times in the misty regions of an unproductive contemplation; on the other side, the doctrine of sensualism, adopted by the French, has led them once already by a rapid descent to the most deplorable effects of a desolating materialism. By reducing every thing to the miserable proportions of our fragile and perishable nature, and trying to explain, mechanically, the phenomena of our intellect, they came to consider, in the end, the noblest faculties of the soul as material and physical gifts. Virtue was no longer the offspring of heaven, refined feeling was owing to weakness of organization, and people fancied that they had discovered, in the predominance of certain fluids in our animal economy, the courage which produces the hero, and the self-devotedness which inspires the martyr. They were on the point of establishing a course of diet and sanitary treatment in order to stimulate or modify talent, of putting a straight waistcoat on the poet, and confining genius in a lunatic asylum. Such a system cannot be favorable to poetry, etc. . . . . . . "

" The French are characterized by their quick intelligence of the affairs of the world, their diplomatic shrewdness and perspicacity, their mobility, their rapidity of thought and of action, by minds alert and supple like their bodies, by a warlike instinct; to which they owe their brilliant laurels, and lastly, by their taste for pompous ceremonies, brilliant festivals, and splendid monuments. Opposed to this existence, wholly external and practical, stands the genius of meditation, which belongs to the nations of the North; a character more grave, more reflective, of a more abstruse nature, an imperative want of diving into one-self, and analyzing the most fugitive sentiments of the soul. Man, in Germany, is a world in miniature, in which, notwithstanding the discoveries already made, there remains still some unexplored spot, some unfrequented and uncultivated nook.

" In France, the rage for politics pervades all classes of society. Proteus like, it assumes all forms, and protrudes into every conversation. But politics fill little space in the ordinary existence of the Germans; they are too careful of their material welfare, too fond of a peaceful and comfortable home, too accustomed to an inward life, to have, generally speaking, much relish for the stormy scenes of public life, for the struggles of the bar, the hustings, and the parliamentary debate. This natural taste of the Germans for retirement, domestic life, and the silence of the cabinet, accounts for their reserve and coolness in the social relations, and for the absence of that free and communicative gaiety which imparts a charm to French conversation. Variety and the desire of pleasing effect greater wonders on the left than on the right bank of the Rhine. We often miss in Germany the elegance of *ton*, the urbanity of manners and of language which are so natural to the French; even the appearance and carriage of the people in the former country is somewhat stiff and starched. But their apparent frigidity is owing to bashfulness, and, instead of a common-place gallantry, they have the true politeness, which is that of the heart ; for it is the nation which has most benevolence and cordiality. The women of Germany are not gifted with that vivacity of spirit and mobility of imagination which render French women so fascinating ; they have neither the prompt repartee of the latter, nor their wonderful sagacity in deciphering the most recondite mysteries of the human heart, nor the tact which gives an original and refined turn to the expression of every thought. But the women of Germany possess other qualities which endear them for ever to those who have once deserved their confidence and obtained a place in their friendship ; they possess a frankness and simplicity of heart, a candour of feeling, and an evenness of temper, owing to a natural fund of indulgence and general benevolence, which is soon perceived in their intercourse with strangers.

" The prevalent qualities of the French are wit and sagacity, but the Germans have more soul and more imagination. The former are more sensible of faults than alive to beauties ; more fond of art than of nature ; quick of impression, they are also quick in shaping their thoughts, but they are likewise, at times, exclusive, wilful, and superficial. The Germans are more reflecting, grave, and conscientious : they conceive slowly, and are circumspect in forming their judgment. Hence it was to be expected that the theory of the fine arts should have assumed a very different character among each of the two nations."— *Introduction*, p. 1—14.

The author, in noticing the various phases of the French critical art, speaks with just praise of Montaigne, Pascal, Nicole, Arnauld, and Fenélon. In the 18th century, however, literary criticism, in France, gave way to a presumptuous dogmatism, an impertinent frivolity of judgment, to which Voltaire himself lent his then paramount influence. Our age has seen the revival of a better taste, in proof of which we may mention Madame de Staël, Benjamin Constant, Guizot, Villemain, Barante, Thierry, with a chosen band of young writers, who follow the track of those, regardless of party prejudice and clamour.

" As for the Germans, (our author goes on to say,) they move on in the front rank of the most forward among the nations of Europe. To criticize the works of the great masters, whether in literature or the arts, is not with them a common vocation, the solution of a mere grammatical or rhetorical problem ; it is an important and almost apostolic mission. They are not satisfied with passing judgment on the creations of accidental genius, but they must re-ascend through the course of ages, and explore the sources of the true principles of the art ; those principles which are applicable alike to all times and countries. . . . A great critic in Germany stands on a par with a great orator or poet ; he enjoys equal respect and equal applause. He feels what he writes, he sympathizes with a noble thought, a fine action, a generous sentiment ; his criticism is lofty, eloquent and inspired. Germany, in short, is the country of æsthetics."—pp. 20, 21.

" There are, in many an obscure town of Germany, studious, hard labouring men, miners of thought, who pass years, sometimes perhaps half a century, in solitary retirement, without their names being heard of. They care little about popularity or fashion ; they work, not for a party, a coterie, a saloon, but through real love of science, supported in their task by their enthusiasm for the good, the beautiful, and the useful—for all that is great and generous in the heart of man—in order to pay what they look upon as a sacred debt towards their country, and towards mankind. Owing to this spiritualism, to this prevalence of the soul over the other faculties, the Germans, even in the midst of the illusions of their fancy, have always bowed with respect to the great dogmas of immateriality and immortality, which form the key-stone of the structure of religion."

Through the remainder of this interesting introduction our author traces the influence of the national character in the differences existing between the German and French styles of conversation, their music, their poetry, and lastly their drama. The whole parallel is remarkably well kept up and clearly defined.

After recalling in the first chapter of his history the scanty memorials of the ancient Germans, drawn chiefly from the masterly sketch of Tacitus, who seems to have been inspired by a kind of instinctive foreboding of the destinies of that unconquerable race which stood alone opposed to Roman despotism and Roman corruption, our author points out the most important distinction between classical liberty and the liberty of the German races. " Among the nations of antiquity, liberty was collective and not personal. The masses were first ranged into independent political bodies, every individual of which was nothing by himself, but acquired importance only as a fraction of the great whole. They were not free-willed men, but citizens, the slaves of their country for life and death." The word " *patria* " had a despotic influence ; it was a sort of divinity to which every thing must be sacrificed, and for which any crime or cruelty might be perpetrated without remorse, and every self-denial or privation endured. There was something grand and noble, at least to the imagination, in this self-devotedness, but it was any thing but individual liberty, the liberty of a rational and responsible being. It was fit for men who had no definite idea of any thing beyond the grave. In our own times, men of a similar mind have sought to revive this classical liberty, with the magic words *patria*, glory, &c., with which they have certainly effected astonishing, but unprofitable and merciless deeds, and only for a short space of time ; for they found that the masses were not so docile as those of ancient Rome or Sparta, in their blind enthusiasm and stoic resignation. Men, in our days, are apt to inquire for what they are called upon to sacrifice their lives, their dearest ties, and their peace ; and an empty word does not always afford to them a convincing answer. Christianity has greatly contributed to effect this moral change : it was Christianity that first recalled man to his individuality; that told him that he was a free agent; that he had an immortal and invaluable soul; that he lay under a personal responsibility towards his Creator, a responsibility unknown to the ancients; that he was amenable to a higher and very different tribunal than that of his country, or Cæsar's, or men's opinion. These solemn truths imparted a new and healthy freedom to man's mind; they inspired the Christian convert, whether freeman or bondsman, with a sense of his own dignity; they gave eloquence to the apostle, firmness to the confessor, and holy resignation to the martyr. This spiritual individuality easily allied itself to the old personal freedom of the German nations,—a freedom founded upon individual strength, and a nomade state of society; and from the two together, the modern European notion of liberty has sprung. In this distinction between classical and individual liberty, between the liberty of men, as enlightened moral agents, or the mere political sovereignty of the uninformed masses, which is but another form of despotism, lies much of the solution of the political, religious, and social problems of our own times.

In Chapter II. our author treats of the era of Charlemagne, himself a son of Germany, whose long reign throws a streak of vivid light across the darkness of the ages which intervened between the fall of the Roman empire and the time of the Crusades. With Charlemagne the literary history of Germany may be said to begin.

German literature is supposed, by many foreigners, to be of very recent creation, because it was only in the last century that it became familiar to the rest of Europe. This, however, is a mistake, for, without going back to the ancient war-songs of the German bards, recorded by Tacitus, or to Ulphilas' Translation of the Scriptures, we find poems written in the Teutonic dialects in the age of Charlemagne, such as Hildebrant and Hathubrant, which was republished by the Grimms, in 1811; the war-song on the victory of Louis III. of France, over the Normans; the paraphrasis of the Gospel, in high German, by Ottfried, of Weissemburg, in the 9th century, with another contemporary version in low Saxon; the Annals of the Saxons, by the monk Witikind, and those of the Emperors of Germany, by Dittmar, Bishop of Merseburg, both of the beginning of the 11th century, as well as the Chronicle of Lambert of Aschaffenburg, and the noble hymn in praise of St. Anno, Archbishop of Cologne. Our author gives extracts of these various productions. He leaves out the *Latin* literature of Germany of the same period, to which many of the clergy, both secular and regular, and also some nuns, applied themselves, and which exhibits some interesting productions.

For this branch of information we might refer our readers to the comprehensive sketch given by Mr. Dunham, in his excellent *History of the Germanic Empire,* (Lardner's Cyclopœdia), Book II. *On the religious and intellectual History of the German Church during the Middle Ages.*

Under the Emperors of the Franconian dynasty, Germany distracted by the great struggle between the throne and the altar, produced but few specimens of literary talent. Even the stirring period of the first Crusades could hardly rouse the German mind from its torpor. With the Swabian dynasty in the latter half of the twelfth century, appear the Minnesänger, " singers of love," very different, however, from the Troubadours of the South, to whom they have been compared. The Troubadour is gay, thoughtless, and licentious; the Minnesänger is tender and plaintive, spiritual and lofty. The former sings of love and chivalry, and of the varied incidents of war and *courtoisie;* the latter, although many Minnesänger had been with the Crusades to Palestine, seldom if ever alludes to the adventures of chivalry and romance; he dwells chiefly upon the inward feelings of the soul, upon the refined sentiments and pangs of the tender passion; his strains are chaste and melancholy, they are marked by a disdain of sensuality, and of the corruptions of the world, with allusions to the contemporary history of Germany, and occasional aspirations after the purer joys of another world, and the sublime visions of eternity.

The series of the most celebrated Minnesänger begins with Henry of Waldeck, who was contemporary with Frederic Barbarossa, and ends with Hadsloub under Rudolf of Habsburg, towards the end of the thirteenth century. Our author gives specimens of some of their compositions, especially from Walther von der Wogelweide, who is one of the most interesting of the whole series.—p. 187—202.

The epic muse followed close upon the lyric effusions of the Minnesänger. Its first essays in Germany were borrowed from the then prevailing romances of Arthur and his Peers, and of the St. Graal. Wolfram of Eschenbach, whom Schlegel has greatly praised, wrote Tiurel and Perceval, and the Lohengrinn, or Lorrainer; and Godfrey of Strasburg wrote Tristan and Iseult. But the German poets soon turned to national subjects, and produced the " Book of Heroes," which treats of the exploits of the Goths and other races, and the Niebelungen, which is less historical and more romantic, but in which a gigantic historical figure towers above the mists of fiction; this is Etzel or Attila, " the scourge of God." The author of the Niebelungen is not ascertained. This poem has been styled the Iliad of Germany, as that of Gudruna has been called its Odyssey. Then came Rother, or the Red King, which relates to the wars of the Lombards with the Greeks in Italy, Otnit, Hugh Dietrich, and Wolf Dietrich, which are full of sorcery and magical wonders. These poems are of the age of the Hohenstauffen, a brilliant epoch for German chivalry and romance.

The Meistersänger are another class of poets peculiar to Germany. The epoch when they flourished was about the time of the decline of the Minnesänger. The latter were the bards of the aristocracy, they were chiefly knights themselves; the master-singers were the poets of the municipal towns and corporations, burgesses, tradespeople, and artizans, who formed musical and literary societies or schools, in which a sort of apprenticeship was required; they had competitions or trials of skill, had certain fixed rules of composition, and had their judges of poetical merit. The schools of Mainz, Strasburg, Colmar, Frankfort, and Wurtzburg, were the most celebrated in the fourteenth century; those of Nürnberg and Augsburg in the fifteenth; those of Ratisbon, Ulm, Münich, and Breslau, in the sixteenth; and that of Basel in the seventeenth. Many of their effusions were satires on the vices of society; others were religious, such as paraphrases of the Scriptures, hymns, &c. At the time of the Reformation the master-singers proved a powerful auxiliary to Luther and his colleagues, with whom many of them were connected, and whose cause they embraced.

Germany was at the same time rich in popular songs and ballads. They were of many sorts; religious songs, which are marked by a feeling of sincere piety, free from coarse superstition, a feeling more prevalent perhaps in Germany than in other countries during the middle ages; they had hymns upon the great mysteries of the Christian faith, upon eternity, future life, &c., which are truly sublime in the simplicity of their expression. There were also ballads for the different trades and callings of life, such as the fisherman's, the hunter's, the shepherd's, the husbandman's, of which the melody as well as the words are imitative of the sounds and scenes familiar to each. The fisherman's song is distinguished by a monotonous hollow tune, resembling the moaning of the wave striking against the shore; that of the hunter is shrill and wild; that of the shepherd soft and calm. The songs of the husbandman are varied, some for each season, adapted to the various works of the field. In several towns and villages of Germany, towards the beginning of the spring, winter, represented by a Jack Straw, is driven out by the children, amidst joyous clamours. The vinedresser's song is like those of old, satirical, and somewhat licentious. The miner's lays are among

the best; they are marked by a sort of religious awe; as his labour is among the mysteries of the subterraneous creation; they tell of sylphs and other genii which guard the treasures concealed in the bowels of the earth.

Among the warlike songs of Germany, those of the Swiss on the occasion of their wars with Charles the Rash, Duke of Burgundy, deserve a distinguished place. Veit Weber is the most celebrated among these martial bards of Helvetia; he was present at the battle of Morat, in 1476, and describes with fearful truth the rout and carnage of the Burgundians.

Of the satirical compositions of those times, Reynard the Fox, and the Ship of Fools, the latter by Sebastian Brand, a Doctor of Laws at Strasburg, were the most popular. The former is more of a political and religious satire; it lashes the vices and gross corruption of the clergy and monks of those times, which must certainly have been very great, for chroniclers and poets, novelists and moralists, in every country of Christian Europe, laymen and clergymen themselves, doctors of the Church, and even Popes, have all expressed their reprobation of them. The Ship of Fools is a more general satire on the follies and vices of all classes; the poet lashes the various manias of the times, bibliomania, melomania, dansomania, &c.; he attacks fops, drunkards, gluttons, upstarts, sensualists: who are all shipped together in the author's vessel, in which he also, with great good humour, takes his passage. The gloomy but powerful verses which accompany the well-known series of paintings which were seen at Basel, and other towns of Germany and Switzerland, and which are called by the name of the Dance of Death, may also be reckoned among the satirical effusions of Germany in the middle ages.

The middle ages conclude with the Reformation, and the Reformation boasts as its champion one of the most powerful minds that Germany has ever produced, Martin Luther. In our own times a disposition has shown itself in various quarters, to undervalue that great man. The truth is, that unless a man feels strongly the importance of religion, and at the same time the value of mental freedom, he cannot have sympathy for such a mind as Luther's. Luther considered religion as the most important business of man, and it is because he considered it as such, that he wished to take it at its very source, unalloyed by tradition and human authority. He fought for the right of every man to consult the great book of the law, the Scripture, in order that his reason may be enlightened, and that his faith may not be the offspring of mere servility. He fought for liberty of reason, not for licentiousness; for the liberty of Christians, not for that of infidels; with the latter he had nothing to do. The question between Luther and his antagonists is of material importance only to Christians. To those who do not believe in Christianity it seems of little consequence what Christians do believe, and how and whence they derive their belief. To such men the various communions and sects of Christianity appear but as human contrivances, but even they, were they logical in their reasoning, might at least allow that, in a social point of view also, it is better for men to exercise their own judgment, and to be able to give reasons why they believe certain dogmas, and follow certain rules of morality, than merely to say that they were told so by another man, who had himself been told so by another, and so on. And then observe the result of these two ways of believing, upon human actions. One will believe only what is consistent with the text book; the other may be made to believe anything, and to act accordingly. At the time of the Reformation in Switzerland, a plain-spoken abbot, alluding to the state of subjection in which the peasantry were kept by the clergy, observed that, " had the system continued much longer, we should at last have persuaded the people to feed upon straw." But it is unnecessary to proceed further with this argument. One has only to read the history of the times which preceded the Reformation, in order to see the state to which Christianity was reduced. Catholic writers have acknowledged the deplorable corruption of the Church in that age, and it is not one of the least important results of Luther's mission, that the clergy of the Roman Church have since become much more exemplary in their conduct, more studious and better informed, and more temperate in their sentiments, than they were in the fifteenth century.

It is not, however, our author's object to consider Luther as a great theologian and controversialist, but only to advert to the influence of his writings upon the German mind and literature. Few foreigners are aware of Luther's services in this particular. It was he who gave that impulse towards spiritual philosophy, that thirst for education, that soundness of logic, which have made of the Germans one of the most generally instructed, most rational and moral, and most intellectual nations of Europe. Being convinced that education is the natural ally of religion and morality, Luther pleaded, unceasingly, for that of the laborious classes, boldly telling the princes and rulers, how dangerous, as well as unjust, it was to keep their subjects in ignorance and mental degradation. His catechisms for children are masterpieces in their simplicity; the moral precepts which they contain are exactly adapted to the tender capacities of the readers. His explanations of the Psalms, and of passages taken from the Old and New Testaments, his sermons, and other works, are all full of useful moral precepts; they all bear testimony to the profound religious conviction of the author; they all exhibit his admiration for the works of the creation, and his deep sense of the perfections of the Creator. His penetrating eye dives into the abyss of the human heart, and discovers its darkest recesses. But he is no gloomy ascetic, no contemplative visionary satisfied with deploring evil, or seeing no remedy but in extremes; his precepts are all practicable, his morality is social, and his faith is cheered by hope and charity.

To Luther the German language is indebted for much of its improvement, for its clearness and loftiness, and for that flexibility which distinguishes the works of later writers. The style of Luther is vigorous, straight-forward, and comprehensive; it is not the style of a conceited sceptic, who doubts because he is ignorant, and who renders us as weak and undecided as himself; it is the style of a sacred orator, who affirms because he himself believes, and who believes in obedience to the inspiration of his conscience, and to that divine light which the Gospel displays before him. He employs, at the same time, all the resources of polemical rhetoric to move and to convince; he appeals to the heart, as well as to reason; he mixes passion with dialectics; sometimes even he descends to a vulgar jocularity of manner; he mixes bad taste with genius; and the German idiom, which was still cramped and unmanageable, comes from his pen more ductile and fashioned, though not disfigured, by his genius. Luther's version of the Scriptures, an imperishable monument of his learning and patience, a master-piece of precision, fidelity, and elegance, constitutes his best title to the gratitude and veneration of Germany, for having rendered the Bible popular and intelligible to all classes, and made it the domestic book of the people.

Luther's table-talk and his familiar letters, are enlivened by imagination, a graceful turn of thought, and often by a harmless and pleasing hilarity of manner, which denote that the mind of the writer was happy and satisfied with itself. His religious hymns, on the other hand, have much power of expression, and considerable poetical merit.

Ulrich von Hütten, a poet and a warrior, was a contemporary of Luther's. He is best known for an anonymous Latin pamphlet, styled " Letters of some Obscure Men," which had as much success at the time, as Pascal's celebrated " Provinciales," two centuries afterwards. It is a series of letters attributed to the pedantic supporters of the scholastic method, which then reigned paramount in the colleges and universities of Europe, exposing their ridiculous style, their Beotian ignorance, their hatred of innovation, their intolerance, presumption, and religious hypocrisy. The correspondence was considered for a time as genuine, and the scholastics themselves were deceived. But when the trick was discovered, anathemas fell on every side on Hütten's head, and his book was formally excommunicated by Rome. He wandered about to avoid persecution, and at last died in 1523, in a little island on the lake of Zürich, which is still known by his name—" Hütten's Grab," or Hütten's Grave.

Thomas Murner, a Franciscan monk, and a determined but conscientious adversary of the Reformation, ranks high among the German writers of the 16th century. Although a champion of Catholicism, he did not spare, in his honest indignation, the vices of his clergy, which he lashed, like those of all the other classes in his satirical poems, and especially in his " Corporation of Rogues."

Fischart translated, or rather imitated, Rabelais, but the keenness of his humour exceeded even that of his model. The title alone of the German work is a full specimen of the writer's eccentricity. He also wrote an heroic-comic poem on the expedition of the Zürichers, in a boat, by the Limmat and the Rhine, to Strasburg, where they presented the citizens of the latter city with an enormous kettle of millet soup, which was still warm on their arrival, in order to encourage the Strasburgers to join their confederation, by showing them that the distance between the two cities was not so great as they might have supposed.

In the 17th century, the long struggle, known by the name of the thirty years' war, afforded little encouragement or leisure for the cultivation of literature in Germany. Opiz was, however, a remarkable exception; he wrote many poetical compositions, and a treatise on German prosody, whence he has been styled the father of German poetry. The most distinguished disciples of his school were Flemming and Gryphius. Flemming is known for the romantic adventures of his " Mission to Persia," whither he was sent by the Duke of Sleswig. He died young, soon after his return home, and left a collection of short poems, which abound in tender and impassioned feelings, and with recollections of the strange regions he had visited. Gryphius was chiefly a dramatic poet; some of his dramas are not destitute of merit, and one of his farces is still popular in Germany, for being a caricature of the boastful military jargon which prevailed in that country towards the end of the thirty years' war. The principal character, Captain Horribilicriblifax, is a type of military fanfaronnade. But with these few exceptions, the 17th century may be considered as a barren period in German literature and taste, and with it M. Peschier closes the first volume of his work, which

will, perhaps, prove the most acceptable to readers in general, because it treats of the least known part of the literary history of Germany. In the 18th century, German literature appears full grown, but it did not come forth so at once, like Minerva out of Jupiter's head, as some people seem to have supposed.

We can afford but little space to our author's second volume, which treats of the 18th century, a ground much better known, and which has been already trodden by our predecessors in several articles of this Review. After speaking of the influence of French taste upon German literature, in the earlier part of the 18th century, of which influence the critic Gottsched, of whom Göthe, in his *Dichtung und Wahrheit*, gives such a curious portrait, was the chief supporter, and of the national reaction effected by Bodmer and Breitinger, our author speaks of Klopstock and Lessing as the reformers of German taste, and the champions of a national literature, as Winckelmann was the restorer of taste in the fine arts.

The influence of France extended to the sentiments and opinions, as well to the style and manner of literary composition. The Berlin Academy, the philosophical coteries favoured by Frederic, the influence of Voltaire, and the French encyclopedists, all united to propagate among the Germans a contempt for the past, by sneering at nobility, feudal recollections, and old national songs and romance. Engel, the philosopher, Nicolai, the bookseller, and Bahrdt, the theologian, were among the coryphæi of this coterie, which, in the name of tolerance, exercised the most intolerant sway over the literature of Germany. But they found a stout resistance. Klopstock, Hamann, Claudius, Jacobi, Lavater, Herder, Göthe, formed a powerful opposition against the efforts of scepticism and sensualism. Herder was especially the object of the attacks of the Berlin philosophers; he was a man profoundly impressed with the feeling of religion, and had a genuine enthusiasm for the beautiful, in nature and poetry. He collected the popular songs of the different nations, which he classes into two categories, " Songs of the North," and " Songs of the South," and which form a sort of universal history of the different races of mankind. But his most important work is, " Thoughts on the Philosophy of the History of Mankind." His prevalent idea is, that this world is only a preparation for another existence; that human life is only the bud of a flower, which will open hereafter. The whole history of humanity, according to him, is a struggle for spiritual freedom against the material world by which man is fettered—for the triumph of the infinite over the finite,—for the emancipation of the mind, the reign of the soul. Man is continually struggling against sensual forms; he is continually changing the objects of his worship: at every step the world seems to constrain and embarrass him. He feels the want of a purer and wider sphere to breathe in.

" In vain the ancient East, slumbering on the faith of its symbols, thought of having chained man for ever by mysterious allegories : on the opposite shore, an infant people arose, which laughed at its enigmas, and triumphed over its apathy. In vain Roman selfishness, watching the various forms of religion and society, availed itself of them to enthral the whole ; in the midst of the silence of the mighty empire, a hollow murmur was heard from among the forests of the North, which, growing louder and nearer, scared away the legions that vainly pretended to place an eternal boundary to progress or change ; the stream poured in, destroyed that fabric of unity and slavery which had been reared at so fearful a cost of time, labour, and blood, and new and varied forms of existence sprung up from among the scattered ruins. . . . It is thus that we follow the wanderings of mankind through the history of ages, without knowing what will be the termination of these strange vicissitudes, and when the weary traveller will at last behold the pinnacles of his native Ithaca."

Lichtenberg was a disciple of Lessing, and shared his metaphysical opinions, which led to a sort of spiritual pantheism, very different, however, from the materialism of the Paris and Berlin coteries. Lichtenberg was a natural philosopher, a moralist, and a satirist ; he was the father of the humorist school of writers, of which Jean Paul Richter became afterwards the most finished specimen.

Our author bestows a long chapter on Göthe, which is well worth perusal ; but as this subject has been repeatedly treated in our journal, we will not dwell upon it. He next treats of Wieland, Schiller, Bürger, Höltz, Frederic Stolberg, Hebel, Mathisson, and Salis ; he then passes in review the dramatic writers, Werner, Grillparzer, Iffland, Kotzebue, Kleist, Müllner, &c. Of the historians he notices Schlœzer, Spittler, and Müller ; and among the novelists, Tieck, Jean Paul Richter, Hoffmann, Lamotte Fouqué, and Musæus.

The fifth and last chapter of the work treats of the German literature of the nineteenth century, that is to say, of the writers who have appeared first in the present age, and although, as our author observes, there is no Schiller or Göthe amongst them, still we think that he might have devoted to them more space than a score of pages. He will probably make up for it by adding a third volume to a new edition of his work. He has entirely omitted to notice, with the single and most honourable exception of Niebuhr, a most numerous and most meritorious class of German literati,—the eminent scholars, critics, archaiologists, and illustrators of the works of antiquity, a class for which

Germany stands by far the foremost in Europe. Classical scholars and commentators constitute a branch of literature as much as the historians, and many of them, like Heeren, Böttiger, O'Müller, Boeckh, &c., may be called historians likewise. Several thousands of new works appear now annually in Germany, but most of them resemble in taste the ephemeral productions with which France is also inundated, and serve to feed that craving, not for instruction, but for factitious and transitory emotions, that idle curiosity, that restlessness without an object, which are characteristic of our reading age. Of these abortions of the press we may say, borrowing Dante's words—

" Non ragioniam di lor, ma guarda e passa."

Among the historians our author mentions Zschokke, Schlosser, Raumer, and Rotteck. Of dramatists he notices Raupach, Immermann, Count Platen, Grabbe, and Brentano ; of the lyric poets Koerner, Schwab, and Uhland ; of the novelists, A. Lafontaine, Hauff, Alexis, Spindler, Van der Velde, Steffens, Mesd. von Schopenhauer, and Caroline Pichler, Achim von Arnim, Novalis, and Chamisso, and he speaks very highly of the last three. Of Heine our author observes that—

" The *Reisebilder* contains the whole of his political, religious, and literary faith ; in politics a bitter hatred against despotism, and a warm sympathy for liberty and progress ; in religion a vague and confused Deism ; in literature a total independence of rules and coteries ; but above all that old rancorous feeling of liberalism whose shafts are deadly, and which strikes its enemy to the heart. His satire is full of originality, but he seems to forget at times the rules of good taste, and of literary *convenance.*"

Börne, another champion of ultra-liberalism, has assumed as his peculiar mission to abuse all that is doing in Germany—

" In his bitter invectives against his countrymen, he attacks both sovereigns and people, the learned and the journalists, by bitter and contemptuous sarcasms ; he sneers at diplomatists, charges even violent demagogues with servility, and upon every occasion he quotes France as the model country, as the sun-dial of Europe ; he has entrenched himself within Paris as in a citadel from which he keeps up a constant fire against the country of his birth."—p. 488.

We now take leave of M. Peschier's work, which we can conscientiously recommend to those who wish to form an idea of Germany, its people, and their literature.

119

1st. *German Lyrics. By W. Klauer Klattowski, Professor of German in London.* 2d. *The German Reader. By the same.* Simpkin and Marshall.

3rd. *Klauer Klattowski's German Ballads and Romances.*— Simpkin and Marshall.

4th. *Donatti's German Grammar.*— George and Stephen Noden.

We are glad to find that Mr. Klauer-Klattowski continues to publish well-selected volumes from the rich literary stores of his native country. Within the last few years it has been the fashion for English ladies to study German, and we must consider that they owe much to the labours of this author; for in literature so exceedingly copious as that of Germany is well known to be, the task of selection is an extremely difficult one, if it is left for the student to discriminate among a vast mass of publications the works that are calculated to afford pleasure and instruction. It must, therefore, be evident that selections by an accomplished German must be extremely useful in giving a learner a proper taste for German literature.

We hope the publication of this very pleasing volume will induce our fair countrywomen to persevere in the study of the rich original language from which all that is idiomatic and nervous in our own dialect is drawn. Our knowledge of German poetry is singularly limited, even through the medium of translation. A few lyrics by Goethe and Schiller, with Bürger's Leonore, have been frequently translated, and there the general knowledge of German poetical genius ends. Coleridge's magnificent translation of Wallenstein, and the various translations of Faust, with Körner's spirit-stirring martial lyrics, are rather themes of research and discussion among literary circles, than well known to the reading public, who are chiefly acquainted with them through the allusions and quotations of some of our most popular authors. The reader will find many beautiful lyrics which are unknown in English literature among the present collection. We were particularly pleased with the pretty national song written by Klopstock for his young friend Elizabeth von Winthene, beginning

" I am a German maiden,
   Blue mine eyes and soft my looks."

The students of this noble language will find much in this volume which will repay them for their labours, and induce them to continue the study of the great northern tongue.

It is certain that the knowledge of German in this country is not commensurate with the great advantages it offers, it is possible that the trifling difficulties presented by the difference of type has its effect in preventing the extension of its study. But the extreme legibility of the characters in which all the works edited by M. Klauer-Klattowski are printed, really removes this obstacle; the small letters are as legible as roman type, and half an hour's attention will familiarize any one to the diversity of form in the German capitals. The German type of these works is remarkably clear and beautiful. This is a characteristic of " The German Reader" of M. Klauer-Klattowski, which is published in a series of firmly bound books, and consists of some well chosen dramas and tales; and in them, as in " The German Lyrist," we find notes whereby the difficult passages and idiomatic expressions are well explained. Some time ago several numbers of " The German Reader" were forwarded to us, but through the neglect of a person employed they received no notice in the reviews of this magazine, although well deserving of it; the beautiful edition of Undine is now before us, and merits the highest commendation for the useful explanation of the idioms and for the excellence of the type.

There is a good deal of curious reading in the notes of the " German Lyrist," intermixed with clever instructions for construing, but we must protest against the author's plan of mingling up his opinions regarding European politics with philological information. This mode of proceeding will have the effect of procuring him enemies, and will occasion a large circle who would be happy to avail themselves of his talents to reject his works, to his loss and to their own. Political violence mixed up with any species of tuition gives great disgust to every person of judgment, even though belonging to the very party he espouses. But if he cannot control his combativeness on this point, he would do well to clothe his ideas entirely in German, and then his English pupils will not be prejudiced by such eccentricities until after they have derived considerable benefit from his philological labours.

No. 3. These ballads are selected with the critical taste which we have noticed in our review of the German Lyrics, at page 304, to which we beg to refer the reader; and all the extracts in this bespeak the intimate acquaintance and knowledge that M. Klauer Klattowski possesses of the best German authors. They really open a mine to English authors acquainted with this language, which has never been worked before; as instances, we would draw the attention of the render to the following poems: " The Confession," by Langbein; " The Sacristan and the Peasant," by Pfeffel; " The Benefaction," by Gilbert; " The Dying Father," by the same author; " Peter Abroad," by Guibel; " The Emperor Max," by Von Collin. This last relates to the miraculous preservation from an awful tumble that good emperor got, when hunting on the hills of the Tyrol. Our German scholars will see that new and excellent pasture is provided for them in this work. It is got up to match the sister volume, German Lyrics.

4th. Those who wish to master the difficulties of the German language, without the assistance of an instructor, cannot do better than provide themselves with Donatti's German Grammar; from the perusal of it, we are convinced that an industrious student may translate German, readily, in the short space of six months. The mode of instruction is simple and perspicuous, and does great credit to Mr. Donatti, who, himself the teacher of a large circle, has displayed great attention to those difficulties which are most likely to retard the progress of zealous beginners.

17. TAIT'S EDINBURGH MAGAZINE, n.s. 4 (1837), 23-31. M/H No. 3432.

POPULAR SONGS OF THE GERMANS.

WE have already, on former occasions, in fulfilment of a welcome duty, attempted to place before the English reader, from time to time, some outlines of the poetical literature of Germany, in noticing certain of her eminent authors. All of these having, more or less, and some especially, (as Körner and Bürger,) enriched the popular lyrics of their country, we have been led to make incidental mention of this beautiful and characteristic branch of poetry. On the present occasion, it is proposed to devote a few pages exclusively to the subject; although only to offer a few gleanings from the harvest of a land exceedingly fertile in popular song. A full display of its riches in this respect, tracing the origin and growth of a plant deeply rooted in national character, and shedding continual influence on the soil which gave it birth, would require a longer treatise, and might exercise and and reward a higher criticism than ours. It must suffice, in the present instance, to gather and exhibit such specimens as a passing hand may here and there select from a field of unbounded extent and diversity. This, a long-cherished purpose, has now been mainly called into execution by the appearance of a pleasant little volume, by M. Klauer Klattowsky; which, as the first of a series destined to make the songs of Germany accessible to English students, deserves kind notice at our hands. The selection, moreover, is generally judicious; and, though it does not include many favourite compositions which we looked to find there, it must be remembered that the limits of a little book can but embrace a small part of what is excellent, amidst the profusion offered on every hand. We have, therefore, great pleasure in recommending M. Klauer's " Anthology" to all young students of the language and poetry of Germany.

Lyrical poetry, as Wordsworth justly remarks, demands, as its specific distinction, the presence of musical accompaniment; and such, in the early periods of the art, was never wanting to it. This condition, however, although constituting its very essence, has, in great measure, ceased to be more than an imaginary one in highly cultivated languages, with respect to many productions of a class which are, nevertheless, truly lyrical. The alliance between music and poetry, has been neglected by custom, as each gradually became more artificial; but has not been virtually dissevered. We are now to speak of that class only in which the alliance actually survives—of poetry written to be sung, and living, with the strains to which it is wedded, on the lips of a people to whom music is an element of daily life, as universal and familiar as the common air. The national features of the Germans are, in an especial manner, reflected on the surface of their national song; which, mingling with the current of all their habits, actions, and feelings, imparts to each an appropriate language and an immediate utterance. And when to this it is added that the lineaments thus reflected are, in themselves, peculiarly distinct and original, we may expect to find in the national lyrics, much that is marked and characteristic. Nor will the expectation be disappointed.

In a wit's description of the great European nations, there was assigned to the Briton, the empire of the sea; to the Gaul, of the land; to the German, of the air. Such are the random traits by which one half of mankind learns to characterise the other. It is at once amusing and pitiable to think how many are content to seek no better idea of nations and races than may be supplied by vague generalities or vulgar nicknames. Those, however, who are not so contented, on applying themselves to observe the points by which the character of a people is revealed, will find in the Germans, a nature, strangely composed indeed, but exceedingly genuine, decided, and love-worthy. Prone alike to the affections and enjoyments of life, steadfast in attachment, and strongly disposed to reverence and a certain methodical love of order; simple, nay, homely in manners; combining an uncontrollable imagination, and a propensity to dream and speculate, with a firm hold on the plainest realities; trustful, truthful, and earnest, beyond measure; of indefatigable perseverance, and rather daring in conception than prompt to actual enterprise; with a nature easily moved to tenderness, and abounding in substantial cordiality, but neither sensitive nor apt to assume the polish of conventional refinement; with much poetry, some humour, and little wit; seldom agitated by violent passions, but ever alive to warm domestic and social feelings:—such are the people amongst whom lyrical song has found a welcome and a home.

Nor should we overlook their peculiar happiness, in the possession of a language the true offspring of a nature such as we have attempted to pourtray—a language strong, hearty, and copious; full of point and idiom; equally ready for the subtlest combinations and the plainest simplicity; sonorous, masculine, and expressive, with a certain positive directness of structure which hardly admits of equivoque or levity; and, above all, possessing a marked and very musical prosody, which renders it unrivalled amongst modern languages in the variety of poetical forms which it can assume. And we may further add, to the surprise perhaps of those who know it only by report, that, with the exception of the Italian only, there is no language more melodious in poetry or more vocally adapted for song.

To the nation thus constituted and endowed, poetry and music were a natural birth-right. But to bind these more closely together, a further privilege was added. Luther, himself a very German, and one of the greatest men the world has yet seen, with the same hand that struck at the roots of Papal abuse, and gave his noble translation of the Bible as an imperishable legacy to his country, also engrafted on the new creed the healthy growth of popular song, to flourish with it in perpetual union. The great Reformer, a thorough lover of music, and wisely aware of the aid to be derived therefrom in attaching his doctrine to the hearts of the people, made it an express and prominent part of all elementary public instruction. In all the schools constituted under the reformed system, singing was and continues to be taught with the alphabet: thus a broad foundation was laid upon which to raise a structure overshadowing all the land. This consecration of two noble arts on a soil where the minnesingers and meistersingers had already claimed them as a patrimony, has established them for ever, with an efficacy of which the consequences may be plainly seen. The fruits this inestimable gift has borne to Music, may be shewn by pointing to the names of Handel, Bach, Haydn, Mozart, and, greatest of all, Beethoven.* Nor has the sister art less happily flourished.

* We do not agree with our contributor in this comparative estimate of Beethoven.—*E. T. M.*

To say nothing of the higher branches of poetry—the true lyric, its utterance in song, lives amidst all classes in Germany with a genial vigour, such as no other nation can exhibit. In one class of songs, the French, in another the Spaniards, have each their national advantages; but in neither people is the true alliance of poetry and music so universal and supreme. In the fields, the towns, the villages of Germany, their voice is never mute; wherever three are met together, the chorus is heard. The festival and the holiday, the christening and the funeral, have each their joyful or solemn strain. The soldiers sing on the march, or around the fire of the bivouac; the lover serenades his mistress with a chorus in the twilight;—the year opens and closes amidst songs. Of twenty Germans taken, at hazard, from all or any class, you shall hardly find one that is not ready to bear his part manfully in any of the favourite popular lyrics of his country. Here, indeed, national song has very life and being.

Thus the lyrical poetry of Germany is at once married to music; and, while the compositions generally sung are, for this reason, of a higher class than in countries where music is less supreme, they are at the same time directly modified, in form and tenor, by the application to which they are destined. Where song is either occasional or exotic, the poetry set to music is liable to become worthless or affected, as, with some exceptions, is the case in England; it is only where it is popular and universal that the poet and musician work in entire concert. Hence, in considering the songs of Germany as poems, their vocal purpose must be kept constantly in mind; he that reads them only, has only half of the whole before him. And how much is thereby lost will readily be known by those to whom the unrivalled song-music of the Germans is familiar.

The songs of Germany, moreover, are, in general, intensely popular. They are not artificial things, got up to be exhibited in drawing-rooms, by ladies in ringlets, and amateurs in spotless gloves. They are matters of far more interest and significance—the very expressions of the various emotions, and likings, and manners of a people very earnest in their way, and nowise ashamed of seeming to be so. Of the pretty nonsense verses which pass for songs with us, few specimens will be found amongst them. Their songs are jovial, fond, satirical, or plaintive, as the mood of the singer may require; but all have some downright purpose and meaning, and a flow and energy which bespeak their genuine character. The reader, bearing in mind what has already been said of the people whose nature they reflect, and remembering that, in popular song, the more positive and tangible features will always be the most readily presented, will not be surprised to find them impressed rather with the strong and homely than with the spiritual traits of the national character. In short, these songs, as they are the companions, so will they be found to be faithful interpreters of the Germans' social and domestic life ; and the first of their poets and composers, a Goethe and a Beethoven, will be heard, in these compositions, lending their unrivalled genius to express the popular language of their country's lyrical muse.

A pleasant task it would be to treat of the songs current amongst peculiar classes ; each of which has strains expressly its own, from the nightly ditty of the watchman, to the chant of the soldier or student, or the guild-song of the artisan. But this would lead us too far into detail. For the same reason, a passing word is all that can be given to the popular hymns of Germany, many of which, with their vigorous, simple speech, and noble *chorale* tunes, were composed by Luther. Passing from these, we must begin with the extracts that we have prepared; entreating the reader to bear the preceding remarks in mind, as well as to make due allowance for the insufficiency of the translation.

It may be questioned whether, without woman, poetry would ever have been uttered : to her we certainly owe its lyrical form in song. The main sources of this delightful stream, love and honour, flow, the one directly, the other by a returning course, from the influence of the gentle sex ;—the poetry whose life is passion, obeys the power which rules the warmer emotions of the heart, as the moon commands the tides. The nations whose women are degraded, are destitute of song, as well as of all other of the best privileges of life. And wherever lyrical poetry exists, its current is principally fed by the overflowings of amorous feeling : its alarms and ecstasies, for ever repeated, have a universal charm, which no repetition can impair; choice therefore, no less than judgment, directs us to draw the first selections from the songs dedicated to this paramount theme. At the first glance, the following little morsel of petulance, by Schubart, may discredit the gallantry of our choice—the second will discover that the show of captiousness is merely assumed by the poet. He is one that loves the objects of his whimsical displeasure far too dearly to reproach them in hard earnest. The next smile he meets will melt all this cynicism like May frost.

> Your maidens all are fickle gear—
>   Now so—to-morrow so !
> If but one rosy cloud appear,
>   How glad and bright they grow !
> To-morrow ?   Why, at once you find
>   Change in the wind.
>
> Let but an air too roughly blow,
>   The maiden 's near to die ;
> Her pretty eyes are all aflow,
>   Her little mouth's awry.
> To-morrow ?   See how light she springs,
>   Frolics, and sings !
>
> When maiden greets with loving eye,
>   You trust the cunning glance ;
> And mount, all dizzy, to the sky,
>   In such a blissful trance !
> To-morrow ?   Why, you're hardly known—
>   Vain dreams alone !
>
> So, maids, howe'er you roll your eyes,
>   As fond as you may feign—

> Ay, came ye straight from paradise—
>   I'll trust not one again !
> False things !   To-day, as hot as spice—
>   To-morrow, ice !

But should this be thought too saucy, here is a corrective, in a more cordial strain, professing devout homage to the " angels of life," all and several. It is conceived in a fine catholic spirit of love, akin to that expressed in Byron's noble wish—

> That womankind had but one rosy mouth,
> That he might kiss them all from north to south.

As a song, too, it is effective and vigorous, when provided with a sufficient chorus.

> A fair good health to every gentle maiden,
>   Who still in virgin freshness grows !
> Health to the matron grave, with years o'erladen,
>   Whose temples age has crowned with snows !
>   CHORUS.
> But each give a health, ere he drink to the rest,
> Thrice fondly repeated, to her he loves best !
>
> Health to the princess on her throne of splendour,
>   That well her golden crown beseems !
> To humble maid, with crown that wild-flowers lend her,
>   Whose eye with modest virtue beams !
>   But each, &c. &c.
>
> Health to the child in slumber's sweet caresses,
>   On wakeful mother's bosom laid !
> To her whose heart the lovely nursling presses,
>   Be next a brimming goblet paid !
>   But each, &c. &c.
>
> Health to the sylph whose cheek fair colours, blending
>   With snow the morning blushes, grace !
> To the brown reaper o'er her sickle bending,
>   We drain, as well, one hearty glass !
>   But each, &c. &c.
>
> Health be to her whom love's dear triumph blesses,
>   Who deems her bliss, like Heaven's, entire !
> Nor less to her whom sadness lone oppresses,
>   And love torments with mocked desire !
>   But each, &c. &c.
>
> Health to the maid whom circling graces favour,
>   Who loves the dance, and song, and joy !
> And her, the virgin prone to musings graver,
>   Whom duties, freely sought, employ !
>   But each, &c. &c.
>
> All were vouchsafed us by the heavenly Giver,
>   Our hearts to better and to bless :
> All, all to us shall be the image ever
>   Of good and fair in fairest dress !
>   CHORUS.
> Fill, then, your glasses, your glances uplift ;
> Thank, in glad choruses, Heaven for its gift !

A more homely and a stronger vein of tenderness, without one atom of sickly sentiment, will be found in the delightful Old-German song we shall now quote. It is an utterance of such manly and fervent love as flourishes only in generous natures ; and is expressed with a plainness that enhances its warmth. In the original, there is a rustic earnestness of language which we have in vain attempted to preserve. The author is Simon Dach.

> Annie of Tharau is she whom I court ;
> She is my being, my life, my support !
> Annie of Tharau her heart doth incline,
> Loving or grieving, in answer to mine !
> Annie of Tharau ! my riches, my good !
> Soul of my body, my flesh and my blood !
> Though the storms meet us, and tempests should strike,
> We two are plighted to bear them alike—

124

Sickness, hard usage, and trouble, and pain,
Only the closer our love-knot shall strain !
Annie of Tharau ! my joy, my sunshine !
All mine own being is clasped around thine !

Straight as a palm-tree shoots upwards again,
After some yielding to tempest and rain,
So the love in us grows mighty and great,
After much sorrow and hardship of fate !
Annie of Tharau ! my riches, my good !
Soul of my body, my flesh and my blood !

Wert thou e'er torn from this bosom, mine own—
Yea, wert thou dwelling where scarce the sun's known—
Iron and dungeons, the waste nor the sea,
Armies of foes should not keep me from thee !
Annie of Tharau ! my joy, my sunshine !
All mine own being is clasped around thine !

As a contrast to the above, we subjoin an exquisite little serenade by Goethe, in which the complaint of unreturned affection is breathed in murmurs like the wailing of an Eolian harp. The fanciful tenderness of this strain is no less true than the simple warmth of the preceding one to that passion which moves every chord of the human heart, the lightest as well as the deepest. In this class of songs, Goethe is quite unrivalled ; his melody is inimitable.

Oh ! while the soft dream's o'er thee,
Half listen, as I pour
My love and song before thee.
Sleep on ! what wouldst thou more ?

And as my lyre is sighing,
Stars smile all heaven o'er,
To hallow love undying.
Sleep on ! what wouldst thou more ?

The power of love undying
Uplifts me, and I soar,
From earth's disturbance flying.
Sleep on ! what wouldst thou more ?

The strife of worldly dealing
For thee I long forswore,
Too oft to silence stealing.
Sleep on ! what wouldst thou more ?

Thou bidst me wake thus lonely,
Yet wilt not hear---I pour
Song on thy slumbers only.
Sleep on ! what wouldst thou more ?

This delicate lament is no unfit prelude to one of almost equal sweetness, by Jacobi, the pathos of which is nevertheless deeper ; for its sadness is more than a lover's melancholy. The burden of the song is not the less real for being clothed in poetical imagery. It is a plaintive commentary on the old strain—

Hal hay que fia,
A gente que pasa !

Whither be the violets gone---
Those that bloomed of late so gay,
And, in fragrant garlands strown,
Decked the blooming Flower-Queen's way ?
Youth ! alas ! the spring must fly---
Yonder violets withered lie !

Whither are the roses fled
We so gaily singing bound,
When the brow of shepherd maid
And the herdsman's hat was crowned ?
Maiden ! summer days must fly---
Yonder roses withered lie !

Lead me then the brook beside
That refreshed the violets pale,
And in murmurs low did glide
Downwards to the quiet vale.
Air and sun were scorching sore---
Yonder brooklet flows no more !

Take me then to yonder bower,
Where the summer roses grew ;
Where, in love's confiding hour,
Swain and maiden came to woo.
Wind and hail were pelting sore---
Yonder bower is green no more !

Tell me where the maid is flown---
Her I saw, one summer day,
O'er the violets stooping down,
Lowly flower, as sweet as they :
Youth ! alas ! all beauty dies---
Withered, too, the maiden lies !

Whither has the poet strayed---
He that o'er the chequered plains,
Sung of violet, rose, and maid,
Brook and bower, in pleasant strains ?
Maiden ! life for ever flies---
Withered, too, the singer lies !

But melancholy is by no means the prevailing character of the German's songs. He is no idle repiner by profession ; and if at times subdued by the mournful aspect of life, he is ready at others, to share heartily in its pleasures, and to enjoy a loud laugh at its drolleries. There is no reason why we should refuse to join him in this exercise ; and here is an occasion presented us by honest Klamer Schmidt, in his humorous ballad of the " Fair of Life." The satire has no bitterness, although it be a little rough on the tongue.

I sing you a ballad of life and its fair, sirs :
Full many frequent it, and cheapen bad ware, sirs ;
And, thinking right jewels secured by their choice,
Take home from the market mere tinsel and toys.

There's one !---he's by far the chief fool : how he rages,
All breathlessly greedy, through booths and by stages,
And chaffers and bargains for glittering sand
That Fate the next minute may dash from his hand !

The other's more cunning : he wrestles for places
And titles of honour. They're burdensome graces ;
But this may console, when they weary and vex,
That fame brays aloud, and the mob bow their necks.

The third, he's for beauty so longing and tender,
His life, the whole world, he would gladly surrender,
In eyes that enchant him his heaven to survey.
Ah ! heard he none whisper that charms will decay ?

The price-list of Bacchus' rare blessings entrances
A fourth with its promise. This number he fancies,
And that must be purchased. Alas ! saw he not
The gout as it lurks in the cask of the sot ?

'Tis the fifth that the crown of the merchandise chooses :
The toys that catch others he freely refuses---
His jewel is health ; and his care, to engage
The friendship of wisdom to cheer him in age.

Long life to the Fifth ! the true king of right reason !
Might I visit the fair, as a Fate, for a season,
On him my whole stuff would I gladly expend,
And leave not a rag to the fools that attend.

Having fallen into a humorous vein, we may as well pursue it a little further. Here is the very song we were looking for, in charity to the impatient reader ; who, having doubtless been taught to believe that Germans do nothing else but eat *sauer kraut*, spin metaphysics, and smoke out of immense pipes, has been amazed to find none of these matters hitherto commemorated. In this strain, of no peculiar worth indeed, he will find tobacco sufficiently conspicuous ; although, to render it tractable in an English dress, we have been forced to take some liberty with the name of the magnificent weed—

for which we bespeak the indulgence of the adept.

> Of croaking fools that whine profanely
>   At life's disasters, there's a pack :
> Me grief assails and pinches vainly,
>   Blest with a pipeful of taback.
> But just to-day quite changed the case is—
>   To-day my wonted taste is slack ;
> And gladly for a maiden's graces,
>   I'd pledge my pipe of best taback !
>
> The soldier 'gainst his will a-fasting,
>   The sailor that his grog must lack,
> Beguiles the vain desire of tasting,
>   With help of pipe and mild taback.
> But comes some pearl of pretty wenches—
>   At once his heart begins, tick-tack !
> The joy within him even quenches
>   His smoking pipeful of taback.
>
> For me, I hold the doctrine stoutly
>   Maintained by famous Major Crack ;
> Because, like him, I prize devoutly
>   Both comely maidens and taback.
> By war's outrageous din unshaken,
>   He still kept safe in haversack,
> A picture from his mistress taken,
>   And his dear pipe, to puff taback.

Punch follows tobacco as naturally as rain comes after a south-wester. Here is a punch-song, and—by Schiller!—the philosopher!—the tragic poet ! We see our Glasgow readers already on the alert, *arrectis auribus*. It may be questioned, indeed, whether any, even the most learned, in that city renowned for its brewage of "the materials," have been until now apprized that their favourite compound was a symbol, as well as a mystery ; or that it was typical of the high matters here expounded by the poet. As one of those trifles which betray an affinity of character, this little song tells more of the peculiar bent of Schiller's mind, than a volume of criticism. Here we see the purpose which moulded every object, common as well as sublime, into an image of the ideal. " What !" the reader may exclaim, " even a punch-bowl ?" Let the song answer for us.

> Four primal elements,
>   Inly combined,
> Build up the universe,
>   Fashion mankind.
>
> Press ye the citron's star,
>   Juicy and sour ;—
> Life has an inner heart,
>   Sharp at the core.
>
> Now with mild sugar juice
>   Mingled between,
> Temper the influence,
>   Burning and keen.
>
> Forth let the water gush,
>   Bounding and clear ;—
> Water encompasseth
>   Calmly the sphere.
>
> Now let the spirit drop
>   Trickling adown ;—
> Spirit to life a life
>   Giveth alone.
>
> Ere the fresh perfume dies,
>   Straight be it quaffed ;—
> Only while glows the spring,
>   Quickens the draught.

We suspect that more than one heresy will have been detected in Schiller's doctrine ; but this is said *sous correction*. In the meanwhile, having thus fallen sidelong amongst the cups, we may as well give one specimen (or rather imitation) of a regular German drinking song, and one of the most outrageous of the sort, enough to paralyze a whole bevy of Temperance Societies. It goes to the stirring air—" *Heu ! heu ! ericht mir Nectar*," which Phillips used to sing with such unction and applause some five years ago. The original is not in M. Klauer's collection.

> Fill ! fill a goblet brimming,
> Fit for buoyant mirth to swim in !
> When the wine-god lends me wings,
> What care I for laws or kings ?
>   State and rules
>   Were made for fools—
> He alone is great and free
> Who can drink as deep as we !
>
> Love from sober crews escapes,
> To toy with Bacchus and his grapes ;
>   Laughs, and dips
>   His arrow tips
> In every foaming beaker ;
> Then to timid suitors teaches
> Bold addresses, winning speeches—
>   All that smart
>   By woman's art,
> Drink till pain grow weaker !
>
> Fill ! fill a goblet brimming,
> To the pretty craft of women !
> Let them pout !—its full lip bears
> Kisses quite as sweet as theirs !
>
> Pour ! pour the magic liquor,
> Till the bright thought flashes quicker,
> And the heart exults in song,
> And the pulse of joy beats strong !
>   Lo ! the sprite
>   Of wild delight
> Flutters o'er the goblet's brim !
> Let me quaff, and soar with him !
>
> Fill ! fill a goblet brimming,
> Fit for dancing souls to swim in !
> All the gems of Fancy's mine
> Borrow brighter hues from wine !

It is time to turn to inspirations from a nobler source ; and, in so doing, let us first pay a willing tribute of gratitude to Tschokke, author of the following patriotic song, and of a little book, but one that will survive many works of more pretension—his " Switzerland's History." This is indeed a precious volume, full of simple, manly eloquence, worthily employed in recording the noblest story that the world has yet heard. It is a book that makes the heart beat and the eye swim as you read it ; in a word—and what higher praise can be given ?—it is worthy to be read by grey-haired men to their children, on the very hearths which, in old time, sent forth the men of Grütli and Morgarten, to consummate their noble sacrifice in the face of Heaven, and on the majestic altar of their native mountains—a light and an example to all ages ! This is a digression ; but it is to pay a debt, long owing, for pleasure enjoyed and good received—a duty so nearly religious as to supersede trifling considerations. The following song is one of warning and appeal. It is still customary, in several German towns, for the watchmen to chant a rugged stave, generally containing some trite adage or commonplace moral, as he calls the hour at night. Alluding to this custom, the poet personifies the servile party in his country, as one of these night-birds, groping about in the sunshine, and seeking to persuade his neighbours that all are as dark as himself. The moral, we fancy, might suit other countries as well as Switzerland.

Hear, gentles all ! I give you warning,
  The hour is late, the night is deep ;
At such a time, so far from morning,
  Who'd still be wake ?—'tis well to sleep !
  —The fool through dusty glasses blinking
    Sees not the sun in open day !
Let him be hush, that will go winking ;
  He dotes that shuns the golden ray !
But croak the dotards as they will—
In Switzerland 'tis daylight still !

Hear, sirs ! Your psalms of penance patter—
  They're safe, and none suspected make :
But still the sound of beakers' clatter—
  The sun is down—suspicion's 'wake !
  —When Switzers glad carouse together,
    And friends to friends their hearts resign,
Ne'er sinks the sun, nor darkens either—
  It shines in Heaven, it beams in wine !
So let the mole grub where he will—
In Switzerland 'tis daylight still !

Hear, gentles all ! Till morn be dozing,
  Draw nightcaps o'er your ears, and snore---
On me and mine your trust reposing,
  We'll gladly watch at fold and door.
  —The Swiss is still his own best warder---
    In his own house the lord he stands ;
And, of his native land the guardian,
  Entrusts it not to strangers' hands !
So, warn the stranger as he will—
In Switzerland 'tis daylight still !

Hear, gentles ! Seek to live securely ;
  For waking calls for thoughtful pains ;
And thinking leads to danger, surely—
  So quench your lights, as use ordains.
  —Though all around, behind, before us,
    The brains of men to blocks ye wrought,
We, Swiss, will laugh and sing in chorus—
  " Who dares think freely, well has thought !"
Let light-destroyers preach their fill—
In Switzerland 'tis daylight still !

Hear, sirs ! With backs so little supple,
  You ne'er may Fortune's grace expect---
Bow then, as bend your neighbours, double ;
  And live as modish arts direct.
  —Begone, with foreign modes and favour !
    Ours be the virtues strong of yore ;
Were Freedom crushed, with none to save her,
  The earth would find the Swiss no more !
But sons of night may groan their fill—
In Switzerland 'tis daylight still !

Having now extracted pretty liberally from M. Klauer's " Anthology," we may continue our specimens of German song from other sources. The next shall be one of the many martial strains which were rife during the war of liberation. Some of these, by the lamented Körner, have already been introduced to the reader;* the following —" Blucher's Song"—written by Arndt, is one of the finest of his numerous stirring lyrics, and deserves the popularity it has acquired. During the period when the strife was actually raging, a song like this was worth an army ; even now, as we read it by the fireside, we seem to hear the blast of the trumpet, and see the fierce old warrior charging at the head of his squadrons.

* No. VI. Old Series of this Magazine, for Sept. 1832.

And heard ye not the trumpet call ? Up, troopers all to horse !
'Tis he, the old Field-Marshal, spurs like lightning on his course !
How proudly and how joyously his noble horse he rides !
And, ho ! with what a biting sweep his good broadsword he guides !

CHORUS.
Up, hearts ! and away ! 'tis the Germans' array---
The Germans are riding and shouting " huzza !"

Oh, marked ye but his clear blue eye, like kindled beacon glow ?
Oh, saw ye how his snowy hair is waving round his brow ?
Right strength and heat, like generous wine, his age doth still retain,
And so to conquer shall he ride o'er many a battle plain.

He was the man, when all was lost and every heart dismayed,
That still to Heaven, in steadfast hope, upraised his shining blade ;
Then swore he by its biting edge, right wrathfully and stern,
That he some German fashions would make the Frenchmen learn !

He kept his oath ; and when abroad the royal summons rang,
Oh, how the hoary stripling up to the saddle sprang !
Then he it was that fairly put the vermin to the rout,
And with an iron besom clean swept the land throughout.

By Lutzen on the meadow, there kept he such a coil,
Some thousands of the enemy lost breath in that turmoil,
And thousands from the battle-field right speedily did strain,
And full ten thousand lay them down that never rose again !

At Katzbach, on the Weser-stream, likewise he kept his oath ;
For there he taught the French to swim---to learn they were but loath.
Good night, Messieurs ! sail pleasantly down to the Baltic sea !
The swallow of a northern whale your proper bed will be !

At Wurtemberg, hard by the Elbe, how hotly he pressed through !
Nor ditch nor bulwark saved the French, although they were not few.
No choice had they, but rose and ran, like hares across the bent,
And after them the stout old boy a hearty " holla !" sent.

By Leipsic, on the Plauen-stream, oh, 'twas a glorious fight !
There did he dim the Frenchman's star, and crush his power outright ;
There still enough the spoilers lay---he finished their campaign !
And there he won his marshal's staff upon the smoking plain.

Then blow the trumpet lustily ! Up, troopers all ! to horse !
There speeds the old Field-Marshal, with glory, on his course,
Upon the Rhine, beyond the Rhine, the German arms to wield---
Go on ! thou tried and valiant sword ! and God shall be thy shield !

If this be not the true tones which rouse the heart of a people, we know not how the chord that shall stir them may be struck. To us every note seems full of the right harmony—the energy, the rough scorn, the swiftness and exultation of the several strains, each alike genuine and excellent.

127

The Burschen-Lieder, or songs current amongst the students at the German universities, form a class by themselves. With a good deal of slang and froth, such as might be expected in the ditties of these very uproarious sons of learning, there are many capital things in the *Commers-bücher*, which contain their settled favourites; and the music is generally excellent. We must give one specimen; premising that the term *Philister*, now almost become part of the German language, was invented by the students, and applied to those, not of the university, whom it was their pleasure to consider hostile or unworthy. Here is their own description of the cognomen :—

> Know ye a Philistine at sight ?
> I'll paint him to a tittle :---
> Where'er a cautious, sullen wight
> Creeps as if stones were brittle,
> And roofs an empty pate with thatch
> Of caxon, periwig, or scratch :
> 'Tis he !---Sir Philistine we call him—
> The Devil and his beadle maul him !
>
> Who, when the grape's-blood from the Rhine
> In manly bosoms tingles,
> That drink of gods, with gander-wine,
> In puling tipple mingles ;
> And, where rejoicing songs arise,
> Makes faces sour, and groans and sighs :
> 'Tis he !—Sir Philistine we call him—
> The Devil and his beadle maul him !
>
> Who evermore of times of need
> And state diseases snivels ;
> And every bold and manly deed
> With vulgar scoffs be-drivels ;
> And calls the muses' art a curse,
> Because they will not gorge his purse :
> 'Tis he !—Sir Philistine we call him—
> The Devil and his beadle maul him !
>
> In short, whoe'er on earth looks down,
> With dullard pride inflated,
> As though for his great self alone
> By our good God created ;
> And looks, in stupid arrogance,
> That when he whistles, all shall dance :
> A Philistine we ever call him !
> The Devil and his beadle maul him !

Were it not for the unchristianity of the thing, few would be disposed to refuse an " Amen !" to the wish so heartily expressed. The song altogether is full of character and effect ;—tameness, indeed, is not the besetting fault of any of the Burschen songs.

We have purposely reserved to the last, our mention of a most delightful class of lyrics, in the manner of the ancient national ballads, which several of the modern poets of Germany have imitated with exquisite success. The stock of genuine originals of this kind, in the different dialects of the country, is exceedingly rich. At present, we must restrict ourselves to later imitations. Some of Goethe's beautiful ballads have already been rendered into English ; we shall, therefore, prefer taking our selections from less celebrated authors. Without offering any comment on the following—for, surely, they will not be thought to require an express recommendation—we may begin with this wild and touching strain by Chamisso. It is from the Lithuanian :---

THE WIDOW'S SON.

The swans with war songs came sweeping by ;
" To horse ! to horse !" was the grating cry.

The youngest sons to the host were bound—
They rode from all the castles around.

We bear great sorrow, and sore complain,
When one goes forth there's none will remain.

My bridegroom ! my brother ! my son, my son !
Thou art gone, alas !—to the wars art gone !

We women the man-at-arms must dight---
Thy bride must fasten the plume aright.

Thy sister leads out the war-horse great ;
The mother unlocks thee the court-yard gate.

Oh, when, my bridegroom ! my brother ! my son !
When comest thou back ? Now quickly make known !

When air, and water, and land are freed,
I stay no longer : then come I with speed.

And air, and water, and land are free---
Why tarries he longer ?—why comes not he?

Now forth to meet him, we women will ;
And see him coming afar, from the hill.

There wait the women, watching the way
Along the vale, where the sunbeams lay.

And the sun rose high, the sun sank low ;
They spy no horseman riding below.

Now smokes the dust, now comes at speed
A war-horse onwards—none rides on the steed !

They up and caught him, and question near---
My horse, what brings thee masterless here ?

Base jade, hast left thy master alone ?
Where tarries my bridegroom, my brother, my son ?

They struck him down in the battle keen ;
They made his bed in the valley green ;

They left me loose, to run as I might ;
I have brought the tidings in woful plight.

There flew three swans with wailing song ;
They're seeking a grave the meadow along.

And, when they found it, each lighted down :
At foot, and head, and side, stood one.

At head the sister, at foot the bride ;
The grey old mother stooped at the side.

Oh, wo and alas ! we three forlorn !
Is none will join us while thus we mourn ?

Then, stooping him down, the sun 'gan say---
I'll bear my part as well as I may :

Nine days I mourn in a misty pall ;
The tenth, I will not be seen at all.

The bride mourned on till the third week passed ;
The sister's mourning three years did last ;

The mother her mourning kept alway,
Till, all outworn, in the grave she lay.

From the pathos (we had almost said ghastliness) of this dirge-like chant, let us seek relief in the milder strains of Uhland, whose ballads are almost the sweetest things in the German language. He has the gift by inheritance, as a Swabian ; and the minnesingers of his native kingdom would have no reason to be ashamed of their successor. Here is his " Lay of the Goldsmith's Daughter :"—

> There stood a goldsmith in his stall,
> Around him gems and pearl :---
> " The dearest of my jewels all
> Art thou, my daughter Helena !
> My well-beloved girl !"
>
> A buxom knight came stepping in :
> " Now save thee, maiden fair !

17. continued

And welcome, trusty goldsmith mine!
Make me a precious coronal
For my sweet bride to wear."
And when the circlet all was wrought,
And quickly glinting shone,
Fair Helen hung, in mournful thought—
When none, be sure, could see her—
On her white arm the crown.
" Alas! the bride how blest is she
On whom this band may shine!
Oh, gave yon gentle knight to me
A wreath of common roses,
What joyful heart were mine!"
Eftsoons, the knight came stepping in;
The gaud he strictly eyed :---
" Now set me, trusty goldsmith mine,
A ring with precious diamonds,
For my sweet plighted bride."
And when the ring was rarely wrought
With costly diamonds bright,
Fair Helen drew it, sad of thought—
When none, be sure, could see her—
Half on her finger white.
" Alas! the bride how blest is she
For whom these diamonds shine !
Oh, gave yon gentle knight to me
From his brown locks one ringlet,
What joyful heart were mine!"
Eftsoons, the knight came stepping in ;
The ring he closely eyed :—
" Thy cunning, worthy goldsmith mine,
Has wrought these presents rarely
For my sweet plighted bride.
" But now, to see how fit they be,
Come, fairest maiden, now,
That I may know approved on thee
My true love's bridal jewels ;---
She's even fair as thou!"
'Twas early on a holiday,
When that sweet maiden was
Bedight with special care alway,
All in her bravest garments,
As she was bound to mass.
With lovely shame, all burning red,
Before the knight she shook.
He set the frontlet on her head,
The ring drew on her finger,
And then her white hand took :---
" Sweet Helen ! Helen dearly tried !
The time for jest is spent—
Thou art of all the fairest bride,
For whom the golden coronal,
For whom the ring was meant."

Of the following ballad, by the same author, (the last we can give,) we must not say all that is in our heart, lest sober readers should condemn the praise as exaggerated. In the original, to our eyes, it is faultless. Nearly all that can be sought in this class of lyric—a simple yet striking and touching theme, vivid and dramatic narrative, and a melody like the sound of silver bells—are united in this delicate little treasure, with a certain wildness that seems borrowed from a time immeasurably remote. We have taken more pains in translating this than with all the others put together—and the version is a failure after all !

Three maidens stood on the castle wall,
They looked adown the vale ;
Their sire came on his charger tall,
Beclad in coat of mail.
" Welcome, Sir Father ! a fair welcome !
What hast thou brought thy children ?
All we were meek at home."

" My daughter in the yellow vest,
I thought of thee to-day.
Rich garments ever please thee best,
Thy joy is brave array :
This chain of ruddy gold I tore
From a bold knight and haughty ;—
Gave him his death therefor."

About her snowy neck apace
The lady clasped the chain ;
And down she went unto the place
Where she descried the slain :—
" Thou liest like any felon here !
I art a knightly noble,
And art my true love dear !"

She raised him in her arms, and bare
To the house of God adown ;
In his father's tomb she laid him there,
With much lament and moan.
The chain that on her neck was tied
She straitly drew around it,
And sank the grave beside.

——

Two maidens stood on the castle wall,
They looked adown the vale ;
Their sire came on his charger tall,
Beclad in coat of mail.
" Welcome, Sir Father ! a fair welcome !
What hast thou brought thy children ?
Both we were meek at home."

" My daughter in the grassgreen vest,
I thought of thee to-day.
The hunter's sport delights thee best
All in the greenwood gay:
This spear, with golden bands, I tore
From the wild huntsman yonder ;—
Gave him his death therefor."

The spear in her lily hand she bent---
The spear her father brought ;
And to the forest green she went---
Death was the chase she sought.
There lay, beneath the linden-shade,
With his true blood-hound near him,
Her love in slumber dead.

" I keep the tryst beneath the tree,
I promised, true love dear !"
Then in her heart all suddenly
She plunged the pointed spear.
In that cool shade they slumber well—
Small wood-birds warbled o'er them,
Green leaves upon them fell.

——

One maiden stood on the castle wall,
She looked adown the vale ;
Her sire came on his charger tall,
Beclad in coat of mail.
" Welcome, Sir Father ! a fair welcome !
What hast thou for thy daughter ?
All meek I kept at home."

" My daughter in the vest of white,
My thought of thee has been.
In flowers thou ever didst delight
More than in golden sheen :
This bloom, all silver bright, I tore
For thee, from the bold gardener ;—
Gave him his death therefor."

" Alas ! how grew he so perverse ?
Why didst thou slay him there ?
The flowers that he was wont to nurse
Will pine for want of care !"
" He bore him strangely bold ; and said,
The fairest flower that blossomed
He kept for his own maid."

The flower that gentle lady laid
Upon her tender breast ;
She went and sought the garden shade
She ever loved the best.

129

There rose a freshly-turfed mound—
  There, midst the pale white lilies,
She sate her on the ground.

" Oh, could I die this very hour,
  Like my dear sisters all!
I cannot wound me with this flower,
  So soft it is, and small!"
All pale and sick at heart, she eyed
  The small flower, till it faded—
Till she sank down and died.

We have, we fear, exceeded our limits, and yet it seems as if we had barely made a beginning. The subject is nearly inexhaustible ; and, if the examples we have given should occasion the wish for more, we shall not be at a loss for means to gratify it. The only difficulty will arise from the rival claims of so many favourites, each demanding the preference. What would have been the " Judgment of Paris" if the contest had lain between, not three, but three thousand beauties?

                             V.

MERCK'S CORRESPONDENCE.*

" This was a man who exercised the greatest influence upon my life."
GOETHE.

We were very grateful for Mrs. Austin's characteristics of Goethe as a piece of most sterling, well-meant, and honest work in the great field of international civilization ; but we must say withal that that work was in respect of time premature, and in respect of execution very imperfect. Premature it certainly was, for since its publication we have received certain voluminous Weimarian memorials from Germany, with which it is indispensable that the future biographer of Goethe or historian of

German literature should be familiar. Imperfect it also was, as appears from the very plan of the work, (a sewing together of patch-work) and from the confession of the modest and talented editor herself, who in the very outset of the work, instead of like a benignant Pallas removing the mist from our eyes, very reverently spreads a veil of mystery over the whole ways and doings of the great poet. This, we think, was bad policy in the first place, for Englishmen hate mystery, and will not be

* Briefe an Johann Heinrich MERCK von GOETHE, HERDER WIELAND and anderen bedeitenden zeutgenossen: mit Merck's biographischer Skizze herausgehen von Dr. Karl Wagner, Lehrer am Gymnasium zu DARMSTADT. *Darmstadt*, 1835.
Der Deutsche Merkur. Jahrgänge, 1776-1790.

We wish Thomas Carlyle would leave his Gallic monsters, his Dantons, Mirabeaus, and other fearful wind-blowing and fire-spitting γηγενεις of the moral world, and come back to his native Germany, and that quiet Weimar from which he sucked the milk of wisdom in his youthful days. Here is a field for his comprehensive intellect, in which there is much to do, and absolutely nothing done. The few stray translations that we have, are merely cabinet specimens chipped off from the living rock of Teutonic thought ; but where is the man with a British name and surname, that has yet attempted to give us a scheme of the geological genesis of this mighty country ? We mean that there is no such thing as a philosophical and a well-digested history of German literature in the English language,* though from the character of the time and the daily increasing humanization of intellect, it is manifest that such a work is much wanted, and cannot long be dispensed with. Wolfzang Menzel's work, " *Die Deutsche Literatur*," is excellent in its way, but it will never do for us, being written for and specially addressed to the German people. Besides, were it less German in its topics than it is, it is too polemical, and for some most

mystified even by a great German poet ; and in the second place, it was quite uncalled for on the occasion, as there is really no mystery about Goethe which any honest man (though perhaps not every *woman*) may not see through without spectacles. The "characteristics," however, have done their own allotted portion of good in their own allotted day ; and this is all that the best of us can do. What remains is for them that come after not to be idle. If the temple cannot yet be erected, we may at least gather some stones together for the masonry. The cement is to be found in the mind of some honest thinker, perhaps not yet born. The work which heads this page is, in our judgment, no barren quarry, one out of which many stones may be hewn for the future edifice of German literature, when any Englishman shall arise bold enough to attempt the work. Our present duty is to look a little into this mine, and to tell the English student of poetry what it is, and that it is *there*.

important points, too instinct with the spirit of partizanship to satisfy an unprejudiced mind. Nothing then remains for us but to put our own hands to the plough and work ; and if Thomas Carlyle, or some substantial man, would give us a " Life of Goethe," or something to that effect, much might be done to quiet the vain jabber, that critics of German literature still frequently din us withal. Only let Mr. Carlyle or other Weimarian historiographer bear in mind that Goethe is a man, and not a god ; for blind admiration, though not in itself worse than ignorant contempt, is often, by a never-failing reaction, not less disastrous in its consequences. In the meantime we must gather together our scrape and fragments as we best may, and till the " *opus desideratissimum*" that we have hinted at, under whatever shape, make its appearance, we must be content to shape to ourselves such imperfect outlines of the Goethes, the Wielands, and the Herders of the last century, as the scattered lights of stray memorials afford us.

Of these memorials, which are now so numerous that a neat " Bibliotheca Weimariana" might be composed of them—not one of the least interesting is Merck's correspondence. Most of our German readers have heard of Merck — Mephistophiles Merck, as Goethe used to call him—but we believe the knowledge even of professedly German students as to this worthy man, scarcely goes beyond the name, and therefore we must explain ; but we shall do it shortly. John Henry Merck was born in Darmstadt, in the year 1741, where he lived and died, War Councillor by title, though in reality only Paymaster to the Grand Ducal Government. There is nothing in his internal life worth commemorating ; but he was possessed of an intellect so remarkable for activity, acuteness, strength, and comprehensiveness, that he soon became the intimate friend and enjoyed the love and esteem of all those master-minds, who in the middle of the last century, created the polite literature of Germany. Goethe, Wieland, and Herder, exercised an honourable rivalry, in acknowledging and calling forth his talents ; with Wieland especially he continued through life in terms of the most intimate friendship,

* Professor Wolf's sketch, in the Athenæum, is excellent so far as it goes ; but the writer's business being with the 19th century only, he was obliged to run over the principal part of German literature by way of introduction.

and was, indeed, his principal *collaborateur* and right-hand man during the many years that he conducted that celebrated periodical (the Edinburgh Review of its time and place) "The German Mercury." But Merck's intellectual activity was not confined merely to polite literature. In clever sketches of character, and acute and pungent criticism he excelled ; but in his latter years he devoted himself principally to science, and pioneered to Cuvier in opening up the vast vista into antediluvian times with which geology now delights us. On the subject of fossil bones, Merck published three letters* in the French language, which are yet referred to as forming an epoch in the History of Comparative Anatomy ; and the correspondence now published contains many interesting letters from Blumenbach, Soemmering, Sir Joseph Banks, Peter Camper, the most celebrated naturalists and anatomists of the day, on the then new subject of pre-adamitic worlds. Merck was also a great connoisseur of the fine arts ; his knowledge in this department having been universally considered in Germany as profound, and his judgment as true as in the development of *Belles Lettres*. His personal character was noble and manly, but not without some rather harsh peculiarities which gave occasion to the surname of "Mephistophiles" with which Goethe has baptized him. In his views of human nature and human things, there is always found with great strength, comprehension, and acuteness, a certain tone and tinge of that cutting, critical, and sarcastic disposition which is the characteristic of "the spirit that always denies." But with all this Merck is a generous and kindly man ; and of this the love with which he is cherished by the amiable Wieland, is the best proof. His literary compositions being mostly scattered through periodical works (the Mercury especially), are, of course, little, if at all known in this country ; but they all bear marks of a strong, clear, truth-loving intellect, and are all seasoned with a sufficient proportion of keen wit, and biting sarcasm. It is not our intention in this paper to

enter at length into Merck's literary merits, which we are afraid would possess little interest, even for our professed German students. We shall only briefly refer to the short critical essay on the spirit of German literature in the 26th, and the characteristic sketch from real life, entitled "Lindor" in the 35th volume of the "German Mercury," as two specimens of as vigorous and healthy writing as we know in the German language.† There is much in the style and character of these short essays, very like the writings of an author, who, at the present moment, is exercising a great influence in the critical world of Germany—we mean Wolfgang Menzel. There is also in these productions very little of what we are accustomed to call "German." A strong, clear, practical intellect without mysticism, without smoke, without floundering, leads us along the king's high-way, and shews us what is to be seen with eyes that see it as it is. Merck, in short, is a man of strong sound sense, and that is a quality which cannot be predicated of all German writers, even among those who stand highest in public estimation. Though he occupies but a very subordinate place in the literature of his country, we would advise all persons who wish to obtain from original sources, a "genuine insight" into German literature, to study carefully Merck's critical papers in the Mercury. We have already given our reasons why we do not think Menzel, with all his commanding talent, to be in all things a safe guide. Merck is an equally clear and sharp-sighted, and in many things a more impartial, and what is of importance, a contemporary observer ; and if we make allowance for a little over-severity in witty and satirical sallies we shall for the most part find with Wieland, "that no cloud can cover from his cursed penetration, and no illusion can stand before him."

Our present business, however, is not so much with Merck as with his correspondents. Those students of literature who may think the literary paymaster of the Hessian army beneath their attention (how wisely we say not,

for the planet may be best observed from its satellite, and the valet often tells secrets that could not be extracted from the master) will nevertheless be willing to seek edification from the words of great men that came to him, as to the focus of an acoustic chamber from all parts of Germany. Doubtless there is much trash among the letters of their great men, which the Germans have lately been publishing in such profusion ; but he who cannot find the primest jewels amid that rubbish, has no eyes for literary history. There is, besides, a certain air and atmosphere about the most trifling letters, as about the most trifling conversation of a great man, from which an accurate observer can glean more profound insight into his character, than can be obtained from the study of his most perfect works, or the witnessing of his most important public exhibitions. If you wish to know what sort of a man the actor is, you must go to the green-room, and not to the stage. You must see him in dishabille, lying upon a sofa, smoking a pipe, eating a good dinner, fighting with a bad digestion, or croaking with a bad cold. Any man who is not a very clod may be a hero once in his life, when a heroic occasion excites him ; but shew me a man who on all the small occasions of life, the domestic πραγματα, and περι πραγματων that are not sung in any Iliad, and I will shew you, once in your life at least—a thing worthy to be seen—a true Christian, and a great philosopher. Even so in letter writing. If a man does not let out the cloven foot now and then to his familiar friends and confidants in a private time and place, then most certainly he is not a devil. Much, for instance, has been said and written against Christopher Martin Wieland, by people of nice and prime moralities. Of this much we are free to say for ourselves, that we never believed one word ; but if any man will sit down in a Christian spirit, and read the threescore excellent letters, from the poet of Oberon, that this correspondence contains, and after that still continue to believe that Wieland was a sensualist and a bad man, some Œdipus may explain what he understands by Christian love and charity, for we cannot. Narrow-souled pedantry may

lace itself round with a double wall of circumvallation ; but honest men will walk in the bloomy vale of human charities, and trample upon no flower. It is time, however, that we should proceed to business. Here is a letter from Wieland, very interesting and very edifying in more respects that one : for it tells us something, not only about himself, about human nature, and about the nature of Critics and Reviewers, but also something about Goethe and Herder, which may afford matter for useful meditation.

"Weimar, February, 1777.

"Your letter, dear friend, could not have come to me more opportunely. This cursed opera, Rosamond—half too good, and half too bad to see the light, which, however, *nolens volens*, I must bring to a conclusion—has check-mated me altogether, and I sit here and eat my thumbs, cursing the day, and the hour, when I was seized (no doubt as a punishment for my sins) with the idea of trying to do what I do not understand, and what all masters of the craft tell me I have no turn for. Besides this, dear brother, I am much in want of a *present friend* to help me on my way ; for, of my excellent worthy friends, here, there is not one who can communicate to me heat enough for the laying of two eggs. Even Goethe and Herder are, for me, as if they were not. With Goethe, when he first came here, what a year of blessed hours and days did the gods gift me withal ! Now, however, the court relations in which he has encircled himself seem to have extinguished his genius altogether—his fancy is dead—*the all-animating warmth that used to go out from his presence, has been succeeded by a political frost.* He is always good and harmless as of yore ; but he is not communicative, and one can make nothing of him. We see one another seldom ; although I am quite convinced that he has no objections to me, and is convinced also that I love him. As to Herder, everything that you prophesied to me has gone into complete fulfilment. The particular circumstances of my various collisions with the learned dean,* I shall reserve till we meet. In the meanwhile, matters lie thus ;—my love and good-

---

* Lettre a Mr. de Cruse, sur les os fos seles d'Elephans et de Rhinoceros qui se trouvent dans le pays de Hessen Darmstadt. Darmdst. 1782.
  Second Lettre a Mr. Cruse, 1784.
  Troisieme Lettre a Mr. Forster, 1786.

† The German titles are :—
  1.—Anden Herausgeler des Deutsche Merkur's, vol. 26, p. 25.
  2.—Lindor eine, bürgerliche Deutsche, vol. xxxv. p. 107.

* "Of all authors and men Herder had the greatest partiality for Dean Swift, and we were therefore willing to baptize him, *Der Dechant*."—GOETHE, *ans, m. l. thl.* III. *s.* 111. Herder himself seems to have been conscious of a certain likeness between his own character and that of Swift. In a letter to Merck, (p. 37,

heartedness, of which I was sufficiently lavish at first, in the eyes of his eminence, being nothing but weakness, I have packed it all up again, and drawn back my beams with great self-complacency. *This man is an electric cloud; at a distance the meteor makes a very fine effect ; but may the devil have such a neighbour hanging over his head.* No person is more ready than I am to acknowledge and rejoice in all the excellence and goodness that may be in a man, and count myself as nothing in the presence of superior intellect. But I care for my soul ; and cannot away with it when a fellow is possessed with such a habitual high esteem of his own worth; and, to crown the jest, when a strong giant of an intellect seems to have no other pleasure than pinching other people, and pulling their noses, then may God heap up a thousand Pyrrenees between me and his excellency ! But all this *entre nous.*

As to the *vanitas vanitatum* of reviewing and authorship, the *immensum inane* that dwells behind the most splendid thunder-lightning-and-hail-manifestations of our geniuses, and men of esprit—the great truth that in human affairs everything depends only on light and shade—the still greater truth that it is matter of tears more than of laughter, to see how piously the public allows itself to be cheated by us authors ; and how, finally, we are all employed *nolentes volentes* in throwing dirt upon one another—as to all and much more that Mephistopheles might sermonize upon, you and I, I suppose, are pretty much agreed. But, with all this, we must never forget that we are no better than our fathers were—that we must, willing or unwilling, bear the burden of our age, as better people have done before us ; and, finally, that these very things of which we have most cause to be ashamed (and, for the most part, most ashamed when the simple folks are bawling, *Euge! Bene!* most heartily) do with all their pettiness, often give us occasion — be it illusion or not — to cradle ourselves through many a pleasant moment ; and that, without these things, we ourselves, *relativè*, would be nothing in the world. For example— you yourself, in the very moment that you Philippize (most justly I confess) against reviews, and reviewers, send

me, with the same post, a pair of reviews, which I count master-pieces, and which, be they bad or good, have at least, given me great pleasure in reading them."

———

This letter runs on in that pleasant, playful, easy flow, which gives such a charm to all Wieland's writings, even when he is most prosy, and most diluted. Doubtless, of all the great men of Weimar, Wieland was the most amiable, and the most agreeable. Herder, perhaps, had a more commanding intellect ; Goethe unquestionably stood high above him ; but the acerbity which mingles with the enthusiasm of the one, and the senatorian distance, and scientific formality that sometimes showed themselves along with the dignity of the other, were certainly not the most agreeable of *personal* qualities. It is an undeniable fact, indeed, and most important to be noted by the historian of literature that the most clever writer is not always (perhaps is seldom ?) the most agreeable man. Minds of a high and aspiring character are apt to feel irritated by the many crosses that base and foolish men are continually throwing in their way—and to become impatient of the many incumbrances that selfish and interested persons are daily raising up to dam the progress of what is truly great and good.. "The external world," as Goethe said, "is a thorn in the side of every man of genius." This thorn seems especially to have harassed the flesh of the great Herder. To the small weaknesses, triflings, and follies that are often inseparably connected with the virtues of the best men, he seemed willing to allow no quarter, and the consequence of this was what might have been expected, that, with all his noble enthusiasm, his gigantic erudition, and his unwearied energy, he pleased few people, and few people pleased him. In Weimar he lived almost alone. Goethe again, was of a more tolerant and more social character. The formality and distance of which Wieland here complained, was in some part only occasional, and even in so far as it might be permanent, only external. That it did exist, however, there can be no doubt ; but it is to be ascribed not so much to the peculiarities of his

literary character, as to his situation as a courtier and a minister, combined with the quiet contemplative scientific character which afterwards distinguished him more than that exuberance and playfulness of feeling and fancy which we expect in a great poet. Notwithstanding all this, however, Goethe was a man, as Burke said of Fox, "made to be loved ;" and we find that Wieland and he soon broke down any thin wall of separation that might at first stand between them, and lived together for more than forty years in the most cherished and affectionate friendship. The following letter from Wieland, written immediately after the publication of Oberon, shews that the ice had already melted, of whose freezing influence he at first complained. We find in the letter also a valuable remark on Goethe's genius, as contrasted with Shakspeare and Homer, which they who wish to join Goethe in a literary triad with these two greatest poets, would do well to take to heart. Wieland himself more wisely chooses to compare his brother to Xenophon, a parallel which is new to us, but which, in respect of Goethe's prose, at least strikes us as very happy, and capable of being carried successfully into detail.

"Weimar, April 16, 1780.

"May Oberon and Titania shower blessings on you for the friendly way in which you speak of my *opus* Oberon. I know well that a man of your wit and humour must see faults enough in my work to make both it and me appear ridiculous ; but I am glad when any thing that I can do pleases those whom I wish to please. Goethe also has been shining most benignantly on me ; and I cannot express to you how much I am now pleased with all that he says and does—with his whole manner of existence. Of the duke I may say the same. Of course I speak only of things as they affect my own comfort. I neither know nor care to know the relations of the powers that be among themselves, but I think I may safely say that things are now going on more smoothly than at first, and I begin to perceive in Goethe's public bearing, a *συμφωνία* that rubs down all rough surfaces, and gives us a happy assurance that things will now go on as well as we can rationally expect.

"His description of his tour through Wallis, over the Furka, and St. Got-

hard, which he lately read to us at the duchess dowager's, is, in its kind, as great a favourite with me as the *Ανάβασις,* and truly the tour was properly a campaign against whatsoever elements ventured to oppose him. The thing is one of his master-pieces, and instinct with that spirit of calm grandeur which is so peculiar to him ; the hearers were enthusiastic on the 'nature' of the thing ; the sly *art* of the composition which lay concealed from them, gave me more pleasure. It is a true poem, however little the outward form of the *art* poetic appears. *But the remarkable thing is this, and it is a peculiarity which distinguishes him on all occasions from Homer and Shakspeare—that the 'Ich'—the 'Ille ego' shimmers through the whole—without arrogance, however, and with infinite fineness.* The duke is kept, with the same delicacy, for the most part in the back ground ; but, when he is mentioned, the traits of a noble and princely character are brought out with so much tact, that if I were the duke, I should feel more flattered by it than with the loud bepraisings of twenty Laureates.

. . . .

The self-complacency and confidence, *vulgo* vanity, which you recommend to me, as a wall of defence against the rude attacks of public opinion, were no bad thing. It is an excellent purifier of the blood ; but there is one evil attending it ; the thought is apt to come across us that the most miserable dunce that ever blotted paper—the most stupid Gottsched, as well as the most clever Horace, can, with a consciousness of merit 'equally triumphant, bawl out, '*Exegi monumentum acre perennius;*' and this thought poisons the whole dish. What! can I be helped by a consolation that fits as well to the make of every mechanical scribbler as to the inspirations of genius. Truth to say it is impossible for a man of real genius ever to indulge in much self-complacency ; for the image of that thing which we may attain, but have not as yet attained, continually hovers before us. I, for my part, see only one thing that can defend me against the injustice of my contemporaries, and the misfortune of being born a German, and that is, *dulces ante omnia Musæ;* the love of my art, and what I said in my own stupid Biberach twelve years ago,

"' *Du machst, O Muse, doch das Gluck von meinem Leben,*
Und hört Dir Niemand zu, so singst Du mir allein.'

of this correspondence,) he says, "In your criticisms you are always Socrates-Addison, Goethe—a young, haughty English lord, scraping magnificently with cock's feet. And I, when I come among you, am the Irish dean, with the lash."

And herewith enough. We have always, at least, this private joy, to count on our fingers the name of half-a-dozen sensible men, and another half-dozen amiable women, who are ready to cry, *Euge! Bene!* to our honest exertions, and what is much more pleasant to me on whom we have been happy enough to produce the effect which it was our intention to produce. But, come of Oberon what may, and I hear preparations are already making for divers minings and batteries, I here give you my mouth and hand to it, 'and by the name be it sworn that even spirits dare not name,' that—however much nonsense may be written against it—however oblique and purposely perverse men's vision may be—I will not give a single word in reply, whether for explanation or defence; but, *mir nichts, dir nichts*, go quietly on my way, as if no Oberon or Titania were in existence. In the meanwhile, thou, my dear brother, do not desert me and the Mercury; for, if we can only keep him afloat, even in his present *aurea mediocritas*, it is always more profitable for the finances to write six sheets of criticism every four weeks, than in the same four weeks to produce one or two dozen stanzas, which, when they are produced, will bring to a starving man nothing more than the salt to eat his meat with. And now, adieu! God bless you, and continue to love me. I am always the same, '*dum spiritus hos regit artus.*' Amen."

The sentiments expressed in the latter part of this excellent letter coincide with those which Walter Scott so early formed, and so long continued to act upon, with regard to *literary polemics*. Wieland, Goethe, and Scott, seem to have instinctively agreed upon this point—a philosophical indifference is an author's only mail against the rude rubs of public opinion. Popularity, indeed, as this world goes, is a thing *not* always to be received with thankfulness, and never to be sought after; for, of those who do make a business of seeking after it in the literary as in the religious world, it may be said—"Verily they have their reward." How little Wieland worked for the mere popularity of the day, appears beautifully in the following letter to Merck, written while the poet was engaged in the composition of Oberon:—

"Weimar, March 1, 1779.

"————Since you must have it, I will tell you how Oberon is getting on. I am just finishing the tenth canto; and, after that, 180 or 200 stanzas will finish the business. Of the labour that I have employed on this *opus*, I believe no poet or poetling in the holy Roman empire has any conception. Most of our poetical gentlemen (with a few exceptions) have made their tasks as easy for themselves as possible. I have this time, at least, made it as difficult as I could. The very mechanism of my octave measure, the nature of the Iambics, and the bareness of our language in rhyme, have caused me more perplexity than you can have any idea of. I assure you, dear brother, that I have worked for two days and a half of this week at a single trophe, where I wanted nothing but a single word, which I could not find. I turned the thing round and round in my brain, but all to no purpose. When I have got a clear picture of a thing in my own mind, I of course desire to bring as clear a picture before the minds of my readers; but this, *ut nosti*, is not always such an easy affair, for a single line, or shade, or tint, not always perceptible at the first glance, and not very tangible to earthly fingers, often works the whole magic. Often, indeed, with all my honest endeavors, I make nothing of it, and hit the wood instead of the nail. Verily, true it is, that the greater part of my respectable readers will not be apt to inquire curiously how the stroke falls, provided it is a stroke; but that is a poor consolation. He who does not see where the dog lies buried, and where he is not buried, has no eyes for the true excellence of wit, and for his praise I do not write."

We have made these extracts from Wieland's letters as full as possible, because they really form the gem of the correspondence; and no admirer of Oberon, we are sure, will fail to thank us for this last quotation. The letters from Goethe, again, are neither so numerous nor so interesting as those of Wieland. The mind of this extraordinary man (whom many Englishmen only know or dream of as "the celebrated author of that singularly wild and beautiful poem, called Faust") seems to have been so much occupied with scientific observations of Nature—mineralogical, botanical, and osteological—that he had no time to indulge in that playful interchange of thought on which the great charm of letter-writing depends. We have noticed this, not only in the present but in

other collections of Goethe's letters. In the correspondence with Zelter, for instance, of which six volumes have been published, Zelter's letters are by far the best; and in "Goethe's correspondence with a child," the philosophical "Geheim Rath" is a complete blank before the exuberance of fancy and feeling that is poured out from the poesy-intoxicated soul of Bettine Brentano. The letters to Merck in this collection, though not so laconic, have a great deal of the same calmness which looks like coldness; and instead of warm effusion of feeling between friend and friend, we have merely formal commissions from a man of science and a connoisseur, to a mineralist and a picture-dealer. But even in these communications the student of Goethe's works will find much that characterises the most remarkable man of his time. Nobody will thoroughly understand Goethe who does not also understand a little of mineralogy, and geology, and botanical metamorphosis, and the world-renowned "intermaxillary bone" which Peter Camper most stoutly asserted that he could never see, and Goethe as stoutly asserted that it must be *there*, though it could not be seen. Some light on this mysterious subject may be borrowed from this correspondence; particularly from Cowper's, Soemmering's, and Goethe's own letters; but he who wishes to understand it thoroughly must consult Mr. Whewell's "History of the Inductive Sciences," vol. iii., where "the poet Goethe" is allowed most magnificently to figure among scientific men (Cantabs and others), and that in the face of the fact that he was *not* a *mathematician*, and that he *was* a great *philosopher*.

Our limits do not permit us to enter largely into the very miscellaneous correspondence before us; but we cannot deny ourselves the pleasure of making one other extract—a most characteristic one from Fuseli—a man whom we all know very well, and whom, therefore, we may at once introduce upon the stage without making any elaborate apology for the madness and the nonsense that was so strangely jumbled in him with much sense and extraordinary genius:

"Rome, March 17, 1775.

"Thanks for the books, and have, in return, a little prattle. I knew the best of Klopstock already, when he was less artificial than he now is, and I admire in him as much as the connoisseurs of all ages and all feeling hearts will admire. But his cloudiness and sublime sentimentality I cannot away with. It is images, pictures, substantial imaginative creations that we find in Homer; and these pictures make the poet. You—you German and Swiss, I mean—may despise them if you will. Homer, and the Song of Deborah, and the book of Job—these give a staple habitation and a living root to feeling. An effusion of true individual feeling, incorporated in a living picture, strikes all hearts through all ages; while a false and local and individual feeling pleases only a few, at a particular time and place, and confounds every one else. What a nameless difference is there between the truth and energy of feeling in Sappho's "φαινεται," and the milky confusion and ecstatic dreaminess that characterise your feigned longings for Cidli. The *facultas lacrymatoria*—the beauty-plaster of German poetry from Klopstock down to Dusch—the telescopized eyes, unnameable looks, and the whole theological hermaphroditism, are more perishable rags than the paper on which they are printed. Feel these ecstasies if you please; I, too, had my own experiences of this kind of nonsense when I was a boy; but it is the height of egotistical impudence to drum it up before me; and though it should make the staple of your sacred epos and your holy liturgy, I can have no mercy with it, but say, with Göz von Berlichingen—'I have all possible respect for the dignity of religion, but as to you, Sir Captain, and your hurdy-gurdy solemnities, you may——and here, sir, is the way to the door!'

"As to Klopstock's patriotic poetry, I except 'Hermann and Thusnelda,' and 'the two Muses'—and to the rest I say—go to the devil! I might as soon explain the Talmud to a Jewish synagogue as bring any intelligible poetic shape out of these.

"To distil away such a talent as Klopstock undoubtedly has, after this fashion, is too bad. Lycophron, a prophet by profession, and a Greek, is clearer than this riddle of bardism. What Klopstock writes in these flights of solemn exaltation is not language; it is sandfull of bones, and wrecks upon the sea shore, which the first flood will wash away. As for the Messiah, the ten first books are the song of a swan, the ten last a crow-concert. Chriemhilde's revenge is far above the Messiah—it is the first of all national German poems.

"The contempt that I have for Klopstock's opinion of German painting is only equalled by the arrogance with which he speaks of the English. His ignorance of their poetry is ridiculous. And as to his eternal 'fatherland,' 'freedom,' 'citizen,' and so forth —if he were only a Swiss—but where is the fatherland of a German? Is it in Swabia, Brandenburg, Austria, Saxony? Is it in the marshes that swallowed up Varus and his legion? Did Rome ever lose a battle when it fought on good solid ground, and on equal terms? What, then, does all this ode-building about Hermann and Velleda come to? A Frenchman (curse him!) has more right to 'fatherlandize' than any miserable Quedlinburger, or Osnabrucker,* or any other blown-up frogs that creep about between the Danube and the Baltic. A slave—what has he to boast of? his master's livery?—and which master? the first, the second, or the third? 'Freedom! God!' Freedom from the flatterers of Christina? And then, as to his Anglomania, the English do not boast to have produced a single poet in the present century—except, perhaps, Richardson. Thomson's tame catalogue—which you have so often translated—Young's pyramids of doe, Pope's cadenced and rhymed prose— these they do not dignify with the name of poetry any more than the sweet tears and confections of Wieland and Gesner deserve that name. This is all I have to say on this theme, and may God help you to something better!

"You mention to me a host of painters and crayon-men that I know nothing about. Give me your thoughts on sensible themes. Greet Bodmer, and love me!

"P.S.—*Tres celebre*, before the *painter*, you must leave out. That is German foolery."

We have inserted this long extract from Eusdis' letter, as being a most curious characteristic of one of the most clever madcaps that the profession of painting ever had to boast of. There is much truth and much sense in every line of this fiery effusion; but then it is unregulated and unqualified to such a degree that no gigantic truth marches out without twenty minions of falsehood in its train. Fuseli is a man who never fails to hit the nail on the head; but he hits it so hard that it splits the wood, and plays the devil with the box and what is in it. To make any criticisms on the multifarious topics touched in this very original epistle, were here out of place. The reader can make the necessary corrections and qualifications for himself.

We have only to add, in conclusion, that we hope such collections of letters and original sources of literary characteristics as that from which we have here given a few extracts, will be more and more attended to by our students of foreign literature. It is only this minute and accurate study that can dispel the nimbus of a false saintship which the "*omne ignotum pro magnifico*" raises around the characters of distinguished foreigners. We do not wish to detract a single iota from the measure of true greatness; but we wish to see things as they are, and to substitute a discriminating admiration for the blind idol-worship of an "unknown god." With regard to German literature, indeed, matters are improving daily; and a provincial newspaper would now be ashamed to broach such crudities on the subject as some of our leading quarterlies sported not twenty years ago. The flippant ignorance which once characterized our criticisms on foreign literature has now almost vanished; and the excessive admiration and mystic worship which succeeded it—never very deeply rooted among our practical-minded countrymen—is now also run through and laughed at. A just estimate of foreign excellence is what we must now aim at; and the day is hopefully not far distant when the rough irregularities of national peculiarities (so far as these peculiarities are offensive) will have rubbed one another away, and all men of all nations will rejoice mutually to recognize in one another that which is most noble and most excellent in MAN.

---

* Alluding to Klopstock and Möser, the author of "Patriotic Phantasies," by their birth-places.

Art. IV.—*Germany : the Spirit of her History, Literature, Social Condition, and National Economy; illustrated by reference to her Physical, Moral, and Political Statistics, and by comparison with other Countries.* By BISSET HAWKINS, M.D., Oxon, F.R.S. London: Parker. 1838.

IT has never been our fortune to light upon a book in which such a multiplicity of facts, such a variety of details on every important subject, were brought together within so narrow a compass, or stated with greater clearness and perspicuity. We have here in a single volume of less than five hundred pages, a mass of information which we must have sought for through as many volumes, without having the additional advantage—even should our research prove successful—of finding it sifted, classed, and compared, so as to render it doubly valuable and immediately available. There is not a single feature of Germany—historical, literary, social, or political—which has not been traced by Mr. Hawkins with remarkable brevity and precision. That a work which should place before our eyes the whole German empire, with all the intricacies of its petty subdivisions, was a desideratum in literature nobody who has listened to the conversations of returned tourists, or who has turned over the leaves of their printed inanities, can for a moment doubt ; and it is a matter of no small satisfaction that it has been executed in a very masterly and unpretending style. It may be said, indeed, that it is a mere compilation from other and better works, but it is a compilation judiciously executed—embracing all the most essential subjects which are necessary to give us a clear and comprehensive view of the German empire.

In England our general ideas of Germany are, that it is a romantic land covered with fine old castles and peopled by various races of bookmakers, musicians, and metaphysicians. Besides, it is the manufactory of kings and princes, exporting annually some scores of the latter and the smaller fry of barons and counts, to dazzle the eyes of the " nation of shopkeepers," with their high sounding and unpronounceable names, their red ribands and glittering stars. We laugh at their pretensions while we envy their good fortune. Noble blood is to them Fortunatus's cap ; it procures them all that the most ambitious of us islanders would aspire to, and yet we find a curious historical fact related of these high mightinesses, which might leave us at a loss to distinguish them from the descendants of a privileged " swell mob" of the middle ages. In 1215, Frederick Barbarossa exacted an oath from his nobles not to coin bad money, not to levy extraordinary tolls, and not to steal on the highway. A pretty idea of nobility, truly. An oath to coiners and highwaymen that they will neither coin nor rob is a very gentle restraint ; but taking into account the religious notions of the

period, we admit that many a man would empty his neighbour's pocket without remorse, who would have shrunk from the idea of superadding perjury to a comparatively trifling offence. In the fourteenth century we find the Bavarian nobles accusing their monarch of conferring court dignities on foreigners, of chicanery towards his own nobility, to whom he was difficult of access, and of depriving them of their ancient rights of hunting. They specify instances in which the members of their own body had been seized and carried off by night, and their daughters forcibly married to foreigners. Heavy charges, certainly, and which give us a pretty fair idea of the relations which then subsisted between the monarch and his nobility. In fact, they lived in a state of open hostility ; the monarch using his endeavours to weaken the power of his nobles, the latter leaguing together and attacking their sovereign. In their endeavours to crush the power of the nobles, the kings were powerfully seconded by the knights, between whom and the lords (Herrin) the greatest enmity and jealousy prevailed. In the lesser German states feuds between noble and sovereign were things of common occurrence.

In 1520 a league of the nobles of the family of Salder was formed against the Bishop of Hildesheim. The adverse armies met at Soltau, and the nobles were defeated after a sharp and bloody contest. About the same period the Bishop of Wurzburg was murdered by some noblemen, incited by their chief, Von Grumbach, who, after a protracted resistance, was at length brought to justice. The accession of the family of Luneburg to the throne of Great Britain was favourable to the power and pretensions of the Hanoverian nobility. From that period they have been celebrated in Germany for their lofty deportment and their attachment to their order. The reason is, that they have had the government almost entirely in their own hands, which the nobles of other German states have been obliged to surrender to their princes. The nobility of Brandenburg was quite lawless and independent before the ascent of the house of Zollern to the throne. They had possessed themselves of the sovereign's domains and of the public revenue, and hence a continued contest was carried on between them for these prizes. During the reign of Joachim, the noblemen who filled offices at court amused themselves with highway robbery during the night. Von Lindenburg, the prince's favourite, was found guilty of this crime, and to the honour of the prince, his influence at court was no protection for his forfeited life. His execution served to irritate the nobles to such a degree, that one of them, Von Otterstaedt, had the audacity to write over the door of the prince's chamber—" Joachim, take care of yourself, for if you fall into our hands, we will hang you." While attempting to carry his menace into execution, Von Otterstaedt was seized, and underwent the punishment he had promised Joachim.

In 1568 we find Albert Frederick harassed and tormented into insanity by his nobles, and as they allowed him no medical relief, he remained so to the end of his life.

During the Thirty Years' War, which desolated and impoverished Germany, impoverishing the peasants, and reducing the princes to utter insignificance, the nobility alone managed to escape the deluge of misfortune which bore down the other orders of the state. In Prussia, their excesses continued unrestrained until the accession of Frederick the Great in 1640. This prince saw at once that the only remedy for these evils was to be found in a formidable standing army, and he applied himself vigorously and unremittingly to the organization and discipline of such a force, until at length he was at the head of the most effective military establishment in Christendom. The tall grenadiers of this great master of the art of war were an overmatch for the fierce and licentious nobles. He set the diet at defiance, abolished the freedom of taxation which the nobles had hitherto enjoyed, gave the peasants a legal protection against their oppression and caprice, and abolished such of their privileges as were inconsistent with good government. Thus a nobility which but a few years before had trampled upon the sovereign power became slavishly submissive to its will. Being no longer exempt from taxation, they were forced to seek distinction in the civil and military services of the state. In this new capacity their ancient chivalry broke forth in the campaigns against the Swedes and the Turks, on the Rhine and in Poland. The peace of Westphalia made this change general throughout Germany. Standing armies were everywhere introduced, and all the German governments verged towards a purer monarchy.

In addition to the monarchical tendency of the peace itself, in the seventeenth and in the early part of the eighteenth centuries, several princes mounted foreign thrones and brought their newly-acquired power to bear upon insubordination at home. The splendour of the court of Louis XIV began to be felt in the petty courts of Germany, and those nobles who before sought distinction as leaders of armed retainers moltened into silken performers in court ceremonies and pageantries of state. The French language, French manners, and French morals were introduced at all the courts beyond the Rhine. The country nobility (der Hof und der Landadel) held themselves aloof from this invasion of effeminacy. The Gallomania was of short duration. The morality of the Germans was too deeply interwoven with their national character to afford a permanent hold to French example. The latter part of the eighteenth century saw it give way, even in its strong holds, until it ultimately disappeared. Princes ascended the throne whose personal character was strong enough to introduce an effective reform. The nationality of the Germans awoke as from an unhealthy slumber. A new literature was created, and science was cultivated in a new spirit. The

middle classes asserted their rights against the privileges of the nobles in a bold and determined tone. The nobility they said were alone eligible to civil and military posts, they were still in possession of monopolies, and the services exacted from their vassals were incompatible with justice and humanity. These remonstrances the nobility met with indifference and contempt, and in this relation did the two parties stand until the breaking out of the French Revolution.

The enthusiasm which was kindled throughout Germany by the first successes of the democratic party, was soon quenched in the deluge of blood which succeeded them. These saturnalia were fatal to the cause of freedom. The most upright and purest friends of emancipation from feudal thraldom, were startled at the price of blood and crime at which it was to be purchased. The nobles became the defenders of the throne, and the prince would listen to no accusation against them. But the French invasion precipitated them at once down the precipice they so much dreaded. The left bank of the Rhine was annexed to France, and the nobles of course lost all their privileges. The peace of Luneville abolished at a blow the diets in all the states which it concerned. The Rheinish confederacy were further empowered to deal as they pleased with the privileges of the nobles ; a power, of which all but the King of Saxony and the Dukes of Mechlinburg thought proper to avail themselves. The religious endowments, with the single exception of those of Austria, were everywhere confiscated. The nobility were deprived of their privileges, and even rendered subject to conscription. In Prussia the necessity of making head against the invader, forced the government into the adoption of similar changes of policy. Servitude was abolished, the plebeian was allowed to purchase the estates of the noble, the latter was declared liable to conscription, and birth was declared no longer necessary for promotion in the army. After the peace of 1814, the nobility fondly hoped to recover their lost power and importance, but the middle classes had risen into importance,—to retrograde was impossible. The absolute monarch supported by his army and beloved by his people, was no longer disposed to admit the aristocracy to a share of power ; and the Congress of Vienna contented itself with securing to the latter all the privileges which it could exercise without prejudice to the other classes of society, and without infringing on the Sovereign power. Their present position and numbers are thus estimated by Mr. Hawkins :

" The ordinary nobility in the different German states, is subjected to the respective sovereign powers. In no two countries is its position the same. It has almost everywhere lost its exemption from taxation, and its remaining privileges are rather forms than solid advantages. In the constitutional states, however, it takes part in the government as a legislative chamber, and in several it still continues to administer justice in minor affairs on its own domains, and to exercise the right of church-presentation,

On the whole, however, its position is rather to be ascribed to the respect which it inspires, than to the privileges to which it is legally entitled.

" The king of Prussia, and, I believe, some other German potentates, now require an university education, and certain preliminary tests from all candidates for office; this circumstance alone will probably tend to elevate the character of the German nobility, because they will be compelled to undergo a regular educational discipline, and to sustain competition; but they have also a still more difficult trial to endure in Prussia, in a struggle against increasing poverty.

" The number of noble idinviduals in Austria was estimated by Lichenstern at 475,000. But Hassel believes that this calculation falls far short of the truth. In 1785, the nobility of Hungary alone were estimated at 162,495; and in 1816, the male nobles of Milan were reckoned at 3,859. The number of nobles in Prussia was computed by Hassel, in 1822, at about 200,000. Spain has been estimated to possess the most numerous nobility; Poland, probably, is at least equal in this respect; Austria and Prussia follow, then Russia, then France, next Sweden, and England stands, perhaps, last; Italy is less known."

From the foregoing estimate, it appears that Germany is rich enough in all conscience in noble blood, sufficiently so indeed to furnish a supply of that commodity to the other States of Europe. We are no longer amazed at the crowds which it sends forth to glitter for a while in our *beau monde*, like the swallows that come to revel in the sunshine of our summer. It is not our intention to follow Mr. Hawkins through his masterly chapter on the literature of Germany. In our Review of Mr. Taylor's powerful " Survey" we have already treated the subject at ample length. The various periodicals have, moreover, devoted a large portion of their columns to the work of popularizing the best productions of the several German schools, and of making the public acquainted with every point of interest connected with their writers. Those who have not had access to those sources of information, will find in the rapid sketch given in the present work all that is most deserving of attention. The exposition is clear, and the criticisms impartial and acute, for Mr. Hawkins is as judicious a critic as he is a careful and accurate statistic. As men of letters the Germans are pre-eminent. As Theologians they are not to be regarded with such cordial respect. In the cultivation of systematic geography, and of statistics, they are unrivalled. Busching, Hassel, Stein, Ritter, Crome, Meusel, Malthus, and a long array of celebrated names, have won honourable distinction in this field of science. Political philosophy and state economy have been cultivated with similar ardour, and the names of Schubert, Pœlitz, Von Rotteck and Welcker, and not a few others, have become illustrious by their success. In no country is the philosophy of legislation more sedulously investigated, and nowhere are more learned lawyers to be found, while in all that relates to the literature of their science the German medical men are confessedly the best read men in Europe. In the branches of forensic medicine, medical police and ophthalmic surgery, they 'stand at the head of their European brethren. Their superiority in theoretical pharmacy, in medical botany and dietetics, stands uncontroverted; while the obscure and unpromising study of animal magnetism is peculiarly their own. In natural philosophy the names of Herschel, F. H .A. Von Humboldt, Gauss, Oken, Schœele, and Cuvier, who was born at Montebeliard, in the duchy of Wurtemberg, and received his education at Stuttgard, are in the mouths of all Europe, and shed a lustre over the land of their birth. The cultivation of the arts keeps pace with the cultivation of letters. A rapid progress has been made in architecture; in sculpture, Rauch and Tieck, Schadow and Ohmacht have attained considerable eminence: of Rauch and Tieck Mr. Hawkins speaks thus :—

" Christian Rauch, Professor to the Academy at Berlin, is remarkable for the truth, grace and power of his execution. His works prove him to be a man of great penetration, and, at the same time, of an imaginative mind. He possesses the secret of giving a dignified effect to modern costume. He has recently executed busts of Zelter and Schleiermacher, a colossal statue of Frederic William I., at Gumbinnen, and a monument for Franke, the founder of the orphan-asylum at Halle. Amongst his other works are an admirable little figure of Goëthe, but above all a monument to Queen Louisa of Prussia, and to Maximilian Joseph, of Bavaria.

" Christian Frederic Tieck, Professor of Sculpture to the Academy of Berlin, was born in that city in 1776. This artist has studied nature profoundly, and is well versed in classic art. His execution is singularly perfect and harmonious. His Ganymede and his Shepherd are admirable works of art, and worthy of a Grecian sculptor. He has recently executed busts of the crown-princess, of Niemeyer, and of Milder the singer. Several scholars of the Berlin Academy have distinguished themselves in sculpture, as, for instance, the brothers Wichman and Rietschell."

The modern German school of painting springs from the year 1810. Its principal supporters are Overbeck, Cornelius, the Veits, W. Schadow and Sheffer: it addresses itself to the religious feelings of our nature, and prefers simplicity and force to ornament and grace. Cornelius is the great boast of this school. Regarding religion as the proper field of art, he made those painters whose works were especially imbued with it his peculiar study. He is established at Munich, to which city the munificent encouragement of the King of Bavaria has attracted numbers of the most eminent artists of Germany. With resources less abundant than those enjoyed by many individuals in England, this prince has done more for his small capital, and raised more noble monuments to the fine arts than any monarch of our own time. Munich is now the resort of strangers from all parts of Europe; its artists are obtaining a wide field for exertion, and from the rank of a third rate capital it is now rising to a level with the first. In the matter of music we shall quote Mr. Hawkins's own words.

"In the cultivation of that most delightful of all fine arts, music, the Germans stand, by common consent, at the head of all the world. There the science and practice of this solace of life are carried to a perfection, and pursued to an extent, which it would be vain to seek in any other part of the globe. Those who, from old prejudices, expect to find a rival in Italy, will be grievously disappointed. In the village schools of Germany, singing is taught as a branch of education; a group of peasants, or a regiment of soldiers, will there execute choral music in a better taste than some of the professional choirs in other parts of Europe. In most of the large towns are academies, at which instrumental and vocal music are gratuitously, or almost gratuitously, taught. It forms the staple amusement of every bathing-place, of every public garden, of almost every society. Good music is sought and prized, from whatever quarter it may proceed,—not merely the composition and performance of noted names, not merely that which is new, but the truly good of all times, climes, and persons, is estimated at its just value. I shall not pause to inquire how it happens that in the more southern parts of Europe, the pretended genial soil of melody, the true musical genius is comparatively so barren, and the taste and mechanism in proportion so scanty, and so partial; but whatever may be the cause, not only is Germany the most methodical and the most learned, but she alone appears endued with the true enthusiasm, the full temperament of melody. To enumerate the great musical authors of Germany, would be to repeat a host of names familiar to all who honour sweet sounds; a small triumphant band will suffice, at the head of whom stand Handel, Gluck, Haydn, Mozart, and Weber, who have translated their art into a new language, pouring out at one moment rushing torrents of sublime eloquence, and at another gently gliding into the heart in sportive or murmuring streamlets.

"As to the instrumental performers of Germany, their names abound in the catalogue of every orchestra and concert in Europe. Of great singers she has not been so fruitful, although many such have been born of German parents established in foreign countries; and I believe that the impediment of language, and the vogue of the Italian school, have contributed to keep others in obscurity. In our own time, Sontag and Schroeder Devrient have elevated the national claims to vocal distinction. Even in the sister art of dancing, which some may, from prepossession, infer to be uncongenial to the soil, there are some most successful candidates for fame, such as Heberlé and the two Elslers; and in short, as Germany is the home of music, so also is it the only land in which, in these later and sadder days, the dance maintains its footing as a thoroughly national pastime."

In Germany as in every other country in Europe, the opera, musical farce, and splendid decorations have driven tragedy and comedy from the stage. There too, as in other countries, it is remarked that the theatre is less attended by the higher and more frequented by the lower classes. The drama, however, still maintains a firm hold, and forms an integral portion of daily existence to a large mass of the population. But the opera is in the ascendant,

which Mr. Hawkins says is nowhere else so faithfully and so earnestly exhibited, and nowhere else so judiciously appreciated.

The following statistics of German publication as compared with that of France are curious and interesting.

"We perceive that the number of new publications was formerly much greater in Germany than in France, from the following comparative number of books published in the two countries.

In the Years	In France.	In GERMANY.	
		At Easter.	At Michaelmas.
1814	979	1490	1039
1815	1712	1777	973
1816	1851	1997	1200
1817	2126	2345	1187
1818	2431	2294	1487
1819	2441	2648	1268
1820	2465	2640	1318
1821	2617	3012	985
1822	3114	2729	1554
1823	2687	2558	1751
1824	3436	2870	1641
1825	3569	3196	1640
1826	4347	2648	2056
	33,775	32,204	18,099

50,303

In France 33,775

Balance in favour of Germany . . . 16,528

"Latterly, however, the French press appears so have gained some advance, as in 1828, when above 7000 publications are said to have been printed in France.

"Our excellent ' Foreign Quarterly Review' states, that the number of periodical works enumerated in the Leipsic catalogue for 1836, is 297. The names of 530 publishers are given in this catalogue. An Augsburg journal has lately affirmed, that on a moderate calculation, 10,000,000 of volumes are annually printed in Germany; and as every half-yearly catalogue contains the names of more than 1000 German writers, it has been assumed that there are now living in Germany, more than 50,000 persons who have perpetrated one or more books. The total value of all the books published annually, has been estimated at from 5,000,000 to 6,000,000 of dollars.

"To illustrate the increase of the book-trade during the last hundred years, we may cite the fact, that Leipsic contained in 1722 only 19 bookselling establishments, and 13 printing-offices; while in 1836 it was in possession of 116 of the former, and 22 of the latter.

"The book-trade was thirty years ago in the hands of only 300 booksellers or publishers; at present there are more than 1000. Throughout the whole Germanic Confederation, there is one bookseller to 93,000 souls, but in Austria one only in 122,222. Saxony furnishes the greatest number of new publications, next Prussia, and then Austria, but Austria is far behind in point of numbers. The number of booksellers in London has been computed, we know not how correctly, at above 800."

On the subject of religion, it is the settled conviction of Mr. Hawkins, that scepticism is making rapid strides over the whole fabric of society in Germany as well as in other countries of Europe. The tone of popular writers, the spirit in which religious matters are handled in society, and the feelings manifested towards the clergy, are some of the signs which he instances as being indicative of this result. The clergy themselves marshal the way to the precipice. Their Socinian mode of interpreting the Scriptures is laying the foundation of a popular creed of rationalism, which appears to the eyes of the orthodox Mr. Hawkins as the darkest cloud that menaces the state. The doctrines of the Rationalists were collected into systematic order by Röhr, now clerical superintendent of the grand duchy of Weimar, in his *Briefe über den Rationalismus*, and Weg-schneider in his *Institutiones Theologicæ Christianæ Dogmaticæ;* from which we collect that the fundamental doctrine of rationalism is, that the mission of Christ and the whole scheme of revelation were merely intended for our instruction in certain principles, the truth of which human reason alone, without the aid of inspiration, would in process of time have been able to establish. Hence the fundamental truths of Christianity are totally slurred over or absolutely rejected. Gesenius, the celebrated Hebrew scholar, Schleier-macher and De Wette, are the most noted apostles of this doctrine of "accommodation" as it is technically termed, because it accommodates the wonders of revelation to human reason. Opposed to these are the "Supernaturalists," who maintain the necessity and reality of a revelation, while they deny the doctrine of original sin. Their opposition is not of a very decided cast, and they have given in more or less to the accommodation principle. The education of clergymen both Catholic and Protestant is conducted with the utmost care, and their sufficiency is tested by frequent examinations. The following affords a view of their comparative numbers, and their proportion to the population.

" *Prussia.* We have not been able to discover the number of the Protestant ministers. The Catholic population amounts to 4,816,813, and there are 3,200 Catholic parishes; thus there are 1,505 persons to each parish. *Saxony:* In this country there is one Lutheran minister to 1,600 inhabitants, and one Catholic minister to 432. In *Saxe Altenburg,* there is one minister to 800 inhabitants; in *Hanover,* one to 1,146 amongst the Lutherans, one to 940 in the Reformed Church, and one to 710 amongst the Catholics. In *Wurtemberg,* there is one Lutheran minister to 1,300 inhabitants, and one Catholic to 628. In Catholic *Austria,* there is one ecclesiastic to 500 inhabitants; of the Reformed Church there are 2,035 parishes, and 815 persons to each parish; of the Lutherans there are 807 parishes, and 1,400 persons to each parish; there are 50,000 Unitarians, who have 111 ministers, which is one minister to 459 individuals. In *Bavaria,* there is one minister to 1,000 inhabitants among the Catholics, and one to 914 among the Protestants.

" *Church Property in the Protestant States.* A considerable part of the church-property in Germany was seized upon by the governments when the monasteries were secularized at the Reformation; another portion, consisting of ground-rent, has, for some time, never been realized, and, finally, a part has been expended (as in Saxony,) for the establishment of schools, and on the relief of the poor. However, the little landed property belonging to each parish-church, has, for the most part, remained in the possession of the clergy, and is now the principal source of their income.

" In most livings, there is a parsonage-house, surrounded by gardens and orchards. Tithes are very common, and the value of them sometimes equals that of the church-lands. The clergyman has also certain fees, on the occasion of marriages, baptisms, burials and confirmations (these are called *Accidenzien*). Where the income from these sources is too limited, the government makes up the deficiency. In some parts, and particularly in the north of Germany, it is customary, at certain periods of the year, to make presents to the clergymen. On the whole, in Protestant Germany, the incomes of the country-clergy vary from 350 to 800 dollars; some have less than the former sum, and some as much as 1,000, 1,200, or 1,600 dollars. The value of a living often depends on the price of corn, and on the profit which the clergyman is capable of drawing from his glebe-lands. The livings in town are somewhat more valuable, varying from 450 to 1,000 dollars on an average. The two most valuable livings in Saxony are of 4,000 dollars a year, but, in both cases, this income is chiefly derived from fees.

" In no part of Germany has the church-property been better preserved from spoliation than in Hanover, where, consequently, the clergy are better paid. In Wurtemberg, the property of the church has been consolidated, and applied not only to ecclesiastical purposes, but to the establishment of schools, and to the relief of the poor. Moreover, in 1806, it was united with the royal domains, and subjected to the same administration. The lands attached to the country-churches have not, however, shared this fate, but are under the control of ecclesiastical commissioners. In Nassau, the average value of livings is from 600 to 1,800 florins, of deaneries from 1,300 to 1,800; the Protestant bishop has an income of 3,000 florins. In Prussia, the government pays out of the treasury to the support of the church, 2,326,000 dollars annually.

" *Church Property in Catholic States.* In Austria, not only are the clergy taxed in common with the lay citizens, but particular imposts are laid upon their body. The value of the church-property in this empire is 200,000,000 florins; besides a fund called the *Religious Fund,* constituted by the purchase-money of church-property (monasteries, &c.) sold by the Emperor Joseph, the annual interest of which is two and a half millions of florins. In Bavaria, the archbishop has an income of 20,000 florins, and the bishops of from 12,000 to 15,000 florins."

The greater number of Church presentations are in the hands of

Government, a fourth part only being in the hands of private individuals.

"In most Protestant states, the Catholic and the Established churches are placed upon the same footing. But as the ministers of the former persuasion are more numerous than those of the latter, and as, owing to the practice of celibacy, their wants are fewer, their incomes are generally less. On the other hand, the Catholic dignitaries are much better paid than the Protestant ones. In Rhenish Prussia, the Catholic archbishops have an annual income of 12,000 dollars, the bishops of 8,000, the deans of 1,800, or 2,000, the canons of 1,000 or 1,200. This money is now paid out of the Treasury; the estates from which these dignitaries formerly derived their incomes having all been secularized. In Saxony, where the ruling family is of the Catholic religion, though the great mass of the population is Protestant, the clergy of the former persuasion are so well paid, as to cause great jealousy amongst those who are followers of the latter. In Hanover, and in Hesse-Cassel, the Catholic clergy are equally well paid with the Protestant, though this is not the case in Wurtemberg and Baden.

"In Austria, the Protestant clergy are provided for by their congregations, which have also to pay the *jura stolæ* to the Catholic priests. In Bavaria, the expenses of the Protestant church are defrayed by the government.

"We believe that the Jews throughout Germany are obliged, themselves, to defray the expenses of worship.

"There exist no general rules respecting the support of the clergy. Only the incomes of the higher Catholic clergy are fixed by the bull *De salute animarum*, namely, for the archbishop and prince-bishop of Breslau at 12,000 Prussian dollars; (about 1,750*l.*); for the other bishops 8,000 Prussian dollars, for the dignitaries of cathedral chapters respectively, 2,000, 1,800, 1,400 Prussian dollars; and for canons or prebends, respectively, 1,200, 1,000 and 800 Prussian dollars, besides house-room. The incomes of all other livings, either of the Protestant or Catholic church, are very different. The clergyman receives his income either in kind or in money. It is paid in kind when it arises from a real estate belonging to his benefice, which he manages himself, or when it is rendered to him by landed proprietors. Of the same kind are tithes, rents, and other payments from land. The money-income of the clergy arises partly out of the public revenues of the crown, or of the parishes, either as a salary or compensation for appropriated lands or ground-rents, or as rents from private estates, or from endowments laid out at interest. The crown has undertaken the above-mentioned payment of the Catholic dignitaries, since their landed property had been appropriated to the public revenue. In the Trans-Rhenane part of the kingdom, where, during the French sway, the church property was seized and chiefly alienated, the crown pays a salary to the clergy, as a compensation, according to a *concordat* entered into by the French consular government with Pope Pius VII."

In the matter of education no country presents a subject of such interesting investigation as Germany. In no country is there to be found so ample a provision for the instruction of the people in all sciences and arts. Hence, there it is that the results of education may be most advantageously weighed. The inferences drawn by Mr. Hawkins are not so very favourable to the predictions of our propagandists.

"The facility with which the highest education may be obtained in Germany, naturally introduces into the arena of life an immense proportion of candidates for its higher prizes, too many of whom finally obtain disappointment, if not entire destitution, while not a few bury their obscure heart-burnings in the chance pittance afforded by foreign countries, already overstocked with aspirants of indigenous origin. Thus, in the course of ten recent years, the number of Protestant clergymen has doubled in Prussia, and the Roman Catholic priesthood has tripled; the lawyers have increased one-fourth, but the doctors in medicine only one-seventh. At the beginning of this period there was one lawyer in 12,600 inhabitants, at the end there was one in 8,562; there was one doctor of medicine, at the beginning, in 27,000 souls, and at last one in 25,205. In consequence of the increase of students in the late years, there was recently in Prussia so many as

One student of theology in 442 inhabitants.
" "   law in   822 " "
" "   medicine in 5,660 " "
But the state in Prussia only requires—
One clergyman for . . 1,250 inhabitants.
One lawyer for   . . . 822 " "
One doctor of medicine for 3,516 " "

How many of those now employed must accordingly die or retreat, in order to make room for the forthcoming! In the smaller states of Germany the prospect is still more disheartening. In the duchy of Baden, only eight vacancies annually occur of offices in the law, enjoying a fixed salary, while so many as forty-six candidates present themselves annually for examination; and there are already so many as two hundred and fifty-one candidates examined and approved, and awaiting the long-deferred turn."

The Prussian system is as everybody knows the most perfect in the world. Alluding to its operation on the mass of society, Mr. Hawkins says,

"I am the last person to attach much weight to my own observations, but, in default of the remarks of others, I have not succeeded in discovering that the Prussian peasant or artisan is better informed, or more moral than his neighbours; his manners are not superior, nor does he appear to solace his hours of leisure more than others, with study, or books. But the formation of character is so intimately blended in Prussia with the military system, which converts every man into a soldier, for a certain period of his life, that it is difficult to ascertain the respective share which is to be ascribed to the various elements which combine to mould the individual. The most intelligent and best informed peasant in Europe has appeared to me to be the Scotch, while the Austrian rustic is perhaps the happiest."

In the building and discipline of prisons, great improvement has taken place in Germany within the last half century. The prisons are conveniently constructed, well aired, and well regulated. The silent system is almost universally adopted and enforced by the bastinado. The latter infliction has been much complained of, but after all, it is not worse than forced labour. Mr. Hawkins gives a detailed account of the discipline and regulations peculiar to the prisons of every particular state; but to follow him in this subject, in which he seems quite at home, would be more than our limits would allow of. We shall merely notice the *labour* executed by culprits in the German prisons, as we consider it particularly deserving of attention.

" The prisoners at Munich are employed in an excellent manufactory of cloth, and as tailors and shoemakers. The cloth alone, which is of the quality worn by the higher classes, produces a revenue to the government of more than 50,000 florins yearly. The prisoners in Holstein are still, for the most part, unemployed; but not so in Schleswig, particularly at Glüdkstadt, where each prisoner is bound to do a certain quantity of work, which if he neglects he is punished; if he does more than is required, he is paid for the surplus. The prisoners are employed in spinning, carding wool, knitting stockings, weaving, making pipes for fire-engines, and sail-cloth.

" At Dresden the prisoners are employed in cleaving wood, breaking stones down to sand, and dragging coals through the town. The inhabitants can obtain the prisoners to do any sort of work for them, by paying five groschen per day to the establishment.

" At Plessenburg there is a cloth manufactory and a bakehouse in the prison. The prisoners are allowed to work a little for themselves. The managers of the prison allow culprits who have been liberated to become the superintendents of the others when at work.

" At Mannheim the employments of the prisoners are dressing hemp, weaving, knitting, making cloths, shoes, and lately, manufacturing list. The superintendents of the different kinds of works receive four hundred florins a year. Some of the prisoners are employed in making the furniture of the establishment, and others are employed by the inhabitants, at their own houses, to cleave wood. At Frieburg the prisoners are employed in stone-cutting, weaving, carpenter's-work, and as masons, shoemakers, tailors, locksmiths, and clockmakers. At Cologne, a certain number of prisoners are without occupation, those, for instance, who are condemned to a short imprisonment, debtors, and those of the untried who are not likely to remain long. Trades of all sorts are carried on by the rest of the prisoners; amongst others, lithography.

" In Austria, the daily task allotted to each prisoner is such, that the very industrious have a little time to work for themselves. The half of what the prisoner earns for himself is set apart to be given him at his liberation; the other half he can spend in buying bread, beer, or broth. In order to appreciate this privilege, we must remember that the Austrian prison has, for three days of the week, only a pound of bread for all provision.

At Naugard, the prisoner has first to pay for his support by his labour, before he receives anything extra. What he saves, is placed in the Savings'-bank at Stettin, and should he die in confinement, it goes to his heirs. On his quitting the prison, he not only receives his extra earnings, but he is duly recommended where he is likely to obtain employment. In respect to their gains, all the prisoners are put as much as possible on the same footing; and half is at their disposal for the purchase of provisions, a little brandy, and, on Sundays, of tobacco for chewing.

" At Dresden, the sum accruing from surplus labour is never placed at the prisoner's disposal until his liberation.

" At Hamburg, the system of surplus labour has not been adopted; but a part of what the prisoners earn reverts to them.

" The other German prisons resemble more or less the above, in the arrangements they have introduced respecting the employment of prisoners."

In most of the prisons provision is made for the religious and elementary instruction of the prisoners, and a most praiseworthy care is taken of them by the respective governments after their liberation. At Hamburg it not unfrequently happens that the prisoner receives on his liberation a sum of from 200 to 300 marks as the produce of his labour. When a prisoner has conducted himself well, exertions are made to establish him honestly. In Nassau, if the prisoner's gains do not amount to a certain sum, the deficiency is supplied by the government, and care is always taken to replace him properly in the world, to prevent him from returning to his former courses. In this respect, their conduct is decidedly superior to that pursued in England, where a prisoner is turned forth upon society without any means of subsistence whatsoever, or any opportunity of earning an honest livelihood.

We come now to the social condition of Germany as expounded by Mr. Hawkins, and with this we shall close our observations on the subject. The partition of Germany into a number of small states, gives to individuals advantages of a higher degree than are enjoyed by those of any other European states. Thus the numerous states have their respective cabinet ministers, convoys, generals, and civil officers of various denominations. An office which in England is filled by a single person, gives employment to twenty in Germany. For instance, England sends out one ambassador to France, while Germany sends no less than thirteen. Then again in literature, there are thirty German universities to five British; and moreover a German university has double the number of professors of an English one, besides their Gymnasiums, Pedagogisms, and innumerable schools, with their quota of officers. Another advantage accruing from this system is, that every sovereign, how petty soever he may be, is anxious to embellish and distinguish his territory. Hence, museums, picture galleries, gardens, libraries, academies; and thus for one of such institutions in England, we shall find twenty in Germany, all open to the public; nor does it appear that the German is more heavily taxed for the procurement of such privileges than his neighbours; besides, as every palace, garden, gallery, and park is open, the money which is received from the subject is returned to him in the form of mental and bodily amusement. The gracious and cordial familiarity which prevails between the higher and lower classes is also worthy of imitation. There is no shrinking from contamination, no shuddering at impure mixture as in England. The use of the Murchaum has been severely reprehended. All that can be said is, that it disposes the mind to serenity and quiet contemplation, and is much better than gin-drinking. "The German labourer," says Mr. Hawkins, "seated at a table in a public garden, quietly smoking his pipe, listening to excellent music, and surrounded by his family, is no mean specimen of human happiness and respectability." The Germans are less the slaves of fashion and exclusiveness than any people in Europe, each considers his own means and inclinations, and pursues them without deference to others, and without offence. No one stares at a bad coat or negligent costume, and everybody is at liberty to do and dress just as he pleases. The chief gratification of the higher order in addition to the theatre, consists in a summer visit to some of the many watering-places, where they live almost entirely in public. In the smaller towns, the men of learning shut themselves up in their cabinets, and in the intenseness of their studies the extent of their acquirements and the simplicity of their manners are distinguishable at once from the rest of their European colleagues. The Cosmopolitan man of learning, says Mr Hawkins, who understands most of the European and some of the Oriental languages, while he is conversant with almost every science, is, perhaps, only to be found at the present moment in Germany. He differs from most other specimens of the same class, not only in his attainments, but in his scrupulous sanctitude—in the concientious manner in which he weighs evidence and records every minute shade of fact, and also in his impartiality and that genial love for his calling which enables him to disregard pecuniary profit, and confines his anxiety to the noble ambition of instructing his brethren, of conciliating the suffrages of the wise, and of laying the foundations of a posthumous fame, which, alas, is too rarely completed into a lasting edifice. Frankness, honesty, simplicity, modesty, and diffidence, are the chief qualities of the national character of the Germans. They are the great assertors of a truth of invaluable importance, that all are to be treated with respect, and that no superiority of rank or fortune can warrant arrogance of demeanour or pride of speech.

In addition to the general view of Germany, each of the larger states has a chapter exclusively devoted to itself. There is not a single item which may claim connexion with the statistics of each state which is not noted down with an almost tiresome precision. Thus we have the number of lodging houses, and of arrivals and departures in a given year; the number of each particular trade, profession, calling; the number of sheep, oxen, and stock of all kinds; besides revenues, population, deaths, births, marriages, and all the numerous *et cætera* that can possibly engage the attention of the compiler of statistics. We are only surprised Mr. Hawkins did not attempt to count the trees, or the farming implements in each state. It is impossible for us to give any adequate idea of this huge and compact mass of statistical information; some facts, however, there are connected with the moral condition of a country, where education is so widely diffused and so systematically conducted, which we cannot pass by without an observation.

The annual number of births in the Austrian dominions (Hungary not included) is estimated at 764,290; of marriages 167,704; and of deaths 688,763. There is one marriage annually to 130 individuals. The number of female to male births is as 1000 to 1,602. About every tenth child is illegitimate. The Bohemians are much more prolific than the inhabitants of the other provinces. Amongst them, in every eight births one is illegitimate. In the Foundling Hospital at Prague, 1,125 children were received in the year 1827. The number of marriages in the same year was six to one. In Prussia, the illegitimate births are one in twelve. The number of prostitutes in Berlin, whose names are inscribed upon the books of the police, is only 273, almost an evanescent quantity, when we compare Berlin with Paris, where the registered number amounted in 1834 to 3,816, or to London, where their name is Legion. But this apparently small number is by no means an argument in favour of the superior morality of the Berlinese, but is entirely owing to the compulsory and vexatious interference of the police. Another strange fact connected with Prussian morals is, that the law allows them a facility of divorce, of which they are not at all backward in availing themselves. The number of divorces is one in thirty-seven marriages: this is a most startling fact. In Saxony, the number of married persons is calculated at about one-third of the population, or 277,813 in round numbers; of these, 11,213 were living *separate*, and 3,793 were *divorced*. The number of illegitimate children in the same state was in 1831, one in six. The houses of correction at Spandau and Brandenburg in Prussia, contained, in 1833, 1,458 prisoners; and in 1835, 1,0134 persons were arrested in Berlin, so that one in twenty-five persons spent a portion of the year in prison. In the rural districts of Bavaria, the number of illegitimate children exceeded the number of those born in wedlock, a circumstance without parallel, even in the most dissolute cities in Europe. In Munich, the number of children born out of wedlock, almost exactly balances that born in wedlock, the illegitimates being in 1823, 998; the legitimates 1,030. In 1834, the illegitimates mustered 1,291, while the legitimates did not exceed 1339. So much for the Utopian theories of the ultimate perfectibility of mankind. So much for the diffusion of education and the reading of the Scripture serving as a check upon the passions. It is notorious that in Ireland, where the absence of the education that exists in Germany is so much deplored, the number of illegitimate children in any district is a mere fraction on the amount of population; and that in most districts it does not equal even a fraction. Perhaps, when the Irish become as enlightened as their German prototypes in learning, they will be equally regardless of the slender restraints of conventional morality.

20. BLACKWOOD'S MAGAZINE, 45 (1839), 247-256. M/H No. 3499. *Cf.* Carré, p. 114. By James White.

A DISCOURSE ON GOETHE AND THE GERMANS.

How glad I am, my dear Mr North, to have found you at home!—charming snuggery!—famous fire!—and I declare there's a second tumbler on the table, as if you expected me. Your health, my dear friend!—good heavens, what intense Glenlivat!—I must add a little water; and now, that at last we are cozy and comfortable—feet on fender, glass in hand—I beg to say a few words to you on the subject of German morals and German literature.

Sir, unaccustomed as I am to public speaking, I must crave your indulgence—more sugar, did you say?—while I dilate a little upon the many trumpet-blowings and drum-beatings we have heard on these two subjects for the last fifteen or twenty years. Morals!—oh the good, honest, simple, primitive, Germans! Literature!—oh the deep-thinking, learned, grand, original-minded Germans! Now, the fact is, sir, that the Germans have neither morals nor literature. But, as I intend, with your permission—your bland countenance shows your acquiescence—to demonstrate by the thing they call literature, the notion they entertain of the thing they call morals, I need not trouble you with a double disquisition on these two points, as in fact they are, like the French Republic, one and indivisible. Fifty years ago, they themselves con-fess, they had no literature. The capabilities of their noble language were yet undiscovered; their scholars wrote in Latin; their wits wrote in French. Poetry was defunct, or rather uncreated; for, on the top of the German Parnassus, such as it was, sat in smoke and grandeur the weakest of mortals, the poorest of versifiers, the most miserable of pedants, John Christoph Gottshed. Was he kicked down from his proud eminence by the indignation of his countrymen?—hooted to death by their derision?—and finally hung in chains as a terror to evil doers? My dear sir, the man was almost worshipped—yes—he, this awful example of human fatuity—a decoction of Hayley and Nathan Drake—was looked up to by the whole German nation, as an honour to the human race. It will not do for them to deny the soft impeachment now, and tell us that they look down upon that worthy. I dare say they do; but whom do they look up to between the days of Gottshed, and the first appearances of a better order of things in the persons of Wieland, Klopstock, and Gesner? To the other members of the Leipsic school, Gellert, Rabener, and Zacharia!—pretty men for a nation to be proud of!—No sir, you need not shake your head. I am not in a passion, I assure you, but only a little nettled; for can any thing be more provoking than to have one's ears tormented incessantly with praises of every thing German, by a set of blockheads, male and female, who know nothing of the subject, and take all that the Germans themselves advance for gospel? Depend upon it, sir, hundreds of young ladies can repeat stanzas of Gleim and Utss, who never read a line of Spencer in their lives. So let us go back to Gottshed. Did you ever meet with his collection of plays called the *German Theatre?* A lucky man if you haven't, for such a load of trash was never before brought together in one heap since the days of Augeus. Translation, or more properly, as they themselves call it, " oversetting," is the loftiest of their flights. And such translations! Corneille, Racine, Germanized, and by the hand of John Christoph himself; hand more fit to stuff sausages than translate the *Cid* or *Iphiginie*. And even in this cabbaging and pilfering how limited was their range! The Danish and French seem to be the only tongues they had the command of. English was a fountain sealed, and a well shut up from them, till some French depredator had first melted the wax and picked the padlock. But, gracious heaven, Mr North, how they dirtied the water! And who was it, after all, whom they translated or imitated? *Not* Johnson—*not* Shakspeare—nor even glorious John. Who then? Addison! —*The Drummer,* which even in English is a wonderfully stupid performance for the creator of Sir Roger de Coverly, is tortured into more Teutonic dulness in a close translation; and Gottshed founds his claim to supremacy as an original author on his tragedy of *Cato.* Stars and Garters! bob-wigs and shoe-buckles! what a Cato! Addison's is poor enough, and spouts like a village schoolmaster in his fifth tumbler; and virtuous Marcia towers above her sex like a matron of the Penitentiary; but Gottshed's Cato is a cut above all this. Shall I give you the *Dramatis Personæ?* Here they are in my note-book.

" CATO.
ARSENE or PORCIA.
PORCIUS, *Cato's Son.*
PHÆNICE, *Arsene's Confidante.*
PHOCUS, *Cato's Attendant.*
PHARNACES, *King out of Pontus.*
FELIX, *his Attendant.*
CÆSAR.
DOMITIUS, *his Attendant.*
ARTABANUS, *a Parthian.*
Cato's suite.
Cæsar's suite.
" The scene is in a hall of a strong castle in Utica, a considerable city in Africa. The story or incident of the whole tragedy extends from mid-day till towards sunset."

What do you think of that, sir? And what do you think of Arsene who has been brought up by Arsaces, and by him been made Queen of the Parthians, turning out in the third act to be Cato's daughter, and shockingly in love with Cæsar? Think of all this, sir, and of the prodigious orations between the two heroes in rhyming Alexandrines, and you will rejoice as I did that the long-winded old patriot put himself to death. It is the only consolation one has all through the play to know that in the fifth act justice will be executed on all and sundry; for Gottshed does not spare an inch of the cold steel.

But why do I lay such stress on poor old buried and forgotten John Christoph?—I'll trouble you for the kettle.—The reason is very plain; I want to find out some excuse for the Germans having formed such an exaggerated estimate of their present school—and I think I have found it in the profundity of the abyss they were sunk in before it made its appearance. People in a coal-pit see the smaller stars at mid-day as plain as if each of them were of the first magnitude. The deeper they go down, the brighter shines the twinkler; so that when the Leipsic public had fallen into the depths of Gottshedism, no wonder that, on the first rising of Wieland, they considered him the sun in heaven. Then shone Klopstock, Lessing, Schiller, Goethe forming—as seen from that subterranean level—a whole planetary system. But for us English, sir, to look up to such lights—to talk of them in the same century with our own—or to think they are fitted to be classed with those glorious constellations that illumine the British sky, and shed their glory over all lands—the thing is beyond joke—'tis monstrous. Contrast them,— Klopstock—Milton; Schiller—Shakspeare; Lessing—Dryden; Goethe— Walter Scott; and as to their small fry, Sam Johnson would have swallowed them all.—Let me turn the cock, sir; I admire your hospitable plan of the cask and spigot, it saves so much trouble in drawing corks—is the water boiling ?—So let us hear no more talk of the vast treasures of German literature. There are not six of them authors worth reading, in what is properly called literature. Learning and antiquities I leave out of the question—they are industrious moles, and grub excellently well—and yet it will take many millions of moles to make a Bentley. In history they have but one name worth mentioning—John Von Müller—and he is one of the sons of Anak, and will sit in the opposite scale to Gibbon, and move not an inch towards the beam—their tribe of gentlemen who write with ease—their story-tellers, romancers, parlour poets, and so forth, are utterly below contempt. Our annual bards and authors are worth them all put together ; and as to our novelists, properly so called, taking them as painters of life and manners, who would think of comparing our second, third, or even our fourth-rates with the miserable Tromlitsses and Van der Veldes, or Hauff's and Spindlers, who rule the roast in their own country, and tempt good-natured young lords to introduce them here ? Did any human being ever succeed in getting to the end of a German novel of ordinary life, without a weariness of the flesh that suggested indistinct thoughts of suicide ? Not one : I have tried it a hundred times—and this is what I have been aiming at—their books, my dear sir, are not only stupid but disgusting—I have met with very few that were not positively shocking from the insight they gave me into the depravity of a whole people. The French, heaven knows, are bad enough; but with them it is a paroxysm, a fever of impropriety, that is limited to a certain set and will pass. Besides, the French abominations are *intended* to be abominable ; an unnatural state of manners is chosen as the subject of representation, and accordingly it is treated in as unnatural a way as possible. For the horrors and iniquities, of a kind that shock and disgust us so much in their performances, are limited to the romantic school—the insane men of perverted genius, like Victor Hugo, who, instead of exhausting old worlds and then imagining new, begin the process by imagining a new

world, and peopling it with the creations of their distempered fancies. But nobody meets such things in the novels purporting to be stories of *real* life. Paul de Kock himself is a humorist, gross, coarse, and "improper," but he sets out with the intention of describing gross, coarse, and improper people. There are thieves, drunkards, dissolute men, and naughty women, in all countries ; we may wonder at people's taste in painting such manners and modes of thinking, but we are not to blame any one but the individual who chooses to bedaub his pallet with such colours. The Germans, on the other hand, are more revolting in their novels of common life than in their more ambitious imaginings. The light is let in upon us through chinks and crannies of the story, enabling us to see the horrible state of manners into which the whole nation is sunk ; for observe, my dear sir, I don't allude to the scenes brought forward in their books to be looked at, shuddered at, and admired as pieces of sublime painting ; what I mean is the unconscious air with which such revelations are made,—the author seeing nothing strange in the incident he is describing ; and talking of it as a matter perhaps of daily occurrence. And these are the people that have written and roared about themselves, till they have persuaded all Europe, or, at least, the rising generation in England, that they are an honest, and pure, and innocent people ; simple in all their habits ; and, in fact, only a better specimen of what was once the character of our Saxon ancestors. German integrity, German truth, are the constant parrot song of every national author. They have even made a substantive out of the word German ; and with them Germanism or Deutscheit, means every virtue under heaven—modesty, I have no doubt, included. You nod, my dear sir, as if you approved of that —and in itself any thing that gives a strong national feeling, a pride in one's own country, a zeal to maintain its honour—is an admirable thing. I have not forgotten the thunders of applause that followed the clap-traps at our theatres about British courage —British power—hearts of oak, and things of that kind : admirable clap-traps they were—but *they had their effect*, sir. There wasn't a god in the gallery that wouldn't have licked three

Frenchmen the moment he had done clapping the aforesaid magnanimous declaration ; for who would have cared a halfpenny for a million of Bonapartes after shouting in chorus, till their throats were dry, "Britons never, never, never will be slaves ?" But the records of the last war will let us see the patriotism of the Germans. Every little principality and power seemed to run a race who should first truckle to the invader. The Confederation of the Rhine is a death-blow to their boasts ; and, to go back to their literature, is there a single man among all their authors, except poor young Körner, that showed a spark of Tyrtæan fire ? What said Goethe ? He made the campaign against France in 1792, and wrote an account of it—are there any spirit-stirring appeals in it against oppression ? Not a word— but a great deal about the comfort of a blanket with which he kept himself warm on the march ; and throughout the whole reign of Napoleon his muse was mute, or admitted to a place at court. And yet Thomas Carlyle,— let me propose his health, sir, hip, hip, hurra !—almost worships that cold-blooded, selfish, sensual old man ; and this idolatry before such a shrine, the reputation of the Laird of Craigenputtock goes a great way to perpetuate.

Such clouds of word praises, in which, I feel sure, the heart has no place, have been spread around this idol, that it positively needs a man to have very good eyes to see the paste and pasteboard it is composed of. Faust ! Faust !—every human being, from about eighteen up to five-and-twenty, and some, even, who have come to years of discretion, have got into a perpetual sing-song of wonder and awe about the depth, grandeur, sublimity, and all the rest of it, of this inimitable performance. Did they ever think of extending their enumeration of its merits, so as to include its profanity, coarseness, vulgarity, and unintelligibleness ? What are we to think of a work, sir, that, in the life-time of the author, needed commentaries on almost every passage,— on its general scope and tendency,— on its occult significations,—while, all the time, the author himself seemed to gape with as total an unconsciousness of its secret meanings as any one else. I will answer for it, at all events, he would have found as much

difficulty as either Carus, or Enk, or Duentzer, in explaining its "einiea and ganzheit," its oneness and almost. Read his own continuation of it— never was proof so complete of a man's ignorance of what he had meant in the former part of the work ;—that is to say, if you give him credit for having had any meaning in it at all. Recollect I don't deny that the man was clever. He was as clever a fellow as the world may often see ; for, do you know, Mr North, I have a prodigious respect for the abilities of successful quacks. Success, itself, is the only proof I require. The less *a priori* grounds there were for expecting their triumphs, the greater credit they are entitled to. Therefore a bumper once more, if you please, sir, to the immortal Goethe.

With no one element of the poetic character in his whole composition ; without enthusiasm, without high sentiment,—with no great power of imagination, the man has persuaded his countrymen, and they have persuaded all Europe, that he was one of nature's denizens—the God-inspired —in short, a Poet. Then, again, with no knowledge of life, abstracted from German life, without even the power of entering into a pure or lofty feeling, much less of giving birth to one, he has persuaded his countrymen that he was an imaginative life-describer, bareing the human soul, and tracing every thought to its parent source. Oh ! paltry, foul, and most unnoble thoughts which Goethe had the power of tracing. Oh ! fallen and sinful human soul which Goethe had the power to lay bare ! No, no, my dear Mr North, there is but one light in which that old man purulant can be seen—in the colours his countrymen have bedaubed him with. As a shrewd note-taker of their habits, as a relater of their every-day modes of thought, he is entitled to all the praise they give him,—but, oh German innocence !—*oh pietas !—oh prisca fides !*—what habits of life are these— what modes of thought !

With the help of a first-rate style, full, clear, and satisfying, both to ear and understanding ; and with a perfect mastery over the most flexible and graphic of all modern languages, it will be strange if, amidst all the unencumbered writings of this most laborious of the paper-stainers of his laborious and paper-staining country, one or other may not be worthy a sensible man's approbation. But, heavens, sir! there is not one that not something or other so revolting to all good taste as to destroy the pleasure you might otherwise have in the performance. And over all is spread such a dung-heap of vile sensualism and immorality, that you fear for the health of the surrounding inhabitants; for such nauseous exhalations must bear pestilence in every breath. There, sir, is a novel of this kind which I intend to substantiate every one of these assertions,—and, by way of keeping my assertions more fully in mind, I will reduce them to these:—Goethe is a coarse-minded sensualist, and the laxity of German manners is most revolting. The Wahlverwandtschaften, or, as it may be translated, the affinities of choice (as opposed to the affinities of blood), is a novel of common life. A certain Baron, who is presented to us by no other name than Edward, in the prime of life (which other circumstances make us fix at about forty-three), rich, polished, and happy, is the hero of the tale. Married within a year to a certain Charlotte, and retired to his estate, no two people apparently can be happier. Building bowers, laying out plantations, and getting up duets on the flute and harpsichord, with books and other appliances, make time glide pleasantly enough; but, in an evil hour, Edward determines to have a spectator of his happiness, and launches out on the comfort they would derive from the society of an anonymous gentleman, who flourishes all through the book under the convenient designation of " The Captain." Charlotte, like a sensible woman, objects a little at first; probably as she is aware that all captains are dangerous inmates; and she has also some little regard for the morals of a young girl of the name of Ottilie, who is at present at school, but whom she intends to send for and make a sort of assistant housekeeper. You will observe, sir, both our friends —Baron Edward and the sensible Charlotte—were no chickens, and had had considerable experience of the married life before. Like certain communicative personages on the stage, who generally relate the whole story of their lives, either to themselves or to some person who knows every incident as well as they do, Charlotte takes an early opportunity of informing her husband of various events which it is highly probable he was not altogether ignorant of. " We loved each other"—she says to him—" when we were young, with all our hearts. We were separated;—you from me, because your father, out of an insatiable love of riches, married you to a wealthy old woman; I from you, because I had to give my hand, without any particular view, to a very respectable old man that I never loved. We were again free—you sooner than I was, your old lady leaving you a very handsome estate. I a little later, just when you returned from abroad. We met again—our recollections were delightful—we loved them— there was no impediment to our living together. You urged me to marry. I hesitated at first, because, though we are about the same age, I am older as a woman than you as a man. At last I could not refuse you what you considered your greatest happiness. You wished to refresh yourself at my side after all the troubles you had gone through in the court, the camp, and on your travels;—to recall your recollections—to enjoy life—but all, with me alone. I sent my only daughter to a boarding-school, where, indeed, she learns more than she could in the country; and not only her, but Ottilie also, my favourite niece, who would, perhaps, have been better as my assistant in household concerns under my own eye. All this was done with your perfect approval, solely that we might live to ourselves, and enjoy our long-wished and late-gained happiness undisturbed."

Isn't this a charming mother, sir, and careful aunt?—Why, Mr North, you've filled up my tumbler without my seeing it!—you see how affectionate she is to her only daughter; how tenderly she talks of the respectable old man she could never love,—and what purity of mind there is in the whole description of the double wedding and double widowhood. But a bit of private history comes to light, a little after, viz., that the Captain and she had intended to hook Edward, the rich widower, into a marriage with the aforesaid Ottilie, Charlotte modestly supposing that she was now too old to attract his observation. Now, suppose Edward was two-and-twenty when he St Albansed himself; Charlotte married her " respectable old man " " without any particular view," say in a year after she was deserted; her daughter is now seventeen, so that we can guess pretty nearly how old is our inflammable friend Edward. He ought to be ashamed of himself! But I am hurrying on too fast; I haven't told you what a middle-aged Don Giovanni the rascal turns out.

The Captain came; the Captain did this, the Captain did that—was so deep, so learned, so witty, so genteel, he might have passed for Captain O'Doherty. Ottilie also comes, " fair as the first that fell of womankind," that is, according to Goethe's notions of fairness; full and round as a Hebe, very young, very innocent, and a little stupid—planting, building, digging lakes, and creating scenery, go on more charmingly than ever, and in the course of a very short time, the Captain and the sensible Charlotte are burning like a couple of phœnixes, and Edward and Ottilie are over head and ears in love. To trace the windings and effects of those two passions is the task the delicate-minded author has chosen—his readers' sympathies are enlisted as strongly as possible on the side of Ottilie and Edward—their walks, their conversations, mingled with much crying and kissing, according to the German recipe for love-making, occupy the greater part of the book. But not the whole of it.—Bless you, my dear sir! there are very few subjects that do not receive a moderate share of notice in the course of the story, particularly the proper mode of educating young ladies; with hints to mistresses of boarding-schools, and the masters engaged for the various accomplishments. But you seem to look incredulous. True as gospel, I assure you; for I beg you to observe—and that was the thing I started with, two tumblers ago—that the monster has not the remotest idea that the personages of his story are vicious or immortal. They are all four held up to us as paragons of perfection. Their modes of going on are spoken of as nothing out of the common way, indeed they are rather pointed out to us as miracles of chastity and decorum; for Ottilie and Edward, resolving to be united according to law, confess their attachment to Charlotte, and beg her to separate from her husband, and by so doing make the Captain and Edward happy at the same time! With an effort of virtue almost super-human —at all events super-German—she refuses—and Edward, not to be outdone, determines to exile himself from his own house, on condition that Ottilie and Charlotte remain in it as friends. There's a sacrifice, sir!— What have the Romans to show that can compare to this? His domus et placens uxor, and his children—for the hero is a father as well as a husband—are all left behind. But, though we hear of his children, we are only made acquainted with one of them; and a history more full of horror and debauchery never disgraced any of the French novels that the world has united in condemning. As near as I can tell you the details, without making your venerable cheeks purple with shame, I will trace out the fate of the poor child.

The four lovers—the Captain and Charlotte; Edward and Ottilie—are interrupted in their quiet enjoyments, by the visit of a certain Graf or Count, and a certain Baroness. On the arrival of the letter announcing their approach, the Captain enquires who they are? Listen to the answer, and then talk of Goethe's prolific imagination. 'Tis Edward's story over again.

" They had for some time, both of them being married, been passionately in love. A double marriage was not to be broken without trouble; a separation was thought of. The Baroness succeeded in obtaining one, the Count failed. They were therefore forced to appear to live apart, but their connexion still continued; and, though they could not live together in the capital in the winter, they made up for it in summer at the baths, and in pleasure excursions. They were both a little older than Edward and Charlotte, who had never cooled towards them in affection, though they did not quite approve of their proceedings. It was only now that their visit was disagreeable; and if Charlotte had examined into the cause of her dissatisfaction, she would have found that it was on Ottilie's account. The innocent darling child should not so early have such an example set before her.

Not so early?—quære, at what age are such examples thought useful?— But you will find, sir, that the " innocent darling child" was very forward

...her age, and derived as much bene-fit from the pattern as if she had been ten years older. So this then, is a picture of German manners. If it is not, where is Goethe's fame as a painter of life? If it is, what is the meaning of the word Deutscheit? What the devil are you grunting at, Mr North? Do you think I don't know that what are called our own fashionable novels depict a state of manners not much more pure? In the first place, the novels so called are lies and libels—in the next place, where do you find adultery held up even in them as any thing but ruinous to reputation and entailing banishment from society?—In Germany, sir—if we are to believe this book—written, you will remember, not by some footman out of place, or discarded waiting-maid, as our tales of high life generally are, but by the first author of his country, the great arbiter in arts and literature, himself a courtier and mixing in the highest circles—if, I say, we are to believe this book, the marriage tie is of much easier solution than the gordian knot, and acts, even while people condescend to submit to it, as no restraint on the wildest passions, but rather as an argument for falling in love with other men. No loss of station attends detection—ladies and their paramours are received as honoured guests; and our friend Edward, who is the *beau-idéal* of a German hero, thinks it no degradation to enact the part of Sir Pandarus of Troy!

You start, my dear sir—I hope you are not turning sick? The facts, I assure you, are as I have stated. Let me read you a part of the eleventh chapter.

" Edward accompanied the Count to his chamber, and was easily tempted to spend some time with him in conversation. The Count lost himself in the memory of former times, and raved of Charlotte's beauty, which he dwelt on with the eloquence of a connoisseur. ' A handsome foot is among nature's best gifts—years leave it untouched. I observed her to-day in walking. One might even yet kiss her shoe, and renew the barbarous but deep-feeling mode of doing honour among the Sarmatians, who used to drink out of the shoe of any one they loved or honoured.' "

But their observations did not continue limited to the foot. They passed on to old adventures, and recalled the difficulties that had long ago hindered the meetings between Edward and Charlotte. The Count reminded him how he had assisted him in finding out Charlotte's bed-room, when they had all accompanied their royal master on a visit he paid to his uncle; and how they had nearly ruined all by stumbling over some of the body-guard who lay in the ante-chamber. But while they are deep in this highly edifying recollection, the clock strikes twelve. " ' 'Tis midnight,' said the Count, smiling, ' and just the proper time. I must beg a favour of you, my dear Baron,—guide me now as I guided you then; I have promised the Baroness to visit her to-night. We have not spoken together all day, and 'tis so long since we have seen each other! Nothing is more natural than to sigh for a confidential hour or two.'

" ' I will be hospitable enough to show you this favour with much pleasure,' answered Edward; ' only the three women are together in that wing—who knows but what we may find them with each other?'

" ' Never fear,' replied the Count, ' the Baroness expects me. By this time she is in her chamber and alone.'

" ' Then 'tis easily managed,' said Edward, and, taking a light, conducted his friend down some secret steps which led to a long passage. They mounted a winding stair. Edward pointed to a door on the right of the landing-place, and gave the Count the light. At the slightest touch the door opened, and received the Count. Edward was left in the dark."

And a more pitiful scoundrel than this hero of the great Goethe, I'll bet a trifle, never was left in the dark before, whether by putting out the candle or being hanged on a gallows-tree. Don't grasp your crutch so convulsively, my dear sir. The philosopher of Weimar would have had his skull cracked on an infinite number of occasions if he had been within your reach. But there are no Christopher Norths in Germany. If there were, would the scene that succeeds this have been suffered to exist? Yet, shocking as it is, I must give you some idea of it, to support my main assertion, that the author was the coarsest-minded of men, and the nation the most flagitious of nations.

" Another door on the left led into Charlotte's bedroom. He heard voices within, and listened. Charlotte spoke to her waiting-maid. ' Is Ottilie gone to bed yet?'

" ' No,' replied the other, ' she is down-stairs writing.'

" ' Light the night lamp, then,' said Charlotte, ' and retire. 'Tis late—I will put out the candle myself and go to bed.'

" Edward was transported with joy to find that Ottilie was still writing. She is busy on my account, he thought, triumphantly. He thought of going to her, to gaze on her, to see how she would turn round to him. He felt an invincible desire to be near her once more. But, alas! there was no way of getting from where he was to the quarter she lived in. He found himself close to his wife's door. An extraordinary change took place in his soul; he tried to push open the door; he found it bolted, and tapped lightly; Charlotte did not hear.

" She walked quickly to and fro in the large adjoining room. She thought again and again over the unexpected offer of a situation that the Count had made to the Captain. The Captain seemed to stand before her! Now he seemed to fill the house—to enliven the whole scene—and to think that he must go!—how empty would all things be! She said all to herself that is usually said on such occasions. Yes, she anticipated, as people generally do, the miserable consolation that time would mitigate her sorrows. She cursed the time that it needs to mitigate them—she cursed the deathful time when they would be mitigated. She wept at last, and, throwing herself on the sofa, gave way to her grief.

" Edward, on his side, could not tear himself from the door. He knocked again and again. Charlotte heard at last, and stood up alarmed. Her first thought was, it must be the Captain. Her second, that that was impossible. She went into the bedroom and slipt noiselessly to the bolted door.

" ' Is any one there?' she asked.

" A low voice answered, ' 'Tis I.'

" ' Who?' she enquired, for she had not recognised the tone. She fancied she saw the Captain's figure at the door.

" The voice added in a louder key, ' 'Tis I, Edward.'

" She opened the door and her husband stood before her."

I can't go on, sir—one other tumbler, but this *must* be the last—for the horrors related by the pure-souled Goethe, and published for the edification of boys and virgins, must be left in the fitting incognito of a German dress. I must just give you to understand as delicately as I can, that by a certain process of ratiocination known only to the thinking nation, each of these unhappy persons is persuaded that the object of their passion is before them; Charlotte sees nothing but the Captain, and Edward clasps Ottilie in his arms; and the effect of this strong effort of the imagination will be best shown by going on in the story till Charlotte is again a mother. Recollect, my dear sir, that the whole house has, in the mean-time, been turned topsy-turvy; Edward has gone off to the wars, the Captain has taken possession of his new office, and Charlotte and Ottilie—each being conscious of the other's inclinations—have remained alone. The ceremony of the baptism was therefore shorn a little of its proportions, but still it was got up in a style worthy of the rank of the parents. " The party was collected, the old clergyman, supported by the clerk, stept slowly forward, the prayer was uttered, and the child placed in Ottilie's arms. When she stooped down to kiss it, she started no little at sight of its open eyes, for she thought she was looking into her own! the resemblance was so perfectly amazing. Mittler, the godfather, who took the infant next, started equally on perceiving in its features an extraordinary likeness to the Captain! Such a resemblance he had never seen before."

This, sir, is one of the touches of a supernatural sagacity for which Goethe has credit among his countrymen, and will, no doubt, be quoted in medical books as an instance of the power of imagination, as if it were a real event. But, seriously speaking, can you recollect any scene in a French novel or opera so utterly revolting as this? If you can, your acquaintance with unnatural literature is more extensive than mine; but I am ready to bet you a pipe of Bell and Rannie, you never met with any thing to equal the dénouement of this poor infant's story. What do you think of a man trying to gain his reader's sympathy to Ottilie's love-tresses, by painting her kindness to Charlotte's child, and by describing a meeting between Edward and Ottilie, filled with all manner of embracings and declarations, with that child sleeping on the grass beside her. But worse remains behind. Edward has persuaded the Captain to make another effort to obtain Charlotte's consent to a divorce. That highly honourable specimen of the military profession has gone on to the castle, leaving Edward lurking about his own domain, waiting impatiently for his answer. On that particular occasion, Ottilie has carried out the child to the side of a lake, and is engaged in reading. And, as we are told it is " one of those works from which gentle natures find it impossible to tear themselves away," I conclude it was some book of a moral and religious tendency, like this one—probably the *Sorrows of Werther.* Edward, prowling about, sees her; she sees him. He seizes her in his arms—she points to his child;—he gazes at it, and sees the aforesaid likenesses, and makes sundry remarks on the occasion, worthy of his refinement and honourable feelings.

"Hark!" at last cries Edward, springing up, " I heard a gun, which was the signal agreed on with the Captain——'twas nothing but a gamekeeper." So the conversation is renewed. It begins to grow dark. Ottilie springs up, alarmed, but the "hope (of a divorce) shines out of heaven upon their heads. She clasps him in the tenderest manner to her breast. They fancied—they believed that they belonged to each other; they exchanged, for the first time, decided—free kisses, and separated with agonies of grief."

For the first time, the old goat?—why, there is not a page of his book where they are not kissing and hugging —but, perhaps, he has some peculiar meaning in the epithets—decided and free. What is a decided kiss, Mr North?—what is a free kiss?—Perhaps he intends to state, that her conduct was on this occasion decidedly free, and, there can be no doubt, it was a good deal freer than would have been allowable in the vestal virgins. But whether free or not, Edward has retired without casting another look on his own child, and Ottilie hurries off, as she is afraid of alarming Charlotte by being absent at such an hour.

The way round the lake is long—she is a perfect Ellen Douglas in her management of a boat, and steps into a skiff to cross the water—" She grasps the oar and pushes off. She uses all her force and repeats the push; the boat reels a little, and moves from shore. The child is in her left *arm*, the book in her left *hand*, the oar in her right, she reels also, and falls in the boat. The oar leaves her hand on one side; and, in spite of all her efforts, the child and book fall from her hand on the other—and all into the water! She siezes the child's frock; but in her position she finds it impossible to rise. Her unoccupied right hand is insufficient to turn her round and raise her up. At last, she succeeds in drawing the child from the water; but its eyes are closed—it has ceased to breathe!"

Yes, Mr North, this, I assure you, is considered a highly affecting incident, and the death of the innocent little creature is approved of by certain judges, as raising a new obstacle to the course of Edward's true love, and *therefore* exciting the reader's sympathy to a still tenderer point with the love-lorn Ottilie. In this country, I am happy to say, the " Shirra" would have held a precognition, which would not very materially have enhanced the reputation of that delicate-minded young lady.— An English coroner would have levied a deodand on the boat, presenting a bill, at the same time, against Ottilie for manslaughter at least. But in Germany things are much more comfortably managed. The Captain arrives at this very time on his embassy from Edward. This embassy, you recollect, was to persuade Charlotte to consent to a separation from her husband, and thus open the way for a marriage with Ottilie; the Captain at the same time succeeding Edward, and the " respectable old gentleman she had never loved," in the possession of Charlotte. He is shown to a room where he finds a single waxlight burning. In the gloom he perceives Ottilie senseless, or asleep, resting on Charlotte's lap, and the poor little dead child in grave-clothes, on a sofa at her side. It is in this state of affairs that he pleads his cause. And he succeeds!!! Charlotte consents to the separation, on the rather anti-Malthusian plea that she is called upon to

do so to afford Ottilie an opportunity of supplying the place of the child she has been the means of losing, with another of whom Edward may be fond. And with this answer the Captain betakes himself to his principal.

Ottilie, however, has some conscience left, and objects to marry Edward, though her love to him is great as ever. Many pages, and much fine writing are bestowed on the heroism of her behaviour. She has a meeting with Edward at an inn, where she stops, on her way back to the boarding-school, where she had resolved to devote herself to the education of young ladies—on what principles it is needless to enquire. The consequence of this interview, which consisted of vows and protestations on one side, and of absolute silence on the other, is, that she gets into the carriage in which she came, and returns to the castle, Edward following her on horseback; and so, after an absence of more than a year, the *dramatis personæ* are reunited in the scene of their first appearance.

And now comes the death scene; a subject which seems peculiarly agreeable to Goethe, and which he therefore describes with all his heart. Think, Mr North, of the eloquence of Charlotte and the Captain conjoined to the prayers and entreaties of Edward himself, being of no avail against the inflexible resolution of the pure and innocent Ottilie! She persists, in spite of all they can say, in maintaining a profound silence; and in eating in her own room; the mention of which peculiarity suggests dim images of coming evil to the attentive reader. In fact, she starves herself to death, except that the finishing blow is struck by a meddling old gentleman delivering in her presence a very inopportune lecture on the sanctity of the seventh commandment. The whole neighbourhood is struck dumb with grief at the death of the youthful saint, and great care is required to hinder the

common people from worshipping her relics. A dark cloud of sorrow and regret settles heavily over the castle; and at last Edward is found dead. To the very last, sir, the diseased moral sense of Goethe and his admirers sees no impropriety in the whole transaction. The lovers are lamented as if their attachment had been as innocent as that of Paul and Virginia, and the strange eventful history concludes, after describing the burial of Edward, next to his beloved in these words : " So the lovers rest near each other ! Peace hovers over the scene of their repose. Bright-clothed angel forms look down on them from the vault, and oh ! what a blessed moment will that be when they shall awaken together ! "

What do you think now, of what I began with, Mr North ? But, before you decide, remember, my dear sir, that the state of manners described here is the same exactly as we trace in all the works of the same author. His *Wilhelm Meister*—his *Young Werther*—all agree in representing the most appalling laxity of morals as universal in the land. In heaven's name, is the man a libeller of his father-land as well as a corrupter of youth ? But no, sir, the universal popularity of his novels, the herd of imitators he has given rise to, the silence of his own countrymen on the subject of his false representations of life and manners, are too convincing proofs that he holds the mirror up to nature.

On this occasion, I have said nothing of the absurdly exaggerated claims which are made every day on behalf of German originality. What I have limited myself to, has been the character of the people, as seen in their every-day literature.— And, what a view we have had !— Phaugh !— I must have an " eke" just to put the taste out of my mouth. Sugar, if you please ;—hold—hold—and now, Mr North, I will favour you with a song.—Hear, hear, hear !

Art. VI.—*Histoire de la Litterature Allemande, d'apres la cinquième edition de Heinsius.* Par M. M. Henry et Apffel, avec une *Préface de* M. Matter. 8vo. Paris, 1839.

It is not very long since, in our 39th Number, we noticed with approbation a work similar to the present in its subject and treatment; but the topic is so generally interesting, and the taste for German literature, as it exists at this day, is so widely spread and spreading, throughout our own land and through all Europe, that every notice of its progress in other countries becomes more and more acceptable to the readers of our journal.

It can scarcely be surprising that the peculiar system of thought and study pursued in Germany should make but a gradual progress amongst the French, their very antipodes in almost every thing, but position. Yet it was the eager curiosity of our more lively neighbours for all that bears the stamp or even semblance of novelty, that at length produced the first overt act of acquaintance with German literature, and its first general introduction, through Madame de Stael, to the notice of Europe. The beams of the rising sun had however penetrated long before through the misty atmosphere that envelopes our own insulated comprehensions, when the Sorrows of Werter, the Robbers, and the criticisms of Heyne, excited so strong a sensation, and so much stronger a doubt as to the quantity and quality of reason as developed in the German mind. The rays that reached us were, to return to metaphor, deemed promising in themselves and indicative of considerable power in the planet that scattered them so far; but some doubts were entertained, and not altogether unreasonably, that the mists through which they struggled were not entirely those of English mental obscurity; and that a haze of no ordinary intensity dimmed and concealed the far greater portion of the rising orb of glory in its native land.

We are far from considering this suspicion erroneous; and however long and successfully we ourselves have toiled, with an almost German devotion, for the object of rendering German literature popular here, and transplanting to the best of our means the strongest shoots and fairest flowers of that soil, and importing the lavish wealth of its opened mines of learning to adorn and improve our national mind, we yet are tempted at times to think that the general feeling, and certainly on some points, has run of late too violently into this very extreme; that led and seduced by the labours and talents of some of our own most eminent writers and poets, we have given without due reflection into a species of Germano-mania, and transferred the praise due undoubtedly to their erudition and scholarship, into an undiscriminating admiration for every thing that bears the impress of Teutonic peculiarity of any kind.

That such a state of feeling is a serious error, we do not hesitate distinctly to pronounce. However profound or important a course of abstract thought or inquiry may be in itself, it cannot from its very nature be adapted to the general mass of mankind. It is no answer to say that this mass are not the parties for whose immediate benefit it is intended; and that the stream must first flow through the usual narrow channels of more cultivated intellects, before it can be made available for the world at large. A mental system which requires a long, so to say, chemical process of precipitation, sublimation, and combination with foreign properties before it can be turned to general account, must of necessity be generated by certain peculiarities of home growth: as shadowy, subtile, and meditative, it answers admirably for inhaling in the calm repose and contemplative philosophy of German universities and abstract speculations; but brought into contact with the coarser and bolder practicality of every-day life and action in England and the rest of the world, its very subtility marks a degree of rarefaction unfit for common purposes.

The care that analyzes mental properties into hypothetical classifications and contrasts purely speculative and metaphysical, as if spirit were capable of being fully comprehended by human nature; and indeed as if mind were utterly independent of matter, and did not exist except by combination with it; is clearly a labour of excess: the linguist, the man of science who dives into the secrets of nature and the arcana of the past, and is satisfied to live for these alone, must also be satisfied to remain as the miner, the mere pioneer of a more popular and superficial research: and the poet and the popular writer who constantly chronicles every act and idea that visits him in the retirement of his study and the unvarying routine of domestic life and intercourse, is apt, and with justice, to be regarded by the public at large as tedious or trifling and overlaid with puerilities. It is these qualities in excess that deteriorate the literature of Germany. Her writers are not satisfied unless their readers know all they have done and dreamed in the progress of their labours towards any one point: every portion of their course is held to be of equal importance; every turn and gesture of the inner and the outward man equally deserving the reader's most anxious admiration: and thus the secluded sage, the man of the closet, comes forth before the world, and begs in the unsuspecting innocence of his literary vanity, that all shall respect his shuffling gait and his night cap, the slippers and morning-gown he wears in public, because in his study they have been associated with the pen that has wrought so many marvels of intellect.

With these amusing peculiarities and positive drawbacks upon the real value of their elaborate researches, it will scarcely be expected by any but the most enthusiastic admirers of German authorship, that such can escape that strong turn for the ludicrous inherent in the mind of our Gallic neighbours, and not to a certain extent act as a preventive upon the continuous adoption and imitation of German habits of thinking and writing among them. With our own less mercurial and more kindred temperament these habits have largely affected a considerable portion of our writers; and the very faults and excrescences of German taste have been urged as beauties, and expatiated and insisted upon to the utmost limit of our own reason and forbearance.

In thus unequivocally expressing our opinion as to the absolute defects of the German writers, we must distinctly repudiate any the slightest intention of depreciating the real value of a literature that has made such rapid progress in so short a period, and is daily becoming more important to Europe, having already possessed itself in undisputed sovereignty of the highest classic ground. The very faults indeed of German authorship spring, like all others, from the same source as their excellences; namely, the peculiarities of their position, political and individual. The abstraction from practical life that renders them ignorant of how much that each man considers to be his own immediate discovery is, and has long been, thoroughly known to the world; so much so indeed as to be always taken for granted and to require no announcement; and the utter unconsciousness of the ridicule that, in more active states of society, follows the minute chronicler of intermediate shades of thought and infinitesimal puerilities of action or emotion; these practical defects also and at the same time engender, and are fed by, that insatiable hunger for knowledge, that unwearied labour of examining and exhausting every store of information, which amasses every heap of learning into one huge memorial, as mighty perhaps and scientific as a pyramid, but almost equally hopeless, isolate, and obscure. Digestion sinks in the universality of appetite.

This, the great error of German learning, is nourished by the more natural error of foreign ignorance. We wish to cast no slur upon the former, and little upon the latter; and therefore, conversing the sarcasm, would say

Un savant trouve toujours un moins savant qui l'admire,

and to this subject must address a few words.

The German language is in itself difficult, far more so than the French or Southern European tongues; and its terminology is so various, so compound, and consequently so full of epithets conjoined, that it acts upon the mind through the ear somewhat as the Chinese does through the eye, forming at once in each combination a picture to the sense. But between these two modes a great difference exists: that which is actually pictured in lines acts directly, that which is expressed in words indirectly and through the understanding, upon the senses. The second, then is a less simple process than the former. A language which admits these combinations of terms, admits also their production to excess; and in all these the process of the thought that frames them is more strongly displayed to the reader than the result of that process; as in English. The German gives all the parts, the English the undivided whole. And we cannot wonder at the partiality of learners and students for the former course in preference to the latter, for it brings the reader into the workshop of the writer's mind, not merely into his show-rooms, and has precisely the same effect that he who enjoys the landscape along the road feels, and advantageously, over him who merely travels it. But which more directly reaches the end? He whose mind is however slightly, yet incessantly and eternally diverted from the right line, or he who proceeds in this simple sense?

It continually happens too that this very facility of hinting rather than speaking out, of intimating imperfectly rather than being bound to definition, prevents the writer from closely attending to the accuracy of the thought, since he can dispense with the precision of the term. The former, in truth, he has only shadowed out, not determined; and hence, as in the Shemitic writing, there is always, doubtless, a meaning, but there is always also a doubt; and when a first-rate metaphysician or poet has written a word, each of his admirers writes a book to inquire what it means. Owing to the different formation of men's minds every angle from which it is viewed affords a somewhat different combination; it is gold or silver for the tilting knights, and must be settled by the point of the lance; and Goethe himself was puzzled when his commentators proved to him how much he had intended which he never imagined.

This peculiarity of thought and words acts of necessity upon mind and language. The end is lost in the means in both cases: instead of a common tongue each writer has his own secret alphabet; instead of seizing a thought and stamping it into a perfect idea, a solid form of judgment obtained from casting down the previous fusion of fancy, we are presented but with the components: it is the analysis given for the result; the anatomy of the body, not the body itself, produced. And in proportion as the plastic power is imperfectly used the results are likewise imperfect. Like the intellect too the language gains nothing definite ; no new word, but fresh combinations only of the old : but this is less an advantage than a defect : it may remain essentially German, it never can become universal. It may be less profound than it seems, and it certainly becomes more difficult.

Yet it is this very difficulty that has, in our opinion, obtained for the tongue itself and the writers in it so ample a share of admiration. Men do not like to throw away their labour ; they do not even like it to appear thrown away ; and when the scholar of German, as of Sanscrit, feels that he has mastered the tremendous difficulties of its highest range, he is not only capable of an enjoyment denied to the many, but he is apt to overate the new world into which he has entered, and which is the more enticing as it is more subtile and imaginative ; ideality rather than substance. The basis of reason upon which life reposes, the practicality, that tests all things in the material world, are left behind him as he enters this dreamy sphere ; and he takes the Mephistopheles of subtlety at his elbow for a judge, and the Will-o'-the-Wisp for his guide, and dances through the May-day night of the mountains with the rocky Hartz for his green-sward, and every mocking phantasy for his partner in the maze.

Now there is no occasion for all this : it may be very well for a pastime of the sage ; and if our English literary Fausts are determined to do it seriously, let them remember where their prototype finally went, as Marlow and Goethe inform us. There, they may rely upon it, they themselves will follow, so far as this country at least is concerned. England is too practical in all her habits, too constantly kept by her insular position and political system in strait-forward vigilance and bold existence to allow time to any extent for metaphysical niceties. In her constant collision, forcible or friendly with the whole world, all the currents of thought, all the fancies, cravings, desires, all the elements of material life and action are so unceasingly whirled together, combining and conflicting in the crucible of a positive chemistry, that the lighter vapours, the sublimations and sublimities of alchemical expectations float away into air, the caput mortuum is left at the bottom, and the general extract alone retained for practical purposes.

Nearly the same effect, though from widely different causes, obtains in France ; and has prevented, and will probably prevent anything more than a passing mania for German and exotic mystification. It is to this and this alone we refer in our remarks, for it is simply the prevailing tendency to this in German feeling that robs its literature of the due consideration it deserves on many points. The genius of Germany is too vast to be exhibited by the microscope of one portion of its admirers, or puffed by the bellows of another into ballooning it through the clouds : it wants no mists and haze to exaggerate its real dimensions ; and if it means to meet the sympathies of man, it must be, not ideal but positive ; not confined to its own country by narrow peculiarities, but universal as the globe over which it would range.

The truth of our remarks is borne out in great degree, not only by the fate of those eager enthusiasts of German literature in England, whose praises are heard and suffered to sink in the mysticism that envelopes them ; but also among the Germans themselves. Their warm aspirations for political institutions after the fashion of England or France was the first symptom of the taste for the practical ; and when the leaven is once introduced, even if ill-judgingly at first, it gradually corrects and leavens the whole. An adoption of foreign terms, however few, and a disposition to act upon reasonings instead of abstracting them, is rapidly producing a change in the spirit of the Germans ; whose authorship we trust will soon, as its progress seems to announce, hold another empire than the air, and take its place in the field with England and France for all active purposes, as it has long done in speculation.

With this distinct avowal of our opinions, and which if at all novel in print are more especially so in this journal, and yet, so far as we can see, they are fully borne out by, with some few exceptions, the general sense in England ; with this avowal, we repeat, we must couple a reservation in favour of some of the highest names in Germany. The question of classical or scientific literature, we do not touch upon in this paper. Our remarks in truth refer less at the moment to the range of intellect than to the medium of communication ; bearing in mind however the connection between the two, and which is so close that the one materially affects the other. Clearness and simplicity of thought will always induce with the least practice a corresponding clearness and simplicity of diction ; and according to the imperfections of the latter we can determine with sufficient accuracy whether the mind that puts it forth is turgid or verbose, confused, multifarious, and indefinite ; inert from indigestion of over-crowded reading, or thinking, or smoking ; elaborately heavy or elaborately light, pompous, dictatory, or finical : the merely superficial seems unknown in Germany ; but this we ourselves can amply supply. The froth and scum of English literature is easily thrown aside, but we cannot so willingly, or so lightly, dispense with the mass of information buried in German scholarship. But the last should bear in mind that all complication is counteractive, and all simplicity energetic in its kind : the five hundred mirrors of the

French mechanical experiment could not set fire to a boat at one tenth the distance effected by the single machine of Archimedes.

M. Matter remarks the fact that the southern languages of Europe came into notice long before those of the north. This circumstance was fortunate and was also necessary, as the result, if so alone, of geographical position. Wherever they spread, the northern nations were in earlier ages the predominating race; and thus they preserved in so great a degree not only their original customs and feelings, but were also enabled to engraft, upon otherwise unvitiated modes of thought, in themselves simple, original, and forcible, the dark, wild, and gloomy grandeur of fearful superstitions, rugged manners, and solitary and undivided thought; a fount of masculine and perennial freshness that at a late period invigorated and supplied with novel energies the exhausted and stagnating currents of literatures more feeble but more refined.

In France this error of weakness has been long apparent, and universally felt of late years, if not confessed, by the nation itself. To England, that had so often borrowed from her, France applied in her turn, and admitted with secret pleasure and obvious reluctance the gleam of "barbarian genius" that in Shakspere and his descendants was enlightening the wakening intellect of the nation. That the first dislike was converted at length into an absolute mania, was no more than could be expected in the nature of things, and the nature more especially of French constitutions. But every passion exhausts itself; every novelty tires at length; and now the current has set in the direction of Germany; though not yet with the impetus characteristic of Gallic emotions. It is however a movement not of whim but necessity; an absolute want of oxygen in the exhaustion of the literary atmosphere of both countries; M. Matter well observes

" Yet the progress we ourselves have made has probably approximated us to the north as much as this has approximated towards us. In truth if our literary desires turn now to England and Germany, it is not a mere caprice of taste but a movement of intelligence. In these two countries moral and political studies have assumed so glorious a course, and we ourselves are in a social condition so analogous to that of our neighbours, and so different from the past, that our literary sympathies are established by the force of circumstances, the community of wishes, the fraternity of all thought.

" With England we have been for more than a century united by the noblest labours of the human mind, those of legislation, philosophy, and general politics."

After remarking that for a long time these subjects were merely matters of speculation in France and are now become practical, and that her institutions and views of the social future are abso-lutely at present those of England, M. Matter observes that the difference now consists in forms and manners, and that these will be permanent, though the principles are the same.

With regard to the German, he notices and with justice that it does not possess for his countrymen the same claims to attention, and is not for them in the same degree an object of study, though it offers for many classes of society a powerful interest. It presents to all advantages and inducements which the English has lost by having become familiar in France.

" The German is not only the language of erudition and metaphysics, it is particularly the language of the moral sciences, the study of which is so important for us in the social state wherein we are placed by so many revolutions of manners and ideas. It is in fine the language of a million of Frenchmen.

" The German has also points connected with higher considerations. It is a language of astonishing variety. The English is bounded; the French can in future but exhaust itself. The German since it has become classical, is in its third phase, and seems susceptible of still farther transformations.

" Thus does the German daily gain ground amongst us."

And the writer conceives that it is destined to play a great part in the new epoch into which the French tongue is about to enter; that is, its struggle with the northern idioms, after having so gloriously sustained a contest with the languages of the south, and after profiting so well by the education bestowed on it by the ancient tongues.

From the language to its literature the transition is easy; and in regard to the German, a phrase of very common acceptation, namely, that its literature is but very modern, and of to-day, seems to require some explanation. It is not in truth very clear what is the received sense of this saying, at least if we are to view it in a different light from that of the literature of any other nation of Europe. All differ essentially in their modern from their ancient phases; and yet Herder, if we remember rightly, seems to countenance the general opinion just alluded to, though only in part, when he speaks of the youth of the German muse in her race with that of Britain.

The writers of the volume before us do not appear to uphold the opinion in question in their general estimate; for they affirm of the German,

" This literature is, without question, one of those deserving the most to be studied. It is ancient, it is original, it is rich, and little known out of Germany. Its especial distinction is great vigour of conception, a high degree of ideality, a sort of worship of nature imposed by profound sentiments of religion. Like the country which produces it, it forms a real transition between the literature of the east, of which it possesses all the gravity and mysticism, and the literature of Scandinavia, more pompous, more dry, and more severe."

According to the same authorities, its poetry, like its prose, has fused several kinds into one to form a novel style, commonly termed the romantic. This we are strongly tempted to question though it is the general opinion; for did the romantic originate in Germany? Are not the ballads of the South a sufficient answer, and were not they the progeny of the proper East, and marked more distinctly with their present characteristics than imbued with the tints of the North? Germany has a rightful claim undoubtedly to her own peculiar romance, and this we would especially reserve: but for the epithet itself it is perhaps too general and undiscriminating to be referred so freely as by our authors to that one sole source. "It is thus," they tell us, "that in appreciating this literature we see combined at one time and confounded in mutual embarrassment, the devout and gallant spirit of the Provençal troubadours, the dreamy and mystical imagination of the Oriental poets with its pomp and dazzling splendour, and the sombre genius of the North, that lives in tempests and presides at those gigantic battles where the bravest of warriors fight hand to hand with the gods themselves." Our readers are however aware that this form of romance is to be found, though in more polished shape, in the ancient pages of Hesiod and Homer, and the more modern tales of Ariosto. Whence then came all these? From the earliest East undoubtedly; and they are only modified, not created, by Scandinavian or Teutonic genius; more severe, more stern, more simple, and more shadowy in the latter; a different species, though the genus is the same: the drapery of classic grace or Oriental effeminacy was unknown or despised, and the genius of the north robed his form but in the clouds of his own domain, or presented it, ample and bare, in the sole might of its colossal dimensions.

The History of German literature is divided by our Author into seven periods.

1st. The Gothic, from the earliest times when barbarism dispersed the remains of Roman civilization, down to the reign of Charlemagne (768).

2d. The Frank, or period before the Hohenstaufen, 768—1137, when the light thrown by Charlemagne sank in the obscurity of his successors.

3d. The Suabian; from the rise of the Hohenstaufen race to the origin of the German Universities, 1137—1148; the time of the Crusades, Troubadours, and Minnesangers.

4th. The Rhenane, lasting till the Reformation, 1348—1534; when science raised her head above literature; when the tourney and chivalrous combats disappeared, and Cologne, Erfurt, Leipsic, Rostock, Basle, Treves, Mayence, Wittenberg, &c. successively rose in imitation of Italian institutions; when Guttenberg invented printing at Strasburg; when knowledge became popular; and when, finally, Luther appeared on the scene.

The 5th, or Saxon period, embraces the school of Luther to that of Spitz, 1534—1625; the most important portion of the 16th century—the epoch of regeneration, of religious wars, of conquests in America and Asia. Literature flourished by the religious controversies: poets and men of genius cultivated science and the belles lettres, or refined the Minnesanger lays into the strains of the Master Singers, amongst whom was the celebrated Hans Sachs. Luther, reforming religion reformed also the language; by fusing, we should say, like Homer under a somewhat similar change, the two principal dialects in use into the type of the modern German language.

The 6th period, Silesian and Swiss, comes down to Klopstock, including the interval from 1625 to 1750. Spitz, the founder of the Silesian school of classicists, then opened the way for foreign literature. France inundated the soil with new ideas and fashions of thinking and writing, literary societies were formed every where to assist or oppose the innovations, and from this conflict of principles sprung the new work of German classical literature.

The 7th period reaches from Klopstock down to our own days; i. e. 1750—1838; when, as our author somewhat fancifully remarks, "the most illustrious pleiad that ever shone on ancient Germany appeared in Klopstock, Schiller, Göethe, Engel, Burger, Wieland, and so many others." These last, unnamed, being too many for the constellation in question, form, we presume, the Milky-way; and it must be owned that some of them have supplied the world with that nutritive diet in rather larger quantities than accords with the matured state of European developement; and, we speak it reverently, aided by one at least of the labours of Göethe himself, have raised a sort of bread and butter school, greatly relished in our infancy throughout the nurseries of Europe.

We turn from the Volume before us to notice with our warmest commendations, a work on the actual state of Germany by an English Scholar of deserved reputation. To those who seek to know more of that remarkable, and rising, but half undeveloped land than can be learned in a hurried tour, or inferred from the passing notices of newspapers, we would earnestly recommend

21. continued

this book,* where may be found the real position of Germany, its resources, political and industrial relations, its progress in the sciences and arts, and in literature, with all the details that are necessary for a thorough comprehension of the subject, and of the great political and moral question that is to be solved perhaps in our own days, by the prodigious advances of the German every way. To the work itself generally we can confidently refer our readers, but our more immediate business is with the literary portion of it; and the opinions in this department are so fair and so candid, that they give, better than any thing we have seen, an idea of German literature as it really is.

We select amply from this part of the work.

" The early literature of Germany did not represent the national mind, nor did it tend much to enlighten nor to move it. It principally consists in treatises, more or less elaborate, on matters of theology, jurisprudence, natural history, physics, and medicine, with no small sprinkling of alchemy, astrology, and metaphysics. These were almost all written in Latin, which appears to have been almost a second tongue, used familiarly in conversation, and still more familiarly in composition.

" The modern literature of Germany may be said to commence with Gottsched, who was born in the year 1700, and who died in 1766. He was educated at Königsberg, where he took the degree of Master of Philosophy in 1723. He was shortly afterwards obliged to quit Prussia, where his stature exposed him to the risk of being forced to enter the ranks of the king of Prussia's giant-grenadiers. He took refuge at Leipsic, and was elected professor at the university there, in the year 1730. Gottsched claimed the character of an universal genius, which he was far from being able to support. He attempted to play at once the philosopher, the grammarian, the critic, and the poet. But he survived his own fame, and is now consigned to a degree of oblivion which he certainly does not deserve.

" He did not occupy himself with style and form exclusively; he may be said to have founded the periodical literature; he encouraged numerous young authors, and placed the learned world on a better footing with the booksellers. With the assistance of a number of scholars, whom he had gradually gathered round him, he published a translation of Bayle, whose work, from its free and novel cast, produced a great sensation in Germany. Though a grave professor, he did not disdain to interfere with the theatre, and his criticism succeeded in driving away the Merry-Andrew (Hanswurst) from the stage. A Leipsic lady assisted his reforming career by the introduction of feeble translations from the French. The influence of the pseudo-classic rules of France on the German drama lasted till the criticism of Lessing demolished it at a blow, and rushed

* Germany; the Spirit of her History, Literature, Social Condition, and National Economy; illustrated by reference to her Physical, Moral, and Political Statistics, and by comparison with other Countries. By Bissett Hawkins, M.D. Oxon, F.R.S., London, 1838.

unfortunately to an opposite extreme. The period of Gottsched's glory was between the twentieth and fortieth years of the last century. He legislated for the literary world with a dictatorial air; but into the nature of man, where alone the laws of criticism are seated, he never deigned to cast a glance. Aristotle he misunderstood, and his imitation of the French was clumsy and imperfect. Göethe has left us a highly amusing account of the first visit which he paid to Gottsched. By mistake he was ushered into the dressing-room of the Professor, who, as he entered, clapped on his wig with great dispatch, then boxed his blundering valet's ear with one hand, and received his guest with the other. Gottsched's system of criticism is particularly open to the charge of superficiality and weakness.

" Hagedorn and Haller were eight years younger than Gottsched; they were both born in 1708. In classing, then, these poets together, we only refer to some similar points in the character and tendency of their works. They commenced an indirect opposition to Gottsched, and as they overthrew him, without expressly aiming at him, they rendered his overthrow the more complete. The criticism of the Leipsic Professor was entirely negative. He had prescribed only sobriety of expression, and such poetical enthusiasm as could help itself just as well with prose as verse. Haller introduced the freedom of English literature into Germany. He, at first, took Pope for his model; but if he excels him in depth and solidity, he is his inferior in point of style. Haller deserted poetry for physiology at thirty, and would fain apologize afterwards, for having devoted so much time to the Muses. It is a common prejudice, that a man cannot distinguish himself eminently in two departments. The philosophic reputation of Haller has injured his fame as a poet. To his scientific eminence, he owed his professorship at the university of Gottingen. Here he was an active contributor to *Der Gelehrte Anzeiger*, at that time the most famous periodical in Germany. In estimating the comparative worth of Haller's works, we must never forget that he was without German models. He had the classics certainly, but their sphere is too remote for the imitation of a genial poet, who feels the necessity of giving expression to life as he breathes and feels it. Haller wrote odes, but in imitation of the French—of Baptiste Rousseau, for instance. These compositions instead of being poetical, are a collection of rhetorical rhymes. The criticism of our poet-philosopher is not of much value; for to criticise a literature which is without models is to thrash empty straw.

" Notwithstanding the exertions of the Swiss school, Leipsic continued even after the expiration of Gottsched's popularity, to be the metropolis of literary Germany. In the middle of the last century, it was the residence of Gellert and Klopstock, of Kramer, Rabener, and several others, whom we shall not have space to dilate upon. But somewhat earlier than these, flourished J. E. Schlegel, who was born in 1718, and who died in Denmark, in 1749. He was the first who gave a character to the German theatre, and is, therefore, in his relation to German dramatic literature, especially worthy of notice. He commenced his career by translating some tragedies of Sophocles and Euripides into German

154

rhyme. Though he abandoned the French school of tragedy, he was not quite free from its influence. The favourite plays of the æra we are now considering, were of the kind technically called characteristic, in which a character made up of extremes, whose vices might be either moral or mental, was put to all sorts of trials, through five tedious acts. Schlegel brought on the Copenhagen stage, "The Dumb Beauty," a rhymed comedy in one act, which is admirable of its kind. From this author, the influence of French taste on the German drama dates its decline; all subsequent attempts to modify French plays for that stage have been decided failures. If these productions are of any worth, it lies in their consistency and unity, which are destroyed as soon as they are altered."—pp. 78—85.

The fame of Shakspere renders the following interesting.

" For some time after the period of which we are now treating, Shak-speare seems to have been unknown in Germany. Bodmer quotes him under the name of Sasper, and a bibliopolist of those days tells us that he had heard a great deal about him, but that he had been unable to obtain any of his works."—p. 86.

We need only select a few passages in passing for our readers.

" Gellert is one of those authors, who, by a prudent management of very little talent, earn considerable fame. The public has confounded the man with the poet; and his literary insignificance was forgotten by those who admired the goodness of his heart. Fame, however, seems now determined to vindicate its impartiality, and is consigning poor Gellert to undeserved neglect. His comedies are the weakest of his works; one finishes perusing them, really without knowing what all the five acts have been about. His tales and fables are much too similar; he seems to have confounded the species. The 'Letters' of Gellert were received with great applause, and have survived, in general estimation, many of his works. But it is impossible that a book, the interest of which is but local and temporary, should take its stand amongst the classics of a nation.

" Klopstock came to Leipsic in the year 1746, when he had already commenced his great poem, ' The Messiah,' and was full of plans for its completion. It would be useless to deny, that in some parts of it he has imitated Milton, but on the whole he pursued an original path.

" Klopstock had no ability in rhyming; his muse was neither docile nor pliant. On this score, he was at first considerably embarrassed, being far from decided as to what measure he should choose for his verse. He intended, at first, to write in rhymeless Alexandrines—the worst form he could possibly have chosen. Fortunately, he hit upon the hex-ameter, in which his success was signal and complete. The first cantos of the Messiah were published, 1748, in a periodical which issued from the Leipsic press. The effect which it produced upon the public can-not be measured, even by the greatest possible sensation which a work can now create.

" In speaking of the Wieland of this period, we must not confound him with the Wieland who dazzled Germany in the year 1763. They are one person, it is true; but the one person underwent a complete metamorphosis. At this period, he espoused the cause of Plato against that of Epicurus, and wrote a poem to refute the "De rerum Natura," of Lucretius. Besides this, he composed Scriptural epics, in unwieldly verse; as, for instance, *Der geprufte Abraham*. Sulzer was the scholar of Bodmer in poetry, and of Leibnitz in philosophy. Or, rather, the creed which he professed, and which was very popular just at that period, was an amalgamation of all possible systems.

" Kleist's ' Spring,' is an imitation of the ' Seasons ' of Thomson, which is composed of a series of pictures drawn with truth and feeling, but in no definite form, and with no general spirit pervading the whole. He has all the faults, and, it cannot be denied, all the beauties of his model; but poetry is not entirely a descriptive art. The works of Kleist were disfigured by the corrections of Ramler; and it is only lately that they have been published from the original manuscripts. Ramler has the credit of having tamed whatever was original and energetic in the poetry of his period down to his own standard of correct mediocrity. In his old age he versified the Idylls of Gesner, which had never pos-sessed great merit, but which he deprived of all they had. Gesner, after having been educated in the principles of the Swiss school, came to Berlin about the year 1750, to learn the trade of a bookseller. Dis-gusted, however, with this occupation, he took to painting, for which nature seems to have intended him. He had received no instruction in the art, and he painted, at first, a number of landscapes with common oil, so that they would not dry. It was his distress on this account, which led him to seek and ask the advice of the Professor of Painting. The talent of Gesner was now soon recognised, and his landscapes have always been very justly praised. Unfortunately, we cannot say as much for his literary publications. His Idylls are landscapes, as far as he could make them such with pen, ink and paper. His characters are like those of Ossian,—speaking spirits and shadows, drawn on a coloured horizon, and sweeping along luxuriant ground."—pp. 86—90.

We cannot we confess discover the similarity or aptitude of the last illustration.

" Herder was a critic, and in the best sense of the word,—one who was fonder of dwelling upon beauties, than of searching out defects. He was of a pliable, plastic susceptible nature; at last, perhaps, he verged towards the undecided and indefinite; and even in his best years, we too often miss in him the strength and acuteness of a master-mind. He first gave to German literature that cosmopolitical tendency, which has in-creased since his time to such a degree, as to have become its peculiar boast. Herder was a poet, but not a philosopher;—rather a literary than a learned man. He had the faculty of happily divining where he could not see very clearly. Though acquainted with many languages, he had not a thorough knowledge of one. His researches on the subject of popular and legendary poetry seem to have led him to the conclusion, that the Muses can only be successfully cultivated by their rudest votaries. But this is a grand mistake; Art is natural to man, who cannot, even in his wildest state, be lost to a love of it; and why should poetry be deprived of its aid ? We do not disgrace the heavenly guest by clothing her in a costly dress ; we rather heighten the variety of her beauties, and of our own enjoyment."—p. 103.

We take some portions of the remarks on Goethe.

" In his first works, Goethe was the advocate of that which he felt to be Nature, against that which he thought to be Art. His ' Götz von Berlichingen' was written in defiance of all the old dramatic laws ; and in ' Werter' he would seem to to have aimed at the abolition of the conventional and artificial, and at the recognition of what was called the voice of nature in their stead.

" A year after Götz, appeared ' The Sorrows of Werter,' which produced an incalculable effect upon the public, by whom it was tumultuously received. This book is a singular mixture of truth and fiction ; to a certain extent the author identified himself with his hero, and then superadded the misfortunes of a young man named Jerusalem, whose suicide, the consequence of an unfortunate passion, made at that time considerable sensation. As far as the sentiments and feelings of Werter are concerned, we may take the identification to be complete ; though how far the author was conscious of it at the time of writing is uncertain.

" Of the attacks which this work met with at the hands of the critics, Goethe took no notice ; but he subsequently added one to their number, in his ' Triumph of Sentimentality.' With this latter word, ' Werter ' was the first to make us acquainted ; great as is the part which it has played in our time, we may search for it in vain before the days of Göethe. The feeling, though now naturalised in Germany, is of foreign origin. The *Nouvelle Heloise* of Rousseau first perfectly incorporated it, and is composed of little else ; it is more artificial, but less morally objectionable than ' Werter.' In England, Sterne had touched the same chord, but with a steadier hand and healthier result. The work, however, which mainly contributed to establish the fashionable feeling in Germany, was the ' Ossian' of Macpherson, in which the morbid refinement of the moderns is pictured to have existed at an age, and amongst a people, where no refinement whatever was known.

" ' Stella' he entitled a tragedy for lovers, but a good tragedy cannot be usurped by any class ; it addresses itself to mankind at large. The hero is a worthless character, who is subject to every feeling, and faithful to none. Discontented with ordinary felicity, he sets out in search of something more than happiness. After deserting his wife and daughter, and uniting himself to the innocent and lovely heroine, without any diminution of his passion for the latter, remorse seizes him on account of his treatment of the former, and he hits upon the convenient idea of arranging the matter so as to be able to live with both, in a way of his own, somewhat repugnant to conjugal institutions. In these plays, Goethe allows all emotions and feelings to have their course, without disturbing them by even the mention of morality ; but such a system undermines all strength of mind, all dignity of character, and instead of having a right to our sympathy, it demands our contempt.

" Shortly after the publication of these dramas, a metamorphosis began to take place in the literary character of Goethe ; he recognised his errors, and was one of the few men of his time who rescued himself from the influence of his works ; he withdrew to study and self-examination, and all that was heard of him for some years, was an indefinite report of his being engaged in the composition of ' Faust.' In 1788, he published ' Egmont,' the most theatrical of his tragedies, in which he is no longer true to his theory of the natural, for the language, instead of being the prose of common life, rises often to the poetical.

" At this period Goethe made a deep study of the Greek tragedy, and recognised the poetical foundation on which Shakspeare's world is built ; the result of this is to be traced in his ' Iphigenia in Tauris ;' and ' Egmont ' is a sufficient proof of the progress he had made in the comprehension of the English dramatist. The idea of making Tasso the hero of a play, occurred to Goethe during a journey through Italy. His drama of this name has a certain incidental interest, inasmuch as it doubtless, to a certain extent, describes his own situation. The love of a poet for a princess, and the embarrassing circumstances with which it is accompanied, were subjects with which he was not unacquainted. The elegance and correctness of diction in this poem, cannot be surpassed ; but it had faults which no one had anticipated in Goethe : it was too cold, too artificial. He had not only undergone a change, but he had passed to the opposite of his former self.

" In 1794, Goethe published his ' Wilhelm Meister,' which was received by the public with indifference ; the literary world, however, prepared its ultimate success by enthusiastic laudation. The style of this work is admirable ; the clearness and depth of thought it displays, are alike remarkable, but it has the one great fault of its great author— it is an imperfect whole. It does not solve the problem which forms its foundation ; it is but an introduction, a beginning without an end.

" During the early part of his career, Goethe had paid but little attention to versification, though some of his most durable fame rests on the versified productions of his youth—his ballads and songs, which for melody and depth of feeling, are truly singular. He now, to exercise himself in the composition of hexameters, composed an excellent version of Reynard the Fox, in that form, of which he shortly afterwards showed himself a master, in his ' Hermann and Dorothea.' This work regained for him, in a great measure, the favour of the public ; its genuine warmth of feeling, and poetic truth, were universally applauded.

" The tragedy of ' Faust,' was one of Goethe's earliest and latest labours ; the first part was published in 1790, and it was not finished till 1831. This is one of the most genial works of the greatest German poet, but it is not a philosophic whole. It displays dramatic talent, but its different scenes, the force and beauty of some of which are perhaps unequalled, were nevertheless not composed with any determinate view of their ultimate position. The idea of finding a philosophic system in this poem is ludicrous, and the volumes which have been published with that intention are only valuable as curiosities.

" Goethe did not shine in a critical capacity ; he prescribed to all artists a strict imitation of the ancients; but this is at once a narrow-minded and discouraging doctrine, for every age, unless it be worthless, must have a character of its own.

" Goethe has almost invariably been described in the language of unqualified panegyric, and his character as a man is little known to foreigners. Menzel, in his ' Deutsche Literatur,' has done some service in probing thoroughly the pretensions of Goethe; perhaps he has been somewhat rough in his manipulation. Genius is a gift of nature, but the use which we make of it is our own, and for this we may justly be brought to judgment. Goethe possessed more *influence* than any writer ever enjoyed; idolised by his countrymen, caressed in palaces, and sung in the cottage, he might have done something more than amuse. No one was ever improved by his works, none ever became less sensual, less worldly, less intriguing, less profane. Although he has touched every string of literature, nowhere does he rouse to patriotism, to religious reverence, to the domestic duties; one almost confounds the notion of right and wrong in reading his works, all seems blended and confused—amusement and the fine arts, theatres and critics, the passions and the cleverest modes of gratifying them, appear the great object of life. Let one short trait suffice: when Napoleon entered Berlin in triumph, Müller wrote a Discourse in French (De la Gloire de Frederic), in which he compared the Conqueror to the old Prussian hero; Goethe translated it into German; and at another time, wrote an Epithalamium for this evil genius of his country."—pp. 104—109.

Of Schiller we learn with much fairness,

" Nothing could possibly be more galling to a mind like his than the arbitrary regulations of the military institution at Stuttgard, in which he was educated. Here he wrote his Titanic poem, 'The Robbers,' which indicates sufficiently the wild force of his character, and the despotism of the circumstances which had almost driven him to madness. This work is worse than ' Werter,' because more unnatural: with loud pretensions to originality, it bears prominent marks of imitation.

" Francis Moor is a prosaic Richard III., exciting equal hatred, but demanding no admiration. The fame which this play obtained for him, freed Schiller from the shackles of his situation, and he now was appointed to a post in connexion with the theatre, at Manheim, where he published his ' Fiesco' and his ' Cabal and Love.' Perhaps the peculiar feature of the former is its political bearing; which forms its chief claim to originality. ' Cabal and Love' abounds in convulsive demonstrations of passion. To his first career of enthusiasm succeeded, with Schiller as well as with Goethe, a period of self-examination and study. His next production was ' Don Carlos,' of which the outline is good, the plot powerful, and the execution a manifest improvement on his former works. Its versification, however, is indifferent throughout: the style keeps a middle course between his former extravagance and the lofty rhetoric of the French; the political philosophy which pervades it, is as foreign to the century which it represents, as it would be to the most distant we can imagine. It professes to be an historical picture, but it is, in fact, a work of invention; and the rude features of the poet's

former muse, break everywhere through the more civilized mask he had now attempted to assume. A year after the appearance of ' Don Carlos,' Schiller published his fragment on the history of the insurrection in the Netherlands; a subject which he had not studied very profoundly, and which he did not know how properly to treat. The duty of the true historian is, if the expression may be used, to reflect events, and not to reflect upon them. Our author now essayed the 'History of the Thirty Years' War,' and showed that he had made considerable improvement as an historical writer; indeed, his whole life was a series of improvements.

" In 1798, appeared ' Wallenstein,' a play in three parts, of which the first is not connected with the others, of which the second has no end, and the third no beginning. About this time, Schiller avowed himself a disciple of Kant, whose terminology imposed on the public to such an extent, that it was thought he had found a key to all the difficulties in the arts and sciences. Our author's philosophical disquisitions were more than ordinarily successful, because he was, at any rate, either intelligible or elegantly obscure; but he was too abstract and refined to produce any more than a temporary impression. The negative axioms of Kant's philosophy were true, though the positive were shadowy and unsatisfactory; indeed, his whole system was sceptical, though his followers long persisted in boasting of its constructive powers.

" After the publication of ' Wallenstein,' which was enthusiastically received both by the reading and the theatrical public, Schiller devoted himself more exclusively to the drama; and he now struck into a path which was to be intermediate between the classic and the romantic, though, in fact, it was only situated between both without being allied to either. Of his subsequent plays, ' Mary Stuart' is one of the best; its representation is very effective, though partly at the expense of historical truth. In his ' Maid of Orleans,' considering the romantic view which he took of the character of his heroine, the colouring of the execution was too faint; for Schiller, though of a bold and uncompromising nature, was timid and misgiving as an artist.

" The ' Bride of Messina,' and its preface, may be looked upon as a confession which Schiller was at the trouble of making of his own imperfections; and from the latter, which betrays a complete confusion in his ideas respecting the theory of the drama, we may gather that he understood the classic principle which he sought to imitate, no better than the romantic which he wished to avoid. It is impossible to imagine a costume for this play. The chorus differs from that of the Greeks, in being divided into two interested parties, who do every thing but come to blows for their leaders. But the Greek chorus is essentially an impartial whole; and represents the ideal, contemplative spectator of the drama.

" Even the last and best play of Schiller, ' William Tell,' is not free from a trace of his love of tragic antithesis; the murder of the emperor Albert is something quite foreign to the liberation of Switzerland; and it is evident that the murderer is merely introduced for the purpose of being contrasted with Tell. The local truth of this drama is extraordinary, particularly when we recollect that Schiller had never been in

Switzerland : he was indebted for it, in a great measure, doubtless, to the admirable history of John von Müller.

"The lyrical poetry of Schiller has been eminently successful, both at home and abroad; and his ballads have been held up as perfect models. But in truth, this is his weakest side, and his ballads are among the worst which we possess. All his works are more or less imperfect, but these are glaringly faulty; for everywhere, even in the simple legends of old which they profess to revivify, we are troubled with his philosophic reflections and the discord of a modern nature. Had he lived longer, it is uncertain how far he might have been successful in correcting all his faults; some of them appear too deeply rooted to have been ever thoroughly eradicated. But let us conclude justly, by remembering to praise the candour which rendered him alive to his defects, and the genuine modesty which always restrained him from great pretensions."—pp. 111—114.

We cannot conclude our notice of this part of the subject, and of men so celebrated as the writers before us without entering our protest against the excessive exaggeration of praise that has followed the name of Goethe wherever it has been pronounced. If encomium from all quarters is a proof of excellence it must be a free and unbiassed encomium; but we deny that such has been the case in this instance. Of the plaudits of Germany there can be no question; and as a German writer we are happy to allow Goethe all the praise he can obtain at home. As a delineator of nature, manners, sentiments, opinions; as the first great reformer of the rugged style of the older poetry; as a man of vast acquirements in any or all departments of knowledge, even as a man of very high genius we concede him every possible admiration. But we must be distinctly understood to refer to these, and any other points on which he really merits our sympathies, with a positive reservation. He is national, not universal; exquisitely elaborate rather than overflowing, the trace of study appears in every step : a giant perhaps, but in national peculiarities; a genius certainly, but of artificial life; an artist of nature, not her worshipper, that must make and fashion her image before he could adore it.

We pass over the dull, unsympathizing obscenities that disgrace some of his works, written it would seem, for their especial display : we pass over, and with sorrow and shame, the utter inability, incapacity to comprehend one single trait of delicacy, decency, and morality, that is obvious to every eye but his own. In manners and morals every nation has in its writers occasionally violated the proprieties : but all these, all worth noticing at least, were conscious of the wrong : when they lead astray their reader it is by turning him out of his direct course, into some nook or corner, and raising the veil that covers for him and them the form of corruption : the light they throw is artificial, and

passes through a medium coloured by the passions, in order that he may not by the presence of purity be reminded of grossest impurity, by unsophisticated calmness of feelings of their most atrocious perversions : the pulse of shame is not extinct in their breasts, that they can rely upon the reader's callousness as confidently as on their own. We would ask, Is this so with Goethe? Is not the very basis of some of his works the very theme most avoided by other writers? Does he ever hesitate to picture depravity? Has he ever shown that in painting it he was aware that the picture could not be hung up in open day, nor exposed to the public eye? What maid, what wife, what woman of all the sex could be so lost to even conventional forms as to hear the outline even of these elaborated infamies? What man, deserving the name, does not feel his judgment insulted and his pride of honour debased by being asked to dwell upon these loathsome carcases of putrifying abomination, these nauseous public gloatings and laboured delineations of vice, so fondly dwelt upon by this spiritual dotard of sensuality.

We must avow with sincere satisfaction that the first blow has been struck at this system by a periodical of the highest rank in England. The notice there given of the " Elective Affinities " may be fairly extended, and we have the less occasion to pollute our pages with reference to them. But if we do not envy the intellectual construction of those who can wade through the degrading mixture of filth and sluggishness, insipidity and grossness that in such works debases the name of one born, we could have hoped, for better things; and if we are to excuse them, as alone we can, by libelling his whole nation in supposing they could possibly afford him prototypes for such displays, what are we to think of those who, in evil hour for their own name, have sought to pander to England and Europe by praising and translating those works?

And what is the atonement for these? In what does Goethe so far excel the world as to claim from them its worship for him who could " call evil good and good evil?" If the obliquity of his moral sense was such as to turn early puling into matured abomination; if seduction through the medium of the senses was his desire in youth, could the sentimental sage find a happier parallel in warping feelings into crime than by converting pathos into puerility? his love of another's wife shared with love of bread-and-butter, while the tragic muse weeps over an out-of-elbows' coat! glories shared with our own Liston in his personation of Werther.

But we are reminded of FAUST.

In what does the marvel of this consist? In what is Goethe's claim borne out to the title of the German Shakspere? We utterly deny the epithet's correctness in the usual sense, unless the term German is to be understood as a modification. Shakspere ruled the heart and swayed the sympathies of mankind. His thoughts lay open the intellectual world of man; his aspirations ennoble the mind. The most that Goethe does is to surprise: where he talks of feeling, it is to drone or to sneer; his powers are fantastical, his imagination half cold. The scenes of nature, actual or imaginative, the pulse of the heart, the yearnings of emotion, all are merely elaborately beautiful; all are perverted from simplicity to artificial life.

We are far from denying a high degree of merit to this poem; but we contend it is not so pre-eminent as it has been made to appear by injudicious praise on the one hand and weak consenting credulity on the other. We are well aware of the praise of real judges as bestowed on this performance, and of none more than Mr. Hayward, a scholar, a critic, a man of unquestioned taste and genius. But though our Journal has been warm in commendation of the Faust, we must admit that there are material drawbacks; to the eulogiums we ourselves would bestow much has been added by others, and much too that requires serious modification. We have already stated that artificiality is Goethe's forte; and however repugnant we must feel to strip, even if able, one leaf of laurel from the Mighty Dead, and such in truth he is, our task, since we have undertaken it, must be done, so far as our space will allow in the present paper.

We shall take, too, our own version, since the close and spirited translation of Blackie is not before us, and that of Tracey is at times, though not often, an improvement, may we say it, on particular passages. As to Anster's, so constantly praised, it is one half at least the translator's own; an absolute paraphrase, and a very excellent one in general, but still a paraphrase of the original; some of its passages running to nearly, and sometimes more than to, double the length of the German. Thus substituting beauty for conciseness.

Nothing can well be more beautiful than the original dedication. The man of genius and the artist are both at the summit of their craft in this.

DEDICATION.

" Again ye swarm around me, shadowy train !
　　Once wont in youth this sorrowing gaze to meet;
And will ye now, for my behest, remain ?
　　Still shall my heart's forgotten pulses beat?
Ye throng me round—well, rule me once again,
　　Since thus thro' mist and gloom my soul ye greet:
While drinks my breast again, with youthful bound,
The magic breath your presence breathes around.

" Ye bring with ye the forms of other days
　　Where many a cherished image glads my eyes:
And still, like faded, half-remember'd lays
　　Past memories of love and friendships rise.
Each pang renewed, each plaint recalled, betrays
　　What labyrinths wandering life supplies;
And mourns the loved of brighter hours, o'ercast
And shorn of bliss, who leave me, here, the last.

" They hear no more these closing notes of song,
　　The hearts for whom I waked its earlier lay;
For ever cold that sympathizing throng,
　　And ah ! th' applauding echoes died away.
My sorrows mourn a stranger-crowd among,
　　Whose very praises sadden and o'erweigh;
And all to which my strains had gladness borne
If yet surviving, far asunder torn.

" And now my soul unwonted yearning owns
　　For that still calm, the spirit's phantom-reign:
And float and fall in undetermined tones
　　My feeble numbers, like th' Eolian strain.
A cloud comes o'er me ; tear on tear bemoans,
　　And yielding manhood's pride of soul is vain.
All that is left me, distant seems to be,
And all I've lost,—my sole reality."

We take the next passage as an instance of the artificial: the Poet here speaking is not, we should say, a Poet in the best sense of the word. He speaks artistically, and beautifully doubtless, but he is the mere craftsman throughout the speech: a sense of nature pervades the whole; but the error, and this reigns in every line, is that, unlike the real poet, the true man of genius, he converses the order of things and perverts the real feeling; for he everywhere turns nature into the artificial, while true passion and genius turn the artificial itself into nature.

THE POET.

" Oh tell me not of that detested throng,
　　The scattered senses flee their very gaze:
But hide me from the crowd, that bear along
　　The soul reluctant in unending maze.
No, bear me where beneath unchanging Heaven
　　Untainted joys alone the Poet sate:
Where love and friendship to the heart have given
　　The Godhead's power—to summon and create.
Ah ! all that gushes from the spirit's deeps;
　　All that the lip's low-murmured ordeal tries;
All it rejects perchance, and all it keeps,
　　Too oft in some unguarded moment dies.
Oft too for years th' unformed conception sleeps,
　　Then waked to full perfection meets the eyes.

The brilliant for the passing hour is made :
The pure remains, thro' ages undecayed."

This it may be answered, is in character; it is so, but this is our proposition; it is too much in character for the truth of genius: and it is the mere artist alone that looks on Nature only with an eye to art.

The next extract is liable to precisely the same objection. Again the glory of nature sinks down after the tenth line to the bathos of art; and though the skill of the writer elevates the subject to the close of the specimen it is only to the praise of THE ART.

Nor can it be efficiently objected to us, we conceive, that it represents art as triumphing over nature: because the former is ever compelled to work by means of the latter; its only power is to detect the powers of the last, and to bring at best one of its forces to direct another. As a whole, nature must be more grand than art, for it includes art. To pass from the first, then, to the second, is to lower the tone.

THE POET.

" Begone and seek thee out another slave—
What, shall the Bard his proudest duty wave !
   The sacred right of man, by nature lent,
Resigning basely to thy will's control !
How rules he every subject soul ?
   How does he govern every element ?
Is't not that harmonies, his breast o'erflowing,
Sweep the world back with them when homeward shewing ?
When nature her eternal length of thread
   Spins heedless on, to keep the spindle going ;
When Being's inharmonious mass is spread
   Confused, rude discords only throwing ;
Who portions out the ever-flowing strain,
   Infusing soul, with rhythmic art restored ?
Who bids each bosom own the general reign
   Of consecration, in one proud accord ?
Who bids the storm with mortal passions rave,
   The sun-set dyes in sacred feelings glow ?
Or heaps the lovely flowers spring largely gave
   But in the loved-one's path to throw ?
Who from the green unmeaning leaves has given
   A wreath that every merit well repays ?
Who grasps Olympus ? who unites with Heaven ?
   'Tis Man—whose might the Poet's soul displays."

Our next extract is far more strongly illustrative of the same tendency. The Poet does not feel as other men would: it is again not nature that swells in his bosom, but the sacrifice of this to his craft. Every man but Göethe would have made the native feelings the first and leading object: with him it is the second. He is the mere artist and forgets the " celare artem," the concealment of his object. The man would have recalled the crowd of pulses, the artist only could have talked of them as a crowd of songs. The burst of youth would never have done this; still less the remembered enthusiasm of after-life, that would have felt how poor and cold and vain and artificial were even the most impassioned themes, in comparison of the overflowing gush of feelings that struggled, and how vainly do they struggle! for utterance even then. The close is far superior, and confessedly so, for it returns to the one mighty impulse.

THE POET.

" Oh ! give me now once more the days,
   Th' enlarging senses youth bestowed ;
When from their fount th' o'ercrowding lays
   In one unbroken freshness flowed.
When the world lay in mist concealed ;
   Each bud with marvel-promise sheening ;
   And I the thousand flow'rets gleaning
So richly decking every field.
   Nought then was mine ; I wanted nought ;
Truth my sole wish, a dream in every thought !
   Give all th' unbounded pulse to rove ;
   The ecstacy, o'erwrought to pain :
   The strength of Hate—the might of Love—
   Oh, give me now my youth again !"

Of the charm of these passages in the original, (any more than of our own feebleness in rendering them) we can entertain no doubt; they are beautiful, they are artistical, but to the breast of man they should have been UNIVERSAL.

The next passage is elaborately gorgeous: but if the wonders of Creation were the theme, why confine it to the mere terrestrial phenomena ? The opening would indicate the necessity of more: but it opens so only to disappoint us. The planetary and other systems were known fully at the time this was written, yet they are not referred to.

RAPHAEL.

" The sun prolongs, with wonted force,
   Thro' sister-spheres the choral song ;
And, circling his appointed course,
   He rolls in thunder-sweep along :
The angels hail th' inspiring sight,
   Nor strive to scan unfathomed sway ;
Thy mystic works proceed in might
   Supreme, as in their earliest day.

GABRIEL.

" And swift, beyond conception's range,
  Swift-circling whirls the glorious earth ;
And paradisal splendours change
  To night's deep glooms and phantom-birth.
The foaming ocean's boundless flow
  Heaves the fixed rock and depths profound :
Yet rock and ocean onward go,
  Borne on the sphere's eternal round.

MICHAEL.

" And rival storms, from earth to main
  From main to earth contending hurled,
Weave, in confounding strife, a chain
  Of giant ferment o'er the world—
And devastating lightnings glow
  Before the thunder's fated way ;
But, Lord ! with Thee thy servants know
  Alone the calm of changeless day !

ALL.

" The angels hail th' inspiring sight
  Tho' none shall scan thy viewless sway ;
And all thy works proceed in might
  Supreme, as on their earliest day !"

There is nothing here like the grandeur of

" The cloud-capped towers, the gorgeous palaces,"

even of Shakspere's age, and still less of his genius.

We have only room for Margaret's song, exquisite in its simplicity, elaborate, and perfect throughout. We will not ask, Is simplicity so simple as never to rise in the breast of enthusiastic devotion to anything beyond the idiomatic phrases, matchless as they are of the kind, which Goethe has selected ?

MARGARET—alone.

" My peace is gone
  My heart weighs o'er ;
I regain it never,
  Never more !

When he is not near
My grave seems here :
And Earth, and all
It offers, gall.

My wretched head
  Is agony :
My drooping spirit
  Sinks in me.

My peace is gone ;
  My heart weighs o'er ;
I regain it never,
  Never more !

From the casement sole
  My glance would greet him :
And out I wander
  But to meet him.

His stately tread ;
  His bearing high ;
His mouth of smiles ;
  His might of eye ;—

His voice, entoning
  Music's bliss ;
His hands' soft touch ;
  And oh ! his kiss !

My peace is gone ;
  My heart weighs o'er ;
I regain it never,
  Never more.

For him my bosom
  Will fondly glow :
Then could I clasp him,
  Embracing him so :

Still kissing him
  How fain would I,
Lost in his kisses
  Die, oh die !"

We cannot go further now. But the distinction between Shakspere and Goethe is boundless. Great as he was in art, great in German niceties and peculiarities of feeling, Goethe was the great artist after all : his very May-day night contains nothing beyond this ; it refers to life rather than to nature, and by preference. His simplicity, delicacy, and skill are wonderful, and his sweetness and mastery over his own language perhaps unsurpassable : but his various studies, niceties, and affectations of universal learning, and of universal wisdom dropping hourly from his mouth, overlaid the real powers of the German. He could not contain everything in one. Goethe was only the Shakspere of artificial life ; and Germany we think will surpass him yet.

WOLFGANG MENZEL.

IF a man were to write an account of a whale suddenly become human, and retaining in its new form the feelings and propensities of its former shape, with a multitude of such incidents heaped together as might be supposed to result from this absurd combination, he would probably write a very stupid book, but it would be intensely German.

All the admirers of that peculiar sort of originality to which our neighbours lay exclusive claim, would break out in a chorus of applause. The man-fish or the fish-man would be the *beau ideal* of what can be produced by an exuberant imagination; his memory of northern seas, and the delight he used to experience in refreshing himself in hot weather, by rubbing his back against an iceberg, would furnish ample scope for the grotesque, by bringing the two modes of existence into juxtaposition; and, in fact, we venture to insure the most complete success to any one who will take this as a subject, and work it out with the necessary amount of horrors and incongruities. This would be a novel of active life, where our sympathies would be enlisted on the side of the living and moving personages of the drama: but if the author wished to Germanize in another manner, he would have nothing to do but to invest some inanimate object with thoughts and feelings, but without endowing it with visible life; say, for example, a milestone, and let it love, fear, hate, reason, poetize, or philosophize to the best of his ability. This style of writing appears to a great number of people, who have never taken the trouble to analyse the nature of it, to require a very high degree of fancy in the author. But never was such a mistake committed. It is from a *want* of imagination, and not from the excess of it, that our neighbours have betaken themselves to their mysticism and magic, to their double-gangers and Peter Schlemihls. A very natural anxiety to escape from the imputation which for centuries gods and columns had cast on German genius, that it was plodding, careful, mole-eyed, and unimaginative, has been the main inducement to the convulsive efforts they now make to astonish and perplex.

But they ought to be aware that no man has a right to imagine new worlds till he has exhausted the old ones. It is only in favour of Prospero and Miranda that we make allowance for Ariel and Caliban. See what effect those creations would have unless they were presented to us along with the deep human interests and delicate shadings of character which we trace in the other *personæ* of "the Tempest." Would a whole play of Calibans and Ariels, or even a play in which they were the principal figures, and not the mere accessories and excrescences, impress us with such ideas of an author's *imagination* as if he had called Hamlet into being, or clothed the passion of innocent love in flesh and blood, and called it Juliet, or awakened the horrors of conscience in Macbeth? The mistake of our Gothic cousins in believing that whatever is *not* in nature *must* be a proof of fancy, is much the same as the very common one among some of our youthful bards, of considering that whatever is not prose must be poetry. A ring that makes its possessor invisible, a key that opens a terrestrial paradise filled with Mahommedan Houris, an enchanter, a vampire, or a ghost—these are the great instruments with which to concoct a national literature, unless, indeed, the author adopts the still easier expedient of filling his three volumes with all manner of inexplicable incidents, and then loosing the knot he has so artfully tied by exclaiming, like good John Bunyan, at the end of all, "and I awoke, and behold it was a dream." For, depend on it, there is no *deus ex machina* equal to a nightcap. But this striving after the new is not limited to the dealers in novels and romance. It is the characteristic at this moment, and for several years past, of every effort of the German mind. Their scholars give new views of history, their theologians new views of divinity, their philosophers new views of man, his faculties and final destiny. But by new views, think not that old things are merely put in a new position, and fresh light poured on them from the naphtha lamps of those sages. This would be a labour too low, too poor, for their ambition. The first

step they take in their search for novelty, like the diggers for fairy treasures among their own old castles, is to shake down the whole fabric by removing the foundation on which it rested. Out of the ruins they contrive to build up some fantastic tower according to their own taste, and try to train the old ivy over it again, to give it the appearance of antiquity. But the ivy has been rooted up, and refuses to hide the modern masonry. Oh, Romulus! Oh, Remus!—Oh sacred Capitol! towards which had marched so many triumphant heroes, and over which hung such a glory that Rome was indeed the Eternal City while it rested under thy protection—are ye all things that never were? or so different from what we have been taught to think you, that you are, in fact, mere fancy pieces woven into gossamer tapestry by Livy and the ancient chroniclers?—or was Niebuhr a dull, dreamy, fusty, old pedant, denying all these, and fifty other things and incidents, which we had been ready to swear to for fifteen hundred years, merely to obtain a name for himself? The man was utterly unjustifiable, even if his discoveries were true, in laying sacrilegious hands on what had been so long believed that it had *grown* a truth; in depriving of life and glory time-honoured Cincinnatus, treating great Camillus as an impostor, and slaughtering with a more intolerable slaughter the white-haired senate, seated on curule chairs, whose majesty had restrained for a season the enmity and ferocity of the Gauls. For our own part, we believe in all the early history of Rome; and have as yet had no sufficient proofs offered us of the existence of Niebuhr to convince us that he ever lived. We therefore are ready to make our solemn affirmation, that, to the best of our knowledge and belief, Remus leapt over the walls while they were yet only three feet high; and that the person or apparition assuming the name of Niebuhr was a phantom, and no man.

Theology is too sacred ground for us to tread upon, farther than to refuse to be guided first into labyrinths, (which are not to be found in the Bible,) and then out of them, by such misty guides as Tholuck, Baur, and even Neander. As to Strauss and the other infidels, we name them not without disgust; for if fancy can conjure

any image more revolting than another, it is that of a German Voltaire, with all his venom and audacity, and not a particle of his wit. Their philosophy, however, is protected by no such sanctities; and we repeat that the whole effort of their metaphysics has been to strike out some *new* path—to dazzle us with strange speculations, and puzzle us with unintelligible paradoxes. Let us not fall foul of Kant on this particular occasion; for that unpretending-looking syllable, whether spelt with *k* or *c*, has powerful patrons in these degenerate days, whose slumbering venom it might be dangerous to wake. Let us go to Herder himself, one of the greatest names in German literature—a poet, a scholar, a philosopher; yet tainted so deeply with the spirit of his class and country, that his design is evidently rather to astonish than to instruct. So irrepressible is genius, that it cannot continue hidden even under the mummy-like integuments in which a very undivine philosophy endeavours to envelope it—like light in a tomb, it flashes out amid the most gloomy and unpromising scenes, and beautifies, with its lustre, the uninviting objects on which it shines. Herder was undoubtedly a man of genius—he shows it in all his writings; but in them all there is no mistaking the great aim we have alluded to—to startle, to delight; but not to inform. We shall take notice of but one passage in his "Ideas on the Philosophy of the History of Mankind," because we propose to go at greater length into a work of a follower of Herder, (and no unworthy follower,) of which we think our readers will be glad to accompany us in the examination, as illustrative of the present tendencies of the German speculative philosophy; we mean "The Spirit of History" of Wolfgang Menzel.

The philosophers of Herder's day had kindly taken the other planets into their charge, and entered into laboured disquisitions on the state and prospects of our neighbours in the Milky Way. In his admirable "Ideas" he alludes to the vain dreams of Kircher and Schwedenborg on such subjects, and the utter groundlessness of all the guesses and suppositions of Hugens, Lambert, and Kant; but the temptation is too great. He guards himself, indeed, with the convenient go-between "perhaps," but propounds the ingenious doctrine, "that the proportion that exists between the velocity and distance of the different planets, holds good also between the intellects and faculties of their inhabitants." The relation of our matter to our spirit may be regulated by the relative length of our days and nights —the rapidity of our thoughts is in the proportion which the revolution of our planet round itself and round the sun bears to the quickness or slowness of other stars—so that as Mercury performs his daily revolution in six hours, and his annual course in eighty-eight days, the inhabitants of that favoured planet must be clever beyond belief. On the other hand, it is pleasing to reflect how the dullest of men would be looked up to among the dunderheads of Saturn, who gropes his way almost in the dark round the sun, and takes no less than thirty years to perform the journey. Gods! what a poet would be M'Henry!—how inconceivably " quick in the uptak" the late Lord Newton, who used to find out at breakfast the point of Harry Erskine's witticism of the previous day ! " I hae ye noo, Harry!" would be the proof of the most rapid comprehension, though uttered at the end of a month. This, however, is supposing the possibility of a Henry Erskine in such a world ; which is only admissible in consideration of the extraordinary activity it displays in spinning round itself, a feat which it performs in about seven hours. Perhaps, after all; this wonderful speed in one revolution may make up for its dilatoriness in the other ; and there may be an Athens in Saturn as well as in Scotland.

This, however, is only one of many equally gratuitous exercises of the fancy contained in Herder's work, which, be it observed, having for its subject the philosophy of history, should have been strictly limited to an induction from facts. But inapplicable as such flights were in the midst of such a dissertation, what are we to think of Wolfgang Menzel, whose whole work is composed of nothing else ? Now, Wolfgang Menzel is not a man to be passed lightly over in our estimate of German intellect. There is no higher name in the living literature of his country. His " History of the Germans " is

eloquent and popular at the same time ; as a critic, he is distinguished for sound judgment and clear discrimination, joined to a fearlessness and true-hearted disdain of the hollowness and affectation that reigned in the most admired writings of the greatest authors of his land, that drew on him the unmitigated hatred of the followers of Göthe and Voss. His two excellent tales,"Rubezahl" and "Narcissus," are well known: and as a poet he has shown much talent and a great deal of wit. It was accordingly with no slight anticipation of enjoyment that we opened a little pamphlet, published at Stutgard in 1835, entitled " The Spirit of History." Here, then, we thought, we shall have admirable writing and extensive information. Here the great empires of the past will unfold their buried majesty, and point with warning finger to the present or the future. Here shall we see the footmarks of Providence traced amid the ruins of crumbled monarchies. Here we shall—but a truce to our expectations. We pulled the candles closer to us, fixed our feet more resolutely on the fender, and turned to the preface :—

" The following sketch is intended merely to show the impression which, in a long-continued study of history, the powerful spirit that lies in it has made on one not insensible soul. In this I do not scruple to let my heart have its full play. The man whose feelings are unmoved when he considers the fortunes of his kind—whose inmost soul is not excited by the presence of the spirit that animates the world, will never be able to comprehend them. The calmest enquiry, the most dispassionate observation, enable us to *discover* truths, the knowledge of which, nevertheless, leaves the deepest impression upon our hearts. And is istory, then, something unconnected with us, to which we can continue indifferent? Are we not in the midst of it ?—do we not fight the great fight along with it ? Is not each of us destined to take a part in its tremendous drama: as hero fighting for some holy object, or as base wight who helps to bring about the tragic catastrophe? No one is so inconsiderable that he cannot, by magnanimity or the reverse, add to the number of the good or the bad in the world ; that he does not help to make the beautiful shine more clearly—or make the base more

hateful. Moreover, knowledge is given to us not to destroy sentiment, but to inspire it."

Very good, said we ; feeling is a very good thing ; and Wolfgang, we perceive, is going to give us the plain, unvarnished tale of the sentiments awakened by man's fate and destiny in the mind of a man of talent and sensibility. Proceed—

" History is man's life on earth confined to a few thousand years, and to one small planet. Beyond these limits, however, are spread immeasurable space and infinite time, and in them reigns an inexhaustible world-life. But in the same manner as our earth stands in close relationship to other heavenly bodies, it is probable that *our* history is connected with the history of all beings ; *our* life with that great world-life. We find it impossible either to restrain, or to satisfy the inclination to be informed on these points. It would appear that the mere anticipation of a higher existence is fitted to have an animating effect on our present life ; whereas a clear vision of those loftier things would destroy our earthly illusions, and tear us away from the circle of existence in which we are placed. The explanation of the mode in which our earth is connected with the great world of stars, and how our temporal life is connected with the eternal life of the world, remains a problem, a riddle unsolved and unsolvable, and yet which *must* furnish us with employment." Why ?—we do not see the least necessity for troubling our heads about such unprofitable enquiries. We think, at the same time, we could suggest a book to our philosopher that would go some way towards appeasing his curiosity. But we fear that a person who puzzles himself with finding out our connexion with the *eternal life of the world*, would not attach much weight to the volume we refer to.

It appears, then, that a portion at least of our friend's employment will be to guess at such high and wondrous mysteries ; and if it be really so, we do not exactly see how any strong sentiment or deep feelings can be excited by such an occupation in the most susceptible hearts. But let us go on, and see how he makes good his case.

He divides his subject into five " Problems ;" an Astronomical Pro-

blem ; a Theological Problem ; a Mythological Problem ; a Genealogical Problem, and an Historical Problem. We shall give a short abstract of each, and as we have no intention of detracting in any way from the merits of Wolfgang Menzel, we shall at once allow that many beauties of expression are lost in our translation. We merely profess to give the meaning as closely and literally as the two tongues will permit, begging the reader not to impute to the original the stiffness or baldness he may discover in our version.

"ASTRONOMICAL PROBLEM.

" Our earth is a planet, and belongs to the small family of planets, eleven in number, which circle round the sun, and receive from it their light, their daily and annual seasons, and all existence which depends on light. The astronomical relationship of the other planets to our earth, justifies us in the supposition, that they are inhabited by beings resembling man, and that these also are as near akin to each other as the planets themselves. If a decision on such points were allowable, we might conclude, that in the same way as our earth holds a middle rank among the other planets, in regard to distance from the sun, size, &c., so we men probably hold a middle station between the beings of the different planets, and are therefore a more complete representative of the whole species inhabiting our planetary system, than the inhabitants of Mercury or Uranus, who perhaps express the two extremes of the human system, as their planets express the two extremes of the planetary system. In the same manner, we cannot give up the notion that all the inhabitants of our planetary system, however much they may differ from each other, are still only one *species* of beings, with several subdivisions, perhaps, as we ourselves are divided into separate races. In that case it would be particularly interesting to discover what relation the inhabitants of the planets bear to those of the sun. If there are other systems of planets which revolve round a sun of their own, the idea occurs directly, that they stand on a parallel step with our planetary system. This step, however, appears to be one of the lowest in the great ladder of existence. The relation of the planets to the sun is that of slaves.

"On a higher step stand the double stars, of which many thousands are already discovered, two suns, both self-lighted, which move at no great distance round each other, and by this means express a relationship of freedom and equality, of friendship and voluntary connexion, which is of a far higher and nobler kind than the servile relation of the planets to the sun. Must not, therefore, the inhabitants of the double stars stand on a higher step than those of the planets? But we must now be allowed to assume, that these little planetary systems and double stars are again united to a loftier whole, to a great group of stars; and it is not improbable that the multitude of stars surrounding us are only a portion of the Milky Way to which we jointly and separately belong; and which again is separated, as one perfect whole, from other milky ways and groups of stars, still farther removed from us. And as it is said in the Bible, ' In my father's house are many mansions;' and space is infinite; the fancy has ample room wherein to imagine the milky ways as numerous and as diversified as possible.

"That the mind might not grow giddy, some resting-place, some firm centre amidst the infinite has been sought; but this it is impossible to imagine, without, at the same time, giving up the very idea of infinity. We have assumed a central sun, we have believed that the milky ways move in circles round each other, or that they touch, in parabolic paths, like a number of cones with united points, &c.; but all this can, at the utmost, make only one great starry configuration in the expanse of heaven, but cannot represent that *whole* expanse itself, which, being absolutely immeasurable, can have no figure. But to descend from this height to our little earth again — my intention in this exposition has been to show that, at all events, our earth is but a very subordinate heavenly body, and that what we call the history of the world is but a very small portion of universal existence.

"Although the earth, attracted by the sun, revolves around it, yet she always turns her poles to the congenial quarters of the heaven; that is to say, her north pole, round which most *land* is collected, to the north side of the heavens, in which there are most *stars*;

and her south pole, where she is deficient in land, to the southern quarter, which is deficient in stars. In this, therefore, we recognise a law of the earth, consonant with the law of the whole visible starry world, and which must be older than the law which binds us to the sun; because the sun, with his equatorial tendency east and west, could only produce a preponderance of the equatorial force over the polar force, and a contrasting of east and west, but could not produce a preponderance of the north pole over the south pole, which are indeed equal, so far as concerns the sun, and are indebted for the difference that exists between them to some higher cause. But that this cause is the same which heaped the stars in greater number on the north side of the heavens is clear; and we must accordingly seek the point of gravity of our visible world in the direction of the north pole.

"With the exception of this direction of our earth's axis, and the correspondent collection of dry land on the north side, there remains little peculiar on the earth which does not appear either as a consequence of the influence of the sun, or as a reciprocating power with it. Over all advances a victorious sun-god, who either chains up the old earth-gods as furious Titans, or rules the wife-like earth with the strong authority of a husband, and, as Eros, impregnates the maternal night with a beautiful world of light.

"All existence, therefore, upon earth depends upon the sun, and is its work. Even the metals, the embryo world in the deep womb of earth, bears the image of its golden sire; for the metallic veins run parallel with the equator, and not with the earth's axis, and the noblest are found in considerable quantity only beneath the equator itself. The same is the case with the ˅tanic and the animal worlds, whose n st perfect types are found under the eᵩ.ator. And as space is subject to the solar progress, so also are times and seasons; the growth of all organization; the period of existence. To this sun-service, man, the loftiest of terrestrial beings, forms a remarkable exception, and recurs to that primal earth-service, or rather star-service, which is older than the sun. Unlike the metals, plants, and animals, the human race follows not that confused

zodiacal circle which the sun has drawn around the earth, but follows rather the progress of the pole; and man, in his noblest development, is found on the north side of the earth, his head pointed, not towards the sun, but to that mysterious pole-star hidden in the darkness of old night. If he enters the region of the equator, he becomes brute-like, as have the Negroes, the Malays, and the West Indians; and as little is he the creature of the seasons, for in his principal intellectual and animal functions he is independent of the position of the sun.

"All this proves that man, as the quintessence of the earth, has received of that oldest and star-like earth power which is independent of the sun, or indeed hostile to it. And hence the wonderful contrariety we find in men, and in their history, is the result of predisposing natural causes.

"Whatever connexion may exist between the powers that operate on our planet; on the one hand, of the *universal* stellar and cosmal influences—on the other, of the *individual* solar influence; still our planet preserves its integrity in its isolation in the freedom of space, and has, as it were, emancipated itself. Never have the inhabitants of other heavenly bodies come down to earth, nor any of its inhabitants ascended. If higher powers operate in them, those powers have transmigrated here into an earthly nature; and though they may originally have been widely separated from each other, here they have both become earthly flesh—*one* child of two dissimilar parents. The earth—child of the star-night and of the sun—has her own physiognomy, her own life, and her own heart's pulse, and must be considered, along with mankind and his history, as one whole; nay, in some degree as a characteristic individuality, how strangely soever the double nature of the parents is changed in it.

"This earth-unity, this earth-character, this earth-principle, gives to all earthly nature its regulated order, and also to mankind and to their history. It is a particular seed from which this natural form and this historical sequence must *necessarily* spring. Another seed, in other heavenly bodies, produces a *nature cognate* perhaps with ours, but of a different organization, finer or coarser,

and a history richer or poorer than ours, as the beings inhabiting them may be higher or humbler than we.

"As nothing in our world seems grouped together without design, and as in the mineral, vegetable, and animal kingdoms this grouping arises from relationship and family resemblance; so there seems a certain family connexion to exist between the earth and the other planets, which form between them but one individual system, whose limbs and existence are subjected to one law.

"This law of existence, which the planets have in common, is most observable in their regular revolutions round the sun, and must have had a fixed cause and origin. And perhaps, as being nearer to this beginning, the memory of this common connexion, *i. e.* of the earth and the other planets, was more vivid among the first generations of men; nor is it unlikely that, towards the conclusion, it will again be more visible. In the legends and religious systems of the oldest nations, the stars and the harmony of the planets hold a prominent place, and the ancient notion that the life of all the planets began while they were in a certain position or constellation; and that, after they shall have finished their assigned circuits, they will revert to that constellation again, is, in an astronomical sense, perfectly reasonable; and as, indeed, every thing finite must have a beginning and an end, the notion seems indubitable. But over the duration of this period, and over the connexion between the astronomical and the historical, between the alternation of stars and of events, human reason has often puzzled itself, and has never yet seen its way clearly, and will find it difficult to do so; for history, among its other good qualities, has this, that it never allows itself to be fixed beforehand, but, with its wondrous revelations, constantly strikes us with surprise."

And here ends the Astronomical Problem of a philosophical historian, of what Thomas Carlyle calls "this nineteenth century of time." But our history is only a portion of the history of Georgium Sidus and Mars; that the earth was originally on more familiar terms with her neighbours, and probably will become intimate with them again; that people have never yet found out—either in the plains of Chaldea or the tents of the Gypsies—the influence of the stars on human events ; and that even Francis Moore, physician, will *not easily* do so, because history likes to astonish ! All this is conveyed in the first department of this work, of which we have given a larger specimen than we shall do of the succeeding problems, as we wished the reader to see with his own eyes the struggle to be original and startling, which, as may naturally be expected, ends in being childish and absurd.

We were in hopes that in the next, or Theological Problem, we should have something more tangible than such vague wool-gathering among the stars ; but when the fit comes on him, it is not so easy to bring such an ethereal voyager down to common sense and this plodding world. The third paragraph is somewhat odd. " There exists, however, an extraordinary resemblance between astronomy and theology. " Some " wicked allusion," we thought, to the Inquisition and Galileo. But such trivial matters never entered into the author's head. " As astronomy," he continues, " points out to us a tendency of the earthly to ascend beyond the solar circle into infinite space, so theology points out to us a tendency which leads beyond this narrow sphere of existence into infinite time, or eternity ; and as that corporeal space-tendency was attached to the north-south polarity of the earth's axis, which stands immovably firm in spite of the east-west action of the sun, so also we perceive that each individual's path intersects, in a perpendicular direction, the horizontal stream of earthly history, and seeks its goal upwards in the Deity.

" History moves in an horizontal line, from Adam right onwards to the end of time. Each individual, however, only enters on this line to leave it immediately, and seek his loftier destiny in a higher existence.

" An irrepressible feeling tells us we struggle upwards from this paltry world into an immortality in the great eternal realm of spirits. But the connexion between that future life and our present state, is as much hidden from us as the connexion between the external firmament and this miserable planet. We must confine our efforts to the present life, and not interfere

with another. We are immortal, that we may see and learn more in the world to come ; but here all we can see, and all we can learn, is of the earth, earthy. Much has been said about the connexion of this life with a future, and indeed with a past. The most ancient nations, as do still the people of Eastern Asia, imagined we were fallen angels,—beings condemned for their crimes to inhabit this mortal body. Others imagined we were endowed with freedom of will ; and by virtue or vice could choose between heaven and hell. This grand and happy view began, along with all spirited and chivalrous life, among the Persians, and attained its full triumph in Christianity. But in this faith there is nothing *real* except the effect it has on us, in so far as it inspires us to great deeds and with noble thoughts. Nothing is more foolish than from our earthly state, and with our proportionately contemptible intellects, to try to find out the depths of the divinity, and of the infinite realm of spirits. That depth is as immeasurable by our spiritual vision, as the starry heaven is to our bodily eyes. But the relation man bears to God, eternity, and a future life, has nearly the same weight and influence on his history, as the relation which the earth's axis bears to the heaven of stars, has upon terrestrial nature. If the magnetic attraction of the north pole of the heavens did not produce a counteraction to the solar influence, the whole earth would be nothing but the slave of the sun ; if that spiritual attraction which conducts man into the lofty ideal did not exist, history would be nothing but the slave of sensual nature,—man would be nothing but an animal. Notwithstanding the interest we necessarily take in the concerns of the world, still there is always something apart from us, as it were, in all our temporal joys and sorrows ; and a gentle monitor whispers to us of something higher. It is in this suggestion that Christianity finds its influence. It dashed to atoms the heathenism of old days, in which the sun drew his spiritual circle round the world ; and clear, amid the darkness of night, rose up that star which was the handwriting of Heaven. But Christianity has become crumpled ; the star has been hidden in clouds, and so it seems impossible that there

ever should be fulfilled on this side of the grave a prophecy of rest and happiness, which is expressly limited to the other world. Yes, only in the other world ! for it is vain to hope for the kingdom of a thousand years, the republic of virtues—Utopia ! The struggle will still go on, and grow loftier as it continues ; but in the struggle we shall succumb—our victory will not be *here*—our triumph will be above. As death overcomes all physical existence here below, so will evil overcome all moral good. 'Tis only in the struggle that man ennobles himself, and his wondrous history is perfected. But the hostile principle conquers him at last, and therein alone lies the majestic beauty, the tragic charm of history. Without this appalling catastrophe history would be child's-play, a flat, unprofitable tale. No, there pervades her a deeper earnest ; and as only the boldest and longest struggle is worthy of her, so also is only the end which the Apocalypse reveals. The earth will not go to sleep in peace and awake in heaven ; she will be destroyed in glowing fire. Men will not be perfect in virtue, wisdom, and felicity, and be wafted, like Elijah, to heaven without knowing death ; they will go on multiplying themselves without end ; and all at once, insanely pouring out their strength in colossal depravity, they will expire amid the terrors of nature, in universal slaughter, when the last days shall come."

And this is the " Theological Problem " of a learned inhabitant of Christendom, though we cannot call him a disciple of Christianity. But we will not waste another drop of our good black ink (blue we hold to be a humbug) on such drivelling. Proceed we to the Mythological Problem, and see if he makes any sense out of fable, now that he has made such miserable nonsense out of the truth. But, alas ! alas ! before we get many pages into his mythological lucubrations, we find them every whit as ludicrous as his theology.

" The small portion of the older legends which can be considered as really historical, must be tried by the universal laws of nature and reason before it obtains our belief. The most interesting to us are those of Paradise and the first human pair. According to the Indian legend, the earth was in

the beginning covered with water till it gradually raised itself, and the summit of the mountain Meru (it retains the name still, and is the south-western point of the Himalaya range) first made its appearance. This was the Paradise where the first human pair were placed ;—originally an island till the rest of the continent uprose, and then it sent forth the four rivers of Paradise, (the four well-known great rivers of Asia.)

" With this the Mosaic legend agrees, as do the Persian, Greek, and Scandinavian. The legends of all Western nations point towards the original sacred mountain in the East. The Chinese legend, in exact agreement with this, points to this mountain in the West, because the Himalaya lies westward from China. In short, this Indian legend of the elevation of the earth from the water, constantly recurs among most of the ancient nations.

" To this natural history has nothing to oppose. The form of the valleys over the whole earth, and petrified aquatic animals discovered on the loftiest mountains, are still proofs that the earth was originally covered by the waters. And as the Himalaya is really the highest mountain, and lies in the centre of the broadest and oldest continent ; and as the plains beneath it are the home of all domestic animals necessary to man, and of all kinds of vegetable food, this oldest of all popular legends, when viewed in this light, derives additional confirmation.

" The mythos also of Paradise is still one and the same. Many of the ancient nations have, no doubt, treated it in a childish and almost ludicrous manner. Wherever polytheism was established, the first man is lost in a crowd of gods and deified animals, and is crushed by the weight of symbolical monsters.

" It is only the Mosaic legend which has conceived the idea, at once lovely and majestic, of a beginning, a first childhood of the human race. The first man ! a captivating, most important, inexhaustible thought. How rich in all his relations to God, his Creator ! —to Nature, his cradle, his theatre, his grave !—to the great human family, his children ! — and to their tremendous history ! In all these relations the Mosaic legend satisfies at once the enquiries of the deepest mysticism, and of the plainest understanding.

" In all other legends the first man appears dependent upon nature ; in the Bible alone he is represented as nature's lord. Adam gives names to all creatures : all creatures obey him till, by sin, he falls under the dominion of the powers of nature.

" The Mosaic legend connects the first hostile separation of mankind immediately with the first pair. The eldest born of men murders his brother, and wanders with the mark of Cain upon his brow into distant regions. Is there not in this mythos, however deeply hidden, a trace of the first mysterious division into the different races of mankind ? It is of little importance to enquire whether the legend of Noah be a totally new one, or only altered from that of Adam. To us it is of no manner of consequence whether the world began to be peopled by one or by the other. As soon as history becomes a little clear, we find mankind already divided into five great families, which answer to the five great portions of the world, and having already adapted themselves to the climates ; the white race in Europe and Western Asia, the yellow in Eastern Asia, the red in America, the black in Africa, and the brown in Southern Asia and Australia. The later dispersions at the Tower of Babel, at the destruction of Troy, and at the oppression of Dacia, whatever their effects may have been, belong only to the white Caucasian races, and to a recent period. But all this gives no explanation of the causes of the differences between the races ; and as long as we remain ignorant of them, all those tales and legends can only be regarded as memorials of other separations within the white race itself. Here, then, we must summon the natural sciences to our aid ; for all legends must be tried by geography and physiology."

The fourth, or Genealogical Problem, accordingly commences with an enquiry into the effects of climate in altering the colour ;—then, as to whether it is probable that the Fall had any influence in making mankind black ;—and after suggesting an original solution of the difficulty, by supposing it not impossible that this diversity of colour was originally implanted in Adam's organization, and took some time to develop itself—as

many new faculties seem to make their appearance from time to time, (such, for instance, as animal magnetism,) while others disappear,—he honestly confesses, that the difference of the races continues as great an enigma as the origin of the human race itself. But our worthy friend likes it all the better on account of its being an enigma ; being a gentleman only inferior to Billy Black in finding out a puzzle. And the following short sentence soon gave us note of preparation for another of his flights. " Here, then, we must again have recourse to astronomy"—To astronomy, to discover why there are niggers in Africa ?—Shiver me ! what will the fellow do next ?

" Let us remember the great astronomical opposition of an earth-power north and south, to a sun-power east and west, and we shall find the same opposition recurring in the development of mankind on the earth. Strictly speaking, there are only two positively opposed races of men, the black and the white. But the whites are evidently children of the north, under the influence of the great fixed-star heaven ; under the law of a higher world-regulation, endowed with spirit and activity, and, so far from submitting to the mere power of nature, that they have, through the whole course of history, aimed at making themselves independent of it. The blacks, on the other hand, are children of the south, under the influence of the sun, eternally subjected to the animal desires, without self-consciousness—without historical recollections —without an object of endeavour, and living but for the morrow.

" The third great family is the yellow—Mongol-Chinese.

" If the blacks represent the sun, and the whites the great fixed-star heaven, the Mongols would seem to be the earthly representatives of the moon. There is something about them grey, pallid, and faded, and isolation is their peculiar characteristic. In the midst of the world, they make up a little world of their own, perfectly detached and separate. But this little world, although perfect in itself, is only a shadow of the rest—a lifeless, cold imitation. In physical conformation, the Mongols are even less different from the whites than are the blacks. And on the difference be-

tween these three races, the legend of the three sons of Noah may be founded. The Negroes, indeed, have a legend of the three brothers, and they expressly refer to them the white, the yellow, and the black races of mankind. The two other principal families may have arisen from admixtures of the other three. The brown Malays, from a junction between the blacks with the Indians and Chinese. The red Americans appear also to be a kind of mulattoes, a combination of the Mongol and Malayan races, and probably also of the Gauls, Finns, and Wendæ, who are undoubtedly of Indian origin, and may have peopled the north of Europe and Asia in the earliest times, and have passed over, via Greenland, to America.

" The coloured races have certain points in common, notwithstanding the differences that are to be found among them. I allude not only to the darkness of their colour, but to a corresponding darkness and contractedness of the understanding. The stereotype character of *earthly* nature, under the annually recurring influence of the sun, is shown in their whole life and bearing. They either have no history at all, and have made no progress towards a higher civilisation for thousands of years—or they remain on a very low step of civilisation, and have hindered the farther improvement of their descendants. The first holds good of the Negroes—and the last of the Mongols.

" Europe, from its peninsular shape, is particularly adapted for maritime pursuits, and this led her to make conquests in other quarters of the world. The Dutch-Roman races (the Portuguese, Spaniards, Hollanders, French and English) colonized all America, and made themselves masters of the coasts of Africa and all the Australian islands. With this commenced a new intermixture of the white and coloured races. A great discovery was made in the course of these commixtures, namely, that though they take place in equal *quantity*, the *quality* is in favour of the whites. If, for example, ten whites and ten blacks unite, the descendants in the eighth generation will be white. It has also been observed, that the white mulattoes of the eighth generation surpass their progenitors on both sides in every re-

spect ; they attain the pure complexion, noble sentiments, and lofty spirit of the whites ; and, at the same time, have the plastic forms and sound health of the dark races. May not the splendid qualities of the Greeks and Romans have arisen from a similar combination of the Thracian and Semitic families ?

" It may be asked whether, at some future time, the rest of the world may not be flooded with Europeans from the East Indies, from the Cape, and from Botany Bay, and by this means (though it may take hundreds of years in the performance) a universal commixture take place, as it has in America ? Or whether there may not occur a reaction of the original coloured inhabitants against the colonists—and in that event, whether those coloured races would remain, as hitherto, in their lethargic stupidity, or, of their own accord, would embrace Christianity and European civilisation ? It would be a strange phenomenon in the history of the world if the rigid crust of those ancient nations were to soften all at once, and after remaining immovable for six thousand years, they were instantaneously (as by the touch of magic wand) to be endowed with the soul of the white races. I do not believe it. I believe rather that the final complete triumph of Christianity and of civilisation will be the consequence of an entire fusion of the whites and blacks. Australia must speedily have the same fate as America has had. There the aborigines are thinly scattered, and cannot resist the aggressions of the trading colonists, who will go on increasing rapidly as the Indian trade acquires additional expansion through the prosperity of the American States —the emancipation of the East Indies—and the extending colonization of the Cape. Africa will soon follow. The time is not far distant when Northern Africa will be subject to Europeans. And Egypt also must in future play a distinguished part, either by the restoration of an Arab kingdom, or by European conquest ; and colonization will go forward slowly, but surely, from the Cape. The Negro tribes in the interior seem incapable of offering any effectual opposition, and will sooner or later be reduced to the same situation as the North American Indians.

166

"As to Asia, the same processes secure a similar result. In the East Indies the elements of a mighty kingdom are collecting, and European cultivation widely diffusing itself. The Indians are so ready to receive it, and so thankful for the instructions of the English, that I do not dream of their ever being expelled the country.

" New sects will arise in Arabia, which will approximate the old faith to Christianity. China and Japan will offer more resistance, inasmuch as in material cultivation they are already so near the Europeans; and it would be impossible to modify such immense masses of people by intermixture, like the blacks, or root them out, like the North American Indians.

" Whatever, therefore, may be the result, whether at any future time the whites, by intermixtures, may swallow up all the other shades, it is, at all events, certain that population will go on increasing in a greater ratio than ever. Nothing has yet set bounds to its progress. Great nations have disappeared, the whole American race is on the point of expiring, and yet the numbers are replaced tenfold. Mortality in China is prodigious. Millions are swept off by a war or a pestilence, and yet that is the territory in the whole earth where population is most dense. It is, therefore, no idle question what will happen in some thousand years, when every corner of the earth is inhabited. In this question lies matter for the most awful page in the world's history. The means of supplying such prodigious numbers are above our present faculties to imagine — or is that the time for the angel of destruction foretold to us in the Revelations?"

We find we have left ourselves little room to give any account of the fifth or Historical Problem, and our readers may perhaps be of opinion we have devoted quite as much space to the others as they deserve. But we explained, when we began, our reason for doing so; and we feel persuaded they will not now dissent from our proposition, that the present school of German philosophers has a much greater tendency to the absurd and grotesque, than to the useful and the true.

Following in the steps of Herder and Schelling, Menzel discourses very learnedly on a certain " parallelism of nature," taking for his text this somewhat astounding proposition, which is the received doctrine of the modern philosophers, " That history forms one great self-connected life in time, as nature does in space." He agrees also with Schelling, that all the appearances we are acquainted with in nature compose oppositions or antitheses; and that the antithesis is, therefore, the only form in which nature reveals herself to mankind."

We shall not follow him in his exemplifications of this theory, although we confess that his Historical Problem shows as much information as ingenuity. We have now done all we intended, and, after wading through a hundred and ninety-five pages of such wonderful speculations, (which, we confess, have astonished us the more, as proceeding from the author of the *Deutsche Literatur,*) we cannot part without promising, on some future occasion, to restore him to our own good opinion, and that of our readers, by giving a view of him in some of his better works—his stirring history of his own land, or his noble assaults on literary quackery and imposture.

SOME REMARKS ON THE PRINCIPLES OF TRANSLATION;

Followed by Specimens from the German Lyric Poets.

SPECIMEN I. SCHILLER'S " SONG OF THE BELL."

TO THE EDITOR OF THE NEW MONTHLY MAGAZINE.

SIR,

The immediate occasion of the remarks which I have the honour to address to you is the notice which has been taken (in the October number of the *Quarterly Review*), by a far from unfriendly critic, of two small volumes, recently published, of my collected poems ; and the subjoined specimen is one—the most considerable in length—of several versions attempted during the leisure of the late summer vacation, as incidental to my main object—that of becoming acquainted with the noble language of the original. Whether the reasons I shall have to allege be of sufficient force, or the version itself of sufficient distinctive merit, to induce you to give insertion to this new performance of what has been so often before undertaken, I must leave to your decision ; and, if that should prove in the affirmative, you will perhaps not object to receive a succession of similar contributions, most of which, I believe, will be found to possess the recommendation of not having been previously known in an English dress.

I am, Sir, your obedient servant,

J. H. MERIVALE.

Nov. 13, 1839.

To be assured of having succeeded in the endeavour to render into English some of the first passages in the greatest of modern poems (the *Divina Commedia*), with the aid of a metre peculiar to its original language, the presumed difficulty of which, in our own, is such as to have deterred (except in two or three short instances) all former translators from attempting it, is praise sufficient to satisfy a more inordinate vanity than I would willingly own myself to possess. At the same time, I am far from considering that this praise, even if well-deserved, is of such a nature as to entitle me to the rank of a victorious competitor, where no competition was ever intended ; and the problem rests wholly unsolved (and is one, the solution of which I frankly declare I should myself shrink from attempting, even if I had years before me, and time at my command, more suitable) whether an English version of the entire poem in *terza rima* be practicable, or if practicable, whether not calculated to fatigue, rather than gratify, the unaccustomed ears of transalpine barbarians ? At all events, since the experiment has not been made, I must, in common humility, disclaim all notion of rivalry ; and, having said thus much, will proceed to suggest a canon of criticism, the reception of which I feel to be important, not only to my self-justification, but

to the encouragement of other translators, past, present, and to come —namely, that as the painter from nature witnesses many effects both of shade and colour, which even a Claude or a Rubens would despair of being able to transfer to his canvass ; so, in poetry (and which, moreover, is the truest test of originality in the artist) there are many hues and tints which it is utterly impossible to imbody in a translation, however laborious or skilful, for the absence of which it follows that a translator is no more justly chargeable than for any of the various imperfections of human language which are necessarily derivable from the confusion of Babel. It does not follow that a translator may not, even in the most unavoidable deviations from, actually surpass his original ; and in those instances where such is the case, he is, in strictness of speech, no longer a translator, being himself an original poet. But still, in all of the highest order of poems, there are passages of transcendent force and beauty, which cannot be surpassed—which can only be imitated at a most humble distance—and where, though some deviation is, in the very nature of things, unavoidable, *all* deviations must (alike unavoidably) be for the worse ; and it is very possible that the six exquisite lines, at the conclusion of the episode of Paul and Francisca, my version of which is pronounced to be a failure, may be of this description. Indeed, the critic himself has perhaps signed my acquittal in merely writing them down as " *inimitable.*" The interpolation of the words " fired with passion," I acknowledge as a fault only to be justified by the case of necessity to which I have already alluded. Still it only amplifies—it does not (at least that I am conscious of) either alter, or dilute, the sense of the original. The " trembling o'er, *like his*," I cannot attempt to justify, inasmuch as it introduces a new idea, unwarranted by the original—a case of obvious distinction.

But there is a third instance in which I am accused of having erred, by omitting one great beauty—the prayer,"

" Questi che mai da me non *sia* diviso.'

As to which I plead boldly " not guilty," and retort on the critic the charge of having allowed himself to be blindly led into the adoption of a most unaccountable error of Mr. Landor, who makes one of his interlocutors ask, " Are we not impelled to join in her prayer, wishing them happier in their union ?"—to which the other is supposed to answer, " If there be no sin in it,"—whereas, in fact, there is no prayer whatever—the word not being *sia* but *fia* ; the reading to be found in the earliest as well as the latest editions, and never (I believe) disturbed or questioned. *Fia* for *Sarà*—so say the commentators—and accordingly so rendered by Byron,

" He who from me *can* be divided ne'er"—

by Cary,

———" he who ne'er
From me *shall* separate—"

and by Wright,

" He who from my side *will* ne'er remove."

Nay, I will venture to say further, that the *sia*, imagined by Mr.

Landor, would have been wholly unlike Dante—so unlike, as to induce a suspicion of the accuracy of the text if it had been found there—a mere prettiness, unworthy of his severe simplicity even if suitable to the occasion ; but (moreover) altogether unsuitable to it, since there was no manner of reason for those, the peculiarity of whose punishment consisted in their eternal union, to utter a wish that they might never be separated, as if one of the Siamese brothers were to breathe a sigh that he might never lose the society of his inseparable companion. In short, the mere suggestion is downright nonsense; affording a proof that critics have their besetting dangers, no less than poets and translators of poets. After all, I have now to propose that the version of the entire passage may be given as follows :

> " ' For, when we read the smile, so long desired,
>   Which to the lover's kiss her answer bore,
> He who can ne'er from me be parted, fired
>   With passion, kiss'd my mouth, all trembling o'er.
> Galeot the book—and who the story wrought.
>   That day in the pandar page we read no more.'
> —Thus, while the one disclos'd their secret fault,
>   That other spirit wept ; till, with the swell
> Of pity, all my sense was quite o'erfraught,
>   And, as a lifeless body falls, I fell."

And now, a few words only, by way of introduction to the following version, and at the same time of apology, for its being offered after so many previous attempts, and some by authors of no mean celebrity—for instance, Lord Francis Egerton and Mr. Sotheby. It would, indeed, be inexcusable to submit a new translation of the same poem to the chance of public approval, unless in the persuasion that something had been left unaccomplished by former adventurers in the lists, and in the confidence that some improvement has now been made on their efforts. A more recent version than either of those already noticed—that of Mr. Pym Johnston—will, I think, be found to have exceeded both the former in point of accuracy, though, perhaps, not in respect of poetical expression, or felicity of versification. I must add, however, that this last-mentioned version was alone before me at the time of my performing the task, and I have accordingly noticed in the margin those passages in which I have to acknowledge myself principally indebted to it. In all others, I have endeavoured (however unsuccessful may be the attempt) to improve upon it, in both the combined requisites of fidelity and poetical spirit ; and, upon a subsequent comparison with the labours of my other predecessors, I do not feel discouraged from the design of presenting my own as a supplemental contribution. The portions of which I am most diffident are the linking stanzas descriptive of the operations of the foundry ; and it is in these that I have chiefly availed myself of the resources afforded by my precursors.

"THE SONG OF THE BELL."

(SCHILLER.)

I. 1.

FAST immur'd in solid earth,
    Of well-bak'd clay the model stands.
To-day the Bell must have its birth,
    Brisk, comrades! ply your ready hands !
        From the burning brow
        Must the sweat-drops flow :
Our work the master's skill may prove ;
But the blessing's from above.*

I. 2.

Well befit the words of Reason
    That grave task we've now begun.
If sage discourse the labour season,
    Smoother will the minutes run.
Then let us mark with watchful eyes,
    What ends from our weak efforts spring,
And the dull peasant-slave despise,†
    Who heeds not what his pains forth bring.
'Tis this that most adorns our race—
    For this was Reason's power assign'd—
What with our plastic hands we trace
    To fashion in our inmost mind.

II. 1.

Splinters of the fir-tree take—
    But well-season'd be they—so
Shall th' imprison'd fiery flake
    Fiercer in the furnace glow.
        Quick ! pour your tin !
        Cast your copper in !
Let the Bell's thick gruel‡ be
Stirr'd to an apt consistency.

II. 2.

What in the mound's deep concave hidden,
    The hand by aid of fire brings forth,
High from the steeple's belfry, bidden,
    Shall witness loudly to our worth—
Bidden—to peal through many a morrow—
    The ears of many a race to shake ;
To sooth the mourners in their sorrow,
    Devotion's choir to rapture 'wake.

---

* Since the period of original composition, I have new-fashioned this introductory stanza after comparing it with Mr. Sotheby, to whom I am accordingly indebted for much of its present structure.
† " Why, what a wretch and peasant slave am I !"—*Hamlet.*
‡ *Glockenspeise*—literally, Bell-fodder.
    " Make the gruel thick and slab."—*Macbeth.*

What fates the womb of changeful Time
  For earth-born man may yet be breeding,
Loud from its brazen crown shall chime
  Through many an age, to age succeeding.

III. 1.

Bubbling white th' ingredients thicken,
  And the molten masses flow.
Now, our foundry task to quicken,
  In the chymic cinders* throw!
    But from scum let be
    The heaving mixture free!
So the metal, bright and pure,
Will a clearer tone ensure.

III. 2.

For now the Bell, with festive sound,
  Begins thy silent hours to number,
  Sweet babe! who in the arms of slumber
Hast enter'd life's enchanted ground.
  Still sleeping lie, in Time's dark womb,
  Thy lots of brightness and of gloom.
Fond mother's love, with wakeful warning,
Attends to guard thy golden morning—
  With arrow speed years circle round.

III. 3.

Wild starts the boy from the young girl's† side,
  And eager for Life's journey burns;
Roves through the world—his staff his guide—
  A stranger, to his home returns—
Then, flush'd with manhood's graceful pride,
  Sees, like a beam from Heaven shed o'er him,
Her bashful cheeks in crimson dyed,
  The ripen'd virgin stand before him.
Now nameless thoughts, in tempest rushing,
  Possess his soul; he roams alone;
Tears from his eyes unbidden gushing,
  Shuns each gay sport his youth had known;
Pursues her footsteps, trembling, blushing;
  Basks in her smile divinely blest;
Scouring the mead, the woodland brushing,
  For fairest flowers to gem her breast.
Ah! tender longings, hopes endearing,
  Love's golden prime encircling round;
Heaven to our gaze unveil'd appearing—
  The heart in floods of rapture drown'd!
Ah! might its verdure ne'er decay—
That brilliant hour of Love's young May!

---

* *Aschensalz*—Alkali—Kelp.—*Dict.*
† *Vom Mädchen.* Surely this means the female playmate, whom he leaves a frolic child, and, returning, finds grown into a blushing maiden. Sotheby, and (I think) Lord Francis Egerton also, refer it merely to female guardianship, converting the young playfellow into an old nurse. But, if there were any doubt as to the true meaning, it would be set at rest by comparing the exquisite lines in the " Piccolomini."
     " Und schambaft tritt als Jungfrau ihn entgegen,
      Die er einst an der amme Brust verliess."

IV. 1.

The pipes already seem to brown,
  See this rod!—I dip it in!
Is the surface glassy shown?
  —Then the foundry may begin.
    Brisk, comrades, haste!
    Let's prove the cast.
If soft and brittle well combine,
This we may count a lucky sign.

IV. 2.

For as, when strength with weakness blending,
Stern force on ductile softness tending,
  The metal yields a clearer tone;
Prove ye, who seek Love's mystic union,
If heart meet heart in true communion.
  Repentance 'bides when rapture's flown.

IV. 3.

'Mid the bride's dark tresses stealing,
  Gleams the virgin chaplet bright;
While the church-bells loudly pealing,
  To the festive bower invite.
Ah! Life's sunniest holiday—
  Must it end like summer's tale?
  With the girdle—with the veil—
The fairy-charm is torn away.

IV. 4.

The passion flieth—Love must survive:
The blossom dieth—the fruit must thrive,
The man must a-field, where foes are alive;
    He must struggle and strive;
    Be sowing and hatching,
    Contriving and snatching;
    Must wager and dare,
    Fortune's gifts to insnare.
Then riches in torrents abundantly pour;
His granaries groan with the weight of their store,
  And his roof stretches widely its sheltering shield.

IV. 5.

    And thereunder, supreme,
      Sits the virtuous housewife,
      The tender mother,
    O'er the circle presiding,
    And prudently guiding;
    The girls gravely schooling,
    The boys wisely ruling;
    Her hands never ceasing
    From labours increasing,
    And doubling his gains
    With her orderly pains.
With piles of rich treasure the storehouse she spreads,
And winds round the loud-whirring spindle her threads:

23. continued

She winds—till the bright-polish'd presses are full
Of the snow-white linen and glittering wool ;
Blends the brilliant and solid with constant endeavour—
    And resteth never.

IV. 6.

And the Father, with triumph swelling,
From the roof of his prospect-dwelling,
    His flourishing stock counts o'er;
His piles of timber, tempest braving,*
His fruitful fields, like billows waving,
    And his barn's o'erladen floor.
Then shouts with exultation—
"Secure as earth's foundation,
Against the assaults of fate
I've fix'd my proud estate!"
But ah! with fortune's powers united,
No lasting league can e'er be plighted!
    Disaster strides at giant rate.

V. 1.

Well! the torrent now may gush—
    Fairly is the sample broken.†
Yet—or e'er we let it rush,
    Be some pious sentence spoken.
        Out the spigot drive!
        God keep the house alive!
Reeking in the handle's bow,
See the fire-brown billows flow.

V. 2.

Fire lights a mild benignant flame
While men its power control and tame:
Whate'er we shape—whate'er produce—
Is by its Heaven-directed use.
But different far the Fury burns,
When man's restraint she madly spurns,
And walks, as monarch of the wild,
Boon nature's free and lawless child.
Woe! when loos'd from dungeon bar,
    And with fearful speed advancing,

Thro' the streets, where tumult rages,
    Comes the uncouth monster dancing;
And in elemental war
Heaven itself 'gainst man engages !*

V. 3.

From the welkin blessings pour—
    Streams the shower.
From the welkin, unaware,
    Lightnings glare.
Hark! shrill whistling round the steep,
    Tempests sweep.
        Red as blood
    The heaven is glowing—
(Not with daylight's golden flood)—
        And the street,
As wilder still the tumult's growing,
    Steams with heat.

V. 4.

Flickering thro' the lurid skies,
See the flaming column rise !
On the wind's swift wings it flies.
See! it reddens, furnace-bright.
Pillars tumble, rafters break,
Door-posts crackle, windows shake ;
Mothers straying, children moaning,
Beasts beneath the ruins groaning ;
All is bustle, terror, flight !
—Clear as noonday shines the night.†
Lengthen'd files in labour vying,
From hand to hand the bucket flying,
High o'er head, in concave bending,
Mark the water-spout descending !
Louder howls the tempest, blending
With the flames in hideous roar ;
Wastes the corn-field's arid store :
In the smoking granary preys,
Mid the serried timbers strays,

---

* I had first written these lines as follows :
        His broad oaks, tempest braving,
        His fruitful corn-fields waving,
having mistaken the sense of the words in the original,
        " Der Pfosten ragende Bäume,"
and I thought of justifying my mistake in the manner following :—To survey the mere contents of his farm-yard, a man needs not mount to the roof of his far-seeing mansion —" Das Hauses weitschauenden Giebel." Besides, the rows of timber are placed in opposition to the fields of corn ; and, as the last are unreaped, so it seems more fit that the former should be represented as still standing.
    However, it is better to correct an error, when discovered, 'than to attempt its vindication, and I have still to confess myself amenable to criticism by retaining a favourite epithet not to be found in Schiller, who, however, would not, perhaps, have scrupled to use it, if his rhyme or metre had required it.
    † This line is Mr. Pym Johnston's. I trust in him for the technicality of the expression.

* In these verses I must confess to another freedom with the original ; owing, at first, to mistake arising from my imperfect acquaintance with the language ; retained, because, like the foam on the dog's mouth in the picture, I became pleased with the effect my error had produced. Mr. Johnston has, more literally,
        "Woe! when, independent grown,
        Increasing, 'spite of all command,
        Thro' the thickly-peopled town
        She hurls the all-consuming brand."
    But where is the magnificent epithet, "ungeheuren," which I had ignorantly transferred to the "free daughter of nature" herself?
    "There be spirits," says the son of Sirach, "that are created for vengeance, which in their fury lay on sore strokes; in the time of destruction they pour out their force, and appease the wrath of Him that made them. Fire and Hail, and Famine and Death, all these were created for vengeance. Teeth of wild beasts and scorpions ; serpents, and the sword, punishing the wicked to destruction. They shall rejoice in his commandment ; and they shall be ready upon the earth when need is ; and, when their time is come, they shall not transgress his word."
    † I am indebted to Mr. Pym Johnston for several of the above lines, which are utterly unsusceptible of any improvement.

171

23. continued

And—as if its breath had power
To whirl the solid globe away,—
Raging still with mightier sway,
Braves, in giant strength, the tower
Of Heaven's height.
—Hopeless quite,
Man bows him to the afflicting rod ;
And wondering looks, with vacant stare,
At the wide-wasting work of God.*

v. 5.

Burnt and bare
Lies the ruin'd mansion spread—
The wild storm's rugged bed.†
In the empty window-cells
Horror dwells ;
And peers in, from its throne on high,
The cloud-wrapt sky.
One look—his last—
Doth he cast,
Of grief and dread,
On the spot where his wealth lies sepulchréd ;
Then takes his staff—and away ! 'tis past,
For, whatsoever the flames have 'reft,
One sweeter comfort still is left—
—He counts the heads of his lov'd ones round,
And—joy ! not one is wanting found.

vi. 1.

Now the ore is deep in clay.
Now the mould hath drunk its fill.
Will it well come forth to-day ?—
Well reward our toil and skill?
Should the foundry fail !—
Should it burst the pale !‡—
Ah ! while most we hope, belike,
Mischief is at hand to strike.

vi. 2.

To holy earth's dark womb we trust
All good that we from Heaven implore.
So hoping, trusts his seed the sower,
To see it blossom in the dust,
By blessing from the Great Bestower.

---

* I suspect, here, another error from ignorance, but am again loath to correct it. The compound word " Götterstarke" is referred by Sotheby (who I imagine is right) to the power, not of God, but of Fire personified—
" Beneath its Godlike strength man bows," &c.
But, if my interpretation be wrong, Mr. Johnston has partaken my error.
† " Burnt and bare
The homestead lies,
The wild storm's prize.
In the empty window-frames
Horror reigns," &c.—P. Johnston.
‡ " Now the metal in the clay
Rests happily—the mould is fill'd,
Will it fairly face the day,
And profit for our labour yield ?
Should our efforts fail !
Should it burst the pale ?"—P. Johnston.

But in the Mother-lap, with mourning,
A seed more precious we entomb,
In hope that, from its rest returning,
'Twill flourish in immortal bloom.

vi. 3.

From the steeple
Hark ! the bell
Hollow booms
A funeral knell—
Seems the dull peal, so solemn swinging,
On his last road some pilgrim bringing.
Ah ! it is the wife beloved—
Ah ! 'tis the matron, faithful proved—
Whom the Prince of Shades, unsparing,
From her mate's fond arms is bearing,
From the offspring of her womb,
Which she bore him in her bloom,
Which she, on her constant breast,
Hush'd, in mother's joy, to rest.
Ah ! the ties for ever parted,
Late that bound the house in one,
Now the true—the tender-hearted—
To the land of shades is gone !
Now her gentle rule is ended,
Now her cares no longer wake,
And the Orphan House, unfriended,
Must a stranger guardian take.

vii. 1.

Now, then, while the metal's cooling,
Let us seize the vacant time !
As the schoolboy quits his schooling
When he hears the vesper chime,
So, when stars appear,
Then, from labour clear,
Let each be free, like bird on tree—
The master still must burden'd be.

vii. 2.

Now the evening shadow thickens
In the forest's deep'ning gloom,
And his steps the traveller quickens,
Hasting to his cottage home.
Bleating flocks are fold-ward going ;
Distant-lowing,
Herds of cattle, broad-brow'd, sleek,
Their accustom'd home-stalls seek.
Heavily, with thundering din,*
The corn-pil'd waggon totters in :

---

* " Heavy laden, from the field
The corn-pil'd waggon totters in.
Bright with variegated leaves,
On the sheaves
The garland lies," &c.
P. Johnston.

172

On the sheaves the garland lies,
Bright with variegated dies:
Youthful reapers to the dance
    Brisk advance:
Street and market's busy hum,
    Now is dumb.
Where the friendly lamp is burning,
    Social circles gather round,
While the city-gate, slow turning,
    Closes harsh with jarring sound.
        Clad in sable
        Is the earth;
But no nightly fears are able
    To disturb the burgher's mirth.
When wakes the eye of justice, then
None evil dread, save guilty men.

VII. 3.

Holy Order, blessing-fraught;
Heaven's own daughter, wisely taught
To bind in strict equality
The light, the happy, and the free;
On surest base to elevate
The social fabric of the state—
The savage of the woods to tame,
His lawless passions mild reclaim;
To light the cheerless haunts of man,
And mould him to thy gentle plan;
And, last, to weave that holiest band—
The sacred Love of Fatherland!

VII. 4.

Thousand active heads combining,
    Help the work with friendly strife;
And, the lengthen'd cord intwining,
    Bring man's noblest powers to life.
Lord and servant join to prove
    Holy freedom's firm alliance:
Each, as all in concert move,
    Bids the mocks of scorn defiance.
Labour fits the burgher's state;
    Useful toil brings blessings down;
The king is honour'd by his crown,
    We by the works our hands create.

VII. 5.

Peace benignant! Concord sweet!
    Yet awhile—yet awhile—
Rest ye in this cherish'd seat!
Far from this silent valley—far—
Be the rugged hordes of war!
May we ne'er the day descry,
    When the sky,
Now with evening's softest red
    Overspread,

Shall reflect the fearful burning
Of tower and town to dust returning!

VIII. 1.

Break we now the mould asunder,
    Now the purpos'd end is won;
While we gaze, in joyful wonder,
    At the work our hands have done.
        Sway the hammer, sway!
        Till the crust gives way!
When the bell ascends on high,
Must the form in pieces fly.*

VIII. 2.

The master may destroy the mould
    When the season fit shall be;
But woe! when raging uncontrol'd,
    The burning ore itself sets free!†
In floods of fire, like thunder roaring,
    It blows in air the bursten shell,
Wild destruction hot out-pouring
    As from the open jaws of hell.
When untam'd towers chaotic jangle,
No order'd shape can disentangle;
When senseless mobs for mastery strive,
No commonwealth may hope to thrive.

VIII. 3.

Woe! when in the city's veins
    The heap'd-up fuel smouldering lies;
The madden'd people bursts its chains,
    And, fiercely to self-succour flies.
Now from the bell-ropes, tempest-shaken,
    The uproar swells, with hideous jar;
And, meant the notes of peace to 'waken,
    They clung the alarum peal of war.
    "Liberty! Equality!"
Hear ye not the watch-words howling?
    To arms the peaceful burghers fly;
    The crowded streets and halls reply,
While banded murder round is prowling.
Women no more—hyenas, daring

---

* " Sway the hammer, sway!
    Till the crust gives way!
  When the Bell is fit to rise,
  Then the mould in pieces flies."
                            P. JOHNSTON.
  " Wenn die Glock soll auferstehen,
    Mass die form in stücker geben."†

"The master may destroy the mould
    With prudence and with certainty;
  But woe! when raging uncontrol'd,
    The burning ore itself makes free."
                            P. JOHNSTON.

To laugh 'midst horrors—jest at woe ;
And now, with fangs of panthers tearing
 The quivering entrails of the foe.
No longer aught is held for holy ;
 All bonds of solemn reverence fall :
Virtue gives place to rampant folly,
 And crime wide ranges, free from thrall.
'Tis dread, the lion to awaken ;
 To cross the tiger on his path ;
But, dread of dreads, when, phrensy-shaken,
 Man rises in vindictive wrath.
Beware, on eyes long darkness-shrouded,
 To pour the full meridian blaze :
It fires—not lights—the sense beclouded,
 And towns and states in ashes lays.

IX. 1.

Heaven the work hath prosper'd well.
 See ! how like a golden star,
Bright and polish'd from its shell
 The metal-kernel gleams afar !*
  From helm to crown it dances
  Like the sun's bright glances ;
And trophies on the blazon'd shield,
Due tribute to the founder yield.

IX. 2.

 Come in ! come in !
All good comrades, close the ring !
The Bell must have its christening.
Concordia name it ! so begin.†
Henceforth, with brother's love, and heartfelt union,
May it assemble all in sweet communion !

IX. 3.

And oh, be this its glad vocation—
The destin'd end of its creation !‡
High raised above this nether world,
 In Heaven's blue canopy to swing ;
And, where the thunderbolts are hurl'd,
 Its loud responsive voice to fling.
There shall its clear-ton'd notes resemble

The hymning of the starry choir,
Round which the planets move and tremble,
 In praise of the Almighty sire,
While, listening to the angelic song,
They lead the wreath-crown'd year along.*
To themes eternal welfare bringing,
We consecrate its brazen chime,
As, hour by hour, its hammer swinging,
Shall touch the flying wings of Time ;
Shall lend its tongue for Fate to borrow,
Itself unfeeling joy or sorrow ;
Still with its solemn voice attending
Life's changeful drama to its ending.
And as each clang, so hollow sounding,
 Dies faintly on the listener's ear,
Oh, let it teach, his pride confounding,
 That nothing is perpetual here.

X.

Now, then, with the strength of rope,
 Let the Bell be hoisted high,
Where it shall well fulfil our hope,
 Responding from the vaulted sky.
  Pull now ! pull away !
  It moves with steady sway.
" Joy to our city !"—be its token—
" Peace !"—be its earliest accent spoken.

---

* " So let it seem a voice above,
 Like the bright planets' dazzling throng,
 Which praise the Maker as they move,
 And lead the wreath-crowned year along."
       P. Johnston.

---

*'Heaven the work has prosper'd well.
 See how, like a golden gem,
 Bright and polish'd from the shell,
 The metal kernel darts its beam."
       P. Johnston.
† " Come in ! come in !
 Companions all, close the ring !
 The Bell must have its christening—
 Concordia shall its name be called," &c.
       P. Johnston.
‡ " Be this henceforward its vocation—
 For this I watch'd o'er its creation," &c.
       Sotheby.

24. NEW MONTHLY MAGAZINE, 58 (1840), 319-330. M/H No. 3642. By J. H. Merivale.

SPECIMENS OF GERMAN LYRIC POETRY.—NO. II.*

BY J. H. MERIVALE, ESQ.

In performance of my undertaking to furnish a series of translated specimens from the lyric poets of Germany, I wish to make a few more preliminary observations on the style and method adopted, without which I should be held to do little else besides adding, perhaps superfluously, to the streams of German translation with which some very respectable portions of our periodical press have recently been irrigated almost to overflowing. So many, and of such various degrees of merit, have been these contributory rivulets, that I cannot take upon me decisively to pronounce whether in all the particular instances which I shall have to produce, the same originals may not have already, once, or more than once, been copied (and perhaps more successfully copied) by other artists. I can only undertake to say, that wherever I am aware of having had a precursor, I shall either withdraw my own attempt; as being conscious of its inferiority, or freely indicate the rivality, and point out in what respects I presume to consider my imitation as preferable. In no case shall I be deterred from presenting my own performance, by the mere circumstance of having been preceded by others;

* Continued from No. ccxxix., page 139.

because I hold it a tribute due to original genius, not to relax in our efforts while it appears possible for the copyist to produce a more perfect resemblance.

It is in following up this principle that I submit the two following pieces of Schiller—the first strictly lyric—the other of the ballad species. I was not aware, at the time of attempting either, that it had been the subject of previous translation ; and with regard to the first of them, I feel some knightly diffidence in entering the lists with a lady—nay, more, a champion of such deserved renown as Mrs. Hemans—the very Clorinda of the field of poetry. But, superior as her version may be in other respects, she has not attempted that which I hold to be an indispensable requisite of translation—especially from a language so cognate with our own as the German—namely, to retain the peculiar metre of the original—or, in failure of that, to adopt another as nearly corresponding to it as the genius of the language will permit. And here I must be allowed to observe, once for all, that the peculiarities of versification and rhythm, however *secondary* they may be regarded by some, I hold to be among the *primary* observances in the catalogue of a translator's duties—an opinion I have before pronounced when apologizing for a new version of Dante, after the labours of Wright and Cary had rendered it, in the judgment of many, superfluous. Few, indeed, who have *not* practised (few even of those who *have* practised) the art of translation, seem to be aware how very much of the *essence* of poetry is combined in these most important requisites. The little poem I am about to present—which might perhaps, in itself, be called a mere poetical trifle—becomes with reference to this its chief characteristic, a gem of the first water. Its metre, uncommon to an English ear, is not so very unusual, though still peculiar, in German ; and this must be recollected by those who may be otherwise disposed to censure it, when presented in English, for affectation, or (perhaps) harshness. But to me, there is something remarkably pensive, and, as it were, dreamy, in the construction ; which is therefore not on any account to be neglected in the attempt to give an English dress to the original composition.

One of the difficulties of which an English translator from the German is most conscious, and which he is therefore too easily prompted to evade by changing altogether the frame and structure of the stanza, arises from the inferiority of our language, *as spoken*, to that of our Teutonic cousins, in dissyllabic terminations. But this, it should be recollected, is an inferiority resulting from vernacular corruption ; and therefore, in translating from the German, I hold it to be not only permissible, but highly praiseworthy, to have recourse to our own old Saxon infinitives and participles, at the risk of whatever censure, rather than sacrifice what in any instance constitutes a peculiar grace or feature of the original, by the weak effort of accommodation to a corrupt popular idiom. It is under this impression that I have chosen to retain the good old English participles " bounden" and " founden" in the third stanza of the ensuing specimen. And now, having expounded my principles of translation, I proceed to the subject of the poem, in itself strikingly illustrative of the prevailing cast of German thought and expression.

Every body who has read Wallenstein (and who has not done so, at least in Coleridge's splendid version of the two last of the three pieces into which the whole drama is divided ?), must remember the exquisite lyric effusions which are put into the mouth of that most graceful of heroines, Thekla ; as well as her sudden disappearance after the report of her lover's death, and the uncertainty in which we are left as to her after fortunes.

A lady of Schiller's acquaintance once complained to him of this uncertainty, in the guise of a fiction—saying that, in ruminating on the subject, she had seen the shade of Thekla pass before her eyes ; but that it vanished on her attempting to question it. The poet undertook to *answer* for the spirit ; and, for the sake of the peculiarity already noticed, I may be excused for presenting the original appended to my translation.

THEKLA.

THE VOICE OF A SPIRIT.

"Where I dwell ?—or whitherward I wended,
     When my flitting shadow swept thee by ?"—
Had I not my task foreclosed and ended ?—
     Loved and lived ?—what was there, but to die?

Seek the nightingale's sequester'd bower ;
     Who with her soul-melting melody
So bewitch'd thee in the vernal hour.
     When she ceased to love, she ceased to be.

"Him—the lost-one—whether I have founden ?"
     Trust me, I with him united go,
Where those ne'er shall part, who once were bounden—
     There, where mourners' tears no longer flow.

There, too, even thou again mayst meet us,
     When thy love hath learn'd to equal ours :
Freed from sin, my sire is there to greet us,
     Where no cloud of blood-stain'd murder lowers.

Now he knows, his sight no phantom cheated,
     When he upward gazed into the sphere.
As each metes, shall there to him be meted.
     Who believes—to him is Heaven near.

Faith is kept, in those bright mansions yonder,
     With all trusting souls who there resort.
Be thou free to dream, and free to wander !
     Meaning deep oft lurks in childish sport.

THEKLA.

EINE GEISTERSTIMME.

Wo ich sey, und wo mich hingewendet,
Als mein flücht'ger Schatten dir entschwebt ?
Hab' ich nicht beschlossen und geendet ?
Hab' ich nicht geliebet und gelebt ?

Willst du nach den Nachtigallen fragen,
Die mit seelenvoller Melodie
Dich entzückten in des Lenzes Tagen ?
Nur so lang sie liebten, waren sie.

Ob ich den Verlorenen gefunden ?
Glaube mir, ich bin mit ihm vereint,
Wo sich nicht mehr trennt, was sich verbunden,
Dort, wo keine Thräne wird geweint.

Dorten wirst auch du uns wieder finden,
Wenn dein Lieben unserm Lieben gleicht ;
Dort ist auch der Vater frei von Sünden,
Den der blut'ge Mord nicht mehr erreicht.

Und er fühlt, dass ihn kein Wahn betrogen,
Als er aufwärts zu den Sternen sah,
Denn, wie Jeder wägt, wird ihm gewogen,
Wer es glaubt, dem ist das Heil'ge nah.

Wort gehalten wird in jenen Raümen
Jedem schönen, glaubigen Gefühl.
Wage du zu irren und zu träumen ;
Hoher Sinn liegt oft in kind' schem Spiel.

To those who are familiar with Schiller's immortal drama, the allusions in the three last stanzas, to the astrological distemperature, the gloomy forebodings, and midnight assassination of Wallenstein, will be sufficiently obvious.*

---

* The germ of certain expressions, which, taken by themselves, appear somewhat enigmatical may be detected in the following lines of the concluding part of the drama :

     " fur ein liebend Herz ist die gemeine
     Natur zu eng ; und tiefere Bedeutung
     Liegt in dem Mährchen meiner kinder-jahre
     Als in der Wahrheit, die das Leben lehrt."

Again, the entire sentiment of the poem is comprised in a single couplet of the drama.

     " An dem Sternenhimmel gebn sie jetzt,
     Die sonst im Leben freundlich mitgewandelt."
                                        WALLENSTEIN's *Tod*.

The next of my promised specimens must be, as I have already declared it to be my intention, of the romantic, or ballad class of poetry; in which Germany has, for the greater part of a century—since the days of Burger—been extraordinarily prolific, and does not seem, even yet, to have exhausted her productive powers. As contrasted with works of the same species which have, during an equal space of time, issued from our own native brain—of which Scott and Southey may be regarded as having furnished the most illustrious specimens—those of the Teutonic school are, I think, chiefly distinguishable by the characteristic which I have before ascribed to one of its lyric effusions, and which I cannot designate by a more appropriate term than that of *dreaminess*—mystifying the hearer's senses, and making him feel doubtful whether he is himself awake or asleep, while listening to the strains of enchantment. And this is equally the case, whether, as in the instance about to be submitted, the recital be founded on some already existing local tradition, or be the pure coinage of the writer's imagination.

And now, without further preface or apology, I beg to introduce my readers to

RITTER TOGGENBURG—THE KNIGHT OF TOGGENBURG.

> " Ritter, treue Schwesterliebe
> Widmet euch dies Herz.
> Fordert keine andre Liebe,
> Denn es macht mir Schmerz," &c.

" Take, oh take true sister's love !
  Ask me not for more :
Other that thou bidd'st me prove,
  Think it grieves me sore.
Peaceful let me part from thee;
Peaceful learn to think of me :
And, in pity, oh forbear
Wishes that I must not share !"

Mute with sorrow, from her sight
  He rush'd with desperate speed ;
And buckled on his armour bright,
  And vaulted on his steed :
Then sent he round to all his band
Of followers in the Schweitzer land,
And bade them arm, and with him bear
The cross to the Holy Sepulchre.

And nobly that valiant band behaved
  When the battle raged most high ;
And proudly the good knight's banner waved
  O'er the Paynim chivalry :
And much the Paynim warriors fear'd
When the name of Toggenburg they heard :
Yet nothing could yield his pain relief,
Nor ease his heart of its heavy grief.

He has born that load a tedious year,
  And sought for rest in vain ;
Until he can no longer bear—
  So quits the battle-plain.
He speeds his bark from Joppa's strand,
And steers him to his native land;
In hope to breathe more freely there,
Because *her* breath is in the air.

Already at her castle-gate
  The pilgrim's fingers knock ;
And to his touch it open'd strait,
  With words like a thunder shock.
" Her whom thou seek'st a veil doth hide ;
Not thine—but Heaven's elected bride.
But yester eve, in the cloister's shade,
The solemn vow to God she made."

Oh then he left, and left for ever,
  His father's ancient hall ;
His arms to behold again—no never !
  Nor his steed best loved of all.
Down from Toggenburg, alone,
He descends—a man unknown ;
His limbs, for knightly harness, drest
In a monkish, hair-cloth vest.

He builds him a hut in the silent glade,
  On the spot where first he sees
That convent rise amidst the shade
  Of the gloomy linden-trees—
Tarrying there from morning light,
Until the shades of coming night,
—Silent longing in his face—
Fix'd he sat in that lonely place.

Thence towards the convent's wall above
  For hours he bent his look,
And towards the window of his love—
  Until the casement shook ;
Until he saw his love appear,
And then beheld that form so dear,
—Mild as holy angels show—
Bend downward o'er the vale below.

Then joyfully he down him laid,
  And sank in sleep profound,
Till another morn dispell'd the shade
  That night had cast around.
And thus he sat, till many a day,
And many a night had pass'd away ;
Still waiting, without plaint or pain,
For the lattice-bar to clink again ;

When the loved-one might again be seen,
  And her dear image throw
Again its angel glance serene
  Over the vale below.

And thus he sat, till the morning ray
Once dawn'd upon his lifeless clay.
Yet that long gaze—now mute and chill—
Was fix'd upon the casement still.

What a picture for our next annual exhibition ! The high convent-wall overhanging the precipice—with the casement, and the " angel face," casting a gleam of mild radiance over the gloomy depth below—there, in dim perspective, the linden grove, the cell, and its rapt inhabitant—his glazed eye fixed, in dying ecstasy, on the object of its enchantment. The difficulty of the painter, however, would be found to consist in the necessity of devoting so large a space of his canvass to the mere landscape, as to leave scarcely scope for exhibiting the human features of his subject in due proportion ; for though a Poussin and an Albano may have combined in giving effect to a classical representation, we have no instance of a Guido uniting with a Salvator, least of all of such an union to be imagined upon terms of equality in point of expression. But it is otherwise, as to its capability of pictorial illustration, with respect to the subject of the poem, which I mean next to submit in the garb of translation which, so far as I know, it has never yet been invested with. Its author is Uhland—one of the most successful of living lyrical poets—founder (as I apprehend he is esteemed) of the peculiar school designated by the name of " the modern Swabian," and who (as far as I am able to form a judgment) has received rather unfair treatment from English critics, as well as from English versifiers. At least the few specimens which I have met with of the *latter* class of conspirators against his reputation, are among the worst of what are miscalled translations from the German ; while the *former* class—that of the critics—seem to have combined in charging him with weaknesses, into which some of his compatriots had previously fallen, but from which he has laboured, by no means unsuccessfully, to liberate the national genius. In saying thus much, it is not my design to attempt a task, for which my recent and slight acquaintance with the language so little qualifies me, as that of vindicating the object of censure. I shall merely observe that, after a perusal of no small portion of the volume containing his collected poems, I am myself more inclined to coincide in opinion as to its merits with one of his own countrymen, whose judgment few will be inclined to dispute who have enjoyed the benefit of his instructions, or even observed the effect which they have produced upon others who have been his disciples—I mean Professor Bernays, who in the preface to his little volume, entitled, " German Poetical Anthology," writes thus concerning the poet, and the circumstances which called his genius into action :

" The enthusiasm which roused the German nation, in 1813, to cast off the French yoke, seemed to supply for a time a noble theme to the poet, to speak from the heart and to the heart ; and the war-songs and other national lays which were written at that period, afford ample evidence of the high powers, both of the German mind and the German language, for the loftiest strains of poetry. But, strong as was the excitement, and fervent the hope [which stimulated such spirits as Körner, and others, to combine the soldier and the poet at that memorable era], the recoil was yet greater when the congress of Vienna dashed down the hopes and expectations of the chivalrous men who had survived the struggle, and in their enthusiasm had dared to dream of the establishment of a German empire, united and free within, and powerful without. Poetry now became political and polemic, or at best assumed an elegiac turn, which often indicated broken spirits, and hearts despairing of faith and truth. The calmer minds, and stronger hearts took refuge in science and historical investigation, or strove to elevate their contemporaries by a revival of the national poetry, and recollections of the middle ages. Hence arose, in particular, what is now often called *the modern Swabian school*, with Uhland and G. Schwab at its head. But we perceive, even among those whose compositions at first betrayed the gloomiest despondency, a glowing calmness, a development of strength, which promise high results. The public calamities they have experienced, seem to have filled them with a seriousness which raises them above the sentimental dalliance of their predecessors. The present poets are no longer sighing shepherds, but armed men, fighting the battle of humanity. Their glances into outward nature, as well as into the soul of man, are often vast and profound ; and although some do not yet seem to have arrived at that state of perfect repose, which springs from a steady faith in the things unseen, yet there is in many of them a heavenward tendency, and a growing conviction that Eternal Love *has* prepared a refuge for the agonized spirit beyond the limits of time and space ; and they are nobly pressing forward to reach this sacred haven."

———

DER BLINDE KONIG—THE BLIND KING.

" Was steht der Nord'schen Fechter Schaar
    Hoch auf des Meeres Bord ?
    Was will in seinem grauer Haar
    Der blinde König dort ?

    " Er ruft, in bitterm Harme
        Auf seinem Stab gelehnt,
        Dass über'm Meeresarme
        Das Eiland wiedertönt."

Why throng the northmen's warrior band
    To the sea-girt cliffs ?—and there
What makes the Old Blind King to stand
    With his silver-streaming hair ?
        On a staff his limbs supporting,
        He shouts with fearful cry ;
        And across the channel'd waters
        The cavern'd isles reply.

" Give, robber, from her rocky cell,
    My child to me again !
Her song so sweet—her harp's wild spell—
    Were the balm of my age's pain.
        From the dance on the sea's green margin,
        Thou hast her borne away ;
        And my head is bow'd in sorrow,
        With its locks all hoary gray."

Then fiercely from the rocky mound
Stepp'd forth that robber knight,
And swung his giant falchion round,
And clash'd his buckler bright.
"Thou keep'st full many a warder—
Why did they let it be?
Thou marshal'st many a champion—
And none to fight for thee?"

But all the champions were astound;
Not one steps forth—not one :
And the Blind King asks, as he turns him round,
"Then am I all alone?"
His youngest son has caught him
By the right hand so warm—
"Oh suffer that I the battle try!
There's strength in this mine arm."

"O son! the foe is giant strong—
There's none can him withstand:
But to thee doth noble blood belong,
And I feel how firm thine hand.
Now fetch me my trusty falchion,
The prize of the Scald-men old;
And, if thou fail, may the billows
O'er this gray head be roll'd!"

And hark!—it bounded and it hiss'd—
The pinnace—o'er the deep:,
The old Blind King, he stood to list,
Till all seem'd hush'd asleep.
Then rose across the water
The clang of sword and shield;
And the hollow caves re-echo'd
The roar of the battle-field.

The old man shouts with fearful joy—
"Say on! what have ye seen?
My sword I know by the sound of each blow
It gives—so shrill and keen."
—"The robber lies extended—
The price of blood is won.
Hail to thee, first of heroes!
All hail, thou true king's son!"

Again 'twas silence all around—
The king stood by to list.
"It comes—it comes—I hear the sound;
Their oars have the waters kiss'd."
—"Yes—onward come they rowing—
Thy son, with sword and shield;
And with sun-bright tresses flowing
Thy darling child, Gunilde."

"Right welcome!" from his beacon stone
A shout the old man gave—
"Now may mine age glide blissful on,
And glorious be my grave!

Then, son, by my side, remember,
Lay my good sword along :
Gunilda! thou, my freed-one
Shalt chant my burial song."

———

The next specimen has more of that *dreaminess* of cast which I have already remarked as peculiarly characteristic of the German romantic ballad, but for which I do not know that those of the school of Uhland are more properly chargeable than many of an earlier, and what some of our critics are pleased to denominate, a better period. It is, perhaps, more justly obnoxious to the charge of plagiarism—Burger's "Lenore" being somewhat too obviously the model which the author had placed before him; and which, moreover, may serve as a key to its right interpretation—otherwise, apparently, somewhat doubtful.

In the present version I shall be found to have deviated a little from the structure of the original stanza—and *that* contrary to my own canon of taste; but I do not think that the English ear is adapted to a blank verse termination, when the preceding couplets are in rhyme. In order that the reader may judge for himself, I prefix the first German stanza of this, as I have done of the previous poem.

DER TREUE WALTHER.

"Der treue Walther ritt vorbei
An uns'rer Frau Capelle.
Da kniete gar in tiefer Reu'
Ein Mägdlein an der Schwelle.
Halt an, halt an, mein Walther traut!
Kennst du nicht mehr der Stimme laut,
Die du so gerne hörtest?"

True Walther rode him forth alone
By our Ladye's chapel door :
A maiden knelt on the threshold stone
The holy shrine before.
"Now hold, how hold, my Walther dear!
Remember'st not that voice so clear,
Which once thou saidst 'twas joy to hear?"

"Whom see I?—her of broken oaths,
Who once—(ah once!) was mine?
Why hast thou cast thy silken clothes,
Thy gold-and-jewel-shine?"
"Woe's me, that e'er I broke my plight!—
Now lost is every false delight :
My joy is only in thy sight."

By pity moved, that maiden young
Upon his steed he placed;
And with her white soft arms she clung
Full closely round his waist.
"O Walther dear—my joy! mine own!
This heart that beats for thee alone,
It beats against a breast of stone."

They enter'd Walther's castle mound—
  Within 'twas empty space:
His knightly helmet she unbound,
  And mark'd his clay-cold face.
" Thy cheek so wan—thine eye so sere—
Adorn thee most, thou dearest dear!
To me they never shone so clear."

Then loosed she from his troubled breast
  The armour he had on :
—" What see I ? Ah ! a sable vest ?
  What dear-loved friend is gone ?"
" For one most loved I grieve full sore ;
One whom on earth I never more
May find—nor after life is o'er."

Down at his feet she lowly bent,
  With arms outstretcht to Heaven :
" Here do I lie, poor penitent,
  And pray to be forgiven.
Oh, raise me once again to bliss !
The cure of all our woe be this—
One fond embrace—one true-love's kiss.

" Rise up ! rise up, thou hapless maid—
  It is my last behest.
My stiffen'd limbs refuse their aid,
  And lifeless is my breast.
Mourn thou, as I have mourn'd before!
Our love is o'er—our love is o'er—
'Tis gone—and will return no more.

With the foregoing specimen I close my present series of contributions from the romantic school of poetry, though I may perhaps be inspired with the inclination to return to it at some future period. My next paper will probably be devoted to pieces of a more strictly lyrical species. But I have not yet done with Uhland, and have still to add some specimens of Schwab, whose name is coupled with his in the manner already noticed.

P.S.—In the last number of *Blackwood's Magazine* (February, 1840), and in a very able article on the " Poetical Translations of Faust," are laid down certain rules of criticism, which may be thought at variance with some which I have ventured to promulgate. Against so much of those canonical regulations as may appear to derogate from the rights and privileges of rhyme and metre, by treating them as *non-essentials* in the laws of poetical translation, I beg, in this place, to enter my solemn protest. At the same time, I wish to be understood as by no means intending, by any thing I may have said or sung, to underrate the paramount necessity of a strict *substantial* adherence to the *sense* of the original ; and this necessity it is, which, with respect to the works of poets like *Goethe* and *Dante* (who may fairly be classed together with reference to this question), almost every word in which has its peculiar meaning and appropriate collocation, renders the task of the translator so very difficult, and (indeed) *impossible*, of scrupulously-faithful performance.

What may be the merits, in either or both respects, of the particular translation to which the following letter refers, I am unable to form any judgment, it never having been my fortune either to meet with the volume in question, or to have heard the name of the party who has done me the honour of opening a correspondence on the subject of it. But, as his letter seems designed for publicity, and as it more immediately relates to a passage in my own former communication, besides that it confirms me in the ground of defence I had taken, I make no scruple of soliciting its insertion.

" January 23, 1840.
" In a communication of yours, which appeared in the last number of the *New Monthly Magazine*, you have asserted that the Tertian rhyme in which Dante wrote his great poem, had not been adopted by any of his English translators, except in a few brief specimens. In making this assertion, you were of course unaware of the fact that the latest translator of " The Comedy" into our language, has actually adopted the *terza rima* of the original ; and has, in his preface, insisted on the necessity of using that very impressive kind of rhyme, in any endeavour to convey an accurate idea of the great poet of the middle age. It is not at all strange, sir, that you should have been ignorant of the existence of the translation in question, as, owing to certain unlooked-for circumstances, the book which contains a large portion of it, with the preface, was never advertised in England ; and was, apparently, not even looked at by any of the reviewers, quarterly, monthly, or weekly, to whom copies had been sent, as I believe. I confess that I was foolish enough to be somewhat surprised that none of those critical gentlemen would condescend to say one word of my book, especially as the second of the original poems which it contained was, under its first title of ' Giuseppino,' most confidently attributed to Lord Byron by at least one critic (see *Literary Gazettes* of the 17th and 24th of November, 1821). It was also reprinted in America, and largely circulated as the work of his lordship. I venture to hope that, as you are interested about Dante, you will look at the specimen of my translation (10 cantos) with some attention. The volume of which it forms the concluding part, is entitled ' Arnaldo, Gaddo, and other acknowledged poems by Lord Byron and some of his contemporaries : London, Groombridge ; Dublin, Wakeman, 1836.' This title was, perhaps, unfortunate. I had heard, in fact, of a volume called ' The Rejected Addresses,' which went through many editions, and I knew that at least one of my poems had been thought to be identical with the style of Beppo ; and therefore merely for the purpose of attracting some notice to the work, I prefixed to it the name of Lord Byron,—not specifying whether the late lord or the present. This may, perhaps, have struck the critics dumb, as a prodigiously bold attempt at imposition, though the preface would have shown that none was intended ;—and thus the larger and better portion of my poetical doings has remained unnoticed and unknown.
" Permit me now, sir, as one who has studied Dante long and deeply, to assure you that your version of the line,

'Questi che mai da me non fia diviso,'

is perfectly correct. It is really impossible that Dante could ever have written the line as Mr. Landor and the *Quarterly Reviewer* choose to read it. I am convinced that there is not the authority of a single MS. or edition for that reading, as the spirit of the entire *Cantica* is against it. The punishments in Hell being described, of course, as unchangeable, Francesca could not fear a separation from her lover. It is, I think, very strange that so admirable a writer as Mr. Landor, and one so deeply read in Italian literature, should have fallen into such an error. Hoping that you will correct the slight mistake into which you have fallen,

" I have the honour to be, Sir,
" Your very obedient humble servant,
" EDWARD N. SHANNON."

25. NEW MONTHLY MAGAZINE, 59 (1840), 118-123. M/H No. 3645.

REMARKS ON THE PRINCIPLES OF TRANSLATION, WITH SPECIMENS OF GERMAN LYRIC POETRY.†—NO. III.

BY J. H. MERIVALE, ESQ.

I HAVE hitherto been prevented, by various avocations of a very different nature, from the further performance of the intention announced, and partly executed, in two former numbers of this year's Magazine (those for January and March respectively), of illustrating the principles of translation by specimens from the German lyric poets. The design is perhaps altogether too daring for a novice in the German language and in German literature ; and I have accordingly found it necessary to devote some time towards improving my qualification in both respects, previous to any thing like a regular recommencement of my projected series. But, in the mean time, I have been favoured by my ingenious, though in some respects unlucky correspondent, Mr. Shannon (the now self-revealed author of a volume mystifically entitled " Arnaldo, Gaddo, and other *unacknowledged* poems, by Lord Byron and some of his contemporaries")‡, with a copy of his mystifying publication ; and this, in addition to many very distinguished merits of the poetical order, contains, in the second portion of it, by way of preface to ten cantos printed as a specimen of an intended

---

† Continued from No. ccxxxi., page 372. The complete title-page is as follows : " Arnaldo ; Gaddo ; and other unacknowledged Poems. By Lord Byron, and some of his contemporaries. Collected by Odoardo Volpi. *Dublin*, Wakeman ; *London*, Groombridge. 1836."

‡ See March number, p. 330.

translation of the entire " Divina Commedia," such ample confirmation of the views entertained and expressed by myself on " the Art of Poetical Translation," that I cannot refrain from requesting the insertion of some passages in aid of my own suggested opinions.

After observing that " English literature has been already in some degree enriched with one translation of ' the Comedy,' " by which he means Mr. Cary's, not, it seems, having that of Mr. Wright immediately before him, though he afterwards proceeds to notice it also : the veiled author thus proceeds under his assumed style and title of " Odoardo Volpi :"

" To me it appears to be an imperative duty of a translator to copy, as far as possible, not only the imagery of his prototype, but likewise to convey as clear an idea of the *manner* of his original—especially if that manner be remarkably appropriate to the subject treated. Now there never was an author whose manner was more peculiar to himself, or more fitting for his subject, than that of Dante, and I think every person of taste, who is acquainted with the great poem of the Florentine, will readily acknowledge that the Tertian Rhyme in which it is written possesses a solemn harmony and grandeur of cadence which impart, as it were, an oracular dignity to the verse ; and that this is, of course, the best form which the poet could possibly have selected in the composition of his sacred allegory."

" There is, besides, another quality in the poem of Dante which should, I think, have prevented his translator from making such a choice," viz., that of blank verse for the medium of translation.

" It is, most truly, a Gothic poem : in other words, it is completely characteristic of the middle age in which it was produced, when all poems of all kinds were written in rhyme, and long before the invention of blank verse in modern language. If an Italian were to render the poetry of Chaucer or of Spenser into *versi sciolti*, I imagine that his bad taste in doing so would be very evident to his English readers ; and yet the different kinds of rhyme in which these poets have written, are much less fitly adapted to the subjects they have chosen, than is the Tertian Rhyme to the subject of Dante, whose form bears the same relation to the classic remains, as a Gothic cathedral has to a Grecian temple. It was probably the great difficulty of this intricate species of rhyme which deterred Mr. Cary from endeavouring to bring the great Tuscan before us, clad in the dark but embroidered garments which he wore, rather than in a scanty and inappropriate imitation of the classic robes of antiquity ; one, in fact, not possessing the ample folds and graceful flow of the ancient, nor the rich adornments of the romantic garb. And I confess that, even after I had versified some cantos of the following translation, I was, from the same consideration, about to relinquish the task I had undertaken, when I was urged by particular circumstances to proceed as I had commenced. *In doing so, I have been really surprised to find the obstacles to my attempt disappear in a great degree.*"

I have marked this last sentence for printing *in italics*, because it so remarkably corresponds with the result of my own experience—that experience having taught me the folly of being deterred by seeming difficulties in the structure of the English language from attempting even so formidable a task as the translation of Dante in corresponding metre. I feel, on the contrary, inclined (after making no inconsiderable trial) to pronounce it the most easy, as well as the most satisfactory, mode of transfusing into our own vernacular dialect the sense and spirit of the original ; and I am the more inclined to lament that my friend, Mr. Wright,* who possesses the undeniable merit of both understanding and feeling his author, did not (as he might have done almost at the outset of his great undertaking) follow my suggestion of abiding by the Terza Rima. Of this I am at least certain—that he will not deny me the credit of having endeavoured to enforce it upon him before I myself made the experiment. At present I shall merely add, that I still think an entire version of this great poem in the metre of the original, a great desideratum in English literature—that, with more years, and more abundant leisure before me, it is one which I would not have shrunk from attempting, and that Mr. Shannon, who has given abundant proof of his own qualification for this " labour of love," ought (I think) on every account to be urged to its completion in the style in which he has already commenced it—with however only one reservation—namely, of a protest which I find myself bound distinctly to enter against his doctrine of *assonance* in substitution for rhyme—a doctrine which, though he may have persuaded himself that it is founded on principle, he will, I am certain, have to regret the promulgation of (at least if he persists in the attempt to practise it) as being too violently opposed to the orthodox standard of modern usage.

Thus it is quite impossible for a poet of the present day to persuade the directors of our literary republic to admit such a word as " great" into partnership with " faith" and " saith ;" and though I have myself no objection to receive our archaïc " wold" (for " would") into terms of alliance with " bold" and " cold," or even " wooer" with " endure" and " ensure," I cannot but repudiate the endeavour to force the *plural* " zones" into an unnatural union with the *singular* " alone"—" gnash" with " harsh" and " marsh"—" together" with " other"—not to add other instances, somewhat thickly sprinkled, of the same species of licence. Rhymes, which are merely defective, can never be justified, though if very sparingly indulged, they may sometimes be excused, for the sake of the exigencies of the sense, and the natural deficiencies of our language ; but they can be tolerated only as an exception, and in instances where the hearer may safely feel assured that it was impossible to find a legitimate substitute. Mr. Shannon, I am constrained to

---

* Of Mr. Wright's version, Mr. Shannon says in a sort of postscript (and I think justly) as follows :

" Since this preface was written, Mr. Wright has published his version of the Tuscan ; and his labours have obtained a critical notice in each of the leading reviews. In the *Edinburgh* he is declared to have made a much nearer approach to excellence than Mr. Cary, as a translator. In the *Quarterly*, he is advised not to proceed further with his version. Thus it would seem that there is still room for another candidate, who may be ambitious of the high honour of representing Dante. As to my own opinion, judging only from the specimens given by the reviews, I must say that, though Mr. Wright has by no means reached the standard of excellence which I would myself endeavour to attain, he has nevertheless produced a work very creditable to his taste, and much superior to any previous translation of Dante which we possess."

add, is too frequent and unblushing a sinner against this article of the poetical code ; and I can urge the completion of his task on condition alone of his not merely carefully revising and correcting in this respect the ten cantos he has printed, but prescribing to himself more rigid exactness in what is yet to come. That he is a deep and diligent student of Dante, I think unquestionable from several parts of his present version ; and, by way of evidence, I take leave to extract the following passage from a letter he has lately addressed to me ; alluding to the famous riddle which is thus printed in the early edition of Landino,

' Pape Satan, Pape Satan Aleppe ;'

and rendered by Mr. Shannon,

' Pope Satan has the sword, Pope Satan dread.'

" You have doubtless remarked," he writes, " the way in which I give the first line of the seventh canto. The original is one of the many enigmas intended by Dante to puzzle the uninitiated ; and, Heaven knows, it has given the commentators full occasion to display their ingenious dulness. I think Landino and other early expositors certainly understood the line ; but they were afraid, of course, to interpret it truly, and therefore wrote mystifying nonsense about it. The words are, *apparently*, a specimen of the unknown language of fiends ; but I think they are *really* a sentence of intelligible French written disguisedly. Thus they will read,

' Pape Satan, Pape Satan a l'épée ;'

instead of being as we are told, a jumble of Latin, Greek, and Hebrew without sense. Plutus tells Dante that Pope Satan has the sword to terrify him ; and accordingly we find Virgil telling him immediately not to be dismayed, and rebuking the fiend. *Plutus speaks French because the then Pope was a Frenchman.*" And he proceeds to justify his tradition of " sospetto" by " dread" as strictly conformable to ancient usage.

This is, at the very least, another of the many ingenious conjectures to which this problematical line has given birth ; though I cannot for my own part but hold to the impression I first entertained, viz., that the word " Aleppe" is nothing but the first letter of the Hebrew alphabet used in the sense of " Princeps" or " Primarius," and that the true reading is,

" Pap' è Satan—Pap' è Satan, Aleppe"—

to be literally rendered,

" The Pope is Satan, the Pope is Prince Satan."

The early-printed reading " Pape" instead of " Pap' è," was probably intentional—to veil without absolutely concealing the sense.

I now dismiss Mr. Shannon and Dante ; but with a strong hope that what I have said of the volume from which the foregoing remarks are extracted, may produce the effect of drawing the attention of the critics, and (through them) that of the public, to the remaining contents of it. Notwithstanding the unfortunately selected *pseudonymy* in the title-page, the poetical merits of the book are such as justly to entitle it to a better fate than that of being condemned to the

"Vicum vendentem thus et odores."

However, not to close this short paper without returning to the subject of "German Lyrics," so far (at least) as to keep up my claim to the insertion of future contributions, I here beg to subjoin a single specimen, of an earlier date, and in a very different style from any I have yet brought forward. The original is a poem of the religious class, more common, perhaps, in the seventeenth century then in the present, and by no less distinguished an author than Antony-Ulrich, Duke of Brunswick Lunenburg, who lived from 1633 to 1714. The version, which is none of mine, I found among the contents of my portfolio; it is somewhat defective in close adherence to the peculiar rhythm of its model.

"AUFMUNTERUNG IM UNGLUCK.

"Lass dich Gott',
Du Verlassner! still' dein Sorgen;
Deine Qual und deine Noth
Ist dem Höchsten unverborgen.
Hilft er heut nicht, hilft er morgen.
Lass dich Gott'!"

ENCOURAGEMENT UNDER MISFORTUNE.

Trust in God!
Thou forlorn one, cease thy moan:
All thy pain and all thy sorrow
Are to God, the highest, known.
He leaves thee now, but helps to-morrow.
Trust in God!

Hold to God!
The blows he deals in love are given,
That thy soul's health may better fare:
So may'st thou know the fear of Heaven.
Confide in His paternal care!
Hold to God!

God is nigh,
Ev'n then when far away he seemeth.
When hope of freedom none appears,
Believe so best for thee He deemeth:
He in His time will dry thy tears.
God is nigh.

God is thine,
If all thy heart to Him thou yieldest.
Thy bitter grief to sweet shall turn,
If most on Him thy love thou buildest,
Nor darest in rage His will to spurn.
God is thine!

Teach not God.
How or when He wills to hear thee,
Still His eye is on thee bent.
Though long thy cross last, bravely bear thee!
Its weight at length shall be forespent.
Teach not God!

Lovest thou God?
Walk'st thou firm, His path pursuing?
Nor bitter cross, nor woe, nor death,
Shall aught avail thy trust undoing,
But all in blessing crown thy faith—
So lov'st thou God.

A very strong resemblance in our own language to the above and similar poems of the same age and class in Germany, is to be found in Quarles, Withers, and other English contemporaries—enough to evidence that they were nourished by the same spirit, rather than that any were imitators of the rest. It should he remembered that the religious excitement produced by the long civil wars both in England and Germany, had not yet subsided, in either country, at the time they were probably written.

The mention of so illustrious a name, among the poetical fraternity, leads us naturally to that of a young and living poet, at least equally illustrious, and bound to our nation by ties of peculiar love and reverence—one of whose pleasing ballads has found place at p. 428 of the number of this Magazine already referred to; accompanied by a version which does not do it justice. May I venture to suggest the following as somewhat nearer to the sense and spirit of the graceful original?

Come, loved one, come! The moonbeams play,
And fresh the gale breathes near thee,
And swiftly o'er the slumbering bay,
My slender bark shall steer thee.
Come, loved one, come!

Come, loved one, come! thy fears forsake—
My heart could ne'er dissemble—
Thy mother sleeps—but Love's awake.
What's here should make thee tremble?
Come, loved one, come!

German Literature. By Wolfgang Menzel. Translated from the German, with notes, by Thomas Gordon. 4 vols. Oxford, Talboys.

THE growing popularity of German literature seems to call for some comprehensive view of its principal features for the use of English readers. Detached portions of the subject have indeed been presented to them of late years by various competent hands; but, with the exception of Taylor's Historic Survey—which was both prejudiced and incomplete,—no attempt has hitherto been made towards a general summary of the whole. The translator of the work now before us appears to have considered M. Menzel's essay as likely, in some measure, to supply this deficiency; and it must be allowed that the choice was recommended by the comprehensive nature of the treatise, as well as by its lively style and moderate volume. It is moreover a work which has, for various reasons, excited no little attention in Germany; where the author is known as a man of considerable attainments and more than common ingenuity.

These, however, are not the sole requisites belonging to a task of this nature. It is perhaps hardly to be expected that all should be united in an individual writer: the industry to gather and arrange the mass of details; the quickness of capacity to apprehend the character of dissimilar productions; the judgment to select, and the feeling to admire, what is excellent in every kind: and, above all, the clearness of an impartial eye, undimmed by anger or prejudice; and an utter forgetfulness of selfish or personal tendencies. And yet without such qualification no satisfactory performance of the history of a contemporary literature can be expected.

Paradoxical as the idea may seem to be, it may nevertheless be questioned whether for such a task a foreigner completely instructed is not better fitted, in many respects, than a native. The absence in him of any party bias, and his exemption from the heats of literary strife, may more than compensate for his defects in minute and subtle perception; and the very distance from which he surveys the subject renders its larger features relatively more distinct than they appear,

to one who views it more nearly at hand. That the best native histories of literature have been written of the past, by men of retired lives, and independent of other authorship, seems to confirm this view. Such were the labours of Tiraboschi and Antonio; and yet, for general clearness of summary, and liberal criticism, we are disposed to attach a higher value to the productions of men like Ginguené, Bouterwek and Sismondi, who wrote their literary histories as foreigners.

The author of the Essay now under review (for it does not profess to be more), is far from possessing the equanimity which we have insisted upon. His peculiar temperament, and the events of his personal and literary career have made him an enthusiastic partisan; and have inured him to continual warfare. A caustic reviewer, an eager politician, and a sententious essayist, he is not the guide we should implicitly follow in a path which leads us into the midst of those with many of whom he has for the last ten years been at deadly feud. His early vexations as an exile on political grounds have left a soreness of temper, which rankles in all his reflections; and in the various literary contests which have busied him since his return to Stuttgart, in 1826, he has committed himself to opinions which cannot but stand in the way of an impartial notice of his country's literature. It was therefore to be expected that he would compose a brilliant polemic treatise, rather than a faithful history; it is at all events certain that the work now before us cannot be accepted as such. As the production of an ingenious and original mind, remarkable for activity and boldness, it will be read with pleasure—the severity with which he censures and ridicules, and the sarcastic wit which seasons his invective, will render it attractive to many whom a calmer writer would tire: but the work will rather mislead than assist the student, if indeed the colours with which Menzel has depicted his subject do not altogether deter him from seeking to approach it more nearly. The effect of the whole is feverish, abrupt, and discouraging; it is rather an angry lecture, addressed by the author to his own countrymen, than an account from which the foreign reader can derive either comfort or instruction.

This is not the only circumstance which impairs the usefulness of Menzel's treatise. His own disquisitions on the several topics under which he has classified the matter of his book,—religion—education—history—philosophy—poetry, &c.—occupy by far the largest part of the work; and, with very few exceptions, the notices of those who have written on these subjects are hardly more than an enumeration of their names, accompanied with a word or two of praise or blame; so that little can be gathered from them, by one who has no previous knowledge of the authors, beyond a notion of Menzel's own views on the several heads of this classification. Some principal names, such as Schiller, Goethe, Schelling, Tieck, &c., are treated more at length; but even of these he rather dilates on the alleged general character and tendencies, than particularizes their works. There is moreover some apparent caprice in his distribution of notice amongst the authors cited; —a few lines are all that he can spare for Richter—while half a chapter is bestowed on Tieck—and Börne occupies as many pages as he gives paragraphs to Hoffmann or Wieland. In fact, the writers who do not furnish matter for the illustration of his particular views are despatched in general with a very hasty survey, however eminent their literary deserts may have been.

The reference of everything in the compass of letters to his notions of political and social

progress, appears to warp his judgments in a manner which cannot fail to perplex the student. The defects which are lightly touched in some writers, are discovered with little justice in others, and visited with great severity. We do not object to his eloquent defence of Wieland's morality, or to his gentle mention of the levities of Thümmel and Langbein, until he surprises us by harsh denunciations of the immorality of such authors as Goethe and Schlegel; and his unsparing ridicule of the sentimentalists loses credit with the reader, when he finds the absurdities of Justinus Kerner mentioned with respect, and abundant eulogies bestowed on Pückler Muskau!

Amongst the objects of his severity may be cited the eminent names of Voss, the Schlegels, Schulze, Johann von Müller, Hegel, and Zschokke; but he has chiefly distinguished himself by bitter hostility to Goethe, whom it has been his constant labour for many years to depose from the place awarded to him in the general estimation of Germany. In this unsparing warfare, the accusation of systematic immorality —of a want of true original genius—and of almost every defect, redeemed only by beauty of form, are brought against his writings; and the man is denounced as an Epicurean, a hollow aristocrat, as the pattern of political baseness, and a designing corrupter of the health of his country's morals. Nay, he is even made responsible for the most inconceivable matters, such as the vagaries of Bettine, and the suicide of poor Charlotte Stieglitz. The very excess of these denunciations may awaken a suspicion of their injustice; it is however out of our power to examine them here, and it may suffice to say that they have found no echo in Germany, save amongst a few dissolute and worthless men. The accusation of Goethe on the ground of his aversion to political strife, has however been so often, and, as we think, so unfairly urged, that we cannot refrain from quoting his own eloquent words on this matter, uttered a few days only before he closed his long and laborious career. They are recorded by Eckermann, as follows:—

"If the poet will effect anything in politics, he must devote himself to some party—and as soon as this takes place, he is lost as a poet; he must bid farewell to the freedom of his spirit, to his unchained energy; and draw the hood of contracted prejudices and blind aversion over his eyes. The poet will love his fatherland as a man and a citizen; but the home of his poetic energies and actions is the good, the noble, and the beautiful—restricted to no particular region; these he embraces and portrays wheresoever they are found—as the eagle, hovering with a free glance from land to land, asks no question whether the prey on which it swoops may roam in Saxony or in Prussia. And what then is meant by loving your country?—what do you mean by 'patriot labours'? When a poet has toiled throughout a long life, to assail mischievous prejudices, to remove illiberal notions, to enlighten the spirit of his people, to purify their taste, and to ennoble their thoughts and feelings—what better than this could he do?—are not these patriotic exertions?— You know that I commonly take no heed of what they write concerning me; but still it comes to my ears; and I well know that for all the pains and toil of my long life, there are people who count these as nothing, because I have refused to take part in political conflicts. To please them I should have become a member of some Jacobin club, and preached assassination and bloodshed! But let us say no more on this wretched subject, lest in protesting against injustice I should myself become unjust!"

Until it shall be proved that all men, whatever their several proper gifts may be, are bound to labour in the same vocation, we must take leave to consider this vindication as conclusive.

The irregularities and defects of Menzel's book must not, however, blind us to its better qualities. We believe him to be, although passionate, thoroughly sincere, and the fire of his indignation is kindled by what he imagines, however erroneously, to be hostile to the welfare of his country. He has done good service in denouncing the profligate crew of writers styling themselves " Young Germany:" his dissection of much that is sickly, false, and affected in the writers of these and of former times, is no less wholesome than happy; and the warmth of his feelings lends uncommon beauty to the eulogies which he bestows on the few whom he delights to honour, and who, it must be said, are in general worthily chosen. His portrait of Schiller is equally true and beautiful; indeed, there are few pieces in the German language more eloquent and striking than the passage which he consecrates to the memory of that great poet and noble-hearted man. His expositions of the various parts of his subject are in general masterly : the work abounds with lively illustrations and acute remarks; and his style (a rare merit in German prose writers) is concise and pointed. In short, the work, with all its failings, must be mentioned with respect, as the production of an ingenious, sincere, and diligent man, whose very deviations from sobriety and fairness are extenuated by the evident honesty of feeling whose warmth has led him astray. But we must repeat, that he is the last author to be selected as a guide by those who are not already well versed in German literature.

Mr. Gordon's translation appears to be on the whole respectably performed, although in places the meaning of the author is not clearly rendered; and not a few instances of haste or carelessness may be found, especially in the two concluding volumes. The notes which he has appended to the text, chiefly describing the authors cited, would have been a useful addition, but for the gross inaccuracy of the printer, who has made such havoc, with dates especially, that no reliance can be placed on them. There is hardly a foreign word or quotation which is not wrong printed; and the execution, as far as correctness is concerned, is altogether discreditable to the press in an university town.

27. ATHENAEUM, 14 (1841), 304-305. M/H No. 3659.

Household Treasury of the Poetry of the German People—[Poetischer Hausschatz des Deutschen Volkes]. Edited by Dr. O. L. B. Wolff. 8vo. London, C. & H. Senior; Leipzig, Wigand.

This is a very complete and judicious compilation; the most comprehensive, indeed, which, as far as we know, has hitherto appeared. The name of the editor (to whom the *Athenæum* was indebted for the Essay on German Literature, published in 1835) was of itself a guarantee for the taste and discretion with which the new task would be performed; and we have not been disappointed on examining his work: which, as containing sufficient and well chosen specimens of all the several kinds of German poetry, from its infancy until the present day, will be especially valuable to the English student, and supply a want which he must have often experienced. The compass of the poetical literature of Germany is so wide, that a judicious selection of this sort cannot but greatly assist the reader on his first entrance into the field: many of the sources from which the materials for the work before us have been drawn, are in this country all but inaccessible; while, as respects the poetry of an early period, it is sufficiently exhibited for general purposes, in extracts which it would cost the student much labour to gather for himself. The specimens of a later time are copious enough to direct the reader in his further pursuit of the styles and compositions which may most attract his liking: and the editor has prefixed to the several heads of his selection, brief but sensible prefaces, which will be read with advantage. A list of the authors cited in the volume, with the dates of their appearance, and an index of the contents, complete the work; a closely printed volume of 1163 pages: a very *multum in parvo*, creditable alike to the industry of the editor, and to the care and enterprise of the publishers. We have no hesitation in recommending this 'Treasury' to all who have betaken themselves to the study of German literature.

The daily increasing number of this class, not in England only, but wherever letters are held in esteem, may suggest matter for reflection. It seems but yesterday that the very name of the language was a signal for ridicule and peremptory disbelief of the most modest assertion, that any good thing could be found therein. The student who had ventured to inquire for himself if these confident scoffs were just, and who had seen reason to think otherwise, was made aware of the necessity of keeping his own counsel, if he wished to avoid a share of the prevalent contempt. It was popular and fashionable to decide that German books and German writers were all misty, diseased, and unprofitable; and those who knew least were generally the loudest in their disapprobation. This was not the injustice or ignorance of a few,—it appeared in the highest places of our literature; and the popular prejudice is not to be wondered at, when they who professed to be our guides and instructors were the foremost in condemning what they rarely had troubled themselves to understand. It was difficult for those who had gathered knowledge and delight from this literature, to repress the anger which the repetition of such unfair and presumptuous censures was apt to provoke. But one thing was nevertheless clear. Whatever has in itself a principle of genuine truth and life, cannot be extinguished by any coxcombry of criticism, nor slain by sentences, nor drummed out of the universe at the will of any school or guild of literary craftsmen whatsoever. This vitality they believed they had found in the poets and thinkers of Germany; and therefore they were content to wait and observe their fate. It now appears to have decided itself in a manner sufficiently positive, although doubtless to the dissatisfaction of those (many of whom are still extant) who would fain have persuaded others to shut their eyes and ears, as they had themselves most effectually done. Without exceeding the limits of sober assertion (for we do not wish to urge the reaction which is apt to be produced by all undue violence), it may be affirmed that Germany is now allowed by the most cultivated minds of Europe, to be the possessor of a literature singularly rich, various, and original: especially abundant in the utterances of poetry and thought, and in its graver productions distinguished by the combination of studious diligence with profound and ingenious speculation. Her poets and philosophers are now familiar to all who pretend to liberal education; and in one eminent department (historical composition) her authors, daily growing in numbers and importance, have occupied a position which no others, of our day at least, can venture to approach. Truly this is an occasion on which we may, with peculiar emphasis, repeat the old exclamation, "*magna est veritas, et prævalebit.*" Some such observations, although not immediately connected with the work before us, could hardly fail to occur, when contrasting the opinions of a time we can well remember, with those which now afford encouragement to the publication in England of a collection of mere German poetry: which ten years since, had our literary judges wielded secular as well as spiritual powers, might have run the risk of condemnation to be burnt *in terrorem* by the common hangman.

In one sense, the literature of Germany may be called more modern than any other that is now distinguished in Europe. The authors by whom it has been rendered celebrated have appeared in rapid succession almost within the limits of the present era; and none of them before the latter half of the eighteenth century. But it is far from being true, that all who belonged to an earlier period were undeserving of notice. A succession of learned and laborious writers has never been wanting since the close of the Thirty Years War: and in High German poetry the chain may be carried back at least to the time of the Reformation. The popular strains in various other dialects, of great antiquity, the several *Heldengedichte*, or heroic poems of the Middle Ages, and the lays of the Minnesingers, are perhaps hardly to be numbered amongst the component parts of High German literature in its modern description: although they form a body of poetical materials which gave abundant promise of the structure to be raised in a subsequent age. But from the time of Luther downwards we have a continual series of poetical compositions which belong to the German as it is now spoken; exhibiting a degree of cultivation by no means contemptible, and deserving of far more attention than is commonly given to them. They have been eclipsed by the brilliancy of a later day;—bu. ... ... still sufficient to rescue the nation from the charge of lethargy and barrenness in the years which preceded that remarkable epoch. Of this the specimens contained in the Anthology now under review give abundant proof: and they who have imagined that Ramler and Klopstock were the first writers of readable German poetry, will discover, with some surprise, in the lyrics of Tauler, Opitz, and Flemming, in the sixteenth and seventeenth centuries, a frequent happiness of thought and fluency of versification, which will still reward the labour of perusal, and bespeak no scanty measure of genius. The noble hymns of Luther it is needless to mention; since many of them have fixed themselves in the hearts and on the lips of the people, and will there remain as long as the language itself. To revert to a still earlier period, there may be found amidst the manifold rubbish of the worthy Hans Sachs a plentiful store of poetical matter, although in a homely and rugged form. His endless diffuseness has deterred many from an examination, which would place him in no disadvantageous relation with most of his contemporaries either in England or France.

The works of Opitz and Andreas Gryphius—both of whom flourished in the first half of the seventeenth century—are deserving of respect, and are the first specimens of an advance towards still higher regions of poetry. They consist of odes, lyrics, and dramatic compositions,—of which the tragedy by Gryphius on the fate of our Charles the First, is deservedly distinguished as falling little short of high excellence. There are passages and scenes in this play alike vigorous in dialogue, and full of genuine tragical pathos; and nothing superior to it appeared until the days of Lessing. The interval between 1650 and 1750 is the least abundant in genuine poetry, although far from being destitute of numerous productions; a certain feebleness and affectation, derived from attempting to copy foreign, and chiefly French models, renders them languid and tedious, in comparison with the ruder and more genial strains of the previous century. Among the most considerable of these writers may be enumerated Gottsched, Conrad Schmid, Hoffmanswaldau, Lohenstein, and Rabener, with the elder Kleist, and Gellert, many of whose productions, as well as those of Gleim and Ramler, fall within the period in question. The last-mentioned writers, however, had already made rapid strides in advance of their predecessors, and prepared the field for the greater labours of those eminent men who began to appear towards its close.

With Lessing and Klopstock the classical age of German poetry was born; and its rapid development by a host of succeeding names, proceeding from Voss, Bürger, Götz, and Hölty, followed by Wieland, Jacobi, and Herder, to Goethe and Schiller, the Schlegels, Tieck, and many other bright but lesser stars that surrounded and have succeeded these signal-lights of their nation, it is hardly requisite to dwell upon, as this portion of its history is the most generally known. In the collection before us, besides the works of these chief poets, will be found many by contemporary authors, less known in England, who deserve more than a passing notice. Among these we may name Schmidt von Lübeck, Ernst Schulze, Rückert, Hölderlin, and Uhland; the last a true descendant of the Minnesingers of his native Swabia, and one of the sweetest lyrical poets that Germany has ever produced. To particularize the lesser but still respectable names would be a hopeless attempt; the list is interminable: and an inspection of the index to this "Treasury," followed by the most cursory glance at the various poems which it contains, will give the reader a respectful notion of the abundance with which poetry of no vulgar kind has flowed from the Teutonic Parnassus. And now that the older languages of Europe have in some degree lost their freshness, it may not be an unprofitable task to turn to sources which are less familiar, with the assurance that in these a new and genuine spring of enjoyment may be tasted. The work which we have thus briefly reviewed will afford considerable assistance in the pursuit, and may be commended therefore, with our best wishes, to all who desire a nearer approach to the fountains of German Poetry.

Fragments from German Prose Writers. Translated by Sarah Austin. Illustrated with Notes. Murray.

WITHOUT plan or arrangement—a mere collection of fragments, as its title imports—this is, nevertheless, a delightful volume. The readers of the *New Monthly Magazine*, we know not how many years ago, will not fail to remember a series of extracts from German writers which appeared in successive numbers of that publication, commanding attention by their own intrinsic beauty, and the perfect translation which they displayed, and leaving only the regret that they should be so few and fragmen-tary. These specimens greatly extended, but still without a view to system or selection—the results of a wider but yet desultory reading—compose this volume, which Mrs. Austin has rightly thought might gratify the increasing curiosity evinced by the English public respecting German literature—and contribute, by their very range and miscellaneous character, to correct the extravagant notions which are current in this country, as to its general form and tendency. " In some places," says Mrs. Austin, " it has been represented as all composed of cloudy philosophy, dull pedantry, or romantic horrors ; in others, as deformed, throughout, by whining sentimentality, impurity, or irreligion. That, in the multitudinous offspring of the German Press, *some* of each of these misshapen productions are to be found, we shall be little inclined to doubt, if we consider the disgusting shape assumed by portions of our own literature ; but that a sound-hearted and intelligent country gives birth to nothing else, is as little consistent with probability as it is with truth." Here then, in this agreeable volume, and without any of the characters or formalities of essay-writing, a notion is conveyed to the English reader of the prevailing tendencies, diffusive range, and rich and picturesque forms of the literary genius of modern Germany, more lively than could readily be communicated by any labour of professed teaching. The choice of the passages which compose it, the author says, " has been determined by considerations as various as their character and their subjects. In some, it was the value of the matter, in others, the beauty of the form that struck me ; in some, the vigorous unaffected good sense—in others, the fantastic or mystical charm. Some recalled familiar trains of thought, which meet one in a foreign literature like old friends in a far country ; others suggested ideas altogether new and strange. My readers must, therefore, apply measures as different as those which I have used, and by no means ascribe to me the intention of recommending every opinion to their unqualified assent, or every passage to their unqualified admiration."

The two characteristics of German literature, which Mrs. Austin considers as the most predominant and striking, are earnestness and suggestiveness. The lighter literary moods in which their French neighbours excel, sit ungracefully upon the writers of Germany ; but passion that awakens passion, and thought that suggests thoughts, enrich and ennoble their pages. The literature of Germany is remarkable as much for its *foresight* as its *farsightedness*—for a sort of prophetic view of yet undeveloped truths—glimpses into strange and original fields of speculation which it has not yet had time to explore — utterances that seem like oracles, pregnant with ultimate meanings, but which have, in their tentative and imperfect expression, the vagueness and dimness of oracles. Leaving the ancient worn-out tracks in which European letters have travelled so long, it points onward to new intellectual combinations ; and crossing the Line by which the old academical adventurers have hitherto been circumscribed, sees new constellations come up the heaven of thought, whose motions have yet to be examined and ascertained, and the philosophy of whose relations it will be the work of its young and vigorous energies to explore. Besides the passages of lengthened beauty, of various kinds, in which these specimens abound, they contain examples of single sentences which involve, as the acorn contains the oak, a world of thought—point the spirit, like intellectual guide-posts, up long dim avenues, into the remote retreats of wisdom. We cannot afford, here, to illustrate our meaning by such striking examples as would tempt us farther into the pleasant paths of speculative philosophy, but will extract a few of those thoughtful or epigrammatic passages, which will help to explain what we mean, when, with Mrs. Austin, we ascribe the qualities of earnestness and suggestiveness to the modern literature of Germany :—

" The last, best fruit which comes to late perfection, even in the kindliest soul, is tenderness towards the hard, forbearance toward the unforbearing, warmth of heart toward the cold, philanthropy toward the misanthropic."—*Jean Paul Richter.*

" It is only necessary to grow old to become more indulgent. I see no fault committed that I have not committed myself."—*Goethe.*

" The critic of art ought to keep in view not only the capabilities, but the proper objects of art. Not all that art can accomplish ought she to attempt. It is from this cause alone, and because we have lost sight of these principles, that art, among us, is become more extensive and difficult, less effective and perfect."—*Lessing.*

" We are near waking, when we dream that we dream."—*Novalis.*

" If the world is to be held together by lies, the old, which are already current, are just as good as the new."—*Lessing.*

" Salt is a very good condiment, but very bad food. Never do I feel more refreshed by serious passages than when they occur amidst comic ones ; as the green spots amid the rocks and glaciers of Switzerland soothe the eye amid the glare and glitter of snow and ice. Hence it is that the humour of the English, which is engrafted on the stem of lofty seriousness, has grown so luxuriantly and overtopped that of all other nations. A satire on everything is a satire on nothing ; it is mere absurdity. All contempt, all disrespect, implies something respected, as a standard to which it is referred, just as every valley implies a hill. The *persiflage* of the French and of fashionable worldlings, which turns into ridicule the exceptions, and yet abjures the rules, is like Trinculo's government—its latter end forgets its beginning. Can there be a more mortal, poisonous consumption and asphyxy of the mind than this decline and extinction of all reverence ?"—*Jean Paul.*

" Among literary men, the gift of bearing to be contradicted is, generally speaking, possessed only by the dead. I will not go so far as to assert that, for the sake of possessing it, we ought to wish ourselves dead, for that is a price at which perhaps even higher perfections would be too dearly purchased. I will only say that it would be well if living authors would learn to be externally somewhat dead. The time will come when they must leave behind them a posterity who will sever everything accidental from their reputation, and will be withheld by no reverence from laughing at their faults. Why can they not learn to endure by anticipation this posterity, which every now and then reveals itself, heedless whether they think it envious or unmannerly ?"—*Lessing.*

" One solitary philosopher may be great, virtuous, and happy in the depth of poverty, but not a whole nation."—*Isaak Iselin.*

" Be and continue poor, young man, while others around you grow rich by fraud and disloyalty ; be without place or power, while others beg their way upward ; bear the pain of disappointed hopes, while others gain the accomplishment of theirs by flattery ; forego the gracious pressure of the hand, for which others cringe and crawl. Wrap yourself in your own virtue, and seek a friend, and your daily bread. If you have, in such a course, grown gray with unblenched honour, bless God, and die."—*Heinzelmann.*

" Of all thieves, fools are the worst ; they rob you of time and temper."—*Goethe.*

" This Ranz des Vaches at once awaked his blooming childhood, and she arose out of the morning dew and out of her bower of rosebuds and slumbering flowers, and stepped before him in heavenly beauty, and smiled innocently and with her thousand hopes upon him, and said, ' Look at me—how beautiful I am ! We used to play together. I formerly gave thee many things—great riches, gay meadows, and bright gold, and a fair long paradise behind the mountains : but now thou hast nothing of all this left—and how pale thou art ? Oh play with me again!" Before which of us has not childhood been a thousand times called up by music? and to which of us has she not spoken, and asked—'Are the rosebuds which I gave thee *not yet* blown?' Alas! blown indeed they are—but they were pale, white roses."—*Jean Paul.*

"Modern poets put a great deal of water in their ink."—*Goethe.*

"Notes to a poem are like anatomical lectures on a savoury joint."—*A. W. v. Schlegel.*

"He who can take advice is sometimes superior to him who can give it."—*Von Knebel.*

"Character is a perfectly educated will."—*Novalis.*

"Formerly it was the fashion to preach the natural, now it is the ideal. People, too, often forget that these things are profoundly compatible; that in a beautiful work of imagination the natural should be ideal, and the ideal natural."—*A. W. v. Schelegel.*

"Men find it more easy to flatter than to praise." —*Jean Paul.*

"The illusion of a past golden age is one of the greatest hindrances to the approach of the golden age that should come. If the golden age is past it was not genuine. Gold cannot rust nor decay: it comes out of all admixtures and all decompositions pure and indestructible. If the golden age will not endure it had better never arise, for it can produce nothing but elegies on its loss."—*A. W. v. Schelegel.*

"There are ideal trains of events which run parallel with the real ones. Seldom do they coincide. Men and accidents commonly modify every ideal event or train of events, so that it appears imperfect, and its consequences are equally imperfect. Thus it was with the Reformation; instead of Protestantism arose Lutheranism."—*Novalis.*

"There are so many tender and holy emotions flying about in our inward world, which, like angels, can never assume the body of an outward act,—so many rich and lovely flowers spring up which bear no seed—that it is a happiness poetry was invented, which receives into its limbus all these incorporeal spirits and the perfume of all these flowers."—*Jean Paul.*

"I hate all people who want to found sects. It is not error, but sectarian error—nay, and even sectarian truth—which causes the unhappiness of mankind."—*Lessing.*

"Love one human being purely and warmly, and you will love all. The heart in this heaven, like the wandering sun, sees nothing, from the dew-drop to the ocean, but a mirror which it warms and fills."—*Jean Paul.*

"There are in certain heads a kind of established errors, against which reason has no weapons. There are more of these mere assertions current than one would believe. Men are very fond of proving their steadfast adherence to nonsense."—*Von Knebel.*

"I would fain know what music is; I seek it as man seeks eternal wisdom. Yesterday evening I walked late in the moonlight in the beautiful avenue of lime-trees on the banks of the Rhine, and I heard a tapping noise and soft singing. At the door of a cottage, under the blossoming lime-tree, sat a mother with her twin babes; the one lay at her breast, the other in a cradle, which she rocked with her foot, keeping time to her singing. In the very germ then, when the first trace of life scarce begins to stir, music is the nurse of the soul: it murmurs in the ear, and the child sleeps; the tones are the companions of his dreams,—they are the world in which he lives. He has nothing; the babe, although cradled in his mother's arms, is alone in the spirit; but tones find entrance into this half-conscious soul, and nourish it as the earth nourishes the life of plants."—*Bettina.*

Mrs. Austin is so well known to the public as a translator from the German, that we need not remark here upon her power in that respect, which seems to transfer the original thought bodily and spiritually—in all its integrity of form and essence—into our literature. But the volume has a yet more valuable feature in an appendix, containing biographical details relating to the authors from whom the specimens are taken, with short original criticisms on their style and works. The former of these, slight as they are, are so useful and satisfactory, and the latter executed with so much taste, judgment, and good faith, as to make us wish that Mrs. Austin

would devote her intimate acquaintance with, and fine apprehension of, the spirituality of the German writers to the production of some work less desultory and more important than the present. Two short passages from her notes—on Goethe and Tieck, respectively,—will give a notion of her manner of treating this part of her subject:—

"There are a sort of people in this country, who continue to speak, and even write, about Goethe and Kotzebue, which to a German ear sounds very much as Shakspeare and Colman would to ours. Others talk of Werther, that fruitful subject of ridicule, as if Goethe had written nothing else. Others, again, think of him only as the author of 'Faust'—that untranslateable poem which every Englishman translates. But in order to form any idea of Goethe's merits, it is necessary to read his criticisms on literature and art, and his remarks on men and events. * * This is no place for entering into the question of Goethe's merits generally. Some of his works are open to serious objections, and though they do not want able and conscientious defenders, it is a discussion in which I have no desire to engage. My own impression is, that there are none from which a mature and disciplined mind may not draw lessons of wisdom of a very high order; but I am aware that the question is not answered so,—nor do I mean it as an answer. * * I shall have to speak of the difficulties of translating Jean Paul. They are great, and I think obvious; for they arise from the uncouthness, irregularity and oddness of his style (sometimes, I ought to add, from its powerful eloquence)—the chaotic profusion and confusion of images and the deep-dyed local colour—to borrow a French phrase. But in Goethe's style it is not quaintness or singularity that reduces his translator to despair; it is its perfection: one sees that every change of form must be for the worse. He was, I think, the most consummate master of *form* the world has seen since the days of Virgil and Catullus; and how difficult is it to reproduce form! The perfectly apposite words, which hang together like a string of pearls; the ease, the euphony; the adaptation of the style to each of the innumerable subjects he wrote on—these are merits which elude the hand of the most scrupulous or the most successful translator."

Again,—

"Tieck's stories appear to me so enchanting, that their small success in England is a riddle I cannot explain upon any hypothesis flattering to the taste of the country. The 'Pictures' and 'The Betrothing' were translated and published in one volume by the Rev. Connop Thirlwall, the present Bishop of St. David's. 'The Old Man of the Mountain,' 'The Love Charm,' and 'Pietro of Albano,' in another, by the Rev. Julius Hare, now Archdeacon of Sussex. Several, if not all, of the tales in the 'Phantasus' are to be found in Mr. Carlyle's 'German Romances.' Yet in spite of these efforts of the most accomplished translators to make Tieck known in England, his popularity is very far from approaching to his merits. These are altogether peculiar. The fantastic grace, the mysterious charm, of his 'Märchen' are unrivalled. They seem written not only about, but by fairies, and 'creatures of the element.' He manages 'to combine a sort of infantine simplicity with the gorgeousness of eastern imagery, or the dimness of gothic superstition. They have the engaging naïveté and the daring invention of the old stories that lived in the hearts and on the lips of the people. Higher praise than this it is not in the power of words to express; though the unfortunate children of these days are taught to consider them as beneath their notice. I know few writers who more powerfully stir the fancy than Tieck. In this respect he reminds one of Chaucer. His descriptions of nature, like those of our great poet, 'breathe a spring freshness.' All that makes up the charm of a wood, for instance, —its verdure, coolness, fragrance, and dreamy music, seem brought before our very senses by an art which it is extremely difficult to define. The musical element in nature is, indeed, the one which seems to predominate in his soul; it flows, like the murmuring of water, through all his works. As Goethe's genius manifested itself pre-eminently in the plastic, so does Tieck's in the musical: his words bring sounds to the ear, as Goethe's do form to the eye."

In dealing with the intellectualities of the German school, and its female professors particularly, Mrs. Austin takes more than one occasion to allude, in terms of indignant satire or earnest remonstrance, to the frivolous character and pursuits, in the upper ranks of society, of that sex for whom her womanly sympathies are naturally concerned, and the misapprehension of its mission, by the other, which is in a great degree their cause. Such appeals as the following, from one of the sex most deeply concerned, will not be without their effect, we should hope, on both:—

"The influence of women on society, however, will never be worth much as long as the reign of the sneerers, whose express business (mission, to use a fashionable word) it is to crush aspirations and to keep society at a dead-level, lasts. Women of the leisure classes, unfortunately for them, come within the department of aesthetics rather than of ethics. They are objects of taste. This evil is inseparable from their nature and destiny. But it might be extremely mitigated if the taste by which they are tried were elevated, refined, and subjected to reason. At present it operates as a check on all the higher qualities of the mind. The poor bird must not spread its wings, for fear the free winds and the fertilizing rains of heaven should ruffle its pretty plumage. Whenever women are permitted to think justly and to feel truly; whenever they are taught to consider that, whatever their station or their gifts, they are bound to pay in, each her own particular contribution to the great fund of human improvement and human happiness; whenever they cease to regard 'the Great Whole as a nursery or a ball-room,' then, and not till then, they will become the nurses of great thoughts and noble actions in men—they will *really* refine and elevate, and harmonize society. Then too the world will hear no more of the 'emancipation of women,' or of preposterous schemes for bringing them into a sort of competition with men—God knows at what disadvantage! The completeness of the human being rests upon that 'most unlike resemblance' which Jeremy Taylor speaks of. Hitherto men have delighted to cultivate the 'unlike' qualities, to the almost entire exclusion of the resembling. Now, by one of those reactions which are in the common course of human affairs, there are indications of a desire to obliterate the unlikeness, and to try to force an unnatural resemblance. Whenever the equipoise is found, the great problem of social life will, I think, be solved. But that can only be effected by the consent of reason; and not by the conflict of love of power with vanity, of a determination to maintain established rights with a passionate sense of supposed wrongs; and, in short, by the conflict of those who have, with those who want to have, power, which is now stirring society in all its deepest depths."

But, far more influential than her language of remonstrance, must be the example of such women as Mrs. Austin: they inevitably "leaven the whole lump" of the society to which they, individually, belong: and the increasing number of such women honouring their sex by the display of mental cultivation, finding dignity in its duties, while they know and assert their intellectual worth, is amongst the hopeful signs of the times.

29. BLACKWOOD'S MAGAZINE, 50 (1841), 143-160. M/H No. 3676. By J. S. Blackie.

TRAITS AND TENDENCIES OF GERMAN LITERATURE.

LITERARY criticism, when plied regularly as a business, and allowed to become a habit, is a very barren and also a very dangerous affair. For as we do not live to anatomize our bodies, or eat to understand the chemistry of chyle, so we do not read books or look at pictures for the purpose of criticizing, but for the purpose of enjoying them. A sensible man, indeed, may—must make his remark on what he sees and feels ; but he will do so accidentally as it were, and without pretence, not formally and in the style of a separate business. It is not every man, moreover, who is entitled even to drop casual remarks on what he sees ; we must first serve a long apprenticeship of seeing and comparing before our speaking can serve any purpose but to publish our own folly. " Judge not, that ye be not judged." The spirit of this grand precept applies to intellectual almost as much as to moral judgments. Young minds beginning with criticism, generally ripen into conceit, and end in ignorance; as the most that criticism can achieve, even with those whom it does not utterly pervert, is to give a sort of dialectical nimbleness to the mere understanding, while it leaves the general intellectual character destitute of all real basis, and barren of all vital grandeur. A clever critic takes up an idea like a sword, and fences with it to the admiration of many ; a great man enters into every idea as it were into a temple, and worships ; and, like all true worshippers, worships oftentimes best when he worships in secret and in silence. With small ideas a clever critic may succeed in playing off a fine game of words to inferior men ; but when he attempts to lay hold of large thoughts, he is like a dog snapping at the air. In vain, indeed, do we apply criticism of any kind to the highest creations. God gave us these like a sea to swim in ; and when we swim not in them we are intellectually dead, and have only a name to live, how learnedly soever we may talk. Literature in itself, apart from life and nature, of which it is the mere reflection, is a thing altogether unintelligible ; and a literature of literature, a systematic science of criticism, a formal architecture of the rules of the beautiful, attempted to be raised up by the mere understanding out of written books, will at best represent a botanist's *hortus siccus*, which a learned eye may microscopize to all eternity, and never be able to gain the simple conception of a green field. All attempts to explain literature out of literature alone, will never lift a man above the perfection of a delicate fingering : a mere critical, a mere literary man, we may say, is merely—a pedant. No man ever got from a book the key to understand a book. Biblical criticism has saved few souls, and literary criticism has made few poets. The most that the one can do is to clip the noisy wings of a rambling religiosity ; the most that the other can do is to prevent sounding sumphs from deceiving themselves and the public into the conceit, that they are sage singers ; and now and then, also, to give a friendly hint to a real artist, that he do not look so strenuously upward as to forget the stone at his feet, on which he is about to stumble. Such is the humble office of criticism.

It is one of the most ominous and least healthy symptoms of modern German literature, (for we exclude the Niebelungen and the Minnesinger as belonging to a practically isolated world,) that as it ushered itself into existence some eighty years ago with Lessing's lancet, so now it seems hewing itself to death with Menzel's hatchet ;—not that either Lessing or Menzel are personally to blame in the matter ; they were both of them made for better things, and have, in fact, achieved better things than mere criticism ; but their literary battles have been forced upon them, like Napoleon's wars, by a peculiar train of circumstances ; only we must say, that the circumstances which forced such bloody work were necessarily bad. In Lessing's case the cause of the evil is manifest. Germany had lain bleeding and exhausted, the victim of her own dissensions, since the unsatisfactory peace of Westphalia. She had no native strength to do any thing, and, of course, fell an easy victim, intellectually as well as physically, to the dazzling superiority of Louis XIV.: in this palsied and enfeebled condition Lessing found her, looking, nevertheless, very dignified—a starched caricature of French courtliness—utterly insensible to her own native worth, utterly false to her own native character. There was no remedy left but the surgeon's ; " *mittatur sanguis pleno rivo*,"—out with the old corrupt blood, that there may be room for the new. Lessing was forced to waste a great part of his vigour in cutting down gigantic dolls, in unrobing lay-figures, solemnly frilled and furbelowed, to look like breathing men. He protested the first in Europe, and with true old Teutonic independence, against the French dynasty of Voltaire ; in that man he annihilated all clever shallowness : in numberless adversaries at home, he caused pretenceful pedantry, if not to blush with shame, (for of this it is seldom capable,) at least to roar with ineffective rage. Menzel, again, in these latter days, had a nobler, but, in some respects, not a less dangerous enemy to contend with. He found the poetry of petty princedom, the true German ideal of the eighteenth century, incarnated in Goethe ; and two-thirds of the German people in the nineteenth century blindly worshipping t is incarnation. As a genuine son of this new century—as a man in wh m the grand national inspiration of 1813 had found a literary representative Menzel was impelled to a *debu* in the shape of a rude, slashing anti-Goethian criticism, more beneficial to the public mind of his nation, than favourable to the healthy development of his own intellect, or calculated to impress strangers with large ideas of what was to be expected from the young German genius of the present age. He has, however, like Lessing, laboured manfully for more durable laurels than those which a polemical criticism, however noisy and however clever, can earn. In his " History of the Germans," we delight to recognise a national work, in spirit and in execution second to none, perhaps, of which any people can boast.

There is one good thing which characterizes not only Menzel's criticism and leanings, but Frederick Schlegel's, Herder's, and indeed German criticism generally. It is essentially a searching criticism : a criticism of men, not of books ; of the spirit, not of the letter ; of the inward soul, not of the outward lines ; of great general tendencies rather than of particular artistical results. One may indeed become vague in this region ; and, what is worse, distort things fearfully if one idea happens to master the mind, as the idea of the middle ages mastered Frederick Schlegel, and the idea of Germanism generally, as opposed to petty princedom, masters Menzel ; but the criticism of tendencies when carried out by men who are something more than mere praters, always ensures a certain comprehensiveness in the spirit, and a certain philosophy in the tone of enquiry, which we shall seek for vainly in the works of those writers who are fluent to discourse of the creations of art, as isolated products apart from the informing genius of the producer. One may make a cabinet of shells and stones, but not easily construct a cosmogony, without a God. And, as for the one-idea men, your Schlegels, Owens, Urquharts, *et hoc genus omne*, political as well as literary, they are dangerous only to a few fools ; for the many, led by the healthy instincts of nature, disregard them utterly ; while a select few, whom the world call philosophers, find, that by allowing the extremes of all nonsense to work quietly together, by a sort of wise chemistry of the brain sense is invariably the result. The fact of the matter is, that the German critics are, of all species of that ill-favoured genus, the least to be suspected, because they criticise, for the most part, with the heart as much as with the head, by a grand speculative intuition more than by a precise hair-splitting understanding, with a glowing imaginative sympathy as much as with that nice, fastidious, priggish thing which we used to write essays on, called TASTE.

(1.) Die Deutsche Litteratur, von WOLFGANG MENZEL. Stuttgart, 1836. The same, English, by GORDON. Talboys, 1840.

(2.) Æsthetische Feldzüge, von LUDWIG WIENBARG. Hamburgh, 1834.

(3.) Deutschland's Jungste Litteratur und Cultur Epoche, Characteristiken, von HERMANN MARGGRAFF. Leipzig, 1840.

Another thing that deserves to be noticed in respect of German criticism is this, that their "æsthetical" discussions are a sort of parliamentary debates which they indulge in, *de omnibus rebus et quibusdam aliis*, to compensate for newspapers and a house of commons, which Prince Metternich and the King of Prussia, putting a politic interpretation upon the 13th and 18th articles of the act of Confederation, are agreed that they are not entitled to. We are not, therefore, to be surprised if, in books of German criticism, instead of the standard topics in which Blair and Kames delight, a strange jumble entertains us. Aristocracy and democracy, feudalism and citizenship, as variously handled from Montesquieu to Tocqueville, the Archbishop of Cologne, and the Archbishop of Posen, old Lutherans in Liegnitz, and new Pietists in Dresden, the King of Bavaria's architectural mania, and the Elector of Hessia's civil list, the King of Hanover's Prusso-mania, and the European Russophobia, the emancipation of the Jews and the emancipation of women—and tossed through these sublime themes a battledoor and shuttlecock game of "genial" personalities touching Henry Heine, Ludwig Börne, Ludwig Wienbarg, Karl Gutzkow, Wolfgang Menzel, and all the other scribbling notabilities of the hour—all this belongs to the wide province of *Deutsche critik*—and, however crude the conglomerate may appear, it is certainly more edifying to hear plain Herr Herrmann Marggraff philosophizing on the social condition of women, than Herr Augustus Wilhelm *von* Schlegel criticising a bad rhyme in Schiller.

There is one unfortunate accident, however, of these recent German writers on German literature; their discussions are so completely what we have termed them, a substitute for native newspapers and parliamentary debates, and partake so largely of the polemical, local, and ephemeral character of such productions, that it is not easy for strangers to understand the position from which they are written, or the references and allusions with which they are replete. One must have lived long not merely in the literary, but also, and mainly, in the political element of German life, in order to understand Menzel, and to be able on so many necessary occasions to temper wisely his judgments when they are violent, and to correct them when they are distorted. So with Gutzkow, Wienbarg, Marggraff, &c., a thousand personal literary feuds, as well as complicated political relations interfere between the English reader and the true state of the case. We have thought it better, therefore, in attempting a rapid outline of the main traits and tendencies of German literature, to shake ourselves free from our recent German guides altogether, and endeavour, from our own English position, to give an independent survey of so disturbed a region. The attempt on our part, we are aware, is not without rashness; but the daily increasing number of German students, many of whom know neither what nor wherefore they are studying, and the facility which our periodical press affords of propagating partial and imperfect views of so important a subject, have induced us to attempt giving the enquiring student a sort of birds'-eye view of this province, which may be of use till the literary world is favoured with something more satisfactory. We scarcely think that we are attempting a work of supererogation; for of the two writers who have done most to enlighten the English mind on this subject, Thomas Carlyle is at once too scattered in his form to be within the reach of the many, and too much enveloped in the atmosphere of Germany to be capable of exhibiting it impartially, or even intelligibly, (in some respects,) to the English intellect; while Professor Wolff's admirable essay in the *Athenæum* is still the work of a German, who cannot be supposed perfectly to understand the necessities, or to appreciate the sympathies of an Englishman in reference to so complicated a matter.

Of the four grand influences which affect a literature—race, geography, church and state, we shall proceed from the last, because, in the present case, it is the most potent, and the most pregnant in contrasts and characteristics.

"Of all things in the world," said oracular old Goethe, "the most uncongenial to art are politics and theology: such characters as Plato, Luther, and Coriolanus, make me shrink back with a mystical repugnance." O the arch old German! Who said that he was a Greek? Æschylus wrote *The Persians;* but he also fought at Salamis, and was a practical politician and patriot of the best kind. Not so Goethe, the German, or rather the Weimarian, for he knew and acknowledged no Germany; and his patriotism consisted in preaching Johann von Müller's gospel, that Napoleon was a δαιμων, not to be conquered by mortal men, and in making profound obeisances, and looking sublimely submissive before every titled baronial or ducal *Von* in the Holy Roman Empire; while Beethoven, with most un-German impudence, crushing his hat on his head, buttoning his coat, and joining his hands behind his back, marched up at Töplitz right on to the face of Kaiser Franz, and all the starred dignitaries of Vienna. The state in Germany is supreme, and the reverence of the state in the minds of men supreme, accordingly; so Goethe, when he expressed his horror of Luther and Coriolanus, however ridiculous the conjunction may appear to us, merely expressed the arch loyalty and religious submissiveness of his German nature. There is nothing goes deeper into German character, and into German literature, than this. Statesmanship in Germany is a science practised exclusively by men thereto systematically trained, as lawyers with us are trained to the practice of the law; and a regular German, like Goethe, will no more think of intermeddling with politics, than a sensible man in this country would dream of writing out the title-deeds to his own estate. The working of this on German literature is most manifold, and most penetrating; for however we may refuse to have any thing to do with politics, politics will unquestionably have to do with us. Church and State contain all men, and bind them down with a strong grateful necessity, as space and time contain and limit the universe. How then do the absolute governments, the exclusive court, and aristocratic influences of Germany, mould and modify the national mind, and with it the national literature? First, manifestly by exclusion from a pre-occupied sphere. Politics, and whatsoever smacks of them, being reserved for the special practical science of the statesman, is necessarily excluded from that common floating capital of ideas which we call literature. Nothing, accordingly, will be found better deserving of study, than the German law-books—the Aus-trian and Prussian particularly—nothing more trifling and inane than a German newspaper. No man who habitually reads and digests the contents of an English newspaper, can be called an uneducated man. The daily reading and talking about public affairs is the best practical education which the mind can receive; and because practical it is manly, practice being the end of all manhood. But the evil does not stop with the newspapers;—memoir writing, and contemporary history, and history generally, by indirect operation is powerfully modified, weakened, and sometimes altogether annihilated, by the influence of the German system. For, when the principle of government is, that to allow popular interference in matters of government is only to admit bungling, it is a necessary consequence, that not merely babbling Parliaments shall not be allowed, but babbling fools in other public places also shall cease; i. e., without the censorship of the press, an unlimited monarchy is inconsistent with the principle of its own vitality, and can hardly exist. Accordingly, we find that in Prussia and in Austria, a very strict censorship is constantly exercised; and that the greater freedom in this regard which may exist in Berlin, in Wirtemburg, and in Saxony, is continually liable to be curtailed; and has once and again, during the last twenty years, been most sensibly curtailed by the overriding influence of Austrian and Prussian counsels at Frankfort. The effect of this system upon historical literature deserves to be well noted by the student. For the public men in many cases will not speak, ("I have an office merely, no opinion,") and the private men dare not speak; so that between these two negatives, it is often only by the aid of cunning combinations, and shrewd genius, that a person not personally concerned in any recent matters of German history can arrive at the truth. No man can blame Prince Metternich for giving a deaf ear to the proposal which has more than once been made to him, that the proceedings of the Frankfort Diet should be made public in detail;—enough that the result be published; it were the most absurd and preposterous conduct to create a talk and a discontent about that which has previously been fixed irrevocably in secret council;

191

the aim of government is not to supply publicists with the most easy materials for writing learned folios, but that the people may be well governed; and as there is nothing more hostile to good government than the conceit of the uneducated many, that they are entitled to call to account the decisions of the skilful few, so nothing would be more pernicious to Germany than the publication of the papers laid before Münch Bellinghausen, and his coadjutors, at Frankfort. So argues Prince Metternich; and it is impossible to deny, that on German principles, he argues with perfect justice. Meanwhile, however, German history languishes both at home and abroad; state documents are bottled up, and private memoirs, (witness Arndt, and von Ense,) are generally blank on those very points where we wished them to speak out. Nor does this affect contemporary history only; it is not fitting and proper that the Prussian youth should be told in some popular Plutarch, that one of their kings was a stiff old Calvinist, and a drill sergeant of grenadiers; that another began his life with most unchivalrous robbery, ended it with most base theft, and was all the while a cold, loveless infidel; that a third was a believer in ghosts, and a worshipper of lewd women; and that a fourth (just departed) might have been most respectable in a private station, but, as a king, was great only once in his life, when necessity forced great men on his counsels. If therefore Forster, or any other refurbisher of ancient papers, shall publish a work revealing the secrets of the first King of Prussia's tobacco-room, and the second king's sentry-box, it is not to be expected that such boldness shall pass without reprimand. And if the Chancellor Hardenberg dies in the year 1821, leaving behind him valuable memoirs of the state of things in Prussia, between 1801 and the peace of Tilsit, the state seal is immediately clapped upon them; and it is ordered that they shall not be opened till the year 1850 —and only then, (we may suppose,) if convenient. This state of things, no doubt, has its excellences; it excludes irreverential gossip, scandal, and evil-speaking—and calumny, which is the devil, (διάβολος;) but it also excludes truth; and we, on this side of the water, whatever we may be in

other matters, are certainly not " one-sided," in our habit of estimating public characters. Fair play and a free field are the only tactics, in these matters, which John Bull acknowledges; and he canonizes no political saint, (according to the pious ecclesiastical practice,) without hearing both *advocatus diaboli* and *advocatus Dei* fully out.

But are not the Germans great in history? what have Talboys and Mr Murray been doing but translating German histories for the last dozen years? Niebuhr, Heeren, Ranke, Rotteck, Neander, Menzel—are these men nothing?—Is it not plain, that while we, with our blessed constitution of checks and drags, bawling and battling, tugging and tearing, are succeeding only with the most painful exertion to act history after a bungling fashion, the Germans alone have time to write it? Can a man both fight the battle, and paint a picture of it?—No! the Germans are, in fact, better historians than ourselves, and must be so; for they alone have leisure and impartiality,

This other view of the matter is perfectly true; for in literature, no more than in science, are opposite views always, or for the most part, contradictory. He who has no newspapers to read, and no speeches to make at political dinners, can afford to become more profound in Tacitus and Thucydides. And as a living Protestantism and a high-pressure educational machinery unite in the north of Germany to produce an extraordinary activity of brain, the inquirers into any region of human fates will seldom take up a Leipzig catalogue without finding something (often in the shape of the vulgarest thesis) that will materially lighten his labour. In history, a German is at home every where except at home.

The operation of the censorship in Germany is somewhat various and complicated, and is influenced by a number of considerations that tend practically to make the yoke tolerable. Herr Marggraff says, that a man may print any thing he pleases in Germany, for if one state will not allow the publication, another will; and this is so far true, that many books are published daily in Baden and Wurtemburg, of the most anti-absolutist, and even republican character, which,

were the Prussian or Austrian police omnipotent over the whole confederated territory, never could have seen the light. To judge by the sweeping terms of the Carlsbad decrees in 1819, and the Frankfort ordinances in 1832, a stranger might imagine that the historico-political literature of Germany was a thing altogether as narrow and one-sided as the religious literature of the Roman Catholic Church in Italy and Spain. And, with regard to Austria, this notion is no doubt practically correct. But in Prussia we have Protestantism, which by a silent salutary operation widens the sphere of licensed thought considerably, in spite of government theories: then comes Frederick the Great, by no means an advocate of a free press in political matters, but too enlightened and too sensible a man to dream of ruling an educated people by a forcible suppression of free thought in every character: theology, literature, and philosophy he left free; and through these regions, it is no difficult task for a willing man to enter into politics. After him came, as was natural, under Frederick William II., a smart reaction of religious bigotry; but the bookselling trade was already too strong to be put down; it was a very hydra and a Briareus. A new phasis of developement appeared after the battle of Jena; Napoleon was then the censor, and Davoust his prefect of police; but neither Napoleon nor Davoust could read German: and thus many works were published (witness those of Arndt) instinct with the strong glow of freedom and the native pith of independence. In 1813 again, the King of Prussia himself, by calling on his people to strike for him, of course allowed them to speak; and Marshal Blücher, in fact, celebrated his arrival in Dresden by a public proclamation, to the effect that he had come to restore to the axons the liberty of the press! In accordance with the same spirit, the Congress of Vienna promised to the Germans that the Diet would take this matter into consideration at the first convenient opportunity. No doubt what the Diet has hitherto done in the matter sounds more like slavery than liberty of the press; but we mention these facts in order to show that practically the Germans, and even the Prussians, have been so long accus-

tomed to a certain latitude in the worst times, that it would not be wise in the Prussian or Austrian governments, whatever their wishes may be, to attempt carrying matters with too high a hand against the literary and publishing interest. Accordingly, we find that a history of the world, in nine volumes, by the famous Rotteck, recently deceased, inspired throughout by the most decided democratic and republican principles, has reached a fourteenth edition, and traverses the length and breadth of Germany (Austria perhaps excepted) without challenge. Menzel's history of the Germans, also, a work carried up to the most recent times, and though moderate and rational in its tone, yet decidedly opposed to the principles on which the Diet and the Governments have acted since the peace, is in every body's hands. In fact, with a little management, a German historian, even of the present moment, though he does not over loudly trumpet, may contrive to let the truth, in political matters, peep out significantly enough for such readers as have their senses exercised to discern between good and evil. Political pamphlets, however, directly attacking public persons or Government measures, are forbidden in all the states. A man may say many things in a folio that would be dangerous in a duodecimo. In general, the works that are positively forbidden are comparatively few, and one may have even these with a little caution and trouble. But the grand operation of the censorship, so far as the present writer has observed, consists in the confined and artificial atmosphere which it causes the historical writers of Germany generally to breathe, and in forcing men of keen and discriminating senses, in these matters, to content themselves with dubious and cloudy generalities where a smart stroke of detail could alone bring out the truth. This, of course, with regard to modern and native history only: in this region the Germans are mostly puerile or consumptive, blind, bigoted, or pedantic. Far away in time and space, they are giants: the records of limbo (where the fathers and the infants dwell) would supply the most innocent materials for their historians; and a Plutarch for the moon were the safest work to be undertaken by a prudent Berlin biographer.

The next literary growth that the system of absolutism not only blights and palsies, but absolutely annihilates, is eloquence: the eloquence of legislative assemblies, which is the highest; and the eloquence of public jurisprudential discussion, which is the next honourable. For the eloquence of the pulpit, in variety of theme and in cogency of interest, can compete with these two only on great and singular occasions. Martin Luther and John Knox, with their protestations and their preachings, were the sublime thunder and lightning of God to purify the moral world, in the sixteenth century; but the candles of the church, in common times, burn quietly to quiet worshippers. We prevail, indeed, in Scotland, with our democratic church, to open our mouths and make a noise by virtue of the General Assembly; but they have no such thing in Germany: and there being no states except in their infancy, and crippled by Austrian and Prussian influence, or only provincial ones for matters of paltry detail, (as in Prussia,) and no bar except in the Rhenish provinces, where it is very closely tied in Prussian laces, and a little asthmatic, it follows necessarily that there is no grand popular eloquence in Germany; that the most they can boast of is a few Zollikofers and Schleiermachers—elegant preachers,—but that, as a people, they are not eloquent, and their literature here is almost a blank. One consolation they have, and a great one: It is a good thing to be Orpheus taming the wild beasts with divinest music; but it is a better thing to have no beasts to tame, or to cage them up beforehand, where they may be either tamed or not as they please, but can do no harm, especially as we see that when the bears and grunters of an English mob are once up, the wisest Orpheus of Lords and Commons will often charm in vain to soothe them.

Another matter is style. The Germans cannot speak, and for this reason mainly, they cannot write. If the late King of Prussia, instead of a university at Berlin or Bonn, had, or could have, established a national parliament in the capital, we should not have waited long for a philosophy more intelligible than Hegel's, and men would have written history less profoundly, perchance, but more legibly than Niebuhr. Goethe said (in

one of his edifying discourses to Eckermann) that an Englishman, quâ Englishman, always writes well; that is to say, he writes clearly, distinctly, and energetically—which are the main qualities of a good style. It is notorious, on the other hand, that the Germans, as a nation, cannot write. How comes this? First, no doubt there is something weighty and elephantine in their whole nature, which strives in vain to attain the graceful agility and strength of the squirrel and the tiger. But we Britons are also of the Teuton stock. So we must even come back to the great want in Germany, the want of public life, of free independent action in society, as the real cause of that heavy, painful wading which so many of us have felt in our first experience of German books. In a university a man will never learn to write. It is our newspaper wars and our hustings speeches that have taught us to use the pen. To speak to or write for the masses, you must express yourself intelligibly at least, which is more than many famous German authors have done, or endeavoured to do; above all, you must speak directly at the thing, without circumlocution or involution of any kind, with quarterstaff or smallsword, or simply boxing, which is one of the most characteristic of English things, and believed in Germany to be as essential to a John Bull as a horn is to a natural bull. Also, when we speak to the masses and to the general human heart, we must speak dramatically, and eschew abstraction. Hence our Scotts and our Shakspeares—hence the raciness, briskness, freshness, vividness, energy, and power, not only of our common novelists and romancers, as compared with the Germans, but of our daily talk, and of our vulgarest newspaper paragraphs and cheapest magazine articles. On the other hand, consider the German style; the style of university men and tenth-heaven philosophers. Observe the dense smoke coming out of that funnel; with what sublime (truly sublime) voluminosities it winds and wreathes, and whirls, and rolls, and then disperses into—nothing! Something such is the similitude of some German styles, and the result of some German philosophies. But it is not always so pleasant, or so poetical. What throes would it not cost a plain-spoken direct

Englishman to construct some of Immanuel Kant's sentences in the Critik, labouring, as they do, like an ill-constructed steam-engine, grandly clumsy, trailing slowly along like a half-created antediluvian crocodile, separating itself scarcely from the primeval slime; with a soul in the body most uncomfortably lodged, staring stonily, or with a stiff petrified frown, like the creature in Frankenstein, which the impious bungling of man made, and not God! Oh, if our German neighbours would only learn to write short sentences! Some of them do, thank God! there is a visible improvement latterly. Menzel writes like an Englishman; and Varnhagen von Ense might decorate the heads of all the tobacco-pipes in Heidelberg with Julias and Matildas, so neat is his pencil; but as for the Germans generally, you might as reasonably expect that the English lawyers should frame their counts with the epigrammatic neatness of Beranger's stanzas, as that a German professor, beneath folios and fumes, and beneath the eye of the censorship, should write books which an English gentleman will delight to read. As eating much makes a heavy body, so reading much makes a heavy soul. These professional erudites stuff each sentence violently with every thing that can go into it, and a few others, as the clown stuffs his breeches-pockets in the pantomime. No wonder that they are clumsy and inelegant, heavy as a carrier's wain, and moving along as awkwardly and uncomfortably as a cow with a stick leg.

We have said that the style of German writers generally is not dramatic; and we are inclined to go a step further, and say, that the acknowledged inferiority of the German drama, as a branch of art, is to be attributed, in some considerable measure to the same cause that gives their literature generally, and their style of writing, a university rather than a popular cast. To write drama well, a people must live dramatically; the great dramatist must be trained on a great living stage, and amid the bustle and collision of great living interests. Now, not only is there a manifest want of popular activity and energy in Germany, caused by the organizing principle of the Government, that the people shall be allowed to do nothing for themselves, or as little as possible,

but, unfortunately, there is no German nation (as Madame de Stael wisely remarked) in any shape, no grand German interest to create a grand German stage. And no one, accordingly, can read Goethe's classical pieces—Iphigenia and Tasso—without feeling instinctively that these are pattern works for a Saxon duchy, but not for a German people. So Schiller has hinted himself; and no doubt he felt it painfully.

"Give a grand object, if thou wilt upstir
The deep foundations of humanity;
A narrow sphere doth narrow in the soul,
A larger prospect makes more large the
    sense."

And Goethe, also, in his ripest production, Faust, where he handles a truly national legend, shows the undramatic character of his nation in another regard—he wants action; he floats where he ought to strike, and discourses on an easy chair with all complacency, as if the audience to be moved were some decent devout John Peter Eckermann, and not the pit and the gallery. Faust, even the first part, is not a good acting play; and in the second part, the old gentleman sails about with the most playful indifference—and piles up a magnificent circus of fairy palaces, through which Dr Faust, or the reader, or the devil, are led, in confused bewonderment, to stare. Altogether—whether the military system, or the petty princedom, or the university aristocracy, or the beer, or the tobacco, or all, be in fault—there seems something too formal, too systematic, too architectural on the one hand; and, on the other, something too vague, cloudy, and floating in the German mind, for the attainment of high excellence in the drama. Take Schiller's Wallenstein, for instance, one of the most obvious, and, we presume, also one of the most esteemed masterpieces of the German stage; it is in too many places literally a "building up" of rhyme,—lofty, indeed, but heavy. The genius of Schiller may, in this respect, serve as a representative of the German genius generally. Without vivacity, rapidity, and salient point, in some degree, (though we English may, perhaps, overdo this,) no high dramatic excellence is possible; and it is needless to say that these are the very qualities of mind in which the German intellect is, and has been, particularly deficient. Schiller seems to have had a secret consciousness that his great work was too prolix by much, and might prove wearisome :

" Forgive the poet if, with rapid pace,
   He rush not to the fateful goal at once ;
   But, scene by scene, with studious care unrolls
   The earnest pictures of the mighty past." *

We do forgive him, because he is a German, and because he wrote his play for a Weimarian, not for a London audience. We do forgive him, because the banks of the Ilm were necessarily less fertile in dramatic incident than the quays of the Thames, and because it was naturally a much more simple thing to satisfy, with a grateful titillation, the " æsthetical " sensibilities of a petty or "grand" German duke, than to command the heart of a mighty people. The latter is the great feat that a dramatist in England has to achieve—a hard granite quarry, in which to work to any purpose there must be a long laborious wedging and boring, of which the noblest chamber-enthusiasm is not capable. But a German PEOPLE has yet to be created ; and whatsoever good (or evil) may have been effected by Münch Bellinghausen and his diplomatic coadjutors at the Diet since the year 1816, in the present aspect of things we are likely sooner to see a Prussian national stage in Berlin, and a Hungarian one in Pesth, than a German one in Frankfort.†

Thus far we have traced, or rather hinted, the influence of political condition on German literature, some-what unfavourably at the first blush, both for absolutism and for German literature, we must confess. But there is another view of the matter, bright and sunny ; and to this we shall now turn.

In the remarks which we have made above, we should by no means wish to be understood as hazarding any sweeping proposition with regard to the necessary connexion between certain forms of government, and certain forms of literary development. We only state that, in fact, certain influences of the state on literature are observable in Germany, according to the best of our judgment ; and we think, also, that some at least of these influences in the general case (open, however, to countless modifying circumstances) are necessary. We think, also, that a limited monarchy, such as the British, is, on the whole, a better atmosphere for a healthy literature than an absolute military government, and a strict centralizing system such as that of Prussia ; or a petty aristocratizing princedom like Weimar, where Goethe was cherished with artistical delicacy, as rare plants are in a hot-house. But we will not say, with certain shallow writers, that any of the avatars of Vishnu is profane ; or that, of the various political and religious forms that embody the soul of social life on the face of the earth, any one is exclusively the church of God, and all the rest unlicensed chapels, dedicated to the devil. God is every where, and with God, good ; and the good that is in German literature, despite the weaknesses noted above, is manifold.

In the first place, the German intellect, being excluded altogether from the dissipating influence of the moment's gossip, and the narrowing influence of urgent present interests, applies itself with undivided energy to the collection and arrangement of all recorded facts in most remote space and time ; and thus arises that famous German ERUDITION, a thing which only a shallow coxcomb and a paltry merchandizing pedant will despise. Take your host of wits and witlings away, in God's name, who whisk their pools of frothy feeling into a fashionable cream, and call it poetry ; and give us in exchange a German polyhistor, a Herrmann Conring, a *σχολως* of the old soldiership, a mind written "literally within and without," with all the *mirabilia mundi* encyclopædia ever contained. If there is any man that wishes to be a scholar, that is to say, not merely an Oxonian or a Cantab, cunning to hunt old anapests out of, and new iambics into *Æschylus;* but a man learned generally in the history of his kind—Greek, Roman, Indian, Egyptian, and Kamschatkan ; let him study German by all means, and before every thing ; for the Germans have compiled, so to speak, with most lawyer-like accuracy and completeness, the very ancient year-books, and the most modern *Barnwell* and *Creswell* of human experience. It is, indeed, an admirable thing to behold, and a more admirable thing to know and to use the works of German scholarship. A man is literally a fool who will employ a French or an English book on subjects of vast erudition, when he can get a German one. And there is another matter to be considered here, of no secondary moment. The Germans not only compile the best works on all subjects from the best authorities, but they also, of the best works in all languages, ancient and modern, make the best translations. Were it for their literature of translations alone, the language of the Germans deserves to be studied by every man who aspires after comprehensive scholarship. They have already, in a great measure, remedied the evil that was brought in by the men of Babel. One may trust to a German translation ninety-nine times in every hundred ; to an English translation in every hundred only once ; and that for several plain reasons.—The Germans make a business of translation ; they study it as an art ; they may well do so, for they can boast a language equal to the most difficult pranks of that difficult art ; and they are honest also, conscientious, and self-exenterating in the matter, which we English, because of our habitual occupation with other matters—because of the less flexible character of our language, and because of our strongly pronounced one-sided nationality, can seldom afford to be. Let us, therefore, study German for its erudition more even than for its poetry and its philosophy ; we have infinitely better poetry at home in every genus ; and as for philosophy, of that immediately. Let them be our quarrymen, our falcons, our hounds, our balkers—"herrings a-head, ho !"—if we are too proud to give them a higher dignity. But it is vain for us to pretend that the learned Germans are not architects also, as well as masons. We are no advocates for *mere* erudition ; for what can Latin, and Greek, and Hebrew, piled up mountains high, do for a man, but to weigh him down from the upper story, and make him clumsy and baker-legged ? The Germans are learned, but their coacervated facts are organized by ideas ; and it cannot be said of Böckh and Müller as Mephistopheles says of the chemist, that they

" Count the parts in their hand,
   Only without the spiritual band."

Nay, rather, in respect of plastic and organizing ideas, our trans-Rhenane neighbours do shoot as far beyond us, for the most part, as in respect of accuracy and comprehensiveness of erudition ; and this brings us to the second good thing that is in German literature, chiefly by virtue of absolute governments and of the censorship of the press. This thing is—SPECULATION.

"Thou hast no *speculation* in those eyes !"

By virtue of speculation the soul stands upon a watchtower, and looks out, and, " with preparatory blast of cow-horn," (in the special case of German speculation,) proclaims the travail of the time and its own (for " the whole creation groaneth ") to the general ear. Speculation is not metaphysics ; but metaphysics is a part of speculation ; and as this word of the species is an ancient one, notwithstanding that it is ungrateful to Eng-

---

* We have contracted the *five* lines of the German original here into *four*, and think we have improved them. So, throughout the whole drama, as Coleridge well remarks, to curtail is generally to improve. In the tragic verse of Wallenstein, there is a great want of variety, breaking up, and accentuation. In Schiller's earlier plays, again, we have fire and impatience, and glaring dramatic points enough ; but here there is a want of that calm strength which, in the midst of bustle, characterises manhood. Altogether we are inclined to think that, as a dramatist, Schiller never attained to the proper balance between youth and age—between passion and reflection, and, we may say also, that a want of balance is the main want of German poetry generally.

† As we shall not have occasion, in the present rapid sketch, to refer to the German drama again, we request our readers here to note, that the observations he will find below on the emotional and the imaginative, applied more particularly to lyric poetry, apply also in a considerable degree to the quality and expression of passion in the drama.

lish ears, we shall beg leave to retain it also. In speculation the Germans are known to be particularly strong, and have pursued it even to pedantry, as we in this country have done classical literature; for nothing is more barren than logic and metaphysics, *when they have nothing to work on :* when beardless boys are set systematically to finger the stamens and pistils of the soul, at the perilous season when the small innocent bud is only now slowly, it may be painfully, opening to the blessed influences of the sun —a very torture, and a martyrdom, and a mind-murder, the contemplation of which we are not surprised to see delighting the satirical malignity of Mephistopheles.

" Redeem the time, for fast it flits away ;
Use order ; rule the hour you cannot stay :
And thus 'tis plain to common sense,
With a course of logic you must commence.
There will your mind be trained circumspectly,
Dressed up in Spanish boots correctly !
That, with caution and care, as wisdom ought,
It may slink along the path of thought,
And not, with fitful flicker and flare,
Will-o-the-wisp it here and there.
You must be taught that a stroke of thinking,
Which you had practised once as free
And natural as eating and drinking,
Cannot be made without one ! two ! three !

" True, it should seem that the fabric of thought
Is like a web by cunning master wrought,
Where one stroke moves a thousand threads,
The shuttle shoots backwards and forwards between,
The slender threads flow together unseen,
And one with the other thousand-fold weds :
Then steps the philosopher forth to show
How precisely it must be so ;
If the first be so, the second is so,
And therefore the third and the fourth is so ;
And unless the first and the second before be,
The third and the fourth can never more be.
So, schoolmen teach and scholars believe,
But none of them yet ever learned to weave."

In which admirable passage Goethe sufficiently exposes the pedantry of that department of speculation called logic, as it was expounded in German universities in his burschen days.

And it is true now, as then, that the systematic classification of the necessary forms of thought, will never teach even a ripe man to think to any purpose, much less a beardless boy ; for form without substance is nothing. Metaphysics, again, strictly so called, has more body, and may (when healthily tinged with love and poetry) be indulged in properly and profitably by young men when their beards are sprouting ; but it also is sadly liable to abuse, and has been most sadly abused in all times and places, particularly in modern Germany, as Mephistopheles, in the same discourse, testifies :—

" After logic, first of all,
To metaphysics stoutly fall ;
There strive to know what ne'er was made
To go into a human head ;
For what is within and without its command,
A high-sounding name is always at hand."

Which few verses pretty completely comprise the sum and substance of an Englishman's estimate of GERMAN METAPHYSICS.

" Dat Galenus opes, dat Justinianus honores
Sed nos philosophi turba misella sumus."

" Physic gives wealth ; Law wealth and honours—You
Philosophers !—who the devil cares for you ? "

But the matter cannot be dismissed altogether so expeditiously as gentlemen in haste to make money might wish. For whatever phases or phrases of the thing particular persons or peoples may choose to legitimate, a man may in fact as soon hope to escape from his own soul as from metaphysics or speculation in some shape or other. A system of theology, for instance, (of which we have many,) built upon such a book as the Bible by Christian thinkers who are not Rationalists, is a system of metaphysics, of which, while the materials are believed to be furnished by GOD, the form is supplied by man ; for every man who reads the Bible, must either read it with the naked eyes of his own understanding, (Protestantism,) or with hierarchical spectacles, (Popery.) He cannot ride out of his own skin ; and the word of God most implicitly believed is still the belief of man ; and man's belief, whether worked out by independent isolated speculation, or received by historic tradition and cus-

tomary enspherement, is man's metaphysics. Thus are we all metaphysicians, consciously or unconsciously ; though conscious metaphysics is that only which we commonly dignify, or (according to our English use) reprobate with the name. " O wonderful ship, but wonderfully ill-rigged ! how grandly it plunges through multitudinous, monstrous, self-created billows ! but having no back-stays, down suddenly pitches the main mast ; and the mizen reels ; and the vessel is on her beam ends !" So we English, with kindly contempt and a friendly feeling of superiority, are wont to apostrophize German metaphysics ; sitting the while coolly by, and from the warm windows of our snug beefsteak club-room, beholding the sad wreck of another, and yet another systematic dream—of another, and yet another " Teutonic philosopher." But, O Englishman, who boastest thyself to be alone wise, because thou art alone practical, and despisest idealism, and mysticism, and Germanism, in every shape, consider whether thou that accusest another doest not the same things—in a different guise. Consider whether, in unquiet times, (and the present particularly,) a man should in magnanimity—can in possibility, remain quiet ? Consider that the world, however pleasant it might be so to picture it, is not one vast beef-steak club, and that the mind of man is not one grand steam-engine—what James Watt may construct, and Adam Smith may calculate. Consider that thou also art a man, and sharest the blessing and the curse of thy kind : on that vast ocean of speculation thou hast been tossed in times past, and wilt be tossed again. Nay, is it not certain that thou art tossed even now ? Consider PUSEYISM, that grand miracle of these latter times, (in England verily a miracle, in Germany it were nothing strange)—concerning which, we shall not say at present how muc' truth or how much falsehood it may incarnate ; but it is certainly a product, a stately, imposing product of British speculation ; a phenomenon which proves at least one thing, that the English Church at the present moment is a-stir and alive—that her clergy are in earnest, and that they will no longer permit Christianity (or even Episcopacy, of which they are the special wardens,) to be greeted of

all men in name supreme, but virtually to sit like an old man in the back galleries of intellectual worship nodding. " Out then with Christianity ! out, I say, out !" as a thinking man lately wrote ; and if this is to be the watchword, we must consider that Christianity cannot be brought out to any purpose without speculation and without metaphysics. Puseyism is, in fact, a sublime crystallization of ecclesiastical metaphysics ; for there are only two kinds of metaphysical results possible, of which the one at the present moment is preached most publicly by the Puseyites, (not as Episcopalians, however, but as the most prominent advocates of the extreme positive and historical in Christianity,) the other by innumerable champions—but we may take as their main prophet, GOETHE. A man must either believe with a firm faith, that he has received at least the whole materials of his metaphysics externally, and by historical tradition from God, and God's messengers, as opposed to man, and the invention of man ; or he must throw himself back on the great sea of healthy human instincts, finding in himself alone, and in the sympathies which he is compelled to share with his brother, whatever best spiritual polarity he can. The one is the metaphysics of divine institution, the other the metaphysics of mortal striving. The one is revelation, as we understand the word strictly in England—the other naturalism, or rationalism. Puseyism is merely a grand ecclesiastical architecture, and projected stereotype of Christianity in a definite form ; and whatever a Christian man may think of the taste of the columns and the cornices and the mouldings, and of the security of the foundation-stone of the temple, he can have no doubt for a moment what worship is celebrated there, and that it is a magnificent building. We English, therefore, and Scotch, in so far as we either acknowledge a supernatural Christianity and a Church, or swear by Goethian naturalism, or something to that effect, are metaphysical at least in the *result* ; or as to the thousand windings and byrinths, climbings and tumblings, epings and turnings, by which a thinking man arrives at this result, or that, it were endless to talk of them. Only two things we shall say. First, that metaphysics, to be of any value, must begin and end with poetry ; and, second, that metaphysics as a mere *means*, that is to say, the dim feeling and floundering through metaphysical systems, must cease before a man is five-and-twenty, or, at the very utmost, before thirty. For, without poetry and the lustihood of a vital enjoyment, to wade through Hegel, and Immanuel Kant, and half a dozen more, is merely to grope and grabble, and to gnaw at the root of one's own growth perversely, to ply busily the treadmill of nothing, and to dig a man's own grave. O premature speculator, smooth-checked meditator, that would be metaphysical, and art yet scarcely physical, " be not wise overmuch ; why wilt thou destroy thyself?" Why wilt thou violently withdraw the veil on which life's divine magic is painted, charming thee with countless witcheries, to discover in the uncomfortable abyss below, not God, as thou vainly deemest, but darkness only and vacuity, with not even a gnome or a goblin for thy companionship? Speculate by all means ; but from a high tower and on a fair landscape. Is divinity a spider, is nature a toad, that she should sit in the dark centre of things moping, to hold converse with metaphysicians? Remember Doctor Faust and the devil. Remember Samuel Taylor Coleridge, and the thousand sunny poems that he should have written, had it not been for that unhappy itch of anatomizing the smallest fibres of his own heart—(" *so gehts mit Dir, zergliedcrer deiner freuden!*")—as if it would beat one whit the healthier for that. Sir William Hamilton himself told the metaphysical youth of Edinburgh that his " first philosophy" and queen of all sciences was useful merely as a gymnastic of the soul, an expert fencing and pleasant somerseting of the inner man. We are inclined to go a little beyond this, and say, that metaphysics, pursued as a study, is useful as a survey and a sounding of the human capacity, teaching us, to a reasonable certainty, what we can know, and what we can *not* know: a great blessing this last ; for a bird in a cage, being once convinced that it can't get out, may make itself very happy. Up to five-and-twenty, then, or even thirty, (if there be time,) let the trout swim about in the pond, plash violently, and

make many transcendental plunges, all as German as may be : for the English are blunderers here, piecers and patch-workers ; the utmost they can do is to prevent your snout, in a fit of explorativeness, from being snubbed by the impudent claws of a gritty rock, which is a benefit, no doubt ; but if you will swim with buoyant bladder, plash with muscular tail, oar with gallant fin, and roll and spout like a porpoise in the ocean (or pond, as you may deem it comparatively) of human thought ; if you will become a true intellectual gymnast, according to the idea of Sir William Hamilton, you must hire a German master, as we hire French masters to teach us the gymnastics of the body. But beware always lest this pleasant game be protracted unduly : bring out a result ; come to a decision ; take a side ; act a part ; *do* something, in God's name ; for " the harvest truly is plenteous, but the labourers are few."

So much for German erudition and speculation ; and we may say here, in a single sentence, as the result of various German studies carried on continuously through many years, that the erudition and speculation of the Germans is both the best thing they have, and a thing perfectly *unique*. None but a very Teutomaniac will maintain that German poetry—or literature, more strictly so called—does in any branch rival, much less surpass, our own. It is less masculine, less tasteful, less healthy, less rounded, less national than the Greek ; no impartial person will even say, that, in respect of grace, vigour, and a well-rounded totality, it is not inferior to the Italian and to the French, not to mention the poetic richness of the Sanscrit, the Persic, and oriental literature generally. But if we look on the German erudition as a grand intellectual quarrying, and on their speculation as a sublime boxing the compass of human thought, sounding the lowest depths of humanity, and ballooning heavenward as high as the increasing rarity of the air will allow, we must confess that the world nowhere, not even in Greece, beheld a nobler spectacle ; for though it is not given to man to solve the problem of the universe, it is given to him—nay, he is necessitated—to attempt the so-

lution :* he *must* go as far as he can go, for so soon as he stops he becomes a mere huddle and conglomeration of chances, and an utter vacuity ; he must assume a keystone to his thoughts if he cannot make one ; he must hope and believe the best, if he cannot prove it. Praise be to the Germans for their Titanic achievements in this region! When a man is tormented with inward questionings that will not be blinked, let him not deceive himself with neat stitches and smooth painting, according to any respectable standard of local orthodoxy ; but let him take the Bible and Shakspeare, and Kant and Schelling, into the green fields, and work these thoroughly and conscientiously in his soul till they rise up with spontaneous elasticity into one harmonious architecture of manifold spiritual organism. Thinkers and theologians ought all to be proficients in German ; and not this only, but all the professors of natural science who are not content to pare the nails and to curl the hairs of nature, and to tell her items curiously, as religious Jews number every Dagesh and Mappik in the Hebrew Bible. We do not value Kant and Schelling, indeed, for anything they are in themselves, so much as for the spirit with which they animate the sciences of material detail, which, without such spirit, sink invariably into puerility and pedantry. Facts, the framework of speculation ; and speculation, the plastic indwelling spirit of facts ; and a glowing heart, to billow both buoyantly before God—this is the grand triad of functional intellect, the well-poised union of which alone makes great scientific MEN ; and they who know science and know Germany have ever been forward to attest, that in no other country has it been more successfully or more wonderfully achieved.

There remains now, to complete our survey, the whole region of the emotional and the imaginative, ex-

cept in so far as it has been already touched on incidentally. Here, however, having somewhat cleared our way, and adjusted our whereabouts, we can afford to be more brief. The Germans are strong in sentiment, so strong as to tumble over into weakness ; strong also proverbially in imagination, so strong as oftentimes to jerk away into madness. Oh, there is something kindly and almost motherly in the character of a real German! Börne, with his fierce glowing political fanaticism,—a pillar of cloud and a pillar of fire in one,—was a Jew in this respect, verily, and no German. We never looked into one of those blue eyes,—genuine old Saxon, which the men wear as much as the women, —without being softened down, for the moment at least, into perfect gospel. O singular people, whom we may justly censure as less manly, but justly also envy as more happy! Absolutism, again, with its blessings, by God's grace more potent than its bane, comes in here, and works mightily ; for why should the Austrian Teut be careful when good Kaiser Franz cares so well for him ? Why should a warm Suabian heart not feel, not float in sentiment, not bathe in sentimentality, (as you hard Birmingham Britons will phrase it,) not sway in upper air, for a season at least, pleasantly in Ludwig Uhland's crescent boat, and see bright visions—blue spirits and green, red spirits and grey—through a rainbow of pious tears with Dr Justinus Kerner, when there are no Whigs and Tories below (Rotteck being dead and Menzel dumb) to beat one another with clubs daily ? It is even so ; we may take it in jest or we may take it in earnest, but the Germans overflow in all their writings with the purest milk of human kindness, swim in the most billowy intoxication of enthusiasm, melt, even the most manful of them, on common occasions, into womanish tears, and are otherwise "sentimental" and "*very German.*" It is

---

* " Man is not born for the purpose of solving the problem of the universe, though he certainly has the vocation to seek the point where the problem begins, and then circumscribe himself within the limits of the intelligible. To measure the operation of the universe is a work far beyond our capacities ; and to inoculate our reason into the mighty whole, is, from our present terrestrial point of view, a most vain endeavour. The reason of man and the reason of God are two very different things."—GOETHE, (*Eckermann.*)

a fault, a disease, or, say more charitably, only a want of proportion and balance ; it is a superabundance of a pleasant fountain, which, with us broad, brawny, practical Englishmen, is rather apt to run scantily. We might borrow from them in this case profitably ; but it is not easy: the instruments are tuned differently ; the whole intellect is braced differently. Where one man laughs and another weeps at the same thing ; where one caricatures and the other preaches ; where one trifles and the other worships, there is an immense gap—not to be filled up by a whole colony of masters of languages—by a whole army of translators of *Faust*. The German lyric poetry is the richest, perhaps, in the world ; in some points perhaps the best : *but it is not for us.* Individuals may be benefited by it—but the nation will not relish it. It is too cloudy, too tearful, too shadowy, for the beef-eater. It wants brawn—ay brawn, and blood, and lustihood ! So Lessing said, a hundred years ago, and it is true still. They cannot name the man whom we should deliberately prefer to Burns—to Beranger. But let us confess, further, that the political palsy under which the Germans suffered for so many centuries, and from which they have not yet recovered, the petty princedom, feudal aristocratism, and rotten Louis Quartorzism which narrowed the sphere of their sympathies, and clipped the wings of their aspirations, give—at least, for the greater part of the last century—a smallness to the objects, and a childishness to the fashion of their feelings, the very reverse of that breadth and grandeur of thought which is an essential element of the classical. The Germans, even at the present day, are continually making a fuss about small matters : there is too much ado about literary nothings ; notability is too cheap. Over the dead carcass of every dog, and cat, and house-sparrow, they raise up a baldachin, pillared and purpled, and bear it about with much pomp, and scatter incense, and sing psalms, and with chaunt and counter-chaunt contend, till you believe, in very deed, that the pope is there, and *Corpus Domini*, and with the foolish worship foolishly. Were there any grand practical national interest habitually to occupy the German mind, literary lions would require to roar

louder in order to be heard—(so it is in England, where genius must practise, like Demosthenes, and learn to vanquish the sea ;) but now the things which they call lions in Germany appear to us rather to be pug-dogs ; and most certainly no Ludwig Uhland, respectable as he is in his way, could go through five, ten, and fifteen editions in England with or without the help of Sergeant Talfourd's bill.

We must consider again and again, for it is the main regulating idea from which the present observations branch, the influence of the state and of public life on German literature. Where there is no House of Commons, every man will make more ado with his own house: and where there are no processions of Chartists, and no Whig and Tory dinners, papa and mamma will walk the more complacently by the river side ; and some John Henry Voss, ambitious to be the German Homer, (as Klopstock is the German, the "*very German* Milton,") will tell in sounding hexameters the epos of a pic-nic. And there is in fact nothing more truly German and pleasant to read than that same parsonage and pic-nic epos of "*Louisa.*" There the poet, slippered all the while no doubt, and smoking quietly, sings how, after dinner, the venerable parson of Grunau sits in the cool shade of two broad-leaved lime-trees which overshadow the manse from the south, beside a stone table, and on a hard-bottomed chair, which his old cunning-headed servant Hans, in the weary hours of winter had carved curiously and painted white and shining green ; and how, with edifying discourse and pleasant tales of olden time, he delighteth the heart of his wife and his daughter—and how the beautiful Louisa all the while feeds the chickens and the guinea fowls benevolently with crumbs, while, in more respectful distance, the proud cock, strutting like the sultan with many wives, snatches the wandering morsel, and the pigeon comes tripping by, and the turkey cock gabbles, and the dog Packan in an adjacent corner is gnawing a bone, and watching the cat, and snapping at the buzzing flies: and how then the sensible housewife unfolds the plan of the pic-nic, and sends Hans off on nimble legs to have the factor's boat ready to ferry Louisa and her intended Walter, and the little Graf Charles,

across the lake to the wood—and how, under the hanging greenery of the white-stemmed birches, dry sticks are gathered together, and a light is struck, and the coffee-pot is brought forth, and the coffee is boiled ; but the little Graf, Charles, whose education has been too delicate and aristocratic, will have no coffee at all, because it sets his blood in commotion ; whereupon, up rises the venerable pastor of Grunau, and holds a discourse on Divine goodness, and on the goodness of the dinner which they had just enjoyed, and insists that Charles shall behave like a good boy, and not like a spoiled Graf, and drink the coffee nevertheless.

" Fie on the foolish excuse ! was the rice soup burned ? was the wine not
Good and strong ? were the peas not young and fresh ? and like sugar
Sweet the carrots ? the goose and the herring, in what could you blame them ?
Better lamb could you find ? and with bright bird-pepper besprinkled,
Surely the sallad was good ! the vinegar, was it not pungent ?
Sweet as balsam the oil, and sweet the cherries ? the butter
Sweeter than kernels ? and say, Oh, were not the radishes tender ?
What ! and the nurturing bread so white, and so light ! it is shameful
God's good gifts to reject, and to call the rejection good breeding,"

And so on, from the anti-teetotal dinner in the parsonage to the pic-nic in the wood, and from the pic-nic in the wood to the end of all great epic changes that do not end in death—marriage. Goethe improved upon this in Herrmann and Dorothea ; but Voss's Louisa is an original and a real true natural picture ; and Voss himself is perhaps *the* German Homer, more creditably so at least than Klopstock is the German Milton. Holstein is a pretty country, with woods and lakes, and sandhills ; but no Ida, and no Olympus.

Of German imagination, so famous for all sorts of devilry and witchery, imps and elixirs, bodiless bodies and shadowless bodies, we shall spare ourselves saying any thing. It is the twin-sister of emotion, (fears and phantoms being constant fellows,) and subject to the same laws. Imagination with us is prematurely nipt by paltry, political pettifogging here, by the love of money there, which is the root of all evil, and by the worship of rank, which is idolatry. In Germany, absolutism, setting up a Chinese wall between the governors and the governed, gives free rein to the fancies of literary men, and creates an artistical world apart, where some pious yogees of the pencil and pen may sketch bloodless arabesques at their pleasure, (Goethe,) while others jerk, and shoot, and dive, and plunge, and toss themselves wantonly, and create a strange dance of not unmeaning figures in the optic chambers of their brain, (Richter,) which, were they only clearly, and in some decent Christian order, set before him, plain John Bull,

who has a sound enough instinct (not a philosophy) in these matters, would not be slow to admire. Petty princedom, again, having no grand interests to exhibit, vulgarizes imagination, and teaches fancy to be trivial. Nothing on the whole is more perplexing to an Englishman than German imagination ; for it intrudes everywhere most impudently, disturbing the Augsburg Confession and the Heidelberg Catechism with no greater ceremony than the stamens and pistils of the Linnæan botany. It is an exuberant thing, and full of rampant vitality—happy beyond its own proper blessing in this, that God, who created it, has created also Englishmen to prune it.

One general remark we may make on the whole emotional and imaginative development of the German mind, whether exhibited in literature or in the fine arts—and it is a pure praise belonging to absolute governments—viz., that there pervades cultivated society in Germany an atmosphere of artistical enjoyment, that there is found more or less, in all classes, an habitual aptitude for the beautiful, which is not found in England. The artist stands higher in public estimation—infinitely higher than with us. We estimate artists, whether actors, musicians, or painters, not so much because they are artists as because they are lions ; hence the immense gap between the few stars and the οἱ πολλοί of our artistical class. The Englishman pays a first-rate artist with guineas and with much staring, a vulgar one with scanty pence—the German pays both with reverence. This is the best thing in Ger-

197

many, better even than the folios—a reach of emotional purity, in the region of the beautiful, which it is to be feared our rude political battlings, our pride, and our pelf, may long hinder us to attain.

On the German Church, and its influence on literature, we have few remarks to make, and these we have mostly anticipated. The ecclesiastical corporation in Germany has no independent *status*, is altogether subordinate, and, properly speaking, built into the state, both in Catholic Austria and in Protestant Prussia. As a Church, therefore, it can play no prominent part. With regard to the state of religion and theology, two remarks will suffice:—First, in respect of religion, it is universally acknowledged that the Germans are the most religious people in Europe—that is, the most instinct with devout feeling, without particular reference to the object of devotion. This, the tone of their literature and of their music equally testifies; and so, indeed, they must have been, unless by some peculiar interposition of the devil the emotion of reverence alone had been stunted where all other emotions are so luxuriant. The state of theology, again, we have explained already under the heads of erudition and speculation; and so it also must have been. Nothing was more natural than that, when the political censorship had forbidden men of active intellects to occupy themselves with the affairs of the present life, they should give themselves up with more undivided devotion to pry into the mysteries of futurity. Add to this, the memory of Huss, Luther, and Melancthon, and the forty years' reign of Frederick the Great, and you will see clearly how the German theology has risen to that Cyclopean vastness which we admire—is instinct with that transcendental magnetism, disturbing the ecclesiastical needle, which we fear. It is quite certain, that to be a profound theologian now, a man must know German, as it is indubitable that a good knowledge of that language will bring a man further, in most theological investigations, in a month, than could be managed without it in a year. One

caution, however, is necessary to a young man entering this region. He must be able to stand firmly on his own legs, and to see clearly with his own eyes; he must have courage to look truth in the face, whatever shape it may assume; he must be proof against intoxicating gas of all kinds—proof against strange stenches multifarious; otherwise he is certain to faint, and fall into the arms of the good old pope, or die floundering in the mud, like a foolish fat sheep, helpless, hopeless, on his back.

The reader will now understand sufficiently, from the whole tenor of these observations, why we commenced with the state, and indeed have carried this one idea through our whole discourse. The state is every thing in Germany, overrides all, moulds all, controls all—in fact makes the national literature run in a certain channel, as certainly as the geology of a country shapes the course of the rivers. With us, as we have repeatedly stated, there is no state, no government, no permanent superinduced mould; but a mere battle of parties trying to govern, and keeping one another from governing as much as possible. We are trees growing wild; strong and lusty, as befits the mountain child; chance-sown and educated by buffets of unpolite Boreas; stems of God, as the old Hebrews would have said: by nature every thing, by art nothing. The contrast is in every respect so complete, that we have not been able to find any point of view from which we could at once more strikingly, and more comprehensively, attempt a rapid bird's-eye view of the general traits and tendencies of German literature. We have said nothing formally, though here and there incidentally, of the great characteristic traits of the Teutonic character, as distinguished from the Celtic, the Sclavonic, and other European races; but we are Teuts ourselves; and, though an interesting paper might have been written with this leading idea, it would scarcely have been so fertile in instructive contrasts as that which we have chosen.*

To conclude. Germanism is a fashion of the day; and we wish it well.

It seems to us that there are four languages which must soon become universal over the globe—English, French, German, Russian. These are the languages in which the history of the future will, in all probability, be written; these are the languages with which every thinking man who sympathizes with the progress of his kind must court acquaintance. Greek and Latin are good; but if they are pursued with a prim, perverse pertinacity, as if a man had only one eye, and that on the back of his head, then we think truly it is time to apply the text of the gospel—*let the dead bury their dead!* German, in particular, we *must* study; for, like Goethe's magical apprentice, having set the imp agog after waterbuckets, he threatens to swamp and drown us altogether, unless we get hold of the word which he will obey. Nor is it from Germany only by external importation that the deluge floods in; we have a sort of indwelling Germanism at home, which is very powerful, and has many names. Undeniably Coleridge was a German, and that not only in the grand healthy speculative and imaginative excellencies of the German mind, but in the excess and the disease of these, and in that he once—

"Soared to eulogize an Ass,"

as Byron, with his true British instinct, did not fail to note. Wordsworth, also, in his calm architectural meditativeness is a German, braced, however, with a British atmosphere, and girt round with British strength; so that there is no danger of his dissolving into clouds and melting into mere tears, as the Germans sometimes do. A German of the Germans was Percy Bysshe Shelley; German in his pure incorporeal idealism; German in his pantheizing poetry and poetical pantheism; British only in his pride. Southey is a German, not only in the main character of his mind, but in the whole style of his life; in his single-hearted devotedness to the priesthood of literature; in the systematic com-

prehensiveness of his studies—in the wide grasp of his erudition—in his pure idealism—in his grand architectural constructiveness: thoroughly English, however, in the historical definitiveness and decision of his religious convictions. Finally, Thomas Carlyle: who will doubt that *he* is a German? more than Coleridge—more than Shelley; a German both by perfect nature and perfect inoculation; a mind grand in all the virtues, equally grand in all the vices, of Germanism. In this man, we wish the reader may see a living epitome of all that we have ramblingly discoursed on this subject—a breathing incarnation of the modern Teutonic spirit, as it is fast marching over to amalgamate with and complement the old Saxon stock isolated here, in this "snug little island," from some good as from much evil—though we must say, in justice, that he is at the same time something better than a German; his sturdiness, his raciness, his dramatic breadth of brush, seem thoroughly English. Carlyle is a man that, above all others, the German tyro should assay; if he finds nothing that he can sympathize with in the "Tailor re-tailored"—that most German of modern English books, then, most assuredly, German literature (the soul of it at least) is not for him. But let not the plain, straightforward English reader take offence hastily, at the first ungainly aspect either of Thomas Carlyle or of German literature. Why an ugly porter should be oftentimes placed at the gate of heaven, we cannot tell; but so it is. With Carlyle and the Germans, you must be content to wade a little while painfully at the bottom of a deep, heavy, sometimes gusty sea of smoke; but keep your breath till you reach a certain height, and you will see notable things—perchance encounter gods. In this outlandish region, as elsewhere in God's world, the good (when a good man holds the balance) is found immeasurably to outweigh the bad.

* For a general view of the more prominent traits of the German character, we cannot do better than refer our readers back to Herr Weber, in our July Number last year.

Art. IV.—*Encyclopädie der Deutschen National-literatur*, von O. L. B. Wolff. (*Encyclopedia of German National Literature*, by O. L. B. Wolff.) 4to. Leipsig: 1834–40.

THE treaty of Westphalia, concluded in 1648, was a precious boon to Germany. After a contest of thirty years, which had spread desolation over the surface of that once-flourishing country, during which whole districts had been devastated, and the track of War,

> "doomed to go in company with pain
> And fear and bloodshed, miserable train!"

was marked out by the ruins of entire towns and villages, and by cities half-depopulated, it brought a breathing-time of repose and restoration, as necessary to the well-being of her people as it was precious and welcome. The air, which the brute clangour of the war-bugle had violated, was filled with songs of cheerfulness and gratulation; the field, rent by the hoof of the charger and the artillery-wheel, now bore but the trace of the productive plough; and to the rapid and destructive evolutions of a licentious soldiery, Pappenheimers and Pandours, Frank and Swede, "blue, white, and red, with all their trumpery," now succeeded the movements of the thoughtful scholar, the enquiring traveller, the toiling husbandman, and all the tranquil and humanizing interchanges of commercial and social activity.

All the curses of war, however, (that sacrifice of abomination that man offers to the evil one), cease not with it; such, as the punishment of our wilfulness, is the law and constitution of the thing by the decree of heaven. The foot of the stranger no longer oppressed the soil of Germany,—" peace was within her walls, and plenteousness was in her palaces,"—but a subtle and wide-spreading infection had shown itself, that threatened to eat into the very core of the national heart. This arose from the extensive influence the French had acquired in the affairs of Germany at the close of the war. This ascendancy soon made itself felt in the manners and literature of the country, producing the most injurious effect on its moral and intellectual life, and fatal for some period to the free development of the vigorous mind, honest character, and national spirit of her people.

Among all classes but the peasantry, instigated by the nobility, a taste for everything French was diffused; customs, dress, amusements, in the habits of domestic, and the proceedings of public, life. A writer* of the time thus reproaches his compatriots:—" There is no doubt, which many have remarked, that if our forefathers, the ancient Germans, could rise from their graves and revisit Germany, they would never believe that they were in their father-land among their own countrymen, but suppose themselves to be on foreign ground, amidst unknown and very different men; so great are the changes which have occurred—I will not say in a thousand, but in a few hundred, years. Among these not the least is, that the French (who by these Germans were not held in any particular esteem), are now everything with us. We have French attire, French dishes, French furniture, French language, French manners, French vices, and even French diseases are most abundant. These ancestors, instead of beholding in their beloved Germany men resembling themselves, would find it occupied by German-Frenchmen, who have so completely departed from their ancient customs, that nothing remains indicative of the past. They would regard us as changelings and bastards; and, with our Frenchified little beards, would rather deem us weak and cowardly women than sightly and brave men. They would pour on us their rough and energetic reproaches, or, not esteeming us even worthy of their scorn, with bitter mockery cast us from them." The native language, already extensively corrupted by the introduction of a multitude of foreign words, making it resemble, as Jean Paul afterwards described it, "a Prussian regiment, which contains deserters from all nations," was cast aside, as unworthy and unfit for literary purposes. Latin was employed by the learned, while French was the language of courts and high society; and the literature of the country was modelled upon the showy, but lifeless, specimens, destitute of all internal feeling, all fervour and force of imagination, of the so-called golden age of Louis XIV.

A nation like the Germans, radically of so much native vigour and intellectual aspiration, however seduced by the

---

* Thomasius, born 1655, died 1728, who vigorously attacked the perverted taste of the day. He lectured at Leipsie in 1688, where he excited the indignation and virulent opposition of the cotemporary literati devoted to the then unnational system, by publishing the programme of his lectures in the vernacular language of his country; by his innovations in many of the vitious usages of the day; and his determined freedom of thought and expression. He deserves lasting honour for his exertions to procure the abolition of torture, trials for witchcraft, and other inhuman and ignorant practises of that time.

selfish policy and mischievous example of their aristocracy, and the glare and glitter of the hollow refinement of France, would not be content to remain in a position so degrading. The wise and patriotic citizen would lament to see how little respect for the individuality of the national mind, the root of all its greatness, such servility displayed. It would be a yoke which his spirit would loathe—a subjugation which would be torture to a free mind. Deeply would he feel with the poet,—

> " There is a bondage which is worse to bear
> Than his who breathes, by roof and floor and wall
> Pent in, a tyrant's solitary thrall :
> 'Tis his who walks about in th' open air,—
> One of a nation who henceforth must bear
> Their fetters in their souls——"

and against such a state of things every true German spirit would arouse itself, and struggle for emancipation. There were not accordingly wanting many authors, truly national in spirit and noble in purpose, who sought to resist this fatal domination, and introduce juster standards, and more free and enlightened aims. Among these were Spencer and the other pietists ; but not being recognized as philosophers, or persons of quality, who alone gave the tone to things, their exertions were almost ineffectual. The religious works of these men had this beneficial result : they nourished a taste for their own genuine and profound language, in all who loved their mother-tongue ; and, however objectionable to some the system they advocated, however pitied by the faithful, or smiled at by the rational, by leading the attention of the people to subjects connected with the spiritual and the eternal, they counteracted that tendency to the sensual and the finite, which was the contaminating result of the French literature and philosophy. Thomasius made use of his native language in his criticisms, in his monthly German discourses, and his lectures on reason and morals ; and handled all branches of philosophy in a popular manner. Confined and imperfect as was his philosophic scheme, and distorted and confused as was his prose style, intermingled with Latinisms and Gallicisms, yet his effort was one of the most cheering appearances of the time, in German literature. He loved his native tongue, and the unsophisticated modes of genuine German life ; and with a clear insight into the errors and wants of the social condition, he combined much wit and humour, and was, to no incon-

siderable extent, well qualified to take the field against the failings and prejudices of the age. He attacked the false, but fashionable style, "the glory of the literati, and their shame," contributed much to the preservation of the national character, embittered the triumphs of the learned champions of the adverse party, and incessantly directed public attention to the matter. From his time, German began again to be employed for literary purposes. Wolff did much, in his philosophical essays, to improve the structure and expressiveness of his country's language, and maintain its reasserted importance. Baumgarten, an acute and clear thinker, who wrote much on æsthetics, and to whom we owe the very term now so familiarized and serviceable, continued the struggle. The dull and pedantic Gottsched also did some service to this truly national cause, in condemning the disfigurement of the language by the use of foreign words, and opposing the taste for bombast in poetry then prevalent. His zeal for the purification of the German was of great use ; and he at least perceived its genius, though deficient in the requisite talent to exhibit its powers in his own productions. But to Lessing, himself one of the most distinguished German authors, and whose language is a model of German prose, are his countrymen most indebted for the regeneration of their literature.

In the midst of the intellectual meanness, perversity and false taste, which then reigned, Lessing grew up. He vehemently rejected the yoke, boldly withstood the prevailing commonness of thought and style, vigorously attacked and discomfited the much-lauded French taste, and spread far and wide in his numerous writings the elements for the improvement of German literature. He sought utterly to annihilate the imitation of French errors. He looked upon the age of Louis the Fourteenth as weak and contemptible. The ancients he honoured from the very bottom of his heart, and earnestly recommended the study of them to his countrymen ; but his admiration was grounded on a true insight into the nature and merits of the classic master-pieces,—while for the French perversions and improvements, as they were denominated, he had the most intolerant scorn. With all his reverence for the productions of the past, he was not one-sided, as he had a keen and just appreciation of the literature of England, Spain, and Italy, then but little known to Germany, so dissimilar from that of Greece and Rome ; and laboured to introduce an acquaintance with its best works, as an antidote to the feeble and artificial exhibited by that of France, and as specimens of vigorous thinking, lofty imagination, and pure taste. He brought the powers of a sound and enlarged philosophy, and an acute and forceful intellect, into play, in this endeavour. The effort was an arduous one for a single individual, however richly gifted; but the success was as great, or perhaps greater, than could have been anticipated. In his hands, the struggle, begun by earlier writers, who were the pioneers to his manœuvres, was finally successful. Mighty Germany,

" She of the Danube and the Northern Sea,"

saw the dawn of a national literature, breathing a language worthy of a great people, vigorous and supple as an athlete, distinct, majestic and impressive, and which, casting off the childish things which, in the moment of her weakness, had dazzled and corrupted her, promised to place her, at no distant day, on a footing with the noblest of European nations.

Of the intellectual wealth of this literature, as exhibited by one class of its writers—the poets—we do not now intend to speak. Goethe, Schiller, Herder, Tieck, and many others of the brotherhood of song, have earned a just and noble reputation; and we shall take another opportunity of directing our readers to their merits and characteristics. It is of some of her prose writers that we have now to make mention, partly because they are rated as writers of distinction by their countrymen,—because they are but little, if at all known, save by name, to the English reader,—and as they are striking examples of the vigour, fancy, humour, and originality of the German mind. The samples that we shall tender will not be the best perhaps of their respective bulks, as both time and space, as well as the nature of our vehicle, do not admit of the fittest selection; but they will not fail to convey a strong impression of the value of the stock from which they are taken, and convince the inspectors that the article is worthy of their further consideration. We moreover desire to convey some notion of the life and productiveness that the German mind displayed, when it threw off the gilded fetters of the French infatuation, and cultivated those talents which Providence bestowed for their own and others' elevation. War, commerce and adventure, are not the worthiest records of a people's activity; it is by its books only that the soul of a nation is best made known. They are the noblest and most engaging chronicles, and most adequately show how it lived, and moved, and had its being.

The *Iliad*, the dramas of Shakspeare, the *Paradise Lost* of Milton, the *Inferno* of Dante, the *Quixote* of Cervantes, will be monuments of the greatness of those lands where they were produced, and outlast tablets of stone or columns of brass. The pillars of Hercules are but a name; but " the blind old man of Scio's rocky isle" is of undying vitality—an immortal creature, a possession for ever!

We are further induced to proffer these specimens of German literature, as an erroneous notion has been formed, and disseminated by many, that its productions are of a stiff, pedantic, and obscure character;—that it is replete with contributions of misty metaphysics, subtle refinements, æsthetic jargon, and maudlin sentimentality. Of the despised metaphysics of Germany we will say, in passing, it would be well if England knew more. The unspiritual philosophy of Locke, and the flagrant morals of Paley, would cease to be the textbooks at her two universities; the teachers and expounders of their religious dogmatisms would be compelled to seek other sources of purer and more elevating character than these erroneous guides, and to abjure that " noble inconsistency" by which their conclusions are now made so awkwardly to square with their premises; her people would then be something more than a nation of shopkeepers. But this result we have yet to hope for, and we fear at no early period, unless some mighty event should strike and quicken the national mind, and raise it from that worship of prejudice, bigotry and mammon, which now engrosses it. To go back, however, to our German brethren:—the above conception of their literature is far from being in accordance with truth. Dulness, pedantry, and enigmatical darkness, is to be found among it, as among all other literatures, enough and to spare. A whole Dunciad of lesser men has not been able to eclipse the light cast upon the literary history of his country by one Pope. This unfounded conception is of long standing, and not confined to our own country. The Père Bouhours launched the adventurous and uncomplimentary proposition, " Si un Allemand peut être bel esprit?" The dialogue is maintained some time on this subject. The worthy father is strongly impelled to determine positively in the negative, believing a German bel-esprit to be a nonentity, a pure chimera,—but finally sums up thus: " C'est une chose singulière qu'un bel esprit Allemand ou Muscovite; et s'il y en a quelques uns dans le monde, ils sont de la nature de ces esprits qui n'apparoissent jamais sans causer de l'étonnement"!

Against this verdict we decidedly protest. In justice, however, to the worthy Frenchman, we are compelled to own, that it might be difficult to disprove his assertion by examples with which he could have been familiar; as the earliest which we intend to produce (Abraham à Santa Clara) was cotemporary with Bouhours in his old age. Had he lived to be acquainted with those specimens of German humour and vivacity which we hope to produce, we think he might with a safe conscience have retracted his sweeping censure.

Abraham à Santa Clara was born in 1642, in the Swabian village of Kräkenheim. His worldly name was Ulrich von Megerle, of a noble family so called. In his eighteenth year, he entered into the order of Augustin friars, became afterwards preacher in Bavaria, and finally court-chaplain at Vienna, in which capacity he officiated forty years; was appointed *definitor provinciæ*, and died there in 1709. His works have all singular titles, somewhat in accordance with their contents, such as *Judas, the Arch-Scoundrel; A well-filled Wine-cellar; The Chapel of the Dead; A Shop for Spiritualities; An entirely new-hatched Nest of Fools; Wholesome Hodge-podge.* They are a real mine of wit, fancy, and humour; although, from a continual bantering play upon words, the homeliest illustrations, and an unrestrained vivacity of expression, they would be deemed offensive by the taste of the present day. These and his pulpit discourses are distinguished by odd, rough flashes of wit, grotesque but significant thoughts, and an intellectual activity that is most extraordinary. In these he does homage to whatever soundness of views was displayed by his age; while he chastises, with the most biting satire and indignant sarcasm, the vices and follies of his cotemporaries, particularly the court. In spite of his extravagant humour, and daring originality of expression, they are of engaging interest, as they are replete with a keen spirit of observation, and knowledge of human nature, "quips, and cranks, and wanton wiles," with touches of true eloquence, noble sentiments, and sweet and graceful fancies. His style, bizarre, energetic, and witty, was cleverly parodied by Schiller, in the well-known capuchin's sermon of *Wallenstein.* Discourses like those of the good Abraham à Santa Clara would be strangely received now-a-days; but we would willingly dispense with the narcotic drenches or the spiteful tirades so often endured, to have a dash of his liveliness and raciness, his honest detestation of hypocrisy and wrong-doing, and his warm-hearted love of mankind.

The following is an extract from his *Judas;* which we present to the misogamist for his justification, to the old maid for her comfort, and to those about to marry for their consideration.

" The confect which our first parents, acting like very step-parents, eat of, on which eating repentance followed, was, according to the statement of some divines, no apple, but an Indian fig, which even to this day is called Adam's fruit. It is, however, little like the fig of our country. but quite round, and of an aspect of extraordinary beauty, as if it had borrowed the hues of the rainbow. When this fruit is plucked, there is found therein an accurate resemblance of the cross of Christ, with all the implements of the passion, which, verily, is to be marvelled at ; and this is the very same fruit of which Adam so inconsiderately eat. This fruit is an exact emblem of the marriage state, which, outwardly, has the appearance of being nought but sweetness ; yea, a very sugar-sphere, a honey-vessel, a heart-feast, a wine press of joys, a Kermes-box, a pleasure garden ; yea, a heavenly mouthful of dainties ; but, but, and again and again but—the interior does not correspond with the exterior, for inwardly, in the married state, nought is found but crosses and sufferings. Dear World-Ape,—excuse me, my friend, for conferring on you a title,—go forth with me in the pleasant season of summer, to enjoy the genial air ; there you will hear the many-toned flutings of the nightingale, the homely filing of the chaffinch, the quail with its resounding throat-clock, the cuckoo with its rustic forest-cry, the ousel with its popular waltz-melody, the lark with its ' Te Deum laudamus,' the goldfinch with its *passarello,* &c. There you will behold the embroidery of the meadows, the silken-green tapestry of the sward, the abundant fruitfulness of the fields, the jocund dancing of the forest foliage, the happy resurrection of all earth's productions, the marriage pomp of the wide world's countenance ; go onward, and enjoy the golden tide to thy heart's content : let us wander a little along the verdant bank of the purling stream, which flows towards us like a bright mirror in a verdant frame, and like liquid chrystal ; in this water we may see the beautifully painted clouds, the beautifully radiant sun, the beautifully blue cirque, the beautifully bright vault, the beautiful heaven. Thereupon, my dear brother, hast thou a yearning for heaven, plunge in, and, from delicate consideration for me, send a *staffetta* of what things come to pass in heaven. On which the other replies, that, in such a game, he takes care to miss his turn, as he would no doubt sink to the bottom. The very river would lose its name, and be henceforth called stock-fish sauce, in commemoration of his folly ; for in these waters was no heaven, only a mere semblance of it, and, verily, instead of tasting thereof, he would have but foul water to gulp, and his days would be cut short for ever. There are so many unadvised children of Adam, who, when marriage is spoken of, prick up their ears like the nag when he sees the haversack shaken ; their pulse beats when the least mention is made of a wedding. They deem the married state to be one of unbroken felicity, a pure heaven. Oh heavens, they are much mistaken,—it is but mere appearance ; there is nothing to be found therein upon which to lay any foundation, but foul water, affliction, and opposition."

The following is a handful of gleanings which we have picked up, that will give some notion of the vigour of the soil, and the healthiness of the seed :—

" The sons of Lamech, Tubal and Tubalcain, were inventors, the one of music, the other of the art of working in metals. If these brethren dwelt in the same house, there must have been a sad noise and discordance. In the upper story sang Tubal, in the lower hammered Tubalcain ; above were the bellows for the organ, below for the stithey ; there resounded flutes, and here hammer-strokes and the rasping of files. Not unlike such a dwelling is the sinner who prays : in the upper floor music resoundeth from his mouth the praises of the Lord ; in the lower one—in his heart, sin is busy, with all its attributes ; above, hymns of praise are sung, below, there are sacrifices to Belial ; there the tongue chaunts with St. Cecilia, here the heart dances with Herodias."......

" Build thyself, like the fratricide Cain, a stronghold, and shut thyself up within it : nevertheless, the mute 'who goes there ?' (the conscience) will make thee tremble. All thy breastworks, bastions, bulwarks, towers, gates, avail thee not. The enemy is within the town—thou bearest him in thy bosom. Thou canst not save thyself by flight ; everywhere the dumb ' who goes there ?' calls to thee. Creep, like Caligula, under thy couch, shelter thyself behind the impervious shield of the godless Artemnon, withdraw thyself to a closed and well-fortified island, like the tyrant of Syracuse, the tongueless ' who goes there ?' is ever at thy side. Let thyself be enclosed within a chest, like the poetical tyrant Elearchos, yet thy eternal companion is again with thee,—dread, accusing, and abiding."......

" Beauty is like a flower—to-day before the bosom, to-morrow before the besom."......

" Friends are plentiful enough, but they resemble the sun-dial, that only yields its services so long as the sun is above the horizon. Friends are plentiful enough, but they resemble leeches, that only attach themselves until they are satisfied."......

" Of the Franciscans there is an innumerable host in heaven. The world, however, is mostly frankish ; heaven mostly Franciscanish."......

" As the night-violets in their retirement only open their chalices in the obscurity of night, and impregnate the air with their divine odours, so should man, as much as possible, only in secret deal out his benefits to those who need them."......

" The dissolute seek pleasures, but when they have obtained them, they soon discover how miserably they have made their bed. The *Venus vulgivaga* delivers a lively prologue, but the epilogue is the more sorrowful that follows."......

" Opportunity is the greatest thief,—a devil above all devils. It befools the wisest, enervates the strongest, pollutes the most modest, circumvents the most heedful, and corrupts the most saintly."......

" We are poor starving wretches : let no one over-rate himself : whatever we have, is a possession we derive from some other source. If the earth required of us its metals, the sheep its wool, the silkworm its silk, the ox its hide, the field its flax, how poor and needy should we stand there. But one little lamb has man, which grows up with him, eats with him, sleeps in his bosom, and is dear to him above all other things, or, at least, should be so. This is called *honour*—an honest name. This alone appertains to him. Meanwhile comes some one, and steals this lambkin from him—robs him of his honour. Must not this pain him ? An honest name is the best of jewels, the best leader, the best treasure, the best of joys, the best of blessings."......

" The poets represent Argus as a warden with an hundred eyes. What in this instance is but a fable, is truth in relation to God. God's eye is over all, watches over every creature."......

" In Paradise, certainly, there was one happy man. His titles were, by God's grace, Adam the First, Mighty King of all earth's circle, Archduke of Paradise, Duke of Womanheight (*Frauenberg*), Count of Joydale, Lord of Cheerfulness, &c. He had a superabundance of all things, and a splendid court. The four elements were his chamberlains ; the lion, the tiger, the stag, his servitors ; the birds his orchestra ; the raven was the *basso*, the ouzel *tenor*, the finch *alto*, the nightingale *treble*, the chaffinch played the violin, the magpie the castanets, and the woodpecker the cymbals."......

" A library is an apothecary's shop, from which the most approved medicine may be obtained."......

As one solitary example, however weighty, may not be sufficient to establish our demurrer, we shall proceed therefore in our roll-call of witnesses, and summon Christian Liscow into court. He was born in 1701. Of his childhood and youth but little is known. We hear of him first as private tutor at Lubeck, in 1730. In this year he was appointed secretary to a public functionary in Holstein: some time after he resided at Dresden, where, in 1744, he was secretary to the minister Von Bruhl. This post, however, he was soon compelled to relinquish; as, by his satirical attacks, he had excited the enmity of many, particularly of the English minister resident there. We are sorry to hear this of our countryman, whose skin must have been of most morbid irritability and of singular extenuation. An ambassador should be as impervious to sarcasms and jokes as the rock of Gibraltar to a cannonading. After his departure from Dresden nothing is known of his movements: he died at Erterberg, in 1760, in confinement, it is said, for debt. He is superior to many of the satirical humourists of his country, in the energy and purity of his style and the ease and vigour of his language. His irony is most keen and well-directed, and his exertions were constant to sweep away the mass of folly, imbecility, and pestilent false taste that defaced the literature of the day. He is deficient, however, in an enlarged knowledge of human nature, and a correct judgment of the complicated relations of life. His writings have fallen into some neglect, as many of them were directed against dunces long since forgotten, and subjects which have now lost all interest. A collection of his works was published at Leipsig, in three volumes, in 1739: the best of them is an essay *On the Value and Necessity of Miserable Authors;* from this we shall give some extracts. He states that if the race of worthless scribes were extinct, the whole tribe of booksellers and printers must go a-begging, as they could not expect to gain a livelihood from the works of superior writers; as among the six thousand annually published, he had, after a very accurate investigation, been able to find only three of any merit. He then proceeds:—

" Our enemies are fertile in lively and ingenious sallies. They have an active propensity for ridicule, and we are the parties who furnish occasion for their witticisms, and for the gratification of their censoriousness. How would it then comport with their health if we were defunct? What subjects would they find for their lively fancies? They must not believe that I am joking; for a suppressed joke is no child's play. It causes many pains and tormenting twitches; suppressed wind is not half so dangerous. One instance only has occurred in my life when I uttered a witty flourish, which, considered as the solitary joke of a despised and

miserable scribe, was tolerably clever. But I must keep it to myself, and the knowledge of the pangs its gestation and delivery caused me. I would not wish my bitterest enemy to experience them. If, then, a single joke, of which I was happily delivered at the proper time, caused me such distress, what would not be the sufferings of our meritorious writers, who are so fruitful in clever sayings, if we did not furnish them with occasions to unburthen themselves? Their flashes of wit and brilliant sallies would eat inwards to the heart; for Ennius long since declared to his contemporaries, that a sage would rather hold fire in his mouth than suppress a witty remark; '*flammam a sapiente facilius ore in ardente opprimi, quam bona dicta teneat.*'* Our enemies would therefore certainly burst if we were not in existence. Why, then, do they wish for our extinction, with which their own is so nearly connected? Let it be admitted, however, that it is possible they might survive us, the world would then have little more good of them. For we are the very persons who force from them their most ingenious essays, in which men so much delight. Where, then, would be found the subjects of so many excellent satires, if our opponents had no one whom they could ridicule? And what would not the literary and cultivated world then lose in us? It is true we cannot furnish it with meritorious writings, but the ancients have already remarked that, 'although the ass does not possess the best of voices, and is extremely awkward at music, men, nevertheless, are able to make the best flutes from his bones.'† And our efforts, however miserable they may be, are, nevertheless, occasions of so many profound refutations and ingenious lampoons, of all which the world would be deprived, if there were no one who wrote wretchedly and ridiculously.

." This is the smallest advantage that the world reaps from us, as this only extends itself to the learned and the enlightened. The benefits which we confer on the whole human race are of greater importance, and prove our necessity more strongly. We are those persons who crush reason and sound sense, which are so detrimental to the peace of churches and states, and the prejudices which are so indispensable to a peaceful, easy, and pleasant life. We defend antiquated notions, and purge Churches of heretics. It is true that our enemies do the latter also, but very rarely; and when they do so, it is achieved by rational arguments, and that is good for nothing. Without us, reason would prosper wonderfully in the world, and our foes would pervert everything. Who would have been bold enough to resist the dangerous innovations of a Puffendorff, a Thomasius, a Leibnitz, and their disciples, if we had not stepped forward to the breach? This alone is sufficient to prove how ne-

* Plutarch in Convivio, ex vers. Xylandri.   † Cicero de Oratore.

cessary we are to the world. Our merits are so great, that we deserve the reverence of all mankind; but, unfortunately, no one will recognize them. Men recompense us with ingratitude; and it has, alas! come to this;—that to ridicule us and our understandings, is considered an undoubted proof of an acute understanding. Nevertheless, * * * our grievous cross, which we only are capable of bearing, has its advantages also; and, I think, it is peculiarly fitted to place our necessity beyond all doubt. Our opponents, the authors of merit and talent, discover follies everywhere, or, at least, they imagine so; and it is impossible that they should not laugh at and ridicule that which appears to them foolish. If, therefore, there were no wretched scribblers upon whom they could vent their malice, no worthy man could be safe for them. They would, as they must always have something to censure, attack everything great and honourable in the world, and by their satires distress the peace of both Church and state. We may therefore boast, that we, in consequence, sacrifice our own well-being for the common good, and, without arrogance, say that we are indispensable to a state.

"I wish from my heart that all Christian rulers may take what I have written into mature consideration, and humbly beseech in particular his Imperial Majesty, and all electors, princes, and ranks, of the holy Roman empire, right-illustriously to conceive how worthy those persons are of their protection, who have so long served the state as a bulwark against a restless host of malaperts. The time, I think, has arrived that some remuneration for our important services should be thought of, or an effort to secure for us, in some measure, a cessation from the attacks of our enemies, and put a bit in their mouths. How have we deserved, that, although other respectable persons are protected from evil doers, we are delivered over to the wilfulness of our persecutors? We suffer for the security of others. I know it well. But why should we bear the sins of our fellow-citizens? I discover no reasonableness in this, and doubt not but that my judicious representations will have the effect that I desire. Should, however, the great ones of this world, misled by the pitiful chattering of our foes, presume that our miseries deserve not consideration, and are not of that magnitude as to call for the use of the temporal sword, then I turn to those who bear the spiritual sword, and implore them, most respectfully, to manifest the same zeal against the base proceedings of our opponents that duty demands. I do not expect this from the more able clergy, for these gentry are, to their disgrace, in combination with the mockers. But I shall be content if the duller portion will lift up their voices like a trumpet, and inculcate, with their accustomed eloquence, at least, to the common man, that it is a great sin to laugh at ridiculous things. They must not think that it is a difficult or an impossible thing to maintain so simple a proposition. I must inform them, and they may believe it, that Girard, in an essay,

which after his death was found among his papers, has established, with six hundred weighty proofs, that there are but few greater sins than that of writing a satire. I am so convinced of their ability, that I firmly believe they can accomplish more than this. I hope, therefore, that they will have the goodness to contend as boldly with their tongue, as I with my pen, against our foes, who are no friends of theirs......

"What have I done then? I have told the truth to many wretched scribblers, laughingly, who suffered themselves to believe they were something which they were not. Is this so great a crime? I will believe it when it shall have been proved that Providence has taken this species of men under His especial protection, and given them the privilege of tormenting mankind with their silly writings, without other, and respectable, persons having the right of saying to these intolerable scribblers, What are you about? Let it not be said that a Christian should patiently tolerate such scribblers, for Christian patience does not impose on us insensibility. We capture fleas without it being deemed a crime, we take the life of gnats, we annihilate flies. The saint does so as well as the sinner. Why, then, should we make it a case of conscience to destroy literary vermin? Those who are blessed with so thick a skin that they are insensible to the bite of these creatures, are fortunate; but it is unbecoming in them to condemn those whom nature has provided with a tenderer cuticle. It is earnestly to be desired that men were more sensitive, and took more pains to free the world from these noxious animals. The grievance gathers strength every year, and I know not what will be the result. The enormous host of these wretched scribes is as fully qualified to introduce barbarism as the swarms of Ostro or Visigoths, and yet men hesitate about opposing their increase."

Similar in kind and object, but somewhat different in quality, are the writings of G. W. Rabener, who vigorously maintained the contest for good taste, sound morals, and the improvement of the language and literature of his country. He was born of a highly-respectable provincial family at Wachau, near Leipsig, in 1714; studied afterwards at the university there; early distinguished himself for his enlightened views, lively wit, and active understanding, and won the friendship and esteem of all cultivated minds. He first appeared as an author in 1741, in a periodical work, and subsequently in the *Bremen Essays*, a work of much celebrity at the time. In this year he was appointed first to a responsible station in the tax department of the Leipsig district, then to a higher one at Dresden. He was most just, diligent, and exemplary in the discharge of his official duties, and displayed so much wisdom in the arduous task of harmonizing the interests of the taxed with those of the state, that nothing was ever uttered against him save a sportive epigram by Kastner, which we hastily translate thus—

> " To ridicule, as well as fleece us,
> Engages Rab'ner's two-fold wit ;
> He makes the nation sigh and whimper,
> While he doth ever laugh at it."

In the bombardment of Dresden, in 1760, his house was destroyed, with all his furniture, library, and manuscripts. This, however, did not deprive him of that calmness and serenity of mind, arising from a happy temperament and resignation grounded on a sincere piety. In a letter to one of his friends he relates the circumstances of this loss, in a style replete with the submission of the Christian philosopher and the humour and fancy of a *bel-esprit*. It is some satisfaction to know that the peace which followed brought to him, with a restoration of his duties, a remuneration from his sovereign. We rejoice when they who are cheerful and virtuous themselves, and strive to make others so, participate in the bounty of princes. His writings are full of fine and varied observations, showing a deep acquaintance with men and their weaknesses ; painting to the life, with much freedom and vigour, their follies and errors ; but far from being impressed with any misanthropical sentiment, they breathe a most amiable gaiety, a firm love of mankind, and an unhesitating belief in their greatness and ultimate elevation. He was the intimate associate of Klopstock, and did much in the early part of the latter's career to protect and aid the awakening genius of his friend. He died of apoplexy in 1771. Several of his writings, like those of Liscow, had relation to more temporary circumstances, although many possess a more permanent and universal interest. To these belong his *Satirical Letters*, and his essay *On the Construction of a new German Dictionary ;* of which we shall now offer specimens :—

" I solicit," he says, " the contributions of my countrymen for this dictionary. The work is too vast for my own powers. Perhaps I am too candid in making this admission. With those who refuse the title of learned to him, who has not published at least six folios, I shall sink into small esteem for this modesty. Be it so. When my dictionary is published, it will be seen whether these laborious creatures will continue to be denominated learned without doing violence to language. If it should be thought that, in some instances, I have been too prolix, and have introduced subjects which transgress the purposes and limits of a dictionary, I am content rather to submit to this reproach than to cancel any part. I can point out an hundred articles in Bayle, which clearly prove that the title of the article stands there for the sake of the comments, and yet it is Bayle's Dictionary."

Then follows the words with their definitions. We select the term "eternal," with all its satirical and bantering explications :—

" ETERNAL is a word which every one uses according to his own opinion, and as it is most advantageous to his interests. To vow an *eternal* constancy is commonly heard from the newly betrothed, four weeks before marriage, but this eternity ordinarily does not endure, at the utmost, beyond four weeks after it ; and last autumn I was acquainted with a young bridegroom whose eternal constancy did not quite survive twenty-four hours.

" *Eternal* love is still more transitory, and properly but a poetical figure. Occasionally this is yet to be met with amongst unmarried persons, and it very much depends upon the female sex how long such eternal love shall last. For many know, from numerous examples, that such eternal love terminates as soon as the lady has ceased to be indifferent, and begins to feel an eternal antipathy.

" As with love, so is it very frequently with friendship. I remember being present in a society, where the bottle circulated freely, when three *eternal* friendships were outlived during the evening's sitting. When the parties are elevated, such eternal friendships do not hold together longer than the intoxication which begets them, for—*cessante causa, cessat effectus.*

" To conclude an *eternal* or perpetual peace is a Gallicism, and has the same interpretation in the French language as a truce has with us, and it is in fact a peace which lasts no longer than the parties see their advantage in maintaining it.

" To *eternalize* one's-self is, among literary men, a certain motion of the right hand from the left side to the right, which, without aid from the soul or the understanding, inscribes something on white paper, and afterwards transmits it to the printer. The keys of immortality are thus in the hands of the compositor, and they consist of certain little leaden alphabetical signs, which are smeared over with a dark-coloured material, and then impressed on clean paper.

" To aspire after *eternity* (*vide* Immortality) is a certain malady which is not only troublesome to the patient himself, but still more so to others. It commonly attacks young persons, abates in virulence with increasing years, but it sometimes happens that old men are attacked by it, in which case it is not only more dangerous, but, which is the more insupportable, such patients cannot be cured. Violent remedies against it are not to be recommended, as the paroxysm thereby becomes more severe and convulsive ; and in this particular those so attacked resemble crazy persons, whom we cannot venture to contradict without increasing the excitement of their disordered brain. The best remedy to be employed is, whenever such pitiable persons are met with in society, in spite of the very great obtrusiveness which is inseparable from, and a diagnostic of, this malady, the spectator should utterly neglect them, seeming neither to hear, to see, or have the least knowledge of them ; by no means to mention their names, in fact to say nothing whatever respecting them, either good or bad. This *recipe* may be found serviceable. Physicians are not yet agreed respecting the specific causes of this disease. Some, on account of the extraordinary gestures which the patient exhibits, and as, like other epidemics, it recurs frequently and at certain intervals, consider it a species of falling sickness, as they have remarked, that if the right thumb of the sufferer is seized and twisted, the convulsions are checked, as is the case in that disorder. Others are of opinion that it arises from vitiated bile. Galen considers it nothing else than a violent *cardialgia*, and the deceased Hofmann, in the third chapter of his treatise on literary infections, denominates it the author-fever."

In this humorous style he runs through the definitions of several other words, such as *compliment, oath, learned* (under this his last comment is, "a *learned* woman is a problem"), *enemy to mankind, enemy. foe, duty, understanding ;* holding up to ridicule the imbecile imitation of foreign manners, the servility, the pedantry, want of patriotism, the corrupt administration of justice, and the cupidity of his countrymen.

In his *Satirical Letters,* among other evils, he attacks the shameful abuse of their patronage which the patrons of livings committed, in appointing to the pulpits of the Reformed Churches men who were unfit to tend the cattle of the parishioners. He protests against any misconstruction of his object, as in using the sportive language of satire he affirms that his only purpose is to disgrace the reckless patron and the incompetent parson, and to make those more venerable who are faithful to their duties and ornaments of their profession. For this purpose, in one instance, he gives us a letter from the colonel of a regiment to his brother, a provincial noble, and the application of the wretched candidate to the said colonel for his interest with his brother. The following is the colonel's epistle :—

" DEAR BROTHER.—I am very glad that thy old fellow has walked himself off at last. His confounded reproofs were interminable. I wonder whether these fellows imagine that we give them preferment and bread, in order that they should preach to us every Sunday their bitterest truths, and send us all to the devil out of revenge. For the boors that is all well enough, and, if I were one, I should perhaps live religiously, as otherwise I should have nothing else to do ; but for men of condition, and us, who are the ancient gentry of the land, a sanctified drooping of the head looks extremely silly. If you had followed the directions of your old grumble-head, you would have become a worthy, pious, Christian citizen, and universally ridiculous to the whole *noblesse.* What think you, my dear brother, which is the more commendable, to take your nap during the sermon or over the drinking-glass ? Let the parsons pray for us, we will drink for them. Each one according to his calling. But after this fashion, you act like your cattle, said your old growler. Good ! Who knows if this be true ? If we profess to be the representatives of our forefathers, we must act like our forefathers. Devil take me, are there not yet whole nations who think something of their ancient nobility ? Every country has its own manners. A good, old, honest German must have little love for his fatherland, if he should visit France to learn to drink water. But to come to the main point. You are in want of a new parson. I have to propose one to you that is an accomplished fellow. He has campaigned it about with me these ten years, as chaplain in my regiment, and he is just the sort of man I like. He has written to me, and begged me to recommend him to you. There, read his letter yourself. I part with him unwillingly. He is a man after your own heart. If you do not choose to frequent the church at all, he is not the man to grumble. Give him a good dinner twice a-week, and you will find him as gentle as a lamb. You will have fine fun with him. He will drink you, and all your right honourable and noble guests, under the table, and when he has cast off his canonicals, he will swear like a corporal. Take him, my dear brother, you will not repent it. He has not studied at all, but I'll be hanged if he will not preach to you after a fine fashion, and the hypocrite stands as sanctified in the pulpit as if he were about to take flight to heaven. My Catharine liked him extremely. Now brother, as I say, take him. As far as he is concerned you may live any life you like, and if you should drive to the devil to-day, to-morrow he drives after you. He is a jolly fellow. Greet thy people for me. Adieu."

Then follows the letter, referred to by the friendly colonel, of this precious candidate for the cure of souls ; establishing, past all dispute, the character and qualifications stated by his noble commander :—

" MOST WORTHY COLONEL.—There is an incumbency vacant in

the gift of Herr——, and I should very much like to have it. Catharine tells me that you are on the best terms with him, and can easily procure it for me. I am tired of a wild life, and earnestly desire to have a flock and a wife of my own. Have the kindness to interest yourself for me. I have heard that the old clergyman lived on the worst of terms with his patron, but the fault was his own. I know how to deal with gentlemen. If he gives me my due he may live as he likes. You gentlemen are not made more religious by grumbling and preaching. You are too elevated in station for you to live a devout and Christian life to please us, and, between ourselves, little results from the continual pother. Increasing years work great changes. It is sufficiently annoying when men of condition are in attendance at court, and compelled, for a couple of weeks, to live seemly : must we in addition sour their lives when they are with their regiments, or residing at their country-seats? I know the world better. Drinking and such like are the only means, independent of your rank, by which gentlemen of your station are distinguished from the common rabble. Excuse this pleasantry,—I speak as I think. You know me before to-day. In one word, most excellent Colonel, get the incumbency for me, or, upon my soul, I will never drink another glass of wine in your company. In the hope of this, I remain, with all esteem, most gracious Colonel, &c.　　　　N. ——, Chaplain."

This satire may seem unduly severe, as it will be doubted if German society, at that time, exhibited a malady so lamentable as to call for such remedy. The grievance, however, was extreme, and of frequent occurrence; requiring unsparing vigour in the treatment. Rabener felt, like every patriotic and right-minded man, that clerical functionaries so base deserved no mercy. An unjust king, a disloyal liegeman, a faithless advocate, are dishonest and contemptible beings; but the falsest and most despicable of all things, is a false priest, who should be held up to universal scorn and reprobation. He lived in an age in which the specific evil was rife ; he had a painful experience of the moral corruption of his time ; and, recognizing his duty as a satirist, dealt with it as it deserved; which was to exhibit in the most striking manner the deficiency of the actual, not only, thereby, shaming the backsliders, but necessarily suggesting the ideal, the highest reality, as a contrast and a true means of working prevention and rectification. To satirize the evil does no dishonour or detriment to the true and the good; on the contrary, it elevates and strengthens it, for by an inevitable association it is presented to the mind in all its purity and excellence, which instantly offers it the homage of its earnest

reverence. Who can read this witty and bitter sketch, without having the image of the true churchman, the faithful pastor, presented to him ; of him whose doctrine and conduct teach the fear and love of the Being of all beings; of him round whom a Christian combination of the august and paternal sheds a most beautiful and engaging light ; who, in all his actions displaying purity of soul and innocence of heart, exhibits himself as a genuine child of God for the edification of all men. Oh heavenly task! Oh felicitous duty! To bear the charge of the everlasting gospel to all men ; treading among the world's miry ways with feet sandalled with truth, more glorious than the diadems of Asian kings ; with hands laden with precious balm for all the soul's dire woes and maladies; severed from earthly ambition by the happiest of destinies ; endeared to the lowly by his consolatory commission, honoured by the lofty for his power and dignity; strengthening the weak, solacing the broken in heart, "proclaiming liberty to the captive and the opening of the prison to them that are bound;" restraining the strong, reproaching the sinful, sustaining the penitent; teaching to sovereigns, with authoritative voice, justice and mercy; to the noble, " that gentilesse cometh from God alone ;" to the burgher, that he has to keep watch and ward over a celestial city ; to the peasant—on whom the misrule of proud and worldly men presses so sorely—cheerfulness and content; unto all, love, peace, and joy, faith, hope, and charity, and all spiritual graces, the gems of that crown which alone should adorn the brow of the Christian. That he who is honoured by this high and weighty calling should lower his soul down to the vices and foul pleasures of sensual life, is an abdication that must awaken the indignation and call for the chastisement of every virtuous man. The pen is then rightly employed as a scourge, and should be wielded in a stern and inflexible spirit; and the guilty recreant should be made to feel that it is sharp as a serpent's tooth or scorpion's sting.*

* Before quitting the subject of Rabener's writings, we may mention that in the second volume of " the Friend," pp. 315-319, of the edition of 1818, Mr. Coleridge has copied, *verbatim*, with the exception of some of the names (which he has changed to give it a greater political application), the story of "Irus and Ceraunius," as it will be found in Rabener's works ; and, so far from intimating that he has borrowed it, he calls the reader's attention to the circumstance that it was " *written and first published at the close of* 1809." Much has been said of the plagiarisms of Coleridge, and in the observations made by his friends, in

From Rabener we pass to one whose works alone do much to establish the claim of our German friends to have the verdict of Bouhours reversed; to Theodore Gottlieb von Hippel. He was born at Gerdauen, in East Prussia, in 1741, where his father was rector of the public school. To him he was indebted for his earliest knowledge of languages and the sciences, as well as many peculiarities which he afterwards displayed; his love of solitude, his mode of study in his youth (lying, as he himself states, whole weeks in bed, in order to give an uninterrupted application), his mysticism and his notions of the spiritual world. In his fifteenth year, at his father's desire, he devoted himself to the reading of theology, philosophy, and mathematics, at Königsberg. Here he acquired the friendship of a Professor Woyt, with whom he resided as companion and tutor to his son. His intercourse with this person, a scholar and man of the world, was particularly serviceable and instructive. In 1760 he accompanied a Russian officer of rank to Petersburg. This introduction to the great world gave birth in him to new ideas, plans, and desires, which had a decisive influence on his future life. Here favourable prospects were opened to him, but his attachment to his native country, an ardent love of knowledge, and a philosophic and contented mind, induced him to return home, after a short sojourn, where he accepted the office of tutor in a noble family. He soon after strenuously applied himself to the study of jurisprudence, a taste for which had been enkindled in him by Professor Woyt. The hope of attaining a distinguished sphere of action, combined with wealth and station, was long nourished by him in solitude. His attachment to a lady of property and distinguished family, so irresistibly increased this, that in 1762 he relinquished his duty as tutor, and, overcoming all the obstacles which his poverty and want of connexions interposed, with incredible sacrifices and extraordinary zeal, entered upon his

relation to those pointed out by Mr. De Quincey, we think they forgot what was due to the latter, both as Coleridge's liberal critic and most sincere and munificent friend. We yield to no one in the deepest admiration of Coleridge's genius, and the acknowledgment of his vast powers; we loved him as a man, and venerated him as a sage; but nevertheless we declare, that with a knowledge of his productions, it is impossible to read to any extent in German literature of the last hundred years, without discovering the numerous unavowed instances in which he has been indebted to many of its writers. With his great and original mind this fact is difficult to be accounted for; but without fear of disproof, we do not hesitate to affirm it.

legal career. From this time he became publicly known, as a man of great talents, unusual perseverance, and practical ability; succeeding in all that he willed and undertook. He gratified his ardent desire for honour and wealth, obtaining both. He gave up his union with the woman he loved, and lived single all his life; that, in that independent state, he might apply himself with undistracted mind to his beloved studies, and be able to pursue the plans of public and private utility which he had formed. He rose to a high rank in his profession, after passing through various offices, in all of which his judgment, expertness, activity, and rectitude, were conspicuous. Late in life he obtained from the emperor a renewal of the nobility of his family, as a means of facilitating the advancement of his children, as he called his nephews, in the military profession. He died at Königsberg, in 1796, aged fifty-two.

The events of his life, for about the first twenty years, are to be found beautifully detailed in an autobiographical fragment left behind him at his death. The remainder he intended to have finished, of which many detached portions were found among his papers at the time of his decease.

Nothing was common or ordinary in the man. With the excellencies ascribed to genius he also possessed many of its faults; with a vigorous and enlightened understanding were combined in him a proneness to fanaticism and superstitious weakness; piety, pushed at times to bigotry, and an intense inward love of virtue and duty, with frequent surrenders to sensuality and worldliness. His enthusiastic feelings of friendship did not exclude his premeditated withdrawals from those who appeared most dear to him. A warm-hearted humanity was associated in him with despotic severity; a passionate love of nature and her simplicity, with artfulness in his actions and demeanour.

With all these extraordinary contradictions and deficiencies in the man, it is not our present purpose to interfere. The spiritual and animal faculties were of singular force in him; and against his evil inclinations he struggled with a strong, if not always a successful, will. *We* are not to judge him. The soul of the man was by nature lofty, noble, and clear; a brotherly love of mankind, a reverence for God and the godlike, a thorough appreciation of all the graces that make up the Christian character, a piety the most winning, a zeal for virtue and the elevation of humanity, united with a fulness of worldly knowledge, profound and original ideas on man, nature, and society, and with a rich vein of humour and wit, are to be found in his writings.

The most celebrated of these are two novels, the *Lebensläufe*, and the *Kreutz und Querzügen des Ritters A—Z*. In the first, many events of his own life, and of those of his friends, are represented; and it abounds with sketches of the rarest idyllic beauty and most touching interest. In the latter— now in sportive, now in severe, irony—he ridicules the pride of nobility, wild fanaticism for liberty, eagerness for the formation of secret societies, and trading in mysteries, of his day. In both is to be found much that reminds us of the sweetness and tenderness of Goldsmith, the humour and pathos of Sterne, the wit and mockery of Swift, the fancy of Bunyan, the knowledge of Fielding, and the inward life and spiritualism of William Law. Next to these is his book upon marriage, *Uber die Ehe*. A full and systematic treatment of the subject must not be looked for in this work. It is rather a collection of fine, humorous, and original observations, ideas, and paradoxes; the result of the experience of an acute and philosophic observer of mankind, put forth in the liveliest garb, plentifully besprinkled with the laughing flowers of wit. His other writings are a treatise on the *Bürgerliche Verbesserung der Weiber*, some dramas, spiritual songs, and several treatises on questions of jurisprudence, of considerable merit and originality. All that he wrote appeared anonymously, and so strictly was the secret of the authorship (known only to two confidential friends) kept, that they were ascribed to several distinguished men of the day; among others to Kant. Several incomplete dramas, sketches of romances, and other materials, to be interwoven in future works, were found among his papers; of which only the delightful biographical fragment before-mentioned has been published. It is no slight recommendation of his works, to say that they were the delight and the study of Jean Paul Richter; and the extent to which they influenced the style and method of the latter, will be instantly perceived by the reader who is acquainted with the productions of both these original men. Hippel himself noticed it; for when the *Invisible Lodge* of Jean Paul (the work which first established his reputation in Germany) had been perused by him, he said, in returning it to a friend, "He is either a son of mine or we are brothers in authorship."

From his book on marriage, many times reprinted in Germany, extremely popular there, and deservedly so, from its wit and its wisdom,—in which he declares that "neither sex has the least worth without the other, but united they make up the complement of humanity,"—we make the following extract: it is addressed to the softer sex on the choice of a husband:—

"Which of you desires to have a learned man as your husband? You, perhaps, sweet sprightly maiden. Well, then, play the illiterate. Read nothing yourself, or if you should have read much, act as if you had not done so, but listen complacently. If you must converse, entertain him with little tales, and mere simple stuff. The gossip of the town can do no mischief, but there must be something grotesque and piquante in it. Play some street melodies, or strike up such common airs as 'Our mother has geese.' An astronomer, I know, will as little suit your taste as a night-watchman; but, between us, why select a learned man?

"Will you have one who lives expensively? then marry an able and dexterous man who has no means, but who will be able to acquire wealth without extraordinary difficulty. All *great* impediments only make such persons covetous, and if they have once paid homage to the idol Mammon, they sacrifice every thing to it. However, it is generally better to marry some one who has the prospect of becoming rich, than one who already is so. Well earned possessions are better than those inherited. Be careful, however, to obtain, during his life, a provision for your widowhood, otherwise, at his death, you would be the laughing-stock of the whole city.

"Will you have rank? I pity you. The very best of colours suffer from the sun. Not only are the keys of St. Peter's said to cause men to go bent before they are picked up, but all people generally stoop who seek something. A man who is conscious of his own superiority holds it unnecessary to receive honour from others, and unseemly to seek such attention. One greedy for honours cringes before those above him, and considers all that are equal to him, consequently his dear helpmate, but as dependents; those who are inferior as slaves: if a countess looks favourably on him he can deny her nothing,—to please a princess he would hang himself.

"Is a rich man your object? A girl that marries a young man only on account of his wealth, cannot fail to degrade herself; if she marries an old man, she has hired herself to him as his servant. Children destroy everything; people of years, or old children, are saving in all things, and wish, if possible, to immortalize every possession. If you reside in a palace, you occupy but one room, the remaining chambers are for others. If you secure riches, who will guarantee you against avarice or extravagance? In one case you mount guard, in the other you go a-begging. A trivial circumstance oft changes the temperament, and, as consumption may terminate in dropsy, so may a profligate be converted to a niggard.

"Will you have a poet? An extraordinary question! I have nothing to object to a poet, but, believe me, in the married state, sound healthy prose is better than poetry. Difficulties in love turn people into poets * * * A poet has no existence but in the realm of imagination, and marriage is right well fashioned to clip the wings of the imaginative power, and to bring us down to earth. The history of Pygmalion who loved a statue, and Narcissus a shadow, are no recommendations of persons who exist only to give indulgence to their fancy. Poesy is like alchemy, which ennobles the metals. If the poet makes good verses, he has, you may be sure, some maiden in his eye; a poem on his wife will not speed him, unless upon her death. The wife, nevertheless, acts wrongly in being jealous of her poetic husband; unless his imaginative power is on the stretch, he is inactive, and a mere bungler. Some inspiration he must have; but this inspirer need not be more than ideal; and need not justify the smallest jealousy. The most common things, even his mother-tongue, he is ignorant of, if his fancy be not enkindled. From his poetic vocation, he has accustomed himself to this, and no falling-off need be feared, as a consequence of this, in any of his customary operations. Why then, my dear lady-poetess, would you compel him to ride without spurs, and to spend a whole day on one road, which he may sicken of in an hour? To write prose generally signifies to journey often with six, oft with four, oft with two, sometimes in an open carriage, sometimes in a common cart: poesy is on horseback. He who cannot count syllables is but a small light among the equestrian order. It is said of many of these gentlemen, that when the horse does not prance high enough for them, they would mount aloft in the gondola of an air-balloon. Without doubt, Pegasus must disapprove of such poetic licenses. Bucephalus and Pegasus yoked together, and lord knows who in the chariot,—that would be a journey! Between us, madam, all the excesses of that darling of the nine sisters, your husband, however evil they may appear upon paper, are but nonentities, mere poetical figments."

With respect to places of residence, he says:

"Great cities are for lovers a purgatory, for the lofty thinker an hotel, for the ignorant a theatre, for philosophers a sepulchre, for witlings a lecture-room, and for physicians (*dat Galenus opes*) a pest-house or a mine."

The following is a humorous description of the criterion to be used by parents, to ascertain the capabilities of their children in works of prose or verse:

"Wouldst thou know, respected friend, whether thy clever son will gather palms in prose or in verse? *Recipe;*—a glass of physic, of which sixty drops are to be taken every hour, in any liquid one chooses. Let him measure himself this prescribed quantity, and if he let them run, drop by drop, he is a broken-winged prosaist; if he lets them flow freely, and counts during this shower, one, two, three, to sixty, he is a poet. If he can eat immediately with the spoon, he will be able, if he and the public will, to write *methodo-mathematica*; if, however, for twenty-four hours he cannot bear the sight of the spoon, then he will be a lyrical writer; should he not be able to use the said spoon for six days, without a cold shuddering, educate him accordingly, and, if fortune be favourable, he will become a Homer."

In this work are scattered some fine and original thoughts on education, remarkable for their keen insight, their practical worth, and their cordial humanity. In fact, from his various writings a *cento* of profound and invaluable truths on this momentous subject, this finest of the fine arts, might be selected, worthy of becoming a manual to all who take an interest in it. We select at random the following, as specimens:

"There was a time when teachers did nought but punish or caress, soothe or manœuvre, and called these alternations education. The human being is not destined to extremes,—such festivals of joy and periods of lamentation,—but to the daily bread of ordinary life and steadfastness. Posterity will not be the first to garner in the benefits of this education-chemistry; the advantage has already exhibited itself here and there, and it is in the very nature of the thing that it should reveal itself immediately. We use the body for action, and man is born for action, and education requires tongue, heart, word, deed, and truth."......

"He who teaches the child only to command and not to obey, has neglected it. He may perhaps have instructed it for the duties of a prince, a noble, a citizen, a peasant, but not for that of a man. Only by self-denial, by labour in the sweat of his brow, by heartiness, by respect for others and their rights, by contentedness with what God has given him, and a firm renunciation of all that the juggling fancy presents as necessary, and, by a wise and Christian enjoyment, will man find life endurable, and learn, above all, that humanity is not an alien thing."......

"Educate the child, I pray you, not to fulfil the offices of youth, middle life, or old age, but of the *entire man*; not for the fragmentary but the Catholic, the complete.* Teach him those methods by which he may be able to discipline himself, principles which are eternal and unchangeable; occasionally resign him, in certain cases, to himself, for soon you will be compelled to resign him entirely to his own control, and how sad would it be if he possessed a knowledge of all other things, but none of himself. Exact not a formal display of positive virtues, but from the first endeavour to preserve the soul of the child pure and uncorrupted by ignoble passions; all good qualities will then spring up within him, without your cooperation, and his heart will shut itself against all selfishness."

The jury we have empanelled in the cause of Bouhours versus German wit, begins, we trust, to be satisfied with our defence; and we hope that the plaintiff's advocate has ceased to look for a verdict. Before, however, we close the defence, although the evidence may be superfluous, we shall take the liberty of calling one more witness, who, in combination with those already cited, will destroy for ever, we think, the libel, "pleasant, but wrong," launched against our German friends. One powerful testimony, our much-loved Jean Paul, we leave unsummoned, for certain reasons,—who would have been something more than Cerberus, "three gentlemen at once," but equal to any threescore of the very best French wits that ever enlivened either drawing-room or duodecimo. The last that we shall introduce is George Christoph Lichtenberg, born in 1742, at Oberramstädt, a little village near to the town of Darmstadt. He was the eighteenth and youngest child of his parents. His father resided some time as pastor of the place, and died subsequently as superintendant-general at Darmstadt. Until his eighth year, our young Lichtenberg possessed a well-shaped person, and good health; at which period a spinal distortion, the result of some accident in nursing, showed itself, and rendered him humpbacked for life. This mischance not only affected his bodily shape, but had a powerful influence on his health, which was henceforth continually deranged and unsettled. From early youth he devoted himself to the acquisition of physical and mathematical science with ardent zeal, and laid the foundation of that knowledge which afterwards so eminently fitted him for that scientific and literary career in which he

pre-eminently distinguished himself. In 1763 he went to the university of Gottingen, where, with the most unwearied diligence, he applied himself to the whole circle of studies pursued there. In 1770 he was about to accept a professorship at Giesen; but at Gottingen, where the merit of the young student was recognized and appreciated, an extraordinary professorship was offered to him, which he accepted. He subsequently accompanied two young Englishmen of high family to England, where he became acquainted with many celebrated men, particularly with those to whom the tendency of his scientific pursuits would bear him,—namely, the great mathematicians and astronomers of his day; and had the honour of being presented to George the Third. His sojourn in our country was not of long duration; but his love of England, her literature and learned men, induced him again to visit it, a few years afterwards, where, among the many additional friendships he formed, not the least interesting were those of Sir Joseph Banks, Johann Reinhold Foster, the companion of the celebrated circumnavigator Cooke, and his son, George Foster. The next year, with much enlargement of his intellectual acquirements, he returned to Gottingen, and in 1788 he had conferred on him the dignity of Hofrath. Here he entered upon an active discharge of his official duty; his lectures upon experimental physics were of most distinguished merit, and his apparatus for operation and illustration was princely. His vigorous and original intellect, applied to the consideration of physical subjects and matters of scientific comprehension, had the most beneficial result in enlightening and advancing these studies. But not to subjects of such abstract and philosophic character was his activity confined. He soon became involved in learned controversies, in which he brought the force of his vigorous and peculiar humour, and keen wit, to bear in such a manner, as always to come off triumphant. Amongst others, he attacked the new physiognomical views of Lavater, then making much noise in the world; in which, if the argument was not always on his side (and it was rarely that it was not so), the laugh never failed to be. In a multiplicity of minor essays and fugitive writings, scattered in the *Gottingen Magazine*, and other similar works, such as his "Patriotic Contribution on the Methyology of the Germans, with a preface on methyologic study, or the art of getting drunk;" "On the particular estimation of women among certain

---

* "Remember still
Thou must resolve upon *integrity*.
God will have *all* thou hast, thy mind, thy will,
Thy thoughts, thy words, thy works."

212

nations;" "On Christian names—a contribution to the history of human follies;" "On the varieties and uses of cudgellings, ear-boxings, and thrashings, among divers nations;" "Consolations for those unhappy ones born on 29th February;" "Speech of the Number 8, in the last day of the year 1798, at a grand council of all the numerals," when "the cipher, as usual, was in the president's chair;" and many other writings of similar character;—but, more than all, by his admirable commentaries on Hogarth, he has acquired a conspicuous place among the humorous authors of Germany; and his productions of this class are ranked among the foremost in his countrymen's estimation. In the latter years of his life, from increasing bodily distortion, and the derangement of his health, this able man suffered much from attacks of hypochondriasis, so that he almost entirely confined himself to his chamber, and, except the society of a few confidential friends, lived apart from the world. A series of nervous attacks continually tormented him; fancies and notions the most absurd and extravagant, which, like Nicolai, a similar sufferer, he felt to be delusions, and which present to the psychological and physiological enquirer a most singular case. Of these a detailed account will be found in a biographical sketch which he published in his lifetime, entitled, *The Character of a Person of my Acquaintance*. These so completely destroyed all healthful functions, as to shorten the career of this original-minded man, and led to his death in 1790, in his fifty-seventh year.

Sickly and deranged as might be the outward frame, the soul of the man nevertheless was sound, vigorous and aspiring, as a forest-tree. In him were united a keen speculative understanding, with a reverence for the supersensual; great powers of humour and irony, with a loving respect for humanity, and a confidence in its essential nobleness; scientific ability, with poetic feeling; and faculties of such opposite tendency were so melted together in him, as to present an interesting and many-sided unity, worthy of study. Not artificially, by gathering and reminting other men's jokes, but as the result of an original individuality, he stands distinguished among German writers in that mysterious but fascinating mixture of playful wit, capricious satire, and deep feeling, which we call humour, and which is much more easily recognised than philosophically defined. Truth, above all things, had a preciousness for him; and in his works he shows himself to be a man whom no new view appals, but who resolutely and honestly sets himself to work, in a praiseworthy spirit of acuteness and justice, to sever the real from the seeming, the veritable from the false.

His detractors have described him, but unjustly, as a mere imitator of Swift. There is much in him that reminds us of the witty dean; in Lichtenberg, however, it was no imitation, but a genuine idiosyncratic affinity; and he has manifested, particularly in his essays on Hogarth, an appreciation of the deep truth and living nature exhibited in the graphic poetry of our immortal engraver, a warmth of heart, and an earnest healthy humanity, that places him in a very advantageous position, in comparison. On the subject of Hogarth, we may observe a stronger resemblance in Lichtenberg to our Charles Lamb, the "gentle-hearted Charles," "alike, but yet how different!" And we may safely declare, that finer commentaries that those of Lichtenberg and Lamb, on these undying productions, have not been written, nor is it very likely that they will ever be surpassed.

We should be much pleased to exhibit to our readers specimens of these illustrations of Lichtenberg; but to do so effectually would demand too much of our space, and we must therefore content ourselves with laying before them the following specimens from his *Remarks on Divers Subjects, Religious, Political, Moral, and Literary*. An edition of his collected works, in nine volumes, was published in Germany in 1805.

"If I should ever write a sermon, it should be on *the power of doing good*,—a faculty which every one possesses. We should be unhappy creatures if the emperor alone had the power of doing good. Every one in his position is *an emperor*."......

"Would but that one-tenth of the religion and the morality which we find in books, existed in our hearts."......

"There is something in the character of every man which cannot be destroyed. It is the osseous frame of his character. To seek to change this, is to attempt to bleach a negro."......

"I am astonished that cats have two holes in their skins exactly at that place where their eyes are."......

"We ought not, ordinarily, to trust a man who, in asserting anything, always puts his hand upon his heart."......

" How happy would many men be if they occupied themselves as little with the affairs of others as their own."......

" There are really many persons in the world, who read on purpose that they may not think."......

" There is no man in the world who, having become a scoundrel for a thousand dollars, would not have remained honest for half the sum."......

" I lodged at H——, in a situation which commanded a view of a small street, that formed a communication with two great ones. It was amusing to notice the change of mien and action in those who passed; how much more they seemed at their ease when they entered the small street, where they supposed themselves less subject to observation. One drew up his stockings, another laughed, a third drooped his head. The young women were thinking of the preceding evening, and smiled; while some of them arranged their ribands, and made a species of toilet, for the conquests they expected to make in the great street."......

" If physiognomy become what Lavater anticipates, they will hang young children before they commit those offences which would make them worthy of the gallows. In fact, every year, it will be necessary to hold a new species of confirmation, a physiognomical *auto-da-fe*."......

" It is singular, and I could not, in remarking it, avoid smiling, that Lavater discovers many more things in the conformation of the noses of our present authors, than the rational world does in their writings."......

" We ought to investigate profoundly the causes which so commonly produce flowers without fruit; and that not only with regard to trees. The same thing occurs with our learned children; superb flowers, but no fruit."......

" There, perhaps, never was a father who did not consider his child as something entirely original. I believe, that amongst parents, the learned are most exposed to this error."......

" If chance did not interfere so much with our education, what would become of the world?"......

" I would give something to know for whom those actions have really been done, which it is publicly said have been performed for our country."......

" There is a certain country, it is said, in which a particular custom prevails. The sovereign, as well as the ministers, are bound to sleep on a barrel of gunpowder as long as the state is at war, and that in the chambers of the palace; and so arranged that every one may see that the night-lamp is not extinguished. The barrels are sealed, not only with the seals of the deputies of the people, but they are attached to the floor with leather bands, which are also sealed. Every night and morning the seals are inspected. It is said, that for a long time that country has not been at war!"*......

" They pretend that, for the last five years, no one has died of joy in our land."......

" It is an opinion somewhat received in Germany (thank heaven, however, only among young persons), that a man should understand the subject thoroughly, upon which he has to write at length. It is quite the contrary. Those persons who do not think, and who write only in order to write, do not know, fifteen days after, what they have written. Heaven preserve us from such writers; but, unfortunately, they are the most common."......

" That which is opposed to the glory and immortality of such writers, (an obstacle more to be feared than the envy and malice of all the gazettes and critical journals together), is this unfortunate circumstance,—they are obliged to print their works on the same material which serves *to enwrap pepper*."......

" There is no merchandise in the world so singular as books. Printed by persons who do not understand them, sold by persons who do not understand them, bound, criticised, and read by those who do not understand them, and often written by persons who do not understand them."......

" I am astonished that no one has ever written a Bibliogeny—a didactic poem, in which might be described the origin, not so much of books, but of a book, from the very springing of the flax seed until it is placed in the library. Many most amusing and instructive things might be said upon the subject. The derivation of rags, the manufacture of paper, the rich stores of waste paper, printing, how one letter is used here to-day, there to-morrow; then how books are written (here would be an ample field for satirical display); then would follow the binder, the titles of books, and finally, the *cornets de poivre*. Each of these subjects might make a canto, at the commencement of which there should be an invocation to the spirit of an author."......

" A philosopher, somewhat impertinent in joking (I believe it was Hamlet, prince of Denmark), has said somewhere, that there were in heaven and earth many things not found in our philosophic compendiums. If this good young man, who, all the world knows, was a little cracked, intended to make any allusions to our treatises of natural philosophy, we might boldly reply to him, 'That is true;

---

* We should recommend the adoption of this custom to our French neighbours.

214

but, as a set-off, how many things are there to be found there, of which there is no trade in heaven or on earth.'"......

" If any one left, by will, ten thousand louis d'ors to the greatest rascal in Germany, I should like to know how many claimants there would be."......

" The skin of man is a soil upon which hairs grow. I am astonished that a method of sowing wool upon it has not yet been discovered; it would be more profitable, as men might then be shorn."......

" Condamine relates that he met with apes in America, who imitated all his operations. They ran to the clock, then to the eye-glass, then they pretended to write. We have many of these philosophers."......

" Oh yes, Doctor —— was a most worthy man; he visited everybody, great and small, were it even at midnight. One might say of him, as of the physician in ordinary of the Emperor Augustus, '*Æquo pulsat pede pauperum tabernas regumque turres.*'"......

" Among those great discoveries which the human mind has made in modern times, the foremost, in my opinion, is the art of criticising books without having read them."......

" If it happens sometimes that a man is buried alive, there remain, in revenge, a hundred on earth who are already dead."......

" When the Goths and the Vandals took it into their heads to make their grand tour in Europe together, the taverns in Italy were so full, that no one could be heard; often three or four of them were ringing the bell at the same time."......

" When any person in Cochin China says '*doji*' (I am hungry), people hasten immediately to bring him something to eat. There are certain districts in Germany where a poor devil may exclaim twenty times, ' I am hungry,' and which would be of as much service to him as if he said '*doji*.'"......

" I have had the journals of last year bound. I have tried to peruse them again; a most tiresome experiment. Fifty instances of false anticipations, forty-seven of false prophecy, three of truth. This perusal has very much diminished my estimation of the gazettes of this year; for what the latter are, the former were also."......

" In the system of zoologists, the monkey ranks next to man, although at an immense distance. If a Linnæus were to classify animals according to their happiness, or the advantages of their condition, there are many men who would be placed below dogs of the chase and coach-horses."......

With the favourable conclusion which will be drawn from the evidence that we have adduced, and the reference to the other written testimonies which we have named, we shall let the case go to the jury of our countrymen, without the usual artful appeal of the pleader, which too often is a tissue of falsehood, blandishment, and sophistry, seeking rather the winning of a cause, than the establishment of any great principle of truth, justice, or public virtue. It will be well if they make themselves fully acquainted with that mass of proof which we have pointed out: friend Bouhours and the calumniators will then have the verdict against them, and they will themselves have acquired indubitable conviction that the literature of Germany, however short of perfection and completeness, is one of which that country may be proud; which other nations, in many of its qualifications, would do well to study and to emulate, as the production of an able and original people, destined to produce a large and important influence on the intellectual condition of the world.

The day of national bigotries and national antipathies is passed, or passing rapidly away. The wide heart of humanity is beating in all its arteries, full of an embracing activity, a yearning hope, a loving spirit of comprehensiveness. Full gladly must we learn;—as gladly teach. Synthesis, not antithesis, is beginning to develope itself as the aim of man's exertions; and as mind is to be the mighty agent in all ultimate union, let us have a right understanding and a reverential appreciation of the mind of other nations.

31. ECLECTIC REVIEW, 3rd ser. 73 (1841), 510-523. M/H No. 3721.

Art. II. *German Literature, by Wolfgang Menzel. Translated from the German, with Notes.* By Thomas Gordon. In four volumes. Oxford: D. A. Talboys. 1840.

OUR readers will recollect that in the year 1837, we inserted a series of articles on the stalwart and vigorous Teuton whose name is appended to the above work on 'German Liter-'ature.' We commenced that series by some account of Wolfgang Menzel himself, and then proceeded to give an analysis of his work, accompanied by copious citations. Those extracts were from the incomplete and now never to be completed MSS. of two friends who had long indulged the hope that their 'translation' might one day be published with their joint names, and stand as a memorial of a long and endeared friendship. But their work was so long delayed by unexpected engagements that, though they announced it, they cannot complain if others have taken the field before them, and rendered it unnecessary that they should take it at all. They have the less reason to complain, inasmuch as the new translator has made honorable mention of his obligations to the series of articles in question, as well as to the articles in the Edinburgh and Foreign Quarterly.*

It is a curious and striking tribute to the merit of Wolfgang Menzel, that while at least two distinct translations were preparing in England, one was also preparing in America; it appeared some little time before that which is the subject of the present article. Of the American version, we have seen only one volume, and that for too short a period to allow us to form any opinion of its merits. We can therefore give no opinion as to whether that or the British translation bears away the palm.

But without attempting to decide which is the better of the two, we have no hesitation in saying that the present translation is upon the whole a very good one. There are some few (as we conceive) misconceptions of the author's meaning, nor is the expression always quite so elegant as it might have been. There are also some cases in which the meaning is not very intelligible; but on referring to Menzel himself, we generally find that such obscurity is but the shadow cast by the original, and that what is dark and mystical in the English, is also dark and mystical in the German. It is true there is much less of this matter in Menzel than in most German authors, yet is he not always entirely free from it. He would not be German, were it otherwise. Upon the whole, the translation is marked by the union, to a considerable extent, of fidelity and elegance—by a close adherence to the meaning of the original with a due regard to the idioms of the language into which the meaning is to be transfused. Of the justice or otherwise of these commendations the extracts which we shall presently make will be the best test. Our author seems to have overlooked no source of information which could by possibility throw light either on Menzel's history or the character of his work; and as already said, he has made diligent yet perfectly fair use of those translations of portions of Menzel's volumes which had already appeared in the English periodicals. We must also mention,

---

* The following is the translator's courteous mention of his obligations to the labors of his predecessors. 'Menzel's *Deutsche Literatur,*' says the translator, 'has been several times reviewed in England, and always very favorably. The following I have met with, which are, so far as I know, the only notices—Foreign Quarterly, vol. xvi., Edinburgh Review, vol. lxiii., Eclectic Review (new series) 1837, vols. i. and ii. The Eclectic contains six or eight articles, almost entirely occupied with translations, principally of portions of the first volume of Menzel. These I have compared with my own; and to them, as well as to the translated passages contained in the Edinburgh and Foreign Quarterly, I have to express my acknowledgments for several expressions adopted.'

to the great credit of the translator, that he has given som account, in the shape of brief foot notes, of all the principal writers mentioned in the course of Menzel's extensive survey; and though these contain little more than the dates of birth and death, place of residence, rank, and titles of principal works, yet they form altogether a considerable mass of matter, and add much to the interest with which the volumes may be perused. We are also glad to see that the German works which have been translated into English have been for the most part carefully distinguished, though here we have noted some important omissions, especially in the cases of Herder, Lessing, Schiller, and Goethe.

At the beginning of the first volume we find a sketch of Menzel's history and character; it contains little which was not already stated in the sketch which was introduced into the first of our own series. One or two paragraphs, however, contain further information, with which we will gratify the reader.

' The following characteristic passage is extracted from the Recollections of Ernst Muench :--

' ' It was upon another fine summer's day that, going to invite my friend Steingass to a walk, I saw an unknown figure sitting at his study table. This was a powerful young man, of slender form and swarthy complexion, with a pair of keenly penetrating eyes; his long black hair parted on his forehead, and cut after the fashion of the Black Forest. His beard was long, according to the fashion of the *Turners;* and he was clad in the shortest black old-German coat I had ever seen. Long did the young man sit before me, uttering nothing but the most indispensable answers, and absorbed in the map of Switzerland. My friend soon appeared, and introduced him to me as Herr Wolfgang Menzel, of Waldenburg, near Breslau, formerly *Vorturner* at Jena and *Bursch* at Bonn, who had thought it prudent to withdraw himself from the immediate presence of the Prussian government, and seek his personal safety in that classic land of liberty, Switzerland.

' I now learned much of the sacred legend of Menzel's early achievements; of his feuds with the Breslau Menzel, Carl Adolph (the historian), with whom he is not unfrequently confounded, but with whom he disowns all kindred; of his dissensions with his parents, who opposed his literary career; of the hard fate of his youth, whence arises the harshness of his manly mind; of his audacious attack upon Goethe's lofty aristocratic supremacy at Weimar, &c. I soon discovered that he was, indeed, an overbearing companion, with whom it was not every one that could live, but richly endowed with intellect, and of a very decided character; in short, that he really was of the wood out of which, if they themselves mar it not, illustrious men are carved.'

It is by no means our intention to enter further into Menzel's history, or to discuss again the character of his mind or the value of his writings. For our views upon these points we must refer the reader back to the series in question, where they will find them fully stated. Neither do we intend to enter into an analysis of the present work; that was also given in the aforesaid articles. We shall merely take this fair opportunity of laying before the reader Menzel's judgments on some important points connected with German literature, to which we had not then an opportunity of referring. They are the judgments of a highly intelligent and honest witness, and his observations are always well worthy of attention, either from the light they shed upon the state and prospects of the literature of his own country, or from their being equally applicable to the literature of every other. Wide as are the points of difference between the literatures of Germany and England, there are not a few in which, at certain epochs, they present considerable resemblance, while in every country, literature, being subjected to the same general laws of development, will pass through radically the same revolutions, encounter the same obstacles, be liable to the same abuses, and will require the same correctives.

The extracts we made were, as our translator says, principally from the first volume, and more especially from the chapters which gave an account of the ' Mass of Literature,' ' German ' Nationality,' the influence of ' School Learning,' the influence of ' Foreign Literature,' the ' Book Trade,' ' Religion,' and ' Philosophy.' From none of these, except the last, do we think it worth while to make any further extracts. In our article on ' philosophy,' we remarked that none could perceive more strongly than Menzel the defects of German philosophers, especially in point of style, and that a disciple of Reid or Stewart might be satisfied with the force with which he exposes them. We remarked that if we had had space we should have liked to cite a few passages on this subject. As space now unexpectedly offers, we will avail ourselves of it. We rejoice to find the obscurity and the mysticism of this class of writers thus freely exposed by a German. We have often been disposed to imagine that their obscurity to an Englishman might be very mainly owing to insufficient acquaintance with the German idiom, and with the meaning of the technical terms employed. At the same time we have certainly often been staggered by the fact that the writings of no other philosophers who have written in a foreign language, ancient or modern, are half so unintelligible, so often utterly baffle the most diligent and clear-headed student, or leave room for such endless disputes amongst their commentators. We are often in doubt about the *truth* of their doctrines—but comparatively seldom about their *meaning*— often feel inclined to reject or modify their views—but are not perpetually in the dark as to what is to be rejected or modified.

31. continued

Of course there are some exceptions to be made; but neither in Aristotle, Cicero, Bacon, nor Locke can we proceed page after page in utter darkness as to what is the writer's meaning. Plato, indeed, to appearance at least, is often mystical enough; but then we must not forget the dramatic form into which he has thrown his philosophical speculations, and the subtile irony which everywhere pervades them, which, independently of other causes, really leave us frequently in doubt as to what is his meaning, or whether he meant what he appears to have said. In many cases he is undoubtedly merely attributing to his characters the sentiments which dramatic propriety dictated, and in as many others, we may freely suppose that the statements of his great master are to be taken as simply ironical. With the German philosophers it is altogether different; their works profess to be plain, didactic expositions of philosophical doctrine, and we do not believe there are any other works of the kind in any literature of any age or country, in which there is so much that is utterly unintelligible. We have heard of one of their philosophers, we believe Hegel, who said when near death, and when it was too late to attempt another unintelligible exposition of what must be always unintelligible, 'Alas! there is but one 'man in Germany that understands my writings—and he does'nt 'understand them.'

We think there is great truth and honesty in the following observations of Menzel in relation to the obscure language in which the German metaphysicians have attempted to clothe their doctrines. We have especially been struck with the justice of a remark, which we have often made, but which we have never before met with either in a German or an English author, that the employment of vernacular terms (signal as is their advantage in point of energy and vivacity, where they are capable of being exactly defined, and the definition is strictly adhered to) is one principal cause of the obscurity of German philosophers. From the great diversity of meanings attached to them in ordinary life, all more or less related (so nearly related, indeed, that for ordinary purposes it often matters little in which out of several the words are employed), it is almost impossible to use them with the requisite precision. Gesenius, we believe, has remarked that German philosophers ought to write in Latin; and that it would be impossible for them to utter such unintelligible stuff in any other tongue than their own. We have heard an amusing anecdote of a somewhat comprehensive erratum arising out of the use of common words in a scientific sense. It is said that a philosopher, having written a volume to expound the distinctions between 'vernunft,' 'reason,' and 'verstand,' 'un-'derstanding,' arrived at the conclusion just after he had finished printing it, that each word more truly represented what

he had attributed to the other, and therefore requested the reader that whenever he met with the word 'reason' he would be pleased to read 'understanding,' and whenever he met with 'understanding' he would be pleased to read 'reason.' But to our extract.

'Scarcely one of our philosophers is understood by the people. They have borrowed a foreign terminology from the Greeks and scholastics; they long wrote in Latin, and even now they take the greatest delight in coining new words. Though this has procured for them the greatest reverence from the people, and lent to their most ordinary commonplaces an air of deep wisdom, yet it estranged the great mass of the public from philosophy, making it be looked upon as altogether an affair belonging to the school. Oken, who is as much distinguished for his patriotism as for his learning, inveighed with the greatest zeal against this foreign terminology, but without effect; nay, even without being himself able to avoid it. The difficulties of philosophical language are rendered still more perplexed by the peculiar and capricious use which each individual philosopher makes of the various terms. If we open their philosophical works, how different are the names which we meet in Leibnitz, Wolf, Kant, Fichte, Schelling, and Hegel. The foreign words, however, are, notwithstanding their diversity, still the most intelligible; the German, with their similarity, and in consequence of their various uses, are (the plainer they are in themselves,) the more unintelligible in philosophy. Whole volumes have been written about the true import of such expressions as *Vernunft* (reason), *Verstand* (intellect, understanding), *Geist* (spirit, mind), *Herz* (heart, feelings), *Gemüth* (sentiments, feeling), *Gefühl* (feelings), &c. Even yet no universal code of language has been adopted. The difficulties of language have kept on an equality with those of thought. The faculty of thinking having effected its release from the old obscurity by immense exertions, and only by degrees, was therefore compelled to create a new language for every new discovery. A tiresome, circuitous, and prolix manner of representation (*Darstellung*) was unavoidable, because it first directed men to simpler notions. Nothing is acquired with greater difficulty than what comes afterwards to be looked upon as a matter of course. The great majority of philosophies, indeed, to a certain extent, all the earlier ones, are merely preparatory studies. The great Kepler had to cover many hundred folio pages with figures, before those simple, well known laws which every one now comprehends without difficulty, were the result of his iron-like assiduity. The same holds good of many German philosophers, especially of those before Kant. Though we neglect, with an æsthetical aversion, the dry and often deceitful calculations of the intellect, yet we must confess that they were necessary. The most striking feature in almost all our philosophies is the scientific form, which takes pleasure in parading systematic tables, sections, and paragraphs.'—Vol. i. 312, 313.

We cannot resist the opportunity of citing the following

31. continued

account of the characteristic features of the philosophy of Hegel. Its absurdities, extravagancies, and impieties are almost beyond belief, and above everything disgusting, if we except the gross adulations of his followers and admirers. What hope is there of the philosophy of any country in which one man can conceive and print such stuff, and ten thousand praise him for it?

'This system is a complete self-deification of Hegel, for he makes no distinction between himself and God; he gives himself out as God, for he says expressly—'God does not know himself, does not exist, until he arrives at a consciousness of himself in men. A consciousness which in other men, for example, in Christ, is obscure, and manifests itself like a model only in representations; and that he arrives at a clear consciousness at the fulness of his being, only in a philosopher who is acquainted with the only true philosophy;' that is, in Hegel himself, in his own person.

'Thus we may have upon the throne of the world, as God, a withered pedant, a stiff, squinting professor, a tiresome, bombastic scholastic, a man filled with feelings of the most repulsive envy, one who takes an interest in the most trivial academic polemics,—in a word, a German pedant. The ancients placed a Hercules or an Alexander among the gods, but no Thersites. Only among the people of the mummies do we find a dogheaded Anubis and a diminutive, withered Horus.

'The whole affair, however, is quite natural. It is not the vanity of Hegel alone, it is a natural consequence of the whole tendency of the age, that a German pedant should pretend to be God. During the age of chivalry, heroes were gods; during that of the hierarchy, God became a second pope; it was therefore to be expected that in the age of learning, he would become a scholar, and that Germany, the land of learning, would produce him. I should be sorry, did my panorama of German literature want this principal figure. Hegel marks the highest point of the misdirected mania for learning, of this great craze of the modern Germans. In him the evil reached its culminating point, in form as well as in spirit; for his language is, by its obscure bombast, its tediousness and stiffness, just as his system is, by its arrogant and contemptuous, yet unsatisfied, peevish, and sickly pride, the most perfect expression of that learned abscess which has now come to a head. Hegel's philosophy would in all probability have attracted but little attention had it not obtained political adherents and patrons. And how did it do so? Did not the god-professor look down upon the kings of this world? I know not; but certain it is, that attendance upon Hegel's lectures was highly recommended, and that the Hegelians were favored in the filling up of situations.

'The Hegelian system presented itself, as a political scholasticism, furnished with almost the same weapons as the ancient ecclesiastical scholasticism. As they had to deal, not with facts, nor with convictions, but merely with notions; as they drew nothing from religion or morals, but all from logic, it was in their power to play with notions

and positions as they chose, to prove everything or nothing. The system became an absolute dialecticism without contents, without object; a mere means of explaining every possible object in any way men chose. In this relation the notorious position of Hegel: 'All that is, is in accordance with reason,' was principally used to prove that our present condition is absolutely the one most in accordance with reason, and that therefore it would be not only revolutionary but even foolish, nonsensical, and unphilosophical to find fault with any part of it.

'This new scholasticism returned even to the old distinction between the initiated and uninitiated. The abstruse language of Hegel, the affected obscurity in which he enveloped even the simplest propositions, in order to stamp them as oracles, were means intended to form an insurmountable wall of separation between the initiated and the profane.

'He has, therefore, made a right and proper use of the folly of those who imagined that they were drudging for their own vanity, while in reality they were promoting that of others. Few have become greater adepts in the art of mystifying. Now that he is dead his disciples dispute about what this or that oracular saying really meant. Something of the same kind has taken place with Schleiermacher, and with Goethe. These men having been often pleased to express themselves somewhat vaguely on the most important questions, the Berliners have always made it their business to admire, with the most serious air in the world, that which they understood least, each, however, making his neighbors believe that he understood it, whilst he himself was afraid that some of them might have really comprehended it. The Hegelians carried their folly so far, as to consider it a mere condescension to the inferior powers of the conception of men, to compare Hegel with Christ, and to think that they did honor to the latter in calling him a forerunner and apostle of Hegel; a subordinate messenger, who, by mere representations and appeals to the feelings, pointed out and foretold, as it were symbolically, the far more exalted Hegel, who was afterwards to come in the might of the notion (Begriff). This folly was carried so far, that Friedrich Förster, a man from whose historical spirit of investigation better things might have been expected, said, at the grave of Hegel, that he was, beyond all doubt, the Holy Ghost himself, the third person of the godhead. To such lengths the vanity of a coterie may lead its members,—yet perhaps only in Berlin.

'It is a striking characteristic of the age, that the Hegelians look kindly and graciously down upon Christ, whilst they look up with reverence to Goethe, as to something still higher. Hotho, for example, in his strange Preparatory Studies for Life and Art, showed that man's chief aim ought to be to immerge into the mind of Hegel, yet that through him an admission to the still higher joys of heaven was to be found in the mind of Goethe. Lerminier, a Frenchman who is, in other respects, far from being silly, and who was then in Berlin, has repeated him, and told his countrymen: 'Si Hegel a consommé la philosophie de son pays, Goethe en a consommé la littérature. En

219

verité, on croiroit avec ces deux hommes avoir abouti à toutes les possibilités de la pensée.'—Ib. 302—306.

One of the most amusing chapters in the work is that entitled ' Die Pädagogik,' on ' Education.' Though we cannot agree in the too moderate estimate which our author appears inclined to form of the indirect advantages resulting from the study of ' philology ' in comparison with what he calls the ' Realia,' there is very much of valuable truth in his observations, and of truth almost as applicable to our own country as to his. There cannot be a doubt, for example, that there are many pedagogues in England who teach the classics less for what they contain than for the language which conveys it—less for the kernel than for the shell—less as the repositories of important fact or impressive fiction than as collections of grammatical constructions and illustrations of the laws of syntax. Let such read the following observations.

' The young who never learn aught but words and forms will never become acquainted with the substance. They are thrust into school, and there subjected to philological drilling. Most of them look upon this drilling as a torment, office as the only means of liberation ; they, therefore, study only for the examination (examen), and try to cram into their heads as much philological knowledge as it will hold, troubling themselves, however, as little as possible about the substance, because an acquaintance with the letter alone is required of them.

' In this manner the greatest minutiæ of grammar became the chief occupation of our learned schools. As if there were nothing of more importance in the world, school-pedants contended about the most useless philological trifles, and compelled the great mass of the young to do homage to this enthusiasm for that which was absolutely nothing. Not only all the realia,—the German language, mathematics, history, geography, and natural sciences, gymnastics, and even religion, were all neglected ; and all the time and all the attention of the pupils were devoted exclusively to the dead languages. I am sure that many of my readers must remember, that the philologists, the teachers of Greek and Latin in the *gymnasia*, exercised such a tyranny, that they appropriated almost every hour to themselves, making over all the other departments to subordinate and despised teachers, so that these departments might at least stand in the lists. They must remember that the grossest carelessness and neglect was overlooked when it related to these shelved departments, and that blunders against Buttmann, Thiersch, and Grotefend, were the faults which were looked upon as sacrilege. Nothing was required of the scholars but to understand and imitate the niceties of the Attic and Ciceronian style, the difficulties of Pindar and Plautus. The chief aim of philology in almost every German gymnasium was, to train scholars who could produce a Greek or Latin exercise so interwoven and refined with artificial difficulties that the very mouths of the professors watered at the sight. Under the pretext that the reading of the pupils must be little, but good, they kept by a few classics, of which scarcely a single one was strictly enough parsed in several years. Yet the pupils, notwithstanding the eternal classicism, had never the advantage of becoming thoroughly acquainted with the classics. That this folly is not entirely done away with, is proved by the Bavarian school plan (schul-plan), the first of which (afterwards modified, it is true) was to make the whole of Bavaria Greek—and that before there was any talk of the election of King Otho I. This Bavarian school-plan excited the whole wrath of the dominant philologists against the oppressed but resisting realists. These stupid philologists have no right to the title of humanists. Humanism was something quite different ; it tended to an universal human culture ; the dead languages were looked upon by it as a means, not as an end. This new *grammato-mania*, however, considers the language as its sole end ; in the dead languages, only that which is rare, peculiar, or difficult. A pedant, for instance, to whom the guidance of an extensive celebrated gymnasium was intrusted, hunted only after rare subjunctives, and had got a precious collection of them. As soon as the pupils opened Plato, Thucydides, or Tacitus, a general bush-beating commenced throughout the whole numerous class. No mention was made of the god-like ideas of Plato, of the profound political philosophy of Thucydides or Tacitus ; subjunctives alone were hunted after, and entomologically arranged, like rare cockchafers.'—Vol. ii. pp. 17—20.

Equally certain it is, that there are not a few schoolmasters at home as well as abroad, who ridiculously pretend to convey an encyclopædic knowledge, and to cram the heads of their young scholars with superficial lectures on subjects wholly unfit for them. We have only to glance at the advertisements in our newspapers to learn at how cheap a rate benevolent schoolmasters pledge themselves to initiate the youth committed to their charge in the mysteries of all science—in how incredibly short a time they propose to send them forth universally accomplished. We commend to them the following sarcastic rebuke of all such empiricism.

' That aristocratic propensity which moves society from below, turning every journeyman tailor into a gentleman, and every cook into a lady, has infected even the simple schoolmasters and preceptors with a desire to imitate the university professors. Did every one know his own place, and maintain it with propriety, all ranks would be really equal ; but in place of their being sensible of their honor as citizens, they strive after a ridiculous and unworthy affectation of gentility. Hence proceeds that hunting after distinction which is so common in our schools. Therefore it is that every one wishes to become an author, to bring forward new theories, or to bring himself into notice by certain scientific hobbies. Is there not in every gymnasium one or more teachers, who are constantly attempting to prove that they ought to have been called to an university ; who are upon their own authority delivering philosophical lectures, or treating of the details of those sciences which happen to be their favorite studies, but which are quite unsuited for mere boys? Thus one treats of the most minute grammatical trifles; another of symbols; a third employs himself with some old author whose works he intends to edit, and thinks more of the *scholia* than of the school; a fourth having trained up two or three pupils to chatter Greek with him, never troubles his head about the others; a fifth is not ashamed to lecture on logic, and puts on a serious academical face when on that subject. The sixth is probably a botanist, and a particular lover of the cryptogamia; his pupils therefore learn nothing but to practice cryptogamy. The seventh, being an ichthyologist, teaches his pupils to number all the scales of all the species of fish on the coast of China. The eighth having a peculiar liking for mineralogy, fills the heads of the children with information about the most wonderful stones. There are even among the realists, many pedants, who, like the subjunctive-hunter among the humanists, enter into the most detailed expositions of their favorite studies to the children, as if this were their principal business.

'Thus, in consequence of the vanity of the teachers, either the subjects which of right should be taught in the higher schools are anticipated, or the valuable time of the pupils is wasted on miscellaneous subjects which have no business in the school. Mere boys are in this way sometimes made arbiters in literary disputes. Stupid professors, after having read to their pupils what they have written against their opponents, say to them, 'Well, have I not refuted him capitally?' I myself know such a learned blockhead, who read in triumph to his scholars what he had written against me.

'The desire to become distinguished at the expense of the young is shown chiefly in the invention of new methods, and in the creating of artificial difficulties, where there are no natural ones. Even the A. B. C. has not escaped this rage for novelty. One, in order to put something new in the place of the old alphabet (which, however, must also be learned), teaches the poor children to hiss, to whistle, to neigh, to coo, to lisp, to growl, and to grumble like beasts. Another attempts to explain the letters out of the archetypical numerals; a third takes the trouble of making the children unlearn their native German, in order to teach them anew, first Mæso-Gothic, then old High German, next middle High German, and lastly, following consistently the same process of development pursued by the nation, the new High German. These are all facts; the individuals are still alive. And can we wonder at them? The late Funke went so far as to teach children to amuse themselves, thus attempting by artificial instructions to render difficult what came to them so easily by nature. This mania for methodizing has infected every science. Look, for instance, what strange plans are constantly devised by the music teachers, who attempt to change the old notes into signs and other nonsense.'

—Ib. pp. 41—44.

Equally amusing and equally worthy of the attention of our countrymen, is the account which our author gives of the ridiculous multiplication of the 'objects of education'—far beyond either the time or the average abilities of the pupils. The struggle between what he calls the humanists and the advocates of the realia (or, as we should say, between those who contend for the advantages of polite learning, and those who would content themselves with what they consider practically useful) often ended in imposing upon the unhappy youth the necessity of studying all that belonged to the multifarious departments of both. We are not sure that the close study of the following remarks might not be of service to some of the members of the Senate of the London University, who, however admirable their general plan of study, have assuredly erred in rendering certain branches universally obligatory. We could have wished that they had not striven so hard to conciliate, as a German would say, the rival claims of ' humanism ' and the ' realia.'

' The multiplication of objects of instruction and the increase of school hours, even in the public establishments, kept pace with that in the establishments for private education and boarding-schools. Both were produced by the necessity for a different course of instruction from that hitherto pursued. The private institutions, therefore, rivalled one another in flattering the parents, and the public ones were determined not to be behind. The former were at first principally schools for teaching the *realia*; but as soon as the state itself founded real schools, the private establishments adopted the principle of humanism, and endeavored, by becoming universities in miniature, by uniting at once all objects of instruction, to surpass the real schools as well as the gymnasia, which did not teach so much. Yet these latter in their turn rivalled the former, and it was even proposed to elevate all public schools to a kind of universalism. The different favorite sciences of the learned, the manifold claims of the parents, and the indulgence of the state, which was quite pleased at seeing the young sitting behind their desks, produced that superabundance of objects of instruction, out of which no proper selection has yet been made......The pedagogues were fortunately divided in their opinion, so that while one tormented the children intrusted to his care with one kind of folly, his neighbor plagued his with another; and thus no child was plagued with both at once. At first they hated one another, and avoided the errors of the others from dislike; by and bye, however, they began to become reconciled, and to adopt each others' errors, thus forcing their unfortunate pupils to experience, at one and the same time, all possible pedagogical fooleries.

· In former times the humanist took possession of one boy, the realist of another; now both take possession of the same boy, and each makes the same claims upon his time and attention, as if it were in his power to devote himself to one alone. Formerly one pedagogue devoted his chief attention to religion, a second to morals, a third to the cultivation of the intellect, a fourth to æsthetics, a fifth to bodily and social training ;—now there are systems of, and establishments for, education, in which the pupil is taught to learn all at once. All the pedagogical rods have been bound together into fasces, and there is only the axe wanting to strike off the head of the poor boy who is utterly stupified by much learning.

'When will the German get rid of his tendency to roam into the boundless? It is true that endless paths lie open to men in every direction, and it would be all very well, did our strength and time allow us, to traverse them all; but 'art is long, life is short; we cannot become everything:' the young, therefore, should not be prepared to undertake everything. It is indeed very desirable that the dear German youths should thoroughly understand Greek, in order to appreciate all the graces of ancient Hellas, and the mild lustre and power of its spirit; I should also like that the good boys all understood Sanscrit, Persian, Arabic, Chinese, &c.; on the other side, life and practical utility, as well as poetry and dead science, must be attended to; it would therefore be well that the young, each and all, understood not only French, English, and Italian, but also Polish, Russian, and Turkish. This holds good still more with respect to the *realia*. Each of the boys should learn mathematics and mechanics, chemistry, natural philosophy, natural history, astronomy, geography, as well as the first principles of medicine, surgery, and pharmacy. But, cry out others, are we to neglect the body in the training of the head? Not at all; the young men must learn to exercise and swim, to ride, fence, dance, dress, carve, &c., thoroughly. But the heart, inquire others, and religion and philosophy? Should not the young be trained up above all in the knowledge of virtue and Christianity? Ought not the heavenly goal, which is exalted far above this earthly life, to be held up to their view? Ought not the human mind to dive into the holy mysteries of the Deity, and to press on to the origin of all existence, in place of sporting on the surface?

'Yes, indeed. Why not? All that and some more. But the gentlemen never consider where we are to get time for all this. It would be very well could it be accomplished, but it is impracticable. The gentlemen must therefore make up their minds to lower their standard of education; they must learn to look not only at what they wish to stuff into the youth, but also at the small capacity of the young, who cannot by any possibility receive everything at the same time.'—Ib. pp. 47—51.

We have no space for extracts from the chapters on 'History,' 'Natural Sciences,' or 'Political Sciences;' though containing much which deserves special mention. By far the larger portion of the work is devoted to polite literature and criticism. As, in our preceding series, we gave Menzel's judgment on Klopstock, Herder, Lessing, Wieland, and Schiller, we feel inclined to avail ourselves of this opportunity of adding a portion at least of his elaborate character of Goethe, who, if not absolutely the greatest name in German literature, is yet that which has occupied most space in the public eye, and has led to most discussion. But our space forbids. Nor must the reader forget that Menzel has long been engaged in hot iconoclastic zeal, against the idolaters of Goethe, and that therefore his estimate, though in the main correct, must be taken *cum grano.*

Though we should much like to extend our extracts, and to add to the portraits already mentioned, those of Jean Paul Richter, Hoffman, Chamisso, Tieck, and some others, we find our space nearly exhausted, and must conclude; merely remarking that the observations of Menzel on the principles of poetry and criticism generally, and on the causes which have ushered in each of the rapid revolutions which have distinguished the brief history of German literature, are often conceived in a truly philosophical spirit, and are quite as valuable as the spirited portraits of individual writers with which they are appropriately interspersed.

Though a work like the present can hardly have a very extensive circulation, we do trust that the students of German literature are sufficiently numerous to reward the diligence of the translator and the enterprise of the publisher. It is but just to Mr. Gordon to state, that though he has nowhere controverted the opinions of Menzel on the subjects of religion, philosophy, or literature, he distinctly begs it to be understood that he by no means always agrees with him. We are pleased to see that he fully agrees with us respecting the dangerous latitudinarianism of some of Menzel's remarks in the chapter on 'Religion,' and enters his protest against them. Menzel, while he has done most excellent service against the rationalists, yet seems in some degree, as might be expected, infected with the lax liberalism of his country and his age. His own opinions appear to be nearer those of the Pietists than of any other school; but while orthodox himself, he certainly seems inclined to exercise his charity beyond the limits of non-essential errors; at least we cannot interpret some of his remarks in any other way.

We cordially commend Mr. Gordon's translation to the attention of the public.

ART. X.—*Neuere Geschichte der poetischen Nationalliteratur der Deutschen.* Von G. G. Gervinus. Zwei Bände. (The Modern Literature of the Germans. By G. G. Gervinus. Two Volumes. Leipzig. 1840--1842. Engelmann.

THESE two volumes form a continuation of the same author's work on the development of the national literature of the Germans, in three volumes. Many of the views and opinions which Professor Gervinus holds are opposed to the sentiments of some of the ablest writers in Germany; but all have done justice to the ability and talent which he has displayed. Independent in his judgment, little caring to flatter the prejudices or even the feelings of his countrymen, his work has the merit, if not of always commanding assent, at least of exciting to reflection. Very different from the mass of literary histories, it is not to be idly skimmed over, nor does it by any means supply the want of a *Conversations-Lexicon.* We do not always learn when a writer lived, but we are sure to be entertained by much ingenious speculation concerning his writings, and the prevailing tone and colour of the times in which he lived. These speculations and a too great love of antithesis sometimes degenerate into mannerism. But although his work will be useless to fine ladies and gentlemen who wish, with little trouble, to chat about German literature, we can strongly recommend it to those who, with some previous knowledge of the subject, wish to follow out their studies in an independent spirit. Omitting the three first volumes (on which we shall probably give an article shortly, since the national MSS. on which they are based are most important,) which, although very interesting, are less calculated for the general reader, we will confine our observations to the two last, which very properly form a complete work of themselves. They embrace the period from Gottsched to the deliverance of Germany from the French yoke. The author closes his work without bringing it down to the present time, for reasons not very flattering to his contemporaries.

"More recently our literature has become a stagnant marsh filled with such noxious matter that we must wish for some hurricane from without. Our literature has had its time; and if German life is not to stand still, we must decoy the talents which have now no object, to real life and to politics, where a new spirit may be cast into new matter. As far as my powers permit, I follow this warning of the time."

His scorn of the present writers warms him into a multitude of expressive epithets which almost defy translation in our colder language. In conclusion he calls up Harry Hotspur.

"Shall I quote his catechism? I find it exceedingly beautiful: those who know nothing may call me a barbarian if they please.
'I had rather be a kitten and cry —— mew
Than one of these same metre ballad-mongers.' "

We have no very great affection for many of the writers of the new school, nevertheless we think this somewhat hard measure.

In a work which consists principally in reasoning and reflections, it is difficult in a limited space to find passages which will convey a just idea of the merits and peculiarities of the writer. Perhaps the following remarks, which form but small part of his observations on Wieland, will show how far superior he is to the majority of writers on similar subjects.

"Wieland defended himself (1775) in The Conversations with the Vicar of * * *, and confessed that he had gone too far; though with his usual *halfness* he tried a hundred excuses, none of which were very happy, whilst the objections against which he advances no answer remain in their full force. He comforts himself for the evils which his tales may have caused by the good they may likewise have produced. Moreover, he says that if he had foreseen such a result, that he would not have written them, although he declares that caution in a poet in a moment of genius is a weakness. He soothes himself with Pope's maxim—'Whatever is, is right;' and 'as Ariosto and Boccaccio already existed, *his* productions would not make the world much worse!' He will not be responsible for the accidental evil which he had produced, but he is silent respecting the necessary evil, which was easily to be foreseen. He would not put his Idris into the hands of his own daughter, but he intended to educate her so that it would do her no harm if she read it. This is in connection with the aristocratical maxim of Shaftesbury, that the heart must be in unison with the head —that the virtue and goodness of man were dependent upon wisdom, true enlightenment the only means of true amelioration; and that a fundamental morality must supply the place of a superstitious religion.
"*Naif* sentiments and innocence exist in Wieland's personal and moral character. In the honey-

moon (since 1765), which extended to honey years, he published his joys in his different writings with antique *naïveté*, but in these writings themselves there is nothing of innocence or of *naïveté*. False guides had corrupted his taste and style, although they could not corrupt his life. Here lies the contradiction in Wieland's conscience—the contradiction between his pure consciousness in his course of life, and the voice of the time—the difference of judgment between his domestic character and his works. . . . . Wieland is always full of moral tendencies even in those licentious tales; and he afterwards brought his poetry into still closer connection with history and philosophy than he had formerly done with religion. But—and this is the grand point—his grace was not real, his art not beautiful; it offended against the nature of the new principle; for, independently of moral allusions, all the above tales, considered as works of art, are thoroughly insipid and contrary to sound taste. Some extreme or caricature, in the beginning of this new direction, would have done no harm, if Göethe's assertion were but true, that they were daring attempts at genius, in which he had tried to compete with Aristophanes!! or if Wieland had had a genius for poetry. But how little this is the case he himself shows in his Excuses to the Vicar of * * *. He expressly opposed his inventions and men to the romances and characters of Richardson; saturated with the nothingness of these figures, which stood in no relation to human nature, he would describe men as they are; he again forgot that the object of art is the Beautiful. He did not even oppose real men to those virtue-heroes of Richardson, but caricatures, if we consider them materially, or beings who, in their ideal and real relations, partook of human nature in his own too peculiar manner. His celebrated knowledge of mankind is far removed from Lessing's knowledge of mankind and of life; it is often derived from the suspicious sources of Rousseau and Voltaire; it is, where it is real nature and experience, only knowledge of himself, and this is the reason why Wieland's personality is a much more interesting subject than his works in themselves."—vol. i., pp. 286—290.

In this tone of philosophic chit-chat our author continues to dilate on Wieland for some thirty pages; but although long, we seldom find him tedious. Although German literature has not till now been treated in this manner, it cannot be denied that it is peculiarly calculated to throw light upon, and, by exciting opposition, to promote a deeper study of, the different writers and their times. For German literature, by which we mean its developments in the last hundred years, has this peculiarity, that it has within a short period gone through those phases which with us extend through a much longer period of time. Contemporary with a rising spirit of criticism and reflection, almost all the writers of note had promulgated their own peculiar philosophical system; and thus acting, as it were, under a double principle, the creative power does not soar so unimpeded; and a striving of the mind after some particular aim diminishes the freshness and singlemindedness (if we may be allowed the expression) which we find in the works of a vigorous but less reflecting and philosophical period. The rapid change of systems, too, in Germany has essentially contributed to lessen the duration of their influence; and of all the elder writers so loudly bepraised in the last century, Lessing is perhaps the only one who still retains a hold on the national affection; and to this he is indebted to the manly vigour of

mind. Our English writers, till within a comparatively recent period, followed rather their inward impulse than the gradual developments of theory, whilst the Germans strove to unite the somewhat discordant characters of poet and critic, each in equal perfection: but it was not given to men to be at once an Aristotle and a Homer. Fortunately for England, she possesses writers of surpassing excellence, who will serve as beacons to recall the nation, after periodical wanderings, to those models that will command admiration as long as our language shall exist. We by no means agree with our author in the desponding view which he takes of German literature; on the contrary, we consider the preceding appearances in that country but as harbingers of a brilliant and perhaps not very distant future.

Fragments from German Prose Writers. Translated by Sarah Austin. Illustrated with Notes. 12mo. pp. 359. London, 1841. Murray.

Some of these fragments have appeared in a periodical publication, and the whole collection, though not formed with any express design or orderly object, is well calculated to afford a taste of the beauties and peculiarities of the principal German prose writers. There is not enough, perhaps, to enable us to frame an opinion of the characteristics of the nation and its literature, but there is enough to mark their distinctions from the rest of the world, and to amuse and inform the readers of other countries. Mrs. Austin considers the prominent quality of Germany to be *earnestness;* and that wit, humour, or persiflage (so eminently French), do not belong to them. The pet phrase "*suggestive,*" is applied to the whole, as well as to Goethe; and a number of biographical notes respecting these suggestive authors adds much to the merit with which our intelligent translator has endowed her desultory and pleasant volume. We have nothing further to offer by way of introduction; and can only quote a few of the shorter extracts as specimens of the rest :—

Lessing.—" If the world is to be held together by lies, the old, which are already current, are just as good as the new."

Merkel.—" Ordinary people regard a man of a certain force and inflexibility of character as they do a lion. They look at him with a sort of wonder—perhaps they admire him—but they will on no account house with him. The lapdog, who wags his tail, and licks the hand, and cringes at the nod of every stranger, is a much more acceptable companion to them."

Novalis.—" The most perfect specimens of ordinary women have a very acute and distinct perception of all the boundary lines of every-day existence, and guard themselves conscientiously from overstepping them. Hence their well-known and remarkable uniformity. They cannot bear excess, even in refinement, delicacy, truth, virtue, passion. They delight in variety of the common and accustomed. No new ideas—but new clothes. Fundamental monotony—superficial excitement. They love dancing,—on account of its light, vain, and sensual character. The highest sort of wit is unsufferable to them—as well as the beautiful, the great, the noble; middling or even bad books, actors, pictures, and the like, delight them."

Von Knebel.—" He who can take advice is sometimes superior to him who can give it."

The same.—" There are in certain heads a kind of established errors against which reason has no weapons. There are more of these mere assertions current than one would believe. Men are very fond of proving their steadfast adherence to nonsense."

Jean Paul. — " We celebrate nobler obsequies to those we love by drying the tears of others than by shedding our own ; and the fairest funeral wreath we can hang on their tomb, is not so fair as a fruit-offering of good deeds."

A. W. v. Schlegel.—" Duclos remarks that few distinguished works have been produced by any but authors by profession. In France, this class has long been held in respect. With us, a man used to be esteemed as less than nothing if he were only an author. This prejudice still shews itself here and there, but the force of honoured examples must in time crush it. Authorship is, according to the spirit in which it is pursued, an infamy, a pastime, a day-labour, a handicraft, an art, a science, a virtue."

The same.—" There are days in which we are in a most felicitous vein for the conception of new images and projects, but can neither communicate nor mature any of them. These are not thoughts, they are only the ghosts of thoughts."

Lessing.—" I hate all people who want to found sects. It is not error, but sectarian error —nay, and even sectarian truth,—which causes the unhappiness of mankind."

Rahel. —" It is indifferent in what condition we are, if we are not in that we wish for."

Oehlenschläger. — " The plays of natural lively children are the infancy of art. Children live in the world of imagination and feeling. They invest the most insignificant object with any form they please, and see in it whatever they wish to see."

Deutsche Amaranten; a Selection of Modern Pieces, in Prose and Verse, by the most esteemed and popular German Authors. By WILHELM KLAUER KLATTOWSKI of Schwerin in Mecklenburgh. With an Engraving from an Original Painting by RETZCH.

The compiler of this collection has had ample range within a vast and most luxuriant field, and has acted his part carefully and most judiciously. Where the abundance of all that is beautiful is so great, the difficulty must have been, not what to select, but what to reject. As every piece here presented to the reader has long secured to itself a lasting reputation, we are spared the necessity of commenting upon them individually. As this is exactly the selection we could have wished for, we have no doubt but that it will receive ample patronage from all the lovers of German literature.

Art. IX.—*History of German Literature, by Wolfgang Menzel.* Translated from the German, with Notes, by Th. Gordon. Oxford: Talboys. 1841.

Mr. Gordon hopes that Menzel's work, although not a history of the literature which it professes to be, will yet be " of much use to those among us who have acquired a desultory and smattering acquaintance with the subject." The book, however, being eminently superficial, random and bold in its decisions, and opinionative in its assertions, can only convey a smattering knowledge, and therefore cannot be of " much use" to persons who have previously acquired a similar extent of acquaintance with German literature to that which Menzel furnishes.

To write a history of the literature of any nation eminent in that department must be an achievement of the first magnitude. To do so in the compass of Menzel's book would be, it appears to us, the perfection of history, and one of the noblest human exploits ; for instead of consisting of a crowded enumeration of authors with slight notices of them, or of the books which these authors have written, with hasty and smart criticisms of them, or even of lively pictures of the national mind at any one particular period, as this writer has done, it would require a profound insight into the progress and vicissitudes of the intellectual and moral development of a people, of social forms and political principles, with the reciprocities and reactions of all of these phases, to be illustrated with masterly skill and selection, by biographical and critical notices, instead of only slightly indicating causes and principles, and making up a book with rash and singular opinions, or imperfect and disjointed sketches of men's lives and characters. Now this last mentioned sort of performance is that to which Menzel can alone lay claim ; and even in its achievement he is verbose and commonplace, smattering though forcible in as far as assertion and expression go.

The society in which Menzel has moved, his reading, and his occupations, have all served to nurture a superficiality and a dictatorial habit, features which appear to have been in no way alien to the original constitution of his mind, and certain natural gifts. At an early period of his life he had the situation of a schoolmaster ; he afterwards was editor of a literary periodical. From the first he was master of a remarkable fluency of language, and therefore, having betaken himself to letters, attended lectures, and caught a conversational acquaintance with everything, he, like all other young *litterateurs*, and especially those who have great facility in composition, readily mistaking fluency of words for wealth and depth of ideas, rushed into print, and dictated with a despotic confidence. No established names and no current principles were exempted

from his attacks. He and others mistook assurance for originality, and dogmatism for genius ; and when it is understood that it was the manner in which he delivered his opinions, and not the matter in them (which was trite and plain), that attracted notice, it will be admitted that he might with shallow thinkers, and impudent pretenders, be readily enough taken as a master critic, the founder of a new school, and the discoverer of the grand principles as well as epochs of German literature. He who was bold enough to assail Goethe in a manner analogous to that of those who have leathern lungs, and who bawl with stentorian voice, would pass with many who dream not that deep waters run smooth, or that noise is not eloquent, for an oracle.

But if held by the half-educated and the superficial like himself to be a high priest, it was not as one who officiates in a temple of mysteries. He was a man of sturdy opinion, rather than a transcendentalist,—of healthy nerve, rather than a mystic and dreaming sentimentalist. It was something of thousands of books which he knew, gathered as hasty reviewers are in the habit of doing, instead of having time or being able to fathom the profundities of any one, digest its contents, and imbibe its spirit. And so far did this inferior attainment work well, that he neither attempts nor pretends mysticism. He is too confident and self-flattered for screening himself amid mists and clouds : he had been too long accustomed to dogmatise to betake himself to effeminate or visionary resources. Accordingly when he comes to speak of that which he had knowledge, derived from observation and reality, fully as much as from slap-dash reading and imperfect study, he not only speaks out like a man, but makes a sensible as well as a clear and comprehensive statement ; at the same time dressing his manly views in a manner that is taking both in respect of language and illustrative points. If this manly and independent tone is anywhere particularly to be admired, it must be when the distracting subjects which politics, local as well as national, engage a writer and critic, and still more when religious differences and opposing creeds are his themes. We shall confine our examples of Menzel's fairness and powers to these perplexing topics, and also with the purpose of conveying to those of our readers to whom Germany, its sects, and its literature are strangers, a general account that is informing.

The portion of the account which we first copy, referring to the political mind of Germany, is limited to the utterance of it by the press. Says Menzel—

" Liberal principles, however, were disseminated by speeches in the Chambers, by articles in the newspapers and local publications, to such an extent, that among so many names we scarcely know which to praise most. Upon the whole, political ideas and the political style have been both wonderfully improved. How astonished would Justus Möser be were he to see the interest with which our burghers and peasants now talk about politics, and to find in every corner of Germany papers filled not only with patriotic dreams, but also of disquisitions on questions of public law, such as we really meet with every day.

"The number of those who read political papers has increased to an amazing extent.

"The papers no longer occupy themselves exclusively with foreign policy; they now enter into questions connected with that of our own country.

"There is in the age, despite the censorship, an invincible desire to make everything public. Even when the censorship suppresses all Liberal papers, the state-gazettes and the servile papers give, in their own way, a publicity to contested political questions.

"Our political public press has already found out by experience, that the controversies of parties have become a kind of routine: some leading questions have been so often discussed, that notions formerly unknown or mysterious have become clear and known to every one.

"After the Rhenish Mercury of Görres of Coblenz, the Balance of Börne of Frankfort, the Franconian Mercury of Wetzel in Hamburg, the Opposition paper of Wieland (the son of the poet) in Weimar, the Nemesis of Luden in Jena, had all ceased to exist, and the Isis of Oken had gone a wandering, no Liberal journal was started after the passing of the Carlsbad Decrees, except the Neckar Gazette of Seybold, which soon became very moderate in its tone, and the German Observer of Liesching of Stuttgart, who was thrown into prison. After the French Revolution of 1830, this ebb was all at once followed by a flow, so that the sudden transition from chains to a wild and unrestrained licence was truly surprising. Wirth in his Tribune, and Siebenpfeiffer in his Western Mercury, some German exiles in the Courier of the Lower Rhine, preached up revolution and republicanism; nay, some of these terrorists went so far as to attack Rotteck, who appeared to them to be far too moderate, and in whom they saw nothing but an aristocrat, while his paper, The Liberal, (*Der Freisinnige*,) was suppressed by the Diet as being too liberal.

"The local papers, those which took an interest in the peculiar affairs of one province or city, and began to criticize in an interesting and intelligent manner their local affairs, were far more numerous and of more influence than those which argued about matters of more general importance. Every one knows best himself where the shoe pinches him. He, therefore, who pointed out and discoursed of those wants of any particular place which were the most particular and pressing, was far more attended to than he who spoke only in general terms. The people of one province or town did not, it is true, take any interest in the affairs of another; but all, though independent of one another, felt the same interest in public questions. Few editors of such papers, it is true, were celebrated, or can be ranked among our distinguished literary men; yet though, on the whole, they had but little influence on the upper ranks, they found means to make themselves of more importance on single questions among the lower classes, where they found a fruitful field which had hitherto remained almost uncultivated.

Our great national literature passed unheeded before the eyes of the mechanic and peasant; this little local literature came home to his interests and feelings.

"The papers which daily started up in incredible numbers were of very different value. In one place they breathed forth a noble spirit, like the Patriotic Fancies of Justus Möser; in another, they were exceedingly vulgar. Here, they were more like political newspapers; there, amusing literary papers. Here, they used the popular style of the older Village Gazette, (*Dorf-zeitung*); there, more of the analyzing language of the advocate. In other cases they were sentimental, pedantic, warning, intrusive; or they took delight in vulgarisms and pointless wit. The papers of enlightened countries, and of a population which was less uncultivated, were much more tolerable; but in no place were they and are they more immoral than in München, where many vie with one another in vulgarity.

"The numerous pamphlets which were written on provincial occurrences were no less influential than the local papers. Holstein alone published above thirty within two years. Hanover, Brunswick, Saxony, produced a great number of them; indeed so did every German province, in proportion as each was more or less subject to violent crises. These pamphlets, joined to the voluminous reports of the proceedings of the legislative assemblies, have increased our libraries so much that we cannot now survey them. Alexander Müller and Dr. Zöpfl attempted to give, in journals peculiarly devoted to the consideration of questions of public politics, a review of the whole; but they could give nothing but fragments; they had not room for the whole. There would be no end to the matter, were we to add the Swiss, with their newspapers and pamphlets. Here, thirty-eight—there, twenty-two states—in each of which questions are put and answered, wishes breathed and satisfied, demands made and refused: with all these we cannot wonder that there is a great noise and tumult."

Menzel goes on to remark that it is the more difficult to compress a review of the whole field of public politics, because the greatest differences everywhere meet the eye; for in one province the same man is a Liberal, who in another would be considered an Aristocrat. Then each petty state possesses an immensely learned and confused code of laws, which Ministers and Chambers vie with one another in making still more unnatural, by additions and amendments." There is a wondrous minuteness of legislation, more than sufficient to perplex every one excepting a few learned jurists. Nor has general attention been yet directed to the affairs of the Confederacy, although a few eminent writers have commented in a purely historical manner upon its constitution, decrees, and protocols;—upon its general relations, and suggested or urged the infusion of new elements. But here comes a paragraph that must not be abridged:—

"Among the many isolated and petty questions which, during the silence on great leading questions, have been thrust forward into notice, that of the emancipation of the Jews plays an important part. A multitude of pamphlets have been written on both sides in almost every state of Germany Riesser of Altona has used the most energetic and talented language. What he, himself a Jew, has said in favour of the rights of Jews, ranks amongst the master pieces of political eloquence. Yet the children of Israel suffer even till this day from the petty regulations of Germany, and they have been granted their poor rights in but very few places. Here men attempt to educate them ; and we see the oldest people in the world treated like a little child which cannot stand on its own feet. There they wish to convert them, with all possible forbearance ; they do not compel them, it is true, to become Christians ; but they cannot claim the right of citizens—nay, scarcely that of men—as long as they are not Christians. Here they are openly hated as a foreign people, upon whom, however, as we are ashamed to kill them, we vent our barbarian courage in another way. There men play the master, the gracious protector ; but they take care not to emancipate them, lest by so doing they should lose the pleasure of playing the part of patron. There are even Liberals who are opposed to the emancipation of the Jews, merely because Christians are not yet in all respects free. We find everywhere that petty pride which ridicules the Jews, tormenting them at one time with refusals, at another with half concessions, at a third with obtrusive offers of instruction. We can scarcely be surprised that men of talent and education, such as have of late years arisen in considerable numbers among this race, should become mad at this despicable ill-treatment. But the wrath of a Borne, the sarcasm of a Heine, will not aid in furthering the Jewish cause, because they foster petty antipathies, and because, under their protecting shield, a brood of commonplace Jewish youths is formed, who load with open scorn everything which is holy in the eyes of the Christian and the German."

This temperate, apparently even-handed, and enlightened account, will prepare the reader for a dispassionate view, if we except an antithetic manner of expression, of both Catholicism and Protestantism as at present manifested in Germany. We had been looking out for information regarding the religious and ecclesiastical condition of certain German states, with the design of presenting a sketch similar to what we have done of establishments nearer home, in some of our late reviews. But a few paragraphs from Menzel's pages, which we now extract, will be more satisfactory, and shall save us the contemplated trouble. First for the Catholics :—

"We must make a few general remarks upon this moderate party before we leave it. It is the younger sister of the Reformation : it has not, however, like it, abandoned its aged mother, but cherishes her with childlike forbearance. It has not deserted the ranks of the regular succession of Catholic centuries, but has returned to the ninth—to the independence of the German Church, and to the purity which doctrine then possessed in the time of Rhabanus Maurus. This party wishes for a German national church, in opposition to ultramontanism, as well as an independent church in opposition to the secular power. It wants an intelligible German liturgy, divested of Latin formulas, a national education in place of ignorance, a cheerful

philosophy instead of gloomy superstition, and toleration instead of persecution. But this party is not yet sufficiently aware of its vocation. Placed half-way between rationalism and ultramontanism, it has not yet gained a firm footing : it inclines most to the former, that is, to the Protestant side. Thence proceeds that wretched prose peculiar to it, the dry morality and the wishy-washy sentimentality, the jejune translations of the Bible, the fear entertained for every play of the imagination, and finally that inclination to political servilism, that liberalism, which so vaunts itself in the affairs of the church, whilst, thundering out its anathemas against Rome, crouches before, and fawns upon the pettiest of the German petty princelings. These traits, which have lately occurred, disfiguring the character of one of our most respectable sects, are fortunately not the prevailing ones : on the contrary, the great majority of this party manifest a certain degree of patient unassuming modesty, a disinclination to except any advice which may happen to be offered, much good sound sense and understanding. The signs of the times shew that the abolition of the laws regarding celibacy will become the watchword of a struggle, which in no distant period will separate this party from the ultramontanists, thus bringing it a step nearer to Protestantism."

Now for the Protestants :—

"It is well known that the Protestant Church became, even from its very commencement, the tool of worldly politics, and remained dependent upon worldly power. The higher the Romish Church had raised itself above the temporal power, the deeper was the dependence into which the Lutheran fell. At first, when a religious enthusiasm and fanaticism still glowed, the Protestant clergymen, acting as royal chaplains, upper court preachers, and diplomatists, naturally played an important part. But this ceased with the age of Louis the Fourteenth. Black coats were supplanted by green coats : the place of the fat father confessor was supplied by jovial hunters and mistresses. The Protestant clergy sunk into the lists of inferior officers.

"It is not long since country livings were conferred by licentious and coarse country squires 'under the apron'—that is, under the condition that the poor *candidatus theologiæ* should marry the paid-off chambermaid or the cast-off mistress. Rabner in his Letters and Thümmel in his *Wilhelmina*, satirically scourged, about the middle of the last century, this disgraceful practice : the most detailed and faithful account, however, of the lamentable state of the Protestant Church at that time, will be found in Nicolai's novel, *Sebaldus Nothanker*. If at that time a poor preacher happened in the slightest degree to displease the whims of a petty princeling or countling of the German Empire, or of his mistress, or of his court marshal, or to contradict a brutal court chaplain or superintendent, he was unceremoniously dismissed from office and employment, and left without support.

"These things, it is true, now no longer occur. The greater decency observed by the Courts and the Government has had a beneficial influence upon the Church. Though church livings and professorships are still given away by petticoat influences, yet only the honest daughters and cousins of the patrons are concerned ; so that all goes on decently.

"But dignity is not always combined with decency : dignity consist in freedom ; and our Protestant Church is now, as formerly, enslaved.

"A hundred years ago, the Jesuits in Dillingen attempted to prove the position, that the Catholic faith is more serviceable to absolute monarchy than the Protestant; but the Pfaff of Tübingen drove them from the field, by proving that no church was more servile than the Lutheran. When a court chaplain at Copenhagen (Dr. Masius) dared to say that princes ought to become Lutherans, not so much from fear of God as from motives of temporal advantage, because no creed but the Lutheran favoured the divine right of kings, maintaining that it was derived directly from God without the intervention of any higher spiritual power, and because in the Lutheran religion alone was the secular prince at once bishop, emperor, and pope,—when Masius argued this, and when the chivalrous defender of truth and right, Thomasius, who can never be sufficiently praised, Thomasius alone, of all his contemporaries, had sufficient courage to censure a publication so blasphemous. All attacked this worthy man, and called his opinion, that religion had other purposes in view than the stengthening the power of absolute monarchy, a *crimen læsæ majestatis·* so that he was compelled to flee from Leipzig, where they had confiscated all his property, in order to escape imprisonment, or perhaps even death; and in Copenhagen his reply was solemnly burnt by the common hangman.

"Such was the state of affairs then; and in all that is essential no change has since taken place. The episcopal dignity is still possessed by the temporal monarch, and the Church is ruled by Cabinet orders. The consistories, it is true, appear to possess some aristocratical power, but this is in appearance only; they are, in reality, the mere organs of the Ministry. From the Cabinet they receive instructions respecting their liturgy, their clerical vestments, their texts, and directions how they shall apply the Word of God in accordance with the circumstances of the times. The subaltern clergy are trained like the other public functionaries. In a word, there are no longer any priests, but merely servants of the state in black uniform,

"The feeble attempts to introduce a Presbyterian form of government into the Protestant Church have always been received with displeasure, and put aside with a degree of ease which proves that it is impossible to form a middle party between the totally servile clergyman and Dissenters, who follow their own path. The Court will never permit the introduction of a democratical element into the government of the Church; and that portion of the people which takes a serious interest in religion will never trust the priests. Thus, our well-meaning Presbyterians always fall between two stools.

"The State will long exercise this power over the Church, for the number of Independent Dissenters is still small. The majority of the people have, as it were, had their fill of religious controversies in former centuries; they no longer take any interest in such affairs; they are engaged in other occupations: the servilism, therefore, of their clergymen, and that vulgar routine which is hostile to every innovation, to every advance in mental power, is quite suited to their condition. People are no longer harangued to, or irritated by their clergymen; and that is what they like. They may believe what they choose; they may go to church or not without being blamed or teased by the clergymen: a state of things quite suited to their present degree of culture. From this proceeds the characteristic mark of the Protestant world—*religious indifferentism.*"

36. MONTHLY REVIEW, 4th ser. 155 (1841), 451-453. M/H No. 3756.

Art. XXI.—*Fragments from German Prose Writers.* Translated by Sarah Austin. Illustrated with Notes. Murray.

An exceedingly miscellaneous collection of striking passages, which have captivated Mrs. Austin in the course of her extensive German reading, and which she has translated with her wonted skill and beauty. There has been no attempt at system in the selection, and the fragments look as if they had been gathered in the most desultory way; although the translator's choice has been guided by certain principles, so as to enable her to range at will over the immense field which German literature and the German mind now occupy; in order that she might exhibit their riches, their variety, their picturesque, and their philosophic, beauties. The fragments, she says, have been taken up on account of considerations as various as their character and their subjects. "In some, it was the value of the matter, in others, the beauty of the form, that struck me; in some, the vigorous un-affected good sense, in others, the fantastic or mystical charm. Some recalled familiar trains of thought, which meet one in a foreign literature, like old friends in a far country; others suggested ideas altogether new and strange. My readers must, therefore, apply measures as different as those which I have used, and by no means ascribe to me the intention of recommending every opinion to their unqualified assent, or every passage to their unqualified admiration."

Mrs. Austin complains of, and ridicules the limited as well as the exaggerated notions current in England, with regard to the character, intentions, and merits of German literature. "In some places it has been represented as all comprised of cloudy philosophy, dull pedantry, or romantic horrors; in others, as deformed, throughout, by whining sentimentality, impurity, and irreligion. That, in the multitudinous offspring of the German press, *some* of each of these misshapen productions are to be found, we shall be little inclined to doubt, if we consider the disgusting shape assumed by portions of our own literature: but that a sound-hearted and intelligent country gives birth to nothing else, is as little consistent with probability as it is with truth." In another passage, when speaking of Goethe in particular, she says, some "talk of Werther, that fruitful subject of ridicule, as if Goethe had written nothing else. Others, again, think of him only as the author of Faust, that untranslateable poem which every Englishman translates. But in order to form any idea of Goethe's merits, it is necessary to read his criticisms on literature and art, on men and events."

We must say, however, that the fragments before us are often dreamy, and are generally speculative rather than real; and it is natural to expect Mrs. Austin to sympathize with a style of reverie which she has studied so long. At the same time her illustrative notes, consisting of criticism and biography, are valuable; evincing judgment, ability, and sound taste; being in truth the most useful things in the volume. Some samples, however, will afford the most satisfactory evidence of the nature of the contents; only further premising that Mrs. Austin considers the grand characteristics of the German mind, as seen in its literature, to be earnestness and suggestiveness.

Many of the examples are mere sentences, and collected on account of their sententiousness: although the truth of the thing uttered is not always so clear as is its point. We begin with very short specimens.—

"We are near waking, when we dream that we dream."—*Novalis.*

"Of all thieves, fools are the worst; they rob you of time and temper." —*Goethe.*

"The illusion of a past golden age is one of the greatest hinderances to the approach of the golden age that should come. If the golden age is past it was not genuine. Gold cannot rust nor decay: it comes out of all admixtures and all decompositions pure and indestructible. If the golden age will not endure, it had better never arise, for it can produce nothing but elegies on its loss."—*A. W. v. Schlegel.*

"There are ideal trains of events which run parallel with the real ones. Seldom do they coincide. Men and accidents commonly modify every ideal event or train of events, so that it appears imperfect, and its consequences are equally imperfect. Thus it was with the Reformation; instead of Protestantism arose Lutheranism."—*Novalis.*

"There are so many tender and holy emotions flying about in our inward world, which, like angels, can never assume the body of an outward act,—so many rich and lovely flowers spring up which bear no seed—that it is a happiness poetry was invented, which receives into its limbus all these incorporeal spirits and the perfume of all these flowers."—*Jean Paul.*

"I would fain know what music is; I seek it as man seeks eternal wisdom. Yesterday evening I walked late in the moonlight in the beautiful avenue of lime-trees on the banks of the Rhine, and I heard a tapping noise and soft singing. At the door of a cottage, under the blossoming lime-tree, sat a mother with her twin babes; the one lay at her breast, the other in a cradle, which she rocked with her foot, keeping time to her singing. In the very germ then, when the first trace of life scarce begins to stir, music is the nurse of the soul: it murmurs in the ear, and the child sleeps; the tones are the companions of his dreams,—they are the world in which he lives. He has nothing; the babe, although cradled in his mother's arms, is alone in the spirit; but tones find entrance into this half-conscious soul, and nourish it as the earth nourishes the life of plants." —*Bettina.*

From the notes we take a passage respecting Tieck.—

"Tieck's stories appear to me so enchanting, that their small success in England is a riddle I cannot explain upon any hypothesis flattering to the taste of the country. The 'Pictures' and 'The Betrothing' were translated and published in one volume by the Rev. Connop Thirlwall, the present Bishop of St. David's. 'The Old Man of the Mountain,' 'The Love Charm,' and 'Pietro of Albano,' in another, by the Rev. Julius Hare, now Archdeacon of Sussex. Several, if not all, of the tales in the 'Phantasus' are to be found in Mr. Carlyle's 'German Romances.' Yet in spite of these efforts of the most accomplished translators to make Tieck known in England, his popularity is very far from approaching to his merits. These are altogether peculiar. The fantastic grace, the mysterious charm, of his 'Märchen' are unrivalled. They seem written not only about, but *by* fairies, and 'creatures of the element.' He manages to combine a sort of infantine simplicity with the gorgeousness of eastern imagery, or the dimness of gothic-superstition. They have the engaging naïveté and the daring invention of the old stories that lived in the hearts and on the lips of the people. Higher praise than this it is not in the power of words to express; though the unfortunate children of these days are taught to consider them as beneath their notice. I know few writers who more powerfully stir the fancy than Tieck. In this respect he reminds one of Chaucer. His descriptions of nature, like those of our great poet, 'breathe a spring freshness.' All that makes up the charm of a wood, for instance,—its verdure, coolness, fragrance, and dreamy music, seem brought before our very senses by an art which it is extremely difficult to define. The musical element in nature is, indeed, the one which seems to predominate in his soul; it flows, like the murmuring of water, through all his works. As Goethe's genius manifested itself pre-eminently in the plastic, so does Tieck's in the musical: his words bring sounds to the ear, as Goethe's do form to the eye."

POEMS FROM THE GERMAN.

BY J. H. MERIVALE, ESQ.

The two following pieces are extracted, with permission, from Sonderland's "Illustrations of German Poetry," to which they were originally contributed by the translator, Mr. Merivale. The first is already familiar to lovers of German literature in the version by Mr. Taylor, (vol. iii., p. 357, of his "Survey of German Poetry,") which, though sufficiently spirited, is not in all respects so close to the original, either in sense or metre, as to supersede another attempt. It has also been made the subject of a poetical paraphrase by Mr. Impey, in his late elegant "Specimens of German Lyrical Poetry," where he has proved its classical origin, or rather derivation, from a fiction of the Byzantine period. But this is an avowed departure from the story as told by Goethe, and so wide a departure as rather to call for, than discountenance, a more literal copy. The singularity of the German poem consists in the form of the narrative—being, throughout, (with the exception of the last six lines which are spoken by the Master-Conjurer,) a monologue in the person of the unlucky apprentice, whose rash assumption of the magician's office, and impotent terror at the sudden failure of his usurped powers and its destructive consequences, may well be applied, with some skilful adaptation, to the case of a certain class of modern politicians, who make no scruple for their own selfish purposes, of evoking an agency which they possess no means of controlling ; and who would be the first to perish in the inundation they themselves have produced, but for the timely restoration of the legitimate power whose functions they have invaded.

Of the second piece, that which relates an adventure supposed to have happened to the celebrated magician, whose name it bears, no other English version has, it is believed, ever appeared, but the present. It may not be known to all readers, that the Virgilius, or Virgil, to whom these magic powers were ascribed by the superstitions of the middle ages, was not the great Roman poet, but a venerable prelate of the Carlovingian period, although the ignorance of the succeeding ages confounded the one with the other, and the stories connected with the name were equally fabulous as respected either—of which that now presented may be taken as a specimen :—

THE MAGICIAN'S APPRENTICE.

DER ZAUBERLEHRLING (GOETHE).

There ! our wise old hag-commander—
He for once is gone away,
Leaving free his sprites to wander.
They shall now my call obey.
Words and works right well,
Have I long been heeding,
And by magic spell,
Need not doubt succeeding.
Wallow ! wallow !
Far and wide,
Let the tide
Still be going
To the bath's capacious swallow,
Be the water still o'erflowing.

Come, thou Broom-stick, old and crazy,
Clothe thee in this tatter'd clout :
Be a long-legg'd knave—not lazy,
To perform my where-about.
There ! on two legs stand—
Cap on head—I've stuck it—
Run ! and in your hand
Take a water-bucket.
Wallow ! wallow !
Far and wide,
Let the tide
Still be going
To the bath's capacious swallow,
Be the water still o'erflowing.

See ! he's at the brink already—
Quick as lightning see him rush !
Back again, boy ! Steady—steady—
Lo the torrent—what a gush !
Now another turn—
How the bason's swilling ;
Every vase and urn
To the brim he's filling !
Stop ! no further !
Five—ten—twenty—
Now, there's plenty.
Stop ! 'od rot 'en !
Ah ! I have it—murther ! murther !
Sure the word I've clean forgotten.

Ah ! the word ! the word, to make him
Now his pristine shape resume !
Who the deuce will overtake him ?
Stop, you old infernal broom !

What! still pouring on?
  Must it rain for ever?
Stop! or ere you've done,
  You'll have drain'd the river.
    No—no longer
    Will I suffer
    Such a huffer.
    'Tis a scandal!
We shall soon see which is stronger—
(How he grins—the ugly vandal!)

O thou villain—hell-begotten!
  Wilt thou all the house be choaking?
All the timbers, sound and rotten—
  See the water-spouts are soaking!
    O thou broom accurst!
    Art thou hard of hearing?
    Be as thou wert first—
    Stick—no longer stirring!
    Wilt thou never
    Cease pursuing
    My undoing?
    I'll withstand ye,
And the dry old broom-stick sever
With my sharp-edg'd axe so hardy.

See! he comes again, slip-slopping—
  Stay: or I'll be down upon thee—
Now, hobgoblin, cease your hopping!
  This good axe hath quite undone thee,
    Truly, well besped!
    Split in twain genteely!
    Now my fears are fled,
    And I breathe more freely.
    Blood and thunder!
    Both to shivers,
    Rain down rivers,
    Rogues eternal!
There they fly—two knaves asunder—
Help, oh help! ye powers infernal!

There they scamper!—deeper! deeper!
  Swells the tide o'er stairs and hall—
Wave on wave—Ah! there's a sweeper!
  Master, master, hear me call!
    Save me, master, save!
    Ere I fall a martyr—
    In this goblin knave
    Sure I've caught a tartar.

THE MASTER.

  " To thy lonely
  Nook betake thee!
  Broom, go shake thee;
  For the master
Calls thee for a goblin, only
When he wants his work done faster."

VIRGILIUS THE CONJURER.

DER ZAUBERER VIRGILIUS (IMMERMANN).

To his snug cot the wise man would repair
  To pass an evening hour of light disport:
No fire was on the hearth—his maiden there
  Sat wringing of her hands in piteous sort.
He raised from off her knee that comely cheek—
She sighed and moaned—and not a word would speak.

He bade her fair her cause of grief to say.
  " My silent fane deserted—tell me why?"
She sobbed—" Alas! that dear unhappy day,
  When first you won me, greeting wild and shy!
Now have I joys enough with thee—but bear
Contempt and mockery for my worldly share.

" The fire upon my hearth was gone and spent,
  Whilst you stood outside, preaching to the wind,
With lantern to the neighbours round I went,
  And ask'd—' A light, sirs—will ye be so kind?'
From door to door thus meek besought them—but
They shouted all, and cried—' Begone, you slut!'

The wise man gently kissed her swimming eye,
  And said, " I'll help thee in a case so cruel,"
Then wink'd, when through the dun smoke curling high,
  Bright burst the flame from gathered heaps of fuel.
" Now get our supper, girl—a fowl for two.
Before the hut I've something yet to do."

Now busily she tends the pot—and now
  With laughter strange he paces through the dark.
The town lies merry on the hillock's brow,
  And every window-pane emits its spark.
Three words he muttered low, of secret might;
And, sudden, all the panes were black as night.

The fowl is ready dressed—the cloth is laid—
  Two plates are there—one glass to serve for both.
The master's lips with mirth o'erflow—the maid,
  Cured of her grief, bends o'er him, nothing loath.
Soon as he stops, she, wondering, hears the sound
Of feet quick trampling through the valley round.

Nigher it rolled—and now are heard full plain,
  The loud hoarse voices of that ribald crew.
" Ah me, unhappy! must that hateful strain,
  Ne'er cease to mock me, even placed by you?"
" 'Tis now," he said, " your triumph must begin."
Therewith the whole town's livery bundled in.

In bundled men and women—young and old—
  And at their head the Burgomaster—He—
Somewhat against his will, it must be said,
  As ill comporting with his dignity.
All scream'd in chorus, to be heard a mile hence—
The great man, full of ermin'd pomp, cried, " Silence!"

233

" O learned Sage and honoured Host !   Of late
  A woful misadventure hath arrived
To this our happy, free, enlightened state,
  Whereby of light and heat 'tis clean deprived.
Nor self, nor friend, can get aught hot to eat,
And none can see a stitch in stove or street.

" Our plain God-fearing brethren, ere the end
  Of evening prayer were forc'd to make a pause ;
Our Sophs are left in darkness to perpend
  On the foundation of a primal cause.
And through the wilderness of shade we wander,
(To say it with respect) like goose and gander.

" We've fetch'd both flint and steel, wherewith to raise
  A flame, as men are wont at day's retreating ;
But not a spark would from the tinder blaze,
  Although they made their knuckles sore with beating,
So, learned Sage, in this our utmost grief,
We fly to you for counsel and relief."

" Go, ask the maid," Virgilius said in turn ;
  " And try if she will grant you your petition.
Her fire burns bright—as bright as fire may burn.
  Belike she'll grant you some, on due submission.
I know no way but this ; nor think 'twill hurt you,
No—not for all your town's immaculate virtue."

Therewith from him to her they trooping go,
  Most like a flock before the boy that drives ;
And all beseeching cry, " Your grace bestow !"
  But most of all the prim, starch, pious wives.
The maid, in sign of concord, waves her hand,
And each one fetches from the hearth his brand.

But now the conjuror 'gan himself uprear,
  And shake the terrors of his bushy crest ;
Then thundered—" Take this warning in your ear—
  Perhaps a stubborn parchment to digest.
Now go—but keep ye from the scoffer's ways,
Unless you'd eat cold mutton all your days.

" Until I hither bent my wandering feet,
  No jolly harvest-home your fields e'er saw ;
Nor should I here have deigned to fix my seat,
  But for a pearl I found among your straw.
Then tempt her not ! awaken not her scorn !
Or all again shall thistle be and thorn."

The reverend guild, low crouching to the rod,
  Abjured all jest for their remaining days ;
The conjuror stands like some acknowledged god,
  Illumin'd by their torches' crimson blaze.
The maid clings to him in a close embrace,
And looks with roguish laughter in his face.

A POET'S NATIVITY.

The moonlight flood was sleeping o'er hill, and tower, and town,
The larger stars were peeping, in light and glory, down ;
There was scarcely left a watcher, save the sage who loves the stars,
And here and there a miser, insecure 'midst locks and bars,
Save in one little chamber, where a taper shed its light,
And a new born infant's wailing pierced the silence of the night.

Poor was that little chamber—a poor man's only home,
Yet as fond hearts were beating there, as 'neath a palace dome—
Hearts that but clung the closer, because of mutual care,
Hearts that but loved the dearer, for the sorrows they must share.
They saw a lowly future, and yet were reconciled,
Though they knew not of the treasure that was giv'n them in that child.

There came a rushing murmur through the cloudless depths of Heaven.
They said it was the zephyr that a stronger breath had given ;
But it was not so—it was not so—though unto earthly eyes
It seemed as if the breezes did with wilder gust arise.
There were angels traversing the space, with one benign accord,
Obedient to the mandate of their Maker and their Lord.

A bright winged glorious angel—all robed in stainless white,
And a darker spirit near it, yet with a gem like light ;
They were searching out the rainbow, from its cavern in the cloud—
They were searching out the lightning, in its dim and secret shroud—
They were catching heavenly music from the planets as they roll,
And all to weave a garment for the little infant's soul.

A spark of life immortal already warmed its breast ;
A gleaming from the portal of a region pure and blest ;
Thus far the Great Creator his own high work had done,
A task too solemn to be made a delegated one—
But he bid them gather thoughts, and dreams, and fancies bright and fair,
And dress the spirit's chamber with glorious hues and rare.

They caught the silvery light'ning, they took the rainbow's rim,
They caught the star-beams, ere they fell through earthly vapours dim ;
And the music of the wood-bird, and the murmur of the sea,
And the breathing of the softest wind that roams the forest free ;
And blending all these lovely things into one glorious whole,
They spread the garment of the *Mind* around the poet's *Soul*.

M. A. BROWNE.

38. FOREIGN QUARTERLY REVIEW, 29 (1842), 172-183. M/H No. 3805. By John Sterling.

ART. II.—*Fragments from German Prose Writers.* Translated by SARAH AUSTIN. Illustrated with Notes. London 1841.

SOME have experienced, and all can imagine, the pleasure of waking in a new long-desired country, with vague wonder and uncertainty how that foreign life would present itself, and then receiving its first greeting from a fair smiling figure, who presents us with a nosegay of unknown flowers, and looks our welcome to the fields they grew in. Such must be to many English readers the interest and joy imparted by this rich and graceful, as well as truly friendly offering; which is at once a garland of fresh flowers and a string of lasting pearls. Perhaps no other prose literature but that of Greece could have furnished the materials of a volume at once so wise, so bright, and so varied; and those old Hellenic books, nearer than any modern can be to the age of primeval awe, and combining, as no other, childish liveliness with mature thought, yet want some of the nobler, the very noblest elements of our Christian world, and the clear complete knowledge of nature and history, which in our time we require, and which the Germans, beyond all other people, have realized. In truth, resembling the Greeks far more than do the writers of any other nation as to elevation and fulness, they have for us the incomparable merit that they are the children and teachers of our own time. At all events whatever may or may not be the value of German literature, it is plain that Mrs. Austin is, of all English persons, the one who has best succeeded in making its worth clear and pleasant to merely English readers. Mr. Carlyle, with his deep spirit and prophetic originality, has been

and will remain we suppose for ever, the great hierophant, disclosing to prepared minds the truly divine wisdom of that modern Holy Land. But it requires to have something of a "foregone conclusion" of Germanism within us, and much of the temper of a devout neophyte, to receive the infinite benefit of his teaching. Mrs. Austin, with the unpretending ease and felicity of her soft, open, womanly nature, interprets to all like one of themselves, in familiar though choice language, whatever can be so communicated of the Beliefs, Images, and Feelings, that the highest and most creative geniuses and most sagacious inquirers of modern times have bestowed upon the world. Let us acknowledge our obligation by sitting beside her—it is no painful position—in the same great school.

Her book is one that hardly perhaps permits, and certainly does not require, any comment. Nor do we propose attempting one. But Mrs. Austin, and her and our readers, will you pardon us if we make it an excuse for offering some remarks on the history of modern literature, and on the place which that of Germany holds among the higher products of Christian Europe? That in the last twenty-five years it has gained for itself a universal importance, is plain matter of fact. The writings of Chateaubriand, of Byron, of Manzoni, have excited a wide and eager feeling; but none of these men, nor any of their respective countrymen, have produced a work, the object of repeated translations and commentaries, like the *Faust* of Goethe. And it is well known that this poem does not stand out from the other literature of its country, as something different in spirit, but only as of greater depth and more perfect execution than most other German books, many of which, besides those of its author, are analogous to it in purpose and tendency.

A little wider survey teaches that, as a matter of European interest, the theories and images of the Germans succeeded immediately to that place which had been occupied just before by the great writers of France; by Voltaire, and especially by Rousseau. It is not only that every cultivated person is expected to know something *about* these Teutonic singers and sages; but their feelings and opinions reappear in the works of their most celebrated contemporaries in all other countries. For instance: among us, Scott and Byron had both of them been anticipated in what is most essential to them by German

authors; though no doubt the Feudalism of the one, and the Suicidism of the other, are more fully developed in them than in any foreigners by whom they may have been influenced. Still more remarkably than in poetry, the philosophical speculations of all Europe are daily learning obedience to the example of Germany. M Guizot is a pupil of those deep and zealous schools. Cuvier was himself by birth and education a German. Coleridge is the genial interpreter of the lore, now of Kant, and now of Schelling. Mr. Wordsworth, who, under the guise of a poet, is pre-eminently a high hortatory moralist, teaches only doctrines (except when eulogizing Archbishop Laud, &c.) which might be found long before his works appeared, even more fully and vividly declared in all the most illustrious masters of our ancestral Teutonic speech.

Some parts of this statement must pass for the moment without evidence, as we cannot now wait to support it in detail. Indeed it will be denied, we believe, by few persons having a wide prospect over the world, that this German literature, or the state of mind which it expresses, has, both in extent and seriousness of influence, a remarkable meaning. This Madame de Staël perhaps rather wished than quite attained to recognize and explain. But mistaken as are many of her notions on the subject, and (we suppose) all her translations from German books, it is evident that she had really felt something great in the minds of that country, something that far exceeded her previous Parisian standard, and was not even included in the large and radiant though spotted orb of Rousseau's genius. Substantially her belief has become that of the intelligent world; and the fear perhaps now is, not so much that German literature may be insufficiently valued, as that it may be prized on wrong grounds and used to mistaken purposes.

We will try to indicate some of the steps by which mankind moved on to the production of that German literature, the worth of which we hold indubitable by any one who, after due preparation, has really searched into the matter.

The combination of urbane and courtly elegance with ecclesiastical power, wealth, and wisdom, produced in Italy the earliest modern literature that can still be called much more than an object of antiquarian study. This glory failing with the wholesome earnestness of the church, whose decay produced beyond the Alps the protestant reformation, did not outlive that great change by much more than the life of one generation. Tasso died before the close of the sixteenth century. The beauteous strength of the Catholic times lingered longer in Spain where it had been slower in unfolding itself, and had been invigorated and hardened by its long conflict against the Koran. Calderon, whose life filled more than the first three-quarters of the seventeenth century, was the last great Catholic poet ; and we may safely affirm, that the world will never see another. Not of course that there may not be great poets born Catholics, and nominally, or even in a certain sense sincerely such throughout their lives : but that the days are long past when the form of feeling characteristic of the middle ages, and filling them with mystic many-coloured glories, can be the atmosphere at once and life blood of a great man.

Long before the death of Calderon, nay, before his birth, the bloom and richness of Europe had shown itself in the remote north under a very different shape from those dear to him. His predecessor Lope, the contemporary and more prosperous rival of Cervantes, was a soldier on board the Armada, which would have invaded England. But no doubt he little knew that in the cold and cloudy land of heretics there was then a burst of thought and imagination, the fame of which in after-times would far exceed his own.

We had at that time among us a combination such as existed nowhere else, of the mental freedom and social vigour of the reformation, with the stateliness and strength of feudalism. The result was the age of Elizabeth and Charles—Shakspeare and Cromwell. It is now clear enough to all Europe, that the England of Shakspeare was one of the chief scenes in the long drama of the human intellect. It succeeded to the splendour of Italian genius ; for at this time German thought was merely theological, and France followed mainly in the same track. Then broke out our civil war : and literature thenceforth became among us a matter either of pedantic research, or frivolous lightness, or practical utility ; not a free and beautiful outpouring of the heart. The material interests of our commercial and parliamentary life occupied the strongest minds so completely, that our lighter works were the productions only of second-rate men, and are, in the history of the world, entitled to but small notice. In truth, there could not be any minds of a very high order, when everything was bartered away that makes men great : enthusiasm, romance, poetry, the ideal in all departments but the useful and luxurious arts.

Now came the turn of France, the age of Louis XIV. Corneille, Racine, Molière, Bossuet, Pascal, and Fénélon, and at last Voltaire, were the representatives of a period in the history of their nation analogous, though not similar, to that of Shakspeare, Spenser, Ben Jonson, Raleigh, and Bacon among us. They gave to modern literature a clearness, precision, and obvious symmetry, which it had never possessed before : and then they died : though Voltaire, indeed, with his eighty years, lived over into a totally new epoch. This latter day may be called that of the French revolution in facts, that of the German revolution in ideas : two great changes closely but not very definably connected, in their causes as well as in their dates. By the German period of ideas, we mean one in which the imagination had far wider and deeper aims, and speculative inquiry a much more serious and more comprehensive character, than in the preceding French epoch ; which, however, had also bequeathed to its successor more of knowledge, elegance, system, and conscious clearness, than had been attained by England in her greatest age.

It may be remarked, that as Tasso lived after the Reformation (died 1595), and was contemporary with Shakspeare and Spenser, so Milton (died 1674) might have seen every one of those great writers of the age of Louis XIV., except by much the latest as well as longest-lived, Voltaire : and similarly Rousseau (died 1778), on the whole certainly the deepest and grandest of the French men of genius, saw, though he knew nothing of, the great outburst in Germany, when Winkelmann, Lessing, and Klopstock, led the way for Herder, Goethe, Kant, and Schiller. In each case there was one memorable chronological link between the departing and the coming period of human strength.

Having thus cast a hasty glance at the mere succession, in order of time, of these great movements, it may be worth considering what were the predominant circumstances affecting the intellectual character of each country shown in its literature.

England, in the hundred years that followed the accession of Elizabeth, was more alive with various hopeful energy than it has ever been since. In physical prosperity, enterprise of all kinds, in stirring thought, poetic freedom and greatness, and moral fervour and heroic conscientiousness, all combined, no similar period in the history of any nation has ever excelled this. Perhaps there have never been two generations in any country comparable to these. In point of mere date, Spenser, Bacon, Sidney, Shakspeare, and Raleigh, might have been brothers ; and Hobbes, Milton, Jeremy Taylor, Strafford, Hampden, and Cromwell, were the contemporaries of their sons. Down to the restoration of Charles II.—the end of this extraordinary age—feudal splendour, commercial activity, rural freedom, catholic authority, and biblical zeal, seemed all blended and balanced ; the rich and golden life of the earlier half of the century gradually yielding to the sterner subsequent forces ; till at last, when all else had passed away, the religious poetry of Milton rose as the peal of a single organ over the tomb of Cromwell, amid the lutes and drinking-songs and oaths of Charles the Second's court.

In fact, in the Stuart portion of this hundred years, though much of learned culture, poetic impulse, and high-born dignity still remained, the materializing commercial tendencies were gradually gaining the dominion which they have now so long boasted ; and were then far more strikingly accompanied than in later times, by that somewhat hard and narrow, but still noble theological dogmatism, which is the only higher kind of power that in recent times seems ever to have allied itself with the activity of Anglo-Saxon trade. Those puritan wars were only the fierce transition to the orderly, stiff, prosaic, aldermanic form of national life, which has prevailed in this country ever since.

Of this state of existence the explanation seems to be, that trade, diffusing wealth and a certain (strictly limited) intelligence, secures what is sometimes called freedom ; that is, representative government ; and gives the character of more or less shrewd and solid but very unheroic men of business, to the mass of the community. On the other hand, all serious human action developes the need of a moral law by which it may be governed. But mere practical life only seeks to have this law made as definite as possible, and enforced by the extremest sanction ; and hence rejects as dangerous all scientific inquiry into human duties and destinies, and shuns all question of the coherence and completeness of its creed, provided only that it be applicable and positive. We must take into account also the political weight of what is once established; and hence the repugnance on the part of constituted authorities to intellectual movement, except within a very definite sphere. The road is made, the toll-gates settled, money paid at them with grumbling, but without resistance: what wonder that all concerned, from trustees down to stone-breakers, feel a sincere public-spirited suspicion of plans for new visionary rail-roads? And these latter once established, as naturally join the remains of the old turnpike interest to vilify the chimera of superseding all roads whatever by the use of wings, seven-league boots, or any other transcendental furniture. On the other side, in behalf of men's nobler tendencies, little is to be said in this case: but that knowledge even in the weary greedy multitude has a certain weak expansiveness; and the wealth which brings leisure and luxury to the few will also ask for intellectual amusement, and will generally let some of the gilding of sofas and chiffoniers overflow on the frames of pictures and the covers of books. Which helps to man's higher culture we are far from denying, though it may be doubted whether they are quite all-sufficient.

In this state of things, then, we are sure to find, 1. An endless repetition of moral and religious common-places for practical use; 2. An infinite bustle of political discussion adapted to the comprehension of all, and therefore to that of the least comprehensive; 3. Scientific inquiries into "matter and motion," such as can be at all connected with money-making; 4. Frivolous literature in a perpetual succession of novelties, made for to-day and gloriously independent of to-morrow. But under none of these heads could we expect to find anything deeper in meaning or wider in survey than an enlightened public can relish. Little could be hoped of true and energetic originality. And genius itself, which comes from Heaven and cannot be prevented by the happiest mechanization of man, would hardly break out except either in some loose and loud subserviency to the multitude; or with fainthearted dishonest adherence to the letter of what is orthodox; or by mad revolt, as in melodious Shelley, against nature and necessity, no less than laws and men.

In France, after the long confusion of civil wars reaching down far later into their history than those of our middle ages, we find social life, and literature which embellished it, assuming under Louis XIV. an elegance, finish, and festal splendour previously unknown in Europe. Everything became neat, and much magnificent; but still, after the manner of courts, all in clear pre-appointed forms, with reason itself appearing only in the shape of *etiquette*. Yet the robust free life of feudalism more or less survived, and showed itself in the characters of many of the marshals and nobles—now plainly, for instance, in the Duc de St. Simon—and even in the writings of the great authors, though under somewhat rigid control, and with a rather obsequious decorum. Literature had its pedantic unproductive side in colleges and monasteries, but, as a public fashionable matter, was fitted to the luxurious tastes of a court and nobility. The middle classes, long before so powerful in England, had not yet in France risen into importance. Hence the prevailing books had neither the plain serviceable utility of our common moral disquisitions, nor their careless manner, any more than the brave liberality and largeness of our Elizabethan age. It was evidently proper that pains should be bestowed on what was meant to amuse and instruct a great king and his highborn nobles. Then too, and long after, very little was to be gained by copyright from the public; so that a terse and concise style, in harmony with the mental clearness and compactness of the race, very naturally came to characterize the productions of Racine and Bossuet. The colleges and ecclesiastical authorities, with their popish traditions and rich endowments, helped to secure elegant culture and finish. But their influence, and the tastes of a court, were alike opposed to any meddling with first principles, and the main elements of all high knowledge were required to be merely taken for granted. These writers show, perhaps, better than any others in the history of the world, how far it is possible to go in the absence of very varied natural life, and of deep and free philosophy. The genius of Molière rose above the pitch of his contemporaries, and in spite of seeming destiny, made him a great original painter of life and a worthy companion of Montaigne and Rabelais, who had preluded, somewhat as Chaucer among us, to the glories of a later age. His *Misantrope* is more truly Shakspearian, more simply, deeply drawn from the realities of the human soul, than anything we have seen of the professedly Shakspearian school now shedding blood by pailsful on the Parisian stage. This play in fact anticipates Rousseau, and stands in a very singular relation between "Hamlet" and "Faust;" and in like manner *Tartuffe* strikes the key-note of much that distinguishes Voltaire.

This author of Zaire and Zadig, with all his bold scepticism, seems only a vigorous and progressive survivor of the age of Louis XIV. He himself hints not obscurely his claim to be the Euripides in a triad of which Corneille and Racine formed the earlier pair. Sentimental emotion and all the refinements of a pleasant life had been the main objects of the authors whose Parnassus was Versailles. Even the state preachers spoke of death and judgment with ceremonious grace, as if to make the Christian pulpit contribute its share to polished entertainments of the court. And they, and all their lettered compeers, seemed to give up a tithe of their worldly amusements in obedience to the church, by way of securing a continuance of the remainder in a future life. Voltaire had spirit and shrewdness to contest the claims of the bishops, for even the fragment which alone they asked. By fifty years of multiform resistance, he made his protest good, and at last had all France with him.

But, in the main, while disputing the commands of the hierarchy, he obeyed without an audible murmur two other recognized powers; the laws of the state, and the rules of social custom. Rousseau arose, and rebelled also against these. Voltaire had mostly aimed only at relieving the world from a priesthood and a faith; letting it last in other respects as it was. Rousseau insisted that men must have a belief, though a reformed one; and that this reform ought to extend to their political constitutions,—nay, to all their habits, tastes, and practical convictions. If, as we ought, we leave out of view whole masses of inane egotism and dialectical paradox, we must own that he combined in his wonderful genius the most impassioned affection and the most earnest reason; and, with all his faults, was more than any man the precursor and representative of the great intellectual revolution which had begun in Germany before his death, and has extended more or less to all Europe.

To Germany, our final object, we now come. It is certainly at first sight a very singular fact that its literature, from the Reformation for more than two centuries onwards, was almost wholly either of a scholastic or commonplace character. Theological, antiquarian, nay, speculative books, there were in abundance; and the great, truly encyclopedic, name of Leibnitz, has hardly a superior among modern scientific thinkers. There were also many works of a practical kind for the people. But of men of lasting eminence, writing classical books in German on matters of general, not purely academic, interest, there was not one till less than a hundred years ago. The want of high and universal worth in German literature, must have been decided enough and known to be so, when Robertson dared confess, with no particular appearance of shame, that he had written the history of Charles V. without being able to read the language of that country which Charles ruled as emperor; the language, by his use of which, Luther in Charles's reign revolutionized Europe.

The slow maturity of German thought is, on consideration, intelligible enough. In the first place, all the other highly civilized parts of Europe were at one time ruled by Rome, and retained always some strong traces of classical culture. In England, indeed, all Roman refinement seems to have been swept away by the northern invaders; and it is the only part of Europe, once Latin, where this can be said to have been the case. But our Norman conquerors, succeeding to the Saxons and Danes, came to us from France, where they had learnt a language of itself half Latin, and many arts and tastes derived from the same noble source. The subsequent long and close connection of our sovereigns, nobility, and clergy, with the more enlightened country they sprang from, had an evident and great effect upon Britain. Here, then, was one means of knowledge and humanity almost entirely wanting to the Germans. Hence, perhaps, mainly it is that in modern times the German courts displayed but little sensibility for intellectual pleasures, till influenced in the eighteenth century by the example of France.

Secondly, of the great European countries, Germany is by far the most inland. Spain and Italy are almost insular; we are entirely so; even France has a land frontier on but one and a half of its four sides; while Germany is open to the sea on but a portion of its northern boundary, and the greater part of that sea-coast looks to the landlocked and remote Baltic. Hence, there were not the natural causes prevailing over all the west of Europe for the growth of a wealthy and quick-witted commercial class. And thus neither courtly nor mercantile refinement arose as early as in Latinized and maritime countries. Rude nobles and poor serfs composed the people of Germany, long after polished aristocracies and rich intelligent burghers had filled other lands with graceful arts,

and brought forth the various national literature of the modern world.

Thirdly, the religious wars caused in Germany by the Reformation, filled the whole following century, and did not end till the middle of the seventeenth. In France, where civilisation was already far more advanced, they occupied but a few years; and in England nothing of the kind occurred till after our greatest intellectual age, and then only disturbed six or seven years, and hardly interfered at all with the progress of the country in the arts of peace.

These considerations may help to explain the fact that Germany, after occupying almost the whole of Roman Europe, and placing her sons on all its chief thrones, and then inventing the printing-press and bringing forth Luther, was yet left far behind by England, France, Italy, and Spain, in the elaboration of that free, varied, and beautiful modern culture, which, in recent times, it has more completely appropriated and perfected than any of its rivals.

But perhaps the very causes which retarded the efflorescence of Germany, also secured that the flowers when at last disclosed should be more abundant and richer. For what was it but the strength, depth, uncommercial quiet and solidity of the nation, that brought out the Reformation among them. And were not these the virtues which, two centuries after, fashioned themselves into the Lessings, Goethes, and Kants? What but the absence of political centralization, the division of Germany into many states, so long gave up the country to wars for religion, which must have ended far sooner had the land, like France and England, been under one government? And this very plurality of states and capitals, with their courts and universities, has been among the most obvious and certain causes of that widespread, varied, unshackled intelligence, which the torpid priestly colleges of England, and the single tyrannical metropolis of France, have alike, though in such different ways, prevented in their respective countries.

This slight, though we believe accurate sketch of a great subject, may possibly seem imperfect for want of any statement why it is that Spain and Italy have done nothing in modern times at all comparable to the intellectual achievements of the three principal northern countries. To this difficulty, also, something like a plausible answer can be furnished. It is

not because they have had no protestant reformation, or, as in France, a revolution of equivalent energy. For we must still discover *why* this has not taken place. The explanation appears to be as to Spain, that the long struggle against the Moors made hatred of heresy the one serious passion of the people, and thus gave them up more entirely than any other Europeans into the hands of their clergy. Then the possession of America rendered the sovereign independent of the nation. And thus king and priest, the natural and reasonable representatives of the highest forms of social life, obtained and used the power to extinguish all national force and health, in slow, shameful decay. Fire, indeed, remained under the ashes, and at last has burst out; nor, we trust, will the blaze be quenched again.

In Italy the mischief sprang from other causes. The consolidation of the great monarchies of France, Austria, and Spain, surrounded that country with neighbours too strong for her divided force to encounter. Her physical structure made it easy to attack her in detail and hard for her to rally round any centre. The power of the Bishop of Rome, inherited from the old civil pre-eminence of that city, set apart one portion of the peninsula under a consecrated rule with which it was impossible for the other states to coalesce. Thus inwardly distracted, nay cloven, and alternately overpowered and parcelled into small despotisms by one or other of her neighbours, Italy, too, sank into a languid imbecility which only now and then utters some detached phrase, recalling her former and still latent strength. Had Rome been governed by any sort of temporal ruler, he would gradually, no doubt, have united all the other Italian states; and then, in confidence of national dignity, every individual citizen would have risen into higher life. But the anomaly of a superannuated old clergyman governing, in the name of God and of the Fisherman, the former capital of the civilized world, was itself enough to make it impossible that, in modern times, he should extend a dominion the foundation of which was thus equivocal.

Taking up our former inquiry into the history of the German mind—what seems most peculiar to that nation, among all those of Europe, is the number and strength of the universities, and, at the same time, their freedom from ecclesiastical trammels. The nature of the land itself with reference to commerce and other particulars, the kinds of government and the political divisions, the diversities of religion established in the several sections, the national character, with its deep and steady fire, and the tranquillity and seriousness of its social habits, all these are important points. But as discriminating Germany from the other great European countries, there is, we think, not one nearly so significant and productive a fact as this of the existence of a great number of bodies of men selected for their eminence as thinkers, and set apart to think, and permitted to declare their thoughts with perfect, or nearly perfect, freedom.

We see, at this instant, an Oxford professor, of unquestioned piety, nearly worried to death for controverting or supporting (we forget which) St.Thomas Aquinas. A German may proclaim his agreement with Plato, Spinoza, or Shaftesbury, and his disregard of all the Fathers and all the Reformers; and in all probability, if he shows sincerity and genius in doing so, will gain an increased salary, the cross of an order, and a larger body of pupils. It is not very difficult to perceive which plan is the more likely to make profound philosophical inquirers.

In England and Italy, even in France down to the Revolution, there was neither any such abundance of institutions for the highest knowledge, nor any such liberty in those existing. Accordingly, in these three countries it has been almost exclusively in physical science, in matters only remotely connected with theological dogma, and therefore exempt from its control, that there has been any steady conjoint progress, any recognized independence of inquiry, and a deference in the government for the opinion of the most competent. In Germany alone has the case been memorably otherwise. We find there an organization of men's highest interests and tendencies, neither crushed by the jealousy of civil rulers, nor perverted by ecclesiastics to serve the purposes—most important, no doubt, but not alone important—of their profession. Perhaps it would not be too much to say, that as the representative institutions of England and America are gradually being adopted by all the civilized world, as the best instruments for arranging men's outward and material concerns, so the day must come when the intellectual progress of mankind will stop, or something like the German universities be everywhere established, and endowed with at least as healthy and noble a freedom as has been allowed in those bodies. In that country—poor as Germany is, compared

with England and France—there may now probably be found the greater part of the generous knowledge and earnest meditation extant on earth. But Oxford and Cambridge, with perhaps more wealth than all the German professors together, certainly do not contain six men who have added a jot to human knowledge, except in the physical sciences; and not more than two or three, if so many, whose names Europe has ever heard of in any department. The monastic spirit of these establishments cannot be expected to produce better fruits; and we must rather pity than blame the individual men, the victims of a system that they fancy themselves bound to defend.

As the total result of these causes and revolutions on the banks of the Rhine and Elbe, what do we find? A modern German literature no doubt, which lies before us and around us, and is studied as the modern French and modern Italian by those who have a taste for polite accomplishments. Something more, however, there is than this. These German books are not merely in a language of their own, but have a whole physiognomy and character distinct, original; not only very unlike either our own or any other writings, but also, perhaps, of a deeper, wider kind.

What then, we would ask, is the word —for there must be one—which more nearly than all others expresses the specific character of the more celebrated German writers during the last half or three-quarters of a century? Let us try some of the more popular solutions:

Is it *homeliness?*

No, they are not more homely than Goldsmith, or Crabbe, or Walter Scott; not more even than Theocritus or Homer. But they combine homeliness with a higher somewhat, which we hardly find elsewhere in this connection.

Is it *affectionateness?*

Scarcely this either; though it is true that their philosophers recognize, and their poets delineate, a warmth and fulness of the feelings, and not merely of the passions, such as other modern writers do not attempt, except in spasms of sentimental exaggeration. But this is not universal in these foreign works, and is not peculiar to them: Shakspeare and Cervantes, Dante, Boccaccio, and Montaigne, abound in the same tone, which is also the familiar music of much of the ancient classical literature.

Is it then *mysticism?*

Surely in no sense of the word can this

be found in the greater part of the poems of Goethe and Schiller. Popularly speaking, the word means nothing but *obscurity;* which, except so far as everything worth understanding requires pains to understand it, is as little a fault of the German writers, excluding Novalis, as of any in all literature. A mystic is properly a man who does not seek to bring his own higher feelings and convictions into as much intellectual clearness as they are capable of, but loves the solemn gloom of indistinct emotion too well to approach it with conscious reflection. In this sense there are perhaps no men having a deep faith of heart so little chargeable with *mysticism* as the more eminent of the German philosophers and even poets.

Is it, then, perhaps the opposite of mysticism, *reflection,* which distinguishes these men from the guides of other nations?

This, more nearly than any of the other characteristics we have tried, might seem to fulfil the purpose. M. Guizot has somewhere stated it as the blame of German literature, that reflection is too prominent and general in its productions; that there is not a sufficiently clear, direct representation, of the outward realities of life. But though there is more of large and accurate meditation in these works than in any other contemporary masterpieces, neither can this be styled their main distinction. We find it indeed as a most important element in their poetic works. But it cannot, at all events, characterize their philosophy; for that must always be entirely and purely reflective; and to say that one philosophy is more so than others, is merely to pronounce it the best. But neither is it, though conceivably of course it might be, the chief singularity of other than their philosophical treatises. There is in the mere descriptive department, in verbal landscape-painting, and the like, a clearness, completeness, and conciseness in much of the writing of these men—as Goethe and Tieck, for instance—to which we can find no parallel elsewhere; and in these two, and Schiller and Jean Paul, a true, free exhibition of varieties and greatnesses of human character, of shades and depths of emotion, which reflective thought could never have revealed to any man who had not either felt them in his heart before his head took notice of them, or found them in human life before he generalized them into a theory.

Shall we then enlarge our phrase, and say that it is *knowledge* in general in which they excel?

In this also there is much plausibility. If we look at their speculative writers, there is an extent of survey, a mastery over the theories that all ages and countries have produced, and the facts that these theories were designed to explain, such as no school among any other people has had the least pretension to. Indeed, directly to translate, or indirectly to borrow from these men, is sufficient to obtain in other parts of Europe, and eminently among us, the somewhat dangerous repute of engaging deeply in the strangest of forbidden pursuits—the black art of thinking. It is also an unquestionable fact, that their poets have had an acquaintance with philosophic speculation, with the theory of criticism, with the history of the fine arts, and with various languages and literatures, such as could hardly be found among those of most other countries. But neither can this be what constitutes the clearly-felt difference between this and rival literatures. The difference is one too deep and fundamental for mere book-knowledge. however large and various, to explain. The whole view of life, and all the little unconscious turns of feeling that meet us in every page of their imaginative writings, spring from a far other root than that either of our popular bravura writing, or of encyclopedic learning.

Do we come any nearer our object in trying if *culture* will satisfy the sphinx ?

So it may seem, for *culture* includes many of the elements that we have already found in the great fact before us. Yet neither will this quite succeed. For culture will do everything for man but give him the original capacity on which it most successfully works. If culture were all, how far had a Voltaire been above a Shakspeare, a Gray before a Burns, a Mengs beyond a Correggio, a Dugald Stewart ahead of a Spinoza ! All which is much the reverse of true.

We require something from which—granting the due circumstances—culture, knowledge, and reflection, clearness and liveliness of painting, the seriousness that will to careless eyes appear mysticism, the affectionateness that fills a life and book with warmth, and the homeliness which is the proof of real interest in all the forms and conditions of human nature, must, as water from its fountain, rise and be manifest. And there is one power in man, which, with proper qualities of other kinds, and under favouring influences, will produce all that and every other good

thing. There is but one. It is *Earnestness of heart.* This we do conceive to be the grand fontal characteristic of the better German writings, as compared with those that other nations have brought forth during these last three-score years and ten.

Here, perhaps, we might fitly stop. For where men have equal natural gifts, and equal circumstances, *Earnestness is all* that makes the difference. As to gifts, the Teutonic race are, in force, fire, and clearness, the masters of the modern world; being indeed the conquerors of it all, and founders of its medieval Christian life. Their circumstances, as already we have partly seen, are not in later times less favourable, but rather more so than those of other countries: for they are in good measure exempt from all-confusing commercial bustle ; and do not shrink under the tyranny of one huge feverish drunken metropolis ; and are amply provided with *seats of free thought*—at once cause, result, proof and furtherance of this faithful national earnestness. Other things being equal, or even not grossly unequal, the most *earnest* people will be the wisest, most melodious, most creative ; and this is what we esteem the Germans to be as shown in their modern books.

In France all or most that is loudly written, and similarly spoken, seems designed for instant effect on a vehement gregarious race. Nearer ourselves we see much of a literature more for household use, and regarded mainly as a convenience for the domestic soul. Each country also shares in the blessings characteristic of the other, and Germany in turn has enough of the same froth and dregs as its neighbours. But it has begotten all the greatest masters of thought produced in Europe since the time of Rousseau ; and Tieck and Schelling are still alive to represent in the flesh a literature, which for compass, loftiness, and enduring beauty, for all that Earnestness must in our modern world attempt and realize, is quite unlike almost anything that either we or our nearest neighbours can boast of.

Happily for us no great European nation has so close a relation as ourselves to these sons of the weird northern Muses. We may largely gain by using those rights of kindred which they have been always proud to insist on. For in varied tones and utterances—of calm reflection, of dramatic personification, of lyric enthusiasm, of epic and idyllic narrative—they teach us that our human life is not only, as it must always

be, a course of hard toil and a mixture of broken joys and sharp sorrows, but full of a divine meaning, and capable of immortal good. With deep meditative wisdom, and in forms of many-coloured beauty, they set before us a lesson which England much needs, but is also most worthy to learn. Our coarse mechanical strength is mingled with a rich and strong element of conscience, humanity, and unwearied hope, but all tortured into maimed shapes, and wrapped in thick gloom. We may again help towards the recovery both of light and beauty among the men who still gloriously consecrate the soil we first sprang from. There are many of us who delight in the manifold glowing world of Shakspeare ; others who have felt the tones of eternal truth in the slow chant of Wordsworth, in some piercing lyric phrase of Coleridge, and in the sweet bewildered wail of Shelley. Many again have stepped more lightly over our toilsome earth in the presence of the bold shadows evoked from the past by Scott. All these living hearts, varied as are their habits and outward interests, will find leaders of their pilgrimage, such as all earth beside does afford, in the great men of modern Germany.

There is one quality of those modern German writers which, it may be as well to warn unprepared readers, will strike them with wonder and perhaps with fear. This is nothing but that freedom to which we have before adverted. The greater of those men have used their fine and robust faculties in looking at life and nature for themselves ; not in order to escape from duty, but to fulfil it more abundantly and on a larger scale than custom would prescribe. There is nothing more common than the sight of persons, the despair of moralists in all ages, the *fools* named in Scripture, who throw off a burden which they are too weak to bear bravely, and disown whatever is high and pure within them that they may sink into inert mean falseness and brutishness. But there is another revolt against popular rules and laws of opinion, having a very different aim from this. The weak man, to get rid of his load, will cut off the arms to which it is tied, and maim his powers to escape his obligations ; but the strong man who refuses to " carry coals " at the bidding of others, claims only to choose his own load, and will bear willingly and with painful fidelity a far heavier one than the public opinion which he disobeys would have dared to lay on him. No taskmaster would have made those women, who carried forth their husbands as their most precious commodities, submit to a burden half so weighty. And thus it is with all who engage seriously in the task of life. Freely they choose, and freely perform, a work beyond the compass of all legal injunctions. For freedom is found at last to be nothing else but the willing choice of those conditions which enable our best, most laborious powers, to exert themselves for the fittest ends. And this is the freedom towards which every noble soul feels, toils, and bleeds, as towards its native and only vital element, as the plant to light and air, the fish out of the net into the fresh unbounded water. This victorious effort it is, which glorifies more or less every truly great man ; and above all in modern times, those of Germany ; whose names we constantly hear connected with the charge of irreligion, licentiousness, and whatever of horrible that stupid tongues can devise to ring in stupid ears. As if profane irreverence, and mad self-willed resistance to reason, could ever be the characteristic tendency of thoughtful, humane, and imaginative minds. There is a freedom far unlike that of the escaped convict, and consisting not in doltish disobedience, but in the sacred and serene obedience of love to the highest rule of duty we can find within us. Not such is the freedom secured by Magna Chartas, and acts of settlement that guard us from the tyranny of kings, but leave us under the yoke of our next door neighbour's eyes and our newswriter's pen. Neither is there any such liberty to be obtained by the most diligent compliance with all the precepts of ethics and theology, in which the heart and strength of a man may be as much confined, as his body if it were chained in a locked church. Divine commandments are but the commandments of divines for him who does not feel that in compliance with them is the only liberation of his soul from death. A man who does not feel this may be gravely wrong, but will not get himself right by tying himself to the letter in which he finds no spirit. The freedom of an earnest mind brings with it laws as strict and holy as any in the pentateuch or the canons, but also has tenfold strength for the performance of the only work on earth really worthy a man. All the rest is the routine of a scourged and hoodwinked heart. Political freedom is a great blessing ; but there is a still better kind known only to the good and wise, and of which

Schiller and Fichte and their compeers are teachers and examples, such as Europe for near two centuries had hardly seen.

Connected, not very remotely, with this matter of spiritual freedom, is the remarkable fact that while, of the population of Germany, considerably more than half are catholics, every man who has gained an immortal fame in that country as a thinker, was born and bred a protestant. As to the right of the greater number of the following names to appear in the list, there can be but one opinion.

Leibnitz	Hegel
Frederick II.	Eichhorn
Lessing	Johannes Müller
Winkelmann	Jean Paul Richter
Klopstock	2 Stolbergs
Herder	2 Schlegels
Wieland	2 Humboldts
F. H. Jacobi	Novalis
Goethe	Tieck
Schiller	F. A. Wolf
Kant	Voss
Fichte	Niebuhr
Schelling	Savigny.

Three of these illustrious men—one Stolberg, one Schlegel, and Winkelmann—became catholics ; the last, it is said, from mere convenience ; the former two, no doubt, with entire sincerity. We might, perhaps, have added Werner, the dramatic poet, as to the purity of whose motives in the same change there seems to be no cause for doubt. But even these converts, all except Winkelmann but second-rate among the great, were formed in the comparative freedom of protestant doctrine. Of the others, many, perhaps nearly all, were very far from what we commonly call orthodoxy—that is, from believing that the creeds of the reformers three hundred years ago, or any one such document, contains the whole and nothing but the truth, as to man's spiritual constitution and destiny. But though mostly heretics in the eyes of synods and consistories, and of our bench of bishops, they were generally far more completely removed from any allegiance to the doctrine of the schoolmen or to that of the fathers ; and the mere artistic and romantic admiration felt by some of them for the times of legend and miracle, was only similar in kind to that which they cherished for the mythological beauty of early Greece, and even of ancient India. Except the two or three persons just mentioned, whose history is not very hard of explanation, there was not one of these men who would not rather have sacrificed his life than the liberty of believing and

feeling for himself in conformity with the promptings of his own soul, and with the spirit of the times that he belonged to. If we remember that more than eighteen millions of the Germans are catholics, this protestant consent of all their strongest, deepest, and most genial minds, is perhaps as significant a fact as any that history presents. Not that it portends any triumph of Exeter Hall over the Vatican, and the Prayer-book over the Missal, but that it exhibits the emancipation of all truly great minds from the bondage of all dead traditions, by whatever name they may be trumpeted.

Strange, moreover, as it may seem, with all their heterodoxy, there are not above five or six in our whole list whose writings do not indicate a far nobler, purer feeling of religion and of duty, than can be found in our Paleys and Watsons, and scores of well-reputed correct British theologians.

We have already stated, that in our view their most remarkable quality, and indeed the root of all their merits, is moral earnestness. It has also been pointed out that this Earnestness is combined with, or seen to issue in, a Freedom, of which the serious minds among us have in general but little conception. If now we further attempt to mark by one expression the *idea* which pervades this literature, and the consciousness of which all sympathizing readers must more or less obscurely derive from it, this may be called the WORTH OF MAN.

This Worth it is which we find exhibited in each of the three great forms assumed by the genius of the Germans—in History, Philosophy, and Poetry. History displays the facts of human nature ; philosophy, the principles that the facts rise from and express ; poetry, the symbols in which the principles are illustrated, and the facts more compendiously and vividly reproduced. In all these departments alike, the Worth of Man, the fellow-feeling that we owe, and the labour that the construction of our life requires and deserves, are shown with a settled strength and complete beauty far beyond the pitch of any other writings we know but those of the Greeks, and superior even to them in depth and compass. We do not forget Dante and Ariosto, Cervantes and Calderon, Shakspeare and Milton ; but among the Germans we have a whole literature, and not merely one or two great minds— we have vast regions of philosophy and history almost unknown, and altogether unsurveyed, by any other nation. And even their poets, being much the latest that the world has produced with anything like equal powers, have, though certainly not an absolute superiority to all their predecessors, yet an extent of knowledge, and, above all, a suitableness for us in this age, which earlier ones could not possibly be endowed with.

But in history and philosophy (*i. e.* what is commonly called metaphysics) the higher dignity with which man appears than that which our popular authors allow him, is far more strikingly manifest. The ancient world especially has been as good as reconquered for us from waste darkness by the race of scholars, with Wolf, the critic of Homer, at their head, whose works are beginning, either by vague rumour or small samples, to make their way into England. Niebuhr, at least, we all know, has re-constructed for us that old, stern, half-Etruscan Rome, which had lain so long buried under the ruins of her own later empire, and chronicled only in supernatural, that is unnatural, legends. To him Man, as he trod five-and-twenty centuries ago the banks of the obscure and marshy Tiber, was still so venerable and dear an image, that a whole laborious life might be well spent in tracing out his faintest footsteps, and deepening the slightest outlines of his story, till ages that seemed as completely lost as if they had belonged to some anterior planet, and whose place had for two thousand years been supplied by fantastic fables, stood again before us with the breath of life, and there, instead of a shapeless cloud, was Rome resurgent "in all her panoply." But it is less this result with which we are now concerned, than the spirit of sincere faith, the feeling of the Worth of Man in his historical no less than his present existence, which makes Niebuhr so remarkable to us, and which has made his fellow historians and philologers a race so different from the earlier verbal pedants and all-believing devourers of old books. If the mythology and history, the thoughts and beliefs of the classical world, and especially of ancient Greece, have a living interest, and coherent intelligible subsistence for us, we owe it to such men as Niebuhr, Wolf, Voss, K. O. Müller, who have penetrated with their sharp eyes and glowing enthusiasm into the tangled, thorny, fruitless wilderness, the sacred haunt of ghosts and schoolmasters.

Thus also it is with philosophy, which in England and France has long attempted little more than to explain away whatever is awful and divine in man, into something, if not mean and bad, yet small and frivolous. Our writers on such subjects, often with the best purpose, but ill-placed and stunted by the tendencies of the world they lived in, like their French contemporaries only sought for the most part to analyze some separate faculty or thing that they found in man. The Germans took another road—made philosophy properly *constructive*, and sought to ascertain and consecrate laws around and above us, from which we and all things spring and become intelligible—and not merely to use the tools of the workshop within us in taking those tools to pieces. The aim of the Germans is at least the nobler one, and elevates, not dwarfs, the soul of him who makes them his masters. There is a godlike within us that feels itself akin to the gods; and if we are told that both the godlike and the gods are dreams, we can but answer that so to dream is better than to wake and find ourselves nothing.

There is one remark which reflections of this kind are almost certain to call forth in a large and respectable class of persons among us, viz., that to assert the Worth of Man is an arrogant delusion, and one that puffs up men with vanity. But this objection implies the absurd mistake of supposing that the loftier the standard by which we judge ourselves, the more and not the less nearly shall we seem to reach its full height. What is all that is held most holy—what all the godlike men whom religious tradition canonizes and glorifies—but forms of a divine idea ever to be kept before us, and approached, though in each individual most imperfectly realized? And when in other words we speak of the Worth of Man, which philosophy explains, history displays in action, and poetry sings of and makes visible to the soul, we but declare that there is a greatness of human nature which rebukes the littleness of each, and yet is the common blessing and support of us all. It is not those that think most lowly of themselves who will protest loudest against the assertors of the experienced and still possible Worth of Man. We have already sufficiently declared that we hold the great German writers to be the chief teachers of this lesson in the present age; and we wish nothing better than that our readers may not take our word for the fact, but examine it seriously for themselves. We believe no one ever thoughtfully studied these masters of modern thought without finding in them more and more of what is best for all men.

Art. IX.—*Geschichte der Poetischen National Literatur der Deutschen.* Von G. G. Gervinus. (History of the Poetic National Literature of the Germans. By G. G. Gervinus.) 5 vols. Leipzic. 1810-42.

This is a very able and very original book, and though of too large a range to admit of due notice in the space we can at present afford to it, we are anxious to bring within view of our readers at once, a work so striking and important.

The writer is a person sufficiently remarkable to claim attention in himself. G. G. Gervinus was born at Hesse-Darmstadt : one of those small places scattered over Germany like the seed of Cadmus, to give forth their yearly produce of armed men and government employés, with hardly a shoot of literature at any time among them. The early life of Gervinus was new proof of what a man may do, with the help of real genius. From the dingy and miserable shop of a German *épicier*, where as an apprentice he passed his youth, he mastered for himself, in an incredibly short space of time, the way to a professor's chair at Gottingen. Gottingen was then in the flower of its literary reputation and influence, and neither of these suffered by the results of this appointment.

But alas! while Gervinus continued to give the fruits of his learning and genius to the students that crowded in his lecture-room, we gave Germany one more prince, in the person of King Ernest Augustus. It is hardly pleasant that our country should be even passively responsible for the sudden, sullen, and hateful storm, which, rising from our English shores, thus burst over unhappy Hanover. It threw down Gervinus at once from the peaceful seat he had occupied so ably and so long. Proscribed by the famous manifesto of his Hanoverian Majesty he left Gottingen ; not the least illustrious of the Seven, who, like the ancient Greek philosopher *omnia sua secum portans*, preferred seclusion and exile to slavish obedience and shameful perjury. He went to Italy first ; and ultimately settled in a beautiful villa near Heidelberg. He lives there now : not belonging in any way to the corps of the University, but solely given up to study. The book before us is the growth of that retirement : a rich, abundant, and wholesome produce.

It must not here be omitted that neither Gervinus, nor the leader of the Seven, Dahlmann, are in any way, save by their superior intelligence, connected with what is called the liberal and progressive party in Germany. No German ever dreamt of calling them liberals. Both were on the contrary rather more than conservative in their political opinions : and universally known to be so by their countrymen. In their opposition to the King of Hanover, it is worth keeping in mind, they followed only the steady and conscientious dictates of upright and truehearted men. As in the tendency of certain learned pursuits, so in the purest type of honesty and honour, Gervinus will bear to be called the disciple of Jacob Grimm, the well-known restorer of the ancient literature and grammar of Germany.

Following Jacob Grimm and his brother, however, in the way of their pursuits, Gervinus arrived at quite different results. The Grimms, Jacob and Wilhelm, set themselves to work to re-create, as we have said, the grammar of the ancient German languages: they pierced to the deepest and most hidden roots of that wonderful tree, pursued it in its different branches, and as the issue of an enormous labour, have given life to the old dialects, have sent forth invaluable editions of the earliest German literature, and completed all needful preparations for the great Lexicon or Dictionary of the German tongue, on which they are now engaged in Berlin. That great task, however, was only half of what was to be done : its supplement and completion we owe to Gervinus.

The work before us is the first history of German Literature, taken as whole, and considered in its relation to the nation and the several ages. We know of no similar work comparable to it in any other country. Gervinus has been the first to adopt, in writing a history of literature, the true historiographical method. The numberless attempts of this kind in his predecessors have been either merely biographical, annexing the history of literature to names and persons ; or still worse compilations of bibliographical notices ; of fragmentary criticisms marked by all the pedantry and prolixity German learnedness has been so proud of ; stuffed out with endless quotations, and, by the effort to make themselves intelligible, hopeless of being ever understood. Gervinus's plan is simple : he starts at the earliest sound of German song, and steadily follows up the course of letters into the time of its highest perfection. This, being a true German, he holds to be an absolute perfection, never to be equalled or surpassed, and he finds it in the time of Schiller and Gothe. The highest reach of German genius is, according to Gervinus, in those two men. At that point we understand him to say, plainly and severely, the task of German poetry is done, and its work over. After Gothe, no more. It is to mislead the power of intelligence and genius to direct it to art and poetry thenceforward. The next duty of the German race is not æsthetical, but political : and in the ideas of State and Church other tendencies must become absorbed. We are stating opinions here : we are not admitting or contesting them.

This is why Gervinus has closed his work with the death of Göthe : only naming what is called the romantic school, Tieck, Schlegel, and their companions ; and slipping over, perhaps with too adverse and scornful an air, the newest revelations of German mind. The part of his labour in which he is most diffuse, is at its outset ; where, engaged on the earlier times, he gives minute account of the different phases German Poetry has passed through. He abolishes the old distinction of periods taken from political history. He overlooks his enormous materials from a higher point of view : one which, at the same time, enables him to show how the literary and poetical development must be ever deeply

39. continued

connected with political life. And in relation to this it is one of his favourite ideas to attempt to prove, that the political disunion of Germany has been as favourable to literature as pernicious to the state and church. The singular merit of the work throughout, is its clear and subtle insight: Gervinus has at all times the whole subject-matter within its view, and is master of the secrets of the composition of German literature. And the sure and unfaltering hand with which, having sketched the outlines of his various characters and placed them in their respective times, he lightens and illustrates the one by the other, is satisfactory and beautiful. His parallels of Schiller and Göthe, Wieland and Klopstock, Lessing and Herder, are masterpieces. His description of the literary revolution of Germany that went on in Göthe's youth (1760—1790) is perfect even in style: not always the best side of Gervinus. His style, it must be admitted, for the most part wants ease and a natural movement.

The history is comprised in five volumes. An abridgement has been very recently issued (by Engelmann of Leipsic), and with extraordinary success. But this, which might have been most valuable to readers here, we are sorry that we cannot altogether recommend to them. Its arrangement is not very happy; and its profitable use is hardly likely to extend beyond those who either know the greater work, or are already extremely familiar with the subject of which it treats.

___

IMAGINARY CONVERSATION. BY WALTER SAVAGE LANDOR.

SANDT AND KOTZEBUE.

Sandt.—GENERALLY men of letters in our days, contrary to the practice o. antiquity, are little fond of admitting the young and unlearned into their studies or their society.

Kotzebue.—They should rather those than others. The young *must* cease to be young, and the unlearned *may* cease to be unlearned. According to the letters you bring with you, sir, there is only youth against you. In the seclusion of a college life, you appear to have studied with much assiduity and advantage, and to have pursued no other courses than the paths of wisdom.

Sandt.—Do you approve of the pursuit?

Kotzebue.—Who does not?

Sandt.—None, if you will consent that they direct the chase, bag the game, inebriate some of the sportsmen, and leave the rest behind in the slough. May I ask you another question?

Kotzebue.—Certainly.

Sandt.—Where lie the paths of wisdom? I did not expect, my dear sir, to throw you back upon your chair. I hope it was no rudeness to seek information from you?

Kotzebue.—The paths of wisdom, young man, are those which lead us to truth and happiness.

Sandt.—If they lead us away from fortune, from employments, from civil and political utility; if they cast us where the powerful persecute, where the rich trample us down, and where the poorer (at seeing it) despise us, rejecting our counsel and spurning our consolation, what valuable truth do they enable us to discover, or what rational happiness to expect? To say that wisdom leads to truth, is only to say that wisdom leads to wisdom; for such is truth. Nonsense is better than falsehood; and we come to that.

Kotzebue.—How?

Sandt.—No falsehood is more palpable than that wisdom leads to happiness—I mean in this world; in another, we may well indeed believe that the words are constructed of very different materials. But here we are, standing on a barren molehill that crumbles and sinks under our tread; here we are, and show me from hence, Von Kotzebue, a discoverer who has not suffered for his discovery, whether it be of a world or of a truth—whether a Columbus or a Galileo. Let us come down lower: Show me a man who has detected the injustice of a law, the absurdity of a tenet, the malversation of a minister, or the impiety of a priest, and who has not been stoned, or hanged, or burnt, or imprisoned, or exiled, or reduced to poverty. The chain of Prometheus is hanging yet upon his rock, and weaker limbs writhe daily in its rusty links. Who then, unless for others, would be a darer of wisdom? And yet, how full of it is even the inanimate world? We may gather it out of stones and straws. Much lies within the reach of all: little has been collected by the wisest of the wise. O slaves to passion! O minions to power! ye carry your own scourges about you; ye endure their tortures daily; yet ye crouch for more. Ye believe that God beholds you; ye know that he will punish you, even worse than ye punish yourselves; and still ye lick the dust where the Old Serpent went before you.

Kotzebue.—I am afraid, sir, you have formed to yourself a romantic and stange idea, both of happiness and of wisdom.

Sandt.—I too am afraid it may be so. My idea of happiness is, the power of communicating peace, good-will, gentle affections, ease, comfort, independence, freedom, to all men capable of them.

Kotzebue.—The idea is, truly, no humble one.

Sandt.—A higher may descend more securely on a stronger mind. The power of communicating those blessings to the capable, is enough for my aspirations. A stronger mind may exercise its faculties in the divine work of creating the capacity.

Kotzebue.—Childish! childish!—Men have cravings enow already; give them fresh capacities, and they will have fresh appetites. Let us be contented in the sphere wherein it is the will of Providence to place us; and let us render ourselves useful in it to the utmost of our power, without idle aspirations after impracticable good.

Sandt.—O sir! you lead me where I tremble to step; to the haunts of your intellect, to the recesses of your spirit. Alas! alas! how small and how vacant is the central chamber of the lofty pyramid?

Kotzebue.—Is this to me?

Sandt.—To you, and many mightier. Reverting to your own words; could not you yourself have remained in the sphere you were placed in?

Kotzebue.—What sphere? I have written dramas, and novels, and travels. I have been called to the Imperial Court of Russia.

Sandt.—You sought celebrity.—I blame not that. The thick air of multitudes may be good for some constitutions of mind, as the thinner of solitudes is for others. Some horses will not run without the clapping of hands; others fly out of the course rather than hear it. But let us come to the point. Imperial courts! What do they know of letters? What letters do they countenance—do they tolerate?

Kotzebue.—Plays.

Sandt.—Playthings.

Kotzebue.—Travels.

Sandt.—On their business. O ye paviours of the dreary road along which their cannon rolls for conquest! my blood throbs at every stroke of your rammers. When will ye lay them by?

Kotzebue.—We are not such drudges.

Sandt.—Germans! Germans! Must ye never have a rood on earth ye can call your own, in the vast inheritance of your fathers?

Kotzebue.—Those who strive and labour, gain it; and many have rich possessions.

Sandt.—None; not the highest.

Kotzebue.—Perhaps you may think them insecure; but they are not lost yet, although the rapacity of France does indeed threaten to swallow them up. But her fraudulence is more to be apprehended than her force. The promise of liberty is more formidable than the threat of servitude. The wise know that she never will bring us freedom; the brave know that she never can bring us thraldom. She herself is alike impatient of both; in the dazzle of arms she mistakes the one for the other, and is never more agitated than in the midst of peace.

Sandt.—The fools that went to war against her, did the only thing that could unite her; and every sword they drew was a conductor of that lightening which fell upon their heads. But we must now look at our homes. Where there is no strict union, there is no perfect love; and where no perfect love, there is no true helper. Are you satisfied, sir, at the celebrity and the distinctions you have obtained?

Kotzebue.—My celebrity and distinctions, if I must speak of them, quite satisfy me. Neither in youth nor in advancing age—neither in difficult nor in easy circumstances, have I ventured to proclaim myself the tutor or the guardian of mankind.

Sandt.—I understand the reproof, and receive it humbly and gratefully. You did well in writing the dramas, and the novels, and the travels; but, pardon my question, who called you to the courts of princes in strange countries?

Kotzebue.—They themselves.

Sandt.—They have no more right to take you away from your country, than to eradicate a forest, or to subvert a church in it. You belong to the land that bore you, and were not at liberty—(if right and liberty are one, and unless they are, they are good for nothing)—you were not at liberty, I repeat it, to enter into the service of an alien.

Kotzebue.—No magistrate, higher or lower, forbade me. Fine notions of freedom are these!

Sandt.—A man is always a minor in regard to his fatherland; and the servants of his fatherland are wrong and criminal, if they whisper in his ear that he may go away, that he may work in another country, that he may ask to be fed in it, and that he may wait there until orders and tasks are given for his hands to execute. Being a German, you voluntarily placed yourself in a position where you might eventually be coerced to act against Germans.

Kotzebue.—I would not.

Sandt.—Perhaps you think so.

Kotzebue.—Sir, I know my duty.

Sandt.—We all do; yet duties are transgressed, and daily. Where the will is weak in accepting, it is weaker in resisting. Already have you left the ranks of your fellow-citizens—already have you taken the enlisting money and marched away.

Kotzebue.—Phrases! metaphors! and let me tell you, M. Sandt, not very polite ones. You have hitherto seen little of the world, and you speak rather the language of books than of men.

Sandt.—What! are books written by some creatures of less intellect than ours? I fancied them to convey the language and reasonings of men. I was wrong, and you are right, Von Kotzebue! They are, in general, the productions of such as have neither the constancy of courage, nor the continuity of sense, to act up to what they know to be right, or to maintain it, even in words, to the end of their lives. You are aware that I am speaking now of political ethics. This is the worst I can think of the matter, and bad enough is this.

Kotzebue.—You misunderstand me. Our conduct must fall in with our circumstances. We may be patriotic, yet not puritanical in our patriotism, not harsh, nor intolerant, nor contracted. The philosophical mind should consider the whole world as its habitation, and not look so minutely into it as to see the lines that divide nations and governments; much less should it act the part of a busy shrew, and take pleasure in giving loose to the tongue, at finding things a little out of place.

Sandt.—We will leave the shrew where we find her: she certainly is better with the comedian than with the philosopher. But this indistinctness in the moral and political line begets indifference. He who does not keep his own country more closely in view than any other, soon mixes land with sea, and sea with air, and loses sight of every thing, at least, for which he was placed in contact with his fellow men. Let us unite, if possible, with the nearest: let usages and familiarities bind us: this being once accomplished, let us confederate for security and peace with all the people round, particularly with people of the same language, laws, and religion. We pour out wine to those about us, wishing the same fellowship and conviviality to others: but to enlarge the circle would disturb and deaden its harmony. We irrigate the ground in our gardens: the public road may require the water equally: yet we give it rather to our borders; and first to those that lie against the house! God himself did not fill the world at once with happy creatures: he enlivened one small portion of it with them, and began with single affections, as well as pure and unmixt. We must have an object and an aim, or our strength, if any strength belongs to us, will be useless.

Kotzebue.—There is much good sense in these remarks: but I am not at all times at leisure and in readiness to receive instruction. I am old enough to have laid down my own plans of life; and I trust I am by no means deficient in the relations I bear to society.

Sandt.—Lovest thou thy children? Oh! my heart bleeds! But the birds can fly; and the nest requires no warmth from the parent, no cover against the rain and the wind.

Kotzebue.—This is wildness: this is agony. Your face is laden with large drops; some of them tears, some not. Be more rational and calm, my dear young man! and less enthusiastic.

Sandt.—They who will not let us be rational, make us enthusiastic by force. Do you love your children? I ask you again. If you do, you must love them more than another man's. Only they who are indifferent to all, profess a parity.

Kotzebue.—Sir! indeed your conversation very much surprises me.

Sandt.—I see it does: you stare, and would look proud. Emperors and kings, and all but maniacs, would lose that faculty with me. I could speedily bring them to a just sense of their nothingness, unless their ears were calked and pitched, although I am no Savonarola. He, too, died sadly!

Kotzebue.—Amid so much confidence of power, and such an assumption of authority, your voice is gentle—almost plaintive.

Sandt.—It should be plaintive. Oh, could it be but persuasive!

Kotzebue.—Why take this deep interest in me? I do not merit nor require it. Surely any one would think we had been acquainted with each other for many years.

Sandt.—What! should I have asked you such a question as the last, after long knowing you?

Kotzebue, (aside.)—This resembles insanity.

Sandt.—The insane have quick ears, sir, and sometimes quick apprehensions.

Kotzebue.—I really beg your pardon.

Sandt.—I ought not then to have heard you, and beg yours. My madness could release many from a worse; from a madness which hurts them grievously; a madness which has been and will be hereditary: mine, again and again I repeat it, would burst asunder the strong swathes that fasten them to pillar and post. Sir! sir! if I entertained not the remains of respect for you, in your domestic state, I should never have held with you this conversation. Germany is Germany: she ought to have nothing political in common with what is not Germany. Her freedom and security now demand that she celebrate the communion of the faithful. Our country is the only one in all the explored regions on earth that never has been conquered. Arabia and Russia boast it falsely; France falsely; Rome falsely. A fragment off the empire of Darius fell and crushed her: Valentinian was the footstool of Sapor, and Rome was buried in Byzantium. Boys must not learn this, and men will not. Britain, the wealthiest and most powerful of nations, and, after our own, the most literate and humane, received from us colonies and laws. Alas! those laws, which she retains as her fairest heritage, we value not: we surrender them to gangs of robbers, who fortify themselves within walled cities, and enter into leagues against us. When they quarrel, they push us upon one another's sword, and command us to thank God for the victories that enslave us. These are the glories we celebrate; these are the festivals we hold, on the burial-mounds of our ancestors. Blessed are those who lie under them! blessed are also those who remember what they were, and call upon their names in the holiness of love.

Kotzebue.—Moderate the transport that inflames and consumes you. There is no dishonour in a nation being conquered by a stronger.

Sandt.—There may be great dishonour in letting it be stronger; great, for instance, in our disunion.

Kotzebue.—We have only been conquered by the French in our turn.

Sandt.—No, sir, no: we have not been, in turn or out. Our puny princes were disarmed by promises and lies: they accepted paper crowns from the very thief who was sweeping into his hat their forks and spoons. A cunning traitor snared incautious ones, plucked them, devoured them, and slept upon their feathers.

Kotzebue.—I would rather turn back with you to the ancient glories of our country than fix my attention on the sorrowful scenes more near to us. We may be justly proud of our literary men, who unite the suffrages of every capital, to the exclusion of almost all their own.

Sandt.—Many Germans well deserve this honour, others are manger-fed and hirelings.

Kotzebue.—The English and the Greeks are the only nations that rival us in poetry, or in any works of imagination.

Sandt.—While on this high ground we pretend to a rivalship with England and Greece, can we reflect, without a sinking of the heart, on our inferiority in political and civil dignity? Why are we lower than they? Our mothers are like their mothers; our children are like their children; our limbs are as strong, our capacities are as enlarged, our desire of improvement in the arts

246

and sciences is neither less vivid and generous, nor less temperate and well-directed. The Greeks were under disadvantages which never bore in any degree on us; yet they rose through them vigorously and erectly. They were Asiatic in what ought to be the finer part of the affections; their women were veiled and secluded, never visited the captive, never released the slave, never sat by the sick in the hospital, never heard the child's lesson repeated in the school. Ours are more tender, compassionate, and charitable, than poets have feigned of the past, or prophets have announced of the future; and, nursed at their breasts and educated at their feet, blush we not at our degeneracy? The most indifferent stranger feels a pleasure at finding, in the worst-written history of Spain, her various kingdoms ultimately mingled, although the character of the governors, and perhaps of the governed, is congenial to few. What delight, then, must overflow on Europe, from seeing the mother of her noblest nation rear again her venerable head, and bless all her children for the first time united!

Kotzebue.—I am bound to oppose such a project.

Sandt.—Say not so: in God's name, say not so.

Kotzebue.—In such confederacy I see nothing but conspiracy and rebellion, and I am bound, I tell you again, sir, to defeat it, if possible.

Sandt.—Bound! I must then release you.

Kotzebue.—How should you, young gentleman, release me?

Sandt.—May no pain follow the cutting of the knot! But think again: think better: spare me!

Kotzebue.—I will not betray you.

Sandt.—That would serve nobody: yet, if in your opinion betraying me can benefit you or your family, deem it no harm; so much greater has been done by you in abandoning the cause of Germany. Here is your paper; here is your ink.

Kotzebue.—Do you imagine me an informer?

Sandt.—From maxims and conduct such as yours, spring up the brood, the necessity, and the occupation of them. There would be none, if good men thought it a part of goodness to be as active and vigilant as the bad. I must go, sir! Return to yourself in time! How it pains me to think of losing you! Be my friend!

Kotzebue.—I would be.

Sandt.—Be a German!

Kotzebue.—I am.

Sandt, (having gone out.)—Perjurer and profaner! Yet his heart is kindly. I must grieve for him! Away with tenderness! I disrobe him of the privilege to pity me or to praise me, as he would have done had I lived of old. Better men shall do more. God calls them: me too he calls: I will enter the door again. May the greater sacrifice bring the people together, and hold them evermore in peace and concord. The lesser victim follows willingly. (*Enters again.*)

Turn! die! (*strikes.*)

Alas! alas! no man ever fell alone. How many innocent always perish with one guilty! and writhe longer!

Unhappy children! I shall weep for you elsewhere. Some days are left me. In a very few the whole of this little world will lie between us. I have sanctified in you the memory of your father. Genius but reveals dishonour, commiseration covers it.

FOREIGN CORRESPONDENCE.

◆

THE novelty and extent of view embodied in the subjoined letter, which our readers will readily perceive, forms one main reason for our insertion of it. The reading ladies of Germany form a class perfectly unique. They are little known; even the celebrated Rahel but partially in England; and we trust we shall be enabled to give in our correspondent's communications not only what is novel, a female view of German literature, but also the thoughts of one, from her high position, connected with all that is great in reminiscence and living reality in her country. Either of these points would be interesting, and when both are united with comprehensiveness of view and a deep penetration that rarely falls to the lot of even her sex to enjoy, they form an aggregate influence that cannot but charm. Female writers dwell generally on the surface points, and describe them with unrivalled excellence. We shall not apologize for the obvious tendency of our fair correspondent's notions. It is the peculiarity of the youthful writers, and of the female writers of Germany especially, to run rather wild on political subjects, which deeper reflection induces both parties to alter, and to see that even Germany is better governed according to the notions of its rulers, than those of literary savans or university professors.

Letter on the State of General Literature in Germany.

(FROM A GERMAN CORRESPONDENT.)

You call upon me to describe the state of literature in this country at the present moment. Do you know, my most respected friend, that you thus urge me in the most friendly manner to a task as difficult to execute as that of the Danaides of old; and that you do this as if a kind of scribbling child's play, a comfortable half-dosing chat, a talk about "all the world and his wife," were the only needful requisites for my communications; as if, in fine, I had but to follow the whim of the moment, and not pursue that definite aim and object, the attainment of which you have, notwithstanding, so expressly desired and required. The theme you have given me is extremely confused, and divided into innumerable branches. I shall therefore be compelled to tax all my faculties to the utmost, and speak as if something *painful* were under consideration.

For our Germany is labouring at present, in a social point of view, under a lingering disease—a disease occasioned by the slow, yet sure advances of an internal and national power of self-judgment; and the very same process of development, with all its changing moods of ebb and tide, of advance and retreat, is repeated at the present moment in the world of literature of the day. We all hope that Germany may, both in a social and literary point of view, attain, ere long, an epoch of virility, of firmness and decision, with an active feeling of nationality and true liberty of thought, word and action. In the mean time we are in an intermediate state of doubt and indecision: we grasp, and then again abandon; appropriate the mental products of other countries to ourselves, and cast away all that we have thus gained. In a word, we find ourselves in an epoch of slow and changeful recovery, during which we exhibit much praiseworthy aptitude, and a strength of which we were not ourselves aware until we had begun to employ it.

One of our best historians, Schlosser, was the first to point out the mutual influences which have ever existed amongst us;—first, of literature on everyday life; and secondly, of the history of the day on that very literature. We have not only confessed the justice of Schlosser's observation, but we have also recognized his " History of the Eighteenth Century" to be the very original propounder and supporter of that principle, which we everywhere inculcate, viz. that the closest connection subsists betwixt the condition of our times and people and the latter's mental and literary creations.

An exception to this general rule will be found in the case of our deeply learned and universally esteemed savans and professors, and the laborious studies of their untiring brains. These men go on their way silently and tranquilly; their four walls being more effectual barriers to them against disturbances emanating from the stranger world without, than the wall of China has ever proved to the people of that antediluvian country. It is only necessary to have been in the company of German "chamber professors" for one quarter of an hour, to know that they are not only a peculiar nation, but a singular species of cosmopolites, who form as it were for themselves, by the mere emission and inhalation of the breath of life, the only atmosphere requisite for their well-being. Of these silent beings I do not here speak; the movement of our times scarcely, if at all, affects them. But our political and belle-lettristical critics—our other thinkers, statesmen, critics, and artists—our geniuses and our legislators,—all these afford numberless proofs of the truth of Schlosser's assertion, inasmuch as all of them declare their times to be restrictive of and unfavourable to the development of eminent "individual talent." We do not even hope for a Schiller or a Goethe from "the present;" and I almost believe that we render the appearance of such a being an impossibility, by our utter want of any real, long-continued and enthusiastic interest or desire. The inward convulsive movements of the body of the State make it altogether useless to attempt producing a lasting and universal effect on our people, although it is easy to excite an ephemeral sympathy; and this impossibility of effecting anything on a great scale increases indeed the general amount of productions, but lessens true nobility of conception, and subjects each separate work to the influences of place, time and fashion.

I shall be compelled to bring long medleys of heterogeneous creations before you in my letters; and I must now call your attention, before I commence my task, to the fact, that the lighter literature of Northern and of Southern Germany, with some few exceptions, is altogether distinct, and has little or nothing in common. In Vienna the names of those books are scarcely known which are all the rage at Berlin. And the same disregard of our neighbours' productions is manifested by us even to a more unjustifiable extent, for the works of a great number of truly excellent poets and authors of Austria never once enter our booksellers' shops.

The only recent means of communication existing betwixt these two parts of our country may be found in the productions, passing current in both, of that fairer sex, universally regarded as all-conquering and invincible. Our writing ladies do not fear the Scylla and Charybdis which, under the forms of poverty and fashion, menace and terrify all our other authors: they write to please themselves, and, strange to say, they seem to please all.

" But what has poverty to do with the applause of the public?" you ask. Much, alas! very much. Our educated middle classes are poor; and thus in those parts of Germany which may be said to form its real core, those books alone are purchased which are absolutely required. The lawyer buys juridical treatises—the economist, essays on agriculture—and the theologist, argumentative productions in his own branch of study. The ladies alone have succeeded— heaven knows how! in procuring a more extended circle of readers for their works. From Rahel and Bettina to Madame de Paalzow and Countess Hahn-Hahn, novels and travelling sketches, by one and all these ladies, will be found in every part of Germany, amongst the highest as well as the middle classes, and even in the hands of our most learned and bookworm professors. They are bought and read likewise universally, and in a word have been till now quite the

41. continued

rage. That the demand for such a literature as this brings no slight evils in its train, I scarcely need inform you. Even in your own country, where all that is classical is so highly honored, how many readers are there who are well acquainted with the celebrated authors of the last century? People cannot read all, and the flimsy and the sterling seldom go together.

But before I speak of the separate books, and the still often important, though not perfectly impartial productions of our female authors, I must allude "en passant" to a class of works almost universally read in Prussia and Saxony, but which never pass Austria's frontier. Twenty years ago our students and our women never dreamt of reading political treatises; they remained exclusively in the hands of statesmen and men in the possession of positive political offices. Even our speculators and merchants scarcely ever looked into them. The newspapers contained all the news of the day; all that it seemed positively necessary to know. Besides, those works were not written in a style calculated to make them popular: none dreamt of influencing by such productions a people not yet sufficiently formed, in a political point of view, either to esteem or to understand them. I think indeed that it may be pretty safely asserted, that the public at large first began to take an interest in such works in 1838, when the professors of Göttingen refused to take the oath of allegiance to the present monarch of Hanover, on the score of his not acceding to the constitution of the country. The pamphlets of " the Seven," as they were called, were read with much eagerness and avidity, inasmuch as these men were regarded as the representatives and champions of the popular cause.

At about the same time the ecclesiastical disputes in the Rhenish provinces attracted much attention. The vicinity of France and the publicity of the courts of justice in these provinces, had exercised an influence over the public mind there which could not well fail to demonstrate itself on such an occasion. Numberless books, pamphlets and treatises made their appearance; people soon began to take an interest not only in the mere naked facts, but also in the causes and tendencies of those facts, and a general craving for information on this subject displayed itself on all sides.

Any and every thing, once begun in Germany, is like the oriental story-teller, almost endless. It continues to advance simultaneously in all directions; and thus is it that we have now not only popular prose authors, who treat of the political interests of State and People, but also poets, who violently oppose what they consider abuses in government and religion. And although these writers are deprived of their offices (when they happen to hold any), and now and then even imprisoned, their works still fly like young and ardent eagles over the frontiers of states and walls of cities.* Auersperg's and Lenau's writings you know yourself. The most remarkable of our *quite* modern works of this kind are Herwegh's Poems, Hoffmann von Fallersleben's " Unpolitical Songs," and Dingelstadt's " Ditties of a Cosmopolitical Watchman."

Herwegh is undoubtedly a true poet; but I do not deny that I could not help thinking a little of Don Quixote when I read his repeated orders and solicitations " to brandish the sword on high! " and heard (in fancy's ear) his undoubtedly musical, but extremely martial trumpets. If, as his admirers assert, his songs are only directed against the abuses of systems, not against individuals—if no blood is to flow after all this parade,—then it does seem to me that Mr. Herwegh might walk about just as well and go just as far in everyday boots, as on those gigantic cothurns upon which he now promenades so furiously, although

it cannot be doubted that his fierce ditties have excited no slight degree of enthusiasm amongst the students of our universities. But as for all this talk about " hewing and hacking," it would be just as well to wait for the time when it may be really needed;—for a war with some foreign nation for instance, when it is to be trusted that we should quickly prove that we yet know how to defend ourselves. However, despite the one cardinal fault attending these productions, of throwing a firebrand uselessly amongst the wild and ardent spirits of our youth, these songs have many real excellences, and it is impossible not to admire the beauty of thought and poetical harmony of versification displayed in them.*

After a more humorous and a more sprightly fashion, but in no less plain and decided terms, does Hoffmann von Fallersleben express his sentiments. The delightful spirit of light, sarcastic humour which distinguished his little Allemanian Poems was only now and then checkered by a momentary display of more concentrated bitterness of soul. In general he amuses at the very moment that he inspires, and thus coaxes his readers, as it were melodiously, into strife, discord and dissension. Still he is not devoid of real power or sense; he is the experienced man by the side of the enthusiastic youth, Herwegh; but at the same time many little weaknesses may be laid to his charge, with vapid commonplaces, such as are the natural attendants on middle age—"everydayisms," enfin—allow me to coin the word, as I know of no better for the nonce.

Dingelstadt's " Ditties of a Cosmopolitical Watchman" are perhaps the most truly " spirituel " of all these productions: they comprise some perfectly beautiful poems, treating of matters of the highest importance, and others so trivial as to be almost beneath all notice. It is not to be understood how an author generally possessed of such clear judgment and common sense could have ever composed such things: but there must be hours in which the poet's genius is wandering far away, perhaps in some other star, even whilst his hand indites: otherwise it would be impossible to explain the existence of such a mixture of the most noble and the most vulgarly vile.

Besides his much esteemed novel, " Under the Earth," and his plays, he has written all the recent articles on literature in the Augsburg Gazette. Unfortunately he in this manner dissipates and all but throws away that talent which he ought to concentrate in some one greater production.

If I were not afraid of wandering too far into the thorny brakes of politics, I should not only notice, but even briefly examine, "the Four Questions" of Jacobi, the pamphlet of Bulow-Cameron, and other similar works which have recently made their appearance. But to do this I should be compelled to deviate too far from the course I have marked out for myself in these letters; and besides, you will no doubt be able to follow the appearance of these works in the Augsburg Gazette, where they are almost all noticed in due order.

I recommend to your readers as an important and attractive work, " Sketches of the War of Freedom"—[1813-14 and 15]—" Lebensbilder aus dem Befreiungskriege," Jena, published by Fr. Frommann, 2 vols.—the editorship of which work is attributed to Hormair. This book indeed presents no historically concentrated picture of the times of which it treats; but the very clearest general view of the separate condition of every State in Germany, in and about the year 1813, may undoubtedly be gleaned from it. The political documents and official letters and communications which will be found therein, particularly the letters of Munster and his friends, give such a deep insight into the aim and active exertions of the leading men of those days, that the reader finds himself able to

* We cannot forbear making one remark " en passant" on our correspondent's observations. We are aware that it may be desirable in some instances to change the despotic governments of Germany and of Europe generally to constitutional monarchies; but we are also aware that this desirable change cannot be effected in a moment, and that it must be retarded by the mad rhapsodies of a Herwegh and men of similar calibre.

* The Leipzic Gazette informs us under the head of Berlin, Nov. 24, that Herwegh has been presented to and graciously received by the King of Prussia, who informed him that he liked his poetry, and added, "that he was pleased by a warm opposition, if founded upon conviction."

249

supply all that may be wanting in the work, from the stores of his own imagination. Hanover's condition—England's sympathy—Tyrol's misfortune—Heligoland's trade in smuggling (employed as a means of transport for government messages)—the separate forms and characters of Munster, Von Dörenberg, Walmoden, Stein, Greisenau, and a host of others,—all these men and things step out from the canvass so distinctly before us, that, notwithstanding our regret at the subsequent comparative dulness and drowsiness of that great era, we find ourselves enabled to follow each separate thread in the general web of fate of the community.

Unfortunately the correspondence is not arranged chronologically, but under the head of each separate writer, and this renders the perusal of the book infinitely more laborious than it otherwise would be. Still this work remains inestimable as a living monument of that moment of time in which Germany assumed its ancient dignity; and this the more especially on account of its containing nothing written with a peculiar purpose or in a vein of cold calculation. The reader therefore does not only read; he seems to live and feel with the characters in the book; and he sees that the present times form as it were the most solemn notes and addenda to the text of the work before him.

There is a new quarterly publication, the "German States' Archive" (Deutsches Staatsarchiv), published by Buddeus, which deserves your attention. Three numbers or volumes of this work have appeared up to the present time. This Archive, which is intended to form a point of union for the practical demands of the age and the claims of science, treats of all interests concerned in the political, financial and juridical government of Germany, and bears no particular party colour; on the contrary, it is an evident attempt at real impartiality. The first number is filled by the discussion of the Hanoveranian quarrels, admirably treated by Stüve. The second boasts of more variety: it contains, besides several official documents on events of the day, an examination into the claims of the Bentinck family, an account of the conduct of State affairs for some years past in the Grand Duchy of Hesse, by Charles Buchner, and several reviews by Bülau, W. Lüders, Buddeus and others. The third number contains a notice of the Commercial Union (Zollverein), in which the real interests of Austria in this union are considered, an article on the Constitution of Prussia, an attack against the Nobility of Germany, and a quantity of important and instructive official documents and reviews. This Archive, and most of our present political productions, are published by Frederic Frommann, whose independent position in the little Grand Duchy of Weimar obviates all possible difficulty in the publication and communication of these works.

A little work which may still be said to belong to this class, although it attacks and assails with less ponderous weapons, has appeared a short time ago at Königsberg, published by Voigt, and in a very few weeks has run to a third edition. It is called "Glosses and Marginal Observations on Texts of our own Times" (Glossen und Randzeichnungen zu Texten aus unserer Zeit), and is composed of four lectures, held publicly at Königsberg by Louis Walesrode. The author observes in his preface, that he spoke before an audience of both sexes, and that the form and tenor of his observations was influenced by this circumstance; and the book fully bears out this assertion, being in truth a clever and highly coloured arabesque. The names of the lectures, which sufficiently reveal their purport, are, 1, "The Masks of Life;" 2, "Our Golden Age," which he thus denominates in his humorous but pleasing strain, on account of the present universal dominion of gold; 3, "Literary Don Quixote's Tournament;" 4, "Variations on favourite National Melodies of the day." The humour shown in the different pictures thus introduced is charming, particularly in the tournament affrays, as, for instance, in the "Liszt-enthusiasm," the "Monument-rage," &c. The lively, bold vein of wit with which the faults and

follies of all classes, from the monarch to the street-sweeper, are here exhibited, displays, despite true humour and great freedom of speech, no real bitterness or demagogical propensities. And for this very reason it is, as I believe, that the book has so universally pleased, and has been so much read and bought. Every person who recognizes himself in this mirror will laugh; nobody will put down the book with the slightest angry feeling.

But let us now proceed to the ladies. I fear that we have already kept them too long waiting. Amongst our German female authors, no one excites more interest at this moment than Countess Hahn-Hahn. Since her volume of poems and her first novel, "Society" (Aus der Gesellschaft), appeared, she has written and published from time to time various other novels; "The Right Person" (der Rechte); "Countess Faustina;" "Ulric,"—the latter in several volumes. Betwixt her novels and her travels (we have two of the latter class) stands as it were a charming little book, entitled "Beyond the Mountains" (Jenseits der Berge), which describes her residence in Italy after a somewhat flighty and sketchy fashion. It contains also two excellent tales. Aristocratic grace and the passionate susceptibility of woman's nature, are so perfectly united and melted into one in this authoress, and these qualities are conjoined with such descriptive power, that the most remarkable whole results from the combination, a whole which cannot fail to amuse and delight the reader.

The only things to be blamed in the book are the criticisms on Art, particularly all which Countess Hahn-Hahn has said of Michael Angelo. The strange peculiarity of her views on this subject has led a countrywoman of yours, Mrs. Austin, to a slight injustice, which I must make it my task to controvert, in her "Fragments from German Authors." Much as I am disposed to concur with Mrs. Austin in her censure of the artistical opinions here propounded, and much as I am disposed to agree with her in thinking that Countess Hahn's own personality is too prominent in all her works, I still can by no means admit that she strives for theatrical effect, and endeavours to produce this result by bizarre and unnatural criticisms.

The Countess's life has sufficiently proved the necessity which nature imposed on her of going her own way through the world: she is no doubt remarkable, often too distinctly different, from the crowd of mortals around her: but were I to point out a fault in her character, I should rather accuse her of caring too little for the opinions of her readers, than censure her for a too direct attempt to secure their admiration or applause. Countess Ida Hahn has so much real sense, such complete freedom of position, such a knowledge of all that education can teach to mortals, that I should think myself justified in calling on her in some degree to modify her violently aristocratic views, in as far as these positively affect the truth of her sketches of character, and in claiming a little more attention on her part to the feelings and desires of the public. She warbles

> "as the blithe bird sings,
> Mid forest branches lord,
> The song, that from his clear throat rings,
> Is still its own reward." (Goethe.)

But it would be undoubtedly far better done on her part, if she were to employ to its full extent that great talent, of which providence has constituted her the possessor.

Her style and colouring have something particularly winning about them; her characters are new, and generally original. In "Ulric" she introduces a perfectly natural and really charming woman, and her description has all the warmth of truth. As lively, as faithful, as fresh, seem most of the scenes in her "Travelling Letters from Spain" (Reise Briefen aus Spanien), in 2 vols., and the account therein given of the effect which Murillo's pictures produced on her is truly masterly. This forcible power of description should lead her herself to feel what it is in her power to effect, and induce her, for instance, to delineate her male characters more carefully, and omit those long genealogical tables which she at present inserts in her letters. Not only does she know all the leaders of our fashionable world; she is also perfectly acquainted with all the faults and good qualities *born* with our aristocracy, and it is thus in her power to give a perfectly faithful picture to future times of our nobility, as it still maintains itself in Westphalia and Mecklenburgh. She has such a singular power of piercing to the depths of the human heart, that she should not confine herself solely to the description of the conversations of fashionable "salons." The picture of the Neapolitan poor, which she draws with such freedom of touch in her "Beyond the Mountains," should induce her to make herself acquainted with the way of life of the poorer classes in her own country. It is to be hoped that she, like Chardin, may be led nearer to reality by her travels, and thus enter on a second period of more general and less individual productivity. A short time ago a new work of her's, describing her travels in the South of France, appeared at Berlin: it is called "Recollections of France" (Erinnerungen aus und an Frankreich), and is published in 2 vols. at Berlin, by A. Dunker. This work I have not read, but my next letter shall give you some account of it.

Madam de Paalzow's novels (the third of which has made its appearance) have created an incredible sensation. All the three have an historical background. The first, called "Thomas Thyrnau," treats of the state of Germany under Maria Theresa. Perhaps she is better acquainted with her chosen territory here than she is, or at least to an English eye would appear to be, in her "Godwin Castle" and her "St. Roche." If the faults of her novels are considered,—the want of deep historical penetration, the deficiency of correct knowledge in the details, the crowding together of "coups de théâtre," the supernatural characters devoid of flesh and blood,—our taste would appear an extremely vulgar one; for Madam de Paalzow's works always run to a third edition, and she is one of the most favourite female writers of the day. If, on the contrary, the nobility of the style and the clearness of the narrative are considered—if we observe her admirable and exciting manner of telling a story, which renders it impossible for us to break off in our perusal—if we think of the many exquisite passages introduced, the general knowledge of the world displayed, and above all, the pureness of thought which is constantly beaming through all these works,—we shall feel well disposed to accord that fame which she has already attained to the authoress under our consideration. She knows how to lead us on irresistibly from chapter to chapter, from volume to volume: her books contain more the suggestions of feeling than those of taste, and on this very account they are more true and produce the greater effect. Unfortunately I have not yet been enabled to procure her third novel, mentioned above, and must consequently, as in the case of Countess Hahn, refer you for an account of it to my next letter. The book has only just appeared.

But as, like all men after dinner in your country, we have adjourned from our political debates to the world of the (literary) fair, ever waxing and increasing as it is in numbers and in novelties, I must now point out to you some of the new stars which have recently flashed on our horizon. In the first place I shall direct your attention to a young lady who has written several much read books, under the name of Thekla, and who possesses a pleasing facility of style. She belongs rather to the Hahn-Hahn party. Her little novels both play in the great world, and are called "Castle (Schloss) Goczyn," and "Marie"—"Sketches of the World of Fashion."

My second star is also anonymous, and writes under the name of Theresa (von V.): she first favoured us with "Letters from the South" (Briefe aus dem Süden). The book has much that is attractive, although it is too personal, too

individual, and displays an extreme want of real knowledge of the world. It is singular without being affected; feminine, yet devoid of sentimentality; and altogether exactly what one would call an agreeable book. The views entertained by the authoress of the countries through which she travels (Italy and Sicily), are free from the prejudices usually entertained respecting them; but she cannot at all get rid of herself; though it must be admitted that she shows her individuality, not designedly, but naturally and unavoidably, in a very amiable point of view. Originally these letters were addressed to her father, the Russian State-Counsellor Struve, and the applause which they met with from all who became in any wise acquainted with them occasioned their subsequent publication.

Authors publishing are—(forgive the ungentle simile, O Theresa!)—like wild beasts who have but first tasted blood. Publicity thus, when once tasted, leads its votaries irresistibly onwards to new attempts of the same kind. The second work of Theresa's, "A Diary" (Ein Tagebuch), is very inferior to the first. To amuse us with an entire volume of aphoristical remarks, views and youthful reminiscences, one must be a Bettina; one must believe unconditionally in one's-self, and feel one's-self inspired by one's own declarations. It appears improbable that the very pretty little stories introduced do not contain half confessions; at least they produce this impression on us; and this very inability of the authoress to leave her own personality greatly injures the book. The style and arrangement of the thoughts are good.

Besides the authoresses already named, several others have a large circle of readers. Amalie Schoppe and Henriette Hanke are still writing. Amalia Winter, Frau von W. and H. Mühlbach, I shall pass over for the present; for I must now hasten to notice a numerous class of not indigenous indeed, but naturalized productions. Amongst the writers which I have as yet spoken of, Countess Hahn-Hahn would probably please the least in England. With the exception of the one single character of Margaret, in "Ulric," the female characters in her novels would not at all meet with the approbation of English readers; and the greater part of our reading public agrees with them in this matter without exactly knowing how or why it does so.

Our national character naturally possesses much that is domestic and naive: we incline also to sentimentality, not of that elevated and tragic kind which people in England think proper to attribute to us, but rather to a sentimentality to which your own inclinations are no strangers, that delights in the little details of every-day joys and pleasures, and would commemorate every prick that the thorns of the briar-rose may give us.

Whilst our aristocratic and spiritually emancipated women describe the fashionable world, with all its calms and storms, its cold passions and frivolous interests, but also with all its charms, the old longing for domestic life assails us even whilst we are perusing these annals of rank and fashion; our hearts crave pictures of family bliss, children that we may nurse in fancy, and all the joys and sorrows of young wedded love, which only seeks to give and to sacrifice. Strangely enough it was left to another nation to satisfy our own native and indigenous cravings and desires. The *Swedes* were to give us what we wanted. Frederica Bremer's novels were translated, and became so dear to us, that they almost drove our own original productions out of the field. Every German whom I ever asked had read Fr. Bremer's "House," her "Neighbours," and "The Daughter of the President." Even those palates which were accustomed to the unnaturally sauced and seasoned diet of France, longed for the simple domestic fare of this Swedish lady's novels. Perhaps the singularly clear, but somewhat diffuse, style of narration of Frederica Bremer is like that of your Miss Edgeworth. She neither describes the storming of castles, nor deals in deeds of death and murder; she only paints domestic happiness, love and married life. Amongst other characters she has drawn a delightful German husband in her " Neighbours," whom his wife dignifies by the appellation of " my Bear."

Even the husbands, too, took pleasure in this bear and his she-bear, and the talent of a Swede was universally acknowledged in all the length and breadth of Germany. The most poetical work of this authoress is probably her " Strife and Peace" (Streit und Friede). It describes the landscapes and customs of Norway, as contrasted with those of Sweden ; and the grace with which she is enabled to depict a poultry-yard and interest us for a grey goose, and the truly charming humour with which she elevates these creatures to a poetry of their own, is undoubtedly peculiar to herself. It is true that the attractive and singular customs of Norway somewhat aid her in her task.

A second Swedish authoress, who is everywhere read and whose books run from edition to edition, is Stygara Carlen. She has more phantasy and feeling, but less power of narration and description, than Frederica Bremer. Through her works, as through those of the latter, run a noble truth and simplicity of feeling, like a vein of pure gold. And it is this which gives a kind of shadowy coolness to these books, in which we gladly rest, and feel as if we breathed anew. According to our German views of amiability, that quality may be learned by our maidens from the characters depicted in these works.

Both of these authoresses have unfortunately paid the usual price of fame—they have written too much. An entire series of volumes has appeared, published by Stygara Carlen. " The Scandinavian Boy" (Der Sejuts-Junge), a novel, *took* amazingly in Germany, because it contained an explanation of what was " according to one's rank" (standesgemäss—there is no English word to express the idea), which was extremely welcome to our poverty-stricken nobility. The Scandinavian boy is of a noble family, and receives a box on the ear because he earns his bread in an honest manner, whilst the aristocrat who gives the blow is not ashamed of running into debts which he can never pay, in order to be able to live "according to his rank."

" The Church's Consecration at Hammerby" (Die Kircheneinweihung zu Hammerby), in 2 vols., has much that is interesting about it, and yet does not answer all the expectations that it excites. The subject turns on the revenge of a young architect for a wrong done to his grandfather. This in itself is somewhat unnatural : but more than this, the revenge is to be taken on a lovely and charming girl, who is betrothed to a descendant of the offender without loving him ; and it consists in an attempt to win the heart of the poor child in order to make her intended bridegroom miserable. There is something very contemptible and almost absurd in this idea. The mixture of noble and equable elements in the character of the "hero," however, is well depicted : a vanity which is natural to him, and a passionate desire to please, come to the aid of his craving for revenge ; and whilst he is doing what is evil and unjust, he prepares his own destruction. But this destruction does not arise from a return in himself of the inclination excited for him in the young maiden's bosom, but from a series of subsequent events, which are not sufficiently accounted for and but imperfectly described. The somewhat spectral conclusion does not accord well with the commencement. The lover, another architect, is, however, a faithful and well-drawn manly character.

And now permit me to conclude my series of parti-coloured pictures for to-day. When my mental eye, glancing backwards, still misses the well-known names of Immermann, Steffen, Spindler, Mosen, Sternberg, Wolff, Mundt, &c., I feel quite giddy at the thought of my undertaking ; and yet to-day you shall neither hear of classic nor of romantic writers, not even of Young Germany ; for I am tired of *writing* : how then should I call upon you not to be tired of *reading* my lucubrations !

ART. VIII.—1. *Geschichte der Poesie und Beredsamkeit seit dem Ende der dreizehnten Jahrhunderts ; von Friedrich Bouterwek.* Bände II. III. Göttingen. 1802-4.

2. *Histoire de la Littérature du Midi de l'Europe.* Par Simonde de Sismondi. 8vo. Paris. 1813.

3. *Lectures on Dramatic Art and Literature.* By A. W. Schlegel ; translated by John Black, with an Introduction by R. H. Horne. 2 vols. Templeman. 1840.

4. *Essays on the Drama.* By Samuel Taylor Coleridge. *Literary Remains.* Vol. II. Pickering. 1836.

5. *Lectures on the Literature of the Age of Elizabeth.* By William Hazlitt. Third Edition. 1840.

6. *Introduction to the Literature of Europe, in the Fifteenth, Sixteenth, and Seventeenth Centuries.* By Henry Hallam, F.R.A.S. Murray. 1838.

OVER so vast a field of literature and art, as that which is comprised in the title at the head of this article, it will at once be understood that, in a single paper, no space can be afforded for details, nor for analytical exposition and criticism. Such a proceeding can only be accomplished by devoting a substantive paper to each country where the modern drama has flourished, and from whose literature illustrative extracts can in that case be made. This series we shall, in all probability, offer to our readers in subsequent numbers of the Review. At present, it will be the sole object of this article to give a synthetical view of the dramatic mind of modern Europe, with such brief comments upon prominent men of genius, and the several schools they followed or originated, as our condensed design will allow. We shall not perplex the reader by going so far back as the early twilight of the dramatic art in modern ages, but will place the commencement with Trissino, in Italy ; Sackville, in England ; Bermudez and Cervantes, in Spain ; and Jodelle and Garnier, in France. The German drama, so far as an art is implied by the term, can scarcely be dated farther back than Lessing.

Before offering our remarks upon the dramatic mind displayed by any particular country, it will be well to show the principles by which we propose to measure their several productions.

Dramatic genius is that class of mind which identifies itself with the passions and thoughts of others, as displayed by varieties of character and circumstance ; and makes the identification apparent through the medium of suitable action, dialogue, and soliloquy. During the moments of composition, a truly dramatic genius loses the sense of its own identity in ideal natures, and, by the impulse of imaginative sympathy, feels and thinks as those ideal natures might really feel and think under the given positions. This peculiar form of genius does not endeavour to copy or imitate individual nature and character, but to *be* that nature and character while it is present on the ideal scene, or to the mind during the progress of the drama. All the work is developed from within. It opens out its diverging rays like a star ; but unlike a star that "dwells apart," it only becomes luminous in proportion as it is projected upon and reflected in the bosom of humanity. Its external appearance and local circumstances are all subordinate to the moving power within. Here, then, is the great distinction between a dramatist, and a descriptive or narrative writer. The former only incidentally paints a scene, and the external parts of character, by brief touches (if at all), whereas the surrounding circumstances of time and place, and the entire physiognomy of the individual and his habiliments, constitute some of the most striking and seductive features of all other poets and writers who deal with imaginary creations. By repeated touches and suggestions, as well as by minute delineations of particulars, the portraitures and scenes are brought before the mind, by the latter class, which gives every assistance to the imagination, and in many cases almost supersedes the need of any effort in that faculty. All this is denied to the dramatist, in his abstract capacity as an artist. He whose art solely depends upon the acting, and its "scenery, dresses, and decorations," is not a dramatist, but a playwright. The higher class of dramatic composition is based on its knowledge of human nature, and its power of evolving this knowledge intelligibly by means of ideal action, which the stage should illustrate, but can never create. The truly dramatic mind understands its severe task, and abides by its requisite restrictions. Its narrow space of words, as of time for their delivery, must be reserved for psychological developements. It cannot afford the long and vivid description of a scene, for the scene is nothing except as it is *felt;* or if it be anything extraneous to the genuine emotion of the particular drama, it is so far a distraction and an injury. Its heart is not to be smothered with illustration, however pictorially appropriate. Its only legitimate appeal is to the imagination,—through the medium of the senses when produced upon the stage,—and when not, it can only appeal to a corresponding faculty in the reader. Hence the comparative necessity of stage representation, in order to obtain the right estimation of any genuine drama; and hence, therefore, the total and very natural indifference of the public to all unacted dramas unless they have been "handed down" with honour from past ages. They are too onerous a tax upon the unassisted imagination and abstract sympathies, to be likely to find at any period either competent understanding or patient study among the vast majority of readers. They have their "fit audience," but few; and this is most especially the case with the unacted productions of the romantic drama, which cannot call to its aid the sympathies of classical learning, and the lofty associations of the heroic ages and mythological lore. How few, even among Spanish scholars, are interested about the dramas of the great Cervantes? Most of them are absolutely lost. Those which remain are scarcely ever read. How few are conversant, even among readers of dramatic literature, with the genius of Webster, whom Charles Lamb regarded as a "more potent spirit" than Ben Jonson? Nay, how few are the readers of the noble Ben Jonson himself, compared with those of any very frequently acted drama? True it is that the latter may only be acted and read by the public for a season; but then, next season, there is "just such another thing,"—and, meantime, Ben Jonson is *not* read by the public. It has never been, nor is it likely ever to be, otherwise.

In one genuine tragedy of five brief acts—soon read, still sooner "scanned over"—how much is contained. The internal history of many lives is there—lives of original characters full of power,—of power mixed with weakness, of nobleness, of depravity, of consistency, of vacillation; the history of passionate emotions and thoughts, with the climax which closes their tumultuous career of doing and suffering. Not for themselves only, as in real life, do the ideal characters of profound tragic creation act and suffer. Their mental history burns in the footways of their departure. It is the revelation of passion by genius; the intimacy communicated through ideal art; it is "the cause, my soul," which turns ignorance and indifference into shuddering comprehension, and dogmatism or levity into solemn-thoughted grief. It is the *knowledge* of all their struggles that finds a way into successive hearts, and multiplies in imagination the fiery aspiration, the love, the terror, the satisfaction or the pity, that attends their doom. We act and suffer with them; *their experience is made ours;* and from the grave of their gone existence the fatal histories of their lives arise, and warn us of ourselves.

"The excess of Life in those whose passionate activity was accompanied by intellect, imagination, designs, and deeds, becomes trans-missible in full action of heart and head from age to age, exactly in proportion to the truth and completeness with which their characters and actions are chronicled, and brought home to the intense abstract interests and individual sympathies of mankind. They present a constant food for study, deep interest, and self-improvement; the food increasing with the extent of consumption. They offer to the student a more varied and profound knowledge of human nature than he can elsewhere obtain (such revealments only accidentally and partially occurring in actual life); while the improvement to those who read in private, or witness in public merely to be amused and excited, is, perhaps, still greater from the unconsciousness of the influence so powerfully and subtly exercised over their feelings and imaginations."

"Tragedy is the exercise of the feelings, the antagonism of all hardness of the heart. The extremity of its distresses softens the obduracy of natures, frequently so hard as not to be otherwise reducible to sympathy; and yet more generally, of natures deadened by the unvarying flow of the common current of everyday business, which is but too apt gradually to petrify the passages to the heart, though the heart itself, when reached, may be one of real kindness and humane capacity. Natures are elevated and instructed unconsciously. Taken unawares, and thrown quite off its guard, the will offers no opposition to the impulse and the course of genuine feelings; the sympathies have free play through the imagination, and experience no repugnance from any sense of compulsion, prejudice, or worldly discretion. We feel with others, and for others, without any interest except the ties of our common humanity. In public representations, large masses of men experience emotions together, which are more generous, more just, and less selfish than under any other circumstances of their lives; and emotions, as Lord Bacon has remarked, are the more readily and strongly experienced when multitudes are assembled together. This latter circumstance is attributable to the enhancement of mental and moral courage under such circumstances; to the increased faith in a common nature; and to the radiation, reflection, and irresistible atmosphere of passionate sympathies.

"The knowledge of man and woman as they are at heart; the insight into the secret thoughts and passions of nature at its most deep and momentous periods of speculation, purpose, and impending action; and the means of comparing all these with the internal state of the individual after the consummation of all their passions and designs, can be obtained with equal completeness from no other source."*

Admitting the argument of Plato, as illustrated by Coleridge,† in speaking of the "Symposium," that it is "the business of one and the same genius to excel in tragic and comic poetry, or that the tragic poet ought, at the same time, to contain within himself the powers of comedy," (but thinking,

* Essay on Tragic Influence. London. 1840.
† Literary Remains. Vol. II. London. 1836.

nevertheless, that though the Greek drama displays this double capacity, the Greek dramatists do *not*,) our design compels us to pass at once to the consideration of the modern comedy, as coeval with the modern or romantic tragedy.

In one genuine comedy of character and action, what an epitome of large masses of social life is to be found. Its chief characters are at once individualized and generalized, so that you see both the man and his class. What a vivid moving picture and portraiture of the external manners and received moralities of the time; local conventionalisms, which sometimes involve universal truths of all times; what a compact and comprehensive field for the philosopher, who goes but little into mixed society, wherein to note the many-coloured currents of onward flowing life! Under this head must be comprised the comedy of wit or of extraneous humour, which is generally meagre in plot and action; the comedy of intrigue, which is so apt to place its vices in a position to be more admired than condemned, and has therefore an immoral tendency; and the comedy of real life, as existing at the time, which has in general a tendency to merge in farcical and burlesque portraitures of known individuals, and (when not supported by genuine wit and humour) is among the lowest orders of the dramatic art.

There are three other species of drama, the product of the romantic age of Elizabeth, which it is requisite to particularize. First, the poetical play, or mixed drama of serious interest, and comic under-plot: secondly, the more expressly poetical and romantic drama, which deals with supernatural agency, and is sometimes pastoral and mythological, sometimes monkish and diabolical in its elements, sometimes dealing solely with the more beautiful enchantments of fairy-land: and thirdly, the chronicle, or historical play, in which the poetry calls upon the imagination to supply the pageantry,—which pageantry being really and profusely furnished, in our own day, has been found utterly to overwhelm the poetry, and to convert the old chronicle play into a gorgeous spectacle. All the other varieties which are to be found at the present time may be comprised in the foregoing; for the opera of Italy is the poetical drama with music, and choruses in "distant" imitation of the antique tragedy,—the French vaudeville is a light comedy, or drama, with incorporated songs, carrying on rather than suspending the dialogue,—and all farces may be regarded as absurdly improbable comedies. If there be any other which cannot so well be included in those classes already described, we should say it was the domestic drama, or direct attempt to represent reality,—in general, the most *painfully* exciting, and therefore the most unartist-like and unelevating of all classes of the drama which pretend to a superior moral tendency.

The earliest history of the drama of all countries is one and the same. They have all commenced with certain rude religious ceremonies, and included a sort of comic character, who was the representative of Vice, and whose comedy chiefly consisted in the kicks and cuffs he received. Our readers will see that we had good reason for declining to enter into the antiquities of dramatic history, and thank our forbearance, when we inform those who may not be aware of the circumstance, that a figure of Punch was discovered on the walls of Pompeii.* But in saying that the drama in all countries had the same kind of primary origin, we by no means intend to infer that any one of them adopted its rude beginnings from the rude beginnings of another. The drama arises out of an elementary principle in the mind of man, which always manifests itself in an early period of civilization. In a comparatively barbarous district of one of our manufacturing counties, there is occasionally to be seen, at this very time, a species of drama among the sect called "Primitive Methodists," or "Ranters," bearing a close resemblance (if it be not precisely the same kind of thing) to the very form in which the English drama had its commencement in the time of Edward III. and Richard II., namely, with "Miracle Plays."† These poor people, few of whom, preachers included, can read or write, who have never seen a play, nor heard of one, cannot be supposed to have gone all that distance into obscure history to imitate the first dawn of the drama. It has sprung up in their own minds and feelings, as it did in other countries ages ago. We pass over the interval of these early struggles, and proceed to the consideration of the first regular dramas which can lay claim to be the commencement of the art in modern Europe.

If the similarity of origin be a curious and interesting circumstance, it is almost equally so, though of more simple and ostensible solution, that the first dramatic work of modern art should also, in every country, have been derived from the same original source. They have all been formed on the model of the Greek tragedies. The first of those imitations arose in

* "The figure of Pulcinello is said to be an accurate resemblance of what has been found painted on the walls of Pompeii."—*Schlegel*, Vol. I. Lect. VIII.
† We learn this from the Second Report of the Children's Employment Commission, Appendix, Part II. Report on *Sedgley, South Staffordshire*.

Italy, where the first regular tragedy, since the revival of letters, appeared. It was the production of Gian-Giorgio Trissino, a poet, born at Vicenza in 1478. The tragedy is entitled "Sofonisba," and was an imitation of the method of Euripides, "but without the genius," as Sismondi truly says, "which inspired the creators of the drama at Athens." It has a Chorus, which constantly occupies the stage, and, by its singing, when the stage is left by the principal characters, fills up the pauses, and divides the tragedy into acts, otherwise not so divided. The tragedy has many long narratives, recitals of messengers, and dialogues, and none of the characters are individualized or interesting, except it be Sophonisba, who is, however, very weak, and an unresisting creature at the mercy of her circumstances. It is not the business of the present article, as we previously intimated, to enter into any detailed criticism, otherwise we should find many occasions for praising the poet in this tragedy; most of its faults being those which are always manifested in the infancy of the dramatic art, while its poetry, particularly in the Chorus, and its general tone of ideality, are his own. Trissino died in 1550.

The next country, in historical order of succession, in which the regular drama arose, was England. In 1561, Thomas Sackville, afterwards Lord Buckhurst, presented the tragedy of "Ferrex and Porrex," (sometimes called "Gorboduc,") at Whitehall, before Queen Elizabeth. It was written by Thomas Sackville and Thomas Norton. It has a "Dumb Show" and a Chorus, but differs from the Greek drama in having divisions of acts and scenes. We can only spare room to indicate a few of its chief features. In its elemental design it mistakes a profusion of murders and slaughter for the tragic principle; and its structure is rendered wearisome by the prodigious length of its speeches and soliloquies. But its poetry and rhythm possess greater merits than are usually accorded to them.

We now pass over to Spain, where tragedy was first commenced by Geronimo Bermudez, a Dominican monk of Galicia, who was probably the inmate of a cloister at the time he wrote his two dramas.* He thought it most prudent to publish them under an assumed name—that of "De Silva."† He chose the subject of Inez de Castro, and treated it after the manner of a Greek tragedy, except that he took no trouble to preserve the unities of time and place. It has a Chorus of Coimbran women. The subject is treated in two distinct tragedies, each

* See *Bouterwek;* and the Introduction to Vol. VI. of the *Parnaso Español.*
† *Primeras Tragedias Españoles,* de Antonia de Silva. 8vo. Madrid. 1577.

forming a drama of itself, and the two completing the tragic history. It is full of long speeches and long soliloquies, and the action frequently pauses. In the first of these tragedies the principal character does not appear till the third act, and her presence has the extraordinary effect of stopping the progress of the story. The fourth act displays pathos and dramatic genius; but the fifth, as Bouterwek says, "is a tedious supplement." The second tragedy, which concludes the history, is too full of revengeful and revolting horrors, under the guise of justice. Some idea may be formed of this from the circumstance of two criminals being executed, amidst the applauding shouts of the Chorus, both of whom are condemned to "lose their hearts;"—and the heart of one victim is accordingly extracted through his breast, and that of the other through his back.

The regular drama commenced in France with an imitation of the external form of the Greek drama, and by the study of Aristotle, and of the tragedies of Seneca. The first of their compositions of this kind, which were acted, were the "Cleopatra" and "Dido" of Jodelle; and they had a Prologue and a Chorus. Jean de la Peruse made a translation of Seneca's "Medea." The principal dramas of Garnier are taken from the Greek tragedies, or from Seneca; and other writers of the time busied themselves in translating or imitating the "Sofonisba" of Trissino.

"Mysteries," or "Miracle Plays," were represented in Germany as early as the middle of the fourteenth century, (See "Eulen-spiegel;" but no regular dramas appeared till the seventeenth century, when a commencement was made by Opiz, and Andreas Gryphius, who translated tragedies from the ancients, and translated or imitated certain productions of Italy, France, and Flanders. The almost interminably lengthy tragedies of Lohenstein followed, as also did more translations by various authors, sometimes from vulgar Danish comedies, but chiefly from the French, till Lessing, after falling into the same errors himself, redeemed the German stage from French models of affected classicality. But Lessing ran into an opposite extreme, and wrote familiar tragedies in the every day, colloquial style, and endeavoured to establish the theory, so infallibly destructive of the higher classes of all the Fine Arts, *viz.,* that nature, as it is, should be exclusively copied, with a view to produce the nearest possible impression of reality. Lessing appeared to possess very little of the ideal faculty, and, therefore, very naturally denied its validity.

We now pass an interval of further efforts, and come at

once to the true strength and rapidly following maturity of the dramatic art. The dramatic mind varies in different countries, not in its essential principles, but in the greater or less degree of purity and directness of its manifestation; not in its substantial foundations, but external form and structure. After the period of classical translations and imitations, each country began to receive a national impulse, an action or re-action from within, according to the force and peculiarity of its own nature and institutions. Spain, England, and Germany, commenced each an original species of drama for itself. Italy and France adopted classical models; into which the first introduced music, and a cold, arid, severe style of tragic composition, all of which were also adopted by the French, at first with energy, and then with the addition of long speeches of wearisome didactic disquisition.

If the only thing requisite in order to originate, to revive, to reform, or to re-create the drama of a civilized country, was dramatic genius; if to possess the faculty and execute the work, as matter of literary composition, were all that was needed to produce the effect, or commence its developement, — then perhaps might the name of Cervantes have stood parallel in Spain with the highest names of our dramatists of the age of Elizabeth. But between original dramatic genius, and its desired attempts, there come three powerful intermediates, any one of which may prevent the very chance of a fair trial, or of any trial at all,—these are the public tastes of the day, influence of capital (or the want of it), and the individual capacities and characters—in fact, the private taste of managers of theatres. The public taste may be good or vicious, its reception of new things is always a doubtful matter; capital is rarely, if ever, embarked upon a new thing of *ideal* pretensions; and to say that a particular novelty of any kind would be to the interest of a manager to produce, might be true, or untrue,—that is not the question, but what he thinks and chooses to do; and whether he be very wise, or very ignorant, he has hitherto been " the law," as to what genius or talent should make its appeal to the public through the medium of the stage.

Cervantes successfully resisted the attempt in Spain to give the antique form to its rising dramatic literature, and wrote some thirty pieces for the stage, few of which were probably ever performed, and they are nearly all lost—the usual fate in those days, in all countries, with regard to unacted dramas. He subsequently composed eight dramas; but "his day" was not with him, and his poverty, if nothing else, was against him. He made an attempt in various interludes and minor pieces, to adapt his genius to the taste of the time, and wrote beneath himself without suiting the public. His genius was too peculiarly his own, and he had no means of creating a taste. Many heavy and uninteresting scenes in his own dramas look as if written under the influence of fatigue and disgust, and seem also to prove that he had not had much opportunity of studying dramatic effect, by witnessing the production of his own pieces, or such scenes would never have been allowed to remain. His highest claim must therefore rest upon his tragedy of " Numantia," which has justly been considered a noble production. " The conception," says Bouterwek, " is in the style of the boldest pathos; and the execution, at least taken as a whole, is vigorous and dignified." It is not an imitation of the style or form of the antique, nor of any other drama; it has no Chorus, and is divided into four acts, termed *jornadas*. He possessed dramatic genius, peculiar, yet of the highest and most refined class, and of this we will offer two instances in illustration, from this tragedy. During a religious ceremony, a solemn sacrifice is about to be made to a presiding spirit; but an *evil* spirit scatters the sacred fire in the dust, and carries off the intended victim. This method of showing that the prayer would not be granted, but disaster would ensue, required the audience to appreciate more than was visibly presented. Still more is this the case, when during a famine which rages in the city, a lover, accompanied by a friend, forcibly enters the enemy's camp, and returns, alone, with a piece of bread tinged with blood, which he gives to his famished mistress, and then dies of his wounds at her feet. Such a scene, as fearful in its suggestions of what lives it has cost to obtain that morsel of bread, besides that life which is laid down at her feet, stamps the genius of Cervantes, but shows at the same time the need of an understanding audience. Spain gave the preference to Lope de Vega, and his two thousand most ingenious levities.

About the same period that an original drama arose in Spain, the regular original drama arose in England. Each may be fairly regarded as a genuine national production, quite independent of the other. Cervantes did not begin to write for the stage till after the year 1581. Chapman, Greene, Marlowe, Webster, Shakspeare, Decker, Ben Jonson, and probably several others, were all born between the years 1557 and 1574; and supposing that they were all writing for the theatres when some thirty years of age, (for there are very few certainties as to these matters), it would bring them all close upon the time of Cervantes and Lope de Vega. Tragedy and comedy were flourishing in England, and chiefly tragedy; in Spain, the whole play-going public was running wild with delight at the prolific genius displayed in the extravagant comedies of Lope de Vega.

In treating of the dramatists of the Elizabethan age, it has been the almost invariable custom of writers, especially of late years, not to attempt to estimate the universality of Shakspeare (a task to which, perhaps, no one man has hitherto been quite equal), nor even to seek to add a single new thought on the subject; but the sole endeavour has been to pile up the admiration to a greater height than all the many immediately preceding writers had piled it, who had themselves all sought to do the same. After this, a few words have been said of Beaumont and Fletcher, fewer of Marlowe, a passing word on "rare Ben Jonson," and nothing at all of Webster, Ford, and the other great dramatists,—partly because, not being "acted," they are scarcely known to the mass of the public, and partly also because the writer had generally exhausted "all his space."

There can be little doubt but that the entire works of Shakspeare comprise more "dramatic stuff" than all the other dramatists of his own, or, perhaps, of any other age, put together. Yet his greatest scenes are seldom greater than can be found in several of the other men of his time; nor can his matchless superiority as the architect of a "whole," in any case, annihilate the genius of his contemporaries. It has been well said that they were "a constellation," although the magnitude of the Star of Avon was such as to make his brothers look far less bright than they really were, and would have appeared, but for his glorious presence.

No one author has done so much to give a synthetical account of the entire dramatic scope of Shakspeare, and of each of his works, as A. W. Schlegel, who has, moreover, the honour of having been the first to do so. The criticisms of Lessing had the precedence, but were by no means so complete. Coleridge and Hazlitt followed, with fine subtle appreciations and disquisitions in the first, and fine illustrative criticisms in the latter. Schlegel, also, does considerable justice to some of Shakspeare's contemporaries, but seems to know but little of others. Coleridge deals only with a few of them; Hazlitt with all the greatest among them; and Charles Lamb has, perhaps, done still more for their memory by his "Specimens of English Dramatic Poets."

"Perhaps the genius of Great Britain (if I may so speak without offence or flattery) never shone out fuller or brighter than at this period. Our writers and great men had something in them that savoured of the soil from whence they grew: they were not French; they were not Dutch, or German, or Greek, or Latin; they were truly English. They did not look out of themselves to see what they should be; they sought for truth and nature, and found it in themselves. There was no tinsel, and but little art; they were not the spoiled children of affectation and refinement, but a bold, vigorous, independent race of thinkers, with prodigious strength and energy, with none but natural grace, and heartfelt, unobtrusive delicacy. They were not at all sophisticated. The mind of their country was great in them, and it prevailed. With their learning and unexampled acquirement, they did not forget that they were men: with all their endeavours after excellence, they did not lay aside the strong original bent and character of their minds. What they performed was chiefly Nature's handiwork, and Time has claimed it for his own. To these, however, might be added others not less learned, nor with a scarce less happy vein, but less fortunate in the event, who, though as renowned in their day, have sunk into 'mere oblivion;' and of whom the only record (but that the noblest) is to be found in their works. Their works and their names, 'poor, poor, dumb names,' are all that remain of such men as Webster, Decker, Marston, Marlowe, Chapman, Heywood, Middleton, and Rowley! 'How lov'd, how honour'd once, avails them not;' though they were the friends and fellow-labourers of Shakspeare, sharing his fame and fortunes with him."[*]

Coinciding in the general tone and purport of the foregoing extract, we may still remark that enough weight is not attached to the *art* and good *judgment* of Shakspeare, as a striking exception among nearly all his brother dramatists; while for the "oblivion" of his contemporaries, we may rejoice that they are now rescued from such a fate. This may be considered as the first period of dramatic literature in England, and its extension and close may be placed about the end of the reign of Charles I., when all theatrical amusements were prohibited by the Puritans.

After the Spaniards had been delighted by the fertile inventions of novel plots of intrigue, striking situations, and excellent sallies of wit in the innumerable pieces of Lope de Vega, there arose a dramatist of far higher genius in the person of Calderon, who fortunately combined with that genius the power of exactly suiting the taste of his time. He is like a poetical spirit rising from the union of the essential powers of Cervantes and Lope de Vega, with the addition of a third power which at the same time renders him an original poet and artist in the drama. His productions are far from being

[*] Lectures on the Dramatic Literature of the Age of Elizabeth.

as numerous as those of Lope, but they weigh more. In the finer kind of conception and invention, Calderon was by far his superior, and also in passion, pathos, and in the general execution, so far as a highly poetical and imaginative style are concerned. He wrote upwards of a hundred carefully finished pieces. They would probably be too high-flown in certain notions of honour, too glowing, glittering, and exotic, to gain a permanent hold upon the taste of northern nations; yet it is difficult to believe but that many of them would prove effective upon any stage. The Spanish drama had but this one period, which may be said to have closed with Calderon. If there be any great dramatist of Spain in our own day, it will be the business of a substantive article on the dramatic literature of that country to discover him.

The Italians never produced but one dramatic genius of the higher order, (however they improved in the art,) who could be considered superior to the father of modern tragedy, Trissino; and with the severe monotony, harsh loftiness, baldness of style, but fierce passion, concentration, and grandeur of Alfieri, the period of Italian tragedy may be said to have terminated. Both Metastasio and Alfieri adopted the French views of simplicity of construction, and the latter their "formal cut" of all the unities; but Alfieri was far more Greek than French, as Metastasio was far more disposed to imitate the ornate and brilliant extravaganzas and effects of Calderon.

In grandeur of design and abstract purpose, in breadth of passion, (though deficient in concentration), and in loftiness and energy, the French drama never had a writer equal to the founder of their tragedy, Corneille. He was not like a Frenchman. Schlegel very truly says, "we might take him for a Spaniard educated in Normandy." But the force of his genius is very much lost by its expansion, and was rather epic than dramatic. Racine brought order, precision, purity of language, elegance, tenderness, and pathos into the national drama; and Voltaire, without adding any original principle, introduced several salutary reforms with reference to the more correct treatment of historical subjects. He also endeavoured to obtain a greater degree of scenic truth and latitude of movement, but with little success. As though for the sake of a perverse inconsistency, and to remove art as far as possible from nature, the volatile character of the nation resolved that at least the abstract forms of its ideas should approach as near as possible to the petrific—and where not so, it should present a courtly immobility of feature. But

if Voltaire was unsuccessful in his attempt to enlarge the bounds of the drama, the climax of national inconsistency is yet more completely perceptible in the fact that Racine was unpopular in his day, and abandoned his dramatic career with chagrin.

The foregoing remarks will of course be understood to apply solely to French tragedy; and with the three great names, just mentioned, closes the first period of their drama, in its higher or more stately walk. In comedy they were always more or less clever,—unrivalled from the time of Molière—and on this species of composition a few remarks will subsequently be offered.

It is a peculiar and amusing feature in the early literature of England,—and especially in the age of Elizabeth,—that, all its writers of imaginative stories laid the scenes in England, and with the customs, habits, circumstances, and associations of their own country, by whatever names they might designate their men and places, and in whatever period of the world. Chaucer speaks of Mars as a knight, of Theseus as a duke, and in one poem actually speaks of Saint Venus. In the noble translation of Homer by Chapman, we frequently hear of knights and dukes—Duke Ajax, Duke Menelaus. Shakspeare's invariable practice in these respects is notorious. Some excellent remarks on this subject, with reference to the dramas of various nations, are made by Sismondi.

"We have observed that Metastasio represents every thing under a conventional form, a state of society ever the same, and whose manners and characters are invariable, in whatever dress he clothes his personages, and whatever name he imposes on them. Alfieri completely banished this effeminate, peculiar, and conventional form, which reminded him of what he most held in abhorrence,—the debasement of his country,—but he substituted nothing in its place. The scenes of the pieces of Metastasio may be said to be in the theatre; but those of Alfieri have no scenes whatever. He accomplished all the five acts without any description, and in those tragedies where the chief passion is the love of country, he has deprived the patriot of his native soil. We may remark that every author, perhaps every tragic poet, has a different manner of placing before the eyes of his fellow citizens events remote in time or place; and, indeed, it is not an easy task to introduce a spectator, often uninformed, to a country and manners to which he is an entire stranger. The French have adopted the easy mode of transferring their heroes to their own capital. If they describe the Greeks, all that is generally known of them is accurately and consistently painted, but for the rest they represent manners as being the same in Greece as in Paris; and the court of Agamemnon does not, in their view, differ much from the court of Louis XIV. The Germans have proposed to themselves another kind of representation, and the spectator has reason to regret, if he be ignorant of the subject. For he will have the more pleasure, the more he is acquainted with the history of the piece. They neglect nothing to make the picture faithful and complete; they sacrifice the rapidity of the action, rather than allow the imagination to remain uninformed of a single circumstance. They rely on vast information on the part of the spectator; and still unsatisfied, they devote a further quantity of time to his instruction; and this not so much in local detail, which lessens the interest, as in philosophical digression, from which the German poets are unable to abstain."

Whether the majority of the admirers of Goethe will admit the possibility of any one having a great admiration of his genius and varied acquirements, yet at the same time believing that he was not an actable dramatist, we do not know; nevertheless, we venture to assert that not only do his dramas belong to no principle of dramatic art hitherto practised, but that (except in detached scenes) they are opposed to every recognized principle. Each of his plays has its ruling design and purpose; but no consecutive structure for combined, progressive, and harmonious effects in action. The criticisms of A. W. Schlegel fully support these remarks, as also does the fine philosophical essay of G. H. Lewes. Goethe was great in single scenes: the rest is foreign to our present subject. The developement of the dramatic spirit of Germany has been delayed, partly by its wrestlings with metaphysics, and partly by having been led astray. The "most admired disorder" of the dramatic method of its greatest genius, did incalculable mischief to the rising drama of his country, because such a man as Goethe was sure to have many imitators, who thought it a fine free thing to write scenes, collateral, episodical, and roundabout a subject, and call that a new method and principle of dramatic art. This influence, however, did not spoil Schiller, who in his steady, consecutive, earnest purpose, practical energy, and eye to action and genuine effect, may be regarded as belonging, by his very nature, as well as method, to the English school of the highest class of drama.

Describing the origin of comedy, in all times, Coleridge says,—"Let two persons join in the same scheme to ridicule a third, and either take some advantage of, or invent a story for that purpose, and mimicry will have already produced a sort of rude comedy." But what striking varieties have been developed from this simple principle by its peculiar application among different nations, and by different writers in the same nation! The classical comedies of Ariosto are certainly

not so animated and comic as those of Macchiavelli, Babiena (afterwards Cardinal), Pietro Aretino and Giambatista Porta, in which latter authors the want of art is supplied by a profusion of unmisgiving indecency. After these the thin, sentimental, unstable productions of Goldoni obtained the first name in this class of literature, and long remained the favourite of the comic stage. Compare all these with the best comedies of Lope de Vega and Calderon, and what a difference in the invention and enjoyment of life do they display. But turn to France, where the vain and perverse notions of tragic art have left comedy uninjured, and let us contemplate the works of Molière. What skill in structure; what truth of character, at once individualized and a class; what humour, animation, and *knowledge!*

Lastly, let us turn to the English stage in 1660, when Charles II. re-opened the theatres. Can it be termed a revival of the drama? Far from a revival of departed greatness, it was rather the rise of a new and spurious spirit, the influence of which in respect of the drama was worse than if the great age of Elizabeth had produced no dramatists at all. It was no genius of the drama that came to life, but the spirit of a licentious court that generated the rank productions that flourished upon the stage. Davenant and the Duke of Buckingham were as much at home in the theatre, as in the gaudy places of another kind patronized by the court. But the crowning impudence of all, as the finishing proof of depraved taste, is to be found in the fact of those worthies altering Shakspeare to their own low standard. Our respect for Dryden makes us pass on to Wycherly, Congreve, Vanbrugh, and others of that class, with whom wit and indecency were the main thing; and who appear to have been so thoroughly imbued with the worst influences of the day, that they were scarcely conscious of the prostitution of their undoubted genius. The only genuine dramatist of the time was Otway; and how well he was estimated, is perceptible by his fate.

How different is all this from the poetical and romantic comedy of Shakspeare and some of his contemporaries, need not be remarked. Scarcely any essential improvement is to be found with Cibber, and not much with Coleman. A new, more genial, and thoroughly English comedy, was attained by Goldsmith and others; though scarcely any of them were so popular as Sheridan with his brilliantly unprincipled wit. But genuine tragedy in its higher walk was no more; nor were there any feebly galvanized remains of its substance much better than the formal and ostentatious dulness of "Cato," and the painful turgidity of "Douglas." The best exceptions would probably be found in Rowe and Young. Nearly all the rest, of tragic pretensions, were of the domestic or familiar kind, so frequently adopted by even superior minds, but which are opposed to all ideal art. On this very important question, a few closing observations will presently be offered.

Recent writers on the literature of Spain take no more notice of the present state of its drama, than if a stage did not exist; nor does anything new appear in Italy except in the way of opera. In Germany, those who are regarded as their best dramatists seldom write for the stage; but whether this perversity is attributable to the authors, the managers, or the public taste, remains to be examined. A new spirit, however, has manifested itself in England and France of late years;—in the former it has found little vent through the theatres; in the latter it has found ample vent, and become both "audible" and visible.

The tragedies of Victor Hugo were a new thing in France; their unscrupulous passion, energy of imagination and action, as well as striking stage effect, have a far closer resemblance to the style of our early English drama than anything ever before seen or expected in "our loving sister." But it is more especially to the *Comédie Française*, and to their charming little *vaudevilles* that we would direct attention. For excellent delineation of character, interesting plot, masterly structure and developement, we have nothing like them; and as to the graceful poetic effect, and ideality (however comparatively trifling in subject), of these *vaudevilles*, with their graphic songs, any one who cannot surrender himself to the amusement of their small yet romantic world, may be assured that the period of his youthful feelings is passed. These amusing little pieces are nothing more than they pretend to be; but what they pretend to be, they are to perfection. In tragedy there may be none to compete with Victor Hugo, but in comedy there are many excellent writers. We have, we trust, sufficiently manifested our estimation of the higher classes of ideal art, not to fear that the extent of our appreciation, which seeks to embrace every form and peculiarity of our subject, will be misunderstood. We therefore wish to give its due praise to the knowledge and skill displayed in the French comedy of the present day, including the lighter pieces by Scribe, Dumas, and others. They are models of their kind; and that they possess a peculiar grace and spirit of their own, is manifested in the clumsy attempts of English playwrights to imitate or "adapt" them to our stage, in which process they generally become vulgarized. But when taste and skill are really displayed by the adapter, then we

find the inadequacy of our actors and actresses to fill such characters.

In our own country there has been a manifestation of the dramatic spirit during the last fifteen years, of a kind which, under its particular circumstances, is quite unexampled in the history of the drama of all nations. Innumerable plays in this and other countries were acted in the early periods, and never printed; but in no country, until the present time in England, has there been a great number of plays written, published, and never acted. As none of these unacted dramas ever meet with any sale, nor, with few exceptions, much notice from the press, the fascination in this species of composition is apparent, and must betoken, at least, a very strong dramatic impulse in the spirit of the age among literary men. Yet how seldom is a new drama of the higher class produced on the stage? Two or three in the course of a season are the utmost; and they scarcely ever appear after that season. The choice was made without good judgment; the least likely to succeed were thought to be most likely. How extremely few are the writers who obtain a trial. About four names would complete the "whole round." Yet there is scarcely a literary man of any eminence in the imaginative class of composition who has not written for the stage, and published his play without its being acted. Most of them are very unskilful in construction, and want dramatic tact and effect. But so do all those which are produced on the stage; for the construction and *desired* effect is arbitrarily supplied or "settled" by the manager or principal actor,—and with what inefficiency is but too perceptible. Even the stage effects are miscalculated.* The dramatists have no means of learning their art in practice; and the rulers of the patent theatres cannot communicate even that, far less those subtler principles with which they are themselves unacquainted; for their "practical knowledge and experience" presents, as its results, a long list of mediocre pieces, unexpected condemnations, and commercial losses. Theirs is the practice of foregone failures; an uninstructed experience.

Amidst the numerous extraneous causes, more or less operating adversely upon the evident struggle of a new dramatic literature to arise in England, there are two fundamental evils —one extraneous, one internal—which destroy the chance of such a developement of the intellect and energy of the

* On what principle of dramatic art (to say nothing of appreciation of high excellence,) could the "Blot in the Scutcheon" be produced, while so fine a tragedy, eminently actable, as the "Return of the Druses," by the same author, is in existence? Or, if this be not thought a sufficient case in point, let us recollect "Plighted Troth."

country. One of these is referable to æthetics, the other to a tyrannical matter of fact. The former is manifested in the invariable attempt to substitute realities for poetical illusion ; * the latter in the patent monopoly. By the former the expense of producing a new five-act drama is rendered prodigious, and, therefore, a serious commercial speculation. By the latter there is a monopoly of Shakspeare, and all the higher class of drama; whereby fair competition is prevented, public taste vitiated with shoals of spurious productions at the minor theatres and saloons of taverns, and a despotism established over all the productive power by managers and actors, be they who or what they may. It argues nothing for the attempt to realize scenery, that great intellects have, in their first experiments in dramatic composition, frequently adopted the domestic or familiar drama of real life ; they have all abandoned it for the ideal, as they advanced. Of the injurious effect upon poetry and true dramatic effect, by overloading it with scenery and illustration, however correct, little need be said, as it must be apparent to every observer who is previously conversant with the drama by previous study and enjoyment. But if a monopoly which provides, by an antiquated act of parliament, that the great majority of dramas shall be illegitimate—that is, of a lower influence, which injures the public taste and morals —a monopoly which denies the great majority of theatres the right to accept and produce the best dramas they can obtain—we feel assured that it only needs one vigorous movement of a member of the legislature to be at once abolished. Lord Lyndhurst gave notice, some time since, that he intended to present a petition to the House of Lords against this absurd theatrical monopoly, which is injurious to all parties, as well as the public ; but before the day arrived he was suddenly called to the Cabinet, and, as may easily be supposed, had " his hands full" immediately. A few months ago Lord Mahon addressed the Commons on the subject, and was expected to present petitions, and otherwise exert himself on the question ; but, from some cause or other, he seems to have faded away. That so ridiculous a monopoly, outraged as it is in all directions, should be speedily abolished, we cannot doubt ; and with it will vanish the unnecessary and suicidal expenses of the stage, and its prodigal love of " real upholstery," minute details, and dioramic scenery, be superseded by pure dramatic productions.

* See Quatremère de Quincy ; " *Essay sur la Nature, le But, et les Moyens de l'Imitation dans les Beaux Arts.*" 8vo. Paris. 1823. Coleridge ; " Progress of the Drama ; and Public Taste ;" " Literary Remains," Vol. II. Schlegel's " Lectures ;" and the " Introduction to Schlegel," and " Essay on Tragic Influence," by R. H. Horne.

43. FOREIGN AND COLONIAL QUARTERLY REVIEW, 2 (1843), 221-234. M/H No. 3892.

Art. X.—1. *Selections from the German of Goethe and Schiller, translated, with Introductory Remarks.* By Anna Swanwick. Murray. 1843.

2. *Translations from the German.* By Henry Reeve and J. E. Taylor. Murray. 1842.

3. *The Blind Wife; or the Student of Bonn: a Tragic Romance.* By Thomas Powell. 8vo. London: W. E. Painter. 1843.

It is with great regret that we feel ourselves compelled to be so ungallant as to deny to the lady whose name appears associated with others in this article any further meed than that of smooth and easily flowing metre. In fact, the spirit of Schiller is fearfully remote from the versification before us. Some passages of Goethe are well given, but we miss the powerful feeling of the author of " Faust." We give one passage from the " Iphigeneia," which is a favourite with us :—

> " Rash combat oft immortalizes man.
> If he should fall, he is renown'd in song ;
> But after ages reckon not the tears
> Which ceaseless the forsaken woman sheds ;
> And poets tell not of the thousand nights
> Consumed in weeping, and the dreary days,
> Wherein her anguish'd soul, a prey to grief,
> Doth vainly yearn to call her lov'd one back."

Messrs. Reeve and E. Taylor have given considerable force to Mickiewicz, and other writers, in their elegant little volume before us. Uhland is also singularly well translated in some of his beautiful minor poems. We give one extract from Dante's " Love :"—

> " And Dante wrote his wondrous love,
> With fire strokes nothing can efface,
> As on the Rock the Brand of Jove
> Graves its imperishable trace.
> Then to his Muse of heavenly birth
> Well may the name Divine be given,
> Who raised his Beatrice from Earth,
> To shed on men the love of Heaven."

From these gentlemen we pass to our third head,—" The Blind Wife; or the Student of Bonn," by Thomas Powell. We shall but rarely venture, even for the sake of those British colonists who love to hear of the literature of their own land, on the enchanting realm of domestic poetry ; but the passages of *sustained* merit in this play are so numerous as to entice us to the task.

Mr. Powell's first promising effusion, the " Count de Foix," was founded upon the last new school of narrative poetry, in the heroic measure that came up some years ago ; but we will venture to affirm that he had caught little of the manner of his prototype, except its rejection of the formality of the later Anglo-French school of versification, and that he had not studied a single one of the principles of its structure. We are disposed to think, in relation to the structure of verse, rhyming or blank, that up to this moment, the words *cadence,* or *rhythm,* or *modulation,* much less *iambics,* or *trochaics,* or the idea of any systematic difference whatever in the styles of Chaucer and Dryden, or Dryden and Pope, or Shakspeare and Beaumont and Fletcher, except with the vaguest general impression, never entered his head. The following is the commencement of the "Count de Foix:—"

> " The hall was fair and large : a noble blaze
> Gladdened the hearth, and sent its cheerful rays
> O'er half the floor ; while at mid distance sat
> Two noble knights, engaged in pleasant chat
> Before a well-stored table, where the wine
> And pasties *told* they were about to dine.
> Right sumptuous was the board ; here fruit was piled,
> And here a haunch,—and there the pasty *smiled* ;
> And as they tossed the draughts of Rhenish wine
> Down willing throats, their eyes more cheerly shine,
> The speech comes freer, and they grasp each other's
> Hands with right cordial pressure like two brothers !
> They tell their boyish freaks, their youthful loves,
> When they penned sonnets, called their ladies doves,
> And did the foolish things all lovers do ;
> And then their manly deeds they both went through,
> From the first fleshing of their maiden swords.
> Right valorous were they ! generous as lords !
> And full of quarrel, yet as virgins modest !
> Indeed they said, and did, the very oddest
> Things that the youthful do : and when they *told*
> Each other very gravely,—they were *old*,
> And not the knights they were, when at a *blow*
> One took the head and helmet from his *foe*,
> And left the bleeding trunk to fall *alone*.
> And Sir John Froissart, too, had nerve and *bone*
> E'er ready for the battle or the bower !
>   And now they went to other things. The *old*
> Grey-headed Sir Espagne de Lyon *told*
> The brave Sir John, that on the morrow he," &c. &c.

In this exordium, by the meeting of extremes naturally resulting from the mere rejection of a principle, and the substitution of no other, the very ease becomes a sort of uneasiness ; the rhymes are forced upon the notice, by the very attempt to take no care of them ; in the third, and fourth, and fifth couplets, the leading sounds of the rhyme are all alike,—all in the vowel *i* ; and in the three closing couplets of the paragraph, as well as in the first one of the paragraph next ensuing, they are all in *o !* with the singular intervention of a solitary verse that has no rhyme at all ! ! *Told, old, blow, foe, alone, bone,* BOWER, *old, told.* Now exuberant rhymes, or overflows of the like terminating sound, as in the old French Fabliaux and the works of Chaulieu, have sometimes an admirable effect, when purposely and joyously indulged in,

as a result of animal spirits ; but in the present instance, they have evidently no purpose at all, and are quite misplaced. In fact, the writer did not think about the matter. Indeed, if he had, the case would have been worse ; for reiterated rhymes do not suit the heroic measure. The rhymes, and their repetition, it may be said, are small things. But they are not so in a rhyming poem. They become an essential part of its harmony or discord. If you see rhymes written upon no principles, you see the rest of the versification written upon none.

The style of Mr. Powell's first play, "The Wife's Revenge," was equally without thought. It is true there are too many modern dramas, which in their same want of all principle of writing, and mistaking a slovenly want of study for freedom, deal in conventionalities and prosaic phraseology.

In his latest and best production, now before us, all these faults are repeated. The versification is left to take its chance, without knowledge : the prosaic phrases and conventional metaphors, though not so numerous as in "The Wife's Revenge," are still to be met with ; almost every thing is done with a hasty will, as if with an avowed intention of taking no trouble. The very first scene of the play commences with a verse that is no verse ; and there are numerous unintentional Alexandrines, or other superfluous quantities. (See pages 10, 32, 42, 49, 72, 111, 115, 136, 142.)

In "The Blind Wife," a year is supposed to have elapsed between the third and fourth acts, and five years between the fourth and fifth. We should have no objection to concede these " Winter's Tale" privileges to a writer who would reverently consider what he needs in other respects ; but they look too much like self-indulgence in Mr. Powell. There is no proper study even of character or manners in " The Blind Wife." The plot, for example, which is soon told, consists of the deliberate murder of a blind and innocent wife by a young man, who is represented as an enthusiast for all that is lovely and generous, and who has obtained a fortune by her, as well as the most affectionate of companions ; and this murder is committed solely for the purpose of marrying another girl, to whom he transfers his enthusiasm ; and the perpetrator commits suicide out of remorse. He is a really generous man, in all other respects ; but the murder, and kind to every body about him. This is not in nature. Such a man would never have thought of murdering his wife, unless out of some hypochondriacal horror of the very fear of doing it, much less would he actually have murdered her, especially in the most paltry and ungenerous manner conceivable, *viz.* by letting her walk, in her poor blindness, over a precipice! Then, as to manners, no blind woman could talk, as she does, of light and colours; of one who attended her like her "shadow;" of a presence like a "brightening dawn;" of "eyes that patience brightens more than love;" and of a terrace "*looking* towards the Drachenfels." All this is owing to Mr. Powell's notion of trusting every thing to "genius," and taking no heed of study, or even common reflection. Yet hence the many misgivings which might have taught him better, and the hysterical semi-jocose anticipations of the critics, as in the preface to "The Wife's Revenge." Hence also a good deal of the evidently unsettled nature of most of his opinions, and a doubt sometimes forced upon the reader's mind, as to that sincerity on his own part, which he is constantly doubting in others. He does not think, except when compelled by his feelings, and then for no final and calm purpose; but only how to get through them at the moment, or work out some crude effect on his critics. In short, he thinks idly of many things not worthy the trouble, and little or not at all of the only means for giving him lasting repute; to wit, study and straightforwardness.

Now Mr. Powell has faculties in him; and though we have felt it to be our duty to follow up our encouragement with the present strong remonstrances (forced upon us by himself, and indisputably necessary to his advancement), yet, provided he studies, reads, and digests those remonstrances, and sets himself heartily to work to render all repetitions of them superfluous, we hold him worthy to be told, what many a less fortunate writer would have given half his subsistence to hear at an early period of his endeavour, in spite of all such drawbacks; and that is, that he *is* a poet, with many intimations of qualities fit to make him a distinguished one. If he has will and stubbornness, he has also passion, in the better sense of the word; if he is hasty, he has also one of the best accompaniments of haste, dislike of the superfluous; and if his style is careless and slovenly, it is at the same time natural, and goes direct to the purpose. If he has read any authors, we should say they have been Marlowe and Heywood. Marlowe pleases his will; and Heywood that belief in truth and simplicity, which belongs to genuine passion; and to which, in his best moments, Mr. Powell shows such a tendency as should save him from all unworthy perplexities. What matters it to him, if half the world are insincere, or even nine tenths of them? Light might as well object to the darkness which it is made to illumine or to adorn. As a man is a great and good man in proportion as he is above weakness and falsehood, so is a writer a great writer in proportion as he gives himself wholly up to truth and nature, without sloth, without misgivings, without trickery. What cares he about having credit given him for what he does not do, or will not take pains to do properly? What cares he for critics and Reviews, except that they should tell him the truth, which he must desire to discover, whether for or against him; and which, being discovered, will make the Reviews think of *him*, instead of his thinking of the Reviews?

To give this gentleman new proofs of the sincerity with which we can praise as well as blame, we proceed to give extracts of passages we admire, from "The Blind Wife." We would fain, in spite of its two ugly "*laids*," begin with extracting the whole of Leonhard's selfish soliloquy, in which he supposes a good wife to be a mere reflection of his own will and conceit; but though an admirable preparation for what follows, it is rather a suggestion of character than a specimen of the author's best writing. In a previous passage, it is hardly so characteristically said of his hero, though it is well and wilfully said, too, that in his fits of philanthropical anger with the world—

> " He would have sent
> The human race, for which he felt so much,
> *To hell itself, to learn humanity.*"—(p. 4.)

In a succeeding passage, continuous flashes of lightning are finely called "showers of terror;" and the storm in which they came, is thus forcibly described:—

> " I took some shelter 'neath a forest's edge,
> And never felt the regal might of God
> So wonderfully grand. The Rhine was lit
> With living fire, its waters turned to flame,
> And the old castles seemed like blazing ruins.
> All was laid bare for miles: darkness and light
> Seemed battling for a mastery, and each
> Had victory by turns,—now day, now night.
> *The thunder seemed the angry tread of God
> Upon the air,* which shrieked with all its might;
> While nature crouched a living battle-plain,
> And shook with dread! My poor steed shivered,
> As though it had an ague. 'Twas indeed a storm,
> Worthy the very Alps.
>   *Bertha.*   You tell it with a force
> As though you gloried in its perilous grandeur."—(p. 35.)

Bertha's expressions of regret at being blind, though they are hardly blind enough, are touching—sometimes beautiful; and Leonhard's reply ends nobly. There is a bit of slovenliness, however, in its second line—a want of a nominative case between the words *but* and *does*.

> " *Bertha.* I have enjoyed your converse much,
> And shall for ever treasure in my heart
> This pleasant ramble.   Would I had a brother,
> Who could like you pour floods of light
> Upon the darkness of my mind, and make
> My happiness twice happier than it is!
> We all owe God a mighty debt, too great
> For words to sum up its amount; but those
> Who have the wondrous faculty of sight,
> Owe him a greater still.   Had I but seen,
> Only for once, the everlasting sky,
> So full of stars, of which I hear so much,
> I could exist upon the memory!
> Or, had I witnessed from the Drachenfels
> *The silent springing of some golden morn*
> *Which brings the world into the midst of May,—*
> For well I know that season by the flush
> Of odours, which upon my senses steal
> Like revelations from an invisible world,
> Even as great Columbus felt he drew
> To the New World, long ere he saw its groves,
> By the land-odours borne upon the wind;
> Or had I gazed upon a human face,
> And look'd but once on Emmeline's kind eyes,
> I think that would content me: but to be
> Shut out from all the glorious works of God;
> And at the keenest and the mightiest sense,
> Sometimes steals o'er me as a fond regret,
> Which leaves a peaceful sadness on my heart.
> And yet could I behold the awful book
> Of Providence, in which my destiny
> Is as a map laid down, I should discern
> A special reason for my deprivation,
> And have another cause to thank my God!
>   *Leonhard.* To the contented mind, all things seem best,
> But does not make them so; yet in your case
> The sense of sight were a superfluous one:
> We can but feel we're happy,—you are so.
> The eye is a tormentor when we look
> On half the things that strew our daily path;
> How else would patient merit know the sneer,
> That loftiest effort of a rich man's mind,

> The offspring of his heart? or feel the cold
> And arrogant smile which strikes into his soul
> Like to an icy wind, *but for the eye,*
> *That instrument of torture?*   It had need
> *Have golden dawns, and night's serene*
> *Magnificence of stars.*"—(p. 44.)

The following extract is of great force.   Count Leonhard has been five years a murderer, and is laden with remorse. He thus soliloquizes:—

> " *Leonhard.* Five years?   Great God! it must be centuries.
> Oh, what a weary length is life!   Yet I
> Have seen but half the years doled out to man.
> *All nature seems to crawl along in pain.*
> I have infected it, and hung a shroud
> Upon the visible glory of the world,
> Changing the stars to ashes.   How the wind,
> That moaning voice of night, howls round the turrets,
> As though it bore a death shriek, stifled in,
> The depths of its unfathomable breast;
> Not an hour creeps but I do register.
> With some fierce pang, that brands its memory
> In fire upon the tablet of my brain.
> Why, one would deem the human heart must stop
> Beneath the weight which hangs on every pulse,
> And that the mind would grow confused and dull
> With this unsleeping vigil of my thought,
> Brooding like Satan on the throne of hell!
> How long is't since I've had a moment's peace?
> And what is peace?   Alas! I only know
> 'Tis fled from *me.*
> I have had feverish moments of delight,
> And lost for some short time the sense of woe,
> By rushing into pleasure; but oh, peace!
> Calm, sweet-souled peace! that left me with a sigh
> Which seemed like parting from a heavenly guest,
> When first I trod the burning path of passion.
> Passion is brief, and dies; but from its grave
> Rises a mighty demon, strong to curse,
> The vampire-fiend—Remorse, which lives on crime,
> Till by degrees the struggling spirit writhes
> Beneath the clinging of its twining flames,
> Like Laocoon in serpent folds fast wreathed.
> Guilt is a leprosy to every thought,—
> Makes memory a hell, and hope a fear;
> Turns daylight into torture, gives to night
> A silence far more terrible than day,

With her accusing voices.
                              My own voice sounds
Like to a judge who on a seat which groans
Beneath the weight of his own conscious crimes
Dooms some poor maddened homicide to die
For blind revenge, while he feels every word
Strike on his heart self-condemnation !
Not midnight yet? Is there no day to come ?
Will an eternal darkness rest on time,
With intermittent flashes of a storm
Alone to show us what we hate to see ?
Faith is a fearless thing.   Once in the night
When, *like a serpent by an angel's side,*
I lay by Bertha, suddenly there came
A tempest roaring through the waste of heaven;
The crash of thunders bursting o'er my head
Scared sleep away.   I started up; a flood
Of fiery lightning rushed across my sight.
I closed my eyes in horrible dismay !
Again the thunder revelled in a roar
Which shook the murky vault.   Aghast I fell
Back on my pillow, like a trembling wretch
Who begs for mercy crouching to a fiend:
While that sweet soul, calm in her innocence,
And strong in faith, said, in her *starry voice.*
' I trust no peasant is abroad to-night !' "

This picture of the strong man, feeble from guilt, and the
gentle female, " strong in faith," lying one beside the other,—he
" like a serpent by an angel's side," and she unsuspecting, ever
loving, and expressing kindly fears for her fellow-creatures
with her " starry voice,"—is extremely beautiful.   It is one of
those domestic, yet passionate and poetical emanations of the
heart, for which Mr. Powell will establish a fame, if he will
but take pains to write all worthily.   " Starry voice" may stand
side by side with the famous " starry Galileo" of Lord Byron ;
not obviously so, or to common eyes,—but with all those who see
into the depths of feeling, and who recognize the true imagination with which the author, by this single word, shows the
immense gulf existing between turbulent earthly passion and
the celestial superiority of goodness.
    Leonhard continues :—

            " Oh ! for some spot
Where I could lie and gasp my soul away
In the slow stupifying drowse of death !
And as my spirit fell into the dark,
Some *gleaming* god would say, with soothing voice,

' The past's a dream ; the future is asleep
Without a dream ; and thou, dead soul, art nothing.'
    (*He takes up a book, turns over the leaves listlessly, and
        then throws it down in disgust.*)
This page I've read to her a thousand times,
And now it *open sprang as though alive,*
To curse me with its presence !   Sorrowful
And vain the labour spent in old pursuits,
However once enjoyed, once prized, once loved,
When a guilt-stricken spirit turns the leaves.
Oh ! what a contrast to the joys that were,
But are not now.   The glow of Poesie
Has died away : Apollo's laurels hang,
All withered, down a sad and tear-worn face ;
His kindling glance has gone, his harp is broken ;
The music has departed, and the voice
Comes like the haunting memories of a ghost,
Which has no rest in an unquiet grave.
Thought rolls on thought, as black and sluggish throes
Which have no shore to rest their toiling on,
No sand to die on, like a weary wave
That ever labouring, moaning, heaving on,
Is part of the eternal, restless sea.
What a glad thing a ragged beggar is !
The man who yesterday asked alms of me,
As I was loitering near the Rolandspeck,
Lost in a vision of my earlier days,
Seemed like *a man :* his look was bold and free;
Joy was a plant firm-rooted in his heart,
Putting its leaves and flowers forth to the sky
And sun-bright air.   I saw it,—marked it well,
By the strong quiet of his steadfast eye ;
And as I flung a golden coin it seemed
A world to him.   Alas ! how little he
Supposed the wealthy donor groaned within
That he was not the beggar !   Rank, power, wealth,
Are but *accumulations of despair*
And active miseries to guilty souls !
Beggars alone are happy."—(p. 120.)

The author, we think, had better have said *sadly* than " list-
lessly," when speaking of Leonhard's turning over the leaves
of the book ; and *despair* instead of " disgust."   " Listless-
ness" and " disgust" are words too capricious, leisurely, and
superior to the occasion.   True wretchedness does not give
itself such airs.   But how beautiful and affecting are the
withered bay-leaves hanging down the dreary face of poetry,
and the truth (to the poor wealthy wretch), uttered neverthe-

less with so much of his characteristic will and pleasure, that "beggars alone are happy!"

Leonhard again resumes, "looking up and fixing his eye on a picture of a German warrior, ancestor of Bertha."

"How terribly that warrior scowls on me!
The torture of that dull and fixed dead stare,
Searching with shrouded gaze into my heart,
Like to a fiend who has *the hate of hell,*—
The justice of a God! A painter there
Stood for a few short hours, and plied his hands,
Active with malice, and upon the wall
Left that dead face to blast me! But I could
Rip it to shreds, and in a moment's time,
With this sharp steel of mine, now bared before me.
And yet I pause: I dare not strike a picture,
For fear of something standing armed behind
That fragile canvas. Ha! the picture moves!
No; it was but my fancy; yet the eyes
Have all the venom of a human look.
  (*Enter* JULIA *in her night-dress.*)
What noise is that? (*Sees* JULIA.)
Bertha! and from her grave! Alive in death!
Avaunt, and spare me! spare your——"

Readers, indeed, who are intimate with the old and modern drama, will agree with us in thinking that Mr. Powell, while he is terribly deficient in the former's constant weight of matter, especially when most needed, and takes no pains to supply it to his dialogue in ordinary, is superior to almost all his contemporaries in his faith in the sufficiency of passion, and the simplicity of its words. When occasion is wanting to him, he is wanting to occasion; but when it comes, he has the very best and most trusting inclination to meet it; he has nothing to do but to go to his studies, possess himself of our noblest writers of all kinds, read the best critics on composition, acquire, in short, all the information that becomes him, and end in being a fine dramatic poet.

But he must do this at once, and with no subsequent effort to escape from the glorious necessity. Neither must he resort to any tricks of propitiation, or of any other sort, with critics, readers, or any body. It must be all true work, plain and above-board, and without any intention or purpose but the love of the task, and the glory of proving it. Does he think any poet ever did without it? There used to be a fancy that Shakspeare did; that he was a "wild irregular genius," coming "staring from the woods," like the Satyr in the poet, seizing a pen like an inspired Caliban, and sitting down with brutish ignorance to write like a god! Why, if any fault be attributable to him, it is that he writes too learnedly; we do not mean in the scholarly sense (though he wrote in that too); but with too incessant a pressure and abundance of thoughts and images, collected from every available source of his time, every book that he could read, every custom that he could see or hear of. The greatest geniuses are precisely those who know that they are nothing in comparison with the greatness of Nature, and who, therefore, in speaking of her, take all the modest pains they can to speak not unwisely. Spenser, to all the learning given him by a University education, joined the accomplishments of French and Italian. So did Chaucer. Milton, before he wrote "Paradise Lost," expressly hoped to do it only by means of "intense study" joined to "natural inclination," and the assistance of Heaven itself. Raphael made study after study before he set about a picture,—studies of bones, studies of muscles, studies of drapery. One of the proofs of this modest industry was to be found in three successive drawings among those which formed the collection of Sir Thomas Lawrence (lost, we are ashamed to say, to this country, now, or at least the greater part of it;—sold to Russians, and to Dutchmen!) Michael Angelo, Leonardo da Vinci, Claude, Poussin, the Carracci, Plato, Bacon, Dante, Ariosto, Tasso, Boccaccio, were studying all their lives. Ariosto wrote the opening of the "Orlando Furioso" twenty times over before he could satisfy himself. Burns has been erroneously called an uneducated man. He was not only as well educated as most of the gentry of his day, apart from those brought up at colleges, but better perhaps than most; for he had a literary tutor; and what he wanted, he did his best to supply with books of his own. His English prose style is even too ambitious.

The first business of a dramatist, (as of any other poet,) supposing him to possess a sufficient portion or promise of imagination and passion to set out with, is to have a subject to which he is strongly inclined, and which is suitable to his genius; for inclination even in genius does not always imply ability. Shakspeare himself did not succeed in narrative poetry as he did in dramatic. His "Venus and Adonis," and "Rape of Lucrece," are rather heaps of reflections than stories. Marlowe made a sad, lumbering, unartistical business of "Hero and Leander;" and Chapman continued it, and made it worse. It is in all probability lucky for Spenser, that his "Comedies" have not come down to us. Pope once had an intention of writing an Epic on Brutus! Most fortunate was it for his reputation that he did not. It would have threatened to cast an unwieldy shade even on the exquisite " Rape of the Lock," Not Addison's " Cato" could have been worse. Addison was a great wit, a fine observer, and had a charming prose style, though a little too much betraying its system. As a poet (though he began with being no unpleasing translator of the " Georgics") he is absolutely worthless, except in one bit of versified wit, and in putting an occasional moral point. But to return to the writer before us. No fault is to be found with Mr. Powell, in respect to the main subject of his dramas. They suit admirably his eager but home-loving turn of mind, and augur well for his choice in future.

The poet's next business is to make himself thoroughly acquainted with character and manner, and every species of verisimilitude. He must neither make deaf people talk as if they heard, nor the blind as if they saw. There Mr. Powell has failed; and it is a notable failure, and such as, we trust, he will never repeat.

Style is the poet's next concern,—a natural and passionate language, expressing images to the purpose, and containing nothing forced, affected, superfluous, prosaical, or conventional. He is not to strain after thoughts, like a schoolboy; the thoughts ought to arise happily from his feelings. He is not to confound the familiar common places and conventional metaphors of every-day discourse with ease and artlessness; neither is he to take a mere contradiction to them for something profound and apposite. It is much easier to over-think a poem than is imagined, and very dangerous. It leads a writer into a slough of irrelevances and errors,—into making a great splashing noise to no purpose,—into missing the end of his journey and disgusting his observers, by the ambition of turning every step into an object of astonishment. The great point is to think *just enough;* and this will be attained if the feeling be true, the acquirements fitting, and the object single-hearted. We have more than once observed, that Mr. Powell's language is of excellent promise, as far as concerns brevity and straightforwardness, and (in his dramas) a total freedom from affectation. Let him but devote two hours a day to study for a year to come, and we shall be surprised if he does not produce, not a hasty bit of a drama in one act, or a mixture of slovenliness and passion in a larger one, but an excellent solid play, fit to meet any critical investigation. But the brevity of concentrated passion, and the haste to get through a task, are two very different things.

We take leave of Mr. Powell for the present, with a couplet from one " Dr. Lluellin," who, from his just idea of what a poet ought to be, deserves to have been better known. May the poet whom our article has been rebuking with regret, and praising with great hope and admiration, hang it up in the heart of his *study* :—

> " A poet's then exact in every part,
> That is born one by nature, *nurst by art.*"

269

1. *Aus dem Leben eines Taugenichts.* (Fragments from the Biography of a Scamp.) By JOSEPH BARON VON EICHENDORFF. Berlin. 1842.

2. *Wien vor vierhundert Jahren.* (Vienna Four Centuries ago.) A Novel in 2 volumes, by EDWARD BREIER. Vienna. 1842.

3. *Der Missionär.* (The Missionary.) A Novel, by A. VON STERNBERG. Leipzig. 1842.

4. *Die Familie Treuenfels.* (A Tale of the Thirty Years' War.) By M. RICHTER. Leipzig. 1841.

5. *Novellen.* (Tales.) By BRUNS HENRICUS. Leipzig. 1841.

6. *Historischer Roman.* (An Historical Novel.) By FR. LUBOJATZKY. Vols. I. and II. Grimma. 1841.

7. *Das Blutende Herz von Christburg.* (The Bleeding Heart of Christburg.) An Historical Novel of the Olden Time of Prussia. By FERDINAND SCHREIBER. Meissen. 1841.

8. *Graf Ladroni, oder die Todtenkrone.* An Historical and Romantic Picture of the Time of the Thirty Years' War. By ERNST SCHUBERT. Leipzig. 1841.

9. *Die Schwarzen Hausren.* (The Black Hussars.) By AUGUST LEIBROCK. Leipzig. 1841.

10. *Xenia, Tochter des Grossfürsten Boris Godunow von Russland.* (Xenia, Daughter of the Grand Duke Godunow of Russia. By J. SARTORI. Danzig. 1842.

11. *Aus der Schule des Lebens.* (From the School of Life.) By A. QUEDNOW. Stuttgart. 1842.

12. *Linchen, oder Erziehungsresultate.* (The Result of Education.) By DR. SCHIFF. Hamburg. 1841.

13. *Der Kerkermeister.* (The Gaoler.) By F. M. WANGENHEIM. Leipzig. 1842.

14. *Die Seelenverkäufer.* (The Soul Sellers.) By F. M. WANGENHEIM. 3 vols. Brunswick. 1841.

15. *Myosotis.* By AMELIA VON SCHOPPE, geborne Weise. Leipzig. 1841.

16. *Die Verwandten in Copenhagen.* (Our Relations in Copenhagen.) By PENSOROSO. 3 vols. Leipzig. 1841.

17. *Ibrahim Pascha.* An Historical Picture of the Seventeenth Century. By GEORGE. Leipzig. 1841.

18. *Die Marquise de Noverre.* By M. DOERING. Leipzig. 1842.

19. *Novellen.* (Tales.) By JULIUS SEIDLITZ. Leipzig. 1842.

20. *Hygea und Eros. Ein Cyklus interressanter Badegeschichten von* BOHEMUS. 3 vols. Leipzig. 1842.

21. *Mein Wanderbuch.* (My Roadbook.) By C. HERLOSSOHN. 2 vols. Leipzig. 1842.

22. *Grenzer, Narren, und Lootsen.* (Borderers, Fools, and Pilots.) By ERNST WILLCOMM. 2 vols. Leipzig. 1842.

23. *Erzstufen für* 1842. (A Collection of Tales.) By IDA FRICK. Dresden. 1842.

24. *Die Bandomire.* By HEINRICH LAUBE. 2 vols. Mitau. 1842.

25. *Die drei Schwestern.* (The Three Sisters.) A Novel, by CHR. LYNX. Leipzig. 1842.

26. *Das Schloss Loevestein im Jahre* 1570. (The Castle of Loevestein in 1570. An Historical Novel of the Eighty Years' War.) By J. VAN DER HAGE. 3 vols.

27. *Skizzen aus der vornehmen Welt.* (Sketches of High Life.) Vol. I. Breslau. 1842.

28. *Abendfahrten auf den Lagunen.* (Evening Excursions on the Lagoons.) An Historical Novel, from the papers of a celebrated Cantatrice, by GEORG LOTZ. 3 vols. Hamburg. 1842.

29. *Das Tyroler Bauernspiel.* (The Peasant Game of the Tyrol.) Characteristic Pictures of the years from 1809 to 1816. 2 vols. Magdeburg. 1841.

30. *Vier und zwanzig Stunden.* (Twenty-four Hours.) By C. DRAEXLER-MANFELD. Leipzig. 1842.

31. *Die Juden und die Kreuzfahrer in England, unter Richard Loewenherz.* (The Jews and the Crusaders in England, under Richard Cœur de Lion.) By EUGEN RISPART. 2 vols. Leipzig. 1841.

32. *Don Carlos, Prätendent von Spanien.* (Don Carlos, the Spanish Pretender.) By H. E. R. BELANI. 3 vols. Leipzig. 1842.

33. *Der Zögling der Natur.* (The Pupil of Nature.) A Novel, by L. MUEHLBACH. Altona. 1842.

34. *Gesammelte Novellen* (The Collected Tales) of FRANZ BERTHOLD. Edited by LUDWIG TIECK. 2 vols. Leipzig. 1842.

AMONG the tales and novels of which the titles have here been enumerated, there are many of which it would be most charitable to say nothing, and of which the only redeeming quality is their brevity. The German novelist is not bound, like his fellow-labourer in London, to the prescribed length of three volumes, but may make his story as short or as long as he will, limiting himself, at his pleasure, to two volumes, to one, or even sending his little narratives out to the world by six or eight at a time, when each is too diminutive to be ushered forth by itself. In the above list, there are but few tales that occupy more than one volume, and that volume is mostly a dwarf compared to the bulky tomes issued in such quick succession from the factories of Marlborough-street or Burlington-street.

The Baron von Eichendorff's Scamp is but a half-and-half vagabond. The German word *Taugenichts* is far too severe for him, for the fellow *is* good for something; he can play the fiddle, and not only earn his own livelihood, but afford good entertainment to the Baron's readers. Eichendorff was hardly the man to paint a scamp; for the worst scamp, in passing through his hands, had certainly been converted into something upon which, though we might not esteem it, we should be sure to look indulgently. Eichendorff has long been an active contributor to the light literature of his country ; and all his works, whether in verse or prose, preserve the same good-humoured, easy-going character that has recommended him to the kindness and indulgence of idle and uncritical readers. The Baron wants vigour, and many things beside; but he has a certain grace and humorous badinage, which appear nowhere to more advantage than in his smaller poems, of which a collection was published at Berlin in 1837. The tale now before us is neatly told ; but, if we mistake not, has been printed before, and that nearly twenty years ago. The present edition has nothing new about it, we believe, but the clever illustrations from the pencil of Schrödter, of Düsseldorf.

Sternberg's ' Missionary ' is a Moravian, who wanders forth on his mission of love to the new world. The scene opens immediately after the death of Zinzendorf, the founder of the sect, who at his death bequeathed his spiritual authority over his disciples to his daughter Sarah. At least the elders of the sect had not been able to gather more than that, from the feeble and imperfectly articulated words of the dying man. Zinzendorf, however, had left three daughters, each named Sarah, and the difficulty was, to know which of them the father had intended for his successor. The elders, after much deliberation, decided in favour of the youngest, a widow residing in Paris, who made her appearance among the plain and unsophisticated flock of Zinzendorf, with a splendid equipage, and a host of servants. The embarrassments of the lady herself in so unsuitable a situation, and still more the embarrassments of the flock, have been woven by the author into an interesting narrative, well worthy of the repute he had before acquired.

Sternberg has now been about ten years before the German public as a novelist. His first work was *Fortunat*, a fairy tale, which has been rapidly followed by a multitude of tales, none of which can be said to betray any marks of the haste with which they must have been prepared for the press. His *Die Zerrissenen* had a great success, and the word itself became a password in familiar conversation throughout Germany. His *Lessing* has likewise enjoyed popularity, notwithstanding its constant violation of local and historical truth. His *Molière*, intended as a companion to *Lessing*, was, comparatively speaking, a failure. But in all his works we find good taste and a fertility of invention, while his dialogues are full of spirit, and often the happiest aphorisms are put into the mouths of his characters. It is in his shorter tales, however, that Sternberg is most happy; when he has attempted to expand his subject into a novel of several volumes, he has seldom been equally successful.

The Family of Treuenfels is from the pen of an author who after a long interval comes again before the public, but with a work by no means calculated to support his former reputation. Something better might have been expected from one to whom we owe the *Old Man of Fronteja*, and *Kurt der Jägerburche*.

Lubojatzky's Historical Novel is a striking and well-drawn picture of the state of society in Paris before the revolution of 1830. The conclusion of the work is yet to come; and though there can be little of suspense as to the winding up of a tale founded on events of such recent date, we must condemn this piecemeal system of publication. Who will not have forgotten the incidents of the first two volumes when the third appears?

Xenia is from a well-known pen, but will not add to the reputation of the authoress. Sartori is only an assumed name; the lady's real name is Neumann.

The School of Life, by Quednow, appears to be the *coup d'essai* of a young author, who possesses information and good perceptive power, but after making an excellent plot, has spoiled it in the working out. There is much that is really promising in this little tale.

Blood, murder, robbery, incest, perjury, seduction, madness, blasphemy, and bombast, are mingled in edifying confusion to make up Wangenheim's Gaoler, a concatenation of horrors suited to the morbid taste of a certain class of readers, but utterly revolting to common sense and good feeling.

Dr. Schiff's novel of *Linchen* deserves notice only on account of the dishonest manner in which the author and the public have been dealt with by the publisher. Dr. Schiff some years ago published a tale under the title of *Lie Ohrfeige*. The thing had no more success than it deserved, but the copyright having passed in due time into the hands of another bookseller, a new titlepage was printed, and the old tale put forward under the new title of *Linchen*. The author published a declaration in the newspapers, with a view to exonerate himself from all participation in so gross a fraud; but the speculating man of trade came forth with a rejoinder, in which he insinuated that the author had been a consenting party to the trick. A

fraud precisely similar has been played by another German bookseller with August Lewald's *Seydelmann und das deutsche Schauspiel*, which has just been brought out as a new book, under the title of *Seydelmann, ein Erinnerungsbuch für seine Freunde*.

Amalia von Schoppe's novels already fill from 120 to 130 volumes, though the lady has scarcely been more than fifteen years before the public; and though she is a woman of talent, it is not surprising that her works should be hastily planned and very imperfectly finished. The collection of tales published under the title of 'Myosotis,' bears the usual characteristics of Amalia's former writings. Her historical tales show extensive reading, and just enough power to make us regret that so little pains should be expended on them. Among her writings none is calculated to excite more interest than the *Erinnerungen aus meinem Leben*, published in 1838, in which there is no doubt, her own history is represented under that of Clementine. If so, she presents herself to the public as a woman of no ordinary character, intelligent, but unimpassioned, of a frank and energetic disposition, and devoid of prudery and false sentiment. A son of Amalia von Schoppe, we perceive, has lately come before the public as a translator from the French.

Mein Wanderbuch is a lively story enough, with some good pictures of modern manners.

Willkomm is a favourite, and deservedly. He is most successful where a bold landscape forms the background to his pictures. His borderers, on the present occasion, are the mountaineers between Bohemia and Lusatia; his pilots are the denizens of the island rock Heligoland.

Ida Frick's writings, so far as literary worth goes, cannot be ranked above the commonplace, but it is impossible not to sympathize with her evident wish to raise her own sex by an improved system of education. She is an advocate for female emancipation, but her object is not a subversion of existing social relations. She envies her male friends the greater freedom they enjoy, but does so only because she sees in that freedom the means of obtaining greater knowledge, and a more vigorous development of mind. This longing to overbound the limits prescribed to the sphere of woman, is in our authoress free from all frivolity, and seems to be the result of a feeling that has manifested itself only at a mature period of life. In the collection of tales here presented to us, there is little either to praise or condemn.

The *Bandomire* is an excellent subject well treated; the story is full of happy situations, and the interest admirably sustained to the last. The provincial history of Courland, where the scene is laid, is turned to good account, but more skill might have been shown in blending the fictitious with the historical portion of the novel. Laube, the author, is one of the writers of 'Young Germany.' He has had the honour of being thrown into prison; and, as all his works were prohibited, they had for several years to be published anonymously; but Laube has outlived the days of persecution, his former offences are forgotten, and he is now known, less as a political demagogue, than as one of the best tale-writers of his time. Among his most successful works are: *Das junge Europa*, *Die Schauspielerinn*, *Moderne Charakteristiken*, and his *Görres und Athanasius*, a pamphlet on the religious disputes raised by the collision between the King of Prussia and the Archbishop of Cologne.

Das Schloss Loevestein is a translation from the Dutch. The novel appeared in Holland in 1839, and its great success there has caused several translations to appear simultaneously in Germany. The work is unquestionably one of very high merit, but there is no probability that it will ever excite anywhere else the interest which has been manifested for it in Holland.

The authoress of Sketches of High Life and of *Schloss Goczyn* may be reckoned among the best living lady writers of Germany. This first volume of a new series comprises the history of a young authoress, who is introduced to us under the name of Maria von Unruh. The scene is laid at the country-seat of a nobleman, where the young lady is expected as a visiter. A strong prejudice is awakened against her. Among some she is disliked merely because she writes; others are determined to keep aloof from her because they expect to find her supercilious and vain. Among those most prejudiced is the young Count of Solms. Maria appears, and her gentle and unaffected manners win for her every heart. The young Count becomes her warm admirer, offers her his hand, is accepted, and then seeks to extort from her a promise not again to write. Maria feels the demand as an insult, refuses to unite her fate with one who thus intimates a condemnation of her former career, and is soon convinced that what she had taken in herself for love, was merely admiration of the Count's personal advantages and agreeable manners. The Count travels away to digest his mortification, and the young lady is soon taught to distinguish between real affection and a passing caprice. Several secondary characters are grouped around the principal personages, and the whole forms an extremely pretty tale.

The works of Georg Lotz are certainly commonplace, but the wonder is that a man who throughout the greater part of his life has been blind and deprived of the use of all his limbs, should not only hold his place among the fertile novelists of the day, but should for several years past have edited a periodical, a great part of which is entirely of his own composition. The constant occupation in which his mind is thus kept, has prevented him from sinking into despondency, and strangers who visit him are astonished at the cheerful and lively conversation of one, who, unable to stir from his chair without assistance, and unblessed with the light of heaven, continues, nevertheless, by his mental exertions, to maintain himself and his family in honourable comfort. It has been the fortune of Lotz to find in his wife, a woman who, since he was overtaken by affliction, has softened the bitter cup by the most unremitting devotion. His amanuensis and his nurse alternately, she passes nearly every moment of the day by his side, and though she declines every invitation that would for a moment remove her from the performance of a never-ceasing task, she does not fail to make her house as attractive as her means allow, to those who by visiting her husband, relieve in some measure the monotony of his life. Lotz's writings, as we have said, do not rise above mediocrity, but who could have the heart to judge otherwise than indulgently, of what has been written under circumstances apparently so adverse to literary composition?

The *Tyroler Bauernspeil* is a work of merit by an anonymous author, who evidently knows the Tyrol well. Andreas Hofer, and the other heroes of the Tyrolese war, are sketched with a bold and animated pencil, and the local dialect and picturesque scenery are turned to good account.

Deutsche Dichter des Gegenwart. (German Poets of the Present Time.) By AUGUSTUS NODNAGEL. Darmstadt: Diehl. 1842.

AMONG the difficulties which offer themselves to the student of a foreign literature, none are greater than that of knowing what is actually going on at the present time, and the opinion which is entertained of modern poets in their own country. M. Nodnagel's book, if continued in the manner in which it is begun (for it is published in numbers) will be found even more useful in England than in his own country. He gives a biography of the German poets of the day, with specimens of their works : illustrated with copious notes, and a *resumé* of all the critiques upon them, *pro* and *con*, which have appeared in the various periodicals. Thus, with a very little trouble, is the reader put into the possession of a quantity of information, which, without such assistance, it would be impossible to obtain. The first number treats of Freiligrath and Eidendorff, and a notice of the most celebrated living poets is promised.

Handbuch des poetischen Nationalliteratur der Deutschen, von Dr. HEINRICH KURZ. (Manual of the Poetical National Literature of the Germans). By Dr. H. KURZ. Zurich. Meyer and Zeller. 1842.

ALL collections of specimens from the masters of a foreign literature are useful in England, if they are made with ordinary judgment. By works of this kind is the student able to take a general glance at the various authors, and to decide on the particular path he will afterwards follow. Dr. Kurz's book is sufficiently large to allow of the glance being more than a superficial one. It is a thick royal octavo, containing selections from the time of Haller to the present day, and concludes with a tolerably full history of German poetry; the dates of births and deaths being given in notes. Most of the pieces are necessarily short, but not exclusively so; as we have the whole of Göthe's 'Iphigenia,' and 'Hermann and Dorothea;' of Schiller's 'Wilhelm Tell;' and of Lessing's 'Nathan der Weise.' The reader who has gone through Dr. Kurz's Manual, will find very few in this country who will rival him in a knowledge of German poetry.

1. *Sieben Bücher Deutscher Sagen und Le-genden. In Alten und Neuen Dichtungen.* (Seven Books of German Traditions and Legends. In Ancient and Modern Poems). Edited by August Nodnagel. Darmstadt. 1839.

2. *Die Volksagen Ostpreussens Litthauens und Westpreussens.* (Popular Traditions of East Prussia, Lithuania, and West Prussia). Collected by W. J. A. von Tettau and J. D. H. Temme. Berlin : Nicolai. 1837.

3. *Sagen und Märchen aus Potsdam's Vorzeit.* (Traditions and Tales from Potsdam's Former Times). Collected by Karl v. Reinhard. Potsdam : Stuhr. 1841.

4. *Schlesischer Historien-Sagen-und Legenden Schatz.* (Silesian Treasury of Histories, Traditions, and Legends). Edited by Hermann Goedsche. Misnia.

5. *Die Volksagen Märchen und Legenden des Kaiserstaates Oesterreich.* (The Popular Traditions, Tales and Legends of the Imperial State Austria). Collected and edited by Ludwig Beckstein. Leipsig : Polet. 1841.

6. *Polnische Volksagen und Märchen aus dem Pölnischen des K. W. Weycicki.* (Polish Popular Traditions and Tales, translated from the Polish of K. M. Weycicki). By T. H. Lewestain. Berlin : Schlesinger. 1839.

7. *Die Sagen der Stadt Stendal in der Altmark.* (The Traditions of the City of Stendal in the Old Mark). By E. Weihe. Tängermünde : Doeger. 1840.

That the people of Germany are essentially lovers of poetry, few readers who devote any attention to the progress of publication in that country, will for an instant doubt. Nor is their fondness for the productions of the divine art limited to the masterpieces of its greatest professors. The nation, like their own Herder, recognizing the voice of the many—the very germ of poetry—in the national songs and traditions of all countries, receive with warmest satisfaction every fresh accession of ballads and legendary lore, which the most persevering industry of their writers can contribute to literature.

Nor are these endeavours made by the German literati to supply that demand which exists for works illustrative of the literature of the people, limited to a careful gathering up of the songs and tales, with which the boundless fertility of the national imagination has stored every corner of the empire; or to translation into the language of their Fatherland of the various collections of national tales, traditions, and ballads, which appear from time to time among the literary productions of foreign countries. Dwelling with affectionate delight on those old wives' legends, with the recital of which they were accustomed in their earlier years to while away the dull, dark evenings of winter, we find the numerous poets and poetasters of Germany ever and anon employing themselves, according to their several gifts, in turning into playful, and sometimes touching stanzas of their own, such favoured portions of the popular literature.

Göthe, Schiller, Tieck, have not disdained the task of marrying to immortal verse many of these wild and imaginative fictions; and it seems to be a favourite practice with the minor poets of Germany to find the themes of their poetic exercises in the legendary treasures of their native land. Some publish these sportive effusions in separate volumes, while others are contented to employ them in giving a varied interest to the numerous pocket-books and periodicals with which Germany is inundated.

The first work before us, is an attempt to collect into one body these fanciful and widely-scattered productions of the German muse : an attempt for which the editor is entitled to the best thanks of all those readers who are content, like ourselves, to find in the innocence and simplicity which characterize them, glimpses of those good old times—those golden days, when 'love and all the world was young.' The collection is divided into seven books, containing altogether nearly three hundred different poems : comprising legends connected with the world of waters, and the nixes and water-sprites who haunt seas, rivers, and lakes; legends of giants, kobolds, and other 'black spirits and white;' fictions which turn upon that supernatural prolonging of human life of which the Wandering Jew furnishes eternal example, and upon the power which some mortals have possessed of revisiting the world; local traditions; poems based upon historical materials; and legends and miracles of the saints.

The other collections which follow M. Nodnagel's book, in the formidable list above this article, are so many testimonials of the love of tradition in all parts of Germany. Sometimes large districts, sometimes cities, have furnished legends that constitute the material of so many separate works. From the Sclavonic provinces of Prussia, from Potsdam, from Austria, from the Old Mark, have these industrious antiquaries come forward with their stores; while one of them makes addition to the legendary riches of his own country by translation from the Polish. The authors have given their legends in every possible form. MM. Tettau and Temme adopt the dry style, and give the tradition itself, true and unembellished. Their object is not to amuse but to contribute to early history; and though their book is not a very readable one, the dark lights which their legends throw on the condition of a race which has now almost ceased to exist, the Lithuanian race of Prussia, are exceedingly interesting to any one who will study the subject. The Polish traditions are given as works of art; the dry legend being worked up into a pleasing tale by M. Weycicki. This collection, which is singularly wild and poetical, is, as a book of amusement, the most attractive of them all. In the Austrian legends, by L. Bechstein, who has considerable reputation as an antiquary, the dry style again prevails; while those of Potsdam form a sort of *juste milieu.* The Stendal traditions are divided into two parts: one containing the legends in verse, and the other following the popular style in which they are told. The 'Treasury' from Silesia fluctuates between the dry and the entertaining. This is a very carefully compiled book : each chapter being headed with a chronological table, so as to show the events of the period to which the traditions refer.

The whole mass of traditions will be most serviceable to the antiquary in northern history and superstition; but we most distinctly warn the general reader that the German is a serious personage, and that when he intends to give information, he does not care to mix the *dulce* with the *utile*. Nodnagel's Collection, the 'Traditions of the Rhine,' and Weycicki's 'Legends,' are all entertaining enough; having been especially adapted, chiefly by modern authors, to the amusement of the modern reader. But with the real grave book of tradition, the case is quite different,—and we can fancy the look of a reader, who having formed his notion of legends on Croker's 'Irish Tales,' or some work of the kind, opens the collection of MM. Tettau and Temme!

Our translation of the following specimens, of which the first is from the pen of W. C. Muller, will serve better than any description to show the manner in which the traditionary materials in Nodnagel's collection are worked up.

THE MONK OF HEISTERBACH.

A young monk once, in cloister Heisterbach,
  Its pleasant garden's furthest paths explored;
His thoughts upon Eternity fell back,
  He sought its meaning in God's Holy Word;

And pondered o'er what Peter once did say—
  'A day to God is as a thousand years,
A thousand years to Him are as a day'—
  Till straight his mind was torn by doubts and fears.

Thus lost in thought he paced each forest dell,
  Yet heedless still of every object there,
Until he heard the solemn Vesper Bell
  Summon him home to join at Even prayer.

In haste he runs to gain the garden door—
  A stranger at the portal met his view—
He starts—yet sees the old church as of yore,
  And hears those holy songs so well he knew.

So in the choir quick seeks his well-known place:
  More wondrous still—a stranger fills his chair—
Nor does he see one old familiar face
  Among the brotherhood assembled there.

Frighted himself, he scatters fear around;
  They ask his name—he tells it, and straight hears
A murmur rise, that throughout Christendom,
  No one has borne it for three hundred years.

'He who last bore it was a doubter, and
  He disappeared once in yon forest old.
Since then the name has perished in the land—'
  He hears them, and his heart's best blood runs cold

He nameth now the Abbot, now the Year,
  They search the cloister's musty records o'er,
And, wondrous! he's the very man, 'tis clear,
  Who disappeared three centuries before.

Withered by fright, and suddenly turned grey,
  He sinks—and sorrow killing him apace,
He dying warns the monks who round him pray,
  'God is exalted above time and space!

'What He concealed, a miracle now clears!
  Doubt not, but warning take by me, who say
I know, a day is as a thousand years
  To God—a thousand years is as a day.'

The next, which is of a more playful character, is by Kopisch, a writer who possesses a very extraordinary facility of versification. We have ventured to make a slight alteration in its title, by turning the 'Wasserman' of the original into a Water Sprite: the more strict interpretation of 'Waterman' being unfortunately suggestive to English ears of nothing more poetical than a saucy man in plush unmentionables.

GAFFER MICHAEL AND THE WATER SPRITE.

Gaffer Michael and the Water Sprite
  Had dealings fair and good,
So well they dealt, they drank that night
  Eternal brotherhood.
What brotherhood with a Water Sprite!
What good can ever come of it?

They ate together from the dish,
  Together drank their wine:
'Gaffer Michael, an' thou likest fish,
  Be thou a guest of mine.'
Ay, eat fish with a Water Sprite!
Who knows what good may come of it?

Gaffer Michael dived beneath the stream,
  Well Michael marked the road;
All glazed with glass, as it did seem,
  Was the Sprite's abode.
He went in with the Water Sprite—
Who knows what good may come of it?

They ate the best, they drank the best,
  Till the Water Sprite was fou',
When Michael boldly him addressed,
  'Thine house pray let me view?'
'Right gladly,' quoth the Water Sprite,
Who knows what good may come of it?

And as they went up stairs and down,
  How Michael stared to see
Jars piled on jars each chamber round,
  'What can this mean!' quoth he.
'Good store of jars, Sir Water Sprite,
You have, but what's the good of it?'

'Why in them,' quoth the Water Sprite,
  And in his sleeve laughed he,
'I keep the soul of every wight
  Who's drowned in flood or sea.'
Thought Michael, 'Now, Sir Water Sprite,
I know there may come good of it!'

The readers of Crofton Croker's 'Fairy Legends of the South of Ireland' will remember the story of the 'Soul Cages.' The song of Michael and the Water Sprite terminates in the same way, and we may here therefore, not inappropriately, bring our notice of these amusing and interesting volumes to a close—without further taxing our rhyming powers, or the patience of our readers.

275

Art. XI.—1. F. L. Z. Werner's *Sämmtliche Werke.* (Werner's Collective Works.) 12 vols. Berlin. 1840.

2. Franz Grillparzer: Dieterich Christian Grabbe: *Dramatische Werke.* Frankfort and Vienna. 1820, 1840.

3. Immermann's *Dramatische Werke. Merlin: Das Trauerspiel in Tyrol* (The Tragedy in the Tyrol): *Alexis. Die Opfer der Schweigens.* (The Victims of Silence.) Hamburg. Hoffman and Campe. 1837, 1841.

4. E. Raupach's *Dramatische Werke: Ernster Gattung—Dramatische Werke: Komischer Gattung.* Hamburg. Hoffman and Campe. 1829, 1842.

5. *Original-Beiträge zur deutschen Schaubühne.* (Original Contributions to the German Theatre. By the Princess Amelia of Saxe.) Dresden. Arnold. 1836, 1842.

7. *Griseldis.* (Griselda.) *Der Adept.* (The Alchymist.) *Camoens.* (The Death of Camoens.) *Ein milder Urtheil.* (A Mild Judgment.) *Imilda Lambertazzi. König und Bauer.* (King and Peasant.) *Der Sohn der Wildness.* (The Son of the Desert.) Plays by Friedrich Halm. Vienna: Gérold. 1836, 1843.

7. Ferdinand Raimund's *Sämmtliche Schriften.* 4 vols. Vienna: Rohrmann's. 1837.

A review of the Modern German Stage is not an easy, and very far from an agreeable task. Since the silence or death of Lessing, Schiller, and Göthe—that is to say, for the last forty or fifty years—no branch of German literature and art has fallen into such undeniable decay. Most others have made admitted progress: the drama alone, the youngest and the most feeble shoot of German genius, has been stunted and discouraged. Perhaps some of the causes lie upon the surface.

There is no central public in Germany: a want which has been of evil influence to many of the national interests, but to none more decidedly than to the proper cultivation and development of a national dramatic genius. The numerous German capitals—every one of them strongly indoctrinated with peculiar and distinguishable tastes; each in some sort playing rival to the other; all existing by their own special laws, manners, and customs; Vienna praising what they are laughing at in Berlin, Weimar not knowing what they admire in Frankfort—have offered little of that settled public guidance to the dramatic poet, without which the highest order of stage success can rarely be achieved. To this are to be added the operation of censorships, more especially fatal to the health of comedy, and the luckless influence of the German governments in every other point wherein they have meddled with the theatre. It was they who cumbered it with its absurdly restrictive laws; who disabled it of its few chances of control by popular influence; who effected that unhappy metamorphosis of the gay, lively, self-supporting actor, into the compelled servant of a manager, or the life-hired menial of a prince; and finally, when some daring dramatist had even braved these dangers, and with them the certainties of mutilation that awaited his work from public censor, from prince-fed actor, from ignorant critic, it was the wisdom of these governments which so ordered the system of his remuneration, as to starve him back, with as little delay as might be, into pursuits he had unwisely abandoned. 'Our pedantry is so great,' said Lessing, when he satirically deplored* this condition of things, 'that we consider boys as the only proper fabricators of theatrical wares. Men have more serious and worthy employments in the State and in the Church. What men write should beseem the gravity of men: a compendium of law and philosophy; an erudite chronicle of this or that imperial city; an edifying sermon, and such like.' But Lessing did not content himself with

---

* Dramaturgie, 1st April, 1768.

---

lamenting or with satirizing; he applied a remedy. When, by his vigorous criticism, he had demolished the slavish following of the French school, and fixed the attention of his countrymen on the great dramatic poet of England, he may be said to have created the German stage. Göthe's influence was less favourable. His 'Goetz von Berlichingen' announced his early inclination to the theatre: but of the pieces he afterwards constructed in that form, 'Egmont' and 'Clavigo' alone continue to be acted; while the greater works of 'Tasso,' 'Iphigenia,' and the incomparable 'Faust,' introduced that dangerous distinction between acted and unacted drama, which was fated to mislead so many in their approaches to the stage. The third is the greatest name in the history of the German theatre. Schiller's influence, its character, and its enduring effects, are known to all; we have lately enlarged upon them.

Once established, and its native claims allowed, a schism broke out in the dramatic literature of Germany, and two 'schools' set themselves in marked opposition: the 'romantic,' and what we should call the domestic. The last-named had its founder in Lessing, who set it up in rivalry to the French classical manner; and whose 'Sara Samson,' 'Emilia Galotti,' and other plays of the same kind, turned Göthe and Schiller in that direction: the one in his 'Clavigo,' the other in his 'Cabal and Love' (*Kabale und Liebe*), and in such episodes of his greater works as the Max and Thekla of 'Wallenstein.' But while this example strengthened the more direct followers of Lessing in the domestic school (the Ifflands and the Kotzebues), the same writers, particularly Göthe, were responsible for influences that tended strongly to what we have called the romantic school, of which the leaders were Tieck, the brothers Schlegel, Novalis, and Arnim. There is no very exact meaning in the term *romantic*, but it was the word in vogue.

The effects of this style of writing, in criticism perhaps more than in dramatic production, were adverse to the progress of the German theatre. The dramas of Tieck and Arnim were impossibilities. The thin, fantastic, cloudy world of elves and fairies, of spectres and of dreams, which had found itself so effective in the tale, the novel, or the song, showed pale and utterly out of place in the compact form of the drama. Tieck's 'Genoveva' and 'Blue Beard' were poems of imagination and a sharp original fancy, but their dramatic form was accidental: not bestowed upon them by

48. continued

qualities of their own, but by the voluntary afterthought of the poet. The same is to be said of Arnim's dramas, a new edition of which has been lately published by Wilhelm Grimm. The only one of this school, indeed, who actually found his way to the stage, was Henrich von Kleist (not to be confounded with the elder poet of the same name, Christian Eweld von Kleist), whose dramas of 'Kate from Heilbronn,' adapted for representation by Holbein, and 'The Prince of Hesse-Homburg,' are acted now and then even to this day, attracting such as have a touch of their own mysticism, but in themselves as weak and sickly as the poor poet had been, who in 1811 took to drowning out of melancholy and despair. But the critics of the school were a more formidable party than the dramatic producers. Friedrich and August Wilhelm von Schlegel, Tieck himself, Franz Horn, and others in connection with them, brought all their talents to bear against the existing German theatre, and proved a formidable impediment to its growth. Young and feeble as it was, they proposed nothing but the very strongest drink for its nurture. Shakspeare and Calderon : these were the only models they would offer for imitation; nothing short of these could be the salvation of the drama. And straightway on this Procrustes bed of criticism, modest and quiet German poets stretched themselves out, to the terrible injury of what limbs they had, and to no earthly production of any they had not. All this wrought but one result : the unnatural excess of effort introduced into the drama a deplorable affectation, a phrenetic, convulsive style, a kind of intoxication of the pathetic, which have to this day depressed and retarded it. And it is worthy of remark that at this very time, in opposition to the violent demands of Tieck, the Schlegels, and their followers, it was reserved for a writer of a more moderate genius and less exaggerated claims to prove with what far more useful results the foreign model might have been brought in aid of the native effort, if a modest, practical spirit had only guided and controlled its introduction. Schreijvogel's * pleasing translations from the Spanish drama are still acted. He was a man, we may add, of very great merit, though little known out of Germany. He was born in 1768, and was properly the creator of the first German theatre, the 'Burg-theater' at Vienna. He died in 1832: one of the first victims to the cholera. His best and most successful translations are 'Donna Diana,' from

* He wrote under the name of West.

the Spanish of Aretino Mureto ; 'Don Gutierre,' after Calderon ; and 'Life a Dream,' also after Calderon.

Meanwhile Iffland and Kotzebue had steadily and perseveringly cultivated what we have called the domestic school, the *bourgeois* drama (*das bürgerliche Schauspiel*). Both these writers are widely known; both are popular to this day with German audiences. Overflooding with his 'comédie larmoyante' every little theatre in the country, Kotzebue was too profuse and immoderate in production to care at any time for progress or elevation. Iffland, himself the best existing actor, and the head of a dramatic school, some members of which are yet living at Berlin, had a practical knowledge of the stage superior to any of his contemporaries : his motives were well marked and effective; his characters strongly individualized : but his plots were in every instance from commonplace life, and that in its most prosaic form. A bankruptcy, a gambling loss, a theft if possible : these were the catastrophes of the plays of Iffland. A generous husband, who forgives his *femme perdue;* an illegitimate son, who reconciles his mother to his father; an uncle, who arrives in the nick of time from the Indies, West or East : these were the favourite heroes of Kotzebue, whom our German friends have the most loudly applauded for upwards of thirty years. Not 'classical' tragedy this, it must be confessed; no need of the cothurnus here, to mount up the actor to the poet's requirements; here are heroes much within standard height of the Prussian soldier, and passions other than those whereat Germany might have wept with Shakspeare, or shuddered with Calderon. It may be further admitted that there is often in these writers more sterility than simplicity, less clearness than insipidity in their intentions, and of the humble much less than of the vulgar in their general scope and aim. But there was some reality to go upon ; something that made appeal to the honest German playgoer on the score of what he had felt himself; and all the idealisms on abstractions in the world went for nothing against it. The 'romantic' school was worsted : and the highest order of genius then existing in Germany was withdrawn from the service of the stage, and unluckily devoted to the misdirection of other talents on their way to it. Success vitiated the *bourgeois* style, of course : but though its fortunes were not without vicissitude, and other modified styles, influenced by the critical sway which the 'romanticists' maintained, be-

came grafted on it, we must admit that it has on the whole kept the victory it won. When we arrive at the most recent date— in the detailed review to which we now proceed—it will be seen that the plays of the two most successful stage writers of the day, the Princess Amelia of Saxe, and the Baron Münch-Bellinghausen* are but the revival, with modern additions, of the principles of Lessing and Iffland.

What the Germans call *das Schicksalsdrama*, the drama founded on the idea of fate *(Shicksal)*, comes first in our review. It was a strange product of the conflicting theories and tendencies of the time : a sort of wild clashing together of the most inflated romantic pretensions, and the most ordinary domestic interests. Here was Calderon with a vengeance, his Christian inspiration, his wild catholicism, wedded to the old remorseless Fate of the Greeks : here was all-sufficient sympathy for the wonderful and mysterious in nature and in man, to please even the most exacting romanticists : and could Shakspeare have been fairly represented by supernatural passions and unearthly fancies, here was a laudable effort to imitate Shakspeare. Superstition, mysticism, or murder, had constant possession of the scene; fright and shudder were the fashion ; pity was dethroned by terror, and this despot ruled alone. Conceptions so wild and irregular must have a special language too : and the passionate rhythm of the trochaic verse, modelled on Calderon, supplanted the steady flow of the iambic. The representatives of this extraordinary dramatic style (which, after all, would never have taken hold of the audiences as it did, but for its points of human interest studied in the school of Lessing) were Werner, Müllner, and Houwald : three men of very different talents, and the first by far the most remarkable. But for him, indeed, there had been little interest for us in *das Schicksalsdrama*. 'A gifted spirit,' as Mr. Carlyle has well described him,† 'struggling earnestly amid the new, complex, tumultuous influences of his time and country, but without force to body himself forth from amongst them; a keen, adventurous swimmer, aiming towards high and distant landmarks, but too weakly in so rough a sea ; for the currents drive him far astray, and he sinks at last in the waves, attaining little for himself, and leaving little, save the memory of his failure, to others.'

Zacharias Werner was born at Königsberg in Prussia, 1768, and died at Vienna,

* Frederick Halm is his adopted name.
† In Carlyle's Miscellanies a paper will be found on the Life of Werner.

in 1823. Impassioned and ill-regulated in his life and in his poetry; without a solid foundation in character or in knowledge; three times married, and three times divorced; now selecting for his dramatic hero the great author of the Reformation, and then announcing himself a zealous convert to the Roman Catholic religion; at Berlin the ruling dramatic author, and at Vienna a preaching, proselytising fantastic priest: Werner, wandering on this earth like a restless shadow, proved, by so many changeful contrasts and vicissitudes, that the wild, irregular spirit in his poetical productions, was at least no affectation, but a truly-felt, remediless, sickness of his soul.

His first dramatic work* was 'The Sons of the Valley,' and, notwithstanding its vague, impracticable, rhapsodical character, it contained more of the chaotic nature and genius of the man than any of his later writings. It is in two parts: the first, 'The Templars in Cyprus' *(Die Templer auf Cypern)*; and the second, 'The Brethren of the Cross' *(Die Kreuzesbrüder.)* Each of these parts is, itself, a play of six acts, and the two fill two thick volumes. The subject is the persecution and destruction of the Order of the Templars: a rich and tragic subject as it stands in history, and presenting a worthy hero in the person of Jaques Molay. But mere history had no charms for Werner. It was the history entirely within himself to which he had resolved to give utterance, and a mighty strange business he made of it. He happened at this time to be a brother, and an exalted one, of the order of Freemasons; and so, behind the full and warlike form of the Templars, to which in the first part of his poem (where their condition before their fall is pictured) he now and then does striking dramatic justice, he places the shadowy power and control of a mystic institution: a new, never-heard-of rival Order, called The Sons of the Valley, half-spiritual, half-real, omnipotent, ubiquitous, and full

of extraordinary schemes for the perfecting and regenerating of the soul of man. Amazing are the plans and structure of this society; but more amazing the expression it affords to the wild, unmanageable thoughts that made up the fever-fit we call Werner's life. It has projected a perfectly novel religion: a syncretistic, universal faith, combining Moses, Christ, and Mahomet, and uniting with Christian devotion the paganism of the ancient times, the mysteries of the oriental countries, and the worship of Isis and of Florus. And how connect it with the Templars? Why, by correcting history. It is not by the King of France, it is not by the Pope, that the Templars are destroyed: neither Clement nor Philippe le Beau had anything to do with it, for the great work was transacted by these Sons of the Valley, and even the good Jaques Molay himself becomes persuaded that the sacrifice is necessary, and is inaugurated into their secrets before he dies.

Such is the strange conception of a poem, which, it would be most unjust not to add, is rich in many characteristic beauties. Besides its gorgeous theatrical effects and show, it contains characters and figures in whose outline there is no lack of either strength or manliness; but the solid foundation in truth is absent, it is without organic connection, and is wholly deficient in progressive interest: matters somewhat needful to a drama. In 'Martin Luther,' Werner again indulged his unfathomable notions, metaphysical and religious. The lesson proposed to be worked out was that the Strength (of human belief) received its highest consecration from Love; wherefore ought both to be, as man and wife, inseparable. Not at all clear in itself, this idea is plunged into the obscurest depths of a mystic plot, in which, notwithstanding some passages of exquisite beauty, the noble and manly figure of the great reformer is certainly seen to disadvantage. Better, decidedly, is the tragedy of 'Wanda, Queen of Sarmatia,' adopted daughter to Libussa, the celebrated mythic heroine of Bohemian tradition. Wanda and Rudiger (Prince of Rugen) had been in love, and pledged to each other, before she was called to the throne of Sarmatia. Since then, she has vowed herself solemnly to her people, when suddenly Rudiger, whom she thought dead, appears and claims her hand. The dilemma is cut through by a battle between Rudiger and the Sarmatians, the latter defending Wanda: he loses the battle, and is himself slain by Wanda, who afterwards drowns herself in the Vistula. The two chief characters are here drawn with some strength

and substance of reality; the collisions of love and duty, and the situations of mutual despair, are painted with masterly success; and there is a unity about the work, wanting to the other dramas of Werner—even to the 'Cross on the Baltic Sea,' which Iffland, struck with the genius there was in it, in vain endeavoured to adapt for his theatre at Berlin. But from these we must pass at once to the work which sent the name of Werner like wildfire through Germany.

This, the most significant for him and for the 'school' it set up, was 'The Twenty-fourth of February,' which found at once incredible success and numberless imitations. It was the first of that long list of dramas, compounded of the mean and the terrible, which excited and degraded the taste of German playgoers. The plot and catastrophe of this piece, Werner took occasion to declare, were merely fictitious. He might, with the exercise of a little more candour, have recollected to add that for both he was greatly indebted to the 'Fatal Curiosity' of our English Lillo. Not that we would not gladly, but for the fact's sake, hand over to Germany the whole credit of the invention, for assuredly the whole is a most horrible and unwholesome nightmare. Briefly, thus the story runs. Kuntz Kuruth, once a soldier now a peasant, lives with his wife, Trude Kuruth, in a solitary valley of Switzerland. Well off in former days, they are grown poor and miserable. Many misfortunes have overtaken them, and now the cottage is to be sold, and prison stares them in the face. Such is the state of things, when Kuntz comes home in the stormy and dark night of the 24th of February, if the cold and empty room in which his wretched wife awaits him can be called a home. You then find by their talk that, apart from even their worst misfortunes, some terrible cloud is over them. Past and present times are alike dreadful to both, the future more dreadful still. The man thinks of killing himself; the wife proposes a theft; when a sudden knock at the door disturbs these domestic confidences. A foreigner is there, who has lost his way, and seeks a refuge in the storm of the night. He has the appearance of wealth; he has brought wine and food; he entreats the starved inmates to partake with him. At table, conversation begins: and such is the interest manifested by the rich stranger for these occupants of a hovel, that Kuntz is moved to tell his story. It runs to this effect. His father, choleric, passionate, and unjust, had never approved his marriage with Trude; and one miserable day—the 24th of February —the old man having grossly insulted and

---

* We subjoin a list of the whole. *Die Söhne des Thales* (The Sons of the Valley): 2 vols. Berlin, 1803. *Der Vier-und-Zwanzigste Februar* (The Twenty-fourth of February): Leipsic, 1815. *Das Kreuz an der Ostsee* (The Cross of the Baltic Sea): 2 vols. Berlin, 1806, and Vienna, 1820. *Martin Luther; oder, die Weihe der Kraft* (Martin Luther, or the Consecration of Strength) Berlin, 1817. *Attila*: Berlin, 1808. *Wanda* (Queen of Sarmatia): Tübingen, 1810. *Kunigunde* (St. Cunigunde): Leipsic, 1815. *Die Mutter der Makkabäer* (The Mother of the Maccabees): Vienna, 1815. The complete edition of his works was published in 1840, by his friends Grimma, and contains in addition to the dramas, the lyric poems and the sermons preached at Vienna. His friend and companion, Hitzig, published his biography at Berlin, in 1823.

ill-treated his daughter-in-law, Kuntz in ungovernable rage and fury flung a knife at him. He had not hit his father, but the latter, to Kuntz's horror and remorse, died almost on the instant, choked with the fright and anger. His last words were,

'Fluch Euch und Eurer brut!
Auf sie und Euch comme Eurer väters blut!
Der Mörders Mörder seid—wie Ihr mich morden thut!' *

Years passed; Trude had borne two children, a boy and a girl; and it was the anniversary of the day of the old man's death. The boy was playing with the girl, and as he had seen, some hours before, a bird killed, it occurred to him, by way of a childish game, to kill his little sister. The father exiles and execrates the child, who went abroad and perished. The 24th of February never returned after this without some cruel misfortune. Everything that lowered them in their lives, had come upon that day; on that fatal day fell the last year's avalanches which made them utter beggars. And now, adds the wretched Kuruth, as he finishes his frightful story, this day is come again.

But it will bring better fortune at last, the stranger hopes. The reader need be hardly told the sequel, or that this day again brings back its crime. The wealthy foreigner is the son, whom his parents had supposed slain in the French revolution: he has come back from far beyond the seas, full of the man's repentance for the child's crime; full of anxious desire to be pardoned by his father; with means to make his age happy at last, and the strong sense that he shall succeed in what he purposes. Persuaded of this, and fearful of increasing to danger the excitement of his father's narrative, he defers his disclosure till the morning. But somewhat oddly, he has taken occasion to say meanwhile—to establish a sort of fellow-feeling with Kuruth, at supper—'I too am a murderer!' He falls asleep. Upon this, Kuntz, excited by the wine and irritated by the turn the conversation has taken, thinks of doing justice at once upon this unknown murderer, but his wife dissuades him. At last he resolves to leave him life, but to take his money while he sleeps. While thus engaged, however, Kurt, the son, awakes, and cries out; when the father, on the sudden impulse, stabs him with his knife. Dying, the son

* Cursed be you and your race! Upon you and upon them your father's blood! They shall be murderers of the murderer—as you murder me.

says who he is, and pardons his father, who rushes from the scene to deliver himself up to justice! And so ends the 'Twenty-fourth of February,' which, with all its faults and its absurdities (for Werner continually walks on the narrow and dangerous line which is said to reach the verge of sublimity) has a deep tragic passion in it, worthy of a better theme.

Adolf Müllner, the first of the two chief followers of Werner to whom we shall here advert, was born in 1774, at Weissenfels, near Leipsic, and died in 1829. He was more of a critic than a dramatist, and became chiefly notorious in Germany by his endless and savage polemics with all the poets and all the booksellers of his age, who paid him back with a nickname that stuck to him, 'The wild beast of Weissenfels.' He had no fancy or imagination of his own; inspiration was a thing altogether unknown to him; but he constructed his scenes very well, and had, on emergency, a tolerably available stock of common sense. He had no special vocation to the drama: but when he took to it, he common-placed Werner, and so succeeded wonderfully. He had probably never taken to it at all, but for the Amateur Theatre he had established in Weissenfels, a very small and dull place, where it was no very vast merit to have turned out the best actor. His first play was 'The Twenty-ninth of February:' a copy, and a very bad one, of Werner's play. But he improved as he went on, and got out a piece at last which forced its way into all the German theatres. This was 'The Guilt' (Die Schuld), acted for the first time at Vienna, in 1816; and perhaps, since Schiller's time, no single drama had found a theatrical success at all equal to 'The Guilt.' Its simple, pleasing, moral idea, is that of a murder expiated by a suicide; but its horrors were very cleverly put together, and there was no higher aim beneath them, no metaphysical wanderings indulged, nothing that plain, sensible lovers of the horrible could not with comfort understand. After this followed 'King Yngurd' (König Yngurd), and 'The Maid of Albania' (Die Albaneserin): superior to the 'Schuld' in a kind of poetical value, certainly—this Müllner himself thought—but on that account, we suppose, not comparable to it in success. Upon which, in high dudgeon, Müllner left the theatre, and from 1820 occupied himself with the pleasing style of criticism before named. He became the terror of German writers and artists, and at his death a common breath of ease and comfort was drawn. His works were published at Brunswick, in

1828, in seven volumes, with supplements. A biography, by Schüts, appeared at Meissen in 1830.

Of a softer complexion, very mild and very sentimental in his way, was Ernst Baron von Houwald: in his poetry, indeed, a true son of his country, the Lusace (Lausitz), where he was born in 1778. He tried a still closer combination than Werner of the Schicksalsdrama with the bourgeois, and gently infusing Kotzebue into Werner, found many friends and enthusiastic applauders. The most successful of his dramas were, 'The going Home' (Die Hiemkehr), Leipsic, 1821; 'The Pharos' (Der Leuchtthurm), 'Curse and Blessing' (Fluch und Segen), 'The Portrait' (Das Bild). But all of them vanished from the German stage after a few years' triumph, and became but the occasional resource of strolling companies, or the recreation of the family circle.

We now come to a poet, nearly connected with the Schicksalsdrama by his first essay, but in aim and genius much superior to all that we have yet named; known too well by his first effort, and unknown for what he did later and better; isolated in his literary position, and almost forgotten by the critics; without contradiction the most original and the most powerful of living German dramatists, though neither the most successful nor the most productive; Franz Grillparzer, born in 1790, and still living at Vienna. He took possession of the theatre in 1816, by his first work 'The Woman Ancestor' (Die Ahnfrau)—a phantom which wandered over every stage in Germany, to the smallest and most remote. Grillparzer, a young man then, visibly formed on the models of Werner and Müllner, and excited by their success, took up the notion of fate in a more ghostly as well as ghastly sense than theirs, and gave the added horror of dreams and spectres to those of murder and physical suffering wherein the vulgar taste rejoiced. But this could not conceal a language of genuine poetry, and a faculty for the dramatic art such as no German had shown to a like extent since the death of Schiller. Hideous, therefore, as the invention was, this 'Ahnfrau' became a general favourite. The critics, indeed, protested energetically. Tieck, in his caustic way, called it a tragedy for the Carribbees; and great, for a time, were the sufferings of select taste. But alas! the greatest sufferer by his success was Grillparzer himself. He was self-degraded by it to a level, from which, the more he attempted to rise, the more his own example served to strike him down.

Thus the better and worthier the work he afterwards produced, the more his reputation declined.

'Sappho' (acted in 1818) was a somewhat strange combination of antique tragedy and modern intrigue; but the chief character, represented by Sophia Schröder, was drawn with exquisite beauty. The main defect was in the relation of young Phaon to the elderly Sappho; while the loves of her daughter Melitta and of Phaon touched the very verge of the ridiculous. His next work was a greater advance. 'The Golden Fleece' (*Das goldene Vliess*), a classic trilogy, containing in ten acts the murder of Phrixus, Jason's expedition, his affair with Medea, the rape of the fleece, the flight and the return of the two lovers, their misfortune, and Medea's infanticide, is perhaps, as to general dramatic conception, and a sustained force of composition, the masterpiece of Grillparzer's writings. 'Ottakar' (1825) was an historic drama, treating the rebellion and the unhappy end of Ottakar, King of Bohemia, and the victory of the German Emperor, Rudolf von Hapsburg. These two persons—the man of force and the man of right; the ambitious vassal and the great sovereign—were here discriminated with wonderful success; but the minor points of invention, the details of the plot, were done less happily, and some of the inferior and mere sketchy groupings of the piece disturb the great impression of its leading features. The later plays of Grillparzer—'A True Servant of his Master' (*Ein treuer Diener seiner Herren*), a tragedy; 'Woe to the Liar' (*Wehe dem der Lügt*), a serious comedy, full of satiric touch, but designedly unsuited to a great public; 'Dream a Life' (*Der Traum ein Leben*), a most tender and graceful play, in which the lyric element predominates; 'The Waves of Sea and of Love' (*Des Meeres und der Liebe Wellen*)—all composed from 1830 to 1840, did not answer the expectations of German audiences, for no better reason than that they were greatly in advance of their means and powers of appreciation. Discouraged by this experience; oppressed by the intolerable obstructions and annoyances of the theatres of the day; the poet has at last given up his unthankful task, and retires into the solitary cell of the Austrian archives, of which the government made him a director. Germany loses in Grillparzer her greatest living talent for dramatic poetry. Future times will be judges between Grillparzer, Immermann, and Grabbe, the rejected of the German Theatre, and such as Raupach, Madame Birch-Pfeiffer, and the miserable translators of French vaudevilles, who have been so long its idols.

Our next group, in this rapid survey, are of no special school or class: being now romantic, now historic or domestic in their tastes, and imitators in turns of French, Spanish, English, and Italian models: but as they kept up in Germany the type of Schiller's form, they may be considered properly as followers and disciples of him in respect at least to the exterior shape of the drama. Körner (1791—1813) is the foremost example of this school, too well known to be more than mentioned here. His heroic dramas, 'Zriny,' 'Rosamunde,' &c., mere exercises in Schiller's style, made sensation for a time, less by their merit than by the personal position of the author, and his heroic death. Zschokke (born in 1771), the famous novelist of Switzerland, produced with some success, 'Aballino,' a sort of bandit tragedy. Gotthilf August von Maltitz (1794—1837), an earnest, excited writer, but without art or study, was author of two successful plays, 'The Old Student' (*Der alte Student*), and 'Hans Kohlhas,' after the excellent novel of Heinrich von Kleist. Uhland (born in 1787, and still living at Tübingen) was too essentially a lyric poet to win success upon the stage, though his patriotic play 'Ernst von Schwaben,' was not without merit. Edward von Schenck (born in 1788, and who died at Munich in 1841, in the post of minister to the King of Bavaria) became popular by his tragedy of 'Belisarius.' But 'The Crown of Cyprus' (*Die Krone von Cypern*) and 'Albrecht Dürer in Venedig,' were not equal to this first success. Auffenberg (born in 1796, and still living at Carlsrube) wrote several plays historical and romantic, and among them adapted one of the romances of Walter Scott under the title of 'The Lion of Curdistan' (*Der Löwe von Curdistan*). 'Pizarro,' 'Xerxes,' 'The Night of St. Bartholomew' (*Die Bartholomäusnacht*), 'Themistocles,' 'Ludwig XI.,' and others, followed. 'Alhambra' is perhaps the best of his dramatic poems, but by its form (it is published in three volumes) unactable. Uchtritz (born in 1800, and still living at Dusseldorf), began by a clever effort, 'Alexander and Darius:' but, somewhat misled by Immermann, he wrote impracticable plays, which could hardly hope to pass beyond the closet. The best of them is 'Die Babylonier in Jerusalem,' a piece of some dignity and elevation of manner. Oehlenschläger, a Dane (born in 1779, and still living at Copenhagen), wrote his best dramatic works in German, and gave, by 'Correggio,' the first model of a special kind of drama, *das Kunstlerdrama*, so called because it celebrates the characters and fortune of great artists or poets. Schenck, in 'Albrecht Durer'; Deinhardstein, in 'Hans Sachs;' Raupach and Zedlitz, with each a 'Tasso;' Halm, with 'Camoens;' Gutzkow, with 'Richard Savage;' afterwards cultivated this model with more or less success. Zedlitz, just named, wrote several dramas, comic and serious: the best of which are 'The Star of Seville' (*Der Stern von Scvilla*), after Calderon; and 'Prison and Crown' (*Kerker und Krone*), treating the death of Tasso.

This is a long list, but with little salt or savour. Not one of the authors enumerated, though all of them in their day very popular with German audiences, produced other than the momentary and false effect of the day. The only one who, with not the least title to original dramatic genius, with less power indeed than the mob we have just named, yet managed by a close and skilful imitation of Schiller, and by the nicest mechanical application of that style to all kinds and varieties of subjects, to keep an almost despotic possession of the stage from 1826 to 1836, is Ernst Raupach: not the least notable person in modern German literature.

This writer was born in 1784. He lived a few years in Russia, as professor at the college of St. Petersburg, and since his return, with the interval of some travels through Germany and Italy, has resided at Berlin. His prolific faculty, since Kotzebue and Lope de Vega, is quite without example. In 1836 the number of his plays had already mounted to sixty; and notwithstanding constant and most energetic critical protestings, Raupach kept absolute possession of every German theatre for upwards of ten years. Let those who talk of the common people of Germany as nothing less than a nation of critics and thinkers, explain how it is that the first German author who merely by the produce of his pen has made a considerable fortune, has become master of large estates in Silesia and a palace in Berlin, is our worthy Ernst Raupach. Alas for the real critics and thinkers! One by one, in an unflagging succession of reviews, have they assured this excellent German public most positively, that Raupach is not in the least a poet, but simply manufactures his plays as the cutler or other trafficker his wares. The good public found him good enough for them. Fine were the decorations of his scene, startling his effects, particularly plain and intelligible the language in which he echoed Schiller's sentiment and pathos, and undoubted the enthusiasm of every audience in Germany for this their favourite Raupach. His first extraordinary ' hit' was, as we have said, in 1826, when he produced ' Isidor and Olga.' The old notion of two brothers in love with one girl, was here renewed ; the scene, Russia, the author thoroughly knew ; but it was the serfdom on which it turned that gave particular interest to the play—one character of which, Ossip, an old bond-slave, with oppressed, revengeful soul, became a parade-horse for all the most celebrated actors. After this brilliant success, Raupach at once, and with incredible activity, established universal empire over tragedy and comedy. To mention even the names of the pieces with which in a few years he inundated the theatres, would be here impossible.

Perhaps his most important work is a continued series of historic dramas (filling some eight or so of mortal volumes!) on the subject of the Hohenstaufen. A great subject, taken from the heroic age of Germany : a kind of colossal idea for prudent Raupach to have laid hold of. But Schlegel in his dramatic lectures had pointed out its dramatic excellence. We do not agree with him. Friedrich Barbarosa, Conradin, Enzio, and Manfred, are probably not bad heroes for the action of an epic, but certainly they are not good ones for the action of a drama. The historical play, even the utmost licence of the dramatic chronicle, must have a certain continuity, if not concentration of purpose. In the works of our own great master in this art, by the special circumstance of the time, often by the mere position of the scene, a continuous solid background to the action is unfailingly supplied. And the very character of French history saves a world of trouble in this respect. Even her old châteaux ; her Versailles, her Fontainebleau, her castle of Peau ; Eu, of old esteem and fresh with recent honour ; the mere places which saw the tragedies or comedies of the French monarchy, supply at once to the dramatic author a scene for his persons, and a kind of solid centre for the interest of his work. In the chronicles of the Hohenstaufen there is nothing of this ; everything is unsteady, dilacerate, torn a thousand ways. Their princes and heroes are now in Italy, now in Palestine, now in Germany : they fight with rebellious vassals, with proud citizens, with arrogant priests : a great, perturbed struggle is their lives, but made up of mere gallant ventures, single and detached : most picturesque it is true, and many ways inviting both pencil and pen, but in no respect harmonious, never with solid agreement in its interest, or with separate lines of action

converging to a great catastrophe. Nor need we add, that as good Raupach found these things he left them. Raumer's historical work had already arranged the materials (another reason that he should take the subject), and neatly cleansed them from the dust of the archives. All the popular dramatist had to do, was to arrange the number of his scenes, and put the facts into easy dialogue. We open the second part of Frederick I. (*Friedrich's abscheid,* ' Frederick's farewell') and find its argument to be simply the various motives and preparations towards his departure for the east. But then Raupach had a splendid decoration in reserve ; and who, when the ship of the emperor with full sails set, hove in view as the curtain fell, could possibly feel the want of any other earthly catastrophe !

This is easy work, and in this Raupach, by long and skilful practice, became so far a master, that five acts of a new play (prologue included) were commonly written much faster than the actors could commit it to memory. The rapid dramatic growth found all encouragement in Raupach's connection with the Berlin royal theatre. Utterly inaccessible to the young and unknown writer, it was always open to him ; who had made, indeed, a regular bargain that every one of his plays should be received, put into rehearsal, and paid by acts as they were handed in. It was an agreement not without advantages to both, the theatre thriving upon it as well as Raupach. Due is it, however, as well to this particular theatre as to the rest of Germany, to add, that here only did Raupach's Hohenstaufen ever grow really popular ; inhabitants, and not mere guests. In the south of Germany, where altogether, perhaps, his name and talents are less recognized, his Hohenstaufen chiefs made but a very short stay, now hardly to be traced ; and even from Berlin itself they have of late nearly vanished with the death of the famous actor Lemm, for whom Raupach was wont to take as careful measure as a first-rate tailor for a coat.

Among Raupach's other tragedies, ' The School of Life ' (*Die Schule des Lebens*), ' Tasso,' ' Corona von Saluzzo,' are the most notable ; and these are all full of fine phrases, faultless sentiments, and good effect ; nay, they have even some happy characters, and here and there an invention worthy of the scene : but to speak of the best portions of them as approaching, by any happy chance, within a thousand leagues of the dramatic elevation of Schiller, or of the calm and solid grandeur of

Göthe, would be ridiculous folly. Certainly a field much better adapted to the second-rate order of his talents, is one he has tried occasionally with better success ; a kind of mixed, sentimental play, of ordinary life and conventional manners. He wrote several of this kind, which we think the best of his works. ' A Hundred Years Ago ' (*Vor hundert Iahren*), dramatizing an anecdote from the life of the general so popular in Germany, ' old Dessauer ' (Frederick the Great's Duke of Dessau), was admirably acted, and exceedingly well received at Berlin, city of barracks and epaulettes. Of the same class were ' Brother and Sister ' (*Die Geschwister*), in which a fire-insurance-office supplied the catastrophe ; and ' The Secrets ' (*Die Geheimnisse*) ; both of which poor Raupach, being at that time especially plagued by the criticism which dashed even his success with bitterness, published under the assumed name of Leutner. It was discovered, and increased the critical storm. But the public came again to the rescue, and when a new comedy with Raupach's name was announced, it received enthusiastic welcome. Comedy, tragedy, history, pastoral : nothing could come amiss from Raupach. He could be heavy as Seneca, light as Plautus.

Of his comedies, we mention the best. ' The Smugglers' (*Schleichhändler*) ; ' Criticism and Anti-Criticism ' (*Kritik und Anti-Kritik*) ; ' The Fillip ' (*Der Nasenstüber*) ; ' The Genius of our Age ' (*Der Zeitgeist*) ; ' The Hostile Brothers, or Homoöpathy and Allopathy ' (*Die feindlichen Brüder*). These have been wonderfully popular, but, truth to say, their wit is of the driest—' the remainder biscuit ' of wit. A kind of hard, ironical satire seems peculiar to the north of Germany, and Raupach's comic muse betrays his birthplace. The gay, good-humoured smile, the hearty laugh, never illuminate her visage. His favourite comic characters are two : the dupe and the quiz : barber Schelle, fool and poltroon, and Tille the mocker, dealer in what is meant for quintessence of persiflage. One would have thought that tender memories of the honest old *Jack Pudding*, whom learned Professor Gottsched had ruthlessly banished, would have interfered with the relish of the one ; and that, possibly, some shadow of the great Mephistophiles might have served to obscure the other. But no, Raupach was fortune's favourite, and his friends, Gern and Rüthling, two excellent comic actors of Berlin, made golden harvest for him and for themselves out of the wit of Tille and Schelle. But the sun of even a Raupach popularity does not always shine; within the last ten or twelve years it has had many dull days; and it has been a part of the man's really clever intellect, and always wonderful tact, to have been, during these years, by almost imperceptible degrees, withdrawing himself from the stage.

Before we speak of those to whom his mantle descended, the present most popular possessors of the German stage, two names occur to us of writers too bitterly neglected by their countrymen to be passed in silence here. Both were men of indisputable talents; neither of them could be claimed by any of the coteries or schools, who have done their best to make a faction-fight of both life and literature; with both the stage was a passion, though an unprofitable and unsuccessful one; and in the midst of a hard struggle, both died young.

Dietrich Christian Grabbe was born in 1801 and died in 1836, at a small place—of course 'a residence'—near Hanover, called Detmold. His life had one unvarying colour, and ended as it began. His parents were miserably poor, and what education he had was self-seized, by fierce gulps and snatches, from the midst of sordid employments. The natural faculty he possessed was early shown, and with some assistance would have worked to a good result: there was genius in him, a wild ambition, and a youthful glowing strength, which with moderate encouragement might have made a really great man, and saved us the pain of speaking of the caricature of one. For alas! he became little more. The German *Philister* is a word, and a man, as untranslatable as the French *Epicier*; but including a cowardice as faint-hearted, and as mean and gross a tyranny. Grabbe could never master the squalid wretchedness in which he first saw life; at Berlin and Leipsic he tried to get footing in the law, and was driven back; at almost every theatre in the country he presented himself with a dramatic composition, and had the door slammed in his face. His 'Duke of Gothland' (*Der Herzog von Gothland*), begun when he was nineteen, is in itself, wild, irregular, and fantastic as it is, ample evidence of the wealth and abundance of his powers. 'You patronise foreigners,' he cried : 'why not do something for me? You idolize and talk nonsense about your Shakspeares; try to make a Shakspeare of me!' There was no notice taken; and he launched forth a treatise against the mania—noticed just as little, though full of lively and admirable writing. (*Uber die Shakspearomanie.*)

Labour as he would, none would listen. The mere names of his heroes and subjects show what a profitless exaggeration of ambition then possessed the man. Even Hannibal, Hermann (Arminius, liberator of Germany), and Napoleon, show pale before his design of setting forth, in one character, Don Juan and Faust combined! Impracticability grew upon him with years and neglect, till poetic beauty as well as scenic possibility were alike disregarded in his plans. Everything must be exaggerated; everything gigantic, enormous, desperate; if a battle, all its details; if virtue, or vice, both in their most violent form; if history, a whole people, a whole period, a whole land, must be dragged within the circle of the poem; and since others wrote fluent verse, he must affect a dry, hard, stony inveteracy of phrase. If the man's life had been less sad, we might afford to laugh at the ludicrous violence which was also assumed in his complaints of this latter period. 'What a to-do about this Faust!' he cries in one of his letters. 'All miserable! Give me three thousand thaler a year, and in three years I'll write you a Faust that shall strike you all like a pestilence!' He died at thirty-five, as we have said; the last few years spent in low scenes of drunkenness (his mother had been a notorious drunkard), and in quarrels with an unhappy wife that he had married. His reason fled before his life. Poor luckless Grabbe! He is not known out of Germany, but even the poor translation of which his rude strength admits, would deeply interest the English reader. *Ex ungue leonem.* The claws, unhappily, are what he chiefly shows. Had proper culture clipped them, we might have had more of the mane and of the majesty.

The name we mention with his, is a worthier and more honourable, and that of one who, though never popular while he lived, and by death removed suddenly from the scene of his exertions, yet did not sink in the struggle as Grabbe did, but mastered much before he died, and kept to the last a proud and noble purpose, a clear and broad understanding. Karl Immermann—of whose extraordinary romance of 'Münchhausen' we recently spoke in this review—was born at Magdeburg in 1796, and died in 1841 at Düsseldorf. His taste turned to the stage with almost his first effort: at sixteen he had written a 'Prometheus.' His passion received fresh impulse with his university career; for, being a student at Halle, he saw the last days of the golden age of Weimar, where the theatre flourished under Göthe. The impression it made

upon him reappeared in after-life, when—having served in the war of liberation, practised as a lawyer, and received some small appointments—he found himself in 1827, counsellor of the provincial court at Düsseldorf, and, with high sanction, resolved to form a national theatre for the performance of the classic drama. He assumed its direction, in which he displayed the most consummate talent. He called to his side Uchtritz and Grabbe, to the latter of whom, if his great scheme had succeeded, he would have opened what had so long and bitterly been shut upon him. Nor were any legitimate means of success left unattempted. No other would Immermann have tried, and might be justified in thinking these most likely to meet reward in a town which boasted to be a metropolis of German art, and which was crowded with artists: the colony of painters, Schadow, Bendemann, and Lessing. He began his task by introducing to his public Shakspeare, with splendid scenic decorations and all fitting costume; Calderon, Lessing, Göthe, and Schiller followed; his energy was unremitting; and he displayed, in every department of his noble task, the most masterly skill. But one year, and the dream was dreamt. Immermann awoke and never again thought of taking the management of a theatre. What he says himself of this period of his life is very striking and full of instructive matter; but so indeed is the whole of his 'Memorabilien.'* Though he gave up the career of manager, however, he did not wholly abandon the stage. He continued, without making any strong or lasting impression, to write for it. It was in truth, though he loved it most and thought it most loved him, not the strongest side of his genius: which did not fully assert itself till it burst forth in two of the most extraordinary prose fictions of modern German literature. We described his 'Merlin' on a former occasion: we shall now simply add the names of his best tragic productions. 'The Tragedy of the Tyrol' (*Das Trauerspiel in Tyrol*), the hero of which is Andreas Hofer; 'Alexis,' an episode taken from the history of Peter the Great; and 'The Victims of Silence' (*Die Opfer der Schweigens*), his last tragedy.

The exciting year of 1830 carried off the rising talent of the country into an opposite direction to the drama, and the interval between that and the five following years is perhaps the most flat and hopeless in the whole range of even the German stage. Mean and poor translations of not very elevated or wise originals, taken wholly from the theatres of France and England, were its meager fare. Its brightest effort was the popular, vulgar 'effect piece,' wherein the Charlotte Birch-Pfeiffers reigned supreme. But there was afterwards a reaction, and within the last seven years original dramatic productivity has been again immense. We shall speak of it as briefly as possible, in its chronological order : since none of it can fairly claim a very marked pre-eminence.

The quiet domestic *bourgeois* style was cultivated with extraordinary success by the Princess Amelia of Saxony, sister of the king, who under the name of Amelia Heiter (Amelia Serene), tried her own Dresden Theatre in 1829 with a piece of the fantastic school, and in 1833 began her successful series of plays and dramas modelled on the style of Iffland. Born in 1794, while her uncle sat upon the throne, she passed her early years in extreme seclusion—'her foot not suffered to touch the ground'—and it was said of her, or of one of her sisters, that her first request when she had outgrown her childhood, was to be allowed to cross on foot the beautiful bridge over the Elbe, on which she had looked daily for all the years of her young life. The reaction of the French Revolution first came with a crash on this seclusion ; and many were the royal feet that then touched the ground—trudging over bridges, ascending scaffolds! The princess shared of course, between her twelfth and twenty-third year, all her family's vicissitudes. She saw her uncle-king twice exiled, and twice restored : a prisoner, and again upon his throne. She returned to the palace of her ancestors amidst the triumphs of 1815, and having refused the hand of Ferdinand VII., was unknown save by her quiet attention to the duties, accomplishments, and pleasures of her high station, when her dramatic career began.

We have mentioned Iffland as her model. Her characters are all taken from common life. With one exception, she avoids the incidents of courts and palaces. The dwelling of the farmer, the counting-house of the merchant, the parlour of the physician, are her scenes. Simplicity and sentiment, which never ascend to passion ; gentle and somewhat feeble characters ; a plain and artless plot ; the manners of good society, and a sound but commonplace moral ; are the leading features of her dramatic muse. Her best points are a certain nicety of humour, some pathos, a strong sympathy in the common emotions of life, and an excellent heart. Her faults are on the negative side : her dramas want variety and relief,

and are constructed too much on Mr. Puff's drop-your-dagger style, some one important secret supplying the beef-eater's function. Iffland she is, but *en beau :* Iffland in the sphere of German tea-parties, and innocent, well-bred modern life. We mention a few of her best productions, and may refer the English reader to specimens lately translated by Mrs. Jameson. Her first was 'Falsehood and Truth' (*Lüge und Wahrheit*), and the most celebrated four that followed were 'The Uncle' (*Der Oheim*), 'The Bride from the Residence' (*Die Braut aus der Residenz*), 'The Farmer' (*Der Landwirth,*), and 'The Pupil' (*Der Zögling*).

The princess found a successor, of equal rank and birth, in the Duke of Mecklenburg, Karl Friedrich August : a 'full-blood Mecklenburg,' and one of the fiercest opponents of German culture and modern progress, who died in 1837, in Berlin. At the close of his life, and under the name of Weisshaupt (*Whitehead*), he wrote a play called 'The Isolated Ones' (*Die Isolirten*), which has some excellent points of dialogue. Other authors hastily followed, as a matter of course, in the same direction. Edward Devrient, an actor of Berlin, produced 'The Favour of the Moment' (*Die Gunst des Augenblickes*), 'Aberrations' (*Verirrungen*), 'True Love' (*Treue Liebe*); and, after a novel of Emily Souvestre, 'The Manufacturer' (*Der Fabrikant*). Johannah von Weissenthurm, formerly actress in Vienna, achieved similar success by many plays and comedies. Robert, in one of the most famous dramas of this modern period, 'The Power of Conditions' (*Die Macht der Verhältnisse*), and Gutzkow in 'Werner,' or 'Heart and World,' in 'The School of the Rich' (*Die Schule der Reichen*), and 'A White Page' (*Ein weisses Blatt*), also wrought with some effect on the same popular model.

Then came forth, in 1836, with a success quite enormous something between the romantic, the sentimental, and the *bourgeois* tragedy—another darling change for the playgoer—'Griseldis,' by Friedrich Halm (so the *Baron Münch-Bellinghausen*, privy-councillor to the Austrian government, and nephew of the president of the German diet in Frankfort, chooses to designate himself.) The part of the heroine in this piece became, on the instant, as great a favourite with the German actresses as Raupach's *Ossip* had been with the actors ; and the performance of clever Madame Rettich of Vienna, was ardently studied by all. No inconsiderable element in a vast popularity. It has been published in number

less editions; translated into the French, Dutch, and Swedish languages; is on the eve of appearance, we believe, in an English dress ; and will speedily make acquaintance, we are told, with the Théâtre Français and Mlle. Rachel. It is ungracious to make detailed objections to the reasonableness of a success of this kind, and the task has been in some sort made needless by an able and well-informed contemporary journal.* We shall, therefore, be brief. The story is, of course, that of *Patient Grissel*, with some striking change. Griseldis is wife to Percival, knight of king Arthur. The tortures and temptations are inflicted by her husband for a wager with Queen Ginevra ; and her moral victory and virtue, contrasted with the pride and selfishness of Percival, is the bright and glowing theme of a series of pathetic scenes, constructed with immense effect, though in language more flowing and effeminate than powerful. She sacrifices her child, delivering the boy to the king's heralds ; she goes into poverty and exile, repudiated by her husband ; she saves his life, seeing him in danger, at her own and her father's risk ; but, all these tortures borne, and the secret of them at last discovered, she does not, as in the old romance, consummate the lesson of patience and duty by returning to her husband, but (and there is a truth in this too !) utterly wretched, broken-hearted, incapable of further joy, and almost of life itself, she elects to return with her father to the poor cottage of her youth. And Percival ? He remains upon the stage, covering his face with his hands, and as his gracious sovereign Arthur reads him a moral sermon, the curtain falls.

Since Müllner's *Schuld*, no such torrents of tears had been shed as these, which bore witness to the pathos of *Griseldis*. It was a success like that we formerly noted in Grillparzer, which could hardly have its fellow ; and though, as his friend and countryman Grillparzer did, Halm has written better since, he has not kept pace with that first success. Particular scenes in all his plays have, notwithstanding, had surprising effect on his audiences. His exuberant flow of verse is at least extraordinary ; and no one can cover a poor invention, even a cruel and unnatural catastrophe, with the perfume of such tender feelings, or beneath the flowers of such soft speech. Since 'Griseldis,' he has produced 'The Alchymist' (*Der Adept*); 'The Death of Camoens ;' 'A mild Judg-

* 'The Athenæum.'

ment' (*Ein Milder Urtheil*); 'Imelda Lambertazzi' (this is a pale and faded copy of 'Romeo and Juliet'); 'The King and Peasant' (*König und Bauer*: a beautiful design after Lope de Vega); and, the latest and greatest favourite after 'Griseldis,' 'The Son of the Desert' (*Der Sohn der Wildness*). This latter piece is a kind of inverted picture to that of 'Griseldis,' and turns on the civilisation of Ingomar, chief of a wild horde of barbaric Gauls, by the Greek maid Parthenia, daughter of an old blacksmith at Massilia. It is the old story of the lion tamed by love, it being a kind of 'Griseldis' who figures in the bear's skin.

Simultaneously with these successes the historic drama found a feeble representative in Julius Mosen, born in 1803, and still living at Dresden. A collection of his plays appeared in 1842, containing 'Otto III.' (the German emperor, poisoned at Rome); 'Cola Rienzi' (Bulwer's hero, and at this time also hero of a grand opera by Richard Wagner, at Dresden); 'The Bride of Florence' (*Die Braüt von Florenz*), a piece of action from the time of the Guelfs and Ghibellines: and 'Wendelin and Helene' (taken from the history of the peasant-war in Germany). But beside these, Mosen has written 'The Son of the King' (*Der Sohn der Fürsten*), founded on the history of Frederick the Great while he was prince hereditary under the strict power of his father, and embodying his friend Katte's tragic sacrifice for him. This was represented only a few weeks ago at Dresden. 'Bernhard von Sachsen-Weimar,' Gustavus Adolphus's great successor, is also another of his heroes: in choice of whom, it will be seen, Mosen shows great intentions. But he wants power and originality. More original is Karl Gutzkow, born in 1811, and now living at Frankfort; but his great strength has not lain in the drama. One of the leaders of young Germany, with all the faults of his school, as we recently showed, but with more than its ordinary merit; a man of energy, a sharp critic, and with a certain degree of power in all he writes; for a dramatist he is too cold, too much of a reasoner. In three years he produced the following plays, which excited attention, and indeed raised hopes that have not been fulfilled: 'Richard Savage,' on the tragic history of the English poet; 'Werner,' 'Die Schule der Reichen,' and 'Ein Weisses Blatt' (to which last we have already referred as bourgeois-dramas; and finally, his masterpiece we think, 'Patkul,' a sort of political tragedy; a work which

dared to offer liberal thoughts and opinions on the stage; a tragedy of actual modern feeling, modern in the highest sense of the word, because inculcating important truths of freedom and nationality. Gutzkow writes all his dramas in prose, after Lessing's manner; and his style is brief, strong, and of epigrammatic force, but seldom of high elevation, and not always unaffected. His friend an associate Heinrich Laube, now living at Leipsic, has also ventured on the stage. He made a lucky hit with 'Monaldeschi,' produced at Stuttgart in 1841; and followed it with a very unlucky one, in the comedy of 'Rococo.'

It was not an exception to the ordinary fate of all German attempts at comedy. Save in the case of Raupach, it has hardly occurred to us in the survey which is now coming to a close, to name a comic effort. It is the barren side of even the classic names of their theatre. But in accordance with the plan of our notice, which not only does homage to the famous, but attends to the neglected and remembers the forgotten, we will single out some names. Perhaps the easiest and most 'gracious' dialogue with any regular pretence to comedy, as well as the happiest observation of commonplace, every-day life, is in the writing of Edward von Bauernfeld, born in 1804, and still living in Vienna. We specify him; and, at Vienna also, Deinhardstein and Castelli; at Hamburg, Töpfer and Lebrün; and at Berlin, Albini, Cosmar, Blum, and Angely—without the least fear that our readers will dream of comparing them with Aristophanes, Goldoni, Gozzi, Vega, Molière, Congreve, Sheridan, or even Monsieur Scribe. Germany will probably have to wait for her comedy, till she gets in the nation social unity, and in the poets literary liberty and personal courage.

Meanwhile she has had, at least in Vienna, a very merry-making and much-loved substitute: what she calls her '*Volkslustspiel, Zauberposse, Localstück, Wienerstück,*' popular comedy, magic drollery, local farce, Vienna piece! How shall we describe it? Sense and nonsense, the false and true, the moral and the fanciful; a world of fairies, demons and devils, mixed in endless practical joke with a world of honest workmen and stupid servants; over all, a dazzling blaze of fireworks and scenic metamorphose and grand pantomime trickery;—how shall we describe what, to the fun-loving childish population of Vienna, more fond of shows and spectacle than any other of the Germans, has always been the source of inexpressible pleasure and delight? Hence came the famous 'Nymph of the Danube'

(*Donauweibchen*); hence 'Caspar Larifari' with his rude, plain joke, happier follower than 'Tille' of honest old Jack pudding; hence 'The Magic Windmill on the Hill;' and all that for fifty years and more has charmed in-dwellers of the merry 'Kaiserstadt.'

But hence, above all, for it is mainly this that has severed it in our thoughts from association with the low and vulgar tastes it has too often subserved—hence came one of the most original and poetical figures, small as it is, that ever Germany possessed: poor Ferdinand Raimund, who was born at Vienna in 1790, and killed himself in 1836, in a sad and sudden access of melancholy and madness. Before him the author-triad, *Gleich, Meizt,* and *Bäuerle* (the last, creator of the famous comic 'Staberl'), had hovered as a steady constellation over the theatres in the Leopoldstadt, and other faubourgs of Vienna; when Raimund came and darkened it by his magic brightness. He was from 1825 to 1836 not only the favourite of his countrymen, but even, sharp and peculiar as was his local school, of all other audiences in Germany. Raimund was himself a most excellent actor, and the brief mention of one of his delightful little works will illustrate at once his genius and his heart. We take 'The King of the Alps and the Misanthrope.' Its argument runs thus. The Demon of the Alps hears of a rich man, who is unhappy, and makes others so, by his selfish misanthropy. He determines to cure him, and with this view takes his figure, his face, his dress, his sickness, his miserable faults, and appearing to him thus, shames him to a sense of his wickedness and folly. By the side of this there is another picture—the contrast of a poor digger in the mines, who with his family lives in the greatest external wretchedness, but in all peace and happiness within. The effect upon the rich man's lot is most charmingly wrought. And such is the moral of nearly all Raimund's plays; the lesson, most prettily and quaintly enforced, that human happiness does not consist in riches and splendour, but in innocence, peace, and love. He was in the best sense of the word a popular poet; plain and intelligible, simple and fanciful; and his couplets are to this day re-echoed, as for years and years they are sure to be, in the streets and inns and all jovial places of German towns. With the faith and truth of a child's pure and unmisgiving fancy, his poetry mingled the world of dreams, of wonders, and of spirits, with an earnest reality; and through all his works, the instructive contrasts and mutual lessons of youth and old age, of love and envy, of peace and dispute, move in charming and simple allegories.

After poor Raimund's unhappy death, his imitators did their best to degrade his memory; and the style he made so fascinating is now represented at Vienna by a series of vulgar, mean, gross farces, in which Nestroy has the honour to excel. In the north, indeed, Karl von Holtei made an attempt to supply his loss by something analogous to the French vaudeville: little pieces with songs (*liederspiel*), in which 'Leonore,' after Bürger's ballad, became tolerably popular:—while in Berlin the lowest and most abject descent was made by introduction of what were called the *Eckensteher Witze*, the jokes and farces of carriers and porters, the humour and enjoyment of thieves and drunkards. Beckmann, actor at the minor theatre, who made it his special study to copy such men after nature, was the first who brought them on the stage. His 'Nante' has been published in upwards of twenty editions, and has numberless imitators. Such is the direction taken now-a-days in Germany by dramatic 'poets for the people!' It has brought us as low as we can require or care to come; and with a few words upon the living actors, we shall bid the subject adieu.

The various interests of the stage are for the most part closely connected. Let the poet, the actor, or the public, fail of what the drama's full support exacts from each, and the failure is adverse to all. Some causes of the decline we have touched upon; but in proceeding to speak of the low condition of the mere scenic departments of the stage, the injustice from which authors suffer cannot be too strongly premised. The brighter side of the history of the German theatre, proves that only by active assistance and direction from men of letters, has success been at any time attained. Hamburg under Lessing and Schröder, Weimar under Schiller and Göthe, Berlin under Iffland, Vienna under Schreÿvogel, Dresden under Tieck: these were the golden times. Their successors have, for the most part, been crown-dignitaries, counts, knights, generals, equerries, marshals. Men whose knowledge of the scenic or dramatic art has been confined to studies of the ballet made at the *coulisses*, have since had exclusive sway over establishments of national art and culture. Hence, among other results directly levelled against the proper influence of the higher order of literary men, the ridiculously low sums to which rates of payment for dramatic authorship have been almost universally reduced.

Even English writers may shudder at them, what would the French do! There are some fifty managements in all. Suppose a lucky dramatist, by some astonishing good fortune, to have mastered his approach to half of them, the other half are pretty sure to remain inaccessible; and his remuneration must depend on a small fee paid by each of these twenty-five theatres, or so many as consent to patronise him, amounting, for a full five-act play, to an average of six or eight louis d'or, which, once paid, gives the right of performance for an unlimited time! Such is the system even in the royal theatres of Munich, Stuttgart, Carlsruhe, and other distinguished 'residences.' The exceptions are the royal theatres of Vienna and Berlin, where, for the former, a hundred ducats will purchase a play, and, for the latter, twenty louis d'or. A play so purchased (we except, of course, such special engagements as those of Raupach), popular to an unexampled extent, and received at every theatre in the country, would hardly bring more than a thousand florins, and could not, in any juncture of circumstances, double that amount. Nor has the author any resource or help from publication. The German law is as disgraceful in this respect as the English was, some years ago. A drama committed to the press, is at once the property of every theatre that may think it worth the acting. Some slight modifications have been lately attempted, but almost universally this is still the law.

As authors have declined, and with them theatres, it was not to be expected that actors should improve. Their great time, as a mere matter of course, was from 1780 to 1820. Long ago had such names as those of Eckhof (Lessing's friend), Iffland, Schröder, and Beil, vanished from the scene: within even the last ten years the losses have been grievous, and in no case supplanted by younger men. Berlin has lost, by death, Ludwig Devrient, by far the greatest genius of his art: Göthe's pupil, P. A. Wolff; Lemm, a survivor of Iffland's time; more recently, the careful and learned artist, laborious and painstaking Seydelmann;[*] and, by madness, Krüger, whom Göthe was fond of calling the *German Orestes*. Vienna has within the same time lost Sophia Muller, the best actress of high comedy; and Raimund, Schuster, and

---

* His best dramatic pictures, all elaborated with infinite care and finish, were Loui. X.; Cromwell; Shylock; Ossip; Marinelli (in Lessing's 'Emilia Galotti'); Carlos (in Göthe's 'Clavigo'); and Mephistophiles.

Madame Krones, the three great supports of its popular drama. So Munich has lost Vespermann, Urban, Esslair (the last great *Wallenstein*); Dresden has lost Paerli; and Weimar is desolate, as well as Hamburg, since the death of Schmidt. Nor, as we say, does youth supply their places. Still, in Berlin, in Vienna, in Frankfort, in Dresden, the old generation is yet the only good one: though alas! lovers are stricken in years; heroes have lost their teeth; and intrigants are so deaf that they hear no one, not even the prompter. Is this a reasonable prospect for a stage? Sophia Schröder has a daughter, the noble singer Madame Schröder Devrient; and if the daughter is quite old enough for *her* performances, what should the mother be for characters younger still? Madame Crelinger, of Berlin, has in like manner, though often not out of her teens on the stage, presented the stage with two full-blown acting daughters. So with the two first of German lovers. The one is a happy grandfather; and the other an old customer, of many years' standing, to the best of Paris wig makers. Korn, the best comic actor in Vienna, is similarly circumstanced. And Madame Lindner in Frankfort, once the most lovely Gretchen in 'Faust,' is grown now so dreadfully fat, that she requires a larger entrance at the wing than is commonly used.

And as these stars set, we repeat, no new one rises. We pointed, at the opening of our paper, to one of the causes that leave the stage to be chiefly recruited now from young men that have nothing better to do, and young ladies who cannot get reasonably married. To such the art presents peculiar attractions, being distinguished from all other arts by advantageous absence of apprenticeship. People laugh at the notion of a school, or academy, or college for scenic studies. Saphir, one of the leading journalists of Vienna, and Edward Devrient, the dramatist and actor of Berlin, have made propositions for some such establishment more than once, but without the least success. It is thought much better and more natural that, as Minerva comes, full grown and appointed out of Jupiter's head, the actor should come finished and full-sized out of his own.

But it is time to close our sketch. We will take the theatres in succession, and mention, briefly and rapidly as we may, their chief histrionic ornaments. And first for the Imperial Theatre of Vienna. Its present conductor, Franz von Holbein, called lately from Hanover to assume the post, is certainly the best existing theatrical manager. He has around him the first talent of Germany, and has already, in the face of all the disadvantages of the modern system, given promise of an apparently zealous wish to recall the days of Schreyvogel and Deinhardstein. His best gentleman-actor in comedy is Korn, who has never had a rival in the Iffland characters, and has lately increased his repute by a masterly performance of Bolingbroke in the translation of Scribe's 'Verre d'Eau.' Next may be named a celebrated stage-lover, M. Fichtner; his wife, as famous a stage coquette; and with these, Louisa Newmann, an excellent natural actress. In tragedy, Madame Rettich, the pupil of Tieck, is not only first in Vienna, but has admitted tragic supremacy through the whole of Germany. Her first performance was Gretchen, in Göthe's 'Faust.' Her great successes since have been Iphigenia, Mary Stuart, Joan of Arc, Juliet (Shakpeare's), and of late years more especially, Halm's Griseldis and Parthenia. She has a majestic figure and an admirable voice, and is a woman of unquestionable genius. In the serious, sentimental parts Madame Peche (whom A. W. Schlegel found at Bonn on the Rhine in the caravan of a juggler, disguised as a wild girl and showing boa-constrictors) is now the best actress, and may occupy the step immediately beneath Madame Rettich. Of the tragic actors the first to be named is Ludwig Löwe, member of the famous family of artists who have made that name eminent in the history of the German theatre; himself son and brother of great actors, husband of a great actress, father to a most promising actress, and cousin to one of the most celebrated of Berlin singers. Löwe is, beyond question, the most versatile of all the living artists. He began his career with comic performances at Prague; at Cassel he played lovers and heroes; and since 1826 has taken first rank at Vienna. His most eminent performances here have been Hamlet, Romeo, the Fool in 'Lear,' Percival in 'Griseldis,' Ottokar (Grillparzer's), and Roderick in Calderon's 'Life a Dream' He is supported by Anschütz, a pupil of Iffland, Wolff, and Esslair; in the old times himself a Lear and a Wallenstein whom Tieck pronounced incomparable; but now, on the score of great age, exclusively devoted to the performance of heroic fathers, and parts of venerable age. With this name we have summed up the strength of the Imperial Theatre. The lower houses are chiefly strong in Carl their director, in Nestroy their writer, and in Scholz their comic person. It is at least impossible to see them, and keep your countenance!

The recent loss of Seydelmann to Berlin, is but feebly supplied by the enormous voice and amazing physical force of Rott. Since this death and those of Wolff, Lemm, and Devrient, the only support of the classic drama in Berlin has been Madame Crelinger. She is the Maid of Orleans; the Emilia Galotti; the Thekla of 'Wallenstein;' the Juliet and Ophelia. She is Mary Stuart; Sappho; Countess Terzka in 'Wallenstein;' and Olga. Lastly, she is the Lady Macbeth; the Lady Milford of Schiller's 'Kabale und Liebe;' and the Lady Macclesfield of Gutskow's 'Richard Savage.' Of the Berlin comedians, it seems only necessary to single out Charlotte Von Hagn: a Dejazet without the coarseness.

After Vienna and Berlin, for the merit of their theatres, come the theatres of Dresden, Stuttgart, Munich, Carlsruhe, and Frankfort. In Dresden, Emil Devrient, the nephew of Louis, is the best sentimental actor; and Miss Bauer is supreme in comedy. In Stuttgart, Döring is one of the few who are masters of a genial and natural force of humour. He excels in characters of common life, and his Jews, in particular, have gone with a wonderful reputation throughout the whole of Germany. Here, too, is the excellent stage-manager, Moritz. Munich has a very fair imitator of Seydelmann. In Carlsruhe, Madame Haitzinger Neumann, wife of the celebrated tenor; in Frankfort, Miss Lindner, and Auguste Frühauf with her pretty French manner; have great merit. And with the deserving name of Julius Weidner, also at the latter theatre, we close this rapid survey, the most complete that has yet been given to an English reader, of the actual condition of the modern German stage.

STORIES, TRANSLATED FROM THE GERMAN. London: Longman & Co. Ryde, Isle of Wight: P. T. Hellyer. 1842. Small 8vo., p.p. 220.

The translator of these novelettes (Mr. G. T. Crossthwaite) confesses to have been rather at a loss for an appropriate title; we wish for his own sake he had chosen one more characteristic. This little volume contains five stories, four by Julius Mosen, a writer who has acquired some celebrity by his epic poem of "Ahasver;" the fifth by Tieck, an author well known to the English student of German literature.

The merit of the stories will be very differently estimated by different readers: writing so thoroughly German requires learning to like, but it is well worth it, 'tis an appetite that grows by what it feeds on. Strange that a people so peculiar as the Germans, in music, in art, in literature, in intellectual and moral character, should have so little *political* nationality. Surely the time is not far distant when earnest, imaginative, truthful Germany will be again a country,—not merely a place for eating, drinking, sleeping—and paying taxes in, but a nation, a people bound together by sympathies, objects, and wishes, common to all. Patriotism may be a prejudice when opposed to philanthropy, but woe and disgrace ever await the country where IT is not. Such is not, cannot be the fate in store for Germany. Her sons are too proud of their father land, too proud of being members of her great family to let us doubt but that they will shortly work out for her a political entity. Perhaps the present congeries of insignificant sovereign states, is merely the transition stage towards a vast, powerful, educated, refined, industrious, peace-loving republic, to be an example and a guide to the monarchies of Europe, and to the oligarchy of Britain. This may appear a wide digression from "Stories from the German," but it is not, for such are the thoughts and feelings which, we doubt not, their authors purposed to excite—such, at least, they have excited in us and others.

The first tale, "Ishmael," is the history of an old man and his sons, who believed himself descended from an Arab family. He had adopted, as a child, a neighbour's orphaned daughter, to whom both his sons became attached; the eldest, Ishmael, the preferred one, is expelled his father's house, and after years of absence the old man goes to the hill top to watch for the return of him whom none may mention; after each disappointment muttering "he is not yet come." At last, on the thirteenth anniversary of his son's departure, he desires to be carried to the spot he can no longer reach, otherwise and from the hill-top his dying eye first recognises in the far distance the long looked-for wanderer. He lives but to embrace him once again.

The next, "The Italian Novel," is strongly characteristic of the nation, which has been aptly compared to its own volcanoes, one moment all peace and loveliness, the next destructive outbreak. We quote the following episode, as illustrative of both author's and translator's style.

"'That Shakspeare is a wonderful being!' exclaimed Egidi, the painter. 'Sometimes he appears to me as the living Spirit of the North Sea. The water fiend, with a little red cap upon his head, now waltzing round and round in loud bursts of laughter with the dolphins, diving up and down with his head above, his head below the waves, like a little wild, mad, good-for-nothing child, squirting water over the faces of the playful nymphs: then suddenly, he becomes hypocondriacal, letting his long hair run down upon his face, covering his forehead with his hand, and muttering melancholy, unintelligible sounds, addressed to supernatural beings in the depths below; but then again suddenly he bursts out wild and maddened, tossing up the waves heavenwards, and casting the sportive ships which he meets in his way upon the rocks, drowning every man and mouse on board. Immediately again he appears to repent the creation of this monster, and with uplifted hands, compassionately bears a poor little fisher boy to a delightful island, and marries him there to some beautiful princess; sometimes he also puts on a Sunday humour, sailing over the sea like a gallant, dressed in a red, aristocratical mantle, flaming with jewels, and a

beautifully curled head of hair ..... such enchanting mustaches, that even the oldest sea-nymphs anxiously sigh at his feet. Then again, in the clear July nights, in love to his very toes, with harp in hand, panting over to Italy, drawing after him the whole starry host of heaven, which, throwing off their dark veil, descend with him into the lowest depths, and just as rapidly flee again in terror, when the wicked sprite, casting away his mantle, his crown, and his harp, again appears like a jolly, true-born sailor, merry and drunk with grog, swears, tears wit to tatters, and utters inconceivable fooleries. Oh, wonderful water-fiend of the North Sea! thy name must be Shakspeare!'"

That the Germans love, appreciate, *understand* our Shakspeare, would almost prove that we are of kindred blood, even were history silent.

"Helena Vallisneria," with its quaint similies, "The Picture of the Mermaid," and "Precipitation," we are reluctantly compelled to pass unnoticed.

OUR LIBRARY TABLE.

The Literature of Germany, by Franz J. L. Thimm. —For those who seek to become acquainted with the literature as well as the language of Germany,— and not only with its past, but its actual literature, —no better guide can be recommended than this "Hand-book." As such, and as a general chart of the subject, it will be found more convenient than many works of higher pretension. The form adopted is that of biographical sketches, in chronological sequence, but also collected into groups, according to the departments of literature in which the respective writers most distinguished themselves. Even the standard authors of Germany are so numerous, that as they are here led before us in procession, only a few rapid glances could be taken of them in a volume like the present: yet if the notices are brief, they are by no means dry. Though mere miniatures in dimensions, the characters are, nevertheless, broadly and spiritedly sketched.

Historical Hand-Book for the Poetical Literature of the Germans—[Handbuch, &c. By G. G. Gervinus. London, Williams & Norgate.

THE Germans are certainly distinguished from ourselves by their larger share of toleration in literature, as in other departments. Any one well acquainted with the subject must remark the fact, that among them many writers of moderate abilities are allowed a share of attention who would be entirely neglected with us. Of course, we admit that their great writers, Goethe, Lessing, Schiller, and others, had genius powerful enough to command an English as well as a German audience; but even these, if they had written for our public, would have felt themselves compelled to become more concise and vigorous in style, and often to compress into a few full sentences the thoughts which they have diffused over many pages. Prof. Sewell (a writer, by the way, generally too hasty in coming to his conclusions) is certainly correct when he says of German authors, "they can think like giants, but they cannot *write*." The English undoubtedly excel their German neighbours in satire, and wit of the destructive species, which has little toleration for fine-spun webs of sentiment and tedious meditations on commonplaces; and, for want of this quality, the kindly frost of literature, as we may call it, the catalogues of Germany are full of weak, sickly plants, of which in England we should soon have cleared the ground. It is certainly strange, when we consider the prolific nature of the German press, how few books can be selected from its voluminous catalogues which would be popular in England; and the student of German literature is not more surprised, at first, by the apparent boundlessness and fertility of the field that lies before him, than he is afterwards by the small number of the productions which are marked by a vigorous originality, able to command a popular interest. In the crowd of minor German poets the greater number are mere versifiers of common-place sentiments. Well might the creative mind of our Shakspeare fill the German students of his works with astonishment, for nothing could afford a more powerful contrast to the sentimental and monotonous strains of their own poetry of the middle class.

Yet, as the poetical literature of Germany forms a connected whole, those who would trace its growth, and appreciate the value of its various branches, must form some acquaintance with its mediocrities as well as its excellencies, and, for this purpose, the Hand-book in which Gervinus has summed up the leading points of his more copious volumes on the subject, will prove a useful guide. The compressed materials of the work render it hardly suitable as an introduction to be placed in the hands of the young student, but useful for those who have already had considerable reading, and to whom, as the author says in his preface, "much may be told in a hasty glance." Gervinus has been accused of some obscurity in his larger historical work, and, with an English jury, we certainly could hardly clear him from the charge. His determination to find a logical connexion between the various developements of poetry, leads him sometimes into mistiness; though we must not deny, that in his attempts to trace the genesis and metamorphoses of the different classes of poetry, his reflections are often as sound as ingenious. His summaries of the old epic and lyric poems contain the results of extensive reading, and those who have endeavoured to search out for themselves the meanings and tendencies of the old Teutonic poetry from the Niebelungen Noth down to the curious didactic lyrics of that Prince of all the Minnesingers, Walther von der Vogelweide, will appreciate the help afforded to such studies by this manual. For the curious student of the passions and manners of generations long passed away, these old lays of the Middle Ages have a peculiar interest, and the researches of Gervinus assist us in gaining an insight into their genius.

Art. IV.—*German Literature, translated from the German of Wolfgang Menzel.* By C. C. Felton. Boston.

In the *Monthly Review* for February, 1841, was noticed Mr. Gordon's translation of Menzel's History of German Literature, and with more disfavour than a repeated perusal in Professor Felton's elegant version has led us to entertain. We shall not, however, return to the work further than to cite from this American translation a few short paragraphs, which may serve as an introduction to one particular subject, the limited theme of the present article; especially as this article has been gathered from a source understood to be identical with the author of the work named at the head of our paper.

Wolfgang Menzel in all his works, but in none more strikingly than in his "German Literature," shows that he is actuated by high moral and religious feelings, that he is a vigorous, clear, and fearless thinker, and that while his critical perceptions are keen and independent, he possesses the gift of illustrating them with power,—often with felicitous ornament. He commences in the following manner, which is neither without sarcasm nor severity: "The Germans do little, but they write so much the more. If a denizen of the coming centuries ever turns his eye back to the present point of time in German history, he will meet with more books than men. He will be able to stride through years as through repositories. He will say we have slept, and dreamed in books. We have become a nation of scribes, and might place a goose on our escutcheon, instead of the double-headed eagle. The pen governs and serves, works and pays, fights and feeds, prospers and punishes. * * * The contemplative German people love to think and poetize, and they have always time enough for writing. They have even invented the art of printing, and now they toil away indefatigably at the great engine. * * * Upon a moderate computation, there are printed, every year in Germany, ten millions of volumes."

It is in the words now quoted that the work opens; while its closing chapter, which has for its subject *Criticism*, contains these passages:—

Criticism itself is most severely criticised. Whether it be just or not, it always makes itself enemies. Still it is indispensable, and exercises great influence. To consecrate its often misused weapons by a right use of them, is a difficult and a noble task.

Genuine criticism has a duty to perform as noble as it is necessary. As thinking is propagated by reflection, so is literature by criticism. Every new book grounds its right of existence only on the criticism of its predecessors. Under the guidance of criticism, one race after another grows up and ripens, and the contest is unceasingly carried on with one hand, and the edifice is building with another, as was done at the temple of Jerusalem.

Criticism, so far as it concerns single sciences, is an integral part of literature. But, beyond and above this, critical surveys over the whole range of letters have become necessary; and this want has most naturally joined itself to that of literary reviews. Men desired to know what had appeared in literature, and what was its value; and so the reviews connected themselves with the booksellers' advertisements: and, as the books were periodically published, they were reviewed periodically: the critical literature became essentially a periodical literature.

But the periodical form and the exclusive attention to what is new, make a partial and one-sided character a condition of this literature. It is by this means withdrawn from the real interest of criticism, and given up to a mercantile interest. A great multitude of new works are undeserving of criticism; but they must be noticed, because they are on the booksellers' shelves. A good book happens to be reviewed unfavourably, or is passed over entirely; and when the moment is once gone, and it is no longer new, nothing more is thought about it. The number and importance of the works by this means forgotten, or falsely estimated, is so great, that Jean Paul was perfectly right to propose a literary journal for the arrears, a retrospective review which should be devoted exclusively to literary rescues, after the manner of Lessing. We must perceive at once that criticism should not be a mere fair, where, amidst the throng and pressure of the present, one cries himself out of breath to praise up his merchandise and supplant the rest. By the aid of bribery, of fashion, or of accident, a worthless book often receives a brilliant eulogium from a dozen journals; and just as often an excellent book is misapprehended, abused, and forgotten. What is old falls out of the course: but can criticism be confined to the interest of the day? Besides this fashion rules with tyrannical sway over the journals. The criticism which should bring all the movements of literature to the test, from a fixed point of view, is itself hurried off into the same careers; for the same interest circulates the books and the reviews among the reading world and seeks purchasers for both.

The reviews are established, more frequently, either for reputation or gain; and whether for one or the other, the reviewing is done like manufacturing. The Universities often publish their journals merely to escape the reproach of inactivity and obscurity; and the sheets are filled up *ex-officio*, with such materials as it pleases heaven. Most of the other periodicals are the undertakings of booksellers, calculated for profit; and here the reviewers formally sit, like manufacturers, and perform their appointed task. This mechanical criticism, then, brings out that monstrous number of reviews which nobody can look over. Manufactories of this kind are everywhere established, and managed by a majority of hungry stomachs and shallow heads, who write at random for the day what no mortal will read the next year.

Thus far from Menzel's "*German Literature*"; his observations of course being specially directed to his own country, although many of them have a much wider application.

We now propose to follow up the subject of Journalism in Germany with the account of German Periodicals, as collected from the "*Deutsche Vierteljahrs Schrift,*" (German Quarterly,) a journal to which Menzel is known to be a contributor, as well as other eminent writers, among whom may be mentioned, Humboldt, Leonhard, Bülau, Fischer, Leo, &c. This journal was commenced at the beginning of the year 1838, and forms an honourable exception to many of the strictures now to be presented; the author of them being, no doubt, Menzel himself, judging not merely from the signature, *W. M.*, but from the vigorous hand easily discoverable in it, and the harmony with the views in his more openly avowed productions. The observations and opinions alluded to, are of the nature, and to the effect, seen in the following pages.

It is matter of surprise, first of all, that there are so many periodicals in Germany; in 1837, according to the booksellers' Jahrbuch for that year, there were eight hundred and sixty-eight. If it be a difficult undertaking for the journals to bring under review everything important, which is thought or done, a general review of the journals themselves ought, at least, to be easier. But what museum or reading-room in Germany, and what scholar who merely devotes himself to a peculiar department, has not been obliged to struggle against the difficulty of overlooking nothing among so many periodicals? Still, it is not so much the multitude of these journals that one would censure, as the unwise division and splitting up of their resources. States which constitute a political power need political organs of the views of the government, and also of the sentiments of the different oppositions, if there are any. Every city, inneed every country town, with its district, requires, at least, an advertising paper for its local interests. Every science, every branch of art should have a journal; and so should trade, manufactures, and agriculture. A multitude of journals, therefore, is necessary; but this number should not be increased tenfold by competition, without necessity.

It is especially to be lamented that the Germans have no great, comprehensive organ of the national mind. Where there is no discussion of local interests, where—in reference to common, national interests, to science and art—the talents which are allied to each other ought to unite, even there local spirits and an utterly foolish rivaly interfere, and dissipate the talents. England and France are much in advance in this particular. In those countries a few great political journals maintain the ascendancy; in these the leading parties concentrate all their energies; they are conducted on a definite and consistent plan, and sustained by the best talents of the party; and thus they are recognized by the nation as the organs of those paaties, and become, as it were, a monopoly by an overwhelming increase of subscribers. Rivalry is possible in such a case only to a very limited extent; it arises on the reinforcement or division of old parties, or the commencement of new ones; new journals originate when they are made really necessary by the changed constellation of political classes. The number of great, leading party papers is always comparatively small. Parties understand too well the advantage of a concentration of their resources; and the public, accustomed to the open discussion of important political questions, will sacrifice neither its interests nor its money without necessity. It adheres to a few commanding journals, though they cost more; it would not habituate itself to many smaller ones, were they to cost less. It must be expeditiously and substantially served. It does not care to know what two hundred ordinary minds,—inexperienced youngsters, who have undertaken an editorship, because unfit for anything else,—and what little cities, in every corner of the kingdom, babble and chatter about; but it must see at a glance, in a few papers, how the best-informed and most celebrated statesmen and organs of the principal parties handle the question. And in respect to the literature which is not political, a few great reviews hold the predominance in England; by means of which it is practicable to survey the entire field, and direct the opinions of the whole nation; while, at the same time, the private sentiments of the critic who speaks through these journals must be accommodated to the national feeling and intelligence.

In this way, one would suppose, journalism would be managed in Germany; and perhaps be led to believe, that deeper characteristics would be developed by a literature, which can not only compare with that of England, but indeed, in internal richness excels it. In Germany, however, the relation of journalism to literature is less favourable. To avoid confusion in a survey of this journalism, let the periodicals be considered in the four divisions of *political, scientific, literary* and *local* journals. The political:—

These have a two-fold character. Some of them present a merely historical account of the occurrences of the day; others defend the interests of an existing political power, or the views of a political party. The oldest papers were all of the first-named class, and were generally issued from neutral free cities. Such were those of Frankfort, Nuremberg, Augsburg and Basle; and such, more recently, was the neutral "*Correspondent*," of Hamburg. Gradually there arose official gazettes and party papers; but they did not supersede the neutral, historically edited papers. These, on the contrary, maintained a commanding influence, as, in particular, the "*Allgemeine Zeitung*" has done, which has survived all the storms of the Revolution and Restoration, and always remained the first gazette in Germany. The reason is obvious. The organs of the great powers hold each other in equilibrium within the domain of the German language. An Austrian Gazette cannot gain the ascendancy, because a Prussian stands by its side, and rivals to both of them are the papers of the smaller states,—all in the same domain of language, all intended for German readers. But the less powerful states offer a neutral territory for a newspaper, which, serving no predominant public interest, presents everything in a simple narrative style. One such gazette Germany must have; and if it were not the "*Allgemeine Zeitung*" at Augsburg, there would be another somewhere else. Party papers are not more able than the official gazettes to force these neutral historical publications from their commanding position. They spring up only in times of excitement, to disappear when the excitement itself has passed away.

Here all the relations are determined, and all the boundaries are laid down. It were consequently unjust to require more from the political journals, than they can accomplish in the circumstances in which they are placed, and do actually accomplish. More than they are they cannot be. The interest of Germany in all the political occurrences of the fatherland, Europe and the whole world, is very great; fondness for writing is perhaps still greater; as to the *industrial* advantages of editing political papers, most are accurately informed.

Hence the imprisoned fluid of political eloquence is ready at any moment, to pour itself forth in the form which shall be opened to it by the turn of the cock.

Nothing but sheer unreasonableness can object to German political journals, that they are not like those of England or France. In those countries the official gazettes are also the organs of powerful parties, because there can be no ministry which does not spring from a majority of the people; and against those are arrayed opposition papers, which are also the organs of large parties. The newspapers are only the continuation of the struggles of parliament. In Germany the official gazettes are only the organs of cabinets; and as opposition papers are arrayed against them, with a frequency inversely proportionate to their own influence, it follows that they can keep back what they please. It is only in the weaker constitutional states that opposition papers produce an occasional commotion; but they are scarcely heard of beyond the boundaries of a small territory, and soon die. Voluntary silence, on the one hand, and compulsory silence, on the other, cannot possibly accomplish what the English and French journals accomplish, as they are governed by a directly opposite impulse,—that of making everything public. Calms and hurricanes are hardly more opposed to each other; in respect to which it may be remarked, that a perpetual hurricane is as unnatural as a perpetual calm.

For some time past it seems to have been agreed, that an unofficial gazette can succeed in Germany only through its neutrality, its historic character. In the place of the departed opposition papers, neutral flags of all sorts meet together, which mask their political insignificance—as to which indeed they are blameless—by copious extracts from foreign journals, profound discussions of topics connected with civil and ecclesiastical law, medicine, commerce, manufactures (the cholera, water cures, rail-roads, beet sugar, &c.), and by occasional elegant gossiping. But, it must be repeated, the age tolerates no deeper political characteristics. And, when looking at the formal side of the gazettes, there must be reckoned as something, at least, the activity with which they observe everything which occurs, and the elasticity of language also must be admired which has elevated forecast and talent to so high a grade. If the gazettes of the present day be compared with those which are more than twenty years old, it must be admitted that they have attained to rare circumspection, tact, and expression.

Scientific Journals:—These must be viewed from an entirely different point. In the wide domain of science, the German republic of learning can organize itself as it pleases. Here there are no gates, no boundaries. Here political interests and considerations cease. The Germans are the most scientific people in the world. In particular branches of science they may be surpassed by the learned in other nations, but not in them all. They have possessed themselves of the richest materials in the widest circuit, and in all departments of science they are at home. It follows necessarily that they should have discovered the means of communicating the ascertained results, in the shortest way, to the entire public; in a word, that a journalism of the most comprehensive and pregnant character should correspond to the richness and depth of scientific literature in Germany.

But the fact is otherwise. Hitherto there has been no central point, from which there has been surveyed all the districts of intellect, like so many compartments. *The Universal Literary Journals, Repertories, &c.*, have indeed been conducted very circumstantially and multifariously, and, in part, very fundamentally; but a completeness of view, a vigorous comprehension and separation of the materials have always been wanting. The subjects were not lucidly arranged; nor was there consistency in the opinions, as they often proceeded from diverse and personal considerations. These journals were frequently mere collections of commentaries, of all grades of scholarship, and of polemic sallies, originating in the casualties of rivalry; in them were mirrored all schools, all stages of scientific development, all learned fashions, the personal position, the old age and the youth of the editor. They resemble a conglomerate of all sorts of stones, great and small, polished and unpolished. Indeed their form, and their immethodical succession of criticisms of all kinds, allow no one to obtain the mastery over them. But their greatest defect is their want of a single, clear, strong spirit to arrange and to animate the whole. Instead of taking their position above scientific literature, they have stood under it, and formed a mere conduit, not always of the purest elements. The best and most important are distinguished solely by their extensive learning,—and this only in particular departments,—and not by an all-comprehensive and all-pervading spirit; and they seek their reputation in the greatest possible remove from practical life, in the most secluded and learned aristocracy, voluntarily renouncing all influence over the great public. One is evidently aiming at the supremacy in the republic of learning. But this journal (the Berliner Jahrbücher) shut itself out from the profane public by its language; nor can it attain its end in the learned circle, because it proceeds from the point of a very one-sided speculation, to which empiricism, rich and conscious of its secure position, has never been less inclined to make concessions than now.

This periodical excepted, it did not occur to the *Universal Literary Journals* to desire a distinctive character. They received promiscuously whatever was learned; and some, whose elasticity has sensibly declined, are no longer distinguished by a profound minuteness; they bring to market not unfrequently some state quarrel of the antiquated heroes of the professional chair. The view, however, that universal literary journals, which are not devoted to a particular department, should not confine themselves to the learned circle, but impart the results of their collected scholarship to the entire public, to the *nation*, has been adopted by none.

The English reviews are certainly less learned, and it is not wished to surrender the pre-eminence of German science, through a blind love of novelty, and a desire to imitate whatever is foreign, whilst, in other respects, the example of these reviews is to be commended. English editors proceed from an entirely different position. They have not learning principally in their eye, but the nation. It behoves them, therefore, to enlighten the nation, to make it at home in the field of literature; and, to effect this, they transplant themselves to the position of the nation, feel and think as the nation does, pronounce in anticipation the opinion of the nation, which it silently confirms through the subscription list. Hence a few confessedly good reviews can, without difficulty, arrogate authority and maintain it. They can and must restrict themselves to leading topics, omitting those minute details which fill hundreds of the quartos of the learned German periodicals. They do not by any means attain to the German thoroughness, but they have another important advantage over them,—great influence and energy, great practical efficiency.

The Germans have often done justice to the national tact of the English, in other respects; why not also in this? Can the so profoundly erudite scholars deny that the old Greeks and Romans—were they to live at the present day, and were they to lay hold of modern civilization—would act like the English? Did not these lauded nations of classical antiquity—which are incessantly set up as an example, without, however, having learned as yet to be as practical as they were,—go forth from the clear consciousness of their nationality; and did they not stamp their national character on every thing which issued from their thoughts and their hands; and was not practical efficiency their only expedient for the safety and the honour of the nation? As soon as they lost the national basis, the classic spirit degenerated into Alexandrine scholarship, full of characterless learning, sophistry, and fancifulness.

The false enthusiasm of religious and political sects, learned speculation, æsthetic fancies dash their motley and changeable waves, with the least inquiry, upon a robust national understanding, and characters which cannot endure any womanish, childish, sickly, or affected extravagance. This is to be seen in England. In Germany alas! the national consciousness has become so much weakened, that these waves frequently dash over it; and men have sought elsewhere a sure foundation and foothold, but always in vain. It seems, indeed, that they must go back to that national feeling, which Britons have never lost; for only in this, surely, can there be found that strong position of nature that cannot be drawn from under the feet; while attempts to restore a national standpoint, by a political, ecclesiastical, scientific, or æsthetic footing, have proved, and must prove, abortive.

If universality, or, as it has been called, cosmopolitism,—to which the German nation is so much inclined,—diminishes the one-sided partiality, and receives eclectically everything from every quarter, there is also an objectionable passivity, an indefatigable accumulation without nice discrimination, a giving way to whatever is foreign, often at the expense of self-esteem. Universality, an interest in everything which lies without, the tolerant and honourable acknowledgment of whatever is foreign, even of that which is hostile,—constitute a distinction which the Germans have before all other nations. But it often borders on the want of character, and is a real virtue, a genuine, noble peculiarity, only when it, in connection with multifarious learning, shows a character, a national consciousness, which takes its place not under, but above the influx of that which is foreign, and not merely loves, admires, imitates everything indiscriminately, but also judges severely, righteously, and worthily, and, in all circumstances, knows how to maintain against other countries its own dignity.

In opposition to the establishment of German periodicals in this lofty style, stands a manifest evil—the learned language. It must be confessed that some improvement has been made in the progress of time; but many of the most intelligent German scholars,—who are perfectly at home in certain departments, and whose communications might be valuable to the entire nation,—still employ a style of writing, which is intelligible and tolerable only to those who are initiated into the same department. Not a few write so designedly. They would think themselves degraded, if they were writing for the so-called people. By popularity they understand an extreme of shallowness and vulgarity, which is by no means to be included in the term. But most write in the tract of a customary pedantry, and can descend to a popular style only when constrained by publishers, who desire to profit by their reputation; and yet even then they do not break away from that prolixity to which they have been accustomed in academical lectures. Some, indeed, in the latest times, aspire to a style which is profoundly learned and at the same time popular; but the number of those that succeed is not large. They often resemble dancers who drag along chains attached to their feet. As learning is striving to become more and more courtly,—a fact that is proved by various extremely pedantic transmutations,—it is to be hoped that the courtliness will react favourably upon them, and that more and more suppleness will be introduced into the stiff links of German scholarship.

Jesting aside, it cannot be denied that German scholars would not only become much more useful, if they would write in a smooth, concise, lucid, and persuasive style, but they would secure much more influence and reputation; particularly if they would not disdain to write, together with their principal works, some leading articles for periodicals (there is meant only the larger journals,) essays in which they exhibit the grand result of their researches for the public incitement and the general good, and if they would stand no longer on a little German professor's chair, but at Athens, before the collected people, that will one day erect for them a statue. While anxious to avoid the expression of a premature opinion, it may be confidently submitted to the future, whether it is not possible to oppose quiet to restraint; a rich and tolerant comprehensiveness, to all sorts of narrow one-sidedness; a clear intellect and illumination, to prejudices and passionate obscurations; a healthy knowledge to sickly science, a display of really new advances of the human mind and of society, to fashionable follies. It seems that in the disagreeable glutting of the market, men look around for an open place where they may be able to breathe once more. It seems that anarchy of opinion having ascended to its highest point, needs at last the opposition of an authority, which will be voluntarily recognised, if it is deserving, and makes itself efficient in the right place and in the right society.

The internal management of those periodicals which are devoted to a particular science, is attended with fewer difficulties; but there are many defects even here. Take a look, for example, at the theological journals. Who will deny that the Germans have a pre-eminence, in this respect, over all other nations? Where is there to be found a more active religious life, where a more anxious inquiry after divine things, and more profound and comprehensive study in all departments of dogmatics, morals, exegesis, ecclesiastical law and ecclesiastical history, than in Germany? In latter years, particularly, the religious spirit—which had become depressed in the time of Frederick the Great, and under the influence of the French Revolution—has risen to new dignity and power; and whatever life and literature introduce anew into this field, is made known at the same time and investigated in the journals. But the wonderful efforts of the periodicals to bring every thing under review, are themselves not to be overlooked; for there are in Germany not less than sixty-four theological journals. Is it indeed possible that the public—even the theological public—can interest itself, at the same time, in all these journals, and look over them all? In consequence of this splitting up, must not many valuable articles escape general observation; and, on the other hand, will not the public be wearied by many long tedious, ordinary essays? Would it not be far better to have a few leading journals, in which the principal parties,—on the Catholic side

52. continued

the Ultramontane and Josephine; on the Protestant side, the Supernaturalist, Rationalist, and Pietist,—should exhibit their sentiments, in which case all the best talents of a party might combine to write solely for such journals? It must clearly be for the interest of each party to have such a powerful organ. A few of these would effect incomparably more than the sixty-four publications now can; in which a few professors and clergymen speak out here, a few there, and a few yonder, and, by their much speaking, only prevent one another from being heard.

But the public would gain the most, if it could possibly place itself in this way, readily and perfectly, on every stand-point of the different parties. One may take five or six great periodicals, but not sixty-four. None are so good as to contain all which will interest and instruct; and none are so bad, especially at the beginning, as to contain nothing which is valuable. But it is desirable that the most important and most interesting discussions should be found in the fewest possible party journals, that they may be easily sought out, and easily surveyed. Before the weighty interests of a party, the little local interests of a province, a university city, a coterie, an individual, must vanish; and the different views of those who belong to a great party in the church, on subordinate questions, can also be unfolded in a single journal, without any risk to consistency in the principal matter. The necessity of a condensed and classical style, in such a periodical, will prevent much superabundance of language; which necessarily repels instead of alluring the reader. In a word, the light which is now diffused everywhere, and dissipated in an immense space, would be concentrated on a few foci, and gain incomparably in efficiency.

If the number of states, provinces, and cities in Germany demands a large number of official and local gazettes, these political arrangements ought not to be transferred to the domain of religion. Is the local, divisive spirit a deeper and more irradicable characteristic of the Germans than of other nations? There are professors who ridicule the rivalries of the smaller states, who, nevertheless, know not how to place themselves above the rivalries of the smaller universities. But the honour of a university cannot compare with the momentous interests of a confession, embracing one half of Germany.

But the large amount of theological journals is to be explained by a reference, not so much to the multiplicity of universities, as to the extraordinary number of different opinions in all the confessions. Here conscience comes into the field. But in order to accomplish something in great things, men must yield to the majority in little things. Without this principle no party can be permanent. The Protestant union, two hundred years ago, was shipwrecked on conscientiousness in trifles. Bellarmine and his school first encountered the Reformers victoriously, when that great party had become divided, in consequence of a too scrupulous conscientiousness, into Lutherans, Melancthonians, Zuinglians, Calvinists, &c. In the present day, the religious passions have cooled; still the affair at Cologne should not have exposed the theologico-philosophical differences, and the hundred discrepant opinions of the Protestants, over which Görres justly triumphed.

But if one-sided stiffness, an aristocratic restriction of opinion, a consistorial despotism, the tyranny of an interim, a formula of concord, a synod of Dort be one extreme which must be avoided, anarchy of opinion is certainly the other. Between the two the proper mean may be found; and if the intelligent theologians of the last century succeeded in overcoming in the estimation of the public that hierarchy, it ought not to be impossible for those of the present century to oppose anarchy with success. But this cannot be done without great and influential journals, which shall concentrate authority and talent. The entire Cologne controversy might have been carried on in five journals, more comprehensively for the public, and at the same time more consistently, than in one hundred journals and two hundred pamphlets, in which it was lost, like a noisy stream in the sand.

There *are twenty pedagogic* journals in Germany. This is an astonishing excess. The teaching class, it is well known, is not in a situation to make important contributions to periodicals; and to only a few of the most favoured, in large cities, is it permitted to obtain access to all these journals. But if all were sent to the house of every teacher, inasmuch as their time is so precious, they could not read them. Most of them, consequently, are useful only within a very narrow circle, although calculated, perhaps, for the widest circulation. How much good which they contain is in this way overlooked, or exerts merely a transient influence upon a few readers! Instead of twenty, two would suffice: especially if they were careful to collect and to communicate to the public only what is most valuable, and if they were sustained on all sides without rivalry.

Of periodicals for *national* and *political economy, administration, justice, police,* there is no excess in Germany. On the contrary, in reference to the comparative anatomy of the body politic and candid criticism on the existing state of the things, much remains to be done.

Philosophical journals have found, hitherto, a very restricted public in Germany; and this only during the culmination of a particular school, which has always been of short continuance. Philosophy having never gone out from the lecture room and the study to the public market, has never become an affair of the people. She has always been too dignified for this, her tone too lofty, her language

295

too obscure. She has thought that she would degrade herself, if she courted the favour of the multitude, and brought an oblation to the general intelligence. She has even boasted that she had done so little to court the favour of the dominant power; and that the noble independence in which she moved, was, in the last century, and at the beginning of the present, her highest glory. More recently, a philosophical school has returned to the long-forsaken path of the old scholasticism which attained to rare distinction, in the service of the then dominant hierarchy, and monopolized the whole business of instruction. But, notwithstanding the great pains which appear to have been taken to establish a similar scholastic authority in the service of the now dominant secular power, it is quite too much opposed to the spirit of the times to compass its end. Instead of outflanking the age, it has been outflanked by the age; and in accordance with the religious and political parties of the present day, has separated into two conflicting sects; one of which defends the existing condition of things in Church and State, and the other advocates a total reformation of faith and society, on the theory of deified humanity. Both have established a journal; but the first has never gained a hold upon the people, and it has maintained itself only with difficulty and with a sacrifice of part of its influence, and the other on account of its extravagance, cannot continue long, and is quite as unpopular as the other.

Of *historical* journals there is no want in Germany. In most provinces, there are societies whose business it is to bring to light antiquities, records, old chronicles, and historical notices of every description. Many of them publish journals, in which they make known their discoveries, with their comments thereon. Still, larger periodicals are required for general historic investigation, especially German historical inquiries. Mone's valuable *Anzeiger* is chiefly taken up with the antiquities of language. The very excellent annuals of Raumer and Hormayr are too small to supply the place of larger journals. The *Archives* of Hormayr was conducted on a very happy plan, but, unfortunately, it is discontinued; and the valuable journals of Schlosser and Bercht are also discontinued. At the same time there is wanting a central organ in the wide field of historical inquiries; and it is very difficult to establish one, inasmuch as the historical societies of particular German countries are not disposed to withdraw their own journals, and send their most important discussions and investigations to a central paper. But in the astonishing compass of historical studies in Germany, in the incalculable richness of new sources, new views, new discoveries which yearly come to light, the want of a comprehensive periodical is hardly to be justified.

In the domain of *natural science* alone, has journalism attained to that elevation on which it should stand, surveying the wide pan-orama of life and literature, receiving from all sides, imparting to all sides, arranging, moulding. Most of the natural sciences have some great journal of undisputed authority, which is conducted by the ablest men in that department, and sought by all their fellow-labourers in the same department. But here, also, there is an excess of competition, which renders a comprehensive survey very difficult, and, perhaps, if certain leading-men were to pass away, would make the authority of the journals a doubtful organ unless preserved by the countenance of the yearly conventions of naturalists.

Of *medical* journals there are forty-three in Germany. It must be granted that different modes of practice require different periodicals; also that medicine, which, in reality, is less a science than an art, and which rests mainly upon observation and experiment, cannot be concise and at the same time intelligible. But forty-three journals are an astonishing number surely. What physician who practises daily can peruse them all, and to what physician who does not practise can they be useful?

The number of journals in natural science can be justified only by the number of particular departments, which are sufficiently important to have a separate periodical devoted to them. Local interests can here establish no competition with propriety, the effect of which is to prevent a desirable concentration. Agricultural, technological, and forest journals alone can be allowed to particular provinces; inasmuch as agriculture and manufacturing interests are very different in different places. But it seems that this natural hierarchy of journalism is penetrated, in many ways, by a rivalry which is unnecessary, and which confounds knowledge.

Literary Journals :—The publications devoted to literature have increased in a wonderful manner. There are fifty of them in Germany,—according to the booksellers' Jahrbuch, already referred to, —and in this number many little local papers are not included, which spring up in the country towns on every side like mushrooms, and which, together with local notices, and the political occurrences of the day, contain novels, poetry, riddles, &c. mostly plagiarized. How modestly these periodicals began in the last century! And with what unparallelled boldness do they now press forward beside and among one another! Specific local wants, which can make so many periodicals necessary, are not to be supposed. The standard of taste is pretty much the same in all German cities. The general diffusion of education, the reading of the so-called German classics, above all, the circulating libraries, furnished with fashionable writings, and the plays published in the Repertory, and differing but little from each other, have brought about this result.

In respect to metrical, particularly lyric poetry, there prevails, in all the literary periodicals, the same tendency to poetic eclecticism.

They copy all known fashions, and receive every new one without distinction. Of the old opposition between the classic and romantic schools, there is scarcely a trace to be found. All live in harmony with each other. In prose, they adopt a new fashion once every ten years or so. A short time since, the manner of Walter Scott had the ascendancy; now it is the generic painting of the French, their frivolous tales and spirited drawing-room chit-chat. There is to be noticed, in this particular, an important transition from the prevalence of the descriptive, to that of the conversational style. In general, prose is endeavouring to become more and more elegant, —exerting all its energies to appear fine and polished.

The amazing number of literary papers, which—with a very few exceptions, and those the older ones—have the same style, is not to be ascribed to different local interests, nor to opposition of taste; but partly to immoderate, unnatural *production* and *competition*. Production far exceeds the proportion which is prescribed by the wants of the consumers; and, in addition to this, rivalry has doubled, nay trebled the natural production.

To speak, in the first place, of *natural production*, no one can deny that there is a prodigious number, yea, too large a number of poets. No people, indeed, in any age, can boast of such wealth in novelists and singers; but while the Germans are proud of this rare favour of the muses, it can hardly be concealed, that in this instance, as in every other, the excess of a blessing becomes a curse. Does the amount of the poetic genius correspond to the multitude of rhymsters?—the quality of the poetry to the quantity of verse?—the maturity of taste and fine feeling for poetry in the public, to the great pains which versifiers have taken to form it? Finally, does the high estimate which is paid to poets correspond with their just and reasonable claims? On the contrary, do not the inward worth and the respect awarded to them, stand almost precisely in an inverse proportion to the multitude of poetic productions; so that many of the few genuine master productions are unappreciated, while the public, sung to from so many quarters, finds no time for reflection; while, on the other hand, much that is ordinary, and even exceptionable, makes its way by impudent bawling?

Thus, while a multitude of literary periodicals is to be regarded as the natural organ of that eager desire of publication which a few journals would not satisfy, there are many more which owe their origin solely to *industry*. The success of some of the older literary periodicals served as a spur to many enterprising men, to open for themselves like sources of profit. Of poetical fellow-labourers especially, there was no lack. Some, who had been tolerably content, at an earlier period, with publishing a few lyric pieces and a few tales, and who, abandoning the rhyming art at the end of the nightingale season, had entered upon a practical calling, were now engaged for a literary journal; and soon the muse, which at first was really a muse, became an acknowledged cow. The natural production made more journals necessary; but the establishment of new journals, undertaken from purely mercantile considerations, made a new production which was no longer natural, and to which the rhyming manufacturer hired by the publisher must constantly address himself.

While some genuine poetic geniuses have really climbed too high, and their too sublime conceptions, their too extravagant fancies, and their too learned wit, are unintelligible to the people; this fact has served as an excuse to multitudes with moderate abilities, to construct a vapid, polite literature, which aims at superficially mannerizing everything original, at rendering common everything tender, at varying every theme to an insufferable triviality, at dissolving every idea of higher poetry, like a homœophatic atom, by ever multiplying dilutions in the ocean of their pretended elegant prose. That admiration bordering on reverence, which the older poets enjoyed, is made up to the writers of elegant literature by the clinking of their wages; and though they renounced at the beginning of their industrious career, every claim as modest professionists, they lived to attain to the happiness, in due time, of being numbered among the poets of the nation by their kind-hearted subscribers, on account of the frequent and growing recurrence of their names.

The Germans have accordingly now a very complete poetry, and, together with this, a still more complete elegant literature. Every spot on the German Parnassus is occupied. There have been many who thought that poetry had come to its completion and its close with Goethe, yet many new poets, who must be regarded as such, have obtained a place on the mount, and the crowd of those who are already celebrated, or wish to be, is suffocating. The writers of polite literature, moreover, have encamped around Parnassus, and put up their booths. On all sides music is to be heard, ninepin-alleys and the jingling of tumblers; and exceedingly friendly hosts deal out a profusion of poetry to all who are thirsty and desirous of amusement, at a reasonable rate; which saves the trouble of first climbing the hill and drinking immediately from the consecrated fountain.

As the poetic department has been for some time overstocked, Hitzig of Berlin, the noble Criminal Director, spoke a word in season, when he cautioned young men against authorship as a profession. Still, new flocks of literary adventures are springing up, and tumultuously demanding a place. These younglings followed, as the third generation, the writers of polite literature, as they again had followed the genuine poets. Hence, one can hardly wonder that the older generation of those richly gifted, or at least ambitious men,—who wrote poetry only for the sake of doing it, without any mercenary aim,—had already passed away from them; and they knew only the second generation of *industrials*, and looked on elegant literature solely from this point of view. But finding the business already so much overdone, they saw themselves in the condition of poetic paupers, and availed themselves of the only advantage which their desperate circumstances afforded. It was for their benefit that they had nothing to lose, and therefore need be less scrupulous in the selection of means; and their spirit of enterprise was sharpened far more than their sense of honour could be offended. To be able to enter the field of competition, they must think upon some new attraction, so as to interest the blunted public in their favour. This attraction they thought they discovered in hitherto avoided personalities. They undertook to place themselves above considerations, which before this had been silently influential, in order to stimulate the public in a new and surprising manner. Now began the so-called characterizing of the nobility of the day, the indiscreet copying of correspondence, the scandalous chase after anecdotes, biographical diversions. They seasoned their insignificant and poetically unproductive pages, with biting remarks, allusions, satires, fabrications, and calumnies, referring to well-known individuals. They brought before the public all theatrical cabals, which till now had been very properly unproclaimed; all the rivalries of artists and authors; and they fattened upon true and fictitious chronicles of detraction. They were not disappointed: a bad report is a gladly seen guest; men are flattered when they hear another aspersed. In the midst of the graceful gardens of elegant literature, hundred-tongued Slander erected her throne, and *improvised* all the vexations, robberies, and little cruelties of war, when there was no sufficient occasion for a war.

The older industrials, of a more peaceful nature, also thought that they must not be left entirely behind the younglings, and began to publish in their turn posthumous collections, letters, biographical notices, characteristics, descriptions of individuals, which they would not have thought of copying before. All the old washkettles and visiting cards of distinguished men were made known; and frequently, for the mere compensation, every feeling of piety was disregarded, and the rights of the dead were assailed in the most indefensible manner; the *privatissime* of deceased women were exposed by their husbands; of deceased fathers, by their sons.

It is easy to understand how this third generation, not knowing what else to contrive, lived only on the stirrup of the robbery of another's good reputation; in particular, how it filled the critical supplements of journals with *feuilletons* and correspondence, and likewise established new and mostly defamatory papers.

Before this there was not too much to boast of in the criticism of the German periodicals devoted to polite literature. In general they were pervaded by an indefiniteness, which at least was not flattering to the national character. The nation should have a decided tone, and criticism should give it a distinct utterance. But Germany has no state, only states; no taste, only tastes; no criticism, only critics. The diversity of opinion has a necessary foundation in the extraordinary diversity of views; and if these were honestly expressed, there should be, without much harmony indeed, many pleasant tones. But alas! there are intermingled so many dishonest opinions, views are so often modified by personal interest. A great part of the criticism is properly only anticritical; the expression of revenge instead of censure; a refusal to acknowledge the merits of another; or coterie praise. In this way many periodicals insure their influence. The unjust censure of merit is even surpassed, in insolence, by the systematic self-praise of the coteries. One reads with wonder how many of the most frivolous writers—of whom nothing has been heard, who have not proved their manhood by a single work of mark—make themselves talked about and lauded; and how, in widely disunited Germany, they endeavour to ape the foppery of the literary saloons of Paris. And yet this corruption of fame by coteries is far from being the worst thing which is to be objected to in literary criticism. In addition to all this, it has become a venal tool of bookselling interests. In one well-known periodical, all the works of the publishing house from which the journal issues must be lauded without distinction; and everything published by another house must be condemned without distinction. This instance, though the most striking, is not the only one. The judgment passed upon rival works is very frequently in inverse proportion to their merit; and frequently the copy is praised at the expense of the original. How often, again, does it happen that conductors, to save the price of their articles, fill their critical pages with reviews gratuitously furnished; in which the author of a work praises himself, or abuses his personal enemies!

The nation is so much accustomed to this state of things, that the most unjust criticism of the most valuable works—which in England, for example, would either excite universal disapprobation, or be palliated only as the device of a political party—is treated in Germany, just as when, on the other hand, the most extravagant praise awakens no enthusiasm. The nation has become used to these extremes, and, in general, the writers are no longer respected. Their contests are not contemplated with wrath and wonder, but merely with that ironical pleasure, with which elsewhere cock-fighting is looked upon. In this depreciation of writers, no one is the gainer except the man who speculates thereon. Unfortunately, it must be said that there are writers who indemnify themselves for the contempt which they inspire, by the compensation which they receive;

and who, moreover, think themselves the gainers, if they bring others, (for only slander, and some of it will adhere,) and the whole fraternity of authors, into discredit. Whoever ventures to oppose this critical enormity is certain of the most clamorous abuse, and finds in the already blunted public literally no satisfaction. Hence many a man who had else been called to the defence of the true, the beautiful, and the good, withdraws from the polluted arena. He knows that no merit, no well-earned reputation will be regarded; and *industry* speaks scornfully of all piety, and there is no way of escaping the slanders of the literary herd, but by letting them alone.

Parties in taste, who contend from conviction, can neither continue nor begin in such circumstances, any more than there could be Aristocrats, Constitutionalists, and Girondists, in the French Revolution, after anarchy had conducted the filth of the streets to the tribune. Whenever, in the present day, a contest of principle has commenced in the department of taste, a desolate cry has deafened it, and everything has degenerated into personalities. A well-known young school gave out an intention to reform polite literature from a new principle. If it had been really so, what a fresh living stream would have run through the morass of elegant literature! But they proclaimed an unrestrained impudence, and placed the lyre of Apollo in the arms of the god of gardens. And even this carelessness was merely a crafty device, a sheer imitation of a French fashion, undertaken as a speculation. The tailor at Lisbon who made a carbonari cloak from stolen cloth, did not put the judge to greater shame, than did these young people the honest critics who imagined their *industry* to be fanaticism. And thus this hope of a new spring of poetry has been disappointed; and people must wait a long time, either till a holy power of youth shall wake up a new and beautiful inspiration, and by its sword cut the gordian knot of criticism, or till the nation, conscious of its worth, and turning to its great interests, shall condemn the miserable *industry*, which fills the periodicals with literary prattle, to eternal oblivion.

Local Journals :—Is it indeed worth the trouble to consider these separately? Single periodicals are not of much importance, but the whole together exert a powerful influence in Germany. By far the greater number of the families of citizens read no other than local papers. These, consequently, exert so great an influence upon the thoughts, manners, and taste, that it is well worth while to bring them into consideration. The local papers were originally nothing more than advertising sheets, designed to publish the regulations of the local government, public appeals, deaths, auctions, &c. Formerly there were often connected with these, partly, political intelligence, partly, tales and poems for amusement. Many of these papers have attained to such a standing, that a man cannot live in a considerable city, without receiving them daily,

as the visit of an old friend. But the deserved respectability of these good papers excited the envy of the industrials. Hence, a great number of new local papers has arisen, nay, an incredible number in a single well-known city; and through the rivalry of these papers in every corner, all the accessible tattle of city women, and all the rationale of taverns, of which indeed one would not have expected to read in print, have been published. INDUSTRY has gone so far as to send its too indiscreet personalities and systematic lies, which could not be received into the journals of the father city, as articles of correspondence to local papers of other cities, to be exchanged for similar productions. Literary vagabonds, not merely the absolutely plebeian, but those who affect to be distinguished, avenge themselves on the cities in which they have not secured sufficient admiration, or have miscarried in some speculation, by defamatory periodical articles, in which the city, its societies, and its curiosities are abused. Another well-known *industry* threatens every actor, on his enterance into certain cities, with biting criticisms, if it is not bought off by naked gold. Theatrical criticisms have become, in this respect, a downright disgrace to German journalism; in praise and blame equally contemptible.

The local papers which seek their public in the humblest spheres of society, have already begun to expose to public scandal the lowest privacies of life. They publish what servant girls say to each other at the wells. They endeavour to please by ambiguous expressions and wanton anecdotes. They publish malicious reports, in order to force the injured to a reply, which is thankfully permitted,—all merely to make themselves talked about. Nothing is rejected which will season their journals. It has already happened in one of the obscure papers, that a student in a gymnasium has openly made war upon his teacher. Fortunately, papers of this description are comparatively rare; but they are constantly increasing in all the larger cities; so that it cannot be superfluous in this place to advert to them, inasmuch as they do not contribute to the moral improvement of the people, especially of the young, into whose hands they are particularly apt to fall.

Whilst the latest times nourish and tolerate this manifestly illegal scandal in the cities, a good old custom has been laid aside which the local papers were called upon to preserve. Formerly, the chronicles diligently recorded every important occurrence, both in the physical and moral world. In this way the knowledge of very remarkable persons and events, extraordinary casualties, crimes, &c., reached the public. But now a false hesitancy suppresses such communications. For twenty years past, there has been known nothing of the most interesting suicides, as the papers contained nothing but simple notices of deaths. Of a few crimes only are the circumstances given. Misfortune, it is said, demands respect;

and yet men do not blush, in the least, to read the defamation of an innocent fellow citizen; and they are amused still more, when wickedness and *industry* combine to destroy the peace of families.

Last of all, cast a look at the *Pamphlets,*—that supplement of journalism, which becomes more and more necessary with the increase of small journals, which have no room to receive larger essays, or are so little known, and have so few subscribers, that the author ventures rather to publish his essay in a separate form as a pamphlet.

If the number of pamphlets which are written in Germany on the subject of homœopathy, railroads, the cholera, the Cologne controversy, &c., be considered, it cannot be denied that the country has too much of a good thing. But this excess is explained by referring to the same fault which has already been viewed at length. Were there a few great journals of acknowledged authority, and conducted by learned and able men in every department, the soundest among different opinions, or the most important of opposing opinions would have been readily and clearly exhibited; these journals, besides what they send forth themselves, would have directed attention to the most valuable greater works in which the most interesting subjects are discussed, and the public would have plainly seen and known what to believe. But the composition of numerous journals, which reciprocally assail one another's authority, has occasioned this excess of pamphlets; in which all the voices that have not been able to speak out in the saloon, have been equally loud before the door; as if it were only important that all should speak, and not rather that all should hear what one sensible man has to say.

In this excess of writing, those numerous publishers have no small share who, merely to speculate on the curiosity of the public, procure to be written, as soon as possible, a pamphlet on every passably important event; summoning thereto the unqualified, to enable debtors in this way to cancel their debts, and for once, to give employment to idlers; and who then force their productions upon the public by striking notices and the hired praise of reviews. Not a few daily papers fill their columns with such notices, wholly subservient to the industry of their conductors. Nor is it enough that such a multitude, at the present time, should believe themselves called to a public expression of their sentiments; but associated with these are many others, who do not precisely think themselves called, but write from pecuniary considerations, pretending to have a pleasant opinion, or slightly changing the opinions of others, patching many together, and such little innocent secrets of production. Thus one is brought back to the same result. Excessive competition is the grand evil which afflicts the periodical and ephemeral literature of Germany.

Already there have been enumerated the most prominent causes of this competition. The political divisions of Germany are reproduced in literature, where no political interests come into play; and though they all write in the same language, and boast that they can all be read throughout the whole circuit of the German tongue, yet they want a great capital, which shall be the undisputed centre of all literary life. They have divided their energies among several centres; and the noble emulation to set forth a whole in parts stands either in no just relation to the disunited energies, or dissipates them altogether; while they are doing repeatedly in different places, what needs to be done only once, or calls forth a jealousy that darkens merit to favour another, or weakens efficiency for the same reason. The partiality which so many scholars show, particularly in political appointments, to this or that state or city, is a great hindrance to this so desirable concentration of the means and resources of journalism. It is very difficult for an influential journal, which happens to arise in one state, to obtain a commanding position in another state, unless the independence of such journal is placed beyond all doubt; and even here other considerations interfere; for it is not every independence which is at the same time invested with that distinction, with which alone great names can associate. It is for this reason that so many pens are idle, which should be employed for the public illumination in the journals. It is for this reason that they devote themselves only to the journals of one state or city. It is for this reason that so many write without system or consistency, now for this, now for that independent periodical, as they succeed in obtaining the honour by flattery or importunity.

The second cause of the unreasonably increased competition is the excessive conscientiousness, or the incompatible subjectivity of many men of science and art. One of the greatest virtues of the Germans here becomes a fault. For the sake of the merit of carrying out a single view, consistently and fully, in all subordinate circumstances, they lose the grand result, the triumph of a fundamental view; to which they might attain, if by yielding in secondary matters, they would secure a numerous comradeship. In general the policy of parties, the art of association, are unknown to Germans. Hence it is that so many scholars write for their own journals, unconcerned about the others. That every one, however, should travel his own road, every one think himself right and no one else, and never look around upon his brethren, has been proved, more than once in great contests of opinions, to be an evil. The correctness of an opinion stands in inverse proportion to the number of rays of heat and colour, into which literary and particularly journalistic light is separated: An old German proverb advises every party to stand as one man. They should write also as one man.

The third cause of corruption is the purely *industrial* speculation, which, never with a generally useful aim, or for the sake of an idea, but simply for the pecuniary profit, betakes itself to the business of journalism. Now, although this sort of thing be only a parasite plant, it has already grown so luxuriantly as to threaten to impoverish the tree by which it is planted. The spirit of mercantile enterprise, and still more mercantile independence, were necessary to open a road, on which those who are chained to a learned clod, as has been the case for a long time with most German scholars, never travel. Hence there are journals which at first were only mercantile adventures, that have called into exercise the noblest talents formerly unemployed, and so become national establishments. But there is a limit to such talents; and they fail at last to suffice for the extraordinary crowd of new conductors, all of whom desired to avail themselves of similar distinguished abilities. *Industry* now resorted to *substitutions*. It has not only reprinted, it has in a more general way, by amplification, imitation, and compilation, appropriated the merit of other men of genius. And finally, it has presumed, without any ceremony, to misuse fame, and to publish fabrications, prepared by anonymous bunglers, as works of genius and excellence.

To the expedient of appropriating the appearance of merit, and of giving to suppositious productions the impress of genuine wares, belongs, among other things, the practice of fictitious oppositions. To all parties *industrial* volunteers have attached themselves; who, having no real interest in the controversies, seek only to share the fame and the readers of honest party men. Occasionally they play the part of martyrs, and proceed so far in their calculations, as to obtain their portion of the sympathy which is paid to those who are actually persecuted. Much that has been falsely ascribed to genuine parties and their convictions, must be charged upon this kind of *industry*. Many caricatures have no other origin.

The public, moreover, has always permitted itself to be led astray, and accommodated itself to *industry*. Its discrimination has not merely been lulled by sly deception; it has also allowed itself to be rudely assailed. It has not only endured authors and literary artists of the worst character, but it has permitted their names to shine by the side of the noblest, which secure the honours of German science and art. It has bought, and read, and admired, when it should have thrust away with the bitterest scorn.

Not without good reason do the *industrials* boast of the favour of the public. The public was prepared for their works; *industry* had nothing to do but to supply a want which lay in the times. So it seems indeed: but the public consists of many ingredients; and precisely those,—on whose unripe judgment, youthful susceptibility of seductive influences, unpolished education and culture, and utterly perverted taste, *industry* speculates,—could not be acknowledged as judges in the last instance, however numerous they might be. Those corrupters of youth, whom the wiser legislation of earlier times punished without pity, dared not pretend that the youth agreed with them. The reading of bad books and journals was no more an original want of the northern people, than was brandy, whose ravages we now deplore. A generally pernicious *industry* first introduced that fictitious want into nature, in the process of corrupting it. *Industry* of itself is not moral. It will spread every poison which finds purchasers, whether of opium in the Orient, or of bad books in the Occident. They will even seek out poisons, hitherto concealed, whenever and so long as the ripened reason and morality of the people impose no restraint.

In conclusion, the humbling confession must be made, that how to avoid the impending evil is unknown, should the anarchy of the public judgment, and the impudence of *industry*, speculating thereon, continue to increase in the proportion as hitherto. Without doubt, every one has a right to speculate with his capital in the book-trade, as in any other business. Without doubt, every one has a natural right to publish his opinions; and the censorship itself does not object, if these opinions do not come in hostile collision with those of the Government. Besides, an unrestrained rivalry is serviceable to the arts and the sciences, because it prompts the emulation of the masters. And what crying abuses, what death of all intellectual life must arise, if literature and journalism should become a monopoly, for which the government, or a caste authorized by it, as in China, should alone be held qualified! But how, on the other hand, shall science and art, nay, society itself, be preserved from the other extreme of the *lex agraria*? For to what else does this competition tend but to an agrarian law in literature, which abolishes every aristocracy of mind and good manners, divides the rights of authorship into numberless little portions among the people?

The natural right which every one possesses, of writing whatever occurs to him, necessarily calls for a restriction in the duty which everyone should impose on himself, either to write only what is good, or to leave the business to those who are called to it. But how can this duty be impressed upon the industrials? Public opinion, which on this point should be decided, has been corrupted by bad journalism; and to free itself from this influence, to ripen the national judgment, will require, perhaps, a shock which cannot issue from literature itself,—an energy of events which rests only in the dark lap of the future.

Thus far, on the subject of Journalism in Germany, have we gathered from Wolfgang Menzel, without at all undertaking to review the judgment which he has pronounced. This indeed would require an acquaintance with the vast field traversed by him, which we are far from having. It must be allowed by all, however, that Menzel is amply qualified to do justice to the subject. It is true, that in several of his publicly acknowledged and more elaborate works, especially his " *German Literature*," there was not merely great boldness of criticism, but startling novelty of opinion. At the same time, without professing to coincide with him in all his views, one is perfectly safe in characterizing him as a writer of the most extensive reading and of high commanding talent. Nothing has been published which gives so distinct a view into the " cloud land" as the celebrated book which has just been named. In fact, there is no work which has taken so comprehensive a survey of the whole field of thought and opinion in Germany. Before its appearance, Madame de Staël's Germany had generally been relied upon as authority in such matters. But that is a genuine romance of history, a mere compound of truths and fantasies, made up of materials that must have been furnished her by others; she had not sufficient knowledge either of the language of the country to enable her to judge for herself. Menzel, on the other hand, observed, reasoned, and decided most independently. He had no occasion to rely on any other sources of information, than those which he possessed in his own mind, and his own knowledge; while there are few among his own countrymen, who unite as many requisites for the successful execution of such a task, as are found in him. In addition to the talent, learning, and flowing pen necessary to give the literary finish to his work, he has what is still more rare, and no less necessary to lend substance and soundness to opinions and views, a practical knowledge of mankind, and a familiarity with the real every-day world, its business and duties. These qualifications, of course, peculiarly fit him for drawing up a large and an accurate account of the periodical literature of his country; nor is it probable that we shall soon meet with anything of the same sort, that is equally full, pertinent, and correct.

Wolfgang Menzel has long been engaged in the department of literary criticism. So early as 1824, when he was but twenty-six years of age, he was appointed editor of a journal to which he continued to contribute many papers. But not to go particularly into his career, we shall merely subjoin that he has acquired fame as a poet, a civil historian, and a writer of travels; nor has he confined himself to the literary arena, for, for many years he has been one of the most active political combatants of the liberal party. Still, although liberal, he is not of the " extreme left," seeing that he vigorously opposed, and openly denounced the association of hotheaded patriots, that arrogantly assumed the name of "junges Deutschland," of which fraternity his former coadjutor in the editorship of the Litterationblatt, and the celebrated Henry Heine, were leading members.

53. ATHENAEUM, 18 (1845), 327-328. M/H No. 4085.

The Moral Phenomena of Germany. By Thomas Carlyle, Esq. "of the Scottish Bar." Painter.

It is necessary to add the particular description quoted, to distinguish the writer from the Scotch historian of the French Revolution and critic on German literature. Their minds and styles are, indeed, discriminated by such broad differences, that the most unsuspecting reader, who might be otherwise deceived, would by the perusal of one page be admonished of his mistake. Our Edinburgh advocate, however, is not unread in German lore nor indifferent to German manners, as his present book evinces. He shows, however, no philosophical insight, but only a pietistic meditativeness; and sees, in speculative infidelity, the root of the practical evils that came to maturity in the French Revolution. He is not the first man who, in the logic school, has put the cart before the horse. With the War of Liberation, Mr. Carlyle recognizes a new era. He sides with the "German pietists" against "irreligion and rationalism," using the last as convertible terms,—a point on which we commend him to read Dr. Arnold. To the moral eminence of Prussia Mr. Carlyle bears honourable witness, and of the present king speaks in the highest praise. He is ready to break a lance for him against all gainsayers, and insists that this monarch has done all that he ever promised, and promised all that he ought in prudence and duty. Constitutional principles in Germany, so frequently arrayed against the king, are, our author tells us, "subversive of monarchy and good order, and associated with infidel illumination." Such principles are well enough for England, but will not bear transplanting. Mr. Carlyle loves the principle of unlimited monarchy for itself, and talks of a king's heart being filled by Heaven "with royal wisdom, as no heart can be filled but that of a king," and advocates the necessity of his being *personally* known and felt in the administration of government. In fact, the paternal system of Prussia is the author's ideal;—while, unfortunately, "the British throne already totters on the base of a salary,"—and, more unfortunate still, "the English are insolent to hirelings." We confess ourselves, however, at a loss for materials to confirm this latter statement; for we believe that, if Queen Victoria and Prince Albert be hirelings as predicated, there have been few holders of dominion as "personal estate" more flattered by their subjects;—nay, courtly adulation among the people has lately been a sign of the times even calling for special remark and censure. We have shown enough to characterize Mr. Carlyle's book, and our readers will not be surprised in finding that, in his opinion, the English likewise are no lovers of aristocracy, and that the Germans are (the members of "Young Germany" excepted); but that it is "one omen of good, that *Young England* would restore what *Young France* and *Young Germany* would combine to abolish." Notwithstanding, however, Mr. Carlyle makes many sound and good remarks on the relations between peer and peasant, nor does he ill distinguish between the different merits of the English and the German noble. His opinions, too, on ecclesiastical matters are decided and intelligible; for he tells us, in a word, that Tithe is the Church. The neglect of this principle he states to be injurious to German society, and deprives the household of that corporate life which he thinks essential. Individualism and Protestantism are alike in extreme in families and institutions; yet "the Bible is more boasted in than read: the national idol, 'Gotte's Wort,' the impersonal foundation and judge of protestants, is, like every idol, barren." Moreover, there is among the Germans a false longing for emotion, by which they have been led to "quaff greedily the cup of Goethe's devilry and Bulwer's licentiousness." We must now quote:—

"No one can fail to admire the strength of domestic affection so frequently and naïvely exhibited among Germans. But where its ardour does not operate as a family bond, the sense of obligation too often fails. With all his apparent hebetude, the German is, to an almost incredible degree, the creature of impulse. And where that impulse runs counter to duty, there lies his greatest danger. While parents and masters fail in due attention to those under them, the relations of children to parents, of servants to masters, bear few marks of any real faith in guidance, or of any self-denying submission to control; and although servants are not so insolent or corrupt, they are more passionate and lawless than in England. The multiplication of the legal grounds of divorce beyond those recognized by the Church, so as to bring the conscientious among the clergy into the most painful dilemmas, show how loose are the domestic ties; how lightly regarded the breach of them; and, on the falsest pretexts, how frequently the postponement of duty to feeling, in accordance with the 'Wahlverwandschaften' of that arch-corrupter, Goethe. It is not uncommon for a man to have been married to six surviving spouses in succession. A lady has been known to sit at a card-table with three successive husbands. So jealous are the Germans of their privileges in this matter, that no proposed law has produced greater excitement among them than one intended to set marriage on its scriptural basis; to limit the grounds and increase the solemnity of divorce; and to stamp with reprobation the offending party. It is even said that many couples, who anticipated an ultimate separation, have hastened it, to avoid the operation of the new law."

Such a statement as this must be taken of course with grains of allowance: there is evidently a bias in the mind of the writer—he treats the subject as an advocate, not a witness. Similar, too, is the spirit in which he brings a railing accusation against Luther, and the Sabbath-breaking habits of his modern disciples, their mammonolatry, and subservience to Jewish influence. In Poland the Jew is, says Mr. Carlyle, "the mortgagee of the earth—in Holland, the receptacle of its gold—in Germany, the astute student of its learning. And whether by relaxations on the part of Christian governments, or by compromise on his part, there is no province of literature, and scarce any of public employment, into which he has not crept, and where he is not felt." Mr. Carlyle's fears in the Jew "stick deep." The "Judaico-Christian literati" are his especial terror. The student of German literature is the member of a recognized republic; yet "it is the hardest thing in the world to transfer anything German out of the region of discussion into that of transaction." But the chief evil is, that the new style of composition is employed by the "coryphæi of liberalism." According to Mr. Carlyle, Hegelism is nothing better than atheism, and, notwithstanding its esoteric abstruseness, calculated for popular acceptance in its exoteric relations. "It contradicts nothing: it confounds, neutralizes, and eliminates all objects of personal faith." Mr. Carlyle is literally frightened;—we are inclined to think, ludicrously so:—

"Germany, with such a volcano in its bosom, stands in two very opposite relations to the countries around it on the one hand, and to America on the other. However oppressive in its character, and extravagant, if not ludicrous, in its consequences, the Roman Catholic tyranny over literature and science was, the controversies of Bonn and Paris between the Church and the University have abundantly proved, that if unlawful exercise of control over learning is an evil, its absence is one still greater. Lawless thoughts need but contact with lawless hands to destroy the world. The German has hitherto dealt with the algebra and logarithms, not with the real quantities, of knowledge. The American, essentially a doer, has sought for principles to realize. Each has found what he sought. The American, without history or pedigree even in literature, unmellowed and unclothed, a *novus homo* in the world, has expressly avoided drawing from British sources, lest his doing so should compromise his liberty, and bring him under bonds to ancient institutions. The influx of American students, as well as English Dissenters and Scottish Presbyterians, into Germany, and their translations of German works, testify how congenial they find the soil of philosophical licence and religious lawlessness. The caricature, compounded of German pedantry and American slang, of words pregnant with classic import bought up by the gross and miskeeped in the 'go-a-head' colloquial style of the new country—the sight of ancient garb and gait, plundered from the owner, and misfitted to the wearer, is not a little amusing. But the German has a secret joy in seeing his thoughts realized abroad to an extent which he dare not even imagine at home. What will come of it remains to be seen; but the marriage is one which augurs an evil progeny. On the other hand, while the German philosophy is rendered more liberal by being transplanted to America, it is that which fosters the liberalism and infidelity of its continental neighbours. The Dane, the Swede, the Frenchman, the Italian, the Greek, the Hungarian, and even the Turk, but most of all the Russian, turns to Germany, in the hope of emancipation from the trammels of ancient prejudice. In Russia, the ruler and the ruled, though with different ends, seek, by a rare coincidence, the same things; the Emperor, seeking to cope with Europe by improving his intellectual breed, as a farmer his cattle; the people, stealthily awakening to a consciousness of their wants and of their power. The education, in search of which the literary emissaries of Russia are spread abroad, has no professed connexion with religion. Indeed it cannot; for it is sought at the hands of heretics. In point of fact, it will soon subvert the institutions it is intended to sustain. Germany is the great magazine for every freethinker and liberal of northern Europe. And this is the more remarkable, when we consider that there never was a time when she was nationally more at antipodes with both Russia and France; hating the duplicity, tyranny, and ambition of Russian character and policy to such a degree, that nothing but the alliance of the courts prevents a rupture; and holding everything French at a discount, to an extent which her increased power now renders safe. It is in vain to imagine that the German censorship, justifiable and expedient or not, well or ill administered, has any efficacy in correcting the evils of German literature. Continental governments, professing to keep the peace of this world only, are generally so careless of the higher interests of man, and so sensitive as to political offences, that the censorship which they exercise cannot be duly directed. Political disturbance is the great bugbear of every continental functionary. In many countries criminality is attached to the use of certain words, even though that use be exactly the opposite of evil; upon much the same principle as that upon which the Roman Catholic finds a warrant for the worship of the saints in Rev. xxii. 8. And if a man, with his tongue or pen, only steer clear of politics, he is accounted harmless. Religious faith and moral principle, being regarded as mere matters of speculation, or as things affecting only the world to come, are exempt from the censor's control. If a book contain one or two political remarks, perhaps useful, it is suppressed; but the most subtle licentiousness, flagrant immorality, subversive scepticism, destructive heresy, and revolting blasphemy, pass by wholesale. The censorship, as the conservator of public religion or morals, truly strains at a gnat and swallows a camel, because the censor himself either is an abettor of the evil, or cannot reach to where it truly lies."

Mr. Carlyle would put all this freethinking under ecclesiastical control for its regulation—or rather, we should add, for its destruction. There are, he intimates, few Coleridges in England, and scarcely any but Coleridges in Germany. There, intellect intrudes into sacred things—theology is separated from religion, instruction from the Church—and talent and learning are idolized. Now, we apprehend that there will be here a difference of opinion, and that Mr. Carlyle will not be permitted to have it all his own way. In brief, though the present be a clever, it is an exceedingly one-sided book. There is scarcely a page in which the author does not pretend to be wiser than Providence, as manifested in historical progress; and, in some passages, he indicates a superstitious temperament which proves him to be an unsafe guide in any argument wherein religious opinions are implicated. The sincerity and zeal which he everywhere shows should make us only more cautious; these qualities, admirable in themselves, belong, unfortunately, as much to the fanatic of error as to the advocate of truth.

The Spirit of German Poetry. By J. Gostick. Smith.

We have here, in the cheap and popular form of 'Smith's Standard Library,' a series of critical and biographical notices, and of translations from the German poets, comprising both the earliest and latest specimens. These chapters on the Teutonic muse contain much information, conveyed in a popular style, though sometimes characterized by a levity of manner which we wish had not been affected; for that it is affectation is clear from their general tone, which is grave and discriminative. Mr. Gostick properly distinguishes between the features peculiar to German and English poetry, and judges correctly when he says, that we may best arrive at a proper appreciation by a fair analysis of their productions. He neither agrees with those who have ranked Goethe with Shakspeare, and classified 'Faust' with 'Othello,' nor with those who have styled Goethe "the master of humbug," and condemned German poetry altogether as mystical, puerile, and sentimental. He acknowledges that many German works are little in accordance with English taste; and adds that, "if we seek for Shakspeare's dramatic vigour and variety, for Milton's grandeur of imagination, or for Byron's gloom and passion, we can find them at home." Of the old popular legends of Germany he speaks also with great respect, and gives, in particular, what was much wanted, a succinct and intelligible account of the ancient epic of the 'Niebelungen-lied.'

"The date of this poem is somewhere in the twelfth century, but in all probability it was founded upon and grew genially out of old tragical ballads of a very early origin. Something more than the slight fragments from misty old times, from which our Macpherson composed his incongruous 'Ossian,' inspired the minstrel, or minstrels, who, even in the palmy days of chivalry, dared to confront the sentimental lays of the period with this grim representation of the stern old times of Gunther, Siegfried, and Hagen. * * Here is the tale of bloodshed: like Homer's story, it begins with a fair woman:—

In Burgundy there flourished a maiden wondrous fair—
In all the lands around none with her could compare.
And Kriemhilde was the name of this most beauteous maid,
For whose sake many warriors brave in bloody graves were laid.

Our heroine had received, in a dream, such an unfavourable omen of marriage, that she had resolved to spend her days in celibacy. But there was one destined to shake the maiden's determination. The fame of her beauty aroused the spirit of Siegfried, son of Siegmund, king of Netherland. Armed with a magical sword, and a cap that made its wearer invisible, besides being rendered invulnerable in body (but for one unlucky spot between his shoulders) by bathing in the blood of a conquered dragon, he considered himself amply prepared for the enterprise of gallantry upon which he set out—to win the hand of Kriemhilde, * * with the attendance of only twelve knights. The queen of Siegelind and her ladies prepared suitable array for the young hero, and he departed, as we should say, 'in excellent spirits.' * * We cannot accompany the hero through all his adventures at the court of Burgundy. Here, having gained the favour of King Gunther (Kriemhilde's brother), by assisting him in the overthrow of many enemies, Siegfried proceeds further in his good fortune by persuading Kriemhilde to lay aside all memory of her ominous dream, and accept him as her betrothed. But we must not thus drily pass over all details of the only *affaire du cœur* which relieves the atrocities of this sanguinary old epic. Here are some pleasant glimpses of true love in a barbarous age:—

The ladies of King Gunther's court inquired the hero's name,
And whence the bold and noble knight, and why he hither came,
So beautiful in person, and so splendid in array—
"'Tis the hero of the Netherland," the gallant courtiers say.

At every game and spectacle the hero was displayed,
Who carried in his heart the image of the maid;
And the maiden, still unseen, though he came her love to win,
Had kindly thoughts for him her secret bosom in.

For when, within the court, the knights and squires would play
With lances, spears, and swords, in battle-like array,
Kriemhilde, through her window, would watch the pastime long;
No better pastime needed she, if *he* was in the throng.

And had he known that she whom he carried in his breast
Was looking from her window, and marked him from the rest,
Or had he met her eye there, I verily believe
He would have been as happy as a man may be and live!

Siegfried had proved himself a genuine hero of romance, by daring to fall in love with an unseen lady. No wonder that he was impatient for an interview. There are touches in the following scene which seem too delicate for the rude rhapsodist of the 'Niebelungen-lied':—

She came out from her chamber: so comes the morning red
Forth from the gloomy clouds ; upon her dress were spread
Bright gems ; her glowing cheeks her secret love confess'd;
Of all the maids on earth she the fairest was and best.

For as among the stars the full moon clearly gleams,
And scatters every cloud with her bright and silver beams,
So 'mid the other ladies Kriemhilde's beauty shone ;
The hearts of many heroes beat high as they looked on.

The chamberlains before her walked, in costly garments dress'd,
To see the lovely maiden the warriors onward pressed ;
As Siegfried stood expecting to look upon her face,
By turns, despair and love found within his bosom place.

Thus said he to himself : "How could I ever deem
That I could win the maid? 'twas but an idle dream ;
But if I cannot win her, than I were better dead."
And with his thoughts his cheeks, by turns, were pale and red.

Said one of the Burgundians,—the chamberlain Gernôt—
"The hero who has fought for us must not be now forgot ;
So let the maiden welcome him before this company,
And give him thanks and praises due for all his bravery."

The servants found the hero bold, Siegfried of Netherland,
And bade him boldly come in front of all the warriors' band :
"King Gunther to his presence is pleased to summon you,
That his sister may salute you, and give the honour due."

His soul rose high within him when he saw Kriemhilde there,
And rosy flushed his cheeks as spoke the maiden fair :
"I bid you welcome, Siegfried, a warrior good and brave !"
The kindly salutation new strength and courage gave.

To thank her for her kindness the hero bowed his head,
And love drew near together the hero and the maid ;
For, as he bowed his head, a stolen glance was cast,
And, suddenly, from eye to eye the tender secret passed.

That he kissed Kriemhilde's hand, upon this happy day,
In the fervour of his love, is more than I can say ;
Yet I cannot well believe he would let the moment flee
Without such proper sign of his love and constancy.

In all the summer season, or the pleasant month of May,
He never had such pleasure as on that happy day,
When he walked beside the maiden whom he came to make his bride,—
When Kriemhilde, whom he loved, was walking by his side !

Soon after this favourable opening of his courtship, Siegfried recommends himself to King Gunther, by assisting him in winning the hand of a tremendous Amazon, named Brunhilde queen of Isenland. This was done by fulfilling the arduous conditions with which this queen proffered her hand to every bold suitor,— by vanquishing her majesty in the sports of throwing the spear, leaping, and hurling a prodigious mass of stone, like one of Homer's heroes on the Trojan plain. As a reward for this assistance, King Gunther gave to Siegfried the hand of Kriemhilde, and their marriage took place soon after the conquest of Queen Brunhilde. But now we have two ladies (and both proud ones) in the plot, and it is no wonder if we soon scent mischief at the court of King Gunther. The queen, Brunhilde, was offended at the apparent low rank of Siegfried, who had dared to match himself with royalty. Moreover, Siegfried had been called in to complete the conquest of the Amazon, who had turned the bridal-chamber into a battle-ground, had almost beaten her royal husband to death, and, after binding him hand and foot with her girdle, had completed the ignominy by suspending him upon a nail in the wall ! Such a conflict, in such a place, was, surely, never described by any other epic poet ; but we must pass over all the grotesque and amusing details. After a very hard fight with the royal lioness, Siegfried left her thoroughly subdued, and meek as a lamb, and bore away, as trophies of his victory, her girdle and her ring. These trophies, in an ill-omened hour, he gave to his wife Kriemhilde. Marvellous to tell, after this seed of dissension had been sown, two years were allowed to pass away in peace ! This, however, may be explained by the fact that the ladies were kept asunder ; for Siegfried had taken his wife to his own country. But Queen Brunhilde, intent on a quarrel, reminded her husband that the hero of the Netherland had neglected to present himself at the court. Accordingly, Siegfried and Kriemhilde were invited to the court at Worms. Here the ladies encountered each other, and, in a little time, materials were concocted for ire more fell than that of Achilles, and consequent battles more sanguinary than any that stained the plain of Troy. Queen Brunhilde and Kriemhilde had not been long together before they engaged on a most dangerous topic of conversation,—the comparative excellence of their respective husbands. What but evil could arise from such a discussion? * * Queen Brunhilde, mad with wrath, soon laid a plot of vengeance, and engaged the fiercest hero of Burgundy, Hagen, the uncle of King Gunther, to revenge upon Siegfried the insult offered by his wife ; though the hero of the Netherland denied, with an oath, all participation in the offence ; and even, to confirm his oath, promised to inflict a severe punishment on his lady. But Hagen hated Siegfried on his own account, and undertook the work of revenge as a labour of love. Having won deceitfully from Kriemhilde the secret of the only vulnerable spot in her husband's body, he invited the young hero to join a hunting-party. * * Hagen cruelly caused the corpse of the murdered Siegfried to be laid at Kriemhilde's chamber-door. Long and deep was the mourning for Siegfried. But now, while Brunhilde felt satiated with revenge, the widowed Kriemhilde, in her turn, began to meditate dire vengeance. She went home with her father-in-law, Siegmund, to the Netherland. Here, after a time, she received an embassy from Etzel, king of the Huns, praying that she would give him her hand. She took a second husband, as an instrument to avenge the death of Siegfried ; and, amid all the splendours of the marriage festivity, her heart was nursing thoughts of destruction for her enemies. After the lapse of thirteen years, she returned the unfriendly compliment of Queen Brunhilde, which had led to the murder of Siegfried, by inviting King Gunther, his brothers, and his uncle Hagen, to a great feast in Hungary. After some doubts and suspicions, this invitation was accepted ; and the king set out for Hungary, with a company of 1,000 knights and 9,000 squires, as ready for a fray as for a feast. Kriemhilde, now the queen of the Huns, began the quarrel by demanding from Hagen the treasure of her former husband, Siegfried ; of which he rudely refused to give any account. The next morning after their arrival King Etzel invited his guests to attend mass with him ; but his treacherous design was avoided by the companions of King Gunther, who went to church in full armour. After mass, there was a great banquet, where Etzel and his

54. continued

knights prudently imitated the guests from Burgundy, and sat at table armed to the teeth. A grim company, where the parties were as ready to spill each other's blood as to pour out wine! The ferocious Hagen, who seemed eager to bring secret ill-will into open strife, cast an insult upon the young prince, Ortlieb, the son of Etzel and Kriemhilde. After this, swords stayed not long in their sheaths. The onslaught was commenced by King Etzel's brother, named Blodelin, who accused Dankwart, the brother of Hagen, as one of Siegfried's murderers. Dankwart answered the charge by striking off the head of Blodelin. And now began a scene of horrible carnage. The Burgundian squires, led on by Dankwart, drove out from the dining-hall the knights of King Etzel; but these, soon returning to the charge with augmented numbers, slew all the nine thousand. Dankwart cut his way through the Huns, and announced to his formidable brother, Hagen, the murder of the squires; upon which Hagen began battle in the hall, where the kings, Gunther and Etzel, with their respective companies of knights, were sitting, by striking off the head of the young prince, which fell into the lap of Queen Kriemhilde. Immediately began an onslaught as violent as that in the squires' hall. King Etzel and his queen were rescued from the slaughter by the stout knight Dietrich, who bore them away in his arms. The knights of Burgundy avenged the slaughter of their squires by slaying the seven thousand knights of King Etzel, and throwing their bodies out of the hall window. But Kriemhilde soon renewed the conflict, by bringing against the Burgundian knights an army of twenty thousand Huns. After a fierce fight, when the Huns had lost great numbers, and only six hundred of the heroes of Burgundy remained, the hall was fired; and, in the madness of their rage and thirst, Hagen and his company drank the blood of their foes. The fire was quenched; and, on the next morning, the besieged knights slew another host of Huns. But now the story becomes monotonous in its catastrophe of carnage. Yet in this part of the old legend of blood-shedding we find the only trait of anything like gentleness and generosity which relieves the crimson of its pages. This is in the character of Rudiger, the Hunnish knight, who had performed the rites of hospitality to the Burgundian knights upon their journey, and was only prevailed upon to join in the slaughter by the earnest entreaties of the king and the queen. Before he joined battle, he supplied Hagen with his own shield; and even this stern man-killer was so far moved by the compliment that he vowed to spare Rudiger's life. But this brave knight fell by another hand, and all his fellow knights, after fighting until the Burgundian heroes were reduced to a few, were numbered with the slain. We hurry over the piles of the dead to the conclusion, where we find none left in the bloody hall but King Gunther and Hagen. Dietrich, at last, after another hard fight, succeeded in binding and carrying captive King Gunther and Hagen. Queen Kriemhilde demanded of the latter the secret of Siegfried's hidden treasure, and, on his refusal to disclose it, commanded the head of her own brother, King Gunther, to be struck off—which, of course, was instantly done. Hagen still persisted in his refusal, and the heroine, unsheathing the magic sword of her former husband, next struck off the head of her uncle! Even King Etzel wept over the death of the stern hero by the hand of a woman. The poem concludes with one hard stroke of poetical justice,—the death of the woman from whose tongue one bitter word had stirred up all this fatal strife! Hildebrand, the friend of Dietrich, not bearing that a hero should perish unrevenged, plunged his falchion into the side of the queen, who fell to fill the number of the slain; and Dietrich and King Etzel are left to mourn and bury the dead. The rhapsodist gives one short moral (and a very *bad* one) to all this murder, saying:—

Thus *love* doth evermore its dole and sorrow bring;—

then breaks off with :—

But what, since then, befel; I cannot sing or say.

Such is the story of the famous 'Niebelungen-lied,' a production which has supplied dramatic subjects to German painters, such as Cornelius and Schnorr, for the decoration of the King of Bavaria's palace at Munich. And, if stripped of its charms of style,

how much better would the bare argument even of the 'Iliad' appear? How far would 'divine' Achilles tower, in true strength and greatness, above the ferocious, bloody-handed Hagen? There is a moral even in this old German epic, though it might be far from the thoughts of the rhapsodist, who poured it forth, evidently, *con amore*. It is a sincere exposure of the old times of violence, the days of heroes renowned for strength, but who were weaker than babes in every true manly virtue. That to forgive injuries, to make peace, to subdue violent passions, is a task proving a greater strength and a sterner courage than all evinced in the carnage of the 'Iliad' or the 'Niebelungen-lied,' was a truth unknown in the days of King Gunther and his hero Hagen. The only interest which this singular old epic retains is in its style. Here it may claim a pre-eminence over many poems, superior in other respects, which have usurped the name of the epic. In the clear style of its narrative, and the *naiveté* with which the old rhapsodist often dashes off a striking picture in a few simple lines, there is presented a profitable study even for some modern poets."

Something of the occasional flippancy of style of which we have complained may be traced in the above extract. The morality of an epic poem is not to be judged of by its final apothegm; neither is the maxim that concludes the 'Niebelungen-lied' to be condemned for either brevity or evil. That " Love doth evermore its dole and sorrow bring," is (and we are sure that Mr. Gostick need not be told of it) the one great problem of our human condition. The morality of such poems, in fact, is the heroic sentiments which, in the midst of all their barbarity, they inspire,—the contempt of wealth and ease, and life itself, in favour of the principle of honour, ill understood but devoutly acknowledged. There are other analyses and translations in this work which do credit to the author—particularly those of Goethe's 'Tasso,' and 'Hermann and Dorothea.' In specimens of recent and contemporaneous German song, the compilation, moreover, is rich, and not superseded by any critical work with which we are acquainted.

55. DUBLIN REVIEW, 19 (1845), 312-331. M/H No. 4125. By C. W. Russell.

ART. II.—*Anthologia Germanica—German Anthology; a Series of Translations, from the most Popular of the German Poets.* By JAMES CLARENCE MANGAN, post 8vo. 2 vols. Dublin: 1845.

POETICAL translations from the foreign languages, especially the German, have multiplied so rapidly of late years, that the English reader is often bewildered in attempting to make a selection. There are at least a dozen English versions of Goethe's Faust; nearly twice the number of Schiller's Song of the Bell; and even the less remarkable poems of both authors have been, in most instances, repeatedly translated. Still the rage for translation seems to have been confined to these and a few other poets; while the public has been left in comparative ignorance of a host of other writers equally original, little less gifted, and, if less prolific, certainly not less necessary for a proper estimate of the national literature of Germany.

The volumes now before us will introduce the reader to many poets who are comparatively unknown, but whose acquaintance notwithstanding, will, we make no doubt, prove little less agreeable than that of the old and traditionary representatives of German literature. The translations, with one single exception, are reprinted from a series of papers in the *Dublin University Magazine.*

man, a Mr. Russell, was subsequently employed in various diplomatic missions, and in after life must have reflected with shame and horror on the frantic excess of such party spirit. So signal an instance of its delirious influence is, and must remain, without parallel; for where could the baneful passion find such a victim or batten on such a prey?—But

> "He who surpasses or subdues mankind,
> Must look down on the hate of those below.
>   *   *   *   *   *
> Round him are icy rocks, and loudly blow
> Contending tempests on his naked head;
> And thus reward the toils, which to these summits lead."
> *Childe Harold.* Canto iii. 45.

For the direful rivalry of the contending factions of that day in America, Washington's Life by Jarred Sparke, vol. ii. p. 49, should be read. But, to the versatility of popular feeling, the never-failing animadversion of historians, may be opposed. Machiavelli's observations on the text of Livy, "Hæc natura multitudinis est, aut humiliter servit aut superbe dominatur," (lib. xxiv. cap. 25,) which transfer the blame, in a higher degree, to the rulers. "Dico adunque, come di quel difetto, di che accusano gli scrittori la moltitudine, se ne possono accusare tutti gli huomini, particolarmente, et massimamente i principi; perche ciascuno, che non sia regolato dalle leggi, farebbe quelli medesimi errori, che la moltitudine sciolta." (Discorsi sopra la prima deca di Tito Livio, lib. ii. cap. 58.)

But the intervals of publication were distant and irregular; the papers were scattered through nearly twenty volumes of this periodical, and the author has done good service to the public in reprinting them in this neat and convenient form, in which they assume, for all practical purposes, the character of a new and independent work. Indeed, we have no hesitation in saying, that the *German Anthology* is destined to take its place in the very highest rank of poetical translations. Mr. Mangan's mind is precisely of that plastic character which is indispensable for spirited and truthful translations. He possesses, in a high degree, the art of thoroughly divesting himself, in his capacity of translator, of every individuality of thought and of manner, and becoming, so to speak, the mere instrument of the author whom he translates. The moment he takes up the pen, he forgets himself altogether; or rather he, as it were, converts himself into his original thinking and writing in a new language; so that not alone the thought, but the words, the form, the style, the manner, the very metre, are faithfully rendered back. With him translation is a mere process of fusion; but the metal is recast in precisely the same mould, and preserves not alone the substance, but the most minute and delicate peculiarities of form which characterised its original structure.

And this faculty is still more extraordinary when exercised, as here, upon an almost endless variety of subjects. That a translator, by long study and fervent admiration of a single author, or even of several authors belonging to the same school and resembling each other in the general character of their compositions, should become thoroughly familiar with that character, and as it were, come to form his thoughts habitually in the same mould, is natural enough, and can be easily understood by any one who has at all studied the art of composition. But Mr. Mangan has tried his hand on more than forty different models, and appears equally at home with all. With that strange faculty of which naturalists tell, his pen seems to take its colour from the food it feeds upon—it is pious and didactic with Hölty or Klopstock—humorous and burlesque with Dunkel—it plunges into the depths of mysticism with De la Motte Fouqué—and laughs at the world with Kotzebue or Bürger. The writer is a complete literary Proteus. He appears to be equally in his element among the fairy tales of Schnezler, and the philosophic reveries of Schill. or Goethe; and after throwing his whole soul into one f the fiery philippics of Freiligrath or Kerner, can return t dream over the melancholy sentimentalism of Tieck, or Simrock, or Rückert, as though he had lived his life long in those dreamy halls,

" Where melancholy music ceaseless swells."

Indeed, we have seldom, perhaps never, met any writer who possesses in a higher degree that mastery over the varieties of metre and the proprieties of poetical phrase. ology, which supplies, as it were, the mechanical tools of the poet. The reader of Anster's Faust, for example, cannot fail to be struck with the evidence of this power which is displayed in that wonderful poem. But if he turn to the original, he will find that this luxuriance and versatility is for the most part Dr. Anster's own—the sparkling and bubbling up of the well-spring of genuine poetry, which refuses to be confined within artificial boundaries. Though his own versification is extremely varied, he seldom follows the variety of the original. But it is not so with the author of the Anthology. To him it appears a matter of complete indifference into what form of metre he may throw his thoughts; and the great charm of his versification is, that throughout all its varieties it preserves its freedom, its liveliness, and above all, its perfect propriety.

We have often, therefore, been tempted to regret, that a writer possessing a faculty so rare among the poets of this country—one too which lends-such a charm to the lighter pieces of our German neighbours—should not have done something in the line of original English poetry, if it were only to prove that the language is not unsusceptible of similar varieties of poetical structure. But we are inclined, on reflection, to doubt whether this extraordinary power of imitation is compatible with great originality of poetical genius. The vine-branch can climb the rock, or creep along the plain—its tendrils will follow the upright course of the poplar, or twine among the twisted branches of the mulberry; but by itself it is helpless and intractable —and perhaps the mind which habituates itself to borrow inspiration from another, and moulds itself into the fashion of another's thought, is only following therein a hidden instinct, which warns it that it was not destined to labour

alone, and is not possessed of resources for great original conceptions.

The Anthology, as we have said, comprises samples of above forty German authors, the greater number of whom flourished within the present century, and many within our own time. Still it is necessary to caution the reader against supposing that it contains all the great names, even of modern German poetry. Indeed we are unable to account for some of the omissions. Probably the religious poets did not come within the author's design, therefore their absence is less remarkable;—but there is not a word from Wieland, from either of the Schlegels, from Novalis, or from our favourite poor Ernest Schulze; not to speak of Bouterweck, or Uz, or Schubert, or above all, King Louis of Bavaria. In these latter days, poetry is so seldom found upon a throne, that a poet-king would seem to deserve notice, were it only as a literary curiosity. But independently of any consideration of rank, King Louis well merits a place among the poets of modern Germany, though his genius is not marked by great originality; and his name is so completely identified with the progress both of art and of literature, not only in his own dominions, but throughout the entire Germanic confederation, that it seems almost unpardonable not to make room for him in the collection. Perhaps, however, it is unfair to take exceptions such as these against a work in every way so meritorious; and indeed we believe it is the very excellence of the translations that makes us regret the exclusion of these and several other authors, for the fame of some among whom, as being special favourites of our own, we are particularly solicitous; and we trust that the well merited success of this first experiment, will induce the author to extend and continue his inimitable translations.

That the reader may judge whether we have formed an undue estimate of the truth, energy, and spirit, which characterize Mr. Mangan's versions, our first specimen shall be from a well-known ballad, which has already been translated by many of our most distinguished poets— Burger's Leonore. The fidelity of the version can hardly be felt, except by comparing it, line for line, with the original. In justice, therefore, to the author, we shall transcribe them in parallel volumes, even at the risk of appearing unnecessarily minute in our criticism.

As the story of the ballad is sufficiently familiar, we pass over the return of the triumphant army—the wild anxiety of the maiden's search for her lover among the throng—her despair when she discovers that he is no more—her mother's unavailing efforts at consolation, and the blasphemous excess of desperation into which the unhappy girl flies in her grief, all of which are rendered with inimitable accuracy and force—to come to the midnight visit of her spectre bridegroom.

So wüthete verzweifelung,*
Ihr in Gehirn und Adern,

Sie fuhr mit Gottes Vorsehung,
Vermessen fort zu hadern,
Zerschlug den Busen, und zerrang

Die Hand, bis Sonnenuntergang,
Bis auf am Himmelsbogen,
Die goldnen Sterne zogen.

Und aussen, horch! ging's trap, trap, trap,
Als wie von Rosseshufen,
Und klirrend stieg ein Reiter ab,
An des Geländer's Stufen,
Und horch! und horch! den Pforten-ring,
Ganz lose, leise, kling, kling, kling!
Dann kamen durch die Pforte,
Vernehmlich diese Worte:

"Holla, holla! thu auf mein Kind!
Schläfst, Liebchen, oder wachst du?
Wie bist noch gegen mich gesinnt?
Und weinest oder lachst du?"
"Ach, Wilhelm, du! So spät bei nacht!

Geweinet hab' ich und gewacht,
Ach grosses Leid erlitten!
Wo kommst du hergeritten?"

"Wir satteln nur um Mitternacht,
Weit ritt ich her von Böhmen,
Ich habe spät mich aufgemacht,
Und will dich mit mir nehmen!"
"Ach Wilhelm, erst herein geschwind!
Den Hagedorn durchsaust der Wind,

Herein in meinen Armen,
Herzliebster, zu erwarmen!"
*   *   *   *   *
*   *   *   *   *
*   *   *   *   *

"And thus, as reigned and raged despair
Throughout her brain, through every vein,
Did this presumptuous maiden dare
To tax with ill, God's righteous will;
And rang her hands, and beat her breast,
Till sunk the sunlight in the west,
And under heaven's ethereal arch,
The golden stars began their march.

"When, list! a sound! hark! *hoff*, *hoff*, *hoff*—
It nears, she hears a courser's tramp—
And swiftly bounds a rider off,
Before the gate with clattering stamp.
And hark, the bell goes *ring, ding, ding!*

"And hark again, *cling, ling, ling, ling!*
And through the portal and the hall,
Thus peals a voice with hollow call:

"'What ho! up, up, sweet love inside!
Dost watch for me, or art thou sleeping!
Art false, or still my faithful bride!
And smilest thou, or art thou weeping!'
'What! Wilhelm! thou? and come thus late!
Oh, night has seen me watch and wait,
And suffer so! But oh, I fear—
Why this wild haste in riding here!'

"'I left Bohemia late at night;
We journey, but at midnight, we!
My time was brief, and fleet my flight,
Up, up! thou must away with me!'
'Ah, Wilhelm! come inside the house,
The wind moans through the fir-tree boughs,
Come in, my heart's beloved! and rest,
And warm thee in this faithful breast.'
*   *   *   *   *
*   *   *   *   *

Schon Liebchen schurzte, sprang, und schwang,
Sich auf das Ross behende,
Wohl um den trauten Reiter schlang,
Sie ihre Lilienhände:

Und hurre, hurre, hop, hop, hop,
Ging's fort in sausendem Galopp,
Dass Ross und Reiter schnoben,
Und Kies und Funken stoben.

Zur rechten und zur linken Hand,
Vorbey vor ihren Blicken,
Wie flogen Anger, Haid, und Land!

Wie donnerten die Brücken!
"Graut Liebchen auch! Der Mond scheint hell,
Hurrah! die Todten reiten schnell!
Graut Liebchen auch vor Todten!"
"—Ach nein!—Doch lass die Todten!"
Was klang dort für Gesang und klang?
Was flatterten die Raben?
Horch Glockenklang! horch Todten-sang!
"Lasst uns den Leib begraben!"
Und näher zog ein Leichenzug,
Der Sarg und Todtenbaare trug,
Das Lied war zu vergleichen,
Dem Unkenruf in Teichen.
*   *   *   *   *

Still Klang und Sang.—Die Baare schwand,
Gehorsam seinem Rufen,
Kam's hurre, hurre, nachgerannt.
Hart hinter's Rappen Hufen,

Und immer weiter, hop, hop, hop!
Ging's fort in sausendem Galopp,
Dass Ross und Reiter schnoben,
Und Kies und Funken stoben.

Wie flogen rechts, wie flogen links,
Gebirge, Bäum' und Hecken!

Wie flogen links, und rechts, und links,
Die Dörfer, Städt', und Flecken?

"Graut Liebchen auch! Der mond scheint hell!
Hurrah! die Todten reiten schnell!
Graut Liebchen auch vor Todten!"

"Ach! lass sie ruhn die Todten!"

Sieh da, sieh da! am Hochgerielit,
Tanzt um des Rades Spindel,
Halb sichtbarlich bey Mondeslicht,
"Sasa! Gesindel, hier! komm hier,

Gesindel komm, und folge mir!
Tanz' uns die hochzeitreigen,
Wann wir zu Bette steigen!"

Soon up, soon clad, with lightest bound
On that black steed the maiden sprung,
And round her love, and warmly round,
Her snow-white hands she swung and flung,
And deftly, swiftly, *hoff*, *hoff*, *hoff*,
Away went horse and riders off,
Till panted horse and riders too,
And sparks and pebbles flashed and flew!

"On left and right with whirling flight,
How rock and forest reeled and wheeled,
How danced each height before their sight,
What thunder-tones the bridges pealed.
'Dost fear? the moon is fair to see!

Hurrah! the dead ride rapidly.
Beloved! dost dread the shrouded dead?'
'Ah no—but let them rest!' she said.

"But see! what throng, with song and gong,
Moves by, as croaks the raven hoarse!
Hark! funeral song! Hark, knelling song!
They sing, 'Let's here inter the corse!'
And nearer draws that mourning throng,
And bearing hearse and bier along,
With hollow hymn outgurgled, like
Low reptile groanings from a dyke.
*   *   *   *   *

"Some spell is in the horseman's call,

The hymn is hushed, the hearse is gone,
And in his wake the buriers all,
Tramp, tramp, come clattering pattering on;
And onward, forward, *hoff*, *hoff*, *hoff*!
Away swept all in gallop off,
Till panted steeds and riders too,
And sparks and pebbles flashed and flew.

"On left and right, with flight of light,
How whirled the hills, the trees, the bowers!
With light-like flight, on left and right,
How spun the hamlets, towns, and towers!
'Dost quail? The moon is fair to see,

Hurrah, the dead ride recklessly!
Beloved! dost dread the shrouded dead?'
'Ah! let the dead repose,' she said.

"But look! on yonder gibbet's height,
How round his wheel, as wanly glances
The yellow moon's unclouded light,
A malefactor's carcase dances!
'So ho! poor carcase! down with thee!
Down, King of bones, and follow me,
And thou shalt quickly dance, ho, ho!
Before us when to bed we go!'

---

* It may be necessary to observe that the original German is not given in Mr. Mangan's volumes.

We must pass by the further career of this fiendish cavalcade ; (though, perhaps, in the whole history of diablerie, there is not a single scene depicted with more terrific vividness and power ;) to come to the denouement.

Rasch auf ein eisern Gitterthor,
Ging's mit verhängtem Zügel,

Mit schwankem Gert, ein Schlag davor,
Zersprengte Schloss und Riegel.
Die Flügel flogen Klirrend auf,
Und über Gräber ging der Lauf,
Es blinkten Leichensteine,
Rund um in Mondenscheine.

Ha sieh! ha sieh! im Augenblick,
Huhu! ein grässlich Wunder !
Des Reiter's Koller, Stück für Stück,
Fiel ab wie mürber Zunder.
Zum Schädel, ohne Zopf und Schopf,
Zum nackten Schädel ward sein Kopf,
Sein Körper zum Gerippe,
Mit Stundenglas und Hippe.

Hoch bäumte sich, wild schnob der Rapp',
Und sprühte Feuerfunken,
Und hui! war's unter ihr hinab,
Verschwunden und versunken,
Geheul ! Geheul aus hoher Luft,

Gewinsel kam aus tiefer Gruft,
Lenorens Herz mit Beben,
Rang Zwischen Tod und Leben.

Nun tanzten wohl bei Mondenglanz,
Rund um herum im Kreise,
Die Geister einen Kettentanz,

Und heulten diese Weise,
" Geduld! Geduld! Wenn's Herz auch bricht,
Mit Gott im Himmel hadre nicht,
Des Leibes bist du ledig,
Gott sey der Seele gnädig !"

" Before a grated portal stand
That midnight troop and coal-black horse,
Which, touched as by a viewless wand,
Bursts open with gigantic force!
With trailing reins and lagging speed,
Winds onward now the gasping steed,
Where ghastlily the morn illumes,
A wilderness of graves and tombs !

"He halts, O horrible! behold—
Hoo! hoo! behold a hideous wonder!
The rider's garments drop, like mould
Of crumbling plaster-work asunder!
His skull, in bony nakedness,
Glares hairless, fleshless, featureless !
And now a SKELETON he stands,
With flashing scythe and glass of sands!

"High rears the barb, he snorts, he winks,
His nostrils flame, his eyeballs glow,
And what ! the maiden sinks and sinks
Down in the smothering clay below !
Then howls and shrieks in air were blended,
And wailings from the grave ascended,
Until her heart in mortal strife,
Wrestled with very Death for Life !

"And now as dimmer moonlight wanes,
Round Leonore in shadowy ring,
The spectres dance their dance of chains,
And howlingly she hears them sing—
' Bear, bear, although thy heart be riven !
And tamper not with God in heaven !
Thy corse's knell they soon shall toll,
May God have mercy on thy soul!' "
Vol. i. *pp.* 140—9.

It is only by following word after word the singularly close and spirited version of this extraordinary ballad, that one can fully understand its merit. Bold and stirring, as though it were struck at a heat from the author's own mind—free and flowing, as if it were the extemporaneous outpouring of his own imagination, it is in reality a verbal and literal transcript of the original, preserving not alone the spirit, but the words, the order, the form, and even the minutest peculiarity of structure. Not a sentiment is changed—scarce an epithet is added or withdrawn—and,

above all, not a particle of that bold and fiery spirit, which forms the peculiar charm of the original, is suffered to evaporate in the process of transfusion.

The same minute fidelity, coupled with freedom and vivacity, distinguishes the ballad of "Gertrude Von Hochburg," and that of the "Demon Hunter;" especially the latter, in which it is really wonderful. But we prefer to give a specimen of another class of composition, and one which displays still more the extraordinary pliancy of the translator's pen. Let it be borne in mind that, throughout all the vagaries of the metre of the following passage from Schiller's "Song of the Bell," the same minute fidelity which we have observed in the last example is uniformly maintained. The passage is from the Strophe entitled the Fire-bell.

> " Woe ! when oversweeping far
> With a fury nought can stand,
> Through the stifled streets afar,
> Rolls the monstrous volume-brand !
> For the elements ever war
> With the works of human hand.
> From the cloud
> Blessings gush ;
> From the cloud
> Torrents rush ;
> From the cloud, alike,
> Come the bolts that strike.
> Larum-peals from lofty steeple
> Rouse the people !
> Red, like blood,
> Heaven is flashing !
> How it stains the daylight's flood !
> Hark ! what crashing
> Down the streets !
> Smoke ascends in volumes ;
> Skyward flares the flame in columns !
> Through the tent-like lines of streets
> Rapidly as wind it fleets !
> Now the white air waxing hotter
> Glows a furnace ; pillars totter—
> Rafters crackle—casements rattle—
> Mothers fly—
> Children cry—
> Under ruins whimper cattle—
> All is horror, noise, affright ;
> Bright as noontide glares the night !

Swung from hand to hand with zeal along
  By the throng,
Speeds the pail.—In bow-like form
Sprays the hissing water-shower ;
But the madly-howling storm
Aids the flame with wrathful power.
Round the shrivelled fruit they curl,
Grappling with the granary stores ;
Now they blaze through roof and floors,
And with upward dragging whirl,
Even as though they strove to bear
Earth herself aloft in air,
Shoot into the vaulted Void,
Giant-vast !
Hope is past :—
Man submits to God's decree ;
And, all stunned and silently,
Sees his earthly all destroyed !"
        Vol. i. *pp.* 9—11.

But, instead of following the translator farther through these well-known authors, we shall select a few examples from poets less familiar in these countries. The translations from Körner are all admirable; especially " The Four Idiot Brothers," " Home-sickness," " The Garden that fades not," and the " Address to Uhland." We can afford space but for a single one, " Home-sickness." It is one of those simple thrilling gushes of poetry, which find their way straight to the heart, and never fail to leave a delicious consciousness of their influence, long after their presence ceases to be felt.

"There calleth me ever a marvellous Horn,
  ' Come away ! come away !'
Is it earthly music fumes astray,
  Or is it air-born ?
Oh, whether it be a spirit-wile,
  Or a forest-voice,
It biddeth some ailing heart rejoice,
  Yet sorrow the while !

"In the greenwood glades o'er the garlanded bowl,
  Night, noontide, and morn ;
The summoning call of that marvellous Horn
  Tones home to my soul !
In vain have I sought for it east and west ;
  But I darkly feel
That so soon as its music shall cease to peal,
  I go to my rest !"—*Vol.* i. *p.* 127.

Uhland is better known ; and the specimens of his poetry contained in the Anthology will add to his popularity. He is, or at least was, till the appearance of Freiligrath, emphatically the poetical representative of German nationality ; and the enthusiasm with which his noble ballad, " Forwards !" (I. p. 105.) is sung by his countrymen is hardly inferior to that of a Parisian assembly for the Marseillaise or the Parisienne. The great characteristic of his political compositions is their manliness and energy.

" As a headlong stream that winter had bound,
  When spring reshowers her beams on the plains,
Breaks loose with a fierce impatient bound,
  From its icy chains !"

But, except the single ballad already alluded to, Mr. Mangan has not translated any of these. The best of his collection are "Spring Roses," "The Jeweller's Daughter," a sweet simple ballad, " Durand of Blonden," and " The Castle over the Sea." This last is a good sample, not only of German rhyme, but also of the dark and mysterious character of the narrative which they introduce in their ballad poetry; telling but half the event, and leaving the rest to be gathered from the vague and indistinct allusions in which they delight.

" 'Sawest thou the castle that beetles over
  The wine-dark sea ?
The rosy sunset clouds do hover
  Above it so goldenly.'—

"—'Well know I the castle that beetles over
  The wine-dark sea ;
And a fall of watery clouds did cover
  Its battlements gloomsomely.'

" 'The winds and the moonlit waves were singing
  A choral song ;
And the brilliant castle hall was ringing
  With melody all night long.'

" 'The winds and the moonless waves were sleeping
  In stillness all ;
But many voices of woe and weeping
  Rose out from the castle-hall.'

" 'And sawest thou not step forth so lightly
  The king and the queen ;
Their festal dresses bespangled brightly,
  Their crowns of a dazzling sheen :

"'And by their side a resplendent vision—
    A virgin fair !
The glorious child of some clime elysian,
    With starry gems in her hair?'

"'Well saw I the twain by the wine-dark water,
    Walk slower and slower ;
They were clad in weeds, and their virgin daughter
    Was found at their side no more !'"
Vol. i. *pp.* 100—1.

As our purpose is to illustrate the less known authors of the Anthology, we shall not delay on the translations from Goethe or Herder. They are all extremely good as translations, though we shall not be surprised if they prove the least popular portion of the collection—at least, if we except Herder's " Erl-king's daughter," and Goethe's "Alder-king," " Irish Lamentation," and " Mignon's Song"—which last has an especial interest in being, as it is generally believed, the germ of the opening stanzas of " The Bride of Abydos."

Rückert supplies five pieces to the collection; three of which—"Eleanora von Alleyne," " Gone in the Wind," and " And then no more"—almost realize the ideal of translation. The first of these is a half light, half stately ballad about a whimsical and haughty beauty, who required as the price of her hand that her suitors should ride around the rampart of her castle, which overhung a yawning precipice. The fame of her wealth and beauty nerved many a knight against the danger of the ordeal. They perished, one by one—

"Till six-and-thirty corses, both of mangled men and horses,
    Had been sacrificed as victims of the fame
Of the Lady Eleanora—
    Stately Lady Eleanora von Alleyne."

At length a knight, the " gallant Margrave Condibert" of Gratz, who takes the precaution of training his charger beforehand for the feat, accomplishes it in safety, and by the grace and gallantry of his bearing wins the love, even to madness, of the haughty beauty ; but in requital of her pride and cruelty, refuses to claim the hand he has won ; and the ballad ends by telling

"That long, in shame and anguish, did that haughty lady languish,
    Did she languish without pity for her pain—
She, the Lady Eleanora,
    She, the Lady Eleanora von Alleyne."

As this piece is too long for publication, we must content ourselves with a shorter one of a very different character from the same pen—tender, plaintive, and full of beauty.

AND THEN NO MORE.

" I saw her once, one little while, and then no more :
    'Twas Eden's light on earth awhile, and then no more.
Amid the throng she passed along the meadow-floor ;
Spring seemed to smile on Earth awhile, and then no more,
But whence she came, which way she went, what garb she
    wore,
I noted not ; I gazed awhile, and then no more.

" I saw her once, one little while, and then no more,
    'Twas Paradise on earth, awhile, and then no more :
Ah ! what avail my vigils pale, my magic lore ?
She shone before mine eyes awhile, and then no more.
The shallop of my peace is wrecked on Beauty's shore.
Near Hope's fair isle it rode awhile, and then no more !

" I saw her once, one little while, and then no more :
    Earth looked like Heaven a little while, and then no more.
Her presence thrilled and lighted to its inner core
My desert breast a little while, and then no more.
So may, perchance, a meteor glance at midnight o'er
Some ruined pile a little while, and then no more !

" I saw her once, one little while, and then no more,
    The earth was Peri-land awhile, and then no more.
Oh, might I see but once again, as once before,
Through chance or wile, that shape awhile, and then no more !
Death soon would heal my griefs ! This heart, now sad and
    sore,
Would beat anew a little while, and then no more !
Vol. ii. *p.* 100, 101.

From August Schnezler there are but two pieces—"The Deserted Mill," and " The Lily Maidens"—but they are so beautiful and so characteristic that we shall give them both. They belong, particularly the latter, to that class of purely German fiction, for which De La Motte Fouqué has procured a foreign immortality by his *Undine;* and which Musäus has brought home to every fireside in Germany by his inimitable Volks-Mährchen.

The former of these pieces needs no introduction.

"It stands in the lonely Winterthal
    At the base of Ilsberg hill :
It stands as though it fain would fall,
    The dark deserted mill.

311

Its engines coated with moss and mould,
 Bide silent all the day,
Its mildewed walls and windows old,
 Are crumbling to decay.

" So through the daylight's lingering hours
 It mourns in weary rest ;
But soon as the sun-set's gorgeous bowers
 Begin to fade in the west,
The long dead millers leave their lairs,
 And open its creaking doors ;
And their feet glide up and down its stairs,
 And over its dusty floors.

" And the miller's men, they too awake,
 And the night's weird-work begins ;
The wheels turn round, the hoppers shake,
 The flour falls into the binns.
The mill-bell tolls again and again,
 And the cry is " Grist here, ho !"
And the dead old millers and their men,
 Move busily to and fro.

" And even as the night wears more and more,
 New groups throng into the mill,
And the clangor, deafening enough before,
 Grows louder and wilder still.
Huge sacks are barrowed from floor to floor ;
 The wheels redouble their din,
The hoppers clatter, the engines roar,
 And the flour overflows the binn.

" But with the morning's pearly sheen,
 This ghastly hubbub wanes,
And the moon-dim face of a woman is seen
 Through the meal-dulled window-panes.
She opens the sash and her words resound,
 In tones of unearthly power,
' Come hither, good folks, the corn is ground ;
 Come hither and take your flour !'

" Thereon strange hazy lights appear,
 A flitting all through the pile,
And a deep melodious choral cheer,
 Ascends through the roof the while ;
But a moment more and you gaze and hark,
 And wonder and wait in vain ;
For suddenly all again is dark,
 And all is hushed again.

" It stands in the lonely Winterthal
 At the base of Ilsberg hill :
It stands as though it fain would fall,
 The dark deserted mill.
Its engines coated with moss and mould,
 Bide silent all the day,
Its mildewed walls and windows old,
 Are crumbling to decay."— *Vol. ii. p.* 102—104.

To render " The Lily Maidens" intelligible, it is only necessary to explain that it is a legend of the Black Forest, and that the Mummel Zee is a lake in that traditional seat of all that is poetical in the German mythology.

"Anigh the gloomy Mummel-Zee,
 Do live the palest lilies many;
All day they droop so drowsily,
 In azure air and rainy.
  But when the dreamful noon of night
  Rains down on earth its yellow light,
  Up spring they full of lightness,
  In woman's form and brightness.

"The sad reeds moan like spirits,
 Along the troubled water's border ;
As hand in hand, linked wreath-wise round,
 The virgins dance in order.
  Moon-white in features as in dress,
  Till o'er their phantom huelessness
  A warmer colour gushes,
  And tints their cheeks with blushes.

"Then pipe the reeds a sadder tune,
 The wind raves through the tannen-forest,
The wolves in chorus bay the moon,
 Where glance her grey beams hoarest ;
  And round and round the darkling grass,
  In mazy whirl the dancers pass,
  And louder boom the billows
  Among the reeds and willows.

"But see ! the Giant-elf anon
 Half rises from the water's bosom,
With streaming beard and head whereon
 Dark weeds for garlands blossom ;
  And fiercely lifting towards the strand
  A naked arm and clenched hand,
  He shouts in tones of thunder,
  That wake the abysses under !

"Then lake and winds and dancers rest,
  And as the water ceases booming,
The Elf cries, 'Hence, ye shapes unblest,
  And leave my lilies blooming!'
    And, lo! the streaky morn is up,
    Dew-diamonds brim each flow'ret's cup,
    And Mummel's lily-daughters
    Once more bend o'er his waters."
Vol. ii. *pp.* 105—6.

It is not without a struggle we consent to pass by "Alexander the Great and the Tree," (II. pp. 114-8.) an exquisitely poetical ode of De La Motte Fouqué, and eminently characteristic of its author. But, unhappily, it is too long for our unoccupied space. We shall rather insert in its stead two noble ballads—the first by Ebert, "The Revenge of Duke Swerting," the only thing of his in the collection; the second by the now popular favourite, Freiligrath. They are both in the long swelling measure, the favourite metre of the great ballad-writers of Spain, and introduced into German ballad poetry by Bouterwek and Herder.

Ebert's ballad is founded on the story of Swerting, Duke of Saxony, who having been conquered by Frotho, King of the Danes, was induced to give his daughter in marriage to Ingel, the son of Frotho, who hoped by this alliance to disarm the hostility of his vanquished adversary. How he failed is told in these swelling stanzas:

"O a warrior-feast was Swerting's in his burg beside the Rhine,
There from gloomy iron bell-cups they drank the Saxon wine;
And the viands were served in iron up—in coldest iron all—
And the sullen clash of iron arms resounded through the hall.

"Uneasily sat Frotho there, the tyrant of the Danes;
With low'ring blow he quaffed his cup, then eyed the iron chains,
That hung and clanked like manacles at Swerting's arms and breast,
And the iron studs and linked rings that bossed his ducal vest.

"'What may this bode, this chilling gloom, Sir Duke and brother Knights?
Why meet I here such wintry cheer—such sorry sounds and sights?
Out on your sheets of iron! Will ye bear to have it told
That I found ye thus, when Danish knights go clad in silks and gold?'

"'King! gold befits the freeman—the iron marks the slave;
So thought and spake our fathers, and their sons are just and brave;
Thyself hast bound the iron round thy proud but conquered foe—
If thy chains had been but golden, we had burst them long ago.

"'But I came not here to hold a parle, or tell a wistful tale,
But to bid the dastard tremble, and to make the tyrant quail.
O strong, Sir King, is iron—but the heart is stronger still;
Nor earth can cast in thrall a people's mighty will!'

"While his words yet rang as cymbals, there strode into the hall
Twelve swarthy Saxon Rittersmen, with flaming torches tall;
They stood to catch a signal-glance from Swerting's eagle eye,
Then again they rushed out waving their pitchy brands on high.

"The Danish king grows paler, yet he brims his goblet higher;
But the sultry hall is dark with smoke—he hears the hiss of fire!
Yes! the Red Avenger marches on his fierce and swift career,
And from man to man goes round the whisper, 'Brother, it is near!'

"Up starts the king; he turns to fly—Duke Swerting holds him fast;
'Nay, Golden King, the dice are down, and thou must bide the cast;
If thy chains can fetter THIS fell foe, the glory be thine own,
Thine be the Saxon land for aye, and thine the Saxon throne!'

"But hotter, hotter burns the air all through that lurid hall;
And louder groan the blackened beams—the crackling rafters fall;
And ampler waxes momently the glare, the volumed flash,
Till at last the roof-tree topples down with stunning thunder crash.

"Then in solemn prayer that gallant band of self-devoted kneel—
'Just God! assoil our souls, thus driven to Freedom's last appeal!'
And Frotho writhes and rages—fire stifling his quick gasp;
But strong and terrible as Death his foe maintains his grasp.

"'Behold, thou haughty tyrant, behold what MEN can dare!
So triumph such!—so perish, too, enslavers everywhere!'
And the billowing flames, while yet he speaks, come roaring down the hall,
And the Fatherland is loosed for aye from Denmark's iron thrall!"—*Vol.* ii. *pp.* 183—7.

The "Phantom Caravan" is from the pen of Freiligrath, whose recent contest with the Prussian censorship created so great an interest, not alone in Germany, but throughout the entire continent of Europe. He is a stern advocate of political opinions which find but scant favour beyond the Rhine; and has attested his sincerity in professions by many considerable pecuniary sacrifices, and by voluntary exile from his country. The following, however, will be more attractive than any sample of his political compositions, which this collection could supply.

"'Twas at midnight in the desert, when we rested on the ground,
There my Beddaweens were sleeping, and their steeds were stretched around;
In the farness lay the moon-light on the mountains of the Nile,
And the camel-bones that strewed the sand for many an arid mile.

"With my saddle for a pillow did I prop my weary head,
And my kaftan-cloth unfolded o'er my limbs was lightly spread;
While beside me, as the Kapitaun and watchman of my band,
Lay my Bazra sword and pistols twain a-shimmering on the sand.

"And the stillness was unbroken, save at moments by a cry
From some stray belated vulture, sailing blackly down the sky,
Or the snortings of a sleeping steed at waters fancy-seen,
Or the hurried warlike mutterings of some dreaming Beddaween.

"When behold! a sudden sand-quake—and between the earth and moon
Rose a mighty host of shadows, as from out some dim lagoon;
Then our coursers gasped with terror, and a thrill shook every man,
And the cry was 'Allah Akbar! 'tis the Spectre Caravan!'

"On they came, their hueless faces toward Mecca evermore;
On they came, long files of camels and of women whom they bore;
Guides and merchants, youths and maidens, bearing pitchers in their hands,
And behind them troops of horsemen following, senseless as the sands.

"More and more! the phantom pageant overshadowed all the plains!
Yes, the ghastly camel-bones arose, and grew to camel-trains;
And the whirling column-clouds of sand to forms in dusky garbs—
Here, afoot as Hadjee pilgrims—there, as warriors on their barbs!

"Whence we knew the night was come, when all whom Death had sought and found
Long ago amid the sands whereon their bones yet bleach around,
Rise by legions from the darkness of their prisons low and lone,
And in dim procession march to kiss the Kaaba's holy stone.

"And yet more and more for ever!—still they swept in pomp along,
Till I asked me, Can the Desert hold so vast a monster throng?
Lo, the dead are here in myriads! the whole world of Hades waits
As with eager wish to press beyond the Babelmandel straits!

"Then I spake, 'Our steeds are frantic—to your saddles every one!
Never quail before these shadows! ye are children of the sun!
If their garments rustle past you, if their glances reach you here,
Cry *Bismillah!* and that mighty name shall banish every fear.

"'Courage, comrades! Even now the moon is waning far-a-west,
Soon the welcome dawn will mount the skies in gold and crimson vest;
And in thinnest air will melt away those phantom shapes forlorn,
When again upon your brows you feel the odour-winds of Morn."
Vol. ii. *pp.* 120—3.

It would be unpardonable to close our notice of this collection without transcribing one other piece—the most national of them all—" The German's Fatherland." It is from the pen of the celebrated Ernest Maurice Arndt. This distinguished writer, who was professor of philosophy at Greifswald during the French invasion, was one of the loudest advocates of a union among the German states against the common enemy, and was banished by Napoleon after the treaty of Schönbrunn. From his exile in Sweden, he never ceased to stir up his countrymen to resistance; and his writings were mainly instrumental in exciting that universal outburst of indignant nationality which drove the invader from the banks of their beloved Rhine, and in the end freed Germany from the hated yoke of France. The following lines represent and embody all the mingled feelings by which this great revolution was effected. It has long been popular in every district of Germany, and the traveller may often hear it chanted on the decks of the Rhine-steamers by the wandering students on their way to or from the university of Bonn, with an enthusiasm which might appear capable of effecting once more the regeneration of their country.

"Where is the German's Fatherland?
Is't Prussia? Suabia? or the Strand?
Where grows the vine—where flows the Rhine?
Is't where the gull skims Baltic's brine?
No!—yet more great and far more grand
Must be the German's Fatherland!

"How call they then the German's land?
Bavaria? Brunswick? Hast thou scanned
It where the Zuyder Zee extends?
Where Styrian toil the iron bends?
No! brother; no! thou hast not spanned
The German's genuine Fatherland!

55. continued

"Is then the German's Fatherland
Westphalia? Pomerania? Stand
Where Zurich's waveless water sleeps—
Where Weser winds—where Danube sweeps ;—
Hast found it now? Not yet!—Demand
Elsewhere the German's Fatherland.

"Then say where lies the German's land?
How call they that unconquered land?
Is't where Tyrol's green mountains rise?
The Switzer's land I dearly prize,
By Freedom's purest breezes fanned ;
But, no! 'tis not the German's land !

"Where, therefore lies the German's land?
Baptize that great, that ancient land!
'Tis surely Austria proud and bold,
In wealth unmatched, in glory old?
Oh, none shall write her name in sand—
But she is not the German's land !

"Say then where lies the German's land?
Baptize that great, that ancient land!
Is't Alsace? Or Lorraine—that gem
Wrenched from the Imperial Diadem
By wiles which princely treachery planned?
No! these are not the German's land?

"Where, therefore, lies the German's land?
Name now at last that mighty land !
Where'er resounds the German tongue—
Where German hymns to God are sung—
There, gallant brother, take thy stand!
That is the German's Fatherland !

"That is his land—the land of lands,
Where vows bind less than clasped hands—
Where Valour lights the flashing eye—
Where Love and Truth in deep hearts lie—
Where Zeal enkindles Freedom's brand—
That is the German's Fatherland !

"That is the German's Fatherland,
Where hate pursues each foreign band—
Where German is the name for friend—
Where Frenchman is the name for fiend—
And France's yoke is spurned and banned—
That is the German's Fatherland !

"That is the German's Fatherland !
Great God! look down and bless that land ;
And give her noble children souls
To cherish, while existence rolls,
And love with heart and aid with hand
Their universal Fatherland !"

It would not be easy to believe that the author of this wild and almost frenzied outpouring of passionate and bitter hatred of France, is Ernest Arndt, the mild and gentle religious poet, whose strains breathe nothing but the tenderest and most sublimated purity. In his latter days, he turned his pen almost exclusively to sacred subjects; and among the numberless glorious hymns in which the sacred literature of Germany abounds, there are few which in sublimity, tenderness, and depth of feeling, can be compared to those which he has left behind.[*]

We would gladly linger over these charming translations, and extract at much greater length from the most characteristic among them. We have still left untouched Tieck, Simrock (whose *Maria Regina Misericordiæ !* is a noble old legend), Jean Paul Richter, Körner, Müller Stolberg (but his finest pieces are not translated), Kotzebue, Mosen, and a host of others. But we have already exceeded our prescribed limits. To those who have accompanied us so far in the examination of the collection, it would be idle to suggest that what remains of it will well repay them the trouble of exploring farther. The pen which produced such exquisite versions, as those which are extracted in the foregoing pages, could hardly, even by accident, produce an infelicitous translation.

---

[*] A translation of one of these most exquisite hymns, " Geh nun hin, und grabt mein Grab !" will be found in a former number of this journal.

Art. III.—*Hans Sachs, ernstliche Trauerspiele, liebliche Schauspiele, selt-same Fastnachtspiele, kurzweilige Gespräch, sehnliche Klagreden, wunderbarliche Fabeln, sammt andern lächerlichen Schwänken und Pos-sen, bearbeitet und herausgegeben von J. G. Büsching.* (Hans Sachs's serious Tragedies, delightful Dramas, wonderful Shrove-tide Farces, merry Discourses, pathetic funeral Orations, wonderful Fables, together with other amusing Tales and Farces. Carefully revised and edited by J. G. Büsching.) Three vols 8vo. Nürnberg.

SATIRE is one of the departments of literature, in which the Germans have successfully distinguished themselves, and in which, no doubt, they would have become more perfect were it not that their political constitution offers the greatest obstacles to their attaining complete mastery over this branch of 'Belles Lettres.' Owing to this circumstance, there is a certain air of embarrassment and an excess of caution in some of the German satirical writings, which not unfrequently almost borders on servility, so as to cause to the reader a rather painful sensation. This cautious and embarrassed tone, this display of an evidently fettered mind, is the immediate result of the iron sway which is exercised over the press, and public opinion in general, by the many rulers of Germany.

What hurts the public spirit in Germany most,—what, in fact, contributes to weaken, if not to destroy its powers and ener-gies, and creates that unnatural apathy, phlegm, and indif-ference so often perceptible in the German character, is, that remnant of popish and inquisitorial invention, the *cen-sorship of the press*. The humiliation of submitting one's literary productions to the scrutiny of censors, who not sel-dom treat works of the deepest thought and inquiry as though they were the exercises of mere schoolboys, submitted for the inspection of their preceptors, is destructive and revolt-ing in the extreme. How often are the terms ' admittatur,' ' toleratur,' and 'prohibetur,' misapplied?—The first permits the book to be read by all classes, the second permits it to be read by the learned only, and the third prohibits altogether its being published. How often have these terms deprived Germany, nay, the world, of works which would have proved an honour to the country that gave them birth, and might have been useful to mankind? Thoughts of a straight-forward and uncompromising character, which would prove the destruction of prejudices and abuses, and shine like lightning in the dark night of universal ignorance, appear to the censors un-usual, yea, dangerous. They, therefore, strike them out, be-cause it is the *safest thing they can do*, since they are answerable for every article which appears in print. Of course, it is need-less to state, that no respectable man, or that no author of any dignity and honour (it matters very little whether a Menzel and others make an exception to this rule) would sell him-self to so degrading a purpose, and that the whole band of censors, generally speaking, is composed of men who either cannot or will not pursue a more honourable line of life, or at all events of such as have made common cause with the government whose creatures they are, by whom they are well paid, and through whom likewise they expect to be raised to some more honourable public office.

How long all this nuisance may last, and what course the German government will have to pursue in the end, cannot be pointed out with any degree of certainty. But judging from appearances and from the changes that have lately begun to take place in Germany, in favour of mental freedom, we are inclined to think that this censorship is decidedly on the decline. The noble examples set by the liberal governments of Prussia, Würtemberg, Saxony, Baden-Baden, and other places, with regard to the freedom of the press, cannot fail to produce a favourable influence upon the other German powers. In speaking thus, we allude chiefly to Protestant Germany. Austria, justly termed the European China, Bavaria, and other Roman catholic parts of Germany, are not yet ripe for the blessing; so at least their ministers, both temporal and spiritual, say. But when will Roman catholic countries, generally speaking, be ripe for the emancipation of the mind? There is but one answer, viz., the moment they cease to be the slaves of Rome and of her priesthood, but not until then.

We have thus far designedly digressed, in order to point out the disadvantages under which German writings in general, and those of a satirical nature in particular, have been and still are produced. We now proceed to the details of the subject in question. But in so doing, we shall in the first place briefly allude to the earliest German satirical authors, and give such specimens as occasion may require to show their excellencies and beauty: and in the next place we shall confine ourselves chiefly to the more recent writers, and among them to such only as have gained a universal celebrity, and whose works have become the fashion of the day. Wherever we can do it with pro-priety, we shall point out the chief causes that gave rise to productions of particular eminence and merit.

The ancient Germans, besides their usual war songs and other poems, such as songs of praise, &c., which were generally composed in honour of their heroes, possessed satirical poems, in which they attacked all those whom they regarded as destitute of courage and honesty. These satirical productions were termed 'Gesanglichter' and 'Mondlieder,' *i. e.*, moon-songs, a term derived probably from the season of the day at which they were sung or recited. The most ancient German satires of any eminence, however, are those which emanated from the Minnesängers,' or love-singers, and the 'Meistersängers,' or master-singers, who followed the former at a much later period, and who were not dissimilar to them.

It was customary in former days for the German emperors, like other powerful princes and barons, to keep in their retinue bards or minstrels, men whose duty it was to perform, in the presence of valiant knights and fair dames, either on the cithern or the harp, and to sing, or rather recite, their so-called 'Minne-sang,' *i. e.* love songs. These bards were distinguished as men of genius and learning, and constituted a corporation of poets, forming a kind of German Troubadours, known in German history as the 'Zunft der Minnesänger.' They were the first, who, under the Suabian emperors, especially Conrad III. (1138), of the house of Hohenstauffen, besides in lyric poetry, made also an excellent and highly successful attempt in satirical composition, and who even at so early a period poignantly though laughingly attacked the pope and the clergy. The most distinguished among them were,—Hartmann von der Aue, Walter von der Vogelweide, Conrad von Würzburg, Wolfram von Eschenbach, Heinrich von Ofterdingen, Meister Heinrich Frauenlob, &c. To this period, among other excellent lyrical and ironical compositions, belongs 'Salomon und Markolf,' which is a kind of novel, and is full of beauty, genius, and caustic wit.

Among the satirical writers who followed these 'Minne-sängers,' was a native of Würzburg, Master Hugo von Trimberg, whose chief production is the 'Renner,' *i. e.* the Runner, a work in which he handles rather roughly both clergy and laymen. Another equally powerful satirist belonging to the same period was Hämmerlin, a native of Zürich, who it seems felt a particular calling to chastise the corrupted monks of that period, by exposing their vicious habits in a severe and spirited manner. But when he himself had unfortunately some time after fallen into the hands of the holy fathers of a Franciscan monastery at Lüzern, they in their turn scourged the unfortunate culprit, who, in all probability, expired under the lashes inflicted on him in their vaults in the year 1448.

Germany, generally speaking, during the middle ages, possessed a great number of excellent satirical writers, almost all of whom at a later period have been neglected, or been totally forgotten. The priesthood, with its immorality, pharisaic hypocrisy, pride, and ignorance, as also the courts, courtiers, pedants, and women, afforded plenty of scope for the caustic wit of many superior and enlightened minds. The language of these writers, it is true, is not unfrequently uncouth, nay, even rude; but this fault, which was peculiar to the age in which they lived, was owing to the liberty then enjoyed. Freedom and rudeness, have been at all times, cousins-german, only with this difference, that obscenity in former times was considered as wit by the generality of people, whereas, in more modern times, it is characteristic of the lowest and least cultivated classes of society. In the days we are speaking of, emperors and princes, nay, even prelates and the heads of churches, did not consider it beneath their dignity to make tom-fools of themselves, and to salute or address each other in terms at once the most foolish and gross. This became still worse previous to and about the time of the Reformation, when not only slothful and immoral characters, especially the priests, were unmercifully scourged by means of the coarsest, yet biting lampoons; but when the pope himself, and the 'Tiara,' became the butt of every kind of wit. What emperors, kings, and popes were unable to do, viz., to abolish the most atrocious and flagrant vices of a monkish rabble, because the whole nation—poor misguided victims—clung to it: all this was achieved by laughing satires. Hence Leo X., who was well aware of their effects, referring to Erasmus, feelingly said :—' Erasmus nobis plus nocuit *jocando*, quam Lutherus *stomachando*.' But the best of the joke was, that the stupid and ignorant monks believed for a long time the ' Epistolæ clarorum virorum,' and many other admirable satires, to have been written in their favour, and even purchased scores of copies in order to present them to their superiors.

Of all such writings produced during the middle ages, the highest rank is due to ' Rynke de Voss,' *i. e.* Reynard the Fox, which is justly considered the *chef d'œuvre* of ancient German political satires. Having recently devoted considerable space to an English version of this remarkable production, we shall not dwell upon it here as we should otherwise have certainly done. We may, however, observe, that there is a most excellent and meritorious continuation of this poem, written by Renner, under the assumed name of Sparre. This continuation is entitled ' Hennynk de Han,' *i. e.* Hennynk the Cock, and is well worthy of a careful perusal.

Another humorous satire, or satirical novel of great repute, belonging to this period, is 'Till (or Tyl) Eulenspiegel,' or 'Tyell Howleglass's Merry Jestes,' (as the ancient English translation of it is entitled). This book so universally admired—though, now and then, it is perhaps a little too free—is less the result of serious reflection and observation, than of a powerful mind and a natural flow of spirits; and contains an inexhaustible fund of humour, fun, and somewhat untutored wit, which, however, very frequently assumes the air of genuine and sparkling facetiousness. The real value of this work becomes enhanced the more, inasmuch as every rank and profession in real life is represented, with wonderful truthfulness and precision; each character, being described with rustic simplicity and great spirit. The following specimen, headed, ' HOW HOWLE-GLASS TOOK UPON HIMSELF THE BUSINESS OF A SPECTACLE MAKER,' borrowed from Mr. Roscoe's work, entitled, ' German Novelists, Tales, &c.,' will show that we have not given the author greater credit than his production merits.

' It happened that the electors were one day at variance in their choice of an Emperor of Rome, and the Count of Supplemberg was finally elected. But there were others who wished to elect themselves by force of arms; and it was requisite for the newly chosen potentate to station himself, during three weeks, before the town of Frankfort, waiting the attack of any who chose to encounter him. Owing to this, a vast concourse of people had assembled; hearing of which, Howleglass said :—' There will be a grand assemblage of lords and great people, who will surely give me something; were it only a silver medal, and most certainly I will go.' So when he arrived near Frankfort, he there found the Bishop of Treves, who observing him so oddly habited, inquired who he might be ?

' Howleglass replied, ' Sir, I am a maker of spectacles; I am coming now from Brabant, but I can no where find any custom; our trade is become worth nothing.' ' I should think, on the contrary,' said the bishop, ' that your business ought to go on daily improving; for, truly men grow more weak-sighted every day. Therefore they ought to apply to you for spectacles.' Howleglass replied, ' My much honoured lord, you say very true; but one thing hurts our trade, which I would mention, were I not afraid of offending you.' The bishop replied, ' Say it boldly, man, and fear nothing; we are pretty well accustomed to hear such men as you.' Then Howleglass said, ' My reverend lord, what most hurts our trade is the apprehension that in future it will be good for nothing. And for this reason, that we observe you and other great lords, along with popes, cardinals, bishops, emperors, kings, dukes, justices, and governors of all lands—all of whom God amend—have got a trick of looking through their fingers (instead of spectacles), and hiding their eyes from the sight of justice, except she come arrayed in gold and precious stuff.

' Formerly great men used to study the laws, in order to learn to whom to administer justice and do right. At that period they wore spectacles, and our business flourished. Priests, too, studied more than now, and spectacles indeed were in great request. At present they read their lessons by heart; and never open a book for weeks together. This fault is so frequent throughout the country, that even the peasants themselves study through their fingers.' Now the bishop could read this text without any glass; so he said to Howleglass, ' Follow me to Frankfort; I will give you my arms and livery ;' and Howleglass remained with him until the emperor was inaugurated, and afterwards returned into the land of Saxony.'

Not less amusing and as great a favourite, is the ' Narrenschiff,' i.e. The Ship of fools, a satire, written in rhyme, which has been translated into many foreign languages. It is the composition of Brandt (1453—1520), formerly a professor of law in the university of Strasburg, and also town-clerk of that city. This Ship of Fools, on which Lectures were delivered by the greatest men of those days, is certainly a splendid production, and one which would have done honour to any age and country. The celebrated Geiler (1445—1510), a ' Pietist' preacher, did not disdain to deliver sermons on themes taken from it. Every. sermon bore the inscription, ' Stultorum numerus est infinitus,' and, in his views, he went farther than even Brandt himself, who enumerates one hundred and thirteen kinds of fools only, at the head of whom he places himself as one of the class he designates the ' Büchernarren,' or, book-fools. Brandt well knew that a mirror of fools would safely and more easily bring every individual of that peculiar class to a better self-knowledge, to an infallible ' Nosce te ipsum,' especially by showing to him in a true light the class, of which he constitutes a member. This, the pious Geiler, seems to have considered as being true, and as being well worthy of an experiment. To it, therefore, we are indebted for a collection of excellent sermons, known under the title of ' Das Schiff des Heils', or, the ship of salvation. These discourses are distinguished for a sincere, though perhaps *mystic* piety and learning, and discover a vein of excellent and brilliant humour.

The best, and most correct, but scarce edition of Brandt's ' Narrenschiff,' is that of 1494; all the modern editions are less free from errors.

The noble-minded Hutten, a man full of zeal for art and science, and one of the greatest supporters of the Reformation, was another satirical writer of eminence. A sojourn at Rome, had produced upon his mind an effect, similar to that which it had upon Luther. To it we owe his ' Vatiscus' and ' Pasquillus exul,' both of which were directed against Rome. Among his other satires deserve to be mentioned ' Aula,' ' Febris,' ' Inspicientes,' ' Fortuna,' and ' Triumphus Capnionis,' some of which either preceded or succeeded those already mentioned. Frösch-

318

lein, or Frischlin, is another satirical writer of this period. The game this clever author was particularly fond of hawking at, were either the *sacrosancti*, or the landed nobility. Against the former he wrote his 'Facetiæ,' a work full of *vis comica*, although its tone is rather unchaste, and against the latter he produced the satire entitled, 'Vita Rustica,' a work which contains many highly witty passages. 'Pharma,' 'Priscianus Vapulans,' and similar other productions, are written more in the form of satirical comedies, and are still favourites with the reading world of Germany. Bebel, an admirable Latin scholar, and superior poet, besides many other satires, wrote his famous 'Triumphus Veneris,' a poem, which is divided into six Cantos, and in which the author collects under the standard of Venus, all ranks and classes of society, and excepts neither popes, monks, nor even nuns. This *exposé*, like all the preceding, is crushing, and must have contributed very much to eradicate the then existing social evils. 'The Narrenbeschwörung, Schelmenzunft und Gauchmette,' written by Murner, a Franciscan monk, of Strasburg, was another great favourite of the age we are speaking of. Folly, roguery, vices of all sorts and conditions, are the butt of the clever author's wit. This production, well illustrated by Waldau, was published in Halle, 1788. 'Der Froschmäusler,' by George Rollenhagen, who lived between the years of 1542 and 1609, as also 'Der Spiegel des Regiments,' by Morsheim, and 'Der Barfüssermönche Eulenspiegel und Alkoran,' by Alberi, either satirize in allegories, or in plain and unsophisticated language. Politics, the abuses of religion, philosophy, and manners, are the chief matter of these satires, which afford much more amusement and instruction than many similar recent productions. It seems, indeed, as though the wits of those days by far surpassed our modern ones in pourtraying and scourging human vices and follies. Hence the immense success which attended their creations.

One of the chief ancient German satirical writers, is Johann Fischart, sometimes called Menzer, (1550—1610). This author, who is not unjustly styled, the German Aristophanes, sometimes discovers an almost boundless vein of humour, and although his language is now and then a little too harsh, which is no doubt owing to the too great liberties he takes in forming the drollest, most extravagant, and lengthened compounds; moreover, though his puns very often show too great a freedom, which has been justly considered as one of the sins of his day, yet his humorous ideas, his pointed wit and pungent satire, observable more or less in all his works, make up for these defects. His 'Gargantua,' written in imitation of the style and satirical humour, of Rabelais, is an admirable production, and well deserves to be read. The 'Bienenkorb des heiligen Reich,' a severe attack upon the Romish church and the priesthood, is masterly throughout; and so are likewise his 'Aller Praktik Grossmutter,' 'Podagramisch Trostbüchlein, and the 'Philosophisches Ehzuchtbüchlein.' Inferior and less happy are the 'Glückhaftes Schiff von Zürich,' in rhymes, and the 'Flohhetze,' i.e., the flea-hunt. The immortal humourist, Jean Paul Richter, was one of Fischart's most enthusiastic admirers.

Hans Sachs (Lautydorfer), the chief of the Meistersängers (1494—1576), another distinguished humorous writer of that period, though, by profession, a shoemaker, has left a rich store of amusing and excellent satirical poems. Carlyle, speaking of honest Hans, says: 'He is not without genius, and a shrewd irony; and, above all, the most gay, childlike, yet devout and solid character.' In another place, the same critic says: 'His best pun known to us,—and many are well worth perusing—is the 'Fastnachtsspiel' (Shrove-tide Farce) of the 'Narrenschneider,' where the doctor cures a bloated and lethargic patient by cutting out half-a-dozen fools from his interior!

There is hardly a department in the range of poetry, in which this ingenious shoemaker has not tried his skill, and in some, too, with signal success. His works, numerous and full of mirth and truth, consist of four hundred and twenty songs, twenty-eight comedies, many tragedies, one thousand seven hundred fables, seventy-three allegories, besides a host of sacred hymns. Those of our readers who may be desirous to know something more about this universal genius, are referred to the work placed at the head of this article, as also to Mr. Carlyle's 'Miscellanies.' The celebrated Wieland speaks of him in terms the most endearing and affectionate. A contemporary of Luther, Hans Sachs was one of his greatest supporters, and most enthusiastic admirers.

Moscherosch, properly Kalbsdorf, or Philander von Sittewald (1600—1669)—thus he styles himself in his works—is the satirist we next have to deal with. This learned man has left a book, entitled 'Die Visionen' (the visions), which claims our admiration, inasmuch as it is a production of great intrinsic worth. True it is partly an imitation of the Spaniard Quevedo's work, which bears the same title; but whilst the latter contains seven visions only, the former has double that number. Besides, Moscherosch's whole style is so highly moral and luminous, his seven additional visions, and the paraphrases of the original passages, are so elegant and refined, that the whole may justly be considered as an original production. Every one of the fourteen visions is devoted to some particular theme or subject, such as hypocrisy, vanity, &c., of which those describing the 'Hofschule,' i.e., court-school, and the 'Soldatenleben,' or, the soldier's life, are by far the best. The whole work, even at the present moment, will be found to be superior to hundreds of modern novels, and similar other 'superfine' creations. This admirable writer was the greatest favourite of his day.—With the authors we next introduce to our readers, a new era begins in the history of German satirical literature. Here, therefore, let us rest awhile, and inquire into the causes that gave rise to the writings published during this period, and those following it.

If we closely examine the character of each of the satires then produced, we shall find that almost all of them are as unlike as can be to similar productions of other countries. One class, for instance, satirizes the silly, yet dangerous innovations, which at one time took place in the church and in the system of German theology, and thus endeavours to counteract their pernicious influences. Another class keeps a watchful eye on the corrupted system of philosophy, which about the same time was forced upon the Germans, and which, in consequence, threatened to destroy every atom of native philosophical inquiry, and moral principle. A third class deals with the abuses practised by a contemptible and imperfect system of policy, which at one period rendered the Germans a nation of slaves. A fourth class deals with the faults and weaknesses of the Germans in general; so that all the classes, too numerous to be mentioned in this place, have separate, and weighty subjects, on which they enlarge with admirable skill and point. We shall endeavour to point out, in as brief a manner as possible, the occasions that gave rise to them. What Luther aimed at, when he achieved the Reformation, was to break, by means of the power of a reasonable faith, the chains of an ignominious superstition, and a contemptible system of falsehood. Reason, so emancipated, was to counteract the machinations of Satan, and destroy the effects of false legends, and of similar other inventions of popery. But scarcely had men begun to shake off that degrading yoke, under which they had been labouring for centuries; and to indemnify themselves by the study of holy writ and of the ancients, for their long deprivation of mental food, when the spirit of destruction made its appearance in Germany, and raged with a fury, unparalleled in history, during a space of thirty years, known as the thirty years' war.

Throughout this period, Germany presented a sad, heart-rending aspect. Devastated and pillaged, with hardly a trace left of her former greatness and wealth, it resembled a country newly conquered by a horde of savages. It had the appearance of a battle-field, inhabited by foreign invaders, who were amusing themselves at the expense of the lawful possessors of the land. With this foreign power were introduced foreign customs. The still existing remnant of the former inhabitants, now powerless and crushed, imitated the example of their oppressors. 'They dressed like Belgians,' says a celebrated German historian, 'ate like Swedes, boasted like Spaniards, swore like Hungarians and Turks, and intermixed in their language,—which was looked upon as the most fashionable and elegant,—as many outlandish scraps as possible.' Under these circumstances, the Germans, neglected, and open to every foreign influence, gave way to the overpowering spirit of French fashion, manners, and language, which at this time were introduced at the courts, and among the nobles, and thenceforth took possession of the whole of Germany. But not only the manners, even the language and the literature of the Germans were, partly beneficially, and partly banefully, influenced by it. Its beneficial influence extended so far, as to improve the then barbarous taste of the Germans, and to promote the study of the ancients, which at that time was zealously pursued in all the schools and institutions of France. But its effects proved pernicious, inasmuch as it led the Germans to imitate French models, without any discrimination whatever; so that the German national literature, especially poetry, philosophy, &c., became wholly *Frenchified*. In the study of the ancients, the Germans became almost entirely imitators of Dacier, Batteux, and other Frenchmen, without themselves possessing a thorough acquaintance with the writers, whom they now made their study. French frivolities, too, were introduced into Germany, and these indeed were at one time so great, and had so firm a hold on its inhabitants, that it was thought proper, and anything but unbecoming, to be devoid of all shame and sense of decorum.

Multitudes of works, without discrimination, were now translated from the French, and whilst native literature was as yet either in a state of infancy, or, if more advanced, in that of languishment and neglect, French literary productions unobstructedly took possession of the minds and sentiments of the people, and thus instilled their pernicious and immoral principles. This unnatural state of things ultimately reached a climax, when a salutary reaction commenced. Nor was it long ere this took place. With Gottsched, who was the last but staunchest advocate of everything French, all this had obtained its highest supremacy in Germany; but with him, likewise, or at least through his agency, began its downfall. It would lead us too far were we

56. continued

to enter upon the minutiæ of this event. For our purpose it may be sufficient to know that the first who dealt the death-blow to it, were the illustrious Lessing, (of whom anon) Brokes, Haller, and many others. An examination of the means used by them and other German patriots, for the eradication of the existing evils, will enable us to judge, and dispose us to admire, the skill and talents of those who were engaged in the praiseworthy enterprise.

A declared enemy of the prevailing hypocrisy, pedantry, and priestcraft, was the lawyer Thomasius, (1655—1728). A lucid intellect, an easy natural grace, and deep learning, as also correctness of style, were peculiar to this great man. In his hand irony and biting jest, were among the most powerful instruments for the eradication of immoralities. But he frequently exchanges irony for gravity, whenever the subject under consideration happens to be of an exalted or otherwise grave nature. A stranger to cringing and servility, he represents human follies just as they are, without compromise, and in a tone of admirable and virtuous indignation. On these occasions he often displays uncommon powers of eloquence. One of the many fine features of this great man, is, his dealing only with the faults and imperfections of individuals, and his utter disinclination to hurt their feelings and private character. Some of his simple fugitive puns have done more good to the cause of morality, than many would-be fine orations. But in his earlier days, Thomasius was also of immense service to the German literature. It was he, who, by his lecturing in the German language, when professor of law at Halle, set the first example to the teachers of all the German universities. The Latin tongue, which until then had been the language of the universities, was now abandoned, and the German was adopted in its place. He moreover, by the wit frequently instilled into his lectures, caused no slight good among his audience, which, besides lawyers, was generally composed of men of all ranks and classes of society, and of almost every profession, except the theologians, with whom he was on bad terms, for the reasons above specified.

Thomasius's satires, in more than one respect, may be justly compared to French salad, which generally contains three times more oil, and three times less vinegar, than that of all other nations. This author seems to have known that cupping, if used with skill and adroitness, does, in many instances at least, as much good as venesection. It is at all events, much more safe, a fact which was apparently well known to Horace, who very properly says,—

> . . . . . Ridiculum acie
> Fortius et melius magnas plerumque secat res.

The style and language of Thomasius, as also his philosophy and mode of arguing, are throughout as brilliant as they are convincing and conclusive. Similar to this author, and strenuously opposed to the immoralities of his age, was Ulrich Megerle, better known as father Abraham a Sancta Clara (1647—1709), who was a Suabian by birth, and a preacher at the Austrian court. One of the cleverest humorists of his day, this remarkable and amiable man, poured forth his moral instructions in a manner quite his own. With him exquisite metaphors, antitheses and sentences, were in as great abundance, as similes and little tales, all of which had their source in a pure and enlightened mind, and in a benevolent heart. His language, though often profuse of poetry, and luxuriating in facetious and elegant forms of oratory, never degenerates into bombast or into a mere flow of empty sounds. His corrections of errors, his advice, his description of a righteous life, as also of its future reward, are as full of charity and grace, as they are good-humoured, witty, and well-meant. Father Abraham has scarcely written a line, which does not contain instruction of an attractive and entertaining character. Few, indeed, are the passages in his numerous works, which do not abound in food and recreation for the human understanding. His tone throughout is manly, bold, and pointed. The works of this famous preacher are collected as sermons, some of which have the strangest titles, as, for example, 'Well filled Wine-cellar, wherein many a thirsty soul may be refreshed with a spiritual blessing of God;' or, 'Spiritual Warehouse, containing apostolic commodities,' or, finally, 'Gack! Gack, or the Journey of Man.' The famous character of the Capuchin monk, in the eighth scene of Schiller's admirable 'Wallenstein's Camp,' is said to be a faithful portrait of this extraordinary man. The admonition to Wallenstein's soldiers contained therein, is considered one of the finest imitations of monkish eloquence.

Among the satirical writers who were prominent in purging German literature from foreign literary rubbish, and who powerfully opposed the various political evils, at that time existing in Germany, was Liscow (1701—1760), who in consequence of his labours, must be looked upon as one of the benefactors of his country. A native of Wittenburg in Mecklenburg, Liscow, very early devoted himself to the study of philosophy and to the composition of satires. Settled at Dresden, he began to produce his most successful works; among others, his 'Gefrorne

321

Fensterscheibe,' 'Die Vortrefflichkeit elender Schribenten,' and the ' Satire on amateurs of natural curiosities.'

With an unquenchable thirst for knowledge, Liscow combined a strong love, we might say passion, for justice and liberty, owing to which, many abuses and political frauds which his countrymen, until then, had been subject to, were wholly eradicated. Although he knew full well that the time had not arrived, when national prejudices, or the follies and vices of the great could be attacked with impunity, yet this noble-minded man did not confine himself to the foibles of the un-educated and lower classes of society, but concentrated his powers in those matchless productions, which were directed exclusively against the oppressors of the people, and the would-be learned class. In consequence of this, Liscow became what is emphatically termed ' a friend of the people,' whose rights and liberties he thenceforth stoutly defended, and an enemy to oppression and the abuse of power. He had but one aim, viz., to disarm all those who were in any way ill disposed towards his countrymen, or who proved themselves their mental and bodily oppressors. Hence his satires could not but prove destructive to vice, and advantageous to the cause of virtue, although he himself, as will be seen presently, perished in the attempt. Herr Teufelsdröckh somewhere admirably says, that ' a thinking man is the worst enemy the prince of darkness can have ; every time such an one announces himself, there runs a shudder through the nether empire, and new emissaries are trained, with new tactics, to, if possible, entrap him, and hood-wink and handcuff him.' We need say little more, but that Liscow, the plain-dealing, honest Liscow, the friend and advo-cate of the people, died in prison in a state of abject misery. *Requiescat in pace!* The famous Kant, who had a fine taste for true wit and humour, besides his love for Erasmus of Rotterdam, was very partial to Liscow's satirical writings. And Johann von Müller, the great historian, in one of his letters to the poet Gleim, says ; ' that no German has been more humour-ous than Liscow, and that he is absolutely an original.'

A leaning towards talkativeness excepted, we are scarcely acquainted with any satirical writer who combines so much keen wit, philosophical genius, grace, natural flow of spirits, sarcastic humour, solid learning, and deep knowledge of the human mind, as this delightful and patriotic author. It seems as though the heart lay open before him, and as though he could read and interpret every feeling it contained. In his ' Vortrefflichkeit und Nothwendigkeit elender Schribenten,' he much resembles our own Smollet. In a style at once refined and excellent, he ridicules the pedantic enthusiasm of some German schoolmen of that time, who in theory were the greatest world-improvers, whilst in practice they were com-pletely out of their element, and as it were at sea. He, more-over, now and then depicts in the most lively colours the German caricature of French scepticism, and gives a lively and valuable picture of the customs of his day. Free from corruption, his works are dictated by a sincere love for truth, and, in conse-quence, spare neither the great nor the low-born. His descrip-tion is highly finished, and his tone is such as leaves nothing to be desired ; his irony, especially when directed against priest-craft, is cutting in the extreme. Hence, were his writings uni-versally decried by churchmen, and in some places even pro-hibited.

The counterpart to this admirable writer was Rabener (1714 —1771). Endowed with powerful satirical talents, possessing, moreover, a goodly share of sound learning, elegant taste, and acuteness of mind, this, otherwise amiable man, had neither the inclination nor the courage of Liscow, to improve the state of his countrymen. Confining himself too much to one class, he never could obtain a comprehensive and thorough view of actual life. Overlooking the faults of the great and high-born, he saw only those of the low, the mean, the ignorant ; and, instead of applying the lash to both parties alike, he chastised those who needed no chastisement, but who only were in want of a kind and considerate friend and instructor. Men without any feeling of shame or remorse, full of presumption and arro-gance, of vain-glory, and an unconquerable hatred towards the rights of the people, were beyond his reach. But woe to the humbler classes ! Woe to the old maiden in the hoop petticoat, and high-heeled shoes ! Woe to the poor country parson, the silly country squire, the proud simpleton, the poor schoolmaster, the poetaster, the coxcomb—et hoc genus omne ! These were the people he liked to deal with ; he was sure to make them the sport of his untimely wit. When reproaches met his ear, as being too one-sided and partial, Rabener had but one answer, viz., ' that it were a boldness to censure the faults of our supe-riors. The province of satire,' he would continue, ' is to chas-tise follies, and that, too, without malice ; taking care, however, never to give vent to our wit or humour, whenever objects sanctified by long custom and ancient usages are concerned.' Acting on this principle, he, unlike Liscow, rarely dreamt of attacking or upbraiding the existing vicious and immoral German aristocracy, or the innumerable titled lordlings, who, reposing in perfumed saloons, within damask curtains, squan-dered the hard-earned means of a half-starved and wretched people. With Rabener, the decoration of any lordling had a meaning, it had a language; but no such a thing had the tear dimmed eye of misery and wretchedness. And here, indeed, we find a most striking difference between the one-sided aristocratic Rabener, and the democratic Liscow, Börne, Heine, and many others. In the eyes of the latter, the rogue is a rogue,—no matter whether aristocratic or democratic,—and is treated as such. With them, the decoration on the breast of an individual, to speak with our favourite Herr Teufelsdröckh, is ' little less and little more than the broad button of Birmingham spelter in a clown's smock.'

To all these circumstances, as well as to the contemptible political system of that day, it is perhaps owing that Rabener's satirical humour could but partly display its powers;—at least publicly, since we have good reasons to believe, that his MSS., destroyed at the bombardment of Dresden, during the seven years' war, contained matter of a far different character from that which he as yet had published, but which, for reasons best known to himself, he withheld from the public. In as far as satirical form is concerned, it is unfolded to great advantage by this author. The sarcasm of Rabener, as must appear evident from this brief sketch, is not so much calculated to attack the human race, or even all his countrymen, as to deal with a certain portion only. The foibles and vices peculiar to this portion, he represents in all their nakedness and innate ugliness. He pourtrays with great powers of truth, and though he is frequently carried away by his benevolence, he is never blinded by it. His satires, if our simile be permitted, are cool yet powerful applications to the diseased parts of men. He very forcibly impresses on our minds the necessity and value of self-knowledge. Among his innumerable works, we only mention his 'Schwiftsche Testament,' 'Klim's Todtenliste,' and his 'Satirical Letters,' all of which being distinguished for breadth and spirit, will afford much amusing and excellent reading.

Zachariae (1726—1777) claims our attention and respect, not only as a powerful satirical writer, but also as one of the reformers of the former insipid German literature. There were at that time few men, who could exercise a healthy influence over the German mind, which was fast sinking beneath the contemptible instructions received from foreign men of learning. Zachariae happily succeeded, by means of his ironical poems, in discrediting the degenerate tone which was then prevalent. From the graphic description given in them, we are astonished at the dullness, coarseness, mean ignorance and pedantry which prevailed; and cannot help pitying those who must have felt the want of good and trustful leaders to direct them out of the

rugged path into which they had strayed. Hence, describing places where the coarsest ton was the fashion; and societies where gossipings, intrigues and scandal making were the most vital elements, it is not at all surprising that his writings should partake of a certain air of vulgarity. And if, moreover, we now and then discover traces of bombast and a silly stiffness, we must bear in mind that all these, combined with a corrupted French etiquette, were the sins of the day.

Zachariae's ' Schnupftuch,' ' Renomist,' ' Murrner in der Hölle,' and ' Phaeton,' written in the style of Pope's ' Rape of the Lock,' are distinguished for genuine humour, drollery and truth; and unlike many similar productions, are not so much calculated to excite risibility as to improve morals and to warn against error. Zachariae not unfrequently assumes a rather grave tone, and not seldom exaggerates in his delineations of character, in order (so it seems) to make his picture the more striking and interesting. Exaggeration, indeed, is one of the prerogatives of the satirical writer, since, without the aid of this powerful microscope, much would remain hidden from the view of short-sighted mortals. The interest we feel in whatever this author describes is enhanced by his dry but crushing sarcasm.

' There was one man among the reformers of Germany,' says the historian Schlosser, ' and, next to Goethe, unquestionably the greatest among them, who, although he did not, like Goethe, properly speaking, write for the great public, yet was eager to devote himself to the religious improvement of the people. This man could be no other than Gotthold Ephraim Lessing.' And Mr. Carlyle, speaking of the talents and powerful mind of this illustrious German, says: ' Among all the writers, of the eighteenth century, we will not except even Diderot and David Hume, there is not one of a more compact and rigid intellectual structure, who more distinctly knows what he is aiming at, or with more gracefulness, vigour, and precision sets it forth to his readers. He thinks with the clearness and piercing sharpness of the most expert logician; but a genial fire pervades him, a wit, a heartiness, a general richness and fineness of nature, to which most logicians are strangers.' A little further on, he continues: ' We confess we should be entirely at a loss for the literary creed of that man who reckoned Lessing other than a thoroughly cultivated writer; nay, entitled to rank, in this particular, with the most distinguished writers of any existing nation. As a poet, as a critic, philosopher, or controversialist, his style will be found precisely such as we of England are accustomed to admire most; brief, nervous, vivid; yet quiet without glitter or antithesis; idiomatic, pure without purism, transparent, yet full of character and reflex hues of meaning.' Horn, a German author of celebrity, speaking of Lessing's genius and style, observes: ' Every sentence is like a phalanx; not a word wrong placed, not a word that could be spared; and it forms itself so calmly and lightly, and stands in its completeness, so gay, yet so impregnable!' It is, indeed, true that the noble-minded and philosophical Lessing (1729—1781) was one of the greatest intellects of his age. That man must have had a powerful mind, indeed, who by himself could oppose and tri-umphantly defeat a whole body of the most erudite polemical theologians Germany at that time boasted of! Lessing had as profound and exact a knowledge of ancient as of modern literature, and was as acquainted with the Fathers as with the heathen and modern philosophers. In fact, he was acquainted with the branches of almost every art and science!

The greatest antagonist of every thing French, he dealt the death blow to the prevailing taste in favour of all that belonged to France, especially in matters regarding lite-rature. He ruthlessly attacked everything bordering in any way on the unnatural or on mannerism. Clearing the German ground of its foreign poisonous weeds, and freeing it from its accumulated rubbish, he incessantly laboured to introduce the healthful spirit of the Greek, Roman, and English literature. Ancient customs and coarse habits soon gave way to a better system and improved state of learning. Lessing, indeed, was among the first, if not THE first, who taught the Germans to think and write logically, nay, he himself set them an example in numberless admirable productions, in almost every department of human knowledge. This, however, is not the proper place to discuss so mighty a subject, to revise the character of this extraordinary man, who, as Menzel says, ' combined in himself the study and culture of all the schools of his age,' or to estimate the incalculable benefits conferred by him on his country. We may, sometime or other, recur to this interesting matter; at present we confine ourselves to a few remarks, respecting Lessing's style and language as a satirical writer.

With the exception of some controversial articles in prose, written in a style of the highest eloquence and bitter irony, and directed against single individuals, he has chiefly—we might almost say, exclusively—confined himself to fables and epigrams. His fables, written in prose and poetry, as also his epigrams, were chiefly distinguished for power, purity of language and elegance, as well as for pointed wit, delicacy and nobleness of feeling, and were considered the finest and most perfect specimens of the kind existing. Every trifle from the pen of this master contains within itself the marks of true genius; and of the playfulness with which he gave birth to all his most exquisite works. With him, every thing is in perfect keeping and harmony with decorum and good taste. The reader is never offended by expression or subject; on the contrary, he feels that the whole is the produce of a mind totally unacquainted with immorality and servility. Indeed, the first and last impulse of this author seems to be to act the part of a moral and free, or independent being. Hence that freedom which we discover in all his writings; hence the lovely garb or form of morality which every line wears, and which is truly refreshing to the heart and cultivated understand-ing; and hence, also, the wonderful and beneficial effect he pro-duced upon the minds of all classes of readers. What Madame de Staël has said concerning Schiller, viz., that, ' Ses écrits sont lui,' might with equal truth be applied to this inimi-table writer.

The following is an extract from one of his 'Controversial satirical writings,' generally known under the title of the ' Eleven Anti-Götzes,' i.e., replies to attacks made upon him by a clergyman named Götze. Each of these replies bears the inscription, 'Anti-Götze,' and is distinguished from the rest by a number contained on the first page. The extract we give is from No. 5, and has been borrowed from Schlosser's History of the eighteenth and nineteenth centuries.

' O happy time! when the clergy were all in all,—thought for us, and ate for us! How willingly would the chief pastor have brought you back again in triumph! How eagerly does he desire that all the rulers of Germany would unite with him in his salutary views! He preaches sweet and sour, sets heaven and hell before them! If they will not hear, they may feel! Wit and the language of the country are the dunghills in which the weeds of rebellion sprout up so readily and so quick. To-day a poet, to-morrow a regicide; Clement, Ravaillac, were not formed in the confessionals, but upon Parnassus. I shall return, however, to common-places of the chief pastor upon another occasion; at present, if it is not clear enough already, I shall only make it perfectly clear, that Mr. pastor Götze does not grant what he appears to grant, and that these are the mere claws, which it provokes the tiger so much only to be able to strike into the wooden railing.'

These fugitive pieces against Götze, and a letter, written by the celebrated Lichtenberg are the most perfect specimens of satire and annihilating language the German literature pos-sesses.

324

CENTO.

German Ballads, Songs, &c. Translated and Original. Pp. 201. London, J. Burns.

ONE of Mr. Burns' cheap and acceptable contributions to the general literature of our time; and embellished in the Germanic style, which, if he did not make, he has much helped to make, the fashion. Here, at any rate, it is appropriate, and adds considerably to the interest of the little volume.

The volume itself is composed of new translations of popular legends, ballads, &c., from Schiller, Uhland, Bürger, Goethe, Körner, Becker, Fouqué, Chamisso, Freiligrath, and Von Stolterfoth; and of some twelve or fourteen which seem to be original compositions, of similar kind with the selections. The whole afford a good idea of the German mind as cast into this species of production; and from the strangeness, romantic wildness, and religious feeling with which the different pieces are more or less impregnated, will be perused with pleasure by the majority of readers, young and old. There are also a few of the grotesque and humorous cast; and one of them coming so near the style of our lamented friend Barham, that we offer no excuse for adopting it as a specimen.

"The Enchanted Net.

Could we only give credit to half we are told,
There were sundry strange monsters existing of old;
For, without our disturbing those very large bones—
Which have turned (for the rhyme's sake, perhaps) into stones,
And have chosen to wait a
Long while hid in strata,
While old Time has been dining on empires and thrones—
(Old bones and dry bones,
Leg-bones and thigh-bones,
Bones of the vertebræ, bones of the tail,
Very like, only more so, the bones of a whale,
Bones that were very long, bones that were very short,
They have never as yet found a real fossil merry-thought,
Perchance because mastodons, burly and big,
Considered all funny bones quite *infra dig.*)
Skulls have they found in strange places imbedded,
Which at least prove their owners were very long-headed;
And other queer things,—which it's not my intention,
Lest I weary your patience, at present to mention,
As I think I can prove, without farther apology,
What I said to be true sans appeal to geology,
That there lived in the good old days gone by
Things unknown to our modern philosophy.
And a giant was then no more out of the way,
Than a dwarf is now in the present day.

Sir Eppo of Epstein was young, brave, and fair;
Dark were the curls of his clustering hair,
Dark the moustache that o'ershadowed his lip,
And his glance was as keen as the sword at his hip;
Though the enemy's charge was like lightning's fierce shock,
His seat was as firm as the wave-beaten rock;
And woe to the foeman whom pride or mischance
Opposed to the stroke of his conquering lance.
He carved at the board, and he danced in the hall,
And the ladies admired him—each one and all:
In a word, I should say he appears to have been
As nice a young 'ritter' as ever was seen.

He could not read nor write,
He could not spell his name;
Towards being a clerk, Sir Eppo his + mark
Was as near as he ever came.
He had felt no vexation
From multiplication;
Never puzzled was he
By the rule of three;
The practice he'd had
Did not drive him mad,
Because it all lay
Quite a different way.
The asses' bridge, that bridge of sighs,
Had (lucky dog!) ne'er met his eyes.
In a very few words, he expressed his intention
Once for all to decline every Latin declension,
When persuaded to add, by the good Father Herman,
That most classical tongue to his own native German.
And no doubt he was right in
Point of fact, for a knight in
Those days was supposed to like nothing but fighting;
And one who had learned any language that is hard,
Would have stood a good chance of being burned for a wizard.
Education, being then never pushed to the verge ye
Now see it, was chiefly confined to the clergy.

'Twas a southerly wind and a cloudy sky,
For aught that I know to the contrary;
If it wasn't, it ought to have been proper*ly*,
As it's certain Sir Eppo, his feather-bed scorning,
Thought that *something* proclaimed it a fine hunting morning;
So pronouncing his benison
O'er a cold haunch of venison,
He floored the best half, drank a gallon of beer,
And set out on the Taunus to chase the wild deer.

Sir Eppo he rode through the good green wood,
And his bolts flew fast and free;
He knocked over a hare, and he passed the lair
(The tenant was out) of a grisly bear;
He started a wolf, and he got a snap shot
At a bounding roe, but he touched it not,
Which caused him to mutter a naughty word
In German, which luckily nobody heard,
For he said it right viciously;
And he struck his steed with his armèd heel,
As though horseflesh were but iron or steel,
Or any thing else that's unable to feel.

What is the sound that meets his ear?
Is it the plaint of some wounded deer?
Is it the wild-fowl's mournful cry,
Or the scream of yon eagle soaring high?
Or is it only the southern breeze
Waving the boughs of the dark pine-trees?
No—Sir Eppo, be sure 'tis not any of these:
And hark again!
It comes more plain—
'Tis a woman's voice in grief or pain.

Like an arrow from the string,
Like a stone that leaves the sling,
Like a railroad-train with a Queen inside,
With directors to poke and directors to guide,
Like the rush upon deck when a vessel is sinking,
Like (I vow I'm hard-up for a simile) winking,
Sir Eppo sprang forward, o'er river and bank all,
And found—a young lady chained up by the ankle,—
Yes, chained up in a cool and business-like way,
As if she'd been only the little dog Tray;
While, the more to secure every knight-errant's pity,
She was really and truly excessively pretty.
Here was a terrible state of things!
Down from his saddle Sir Eppo springs,
As lightly as if he were furnished with wings,
While every plate in his armour rings.
The words that he uttered were short and few,
But pretty much to the purpose too,
As sternly he asked, with lowering brow,
'Who dared to do it?' and 'Where is he now?'

'Twere long to tell
Each word that fell
From the coral lips of that demoiselle;
However, as far as I'm able to see,
The pith of the matter appeared to be,
That a horrible giant, twelve feet high,
Having gazed on her charms with a covetous eye,
Had stormed their castle, murdered Papa,
And behaved very rudely to poor dear Mamma,
Taken french leave with the family plate,
And walked off with herself at a terrible rate;
Then, by way of conclusion
To all this confusion,
Tied her up, like a dog,
To a nasty great log,
To induce her (the brute) to become Mrs. Gog;—
That 'twas not the least use for Sir Eppo to try
To chop off his head, or to poke out his eye,
As he'd early in life done a bit of Achilles
(Which much better than taking an 'Old Parr's life-pill' is),
Had been dipped in the Styx, or some equally old stream,
And might now face unharmed a battalion of Cold-stream.

But she'd thought of a scheme,
Which did certainly seem
Very likely to pay—no mere vision or dream.
It appears that the giant each day took a nap
For an hour (the wretch!) with his head in her lap:
Oh, she hated it so! but then what could she do?—
Here she paused, and Sir Eppo remarked, 'Very true;'—
And that during this time one might pinch him or shake him,
Or do just what one pleased, but that nothing could wake him,
While each horse and each man in the emperor's pay
Would not be sufficient to move him away,
Without magical aid, from the spot where he lay.
In an old oak-chest, in an up-stairs room
Of poor Papa's castle, was kept an heir-loom,
An enchanted net, made of iron links,
Which was brought from Palestine, she thinks,
By her great Grandpapa, who had been a crusader;
If she had but got that, she was sure it would aid her.

Sir Eppo, kind man,
Approves of the plan;
Says he'll do all she wishes as quick as he can;
Begs she wont fret if the time should seem long;
Snatches a kiss, which was 'pleasant but wrong;'
Mounts, and taking a fence in good fox-hunting style,
Sets off for her family seat on the Weil.

The sun went down,
The bright stars burned,
The morning came,
And the knight returned;
The net he spread
O'er the giant's bed;
While the eglantine, and hare-bell blue,
And some nice green moss, on the spot he threw;
Lest perchance the monster alarm should take,
And not choose to sleep from being too *wide awake.*

Hark to that sound!
The rocks around
Tremble—it shakes the very ground;
While Irmengard cries,
As tears stream from her eyes—
A lady-like weakness we must not despise—
(And here, let me add, I have been much to blame,
As I long ago ought to have mentioned her name)—
'Here he comes! now do hide yourself, dear Eppo, pray;
For my sake, I entreat you, keep out of his way.'

Scarce had the knight
Time to get out of sight
Among some thick bushes, which covered him quite,
Ere the giant appeared—oh, he was such a fright!
He was very square built, a good twelve feet in height.
And his waistcoat (three yards round the waist) seemed too tight;
While, to add even yet to all this singularity,
He had but one eye, and his whiskers were carroty.
What an anxious moment!—will he lie down?
Oh, how their hearts beat!—he seems to frown,—
No, 'tis only an impudent fly that's been teasing
His sublime proboscis, and set him a-sneezing.

Attish-hu! attish-hu!
    You brute, how I wish you
Were but as geenteel as the Irish lady,
    Dear Mrs. O'Grady,
Who, chancing to sneeze in a noble duke's face,
Hoped she had'nt been guilty of splashing his grace.

Now, look out. Yes, he will! No, he won't!—by the
    powers!
I thought he was taking alarm at the flowers;
But it luckily seems, his gigantic invention
Has at once set them down as a little attention
On Irmengard's part, done by way of suggestion
That she means to say ' yes' when he next pops the
    question.

There! he's down! now he yawns, and in one minute
    more—
I thought so, he's safe—he's beginning to snore;
He is wrapped in that sleep he shall wake from no
    more.
From his girdle the knight took a ponderous key—
It fits—and once more is fair Irmengard free :
From heel to head, and from head to heel,
They wrap their prey in that net of steel,
And they weave the edges together with care,
As you finish a purse for a fancy-fair,
Till the last knot is tied by the diligent pair.
At length they have ended their business laborious,
And Eppo shouts, ' Bagged him, by all that is glorious!'

    No billing and cooing,
    You must up and be doing,
Depend on't, sir knight, this is no time for wooing;
You'll discover, unless you progress rather smarter,
That catching a giant's like catching a Tartar :
He still has some thirty-five minutes to sleep ;
Close to this spot hangs a precipice steep,
Like Shakespeare's tall cliff which they shew one at
    Dover ;
Drag him down to the brink, and then let him roll over;
As they scarce make a capital crime of infanticide,
There can't be any harm in a little giganticide.

' Pull him, and haul him ! take care of his head!
Oh, how my arms ache—he's heavy as lead!'
' That'll do, love,—I'm sure I can move him alone,
Though I'm certain his weight is a good forty stone.'
Yo, heave ho! roll him along,
(It's exceedingly lucky the net's pretty strong);
Once more—that's it—there, now, I think,
He's done to a turn, he rests on the brink;
At it again, and over he goes
To furnish a feast for the hooded crows;
Each vulture that makes the Taunus his home,
May dine upon giant for months to come.

    Lives there a man so thick of head
    To whom it must in words be said,
    How Eppo did the lady wed,
    And built upon the giant's bed
    A castle, walled and turreted ?
    We will hope not ; or if there be,
    Defend us from his company!"

Having given this long sample of the amusing, we cannot afford much room for the serious ; and, indeed, we think we had better content ourselves with simply, but cordially, recommending it to the public. We like, however,
to shew that we have line by line gone before
it ; and to prove this, would ask the poet by
what art of dye (we see several advertised in
the newspapers) he contrived to make the lady's
hair, in "The Hermit and the White Wolf," so
soon acquire the desirable glossy black; for in
page 138 it is—

" Through her golden locks;"
and in page 142—

" She shook her tresses black ;"
quite the reverse of Hudibras's daybreak—

" When, like a lobster boiled, the morn
    From *black* to *red* began to turn!"

58. NEW QUARTERLY REVIEW, 6 (1845), 304-332. M/H No. 4192.

ART. II —1. *Gedichte von Karl Simrock, Leipzig. Layen-Brevier, von Leopold Schefer, Berlin.*
2. *Gedichte von Wilhelm Smets, Elberfeld.*
3. *Gedichte von Wilhelm Wackernagel, Zürich.*
4. *Gedichte eines Lebendigen, von Georg Herwegh, Zürich.*

THERE seems to be a very general prejudice, how far founded on truth we will not absolutely decide, to the effect, that the English nation is a prosaic or at least decidedly an unimaginative nation, too active within the sphere of reality, either to find time, or gain faculties for the enjoyment of the highly fanciful; too matter-of-fact, in fine, to attach much importance to the world of visionary delights. As general an opinion prevails also, that Germany is the land of wild fancy and high bounding imagination, the clime of sublimated and enchanted poetry; the abode, in fine, of the Ideal, where blossoms are as bright as the pineforests are romantically dreary, and all is gnome, or fairy-like, by turns. Now, strange to say, it so happens, that English poetry is infinitely more fanciful, and perhaps more imaginative, than German lays,—that our poets have a thousand glowing similes and "fairy beauties" for one in the German bards; and that our voice of song seems to soar to a higher sphere, while the Teutonic muse delights most to dally with the joys and woes of every-day existence. So far is this tendency sometimes carried on the part of our continental brethren, that the "thorough" Englishman, who has delighted only in our own bold lays, will often regard with contempt the most valuable offspring of German inspiration, considering them too commonplace, too "bathotic," in fine, (to coin a word for the nonce,) to deserve any attention as poetical outpourings. Even our simplest bards, who write almost exclusively on themes connected with domestic life,—a Burns for instance,—have generally much fancy, and interweave many poetical adornments, many fairy blossoms, with the bay-leaf garlands of their lays. Not so the very greatest German authors. Let us turn for an instant to Bürger, the German Burns, and compare him to his Scottish brother of song. Of course of the comparative merits of these two bards there can be no question: Burns is so infinitely the superior. Not that the German poet has not great merits also; earnestness, a certain downright roughness, a power of describing "horrors" with great effect, and a passionate, but sometimes coarse, strain of eager love. But then,

he has little or none of the sweet fancy, the healthy imagination, the bounding, frolicsome, and yet truly loving spirit of the Scottish bard. As Schiller has very justly remarked, Bürger, when he praises his beloved, knows no better course than to compare her in turn to each of the heathen goddesses for some peculiar grace or elegance. He descends to a positive catalogue of charms, and does not let you off for a single feature. Burns, on the contrary, by one happy expression, often seems to convey volumes, and has a thousand sweet fancies illustrating the beauty of his maiden, which have none of the catalogue spirit in them; but seem sparkling wavelets, leaping lightly, merrily, down from the crystal fount of Helicon. Many further illustrations of the justice of our remark would be needless. The whole poetical range of literature of the two countries confirms it. The greatest of England's bards, or indeed of the world's, Shakspeare, is also the most imaginative; rich is he in fairy lore, rich in all poetical and spring-tide imaginings. Quotations in support of this truth would indeed appear absurd. Schiller and Goëthe, on the contrary, (to mention one simple fact,) throughout the whole range of their lyric and dramatic works, have given us scarcely a single comparison; have pointed out scarcely a single analogy betwixt the works of nature and the workings of men's minds. This absence of fanciful beauty may be perhaps extolled in plays. In these we, no doubt, often err in the opposite extreme; but poems, according to our English idea at least, should boast the adornment of both gems and flowers. Not thus think our German neighbours—not thus thought even our own great Southey—according to them, the sparkling elfin fancies alluded to, so very common in all English poetry, the highest and the lowest, are mere "concetti," which should be very sparingly introduced. Feeling is the predominant agent they employ to produce their greatest effects; imagination (in our sense of the word) they seldom display in the conception of their subjects; or rarely at least in the execution of them. We will not deny, that there may be much truth and justice in the theory, which has originated this perhaps severer strain of bardic melody. We cannot deny, that English poets have carried their power of imaginative and fanciful illustration to too great an extent. Even the mighty Shakspeare is not faultless on this point; yet such an error appears, for the most part, an error arising from excess of richness, from fertility of thought and imagination; and may therefore be lightly forgiven by the true lover of the "lyre," though not always commended, or even imitated, *when possible.* Moore may be named as an instance of the exaggeration of such fanciful beauty; not that he has not also given us much of the truly beautiful; but that his analogies have in sooth ofttimes descended to the sphere of mere "concetti," and so justified the condemnation of our Teutonic brethren. The fact is, that a Catholic taste is here, as elsewhere, to be most commended. The beautiful is always the beautiful, whether it be received through the medium of imagination, of fancy, or of feeling; we enjoy the German bards, despite their comparative dearth of blossom, like spring-tide imaginings; and this enjoyment is a convincing proof of their true merit, even could we assign no sufficient reasons for our admiration. Let us not be mistaken! German poets have imagination too; but of a less luxuriant, perhaps less delightful order; they conceive wild legends of horror, and sometimes also light and airy strains of fancy; yet even these latter are *simply treated*, as a quotation or two shall testify. Let us turn to Schiller the poet, "par excellence;" for he was but a confused reasoner, while Goëthe's prose is as immortal as his lyric music. Let us see how this, in some respects imaginative, bard, treats the most fanciful subjects! In sooth, after the most matter-of-fact, though no doubt very delightful, fashion. High and noble feelings we indeed find scattered in profusion through his pages, as through those of our own beloved Southey; but fanciful flowery imaginings, delightful similes, luxuriant images,—of these we shall find few or none. Why is this? Much may be attributed perhaps to the sterner theory alluded to, which inculcates the necessity of being "true to the text," explicit, straightforward, not childishly fanciful, after the old Italian fashion, looked upon as degenerate and "Claudianic" in its nature; but much also arises no doubt from the absence of those more joyous and hope-inspiring faculties which revel in the beauties of nature, and feel a mysterious analogy with the outward world of light and loveliness, which they then hasten, more or less vividly, to express. Something also in the case of German poets may be attributed to the lengthiness of the German language, which renders the introduction of many images and similes most difficult in connexion with true elegance, or even tolerable conciseness. Difficult, we say, yet not impossible; as the translations of Shakspeare made by "August von Schlegel," and "Karl Simrock," (whose name we have placed at the head of our list,) most abundantly testify. But, to cut short this disquisition, which might truly be carried to an almost interminable length, without arriving at any positive result, respecting the comparative merits of these diverging schools of poetry, let us see how Schiller, in his far-famed Dithyrambe has treated a most fanciful subject; remarking beforehand, that this is one of the most richly imaginative of all his shorter lyrics, though yet far less flowery than an English author's treatment of the same subject would probably have been:—

" Never, believe me,
  Appear the Divine ones,
  Never alone.
Scarce hath gay Bacchus beside me reclined him,
Follows young Amor with roses to bind him,
Phœbus with smiles of light hails me his own.

        To wake me, to joy me,
          Their glances are given,
        And earth's hall is thronged by
          The dwellers in Heaven.

How shall the mortal,
The weak one, receive them,
Those Beings Divine?
Give me your birthright, Eternity's treasure!
Poor to ye Gods must be earth's sweetest pleasure;
Oh, let the joys of Olympus be mine!

        Love's torches, light's fountains,
          There ever are glowing:
        Oh, mine be the Goblet
          With Nectar o'erflowing!

His be the Goblet!
Fill for the Poet,
Hebe, fill high!
Raptures of Heav'n to his bosom revealing,
Far the dark Styx from his glances concealing;
So shall he dream him a child of the sky.

        Now forming, now beaming,
          Heaven's fountain entrances;
        The breast gently trembles,
          The eye brightly glances."

In this beautiful poem there is much imagination of a certain order, but little or no *fancy* whatever. The thoughts are lofty and inspiring; the request of the poet for "eternity's treasure" is nobly and boldly conceived, and the reply of Jove is magnificent in its kindly condescension, more especially in its assertion that the poet may thus deem himself an immortal. "So shall he dream him a child of the sky." Yet we have no image, nothing purely fanciful here; the only approach to anything of the kind is the picture sketched above of the approach of the boy Amor to wind his roses around the youthful, dozing Bacchus;

but alas! this is not to be found in Schiller at all. *We* must plead guilty to the introduction of the thought. Thus runs the German, literally, " scarcely have I Bacchus the merry, when Amor also comes, the smiling boy, Phœbus, the admirable, makes his entrance." Now this, as all English lovers of poetry will at once feel, would not seem poetical in English, but a mere matter-of-fact, unvarnished statement; yet it reads poetically in German, owing partly to the exquisite beauty of the rhythm, partly to the fact, that in reading German poetry we do not expect the fanciful, and are therefore not disappointed by its absence. Here we may be permitted to remark, that an English translation of a German poem, to convey any idea to the English reader of the beauty of its original, should almost always be more or less " adorned." The very genius of our language seems to demand this; and it is an undoubted fact, that literal versions of German poetic works must almost invariably appear bold and frequently unpoetic in the extreme.

Pass we to the great Goëthe. He, be it at once admitted, has more of light fancy, of pleasing and ardent imagination, than his exalted contemporary; and yet even in him, upon the whole, feeling predominates, and his very fancy seems to lie more in the conception of pretty subjects, and the invention of the most exquisite and bounding rhythmus, than in the introducing of many fanciful *thoughts* or " spring-like imaginings," as we may not inaptly term these characteristic adornments. Let us, however, place before our readers, in an English version, one of the most fanciful of Goëthe's ballads. It is well known, yet can always be heard again; nor have we cognizance of any existing translation which supersedes the necessity for a new attempt :—

"THE VIOLET.

A Violet on the meadow lay,
And dreamt its youthful hours away;
It was a lovely blossom.*
And o'er the lea a shepherd-maid
In joyous mirth so lightly stray'd;
Across, across
The lea she tripped, and sang.

Ah! thought the Violet, would I were
The fairest flower of Nature fair,
To deck yon maiden's bosom:

* A very poor expression of the German exquisite " herzig's veilchen," which is indeed untranslateable.

That she might pluck me from my rest,
And I might die upon her breast;
Yes there, yes there,
I'd fade without a pang.

The maiden came, but—tale of woe!
She mark'd not there the violet low,
But crushed its gentle blossom.
It sang, and died without a sigh,
" And if I fall, at least I die
Through her, through her,
Beneath her feet I die."

Now there is much fancy in this—in the conception at least of the ballad—and, even to a certain extent, in the execution. There is sweet fancy in the analogy here shadowed forth betwixt the dying flower and hopeless uncomplaining love. The extravagance of the image thus conveyed, (the crushing and annihilation of the heart by passion, as the flower is trampled down by the maiden,) this even adds to the general effect, and creates a pleasurable sensation by so over-estimating the usual dangers of love as to induce us to regard them from a mirthful or at least happy point of view. In fine, the whole little poem is a true gem of the first water; yet it is extremely simple, and has no imaginative adornments whatever. In fine, it is characteristically German, though very beautiful; and few English bards could have combined such beauty with such simplicity of imagery and thought. To bring this long preamble to a close, let it be received as undoubted truth, that there is a poetry of thought and feeling, as well as a poetry of imagination, equally beautiful and enchanting of its kind. A living English poet, Leigh Hunt, in his late work on " *Imagination and Fancy*," seems to lay down that *these* are the very essence of poetry, which in one sense may be admitted to be true; but then there is an *imagination of the feelings*, as well as the more fanciful upward flight; and this latter, in combination with the poetry of thought, is what peculiarly distinguishes the works of Southey, and some few others in a less eminent degree, amongst ourselves, and of the German poets " en masse," with very few or very partial exceptions.

Pass we to the more immediate subject of our this day's converse—the living poets of the Teutonic World. On a former occasion we introduced Rückert, Heine, Freiligrath, Lenau, Immermann, and Betty Paoli, to (we trust) an " admiring British public." At present we have a list of almost equal length before us, to which might be added, Chamisso, Karl Beck,

Count Anserperg, or Anastasius Grün, with others, whom we reserve for a third occasion. Longer tarrying on our way is therefore incompatible with the interests of our readers, (who will have enough of us if we hold our course straight onward,) and shall therefore be forthwith abandoned by us. Karl Simrock, the first on our list of living bards, is a true German and a true poet. He is sometimes rugged in thought and in rhythm, though, when he chooses, no man seems to have the melodious measures of the lyre more fully at his beck and call; he is always honest, straightforward, plainspoken. Occasionally we might wish for a little, a very little more *delicacy*; for, like the great master, Goëthe, Simrock sometimes treats rather unpleasant subjects. There is a certain analogy betwixt Simrock and Goëthe. The former himself alludes to this in a very charming poem on Goëthe's birthday, which happens also to be his own, wherein he styles the mighty master the greatest, and himself the least, of German bards. But this poetical exaggeration can indeed impose on none; it even belies itself—let us not be mistaken! There is nothing approaching to the nature of "Goëthian" imitation amongst the poems of Simrock; the latter are less elegant, less sweet, altogether indeed less delightful; and yet they have a similar freshness and truthfulness; they seem also outpourings from the inward soul, and they are often very beautiful within their own sphere.

Karl Simrock may be regarded as a relic of the Saxon middle ages: he has all the fire, and honesty, and roughness too, of the robber knights of old, who were at the same time most benevolent in their domestic relations, and hospitable to all the world save " bacon-fed knaves," such as Augsburg merchants, and the like. Simrock has indeed revived the greatest poem of the middle ages, " Das Niebelungen-Lied;" on his version or rather reproduction of which, in modern German, Goëthe bestowed the very highest praises. Wolfram von Eschenbach's " Parzival," a very long poem dating from the 15th century, and redolent of knightly courtoisie and faithful love, has also been " renewed " by our living bard most admirably. Again he has reproduced the famous " Reynard " in his original metre, which lately received so admirable an English dress in the version of Mr. Samuel Naylor, which we had occasion to commend as " inimitable " of its kind. Still more valuable, however, in our estimation than his translations, is Simrock's own " Amelungen-Lied," the third volume of his great " Helden-Buch," and an original continuation of " Das Niebelungen-Lied." This is unparalleled for its fresh and healthy beauty: very superior in truth, as we scruple not to declare, to its Nie-

belungen prototype; nor can this appear wonderful. The old poem gives us indeed many descriptions of character, and is sometimes very vivid in its portraitures, still the human heart is better known now than it was in the dark age alluded to, or at all events, its foibles can be better described. " Wieland der Schmidt," which appeared some years ago, and excited a great sensation, was only a fragment of this glorious " Amelungen-Lied," to which we call the attention of all readers of German who delight in noble deeds of knightly bearing, and the annals of true chivalry and love. The invention of our poet appears boundless. There is a foundation indeed for all the stories he narrates; but their mere skeletons existed,—he has clothed them with beautiful forms, and given them light and life. The intention of the poet was to complete, in this " Heldenbuch," one volume of which is occupied by " Gudrun," and other ancient " Sagen," the whole series of German legendary history, comprising a period of from about the year 500 to 800, A.D. But this intention, though most successfully carried into effect, is entirely subordinate, in our eyes, to the extreme beauty of Karl Simrock's separate original contributions, which will be found to deserve even more than all the praises we have at present bestowed on them.

Of course we need scarcely say that these narrative poems are not fitting subjects for quotation. We pass rather to our immediate theme, the minor " Gedichte " of this true bard. These are now published, in one volume, by Hahn, of Leipsic; and that volume is truly worthy of the most extensive circulation. Many of the poems inserted in it had seen the light before in the pages of Simrock's " Rhine Legends," (Rhein Sagen,) which book has so speedily passed through an unprecedented number of editions. We will quote one of these poems, illustrating the ancient legend of the Lurley; in which the said Lurley is typified as the German Muse, looking for the great patriot poet who shall redeem his country, while Goëthe is introduced as one rowing down the stream, who *might be* the destined hero, but who fails from want of decisive purpose. It is well known that Goethe expressed little sympathy with his countrymen during the long series of their struggles against French oppression; wrote, in fact, no single war-song for them, nor at all berhymed the subject until all danger was past, and Napoleon had fallen; when, in his " Epimenides' Erwachen," (written to please the monarchs of Germany and of Europe, before whom it was performed,) he shadowed forth the resurrection of Teutonia from the grave of foreign slavery. Yet however this may be, Simrock, if we are to judge from other poems of his, has changed his opinion respecting Goëthe, and now regards him as "*the German Poet.*" True it is, that he is in some respects essentially German—German, we fear, in that very absence of ardent patriotism, which is here, in our opinion, condemned with so much justice. Now for the poem, the rhythm of which being very singular, should be especially remarked.

"BALLAD OF THE LURLEY.

What magic strains come stealing through the air?
Our boat sails slowly down, and lingers there.
The boatman spoke, Lo! sings the Lurley fair.
There on yon rock hath she as fairy crown'd her,
Thence beam her golden tresses on the Rhine,
And spirits' choirs, in harmonies divine,
Her praises sing, 'mid yon green vines around her;
But, as yon star bursts through the mists that bound her,
So steal the Fay's own warblings through the air.

In rival sweetness, now to pain, now pleasure,
Her strains excite the hearts of all that hear;
They bend in homage to that mistress dear,
And in their breasts those lays of magic treasure.
Thenceforth they chant her soft melodious measure,
And live and die the slaves of Lurley fair.

Ne'er yet hath she her love to mortal given,
Although on many she by turns hath smiled:
A bold knight once alone, by lays beguiled,
By force to gain that beauteous pr... hath striven:
Then rang the horn, and up yon mountains driven,
His vassals rush'd to seize the Lurley there.

Up, up she climbs, to highest heights ascending;
Follows the knight; he grasps her garment now;
When, lo! she springs from off the mountain's brow,
And far below his bones with dust are blending.
She sings, her course across the billows wending,
'No force can gain me: I am free as air!

Him who would crave my love, my passion's madness,
Must harmony surround in childhood's hour;
Full many a strain, inspired by inward power,
Must wake the echoes of his youth to gladness:
Soon shall he come, a youth who laughs at sadness,
And him will I my bosom's lord declare.'

At last he came, and down the river bore him
From the main's golden shores, a vessel bright;
Then roved she o'er the stream with footsteps light
To hail her love, and love and bend before him;
But ah! wild eastward breezes onwards tore him,
And she was left alone in sadness there.

'Alas! he ne'er shall come again: no morrow
Will lead him hither, and no prayers will move.
Fade, wreath of joy, and down yon billows rove.
Yet no!—Once more the tints of gladness borrow!
On yon lone rock I'll pine long years in sorrow;
At last one poet-youth shall find me there.'

Tell, Ballad, thou, how vainly men would dare
By force the gentle Muse's smiles to share:
Come soon, young lover of the Lurley fair!"

This will be admitted by all, we think, to be a very beautiful poem. The rhythm, which we have preserved, is very original and flowing. The expression of the Lurley's regret, with her anticipation of some future worthy woer, in the two lines rendered,

"On yon lone rock I'll pine long years in sorrow;
At last one poet-youth shall find me there,"

appear to us to have a touching and half mystical beauty, the effect of which can only be felt, and not conveyed through words. These Rhine and German legends are indeed, upon the whole, most admirable; not as delicately told, in general, perhaps, as the one we have selected, but more freshly and clearly. We would name as amongst our special favourites, "Drey Bitten," "Kater 'Freyer," "St. Ritza," "Der Schelm von Bergen," "Des edlen Brennberger's Leben und Tod," "Das Ave Maria," "Die Frau von Stein," and "Der arme Leonhard;" but almost all please us in a greater or lesser degree. They are couched in a Christian spirit, of which "Das Christus-Bild zu Wien," is a special instance. They are also Roman Catholic and mediæval in their bearings, but this after so legendary a fashion, as to show the poet's creed, for the most part poetical; though Southey's tone of kind-hearted, cordial humour is not here habitually adopted. We must pass, however, from these legends, (of one of which, by the bye, "The Jesuits' Church at Bonn," we gave a translation in a short notice of our poet, if we mistake not, in our last April Number,) to the other narrative ballads, many of which positively delight us. We may name as our special favourites, "Der junge Veteran," "Das Gebet," "Die Loffenden Thoren," the untranslatable, yet charming, "Zwist und Sühne," "Die Befreiung," "Der Todder Poesie," and "Der Neue Odysseus;" the last of which we will now lay in an English version before our readers. It is a very simple poem, in which feeling, not fancy, predominates, and its beauty may therefore, we trust, be felt by all.

"THE NEW ULYSSES.

Long did I, all danger spurning,
    Over vale and mountain roam;
And I now am back returning
    To my well-loved native home.

And whilst sunbeams shine so brightly,
    Well known tones around me soar:
' Forward, youth, for this day lightly
    May'st thou reach thy father's door.'

Yes, my childhood's bright dominions,
    Vine-clad hills, their forms display:
Sweet Desire, with zephyr's pinions
    Speed me on my homeward way!

Well-loved woods, ye seem to know me:—
    Lo! at last I reach the height,
Whence my home I view below me,
    Smiling in the moonbeams' light.

Down I hasten, joying madly—
    Stand my father's house before—
Knock, and knock, and call so gladly,
    But no loved one opes the door.

Long in vain I moments number—
    Seat me on the steps so cold;
And the pilgrim sinks to slumber
    On the stones he loved of old.

Whilst strange visions vex and scare me,
    They within to greet me come:
Up the steps they gently bear me
    To the well-loved father's home.

And when woke I on the morrow,
    Round me father, mother, bride,
Smile with eyes that mock at sorrow—
    Oh, how flows sweet rapture's tide!

Thus, when life's last sleep hath found me,
    Closed the pilgrimage of time,
May I wake, such friends around me,
    In the Eternal Father's clime!"

We know few poems more simply touching than this. There is a certain air of half mystery thrown over this little poem which is peculiarly German, and adds greatly to its effect. We must remark, however, that our own line, "While strange visions vex and scare him," very badly supplies the place of "Doch vernommen ward mein Rufen," and in fact disturbs the effect. "Smile with eyes that mock at sorrow," is also very inferior to "Scherzend mir entgegenlachen;" and "bride," which only means "betrothed," in German, has a doubtful bearing in English, and may signify "wife," an idea which does not harmonize with the supposed age of the wanderer. But enough of this verbal criticism. They who like this poem will like good German poetry generally. It has seldom more of fancy than this.

But we linger too long in the society of our good friend Simrock, and must hasten to give our last sample of his effusions. His lyrics are, perhaps, scarcely equal to his ballads; and yet, while we say this, we doubt, remembering the exquisite "Schweizer Reise," three divisions of which—the fifth, the eleventh, but more especially the twelfth and last, are really unrivalled for their peculiar naïve but truthful beauties. We will not venture on a version of either of these, fearing to do injustice to the originals, to which we refer our readers. A less beautiful, but also very pleasing little poem, "Mit Liebchen," a good specimen of Simrock's peculiar lyric powers and style, shall form our last extract from this delightful author.

"WITH MY LOVED ONE.

And comes the evening, soft and mild,
    Old customs follow we;
Each lover, with his maiden child,
    Roves forth o'er wood and lea;
Where flowers have oped and flowers have furl'd
        Will we together wander—
As henceforth through the world.

A gentle pair for kisses wooes
    In every pine tree's shade;
Each star its sister orbit sues
    For smiles by fondness sway'd:
The moon herself, in beauty pale,
    In sweet, yet lovely envy,
Looks downward on the vale.

The streamlet from the rocky height
    That leaps in glad surprise,
The bird that in its heart's delight
    Is chanting as it flies,
The evening winds that gently rove,—
    What seek they all in concert,
But sympathy and love?

Here on our mossy height we rest:
    Why need we further stray?
The goal of all the others' quest
    Is ours, this eve, this day:

58. continued

> The bond that heartfelt bliss inspires,
>   And in one other's being
> Our own dear, dear desires.
>
> Now let Love's kiss, Love's trembling sigh,
>   Awake the echoes round :
> Ye stars that twinkle in the sky,
>   By you like bliss be found !
> No higher joy can earth bestow
>   Than Love's most sweet embraces,
>   Elysium here below."

And with this simple love-ditty we bid farewell, for the time-being, to Karl Simrock. And yet one moment must we pause to call our reader's attention to his translations from Shakspeare. These appeared, for the more part, in a Leipsic edition of Shakspeare in a German dress, of which Simrock translated two tragedies—" Hamlet" and " Cymbeline"—as well as some historical plays and several comedies, all of which, with the exception of " Hamlet," had not been rendered by August von Schlegel. The union of Simrock's translations with Schlegel's, in one volume, would be an invaluable gift, we should say, to the German public. Tieck's versions are altogether unworthy of the honour of such union, being awkwardly literal and ofttimes incorrect; this delightful writer thus affording us another instance of the fact, that a man may be a true poet himself, and yet an execrable translator of the poetry of another. Karl Simrock's versions are more literal, on the whole, than those of Schlegel, and yet they are truly German. His renderings of the various comedies are really unrivalled, and we question whether anything could be at all found to match with them. Simrock has also published, at Bonn, " Macbeth," with the English original and the German translation on opposite leaves.) This might be valuable to students of German, as Simrock is at once very literal and idiomatically German and poetical. But we must hasten to leave this subject; once more assuring our readers that the further acquaintance they may form with Karl Simrock's works, will never occasion them regret; nay, that the majority of them will feel grateful to us for having directed their attention to this truly admirable author. Pass we now to Leopold Schefer, author of the " Layman's Breviary," and certainly a most remarkable sign of the times. This poet, if so he can be rightly called, (for though he has written some beautiful poetry, he is yet more of a philosopher than of a poet, and more of a Hegelian than a philosopher,) has created a great sensation by the publication of the novel alluded to, as well as by that of tales and other works setting forth the same views and advocating the same principles. He is the representative in the poetical world of the so-called Hegelian philosophy, for which, we are bound to say, that we entertain very little respect. Hegelianism, in its present developments, seems to be little more than a word for very unmeaning Pantheism, which wrapped up in a mystic veil of words, is, in point of fact, no more than a confusion of the Creator with the creature—of God with the world. Atheism is far more straightforward and honest than this. Every Atheist will admit that there is a motive power in creation; an origin of creation, which he will call either God, or Nature, as you may think fit; but he asserts that that power is not separate from and above creation; that it combines not, in fine, omnipotence with *individual volition*. Now this is precisely what the Pantheist also denies; and herein do both differ from the Christian, or indeed even from the Deist—if what is called pure Deism has been ever held firmly by any mortal without degenerating into universal doubt and infidelity. The Christian, reasoning from analogy, infers that as the union of individual will with reason or mind has been ever an essential during the memory of man to obtaining any fixed result whatever, whether the working of a problem or the construction of a wheel, so the same union must have been requisite for the attainment of that great result, creation; for the construction of that mighty machine, the world. He thus sees the necessity for the existence of an anterior and independent Power, combining will and reason in the highest possible degree, and therefore worships what has been termed " *an individual* GOD." Not so the Pantheist. He confounds, like the Atheist, the Maker with the Made, and in real truth denies the existence of the Godhead altogether.

As we have said that Leopold Schefer is a Hegelian, and given such an account of the views of his school, it will easily be supposed that we cannot do otherwise than condemn most decidedly the tendency of many of Schefer's effusions. Yet, be it remarked, that the extreme obscurity with which the simplest " would-be " truths are enveloped by the employment of Hegelian phraseology, acts as a general safeguard against any deleterious effects resulting from the perusal of these poems. For the majority of readers who *might* be injured by them, will be probably unable to understand them; while those whose capacities enable them to fathom the depths of Hegelian philosophy, will, in all probability, have too much sense not to see the wretched logic and inconsistency of this system. At least, propounded in the form of poems, we think that it cannot do

333

much harm. The German mind is attached to mystery for the sake of mystery. It hates a definite result, which it always stigmatizes as the offspring of empiricism. It is contented to devote many years to the study of a so-called " philosophy" which it knows will conduct to no absolute truths whatever. It is contented to receive any hypothesis, no matter how absurd, for the sake of the beautiful "system" reared upon it, on the condition, namely, that it be permitted to hold any other hypothesis with the same " philosophical faith," and at the same time, if it should so consider fit. Thence, in great part, arises the infidelity of Germans. They cannot bear the plainness and decision of Holy Scriptures. " Is everything to be explained?" they exclaim. "Shall even the truth be forced upon us ? No, rather let us choose falsehood for ourselves." Such is at least the spirit which now animates, and has long actuated, our continental brethren. May we trust that better days are dawning ? Christianity has its mysteries too ; and perchance the hour will yet come when these will be the chief topics of consideration with the German national mind ; when mystic theology, and not false mystic " philosophy," shall be the field on which the greatest German intellects shall display their powers, and exercise that love for deep and mighty themes which is so peculiar to the Teutonic race. In the mean time return we again to Leopold Schefer, and his "Layman's Breviary," two of the leaves of which we shall lay before our readers; choosing for that purpose the most simple and straightforward samples we can meet with, which cannot well fail to be understood. The first of the twain has somewhat of casuistic pride in its bearings, and yet conveys a substantial truth to the mind. Let our readers judge for themselves.

I.

" Stand on this earth with dignity and force,
  And let no giddiness assail thy senses !
  No dizziness when thoughts of distant ages
  Pass o'er thee; of the great, the hallowed past,
  Of which the ruined temples yet exist
  In silent majesty,—like lofty rocks
  Rising from out the bosom of the ocean :—
  In truth, that past is twin-born with the present !
  No dizziness when thou beholdest depths
  Unfathomed, or survey'st the endless realms
  Of starry space, the mazy path of worlds,
  The suns of ether : though our sun be bright,
  Let it not make thee bend before its splendour !
  Earth is co-equal with the proudest stars,

And thou, ay thou, art man upon that earth.—
No dizziness when thou beholdest men
Of might or genius,—who, with others' hands,
Or with the chisel, or the badger's hair,
Or their own inward spirit, have perform'd
Most wondrous works. They, in the course of nature,
Have but their own completion perfected.
Then prove and sunder ! for the greatest man
Is but a mass of well-assorted trifles.—
No dizziness when those appear before thee
Who sit on golden thrones in robes of purple :
The loftiest throne for man is on the turf,
The sod of earth, to which the Deity
Has raised him, o'er the land and o'er the ocean !
Then stand on earth with dignity and force,
And let no dizziness assail thy senses,
Not even when thou ponderest on THYSELF !"

We can trace much of the evil spirit of rebellion, and corrupt self-will in this effusion. It is true that the greatest man is but a mass of well-assorted trifles ;—this should make him humble before his God ; but still he *is* great, by whatever means : and a creature " of less well-assorted trifles " should not indeed crouch before him, (freedom is the birthright of all,) yet in some degree acknowledge his superiority. Equality is a day dream, which cannot be too speedily dispelled wherever that misty exhalation exerts its influences. We should therefore duly reverence all those who are set in authority over us,—and it is not true that the sod is higher in God's sight than the throne. Such distinctions are appointed by Providence, and none but the unbeliever can dream of cancelling them. Still it is true that man never should wholly lose his " self-possession." Man is justified in a certain noble pride, since his Lord and Saviour has died for him. Schefer is therefore right in rebuking that false philosophy which impelled Pope to teach, that God

" Beholds with equal eyes, as Lord of all,
  A hero perish, or a sparrow fall."

In direct opposition to the words of Him, who taught that man was " of more value than many sparrows."—He is also right in asserting the superiority of one immortal soul to myriads of mere material worlds, *as such*. This " Meditation," regarded as poetry, must be admitted, we think, to have a stately and high-sounding march, and really to show vigour of thought combined with not ignoble imagery. Let us pass, however, to our second and more poetical " Meditation," to which we shall have little objection to make on the score of moral truth, and which we ourselves consider one of the most beautiful didactic poems that it ever was our good fortune to meet with.—May our readers share our opinion!

II.

Like to a mother, who has given away
And parted from her last and dearest maiden,
And then, after long years of ceaseless toil
From her own nuptial day commencing, sets
Her down to rest, her work on earth concluded,—
Even so the endless mother, Nature, rests
In fading autumn, from her work of toil.
Full many a gentle daughter, flowers and blossoms,
Hath she in robes of graceful beauty deck'd,
And at the dawn of day and fall of eve
Bedew'd their smiling buds :—and has she not,
When those fair buds to maiden flowers expanded,
The festive nuptial rites of each and all
In silence, 'neath the moon's pale rays, directed?
Has she not tended all her children dearly ?
Has she not changed the tree, erst deck'd by blossoms,
So that its sportive children, golden fruits,
Most gaily wanton'd round it ? Warm'd she not
Beneath the kindly influence of the sun
The very serpent's eggs, and gave to her
A golden new year's dress ? Has she not painted
The butterfly with flowerdust, filled the vine
With juices sweet, and kiss'd with loving lips
Each tender reed of corn and wave of ocean ?
Yes, all was gay, and fair, and beautiful,
In land and sea, in plain and field, and forest;
Nought ask'd, yet all received. Oh, happy mother!
How great must be thy joy, to see thyself:
To enter thine own spirit, and delight
In all thou hast created and perfected !
Even man, though great himself, is but thy child :
Thou art the mother of all life and light!—
But she of whom I spoke, the mortal mother,
Whose last and dearest maiden I myself
Have taken from her, she sits there alone,
And weeps for the beloved and the departed!
She looks upon her aged weary hands,
And tears bedew them ; she is past and gone !—
There in the house of age she sits, the heaven
For ever bright, for ever blue, above her :
Now in her hand yon leafless branch she takes
In silent wonder—deck'd by knotted buds,

Which in the coming spring will bloom again,
And bear their wonted fruits—but she, no more.
' Man is a bud upon the tree of life,'
She thinks, half smiling and half weeping, whilst
The insects of the fading day fly round her,
Who yet would quickly live ere night approaches,
And trembling flow'rets bloom beside her path,
Who yet would quickly celebrate their nuptials
Before the icy winter comes :—and lo !
The silvery moon is rising o'er the mountain,
Casting her light on autumn's fading scene.
As in a legend of long gone-by times,
That once in childhood's days seem'd true, the stream
Is murm'ring, and grey clouds are passing,
As in an aged tale of wonder. With
Her scanty hair the autumn wind is playing,
Which finds no flowers, nay, scarce a leaf, to kiss.
And she, the ever diligent, is startled,
And trembles at that dim monotony.
Now she arises ; on the spreading vine
One solitary grape beholds, and joys
Within her heart to find it : then she turns
To gaze once more on heaven and earth, and slowly
With downcast eyes and faltering steps she enters
Her all-deserted Home ! . . . .
. . . .
This is the fate of man, and of the mother !"

We have said that there was nothing positively objectionable in the morality of this poetry. That morality will be seen, however, to be very deficient, inculcating, as it does, a mere melancholy resignation, uncheered apparently by any certain prospect of a future better existence. That life, without the hope of immortality, would indeed be a melancholy delusion, an altogether useless bubble, we are perfectly ready to admit. Such life we would ourselves reject were it proffered to us. The idea is, however, so totally inconsistent with the whole visible scheme of creation, (which teaches, that as there is no effect without a cause, so also there is no effect without a purpose,) that it needs no refutation here. We only name it to brand it as equally childish and mournful. Perhaps, however, this denial of a future state may not be absolutely involved in the poem we have just given : and certain it is that from a literary point of view, the poem is most beautiful. A playful and cheerful spirit displays itself in the description of the works of " nature ;" a term, allowable in itself, because sanctioned by custom, and known to be the mere exponent of the Godhead. The allusion

58. continued

to the " very serpent's eggs " and "golden new year's dress,"
is peculiarly charming. The lines, again, commencing, " Has
she not painted—The butterfly with flowerdust," can scarcely
be too highly praised. The description of the deserted mother
and the autumnal scene, has, however, even still more poetic
beauty. We know few things more mystically and grandly
German, after its fashion, than the whole sequel of the Poem,
beginning at—" And lo ! The silvery moon is rising," &c.—
Almost awful in its quietness is the—" As in a legend of long
gone-by times, *That once in childhood's days seem'd true*," &c.
The whole picture is most artistically developed. Not a
feature of interest is omitted. The deserted cottage—the fading
blossoms of the lovely garden—the darksome hour of eve—the
melancholy winds—the grey clouds passing athwart the moon
—the grey locks of the abandoned mother, all these combine
to form a whole, which is at once affecting and almost thrilling
in its effect. The poem is indeed what is generally denominated " High German," but it is a most happy sample of the
class alluded to.

Let us leave now Hegelianism behind us, and haste to the
consideration of the merits of Wilhelm Smets: but, turn to
whom we may, we cannot avoid the introduction of themes
of higher import than the mere discussion of any literary beauties, however surprising. We do not seek these topics ; they
meet us, as it were, more than midway, and we know not well
how to avoid them, if we would. Wilhelm Smets then is a
Roman Catholic Priest, as well as a poet ; now, if we mistake not,
Prebendary of the Cathedral of Aix-la-Chapelle. He belongs
to the rationalising party within the German Roman Catholic
Church. We do not mean to uphold him as an infidel : far
from it. But his faith is not perhaps as ardent, as enthusiastic,
as it might be. He belongs, in fine, to that class of moderate
Roman Catholics, who are disgusted by the frauds practised by
their " confrères," but dare not openly murmur against their
"pious" impieties, since they are sanctioned and approved of by
the so-called Father of Christendom, the Pope. The faith of
Roman Catholics placed in this position is naturally in a perilous strait. It is difficult for them to separate the idea of religion from superstition, and duly rejecting with abhorrence the
false, to cling with more reverence to the true. Still we doubt
not that Herr Dechant Smets struggles against his own unor-
thodox suggestions, and strives to maintain a due medium of
faith. Alas ! in what a fearful peril is he of falling from the
truth ! And this danger is shared by many tens of thousands.
On a previous occasion, when we introduced Zacharias Werner,

author of "The Sons of the Vale," to our readers' notice, we
entered more fully upon this subject. At present we can only
say, that the want of uncalculating unsuspicious ardour,
which is scarcely possible within so corrupted a communion
as the Roman Catholic, has acted most unfavourably on Dechant
Smets' religious poetry, of which we will therefore quote nothing ;
still we could not pass over this writer, because he has really
no slight merit, and is besides the representative of a class.
We will quote one sample of his mere worldly effusions, a Triolet, which, strange to say, *appears* at least to refer to love ;
however, our readers may set whatever interpretation they like
upon the lay. The Triolet in itself is excessively beautiful,
and indeed a model of its kind. Before quoting it, we may as
well acquaint those readers who are as yet unaware of the fact,
that a Triolet is a poem of only eight lines in length, of which
one line, the first, must be repeated three times—and another,
(the second) twice, so that there are in reality but five lines altogether.—And now for this strange composition :—

" TRIOLET.

But once I saw thee, once, and after, never,
Thee brightest starbeam on my lonely way :
Vainly I sigh for what has pass'd away ;
But once I saw thee, once, and after, never,
So shall my poet accents mourn for ever,
In many a proud and yet despairing lay,
That once I saw thee, once, and after, never,
The brightest starbeam on my lonely way."

The repetition of the chief line is here most artistic, and appears really perfectly natural, nay, all but unavoidable. That
grief should dwell upon " the beloved thought," none will affirm
to be strange or fantastic.

One word more of " Herr Dechant Smets ;" he is a half-
brother, as we believe, of the famous Schröder Devrient the
singer, and a son by a former marriage of Madame Schröder,
the Siddons of Germany. Talent is therefore hereditary in him,
and can excite no surprise. Once more, let none wonder that
such men as the learned Prebendary, so cautious and philosophising, should be tolerated and favoured within the Roman
Catholic Church. They render themselves highly useful by con-
doling *privately* with discontented laymen on the backslidings of
the Church ; and so hinder their smothered flames of anger and
contempt from bursting into open and undisguised rebellion.
Leave we the painful subject of Romanism and the Romish
Church behind us, and turn we to Wilhelm Wackernagel, the

336

freeborn cheerful poet of Zurich, of whom Simrock often speaks as a true friend in the course of his poems; and who, judging from the character there assigned him, as well as from the spirit breathing from his own effusions, must be a truly delightful and amiable individual : he is also a very pleasing, though not a great poet ; occasionally he waxes polemical, and assails Young Germany with weighty weapons for its saucy emptiness, and would-be rationalising ; but we like him least in this mood. He fights bravely and justly indeed, but he is more a man of peace than of war ;—he is more calculated to persuade than to convince, by the process of knocking down his opponent. Three little lays of his we shall place before our readers ; and as we have already dallied so long on our way, and have yet some work before us, we shall produce them all at once :—First, then, comes a little monitory strain counselling against useless bewailings, and ascetic inaction ;—then follows a little poem on the Calligraphy of Spring, which explains itself ;—thirdly and lastly, we have a Christian's Bridal Song, a little poem extracted from a wreath of poetical blossoms entwined by the poet in honour of his youthful consort, and in emulation of Rückert's hymeneal lays. There is no pretence in these little poems ; and they must be received, as they were written, lovingly, to be at all enjoyed.

"ON THIS SIDE.

Seat thee by the stream of sorrow !
Seat thee there, and sigh, and weep :
But that stream, to-day, to-morrow,
Still its customed course shall keep.

Thus from morn to eve, for ever,
Past thy feet its waves shall flow ;
For with *fears* and *tears* was never
Built a bridge on earth below.''

" SPRING'S CALLIGRAPHY.

Who is he, of scribes the rarest,
On this earth of ours ?
Spring, the gentlest, sweetest, fairest,
Spring with all his flowers.

In soul saddening Winter's crowning,
Who his sceptre sway'd,
Every leaf lay darkly frowning
In the forest glade.

Lo ! approach'd young Spring so gaily,
And, forthwith, in mirth,
Traced his letters, nightly, daily,
On the leaves of earth.

O'er the mountain, in the valley,
'Mid the cornfields too,
Mark him with each blossom dally,
All with tints imbue !

Letters, small and fine, but gleaming,
Azure now, now gold,
On the leaves, the blossoms beaming—
Haste and these behold !

Every lime-tree thus is tinted ;
Read and read them o'er :—
Of the books, by mortals printed,
Pr'ythee, think no more !''

" THE LOVERS.

Like to children playing,
Will we twain unite :
Soul in soul still straying
'Neath the golden sunbeam's light.

From the mead's green bosom,
We, in joyous mirth,
Pluck each youthful blossom,
Red and blue, that decks the earth.

Garlands thence enwreathing,
Bright and fair to see,
Sweetest odours breathing ;
Thou for me, and I for thee.

'Till day's sunbeam fails us,
And 'mid shades of night,
From the ether hails us
In our father's house the light.

Then our arms entwining,
Far from mortal ken,
Where yon house is shining
Haste we to our Father then.

' Lo ! this garland rarest,
Which adorns me now,
All its blossoms fairest
Pluck'd my playmate for my brow.'

Us to glory raising
Smiles our Father there,
And his angels praising,
Fill with songs of love the air.''

The metre of this last effusion is somewhat singular, and its tone is somewhat mystic and German ; and yet there is a truthful simplicity mingled with this half-mysticism, which makes the poem appear extremely pleasing. It is a little parable of wedded love and life on earth, and a happy passage to Heaven, which is conceived in a loving spirit. Pass we to the last on our list, a far less innocent and amiable individual, the Coryphæus of Young Germany, the poetical Stentor of the age, Georg Herwegh; for Prutz, though he is certainly a more thorough-paced "bully," can scarcely be held a poet at all; and as for Seeger, and others of the same crew, they are too valueless to be worth the trouble of either powder or shot.

Young Germany, which after all still continues to exist, though the men who originally founded that sect are no longer members of it, is a very obstreperous and noisy body, of whom it may be said with great truth, that they have as yet only evolved or brought to day "much cry and little wool." Not that we altogether condemn these young gentlemen, as having no foundation whatever for their complaints. No: we are perfectly ready to admit that the dull "Philistery," the cold indifferentism, the utter absence of all generous feeling, high resolve, or deep conviction, which has for some time characterised and still characterises the bureaucratic and other classes of Germany more or less nearly related therewith, called loudly for this reaction against such a system of mere words and appearances, of outward respectability and expediency; such a system, in fine, as some would gladly bring to perfection in our own more favoured country. We have before expressed our conviction, and that conviction we now repeat, that a bureaucratic government is necessarily a bad one in the long run. We are advocates for constitutional monarchies, in which the aristocratic and democratic powers both exert their mutual shares of influence, and in turn obtain the ascendancy. We detest the very notion of equality, save before justice and before heaven. We would maintain the distinctions of noble blood, but under such admirable restrictions as our own constitution has provided, by conferring the title of peers on the eldest sons alone, and that only when they become members of the Upper House, and constantly recruiting this selected body who represent their country's dignity from the ranks of the gentry (often the more noble of the two) and of the middle classes. With this constant ebb and flow no false exclusiveness can long maintain its ground: all the evils of a restricted aristocracy are thus avoided; but all the benefits arising from the influence in the state of a rich and noble body, pledged to an honourable course of life by their public stations, and acting as a due counterpoise to the natural democratic bent for change,—all these are secured and preserved inviolate. A truly honourable and high-minded aristocracy is requisite for the well-being of a country. Without it a high tone of generous feeling will never be preserved in the long run. Money will be the only source of social distinction, and consequently the only theme for thought. In this respect the United States may well read us a lesson. Despotism, as it has been truly said, whether it assumes a bureaucratic or a more absolute guise, is a great leveller. It detests all extraordinary superiority, whether of soul or intellect, and favours only "safe men," whom it may use as blind and will-less instruments. It is the natural foe of nobility of purpose or intellectual genius, of whatever order. It is democratic, in as far as it would level all men *with one another, and with the dust*. It might seem almost needless to recall such facts as these; but, alas! *some members* of our own Young England, honourable as that party must be considered as a whole, have appeared to forget them altogether. They have actually written against an aristocracy, and called our representative government *a Venetian oligarchy!!* We will not waste words upon this most egregious error, which its very propounders must learn sooner or later to be ashamed of. Others, who have been recognized as more consistent, more true members of Young England, have enounced the most contrary principles, and declared their resolution to secure its rights to the aristocratic power, whether against despotism or democracy, the Crown or the masses. To return to our more immediate subject, Young Germany, in revolting against the bureaucratic principle which had wrought decay of faith and of principle throughout the Teutonic realms, had much of right on its side. "Away," it cried, "with your mere pretences! your decent shams!—Either make the truths, as you declare them, handed down to you by your forefathers, *realities*, or else abandon them altogether. Marriage, for instance?—You have twenty causes for the separation of the marriage tie; one is, incompatibility of temper. Now, marriage must be either something or nothing. Abolish it, then, altogether, or abstain from thus degrading it to a heartless mockery! Again, your religion? There seems no verity in it. Week after week your preachers go on teaching a species of Christianity to the *people*, which in your *universities*, 'ex cathedrâ,' they openly deride. Let us have no more of these make-believes!—Truth above all things! Truth for man! Truth for God!" Such, we repeat, was the language of Young Germany, and it found an echo in many hearts: but the young rebels did not stop here. They adopted levelling and infidel principles of the most hateful order, and, at present it would seem, that no extravagance *of words, at least*, could be too great for them. For deeds—these do not at all lie in their department, and we might as well ask the wild boars of the forest to emulate the ditties of Young Germany, as expect Young Germany to show the active resolution and self-dependent vigour of the said boars. But enough of this. We would not speak of Young Germany, but of Herwegh the poet. Only so much be said : we recognise some good in the present movement; for the German " philistery," and dull objectless philosophising of the present day are really "most intolerable, and not to be endured." Now then for Herwegh. This young man seems to have a firm conviction of the justice of his cause. His temper somewhat reminds us of that of our own Ward, though the German is perhaps rather less virulent and spiteful. Indeed Ward has comparatively nothing to complain of, and is evidently one of those rebellious spirits, who always must be on the side of opposition; because the chiefest pleasure to him in life is to calumniate what ought to be most near and dear to him. Whether Ward or Herwegh be most incapable of cool reasoning it would be difficult to decide : the one is blinded by his passions, perhaps even generous, though mistaken; the other by his excess of spite. We return then to " George Herwegh," who, in his first series of poems, and by far his best, " Die Gedichte eines Lebendigen," has most lustily assailed our favourite aversion, Prince Pückler Moskau, a man who has calumniated England's gentry, assuring the German public that they were equal in dignity only to the sheriffs and bailiffs of small German country towns, and has further published and circulated far and wide the most despicable libels on our countrywomen. By-the-bye we would recommend the perusal of this work to the individual above mentioned, who would no doubt find therein much food for pleasurable thought and gratifying reflections. In a short notice of a magazine, in which Herwegh had some share, in our last Number we quoted two verses and a half of this polemic effusion against the Prussian prince. As a sample of German wit (a somewhat rare commodity), we will now present it to our readers, and trust that it may draw a smile even from the most serious.

"TO A DEAD MAN FROM A LIVING MAN.*

Dead knight, and soulless spectre,
    Couch, couch thy lance on high !
For thou shalt be my Hector,
    And thine Achilles I.
Yes, croaking mortal raven,
    I hail thee, with a shout,
Despite thy *crest*, a craven,
    Despite thy *lance*, a lout.

* It need scarcely be stated that Pückler Moskau's first work was published under the title of " Letters of a Dead Man."—*Briefe eines Verstorbenen.*

Thy fame all tongues entrammels,
    All men praise thee alone,
Because such love for—*camels*
    And *coursers*, thou hast shown :
Hence with thy Arab science,
    To Sheiks and Emirs go !
My glove, in proud defiance,
    Within thy tent I throw.

The woes of *Egypt's* nation
    Thou seem'st in heart to share ;
But see'st, with resignation,
    Thy fatherland despair.
Yet never had'st thou holden
    Thy course 'neath palm-groves lorn,
Save armed by ducats golden
    From German coffers torn.

No land to rest hath won thee ;
    World-oceans pierced thy prow.
O, dawn'd it never on thee,
    How small, how small wert thou ?
While o'er Ulysses' island
    Thy footsteps dared to rove,
Appear'd on no stern highland
    His spirit from above :

And cried it not in anger ?
    ' Quit, quit the freeborn main !
Thy base prosaic languor
    Must sigh for chains again.—
To river Pleisse turn thee !
    Back, back to river Sprée !
Not every prince's journey
    Shall make an Odyssey.'—

True, never Hades' portals
    May soul like his receive :
But ne'er less like were mortals
    Than thou and he, believe !
He would not dully falter,
    Like thee, thus idly roam ;
He longed for house and altar,
    For consort, and for home.

In *German* cause, how coldly
    Did'st thou the battle flee !
Yet fought'st thou too—and boldly—
    For—*Turkish liberty.*

Thou'lt die with shield and armour
    For arms *in* shield, God wot!—
Aristocratic charmer,
    Us, us thou charmest not.

Its marble stores Carrara
    In vain for him employs,
To whom e'en Niagara *
    Was nought but smoke and noise :
For him, who worlds before him
    But cross'd, his shame to seal,
And God's stars shining o'er him,
    His stars † more great could feel.

Dead knight, and senseless spectre,
    Couch, couch thy lance on high!
For thou shalt be my Hector,
    And thine Achilles I—
In vain, in vain, would'st hide thee
    'Mid crowds of Eastern birth :
I'll cast thee here, beside me,
    Down, down on German earth!"—

So much for the Prince, who is certainly here most cavalierly treated. Herwegh has, however, ventured on more elevated strains, nor can he be held to have always failed in these. Some of his sonnets strike us as remarkably fine. The following little " Horseman's Song " has excited the musical inspiration of scores of German composers, and of one English one, Howard Glover, the composer of an opera about to be produced at the Princess's, much of the music from which we have heard and greatly admire, and also of a most exquisite *published* song, treating Shelley's far-famed Indian serenata, " I arise from dreams of thee." To return from this act of homage to a young and very talented composer, from whom we expect great things for the honour of England, Herwegh's song has a somewhat revolutionary spirit, and in fact is evidently intended to be prophetic, expressing the feelings with which certain members of Young Germany might be supposed to rush to the conflict with imagined tyranny, in the event of a civil war. We need scarcely say that of tyranny, demanding such an alternative as this, in Germany there is no trace. The great evils there existing, arise from a want of faith *in all things*, and a certainly undue pressure of the bureaucratic system. But to our song, which those, who will, may take in a more harmless sense, and refer to the late Polish revolt against Russian usurpation.

    * He really said this in his flippant Travels.
    † Orders of Knighthood, &c.

" HORSEMAN'S SONG.

The night is round us, far and wide,
In silence dread we onwards ride,
    To death and glory flying.
Cold blows the night wind o'er the lea :—
Quick, hostess, wine!—for drink will we,
    Ere dying, ere dying.

Thou sod, which sleep'st in gentle gloom,
Like rosebuds red thou soon shalt bloom,
    My heart's blood on thee lying.—
The first wild draught, with outdrawn brand,
This drink we to our fatherland,
    Ere dying, ere dying.

Now quick the second draught be mine!
And that for freedom, ray divine,
    In light with sunbeams vying.
These drops still left—for whom shall be?
These, Roman realm, I drink to thee
    Now dying, now dying!

And now, my *love?*—but void 's the glass!
Be thine then, thou my fondest lass,
    My fame, to ease thy sighing!—
Rush on the foe, by stormwinds borne—
O joy of joys, at early morn,
    Thus dying, thus dying!"

In spite of the outcry against political poems as dull and dry, genius can vivify almost any subject, and surely the weal of empires is not one of the least inspiring. Only there is in general so much exaggeration, so little sound sense, such a want of high and noble principle, in these German democrats, that we shrink from many of their works with a kind of instinctive abhorrence. Still, we repeat it, these excesses arise from an absence of due representative government. The useless speculations of " German philosophy" are attributable to the same cause. The human mind *will* find some field for doubt and censure; and if this may not be *political*, it is sure to prove *religious*. Enough of these youthful revolutionists, who greatly hinder the progression of true freedom, by their discordant outcries, and render it almost impossible for the present noble King of Prussia to follow his own heart's dearest wish, and emulate in Prussia our own unrivalled constitution.

We must draw our article to a close. To-day, even, we have seen enough, we think, to show that there is no absence of the true poetic power at present in Germany, though some of its greatest living poets, Rückert, Freiligrath, Lenau, and Uhland, have not been at all quoted. Here we rest for the present. Yet ere we finally bid our readers farewell, let us seize this opportunity to denounce the oft-propounded and preposterous fallacy that the age of poetry is passing away. Never, never shall it pass, while man retains an immortal soul and an eternal destiny; while beauty exists in the outward world of nature and the inward realm of kindliness; never, in fine,

" Long, as sweet passion's power
    Maiden to youth shall bind;
Long, as one flowery bower
    Childhood shall find."—

Germany has now a living galaxy of stars; though we admit that many of these are not of first-rate magnitude. and that the beams of all are somewhat darkened, if not altogether intercepted, by the mists of doubt and infidelity. France has perhaps greater living poets than any who have before adorned her. Not to include Chateaubriand, Victor Hugo, one of the greatest and most fanciful of lyric poets, (whom we purpose soon to notice *at length*), the inexhaustible De Beranger, De Lamartine, and others less illustrious, may now be named as mighty bardic champions for their country's honour. And England too, has she not her bards. Have we then any cause to complain? Certainly not. Obscurity is the reigning defect of our school. This should not be. "Poetry should be written for all, not the few," as Bulwer tells us in one of his clever but far too studied lays. But once more, we repeat it, never let it be imagined that human hearts and souls can cease to admire and acknowledge the beautiful. Some few intellects and feelings there may be, so unhappily constituted, that the arts can exercise no influence, can confer no benefits, upon them. But these are an inconsiderable minority. So may we say, though in a guarded sense, (for true genius *does* strike the lyre already, and *might* win universal fame by stricter attention to clearness and perspicuity,)

" Oh, when true genius chants the lay,
    And strikes the lyre once more,
A myriad hearts shall own its sway,
    And echo back its lore."—

341

59. CHAMBERS' EDINBURGH JOURNAL, 6 (1846), 16. M/H No. 4244.

CRITICISM IN GERMANY.

The following remarks on this subject are from the *Manchester Examiner's* report of lectures on German Literature, delivered at that town by Mr George Dawson of Birmingham :—'One of the most striking things in German literature was its criticism. England was inundated with reviews ; but, until lately, English criticism was an absurdity. At one time the system was to look at the man, and judge of the book accordingly; another system was to look, not at the work, but at the political, religious, or scholastic opinions of the writer ; a third system, the followers of which much-belauded themselves, was that of equilibrium, or impartiality, by which faults and merits were so nicely balanced, that no one could say which preponderated. English criticism had now gotten the dandy spirit of the last age, which wondered and admired at nothing—a coldness of air, a starched-cravatism, which could look on the Coliseum, or walk through the Louvre, without betraying an emotion. These men sat on their icy thrones, dealing out praise and blame ; but they would not acknowledge that anything was new or wonderful to them. After having dwelt at some length on the character of criticism in England, and shown how frivolous and petty were the objections frequently urged against the highest productions of the intellect, the lecturer proceeded to say that criticism in Germany was another thing. There the critics sought not to find out the mechanism of a simile ; they did not weigh and balance a man's character and book ; but they strove to render even plainer than the author had done that which the author had written. A good German critic, of the true order, looked upon a work as the symbolic character in which a great man had expressed his thoughts. He was the interpreter between the author and the public. He explained his symbol, and showed the indwelling spirit and the substance that was there. Even upon Shakspeare there had been no very sound criticism until we imported it from Germany, and since then we had begun to understand the poet better than we did before. If any of the audience doubted this, let them read some of the orthodox notes in the editions of fifty or sixty years since. There they would find elaborate disquisitions on the meaning of a word, as to whether a comma should not be a colon, and so on ; but if this was criticism on Shakspeare, he would rather have him uncomma'd and uncolon'd, so that he might have more time to make out the spirit, and understand the soul of the author. The criticism on "Hamlet" in the "Wilhelm Meister" had never been excelled, and was a sample of what criticism should be. An Englishman would have shown where Shakspeare got this idea, and where he got that idea ; how he pieced them together, and so on ; but the German went up to him as he would to nature. He did not go up to him in the style of a man who, when looking at an oak tree, began to ask why it was not higher or broader, why this branch was permitted to remain, and why the trunk was not French polished, but to expound why it was there—to understand its meaning, to find out the divine idea of which it was the symbol, and so to make it plain.'

New Books.

THE SPIRIT OF GERMAN POETRY: a Series of Translations from the German Poets. With Biographical Notices. By JOSEPH GOSTICK. Medium 8vo. London : W. Smith.

A VERY useful, very agreeable, and very cheap publication. The necessity for every educated and accomplished person, to say nothing of inclination, to be acquainted with German poetry, renders a manual and selection of this kind valuable. Mr. Gostick has, it appears to us, performed his labour very judiciously, and in a manner that proves him to be well-informed on the subject, and with a critical appreciation and analysation extremely serviceable to the reader.

The literature of our own country, in all departments, is becoming so insurmountable, that it is found absolutely necessary to condense it into extracts and beauties, and a very diligent reader now finds it difficult to make himself acquainted with more than the master-pieces of the most celebrated authors. To foreign literature, therefore, but little time can be given, and to be thus presented with a fair specimen of the chief German poets, is a great boon.

There is no necessity for us to enter upon any criticism of the poetry itself ; but we have been struck by two things : first, that after all the immense sensation created by the German writings, that there are so comparatively few poets could claim a place in this collection ; and, secondly, that the tendency of the whole runs so much towards words and sentiments. A great deal more condensation, and a little more reality, would, apparently, vastly improve the whole national poetry, which, from first to last, seems to spring more from enthusiasm than observation. Compared (at all events, by these specimens) with our grand outbreak of poetry in the 16th century, it is comparatively weak and purposeless. It is not fair to make comparisons through the medium of translation ; and, therefore, we shall leave the subject, merely reminding the reader, that in Mr. Gostick's book, will be found an agreeable collection and a valuable guide.

61. ECLECTIC REVIEW, 3rd ser. 84 (1846), 465-478. M/H No. 4272.

Art. VII.—1. *Die Wahlverwandschaften (The Elective Affinities).* By Joh. W. von Goëthe.

2. *Wilhelm Meister's Lehrjahre.* *(Wilh. Meister's Apprenticeship.)*

3. *Wilhelm Meister's Wanderjahre.* *(Wilh. Meister's Travelling Years).* Stuttgart and Tübingen.

THE Germans, next to the Britons, are distinguished as having produced the most celebrated authors in that branch of polite literature, which is generally termed the romance or novel. This assertion will be sufficiently confirmed by comparing, both as to quality and quantity, the catalogues that appear yearly at the fair of Leipzig, and other towns of Germany, and which may be met with in every library of note, both at home and abroad. The mass of books thus produced for the amusement and instruction of the people, is really enormous; and on this account, it almost necessarily follows, that there must be in so large an accumulation a mixture of good and bad productions. In order, however, to form a just estimate as to the real merits of this department of literature, as it at present exists in Germany, it will be well to examine those of an earlier date, to see out of what slender sources the more recent condition of such literature has been evolved.

The German history of fiction, or simply the German novel, may be considered as having arisen out of the multitude of legendary, allegorical, and historical poems, which had been produced up to the close of the fifteenth century. These, with similar other productions, such as ballads, etc., began at this period to be rendered into prose; and it was only within the last two centuries, but more especially within the last sixty or seventy years, that the German novel assumed that moral character and form, which now so favourably distinguishes it from similar creations of other countries, especially those of France and Italy. Up to the former period, the romance in Germany, (with the exception of 'Iwain,' 'Wigolis von Rade,' etc., which are purely German works,) chiefly consisted of stale romances of chivalry, nursery tales and legends, which were translated from the Italian, French, and Latin. Such were the 'Tales' of Troya, Alexander, Amadis, etc.; the favourite books of the day, however, were 'Doctor Faustus,' and 'The Duke of Luxemberg,' which were soon followed by many others, among which deserve to be mentioned, 'Till Eulenspiegel,' or 'Tyel Howleglass,' and 'Ahasuerus, the Wandering Jew.' About the year 1598, there appeared one of those productions, which seem to be wholly unlimited in the sphere of their action. This was a work entitled, the 'Lustige und lächerliche Lallenburg, oder die Schildbürger.' Some consider it in the light of a national satire, whereas others look upon it as an extremely humourous and comic novel. Be this as it may, it is certain, that few romances have earned the praise which has been and still is so justly bestowed on this admirable performance. It affords in the most delightful manner an exquisite and highly correct picture of the governmental constitution, and of the petit-maîtreship practised in those days in every town and village, throughout Germany. It was also at this time that there appeared the so-called 'Adventurous Popular Romances,' a species of light and amusing reading, which has remained even until this day a great favourite with almost all the lower classes of Germany. The most remarkable of these romances are, 'Die schöne Melusine,' 'Herzog Ernst von Baiern,' 'Fortunati Wünschhütlein,' 'Das Buch der Liebe,' 'Die schöne Magellone,' 'Der gehörnte Siegfried,' 'Kaiser Octavianus,' 'Die geduldige Helena,' 'Die heilige Genoveva,' 'Ida Gräfin von Toggenburg,' 'Der edle Finkenritter,' 'Hans guck in die Welt,' which is perhaps the best of the whole; 'Die vier Haimonskinder,' 'Die schöne Historie von den sieben weisen Meistern,' and 'Die über die Bosheit triumphirende Unschuld Hirlanda.'

But a sudden change now took place in the taste of the Germans, which was owing partly to the productions of the Castilian poet, George de Montemajor, and partly to those of Sir Philip Sidney. Through the 'Diana' of the former, and the 'Arcadia' of the latter, the Germans became acquainted with the so-called 'Pastorals, or Bucolics,' which gave rise to Neumark's 'Filamon,' a tale as bombastic and stiff, as it is unnatural, and to 'Herculinus and Herculista.' The latter, written as its author says, for 'modest Christian readers,' appeared in the year 1659, and contains innumerable prayers, and rather good sacred hymns, and was the produce of a pious clergyman named Buchholz. The author's aim was evidently to counteract the mania which raged at the time, for demoralizing 'romances chevaleresques.' An exceedingly flowery, or rather bombastic style, —in those days termed 'brilliant,'—excepted, the book possesses many features, which even now entitle it to a careful perusal. Of a similar character is Samuel Greifensohn von Hischberg's famous 'Abenteuerliche Simplicissimus,' which the author, a soldier, produced during the thirty years' war. In it he has given a superb and exact picture of the state of Germany during that period. Though one of the most stirring novels, yet, like the former, this 'Simplicissimus' is not wholly free from a high-strained pathos, and an unnatural lusciousness of language or expression.

Not long after this change, there arose two men—Hoffmannswaldau and Lohenstein—who, by their productions laid the foundation of 'Heroic' romance. The first novel of this kind was Lohenstein's 'Arminius und Thusnelda,' which had been preceded by 'Aramena' and 'Octavia,' both of which tales boasted the parentage of Ulrich, Duke of Braunshweig, 'Ibrahim,' written by Von Zesen, etc. All these, however, were outdone by the famous 'Asiatische Banise' of Ziegler. This author, who had been the universal favourite, committed the greatest sins imaginable in the way of exaggeration, and attained the acme of bombastic style in this romance, which, with all its faults and exaggerations, may be found nevertheless among the lower classes of Germany, with whom it seems to be an especial favourite. The most fertile novelist of that period was Talander, or August Bohn, who is said to have composed between twenty and thirty novels. Yet these were rather love-stories, and were written especially for ladies, than novels, as may be clearly seen by the title of one of them: 'The Cabinet of Love for the Fair Sex.' From this fact it will appear evident, that love-stories, properly speaking, written for the fair sex, are of a much earlier date than the present day. Another novel writer of the same school, was Happel of Marburg, who produced some of the most insipid and intolerable romantic caricatures possible, with titles so bombastic as to excite derision.

A great improvement in the public taste was produced by the works of Schnabel. This distinguished author, wrote in the early part of the eighteenth century, his celebrated novel 'The island Felsenburg,' a work, which has been very recently edited by L. Tieck, and entirely recast by the great Danish romancist Œhlenschläger. At the time of its appearance it was imitated by a host of German novelists, and subsequently laid the foundation of the so-called 'Robinsonade,' a species of tales, which maintained their rank among the German narratives for nearly half a century, and which thereby gave rise to many very excellent productions of the famous author Campe.

The well-known fabulist Gellert, wrote during this period a novel, entitled the 'Swedish Countess,' which is considered nevertheless a work of very moderate powers. But he, as well as a great many others, was compelled to give way to a mass of British authors, who now, for the first time, were introduced into Germany. Their extraordinary genius was acknowledged by the Germans, and exercised considerable influence over their literature. The greater portion of these writers, if not all, were translated, and their style imitated as closely as possible. The English writers who produced the greatest effect upon the German mind were Shakspeare, Young, Sterne, Smollett, Pope, Swift, Richardson, Fielding, and Goldsmith. Among the Germans who at this period had the greatest influence upon the intellect of the nation, especially that of the fair sex, and above all upon the more educated class of ladies, was John Hermes, Provost at Breslaw. A close imitator of Richardson, his first novel was entitled 'Fanny Wilkes,' which was devoured by all classes of society, and became as great a favourite with the German ladies, as Richardson's 'Clarissa' had been with those of England. The novel itself contains many fine and noble features, and is one of the liveliest and most charming books imaginable, describing in a masterly manner the customs and characters of the age. This was followed by 'Sophia's Tour from Memel to Saxony,' a work of a rather witty turn, containing many admirable views of human life, and traits of the highest practical truths. Some of this author's other novels, such as 'Hermine,' etc. as well as all those in which he especially addresses the daughters of 'noble' extraction, and the ladies generally, were of a similar tendency, whilst others were of a much inferior kind. On the whole, however, Hermes was at that time to Germany, what Richardson had been to England.

Contemporaneously with, and similar in style and powers of invention to Hermes, were Madame La Roche, and Professor Dusch, both of whom wrote for the public with more or less success. But classical novels of the highest order were written at this time by the celebrated scholar Wieland. A pure, flowing, and charming language, combined with much practical experience, cheerfulness, good humour, grace and amiability, are the chief features of his romantic productions. Wieland has been styled the 'German Voltaire,' but this title confers on him in our judgment, no particular honour. Voltaire, may be regarded as possessing more satirical wit and lightness; but Wieland is decidedly his superior in genius and solid learning. In whatever light the Frenchman's creations are regarded, a dozen ideas borrowed from Bayle, constitute all the learning which can be discovered in the course of more than a hundred volumes.

Goëthe and Klinger (of whom hereafter) appeared, and with them the first golden rays of that rising sun, which was to shed its imperishable lustre over the romantic literature of Germany. This was effected by creations of the liveliest, most brilliant and charming fancies. Fire and energy, in works replete with poetic beauties, grandeur, and philosophical truths, combined with a rich vein of humour, and now and then a colouring of a deeper hue, contributed much to wipe away those tears which were the consequence of the unnatural sentimentality then prevailing.

But these great men—at least at first—carried things rather too far, so that their productions, which, in the beginning, were calculated to eradicate prevailing evils, and, to a certain extent, produced that effect, had nearly proved as great a calamity as the existing evils themselves. Germany, overwhelmed by the most unnatural sentimentalism, seemed to have become the prey of the sickliest effeminacy from within, and of a Gallo and Anglomania from without, on which account it was deemed high time that something should be done towards curing a disease which was spreading daily, and which threatened the health of the German mind with utter destruction. Jerusalem, an enthusiast, and intimate friend of Goëthe, and an unfortunate lover to boot, having destroyed himself at a place called Wetzlar, in consequence of an ill-fated attachment, Goëthe, in a state of great mental excitement, which almost involved his own ruin, wrote a work entitled 'Werther's Leiden,' a creation in which, under the name of Werther, he immortalized his hapless friend. For poetic beauties and an enthusiastic spirit, this work has few equals, and at the time we are speaking of, it created quite a *furore*. And well might it have been so. Love, with all its powers and charms, with all its joys and sorrows, expressed in the most passionate and enchanting language, was abundantly suited to enrapture and to unsettle the mind of those already beneath its influence, and to make every one of them feel desirous of an end similar to that of the ill-fated Werther. And yet it was this very work which contributed in no slight degree to a revolution in the world of German letters, and 'belletristic' literature.

We may here speak of the other chief romantic productions of this author, though we shall have again to refer to him. The next romance of note which Goëthe wrote is his celebrated 'Wahlverwandschaften,' a work which may be described as ranking among the finest specimens of its class, and as being perhaps unequalled for its profound and clear ideas, for a pure and disinterested attachment, couched in language as elegant and finished, as it is energetic and powerful. But Goëthe's triumph is a novel entitled 'Wilhelm Meister's Lehr-und Wanderjahre,' which is, beyond all doubt, his master-piece. It is the most elaborate, as well as the most finished, and to a certain degree, a signal triumph of prose over poetry. The invention or plot, order and finish, the characters, incidents and scenery, are as perfect as they are brilliant. The whole work is a mass of the deepest thoughts, of the clearest and soundest judgments, and of the most entrancing eloquence. It is—to use the famous Zelter's expressions—no romance, it is the world, the 'little-great' and 'great-little' world, in which we find ourselves, our instincts, and our follies, pourtrayed in an admirable manner by the pencil of a master. This work, next to Faust, is Goëthe's most original, most perfect production, because it is with all its incidents, practical experience, and philosophical truths, a precise and exact copy of the great man himself.

We have seen how matters stood, at the time that Goëthe wrote the 'Sorrows of Werther,' and the necessity that existed for a speedy cure of the prevailing disease. Musaeus and Trimm, two most brilliant satirical writers, appeared on the stage, the former with his 'German Grandison, or Grandison II.,' and the latter with his 'Marcus Puneratius Cyprianus Curt, called the Sentimentalist,' who, by means of these and similar satirical writings, made a sad havoc among the childish sentimentalists around. But innumerable others, also, both moral and satirical, now began to oppose this overwhelming stream by means of highly meritorious works, which acted most beneficially upon the heroes and heroines of the moon. For, heartily ridiculed, and otherwise laughed at, the number of the Siegwarts and Mariannas (the hero and heroine of 'Siegfried von Felsenberg,' a novel, written by Müller, and similar to Goëthe's 'Werther'), the Herforts and Claras, the Werthers and Charlottes, the Carls and Emilies, visibly decreased daily, or made those love-sick people fall into another extreme, by giving up the phantom of an ideal affection for one of a more substantial character. Whether or not, they have profited by this exchange, it is no affair of ours to determine.

Among the sentimental and would-be historical novels, that were particularly calculated to unsettle the mind of the young of both sexes, were those of the then much admired Professor Meissner, for example, his 'Bianca Capello,' 'Alcibiades,' 'Epaminondas,' 'Spartacus,' 'Cæsar,' 'Masaniello,' and some others, which not unfrequently were looked upon as the *ne plus ultra* of historical romances. That they contain some fair points, cannot be disputed; but on the whole they are very trivial; and it is perhaps for this reason, as Menzel says, that they became popular. There were furthermore the novels, 'Clara von Hoheneichen,' 'Petermännchen,' 'Die zwölf schlafenden Jungfrauen,' 'Benno von Elsenburg,' etc., by Spiess; all of which are scarcely more than a tirade on patience, human sufferings, and human foibles, and yet in those days they were considered as productions of surpassing beauty. But even these, notwithstanding their exaggerations and bombast, contain many original, stirring, and highly poetical ideas, and were not seldom remarkable for great powers of invention. Some of them written after the model of Goëthe, especially after his chivalrous drama, 'Götz von Berlichingen,' were distinguished for a certain wildness and natural sublimity which not unfrequently vary in their mood and character, whereby in many instances they proved in themselves antidotes to their own sentimentalism, and often opposed the narrow prejudices, and stiff, though tame, customs prevailing in those days.

To this period also belongs the venerable canon Tiedge, who among others, wrote the 'Amy and Robert,' 'Urania,' and 'The Wanderings through the Market of Life.' Much resembling the generality of the novel writers of his day, he frequently affects an effeminate melancholy. But though in this respect faulty, he is, on the whole, rather honest than otherwise. Many trains of noble and moral feelings, given vent to in easy and elegant phraseology, are, in spite of the faults just enumerated, to be met with in his writings; and inasmuch as he is serious and sincere in his aim, he sometimes gives birth to profound ideas, among which God, religion, the immortality of the soul, and the freedom of man's will, are plentifully interspersed.

Although alive, and considered as two of the finest of the more recent German romantic writers, we deem it necessary to mention here two female novelists, who have proved an honour to their sex, and to the class of writers of which they constitute worthy members. We allude to Ida Louisa Countess Hahn-Hahn, and to Fanny Tarnow. The former of these, independent of all the writers of the day, has struck out a path for herself which is entirely her own. In her 'Reisebilder,' 'Jenseit der Berge,' 'Cäcil,' 'Reiseversuch im Norden,' 'Ulrich,' 'Gräfin Faustina,' and others, though not unfrequently composed in a style of deep melancholy, and in a certain strain of inexpressible sadness, the countess never closes up her heart: she never denies what sex she belongs to; and in a language at once the purest and the most chaste, gives herself up wholly to her noble sentiments, and openly avows to the world her tender susceptibilities. As a German writer justly observes, far from dipping her feelings seven times in the waters of a stupid and offensive prudery, she permits them to range in all their glow and power.

Possessed in like manner of an affectionate heart, and writing what she feels, Fanny Tarnow has become one of the greatest favourites of the day, and is considered by the Germans as a first-rate novelist. Her best works are 'Natalie,' 'Kleopatra,' and 'Thekla,'—productions, the chief features and attractive points of which consist in natural feeling and feminine tenderness, void of every atom of sentimental prudery or masculine coarseness.

Kotzebue, though more celebrated as a dramatic than as a novel writer, produced two novels—'Leiden der ortenbergischen Familie,' and 'Die Geschichte meines Vaters, oder wie es zuging, dass ich geboren wurde.' But these, as well as his other novels, are so much inferior to his dramatic writings, that they may justly be considered as the mere offspring of a passing humour. Yet they are not without merit, betraying a fine imagination, and great powers of invention, besides a light, graceful flow of spirited language. By far better is Moritz's 'Anton Reiser,' a psychological novel, in which the author describes his own life, as also the lower life in towns as they existed at the time. The whole is a highly interesting production, embodying many noble feelings, and acute philosophical and psychological remarks. A counterpart to this novel is the famous Engel's admirable satirical characteristic painting, 'Lorenz Stark,' which is considered by many as the best description of the higher life in towns then prevailing.

Goëthe, as we have already seen, had produced a highly vigorous drama 'chevaleresque,' embodying the strongest sentiments of political freedom. This was the celebrated 'Götz von Berlichingen,' the sensation created by the appearance of which exceeds description. This work, the good folks of Germany immediately commenced imitating, falling thereby, however, from one extreme into another. If they had been dull sentimentalists and unexampled enthusiasts, they were now suddenly metamorphosed into knights and squires, giving themselves up *con amore e con piacere* to the rudeness and uncouthness of these worthies, and henceforth only dreamt of brimmers and castles, tournaments and combattings, freebootings, donjons, the 'Vehmgerichts,' and such like things. Among the first German writers, who imitated the 'Götz von Berlichingen,' were Babo, the author of the famous novel 'Otto von Wittelsbach,' and the Count Thüring-Seefeld, who wrote 'Agnes Bernauerin,' and 'Kaspar der Thüringer.' In these works, both authors showed how closely they imitated their model, and how strongly they could inveigh (notwithstanding their having written in a style and on a subject belonging to antiquity,) against existing tyrannical laws and institutions. But the work which created the greatest sensation was C. Vulpius's 'Rinaldo Rinaldini, the Captain of Robbers,' a production which may be justly considered as forming the transition from the old honest coarseness of chivalry and freebooting to frivolity. Never did a novel meet with greater success than this frivolous creation, the hero of which, had evidently been modelled after Schiller's celebrated chief of robbers, Carl Moor. It would lead us too far, were we minutely to examine the merits of this work, or consider the mischief it caused. Suffice it to say, that whatever its merits and demerits may be, one thing is certain, viz., that the idea, that one may be a virtuous man and a consummate voluptuous libertine, a man of mark as well as a vain fop, which was conceived by this author, and, if we mistake not, by Göethe himself, is an abstraction to which some Germans are still inclined, and which is perceptible even in some of our own novels of more recent date.

This mischief increased on the appearance of Schiller's masterly performance 'The Ghost-seer,' which henceforth became the model for imitation by numberless scribblers. The result may easily be conceived. Hence it was, that the clever novels of Veit Weber, or G. Wächter, proved refreshing to those who were oppressed by the miserable scribbling of the period. V. Weber's novels are: 'Sagen der Vorzeit' (Tales of Yore), 'Wilhelm Tell,' and 'The Vehmgerichte in Austria.' To these we must add his 'Briefe eines Frauenzimmers aus dem fünfzehnten Jarhundert.' These productions, composed in the spirit of the middle age, afforded relaxation and an agreeable change to those who were already tired of ghosts, chivalry, thieving, adventures, and such-like exhibitions.

Heinse, librarian and reader to the Elector of Mayence, a kind and good-humoured, but rather sensual-minded, man, a disciple of the Wieland school, produced at this time the novels 'Hildegard von Hohenthal,' 'Petronius,' 'Kunst Roman,' and 'Ardinghello.' The last, which much resembles Madame de Staël's 'Corinna,' but which in our opinion is superior to it, together with Tieck's and Wackenroder's 'Franz Sternbald's Wanderungen'—one of the finest novels German literature can boast of—and many other excellent productions, had, with few exceptions, a beneficial influence on the romantic literature of Germany.

Owing, no doubt, to the political storms of the times, and especially to the French Revolution, another change took place in the department of the German romance, which gave rise to the 'Familienstücke' and Familiengemälde,' or domestic novels. The chief authors of this class were La Fontaine, Langbein, Schilling, Friedrich Count von Soden, Anton Ball, &c. The first, who had been chaplain to a regiment, was apparently the head of this school, and was almost worshipped by the romantic world. His writings are divided into 'Unterhaltende' and 'Rührende Familiengemälde,'—entertaining and pathetic family pictures; yet, owing to the striking resemblance which they bear to one another, the difference between them is not very perceptible.

Of the immense number of tales and novels written by Schilling, 'Guido von Sohnsdom,' 'Der Roman im Roman,' 'Die Brautschau,' 'Röschens Geheimnisse,' and 'Das Weib wie es ist,' are in the highest repute. Possessed of great knowledge of the world, a good humoured wit, and a charming conversational mode of expression, he endowed all his writings with an interest, which makes them even at this day pleasant and amusing companions. Langbein, like most of his contemporaries, is somewhat too free; in part from the exactness with which he describes the scenes and characters of that period. In some of his writings, especially in his tales, he moves with much ease and elegance, and in his poetical productions, evinces great powers of invention, a rich flow of spirit, and a certain degree of cheerfulness, which place him by the side of his gifted countryman, Bürger. Dullness, and now and then a little frivolity, are among the distinguishing features of Laun's novels, the chef d'œuvre of which is the 'Citizen of Cöln.' His writings were at one time in great request.

One of the noblest, and in our opinion, finest novelists of that period, is the bookseller, and (Berlin) academician, Nicolai, the intimate friend of the great Lessing, and of Moses Mendelsohn, a man to whom German literature is deeply indebted for the services which he rendered to it. Nicolai incessantly laboured to unite the whole nation, ordinarily separated by political divisions, by means of intellectual and moral ties. This he attempted by the publication of many admirable works, among others by his 'Bibliothek der schönen Wissenschaften,' 'Allgemeine Deutsche Bibliothek,' of both which he had been the editor, and his 'Briefe die neueste Literatur betreffend.' He laboured in his capacity as bookseller and publisher, solely for science and the public good, and seldom from any mercenary motive. Neither the daily labours of his vocation, nor his innumerable other engagements, ever induced him to become faithless to his muse. He very frequently spent whole nights over his books, and regardless of the many attractions which Berlin offered to the man of the world, and of the temptations which surrounded him to spend his time in society, he laboured like the best of his compatriots for the welfare of his countrymen, and the advancement of their literature. The German public had almost become a prey to a haughty and intolerant priesthood, whose evil influences had spread like wildfire throughout the land. Add to this the Anglomania, the Gallo and Greco-mania, in fact 'manias' of all sorts and conditions, especially that of book-making by translation, and the reader will have some idea of the unhappy state into which the country was plunged. The necessity of doing something to counteract these evils, and of aiming a bold stroke at this many-headed hydra, was evident to all. It is beyond our province to say how far Lessing succeeded in freeing the country from these and other evils. A similar task was reserved for Nicolai, and to it he addressed himself right earnestly. Like another Goliath, he appeared with his novel 'Sebaldus Nothanker;' the effect of which was marvellous. His next, 'Der dicke Mann,' or the History of a stout Man, was intended to attack those vain scribblers, who gave themselves more credit for talent and learning, than they in reality possessed. He describes the evil consequences arising from such assumption, and levels many satirical strokes at Kantianism, which at that period was the fashion. But his witty sallies at this system of philosophy in his third novel, 'Sempronius Gundibert,' met with boundless applause. It was a production much needed; a word spoken at the right time, it afforded accordingly no slight degree of pleasure and gratification. Nicolai did full justice to the acuteness and wisdom of the great author of the 'Criticism of Pure Reason;' but what annoyed him was the jargon of the 'Pure Reason.' How could it be otherwise? Cultivating, as he did, the friendship of the greatest German writers of the day, in and out of the Prussian capital, the intimate companion of two such luminaries as Lessing and Mendelsohn, whose brilliant philosophy, good humour, and elegant wit, were truly electrifying, how, we

again ask, could it be otherwise? The Kantians, and among them the great Fichte, were driven to exasperation by the 'Sempronius Gundibert,' which contributed much to free the nation from the fetters in which it had been bound, slavelike, from time almost immemorial.

Nicolai's name will live, not, it is true, in his novels, for these, it is not unlikely, may lose in the course of time much of their interest and beauty, inasmuch as the faults and follies against which they were directed, have long since been blotted out, or laughed away,—but in his many other valuable and excellent works, such as his 'Topography of Berlin and Potsdam,' 'Anecdotes of Frederic the Great,' to collect and arrange which it would have been difficult to find a more suitable individual, since he was at the fountain-head from which only could be derived all the incidents and necessary materials. What an admirable production is his 'Tour through Germany!' The European Chinese, the Austrians, never forgave his boldness in telling them humiliating if not crushing truths. Nicolai, upon the whole, was certainly one of the greatest men Germany has produced, and decidedly one of her best novelists. Klinger, Musäus, and Schummel were very faithful followers of Nicolai. Klinger, the author whom we have already mentioned in conjunction with Goëthe, is a writer of high order. By one of his works, a drama, entitled 'Sturm und Drang,' he laid the foundation of a revolution in the province of the German belles-lettres, a period which Goëthe, in allusion to the drama, has styled 'Die Sturm und Drangperiode.'

The novels of this industrious author, written in a spirit of intense misanthropy, or dislike of the world, are replete with stirring thoughts and incidents, and were (particularly in his days) well suited to counteract the evils that arose from sentimentality, mock enthusiasm, and similar qualities. Klinger's best known novels are: Faust's Leben, Thaten und Höllenfahrt; Geschichte Raphaels de Aquillas (a companion to the former), and 'Der Weltmann und der Dichter.' Musäus, has already been mentioned. Among Schummel's favourite novels deserve to be mentioned his 'Sentimental Journey through Germany,' 'The Little Voltaire, and Spitzbart.' The latter is a masterly comic novel, in which the system of education of the last century, but especially that of the famous Basedow, is held up to derision.

Novels very much admired, and certainly of great merit, are those written by Müller von Itzehoe, of which the following are the most finished, and maintain the highest rank. 'The Ring,' 'The Papers of the Brown Man,' 'Frederick Brack,' 'Selim the Fortunate,' and 'Siegfried von Lindenberg.' The last novel in some degree outweighs the rest. In it, Müller, with much skill and great adroitness, pourtrays a Pomeranian gentleman, whose simple customs but powerful mind come into contact with the so-called modern education, and enlightment. Müller was one of the happiest imitators of some of the English humorous writers, especially of Smollet. A highly polished language, great powers of invention and observation, as also a rather large portion of good humour, though now and then deficient in masculine strength, constitute the chief features of Müller's novels.

Wetzel, whom some consider the German Marivaux, is distinguished more for verbosity and a pompous style than anything else; all his productions are marked by an evident straining after something unusual, which renders them extremely tedious.

One of the most polished German novelists, is Von Knigge, a nobleman by birth, and a man of great learning, of knowledge of the world, and of superior talents. He wrote a great many very interesting novels; among others, 'Leben des armen Herrn von Miltenberg,' 'Reise nach Braunschweig und Fritzlar,' and 'Reise auf die Universität,' almost each of which contains attacks upon the enthusiast Lavater's journeys to Copenhagen. Furthermore, 'Roman meines Lebens,' a work replete with truths and facts taken from the author's biography, 'Peter Claus,' probably Knigge's most perfect novel, and one which has been translated into most living languages, particularly into the French, under the title of 'Gil Blas allemand;' but he is likewise the author of many satires, almost all of a political tendency.

Knigge's writings are chiefly remarkable for acuteness of mind, a thorough knowledge of the subject he deals with, a graceful expression, and a refined wit. It is to be lamented that this author is not more known in our mirth-loving country.

A very prolific novelist of the last century was K. G. Cramer, who wrote between ninety and a hundred volumes of rather smart tales, the most remarkable of which are—'Thirty Acres,' 'Karl Saalfeld,' and 'Erasmus Schleicher.' These, notwithstanding their want of polish and refined tone, are distinguished for depth of thought, a high degree of originality, and a powerful style.

We have dwelt so long on the earlier German novelists (and that, too, we fear, without having done them full justice), that we are unable at present to prosecute our original design, of bringing the more recent writers of fiction before our readers. We must defer this to a future occasion, and in the meantime will simply remark, that the prolific character of the German mind is strikingly shown in the review we have instituted.

It would have afforded us unfeigned pleasure to note a distinctively religious tone in the works we have specified. Even fiction admits of this, and borrows from it a grace and purity which marvellously augment its power. But intellect has too frequently been dissociated from revelation, and the class of publications now reviewed, contributes little to remove the unhappy dissociation.

ART. XXII.—1. *William Tell : from the German of Schiller.*

2. *The Maid of Orleans : from the German of Schiller.*

3. *The Magic Ring, a Knightly Romance. From the German of La Motte Fouquet.*

4. *Marco Visconti: from the Italian of Tomaso Grossi.*

WE have repeatedly spoken of the juvenile publications of Mr. Burns. The series before us, comprising the early numbers of the " Fireside Library," is of rather more elevated mark. The two favourite plays of Schiller with some persons, the " Maid of Orleans " and the " William Tell," are well known. The knightly romance of the " Magic Ring " by the chivalrous La Motte Fouqué, though not equal to his " Undine," is to us as charming as of old, and we hope will never find us more chilled in sentiment to the beautiful visions of sweet and bright romance. In it La Motte Fouqué has embodied the allegory of chivalry, though most persons read it, and we confess we think with quite as much pleasure as ourselves, simply as a romance. We do not know whether the reading of Spenser is much improved in interest by following out his lengthy allegory. " Marco Visconti," the fourth work before us, is by Grossi. Though the powers of Grossi are not great, he has maintained the interest of his story. The death of his sweet heroine, Bice, is, however, unnecessary to the *dénouement*, which is sufficiently tragic in the death of the great leader himself, Marco Visconti. This novel gives us a great insight into this period of Italian history.

THE LYRIC POETRY OF GERMANY.*

THE form of government of the French people, in the days of the great Louis, was said by some shrewd observer to be a monarchy limited by *chansons;* a most just observation : and in the same spirit we may truly say of our Teutonic brethren beyond the Rhine, that, though Europe has yet to learn by what influence their civil government is limited, the character of their intellectual empire may most aptly be defined, LEARNING limited by LYRIC POETRY. A fearful thing indeed it is to unlearned eyes that academic erudition of which Berlin and Bonn, Göttingen and Munich, are the giant manufactories, and Leipsic the loaded emporium ; fearfully heavy in more senses than one, many persons complain. But the evil may practically be reduced to a very small matter ; for, in the first place, no man is forced to read more folios than he pleases ; and in the second place, the biggest books in Germany (which is not always the case in England) have always the best indices ; and in the third place, the learning, as we have just stated, is always tempered by the lyre. These, indeed, are the two great excellencies of Deutschland, which, like charity, may well be allowed to cover a multitude of sins ; erudition unrivalled, even among the Scaligers and Casaubons of a past age, for profundity and variety ; and a spirit of emotional outpouring in the shape of song, issuing equally free and triumphant from wood and glen, and festal board, and from the land of exile in the west, where it is the pleasure of the royal pedant now on the throne of Prussia, that lungs too lusty for his cracked ear-drum should sing to Europe and to the world rather than to Berlin. We may, indeed, assert most characteristically, that the good German Michel loves a song as naturally as honest John Bull loves a joke. 'Tis part of his nationality ; and that is a thing which God causes to grow on every German acre so bountifully that not even the jealous police-monster on the banks of the Spree, with his hundred arms, can root it up.

We propose on the present occasion to give a short sketch of the more prominent points in the rise and progress of Lyric Poetry in Germany, from the middle of the last century to the present time ; and in doing so, by way of illustration we shall throw in a few translations, partly from our own portfolio, and partly from that rich collection which Mangan and others have recently been spreading before us. We begin most properly with Klopstock, (born in 1724.) This is the much-echoed name that first taught Europe to suspect that such a thing as a German literature existed at all, or at least was attempting to exist. Klopstock is unquestionably a famous name in German literature ; he at one time enjoyed a reputation as wide as Goethe's, a popularity almost as extensive as Schiller's : What is his true value? One thing we hold to be certain : "The Messiah"

* I. Anthologia Germanica, by J. E. Mangan, in two vols. Dublin : Curry, 1845.
II. German Ballads and Songs. London : J. Burns.

was a failure, a decided failure. Klopstock has no claim to rank with Virgil and Milton ; his character as a poet must stand on his lyric pieces : "The Messiah," when it is read—which is seldom now—is read only because it is Klopstock's, and for a few isolated lyrical beauties. Neither can we say, much as we should wish to say it, that Klopstock's lyrics are of the highest order. They are not, indeed, without the essential element of all true lyric poetry, strong feeling : they are in no sense lukewarm, much less cold ; nay, they are glowing hot, most outrageously hot, spitting out lightnings and rolling thunders on all occasions, and creating much smoke : there is no measure, no moderation, in their excitement ; therein precisely lies their fault. To be enjoyed, in fact, perfectly, they must be read, as the host of them were written, by a young man ; one in whose brain the evolution of purely internal impulses is yet so eager and so imperious, so overpowering and so monopolizing, that the external world possesses neither clearness nor interest. There is also, as must ever be in this sort of juvenile poetry, an utter want of concentration ; that quality which, when combined with good sense and a happy tone, (as in the case of Horace,) compensates so often for the lack of what is magnificently called genius. But Klopstock is not merely an unripe and an unchastened lyrist. Our own Shelley also wrote poetry, which, in respect of what in more mature years he might have written, may well be called juvenile and unripe ; but the calm blue expanse of his heaven is spangled with a thousand purest lights, altogether of a different temper from those feverish sparks that shoot forth from the rolling pomp of rhetorical vapour in Klopstock. In the "very German Milton" of "The Messiah," the sublime is vast even to inanity, and its terror has a constant tendency to become insane. Shelley wants substance ; so also does Klopstock : but the flimsiness of the one is never without a certain fairy delicacy which delights, while that of the other is ever apt to degenerate into a gigantic confusion which repels. But Klopstock is not merely unsubstantial and vapoury in his matter ; he is harsh and stiff, stilted and affected in his manner. He fell, indeed, at an early age, into the very obvious and shallow mistake, that, to contend successfully with the great ancients, it was necessary for a modern poet to adopt the identical outward form and vesture in which it had pleased them to embody their noble and manly thoughts. He must needs imitate the Romans, as the Romans imitated the Greeks, to the exclusion of those forms of poetic embodiment which were traditionary in his own country. He nourished a pedantic pride in the rejection of rhyme from his lyric measures, as a barbarous modern innovation ; whereas it is merely a pretty ornament, and perfectly inoffensive, except for a few special purposes ; and in the attempt to re-create, for the edification of the modern ear, the lost rhythm of Pindaric strophes and Hora-

tian stanzas, he twisted, and wrenched, and dislocated his good mother Deutsch in such an ungracious fashion, that, in reading some of his sublime strivings, we feel for all the world (as Professor Zelter very happily expressed it) as if we were "eating stones." In no respect, therefore, neither in respect of shape nor of substance, is Klopstock to be accounted a great lyric poet ; not the true German oak certainly, but a gigantic mushroom of tropical breadth and magnificence, and, in a land where there were as yet no green trees, worthy to be looked on not without veneration.

The judgment we have thus attempted to pass on the celebrated author of "The Messiah," may appear harsh to some ardent German student, or to some zealous devotee of what is called "Sunday reading ;" but it is a judgment not a whit harsher than the most grateful of his own countrymen have already more than once passed. There is a well-known epigram of Lessing, the point of which is, that he did not wish his works to be so much admired as Klopstock's, but to be more read ; and Menzel, after a page or two of very generous eulogy, confesses, that Klopstock's grandeur, to be appreciated, must always be kept at a certain distance, for when we attempt to handle it, like one of Ossian's mountain giants, it vanishes into mist. The fact of the matter is, that the bard of "The Messiah" owes his great reputation to three circumstances, none of which have any thing essential to do with first rate poetic excellence. *First,* He was a religious poet ; *Second,* He was a patriotic poet ; and, *Thirdly,* He appeared in an age when there were no great German poets from whom to take his measure. There was no strong pressure from without to keep him in his proper place ; and thus, as, in a pretty experiment of the mechanical philosophers, we see a flaccid bladder in the receiver of an air-pump, on the removal of the circumambient aerial pressure, suddenly swell up into a full distended globe ; so Klopstock, before Goethe and Schiller had created a healthy literary atmosphere in Germany, with his windy inanity occupied a great space. Besides, he walked upon stilts and blew a trumpet : and such men, unless the world is particularly sensible or particularly busy, are sure to be overrated for a season. But Germany, as we all know, among its many excellencies, has never been remarkable for sense : in the middle of the last century also (like the rest of Europe) it lay lolling on an easy chair, with dressing-gown and skull-cap, in a very comfortable state of repose ; it was impossible therefore that the loud trump of the bard of Quedlinburg, swelling portentously with its double blast of piety and patriotism, should not have pricked up the ears of the seven sleepers of honest Deutschland to a very observable height, and that a Klopstock should not have bestrodden the pigmy necks of a GLEIM, a RAMLER, and a John Peter Uz, like a colossus. We have not read the *opera omnia* of John William Ludwig GLEIM ; this we confess honestly : but we have not done so for the reason that we have not traversed Pomerania from east to west, and the Mark of Brandenburg, in search of a hill : common fame and the Gazetteer say that the land is flat ; what we have seen of it agrees with fame and the Gazetteer; and on this agreement we are content to form our opinion. If the Anthologies put their best foot foremost, as it is to be presumed they do, Gleim was a very fair "German Anacreon," a very patriotic Prussian grenadier, a very kind-hearted man, and a very devoted servant of the Muses,—a person of whom, in every view, the good city of Halberstadt, and the old cathedral, had reason to be proud; but a man of that calibre who could not but feel himself called upon to take off his hat in all humility to such a fulminant apparition as the bard of "The Messiah," and who did so in fact most reverentially. Gleim was one of the most ardent Klopstock-worshippers of a time and place in which literary hero worship was habitually pushed to a point that plunged headlong into the ridiculous and the contemptible. But Gleim, in his own region of humble, and healthy. and cheerful mediocrity, is perhaps, after all, a better poet than the mighty Apollo to whom he paid homage; and will be more durable, inasmuch as a tolerable Anacreon (even a German one) is always better than an intolerable Pindar. Gleim, indeed, has written some very pretty little poems, which we cannot but *like*, while the man himself we must *love*; witness the following. We have adopted Mr. Mangan's translation, with some alterations, of which he will easily see the reason.

THE COTTAGE.

A cottage and a green grass plot
Is all my wealth, a happy spot;
A brooklet clear with bickering glee
Comes tripping by; come, see!

In front a fatherly old tree
O'ershades this little cot for me,
And shelters it from rain and storm,
And summer suns so warm.

And from the tree a nightingale
Pours forth so soft and sweet a wail,
That all who pass must linger by,
And love, they know not why.

Dear lassie with the flaxen hair,
Thou know'st me fond as thou art fair;
I go; the rude wind shakes the tree,
Wilt share my hut with me!

Add to this little idyllic picture another picture or two of a different cast, and you have a perfect idea of old Father Gleim himself; who, like a healthy man and a happy poet, died on the 18th February, 1803, at the respectable age of eighty. Fancy him, in the first place, in the month of May 1757, with a pile of letters before him, fresh from the Halberstadt mail-bag, with the news of the battle of Prague, gained by Frederick the Great over the clumsy Austrians; instantly his Prussian blood is up; his keen little eye twinkles ecstatically; his bushy eyebrows perk up as elastic as a squirrel's tail; there is a witching smile about his mouth, (for even when about to indite a warlike dithyramb he cannot be fierce,) the morning pipe is thrown aside; up he starts, and, with the last lingering blast of the German weed, out he puffs the first verse of the lusty German song,—

Victory! victory! in the dust
The haughty foeman lies!
Victory, victory,—God is just,
The insolent Austrian dies.

And though we've lost our brave Schwerin,
He died as a hero dies;
And now he looks on the conquering scene
From his tent in the starry skies!

This is Gleim the Prussian patriot. Then you may see him in his study, or perhaps coming out of it, with a shoe on one foot and a slipper on the other, with a silk stocking on the right leg and a worsted one on the left; going out to meet the sun with a rush-light in his hand; nothing studious of the outward man; a poet plainly, if not a philosopher—perhaps a bit of both; who reads and writes by candle-light when decent people are asleep. Such a man is Gleim, the reader and the maker of books; a genuine specimen of the literary man; one that, besides his pipe and his cup of coffee, and his packet of gossiping letters from half a dozen good friends every morning, requires nothing to make him happy but a book and a pen,—a perfect incarnation of Content, singing his own song visibly, like a living epistle to all men,—

A rich man am I, and I have a good cook,
And Hunger's his classical name;
I honour no man with an envious look,
And find nothing on earth to blame.

Heyne's Virgil, Wolf's Homer, and Elzivir Horace,—
A very correct edition,—
And the Bible by Hans Luft, my bountiful store is,
And the sum of my whole petition.

And finally, to complete the portrait, you have only to see him in his full Bacchantic glory, when he entertains the godlike Klopstock, or, it may be, even the veritable god, Jean Paul Richter. Then it is his glory, in a more vehement style than usual, to trample upon the narrow-minded "Philistines," and to toss up his sunny soul in billows of free sociality; and to cry aloud, with his own Anacreon whom he loves, Θἐλω θἐλω μανηναι—I *will*, I WILL be mad. Then he crowns himself with roses, and calls for the Rhine-wine, and, to the astonishment of the sober host, breaks out into dithyrambic denunciations of water and water drinkers before the cork is drawn.

DRINK STRONG WINE!

Drink! thou lean, thou lemon-colour'd
Sapless water-drinking dullard!
Drink strong wine!
Fill thy veins with lusty vigour—
Both in brain and brawn be bigger
By strong wine.

Gods! we bless you, bounteous ever;
From Elysium rolls a river
Of strong wine.
With what fragrant power it steameth—
With what friendly light it gleameth—
This strong wine!

When a carking care doth teaze you—
When a painful pride doth freeze you—
Drink strong wine!
It will mellow all thy juices—
Ope thy heart in all its sluices—
Wine, strong wine!

Solomon and learned Luther
Spoke thy praise, great sorrow soother —
Wine, strong wine!
Famous heroes, kings and kaisers,
Purple Pantagruelizers,
Drink strong wine!

So much for Father Gleim. A similar influence was exercised by Klopstock on a knot of hopeful young poets at Göttingen, associated under the title of the *Göttingen Bund*, and of whom JOHN HENRY VOSS, the translator of Homer, has had the good fortune to achieve a sort of European reputation. Translators, indeed,—otherwise a no less inglorious than laborious race,—have this privilege, that when they are first rate, they attach themselves permanently to the reputation of their original, and walk through long centuries, sometimes with the larger share of his popularity. So it seems to have fared with Voss, who also has written some songs and hymns that still keep their place in German Anthologies. But our favourite among the many young rhymers of the Göttingen Bund has always been Hölty. This lyrist died young; but there is a delicacy of sentiment in many of his pieces—a sportive play of humour, combined with a fine perception of the peculiar beauties of the ballad style—that will ensure him a permanent niche in the German Parnassus, furnished as it now is so richly with many nobler and more manly names. It is interesting, also, to observe, that while Voss, in his famous epos of a parsonage and a pic-nic, (the "Louise,") applied the sounding pomp of the Klopstockian hexameter to the familiar poetry of strawberries and cream, butter toast, and coffee-cups, Hölty, with instinctive good taste, was content to admire the bard of "The Messiah" without imitating him, and to clothe popular subjects as much as possible in a popular garb. The following piece, from Mr. Mangan's collection, is a good specimen of the tone of Hölty's poetry:—

THE AGED LANDMAN'S ADVICE TO HIS SON.

Oh, cherish faith and truth till death
Shall claim thy forfeit clay,
And wander not one finger's-breadth
From God's appointed way;
So shall thy pilgrim pathway be
O'er flowers that brightly bloom;
So shalt thou, rich in hope, and free
From terror, face the tomb.
Then wilt thou handle spade and scythe
With joyous heart and soul;
Thy water-jug shall make thee blithe
As brimming purple bowl.

All things but work the sinner wo;
For, do his worst or best,
The devil drives him to and fro,
And never leaves him rest.
Him glads no spring, no sky outroll'd,
No mellow yellow field;
His one sole good and god is gold —
His heart is warp'd and steel'd.
The winds that blow, the streams that flow,
Affright the craven slave;
Peace flies him, and he does not know
Rest even in his grave:

For he, when spectral midnight reign
Must burst his coffin-band,
And, as a pitch-black dog, in chains
Before his house-door stand.

The spinners who, with wheel on arm,
Belated, home repair,
Will quake, and cross themselves from harm,
To see the monster there;
And every spinning crone of this
Terrific sight will tell,
And wish the villain in the abyss
And fire of hottest hell.

Old Grimes was all his life a hound, —
A genuine devil's brand, —
He counter-plough'd his neighbours' ground,
And robb'd them of their land.
Now, fire-clad, see him plough with toil
The same land, every where
Upturning all night long the soil
With white-hot burning share.
Himself like blazing straw-sheaf burns
Behind the glowing plough;
And so he burns, and so upturns,
Till morning bares her brow.

The bailie who, without remorse,
Shot stags, and fleeced the poor,
With one grim dog, on fiery horse,
Hunts nightly o'er the moor.
Oft, as a rugged-coated bear,
He climbs a gnarled pole;
Oft, as a goat, must leave his lair,
And through the hamlet stroll.

The riot-loving priest who cramm'd
His chests with ill-got gold,
Still haunts the chancel, black and damn'd,
Each night when twelve has toll'd.
He howls aloud, with dismal yells
That startle aisle and fanes,
Or, in the vestry, darkly tells
His church-accursed gains.

The squire who drank and gamed, pell-mell,
The helpless widow's all,
Now driven along by blasts from hell,
Goes coach'd to Satan's ball:
His blue frock, dipp'd in hell's foul font,
With sulphur-flame is lined;
One devil holds the reins in front —
Two devils ride behind.

Then, son, be just and true, till death
Shall claim thy forfeit clay,
And wander not one finger's-breadth
From God's revealed way;
So shall warm tears bedew in showers
The grass above thy head,
And lilies and all odorous flowers
O'erarch thy last low bed.

For the sake of completeness, we must mention here the name of BÜRGER, one of the most perfect masters of the vivid ballad style that any language possesses; but his merits are too well known in England to require any criticism. Besides, in German literature, his position is too isolated for our present general survey of prominent and characteristic genera. We may refer, however, generally to our own pages, (1835, pp. 328, 378,) and pass on from these introductory preludes, and faint prophesyings, to the full maturity and strong manhood of the German lyre. Goethe was twenty-five, and Schiller was thirty-five years younger than Klopstock. We shall now attempt to state shortly the characteristic merits of these two great Coryphæi of modern Teutonic song.

Nothing, in our opinion, has hurt the reputation of Goethe more in this country, than his having been brought forward principally in two characters, where, whatever be his merits, he is certainly far from first-rate. Goethe is neither a first-rate dramatist, nor a first-rate novelist; and yet any unstudied John Bull, who knows the great Olympian of the German Parnassus by name, knows also that he is the author of "Faust," and of "Werther," and of "Wilhelm Meister;" and knows, perhaps, nothing more. But "Faust," with all its high poetic excellencies, is, as a drama, only a second-rate production. It is pieced together with too obvious coolness in some places, and wants a perpetual current of action, and a continuity of interest. "Wilhelm Meister" the British reader thinks,—and he is no bad judge in such matters,—is flimsy and trifling, and wants a glowing and vigorous reality. So far, therefore, as his current translated works go, Goethe cannot be highly estimated by the general English reader; and the fact of the matter really is, that, like Ovid, Horace, Robert Burns, Beranger, and all great lyrists, Goethe (for he is a truly great lyrist) can be read and relished perfectly only in his own admirable tongue. That *curiosa felicitas* of diction which distinguishes the great and original lyrist from the common congregation of singing birds—that happy combination of suggestive simplicity with the most polished elegance of expression, that marks the practised master of the lyre—is an element too subtle to be transfused out of one material skin into another without injury; and it is precisely in this element that Goethe sways about with the most inimitable ease and grace. That Goethe is great, and very great, as a lyric poet, must now, we think, after the admirable translations which lately appeared in *Blackwood's Magazine*, be evident even to the most un-Germanized Englishman; but the German scholar will, we hope, have no difficulty in agreeing with us, that it is in the capacity of a luxuriant lyrist, and in this capacity only, that Goethe is entitled to take his stand among the great poets of all ages and nations. A first-rate dramatist Goethe was not, and never could be; for he was deficient in one great element of the true dramatist's character, intense moral earnestness, and energetic propulsiveness (if we may so speak) of emotion. He was disposed to paint playfully, and to hint gracefully, rather than to feel strongly and to act decidedly. He feared nothing so much as a strong and billowy current of emotion—shrank from nothing more sensitively than from such characters (to use his own well-known words) as Martin Luther and—Coriolanus! It is plain, therefore, he was not made for a reformer; it is certain, also, he did not possess those stern and stirring elements of character, that would have enabled him to represent vividly any stern and stirring action upon the stage. This acknowledged deficiency in the moral energies interfered, however, less in preventing his achieving the highest eminence in the more playful region of song; here earnestness is justly voted pedantry, tragic passion a hurricane which incommodes us, and morality, if she will not be deemed impertinent, must often be content to be dumb. Goethe, accordingly, stands forward prominently, not only as one of the most varied of graceful lyrists, but also as one of the most profound; for herein, precisely, lies his great virtue, that while he presents the outward aspect of mere oriental ease and epicurean voluptuousness, he is in secret a deep thinker, and a hard worker. He writes a good drinking song, a little more delicate in the handling, and more pregnant in the idea, than good Father Gleim; but if, because you find wares of this kind in his basket, you hastily conclude that he is altogether a mere Anacreon, who pays worship only to smiling Venus, and rubicund Bacchus, you are vastly mistaken. Unquestionably he was a heathen; "a heathen of the heathens," as Rahel says, who knew him well, and admired him much; but he was a polytheist of the most comprehensive kind, and paid worship to all the gods, though to Venus, and the Graces, perhaps with a special preference. But he by no means neglected Minerva; he knew how to combine, as no man did, wise thoughts, and even scientific truths, with the most playful and wanton sports of fancy; and he paid worship also in hard labour and sweat, to the sooty god of smiths, whose subterranean toil burnished the mail and tempered the steel of the celestials. Goethe's lyric poems were in fact the delicate and light blossoms which are evolved as the crowning glory of an ancient tree, only after long years of patient growth, and wide outspreading of healthy branches; whereas the songs and odes of many, are mere fire-wheels, with which idle boys play, or, (what is worse,) blue lights, which, when there is no better ray visible, flicker out their freakish breath from the scum of a putrid pool. To sum up his character in one sentence; Goethe was as great a lyric poet, as pure polytheism, and the philosophy of Epicurus, would allow a naturally great mind to be; what he wanted to make him perfect was, a few chapters of Seneca, and a slight tincture of Christianity.

A very different man was Frederick Schiller, a poet of deep moral feelings, and with Christian and evangelic sympathies decidedly strong; a student of Immanuel Kant, and paying willing homage to the self-dictated law of a despotic ought in the inner man; a mounted equestrian spirit, all eager for the strife of noble, with base emotion, and the triumph which is purchased by the martyr's blood; a warlike angel, as Menzel well says, with a flaming sword in his hand, and an atmosphere of glory for his mantle. Of him we need say nothing; for he is known in this country, and understood now, almost as much as in his own Germany; only this we may remark, that, as in the case of Goethe, so, here, the character by which the poet is most generally known in this country, is not that in which he has achieved the highest and most unquestioned excellence. Schiller's Wallenstein is piled up with too much architectural weight in many places, to be a good specimen of the drama; many of its most attractive beauties, are more lyrical and oratorical, than dramatic; and, generally speaking, we are inclined to suspect that Schiller was both too much of a systematic deliberate German, and too much the victim of exclusive inward intense emotion, to be capable of reaching the highest point of dramatic excellence. As a lyrist, however, after the impetuosity of his first apparition becomes a little more subject to control, we have no fault to find with him; and most justly does he merit that extensive popularity which he has achieved in competition with the master genius of Goethe, by how much the earnestness of moral emotion is a more noble possession, and a more characteristic attribute of man, than that pictorial luxuriousness, and sensuous voluptuousness, of which his great rival was at once the most cunning, and the most graceful of exhibitors.

We subjoin three specimens of attempted translation, from Goethe's various garden; each characteristic of a different phasis of that remarkable man. Schiller's genius is too well-known to require any illustration of the kind; but we happen to have an old version of that unique little gem, the "*Punch Song*," (not at all in the poet's usual style,) which we should like to see in print.

GENERAL CONFESSION.
A CONVIVIAL SONG.

Listen to a good advice,
When 'tis not denied you;
Boldly, ere it be too late,
For the night decide you.
For your faults yet to be mended,
Much begun and little ended,
Soundly must I chide you.

Penance must we do at least,
Once before we die all;
Let us, then, confess our sins,
With an honest sigh all;
To forsake what most besets us,
Care that vexes, freak that frets us,
Let us nobly vie all.

Yes, we have, confess we must,
Waking oft been dreaming,
Emptied not the friendly cup,
When the wine was gleaming;
Many a roving hour have watch'd not,
Many a waiting kiss have snatch'd not,
As was well beseeming.

Often have we sat and gaped,
Silent when we should not;
Pratings of the pedant crew,
When we could, eschewed not;
Listened to their prosy comments
On a poet's happy moments,
That they understood not.

Wilt thou absolution give,
Of all good things giver,
From thy faithful precepts swerve,
Will thy servants never;
And each sorry half-work leaving,
To the good, the lovely, cleaving,
Resolute live ever.

Pedants, while we sit at ease,
To a smile may move us;
Bumpers waiting to be quaff'd,
Shall no more reprove us;
Not with empty phrase harangue we,
But with faithful passion hang we,
On the lips that love us.

PROMETHEUS.

Thy tented welkin, Jove, enshroud
With vapoury cloud,
And, like a boy, with lusty strokes,
Who crops the thistle's crown,
O'er mountain-peaks and aged oaks,
Come blustering down;

Yet must thou yield
To me my earth,
My hut which mine own hands did build,
And mine own hearth,
Whose blazing glee
Thou enviest me.

Nothing more vile the sun below,
Than your host of gods I know!
Ye nourish in most sorry guise,
With tribute base of sacrifice,
And breath of prayer,
Your majesty;
And would starve sheer,
Were there not here,
Children and beggars, a servile crew,
Hopeful fools to flatter you.

When I was a little boy,
And laugh'd and wept, I knew not why,
Up to the sun and to the sky,
Wistful I cast my wandering eye,
As if above there were an ear,
My plaint to hear;
A heart like mine in yonder pole,
To bind the wounds o' the anguish'd soul.

Received I then aught aid from you,
Against the haughty Titan crew?
Who then from death did set me free,
And slavery?
Thyself achieved it with thy inborn art,
Thou holy, glowing heart!
But, young and artless, thou didst pour
Thy gushing thanks (fond fool!) before
The sleeper there above.

I reverence thee! for what?
Hast thou ever in mercy known
To soothe the laden spirit's groan?
Thou ever still'd the tears that start,
When doubts perplex the heart?
Hath not, to the full-grown man,
Forged me Time's all-mighty plan,
And eternal destiny,
Lord both of thee and me.

Deem'dst thou, belike, that I should hate my life,
And into deserts flee,
Because I could not see,
All blossoms of my dreamings rife?
Here sit I, and with life inspire
A race that shall be like their sire;
Who shall know beneath the skies,
To suffer, and to weep,
To enjoy, and to rejoice,
And thee and thine even so despise
As I do!

THE MAGICIAN'S APPRENTICE.

Well! for once he's gone, the sour
Old master of the midnight witches,
And to try his magic power
My adventurous fancy itches.
I have marked them duly,
His charms both great and small,
And the spirits unruly,
Shall obey my call.
Wander, wander
Many a rood!
In full meander
Swell the flood!
In the bath, at my command,
Countless flagons be at hand!

Come, thou ancient besom, thou,
Take this fusty coat and collar;
As thou didst the master, now
Trim thee to obey the scholar.
Take two legs, and stand there,—
Take both head and tail,—
Go, at my command, there,
And bring the water-pail.

Wander, wander
Many a rood!
In full meander
Swell the flood!
In the bath, at my command,
Countless flagons be at hand!

Swift as lightning, lo! it flies!
Now it stands beside the river!
In a twinkling, back it flies,
Like an arrow from the quiver.
Back again (how clever!)
Comes the busy gnome,
Swelling, like a river,
High the waters foam!
Stay thee, stay thee,
Goblin slave!
Lay thee, lay thee,
Surging wave!
Good Heaven! the word! and can I not!
The word!—the word I've clean forgot!

The word, at which its proper form
Must the wicked gnome resume quick;—
Warm it works, and yet more warm—
Would thou wert again the broomstick!
Quicker still, and quicker,
Floods upon me gush;
Thicker still, and thicker,
Rivers on me rush!
No, no longer
Can I allow it!
I am stronger,
Thou shalt know it.
Alack! his wild look makes me quake;
Its fist at me the thing doth shake.

Yield thee, yield thee, imp of hell,
Cease thy labour, cease thy running!
Shall my master's threshold swell
Like the Baltic, for thy funning?
Pert and saucy stick,
Shall I roar in vain quite?
Change thee, change thee quick!
Be a log again quite!
Wilt not fear thee?
Not refrain thee?
Shall I tear thee?
Shall I chain thee?
Shall I take my axe and split
Thy stubborn timber skull with it?

Lo! where limps the thing again!
Imp of hell, wilt thou not hear me?
When thy skull is split in twain,
Gnome, thou shalt have cause to fear me.
Bravo, there I have thee!
Cleft it goes in twain;
My ugly fancies leave me,
And I breathe again.
Wo and wonder!
Toil and trouble!
Into life
It rises double!
Like the fabled Hydra's head!—
Mary mother! send me aid!

And they run! Like ocean's brine
Swells the foaming tide around me!
Help me, help me, master mine!
Help, or I shall surely drown'd be!
There he comes — the devils
Could the learner raise;
But to still their revels,
Is the master's praise.
Get thee hence,
Imp unruly,
Without sense,—
A broomstick truly!
None but the old master merits
The prompt obedience of the spirits.

PUNCH SONG.

Mingle them kindly,
  Th' elements four,—
Mystical Nature
  Works by the four.

Press ye the citron
  Juicy and tart :
Life's inner kernel
  Harbours a smart.

Now with the sugar's
  Mild mellow power
Tame ye and temper
  Wisely the sour.

Pour then the water
  Flowing and clear,—
Water embraceth
  Calmly the sphere,

Now with the spirit
  Charm ye the bowl,—
Life of the living,
  Soul of the soul,

Ere it enhaleth,
  Swift be it quaff'd :
Only when glowing
  Strengthens the draught.

Hitherto we have encountered nothing of political movements, and great social currents, in our tracing of the main stream of German song ; the peculiarities which we have noted, are altogether peculiarities of the individual. Now, however, the times become more troubled ; great movements stir the earth ; and the lyric poet becomes as much the sign of the political, as the cause of the literary movements of his time. Let us state shortly how this great change in the character of German lyric poetry came about. It is a change that is even now working in Berlin and Königsberg, and may soon be productive of the most momentous consequences.

The lamentable peace of Westphalia, in 1648, and the victories of Louis XIV. forty years afterwards, left the German empire so feeble, and so divided, that, when Klopstock mounted his patriotic Pegasus, in the middle of the last century, it is nothing strange if his Germanizing and fatherlandizing enthusiasm proved a sublime inanity ; for there was neither a Germany nor a fatherland then existing to any person who spoke the Teutonic tongue, between the Niemen and the Rhine. Hermann, and Thusnelda, were great names in the Burschen beer-songs ; but in the German public and social life, they had no existence. Goethe, accordingly, with his strong healthy instinct of reality and truth as the living root of all substantial poetry, avoided the patriotic altogether in his lyrics. He saw no German fatherland to sing about, and therefore, on that head was dumb. He could be a minute observer, a delicate anatomizer, and a clear mirror of many-sided nature : but he could not be a German patriot. He knew no German people, no German freedom ; he only knew Weimar and the Grand Duke, In so far as he was not a vague cosmopolite, the author of "Faust" was a satellite of petty princedom, and the humble devotee of frail aristocracy in Germany : nothing more. In this respect, old Father Gleim, in Halberstadt, was infinitely his supe-

rior ; for Gleim was a Prussian. And though there was, and could be no Germany to extol in those days, there certainly was a Prussia ; and if Hermann was an unsubstantial sound, Frederick was a living man, who could both strike and make himself be felt. Gleim, accordingly, as we have seen, with the true heart of a popular poet, seized on the grand popular theme of his age,—the famous seven years' war : but his voice was feeble ; his hero, with all his brilliancy, any thing but a good subject for patriotic poetry ; and the echo of Frederick's astonishing deeds had already become faint, when Goethe, about the year 1770, and Schiller, ten years later, first came forward to stir, with a stronger sweep, the strings of the Teutonic lyre. Schiller, as his "Robbers" sufficiently indicated, was, from his earliest years, a spirit all a-blaze with the glowing emotions that make the patriot and the liberal ; and his latest and most perfect works, "Wallenstein" and "William Tell," plainly testify how great a prophet honest Deutschland would have had in him, had honest Deutschland, in its then state of momently expected dissolution, been a theme worthy to become a great prophet's burden. As things were, however, Schiller also wanted a fatherland ; and the spirit of patriotic song in him, for want of convenient fuel to feed on, burnt like a pent volcano within, and consumed the frail tenement prematurely. Matters were, indeed, after the peace of Basle, in 1795, in Germany so bad, that, to use a common saying, they required to be worse before they could be better. The tremendous blow of Jena, in 1806 ; the public pillory of aristocracy in Prussia ; and the cruel spurs of the "Equestrian Robespierre" for a term of years, were necessary to convince Prussians, and Saxons, and Bavarians, that there was, or ought to be, such a thing as Germany, and that a patriot is a nobler character than a painter. This conviction, however, once gained, out broke the stream of national song, like a 'prisoned ocean ; and Germany, which, to the victories of Moreau and Bonaparte, a few years before, could oppose only a Propertius in Goethe, and a Jeremiah in Herder, now pointed with no vain confidence to her Achilles in Blucher, her Nestor in Scharnhorst, and her Tyrtaeus in Theodore Körner. From the month of March, 1813, when Prussia formally, but substantially the whole of Germany, declared war against Napoleon, a new spirit rushed into the heart of Teutonic poetry. From that day to this it has been, more or less, with varying phases, decidedly patriotic, political, and practical. Of that time, with its genuine epic outline, and vivid lyrical colouring, we have already, in this Magazine, on different occasions, spoken at some length, (vol. i. 1st series, p. 732, and vol. vii. 2d series, p. 409,) There is no name, indeed, in the whole range of foreign literature, which is at once more generally and more deservedly esteemed in this country, than that of Theodore Körner. We shall therefore content ourselves, on the present occasion, with the single historical mention of this great revolution in the character of German song. Perhaps also the reader will not be displeased, if we add here, by

way of passing memorial, a translation of one of the poetic portraits of the great struggle, from the pen of a soldier-bard, whose fame has been almost eclipsed in this country by the extraordinary reputation of his more vigorous compeer. We speak of MAX VON SCHENKENDORF ; and the ode which follows is to the memory of a man to whose years of secret and silent preparation Germany is not less indebted for her political independence, than to the clattering hussar-charges of the hot old Blücher. Scharnhorst, indeed, had he not been prematurely carried off at the very first shock of the terrible struggle which his persevering genius had planned, might, in spite of his modest and most unambitious carriage, have been at this day as bruited a name in Europe as Wellington or Marshal Soult. But God had ordered it otherwise : he fell at Lützen on the 2d of May, 1813, and was carried, wounded, from the field of battle to Prague,—a place famous in the annals of Prussian glory,—where he died shortly after.

THE DEATH OF SCHARNHORST.

In Germania's holy quarrel,
  Prussian land the noblest laurel
    Bound thy gallant captain's brow ;
Deutschland's noon of strength preparing,
Lützen saw his deeds of daring,
    But the spoiler laid him low.

"Hear me, German brethren, hear me,
To the Kaiser's city bear me,
  Prague shall sound the Prussian's knell !
When she sees my red wounds bleeding,
Shall not Austria hear my pleading,
  Let me die where Schwerin fell !"

Prague ! an omen'd cloud hangs o'er thee,
Mighty heroes fell before thee,
  Saints were whelm'd within thy wave ;
Ancient Prague, with awe we name thee,
Holy Prague, with fear we claim thee,
  Tomb of saints and heroes' grave !

Fled from Earth 's the hero's spirit ;
And the angels gently bear it
  To the land that knows no pain ;
There the gather'd Teuton sages,
Great and good from distant ages,
  Gird the throne of Charlemain.

"Greet ye, brethren ! news to cheer ye !
Of her tyrant Earth is weary,
  And the German nations rise ;
See the signs of our succeeding !
Lo ! I bear these fresh wounds bleeding
  From the holy sacrifice !"

Thus the hero spake in Heaven,
And to us the oath is given ;
  Shall we put his words to shame ?
Soldiers whom he train'd so truly,
Swear that ye will keep it duly,
  Let your watchword be his name !

Where the eagle sunward soaring,
Battles with the tempest's roaring,
  Soar'd his spirit loftily ;
Only air of freedom breathed he,
Freedom's sword alone unsheathed he,
  And he died to make us free.

None to Prussia's throne was nearer,
None to German hearts was dearer,
  Scharnhorst was the people's own ;
Sire to son shall tell his glory,
He shall live in common story
  Surer than in brass and stone.

Another verse is sometimes added ; but seems rather to weaken than improve the effect.

63. continued

Waste no more thine eyes with weeping,
For thy sires in glory sleeping,
    Lovely Gräfinn weep no more;
In the stream of song for ever
Flows his fame on like a river—
    Lovely Gräfinn weep no more !

Connected with the poets of 1813, Ludwig Uhland deserves prominent notice ; for he is a true German patriot, and though more retired and cloisterly in his tone, passed by no means (like Goethe) unstirred by the great European blasts with which Arndt and Körner swept the German lyre. Uhland, however, is more properly to be regarded as the lyric representative of that famous romantic and mediæval school, of which Frederick Schlegel was the earnest critical dictator. All Uhland's finest and most characteristic ballads,— Durand, Dante, The Castellan of Couci, The Student of Salamanca,* and the others in the now so popular trochaic rhythm, — belong to this school rather than to that of Körner ; and partake, indeed, not seldom, a little too largely of that tincture of mist and moonshine, of which mediæval romance, in all its avatars, is apt to be so enamoured. In this country, what the Germans call the romantic school has assumed almost altogether an ecclesiastical, or more properly, sacerdotal character, — its most notable product being Puseyism ; and how closely even this English development of the phenomenon is connected with lyric poetry of no vulgar excellence, the name of Keble alone is sufficient to indicate. From Uhland, however, we must reluctantly pass on to the most recent manifestation of the German Terpsichore in the persons of Herwegh, Freiligrath, Fallersleben, Prutz, and others, who have made lyric poetry the vehicle not only of general patriotic appeal, but of direct political attack and party onset. How far the celestial maid may not have been unworthily handled, nay, positively prostituted (as old Goethe would have said) in being thus made subservient to ephemeral and terrestrial purposes, we shall not at present over-curiously inquire. + Let it be enough, so far as Prussia is concerned, to have stated distinctly, that the ruler of that country, having interdicted political excitement from its great legitimate outlet, the daily newspapers, has no right to complain if it seek for itself a new, and it may be unnatural organ, in the pregnant inuendoes of the sportive muse. Poetry can never remain poetry and be substantially waspish: that is plain. But a bee also has a sting ; and such poetic bees, buzzing sportively, and stinging not without dangerous venom, have been observed lately in frequent swarms, hovering about the most sensitive parts of his Borussian majesty Frederick William IV. It is one of the most ominous signs of the times, and deserves to be seriously pondered. Certain good people on the banks of the Spree, among their many theatrical fancies, seem to be tormented with a desire to play Charles I. over

* See Translations in *Blackwood's Magazine*, May 1836 ; and in *The Foreign Quarterly Review*, No. 38 ; and in our own Magazine, 1844, p. 364 ; and *Mangan*, vol. i. 87.
+ But on the connexion between *Politics and Poetry* generally, we refer our readers to our own pages, vol. iv. p. 162.

again ; and do not seem to understand perfectly that such an exhibition in the nineteenth century may possibly be productive of something far more serious than the scenic resuscitation of Sophocles and the Antigone. °It is strange, indeed, what transcendental ideas certain German statesmen seem to have about the power of kings. We read of the Roman emperor Caius Cæsar Caligula, that, having built a bridge of rafts from Baiæ to Puteoli, and covered it with gravel, (to show that he could march over the sea on dry land !) he invited a great number of spectators to witness the extraordinary passage ; but no sooner were the eager multitudes assembled, than he caused a great number of them to be seized, and for his sport thrown into the sea, and drowned. No doubt there were some smooth flatterers at Rome in those days, who showed themselves glib to prove that the divine right of emperors extended also to these recreations. In modern times, Prussia affords a parallel example. For in that famous year 1813, when it seemed to Goethe, and to the aristocratic party in Germany, mere folly to attempt hurling the French despot from his European throne,—in those most problematic and perilous days, it pleased the late King of Prussia to throw himself into the hands of that party which was alone able to restore him to the throne of the great Frederick : the party we mean of Stein and Hardenberg, and those who professed English and constitutional as opposed to military and bureaucratic principles. Many measures, accordingly, of a decidedly popular tendency were introduced and fostered by these men, in the short period between 1807 and 1813. An enthusiasm purely popular was by this means raised. Marshal Blücher came rattling over the bridge of the Elbe at Dresden, proclaiming to the enslaved Saxons, that the allies were come to restore to Germany that LIBERTY OF THE PRESS, of which the tyranny of Napoleon had deprived them ; and under the young and fresh inspiration of these liberal professions, and at that time no doubt honestly felt liberal sympathies, the blood-soaked ground was maintained inch by inch at Lützen, and the hard fought battles of Dennewitz, the Katzbach, and Leipzig, gained. Nay, more than this,—after the peace the same liberal professions were put into systematic legal phraseology, and stereotyped in the Act of the Confederation at Vienna. But the place where these fair speeches were made was of evil augury ; and, in fact, no sooner was Napoleon fairly settled in St. Helena, than the King of Prussia, like an honest simpleton, or a base hypocrite, (we charitably think the former,) in conjunction with a few weak and selfish aristocrats and red-tapists, immediately set himself to enact the part of Caligula, and hurl the spectators of his self-created liberalism into the sea. A general persecution was immediately commenced against all those whose enthusiastic zeal for German liberty had been most instrumental in restoring the king to his throne ; the diet at Frankfurt, by the exertions of Metternich, Gentz, and a few others, was converted into a standing committee, to prevent the growth of those popular institutions which the Congress of Vienna had made a show

of granting ; the free press, wherever it appeared, was gagged ; the parliaments of the several states were forbidden to deliberate on any subject but the granting of the pre-arranged budget, the formation of common sewers, and such like ; independent and manly professors in the universities were deposed and banished ; the students were informed that beer drinking and smoking, and all sorts of licentiousness and dissipation would not be objected to by the evangelic censor of academic morals ; but that politics, and public law, and English newspapers, were the devil. The consequence of all this has been, that the counsellors of the late King of Prussia, and the present monarch who is in the same false position, are, by the idle wits of Berlin, laughed at as mountebanks, by serious thinkers feared as impertinent bunglers in important matters, and by men of manly honesty and independent character, publicly branded as LIARS. The poets of the day, in particular, have become the great prophets of the political opposition, and what St. Paul and the Apostles were formerly, " the ringleaders of sedition among the people." How different from the cosmopolitan, generalizing, and artistic sensitiveness of Goethe, are the plain and urgent political truths of the moment, as they are enunciated in the following pleasant and sportive effusion by Prutz !*

THE STORY THAT'S NOT TRUE.

I climb'd a hill, a goodly hill,
    And what saw I there !
I saw a land, a lovely land,
    Vines on each wall ascending,
And by the throne on the king's right hand
    Bürger and boor attending.
        O, wonderful ! wonderful !
    Were there no lords and earls
    Circling the throne with pearls !
O, wonder on wonder, can this be true !

And higher I climb'd and higher still,
    And what saw I then !
No captain and no corporal,
    Recruiting, flogging, vanish'd,
And standing army none at all,
    The very name was banish'd.
        O, wonderful ! wonderful !
    No barons, dukes, and earls,
    Circling the throne with pearls !
    No taxes ! none to pay
    Soldiers on quarter-day !
O, wonder on wonder, can this be true !

And higher yet I climb'd the hill,
    And what saw I then !
I saw, as far as my eye could see,
    The lusty lads and lasses
On Sunday and Saturday travelling free,
    And nobody asked for passes.
        O, wonderful ! wonderful !
    No barons, lords, and earls,
    Circling the throne with pearls !
    No taxes ! none to pay
    Soldiers on quarter-day !
    Free lads and lasses all,
    Ask'd for no pass at all !
O, wonder on wonder, can this be true !

And higher again I climb'd the hill,
    And what saw I then !
I saw a crowd from lusty lungs
    Disputing and debating,
    With no police to rein their tongues,

* *Gedichte von R. C. Prutz. Neue Sammlung* Zurich and Winterthür, (not Berlin, of course,) 1843.

357

And with no spies in waiting.
　　O, wonderful ! wonderful !
No barons, lords, and earls,
Circling the throne with pearls
No taxes ! none to pay
Soldiers on quarter-day !
Free lads and lasses all,
Ask'd for no pass at all !
Traitorous tongues at large,
And with no spies in charge !
O, wonderful, wonderful, can this be true !

And higher and higher I climb'd the hill,
　　And what saw I then !
Deputies free to bark and bay,
　　In Parliamentary scuffle,
And with no minister's practised play,
　　The great state-cards to shuffle.
　　　O, wonderful ! wonderful !
No barons, lords, and earls,
Circling the throne with pearls !
No taxes ! none to pay
Soldiers on quarter-day !
Free lads and lasses all,
Ask'd for no pass at all !
Traitorous tongues at large,
And with no spies in charge !
Parliaments quite at ease,
Speaking just what they please !
O, wonderful, wonderful, can this be true !

And up I climb'd, and upwards still,
　　And what saw I then !
Science I saw, and Poesy,
　　Flapping triumphant pinions ;
The censorship I could not see,
　　'Twas bound in hell's dominions.
　　　O, wonderful ! wonderful !
No barons, lords, and earls,
Circling the throne with pearls !
No taxes ! none to pay
Soldiers on quarter-day !
Free lads and lasses all,
Ask'd for no pass at all !
Traitorous tongues at large,
And with no spies in charge !
Parliaments quite at ease,
Speaking just what they please !
Authors free, scribbling on,
Censorship nibbling none !
O, wonderful, wonderful, can this be true !

Brisk, and more brisk, I climb'd the hill,
　　And what saw I then !
I saw the wise men, with pen in hand,
　　For truth and justice writing,
And for the freedom of fatherland,
　　The learned doctors fighting.
　　　O, wonderful ! wonderful !
No barons, lords, and earls,
Circling the throne with pearls !
No taxes ! none to pay
Soldiers on quarter-day !
Free lads and lasses all,
Ask'd for no pass at all !
Traitorous tongues at large,
And with no spies in charge !
Parliaments quite at ease,
Speaking just what they please !
Authors free, scribbling on,
Censorship nibbling none !
No doctors, muddy all,
Smoked in their study all !
O, wonderful, wonderful, can this be true !

And up and up I climb'd the hill,
　　And what saw I then !
In the whole land, there was no trace
　　Of mumping methodism ;
And none could creep into a place,
　　By conning his catechism.
　　　O, wonderful ! wonderful !
No barons, lords, and earls,

Circling the throne with pearls !
No taxes ! none to pay
Soldiers on quarter-day !
Free lads and lasses all,
Ask'd for no pass at all !
Traitorous tongues at large,
And with no spies in charge !
Parliaments quite at ease,
Speaking just what they please !
Authors free, scribbling on,
Censorship nibbling none !
No doctors, muddy all,
Smoked in their study all !
No saints, by special grace,
Sneaking into a place !
O, wonderful, wonderful, can this be true !

And now to the top I climb'd the hill,
　　And what saw I then !
I saw each man prove for himself,
　　The eternal revelation ;
With no malignant priestly elf,
　　To thunder down damnation.
　　　O, wonderful ! wonderful !
No barons, lords, and earls,
Circling the throne with pearls !
No taxes ! none to pay
Soldiers on quarter-day !
Free lads and lasses all,
Ask'd for no pass at all !
Traitorous tongues at large,
And with no spies in charge !
Parliaments quite at ease,
Speaking just what they please !
Authors free, scribbling on,
Censorship nibbling none !
No doctors, muddy all,
Smoked in their study all !
No saints, by special grace,
Sneaking into a place !
Bigotry, branded all !
Clergymen candid all !
O, wonderful, wonderful !—but that's not true.

It requires no very profound acquaintance with the history of Prussian politics since the peace, to be able to appreciate this admirable satire. The British newspapers of the day for the last two or three years, and the floating comments of the reviews, supply all that is necessary for its illustration. Only one remark we shall allow ourselves, that the sting of the sarcasm lies in the glaring opposition between profession and principle by which the Prussian government stands so unenviably distinguished. The Czar Nicholas looks like a czar, and speaks like a czar, and uses the knout like a czar, and no man mistakes him ; so also Austria, " honest old Austria," sits spread out with a quiet breadth of contented Conservatism on her green gossiping prater at Vienna, and her likewise no man mistakes ; but Prussia, prating magnificently about her Protestantism, her intelligence, her high pressure education, her Zoll-unions, her Germanism, and Liberalism of all kinds, is, when you anatomize her closely, a hideous compound of pedant, preacher, and comedian, of coward, slave, and LIAR. What is to be the end of these things no man knows. For ourselves, we shall not be surprised if the German Lyric Muse, having now at length, in her youngest incarnation, become decidedly political and practical, should quickly learn to indite in a fluid of a more potent virtue, and more perilous concoction than ink. There were songs, also, and rare ones sung at Paris, in the year of grace one thousand seven hundred and ninety-two.

Art. VII. (1.) *German Fairy Tales, and Popular Stories.* Translated from the Collection of MM. Grimm, by Edgar Taylor. Joseph Cundall. 1846.

(2.) *Village Tales, from the Black Forest.* By Berthold Auerbach. Translated by Meta Taylor. David Bogue. 1847.

'Popular fictions and traditions are somewhat gone out of fashion.' But the volume of fairy tales before us, as well as the many others of its class, that have of late made their appearance, may surely be taken as an indication that this opinion of the translators is a little out of date, and might with more propriety be referred to a past period than to the present; when the more elegant guise in which our old friends present themselves, radiant in their gay bindings, and red and black title pages, would rather intimate that they are becoming very much the fashion: and not only so, but with far higher pretensions than in the days of their former popularity; when their fascinations were usually comprised within some half dozen greyish-white pages, displaying a curious combination of large and small type—the proportion varying according as a story of greater or less length had to be compressed within the same inexorable limits; and adorned with woodcuts, which, as some scribes would say, 'may be imagined better than described.'

Nor are we among those who may be inclined to look with disfavour on this growing disposition to revive the old legendary stores of our own and other lands. However the more cultivated mind of this generation may pronounce upon them, we must not forget that they have been most real things in the world's earlier day. And if among individuals he is held in but light esteem who is incapable of sympathy with his childhood—its griefs and enjoyments—surely it would be no very amiable trait in our national character, were we to look otherwise than with interest and somewhat of fondness on these relics of our comparative infancy, notwithstanding our having outgrown, and in our more vigorous maturity put away such childish things. It has also other and better uses. To the antiquarian it opens a wide field of inquiry and speculation, as illustration after illustration is afforded him, not only of the family likeness which prevails, but of the actual relationship subsisting among the whole tribe of fictional and spiritual beings of the most distant countries, (of their identity even in some cases;) and of the common, though often unassignable origin of their popular traditions. The hobgoblin of the East figures under some freezing alias in the North; the classical legend is faintly discernible through the veil of Saxon romance; while either identity of adventures or equi-

valence, (their different cast evidently the result of their having been moulded by the difference of national customs, modes of thought, and other peculiarities,) proclaims the hero of the story to be one and the same; 'a circumstance,' says Walter Scott, 'which augurs greater poverty of human invention than we should have expected!' And simple as are these fictions, they have yet served to exercise and try the skill of the learned, who, peering into the remote contiguity in which they are enshrouded, have sought, and perhaps not altogether unsuccessfully, to render these apparently mere creations of the imagination intelligible to the understanding, by fixing upon them satiric, historic, or mythological interpretations. In a literary point of view collections of this nature are deeply interesting, as indicative of the early mental, and, perchance, moral characteristics of different nations. Nor must we leave out of sight their own intrinsic merits: the wit, natural humour, keen insights into, and graphic depicting of character, and, not unfrequently, the simple beauty and pathos that mark the fairy tales and quaint romances of the olden time —merits which rarely fail of an intense appreciation alike by young and old.

As to the propriety of these fictions forming any part of a child's amusement or instruction, we are well aware there are widely differing opinions; nor shall we take it upon ourselves to pronounce *ex cathedra* upon the matter. We must, like the Vicar of Wakefield, admit that 'much may be said on both sides.' That singular genius, Adam Clarke, in his most amusing autobiography, after giving a list of his juvenile library, which contained most of the then known stories of this class, Jack the Giant Killer, Tom Hickathrift, Arabian Nights, &c., remarks, that many of them would now be proscribed, as being calculated, especially books of enchantment and chivalry, to vitiate the taste, and give false impressions.

'But,' adds he, 'is it not better to have a deeply rooted belief of the existence of an eternal world,—of God, angels, and spirits, though mingled with such superstition as naturally cleaves to infant and inexperienced minds, and which maturer judgment, reflection, and experience, will easily correct,—than to be brought up in a general ignorance of God and heaven, of angels, spirits, and spiritual influence; or in scepticism concerning the whole? There is a sort of Sadducean education now highly in vogue, that is laying the foundation of general irreligion and deism'. . . . Had I never read those books, it is probable I should never have been a reader, or a scholar of any kind: yea, I doubt much whether I should ever have been a religious man. Books of enchantment, &c., led me to believe in a spiritual world, and that if there were a devil to hurt, there was a

God to help, who never deserted the upright; and when I came to read the sacred writings, I was confirmed by their authority in the belief I had received, and have reason to thank God that I was not educated under the modern Sadducean system.'

We must not here be understood as identifying ourselves with these views, to which objections might be easily raised; but we cite them as an interesting and entertaining specimen of the mode in which this subject may present itself to the mind of one who was certainly not wanting either in learning or piety. And further, for a 'use of instruction,' as old divines say, to exemplify the power which a healthy, vigorous mind possesses of converting into wholesome aliment that, which, to one less happily constituted, would be a mere gratification of the taste, pleasing to the palate, but innutritive, if not absolutely noxious to the system: a power—that of extracting 'good from everything'—eminently distinctive of both mental and moral superiority. There are, perhaps, few who will not own that, *of the two*, an erratic belief in spiritual existences is better than none. Nor, if we may argue from results, are we at all sure that we of the present generation, who have been brought up upon *sensible* children's books, are either wiser, or better in any way, than our predecessors, whose infancy was nourished by so enormous an amount of fiction; whose general bearing, we speak of such of our northern fables as have any reference to morals, is commonly in favour of virtue; indicative of a protective power to watch over the good, and a retributive one to punish the bad. The rich, inexplicable drollery of some of these fictions, which give speech to beasts, birds, and fishes, *may* be objected to by some, as being calculated to convey false impressions of things; but even a child is fully alive to the humour of the thing, which it thoroughly enjoys; and we would venture to say that none ever was deceived by it. While the air of humanity thus given to the inferior animals is likely to have the effect of inducing a kindly feeling towards them in the hearts of children in whom any spark of intelligent goodness is to be found—such a feeling as may prevent their contributing, by thoughtless ill-usage, to increase the burden already laid upon these helpless, innocent sufferers for the sin of man! Great tenderness to all God's creatures would we instil into young minds; yea, a reverence for that life which, derived from the same source as our own, has, with our own, an equal claim to such enjoyment as that of which it, in its lower scale, may be susceptible: nor should the quaint fable, with its irrational interlocutors, be undervalued if it may, in any degree, tend to so desirable an end. For ourselves, grown up, and disagreeable, we must frankly own that stories of this nature have an inexpressible charm, for the sake of the amusement they afford; and, like sensible people, we shall fall to our enjoyment of them, without puzzling ourselves as to its why and wherefore.

For the volume before us, we are indebted to the collection of the indefatigable brothers Grimm, who have done much for this species of their country's literature; not only in rescuing it from the oblivion into which, in more educated periods, such legends are apt to sink, but in bringing to bear upon it a patient research and learning, which transmute what may appear the base ore of mere superstition, into the gold, more or less fine, of historic, or mythologic interpretation. While with these qualities of the *head*, are combined those of the *heart*, a feeling and taste which can deduce the most exquisite moral from that which by an ordinary mind might be apprehended but as the product of a gracefully sportive imagination — beautiful, but purposeless. ' The result of their labours,' says the translator, ' ought to be ' peculiarly interesting to English readers, inasmuch as many of ' their national tales are proved to be of the highest northern an- ' tiquity, and common to the parallel classes of society, in coun- ' tries whose populations have been long and widely disjoined.' Strange to say, ' Jack, commonly called the Giant-killer, and Thomas Thumb,' as a modern critic observes, between twenty and thirty years ago, ' landed in England, from the very same ' hulls and war-ships which conveyed Hengist and Horsa, and ' Ebba the Saxon. The cat, whose identity and London citizen- ' ship, in the story of Whittington, appeared so certain; Tom ' Thumb, whose parentage Hearne had traced; and the Giant- ' destroyer of Tylney, are equally renowned among the humblest ' inhabitants of Munster and Paderborn.' Gammer Grethel, the supposed narrator of the tales, (in twelve evenings, beginning with Christmas-eve,) was a real personage, the wife of a peasant in the neighbourhood of Hesse-Cassel, and from her recital, a large portion of them was derived.

In some of these stories the reader will not fail to recognise, under different names occasionally, many of those familiar to his childhood; we and our cousins-*German* (for so we may with singular propriety term them!) having apparently derived them from one common Teutonic source; unless indeed we must ascend still higher in tracing their origin, and assign to some of them an oriental, in addition to their northern antiquity. The majority of them, as their title imports, exhibit that semi-spiritual, semi-human agency, in which consists our idea of enchantment, witchcraft, and elfin operations generally. And, in passing, we may observe that the wide extent, we might almost say universality, of belief in the existence of beings holding a middle place between material and spiritual, yet inclining to the spiritual, is not a little remarkable, while without attempting minutely to account for it, (which would involve us in longer and graver disquisitions than either our limits, or immediate design permit,) it may be alluded to as an erroneous expression of a great fact,—a catholic testimony to the important truth of spiritual existences: that sort of witness which error often bears to truth by caricaturing it; and yet valuable, seeing the very caricature proves the existence of its original. Various are the forms in which this belief has embodied itself. Some, the very offspring of poetry and romance, which have peopled with aërial creatures the woods and the glades,—the yellow moonbeam, and ' the spangled starlight sheen;' others, that betray gloomier features; and, together with more of the external stamp of humanity, bear the strong impress of the most momentous hopes and fears that can sway the human heart; combining with a recognition of a future state of existence painful doubt and uncertainty as to their ultimate condition; while a third class contains a miscellaneous group of a more homely and prosaic character, the different individuals of which may be comprised under one head, as fairies of all work: and it is with these that our English popular belief has been chiefly concerned. Till very recently it has had a strong hold on the minds of a large portion of our population; though now fast disappearing before the researches of modern science, which in explaining some of the mysterious operations of nature, has sadly shorn witches, fairies, and ghosts of their wonted honours. It strikes us that of late we have not seen the accustomed horse-shoe on stable-doors, though in our wanderings we have looked out for that once familiar sight; and much do we fear that we shall never again (as we did some years ago) see excellent butter sold far below the market price, on the score of its being bewitched! A fact vouched for by the vendor, and undeniably substantiated, since the said butter had, as she averred, taken it into its head to roll along the floor in evident and most unbecoming chase of her, the sorely perturbed dairymaid. Nor should the afflictions, even in the nineteenth century, of our childhood, rurally spent, be forgotten,—the deserted attic in the old house, through whose trap-door entrance none dared to pop more than his quaking head and shoulders, for fear, had his feet followed those more adventurous members, of being snapped up by the reputed ghostly inhabitants of that gloomy receptacle of worn-out and antediluvian furniture. Or, more formidable still, that huge graystone, out lying in the close; whereon whosoever might stand, thrice pronouncing the name of one

who in that vicinity had, as was believed, sold himself to the Evil-one, would inevitably, on its third enunciation, be received into and swallowed up by the yawning jaws of the solid mass, rent by the accursed cognomen of the reprobate. Childish curiosity was wont to carry us through two of these invocations, while childish terror as effectually prevented our venturing on the *experimentum crucis* of a third!

We may smile at these weaknesses of our younger days; yet have they their origin in feelings deeply implanted in our very nature:—a dread, or at least awe, of the pure spiritual. And of this some slight superstitious degree clings to most, whether they care to own it or not. There are few, however sceptical on these subjects they may consider themselves, who would choose to enter, alone, at midnight an old vaulted church, to pace along its hollow-sounding aisles, and thread their way among massive pillars, throwing huge, black shadows across the faint moonlight that just serves to embarrass, rather than guide, their uncertain steps. We have not the slightest hesitation in confessing our own disinclination for such a performance, and for this simple reason,—that we are perfectly aware that at that hour and in such circumstances the imagination is apt to be in the ascendant; and, knowing this, we should not choose to subject ourselves to its freaks. The dullest observer cannot have failed to notice how things, that as objects of terror have absolutely no existence in the clear, cheerful truth-telling sunlight, become invested with strange vitality by the pale shadows of the waning day. How even the lifeless remains of those most cherished,—on whom the ' last enemy' has laid his gentlest hand, stamping on the mortality over which he has triumphed a holy beauty that tells of the glorious immortality to which even that poor dust shall arise; and over which, in the bright morning hours, we have bent with no feeling save that of unutterable grief and tenderness,—how even these, as the shades of evening gather around, become a source of oppressive awe; while a deeper gloom than that of night,—the very shadow of death, seems to fall with silent horror alike over the chamber of the dead and of the living! But these relics of our German neighbours, not our English superstitions, or those common to our nature, are now before us, and to them we must restrain ourselves.

The elfin agents in these tales do not possess much of that vivid poetical character which distinguishes some of the airy creations of the imagination with which we have been made acquainted from the same quarter. They are chiefly just the old-fashioned, every-day fairies; dispensing good and evil to mortals, sometimes arbitrarily enough, at others with a tact and discrimination that do them infinite credit. ' Virtue rewarded, and vice punished,' might generally be their motto. Though in some instances, we must own, their design is but to exhibit the triumph of intellect over physical strength, or that of sheer cunning over simplicity :—amusing enough, but not particularly instructive, save as illustrating that which is of recurrence far more frequent than desirable. Amid so much entertaining variety it is somewhat difficult to make selections ; but as those which are common to us and our neighbours, under slightly varying forms, are, we must presume, tolerably familiar to the reader, we shall have the pleasure of introducing him to some new acquaintances. First, however, to increase his respect for what he may fancy his peculiarly English store, reminding him that Cinderella (the Ashputtel of this collection) is known to the Welsh, the Poles, Servians, and Neapolitans; is alluded to in Scandinavian traditions, and is even made use of by Luther, to illustrate the 'subjection of Abel to his brother Cain'! That Tom Thumb—not the American pigmy, but the old original Tom —flourishes throughout England, Scotland, Germany, Austria, Denmark, and Scandinavia. While some, who have eruditely pursued the small hero's history still further, trace his connexion with the Indian mythology! Jack the Giant-killer, whose adventures are here divided among various individuals, must also claim equal European antiquity.

'The Germans,' says Mr. Taylor, 'are eminently successful in beast stories.' In confirmation of this we might cite several rich specimens. The Waits of Bremen tempts us with its Ass, who, as he had 'a good voice,' thinks he may 'chance to be chosen town musician;' its Cat, 'sitting in the middle of the road with tears in her eyes,' and who, on being invited to contribute her musical powers to the choir, 'was pleased with the thought, so she wiped her eyes *with her pocket-handkerchief!* and joined the party;' and other *dramatis personæ* equally ill adapted for the production of harmony. But we must pass it by, and see how Bruin and the Tits (tom-tits) will make good our translator's opinion.

'One bright summer's day, as Mr. Bruin, the bear, and his friend, the wolf, were taking a walk together, arm in arm in a wood, they heard a bird singing merrily. 'Hist, hist! brother, stop a bit!' said the bear, 'what can that dear bird be that sings so sweetly?' 'My dear friend, Bruin,' said the wolf, 'why, don't you know? that is his majesty the king of the birds. We must take care to show him all kinds of honour.' (Now, between ourselves, you must know, master wolf was a wag, and was hoaxing Bruin; for the bird was neither more nor less than a tom-tit.) 'If that be the case,' said the bear gravely, 'I should very much like to see the royal palace; so pray, come along, and show it me!' 'Softly, my dear friend,' said the wolf, 'we cannot see it just yet, for her majesty is not at home; we had better call again when the queen comes home.''

Soon afterwards the queen came home, with food in her beak, and she and the king her husband began to feed their young ones. 'Now for it,' said the bear, 'the family are at dinner.' So he was about to follow them, and see what was to be seen. 'Stop a little, Master Bruin,' said the wolf, 'we must now wait till their majesties are gone again.' So they marked the hole where they had seen the nest, and went away.

But the bear, being very eager to see the royal palace, soon slipped away, wishing his friend good morning, and came back again, and peeping into the nest saw five or six young birds lying at the bottom of it. ' What nonsense,' said Bruin, 'this is not a ' royal palace; I never saw such a filthy place in my life ; and ' you are no royal children, you little base-born brats!' As soon as the young tom-tits heard this, they were very angry, and screamed out, ' We are not base-born, you brute of a bear ! our ' father and mother are good honest people : and you shall be ' well paid for your slander.' At this the bear grew frightened, and ran away to his den. But the young tits kept crying and screaming ; and when their father and mother came home, and showed them food, they all said, ' We will not touch a bit, no, ' not the leg of a fly, though we should die of hunger, till that ' rascal Bruin has been well trounced for calling us base-born ' brats.' ' Make yourselves easy, my darlings!' said the old king, ' you may be sure he shall have his due.'

So he went out, and stood before the bear's den, and cried out with a loud voice, ' Bruin the bear ! thou hast shamefully slan- ' dered our lawful children: we hereby declare bloody war ' against thee and thine ; which shall never cease until thou hast ' had thy due, thou wicked one !'

Whereupon the bear collects his forces, consisting of all ' the beasts of the earth,' and the insulted tom-tit his, comprising all the birds of the air, with plenty of light troops in the shape of all manner of insects ; and to it they go ! the beasts on the one side, and ' his majesty the tom-tit with all his troops' on the other. Victory is not long doubtful; for once it is *right*, (that of the very unpleasantly phrased tom-tits,) over *might*,—the beasts unanimously take to their heels, leaving the birds masters of the field.

' Then the king and queen flew back to their children, and ' said, ' Now, children, eat, drink, and be merry, for the battle is ' won!' But the young birds said, ' No! no! not till Master

'Bruin has humbly begged our pardon for calling us base-born.'
'So the king flew off to the bear's den, and cried out, 'Thou
''villain bear! come forthwith to my abode, and humbly beseech
''my children to forgive thee for the reproach thou hast cast upon
''them; for if thou wilt not do this, every bone in thy wretched
''body shall be broken into twenty pieces.''

This being a clear case of 'needs must be,' Bruin sulkily complies; and full satisfaction having thus been made for the slur cast on the family honour of the tom-tits, (we cannot but admire the nice sense of it which they evince!) 'after that the cloth 'was laid, and the table spread, and the young birds sat down 'together, and ate, and drank, and made merry till midnight.'

But for pure burlesque, the most extravagant drollery that ever entered mortal's head, commend us to Chanticleer and Partlet; for his introduction of which the translator apologizes, fearing it may be thought too childish; but we beg to assure him that we could have better spared half a score of his other stories, than this witty specimen of unadulterated nonsense, which for ludicrousness of idea, and curt raciness of style, is unequalled. It is too long for us to give the whole, but we must tell the reader, '*How they went to the mountains to eat nuts;*' when, as it was a lovely day, they stayed till evening. Now, whether it was that they had eaten so many nuts that they could not walk, or whether they were lazy and would not, I do not know: however, they took it into their heads that it did not become them to go home on foot. So Chanticleer began to build a little carriage of nutshells, and when it was finished Partlet jumped into it and sat down, and bid Chanticleer harness himself to it and draw her home. 'That's a good joke,' said Chanticleer; 'no, that will 'never do; I had rather by half walk home; I'll sit on the box 'and be coachman, if you like, but I'll not draw.' While this was passing, a duck came quacking up, and cried out, 'You 'thieving vagabonds, what business have you in my grounds? 'I'll give it you well for your insolence!' and upon that she fell upon Chanticleer most lustily. But Chanticleer was no coward, and paid back the duck's blows with his sharp spurs so fiercely, she soon began to cry out for mercy; which was only granted her on her agreeing to draw the carriage home for them. This she said she would do; and Chanticleer got upon the box and drove off, crying, 'Now, duck, get on as fast as you can.' And away they went at a pretty good pace.

'After they had travelled along a little way, they overtook a needle and a pin walking together along the road; and the needle cried out, 'Stop, stop!' and said it was so dark that they could hardly find their way, and the walking so dirty that they could not get on at all. He

told them that 'he and his friend, the pin, had been at a public house a few miles off, and sat drinking till they had forgotten how late it was; so he begged the travellers to be so kind as to give them a lift in their carriage. Chanticleer, seeing they were but thin fellows, and not likely to take up much room, told them they might ride, but made them promise not to dirty the wheels of the carriage in getting in, nor to *tread on Partlet's toes!*

'Late at night they got to an inn; and as it was bad travelling in the dark, and the duck seemed much tired, and waddled about a good deal from one side to the other, they made up their minds to fix their quarters there. But the landlord at first was unwilling, and said his house was full; for he thought they might not be very reputable company. However, they spoke civilly to him, and gave him the egg which Partlet had laid by the way, and said they would give him the duck, who was in the habit of laying one every day: so at last he let them come in, and they bespoke a handsome supper, and spent the evening very jollily.

'Early in the morning, before it was quite light, and when nobody was stirring in the inn, Chanticleer awakened his wife, and fetching the egg, they pecked a hole in it, ate it up, and threw the shell into the fire-place. They then went to the pin and needle, who were fast asleep, and seizing them by their heads, stuck one into the landlord's easy chair, and the other into his handkerchief. Having done this, they crept away as softly as they could, and followed their journey. However, the duck, who slept in the open air in the yard, heard them coming, and jumping into the brook, which ran close by the inn, soon swam off, clear out of their reach.

'An hour or two afterwards, the landlord got up, and took his handkerchief to wipe his face, but the pin ran into him and pricked him; then he walked into the kitchen to light his pipe at the fire; but when he stirred it up, the egg-shells flew into his eyes, and almost blinded him. 'Bless me!' said he, 'all the world seems to have a plot against my head this morning;' and so saying, he threw himself sulkily into his easy chair; but, oh dear! the needle ran into him, and this time the pain was not in his head. He now flew into a very great rage, and thinking it must be the company who came in the night before, he made out their bill for their night's lodging, and went to look after them, but they were all off; so he swore he never again would take in such a troop of vagabonds, who ate a great deal, paid no reckoning, and gave him nothing for his trouble but their apish tricks.'

Unprofitable customers truly! One cannot but sympathize with the poor landlord, regularly victimized by such a couple of accomplished rascals, whose easy assurance and ingenuity of tormenting are inimitable. The introduction of inanimate objects as *dramatis personæ*, is not of very frequent occurrence in stories of this nature. There is something of the sort in our old tale of 'The Old Woman and her Pig;' (of which we are reminded by the third part of Chanticleer's history;) and *this*, it may be remembered, has been traced to a supposed Oriental (Jewish) origin. But its 'hatchet,' 'fire,' 'stick,' 'rope,' which set to work on each other in order that the dame may ' get her pig home to night,' possesses nothing of the vitality and *humanization* of the needle and pin, here so unceremoniously disposed of. However, in his next drive Chanticleer picks up a still more miscellaneous company,—a cat, a mill-stone! an egg, a duck, and a pin,—and off they go to visit ' Mr. Korbes,' an individual who, proving ' very anonymous indeed' to the translator, is rendered the fox; in order, we suppose, to make the story in keeping with the ill-luck generally awarded to Master Reynard. But poor Mr. Korbes, upon whom the same tricks are played as upon the unfortunate landlord, is even worse served than his predecessor. When they got to his house ' he was not at home; so the mice drew the ' carriage into the coach-house, Chanticleer and Partlet flew upon ' a beam, the cat sat down in the fire-place, the duck got into the ' washing-cistern, the pin stuck himself into the bed pillow, the ' mill-stone laid himself over the house door, and the egg rolled ' herself up in the towel.' And then ensues the catastrophe! When Mr. Korbes came home, he went to the fire-place to make a fire; but—

' Henze (the cat,) threw all the ashes in his eyes; so he ran to the kitchen to wash himself; but there the duck threw all the water in his face, and when he tried to wipe himself, the egg broke to pieces in the towel, all over his face and eyes. Then he was very angry, and went without his supper to bed; but when he laid his head on the pillow, the pin ran into his cheek. At this he became quite mad, and jumping up, would have run out of the house; but when he came to the door, the mill-stone fell down on his head, and killed him on the spot.'

After this it seems only poetical justice that Partlet should be choked with 'a great nut;' Chanticleer, like a sentimental rogue, as he was, pining and weeping over her, 'till at last he died too.' The story comprises three; from Paderborn, the Main, and Hesse; but evidently related to each other. Of its date Mr. Taylor says nothing.

But enough of these ' beast stories,' which are supreme of their kind.

Among the tales which bear a resemblance more or less to our own stock, we may notice ' Hans in Luck,' an amusing story of a poor simple fellow, who receiving for his wages ' a lump of silver as big as his head,' purchases a horse with it, which he presently exchanges for a cow; this in turn gives place to a pig, and so he goes on, exchanging each purchase for something of less value,

always with the idea that he has the best of the bargain, till he finishes up with a grindstone, which 'rolls plump into the stream,' and so sets him at liberty, to his great joy, to go home and tell his mother, ' how very easy the road to good luck' is. There is an old song, with which our infancy was wont to be entertained, which this brings to our mind; where the hero, a very Hans in Luck, who begins life with ' six horses to gang wi' the plough,' succeeds, by a series of easy gradations similar to those of our friend above, in reducing his farming stock to a mouse! which, fitting finale, ' sets fire to her tail, and burns down the house.' This in its ' convenient vehicle' of a tolerably lively tune,—considering the doleful strain of the ballad,—may, we imagine, be the similar story to which the translator alludes, as being well known in the northern parts of England, whence we ourselves derive it.

' Rose-bud' exactly answers to our Sleeping Beauty, but is somewhat abridged, ending with the marriage of the Prince and Princess, and differs slightly in details. It is in some parts more drolly told than our own; and this would rather lead us to suspect that it was a more modern version of it. '*Studied* humour of style is rarely of very early date, to which humour of incident more commonly belongs. But albeit a bit of modernism (as we conjecture), the description of the state of the household, fated to share the Princess' hundred years' sleep, is so fine a piece of painting of *still* life, so entirely somnolent, that we cannot resist transferring it, though at the risk of setting the reader a-nodding over our page! The fatal spindle has just been touched, and the princess is—

' Fallen into a deep sleep; and the king and the queen, who just then came home, and all their court, fell asleep too; and the horses slept in the stables, and the dogs in the court; the pigeons on the house-top, and the very flies slept upon the walls. Even the fire on the hearth left off blazing, and went to sleep; the jack stopt, and the spit, that was turning about with a goose upon it for the king's dinner, stood still; and the cook, who was that moment pulling the kitchen-boy by the hair to give him a box on the ear for something he had done amiss, let him go, and both fell asleep; the butler, who was slily tasting the ale, fell asleep with the jug at his lips: and thus every thing stood still, and slept soundly.'

Nor is the general wakening, when the spell is broken, of inferior merit:—

' The moment the prince kissed her, she opened her eyes and awoke, ... and soon the king and queen also awoke, and all the court, and gazed on each other with great wonder. And the horses shook themselves, and the dogs jumped up and barked; the pigeons took their heads from under their wings, and looked about, and flew into the fields; the flies on the walls buzzed away; the fire in the kitchen blazed up; round went the jack, and round went the spit, with the goose for the king's dinner upon it; the butler finished his draught of ale; the maid went on plucking the fowl; and the cook gave the boy the box on his ear.'

Rumpel-stilts-ken we have an idea, though a very vague one, of having heard, in some form or other, when we were a 'careless child.' So 'careless' indeed, that we retain no trace of it save the one line in which the gentleman who cannot keep his own secret betrays himself; and the similarity of which to the couplet quoted by Mr. Taylor in his notes—

> ' Little does my lady wot,
> That my name is Trit-a-Trot,"

would indicate that ours was allied to, if not identical with, the Irish version of the story whence this fragment is taken. The tale is this,—A miller's daughter having been taught by a dwarf to spin gold out of straw, (by which means she becomes queen,) promises him her first-born in return for his good offices; an engagement from which he offers to release her if within three days she can find out his name. She of course sets to work; runs over in her mind all the odd names she has ever heard; Timothy, Ichabod, Benjamin, Jeremiah, Ben Bandy-legs, Hunch-back, Crook-shanks, and so on; to all of which she receives the discouraging answer, 'Madam, that is not my name.' Till at length one of her messengers, whom she had sent all over the land to find out new ones, luckily, in the middle of a forest, stumbles upon the dwarf himself, dancing and singing,

> ' Little does my lady dream,
> Rumpel-stilts-ken is my name;'

which saves the lady any further trouble in guessing. The story is not without its moral for those who care to extract one from it. One does occasionally, in real life, meet with Mr. Rumpel-stilts-ken; indiscreet, chattering people, who cannot keep their own counsel, but let out, and that most gratuitously, precisely what they are most concerned to conceal. One cannot though help feeling for the manikin in the story, at whom, after the discomfiture to which he had helped himself, even 'the nurse 'laughed, and the baby crowed, and all the court jeered, for hav-'ing had so much trouble for nothing; and said, 'We wish you a 'very good morning, and a merry feast, Mr. Rumpel-stilts-ken!''

Master Snip, which is noticed by the translator as having an 'intimate connexion with our oldest northern traditions,' seems to be a near relation of our Jack the Giant Killer; and Tom Hickathrift, if, indeed, he be not these 'two single gentlemen

rolled into one,' and under somewhat humble guise, that, as the name imports, of a tailor. Though our knight of the thimble lacks those treasures which to us have seemed peculiar to Master Jack, the seven-league boots, sword, and invisible coat, *here* found in the keeping of another, Heinel, who, finding the giant quarrelling about them, is requested, as 'little men have sharp wits,' to divide these, their father's goods, among them; and makes good the saying, by taking possession of them himself! In accordance with the compensating principle apparent in these fables—superior strength being balanced (and over-balanced!) by superior wit—the poor giant, as in our own fictions, comes off 'second-best' in his encounter with the tailor. This latter personage sets out on his travels one fine summer morning, with a cheese and a hen in his wallet; and meeting the giant, who sits 'picking his teeth with the kitchen poker!' bids him good morrow, and invites him to join him in quest of adventures. A salutation somewhat uncourteously returned,—'Then the giant looked down, turned up his nose at him, and said, 'You are a poor trumpery little knave.' 'That may be,' said the tailor, 'but we shall see by-and-by who is the best man of the two.'

The giant, finding the little man so bold, began to be somewhat more respectful, and said, 'Very well, we shall soon see who is to be master.' So he took up a large stone into his hand, and squeezed it till water dropped from it: 'Do that,' said he, 'if you have a mind to be thought a strong man.' 'Is that all?' said the tailor; 'I will soon do as much;' so he put his hand into his wallet, and pulled out of it the cheese, (which was rather new,) and squeezed it till the whey ran out. 'What do you say now, Mr. Giant? my squeeze was a better one than yours.' Then the giant, not seeing that it was only a cheese, did not know what to say for himself, though he could hardly believe his eyes. At last he took up a stone, and threw it up so high, that it went almost out of sight; 'Now, then, little pigmy, do that if you can.' 'Very good,' said the other, 'your throw was not a very bad one, but, after all, your stone fell to the ground; I will throw something that shall not fall at all.' 'That you can't do,' said the giant. But the tailor took his old hen out of the wallet, and threw her up in the air; and she, pleased enough to be set free, flew away out of sight. 'Now, comrade,' said he, 'what do you say to that?' 'I say you are a clever hand,' said the giant; 'but we will now try how you can work.'

Then he led him into the wood, where a fine oak tree lay felled. 'Come, let us drag it out of the wood together.' 'Oh, very well!' said Snip, 'do you take hold of the trunk, and I will carry all the top, and the branches, which are much the largest and heaviest.' So the giant took the trunk, and laid it on his shoulder; but the cunning little rogue, instead of carrying anything, sprang up, and sat himself at his ease among the branches; and so let the giant carry stem, branches, and tailor into the bargain. All the way they went, he made merry, and whistled, and sang his song, as if carrying the tree were mere sport; while the giant, after he had borne it a good way, could carry it no longer, and said, 'I must let it fall.' Then the tailor sprang down, and held the tree as if he were carrying it, saying, 'What a shame that such a big lout as you cannot carry a tree like this.'

Excessive simplicity on the part of the 'big louts' seems a characteristic of all these giant stories. Snip again plays on that of his acquaintance, who finally, with the intention of making away with the 'trumpery little knave,' invites him home to sleep, and at midnight comes softly in, and deals such a blow with his iron walking-stick upon the bed, that he exclaims, 'It's all up now with that grasshopper; I shall have no more of his tricks.' His guest, however, suspecting the hospitable intent with which he has been invited, has had the wit *not* to get into the bed; and next morning almost scares the giants out of their wits by presenting himself alive and sound before them. This, however, is vastly inferior to the account of a similar adventure that befals *our* Jack, who, on being asked next morning if anything had disturbed him, coolly and curtly replies, 'Oh no, nothing worth speaking of—a rat, I believe, gave me two or three slaps with his tail, but I soon went to sleep again!' Snip, in conclusion, plays giant-killer, by setting the giants a quarrelling till they kill each other, and the story ends with what might as appropriately conclude many modern memoirs;—'thus a little man became a great one.'

Our other renowned Jack, he of the Beanstalk, seems faintly adumbrated in the Giant Golden-beard of Grimm's collection, or rather of Mr. Taylor's, who has adapted the tale to 'ears polite' by transferring the scene, and the three golden hairs, from the infernal regions, and the beard of the 'gentleman,' (Hamlet is our authority,) who is understood to be the principal personage there. For ourselves, we would rather have the story served up *au naturel*; but must commend the translator's discretion in presenting a milder preparation of it to his young readers.

In the Bear and the Skrattel, (a fiction which dates so far back as the thirteenth or fourteenth century,) we are introduced to a somewhat new element of elfin nature,—the *material* so preponderating over the spiritual, as to render it capable of physical suffering from mortal agency. This Skrattel seems to be of the same order as our Lancashire 'braggart;' taking up his quarters in a woodman's cottage, and there playing so many mischievous pranks, that the family are fairly driven out for a quiet life, and leave him the place to himself. More fortunate than in one of our home stories, where, just as the cart laden with the goods of the worried-out household is driving off, the 'braggart' (to get rid of whom they are leaving,) pops up his head from among them, exclaiming, '*We're* flitting!' an announcement which provokes a rejoinder to the effect that if *he* was going too, they might as well stay. In the present case, however, the creature's attachment is to the house, and not to the family; and having succeeded in turning them out, he makes himself merry enough, till one night when a huntsman, travelling with a great white bear, a present from the King of Norway to his brother of Denmark, takes up his quarters in the deserted house rather than abide the storm outside; whereupon presently ensues a desperate battle between the bear and the goblin, (who attacks him with the spit,) ending in the complete discomfiture of the latter, who, sorely handled, darts out at the door and disappears. Not being seen again for some days, the woodman is in doubt whether his enemy is entirely routed or not; but meeting him on the evening of the fourth day after his flight, the following humorous dialogue occurs between them, which explains the poor Skrattel's mistaken idea of his formidable foe, and assures the countryman that he has nothing more to fear from him:—

"'Hark ye, bumpkin!' cried the Skrattel; 'Canst thou hear, fellow? Is thy great cat alive, and at home still?' 'My cat!' said the woodman. 'Thy great white cat, man!' thundered out the little imp. 'Oh! my cat,' said the woodman, recollecting himself; 'Oh, yes, to be sure, alive and well, I thank you; very happy, I'm sure, to see you and all friends, whenever you will do us the favour to call. And hark ye, friend! as you seem to be so fond of my great cat, you may like to know that she had five kittens last night.' 'Five kittens!' muttered the elf. 'Yes,' replied the woodman, 'five of the most beautiful white kits you ever saw,—so like the old cat, it would do your heart good to see the whole family—such soft gentle paws—such delicate whiskers—such pretty little mouths!' 'Five kittens!' muttered, or rather shrieked out the imp again. 'Yes, to be sure!' said the woodman, 'five kittens! do look in to-night, about twelve o'clock,—the time, you know, that you used to come and see us. The old cat will be so glad to show them to you, and we shall be so happy to see you once more: but where can you have been all this time?'

"'I come?' not I, indeed!' shrieked the Skrattel; 'what do I want with the little wretches? Did I not see the mother once? Keep your kittens to yourself: I must be off, this is no place for me. Five kittens! So there are six of them now. Good bye to you, you'll see me no more; so bad luck to your ugly cat, and your beggarly house.'

'The Schrat, Schratel, Skrat, or Skrattel,' says Mr. Taylor, 'is one of the numerous names for the domestic spirit or elf, ap-'parently limited to the mischievous species.' Hence, may we not presume, the ' Old Scratch,' (or Skrat, for so have we heard it,) of our own *vulgar* tongue !

That most pathetic of all stories, the Babes in the Wood, we can scarcely hope to claim exclusively as our own. Accordingly, we here find some trace of it, nothing more, in Hansel and Grethel—a very fairy tale—in which, however, three stories are combined, the incidents being common to almost every country. The children, Hansel and Grethel, are here led into the wood to perish by the parents of the former—a fate which they escape ; and after undergoing various transformations, finally come into their own shapes again; and, as usual, are married, and ' live happily ever after.' But their wandering in the wood, in vain expectation of the promised return of the woodman, and his cruel wife, at once brings before us the poor babes, hand in hand, awaiting the reappearance of their treacherous protector :—

> ' But never more they saw the man,
> Returning from the town.'

But perhaps the most beautiful specimen of the genuine fairy tale in this collection is the Lily and the Lion—a more poetical version of our Beauty and the Beast; and in which the translator recognises some affinity to the legend of Cupid and Psyche. The first portion of it—the mere Beauty and Beast part—everybody knows; but the thoughtless imprudence of the heroine consigns her prince-spouse again to the power of enchantment; and he is changed into a white dove, which is to fly up and down over the face of the earth seven years, letting fall, from time to time, a white feather, to guide her in following it, that she may overtake and set him free.

'Thus she went, roving on through the wide world, and looked neither to the right hand nor to the left, nor took any rest for seven years. Then she began to be glad, and thought to herself that the time was fast coming when all her troubles should end; yet repose was still far off; for one day, as she was travelling on, she missed the white feather, and when she lifted up her eyes, she could no longer see the dove. 'Now,' thought she to herself, 'no aid of man can be of use to me.' So she went to the sun, and said, 'Thou shinest everywhere, on the hill's top, and the valley's depth: hast thou anywhere seen my white dove?' 'No,' said the sun; 'I have not seen it; but I will give thee a casket; open it when thy hour of need comes.'

'So she thanked the sun, and went on her way till eventide: and when the moon arose, she cried unto it, and said, 'Thou shinest through all the night, over field and grove: hast thou nowhere seen my white dove?' 'No,' said the moon, 'I cannot help thee; but I will give thee an egg: break it when need comes.'

'Then she thanked the moon, and went on till the night-wind blew; and she raised up her voice to it, and said, 'Thou blowest through every tree and under every leaf: hast thou not seen my white dove?' 'No,' said the night-wind; 'but I will ask three other winds; perhaps they have seen it.' Then the east wind and the west wind came, and said they had not seen it; but the south wind said, ' I have seen the white dove; he has fled to the Red Sea, and is changed once more into a lion, for the seven years are passed away; and there he is fighting with a dragon, and the dragon is an enchanted princess, who seeks to separate him from you.' Then the night-wind said, 'I will give thee counsel: go to the Red Sea! on the right shore stand many rods; count them, and when thou comest to the eleventh, break it off, and smite the dragon with it; and so the lion will have the victory, and both of them will appear to you in their own forms. Then set out at once with thy beloved prince, and journey home over sea and land, but be sure and do not delay!'

But, alas! poor Lily forgets one part of the night-wind's counsel—'do not delay !'—in consequence of which the prince again falls into the power of the false princess, who carries him off with her!

'Thus the unhappy traveller was again forsaken and forlorn; but she took heart, and said, ' As far as the wind blows, and so long as the cock crows, I will journey on, till I find him once again.' She went on for a long long way, till at length she came to the castle, whither the princess had carried the prince; and there was a feast got ready, and she heard the wedding was about to be held. ' Heaven, aid me now !' said she; and she took the casket that the sun had given her, and found that within it lay a dress as dazzling as the sun itself. So she put it on, and went to the palace, and all the people gazed upon her; and the dress pleased the bride so much that she asked whether it was to be sold. ' Not for gold and silver,' said she, 'but for flesh and blood.' Then the princess asked what she meant; and she said, ' Let me speak with the bridegroom this night in his chamber, and I will give thee the dress.' At last the princess agreed; but she told her chamberlain to give the prince a sleeping-draught that he might not see or hear her. When evening came, and the prince had fallen asleep, she was led into his chamber, and she sat herself down at his feet, and said, 'I have followed thee seven years; I have been to the sun, the moon, and the night-wind to seek thee, and at last I have helped thee to overcome the dragon. Wilt thou then forget me quite?' But the prince all the time slept so soundly, that her voice only passed over him, and seemed like the *whistling of the wind among the fir-trees !*'

What true pathos is this, and how full of poetry ! Baffled and forlorn, poor Lily is led away; 'and when she saw there was no help for her, she went out into a meadow, and sat herself down, and wept.' But the gift received from the moon recurs to her mind, and this, which displays ' the most beautiful sight in the world,' is again eagerly desired by the false princess; to whom the same answer is again returned—' not for gold and silver; but for flesh and blood!' And again does she design to betray her suppliant:—

' But when the prince went to his chamber, he asked the chamberlain why the wind had whistled so in the night. And the chamberlain told him all; how he had given him a sleeping-draught; and how a poor maiden had come, and spoken to him in his chamber, and was to come again that night. Then the prince took care to throw away the sleeping-draught, and when Lily came, and began again to tell him what woes had befallen her, and how faithful and true to him she had been, he knew his beloved wife's voice, and sprang up and said, ' You have awakened me as from a dream; for the strange princess had thrown a spell around me, so that I had altogether forgotten you; but heaven hath sent you to me in a lucky hour.' And they stole away out of the palace by night unawares, and journeyed home; and there they found their child, now grown up to be comely and fair; and after all their troubles, they lived happily together to the end of their days.'

Refined beauty of idea is here clothed exquisitely by language, pure, tender, simple—nay, eloquent in its very simplicity; for deep feeling does not usually express itself in heroics; and we feel how true to nature is the quiet pathos of the heroine's brief recital of her wanderings, with its touching close :—' Wilt thou then forget me quite?' It is perfect after its kind; nor let it be thought that we are making too much of a mere fairy tale— ' spinning gold out of straw'—if we recognise in this quaint legend a delicate portrayal of the pure, passionate, earnestness of woman's love—a love that ' many waters cannot quench!'

The manner in which these stories are told is exceedingly spirited and lifelike. As may be supposed from their date, they are characterised by a simple energy of style—a breadth and firmness of touch, that stand out in bold contrast with the too elaborate finishing in which we, of this day, are apt to indulge, sacrificing effect to execution, and which unmistakeably stamp them as the work of no modern hand. For an illustration of their graphic felicity, we may turn to the ' Fox's Brush;' where the young prince being invited by the Fox to sit upon his tail, and ' he will travel faster,' does so; and ' away they went over stock and stone *till their hair whistled in the wind!*' Rapidity of transit was, we imagine, never more vividly and succinctly described: we both see and hear it.

It must be admitted that our ancestors far exceeded their

degenerate sons in story-telling. Some of the incidental touches are very amusing. The old king, who ' having just then nothing else to do, amused himself by *sitting at his kitchen window,* looking at what was going on;' the young princess, ' putting on her bonnet and clogs'—like a sensible woman as she was—' to take an evening walk;' the twelve princesses, with whom their papa had so much trouble; since every night ' when they went to bed, the king went up, and shut and locked the door;' and ' was angry at having to buy so many new shoes'— the young ladies dancing each a pair through in the course of the night. While extravagance surely never went beyond ' the great crown, full two yards high;' the ' six fair maidens, each a head taller than the other!' the ' burning lights—the greatest as large as the highest and biggest tower in the world;' and the ' throne two miles high!' which symbolize the various degrees of dignity to which the fisherman's wife attains; and whose insolent ambition at length provokes from the 'man of the sea,' by whose magic influence they had been gained, the concise rejoinder—'go home to your pig-stye again!' The 'hill so big, that all the men in the whole world could not have taken it away,' is good; but still not to be compared with our friend the giant ' picking his teeth with the kitchen poker!' What an idea of a giant it gives me !

It only remains for us to add, that these interesting specimens of the popular fictions of our Teutonic neighbours have found a translator worthy of them. The style is plain, homely, vigorous —everything that it should be. While the volume is enriched with notes, the value and interest of which to the generality of readers, who may not have given more than a cursory attention to the subject, the modesty of the translator can alone lead him to undervalue.

Auerbach's ' Village Stories,' here presented to us in an English dress by Meta Taylor, belong to a different class; yet are they not unmeet to lie side by side with the volume we have just relinquished, seeing they are from the same soil, whence we have of late made such large additions to our literary store, and are designed to exhibit the real life of those among whom these old fictions circulate, and, as we may imagine, find readier credence than in more artificial society. They are confined to a particular district—the Black Forest, and afford us a lively view, not only of customs, manners, habits—which form the outside of life, and that may be depicted with tolerable accuracy even by a stranger, who considers them in a spirit of intelligent observation —but of the feelings, ways of thinking, modes of expression (modelled always by the former), all that constitutes the inner life of a people; and that can be faithfully rendered only by one who is thoroughly acquainted, not with peasant-life alone, but *German* peasant-life also. Simplicity is of course a leading characteristic of rural life all the world over; but then German simplicity and English simplicity are very different things: and it is in the developing of these differences—of this leading characteristic, variously and importantly modified by the agency of political, social, and natural causes, that the main value and interest of such sketches as these are to be found. The preliminary observations will serve to indicate the bearing of such of the tales as have political circumstances for their ground-work, while it affords a brief view of the character and condition of this most interesting and valuable class of the population; in whose features may be recognised some likeness, a *family* likeness, to our own national character; just a dash of our own sturdy John-Bullism, on which we are apt to pique ourselves, and which is excellent—in its place.

Like their subject, the style of these tales is marked by extreme, we might say, excessive simplicity; for occasionally it is overdone, and degenerates into childishness, a very different thing from childlikeness, for which it is sometimes mistaken. Truth to nature is an admirable quality, one which Auerbach exhibits often in a tender, touching degree, that speaks at once to the best feelings of the heart; but it may be carried to an undue extent, when it becomes merely ludicrous; as in the case of one of his village girls, whose tears (she being in trouble) 'fell fast into the wash-tub.' We set up a different standard by which to test simplicity in modern fictions and in those of the olden time; and that is offensive to our taste in the one, which but little discomposes us in the other. Had the ' goose-girl,' or ' Cherry,' or any other of the bewitched young ladies to whom Grimm introduces us, thought proper to cry into the washing-tub, or any other equally familiar household implement, she might have done so with perfect impunity, we should not have felt it to be particularly out of keeping; we should certainly have smiled at it, but not, as in this instance, as a laughable attempt at the pathetic. In drawing from nature, something more is required than a Chinese fidelity in giving every object in the landscape before us its due place on our canvas; and we notice this as an amusing *artistic* error in a tale which bears the impress of acute observation and strong feeling. We must, however, add that we deem it rather an objectionable one. It *seems* to countenance the flagrant and offensive disregard of vice indicated at page 102; and *if* indifference about such matters forms any part of German peasant life, (which we should be very sorry to believe,) we should certainly have preferred being left in

ignorance of so discreditable a fact. We wish a *lady* had not translated it. The incessant craving for fiction ensures an abundant supply, and will continue to do so; at least let us have it pure.

Miss Mitford is the English writer whom Auerbach most resembles, both as to the characteristics of his style, and the general design of these stories, which are chiefly picturesque rather than dramatic; they exhibit little or no plot, merely a transcript of nature in her most unobtrusive guise. And the pleasure which they are calculated to afford is very much of the same kind as that which is derived from a quiet saunter in green fields, with pleasant summer breezes blowing freshly around one. Like hers, this prevailing simplicity of his is varied by great vigour both of thought and expression, and considerable shrewdness of observation; while he indulges occasionally in a sort of freakish humour that reminds us of Dickens. ' The silver top ' of Hansjöeg's pipe is 'shaped like a helmet' and polished so bright, that you could see yourself in it, with the additional advantage of seeing your face *doubled and turned upside down.*'

' Sepper and Tonde' may, perhaps, afford a favourable specimen of the writer's general manner, and the peculiar skill which he possesses of making his rustics speak in character, varied as that may be by age, sex, and occupation. It is a Sunday afternoon in spring, and—

'Three lasses sat quietly under the cherry-tree, with their hands laid in their clean white aprons, and began to sing their songs. Bärbele sang the first part, while Tonele and Brigittle accompanied her by ear. The sounds were heard in a lengthened measure far over the fields, and seemed to accord with the general stillness. Every time the lasses sang, a linnet, perched in the boughs of the cherry-tree, whistled with redoubled glee; and whenever the maidens stopped at the end of a verse, or began chatting together, the linnet was in an instant silent.

'On a sudden a shot was heard: the girls drew close together in alarm, and the linnet flew from the cherry-tree. Presently the gamekeeper of Mühringen leaped over the hedge into the field, with his dog before him, and a dead heron in his hand; then he stopped, plucked a feather, and stuck it in his cap, thrust the bird into his game-bag, and slung his fowling-piece again at his back. He looked a handsome young fellow, as he came striding over the green field.

" ' Surely he might have left the poor thing alive on a Sunday,' said Tonele. ' Ay,' said Bärbele, 'gamekeepers are an unchristian sort of folks; all they are fit for is to get poor people put in prison for picking up a few sticks, and to kill dumb harmless animals. . . . . . I wouldn't marry a gamekeeper: no, not if he promised me I don't know what.'

" ' Old Ursula once told me that a gamekeeper is obliged to kill some live thing every day,' said Brigittle, the youngest of the girls.

" ' If that's the case he never need want for game,' said Bärbele, laughing, and pointing to a troop of ants on the ground.

'Meanwhile the gamekeeper drew nigh. All three girls, as if by a concerted plan, began to sing; they pretended not to notice the gamekeeper, but, from a little embarrassment, they sang in an under tone.

" ' Good day, maidens! why in such a low voice?' said the gamekeeper, stopping to speak to them.

'The three lasses fell to tittering, and stuffed their aprons into their mouths; but Bärbele quickly found her tongue again, and said, ' Thank you, Mister Gamekeeper, but we are singing only for our own amusement, and not forsooth to please other folks.'

" ' Hey-day!' cried the gamekeeper; ' the little lips cut as if they were sharpened on a whet-stone.'

" ' Sharpened, or not sharpened, whoever doesn't like it may do better if he can,' answered Bärbele pertly. Tonele jogged her elbow, and said, half aloud, ' Don't be so rude, Bärbele.'

" ' Oh, I can bear a joke,' said the gamekeeper, putting as good a face as he could on the matter.

'The girls, however, were abashed, but they took the very worst means to escape their embarrassment; they rose up, and arm-in-arm went their way homeward.

" ' May I be allowed to accompany you,' said the gamekeeper.

" ' There is the high road, and the road is broad enough,' said Bärbele.

'The gamekeeper was half inclined to leave the pert young girls to themselves; but he quickly thought how ridiculous he should appear, and felt that he ought to pay them in the same coin, but he could not. Tonele, by whose side he was walking, had so captivated him, that, for the life of him he was unable to make a single smart retort, although it was not his nature to be shy or backward; so he let the lass have her joke without answering a word.

'Tonele, in order to make some amends for their rudeness, asked the gamekeeper, ' Where are you going?'

' To Horb,' said he; ' and if you and your companions like to accompany me, I don't mind treating you all to a bottle of the best wine.'

" ' No, we must stay at home,' said Tonele; and her cheeks grew as red as scarlet.

' We like better to quench our thirst with Adam's wine,' said Bärbele; ' and that we can get, no thanks to any one.'

And so on runs the saucy dialogue; wherein the writer shows himself a perfect master of village jesting, and that species of coquettish warfare in which the rural portion of womankind are not unapt to indulge themselves, at the expense of their heavier-witted admirers; ' misusing, past the endurance of a block,' unfortunate creatures who, like the gamekeeper, have not always the spirit of ' an oak with but one green leaf upon it,' with which to answer their tormentors.

' Ivo ' is a singular tale, of which we find we have not left ourselves space to speak particularly. It exhibits the history of a mind in its progress from infancy to maturity; moulded by the various agencies to which a simple country lad may be exposed; first in his own German village, then during his school education, preparatory to the priesthood, for which he is destined, and lastly those of his early manhood (his being in love is, of course, not the least influential!) that give the finishing to his character, and lead him to abandon the church for secular employment of a more congenial and profitable kind. Of the especial design of the story we are left somewhat in doubt. The sentiments are, at times, such as might become a devout Romanist; while occasionally we have a degree of free thinking about Romish institutions and teaching, that would imply a wish to abate their influence over the minds that may have been subjected to them. The childish thoughts, feelings, and ways of Ivo, are sketched with great truth and tenderness. His innocent questions—' why our Saviour did not make the trees square, instead of round? as they would not have wanted to be sawn;' and ' how can St. Peter ever get into heaven himself, if he has to sit there and open the door for others?' are to the life. There are few who have had children much about them, who have not had such, and far more puzzling queries addressed to them; at times moving a smile, but not unfrequently a sigh, as they may have recognised in the light interrogation, forgotten as soon as uttered, the awful and abstruse questions to which their own spirits, vainly grasping at the incomprehensible, so passionately, but so hopelessly seek an answer; speculations that perplex the understanding and try the faith of the *man*, springing up spontaneously in the mind (all unconscious of their fearful nature), and hovering on the guileless lip of childhood!

It would be unpardonable to pass over Absalom's illustrations. They are singularly pleasing, thoroughly characteristic, and essentially German.

With Auerbach we are certainly not so much captivated as is his translator and countrywoman: perhaps the reason may be found in our harder English head—and heart! Nevertheless, our thanks are her due for some of the pleasing pictures with which she has made us acquainted. But especially do we feel indebted to the translator of Grimm's collection, for rendering us a service which none can fail of estimating, that of making us feel young again! We have of late imported much bad philosophy and worse theology from Germany: good fairy-tales are, in our opinion, infinitely preferable, and we shall be happy, for the future, to receive them instead.

65. ATHENAEUM, 21 (1848), 238-239. M/H No. 4456.

The Peasant and his Landlord. By the Baroness Knörring. Translated by Mary Howitt. 2 vols. Bentley.

IT is to be hoped that the English novelists of the Victorian era are not monopolists: otherwise, irritating indeed must be their present position. "*Those* foreigners" have, beyond all doubt, stormed our circulating libraries: and to make matters worse, too, in English uniforms. What with Amber Witches, Countess Idas and Countess Faustinas, President's Daughters, Wandering Jews ('The Seven Cardinal Sins' of Sue, we doubt not, being already apportioned out among as many paraphrasers), Roses of Tistelön, Black Foresters, Alsatians, Flemings "shown up" by Conscience — orthodox and heterodox "Betrotheds" after Manzoni, Mosaic-Masters of Venice and Mauprats,—what with all these and scores beside,—we repeat that the May Fair loves of Lord William and Lady Adela, or the old English tales of tilt and tournament; the trials of Jockey and Jenny, and the miseries of the poor Irish, bid fair to be elbowed out of our world of novel-devourers. Mrs. Partington herself could not stop the tide; nor Mr. James barricado it out by piling up all the romances which he has written and means yet to write. Were Messrs. Hookham, Andrews, Ebers, &c. &c. &c. bribed to keep every librarian his own Capt. Warner to blow the Bremer back to Sweden and drive the Dumas within the lines of the fortifications of Paris, we see not how May Fair is to be cleared of the invasion nor our country-houses and watering-places given over again to the absolute sway of native fiction. There are traitors among us; and no busier nor more officious opener of the gates to "our enemies" than Mrs. Howitt. She has successively and successfully, too, let in Miss Bremer, Hans Christian Andersen, and Madame Von Paalzow:—and is here again, anxious that we should receive another outlandish gentlewoman to the prejudice of our Gores and Trollopes,—begging us, in an earnest preface, to "do the civil thing" by the Baroness Knörring.

To this we can have no objection whatever —it being premised that the foreign ladies and gentlemen are to be as interesting as the *Dumons* and *Daphnes* whom they displace. Now, the lady for whom welcome is here bespoken deserves it on the score of power. 'The Peasant and his Landlord' is as touching and forcible a drama of common life as most that we have followed to their close. But the remark which we found it necessary to apply to the Alsatian Tales by Weill [*ante*, p. 58] applies also to the invention here. This is not agreeable: a fact proved by the difficulty of telling the story in a small compass without its becoming repulsive. That a peasant should be tricked into believing it necessary for him to marry a servant woman whom his landlord is anxious to get rid of, —that he should discover, too late, the shameful and shameless way in which he has been used as a screen and his honesty imposed upon—these and the steady purpose of vengeance which arises in his mind, are occurrences known to be dismally frequent; and nowhere more so than in those simple states of society which the lovers of class-distinctions are apt to represent as Arcadian — showing on the one side all pure, paternal care, on the other child-like and trusting dependence. But the tissue woven on such a ground *cannot* be a lovely one. The original profligacy must never for a moment be lost sight of; else the virtue of a high and tender-hearted man like Gunnar loses its preciousness, and we cease to feel the progressive torment and temptation which urge on the catastrophe. Let us, however, distinguish. This tale is not written to serve any questionable purpose by prurient description: it is only a picture of events which are too painfully unpleasing for any beauty of individual character or attitude to redeem so far as our taste is concerned.

It is not very easy to select one from among the pictures of life in West Gothland which this tale contains. But the following, which accompanies the portraiture of 'The Village Preacher,' is one of the newest. It has, also, the recommendations of certain dry humour in its manner and quiet wisdom in its moral which make it useful as well as attractive.—

"All the young—and these always constitute the soul of every human mass—had so high an opinion of their pastor, put so much faith and trust in him, that he led them where he would, which was best seen when the so-called 'Preaching Epidemic' approached even this congregation, for there it was upset; not by stern prohibition and the civil power, but by intellectual indifference and coldness to all similar excess unproductive of advantage. Not a single member of the whole congregation fell of himself into this preaching sickness, the cause of which is still unexplained and involved in a wonderful darkness. A few wandering peasant girls only, of doubtful character, were attacked by it, and, singularly enough, found out just one village on the boundary of this parish, where drunkenness and looseness of morals had been ever the most difficult to uproot; and here they settled themselves down amongst an ill-informed people, and began their convulsive falls and preachings, which were witnessed only with a certain degree of curiosity, and found no imitators. The rector at first let the affair take its own course; did not deny his own house-servants to go occasionally to hear 'preaching-girls;' but one evening he presented himself suddenly and unexpectedly amongst a little observant audience, who were listening to one of these preaching peasant maidens. The girl came quite to a stand when she perceived him enter, but he urged her to proceed, which she eventually did, but with great embarrassment, having nothing at all to say but what she had uttered many times before, namely, broken, short, and mutilated exclamations out of the Sacred Writings, as 'Repent ye,'—'make yourselves ready,' —'turn ye.' She called on them to repent, and declared that if her hearers did not do this they would be punished with the most terrible punishments that could be conceived; spoke always of thousands of small and great devils, which she, with an actually astonishing invention, knew how to place and introduce where they certainly had never been before. Thus had she, on another occasion, before the rector heard her, amongst other things, spoken of the village maypole, which, since the primeval times, had its place in the most open part of the village, was furnished with a weathercock, and was in this manner of positive use as a weather-prophet the whole year round, till the Midsummer was again at hand, when the maypole was adorned by the youth of the village and neighbourhood with leaves and flowers and blown eggs, and for the time afforded a great and truly innocent pleasure for the old, and still more for the young. But this poor innocent maypole the preacheress denounced to the lowest root, and into the deepest pit of perdition, declaring that the weathercock only pointed to devils, and that the prementioned empty eggs were altogether choke full of small devils, and that the like sat in the dry leaves and the blown and broken-off flower garlands, and rained down, like a thunder-rain, upon all those who went under the pole. She had, moreover, before the pastor heard her, apostrophized with great disgust, an old disbanded hussar, who was at a loss how to do himself a service except by here and there playing a lively tune to the dance of the young people in the country, upon an old and cracked fiddle, and thereby winning a trifle for the support of himself and children. Him, all imaginable musical places of amusement, and the poor innocent fiddle, she had doomed indiscriminately as the devil's invention and delight, and declared that the arch-fiend would take both player and dancer; that within the fiddle was to be found a whole play-place of mere imps, who there amused themselves, and crept in and out through the sound-hole, scarcely visible to the preacher herself, totally invisible to all her sinful hearers, who all were slaves of sin, and both lived and died, went, stood, lay, and danced, in utter sin, over head and ears. In like manner did she condemn, in a high degree, all crooked combs, and declared that the devil would therewith comb all those who wore such when they came into hell. The consequence of this attack on the maypole, the fiddler, and the crooked combs, had been, that the villagers had sold the maypole to another village for three quarts of brandy; and that the old hussar broke his fiddle—but immediately resolved, in all secresy, to glue it together again; whilst all the village girls went for a little while with their hair carelessly hanging about their ears, having burnt their crooked combs; but that a carpenter soon after prepared dozens of new ones, of the like pattern, made of stained wood, as those were which were burnt. The first act of this drama was already played out some time before the rector became the hearer of this peasant girl. She now perspired dreadfully, was obviously oppressed by her spiritual hearer, and repeated the same thing many times; and when the ideas were altogether exhausted, she took a long psalm, and made her audience sing it from beginning to end, when she began once more to repeat the very same words she had used previously to the psalm. When she had done, she withdrew; and now the rector stepped forward, and asked the assembly if they had heard anything essentially new from the preaching girl?—if he had not told them the very same things before, though in a different order of arrangement?—whether they were dissatisfied with his ministry?—whether he neglected his duty, or ill fulfilled his mission? &c.; and at every query all answered in a breath,—'No! Heaven forbid! far from it! God only grant that we may be able to live as we are taught by our highly respected pastor,' and the like; and on that an old peasant stood forward and declared, on behalf of himself and fellows, 'that the congregation had such ample instruction from their excellent minister, that they had no need to listen to any revival sermons, whether from girls or ranters, but believed they would always be pious enough were they only able to practise all that their venerable rector taught them, both in church on Sundays and on many other occasions, whilst he, both in life and everything else, served to every one as a perfect pattern and reproof.' All, in one breath, acquiesced in this; and, in their enthusiasm for their pastor, the assembled ploughmen insisted that he and no one else should preach to them a little while."

'The Peasant and his Landlord' is a novel rather of scenes and passions than of character. One figure, however, must be singled out as excellent. We mean Mother Ingrid,—who approaches in her homely truth and simple pathos to some of the peasant-mothers of Scott's novels. Elin, the heroine, is too delicate and high-flown for reality. Lena, the shrew, and Olle, the mocking fiend, are touched with greater nature and vivacity,—but the position of both is hateful. The Squire's sister, Ma'msell Sara, is another of those active, charitable, elderly women whom the North seems to produce in such abundance; though in point of character she does not equal *ma chere mère*, nor excellent Miss Rönnquist, nor The Provost's Lady, of the Bremer novels.—To conclude, we should be glad to hear more of the Baroness Knörring,—trusting that the next novel of hers which we take in hand may be on some more cheerful argument.

A Book of Ballads from the German. By Percy Boyd, Esq. Dublin, M'Glashan.

IF a selection of pieces by the best authors, handsomely printed, and decorated with not ungraceful designs, were enough to recommend a volume of lyrical translations, the book now before us might fairly be praised. It has all these merits. But the work itself, although prettily presented, is deficient in those qualities which, after all, give the only real value to such a collection. The poems of which it consists can hardly indeed be termed translations. They are far from being either accurate versions or happy paraphrases of the originals; and this defect is not compensated by the quality of the work viewed merely as English poetry. The versification is careless and often harsh,—and, without any reference to the originals, would not prove the writer a proficient in the poetical use of the language into which he has undertaken to render them.

It is, indeed, no easy task to turn lyrics, of even moderate pretensions to elegance or melody, from one language into another. To succeed in it at all, these conditions, at least, are indispensable :—there must be a complete understanding of the original, a quick sense of its peculiar harmony, and the feeling of those refinements, as well in expression as in thought, which are the very life of this delicate class of composition. There should, besides these requisites, be a perfect command as well of the metrical forms of the new vehicle in which the meaning and music of the original are to be represented as of its poetical resources, to enable the translator where differences of idiom forbid an absolutely literal conversion to choose the best equivalent, and to render both the spirit and manner of the foreign model as well as that difference will permit. On inspecting this ' Book of Ballads,' we cannot report in favour of Mr. Boyd's aptitude for so difficult a task in either respect. He does not excel as a writer of English verses; and he gives few signs of having caught the spirit of the German originals, — frequently disregarding their most essential features,—and appearing at times not to have thoroughly understood their meaning. He has not taken much pains to copy the form of the lyrics he selects; but often paraphrases them in a metre different from that of the originals,—a proceeding fatal to lyrical above all other kinds of translation. So much of the charm of any perfect song is inseparable from the music of its rhythm, that half of its peculiar character must vanish in the arbitrary change to a different mode. In this respect, Mr. Boyd has allowed himself great licence. In only one of the pieces of his collection which we have compared with the German has he preserved the true measure—in many he departs from it so widely that not a trace of the peculiar tone of the original will be found in his version—and, on the whole, we must say that his compositions will give no idea whatever, to merely British readers, of either the substance, the manner, or even the bare meaning of the German poems which he here presents to them. We cannot allow those to be translations, in any admissible sense of the term, that have converted some choice specimens of the best lyrists of Germany into very second-rate English verses.

Of their quality as such, readers of the book can judge for themselves. We shall confine ourselves to the quotation of a few instances of the manner in which Mr. Boyd treats the original text of pieces to which the most studious care would barely suffice to render due justice. The selection, we may affirm, is not an invidious one, as the same process would produce a similar result in any part of the volume.

On looking over its titles merely, we find the contents set down in a way that might suggest doubts as to the close intimacy of Mr. Boyd with this branch of German literature. The names of well-known authors are attached to some of the pieces chosen—others, by the same or equally familiar names, are left without this description, in a manner that can hardly be supposed accidental. One is tempted at first sight to ask how it happens that, while several pieces by Goethe, Uhland, Freiligrath, &c. are ascribed to their authors, others, not less authentic, should be presented as if anonymous: —*e. g.* Goethe's ' King of Thule' (here called ' The King with the Cup'), Uhland's ' Hostess's Daughter,' Freiligrath's ' Freedom and Right,' Zedlitz's ' Midnight Review,' &c.? It looks as if these poems had been taken from some anthology or album, where they may have stood without the author's name, by one who had not sufficient acquaintance with the lyric writers to assign each to its proper owner. If not, how does it happen that while some are affiliated others are left as if the writer was unknown?

The preface is opened by the author with an account, in questionable taste, of an interview with a literary lady at Heidelberg,—and in the compliment which he makes her pay to his skill in translating there is introduced a single word meant to be German, which, however, it is not. This *may*, indeed, have been a printer's error: but such circumstances, trifling as they may be, are rather apt to produce at the outset an impression as to Mr. Boyd's qualifications for his task that is confirmed by further examination of the manner in which he has executed it.—Of this manner we shall give a very few specimens,—which could easily have been multiplied. It will suffice to take, from some of the principal authors, a verse here and there,—literally the first that came to hand,—and, by comparing Mr. Boyd's version with a more literal rendering of the text, to show how he treats his author's meaning and manner. The translations that we give here are not offered with the least pretension to more than a tolerably close adherence to the poet's text and a preservation of the metre.

In Körner's ' Three Stars' Mr. Boyd has kept the proper measure; but how he preserves the substance may be seen in a single verse. We take the second, running thus :—

> In the voice of the song of the poet
> Lives a true and affectionate heart;
> Song gives to all joy a new lustre;
> Song takes from all sorrow its smart.

In the ' Book of Ballads,' the intention and the antithesis of the stanza are alike neglected :—

> For there lies in the voice of sweet singing
> A spell that can banish all pain ;
> And the joys of the past seem reviving
> In our hearts with its glad notes again.

We next turn to the opening stanza of Freiligrath's ' Freedom and Right,'—which begins pretty nearly to this effect, and in this measure :—

> O think not henceforth with the dead she'll lie hidden;
> O think not henceforth she'll forsake us outright ;
> Tho' to resolute speakers free words are forbidden,
> And they get no justice who scorn to indict ;
> No, no ! though the true ones to exile are wending,
> Though others, worn out by oppression ne'er ending,
> Have lanced their own veins in the dungeons they're pent in,—
> Yet Freedom lives ever, and with her the right !
>   With Freedom lives Right !

Mr. Boyd's paraphrase of the stanza preserves scarcely a third of its substance; and he effaces its decided character to put in its place not a very distinct one of his own.—

> O think not she sleepeth with those who have perished,
> In dungeons unnumbered, *by Tyranny's record* ;
> *In the hearts of the free shall her dear name be cherished,*
> Though their lips are forbidden to utter the word.
> Yes ! though lone exiles *by mountain and valley*
> They wander *uncheered by lost liberty's light,*
> There's a *pulse* in the heart of the freeman to *rally,*
> While Freedom still liveth, and with her the right,
>   For Freedom and Right !

Uhland fares no better. His ballad, ' The Hostess's Daughter,' derives its essential tone from an old-world form in which the poet has chosen to present a touching expression of three different degrees of love. The measure of the original is that peculiar two-line stanza common to many of the antique popular lays of Teutonic and other German races; and its manner is purposely kept by the Suabian poet in harmony with those brief and rugged originals. We need only copy a few of the opening lines to give an idea of the style.—

> There went three youngsters across the Rhine,
> And yonder they entered the widow's inn.

Dame! have ye good wine and ale? they said,
And where is your daughter, that fair young maid?

My ale and my wine are cool and clear,
My fair young daughter lies dead on her bier!

And when they went into the room, behold,
In her black coffin the maid lay cold, &c. &c.

Would any one imagine that the following lines were presented as the version of a ballad of this very marked character?—

O'er Heidelberg's old castle
    The morning sunbeams shine,
As journey forth three students*
    Across the silver Rhine.

And they came to a small hostel,
    Where in the time of old,
Rich wine of Asmanshauser
    The good Frau Wirthin sold.

"We know the juice is famous
    Which from the grape is press'd;
Come, then, a flagon give us,
    Frau Wirthin, of thy best."

High in the mantling brimmer
    The rich wine sparkles red;
But she, whose eye was brighter,
    My gentle child, is dead.

Then forth into the chamber,
    They took their mournful way;
Where, like a fair flower withered,
    Frau Wirthin's daughter lay, &c.

Such an insipid piece of prettiness can be truly called only a ballad *from* the German, inasmuch as it is as far as possible from anything to be found *in* the German ballad.

Having none of the better English versions of Schiller's 'Thekla, a Spirit Voice,' at hand, we must beg indulgence for making our own rude copy of the first two stanzas,—in which the elegiac cadence in trochees, and the main substance of the text are, at least, preserved,—to show how Mr. Boyd departs from the one, and overlooks the main features of the other, in one of the choicest gems of German song.—

Where I am, and whither then I wended,
    When my fleeting shade before thee moved?—
Had I not completed all, and ended?—
    Had I not already lived and loved?

Ask'st thou for the nightingales, that trilling,
    Full of soul, their fond melodious lay,
In the days of spring thy heart were thrilling?—
    Only while they still could love—were they!

Which Mr. Boyd thus renders:—

Where am I? 'whither have I wended
    My way? and from thee have I flown?
Is not *my pulse of being ended*,
    And *life and love for ever gone*?

Ask where the nightingales have vanish'd,
    To *what fair realm, far off, above*,
Who *thrill'd in spring, the soul of music*
    Whose very breath of life was love.

This is absolutely all that is given in exchange for the original stanzas, the purport of which may be seen in our rough version. Measure, tone, meaning,—all, in short, that renders the piece what it peculiarly is,—are passed over in this translation; while it will be felt that the verses offered in stead of Schiller's are themselves of no very choice beauty or distinct meaning.†

After such a specimen as this we might pause; having, we think, sufficiently justified the doubt expressed of Mr. Boyd's vocation as a translator of German lyrics. But he has committed something more strange than this on his approach to the highest name in his collection; by turning a ballad of Goethe's in such a fashion as to render it apparent that he has in general shown a want of feeling for the tone of his originals and a licentious treatment of their text. He has in this instance at least misunderstood the bare meaning of the piece,—and that, too, in a way implying no very profound knowledge of the Ger-

man.—The poem that has given rise to this curious display is one of the happiest *pièces d'occasion* known in that language; composed, if we recollect rightly, for the wedding feast of one of the Ducal family of Weimar,—in which an old tradition of one of his ancestors is gracefully carolled forth in the tone of a wandering minstrel: and the close of the old fairy legend is turned in the prettiest fashion imaginable into a symbol of the modern event which it is produced to celebrate. Mr. Boyd does not seem to have had the slightest notion that such was the character of the piece; and presents it, with an entire confusion of the meaning of the text, as if the poet were relating, in the presence of the principal figure of the tale, events that had happened to that personage himself. He introduces the wedding as if it were something independent of the object of the song:—a mere affair to be casually mentioned as having just happened to the *grandson* (so he translates *Enkel*) of the Count to whom he is singing; and he calls this *Wedding Song* 'A Lay of Christmas!'* Such a blunder as this, we apprehend, could hardly have been made by any one sufficiently conversant with the German to discern the true literal meaning of the piece. We need only give one stanza, as it stands in the original, to show the nature of this curious travesty.
'The Wedding Minstrel' thus begins:—

We'll willingly sing of the Count, sirs! and say
    How he *once* was this palace's owner,
Where we meet to drink joy to the wedding, to-day,
    Of *that worthy's descendant*, His Honour.
Now when that good knight from the holy Crusade,
Where long he had fought and great valour displayed,
Came back, and, dismounting, his dwelling surveyed,
    There he found, safe enough, the old castle,
    But within, not a thing nor a vassal!

For which we are offered this opening of 'A Lay of Christmas:'—

We cheerfully sing and *inscribe* our glad lay
    To the *lord of the castle here seated*,
Whose grandson espoused a fair lady to-day,
    And the bridal guests sumptuously *fêted*.
In *the late Holy Wars he* won honour and fame,
By splendid achievements emblazoned his name,
Yet beheld, when adown from his charger he came
    To his mansion, he found it as open as day,
    His property vanished, his servants away!

In the concluding verse, the violence done to the sense of the text in consequence of this mistake at the outset is, if possible, still ruder. But we need not go further. What has already been shown will suffice to prove that Mr. Boyd is not peculiarly well fitted for public appearance as an interpreter of German poetry to English readers:—and he may be apprised that "its mines," which, he says, he hopes to open to their research, have already been not quite so "partially explored" as to afford many chances of success or approbation to such a treatment of some of its best known treasures as this volume of his exhibits. In his preface, indeed, Mr. Boyd lays it down as his opinion that a certain freedom of treatment is necessary to preserve the spirit of poetry translated from a foreign language. Without entering on the discussion of this system of translation, it will be apparent that such liberties as he has taken in practice cannot be justified on any principle whatever; and it will scarcely be concluded from his example that the method he recommends—of closing the pages of his author, and rendering the text from memory—is favourable to the reproduction of either the substantive matter or the more evanescent graces of foreign poetry.

---

* *Bürschen.* This word Mr. Boyd is quite mistaken in rendering *students* here. The university jargon that so applies the word has no place whatever in any poetical style, —least of all in one of this peculiar antique cast.

† It is scarcely necessary to observe that the traits in these opening stanzas which his version effaces are really the key-notes of the whole piece. *Hatte ich nicht geliebt und gelebt?* in the first, expressly recals the burden of Thekla's earlier strain, 'The Maid's Lament'; while the fourth line of the second strophe, left out altogether by Mr. Boyd, contains the answer for the sake of which it is known this lovely poem was written.

ART. VI.—*Vorlesungen über die Geschichte der deutschen National-Literatur, von Dr. A. F. C. Vilmar, Director des kurfürstlichen Gymnasimus zu Marburg. Zweite mit Anmerkungen und rinem Register Vernehte Auflage.* (Lectures on the History of German National Literature, by Dr. A. F. C. Vilmar, Director of the electoral Gymnasium at Marburg. Second edition, enlarged, with Notes and Index.)

THERE are men to whom the sight of a proof sheet is hardly less necessary to enjoyment, than is the sight of his glass to the man accustomed to such companionship. The fascination in the former case often produces a habit not at all less rooted than in the latter. With such men, thought is valuable only as it may be made to present itself upon paper. To live is good, only as it gives a man the power and the space to write. The chief end of the universe is, that there is an objectivity in it about which a man may work out sentences and paragraphs. The past is worth remembering, because it is a something that may be described — something on which man may speculate — a something about which books may be made. History is made for the historian, not the historian for history. Science is made for the author of treatises, not the author of treatises for science. Mohammed was made for Gibbon—the heavens for La Place. Deep and resistless in some men is this love of offspring—of self-reflection in the shape of authorship. Achievement in this form is to them what the gift of speech is to others; both are processes by which men communicate thought and emotion, and the cessation of either would be to the respective parties like the cessation of existence.

In this busy money-getting country of ours, the minds which come to such extent under the sway of this feeling form a comparatively limited class. Not so with our German neighbours.

Judging from appearances, one is sometimes tempted to regard these neighbours as a nation of book-makers. It would almost seem as if the human race had attained to such a state of harmony among themselves, as to have completed a grand division of labour scheme, assigning to the Germans, as their one vocation, the making of books. What less can we suspect in the case of a nation which is said to furnish products of this sort at the rate of ten millions a year? Whether done by steam or by any other power, something like this amount of production is realized, and surely so far as quantity is concerned, the world itself can hardly need anything more. But what must be the passion for production when it takes place to this extent, though the demand to be met, in place of being that of the world, is confined almost entirely to a people speaking one language, and occupying a comparatively small section in one quarter of the world? How mighty must be the impulse in this extraordinary people, which thus promises to augment the number of writers until only a minority shall remain to be described as being merely readers?

For this singular conveyance of so much power into one channel there must be a cause, and, as philosophers say, a cause equal to the effect. Man is an onward creature. Shut him out from one course, and, like the impeded waters, he will force his way into another. Narrow his impulses to one groove, and the rush there will be strong and perilous. It has been thus with Germany. The sword has been consigned to its scabbard for nearly a generation past, but the functions of the state have been everywhere retained as an appendage to the crown. The public spirit called forth by war, has not been succeeded by the public spirit which gives health and progress in times of peace. Political liberty has not been the fruit of military triumphs. The freedom of the professor's chair, and the comparative freedom of the press, have been the only exceptions to a condition of affairs tending to dwarf the nation to a state of passiveness and childhood in respect to nearly everything social. Political feeling, denied all outlet through the forms of a free constitution, has created outlets elsewhere. Religious liberty, proscribed by law, has taken a terrible revenge by indirect means. Action being prohibited, speculation has come into its place. It was very much thus with the old schoolmen. The church without enjoined quiescence on those sturdy thinkers, but the spirit within them could not rest. It was bad enough to doom them to inaction—too bad to prohibit the exercise of thought. The church might chain them to orthodoxy, but it could not prevent them enjoying some degree of freedom in doing real or pretended battle against heresy. If they dared not speculate with any licence themselves, it was something that, in the conduct of an argument, they could freely personate those who did; and often, very often, the demon raised in the shape of an objection, was such as not to be laid by the charm of the reasoning paraded in opposition to it. Thus, the preachers of orthodoxy often became virtually the preachers of something very different. In this manner will nature ever avenge herself. The wise are taken in their own craftiness. To sin against the rights of human intelligence treasures up wrath against the day of wrath. Excess naturally generates excess—superstition is parent to atheism, despotism to anarchy.

Thus has it been in great part in Germany. The Germans are prolific as authors, because doomed to barrenness in so much beside; and if their authorship has often been adverse to liberty and religion, this has happened because the training which rational liberty might have secured to them has been denied them, and because religion itself has too often come before them as a tyranny, more than as a religion. It has not been good for the national mind—for its well-balanced health, that so much power should be thrust away from the practical, and made to converge on the speculative. If its products in other things had been of greater extent, its products in the form of books would have been of better quality. It would have aimed at less in this form, but it would have accomplished more. Its abstractions would have been mellowed by experience, its idealism would have been less divorced from the actual. It would, as the consequence, have exhibited a more robust, a more equally developed intelligence and feeling, and would have learnt to look with a manly contempt on a multitude of conceits which it now lauds as the proofs of genius—as passports to a wonderful immortality.

But this literary productiveness in his country has not sufficed to deter Dr. Vilmar from becoming the author of a book. Much has been written in Germany on German literature, but our author has judged that there was still room for one other mode of treating this large and interesting theme, and his countrymen have confirmed his decision in this respect by the attention they have given to this fruit of his labour. This volume consists of lectures delivered, as the author states in his preface, to an auditory of 'educated men and women,' in the town of Marburg, during the winter of 1843-44. The lectures are sufficient in bulk to furnish matter for two respectable English octavos, and though described by the author as falling far below an adequate exhibition of his subject, they are of sufficient fulness to satisfy the ordinary English reader; while in respect to learning, profound thought, critical skill, the graces of style, and the glow of feeling and imagination, they possess a charm which has secured to the author a celebrity rarely obtained in Germany by a first publication. In the present article we shall submit to our readers some account of the contents of these seven hundred closely printed pages, together with translations of such portions of the work as may enable them to judge for themselves as to the correctness of our critical estimate. The following passage may be taken as the author's explanation of his purpose:—

'The history of German literature, which these pages will set forth, cannot embrace what is usually termed German literature in its widest compass. Even with the most hasty sketches, and the lightest strokes, it cannot undertake to describe the entire literary produce of our people, which throughout, in common with other nations, has had its share in all the sciences relating to it. The subject of these discourses will be the province of German *national* literature, those literary works of our nation which reflect in form and substance its own peculiar mode of thought, sentiments, and manners; which represent its own life and spirit; these alone as constituting the German national literature (or German literature in a more limited sense), will be considered in their rise, nature, consequences, and influence on one another. As poetry has been the most ancient and characteristic language of all nations, so has it been with the Germans, for in it the national character has been most firmly and perfectly stamped in body, soul, and spirit; the poetic national literature of our people will, therefore, be the principal subject of discourse.

'But I shall not be able to present this national literature to the eye of my reader in the form of elaborate descriptions, so much as in slight sketches, which will often be little more than indicative of the subject. Still it would promise but little to the just expectations of the reader, and the dignity of the subject before us, did I not endeavour to unite these sketches into one general, correct, and expressive picture of the connexion in which these individual literary appearances stand to one another, and of the internal necessity through which the one calls forth and limits the other. I must, therefore, beg the reader to accompany me, not merely back to the olden times, but even to the most ancient periods of our history, because it is only in this way that the necessary connexion of literary productions can be made clear—only by a retrospect of the old can the new be thoroughly understood, and submitted to a riper and more penetrating judgment.'

It is in the following terms that Dr. Vilmar speaks of the two classic periods assigned by him to the literature of Germany:—

'Our literature presents a phenomena shared by that of no other nation in the world. It has twice reached the highest bloom of its perfection; twice has it beamed forth in the splendour of a cheerful, fresh, and powerful youth—in a word, it has had two classical periods, while other nations have had but one; twice has it stood the highest of the time, and, in full consciousness of rich vital powers, has reflected, with simple fidelity and generous truth, our inward and outward life in poetic works of art; twice has the purest and noblest life of our nation been poured forth in forms equally pure and noble, natural, and, therefore, perfect. The one of these brilliant periods, which in freshness and fulness of form, in worth and in richness of subject, by no means yields to that which we have lived to see, but in many respects even surpasses it, lies in a region apparently distant and unknown, and falsely regarded as desolate. Perhaps the proper pride in a national pre-eminence, not even shared by the Greeks to its full extent, may not only justify, but even demand a careful consideration of it, and a somewhat more searching treatment of this first bright period of our literary existence. Whose independence has not often been wounded by ignorant persons, who, although acknowledging our Klopstock, Lessing, Schiller, and Göethe, still tell us that we have become what we are only through Voltaire, Corneille, and Racine, Shakespeare, Tasso, and Ariosto; that we have reached our present literary position slowly, and as idle stragglers, long after other nations had arrived at their full growth, urged onward only by the goad of the taskmaster? But when it is shown that our brightest, freshest youth, lay far behind the blooming time of other nations—that long, not only before Tasso and Ariosto, but also before Dante and Petrarch, we had our Walter von du Vogelweide, Wolfram von Eschenbach, our 'Gudrun' and our 'Lay of the Nibelungen'—poems and poets with which foreigners have scarcely anything to compare, and certainly nothing in regard to epic poems—the Greeks alone had an 'Iliad,' and we alone a 'Lay of the Nibelungen;—when it is thus seen that we are not the last, but the first, or rather the first and the last, that, like the eagle and the phœnix, we rise out of the ashes renewed with fresh life—we will not, contrary to the German manner, boast of our performances, but will recognise with high, fervent, and, therefore, silent joy, our rich gifts and distinguished position among the nations of the earth, and unite as the greatest glory of life, the noblest pride and firmest independence, the most simple modesty and silent humility.'

Subsequently these two characteristic stages in German literature are more distinctly marked—

'When our nation first appears in the history of the mental development of man, we see it seized in every branch with a vehement excitement, with a wild passion for wandering, and rude eagerness for battle; tribe on tribe, race on race, press on towards the south and west, so that our primitive tribes threaten to become divided, and to consume themselves in their unbridled rage for war. Then from the south and west, whither the innumerable hordes forced their way, there arose a mighty voice proclaiming aloud the peace of God the Lord, over the restless multitudes, far into the north and east; and it became still in the forests and on the heaths, and the host gave reverent ear to the words of the peace of God. At the cross-ways of the high roads the cross was planted, and the wandering armies halted and raised cottages, and castles, and towers at their foot. The song of the gods of Wuotan, Donar, and of Ziu, were silent; but the heroic songs, the songs of the deeds of their tribes, their kings and dukes, still continued, and mingled with those of the believers, who sang the praises of God the Lord, and of him who was crucified. Former wildness gave way to Christian manners and Christian gentleness; but bravery and fidelity, generosity and gratitude, chastity and family affection, the oldest and most genuine traits of German character, remained undiminished and unbroken. Around the foot of the cross, from that 'living wood,' (as the old Catholic song in this respect, at least, so aptly says,) they derived fresh nourishment, still increasing in strength and splendour. In Christianity, there was nothing strange, nothing to which the Germans were naturally averse; on the contrary, the German character received through it only the perfection of itself; in the church of Christ it became elevated, spiritualized, and sanctified; and if we speak of the struggle of the German nature and manners, at its first introduction, it can only be as of a strife of love. The Apostolic representation of the church as the Bride of the Lord, found its truest counterpart in the German church. Thus, when the union of the German and Christian spirits was completed, this character of love, tenderness, and fervour, which marks in a high degree the poetry of our first classic period—may almost be looked upon as a barrier preventing the present age, so deficient in affection, from fully or rightly understanding these poems, intelligible only to hearts of the same mould, at once wholly German and wholly Christian.

'It was under essentially different circumstances that the second classic period of our literature arose, commencing with the middle of the fifteenth century, and reaching to the eighteenth. This, however, was not, as before, a strife of love, but a war of life and death. During the sixteenth, and still more, in the seventeenth century, our national life and our peculiar character as Germans were assailed; in the eighteenth, Christian independence, and the worth and dignity of the Christian church, were also, for a time, not only conquered, but apparently annihilated. Only after long struggles and hot battles, were we able to recognise ourselves as the masters of the opposing element, and of the rich booty secured from the desolating war of mind. Our second classic period, therefore, bears with it a something specially prepared for war. The yielding affection of the former period is no longer there. In vain we seek for the friendliness and cordiality of the Minnesingers, or the fidelity unto death of the servant towards his master, sung in the heart-stirring songs of our epic poems. Criticism is the constant companion—nay, more, it is the mother and nurse of the greater part of our modern classical literature. The youthful, often touching embarrassment and naïveté of those olden times has been exchanged for the adroitness and intellect of the world. That glance, which was then limited to house and court, the dark forest and green mountain ridges, which surrounded the peaceful towns, now roves freely, far beyond the boundary of the ancestral province, beyond the fatherland, into the most distant regions of the earth, to wander on the shores of China and India, to find equal pleasure in the desolate wastes of the polar sea, or the glowing deserts of Africa.'

Concerning the theology of this extract we say nothing, but during the most ancient period of the national literature of Germany, the period which exhibits the struggle between its heathenism and Christianity, the translation of the Scriptures into the language of the people forms a grand literary landmark :—

'Solitary, and separated by at least three hundred years, from other and later literary productions—the most ancient monument of our literature stands like a giant castle, passed in reverential fear by the dwarf races of succeeding centuries: the translation of the Bible by the Gothic Bishop Ulfilas. This great and memorable work can here meet only with a passing mention, as we treat not of the history of the German language, but of literary works, and the history of German poetry. To pass it, however, entirely by, would be a dishonour to the literature of Germany. Still our remarks must be limited. In our days, an entirely new science, the latest and most perfect, has been raised upon this work—the science of the German language. The historical grammar, and a knowledge of the Gothic language, is a great assistance to the thorough understanding, not only of the old high German, but also of the middle high German poems.

'Ulfilas, a bishop of the Visigoths, died in the year 388, aged 70 years, a point ascertained within the last three years, through one of those happy literary discoveries in which our times abound. A zealous and faithful teacher of his people, even in the grave highly reverenced and prized by his scholars, he crowned his work of Christian instruction among the Goths, which he had pursued thirty-three years, with his translation of the Bible into their language, excepting only the four books of Kings, by which he feared to inflame the warlike spirit of his people. It is not improbable that he invented an alphabet for it, partly old German and partly borrowed from the Greeks. For centuries, this work was held in the highest veneration by the Visigoths, who passed onward into Spain and Italy, and who in the ninth century, still understood its language. Since then, its very existence became doubtful, and only some Greek ecclesiastical writers asserted that an Ulfilas once lived, and that a translation of the Scriptures by him was still extant. Six hundred years had passed, and a vague rumour was spread, towards the end of the sixteenth century, by a geometrician named Arnold Mercator, from Belgium, in the service of the Hessian landgrave, William the Fourth, that one of the parchment-books in the monastery of Werden contained a very old German translation of the four Evangelists. As this astonishing manuscript gradually became known, it reached Prague, and, after the conquest of that town by Count Konigsmark, in 1648, it passed into Sweden, where it is still preserved at Upsal as one of our most valuable literary treasures. The parchment is dyed purple, the letters marked with silver, and through the generosity of Marshal Lagardie, a member of the Swedish family Lagardie, lately become extinct, the whole was bound in massive silver. Two hundred and fifty years later, in 1815, the epistles of the Apostle Paul, in the translation of Ulfilas, were also discovered among the treasures of the Lombardian Convent, at Bobbio, by the present Cardinal Mai and Count Castiglioni. But a few lines remain of the translation of the Old Testament. The language, which speaks to us from these venerable remains of our German antiquity, is the mother of our present high German; and in purity and euphony of the vowels, in strict grammatical construction, in richness of form, variety of accent, accuracy of expression, and more especially in dignity and force, far surpasses her daughter, even though she may not boast of the same fluency of versification. It was as a resurrection from the dead, when this work awoke from its slumber of more than a thousand years, and spoke in a new and wonderful tongue to its grandchildren; first opening to them the real and inward understanding of their own language, raising a new and active life, as we have before said—an entirely new science. In fact, the Gothic language, the most perfect one of our ancestors, though on a first appearance mysterious, yet presently astonishingly clear—strange, and yet at once domestic and familiar—seemingly rugged, harsh, and repelling, nevertheless insinuates itself into our inmost and purest feelings—a something unusually exciting, and one might almost say, heart-stirring —an effect which it has never failed to produce in those who will dedicate themselves to it. After many unsuccessful attempts, an interpreter worthy of the subject has been found in Jacob Grimm.'

Dr. Vilmar denounces, in strong terms, the self-conceit so characteristic of modern taste and modern criticism, which consigns so much of the past, and especially in the earlier history of nations, to oblivion, as necessarily unworthy of study. He has not learnt so to judge of what is called the dark ages, nor of the space in German history which preceded those ages. He does not regard the Germans existing at the commencement of the Christian era, as acorn-eaters and half-men; nor does he think that their language, even at that time, was a wretched ' croaking and snarling.' In his view, even the earliest forms of German poetry are deeply interesting, as an embodiment of the German spirit, naturally the most free from all foreign admixture and the most eminently national. Never, he maintains, was the poetry of the Germans more symmetrical, beautiful, and impressive, than when the cheerful war-song called them up to do battle against their Italian oppressors.

'The stories of those songs through which our ancestors did honour to the fathers of their tribes, their kings, and heroes in the remotest times, still remain. Tacitus tells us, that the Germans celebrated the earth-born god, Tuisco, and his son, Mammus, in old (even then old) songs; that they glorified in battle-songs the god of war and victory, whom he calls Hercules, but most probably the god Sachsnot, or Ziu, the god of war himself. He asserts, not without singular, one might almost say heartfelt sympathy, that Armin, (Hermann,) the deliverer of North Germany, was sung in songs relating to the battle of Teutoburg for nearly a hundred years. These songs have perished, perished probably with the tribes to which they more especially belonged. When the Cheruskans became lost amid the waves of the excited German people, the song of Armin, the Cheruskan prince, was also lost—with it his memory among his people became extinguished, and was preserved only by a romant. The old heroic songs of Berig and Filumer, kings of the Goths, sung by the people in the sixth century, and from which the history of the Goths has collected that which it knows of ancient affairs, have perished.

'There are two, not songs, but materials for songs, remaining from this period, which extend far beyond the accredited national history into the heathen time; certainly beyond the fifth, if not the fourth century after Christ, and in the present day are not only known, but poetically alive. The one, the heroic legend, or Mythus of Sigfrid, the dragon killer, who is still called the horned Sigfrid; the other, the brute-epos,* of Reinhart the fox, and Isengrim the wolf, which has stood in unchanging freshness through all centuries, and which has inspired the greatest poet of our time to remodel the old materials into an interesting poem.

'The tradition of Sigfrid, the brilliant hero who forged his sword, Balmung—whilst still a boy, dwelling in the solitary old forest with the treacherous blacksmith—who slew the treasure-keeping dragon, Fafnir, rescued the Valkyre Brunhild from the castle of flames, and perished through treachery, amid the brightest splendours of his heroic life, refers us to a time in which not only the heathenism of the old Germans continued in unabated strength and life, but when the ancient condition of the people also remained tranquil, not yet having received the shock which manifested itself at the so called migration of nations. By means of this migration, the tradition was conveyed out of Germany to the tribes connected with it in the north—to Norway and Iceland, where it was preserved and written down in its ancient mythic form. Whilst at home, it became modified under the influence of Christianity, and, for the greater part, divested of its heathen mythic character. Under this change, it formed the first part of our 'Lay of the Nibelungen.' We shall consider it more nearly when we come to the analysis of this poem.

* Fables, in which animals are persons, after the manner of Æsop.

'The brute-epos—Reinhart, the fox; and Isengrim, the wolf—shows itself in its general contents to be one to which only the unencumbered natural life, and free, close, almost childlike intercourse with animals, could have given rise. That this story extends into the earliest time, and that it must have been in the possession of the Franks, and by them carried across the Rhine into France, is strikingly proved by the proper name which the fox bears in it—Reginhart, (or, as it is now called, Reinhart, abbreviated in low German, Reineke,—namely, Reinhartchen,) the wise counsellor, the sly. This German name has entirely superseded the old French one, Goupil, and placed itself as Renard instead; a reception which, together with many others, could only be possible in the time when the language of the Franks was general in Gaul, and the meaning of the word still perfectly alive; for, in the eighth century, it was so no longer, at least in Germany. I shall have to exhibit the contents and meaning of *this* story when I arrive at the time at which it gained a firm literary ground, and shaped itself to a brute epic.'

Of the German heroes who made themselves conspicuous during the interval from the first to the sixth century, and of the popular songs relating to their deeds, the following passage may be taken as an illustration:—

'What we have remaining of the songs of this period, (for we still possess them complete, although not in the old language, but in the new form of the thirteenth century,) is limited to three pieces: one in the Latin translation, one in the Anglo-Saxon language, one only exists in the original old high German. For their preservation we are not indebted to the care of Charlemagne, the most important having come to us through a careless, but fortunate accident. The lay of Hildebrand and Hadubrand, belonging to the *Sagen-Kreisze*, (tradition cycle,) of Dietrich von Bern, is composed in this old, high German language, which here and there inclines toward low German. The adventure which this song relates, supposes the same event as the Nibelungen. Dietrich, accompanied by Hildebrand, having been thirty years away from home with the king of the Huns, after the fight in which all the Burgundians, and also Sigfrid's widow and Attila's wife, the lovely and terrible Kriemhild, had fallen; after the conquest of enemies at home, and the appearance of their head, Otacher, (the well-known Odoaker,) returned to his kingdom. The old Hildebrand, who, on setting out, had left behind a young wife and infant, followed him home. Hadubrand, now himself a hero, not knowing his father, makes hostile advances with his followers. Hildebrand, recognising his son, seeks to prevent the combat; he tells him his history, but the son remains unconvinced. 'Hildebrand, the son of Heri-'brand, is dead; from mariners who have crossed the Mediterranean 'I have heard it.' Taking the golden bracelets (the most beautiful and coveted ornament of a German warrior) from his arm, Hildebrand offers them to his son, that he may win his favour, but the young hero boldly answers, ' Sword against sword, and on the point of the lance should the gift be received; thou art a cunning Hun thus to ensnare me that my death may be the more certain.' Then cried Hildebrand, ' Oh, all ruling God, now is misfortune at hand. Sixty winters and summers have I wandered from the land, and now must my own trusted child cut me down with the sword, or I become his murderer? Yet, he who sought to stay thee from the combat for which thou longest, would be the greatest coward amongst the Astro-goths.' Father and son hurled their ashen lances at each other, cutting so sharply that they remained sticking in their shields; then, closing furiously, the champions hewed upon their white shields until their edgings of linden wood became small from the sword strokes. Here the poem, being unfortunately only a fragment, closes. The substance of what remains is not lost, though, of course, nothing can replace the ancient form; the genuine epic material of this poem out-lived all the storms of time. The lay of Hildebrand and Hadubrand continued to be sung 700 years later; in the fifteenth century it still existed in its final form, which, while it will bear no comparison with the original in point of strength, was still by no means unsuccessful. Under the title of ' The Father with the Son,' it has been remodelled, and preserved to us, by a national poet, Kasper von der Roen; at the present time, also, it has found its way into many elementary books, e. g., the well known collection of German poems, by Phillip Wacker-nagel.

' The combat terminates in favour of the father, who then returns with his son to the lonely wife and mother.'

From the poem of Walther, and that of Beovulf, the latter being rather an Anglo-Saxon than a German fragment, the author proceeds to a more general consideration of the heroic poetry of this most ancient epoch, and indicates something of the change which has come over the literary opinion of Germany on subjects of this nature, within the last half-century.

' For a long time many tales were told of German bards of a pecu-liar singer-caste, who were in exclusive traditional possession of poetic art, who not only preserved, but also created the subjects and forms of our most ancient poems, made those old songs, and sang them skil-fully, in their courts or bard-schools. It was the imperfect acquaint-ance with the history of our nation that prevailed during the last century, (an acquaintance fit only for children, except where the most prominent facts were concerned,) which created these bards. This perverted and almost ridiculous opinion was spread by the authority of Klopstock, who was aided by the contemporary enthusiasm for Ossian, and supported for a long time by the *bard-bellowing* of Kretschmann, and others. Amongst the German people no bards ever existed, neither was there ever a caste of singers; the name, and, in fact, the whole is strange to them—they belonged to the *Celtic* races.

' Our old national poetry never was exclusively in the possession of a few, least of all, of a particular class. It belonged rather to the whole people, and to no one person more or less than to another. In those songs whose contents were known beforehand, all took share as they felt inclined. At the courts of kings the harp went from hand to hand, and all joined, if not in the whole song, at least in the most striking passages and refrains. This singing, of which Tacitus has spoken, is a characteristic mark of our nationality, and of the representation and formation of our *heroic*, and particularly *epic* song.

' Poetic subjects, themselves affected by all that is experienced, felt, and contemplated, touched all others in like manner, and, if a single poet appeared, he did not, as in the present day, express a something especially *subjective*,—that is, the effect which the object exercises on the poet, and who must employ himself in trying its influence on his hearers; he was merely the favoured organ through which the common poetic wealth of the people made itself known. He expressed what every listener immediately recognised as his own, and was therefore certain beforehand of the impression it would make, as well as of the pleasurable and lively assent of all the hearers, and sharers in the song. That working upon effect, through which a large part of our modern poetry seeks its strength, is entirely foreign to the ancient art. The legends I have mentioned were nothing imagined or dis-covered by a few persons—nothing that may be discovered or invented, —but partly actual events of the whole nation, like the ' Lay of Hilde-brand and Hadubrand,' which sets forth an historical event that the process of clothing has not altered in any one of its circumstances, not even in the dialogue between father and son; partly, also, the form which certain events had assumed in the common independence and imagination of the people, assumed and maintained at a time in which there were no learned and unlearned; no educated and uneducated; no over refined *haute volée*, and no rude mass sinking in coarseness and filth; at a time when the king not only spoke the same dialect as the lowest of his people, but was most inwardly bound to them by manners, and by perfectly similar views of life, in all that was essential.'

There was evidently a wild force and often a touching beauty in the poetry of these heathen war-songs; as when they speak of the lank wolf from out the forest, hanging on the rear of the army, howling his grim evening song, and waiting for his food; or of the dew-feathered raven, and other birds of prey, as sing-ing among the leaves while waiting for the dead, and as scream-ing over the battle-field rejoicing in their spoil; or of the sword, as darting like a snake upon the foe, and of the bitter bite of the battle-axe as it smites the fainting with death; or of the battle-drops as they fall beneath the death-strokes on the gleaming arms, stained with the blood-fought fountain of life. But this revelling in slaughter, and the pagan spells and superstitions mixed up with these odes, which gave them so much of their character, rendered them obnoxious to the people, especially to the more instructed among them, as their mind became gradually possessed with more Christian ideas. If Charlemagne was at some pains to collect them, Louis the Pious saw nothing to regret in the probability of their sinking into oblivion.

'Many other songs, proceeding from the old mythus, or containing some traces of it, like Sigfrid's early history, have faded, or perished, or were purposely destroyed. Others have been somewhat softened by Christianity, or have, at least, been rendered more agreeable to Christian ideas; as they could scarcely resolve at one blow to extinguish the beloved lays of the glorious heroes of old, they have sought to save and unite, as well as possible, such as could be preserved. The poem of Beovulf, in the form in which it has reached us, retains a large number of Christian additions, easily to be discerned, and often in close connexion with such parts as apparently bear, or have borne a heathen character. Take, for example, the lay of Walther von Aquitaine, which certainly in its Latin translation had already passed through the hands of the monks of St. Gallen. Walther delivers a vehement and bold oration (*gelpf*) at the commencement of the battle, according to the custom of the heroes; this the monks retained, but immediately after make the heroes fall down with out-stretched arms in the form of a cross, and call on God for forgiveness for the bold speech. But the heroic songs gradually disappeared from the world of new Christian civilization, or, as we should now say, from the educated classes, and continued, it appears, to be sung only timidly and secretly by the lower classes, who dwelt with affection on the remembrance of their ancient deities and heroes. In the course of the ninth century, they were entirely lost sight of, and had apparently perished, until three hundred years later, when they arose in new and youthful beauty, old yet young, powerful and yet gentle.'

From the ninth century to about the middle of the twelfth, the literature of Germany, both in prose and verse, was almost wholly ecclesiastical, consisting of harmonious and metrical translations of the Gospels, and other productions, designed mainly for Christian edification. In this respect the history of Anglo-Saxon Britain is the strict parallel of the history of Germany. The Christian element abated the old war passion, without immediately calling any other passion of equal power into the same degree of prevalence. Not that the German people were really slumbering during these three centuries; on the contrary, it was then that their Henrys and their Ottos raised them to a political greatness before unknown in their history; but even this result, though fraught with many benefits, was not favourable to a development of the poetic faculty. The new

combination of power was in a great degree ecclesiastical, and ecclesiastics, if they required poetry at all, required it of another order than had been hitherto supplied by the national spirit. Dr. Vilmar describes the whole space preceding 1150 as the 'most ancient period' in the history of German literature; and the space between 1150 and 1624, as the 'ancient period,' in distinction from the modern, which he dates from the latter point. It will not of course be supposed that our author is content with laying down these broad landmarks. Each of these divisions has its shades of subdivision, which are sketched with much critical discrimination. It was the work of the twelfth and following centuries to call up the Christian hero of the crusades, into the place of the pagan hero of bygone times. This change gave vent to the old national spirit in new forms. Poetry everywhere revived. The old was recalled and new was created. From the ecclesiastical literature of this period, the poet's art was developed and elaborated; but side by side with these productions was the poetry of the people—a poetry from the past, which seemed to find out new affinities to itself in the present, and failed not to receive a hearty response from the national feeling. It is in the following terms that our author discriminates between the two departments of German poetry in the twelfth and thirteenth centuries—

'The *poetry of art* was chiefly cultivated by the nobility. Emperors and kings, dukes and princes, counts and knights, were the singers of art. Songs still remain of two members of the skilful and song-loving Hohenstaufen's; of Frederick VI., the son of the great Barbarossa, and of King Conrad the Young, whose head fell beneath the axe at Naples. We have songs of King Wenceslaus of Bohemia, Duke Heinrich von Breslau, Markgrave Otto von Brandenberg, and the immortal poets Hartman Von Aue, Wolfram von Eschenbach, Walter von der Vogelweide, Ulrich von Liechtenstein, all belonging to the class of nobles. The nearest circle of listeners was that of their companions in rank. Then noble singers sang to their guitars at the courts of princes in the glittering assemblies of brave knights, gentle ladies, and graceful noble maidens. Their province was the ornament of speech; the brilliant, elegant representation; the skilful utterance of new narratives; the story of their own heart's love, its joys and sorrows. In the poems of the people, we are enchained by their artless simplicity and faithful adherence to old subjects and forms; here the dazzling variety, new discoveries, and skilful working of a foreign matter, attract us with fresh and increasing charms. The endeavour of the poets was to deck their subject with all ornament and grace; with lively, varied, and often glowing colours, in which beamed the glad, cheerful life of the chivalrous world, after the variegated splendour of the French and Spanish south, and the wonderworld of the east had been disclosed to the Germans in consequence of the crusades, and their army had become entwined within that magic circle. The poetry of art is therefore also called chivalrous or *courtly* poetry, and as may be easily understood, was early opposed to national poetry — an opposition which afterwards became studied rather than reconciled, as the description of the art of poetry in the next period will prove in all its particulars.'

This poetry of the people, according to Dr. Vilmar, is essentially epic, not so much the work of invention as of history, the function of the poet being not to speculate on the material of his verse, or to overlay it with embellishment, but rather to tell the story of actual events with such natural force and feeling that the humblest may at once understand his drift, and float on with his stream of emotion. But though this poetry of nature is little indebted to the embellishments of art, the mythical and imaginative element inseparable from the condition of a comparatively rude and highly-impassioned people, is a tolerable guarantee that if you look in vain to this kind of composition for the signs of egotism, you are not likely to find it wanting in its own species of strong colouring and impressiveness. The epic is essentially the poetry of passion, of the passionateness of tribe, of kindred, of strong and confederated relationship. Where these are not, or have not been wide-spread and of long standing, true epic poetry is not possible. These observations have their proof in abundance in the two great German epics—'The Lay of the Nibelungen,' and 'The Lay of Gudrun,' which in the form in which they are known to us belong to this period. The great element embodied in these German lays is fidelity, a feudal truthfulness, binding superior and inferior, and proving itself stronger than any appeal that might possibly be made to the human heart either by blandishment or terror. But concerning 'The Lay of Nibelungen,' which comes before us as a poem of large dramatic variety and extent, our learned neighbours, and Dr. Vilmar among the rest, assure us that it existed in fragments over a wide extent of territory, before it becomes known to us in its present continuous and harmonious form ; and their theory is, that these fragments being blended as we now find them, was not the doing of one poetic mind in the more remote times of German history, but the handiwork of subsequent minstrels skilled in such literary dove-tailing. We shall not detain our readers by attempting any description of the erudite processes by which this theory is defended, but shall at once submit to them a few extracts from our author's admirable prose account of the 'Nibelungen Lay,' the poem described by the scholars of Germany as the 'Iliad' of their 'nation,' and the

principal scenes of which are now furnishing subjects for so many beautiful frescos in the apartments of the new royal palace at Munich. It is thus the epic commences—

'In the old castle of the Burgundian kings at Worms-on-the-Rhine, grew the daughter of a noble king, after her father's death, into a blooming maiden, full of loveliness and grace. Soft foreboding dreams hover round the musing head of the lovely Kriemhild, in the still seclusion in which, according to the good old custom of her time, her childhood and early youth were passed. A vision shows her a falcon, which she rears up and tends as her favourite for many days; then two eagles rush upon the tender bird, crushing it with their grim claws before her eyes. Painfully agitated on awakening, she relates the dream to her mother, who thus interprets the sweet and timid foreboding of the daughter. 'The falcon is a noble husband destined to thee in the future; God preserve him, that thou mayest not soon lose him!' 'What dost thou say to me of a husband, dear mother?' replied the daughter. 'Without the love of a hero will I remain, and preserve the beauty of my youth until death, that my love may not at last be rewarded by sorrow.' 'Promise not too much,' said the mother; 'cast it not too far from thee, for if thou wilt ever be glad at heart it will be through the love of a husband. Thou wilt be the beautiful wife of a noble hero.' So this first foreboding of a future unutterable woe rises from the far distance, like a softly echoing sound out of the heart of the gentle maiden, and the shadows of this dream pass constantly through the clear heaven of her life and love; darker and ever darker they hover over the spring days of the sweet first and only love; darker and ever darker over the joyous games and glittering bridal feasts. With a pale fading glimmer the sun shines through the dismal twilight, till it wanes glowing red to its setting, and amid widely radiant and bloody splendour, sinks at last into eternal night.

'Meanwhile, Sigfrid, the son of Sigmund and Segelinda, at Santen-on-the-Rhine, cheerful in joyous youth, strong even while a boy, in fresh manly courage, and powerful in bold might, has grown to a hero, and already passed through many lands in order to prove the strength of his giant frame. He heard the report of the beautiful maiden at Worms on the Upper Rhine, and the most beautiful and strong, the most joyous and glorious of the hero youths of his time, left his home and his men, in order at Worms to woo the most beautiful, and graceful, and modest maiden to be found in any land. A tone of warning misgiving is here also expressed by the lips of the wise father, King Sigmund. A tear of sorrow for the beloved child she fears to lose, falls from the eye of Segelinda upon the strong faithful hand of her son; but the son departs, sent with rich gifts from father and mother. The strangers ride before the king's castle at Worms, like giants in manly and youthful vigour, and with steeds, equipments, and ornaments of unrivalled magnificence. No one knows the warriors, who halt before the king's palace on the shore of the Rhine, or their leader, the youth of kingly bearing. Then Hagen of Tronei, to whom all foreign lands were known, is sent for, but even he has never seen this hero. ' A prince, or the messenger of a prince, it must be,' he says; 'from wherever they come they are noble heroes.' Quickly, however, he added, 'I have, indeed, never seen Sigfrid, but I believe it can be he alone who goes there so stately. It is Sigfrid who conquered the race of Nibelungen, who won the immense treasure of precious stones and red gold from the dark races of Schilbuwg and Nibelung, and took possession of the land of the vanquished and its inhabitants; who tore the invisible-making Tarn-kappe in fierce struggle from the dwarf Alberich. The same Sigfrid who also slew a dragon and bathed himself in the blood, so that his skin became invulnerable as horn. Such a hero should we meet with friendliness, lest we bring the speedy hate of the champion upon us.' Sigfrid is courteously received and sumptuously entertained. Gay tiltings are held at the court of the king. Kriemhild looks stealthily through the window, and at sight of the strong youthful hero forgets all mirth, all pastime with her companions, and all the delicate employments of maiden solitude. But Sigfrid tarries a whole year at the court of the Burgundian king before he once sees her he came to woo. He accompanied, as fellow-warrior and as vassal of the king, the Burgundian heroes and army in many battles; marched the long distance from the Rhine through Hesse far into the Saxon province, whose king, Luitger, with Luitgart, King of Danemark, had declared war against the Burgundians. In murderous struggles Sigfrid is the most powerful and victorious of the heroes. He conquers and takes captive the Danish king, Luitgart; and Luitger, with his Saxons, surrender themselves to the superior power of the hero. Messengers from the army come to the Rhine to announce the joyful victory, and one appears before Kriemhild, knowing or guessing that her heart is in the Saxon war, and not at home in Worms. 'Now tell me good tidings,' said Kriemhild; 'I will give thee all my gold, and if thou bringest a true report, will be kind to thee thy life long.' ' No one has ridden more gloriously to battle than the guest from the Netherlands. The fiercest conflict from the first unto the last has Sigfrid's hand encountered. His strong arm has subdued and sent the hostages which thou wilt see come from Saxony to the Rhine.' Then the king's daughter ordered the golden marks and rich garments to be given the messenger, for the news which was dear to all, but to none dearer than the silent glowing maiden. From that time she stands silently at the narrow window of the castle, looking out upon the road by which the conquerors will return to the Rhine. At length the joyful and victorious knights appear, and the maiden sees the gay tumult before the castle gate, in the wide plain of the Rhine, and amongst the many heroes, he, the hero of heroes, honoured and admired above them all. But his eyes cannot discover the long wished-for object; she has kept herself until now in modest retirement. At length a glittering tournament is held, and two and thirty princes, together with the highest and noblest from far and near, assemble at the cheerful Whitsuntide. Then at the side of her mother, Ute, accompanied by a hundred sword-bearing attendants, and a hundred richly-attired noble ladies and maidens, does Kriemhild, for the first time, appear, rising like the morning red from out the dusky clouds, in the soft tremulous light of youth, of beauty, and of secret love, like the mild glimmer of the moon and stars shining through clouds. Sigfrid stands afar. ' How can it ever come to pass that I should win her? It is foolish presumption; yet rather than leave thee I would die.' Then after the courtly fashion, Gernot calls upon Gunther to command Sigfrid to stand forth and greet their sister. The hero comes forward, and bends lovingly before the maiden. The longing impulse of love draws them one towards another, and they gaze on each other with stolen loving looks. But no word is exchanged, until after the mass with which the feast commenced, when the maiden gives the hero thanks for the brave assistance which he has rendered her brothers. ' That was done in your service, fair Kriemhild,' replied Sigfrid; and now 'after the mouth has also ventured something,' Sigfrid remains for twelve days, the time of the duration of the feast, near the lovely maiden. Then the strange guests depart, and Sigfrid also prepares to set out for home, ' for he dared not woo as he wished.' Through the persuasion of young Giselher, however, he easily resolves to tarry longer, where, as the lay truthfully says, he most loved to be, and where he daily saw the beautiful Kriemhild.'

But the scene now changes. Distant from the court of King Gunther dwells a queen of wonderful beauty and strength, to be won only by the hero who should conquer her in the use of martial weapons. Many suitors had fallen by her strong hand. Gunther resolves to hazard an encounter with this warlike maiden. Sigfrid, on condition of possessing Kriemhild, engages to assist the king in his perilous enterprise. Through the magic aid of Sigfrid, Gunther conquers the heroine. But a mortal hatred grows up in the mind of the vanquished queen, Brunhild, against Kriemhild and her hero husband. It is not, however, until two years have passed that she prevails on Gunther to require a visit from Sigfrid as his supposed vassal. The visit takes place, the queens again meet, and bitter strife ensues between them. Brunhild engages Hagen, a devoted vassal of her husband, to procure the death of Sigfrid in battle. Hagen finds a shorter road to his object. It is discovered that the hero is vulnerable at a certain point in the back, though otherwise wearing a charmed life, and a chase is made to serve the wishes of the queen. How the discovery adverted to was made, and what followed is thus described:—

' The campaign is in full activity; Sigfrid equips. Then Hagen repairs to Kriemhild to take leave of her according to the custom. She has already half forgotten the dispute; not the slightest foreboding that she sees before her the known and eternal foe of her husband who has sworn his death enters her ever unsuspecting heart. 'Hagen, thou art my relation, I thine; to whom in the coming war can I better confide my Sigfrid, than unto thee? Protect my dear husband; I commend him to thy fidelity. He is certainly invulnerable; but as he bathed in the blood of the dragon, a broad linden leaf fell between the shoulder blades, and this, unmoistened part, remains vulnerable. If the war spears come upon him in thick flights, one might strike this place, therefore shield him there, Hagen, protect him.' 'Good,' said the malicious one, 'in order to be better able, sew me, royal lady, a mark upon this part of his garment that I may know exactly how I am to protect him.' Unsuspectingly, in tender love for the lost husband, she embroiders with her own hand, in fine silk, a cross upon his garment—she herself works the bloody sign of death. The next day the campaign begins, and Hagen rides near Sigfrid to see if the wife, in her blind, boundless love, has placed the mark. Sigfrid really wears it, and now the expedition is no longer necessary. Hagen has secured what he wished from the hands of Kriemhild, even more than he expected. The followers are summoned to a great hunt instead of to war. Sigfrid once more sees his wife, she him—*for the last time.* Anxious forebodings, heavy dreams distress her soul, as at first, when blooming from childhood to maidenhood, she dreamt of the falcon and the eagles. Now she sees two mountains fall on Sigfrid and bury him beneath the crashing ruins. Sigfrid comforts her. 'No one can bear him hatred; he has shown kindness to all; in a few days he will return.' What she fears, who she fears, she does not know; Hagen, perhaps the only one she feared, she thinks won—but she parts with the words, 'that thou wilt part from me, that gives me heartfelt pain.'

'The chase is ended, and the heroes, Sigfrid especially, who has slain most deer, are wearied and thirsty with running in the summer heat. But there is no more wine, neither is the Rhine stream at hand from whence to obtain the longed-for cool refreshment. But Hagen knows a spring near by in the wood, and thither he advises them to go. They break up, and already the broad lindens amongst whose roots the cool spring rises, are in sight, when Hagen began, 'No one, it has been said, can follow in running the swift Sigfrid, the husband of Kriemhild; let him now prove it.' 'Let us,' replied Sigfrid, 'run for a wager to the spring; I will retain my hunting dress and sword, my javelin and shield, whilst you shall take off your clothes.' The race commences; Hagen and Gunther spring like wild panthers through the wood clover, but Sigfrid is at the spot long before them. He then quietly laid down sword, bow and quiver, leant the javelin on a linden branch, and placed the shield near the spring, waiting until the king should come that he may let him drink first. For his adherence to this venerable custom he pays with his death. He might easily have drunk before Gunther and Hagen came up, then he would have been again standing with the arms in his hand, and what now happens

would have been impossible. Gunther drinks, and after him Sigfrid stoops to the spring. Then Hagen springs, carrying aside in his hasty leap the weapons which were within reach, and retaining the javelin in his murderous hand, while Sigfrid swallows the last draught, he hurls the weapon, Sigfrid's own weapon, through the cross upon his back, so that the heart's blood of the glorious hero streams over the murderers' garments.'

But the tragedy does not so end. Some years later Kriemhild gives her hand to another king, chiefly in the hope of being some day avenged by his means for the king she has lost. Her new lord is induced to invite her relations to his court. King Gunther, and Hagen, as one of his vassals, make their appearance, with many beside. But all things seem to forebode catastrophe. Superstition is at work. Kriemhild would know why Hagen is of a party which was to consist of her relations; charges him with the murder of her husband; and to be avenged on him employs all her art and influence to stir up the Huns about the court against their Burgundian visitors, and thus becomes the occasion of a strife which ends in a scene of blood and ruin so terrible, that it is difficult to conceive of an element of suffering or horror which is not included in it. The hall of the feast is heaped, and its avenues choked up, with the dead. The building itself is fired, the suffering heroes slake their burning thirst by drinking the blood of their slaughtered foes. Dane and Goth join the Hun in the fray. At length the Burgundians are all slain, the three brothers of Kriemhild, Hagen, Kriemhild herself, and her youthful son, all receive their mortal stroke, and lie amidst friends and foes as part of the great havoc of death. So ends the Nibelungun lay!

The word Nibelungun denotes sons of the mist, or of darkness. These children of night, according to a myth which lies at the bottom of this story, were in possession of a vast treasure. Sigfrid, as we have learnt, had conquered an enormous dragon, and bathed himself in the monster's blood, and is henceforth known as the horned or mailed Sigfrid, becoming invulnerable, except at the point where Hagen thrust the spear. Thus provided, he attacked the dwarfs who had the keeping of the famed treasure of the Nibelungun, and with his good sword Balmung, made the treasure his own. But it is an acquisition doomed to be fatal to all that possess it. It passes from Sigfrid to Kriemhild; from her it is wrested by her brothers, and all come to their tragic end as the consequence. Hagen is the last man who knows where the fatal charm is deposited, and dies rejoicing that he can madden Kriemhild by taking that secret away with him.

Such is an imperfect outline of the Nibelungen lay—a poem

which seems to come forth upon us as a precious vestige from amidst the cloud and disorder of a departing world. Very remote—very shadowy is the region in which the figures of this story flit before us. The life and the races of which they were a part are gone, and their own mysterious place in the world's story is upon the confines which separate between the known and the unknown. Rich, indeed, are these pictures in the truly poetic blending of the ideal with the real, of the mythical with the historical. The action of this poem, it will be perceived, is busy and energetic; but it is observable that, amidst all this motion and excitement, no one thinks for a moment about the poet, every thought and emotion converges on the incidents and the characters. No attempt is made to paint over either the scenes or the actors. The descriptions are direct, brief, simple—the apparent function of the poet being, not as much to create, as to report in the most natural form the things on which his eyes rested, and to which his ears listened. He would almost seem as though laid under prohibition by some terrible deity, not to add to, or take from, the matters which came thus substantially before him. It will be seen, however, that these incidents and characters, though depicted thus promptly, almost as by a single stroke, present a striking variety. As in the Iliad, the story may have its hero, but, at best, he figures only as one hero among many. In some respects, and in some stages of the drama, he may stand forth as chief; but in other respects, and at other times, his place is subordinate. Hence the sympathy of the reader is made to diffuse itself largely through the whole. Even the deeds he disapproves spring from a mistaken homage to fidelity, to which he is himself compelled to do a kind of reverence. Brunhild is not so masculine a person as to possess no womanly claim upon our interest; nor is Kriemhild so feminine as to fail in lofty and self-sustained feeling, or in resoluteness of purpose. Hagen, himself, much as we condemn his treachery in relation to Sigfrid and Kriemhild, exhibits, as he passes on to his fate, a power of self-devotion which rises to sublimity. Nothing can exceed the energy with which hero after hero commits himself to the perils that thicken about him, each joyously choosing death rather than be numbered with the faithless. Everywhere, it is not the existence of a high moral element that is wanting, so much as the wiser culture and direction of a strong but untutored sense of right. Much as may be the harm that has come to this precious relic in the jostling of ages, enough of its substance and form remain to enable us to judge of that bygone life, otherwise hardly known to history, to which it pertains.

After the mention of some smaller lays, all more or less connected with the heroes of the Nibelungen, follows the tradition-cycle of the North Sea, which contains but one poem—the Lay of Gudrun. Next to the Nibelungen, it occupies the highest place in the German epic.

'This poem contains the tradition of three generations: of *Hagen*, the king of Iceland, and his youthful history; and of the wooing of the Fusland King Hettel, for his daughter, Hilde; and, at length, of *Gudrun*, the daughter of *Hettel* and *Hilde*. In the narrative of *Hettel* wooing for Hilde, (as Hagen's history may here be passed over,) we meet, first, with a description of the singing of the Stormarn king, *Horant*, as a celebrated tradition often mentioned and described by the northern tribes related to us, and also by ourselves. The messengers of King Hettel, Horant, and his men, *Frute* and *Wate*, have obtained admission to Hagen, king of Iceland, in order to win Hilde, the daughter so carefully guarded, for their relation, *Hettel*. The two heroes, Frute and Wate, have already won the confidence of the king, and the latter, at least jestingly, the good will also of the royal ladies. Wate, the giant, broad, bearded hero, establishes himself by the ladies, who, as he sits gravely there, with coloured scarfs bound round his head, covered with thick hair, ask him in jest which he preferred, to remain with beautiful ladies, or to fight in hard battles; and the mighty warrior, who rages like a wild boar in the battle, answers, without considering, that to him it seemed indeed good to sit with beautiful ladies, but yet much gentler still to fight with the army in fierce war; then the queens laugh aloud, and ask if this man has wife and children at home? In this manner some favour for the suit is already won. Then Horant raises his wondrously sweet song in the still evening, in the royal castle on the sea-shore; and the birds silence the echo of their evening lay before the lovely tones of the royal singer; and again in the early morning, at the rise of the sun, the wonderful melody sounds through the castle, so that the birds forget also their morning song. All the sleepers awaken, and the king, with his wife, steps out upon the battlements, and the royal maiden entreats her father, 'Dear father, bid him sing again.' And, for the third time, in the evening, the Danish king raises his voice, so that the bells never rang so clearly as his song; the labourers thought they did not work, and the sick thought they were not ill; the beasts of the forest left their food, the worm that crawls in the grass, and the fishes that swim in the waves, stayed in their restless course. The singer wins the maiden for him who had sent him; she steals away, goes with him to the ship, and becomes Hettel's wife.

'Their children are *Ortwin* and *Gudrun*. Hartmut, the son of a Norman king, woos the latter, but ancient hostility between the families prevents the suit from being successful. Then *Herwig*, King of Zealand, appears, and, by fighting, wins the love of the beautiful Gudrun. They are betrothed, and shortly afterwards, Herwig and

385

her father make a campaign into a distant land, and, during the absence of the protector, Hartmut, the rejected wooer, comes with his father, King Ludwig, before the castle, conquers it, and carries off Gudrun. Hettel and Herwig, with their heroes, the first amongst whom is Wate, set out after the robbers, and overtake them at *Wulpensande*, an island in the North Sea. Here, according to the existing testimonies, a bloody battle was fought, which was celebrated in lays throughout Germany. As, after the storm, avalanche on avalanche rolls down the mountain, so fly the spears from their hands; standing up to their arms in water, the heroes fought furiously, till the sea-tide was stained with blood, and waved in crimson brightness upon the distant strand, far as spear could be thrown. Evening approaches; in the sinking sun, Hettel, the father of Gudrun, is slain by the Norman king, the father of the robber; as the evening red dies away in the sky, Wate, furious at the death of the king, kindles anew an evening red upon the helmets of his enemies with his rapid sword-strokes; meanwhile, the darkness of night causes friend to fall on friend, and the battle ceases. During the night, however, the Normans flee with their prey; the king's daughter is threatened with instantaneous death in the waves if she raise one sound of lamentation or one cry for help. The remaining force is not sufficient to follow into the land of the enemy, and Wate is compelled to return forsaken to the castle which he had so often entered with loud cries of rejoicing victory. 'Where is my dear lord, and where are his friends?' demands Queen Hilde, as in terror she sees Wate enter silently, and with cloven shield. 'I will not deceive thee—they are all slain,' is the short answer of the stern hero; 'when the young generation is grown up in the land, then will come the time for vengeance upon Ludwig and Hartmut.'

'In tears and sadness Gudrun sees the coast of the Norman land and the castles on the sea-shore. The old king addresses her kindly: 'If, noble maiden, thou wilt love Hartmut, then all that thou seest is offered thee. At the side of Hartmut joy and royal honours await thee.' But Gudrun replies: 'I would rather choose death than Hartmut. If it had happened thus during my father's life, it might have been so; but now, I would rather lose my life than break my faith.' The words were deep and serious. The wild chief, in wrath at the maiden's reply, seizes her by the hair, and hurls her into the sea; Hartmut springs after her, and can only just catch her fair braided tresses, by which he draws her back to the ship. Had a modern poet invented this situation, he would certainly have done so in order to use the merit of this rescue to Hartmut's advantage; causing the delicate position of the maiden arising out of it to form a chain of other situations, out of which to bring the constant fidelity of Gudrun more glowingly forward. But here, in the epic, not even the slightest *intimation* of such things ensues; it strides rapidly on without tarrying —following only the decisive events, leaving the colouring to the mind of the reader or hearer. I need scarcely observe, that

the enjoyment of those who understand how to enjoy, is in this manner infinitely heightened. A romance of modern time is read out when it is read through; the true epic can, no more than fresh life itself, be read out and hastily used up in the service of idle entertainment. Gerlinde, the mother of Hartmut, at first receives Gudrun kindly; but as she also uses her persuasive powers upon the faithful one in vain, she soon passes on in her 'wolfish' nature to cruelty and ill-treatment.

'She who should wear a crown must now perform the service of the lowest menial—heat the stove, and wash linen upon the sea-shore. But her heart remains patient and her soul true; patient and true through many a year of wrong and humiliation, ever repeated, ever heightened.

'The time at length arrives, when an army can be equipped in Gudrun's fatherland for her deliverance. After a long and dangerous voyage, the Frislandish heroes reach an island, from whose lofty trees they see the distant Norman castles shining up out of the sea. Gudrun, as she has been accustomed for years, goes daily to the sea-shore to wash linen; there an angel is sent to her in the form of a bird, to comfort her; and what comfort does she desire?—her deliverance from disgraceful servitude—from the shameful ill-treatment and strokes of bondage? 'Does Hilde yet live, the mother of poor Gudrun? Does Ortwin still live, my brother, and Herwig, my betrothed, and Horant and Wate, my father's faithful ones?' And no word of her deliverance? Through the long day she converses with her companions of the dear ones at home. But angry scolding from the wicked Gerlinde awaits the comforted one on her return, because she has been the whole day washing; and the next morning, early in the year, before Easter, though a deep snow had fallen overnight, at break of day she must wade barefooted through the snow down to the wild shore to complete her task. On this very morning, Ortwin and Herwig, to gain intelligence, come in a barque near the place where the king's daughter, trembling with cold, in her wet garments, washes linen by the tide streaming with ice, and in the stormy March winds, which throw her beautiful hair wildly round her neck and shoulders. The two warriors approach the maidens, who are already about to fly, and offer them the morning salutation, so long unheard; for with Frau Gerlinde 'good morning and good evening' are scarce. Gudrun they do not recognise in her disgraceful lowliness, dress, and servitude; they question respecting the people and land, hear that it is well-armed and strongly guarded; but that apprehension is entertained only of one enemy — the Frislanders, (Hegilingen.) During the long conversation, the maidens stand trembling in the bitter cold before the inquiring heroes, who compassionately offer their mantles to wrap them; but Gudrun replies, 'God forbid that any one should see man's clothes upon my body.' Then her brother Ortwin asks if a maiden, Gudrun, had not once been carried off and brought hither; and Herwig repeatedly compares the features of the poor serving-maid with those of the king's daughter, who was to be his bride; he also calls Ortwin by name. 'Oh,' says Gudrun, 'if Herwig and Ortwin still lived, they would long since have come to rescue us; I also am one of those carried away, but the poor Gudrun is long since dead.' Then the King of Zealand stretches out his hand : ' If thou art one of those who were robbed, thou must know the gold which I wear on my finger; and with this ring was Gudrun betrothed to love me.' Then the eyes of the maiden sparkle with bright joy; and however she might wish to conceal the disgrace of her servitude, is now overpowered. ' The gold I well recognise, for it was mine before; I also still wear this gold which Herwig once sent to me.' But brother and betrothed cannot believe otherwise than that she has become the wife of Hartmut, and express their horror that, in spite of it, she must perform so low a service. But when they learn why she endured this humiliation so many years, Herwig will instantly take her with him. And does it so happen, we shall ask? No, it does not so happen. The manners of the olden time were for that too firm, too strict, too noble —the manners of a time which we too gladly look upon as one of barbarism. ' That which is taken from men in the storms of war,' replies Ortwin, 'will I not secretly steal away? and rather than steal what I must win by strife of weapon, had I a hundred sisters, they might all die here.' The two princes return to their war-fleet, and preparations are made for storming the Norman castle. Gudrun, however, in proud, awakened independence, and in the joyous expectation of an honourable rescue by hero hands, throws the linen, instead of washing it, into the sea. She anticipates a wrathful reception, and shameful blows from the enraged Gerlinde; and in order to escape the evil treatment, now pretends she is willing to marry Hartmut—in the perfect confidence that, by the morrow's break, all will be quite otherwise at the castle than it now is in the evening. When Herwig and Ortwin return to the army, and announce the wrong which has been done to Gudrun through so many years, the heroes raise a loud cry of lamentation; but the old Wate tells them to serve the daughter of their king in another manner, and dye red the clothes which she has washed white. Now, in the night—the air is clear, the heavens far and wide, bright in the shining moonlight—the storm on the Norman castle shall be begun. The morning star is still high in the heavens; a companion of Gudrun looks through the window, and toward the sea; all the fields are illumined with the bright lustre of steel helmets and glittering shields; and immediately the watchman also calls from the battlements—' Up, ye proud heroes, to arms! lords, to arms ! Ye Norman heroes, up!—ye have slept too long.' The strife commences; bravely fighting, the Norman King Ludwig falls beneath the strokes of Herwig; the evil Gerlinde wishes that Gudrun should be killed, in revenge; and the drawn sword is already above her head, when Hartmut, who from below had known his furious mother's murderous design, nobly averts the crime. Hartmut is taken prisoner, and the wrathful Wate forces his way into the apartments of the ladies, to take the merited revenge upon Gerlinde. As nobly as Hartmut had previously rescued Gudrun from death, she now denies the queen; but Wate knows how to find the right, and strikes off her head, together with that of a servant of Gudrun, who sought to win thanks from the cruel queen by becoming the tormentor of her own mistress; ' he knew,' said Wate, ' how to deal with women, therefore was he chamberlain.' Upon this follows the journey home, reconciliation, and threefold marriages : between Herwig and Gudrun, between the Norman King Hartmut and Hildburg, one of the companions of Gudrun, and between Ortwin and Ortrun, the daughter of Ludwig, the Norman king. The only one in the strange land who had felt compassion for Gudrun, and in her deep injury had stood comforting beside her.'

Among the productions of the art epic, at which we now arrive, those most celebrated are the legends of the Holy Gral, and Parcival, by Wolfram von Eschenbach, the greatest poet of that period, and one of the greatest among German poets generally. He had his place with those poets and minstrels who, at the close of the twelfth century, assembled at the court of the Landgrave von Thüringen ; but little of his personal history has been transmitted to us, and even the year of his death remains unknown. Parcival, brought up by his mother in a lonely forest, is inspired, by the sudden appearance of three armed knights, with an uncontrollable desire to go forth into the world to Arthur's court, and as he disappears in the last deep forest shade, his mother falls to the ground never to rise. His first deed on arriving there is the rescue of the Princess Kouduiramur, whose castle is besieged by her suitors. He marries her, but is soon again driven forth by his restless disposition. In his wanderings, he reaches the castle of the Holy Gral, and there meets with wonderful and interesting adventures, which the poem describes with great beauty. All, however, bear reference to the mysterious legend of the Gral. This Gral was a vessel of precious stone possessed by Joseph of Arimathea; from it our Lord distributed his body to his disciples on the night of his betrayal; in it was caught the blood which flowed from his side for the redemption of the world. It was endowed with many miraculous powers, and preserved in a superb temple under the guardianship of a chosen race of kings. The guardian of the Gral could only be a man perfect in purity, humility, and fidelity. Parcival is heir to the guardianship, but from his haughty, defiant spirit, and his rebellion against God, is unable to take possession of it until the purification of his soul has been accomplished, after which he enters the Gral Castle with his wife and two sons, whose histories are also included in the poem. A few words respecting Wolfram's work may, perhaps, be quoted :—

'No lightly reaped enjoyment is offered us in Wolfram's Parcival; it must be read not once, but many times, in order to be throughout loved and admired, though numerous details interest at the first glance, partly through their tenderness, partly through their power and depth. At the first, or superficial reading, we are disturbed by a mass of material apparently too vast, the number of persons and events which Wolfram has introduced into those pieces designed to represent the brilliancy of worldly chivalry, the adventures of Gaweins, and the length of these passages, will at first appear almost wearisome. Upon a closer investigation of the plan and object of the poem, this earlier objection passes away. The aim of these passages was to set forth *perfectly*, the gay variety, the throng and confusion, of worldly life ; the clear, conscious security of the heroes of this life, who see themselves hemmed in with difficulties, and entangled anew at every step, but who still, through victory over these impediments, preserve their address and ability, directed indeed to the most immediate objects, but with a firm gaze and clear decision.'

The ruling element of Wolfram's poetry is seen in the profound and earnest gravity with which he strove to stem the torrent of worldly desires and enjoyments then so prevalent in France and Italy, and also, though in a less degree, in Germany. The great contemporary poet of Wolfram, Gottfried von Strassburg, presents, in every respect, the most striking contrast to him to be found in the literature of the age :—

'To a child of the world, in so eminent a sense as was Gottfried, the severe, almost holy, gravity, the proud dignity of thought, and the sublimity of a heavenly aim, as we find them in Wolfram, must have been unseasonable, even unendurable. He swims in full current with, even before, the world, its guide to desire and enjoyment; whilst Wolfram, resisting the stream of the world's course, hurls the strong, almost threatening, voice of an instructor—of a prophet, into the universal tumult.'

His chief poem is Tristan and Isolt, a Celtic narrative marked, as are the majority of that cycle, by its recklessness as regards all custom and honour, faith and chastity, but handled with skill, grace, and beauty. Here—

'Divine and human laws, divine and human rights, are trampled upon with an ease and open shamelessness, which astonishes and often disgusts. A most disgraceful mockery of wedded faith is the subject of the poem Tristan and Isolt. Out of the rude mass of colours transmitted to him by the British or French poet, he has created a psychological painting, which in truth and depth transcends all ever composed in a similar manner. But what does he describe—what soul does he breathe into the subject? It is *earthly* love, the glow of love consuming man, and represented as the sole object of life. He himself says the aim of the poem is the *scope of love*.'

After the notice of some antique poems, as Lamprecht's Alexander the Great, Veldekin's Eneas, and others, follow sacred legends and narratives, also the tradition of the brute epic.

'The roots of this tradition lie in the harmless, natural simplicity of the oldest races—in the deep and affectionate feeling for nature experienced by a healthy, vigorous, natural people. As such a nature attaches itself with fervency, with impassioned sensibility to the appearances of natural objects—as it exults with summer, mourns with autumn, and with winter feels itself bound in chains of heavy imprisonment; as it lends to these natural appearances its own form, own human sensations; and as it has cultivated these personifications of natural elements into magnificent myths, clothed in forms, now of lovely kindness, now of fearful splendour, as in Sigfrid and Brunhild,—thus does it closely attach itself to the brute world with which it is more nearly connected. And, further, not only attaches, but opens itself to it, and draws it in to its own life, its own intercourse, as a constituent part of its being, given and necessary, not made, feigned, or invented. The source of the narratives of brutes in the brute tradition and the brute epic, is in the pure, harmless joy of the natural man in animals—in their slender form, their sparkling eye, their bravery and ferocity, their cunning and dexterity—it is the joy in that which he perceives in brutes, and learns from his intercourse with them.'

Concerning the Minne-song, which follows the fable and didactic poetry, we select an extract from the several pages devoted to it :—

'The old heroic song, which sings the deeds of a whole nation, and by the mouth of that whole nation, is followed, among every people, by a song which, instead of issuing from the heart of the whole, proceeds only from individuals,—a poetry celebrating no longer deeds, but sensations and feelings—which sings the grief and joy of one man, and of his own heart. This *lyric*, in the stricter sense, is, however, of a twofold nature—either sensations and feelings common to all, shared by each, and which have moved, and still move, in a similar manner, the hearts of all, are sung, which is the Volkslied—the song of the people; or the exclusive experiences of *one*, which, as they have moved the heart in varied change, now also sound forth in divers forms and deeply stirring lays; they are the joyous notes of the happy and the glad, or they are the mournful melody of a sorrowing and solitary heart, which *seeks* after sympathy, and, through the pure form in which grief and gladness are portrayed in the lay, *wins* the sought-for sympathy. This is the *lyric of art*, which, like the epic in its various forms and grades, unfolds itself during the course of the thirteenth century among the Germans, with unusual richness, bearing the most lovely, delicate blossoms, of ever-varying love and fragrance: it is the *minne-poesie*, (the poetry of love,) the love-song of the glad spring of our poet-life, which once re-echoed like the nightingale's trill in the fresh verdure of the May woods, from every grove, on every heath, in every castle, through every town of our fatherland, in graceful lays from thousands of joyous and longing hearts.'

The most remarkable of the Minne-singers was Walther von der Vogelweide, whose last songs were written about 1228. Scarcely less celebrated than his famed strophe in praise of woman, is one of his political songs, addressed to the Emperor Philip.

In the succeeding fourteenth and fifteenth centuries, we find German fidelity and Christian faith weak and trembling, and German poetry also, as resting mainly on those foundations.

'In the fifteenth century began the so called re-awakening of letters, i. e., the acquaintance with the originals in Greek and Roman literature, and of necessity, beside these, our poetry made the most wretched figure. Now, with the poetry of our fatherland all was passed, passed our national feeling—our national consciousness. Henceforth nothing was valued, nothing read or practised, save *Latin poetry*. Scholars were now, in the strictest sense, ashamed of their mother tongue, and were simple enough to term themselves barbarians, men who had known, had been, nothing—capable of nothing, until the light of the Greek and Roman poetry broke in upon them! The ancient glory of the German emperor, the ancient glory of the German empire, *were forgotten as though they never had existed*. Philological poetry took its place upon the throne, and, three centuries long, ruled the world with fine phrases.'

After touching upon the epic of the sixteenth century, Hans Sachs, Fischart, and others, the first grand period of German literature closes with the prose of Luther and the sixteenth century. The new period commences in 1624 with Martin Opitz. It is distinguished from the old by its striving to blend foreign poetic elements with the German, and as accomplishing its object in the height of the second classic period. From 1624 to 1720, was the interval in which German poetry suffered its greatest deterioration. It then fell under the *dominion* of foreign elements. This last period was followed by a second classic period, as Dr. Vilmar styles it, 'the blooming time of the New Period,' extending from 1750 to 1832:—

'Poetry now unfolds itself, not as in the Old Period, self-dependent, in the perfect tranquillity of a development of slumbering germs and buds, through a secure, firm, natural impulse, conscious of itself—but out of protracted error, deep confusion, and coarse irregularity, it becomes formed on the basis of criticism, through strife and conflict.'

Here follow some remarks upon the contest between Bodmer and Gottsched, which characterized the preparatory stages of this period. Noticing, among others, Gellert, Weisse, and Klopstock, Dr. Vilmar proceeds to remark on the genius and works of Lessing, whom he thus contrasts with his predecessor, Klopstock:—

'Yonder is Klopstock, tranquil, gentle, retiring, confined within himself—here, Lessing, restless, acute, everywhere taking the most lively interest in the life of the world, going forth out of himself, and entering with conscious energy into the spirit of his time; there, a lyric strain of melting softness—here, prose, with the most sober intellect, and the clearest, coolest, thoughtfulness; there, a yielding to matter which becomes subordination—here, a warding off of the same, and authoritative demands upon it; there, the good-natured—let it be, let it pass—here, a keen, sword-like criticism, and a scepticism reaching the highest point; there, a fervent union with Christianity and childlike faith—here, indifference toward revealed religion, and a hostile position toward the church; there, almost all is German and Christian—here, almost all is antique and heathenish; there, the matter overflows the form—here, the most rigid measure and narrow form holds the matter within strictest bounds. Klopstock and Lessing are the great contrast from which grew our new classic period.'

Wieland, Gleim, Jacobi, Tiedge, &c., are followed by Herder, whose universality of genius rendered service to the literature of his country rather by rousing consciousness and elevating mind and intellect, than by the actual creation of poetic works. His immediate successor was Goëthe, who realized and completed what Herder had prepared the way for and commenced. The mental excitement which Goëthe produced has not yet sufficiently subsided to admit of anything purely historic and conclusive being arrived at in regard to him. Of this Dr. Vilmar makes us well aware, yet the pages upon Goëthe's capabilities and performances are among the truest and ablest of the whole work, and bear the marks of far-reaching penetration, of sound judgment, and of careful and scholar-like reflection. A passage may be extracted from them:—

'Goëthe was the poet who united in himself all that which Herder had been able prospectively to recognise, but was not himself able to attain; he was the genius who, with the fullest, strongest, immediate poetic perception, without books, without model, was capable of passing on to poetry out of life itself; who possessed the ability to lay felicitous hold on poetic matter in life, and power and gentleness enough to form the real into the poetic; who sang, as in the old time, (whose oracle was Herder,) not merely upon and for paper, but upon and for the heart, with and for the mouth's living voice. All that was known, made, and artistic, which had possessed its sway in past times, and from which even Klopstock was not altogether free, passed suddenly away. It was an immediate surrender; it was *genius* become reality,—after which the time had hoped and waited in the firm consciousness of its necessity. The supremacy also of matter over the poet now disappeared; a supremacy yielded to by the first poet-genius, Klopstock. This power, on which so many contemporaries should yet founder, crouched down, before the daring, onward, cheerfully victorious energy of the youthful poet who conquered without battle. . . . These qualities, the immediate truth and warmth of feeling, surrounded by clear, deep and spiritual peace; this free and rapid motion governed by the greatest inward tranquillity; this profound and perfect self-merging in the poetic object, in order occasionally to draw the same back into that self, and to mould it according to sure forms and measures; this soft and mouldable objectiveness, and this self-conscious energetic subjectiveness; this ability to conquer in being overcome, and this enjoyment and denial in one act—these are the properties bestowed by nature upon our Goëthe, and which constitute his inaccessible greatness and immortality. Through them he takes his place beside the greatest poets of all ages and nations—beside the Greeks, beside our greatest ancient singers, beside Shakspeare, beside the national lyric—thus remaining but one step behind the *national epic*, the greatest poetic creation of the human mind, unattainable to one individual.

Kotzebue, Jean Paul, Hoffman, and others, here follow, and give place to the successors of Goëthe and Schiller, and to the romantic school, comprising the two Schlegels, Novalis, Tieck, Achim von Arnim, Clemens Brentano, Fouque, Hölderlin, Schulze, Chamisso, Uhland and Schwab, Kleist and Werner, and one or two beside. The romantic school was followed by the Fatherland poets, at the head of whom stands the aged Arndt, the last of these are Count August Platen, and Karl Zimmermann, whose Münchhausen is the only romance known to the present time as of any artistic worth.

We think we have now said enough, and extracted enough, to enable our readers to form their own judgment concerning Dr. Vilmar's publication. We know of no other book so fitted, on the whole, to instruct our countrymen on the interesting subject to which it relates, and we are happy to inform our readers that a translation of the work is nearly completed, and may be expected to appear early in the autumn.

BOYD'S BOOK OF GERMAN BALLADS.*

WE suppose there is no other way of accounting for the phenomena which our recent poetical literature presents, namely, the preponderance of excellent translations over original compositions, except by attributing these results to the universal and all-embracing hospitality of our countrymen, who, though nearly destitute of the common necessaries of literary existence for themselves, still contrive to welcome the wandering children of foreign literatures with entertainments, to which the banquets of Apicius, or even the "noble feast" of O'Ruark himself, were but as the "rations" of a poor-house. Generous and hospitable fellows that we are! while we shudder at the sweet, mournful echoes of our own traditions, as at the wail of the banshee, or, in the philosophical scepticism of the age, disbelieve in the existence of both, we listen with open ears and palpitating hearts to the first breathing of some foreign melody, to which distance lends its ever-potent enchantment. We lapse into credulity out of respect to the Brocken, and warm into momentary rapture to compliment the Rhine; and some of us who would send the poor old "fairy-woman" (the banshee) to the station-house—the "good people" to the public works—and the phookah, or even O'Donoghue's white horses, to a carstand!—introduce the Walpurgis witches to our drawing-rooms, and consider the Wild Huntsman as the most delightful of table companions.

Well, it is better, perhaps, that it should be as it is. It is better, perhaps, that our legends, our traditions, our memories, our national idiosyncracies, should utterly die out, and be replaced by a hardier race, than that they should preserve their vitality at the expense of that respect to which LIFE is entitled, and wanting which annihilation is a boon. Better that their destiny should resemble the fate of the American Red Men, disappear-

ing surely but slowly, and with touching dignity, from their ancestral forests, than that they should increase and multiply but as the objects of scorn, of laughter, or of gain, like the poor despised children of Africa. We have complained of the manner in which our own legends—the materials of a true, vigorous, national literature—have been neglected. We have still greater reason to complain of the manner in which they have been partially used. With but few exceptions, our novelists, our dramatists, our literary tourists, our essayists, our poets, our historians (a few well-known and highly-valued antiquarian writers excepted)—all have treated our most grey and venerable traditions, and most sacred names, in such a spirit of levity, of heartless mockery, and wretched banter, as to render them almost unfit for the serious purposes of a lofty and ambitious native literature. They use them but for the exhibition of that ghastly "fun," which is now so much the rage, or the play of their own bounding humour—much after the manner of the boys at Glendalough, who have converted St. Kevin's Cathedral into a ball-court! This being the prevailing tendency of most of our writers, it is, perhaps, fortunate, that while few among them attempted to raise any permanent memorial of their own genius, or added much to the literary riches of their country, by original compositions of importance, many of them were the means of introducing to the notice of their countrymen, the "interesting foreigners" we have spoken of above; which, if they are often too dreamy and fantastic to serve as models for the rough, simple heartiness that should characterise our native poetry, indicate to us, with sufficient clearness, the mental activity and national pride that exist in other countries; and while silently upbraiding us for our inactivity or incapacity, may spur us

on to exertion and imitation. Not to speak of the earlier writers at the beginning of this century, such as Lord Strangford and the Rev. Henry Boyd (the latter the namesake, and, we believe, the near relative of our author), whose several translations from Camoens and Dante were then so popular—need we call to mind the versatile and wonderful Maginn, the scholar, the wit, the humorist, the poet, the politician—yet squandering recklessly, and, indeed, uselessly, on ancient themes, and modern trifles, and party politics, and denationalizing squibs, talents and acquirements that might have placed him second only to Swift on the muster-roll of our literary giants? Need we mention the gay, the witty, the accomplished "Prout," happily for PIO NONO and the Daily News (and for Ireland too, we trust) still breathing the inspired air of the "Eternal City," whose genius, as if in scorn of the easy triumph of successful English versification, boldly enters the lists, now with Anacreon or Horace, now with Beranger or Parini, and meeting them with their own weapons, comes off unconquered with wreaths and plaudits from the circus. Let him not, however, forget "the pleasant waters" of his native river. The simple ballad in which he has united for ever his own name with that of the "Allua of Song," will be recollected, when all his clever imitations and successful classicalities will be utterly forgotten.

The next of our eminent writers whose name occurs to us, is Dr. Anster—more celebrated, perhaps, than either of the former, as a translator. He has, as every one knows, the rare merit of having produced the best translation of the most world-famous poem that the human intellect has produced since the "Inferno," namely, the "Faust" of Goethe. His work is one of, perhaps, the only four really good, correct, yet spirited translations of lengthy foreign poems, which English literature possesses; the other three being Coleridge's "Wallenstein," Cary's "Divina Commedia," and Rose's "Orlando Furioso." We confess, however, that some of his own smaller original compositions have for us a far greater charm than his more celebrated translation; and had we any influ-

ence with "the good people," we would implore of them to play him some such trick as is recorded in his own exquisite little ballad of "The Fairy Child," but with a difference. We would have them substitute a strong, hardy, vigorous, healthy offspring of his own genius, for the strange, supernatural, though beautiful being he has adopted, and on whom he has lavished so much of his care and affection.

Of Clarence Mangan it is scarcely necessary for us to say anything in this place. Our readers have known him long, and we believe estimate him at his proper value—as, indeed, the public generally seem at length inclined to do, if we are to take the following tribute from a friendly but judicious critic, as its slowly-matured decision on the subject:—"We fear not to say that, in power of versification, variety of rhythmic arrangement, melodious combinations of phrase, vigour of thought, and force of expression, Mr. Mangan is unequalled by any living writer."* This is high praise, in which we cordially concur. We may, however, be permitted to express our admiration and wonder at the spontaneity of his genius, as well as its richness and profusion. Month after month he twirls his poetical kaleidoscope, as if it required no effort but the shifting of his fingers to produce those ever-changing forms of the beautiful and the grotesque in which he delights to indulge. He seems but to breathe on the strange quaint legends and wild melodies of distant lands, frozen up, as it were, by the frosts of a hundred dialects, and lo! as if of their own accord, the foreign harmonies break melodiously on the startled ear, like the tunes in the bugle-horn of Munchausen! If we had not seen him in the flesh, if we had not shook his delicate hand, and been held by "his glittering eye," like the wedding-guest by the Ancient Mariner, so miraculous seems his acquaintance with all tongues known and unknown—so familiar does he appear with all authors, dead, living, and unborn, that we would be strongly inclined to suspect the respectable and prudent publisher of this magazine of having secured, "at enormous expense," the reversion

---

* "A Book of Ballads from the German." By Percy Boyd, Esq. Dublin: James McGlashan, D'Olier-street. 1848.

* Dublin Evening Mail, January 17th, 1848.

of the *Wandering Jew* from M. Sue, now that that famous personage must live by his wits, after being despoiled of all his funded property by those terrible fellows, the Jesuits! However, as we have certified that Clarence Mangan, though unquestionably mysterious, is yet a reality, and not a myth, we can only account for this faculty, by supposing him under the influence of a species of etymological mesmerism, or poetical clairvoyance, before which all languages lie open—fortunately for dictionary-compilers and grammarians, no very common state of mind.

Mr. Mangan has impressed his name upon many a theme, indeed upon so many, that a considerable portion of them must inevitably sink in the river of Lethe, with those medals which Lord Bacon tells us bear the names of the generality of men inscribed upon them. But, fortunately for himself, he has also stamped his name on a few, and those principally his own creation, which we rest satisfied the swans of immortality, also mentioned by the same authority, will rescue from the oblivious flood, and bear to the Temple of Fame, there to be consecrated for ever.

Before proceeding to the beautiful volume which it is our present duty and pleasure to notice, we shall briefly allude to one other language, perhaps more "foreign" to most of us than any of those already mentioned, from which valuable translations have been recently made—we mean the ancient language of this country. In this important department of our literature, several writers have acquitted themselves with great credit to themselves, and advantage to their country. The late Thomas Furlong, Mr. Dalton the historian, and others, in Hardiman's valuable work on the ancient minstrelsy of Ireland; Jeremiah Joseph Callanan, also deceased; Mr. Mangan, and Mr. Edward Walsh, in other publications. But there is one writer who has so pre-eminently succeeded in this particular department, that we cannot refrain from making particular mention of him—

" A casement high and triple-arched there was,
All garlanded with carven imageries
Of fruits and flowers, and bunches of knot-grass,
And diamonded with panes of quaint device
Innumerable, of stains and splendid dyes,
As are the tiger-moth's deep damasked wings."

we need scarcely say we mean Mr. Samuel Ferguson. Although, to us at least, the principal charm of this gentleman's translations consist in their being conceived, moulded, and expressed in the old spirit of this country, to readers of English literature generally, they possess a merit which will be more generally appreciated—namely, their extreme novelty and originality of sentiment, as well as idiom. Discarding the vile gibberish which, from the days of " Lillibulero " to the present hour, is imposed upon our fellow-subjects "in that part of the United Kingdom called" England, as genuine, racy, Hibernian phraseology, in noble disregard of the " cheap and nasty" mock nationality to which we have alluded, and which consists in false spelling, exaggerated mispronunciation, and treasonable grammar, he has given us in correct English, such as Swift or Southey might have used—a style of poetry which, as far as British literature generally is concerned, is perfectly new, and which, in this country, like the blood of the Geraldines, is more Irish than the Irish itself.

Thus having passed in review the several writers who have distinguished themselves in our recent and current literature as translators, we now come to "the Herr Boyd" himself, if we may be permitted to use the language of our author's fair visitor at Heidelberg, as recorded in the lively and pleasant preface to his volume. And first, as to the volume itself. Its external and internal embellishments, its pictorial illustrations, its floral capitals and rustic borders, are all executed with great elegance and care, and reflect the utmost credit, as well on the liberality of the publisher, in projecting, as on the taste and skill of the artist in carrying out the work. As to the binding, we would be at a loss for some suitable comparison, if Lord Byron had not, very good-naturedly, supplied us with one, in his description of the cohorts of the Assyrian—"gleaming in purple and gold," or, still better, that exquisite picture of the casement of the Lady Madeline, as given to us by John Keats :—

And such, dear reader, are the covers of the volume before us. From what has been already stated of the number and merit of the translators who have preceded Mr. Boyd—and we have only mentioned a few of those more immediately connected with this country, to the exclusion of Sir Bulwer Lytton, Mr. Merivale, and many others—our readers will perceive that a new candidate for public favour has certain difficulties and prejudices to overcome, before he can obtain a fair and dispassionate judgment upon his efforts. If he breaks new ground, and attempts to introduce a novel or original style, he will be pronounced presumptuous or eccentric. If he follows in the wake of others, no matter how sweet or perfect the harmony of his versification, he will be condemned for feebleness or imitation. If, as is the case in a few instances in the present volume, he offers a new version of some poem already fixed in the memory of his readers, and familiarized by an earlier English dress, it will be judged of in most instances, not by its closeness to the original, but by its remoteness from that with which the public ear is familiar. Mr. Boyd, however, both in the ballads translated by other writers, of which he gives a new rendering, and in the still greater number which, for the first time, are introduced to the English reader in his volume, can bear the strongest test, and the most stubborn prejudice to which, as we have stated, a new writer must be exposed. Old favorites, indeed, he will not displace; but many will be delighted to hear the strains to which they have been accustomed to listen with delight, breathing from a newer instrument, which, if less powerful or variable than the old, is uniformly more correct in its utterance, and generally more simple and harmonious in its modulations.

The first poem which we shall extract from Mr. Boyd's volume, is one that will recall to many of our readers the happiest and purest moments of their existence. When, perhaps, under circumstances somewhat similar to those so touchingly described by the German poet, their hearts first imbibed the sacred knowledge of God's Holy Word—moved by the divine precepts of the New Testament, as well as by the idyllic beauty of the Old.

It may be hung up in the memory-cabinet of those who recollect the exquisite picture with which Lamartine opens his " Voyage en Orient," of the fine old Bible of Royoumont, which had engravings of sacred subjects in all the pages, and to the early perusal of which, at his mother's knee, he attributed the religious direction of his tastes and intellect in after-life. " There was Sarah, there was Tobit and his angel, there was Joseph, or Samuel; above all there were those fine patriarchal scenes, where the solemn and primitive nature of the East was mingled with every act of that simple and marvellous life which was led by the early men." Now let our readers compare the companion-picture by Freiligrath :—

" THE PICTURE-BIBLE.

" Hail to thee ! time-worn teacher,
    Friend of my childhood's days ;
How oft, by dear hands open'd,
    Thy page has met my gaze—
When from his pastime turning,
    The boy, in glad surprise,
Has seen before him burning,
    The blaze of Eastern skies !

" Wide hast thou flung the portals
    Of many a clime, I ween,
And on thy picture-pages
    Are dreams of beauty seen.
Thanks ! that a new world greeteth,
    Through thee, my wondering eye ;
The palm-tree and the desert,
    And camels gliding by.

" 'Tis thou hast brought them near me,
    Sages and seers of old,
Whose lives inspired prophets
    In burning words have told.
And I see young, graceful maidens,
    Of face and form divine,
Like dreams of rarest beauty,
    Upon thy pages shine.

" Then come the patriarch sages,
    Men of the hoary head :
And as they pass, bright angels
    Keep watch upon their tread.
Their flocks—I saw them drinking
    From the river's crystal flood,
As, wrapt in noon-day musing,
    Before thy page I stood.

" E'en at this hour I see thee,
    Though years have passed since then,
With thy pages open lying
    On the old arm-chair again,

With beauty, fresh and changeless,
Thy pictures still are bright
As when I first bent o'er them,
With all a child's delight.

" Once more I am beholding
Those forms grotesque and strange,
Their colour hath not faded,
Their beauty cannot change ;
For every well-known picture,
By the artist's cunning wrought,
And every bud and blossom
Is with holy meaning fraught.

" Again I stand entreating,
Beside my mother's knee,
And she tells once more the meaning
Of each quaint mystery ;
And my grey-haired father near me,
As I bend my eager brow—
Methinks, still gently smiling,
I see the old man now.

" Oh, times ! old times ! for ever
Pass'd like a vision by,
The Picture-Bible gleaming,—
The young believing eye ;
Those dear old parents bending
O'er the boy so young and gay ;
The true and trusting childhood,
All, all have passed away !"

There is scarcely anything more characteristic of the German ballad than
the delicacy with which the moral of
the poem is conveyed. It is not appended or attached to the body of the
narrative, and separately labelled, as
is generally the case in English with
fables and didactic pieces. It forms
an essential and integral portion of the
composition, although, perhaps, con-
concealed till the very end, when it
gives a new and unexpected meaning
to the poem, and serves as a key to the
entire. In the English and Spanish
ballads, variety of incident, strength of
passion, and picturesque accessories,
both of locality and costume, are generally what are looked for and found.
The story is told for its own sake, and
relished for its incident and sentiment.
In the German ballads, it is true,
many are of this kind, but many of
them, also, have the peculiar characteristic and charm to which we have
alluded, and of which the poem we are
about to quote presents a favorable
example. In this ballad (which would
not form an ungraceful little episode
in " Paradise and the Peri"), the precise manner in which, we conceive,

English and German poetry of this
kind agrees and differs, is pretty clearly
displayed. An English writer, treating this subject, would be very likely
to use the same machinery, introduce
the same incident, and paint the same
result—but only so far as the disappointment of the poor loving soul, and
the inconstancy and infidelity of human
affections were concerned. He would
scarcely introduce the new and beautiful truth with which the German poet
finishes and perfects his work, and
which, like the glance of Nora Creina,
" with unexpected light surprises !"—

" THE POOR SOUL.

" A spirit once lay sighing
Beyond that dim unknown,
Where through long years of penance
The souls of mortals groan.

" ' And still,' sighed the poor spirit,
' A thousand years of pain
I'd live, could I behold once more
Mine own dear love again.'

" From heaven an Angel floating,
With wings as white as snow,
In his arms took up the Spirit,
To heal of all its woe.

" In gentle accents speaking
Full of sweet peace and love
' Come with me, hapless Spirit,
To Heaven's bright realms above.

" But the mournful Spirit answered,
' I'd pass a life of pain,
Could I revisit only
The bright green earth again.

" ' A thousand years of penance
In torture I would dwell,
To see for one brief instant
Him whom I loved so well.'

" A glance of tender pity
In the Angel's eye had birth,
As he bore the weeping Spirit
Again to the green earth.

" ' Beneath the broad, cool shadow
Of the waving linden-tree,
I know mine own love wanders,
Still sorrowing for me.'

" When they near'd the ancient lindens,
Where the pleasant waters flow,
There sat her heart's beloved,
But he loved another now.

" For 'neath the waving shadows
Of their ancient trysting-place,
A gentle maid reclining,
Was locked in love's embrace.

" Then, through the hapless Spirit,
Sharp pangs of sorrow thrill ;
But the bright Angel gently,
In his dear arms held her still.

" And higher still, and higher,
They wing'd their way above,
Until they reach'd the portals
Of heaven's bright halls of love.

" Then sighed the Spirit, weeping,
' I cannot enter there ;
A thousand years of penance
'Tis yet my lot to bear.'

" A smile benign and tender
O'er the Angel's features stole,
As he gazed with heavenly pity
On the fond and hapless Soul.

' Poor Spirit ! all thy sorrows,
Thy woes, are o'er at last—
*In the torture of one moment,
Thy thousand years have passed.'* "

Another not unusual excellence in
the German ballads is, the graceful
manner in which the story is conveyed
to the mind of the reader, rather by
inference than by direct narration.
In English ballad poetry, generally,
except that of the highest order, the
incidents are given too much in detail;
by which means, while the memory
and attention of the reader are over-
strained, his imagination is left totally
unemployed. This is particularly the
fault of young writers, who, being
more fortunate than the " Knife-
grinder," in *having* " a story to tell,"
go as far back for the beginning of
their subject as a Welsh genealogist
for his ancestor. They manage these
things better in the fatherland, as the
following pathetic and simple little
ballad will satisfactorily prove. In it
how many delightful glimpses do we
get of by-gone and happier visits over
the Rhine, made by the three friends,
under the pretence, indeed, of drinking the " rich wine of Asmanshauser,"
for which the little inn was famous ;
but drawn thither in reality, though
unconsciously, by the love which each
of them nourished in his heart—a

secret almost as little known to himself as to his companions—for

" THE LANDLADY'S LITTLE DAUGHTER.

" O'er Heidelberg's old castle
The morning sunbeams shine,
As journey forth three students
Across the silver Rhine ;
And they come to a small hostel,
Where, in the time of old,
Rich wine of Asmanshauser
The good Frau Wirthin sold.

" ' We know the juice is famous
Which from thy grape is press'd,
Come, then, a flagon give us,
Frau Wirthin, of thy best.'
' High in the mantling brimmer
The rich wine sparkles red ;
But she whose eye was brighter—
My gentle child—is dead !'

" Then forth into the chamber
They took their mournful way ;
Where, like a fair flower wither'd,
Frau Wirthin's daughter lay :
And the foremost on her gazing,
As he marked her pale cold brow,
Said, ' Maiden, ah ! I knew not
How I loved thee until now !'

" When the second saw her lying,
Calmly as one that slept,
He turn'd him in the chamber,
And bow'd his head and wept.
But the third, before replacing
O'er her couch the funeral veil,
Bent down, and kiss'd the maiden
Upon her lips so pale :
' To thee the dearest homage
I gave, which heart can pay ;
Stern Death may take thy beauty,
But not my love—away !' "

This poem is illustrated by one of
the best and most characteristic engravings in the volume.
But it is not alone in the gentle
cadence of these ballads of the heart
that Mr. Boyd has succeeded ; he is,
perhaps, even more felicitous in conveying the stronger and more vigorous language in which the German
poet expresses the yearnings of his
own heart, of his country, and of his
age, for " Freedom and Right." It
will be perceived, that in the " Garland of Glory," wherewith the coming
time is to be adorned, " the Shamrock
of Erin" is not forgotten. May it be
a true prophecy !

68. continued

"FREEDOM AND RIGHT.

(FREILIGRATH.)

" Oh, think not she sleepeth with those who have perish'd
In dungeons unnumber'd, by Tyranny's sword ;
In the hearts of the free shall her dear name be cherish'd,
Though their lips are forbidden to utter 'the Word.'
Yes ! though lone exiles, by mountain and valley
They wander, uncheer'd by lost Liberty's light,
There's a pulse in the heart of the Freeman to rally,
While Freedom still liveth, and with her the Right.
For Freedom and Right !

" Till Victory's sunburst shall flash o'er our standard,
No check must impede us—no danger affright—
But, with courage redoubted, the first in the vanward,
Our war-cry will thunder, ' For Freedom ;—for Right !'
These twin ones, the holy, have come, born of heaven,
To earth, by a path track'd in colours of light ;
To the Right let the honours of Freedom be given,
To the Free be the glories ascribed of the Right.
Hail ! the Freedom ! the Right !

" Let this, too, inspire us—they never were flying
From fight unto fight, more exulting than now ;
And the souls which have longest in bondage been lying,
Are stirr'd with the rapture of Liberty's glow.
Oh ! let but one ray of that meteor of wonder,
Burst in through the darkness of slavery's night ;
And like magic the bonds of the serf are asunder,
And the chains of the Negro are rent at the sight.
The Freedom ! the Right !

" Yes ! your banner of crimson floats broad in the vanward,
The nations have gather'd to see it unfurl'd ;
For the motto emblazon'd on Liberty's standard,
Is the death of oppression, that Right rules the world.
What a halo of glory, O God ! they shine clear in,
Like a garland hung over that banner of might ;
There is Germany's oak, and the shamrock of Erin,
And the olive of Greece in that garland of light.
The Freedom ! the Right !

" Though many a heart that now throbs shall be lying
In peace, its last slumber and rest will be light ;
And over their graves shall that standard, far flying,
Tell how they fought for ' The Freedom, the Right !'
To the memory, then, of the brave, the true-hearted—
Fill up ! they have battled 'gainst tyranny's might ;
Nor ceased from the struggle till life had departed :
Hurra ! Right for ever ! and Freedom through Right !
The Freedom ! the Right !"

This noble ballad, which may be considered the cosmopolitan theory or creed of Freedom, is reduced to very intelligible practice, as far, at least, as Germany is concerned, in another poem, which Mr. Boyd has also translated very spiritedly. Although we have already extracted so largely from the volume, *this* one we must give as a practical commentary on the last :—

"THE RHINE.

" No ; they shall never have it,
The free, the German Rhine !
Though, vulture-like, to rend it,
With talons fierce they pine ;
So long as gently floating
Between its banks of green,
A ship shall on the current
Of that sweet stream be seen—
No ; they shall never have it !

" They shall never have it—never !
The glorious German Rhine !
While patriot hearts are bathed
In its generous purple wine ;
So long as the broad shadows
Of tall cliffs o'er it gleam ;
So long as proud cathedrals
Are imaged in its stream—
No ; they shall never have it !

" No ; they shall never have it,
The free, the German Rhine !
While round its graceful maidens
The arms of strong men twine ;
And while one fish within it
Springs glittering from the deep ;
And while soft midnight music
Shall o'er its waters sweep :
No ; they shall never have it,
The German Rhine's free wave,
Till its sacred tide is flowing
Above the last man's grave."

Such of our readers as would wish to compare Mangan's version of this celebrated song with the foregoing, will find it in the number of our Magazine for October, 1841 ; it will amply repay the trouble of the search.

Having expressed *our* opinion of some of Mr. Boyd's predecessors in the pleasant region of translation, and given to our readers a few of the fruits of his experience, and the results of those principles by which he has been guided, we think it only fair that he should be allowed to express his own opinions upon these matters in his own words :—

" Most of the translations with which I am acquainted," says Mr. Boyd, in his preface, " are, in my humble judgment, either too literal or too obscure. In some, the original is followed—word for word, and line for line—with an accuracy ' so excruciating,' that the sense is diluted, and the poem rendered perfectly distasteful to the English reader. Literal translation, especially in poetry, I hold to be impracticable, and the worst of all translators those who pride themselves the most upon a strict adherence to the original : in others, the original is lost sight of altogether, new thoughts and new images are introduced, always to the detriment of the piece ; and—with the exception of the poems of Schiller, which have been translated by Sir E. Bulwer Lytton, with a fidelity and a beauty which cannot be surpassed, and can only be appreciated by those who know the difficulty of understanding this Author—most of the translators have fallen into one or other of these errors.

" In this volume, it has been my endeavour to avoid both extremes. Whether the attempt is fated to be successful, remains to be decided. The object of a translator ought to be, to express himself as nearly as possible in the words which the poet would have adopted, had he been writing in the language into which the translation is made. I do not pretend to intrude these poems on the public as literal translations, but I have not marred their beauty by introducing thoughts which they do not contain. He who would translate well, ought, after reading the poem, to close the book, and then, having reflected upon the subject, endeavour to clothe the ideas in the language into which he translates ; if he is able to adopt the cadence and the rhythm of the original, so much the better."

" It is the opinion of Schlegel that verse translation should be nearer than paraphrase, but less close to it than metaphrase. I quote from memory, but this is the sum and substance of that great critic's maxim : it is, at all events, that by which I have been guided."

Without stopping to question the accuracy of this quotation from Schlegel, which, however, sounds to us more like one of the oracular dogmas of "glorious John," the English translator of Virgil, than the matured opinion of that great German translator as well as critic, whose own rendering of Shakespeare and Calderon might be termed metaphrastic, if, owing to the inferiority of the English to the German language as a medium of translation, we had not become habituated to connect a want of spirit and poetic harmony with this phrase. Without dwelling on this particular observation, we beg leave to express our dissent from the too-sweeping condemnation which our author has passed upon literal translations. Even in the English language, with which he had principally to do, and which, from its comparative want of flexibility and copiousness, presents very great difficulties to the translator as well from the ancient classic languages of Europe, as from the modern Italian, Spanish, and German, we think the attempt has been made with complete success. If Mr. Boyd will look into the translation of " Ariosto" by Mr. Rose, already mentioned, he will find the " soft bastard

394

Latin" of the Orlando "done into" very legitimate and literal English, without any of that "excruciating" torture which he conceives the process necessarily demands. Even the old translation by Harrington, which, however, does little more than preserve the outward form of the original, is better than that by Hoole, which seems written in accordance with the rule laid down by our author, and which to all, except the "mere" English reader, is awfully and tremendously unendurable. The attentive perusal of Mr. Rose's work, side by side with the original, has convinced us that English translators have indolently exaggerated difficulties that industry and a due reverence for their subject might have overcome. Instead of reproducing some great foreign work for the admiration of their countrymen, with the colouring and shading, the proportions, and the perspective of the

original, they have adopted a new standard altogether—changed the character of the composition, and altered its tone, much in the way that a Chinese painter would copy a Canaletti. And thus we have "elegant mistakes," like Pope's Homer—painted or gilded casts from the antique, instead of bronze or marble facsimiles. In German, which, Mr. Boyd must be well aware, is so rich in translations, conscientiously and scrupulously literal, the very reverse of the rule laid down in his preface, would seem to be the one that guided the great masters of translation in that language. However, as Mr. Boyd's practice is so much better than his precept, and as "the right to differ" is not exclusively the privilege of Irish politicians, we shall not further press our own views upon the subject, but take leave of our author and his very beautiful volume, with the following lively poem from Goethe:—

"A LAY OF CHRISTMAS.

I.

" We cheerfully sing, and inscribe our glad lay
To the Lord of the Castle here seated,
Whose grandson espoused a fair lady to-day,
And the bridal-guests sumptuously fêted.
In the late holy wars he won honour and fame—
By splendid achievements emblazon'd his name ;
Yet, behold, when adown from his charger he came
To his mansion, he found it as open as day,
His property vanish'd, his servants away !

II.

" There you stand, noble Count ; you are now in your home,
And more comfortless quarters you scarcely could find ;
Through the chambers neglected the breezes may roam,
And all through the casements loud whistles the wind.
What now can be done on this cold autumn night—
No servant attending—your rooms in sad plight ;
But patiently wait the return of daylight.
In the meantime the moonbeams will show you where best,
On some straw as a couch, you may lie down and rest.

III.

" There, seeking repose, half asleep as he lay,
Something moves about under his bed ;
Perhaps a starved rat may be rustling his way—
For a long time a stranger to bread ;
When, lo! issues forth a diminutive wight—
An elegant Fay in a circle of light—
Who, with action so graceful, and speech most polite,
Thus addresses the Count, as he, drowsily peeping,
Can scarcely be sure if he's waking or sleeping :

IV.

" ' Our festive assemblies we held in this place,
When, your castle forsaking, to war you had gone ;
And as we all deemed that this yet was the case,
We thought that our revels we still might hold on.

So we plead now for pardon, and hope you'll agree
To our giving a fête in good humour and glee,
And feasting the bride of the highest degree !'
The Count, through his dream, as he lay at his ease,
Says, ''Tis still at your service, whenever you please.'

V.

" In an instant, three horsemen, who rode on before,
From under the bed leave their station ;
Next follow a singing and musical choir,
Comic elves of this miniature nation ;
While coaches and chariots came rolling along,
Till the eye and the ear were confused with the throng,
And it seemed as a Queen to the castle had gone ;
At last came a splendid gilt carriage,
With the bride and her suite to the marriage.

VI.

" Alighting, they enter with rapid galope,
And around the saloon take their places ;
To waltzes and polkas they joyously hop,
With partners who dance like the Graces.
There they pipe, and they fiddle, and tinkle, and play ;
They spin round in circles, so noisy and gay,
And they rustle, and bustle, and prattle away ;
Then the count, more bewilder'd than ever, now deems
The whole the effect of his feverish dreams.

VII.

" Thus they clatter, and chatter, and frolic in saal,
Amid benches and tables all prancing ;
Till the banqueting-room offers welcome to all,
And supper succeeds to the dancing.
The dainties so magic, are sliced so fine ;
With roebuck, and wild-fowl, and fish from the Rhine,
While goblets go round of the costliest wine ;
And the festive enjoyments continue so long,
That they vanish away at the last with a song.

VIII.

" But here let us sing of what later took place,
When the revelry ceased and the noise ;
How the pageant, devised by the frolicsome race,
The Count now adopts and enjoys.
So the trumpet is heard, with its musical strain—
A splendid procession moves over the plain,
With chariots and horsemen, a numberless train ;
All cordially joining, so happy and gay,
To honour the nuptials we witness to-day."

395

Art. I.—*Erinnerungen an Wilhelm von Humboldt.* Von Gustav Schlesier. Stuttgart: Köhler.

Reminiscences of William von Humboldt. By Gustavus Schlesier. Stuttgart.

Literature has known a speedy development in Germany, and almost as speedy a decline. Lessing and Klopstock were the first great names. Then followed the graceful Wieland and the serious Herder. Then arose the two great boasts of the German language and nation, the ideal Schiller and the almost-universal Goethe. In the train of these, though partially opposed to them in the literary battles of the day, and ranged under another standard, came the romantic Tieck, the two Schlegels, the mystic Werner, the gloomy Kleist, and last, though not least, the eminently-artistic bard of Austria, Grillparzer. Such names as Müllner, or Kotzebue, or even Körner, cannot be cited in this roll of high degree; nor can we recognize the more modern lyric bards, some of whose earliest creations, however, date from the Augustan age of Germany, as worthy of admission into this category of literary aristocrats. Rückert, though kindly, and sweet, and graceful, has not sufficient power; Freiligrath, though animated, and vigorous, and picturesque, is too deficient in thought; Uhland, though generally pleasing, is too essentially common-place; and neither Karl Simrock, nor Chamisso, nor Gutzkow the dramatist, and still less Herwegh or Lenau, despite their various degrees of merit, can be classed with those masterminds, which wrought together in Germany towards the commencement of the nineteenth century.

It will be seen that we allude mainly to the poets among our Teutonic brethren. But these are also its greatest prose writers, Lessing, Wieland, Herder, Goethe, Schiller, and Tieck, being the classic prosaists of Germany; whilst Frederic von Schlegel has little merit as a bard, and can only live by his Philosophy of History, and other kindred works. In novel literature, however, our friends the Germans are not poor. The names most worthy of citation, besides those already given, including Kleist, are Jean Paul, Hoffman, Fouqué, and perhaps Zschocke; for neither Hauff nor Spindler, nor other moderns, can lay claim to more than a secondary degree of merit. Their historians, including even Johannes von Müller, have not exercised a powerful influence on the national mind; and certainly their philosophers, or pseudo-philosophers, from Kant to Hegel, have not been of much service to German literature.

But to resume. Of all these really great men, (though in writing this, we feel that we are scarcely entitled to honour Augustus von Schlegel with such an appellation, despite his admirable translations,) two alone survive; Tieck, and the author of "Sappho," "The Golden Fleece," and "The Dream a Life," to whom we may possibly on some future occasion devote a special inquiry, one of the most classical of dramatists, severely chaste in design and execution, and yet intensely real, the partially unrecognized, but undoubtedly great, Grillparzer. *He* lives still, and not only lives, but writes: three of his most beautiful dramas have appeared within the last few years; but from various causes, mainly political, which it were too tedious to develop here, they have not attracted that attention, and excited that sympathy, which were due to their intrinsic merits. Grillparzer stands as a giant among a race of dwarfs, apparently more or less incapable to conceive his greatness: he will not yield his homage to all the petty tendencies of the hour; he is not content to swell the vulgar party cry which Gutzkow and his colleagues are shouting at the pitch of their voices; and he is neglected, accordingly, as our own great Southey has too long been among ourselves. Nevertheless, his time will come. But, with this remarkable exception, and that of Tieck, whose last work, "Vittoria Acorombona," has much merit, the great luminaries of Germany now shine only in the reflected glory of those works which have secured their earthly immortality.

We have before us the biography of a man who was the intimate friend, and even counsellor, of both Goethe and Schiller; of William von Humboldt, elder brother of the still living Alexander, author of "Kosmos;" one of the most remarkable thinkers, critics, practical statesmen, and diplomatists of his time, which was that of the great burst of literary genius above alluded to. As critic and thinker he more especially engages our attention: we see in him a contemporary of the greatest German authors, recognized by them as their co-equal; as "ebenbürtig" (the Germans would express it) with themselves. And although the English reader may not pursue the inquiries into the æsthetic value of "the ideal" and "the natural," as philosophically conducted on Kantian and other recondite principles by Humboldt and Schiller, with the same minute attention which German thinkers no doubt bestow on them, nevertheless all who are in any degree interested in German literature cannot but feel pleasure in entering as it were the workshops of the great artists of a foreign land, penetrating into the recesses of their minds, and tracing their creations to their source; all which they may well do in the perusal of the work before us.

Charles William von Humboldt, generally known by the name of William only, was born on the 22nd of June, 1767, at Potsdam. His father was the Baron von Humboldt, a major in the Prussian army, and gentleman of the bedchamber to the king, generally reputed to be a man of sound sense and superior capacity. An interesting account is given of William's education with his brother Alexander. From the first both brothers, but more especially William, displayed an uncommon degree of ability. Their literary tendencies are clearly indicated in the following interesting passage which we accordingly render at length.

"It may be safely asserted, that the education of both brothers was at once singularly many-sided and thoroughly solid. For, although both the desire exhibited for universality of knowledge, and the exactness with which inquiries on any special subject were conducted, were natural instincts of the Humboldts, still such instincts require to be developed by education and guidance, favour and opportunity. By the side of this universality, which went so far in the elder brother, William, that he expressed his wish to leave nothing on earth unknown, the eagerness appears the more remarkable, with which either threw himself upon his own special division of labour, Alexander addressing himself to natural science in its widest sense, William to classical antiquity, art, philosophy, and language. Whilst the former was destined to observe external nature under every form, animate and inanimate, in plants, beasts, and men, William forced his way into the innermost sanctuary of mankind, the spirit-world within, and language, its first creation. Though these territories, in which each of them sought his individual home, may appear remote from one another, yet do they approximate in many ways, and possess one common basis. Thus, if we examine William, we shall find in him also the student of external nature, but with this difference, that such study was to him but *the means* of investigating the internal world and its phenomena."

Subsequently we read:—

"He who heard Humboldt on special occasions discourse with his brother, or even with Goethe, would have imagined him to be a naturalist only; and would have been astounded, indeed, to recognize a spirit of a totally opposed order, when he conversed at other times with Goethe, or with Schiller, or with Wolf, the classical scholar."

William von Humboldt appears to have had much that was English in his character, intermingled, however, with a vast amount of Germanism. In his youth, and even throughout life, a certain tendency to sentiment, which is inseparable from all true greatness, appears to have characterized his heart and soul: but he was habitually cold in semblance, rarely displaying emotion on the most solemn occasions. Thus, when saved from drowning by his friend Stieglitz, he expressed no deep gratitude to his friend, or affection for his distant loved ones; somewhat to the surprise of Varnhagen, who records the fact, and who would have been better pleased had he "made a scene" of it: to our satisfaction, on the contrary, who believe it to be the natural instinct of all men who feel deeply, to conceal emotions on such occasions beneath a playful exterior, and laugh and joke, as Humboldt did on the evening in question. We are not contending for constant reserve in all the actions of life: there are times at which reserve is totally out of place—when we can console or strengthen others. It is out of place, too, when we would convey to others our perceptions of the good, and great, and beautiful, and teach them to admire and love with us; and, more particularly, it is wholly out of place when the prayers of the faithful are to be led, or the devotional affections excited, within the house of God. But to resume: this external coldness, with the depth of affection beneath it, which characterized Humboldt, have certainly something English about them; though, perhaps, we might almost as well say Prussian, or, rather, *Berlinese*.

Few men appear to have combined so many distinctive and almost opposite qualities. "The great susceptibility for the perception of all beauty, which," as Schiller says, "made Humboldt an instinctive critic, in no degree excluded energy and activity from his character: with the utmost sensitiveness of feeling was combined the protective coldness of the understanding; and with the boldest elevation of thought, he coupled the minutest study of the dryest details of science." We cannot wonder that such a man should have been recognized by the very greatest among his countrymen, by a Goethe and Schiller, as their authorized privy-counsellor; or that his career should be deemed worthy of the closest investigation at the present day. As literary creator, he has not indeed left much behind him; but he is universally recognized as one of the most valuable of German critics; as one of the noblest of her statesmen (he was Prussian Minister of Public Instruction for several years); as one of the most successful of diplomatists (he represented Prussia at the Congress of Vienna); and as one of the very greatest linguists of all times and countries. Our readers therefore will not wonder at our directing their attention to the biography of such a man.

No doubt they will inquire, and with reason, was he a Christian? For to us, writing in a professedly and distinctly Christian publication, this must ever be the most important of all questions.

We cannot, alas! answer this question in the affirmative, nor can we altogether negative it. Our readers well know, no doubt, that dogmatic Christianity has been either opposed or strangely disregarded by the majority of German thinkers. Lessing led the attack, and Klopstock was no efficient opponent to Lessing. Wieland, though in his youth a Calvinist, to which fact several of his works bear record, was dissatisfied (as he well might be) with the external coldness and unphilosophical narrowness of his Genevan school, and took refuge in universal scepticism, having, indeed, nothing to turn to but cold and rationalistic Lutheranism, as it then existed, or Romanism, with all its false miracles, and pious frauds, and flagrant superstitions. Goethe followed, and confirmed the antichristian, or at least unchristian tendencies of German literature; he was too self-satisfied to require religion; too selfish, too "bequem," or cosily comfortable, to use his own expression. He has told us in his Auto-biography, that repentance always appeared to him tiresome and useless, since it could not bring back the past. A man who could speak thus was indeed remote from the spirit of Christianity. Even the ideal Schiller had not the courage, or perhaps the power, to stem the tide of infidelity.

We do not find one of these German poets or thinkers grappling with the historical difficulties of the question: they neither ventured to assert that our blessed Lord was an impostor (the only solid ground on which the infidel can stand); nor did they contend, with the more modern rationalists and transcendentalists, the German Paulus, the Englishman Carlyle, and the American Emerson, that CHRIST was totally misunderstood by his Apostles; that they themselves were self-deceived, and imagined they wrought miracles, spoke with tongues, &c., though they did nothing of the kind, eventually dying for a faith which was the phantom of their own fancies; nor had they taken refuge in the still more monstrous hypothesis of a Strauss, that the whole history of the New Testament was a myth, and that those who wrote it, without any mutual concert or intentional deception, imagined themselves to be simultaneously inspired, and placed on record as facts witnessed by themselves what never had any being, save in their own diseased imaginings. In truth, both Goethe and Schiller had too much good sense to be satisfied with such theories as these; and as they would not accept historical Christianity, they consequently contented themselves with placing it altogether on one side—with ignoring it, in a word; no doubt the easiest method to pursue. And thus did Humboldt also act, despite the sound sense, and love for practical reality and positive results, which he was in the habit of displaying on other occasions. His age and country were too much for him.

Let us hear his biographer. As, in his office of Public Instructor, it became his duty to supply the necessary funds, for the state religion, and in many ways influence and control its movements, the question naturally suggested itself, whether he was capacitated for such an office; and thus it is answered in the volume before us, after a very German fashion. "He has learnt little of Humboldt, and has seen little of his writings, who can doubt, whether or no he possessed religious feeling. But it is as certain that his religion always remained at a certain distance from positive Christianity; either because the shell of Christianity" (we suppose its dogmatic teaching) "was offensive to him, or because he feared to lose his spiritual freedom and individuality by yielding himself completely to its influence" (what a small fear!). "In this respect he exactly resembled the men of our great literary era, and though we cannot say that the boundaries of the eighteenth century confined him, we must declare him to have been its constant pupil upon this point. We have this characteristic expression of Humboldt's, 'All true knowledge leads to God.' No one of the philosophical systems of his day, was capable of satisfying his intellectual demands; his natural sense left him remote from all the more modern developments of this science. He was not a mere deist, and certainly not a pantheist." "His belief in the personality of the godhead, in a guiding Providence, and an individual immortality, was deeply grounded in him: and was connected, after a peculiar fashion, in part with the ancient dogma of fate, in part with such thesophic and historic-philosophical views, as have been prevalent since the earliest days among Indians, Greeks, and Germans. But he was not anxious to prove every thing, which he in faith conceived, and gladly fled with his most sacred treasures, into the realms of poetry, where nothing can appear too wonderful." (We translate freely here, the original being very awkwardly expressed.) Once more: "His attitude towards dogmatic religion was coldly reserved, but not inimical. He shunned too close approach to it, as though he feared to desecrate the Holy. And where he could not avoid it, he approached it as something positive, having actual existence, on which we all rest, avoiding closer inquiry."

We think that it will be sufficiently obvious to the thoughtful reader, from these remarks, that Humboldt, if he was indeed what he is here represented as being, would in all probability as an Englishman, have strenuously maintained that dogmatic Christianity which we not only ourselves profess, but of which we are at a loss to understand the rejection, by any man possessed of sound sense and integrity of will, devoting his attention to the subject. The truth is, that the absence of civil liberty in Germany was the primary source of freethinking in theology. Human nature will have some subject for inquiry, for cavil, for possible negation. If politics, the natural food, be denied, religion must be assailed in its place; more especially if literary criticism, as in Lessing's writings, and German literature generally, be rather affirmative than negative. Men questioned the propriety of Divine laws, because they were not allowed to complain of human institutions, and being tongue-tied as to the errors of ministers and kings, they contented themselves with assaults on saints, and angels, and their God. Let Germany receive the representative constitution to which she is justly entitled, and the critical negation and unavoidable "opposition" of mankind will be directed to another and a safer channel. Men will have other things to cavil at besides texts of Scripture. The grandeur, and beauty, and unity of the Christian scheme will be recognized, and all minor objections will be felt unavailable, as opposed to the irresistible internal evidence of truth. Humboldt, however, believing in a personal God, a guiding Providence, and an individual immortality, had secured three of the great verities which Christianity has succeeded in impressing on the convictions of almost all who have come within her sphere; he was, too, a self-sacrificing friend, and one of the best of sons, of husbands, and of fathers. He did not think, with that epitome of absurdity and conceit, Emerson, (the praises of whom in Blackwood's Magazine are disgraceful to that periodical,) that prayer, as a means to effect a private end, is theft and meanness; *supposing* (presupposing?) *dualism, and not unity in nature and consciousness:*" that is, supposing God to be *above* man, and not to *be* man; he did not assert, with this self-satisfied scribbler, that " as soon as man is at one with God he will not beg;" that " men's prayers are a disease of the will, as are their creeds a disease of the intellect." —And here we must be permitted to ejaculate, what a compound of selfishness and villanous conceit this Emerson must be!—On the contrary, William von Burgsdorf tells us of his friend Humboldt, that when at Weimar, enjoying the society of Schiller, with his wife and children, but anxious for his mother's health, who was suffering from a severe attack which ended in death at Berlin, " he rarely retired for the night without first praying for his beloved mother." Thus, again, on his deathbed he said to those around him, his children and others, after a period of intense suffering, " Think often of me, but ever gladly. I have been happy, very happy: yesterday, too, was a beautiful day for me, in your love. I shall soon be with your mother, shall soon understand the ways of Providence."

But we do not strive to make Humboldt other than he was:

we take him as the genial thinker and philosopher, almost unconsciously imbued with much of the spirit of Christianity, with a loving heart and a natural reverence for his God; but wanting that patience for the shortcomings and intellectual weaknesses of his fellow men, which he might have attained in a clearer perception of his own sinfulness before his God. We have now said enough on this subject, and can turn our attention to other things, though want of time and space will compel us to be somewhat hasty in our remarks.

Despite the external coldness, which probably contributed in some degree to extract from Talleyrand the assertion,—" que c'était un des hommes d'état dont l'Europe de mon temps n'en a pas compté trois ou quatre," Humboldt remained an enthusiast ever, for the great, the beautiful, and the true. In his last letter to Schiller he writes, " Be convinced, my dear friend, that my interest, my tendencies, can never change. My measure for things remains unalterable : *ideas* are with me supreme. For these I have always lived, to these I shall ever remain faithful; and had I a circle of operation which included the virtual empire of Europe (like Bonaparte's), I should still regard it as a mere inferior means to a higher end ; and such is the faith of my soul." Such a man, whose words and actions were always self-consistent, we cannot but respect, and almost love.

Our readers may ask for some one sample, however brief, of Humboldt's æsthetic criticism, which should justify the praises of a Goethe and a Schiller. We will quote a few lines from an essay published in 1791, which appear to us at once suggestive and correct.

" Poetry," he says, " is, in one point of view, the most perfect of all the fine arts : but in another, it is the weakest. While it represents its objects with less reality and animation than painting or sculpture, it cannot appeal to the feelings with the power of music. But these defects are soon forgotten ; because poetry, independent of its universality, which has been treated on above, steps as it were nearest to the true man in man, interposes the least shadow betwixt *the thought* and its expression."

Again, he says,

" The Beautiful is a power ; true Taste alone can gather all the tones of being into one entrancing harmony. Taste yields an internal calm and unity to all our sensations, physical, moral, and spiritual. Where Taste is wanting, desire is coarse and savage : Science without it may be deep and even sound, but never fruitful in its application. All spiritual perceptions, all treasures of knowledge, are vain without Taste, without the Beautiful : even moral nobility and strength are rough and displeasing, and void of power to feel or bless."

We should devote some paragraphs at least to the political opinions of such a statesman as Humboldt, particularly at the present moment, when the first principles of all government are at stake, and an European war of democratic propagandism is but too likely to ensue. These opinions are in some respects vague, Humboldt appears to have been altogether opposed to a so called pure or absolute democracy, and to have tended decidedly towards the system of constitutional monarchy; though he saw some advantages in absolute monarchy, which could not be realized under other systems. He was a strenuous advocate for individual liberty, thinking this of more import, than any power residing in the mass or community; but this liberty included so much in his eyes as to be almost equivalent to licence. The state, he thought, had nothing to do with morality, in as far as the sexual relations were concerned, or with religion. Marriage should be a private contract, to be kept or broken at the will of the contractors. State education, under any form, was undesirable, as involving a slavish uniformity of mind on the part of the instructed, who would be taught to be citizens and not men.

We need scarcely say in how far these views are opposed to our own. We hold that the nation or community, or the state as the nation's political embodiment, has a similar right with every individual to distinguish right from wrong for itself, in morals, and also in religion. That is, we think it qualified to recognize marriage as holy and binding, Christianity as truth, and the Church as the Church. With regard to education, we do not believe the fears of the Prussian statesman to be altogether groundless. Yet no state-education, no education at least based on religion, can reduce all children to the same flat level. Mind will always assert its prerogative. We would have whatever religious instruction is afforded in national schools based on that religion which is nationally recognized and established. Children, whose parents wished them to obtain other religious teaching, might retire after the hours of general instruction, and seek it privately elsewhere. We are indeed convinced that any state, not animated by the living spirit of Christianity, would make machines of those on whom it exercised too direct an influence; and thus far we agree with the hero of the work before us.

Despite some crotchets, however, we recognize much sound sense in Humboldt's political philosophy. Thus he demanded, as the editor of this biography says, " Partition of the legislative power betwixt the executive and the people; the utmost possible publicity for all government proceedings; finally, control over the execution of the law possessed by the subject;" involving, we presume, our English trial by jury, and system of magistracy.

Schlesier, our author, remarks: " The principle of the partition of legislative power consists in *this*, that no legal or constitutional change can be effected by either branch alone. This is the theory of counteraction, which daily gains ground in Germany, and will soon obtain supremacy." We are very glad to hear it, for it is the only rational political theory we are acquainted with. However, Mr. Schlesier informs us, *à propos* of another German statesman's praises of the British constitution, as realizing this division of power, that Humboldt could not possibly admire, or, at least approve of, the British system. Why, we are left to conjecture; but, we presume, because our hereditary aristocracy, the peerage, is displeasing to our German friend. He does not see that this affords an additional and, indeed, indispensable security to the balance of power. For that balance cannot be at all maintained, when, as in the case above assumed, the people and the executive are the two only agents of power. We have seen an experiment of this nature tried in France for the last thirty years, and must be by this time, after two revolutions, convinced, that a constitutional monarchy cannot exist without a real and not nominal, a powerful and yet popular, aristocracy. This we have, and have long had, in England; and because we have it, our constitution still exists. The late monarch of France strove to make bribery and corruption, with a very restricted right of franchise, supply the place of an aristocracy. We need not say in how far he has failed.

And now abandoning the stormy field of politics, let us linger for a few moments in the bower of the muses. There is matter for a long and careful essay on the literary relations of William von Humboldt with Schiller and Goethe. Schiller, it should be observed, was his especial friend and favourite. Perhaps, indeed, he admired Goethe most, but he appears to have sympathized far more keenly with Schiller. Let us content ourselves for to-day with a remarkable extract from a letter addressed by Humboldt to Schiller, in which his literary confession of faith will be found worthy of the reader's attention. " The imagination of the Greeks," says he, " was ever subject to the influences of Nature: thence its wondrous calm and clearness; thence, also, from its confinement within the boundaries of the world of sense, its unspirituality, which, contrasted with the most thoughtful productions of the moderns, seems almost poverty. In the moderns this clear response to the external world, this susceptibility to the influences of Nature, will not be discovered; the spiritual intention, taking various directions, is every where manifest. Thence their greater depth of meaning; but also their dissimilarity amongst themselves, national and other indirect causes existing for these various tendencies. Thus, both Italians and English are characterized by poetical imagination, which is gay and sensual in the former, deeper, and nearer allied with feeling, in the latter. In the Germans intellectual intention and true sentiment are prominent: Goethe is especially remarkable in the latter respect, more particularly in his plays, Egmont, Faust, and Tasso, which are neither Greek nor English, but wholely and solely original. In you, my dear friend, the intellectual intention is most visible, but this by no means excludes other qualities." In another place he greets Schiller, for his combination of the spiritual and intellectual with the natural, as "the most modern of all modern bards." There is truth in these remarks, though the German critic must be owned to have claimed, with a perhaps pardonable partiality, the lion's share for his own countrymen. But we also should say, that on the whole, English poetry was more characterized by poetic imagination than any other quality; Spanish by richness and copiousness; Italian by fancy; French by invention, taste, and finish; German by intellectual intention, and feeling; though we are not willing to abandon this latter quality to any foreign nation, remembering our own stores of bardic wealth. And here we may be allowed to remark, that we distinctively claim supremacy for our own poetry, as also for our literature generally, over that of any other country. Every nation, even if national vanity suggested the assertion of its own primacy, would place us second in the roll of degree; nor can we conceive how the Germans even can venture to oppose the few great names which they may muster, to our long series of glorious bardic memories.

Of Humboldt's long and valuable Essay on Poetry and its Principles, in connexion with Goethe's exquisite "Hermann and Dorothea," we can merely say that it is well worthy of the perusal of all students of German literature; and Schiller's admirable reply, in which he maintains the superiority of the creative artist to the critic, who can never thoroughly express his own sensations of delight, and who, with all his writing, never touches the essence, the central core of an inspired creation, must also be dismissed by us with a brief general encomium. We must pause, however, to protest against the somewhat flippant comments of our author, Schlesier, on the later productions of Goethe, whether in poetry or prose, which he declares to be altogether valueless. We should have thought that Goethe's own crushing blows on the little critics who snapped around him in his lifetime, would have silenced such tiresome impertinence for ever. The truth is, that Goethe's prose was noble to the last, though somewhat stiff; that his second part of Faust, published the year before his death, was replete with magnificent poetry; and that his oriental series of lyrics, the so-called "West Eastern Divan," the fruit of his latter years, so far from being an utter failure, is characterized by an almost miraculous freshness of thought, and feeling, and truly Goethian beauty. Writers like Mr. Schlesier should beware of negative criticism in such cases, by which they can only make themselves ridiculous. Nevertheless, we cannot withhold from Mr. Schlesier the general meed of impartiality, veracity, pains taking care, and no small degree of talent. He has conferred a benefit on the literary world, and it would be ungrateful in us not to tender him our thanks for the pleasure and instruction his work has afforded us.

We shall not follow William von Humboldt through his long and honourable career, having already exceeded the space which we had allotted to our labours. One remark let us be allowed to make in conclusion. William von Humboldt is the realization of a noble German character: he is the type of what thousands may become under the influence of that constitutional liberty, the full enjoyment of which should not be delayed another hour. We know not whether these pages will meet the eye of the present Prussian monarch, but here do we warn him that the hour for doubt and hesitation has passed: that if he would not abandon Germany to the almost immediate triumph of democracy, he must deprive the vast majority of the titled class in his country of their titular nobility, yielding them some appellation corresponding to our English esquire in its stead, and, further, form a chamber of peers from the mediatized princes, associated with some of the richest men in the country; the eldest son of each of whom should alone inherit the peerage. Then, having thus popularized the nobility, by an act of absolute but indispensable power, let him share the right of legislation with his parliament and people.

401

ART. VI.—1. *Gervinus's History of Literature; Philosophy of Hegel.* Leipsic.

2. *Works of Lessing.* Hamburg.

3. *Works of Goethe.* Cotta, Stuttgart.

4. *Political and Moral Tales, Essays and Dramas. By Gutzkow.* Hamburg.

5. *Strauss's " Leben Jesu," and " Humanitarianism."*

IN the middle ages, Germany was regarded as the heart of Europe; and even now, it remains so important in social and political bearings to its neighbour states, as to justify a more than ordinary attention on our part to its prospects and its policy. Our immediate design is not to treat of the external developments of German states, and their historic fortunes; but rather to define and examine that national faith, or absence of faith, that character, literary moral and social, which we may denominate the German mind, and to which the existing state of disorder amongst our Teutonic neighbours must surely be attributed.

Though France may appear the loudest and most audacious advocate of Democracy, we are much mistaken if the democratic spirit do not finally prove to have established itself more firmly within the limits of the ancient German empire, and be not too likely there to maintain a broader and a more enduring sway. Willingly would we persuade ourselves to the contrary, but the conviction is strengthened within us from day to day, that the present state of anarchy may too possibly terminate in the consolidation, either of one democratic republic, or of a number of federal states, each possessing a republican organization of its own, and subject to a national congress; and if this end be once attained in Germany, we do not think it will soon yield to the erection of a military despotism; which is obviously prepared for " la belle France."

And indeed, though France regards itself, and is by many people considered, the great agent of the Movement which is going on around us, from authority to equality, from reverence to licence, we cannot close our eyes to the fact, that the influence of the German mind in literature, philosophy, and religion has more real weight, and is far more calculated to promote the advance of democratic principles, at least among ourselves. Voltaire, no doubt, was the first to ridicule Christianity, with seeming success and wondrous audacity; but how much more injury to the faith of superior minds has been wrought by the quiet sneers of Goethe! French philosophy was a pert child that endeavoured with a pin to overthrow the Christian Cross; German philosophy may be compared to a hacker and hewer, who seeks, though with a blunted edge, to lay the axe to the root of the tree. Paris shouts, and yells, and hoots, and proclaims its own omniscience daily, and brings forth some new " Eureka," with every gust of popular fancy: but Germany has been long advancing, more slowly but more surely, towards a democratic goal, and seems moved, as by one consent, to hail the final dawn of the era of equality.

It is not to be questioned that an aristocratic and orthodox party still maintains itself in the north of Germany, more especially in Pomerania and Mecklenburg, as also partially in East-Prussia, Brunswick, Hanover, and even Brandenburg; nor can we deny that many individuals, more or less conservative in their views and tendencies, may still be found in various quarters of the Teutonic empire, as we may yet denominate those states in which the Teutonic mind, in some sense or other, rules supreme. Nevertheless, an apparent ascendancy has been acquired by the friends of democratic and pantheistic or infidel innovation in all the great cities of Germany (Hamburg perhaps excepted), whilst it must be admitted to reign in almost undisputed majesty over the existing literature of that country. There is this great difference betwixt France and Germany: in the former, Paris alone (if even Paris), is decidedly democratic in its views and tendencies; other cities, and the provinces generally, being favourable to the re-establishment of conservative order and a monarchical form of government, whilst even Paris is respectful to religion: in Germany, on the other hand, Vienna, Berlin, Francfort, Dresden, Leipsic, Prague, Munich, &c. are all more or less rife for democratic revolutions, and the mind of the country as a whole is directly hostile to the cause of Christianity. These are melancholy facts: but our present purpose is not so much to mourn over, as to recognize and explain, them. No doubt, if the example of foreign lands could ever induce this favoured realm to barter her liberty for licence, and her religion for rationalism, Germany would be far more likely to incite us to such a course of emulation than France. The literature of the latter has never carried very serious weight with us, and it has lost ground of late in popular, at least national, estimation. German literature, on the contrary, has for some time exercised, and may be destined to exercise, an increasing influence over our own. Some of our most admired essayists and public writers are esteemed for their reflection of its worst peculiarities: many of our deepest thinkers have more or less strongly acknowledged its intellectual power: not only our philosophers, but our very theologians, tend to yield more and more attention to its claims, and become imperceptibly imbued with its spirit. It is a remarkable fact, that several of those, who have of late seceded from our National Church in search of an external infallibility, were first led to feel dissatisfaction with the ordinary evidences of faith, from their study of German thinkers, and philosophers, " so called." The German nation, whatever cause may be assigned for the fact, possesses not a single standard writer, with the exceptions of Frederick von Schlegel and Klopstock, who can be regarded as orthodox in religious views and bearings; and the vast majority of its writers of prose or poetry, within the last thirty years, are more or less openly democratic also. That democracy and infidelity should go hand in hand can appear strange to none: both are equally inimical to that principle of reverence for order and degree, on which the scheme of the visible universe may be said to be founded. No doubt, democrats may here and there be found, who are staunch and orthodox Christians: and again, infidels, such as Hobbes or Goethe, may be essentially monarchical in their political views, and even favourable to despotism: nevertheless the general rule is such as antecedent judgment and consideration would lead us to expect.

Such, then, is the existing aspect of the German mind. Christianity is regarded as effete as a Divine Revelation, devoid of value save such as may yet attach itself to its moral code; equality, or the absolute right to govern of the one direct majority, unhampered by any distinction of ranks or division of authority, is too generally acknowledged as the existing rule of things. Some of our readers may incline to imagine that this statement is exaggerated: we do not speak, however, without mature consideration, or without such acquaintance with the subject as may be supposed involved in a residence of many years, and a careful study of the Teutonic mind in its past and present developments: nay, we believe that the broad facts which now lie patent to the world will suffice to vindicate the truth of our assertions. For democracy, even now when we write, may be regarded as partially triumphant throughout Germany, despite the nominal authority of sovereigns who act as vicegerents to the Francfort congress. In Prussia as in Austria, in the minor German states as well, one democratic chamber exists, each and all of these subject to the central assembly, yet each in itself absolute, elected without any regard to rank or property by the one majority of the entire population. There are no chambers of peers, no second chambers of any order, left in existence, save in one or two nominal instances: there is no virtual check to the supremacy of the democratic will.—An apparent re-action may manifest itself at this moment,—nay, does so, both at Vienna and Berlin. All honour to Frederick William! We forgot, for a moment, the innumerable difficulties of his position, and half-condemned the monarch, whom our hearts have long loved, and with whom our sympathies must aye abide. His Quixotic rashness, in dismissing his defenders after some hours of civil conflict, and throwing himself on the mercy of his foes, we are still unable to approve: but we confess that the error was one of greatness. His haste "to bid for imperial sway" we still regard as unbecoming; and, most of all, are we constrained to blame, his fanning of the popular flame against the rights of his Danish brother. But the vigour and resolution, displayed by him at the late crisis, have partially redeemed him in our estimation, and have again commended him to the prayers of all good men. Austria, too, has awakened from her trance. Democracy has been checked, *seemingly* crushed, by the valour of a Windisch-grätz and a Jellalich. Yet, we regret to add, our convictions are still substantially the same. The destiny of both countries would still appear Republican! The system of one chamber elected by universal suffrage remains intact, and seems likely to do so; and we need not add that *this* is utterly inconsistent with any just balance of power, or the possession of rational freedom.

And, for the national infidelity of Germany, we see not how it can be questioned: here and there, no doubt, orthodox Christians may yet be found, in Brandenburg and Westphalia, and elsewhere: but speaking broadly, the mind of the country is hostile to revealed religion; far more decidedly so than that of France. A popular confirmation of this hostility may be found in the rationalistic tone of the press of Germany, the "Augsburg Gazette" included. Whilst in England, no man, whatever be his personal opinions, dares treat Christianity with disrespect, or avow openly his disbelief of it, in any of our great public organs, the very contrary holds good in Germany, where vast moral courage would be requisite to embolden a writer to profess orthodox views in religion in any of the more widely-circulated journals of the country. In France infidelity might be supposed sufficiently rampant, yet an enormous contrast will be discovered betwixt the tone of De Lamartine, Thiers, Victor Hugo, Alexandre Dumas, Eugene Sue, and even George Sand,—and that of the great lights of modern Germany, Gutzkow, Heine, Sallet, or even the moderate Gervinus.

Let it be the purpose of this essay, then, to inquire, how that existing spirit of irreverence originated and developed itself, which

403

now exercises such potent sway over our German brethren; let us trace the causes of this aversion to all constituted authority, of this licence in politics and rationalism in religion: let us endeavour to pierce to the heart of the seeming mystery, and ascertain, how a nation naturally gifted with lofty devotional instincts and a deep-rooted reverence for lawful authority, has degenerated to this democratic level, and assumed so menacing an aspect to the future welfare of humanity.

Our inquiry is obviously twofold, theological and political; but the two questions are so intimately interwoven that we cannot pursue them separately. We must retrograde some way to obtain a firm footing for our researches.—The aspect of Germany in the middle ages, though it has of course much in common with that of France and England, bears yet a special character of its own, being marked by the absence of that spirit of chivalry, which seems to have mainly attached itself to the Norman banner. German knights were, for the more part, rude and uncouth; honest, but savage, brave, yet devoid of gallantry, in the "trouvère" sense of the term. Despite the close connexion which subsisted for so long a time between Germany and Italy, the Teutonic and Ausonian elements never in any degree assimilated. German art, even, was harsh and stiff, and the ideal was little valued by the sturdy Saxon. Nevertheless, the mediæval development of Christianity, which held sway in Germany as in the rest of Europe, whatever might be its corruptions, was not deficient in romantic beauty, and lent some grace by its influence to the sports and customs of those ages. Germany had, too, a middle-age poetry of its own: its "Niebelungen Lied" with the whole cyclus appertaining to it, dates from the tenth century or thereabouts, and is replete with savage grandeur despite the clumsy homeliness which it occasionally exhibits. Two or three centuries later, in the ages more directly preceding the Reformation, Wolfram von Eschenbach and Walther von der Vogelweide, with Gottfried von Strasburg and other knightly minstrels, arose, and founded a more polished school, which owed no little to the influence of the "Provençal Trouvères," and with much of Chaucer's freshness, combined perhaps more dignity of purpose and breadth of design. Still, the German race, as a whole, despite elfs and witches and hobgoblins, was not at that period poetical. Hans Sachs and his followers, with their dull formality and low humour, are perhaps the most characteristic embodiments of the main bearings of Teutonic mind, within the fifteenth and sixteenth centuries.

The effect of the Reformation on its first development could scarcely be esteemed progressive. Whilst in England it heralded the dawn of a mighty national literature, the Elizabethan, it operated in a negative direction amongst our German neighbours. Few authors of any celebrity arose, and intestine brawls and civil wars ensuing, plunged the nation into a state of apparently hopeless darkness. Thus Germany may be reasonably declared to have been centuries behind the other civilized countries of Europe in developing to a state of self-consciousness, in exhibiting external manifestations of the mind of her people. In the middle of the last century, when Frederic of Prussia came to the throne, whilst Italy, Spain, England, and France, in the order thus enumerated, had long accumulated stores of mental and literary trophies, Germany was the Bœotia of Europe, possessing indeed its universities and its learned professors, who sent forth ponderous controversial folios from time to time to its Leipsic book and treatise-market, yet wholly deficient in the original creations of mind, and destined, according to the then current faith even of its own greatest men, to endure the curse of perpetual sterility. To what should we attribute this state of things? Partly, perhaps, to "a tardiness of nature;" partly, no doubt, to the civil conflicts already alluded to, but, in a great degree also, as we believe, to the direct workings of the German Reformation. This is not an ecclesiastical article, and we are therefore only enabled to indicate the bearings of our argument; but setting all preconceived notions aside, derived from our natural admiration of episcopacy and our own Church institutions, so much may surely be admitted by all reasonable men: religion, however spiritual, should have a corresponding expression in the external world, or it cannot long maintain itself. Now Presbyterianism, as finally adopted by Luther and his followers, is cold and harsh in its forms, hostile to the developments of imagination and fancy, critical, and more or less mechanical. It encourages rather a constant cleaving to the first principles of the faith, than an attempt to carry those principles into action. It is anti-poetical, and consequently sterile. Yet a literary manifestation could only be expected from the Protestant States of Germany. The Roman Catholic, taking refuge in blind obedience to an external infallibility, practically anathematized the intellect as "the accursed thing;" as some of our living teachers would bid us do, "since the intellectual power is so liable to abuse." Neither Austria, nor Bavaria, nor the other States of Roman Catholic Germany, exhibited any symptoms of mental life. What movement there was, was confined to Protestantism: and this, after a period of strict Bible orthodoxy, first warm and real, but even then ungracious,—then cold, but still correct,—finally tended to a moderate rationalism at the beginning of the eighteenth century.

70. continued

There was nothing to check this downward course; no proscriptive reverence for church, or creed, or authority. The poetry of life seemed gradually departing, and a dull indifferentism was substituted in its place. Meanwhile, the monarchs and rulers of Germany, having subdued the manly aristocracy of former ages, and converted them from a horde of steel-clad warriors to a vast body of obsequious courtiers, reigned with more and more absolute supremacy over all their subjects. The so-called bureaucratic system, of privy-councillors and paid officials innumerable, came first to its perfection in this period. This bureaucratic class stood betwixt the people and the throne, possessed of almost absolute power over the former, but with little power or *will* to oppose the most monstrous caprices of their lords. Truly, this was a Bœotian age. All the worst corruptions of French manners and English infidel-philosophy, without any of their attendant graces, were visible in Germany at this period: a multitude of small despotic courts, all boasting the immorality, without the refinements of that of "le Grand Monarque," with mistresses, court-marshals, chamberlains, and pages; but neither poets, nor artists, nor statesmen: and, on the other hand, universities, possessing a hoard of useless learning turned to no account; cold, sterile, lifeless, and impregnated more or less with the materialism and rationalism of the then fashionable English philosophy; which, fortunately for us,—thanks to the influence of our Church,—could never penetrate beneath the surface of our national mind. At the same time, the Lutheran Church itself, practically the creation of the universities, was in no sense striving to retrieve lost ground, to war against the evil tendencies of the age; whilst, as has been suggested, dull and servile, yet despotic bureaucracy reigned paramount over the German people. Can we wonder that a literature which finally developed itself under such circumstances, should be hostile as a whole to Christianity? should have even brought about that state of confusion and general faithlessness, which we now behold in our Teutonic brethren?

For the German mind could not sleep for ever. The influence of spirit on spirit is incontestable. With the advance of civilization, and consequently of art and poetry, in the rest of Europe, Germany could not but strive in some sense to keep pace. Though Frederic persisted in disregarding and despising all the efforts of his countrymen to found a literature of their own, some individual minds did arise, which were fired by a spirit of emulation to the effort of creation. Their first essays were naturally most imperfect. For a long time the awkward Alexandrine was the favourite measure of German rhymers, from their desire to imitate French models. The first individuality after Luther

(a mighty mind, but one confined in its sphere of operation), which exercised a potent literary influence, was perhaps that of Lessing, who formed his intellect principally on Shakspeare and the master-pieces of British literature; and after furnishing his countrymen with a series of essays, which went far to correct their bad taste and lead them from the pursuit of the artificial to truth and nature, concluded by laying before them several original works, of more or less merit, but all deserving the appellation of "classical," for their combination of acute sense with truthfulness, and the spirit of genuine life. It would be difficult to overestimate the literary importance of such a drama as "Emilia Galotti," of such a comedy as "Minna von Barnhelm," or of such a dramatic poem as "Nathan the Wise." These works might be said to teach the German nation, for the first time, that they too had a genius and a national intellect of their own; and might claim their place among their European competitors for the prize of mental greatness. But, as might be expected from the antecedents already noticed by us, the tendencies of Lessing were still rather critical than creative, rather rationalistic than in any sense dogmatic. Nay, he even went so far as to make a direct assault on the very foundations of Christianity: and thus infidelity became, as it were, a mark of literary aspiration, the external evidence of the elevation of mind above the common standard. No doubt, some Christian bards did arise in the train of this literary development, and managed for some time to maintain a respectable position. Of these the greatest was, undoubtedly, Klopstock, who exercised a wide influence for good, despite the occasional Arian bearings of his "Messiade," and his mistaken daring in inventing, though with a Christian motive, the history of wonders beyond the ken of mortal. For this tended, in its success, to give a fictitious colouring or effect to the whole scriptural narrative, with which the poem was so closely connected. Milton has comparatively invented little, and that little is far more generally and vaguely expressed, independent of its being for the more part consistent with what Scripture has revealed to us, and a mere instalment of the almost inevitable efforts of the imagination to supply the links wanting in Holy Writ. But the actions, thoughts, and triumphs of our Risen Lord, as depicted by Klopstock, are further removed from the ken of human gaze, and the whole narrative of his death and passion is so sublime and unutterably solemn, that we shrink from the audacious attempt to blend a mortal's fancies with the revelations of the Eternal Spirit, as from an appalling act of sacrilege. Nevertheless, Klopstock, after his fashion, strove to promote the cause of orthodoxy; and in this he was partially

405

assisted by Gleim, and the author of "The Death of Abel." Kleist, the German poet of the Seasons, and Tiedge followed in the train of these; and though always warring on the defensive and the retreat, for some time they presented a half-front to the enemy.

In the meanwhile, Kant had firmly established his philosophy in the hearts and minds of the *teachers* of Germany; and intellectual *power* resided almost exclusively in the possession of opponents to orthodox Christianity. After Lessing and Klopstock, Wieland was the third great name in German literature, mainly known to us by his "Oberon," but one of the most prolific writers of all ages, and unfortunately a coryphæus of infidelity. In his youth, this author, naturally gifted with a poetic imagination, had shrunk from the cold rationalism of Lessing and Lessing's school of thought: he had even striven to take refuge in ardent Calvinism at Geneva; but this system did not suffice to satisfy the demands either of his reason or his fancy. Romanism of course appeared to him, as it did to almost all the German literary men of that day, a silly and barbarous superstition, not worthy of a moment's consideration: and so, finally, he threw himself back upon classical antiquity, and found a point of rest in the revival of the Epicurean philosophy, which assimilated naturally with the elements of grace and humour, derived by him, in part from nature, in part from a close study of the then modern French standards. Accordingly he was imbued with the spirit of Lucian and Anacreon, and poured forth elegant satires, poems, and tales, in every form, all reflecting the Epicurean creed, or creedlessness. He read, indeed, Shakspeare, whom he translated; but he loved Voltaire, whom he emulated, and, in many respects, surpassed. By nature he was a great poet, and, under more favourable auspices, might have achieved far higher creations. Of course, he either ignored Christianity altogether, in all his chief works, or treated it with good-humoured contempt. The spite of Voltaire was wholly foreign to his temperament. He considered amusement the study of life, and had not therefore sufficient earnestness to essay the overthrow of any system; but perhaps, on this very account, the influence for evil exercised over his country's faith by him, was greater, than if it had been direct and controversial.

Herder, who followed him, was a grave and sober thinker, who earnestly strove to better the condition of his fellow-men, but he was imbued with the Kantian teaching, and consequently prepossessed against orthodoxy. In truth, where was a young German of talent to obtain orthodox views and perceptions at this period? Religion, as presented to him by its Lutheran authorities, was a cold and dry system of dogmatic teaching; regarded not in any sense as the foundation of true philosophy, but as a thing altogether apart from it. Philosophy professed in itself to solve the mysteries of being: Christianity was therefore needless for the instructed man, by the more or less explicit confession of its teachers. And here, let us remark, that whilst political freedom was in Germany utterly unknown, the most absolute theological licence had for a long time prevailed, at least in the Protestant states. The authorities forbad the appearance of any pamphlet, however slight, which trenched on the supremacy of the temporal power: but, inasmuch as the human mind cannot be fettered at all points, as some safety-valve, to use a modern simile, must be allowed for the escape of intellectual steam, the whole field of religious controversy was thrown open to the inquiring mind, and the negative and critical instincts of man were left to develop freely there. The Reformation, too, had established the principle of religious freedom within certain limits; an impulse had been given to man's natural tendency to protest and deny, and it was inevitable that that tendency should be in some sense gratified. In our own country, a re-actionary power resided in our Catholic institutions, in the Divine authority claimed by the Church by right of Apostolic succession, and the mystic and awful value attached to the Sacraments; whilst, at the same time, a due degree of political freedom offered food and occupation to the more restless order of intellects, and made men content themselves with those religious truths which they found consistent with the enjoyment of high political privileges. In Germany, on the contrary, as indeed in France, and more or less generally in continental states, those who were disposed to cavil and amend were confined to this one department, of theological research, and were of course the more likely to misuse their privileges in this. Freedom, properly understood, is the right of man; and, if deprived of it, a tendency to licence will develop itself within him. But we resume.

So far, as might have been anticipated, the awakening of the German mind had been hostile to the claims of Revelation; but one master-spirit arose, on whom a dread responsibility must ever rest; who might have saved his countrymen from the abyss of infidelity, had he turned in faith to his God, and who appears to have more than once hesitated, whether he should do so or not, in the course of his earlier career. We allude, as need scarcely be said, to Goethe! This mighty mind appears to have received a training of an orthodox though cold nature, and to have been endowed with many and warm devotional instincts. He tells us in his "Autobiography," and that, with an obvious half-regret, which must appear strange to his rationalistic followers and admirers, that when in his fifteenth year he went to confession previous to his confirmation, according to the custom of the Lutheran Church, his whole heart was stirred within him; and he suggests in so many words, that had he then been met in a corresponding spirit by his confessor, a cold dry Lutheran, he might have become an orthodox Christian, and have thrown his whole weight into the Christian scale! It is impossible to calculate the consequences of such a decision. It may be said, and perhaps with reason, that this plea was a mere excuse made by Goethe to himself, for having adopted an Epicurean code of selfishness, and having ignored through life a religion, the truth of which he has scarcely ever *explicitly* denied. But is it not a striking fact, that this material and rationalistic thinker, whilst yet in the enjoyment of his intellect's prime, which had only been matured by the experience of some five-and-fifty years, should throw out an unmistakeable suggestion, that so little might have sufficed at one period to give another bearing to his life and literary labours, and constitute him the champion of a religion which he affected to regard as the mere fiction of humanity? Goethe takes occasion to inform us here, that Lutheranism was, in his opinion, wholly insufficient to keep alive the fire of Christianity; and he explains at great length how the Catholic system, as known to him in Romanism alone, met the various needs of the human heart, conferred Divine Grace in the Sacraments, and bestowed all life by the earthly presence of the Divine. He wishes evidently to convey his own impression, that had he been subjected to the influences of this system, he might have remained a Christian.

We will not pause to inquire in how far the superstitions and the pious, or rather impious, frauds of Rome, together with its system of making religion exclusively dependent on its own external teaching, keeping Holy Writ and its evidences in the background, would have been likely to counterbalance in Goethe's case, or that of any other master-mind, the advantages derivable from its possession of the "means of grace:" nor need we do more than indicate that the combination of Catholic spirituality with scriptural reality and earnestness, such as may at once satisfy both *mind* and *heart*, will be discovered in the Anglican Church, according to our sincere convictions; despite our perception of her many practical deficiencies. It suffices for our present purpose to observe, that Goethe could have easily transcended the ordinary difficulties which kept his less-gifted countrymen from the just appreciation of Christianity. German so-called philosophy he never held in great estimation; without running a tilt

against the notions and prejudices of his contemporaries, he never yielded his homage to the systems of Kant or of Fichte, of Schelling or of Hegel, all of which predominated in turn during his long literary empire. He treated all with courtesy, but with a species of polite contempt, never by any accident speaking of them in that tone of involuntary respect with which he met Christianity, even when he ventured to assail it. He saw and recognized the wonderful æsthetic beauty of Revelation; of a Creed, which had reigned so long over so many hundreds of millions, and seemed destined to endure to the end of time. German systems of philosophy, despite their lofty pretensions, he knew to be the creatures of an age, hastening rapidly to decay, and accordingly bestowed very little attention on them. His views, which finally became pantheistic, assimilated with some of Hegel's; and where they did so, he did not deny their likeness, but was never anxious to claim such affinity. We repeat, then, that had his heart been rightly moved, had he been led to love his God, he would have scorned the intellectual molehills which these petty philosophers had thrown up, around the Rock of Christianity. The doctrine of Atonement, as he has told us, appeared to him consistent with the faith of all ages and the experience of mankind. The rationalistic system of explaining away the miracles, and prosaically nibbling at all the external evidences of Christianity, he always held in contempt. His mind was too clear not to perceive, that Christianity must be received or rejected, as a Divine Revelation, and a whole. If true in any sense, he saw it must be true altogether, inasmuch as it was self-consistent throughout. If God was other than the Universe, if He was beyond and above it, if, as Christians maintained, it was only a speck in his infinite glory, if He was the Creator, and capable of Will, what could appear more *probable* than the whole scheme of Revelation? Would it not naturally follow, that He should create man good and happy, yet with the possibility of fall, for the sake of freedom, which *could* not co-exist with absolute and inevitable bliss? And if man *did* fall (as fact evidenced that he *must* have fallen, if he ever *were* in possession of perfect happiness and goodness), what could be more natural, than that God should will to restore his creatures, and effect this by a Revelation, which though supported by many external evidences, should finally appeal to *faith*, and not to absolute knowledge, for the sake of *trial?* And then, the Great Mystery, the centre of the scheme, the Incarnation in some sense of the Godhead, to reconcile justice with mercy,—though this was beyond the understanding of man, the motive to it was perfectly apparent and self-consistent, and, if sufficient external evidence could be procured in support of it, human reason would have no antecedent grounds for its rejection. All this Goethe saw: nay, all this Goethe has either stated or plainly suggested: nevertheless he *willed* (he has not told us wherefore) to reject Christianity altogether. He *has* spoken, however, of the influences which surrounded him; of the many elements which combined against his natural devotion. Making all possible allowance for these, we believe that his master-spirit could have transcended them, and therefore hold him responsible, to a dread amount, for the misapplication of the talents confided to his charge.

He appears for a long time to have laid religion, as well as philosophy, altogether on one side, and to have contented himself with the use and enjoyment of this world. It need scarcely be said, that under such influences he could only ripen into a confirmed and selfish sensualist. The egotism of Goethe is, indeed, his most marked characteristic: the unreality of his best feelings meets us in every page of his Autobiography. We see him sporting with the holiest affections, regarding all things as made for his gratification only, and employing every power bestowed on him without the slightest reference to its effect on his fellow-creatures, Christianity remaining for him a thing apart. In "Werther," in "Wilhelm Meister," every where, save in a few loose epigrams, he treats it with a species of involuntary homage, though he does not subscribe to it. Meantime, he *indirectly teaches* his fellow-countrymen to regard it as something effete, if once beautiful; left behind us in the progress of humanity. He preaches (if so self-satisfied an egotist can ever be said to preach) a morality, or rather an immorality, of his own. He is too comfortable, too "*bequem*" for Christianity; too easy, too cosy, too selfish, too Goetheian. Repentance, he says, is a *bore*, and sorrow for past errors is altogether needless, because it cannot recall what has been: he neglects to observe that it may amend the heart for the future. Finally, rising above the usual rationalistic assaults on Christianity, he feels that its evidences are weighty; that it is next to impossible to account for its existence on the ground either of self-deception, or of conscious imposture in its Founder and Teachers: so, without allowing himself to enter on the inquiry at all, he bars the gate on any Revelation, by proclaiming that Personality must be a boundary, and that the Godhead therefore cannot possess personality; in other words, that It is identical with the All, or is nothing but the Divine principle of nature. This once admitted from antecedent reasoning, all historical evidence is rejected as needless, and Pantheism received as truth infallible. It is not ours here to expose the monstrosity of this system; suffice it to say, that had Goethe's

heart been in the right place, his head could not have failed to reject so poor a syllogism. It is manifestly preposterous for us to proclaim that Personality bounds, *because creature-personality does so. The Creator, who embraces all, need not the less exist, because He is self-conscious.* Divine will and purpose, in fine, are manifest on all sides, and a God who loves us is ever present with his own. Goethe, however, we repeat, might have arrested the torrent of German infidelity; and probably *he alone.* He preferred to help it on, and he and his country must both abide the consequence. His political views are well known: they were rather favourable than otherwise to Absolutism, but had little influence on his nation, which rightly attributed their existence to that egotism which sought for nothing beyond its own personal satisfaction. Goethe agreed with Wieland in regarding man as a being, whose chief purpose should be to enjoy this life; and he thought democracy with its intestine strife unfavourable to social happiness. We pass to his great rival in literary estimation, who according to the popular voice, perhaps, still bears the crown, the energetic and enthusiastic Schiller.

It is not our purpose here, as we need scarcely say, to treat of the artistic and æsthetic merits of the authors we may enumerate, save in as far as these are inseparably interwoven with our theme, the attempt to trace the various causes which have led to the triumph of Teutonic lawlessness; as we may, not too boldly, word it. Without contrasting Schiller with his greater predecessor who yet so long outlived him, we may frankly assume that he would have followed in the former's track, had the bard of Francfort enrolled himself under the banner of Christianity. Schiller's early impulses were directly devotional; and traces of this feeling will be discovered in the great disfavour with which the unbelievers and scoffers, "Franz" and "Spiegelberg" are treated in his first tragedy, "The Robbers." But Schiller, alone and unaided, was scarcely capable of bearing back the torrent of German unbelief; he became a captive to the popular Kantian philosophy of the day, and conceived it his duty to regard Christianity as a worn-out and partial expression of the truth, not worthy even of a careful examination. At an earlier period we find him proclaiming in his "Arcadia" and other poems, that this life is all, and that retribution should not be looked for beyond the grave. Later, he in some degree revolted from this stern conclusion, as his "Thekla, a Spirit voice," "The Lay of the Bell," and his more matured dramas, give us to understand; but even then, he could mourn in his "Gods of Greece" that beauty had flown from earth with paganism, and appears scarcely to have realized the mere *æsthetic* value of Christianity. No doubt, the romantic spirit, which derived its being from Christian sources, was plainly manifested in many of his ballads, as also in " Maria Stuart" and " The Virgin of Orleans." Nevertheless, Schiller has left no such distinct tribute of homage to the genius of Christianity, as was more than once expressed by Goethe ; and in his essay on the " Mission of Moses," he has indulged in an offensively rationalistic strain, which it would be impossible for a Strauss or a Bruno-Bauer to surpass, and which far transcends in evil the corresponding account in Goethe's " West-Eastern Divan" of the children of Israel's sojourn in the wilderness.

It is true, that Schiller frequently expresses an ideal of pure and lofty tenderness of soul, which is essentially Christian in its character ; but, inasmuch as this is given us as a thing altogether apart from and unconnected with religion, its presence could only make his works more dangerous to his admirers. The same remark applies to Goethe, whose pathos and grace, though less prominent to the vulgar eye, are essentially deeper and higher. These two great writers, both in their best prose and poetic works, may be said to have furnished their nation with a moral Ideal, such as a Pagan writer of the fourth century might have been supposed to draw, who had become familiar with Christian virtue, and adorned his own philosophy with its semblance. A morality, however, which is not founded on revealed religion, may never be trusted to ; and thus, that of both these writers will be ofttimes found defective ; so presenting a painful contrast to that of our own mighty Shakspeare. Not the monstrosities of " Stella" only, the exaggerations of " Werther," the flagrant indecencies of the " Roman Elegies" and the " Venetian Epigrams," and the refined immorality of " Wilhelm Meister," are to be blamed in Goethe's works, nor need we call special attention to the yet more dangerous tampering with the social ties manifested in his " Elective Affinities ;" but even his purest works, such as " Torquato Tasso," are not free from evil tendencies : *every where* we recognize the presence of a Pagan code, conveyed in those expressive words, " Whatever pleases be allowed !" Schiller is far purer, but his ideas are frequently characterized by meanness and even hardness of heart. Thus his " Fiesco," though represented, or rather meant, as a hero, acts as the vilest of scoundrels alone could do ; and in his " Cabal and Love," the hero and heroine, despite their mouthing assertions of virtue, are alike impious and graceless. The moral of " The Bride of Messina," if it have any moral, is one of the most awful nature ; directly arraigning, in fine, the goodness and justice of Providence : and his very last play, " Wilhelm Tell," not only studiously advocates cold-blooded assassination, but

throws a sentimental colouring over it, which is most pernicious in its effects, and tends to confuse the first principles of right and wrong. Schiller, then, followed the evil impulse which had been communicated to his country's literature, and carried on the work of ruin.

Yet, all this time, Christianity externally maintained itself: a system based on the Word of God, and dating back for nearly eighteen centuries, could not be overthrown in a day. Infidelity was still confined to the educated classes, and was not even universal among these. Literary men, however, had been gradually led to assume the fallacy of Christianity, not from any examination of its historic or moral evidence, but because it was presented to them under a cold form to which their sympathies were hostile, while they believed themselves to be already possessed of the Absolute, in the philosophy of the schools. The Humboldts, and others worthy of esteem, were all imbued with this indifferentism to vital religion, which they rather ignored than assailed, and taught their nation to ignore with them. A partial reaction manifested itself in the so-called Romantic school, which originated in the desire to re-awaken the buried memories of the middle ages. The Schlegels were the critical leaders in this movement, Tieck being its principal literary representative ; he, however, was satisfied with the externals of romanticism : they pressed on for its reality, which they could only discover in Christianity ; and so, Frederick von Schlegel at least, and his friend and ally, the Count of Stolberg, were driven to take refuge from rationalistic Lutheranism in the bosom of the Roman Church. But the influence of this school on the German nation was by no means considerable ; the bards of Weimar, Wieland, Goethe, Schiller, and Herder, reigning in indisputable supremacy.

However, a more potent aider of the cause of Christianity was provided in the sore need and distress of the German nation under the yoke of Napoleon. In their efforts to achieve their liberties a positively religious spirit once more manifested itself, and quasi-philosophy for a time seemed cast to the winds. Inspired by the Christian, or, at least, devotional strains of Körner, and Rückert, and De la Motte-Fouqué, a pious impulse fired all hearts, and infidelity was silenced by the urgent prayers that arose on all sides from a suppliant nation. Schiller had departed : Goethe withdrew into himself ingloriously, and was for awhile forgotten. Had the German sovereigns seized the hour of victory to fulfil their promises, had they *then*, whilst all hearts were filled with gratitude to Heaven, bestowed representative constitutions on a loving and earnest people, the cause of

409

faith and order might in all probability have proved triumphant: *but this they did not do;* they disappointed the hopes and expectations of their subjects, when these had been wound up to the highest pitch; they re-enacted the laws of censorship and every other restrictive penalty, and converted the German nation into an immense body of malcontents, once more disposed to quarrel with their faith, and bearing a deep grudge to the authority which had deceived them. Thus, what might have been made an occasion of reformation and renovation, was converted into a goad and snare to the most evil tendencies, and the spirit of irreverence once more regained its sway.

There can be no doubt that the German sovereigns had great difficulties to contend with, on the termination of the European struggle in 1815, if their sincere desire was (as they asserted) to assimilate the institutions of Germany to those of our own favoured country: but these difficulties were by no means insurmountable. The great social and political evils of Germany were, the existence of a barren and almost numberless bureaucracy, and the hollow and unpopular position of the untitled aristocracy throughout the land. The first of these was easily to be remedied by the adoption of free institutions, bringing with them, as they must have done, the modified principles of self-government, and rendering the whole system of secret police, censorship, and private administration of justice, a meaningless anomaly. The needful reform of the aristocracy was not so easy to deal with: but, as the danger connected with it was even more alarming, all delay in grappling with the evil could only make things worse. It was obvious that a mere titular aristocracy, many tens of thousands in number, for the most part idle and ignorant, solely employed in the army or the bureaucracy, looking on the wealthiest and most honourable of their fellow-citizens as so much dirt, and consequently hated by all classes, could not safely be allowed to exist in the nineteenth century. The obvious remedy was to effect a reform on English principles, to found a house or rather houses of peers, of which the mediatised princes, at least 150 in number, would have formed the nucleus, to whom all the *heads* of great and wealthy houses might have been added, recruited in some special instances of merit from the plebeian ranks. The remaining nobility should have been deprived of the right to bear any further title than " *Herr von,*" which like our own " *esquire,*" might also have been left open to every great merchant, and even to every larger shopkeeper retiring from business. The youngest sons of peers, also, should certainly not have been permitted to " *sport* " the family title of prince and count to the last descendant of their youngest branches according to the absurd custom of the continent, but should have been restricted without exception to the same simple note of gentle blood. Of course, each man might still have borne whatever arms pertained to him, as in this country, and *could not* be deprived of his inherent nobility. Had this reformation been effected at the period referred to, and had it gone hand in hand with the yielding of constitutional privileges, the present alarming state of anarchy might in all probability have been averted for ever; and—the nation being then favourably disposed towards the faith of its governors—teachers, and bards, would no doubt have arisen, the offspring of the age, and yet in their turn its guides, encouraging and developing all those good instincts, which the Teutonic race had displayed in the hour of trial and danger. But, as it was, the concessions made to the popular voice were few, tardy, and insufficient: representative forms were given here and there, but with little reality attached to them; liberty of the press was still denied; bureaucracy was unmodified; and, worst of all, the aristocracy was allowed to subsist in its unnatural and exclusive position, destined to keep alive the smouldering fires of discontent, which must surely break forth with awful violence at some future not over-distant day. The consequence of all this was, that the ardent and grateful loyalty, both to earthly rulers and the Heavenly Lord of all, which had been called forth, passed away, like " an exhalation of the summer morn." Tieck, Grillparzer, Uhland, Rückert, and others, who would have been prominent in the conservative ranks, remained silent, or espoused the cause of liberalism, and thereby found themselves in inevitable and almost unconscious opposition to all the institutions of their country. No honest man ventured to profess himself a partizan or supporter of the government, whilst that government restricted the freedom of the press. Whoever wrote in defence of the existing order of things was commonly regarded as a spy or a traitor. Hence, the assassination of Kotzebue, from the sympathies with the criminal which it called forth in all quarters, might well be regarded as a national act! But the eyes of " the powers that *were,*" were still not opened: they persisted in delaying the period of political reforms, and thereby rendering the task more difficult and more dangerous from day to day, and hour to hour. As political disaffection became more general and assumed the offensive, the governments conceived themselves constrained to the adoption of more restrictive measures. The malcontents once more flung themselves with angry impetuosity on the truths of Revelation, and found a development for the spirit of irreverence in the field of theology, or rather of neology. Rationalism waxed more audacious than of yore: the very clergy professed its principles openly, in all directions, and were suffered to do so without rebuke. Finally, a school of glaringly immoral and atheistic teaching developed itself, in the lights of "Young Germany," generally individuals of Israelitic origin, Heine, Börne, Gutzkow, and their "confrères," who gave the literary tone of the day.

For the last fifteen or twenty years, the symptoms of an impending revolutionary outbreak, both democratic and antichristian, have been too glaring to be mistaken. The quiet rationalism of a Neander had given way to the audacious denials of a Strauss, a Feuerbach, and a Bruno-Bauer: Goethe and Schiller were neglected as too conservative for the rising generation, and no literature was listened to which possessed not a directly political bearing. This explains the otherwise unaccountable neglect of so great a dramatist as Grillparzer, and the immense reputation achieved by such a man as Herwegh from the publication of a few republican verses. And yet, all this while, the sovereigns of Germany, (we are sorry to confess it,) as a body, persisted in closing their eyes: Austria derided the bare idea of the slightest concession; and Prussia, too, despite many fine words and vague promises, maintained the "statu quo," and, though no doubt animated by the best intentions, made no serious effort to redress evils, which were daily assuming a more fatal aspect. It is difficult to account for this infatuation. The obnoxious censorship, which had the effect of rendering it virtually impossible for a man of talent to espouse the conservative cause, was *known* to have no real power to prevent the publication of seditious works, and was yet obstinately retained. Forbidden poems were in all cases most widely circulated; even where a veil was thrown over the author's meaning to avoid the penalties of the law, that veil was transparent, and attracted the more fixed attention of the public to the design beneath it: mystery yielded only an additional charm, which barbed the arrow of sedition. Then, too, a vain attempt was made to imprison these literary ringleaders; but, the sense of the nation being too decidedly opposed to this, they were speedily liberated, to "renew their revels." What shall we say?—"*Quos Deus vult perdere prius dementat?*"—Matters had perhaps proceeded too far in Germany, Christianity had sunk too low in popular estimation, Pantheism had obtained too firm a footing, for any permanent cure, save that of the furnace of affliction, which we now see prepared for that once mighty nation.

It is obviously too late to hope for the establishment of an aristocracy in the sense of an hereditary peerage, at least for years. Concentration of power in the one numerical majority is held to be the only road to liberty. The only practical immediate remedy is a little sound military despotism.—Nor are we

sanguine enough to believe, that any revival of orthodox Christianity can be looked for at once in the existing state of things. Rather do we expect the total separation of Church and State, both in Protestant and Roman Catholic countries, and the establishment of national heathenism, while the various Churches thus left to themselves may be expected to split into many more or less flagrantly rationalistic sects, following the example of the so-called "friends of light," Ronge and his followers, and the Neo-Catholics generally. We consider the aspect of affairs to be more directly alarming in Germany, than in any other state of Europe. France has still some Catholic instincts, some sympathies with law and order: the countries of the south, Spain and Portugal, enjoy comparative tranquillity: and Italy, though moved from one end to the other by the revolutionary mania, retains a certain external reverence for religion, and is not likely to yield this under any circumstances[1]. The states of the north, Sweden, Denmark, and Norway, though not without many seeds of ill abiding in them, may be looked on as our allies in the conservation of authority and the spirit of reverence. The power of Russia, also, appears as yet unshaken. But Germany is rotten almost to the core, and cannot be saved, we fear, from the consuming fire of *civil anarchy*. For a time every man's hand must be against every man; social strife and virtual atheism must have their day. That there will be a reaction from all this, we doubt not, though we cannot presume to say in what it may consist. Despotism may erect itself on the ruins of democracy: the nations, tired of disorder and disgusted with faithlessness, may demand an Absolute Ruler, and find one of the most fearful order! On this subject we will not speak at present. Rather let us confine ourselves to the strict elucidation of our more immediate theme. Which are then the distinct causes of the downfall of German order? And further, do they exist among ourselves? and, if so, how are they to be combated?

First, then, we have seen that the causes of disorganization and decay among our German neighbours, were religious, social, and political. The dry and unsatisfactory nature of Lutheranism, the existence of an unpopular and practically useless aristocracy, combined with an oppressive and tedious bureaucratic sway, and the maintenance of an odious, yet insufficient right of censorship, together with the refusal of constitutional forms and privileges, all worked together to foment the spirit of rationalism, disaffection, and disorder, and have finally reaped an abundant harvest of

[1] The expulsion of Rome's bishop scarcely modifies our opinion. We still believe the majority of the lower classes to be sincere though superstitious Christians.

411

evil. Had Protestant Germany (for it is *this* which has taken the lead in the movement, and indeed endued the German national mind with its existing peculiarities), had Protestant Germany, then, been blessed with the hallowing influences of Apostolic Episcopacy, with that scheme of sacramental grace which *must* more or less fully attend its development ; had some scope been afforde. to poetic imaginations within the Protestant communions, imaginations liable to be deeply impressed with the awful sanctity of the Christian mysteries, but certain to be repelled and even disgusted by a bare course of dry catechetical instruction ; *then*, in all probability, we should not have seen the theologians of German universities seeking for sources of excitement in rationalistic and neological controversies ; we should not have found the greatest minds of Germany, such as Wieland, Lessing, Herder, and even Jean Paul and the mystic Novalis, imbued with a deep dislike and almost contempt for Christianity, as something harsh and cold, and crude, and only suited for the vulgar, and turning in search of a spiritual ideal, either to the Pagan world of old, or a species of mystic freemasonry, or a vague but transcendental philosophy ; any where, in fact, but to " the fountains of living water" the visible Christian Church, which to them was only the symbol of barrenness, dulness, and weariness of spirit. Again, despite this fundamental deficiency in the religious provision made for the national wants, especially those of nobler spirits, (a deficiency which no mere worldly wisdom could have made good,) had an unpopular titular aristocracy, dependent on court favour, and wholly separated from the people, been converted into a real *peerage*, whilst its younger sons and inferior members had been practically employed and blended with the classes immediately beneath them, so as to bring about a solid union of all, and had at the same time a wise and moderate system of self-government, as understood by us, and evidenced in the cases of country magistrates and juries, taken the place by slow degrees of an overgrown and dull bureaucracy ; *then*, it is possible that the late catastrophe might have been averted, and the German nation taught to value their social institutions. But though we have called these reforms social, it is obvious that they were not to be undertaken apart from the third class of changes, which we may regard as more directly *political*. Had, then, this establishment of houses of peers and partial abolition of bureaucracy gone hand in hand with the accordance of constitutional rights, as expressed by the calling together of representative chambers, together with uncontrolled freedom of the press, it should seem more than probable, that the German nation might have contented itself generally with a mixed form of government, in which monarchy, aristocracy, and democracy, would all have preserved their due influence, so as to maintain " the balance of power ;" in which the equal liberties of all classes would have been combined with just gradations of dignity, useful to all, and offensive to none ; in which, finally, no element of our unrivalled British Constitution would have been wanting, save the action of a visible branch of the Church Catholic, a body gifted with apostolic authority, and, as of necessity, enrolled in behalf of the cause of order and wise conservatism.

The original plague-spot in the constitution of the German realm, at and after the Reformation, was the inefficient working of the Church of God within it. In Roman Catholic Germany the Church was directly hostile to all mental development, and conservative of unmitigated despotism : in Protestant Germany, as we have seen, it was equally powerless to guide the national mind aright. Yet, if the German sovereigns with the elements of disorder and irreverence which the great need occasioned, had ventured at an earlier period on the social and political reforms above suggested, it is *possible* that the spirit of loyalty once awakened, the *Protestant* Churches at least, might have followed the impulse which the present sovereign of Prussia would gladly have communicated to them, and have sought that apostolic ordination at the hands of our Christian bishops, which would have introduced the elements wanting to give them vitality and stability, and have completed and confirmed a Catholic reaction from the absurdities and immoralities of rationalism.

But it is vain to speak of what *might have been*. We have to deal with that which *is*. And is the existing confirmation of evil, which we deplore in Germany, to be dreaded for *ourselves?* Do any of those causes exist among us, which we have found productive of such terrible results ? Is rationalism gaining ground within our Church and nation ? Is our aristocracy, by its very constitution, unpopular, or likely to become so? Do we enjoy, or not enjoy such an amount of rational freedom in our present system of popular representation as is sufficient to meet the just demands of the age ?

Thanks be to Providence, we can answer the first question distinctly in the negative. Rationalism, despite the efforts of an inconsiderable school and the preachments of a certain class of quasi-philosophers, the Carlyles and Emersons of the day, is on the whole becoming more and more unacceptable to the English mind ; is regarded with more and more of contempt, not only by our soundest thinkers, but by the vast majority of the educated classes. Not that it can be denied that a certain class of literary men, of whom (we would not speak invidiously, but all *mealy-mouthedness* on such a subject would be worse than treason to our sacred cause), of whom, then, such a writer as *Douglas Jerrold* may be cited as a fair sample, *do* strive to the best of their ability to unsettle the popular convictions on this score. They dare not openly assail the religion of Christ, for then they would find no readers; but professing their desire to attain an impracticable Ideal, they weigh Christianity, such as they behold it, with its own high standard of perfection, and lead men to understand that the Church which does not realize heaven on earth can be no Church at all. But, despite their efforts, they are ever and anon compelled, as against their will, to do homage to a religion which they assail in its external institutions; to acknowledge the beauty of holiness, and the excellence of prayer and praise. Rarely do we find them carping at Scripture texts or Scripture miracles. Little of the German rationalistic tone will be discovered in their lucubrations; scarcely ever do they presume, like every wretched German scribbler of the day, to treat Christianity as a thing beneath them, an effete and valueless superstition. A Carlyle, indeed, may teach that power is virtue, and call on men to worship success, under whatever form, in Moses or Mahomet, in mediæval superstition or puritan sanctimony: but his unbelief is decently veiled beneath a garniture of high-sounding devotional expressions; which to English ears may indeed appear " profane," but which to German rationalists would be simply " absurd!" An Emerson may go farther, and in a style of mystic blasphemy (the phrase is not too strong) inform us, that man is God, that Christ is only to be honoured in as far as He recognized and proclaimed this truth; that all prayer, therefore, is no better than idolatry as involving " dualism," or the belief that there is a God above man, whilst man is simply God himself:—but his warmest admirers do not dare to allude to these follies in their commendations, and call our attention simply to his recognition of the goodness residing in humanity, and the beauties of external nature. We may take occasion, here, to observe, that Emerson is the most distinct representative in the English tongue of that religion of humanitarianism, or the deification of humanity, which Professor Strauss coolly proposed in his last pamphlet to the Protestants and Roman Catholics of Germany, as a substitute for their present creeds, and the healer of all national divisions. But neither Douglas Jerrold (whom, despite his real humour and occasional kind-heartedness, we must include in this category of evil-workers), nor Carlyle, nor Emerson, nor any of their followers, are likely to effect a serious injury to our national faith, as long as that " Pillar of the truth" is maintained among us, known as the Church Establishment, the most nobly conservative element of our polity.

The Church of England in her wise moderation, encouraging the rightful use of this world, and the development of intellectual power, has exercised the most potent and beneficial influence over the literature of our country, which as a whole is infinitely the most Christian, and consequently the most moral of modern Europe. From Spenser and Shakspeare downwards, with few exceptions, our great bards have been enrolled under the banners of Christianity. In the evil age of licence which succeeded the excesses of puritanic asceticism, even the genius of Dryden was partially led astray, plunged in the quagmire of licentiousness, and finally driven for refuge to the seeming " fair garden" of Romanism, the trees of which " drop poison from their topmost boughs;" but even *he* was a Christian, and has left his manly and vigorous " Religio Laici," and his magnificent version of " Veni Creator Spiritus," (which Goethe calls " Ein Appel aus Genie,") to bear witness to his religious sincerity. Pope, in a cold and barren age, externally a Romanist, and, therefore, not under the direct influence of the Church, was still kept within the bounds of decent reverence, and despite his lifelong halting betwixt two opinions, has hymned some Christian strains, and never insulted the Faith. At a later period, Byron and Shelley can alone be quoted amongst our greater poets as opposed to Christianity; and the former of *these*, even, denied the imputation, and expressed his trembling hope on his death-bed that he might not be cast away; whilst many of his purer strains, such as " The Prisoner of Chillon," and even " The Dream," owe their highest beauty to the indirect influence of Christian sentiment. But, on the other side, what a list of great and worthy names may be enumerated, all more or less directly imbued with the spirit of Catholic reverence and Scripture truth! Let it suffice to name Southey, Wordsworth, Coleridge, Scott, Moore even, in his later works, Crabbe, Burns, Cowper, and Milman: we only pause here, because an enumeration of this nature is needless. In a word, our poetic literature, speaking generally, not only recognizes Christianity as an undoubted objective truth, but strives even to realize it in every subjective form, and is therefore a mighty bulwark to the faith of our nation; the existence of which we are driven to attribute, mainly, to the special influences of the English Church. It has been said, and with justice, that the *songs* of a nation are the most direct criterion and guide of its popular belief: but an examination into every other branch of our national literature would conduct us to a similar result. Our greatest philosophers,

413

our noblest men of science, even our writers of fiction, have been for the more part direct and avowed adherents to Christianity.

We know well that there is a reverse side to this flattering picture; and that it is only by contrast with foreign delinquency that our native virtue can shine so bright: but our present concern is to ascertain and register general truths, and draw results from them; not directly to moralize on our national corruptions and short comings. We repeat, then, the Church of England has kept alive the spirit of faith within this realm, and consequently of reverence to lawful authority. But, let our statesmen look to it! In these perilous days, when the thrones of earth are shaking, when all first truths are questioned, when infidelity and democratic lawlessness seem too likely to triumph throughout the continent of Europe, it will not do for us to foster any seeds of irreverence to the Church of Christ. Above all, no attempt must be made to degrade her in the eyes of the nation to the position of a mere servile minister to the state; or she will lose all her power for political and moral good, and, becoming unpopular in herself, nay, odious, make the cause of Religion unpopular as well. This is no needless caution. Not only have churchmen to complain of perverse ministerial nominations to high offices in the Church, and the indecent attempt to deny the latter any power of protesting against a ministerial error; not only has a deaf ear been turned to all solicitations for the re-awakening of Convocation, a desideratum, however, which cannot, from the nature of things, be much longer delayed; but a tone of flippancy amounting to direct insult has been constantly adopted by the chief ministers of the Crown, in treating of the Church's dearest rights; it has been declared, for instance, that the Government would henceforth conduct the administration of continental and other foreign chaplaincies without any reference to English bishops, and a positive tendency has been displayed to treat the Church as a respectable but somewhat antiquated state functionary, which has no right to have any will of its own. If Lord Palmerston be imprudently suffered by his colleagues to carry out his rash designs, and degrade the Church in the estimation of the nation generally, he and they may be assured, that the storm will burst ere long! a storm, which will end,—contrary, perhaps, to the desires of its first originators,—in the separation of Church and State, and the consequent ruin of the realm!

It is but too evident that a Romanising, and even an orthodox, but impatient and thoughtless body, *within* the Church, desire to effect this consummation, which many of the dissenters also ardently long for. The Church may bear much. The bishops and high dignitaries have obviously worldly interests to consult, which would naturally attach them to the State; but, *if* a certain boundary of State-despotism be overpassed, *if* it be sought to establish permanently, and *to prove*, that the Church is the mere tool and slave of the State, the whole of the clergy may be expected to rise, almost as one man, and demand *that separation*, for which their enemies have so long clamoured; and, in such an event, the bishops, though even against their wills, would be compelled to yield to the popular stream! Here, then, is one of our most pressing dangers; for of this we may be well assured, infidelity and irreverence would receive a direct and most powerful impulse from the heathenizing of the State. Christianity, being no longer received as a *certain* truth, would cease to permeate all our institutions. That sanctity which the State still derives from its alliance with the Church, and which is felt even by those dissenters and avowed infidels who least suspect its source, would wholly pass away. The crown would no longer be held by Divine right. An impulse, in fine, would be given to destructive liberalism and irreverence, which would soon prove fatal to our constitution. This is no vague warning. We cannot linger over the theme; but we once more solemnly assure the leading politicians of the day, and more especially the existing Ministry, that the State must honour and respect the Church, if it would preserve the public alliance with it, and that, without that alliance, it cannot resist the evil tendencies of the age.

But we proceed. Are we burthened with a useless and unpopular aristocracy? Far from it; the British peerage is one of the highest glories of the nation; it is founded on the first principles of nature and policy, and, as long as it is preserved in its present form, must prove one of the most effectual barriers to anarchy and disorder. It is not fenced off like various foreign nobilities, and more especially the German, from the sympathies of other classes. It is fortunately restricted in its numbers to those possessed, for the more part, of vast landed estates, or otherwise holding an important vested interest in their country's welfare. Its younger members constantly enter the ranks of the gentry, where they render themselves directly useful to their fellow-countrymen, and intermarry with members of other ranks. It is frequently recruited, through the army, the bar, or, (as in the case of Lord Ashburton,) even by high commercial greatness, from the other classes of the commonwealth. It stands between the crown and the commons, directly, indeed, representing the aristocracy, but *indirectly representing all*, as do the other branches of national legislature. The wise constitution of things

414

can never be too highly lauded, which renders it next to impossible to declare of any educated individual, whether he is or is not noble. Arms are in heraldry considered the unerring signet of nobility, but these appear conceded to all who occupy a certain position in society. The convenient title of " Esquire" is shared by the descendants of peers and representatives of the oldest and noblest families in Europe with merchants, and manufacturers, and even retired shopkeepers. The so-called landed gentry are of inestimable value, together with the baronetage, as supplying the needful link betwixt the peerage and the lower ranks. By the arrangement thus attained, no man's pride is wounded ; the privilege of gentility is shared by all the educated ; no exclusive barrier is raised betwixt the titled and the untitled ; and it is, in fact, impossible to say, where titles commence, and where they end.

There are all the elements of social stability in such an order of things. At this very period, despite the triumphs of the democratic spirit elsewhere, no aversion to our peerage, *as such,* exists, in any considerable party, not even the most innovating, within this mighty empire. On this point, then, we might appear secure. But it is not so. Certain political changes, already loudly clamoured for, would, if conceded, destroy the balance of power, and thus bring about the overthrow of our undoubtedly most noble aristocracy. Up to the present period, neither branch of the legislature (neither Crown, Lords, nor Commons) directly represents the numerical majority of the nation ; all have their deep-rooted sources of moral influence, which are on the whole fairly balanced ; and thus a just equilibrium is maintained ; not the impracticable equilibrium denounced by De Lamartine as identical with stagnation, but a changing balance, preponderating by turns in various directions, but never altogether overthrown. But were household suffrage to become the law of the land, the House of Commons would thenceforth directly represent a vast numerical majority, and, by an almost necessary consequence, power would be centralized in, and finally monopolized by, it. Thus the prevailing taste or fancy of the moment, whatever that might be, would be almost secure of triumph, and the nation would lose true liberty in the very power of carrying all its conceptions into immediate effect.

It is our business here, in this sweeping summary of our national dangers, rather to indicate great truths, than logically to work them out in all their bearings ; but it appears to us abundantly evident, that the House of Lords would have little real power to oppose the *direct* manifestation of the nation's will, or rather of the will of the majority, who, though they might by

no means morally represent the true nation, would have the power of making laws that might bind that nation for ever. Universal suffrage, a far more honest and self-consistent measure than the scheme of Messrs. Cobden and Bright, would attain the same result, by vesting the real authority in one single branch of the legislature. That branch which directly and exclusively represented the popular will would soon be found to be all-powerful. Vote by ballot would, of course, be a step in the same direction. As Lord John Russell has wisely remarked, it would be impossible to establish a system of secret voting without yielding the right of suffrage to all men ; for, at present, the suffrage is a high and honourable *trust,* and is only to be vindicated on its present foundation as such ; it must therefore be acted up to, in the light of day, not discharged beneath the mantle of privacy, and for any possible private or dishonourable purpose. We need not urge here the more common but equally unanswerable argument against the ballot, " That it would be a direct premium on falsehood ; as none but the liar and the rogue could profit by it ; he, namely, who would vote one way, and affirm that he had voted the other, or who lived a life of perpetual mystification." For the present, we are mainly anxious to establish this great fact, that all who value their country's constitution, in its mingled developments of aristocracy, democracy, and royalty ; who believe power when settled in one individual, or one majority, to be necessarily despotic, and consequently evil ; and who are, therefore, resolved to uphold that balance of power, which a Montesquieu and a De Lolme have commended as the highest goal of political perfectibility, which the sages of all ages have desired, and which our country has now so long enjoyed ; that all these true conservatives, and yet wise progressives, in as far as the social evils of our working-classes are concerned, must resolutely and strongly combine against that false liberal movement, which would tend to centralize power in one branch of the legislature, and so overthrow the equilibrium of the State. This is, perhaps, the most immediately practical danger of the day, and must therefore be recognized and guarded against as such.

The third great danger to our State and Constitution may be discovered in the wrongs and miseries of the working-classes, which can be here but briefly treated of. Our defective political economy has wrought much mischief. Unrestricted competition has been supposed to be the grand panacea for all evils. The aim of our legislature has been cheapness, at whatever cost, and not true plenty. Instead of endeavouring to increase our produce, and more especially our agricultural produce, " the sinews of the State," to a just ratio with our population, we have been

415

led astray by the fatal error that " population must of necessity exceed production," and that it is our main duty to retard the advance of the former. Yet we have seen in Ireland, that misery will not effect this desired result: poverty brutalizes and frees from moral influences. Imprudent early marriages are the almost universal consequence. It is obvious, without entering on the consideration of the many pressing subjects which present themselves, that statesmen, having to deal with an enormous practical evil, *the excess of population over production*, should apply themselves to increase *the latter* to the utmost possible extent; and this, *not* by striving to develop our manufacturing and artificial powers of produce, at least not primarily, *but* by promoting the cultivation of the soil to the extent, if needs be, of millions of acres, both at home and in our colonies! Capital always exists for *reproductive purposes*: and what could be so reproductive, as its outlay for the creation of *substantial national wealth*, such as might render life a blessing to the working-classes? There are, no doubt, great difficulties to the attainment of this end; but our views are not Utopian. The sources of wealth *exist*, and they may be wrought out to far more purpose than the mines of Golconda ever were. But, once more, our object here is not so much to provide a distinct remedy for existing ills, as to recognize the causes of danger, and prepare men's minds to grapple with them: and it is certain, that one of the most serious of these causes is the state of our working-classes. We speak broadly and generally, and by no means wish to imply that the English labourer is ill-fed, ill-clothed, or ill-provided for, if tested by the continental standard. The very contrary is the case. But far more may be done, than is done; and, *as it may be, must be!* The English people are disposed to loyalty. They are conscious that they are in the possession of all the blessings of political and social freedom. Any strong desire for the suffrage is confined to a certain class of political agitators. But men are generally impressed with the conviction, that it resides within the power of government, and is its consequent duty, to amend their lot. Attain this one end, and the last apparent cause of danger to our country's institutions will be forthwith swept away. And let it not be supposed that these political comments on home affairs are naturally unconnected with our immediate theme, the state of "the German mind:" this is only of immediate and practical consequence to us as bearing on our own. We wish not only to satisfy the curiosity of those who may wonder at the prevalence of infidel and democratic notions among our German brethren, though this curiosity *should be* gratified,—but to apply and utilize

our experience, by recurring to our home standard, and realizing its great excellencies and possible deficiencies.

The example of Germany, then, is mainly useful to us, as teaching us to appreciate the institutions we possess, and which that country stood in so great need of; a wisely balanced representative constitution, a popular aristocracy, and a Catholic State Church; consequently warning us, as thinkers, citizens, and statesmen, against any tampering with that constitution, any disrespect for that aristocracy, or any neglect of that Church, or attempt to underrate her just claims and treat her as a mere State-lackey. The spirit of reverence would soon fail, if her hallowing influence were withdrawn from our political institutions; royalty and aristocracy would lose much, if not all, of their beauty and value in popular estimation; and democratic changes would soon be effected in the third branch of the legislature, which would finally centralize indisputable supremacy in that body, and thus give a death-blow to freedom.

One more lesson we learn from German, as from French, "levelling of religious truth with falsehood." These countries endowed various Churches, or religious bodies, *alike* or *equally*:—further, Christianity was not their common statute law, not treated as the basis of all politics. Let us beware of the light of incendiarism this foreign recklessness has kindled,—or of any kindred danger! Let us not stoop to fire our torch at the same volcano, which may slumber in seeming quiet! Let us not endow *two Churches at once;* thus practically professing, that to this nation truth is truth no longer. The false steps we have made in this direction, whatever they be, let us retrace; and at whatever sacrifice. Sternly let us resist all future encroachments of this foreign faithlessness. *Never be Rome's usurping Church endowed within these Sister Isles!* And—as pregnant with danger is the other quasi-liberal measure we are urged to, in emulation of foreign wisdom; to unchristianize our legislature, our state, our nation; to proclaim that for legislative purposes we are no longer "under Christ," to admit the Jew to our Houses of Parliament. Let us not be told by faint well-wishers, they would aid us if we took firmer ground, if we could with any hope of success urge a more definite protest on our representatives. "On the faith of a Christian!" "How vague is this!" urges well-intentioned weakness. We reply, it suffices for all practical ends. We *could* not make the Church's creeds requisite for admission: could not even, perhaps, with justice, admit the Quaker and exclude the Arian. Where then should we stop? We stop within that line, which attests, that Britain receives the Christian faith as truth absolute, not proble-

416

matical, and which imposes silence on the secret infidel who perjure's himself for ambition's gain. More we ask not, need not: but *this is* ALL. Once again, then, solemnly we charge our readers, "Seize not with monstrous folly the very hour of foreign downfall, to emulate its *causes*." Members of the House of Commons, you, in particular, perform your duty; awake to your country's danger; and show Europe that Britain will not be dragged a helpless self-doomed victim in her wake! But *you, Peers*, IF indeed the folly, or weakness, or wickedness of others constrains you to perform your duty, (which we will not believe), then flinch not, but earn, by firmness in this hour of trial, the grateful thanks of children's children! We have spoken warmly; some will think too warmly: let us return to a more sober mood, lest we be stigmatized by the common-place as dreamers. We must not lose sight of our immediate theme.

German literature, then, has of late begun to exercise no inconsiderable influence over ourselves. Let us not be dragged into the abyss after our Teutonic friends and brethren: but let us rather extend the helping hand to them, and, in Heaven's good time, assist in upraising them on a more solid foundation! The German mind is a strange mixture of strength and weakness. With little of positive wisdom, it is capable of profound thought. Its tendencies are to the mystic and ideal, but, like "Euphorion" in "Göethe's Faust," it has sought to soar so high above the practical foundations of this earth, that it has lost itself in the clouds, and finally fallen as a dead weight into the stony pit of doubt and anarchy. As yet, the nobler elements of the German intellect have been almost ever manifested in direct opposition to the Christian Revelation. But may we not trust, that sooner or later, when the bottom of the abyss has been reached, a gradual reaction must ensue? that by slow and toilsome efforts, perhaps, yet in some sort and some way, the German mind will soar from its dungeon of rationalistic darkness? Is it not to be expected, that some gifted individual may yet arise (for by individuals, under God, are nations lost and saved), who may possess the power of Goethe without his indifferentism and egotism; the zeal and earnestness of Schiller, without his infidelity; the devotional energy of the mystic Werner, without his wild rashness and inconsistency; the more tempered wisdom of a Schlegel, without those Romeward tendencies or predilections which rendered his highest efforts barren and almost mischievous; some mighty genius, in fine, who will conjure up a train of noble spirits to follow in his train, and who will teach the German nation practically, that the highest intellects may bow to the claims of Christianity, and that genius is never so worthily employed as when hymning

the praises of the Christians' God! But whether this be so or not, let us see that *our* part be duly performed; that *we* maintain intact our national religion and freedom, though the whole of the rest of Europe be immersed in the vortex of infidel democracy.

It may be, that the evils which we now see on the Continent may prove only "the beginning of troubles." The fiat may have gone forth, that "for a time and times and half-a-time," in the mystic language of Scripture, the powers of evil should prevail. We feel that in treating of so solemn a theme, the true philosopher and statesman will applaud us, for recalling the cheering promise: "When the enemy shall come in like a flood, the Spirit of the Lord shall lift up a banner against him." Soberly and practically we hold and affirm, that the salvation of Europe, morally speaking, the preservation of law, order, and authority throughout the world, will depend on the stand *we* are enabled to make within this British Empire. The issues of the hour are great: greater perhaps than they have been for centuries. Mere state conservatism will *not* suffice us. If we would not be vanquished, the spirit of enthusiastic zeal for right must blend with that of wisdom in our councils. Let us then develop the Church's lawful powers, increase her bishops, and reawaken, if needful, her convocation; warring alike against the superstitions of Romanism and the threatening influences of infidelity. Let as maintain the great institutions of our country, the exclusively *Christian* character of our legislature, and, more especially, our peerage, as one of the main barriers against the ingress of democratic lawlessness. Let us endeavour by every means in our power to better the condition of the working-classes, and render them contented citizens of the state! Finally, let us not work only for ourselves. Let us not seek to isolate our country from the rest of Europe. Let us not leave foreign states without the aid of our sympathy, our earnest counsels, and our warnings; as though we were not well assured of the justice of our own cause, and shrunk from controversy with democratic and infidel licence. Let us tell Germany, that Britain's heart is still with her in the depth of her distress; that we shame not to pray for her, believing the power of God to transcend all human ability; that we regard her pseudo-philosophy and her false humanitarianism with Christian pity and regret. Far be the spirit of boasting, of confidence, and self-assertion from our hearts and lips! What we are, we are through the grace of Heaven alone. With the favourite hero of our greatest bard, Shakspeare's "Henry the Fifth," we recognize "God's hand, not ours," in all our moral and material triumphs. Nevertheless false modesty must not stay us from reminding the fallen German race, that our national intellect *is* clearer and more practical than theirs; and that *that* Christianity is to us a Divine reality, which appears to them a fiction; *that* freedom a noble and glorious possession, which they would sacrifice to democratic lawlessness! It may be that this moral attitude of strength, this preservation of order, amidst the crumbling ruins of disorganized society, will awaken the nations, and Germany the first, (which is intellectually and morally most near akin to us, despite its present fall,) to a sense of their errors and consequent degradation. If we *must* fight the battle singly, so be it! We are prepared, if needful, to maintain the rightful cause against the world. But the north, at least, may learn to rally round us, if we maintain our due position in the coming years; and through our instrumentality may the final renovation be effected, which sages of all kindred and all ages have prophecied and ardently desired; which Scripture has taught us to expect; and which may develop the noblest powers of humanity, in true and universal freedom, under the abiding influence of Heaven.

GERMAN POEMS,

RELATING TO THE DEFEATS OF THE ROMANS IN GERMANY.

TRANSLATED BY JOHN OXENFORD.

THE first of the following poems relates to an event which is said to have oc-curred to the Roman General, Nero Claudius Drusus, father of the celebrated Germanicus. He was the most inveterate enemy of the Germans, and commenced his last campaign in the year B. C. 9. Evil omens had preceded his departure from Rome, but, nevertheless, he hastened to the seat of war, attacked the Chatti (the present Hessians), penetrated to the country of the Suevi, and defeated the portion of the Suevi called the Marcomanni; then turning his forces against the Cherusci (the inhabitants north of the Hartz), he crossed (perhaps) the Weser, and made his way unimpeded to the Elbe. Here, it is said, a woman of more than human dimensions appeared to him, and accosting him in Latin, ordered him to retreat, at the same time telling him that his death was near at hand. Superstition had its effect, and he retreated accordingly. Between the Elbe and the Saal (?) he was overtaken by death, his horse having accidentally fallen upon him, and fractured his thigh. The place where he died was called "Scelerata," or the accursed. Simrock, it will be observed, makes the prophetess appear on the banks of the Weser.

The other poems relate to Hermann—or, as the Romans call him, Arminius—the great national hero of the Germans, whose memory is still held in the highest respect, particularly in times of foreign invasion. He makes his appearance about eighteen years after the death of Drusus, that is to say, in A.D. 9. At that time the Romans had forts in the Danube, the Rhine, the Elbe, and the Weser; and Tiberius Nero having twice overrun the interior of Germany, Varus, a licentious and extortionate man, was left with three legions, to complete the subjugation of the country. Hermann, who was son and successor to Sigimer, chief of the Cherusci, and who had learned discipline while acting as an auxiliary of the Romans, was twenty-seven years of age when he performed the action on which his celebrity depends. He feigned friendship for Varus; and when the Roman ordered his army to march for the purpose of quelling an insurrection, promised to meet him at a certain spot. This was the Teutoburger wood, situated in the present district of Lippe-Detmold. Hermann certainly met Varus, as he had promised, but it was to attack him and his legions, as they were making their way in disorder through the forest, encumbered with baggage, and suffering from the inclemencies of the weather. The Roman legions, with the exception of a small body who escaped, were cut to pieces; all the prisoners taken alive were sacrificed on forest altars to the German gods; and Varus, in despair, fell upon his own sword.

At Rome the news of this defeat produced the greatest consternation, and, according to Suetonius, the Emperor Augustus let his beard and hair grow for several months, and sometimes knocked his head against the door, crying, "Quintilius Varus, give me my legions again." Every year, according to the same authority, he observed the day of the disaster as one of sorrow and mourning.

In the year A. D. 14, the celebrated Germanicus took the command of the legions, and designed to penetrate into Germany by the river Ems. The national party had in the meanwhile gained strength. Inguiomer, a chief who had hitherto fought on the Roman side, joined the patriot; and Segestes, father of Hermann's wife, Thusnelda, had been with difficulty saved from the attacks of his own tribe, because he still adhered to the invaders. The legions of Ger-

manicus, while they rescued Segestes, captured Thusnelda; and it is said that Segestes himself delivered her into their hands. She gave birth to an infant son during her captivity, and was reserved by Germanicus, to appear in his triumph at Rome. The war continued between Germanicus and Hermann; the patriots sustained some severe defeats, and Germany seemed once more at the mercy of the Romans, when the jealousy of the Emperor Tiberius (who had succeeded Augustus) recalled Germanicus, in A. D. 17, and the Germans were left to secure their independence. Hermann, after thus distinguishing himself as the champion of national liberty, seems to have aimed at the possession of absolute power among his countrymen. The people rose against him, and he was slain by his own relations in the year A. D. 19.

I.—DRUSUS. BY KARL SIMROCK.

Drusus, in the German wood,
Made the Roman eagles brood,
While against the sacred oaks
Fell the axe, with impious strokes.

Conq'ring went he through the land,
Stood upon the Weser's strand;
Where he would have cross'd the flood,
Lo! a female figure stood.

More than human is her size;
To the son of earth she cries—
"Fool! ambition dims thy sight;
Quickly turn thy foot to flight.

" Know my country's borders lie
Ever hidden from thine eye;
To life's bound'ry thou art brought;
All thy conquests come to nought.

" Slow the German is, but sure;
Foreign yoke he'll ne'er endure:
Wrapp'd in slumber he may be,
God will wake him presently."

Drusus heard her words aright,
Drusus has commenced his flight;
German groves are groves of dread:
To the Rhine his host he led.

German weapons proudly flash,[*]
German weapons loudly clash;
Now he hears the jav'lin's sound,
Falls, dismounted, to the ground.

Broken is the Roman's thigh;
Thirty days and he must die:
Those who Germans would enthral,
Thus by God's own hand shall fall.

II.—HERMANN. BY HANS FERDINAND MASSMANN.

Old Rome, the greatest, proudest city,
    Queen of the Midland Sea[†] was crown'd;
She swept her sickle without pity,
    And mow'd the nations down around.

With freedom once the Alps were fir'd,
    And brightly glow'd each snow-crown'd head;[‡]
But victims all in vain expir'd,
    The Danube's stream was tinged with red.

And where the Elbe, like silver, marks
    Old Marbod's[§] bound'ry with its stream,
Once swam a thousand blood-stained barques,
    The flood flung back the eagle's gleam.

And from the Rhine-stream's triple source,
    To where its flood is lost in sand,

---

[*] The Romans, during the retreat, are said to have seen supernatural enemies, and it is probably to these Simrock alludes, not to any real attack of the Germans."—J. O.

[†] The Mediterranean.

[‡] Allusion is made to the Roman battles with the Rhœtians, Dalmatians, and Pannonians.

[§] Founder of the kingdom of Marcomanni.

And where begins the Weser's course,
    All was to Rome a tribute-land.

The German heart was cold and dead,
    Welsh* minions hush'd the German tongue;
To Osning's† hills fair Freedom fled,
    And dwelt the hurricanes among.

The groves all echoed with her wail,
    She told her wrongs to each old oak;
Beneath the moonlight she was pale,
    With bitter grief her blue eye broke.

But soon a youthful hero came,
    Enrag'd that mourning form to see;
He swore by Thor and Woden's name,
    To fight the fight of liberty.

The land arose in wild uproar,
    Whelming the army as a flood;
The Forum never saw it more,
    Lost in the Teutoburger wood.

The Emperor, who had never fail'd
    To gain a wish, or act a part,‡
Now at the Nibelungen quail'd—
    The icy north had touch'd his heart.

Down—down the northern cloud has pour'd
    Its rage, in Welshland's golden plain,
The Gothic and the Vandal horde
    O'er nature and o'er man must reign.

The like was never seen before,
    The old Welsh world was doom'd to fall;
'Tis lost—'tis sunk for evermore,
    And Hermann rises over all;—

Head of another race of men,
    Leader of every German deed,
Sower, who sprinkled not in vain,
    With drops of blood, the new-sown seed.

And dost thou ask what seed he sow'd,
    And how much harvest it has brought?
Oh, often as the sword has mow'd,
    While savage Huns and Turks have fought;—

Oft as for faith or liberty
    Mankind has pray'd, mankind has quail'd,
What refuge was there—answer me—
    If German heart or faith had fail'd?

Now German blood and German toil
    Into the wide world's veins have pass'd,
And science, from her mental soil
    Springing, has gain'd her prize at last.

---

* The German word "Welsh" (Welsch), by which the Italians are designated, is retained on account of its national character. The word "Welshland" for Italy will be found lower down.—J. O.
† The row of mountains from Detmold to Osnaburg was once called "Osnine."—J. O.
‡ On his death-bed Augustus asked if he had not acted his part well. The word "Nibelungen" is used a little below, on the assumption that it means an old Germanic race.—J. O.

III.—SONG OF VICTORY AFTER THE DEFEAT OF VARUS.
By F. G. KLOPSTOCK.*

Single Chorus.

Sister of Cannœ, Winfeld's fight!†
We saw thee with waving gory hair,
With the flame-glance of destruction,
Floating among the bards of Walhalla.

Hermann said: "Victory or Death!"
Rome said: "Victory!"
Threat'ning flew her eagles.
That was the first day.

"Conquest or Death!" began
Their gen'ral. Hermann was still,
But struck. The eagle flutter'd.
That was the second day.

Two Choruses.

The third came. They cried: "Flight or Death!"
Flight was not granted to robbers of freedom,
Not to the slayers of infants.
This was their last day.

Two Bards.

None but messengers escap'd to Rome,
The horse-hair crest turn'd backwards; in the dust
Draggled the lance; pale was their face;
Thus came the messengers to Rome.

In his hall sat the Emperor,
Octavianus Cæsar Augustus,
The Penates with wine fill'd the goblet
To him, the greater god.

When the tidings were heard, the Lydian flute was still;
The greater god dash'd his brow
Against the marble pillar: "Varus,
Give my my legions, Varus!"

The conq'rors of the world now trembled
To raise the lance
For their fatherland; and the lot o' death
Roll'd among the tardy.‡

"She has turn'd her face,"
They cry, "the goddess of vict'ry:"
(May it be ever so) but *he* cried,
"Varus,
Give me my legions, Varus!"

---

* This is a chorus, in blank verse lyrics, from one of Klopstock's plays.
† Winfeld, near Detmold, is the probable site of the battle, which is compared to that of Cannœ, in which the Romans were defeated by the Carthaginians.
‡ After the defeat of Varus, the Romans were unwilling to enlist for the German expedition, and Augustus was obliged to enforce military service by the severest penalties. The figure of the goddess Victory is said to have turned her face from Germany to Rome.

IV.—THUSNELDA. By FRIEDRICH HALM.

Thusnelda in the Roman tent lies bound,
    About her is a troop of captives fair;
Tears glisten on the pallid cheeks around,
    And sorrow sports with their dishevell'd hair.

Grief shrieks aloud, and fetters seem to moan;
    But on the realm of woe the trumpet's cry
Dares to intrude with its exulting tone;
    All weep—Thusnelda's eyes alone are dry.

One hope is still reposing in her breast:
    She thinks upon her Hermann's glorious life;
She thinks upon that foeman's friend, Segest,
    Betrayer of his blood in Hermann's wife.

Before the tent, thus silent and forlorn,
    She sits, and to her home directs her gaze;
While glimmering the hopeful light of morn
    Tints her own mountains with its ruddy rays.

Her bosom heaves, her eyes prophetic glow,
　Her cheek becomes suffused with noble blood ;
She hears the waves of Weser as they flow,
　The rustle of the Teutoberger wood.

Then up she starts, and round about her limbs
　Her flowing locks, like liquid gold, she flings;
Forth from her lips prophetic utterance streams,
　And Germany with waken'd echoes rings.

" Oh, do not mourn, my people, in your chains,
　Though ye must bow beneath the tyrant's might ;
A God to punish and to save remains,
　And from all darkness breaks the morning's light.

" No race was yet by endless bondage ground ;
　A day at last arrived—its fetters broke.
No race by endless lethargy was bound ;
　A day arrived, and lo ! its strength awoke.

" Do not despair, although your heart is torn
　By the fierce discord of your sons at home ;
It was decreed, this anguish must be borne,
　That all might feel whence liberty must come.

" On ye the yoke was placed, that ye might learn
　Your freedom as the highest boon to prize ;
That darkness ye might see to day-light turn,
　Exulting in the sun, which glorifies.

" The day will come—'twill come that fated day,
　When round *one* standard all your sons shall meet ;
Then Germany shall to her tyrant say,
　' Our shame is past—thy measure is complete.'

" A day will come, when plainly shall be heard
　The cry of vengeance, as from one great breast ;
A day, when deep despair shall find a word,
　And with the tardy gift of speech be blest.

" A day will come at last, when freedom's breath
　Shall rove about your vales like gales of spring,
Shall pierce the graves, and to your sires beneath
　The joyful tidings of your triumph bring.

" Weep not,—although in chains ye are confined,
　Weep not,—there still is glory in our doom ;
To us the solemn office is assigned
　Of teaching freedom to the race to come.

" What though our blood the Roman's axe may stain,
　Though trampled by his coursers we may be ;
To *us*, through all, this glory must remain,
　While slaves, we dared to hope for liberty.

" With those, who think like us, we still live on ;
　'Tis we that sow ; when ripen'd is the seed,
We are with those who have the battle won,
　We are with those who Germany have freed."

Germany heard, while thus Thusnelda spoke.
　Oh think of this when gloomy days draw near—
Your fathers often burst the cumbrous yoke ;
　Ye bear their name,—like them in strength appear.

Klopstock, Lessing and Wieland. By A. Tolhausen.—This is a brief treatise on German literature, written and published for the benefit of the
German Hospital at Dalston. It begins with the
enunciation of the law that " No nation shall have a
weight in the scales of humanity without having
founded a literature and fought its battles." The
perception of such a law is a cheering fact to the
literary labourer. Germany, though late in the field,
has achieved a literary status which for the last half
century has been recognized, and now commands
general respect. Dr. Tolhausen has in this tractate
chosen to exhibit " three Coryphæs" of German
poetry ; and, in doing so, declares his sense of the
" high vocation of literature in general." His theme is
a noble one; and its illustrators are noble too, though
not the noblest. Germany has higher names—but
the three selected represent a state of transition, the
aspect of which is always interesting. In fact, we
have here a " general survey of German literature at
the time of Frederick the Great." It was a period
of struggle ; and its history is peculiar. Dr. Tolhausen does well in dwelling with emphasis on
Klopstock's Odes ;—their merit is very great, and
rises to far higher excellence than the poet ever
attained in his religious epic. On Lessing's claims
it is more easy to speak. This writer's great aim,
both as a poet and as a critic, was the creation of a
national stage to the Germans. He failed in this,
as he confesses at the end of his ' Dramaturgy,'—
giving the reason of his failure in the fact that the
" Germans were yet no nation;" and this fact he
stated not in relation to their political but to their
" moral character." Dr. Tolhausen considers Lessing
to be " the most original writer of Germany."
Wieland, however, represents most of the difficulties
of the age. Its very spirit passed into his, and accordingly its doubts and its aspirations receive full
expression in his various works.—The reader will find
the Essay before us a pleasing epitome of the argument to which it relates.

German Literature. By Joseph Gostick. Part I. Edinburgh, Chambers.

Tuis is the first part of a work intended, as the preface informs us, "to give in a concise and popular form a general view of the literature of the German people, from the earliest to the latest times:"—a large undertaking to be comprised in two small shilling volumes! The survey proceeds by "periods;" and the part in question brings us to the threshold of a seventh of these divisions (1770-1848), in which all the best productions of German Literature must be included. Certain names and works, indeed, which might have claimed a place in the previous section (1720-1770) with as much right as some that are there discussed,—are postponed to the latter period. Of such we may cite, as a marked instance, the poems of Wieland; of which no word is found in the sixth period,— although he began to write them about 1755, and some of the most characteristic pieces in his later style (e. g. the 'Idris') had been published before 1770. This omission is the more strange, as in other cases the works of authors who began to write later than Wieland have been noticed, although reaching beyond the last-mentioned date. Altogether, both here and in other respects, there is something unaccountable in the distribution adopted, and still more in the relative degrees of attention paid to different authors. Of the more important names the notices are often unsatisfactorily brief,— while inferior figures are described at greater length and exhibited in translated specimens.

This circumstance, and the tenor of such critical remarks as are offered, detract from the value of this essay as a "general view" of German letters:—in which although the author's industry may be fairly commended, it is not easy to admire or to ratify his judgments. He has collected with much pains notices of the names, at least, of nearly all the authors and anonymous writings in German, from the time when the language began to fall into its present shape:—in which task, of course, he has had assistance from the large works of German authors who have treated of the literary history of their country. With several of the authors whom he enumerates he displays a nearer acquaintance; having made and inserted as he proceeds not a few translations from passages of their works. These, if not always well chosen, are often so prettily executed that the taste which they evince makes us wonder the more at the judgments uttered by the essayist in other places when he begins to describe and criticize. Of Bürger, for instance, it is said,

that his poems have no "substantial value:"— what is wanting to this quality in some of the best lyrical ballads that Germany has produced, it would have been as well if the critic had been pleased to state. Wieland's character and performances as a prose writer, one of the most copious of his time—as the author of Agathon, Aristipp, &c. &c.,—we find disposed of in less than twenty lines; followed by half-a-page of colourless extract—about half the space allotted to Rabener or Engel! Hamann, crushed, poor fellow! into a single paragraph,— is declared undeserving of notice altogether on account of his literary merits, and this *because he wrote in a style of studied oddity.* This will be thought rather a questionable reason for thrusting a writer of undoubted genius out of the court of letters; and fatal, if admitted, to not a few besides whose "literary merits" have not usually been questioned — such as Rabelais, Sterne, Quevedo, Richter, and many others.

The part now before us breaks off at the beginning of the "seventh period," in the midst of a notice of Goethe. The promise of what is to follow may be estimated by the assertions here set forth; that his lyrical poems and ballads "are not rich in human interest," —that the interest of 'Herman and Dorothea' "depends in a great measure on the moral reflections interwoven with the narrative,"—and that "the second part of 'Faust' is remarkable only as a specimen of varied and harmonious versification." From criticism of this sort we fear it will not be easy to obtain very correct "views of German Literature:"—and while attesting the diligence, as we have said, with which Mr. Gostick has compiled the dictionary materials of his essay, we are bound to say that we can hardly recommend him as an infallible guide to the understanding of their value, significance, or relative proportions.

74. LITERARY GAZETTE, 31 (1849), 517. M/H No. 4621.

Klopstock, Lessing, and Wieland: a Treatise on German Literature. By Alexander Tolhausen, Dr. Ph.

IF the solemn injunction, not to do evil that good may come, extend to such matters as the writing of books, then has the author of this treatise grievously offended; for he has written an exceedingly bad book for an exceedingly good purpose,—viz., " for the benefit of the German Hospital, Dalston." Klopstock, Lessing, Wieland! what ideas do not these names awaken in the memory, not only from the literary glory which they themselves achieved, but from the might and majesty with which they threw open to the whole world the vast portals of the temple of literature, which had hitherto been shut against all but a few cherished votaries. Were we of the number of hose who hold "omne ignotum pro magnifico," we should hail this production with rapturous applause, for we candidly confess that the more we read the less we understood. The following observation, for instance, may be true to the letter; and yet it is so un-Englishly expressed, that we could well have spared it. " It is in the history of German poets that we meet with so great a variety of character, which to the contemplator and philosophical mind admits of so vast a field of investigation, that it appears almost incompatible with a satisfactory result to encompass the leading principles of several men into one description," p. 48. No man who sets up for an instructor should write in this style. His intentions may be as good as his object is laudable; but we who sit in the judge's chair must dispense justice, not according to each man's motives but his deeds.

A Guide to German Literature; or, Manual to facilitate an acquaint-ance with the German Classic Authors. By Franz. Adolph. Moschzisker, of the University of Leipsic, and Professor of the German Language and Literature. 2 vols. 8vo. J. J. Guillaume. London. 1850.

This book eminently justifies its title; it contains exactly that kind of direction in the choice of books suited to convey a thorough know-ledge of the language and genius of Germany which the learner would expect from a competent and judicious friend. But it contains more than this. It is a learned and comprehensive synopsis of German literature from its earliest dawn in the days of Ulphilas, to its meridian splendour at the period of Klopstock, Göthe, and Schiller. It is divided into seven chronological epochs, which mark the progressive development of the German mind, and exemplify distinct phases in the national literature. The range over which it conducts the reader is immense, leaving untouched scarcely any department of science or art which takes form and expression from letters. Here is an illustrious company of poets, philosophers, historians, and divines. They are pre-sented to the reader, not merely by name; he is informed of the circumstances of their birth and education, of the character of their labours, and of the manner of their death. He receives the brief story of the life of each, with its relations to the lives of others who have moved the intellectual world. Nor is this a dumb phantasmagoria. He hears the marvellous assemblage speak through the medium of an impartial selection from their best productions, and whilst he fami-liarizes himself with their noble tongue, he may revel in their loftiest and most beautiful thoughts. It is surprising how the author has been able to compress so much within such comparatively narrow limits, yet large as is his theme, he has omitted nothing that ought to be included; he even glances at the renowned songs of other lands, and becomingly acknowledges the influence they have exercised on the minds of his countrymen. A short, but discriminating critique accom-panies the notices of the most distinguished writers, and often furnishes the key to the most difficult parts of their works; we would cite as a special example the critical analysis of "Faust," hitherto the great literary puzzle, not only to Englishmen, but even to the Germans them-selves. The book is equally well calculated to serve as Analecta for the beginner, and as a repertory of valuable and elegant extracts for the more mature student.

Considering the extensive and increasing popularity of the German language amongst ourselves, and its growing influence upon our habits of thought and feeling, this Manual cannot fail to meet with a cordial reception. It has the great merit of seeking with integrity and im-partiality to fulfil the promise of its title. The author is evidently a man of high moral and religious feeling, but he has no weak diffidence of the principles to which he has given his faith; he seems willing that they should be thoroughly tested, and, therefore, gives the authors of whom he disapproves, as well as those whom he admires. He appears anxious only that counsel should be heard on both sides. In this we cordially concur as a general principle, and believe it especially ap-plicable to all German questions of opinion. Whatever is impure or false in German literature will never be corrected by the writings of foreigners. There is a peculiar subtlety of thinking and enunciating in the German mind, which, whether we attribute it to training merely, or to an idiosyncracy of the Teutonic race, can alone correct its own aberrations, as the diamond can be cut and shaped by the diamond only. M. Moschzisker has, therefore, rendered good service to the cause of religious and philosophical truth, as well as to the progress of good taste by marshalling and classifying the representatives of all shades of opinion, and describing their leading characteristics, in principle, thought, and style. In the theological field, for example, we have the Neologian doctors, Strauss, Bohlen, Langeske, and Vatke, opposed by the equally stout and resolute champions of orthodoxy—Jacobi, Olshau-sen, Tholuck, and Hengstenberg. In the regions of speculative phi-losophy, too, we find the daring leaders, Kante and Fichte, closely attended and controlled by the accomplished Herder, and the moderate Schleiermacher. Nor is this impartiality forgotten by our author when he enters the realms of fancy. He passes in review before us the Minne-Song, the German echo of the sweet lyrics of Provence, with its monumental Niebelungenlied; and the satyric and didactic Meister-Song, its sly humour and profound observation receiving the most perfect illustration in the wondrous history of "Reinecke Fuchs." The Meister-Song gives place in turn to the deep flood of religious harmony called forth from the German heart by the voice of Luther, and which attained its greatest depth and volume in the grand epic of Klopstock. Here also we find the fascinating but somewhat sensual realism of Göthe met and neutralized by the equally fascinating spirituelle idealism of Schiller.

It is a book to which the reader will recur again and again for the positive advantage of its own contents, as well as for direction to other mines of intellectual treasure. We cannot close our notice of this work without a word of commendation for its clear and beautiful typography. It is, indeed, worthy of the Royal Prince to whom it is dedicated.

76. NEW MONTHLY MAGAZINE, 89 (1850), 513-514. M/H No. 4686.

GERMAN LITERATURE.*

A WORK of this description has long been a desideratum, and is particularly well timed. Not only have the English universities made the acquirement of the German language a conspicuous feature in their colleges, but private and general schools have been obliged to bring it within their routine. And as it is impossible for a boy to follow out the old system to the same extent as formerly, and at the same time be proficient in the new, so it is probable that, as a knowledge of the living languages is gradually superseding that of the dead, that the obsolete Greek will be the first that will have to give way to the study of German.

In making a collection, however, expressly for the student, Mr. Moschzisker has also aimed at far greater objects. He has proposed to himself to bring under one view, comprehensively and clearly, the whole field of German thought; to place before the student her master-minds from age to age, in all their various and relative excellence; so that, apart from the mere lingual advantages of the book, he might, when he has closed these volumes, rise with a just and adequate knowledge of the literature of the country.

To effect this, mere extracts would by no means suffice. Mr. Moschzisker has, hence, introduced every author, not only by a biographical and critical notice, but also by a philosophical analysis of the nature and aim of his creations; and in no instance has a writer's name been mentioned without duly marking every production of any value that has issued from his pen. While these notices are, in some cases, very brief, still it is impossible to over-estimate so valuable an introduction to German literature. Facilities have also been afforded to the student by classifying the works under the different branches of literature to which they respectively belong.

Thus, for example, after an introductory preface on the study of the German language, we have what is called a progressive index of extracts, in three divisions, and then an index of names. We have even an index containing lists of celebrated contemporary foreigners. The body of the work is then divided into epochs, commencing with Ulphila's version of the Bible, the Minnesängers, the Heldenbuch and the Niebelungenlied, which preceded the invention of printing; we next proceed with the establishment of the universities, and the great Reformation, to the epoch between Klopstock and Schiller—Goethe—the dramatists—the humourists, novelists, and tale-writers—the historians—philosophy and theology—the religious systems of Germany—periodical literature, and works of reference. Altogether, a more complete or carefully got-up work of the kind could not be wished for.

---

* A Guide to German Literature; or Manual to facilitate an acquaintance with the German Classic Authors. By Franz Adolph Moschzisker. 2 vols. J. J. Guillaume.

15.—The History of Ancient Art among the Greeks, translated from the German of J. Winckelmann, by G. H. Lodge. 8vo. London: Chapman. 1850.

The Americans of late years have been working the deep mine of German literature with a zeal and perseverance that were hardly to be expected from so extremely practical a nation, towards our deeply speculative and somewhat mystical Teutonic brethren. This is no bad symptom; and if the Germans would only return the compliment, by taking a few lessons in active life from parties so competent to give them, their over-speculative leaders would receive a dose of practical wisdom, which recent events have proved that they need, and the progress of Germany would be greatly accelerated.

This American translation forms the second and most interesting volume of the large work on the history of Ancient Art by Winckelmann, whose learning, taste, and indefatigable exertions during a long life devoted to the arts, are too well known to require comment. Though some discoveries have been made since he wrote —and not a little has been thought, said, and written—this work still maintains its place, and will be read by few who will not thenceforward view Greek sculpture with a feeling and intelligence they were previously strangers to. It should also be observed that Winckelmann is wholly free from what we are in the habit of calling (justly or not) German mysticism.

The architecture of Greece, of which little, or the painting, of which nothing, now remains, are noticed briefly and incidentally, the author having devoted most of his life and work to a critical investigation of Grecian sculpture. Some slight idea may be formed of the nature of the work, from a brief extract of its heads, viz:— Causes of the progress and superiority of Greek art—the essential of art—the conformation and beauty of the male and female deities, heroes and heroines—the expression of beauty in features and action—proportion—composition— beauty of individual parts of the body—animals.

It is not possible to give a correct notion of the work by limited extracts, as the subject is viewed in all ways, from the most general aspect to the most minute details. Thus, the dignified composure of almost all the Grecian statues (notwithstanding that the distinctive character and expression of the personage represented is perfectly preserved, and monotony and dulness are never visible), is frequently noticed, and contrasted with the opposite practice more usual in modern sculpture, which betokens a lower state of art.

" The ancient artists displayed the same wisdom in their conception of figures drawn from the heroic age, and in the representation of merely human passions, the expression of which always corresponds to what we should look for in a man of disciplined mind, who prevents his feelings from breaking forth, and lets only the sparks of the fire be seen."

Again, the statues of a Grecian divinity or hero are found to have, not only a strong general resemblance, but the features of each are remarkably like, and visibly different from those of all other characters. These points of resemblance and difference, so little noticed by the common observer, are most of them very obvious when singled out and illustrated by the critic, though others of them would require acute and practised powers of observation to appreciate fully. The peculiarities of the statues of Jupiter alone, as described by Winckelmann, would require too much space for our insertion; but, to go no further than the hair of the head, the hair of Jupiter "is raised upward on the forehead, and parted; it then describes a short curve, and again falls down on each side," which contributes to the strength and majesty of his appearance. The singular fact is also noticed, that Castor and Pollux, Æsculapius, and the other male progeny of Jupiter, to the second generation, are represented in the Greek sculptures by hair of the same lion-like growth, thus revealing their paternal descent.

These are only a few of the least obvious details regarding the king of the gods. His forehead, eyes, mouth, and other features are taken into account, and their peculiarities stated and accounted for as means of building up the ideal character which the Grecian artists wished to represent.

The translation appears to be fairly executed. It is illustrated by a number of plates, chiefly of heads from the antique, which are referred to in the work.

A Selection from the Poems and Dramatic Works of Theodore Körner. By the Translator of the 'Nibelungen-Treasure.' London, Williams & Norgate.

Free Translations from the German of Gellert and other Poets. By John A. Nuske. London, Whittaker; Farnham, Nuske.

Of the minor German poets there is none better known in England than Körner. His zeal for a great cause, to which he sacrificed favourite pursuits, a happy love, and a life just opening to the most brilliant prospects, won, not in Germany, only a personal interest and the praise of heartfelt truth for those fine lyrics, contained in 'The Lyre and Sword,'—the latest and the best of his compositions—which have already been more than once translated here. Notices of the writer himself, with which these were accompanied, illustrated their poetic meaning and displayed a nobleness and beauty of character more impressive even than the genius that burned in his songs. In this country, his name honoured by a poetic tribute* not unworthy of his memory, has long been familiar to our ears, —as identified with many qualities, each singly

* In Mrs. Hemans's 'Lays of Many Lands.'

precious, and forming, when combined in harmonious alliance, a model such as generous minds love to imagine and but rarely behold. The deepest regrets and sympathies are well bestowed on those rare monuments where the sanctity of an heroic death hallows the splendour of early genius. They are justly and willingly paid, in virtue of both, to the memory of Körner. The poet had besought his countrymen to "forget not the faithful dead;"—nor will he be forgotten in England while anything worthy and bright is held in remembrance here.

Thus, his 'Lyre and Sword' is already well known to us :—of his other compositions, lyrical and dramatic, it may be doubted whether they are likely to reward a translator's pains, at a time especially when the public appetite for poetry, whether cloyed or depraved, is extremely languid. Considered as the productions of a mere youth, Körner's early poems and his tragedies will always be remarkable to the student of literature. While he lived they naturally excited a higher interest, due not so much to their positive merits—which were many—as to the hopes of what maturer skill might produce in one whose unripe years had already produced so much. But, in considering the effect which they may now produce, when introduced in a new language to a foreign audience, this recommendation can of course have no place. They can look for acceptance only in virtue of qualities which they actually embody ; the further hopes that they once awakened are now forbidden to heighten their attraction, even in the land where they were born, by the stern *ne plus ultra* of death. As independent pieces only can they be viewed here ; and as such they hardly possess substantial force enough to make their way to the hearts of a strange and not very excitable public, through the certain disadvantages of translation.

Whatever share of original genius a poet may inherit from nature, he will seldom be found assuming a gait and speaking in accents properly his own at the very outset of his career. If he be precocious, he always begins by copying others. A sense of melody and some force of imagination are the qualities soonest developed in early years. With these, in default of the other faculties which are still dormant, he will adopt, with more or less felicity, the manner and cast of thought of some favourite model. His hour of laying aside this poetical nonage is struck by the first stir of real passion that clearly vibrates through his being, teaching him to feel what he has hitherto been merely repeating from the tones of emotion in others. Thus it is that to love—the passion that soonest comes with any real force upon the dawn of manhood—all very young poets owe the decisive step from imitation to unfeigned and actual impressions. So it was with Körner :—but with him the glow of this feeling had scarcely began to penetrate his compositions with a new and unborrowed life, before another mighty influence —the love of country—came to fan the flame already kindled; and the combined power of these inspirations—the twin genii of lyric Poetry —may be seen in the sudden developement of character, freedom, and self-dependence which distinguishes the songs in 'The Lyre and Sword.' Before it all he wrote was stamped with the influence of Schiller; whom the young poet naturally chose for a model, not only as the favourite of all German youth in his day, but still more as the dear and honoured friend of his father, whom he had been taught to admire from infancy. The tragedies composed at Vienna especially are mere reflexes of Schiller's style; and, in spite of much eloquence and some occasional warmth and power, must on the whole be termed but faint reflections. That

they should have been more than this would have been simply miraculous under all the circumstances. As we know the arduous process by which the originals of these pieces were composed, it can only be matter of surprise that the dramas of the young disciple, in every respect destitute of such preparatory means, did not fall still further below the standard of those great models. Having first seen Schiller's tragedies produced in the maturity of a life wholly devoted to earnest self-culture, long considered, carefully wrought out, and often revised, appearing tardily at distant intervals,—when we note the eager haste with which a poet of twenty, in his raw inexperience, threw out 'The Expiation,' 'Zriny,' 'Hedwig,' and 'Rosamond,' besides several minor dramatic pieces, all in the interval of little more than a year,—we may indeed recognize the force of a talent that could be thus prolific of works of such high pretensions which reach far above mediocrity. But it is no cause for wonder to find them deficient in those qualities which alone can give to productions in this most arduous class of poetry a claim to lasting life. The marvel would have been their possession of true dramatic vitality.

The translator of the 'Nibelungen' gives in the volume now before us a part only of Körner's stage works,—'The Expiation' and 'Antonia' ('Toni'), an early performance little worth preserving, 'Hedwig,' and 'Rosamond,' — with some lesser pieces, in scenes, written for musical accompaniment, which even in the original have no power to please as independent poems. 'Zriny'—to our mind the best of Körner's dramas — has been excluded, because of the discovered existence of a previous translation ; but 'Rosamond' appears, although standing in the same predicament. After the versions of these larger works come the lyric poems. We have not thought it necessary to examine if all are there which formed the collection entitled '*Knospen*' (Buds, not *Blossoms*, as the translator calls them), and published as early as 1810. These shew the precocious talent of the young author,—who gave them to the press while still a student in Leipzig, before he was nineteen years old. But they will be apt to fall tamely on the ears of those who have hitherto known Körner only by his 'Lyre and Sword.' A few of the lays from that series the translator has inserted among those inferior pieces of a previous date.

From the former we shall take one strain, as pretty well exhibiting the extent of this Lady's powers in translation. Her version is generally an elegant, but not at all a strong, complete, or characteristic one. Accordingly, she succeeds better in the comparatively easy task of Englishing the stately iambics and conventional style of the dramas, than in reproducing the warmth or animation and the more idiomatic manner of Körner's lyrics.—

Farewell to Vienna.†

Farewell, farewell! with sad and beating heart
  I greet thee, my beloved ! my duties claim me,
And if one tender tear unbidden start,
  Why struggle 'gainst that tear? it will not shame me.
Whether amid the paths of peace I rove,
  Or where stern death its bloody wreaths preparing,
Still shall that cherish'd form of light and love
  Hover around my soul and fire its daring !

Mistake not, ye good genii of my life,
  The ardent aspirations of my soul!
The same in song as in the battle's strife;
  Of all my hopes, the unalterable goal,
The images with which my dreams are rife,
  My theme of song that would not brook control!
The prize I seek! the wish I fondly cherish,
For freedom and my native land to perish.

Fairer and easier twin'd the wreath of fame,
  Won only by the poet's golden lyre,
But patriot souls know but one single aim :
  For that dear art, I love with youthful fire,

† Written on leaving Vienna, at the commencement of the year 1813; the lines are addressed to his betrothed bride

I will preserve a country! proud and free!
  And though my heart's blood flow in crimson showers,
Yet one kiss more! and though the last it be,
The last? there is no death for love like ours!

If we have misgivings as to the effect which may be made by this part of Körner's literary remains, we can have no doubt whatever as to the reception due to the "*Free Translations*" made by Mr. Nuske from Gellert. This arid writer had once, indeed, some credit—before the golden day of German letters,—while very moderate gifts were still allowed to make rhymed prose current in the name of poetry. But that time has long passed; and to revive this prim and periwigged figure, to hand in his little angular slips of narrow worldly-wisdom, and thin attempts at festivity or slyness, is surely the last enterprise that an amateur could be safely advised to undertake. The author would find but a poor welcome anywhere, however well presented: in a "free translation," which throws away those little accuracies and finesses in style that are among Gellert's chief merits,—it may be feared that doors will be somewhat rudely shut against this nearly forgotten "Philistine." Of the substance of his small endeavours at mirth, and of the translator's "free" way of Englishing the German, which at all events was written with polish and courtly smartness,—a single instance may be more than enough.—

The Ghost

A certain Landlord, as I have been told,
Was much tormented by a Ghost of old,
And felt resolved some potent charm to learn,
By means of which the guest should ne'er return.
Long time he strove without the least success,
Each spell he tried proved wholly powerless,
For still the Ghost all magic art despite,
Paid his accustom'd visit every night.
It chanced a Poet came with him to dwell;—
'Twas then our host, in order to dispel
Somewhat his terror, begged him be so kind
A night with poems to divert his mind.
The Bard complied most willingly, and read
A frosty tragedy replete with dread!
The Ghost came too (and, reader, you should know it,
The Landlord saw him, but not so the Poet),
And listening 'gan to shiver, and—in fact,
Could stop no longer than the premier act;
For ere the second could the tale resume,
He had precipitately left the room.
The Landlord now with hope quite lifted up,
Entreats the Bard next night with him to sup;
He came, and brought with him his tragic store—
Again the Ghost appear'd as heretofore,
But left more quickly, and the Landlord saw
'Twas tragic verse that held him so in awe.
The third night then our much enlighten'd host
Alone determined to await the Ghost,
And lo, the midnight hour no sooner sounded,
Than he again into the chamber bounded!
"Boy!" cries his master to the ostler John;
"Go, fetch the Poet, fast as you can run,
And ask if he the kindness me will do
To bring his Play and read a line or two."
The frighten'd Ghost at this was seen to wave
His hand, as tho' a last adieu he gave,
Then vanish'd, and, as far as I can learn,
Has never since had courage to return.

  Whoever should this wonder read,
    May learn a lesson not so ill:
  A poem may be bad indeed,
    And yet be good for something still.
  For if a Ghost bad verses shuns,
    And seems quite horror-struck to hear them—
  If none *admire*, take comfort dunce,
    There still are plenty that will *fear* them!

We have often doubted the possibility of doing justice by translation to those foreign poets who highly deserve it: yet only such are worth being translated at all. To bring alien mediocrities—especially when faded—to other lands that have enough of the commonplace at home, is perhaps the worst kind of industry in this way that can be thought of. It is sure to be a failure,—it would otherwise be a grievance.

The Romantic School in its Internal Relation to Goethe and Schiller—[Die Romantische Schule, &c.]. By Herman Hettner. Brunswick, Vieweg; London, Thimm.

ALTHOUGH the immediate subject of this acute and well-written essay lies at some distance from non-German readers, it opens a field of inquiry in which the students of modern literature in all countries, as distinguished from those who read for pastime only, are alike interested. The phenomena which it seeks to explain, if more marked in Germany than elsewhere, have been witnessed in France, and are at this moment visible enough in English literature and art. The cause to which their developement is traced, and the principles on which it is judged, are as true in London as in Leipzig; however differences in moral training and civil relations may tend to modify their results here and there respectively.

A brief outline of the treatise is all that can be afforded here. It will suffice to turn to the work itself the attention of those who consider the poetry and art of an era—as types of its higher spiritual tendencies—a fit object for philosophic thought.

One considerable branch of the so-called Romantic school in Germany, after having run through various stages of developement, has now arrived at what may be termed its extreme point. In the embrace of a political and ultramontane re-action, it professes the perverse creed which virtually denies all that modern progress has won,—which declares that society, and those intelligent impulses which are its life, can only be redeemed from their present degradation by falling back on the feudal polity—on the undoubting Catholic faith of the Middle Ages. In other words, that the rules of art and of living must be recovered from the example of times in which the one was helpless and the other rude. The doctrine is absurd enough; but we cannot term it quite a stranger here. Something like this, in various disguises, has, indeed, been preached of late years in our own language.

Such an outcome of the romantic movement, says Hettner, is pitiful enough; and cannot be too strongly rejected by all sane and honest minds. But it is erroneous to say that this was its aim from the beginning. What now appears is but the natural issue in a false direction of a tendency which received its first impulse from a real cause. The primary object of the romantic *nisus* was to supply an actual want—to escape from a condition which was truly felt to be oppressive and inapt for genial production. That it was not a mere caprice in the young authors who founded the school, will be seen, says the essayist, by the operation of the same circumstances which called them forth on minds of a superior order, as shown in a certain period by both Goethe and Schiller. This is displayed with great discrimination by the writer, who traces the contrary effects of the common cause on these dissimilar natures in a very able manner:—showing how it acted on eager, feminine, and sensuous natures—on Tieck, on the Schlegels, and their later followers, on this hand,—and how it was felt even by the higher genius, more robust intellect, and consummate literary training of Goethe and of Schiller on the other.

They all were conscious, says Hettner, of the prime defect of their calling,—of the chasm, namely, which lay between their world of high poetry and art and the common life around them. The seed of any vital literature must take root in the heart of its age; of which it then becomes the living type in perennial forms, — its everlasting, consummate flower. But what nourishment could it then find, in the barren, vulgar, and torpid elements of which German society was composed in that worn-out stage of its existence? In such a soil no spontaneous growth was possible:—the productive enegies of the poet were thrown into some region more or less unreal. In search of the foundation which their own times denied, Goethe and Schiller, each in the way to which his particular genius was most apt, betook themselves to the formal beauty of the antique. The critical deduction of this process, and of its results, from a review of the later works of both these great authors, though severe, is not without substantial truth. The test is applied, indeed, with too much rigour on many occasions; and enough stress is not laid on exceptions, which in the case of Goethe are of peculiar moment. But the general justice of the exposition, as well of the cause as of its effects, can hardly be disputed.

While these superior minds, though preserved by elevated aims and sure perceptions from many dangers of an untoward position, were nevertheless led by it to pursuits of ideal excellence in a path essentially artificial,—its action was less happy on the young and sanguine intellects that had begun their career amidst the excitement to which the success of these illustrious poets had already raised the ambition of the literary world. Partly prompted by temperament, partly tempted by a seductive illusion, they fell upon what seemed a readier way to the free exercise of poetic art than had occurred to its veteran professors. The microcosm of poetry, they said, lies in the poet's brain and heart alone; and, as a consequence of this axiom, spurning the world of reality as altogether dwarfish and prosaic, they fixed his abode in the region of pure fancy. Some of them, carrying out this notion to its extreme, declared open war on whatever was true or tangible in nature; and in fact made the essence of the poetic consist in a state between dreaming and delirium,—where misty and incredible visions took place of living things, and where sickly emotions and a certain sentimental pathos on the one hand, and the grimmest nightmare horrors of feverish imagination on the other, were substituted for the real joys or possible tragedies of human nature. Fable and legend occupied the ground of history:—in the mode of composition as well as in the substance, the emancipation from form and definite rule was the presiding aim. Such at its outset, according to Hettner, was the "romantic school" under its greatest names, Novalis, Wackenroder, Tieck, the Schlegels, &c.

This state could not last for ever. It grew by natural degrees a fantastic leaning to old Catholicism, a morbid admiration of the Middle Ages, — as exhibited by Friedrich Schlegel and others on the ground of poetry and the plastic arts,—now in vehement opposition to the Grecian sympathies and doctrine of the Weimar "friends of art." This condition, however, was far from having yet reached the further developement which it has lately assumed, from having become anything like a practical demand for Popish infallibility and feudal absolutism. It was, as A. W. Schlegel naïvely described it in one of his lately printed letters, a mere *prédilection d'artiste:*—a thing of pure *dilettantism*, in short, such as we have seen preceding more material consequences in circles of art and let-

ters nearer home. Old music, old paintings, old architecture, were thenceforth the objects of exclusive devotion to many. Others betook themselves to legends and folk-lore. The symbolic everywhere thrust out the characteristic. In some quarters, the East began to rise prominently into the foreground; in virtue of its fantastic imaginations, disdain of natural truth, and total contrast to that European life from which it was the business of the romantic to escape as far as possible. The same combination we have seen in our own Young-England romanticists; with this characteristic difference, however, in the case of Germany, that there it led to profound and valuable Oriental studies, which went hand in hand with the poetic worship,—here, it has produced nothing but rhapsodies on the "mystery of the East," flowery journals of Oriental travel, or thin versification in honour of the blessings and beauties of Mohammedan customs and morals.

At the close of this period, after expanding itself in many directions that cannot be pursued here, the impulse given by the better minds in the fantastic school may be said to have worn itself out —as far, at least, as they were concerned. Tieck, the strongest of all, had already drawn back; unable to sympathize with many of its later exaggerations and falsities. In some compositions of his riper age, indeed, he evidently strives to regain his footing on *terra firma*. Weaker heads, in the meanwhile,—like poor Werner's and Hölderlin's, — had given way under their sincere delusions. A period of exhaustion and of disappointment had followed the waste of prepense emotion. It was found that men "had been toiling all day and had caught nothing." The natural consequence was, a relaxation of all that was most productive and genial in the original movement. The further result was, that its field now lay open to poorer natures and more sordid tendencies; which last were not slow in profiting by a condition of things always prone to the admission of abuses: —of the re-action, namely, produced by vain exertions to scale Heaven in a way that only leads to Chaos,—of a sensual craving for excitement baulked of its higher desires, and ready to lend an ear to baser inducements. This, observes our essayist, is the final stage reserved for all attempts to proceed on grounds intrinsically false. The contemplation of the certain result, as traced here along various lines of developement, is worth more than a passing regard. In its clear delineation of the process, and in its endeavour to prove that such is its infallible end, Herr Hettner's essay possesses, as we have said, an interest wider than his particular topic might of itself command in other circles than his own.

We have merely touched on some of its leading points, —and those most slightly. The complement of the outline will be found rich, both in lively references to the best period of German letters, and in acute observations, applicable not to these only, but also to the general pathology, so to speak, of all literary and artistic production. Some of the latter might seem to have been pointed with express regard to certain modern-antique vagaries in this country,—so closely do they apply to their prominent absurdities. But it is ever thus with any faithful and strenuous advance towards the illustration of truth, in whatever department. The lamp carried by the inquirer not only lights up regions immediately before him, but will shine far beyond them;—and may, indeed, as some believe, possess an almost infinite power of radiation.

GERMAN POETS AND POETRY.

A N attempt to compress within the limits of this Paper any thing like a history of the poetical literature of Germany, would only make our pages a catalogue of names and dates; yet we may give, in connection with a few specimens of German poetry, such outlines of its history and characteristics as may afford some guidance to those who wish to read more than our brief review.

If disposed to be critical, we might begin with the question so often asked—" What is poetry?" but we shall take the word in its widest and most popular sense. As the people understand this word "poetry," in Germany as in England, it comprehends all writings in verse which display imagination or invention; it embraces, therefore, such widely-different productions as the homely tales of Hans Sachs and the noble ballads of Schiller; the marvellous dramas of Shakspeare and the rude "Corn-Law Rhymes" of Ebenezer Elliott; and we are not aware that any critic has authority to alter this wide definition. According to the general decision of readers, Homer and Horace, Hans Sachs and Goethe, Shakspeare and Pope, Burns and Wordsworth, must all be received as "poets;" yet how widely and clearly distinct are the minds thus named together! Two poets, both allowed to be great, may have little resemblance to each other, excepting in the fact, that both have written inventively in verse. How wide, for instance, is the interval between Shakspeare, the creator of a dramatic world crowded with strongly-marked characters, and Wordsworth, whose verses give us scarcely the outlines of any character, excepting his own! In this respect, the latter resembles Byron—from whom he is clearly distinguished on all other points—another instance of the manifold varieties of genius comprehended under the name of "poet."

These prefatory remarks are by no means intended to depreciate criticism, (though criticism in England ranks very low in our estimation,) nor to suggest an inference that all judgment on the comparative value of various classes of poetry must be left to individual taste: this is far from our meaning. On the other side, we believe that true criticism or analysis may estimate the value of poetry as truly as we can judge of distances by our recognised standards of measurement. For granting—in accordance with the public decision—that Homer, Horace, Sachs, Goethe, Shakspeare, Pope, Burns, and Wordsworth, must all be classed together as "poets," the questions still remain to be determined by criticism : " How must we recognise the great poet ?"—" How much did he invent ?"—and " What qualities are there of moral truth, spiritual greatness, or human interest, or fine sentiment, or rich humour, or pathos, to impart additional or peculiar value to his poetry ?" In short, we would reject as arbitrary all that style of criticism which once attempted to prove that Alexander Pope was " no poet ;" while we would honour that analysis which shows the distance between such a drama as " Hamlet" and a poem like the " Rape of the Lock."

The application of the above remarks to German literature will be very plain when we state, that the comparative estimates of German poets, even by their own countrymen, are by no means clear and certain. It cannot be said that the reputation of even the most celebrated poetical writers of Germany are as unmistakably established as the characters of our Shakspeare and Milton, or even our Pope and Goldsmith. To prove this, we might quote long passages of enthusiastic praises bestowed upon Goethe, and then contrast them with the low estimates of the same poet given by such writers as Görres and Novalis; or we might quote A. W. Schlegel when he denies " the truth or reality of Schiller's dramatic characters ;" or other writers who have ventured to affirm that " Schiller was no born poet, but only a man of talent, who, by great industry, acquired a certain facility in the use of poetical phraseology ;" or another hardy writer (named Riemer, if we remember well,) who says that " Schiller *stole* all that was good in his poems from Goethe." (!) If opinions can thus differ respecting men of the highest note, then we shall not be surprised to find contradictory assertions with regard to the merits of inferior men—for instance, when we find Wieland, a man widely celebrated in his day, now declared to have been " no poet at all." We have briefly noticed these varieties of opinion to show the necessity of a wide definition of poetry, and also of toleration in our judgments. When "doctors disagree," smaller men should not pronounce their censures as oracles. We must beg the critical reader of this Paper to extend toleration to our opinions if they should happen to be opposed to his own. If, for instance, he finds that we speak in very moderate terms of some writer—say Wieland—whose name has filled a considerable space in German poetical literature, we must respectfully beg that he—the critical reader—will not attribute our comparative neglect of such a writer to ignorance. These remarks will not be thought unnecessary by those who know the vagueness of many English criticisms on German writers, especially if they consider that we must, in this brief review, make several statements for which we cannot assign all our reasons.

Without more preface, we proceed to estimate, as fairly as we can, the value and significance of German poetry: perhaps our best way will be to give some outlines of the history of poetical literature in Germany, and then to attempt something like a classification of its productions.

Of the oldest period, or the times preceding the outburst of chivalrous and romantic poetry in the thirteenth century, we shall say little; for although German antiquaries have indulged in many interesting speculations regarding the poetry of that period, its remains, which have been preserved down to our own times, are few. Yet from these it has been conjectured, and with great probability, that ballads, or fragments of the oral poetry of very early times, must have been preserved by tradition, until they were collected and reproduced in the form of the "Nibelungen-Lied," by some unknown writer of the twelfth or thirteenth century. Of this singular and interesting old epic we need say no more here: for any thing like a fair account of it—such as may be found elsewhere*—would occupy too much of our space. But another, and one of the most precious remains of this early time, must at least be briefly mentioned here: it is the "Life of Christ," or a versification of the Gospel narrative, and was written by Otfried, a monk, in A. D. 863. This was the first German work composed in rhymes, as the more ancient ballads to which we have alluded, were marked by alliteration without rhyme. It is very interesting to trace in this venerable relic the roots of the Teutonic words which we, as well as our German neighbours are now employing every hour—

> " In days of yore how fortunately fared
> The minstrel, wandering on from court to court,
> Baronial hall or royal.

These lines are strictly applicable to the poet's profession in Germany in the thirteenth and fourteenth centuries—the times of the "Minnesingers." So far remote are those times from our modern thoughts and ways—especially in hard-working England, that it is difficult to make their facts appear otherwise than as dreams. The very life of those old times, "wandering on from court to court," devoted to minstrelsy, chivalry, and the praise of fair ladies, was exactly what we in these modern days call "romance;" while our actual life, our journeys through hills instead of over them, and at the rate of some forty miles per hour, our gas-lighted cities, our commonplace crossings of the Atlantic, our Manchester mills, and, perhaps more than all, our telegraph wires, which carry thoughts with something like the speed of thought—would have presented to a minstrel or romancist of the thirteenth century glorious materials with which he would surely have constructed a tale far more wonderful, and, for his contemporaries, a thousand times more improbable than "Prince Arthur." This consideration may perhaps enable the reader now to look upon the life of one of the old minstrels as a reality.

The name of Walter von der Vogelweide may mark the characteristics of this age; for Walter was, like many others, a knight and a minstrel—one whose life was a romance, and whose verses remain to give us some glimpses of the times in which he lived. Sometimes we find him hailing the reappearance of spring after a long winter, and almost imitating the carollings of birds in his praise of nature; at another time he celebrates, in chaste and melodious verses, the beauty and grace of the lady to whom he devotes his songs, but whom he never names; then suddenly, on turning over a page, we are surprised to find the gentle Minnesinger suddenly changed into a stern satirist, denouncing the political and religious corruptions of his times, even venturing to rebuke the "Pope of Rome," and predicting, as many other earnest reformers have done, a speedy ruin of the world. These didactic and satirical verses show that Walter lived beyond the most flourishing times of chivalry and minstrelsy,

* An analysis of the "Nibelungen-Lied," with translated specimens of its style, will be found in the volume on "German Literature" in "Chambers's Instructive and Entertaining Library."

and saw the coming of that cloud which passed over both politics and poetry in Germany in the fourteenth and fifteenth centuries. To speak of the lays of the Minnesingers generally—we might select from them a few which would please even now; but, to tell the whole truth, a fair translation of the greater part would not please modern readers; for both the love-songs and the lyrics in praise of nature would be considered tame. The true characteristics of these old poems are youthfulness of feeling, melodious language, and an almost feminine gentleness. There is hardly any thing like passion even in the love-songs—indeed *minne*, the word by which they were named, does not strictly mean "love," though we can find no other English word for it. In one respect, however, we must commend these lyrics: they served the true purpose of poetry; they were united with the real lives of the Minnesingers; they were written not to be read in solitude, but to be delivered with the living voice; to be sung to the lute, or some other stringed instrument of the guitar kind, in the presence of song-loving men and ladies,

> ————"whose bright eyes
> Rain'd influence and adjudged the prize."

This was a natural use of poetry, and it is necessary now to refer back to such primitive practice that we may learn what poetry ought to be. Nothing but long conventional usage could lead us to tolerate such an artificial thing as a long poem, filling a closely-printed volume, and intended to be read and enjoyed in solitude and silence. The most genuine and natural use of poetry in our modern days is when some friend recites to another some flowing song or lyrical ballad, or when a company unite to listen to readings or recitations from our best poets. If poetry is not to be musical, if the ear as well as the mind is not to be gratified, why do we not turn it into prose at once? We must go back to the origin, the natural history of poetry, to find the best criticism upon it. Through forgetfulness of this many long, prosy, so-called poems have been written during the last half century, which will certainly be forgotten before A. D. 1900. One word more on this interesting point: it may be said that we have still many songs set to music and sung; but we think it might be proved, if we had space here, that the modern style of music is not adapted to bring out and interpret the spirit and meaning of the highest poetry. We believe that fine recitation, or, in other words, the melodious, impassioned, and expressive speaking of poetry, is the highest and purest music to which we can listen!

Into this digression we have been led by the Minnesingers. We must now leave them, and turn from the lays of chivalry to popular versification—from poetry to doggrel. Of course this change did not take place in reality so suddenly as we here represent it on paper; but in sober truth, the fourteenth and fifteenth centuries were as prolific in doggrel or low versification as the thirteenth century had been in poetry. This change in literature was indicative of important changes in society, to which we must now allude. "The code of ethics which characterized the institution of chivalry was too conventional, too much the creature of imagination, to bear the test of time, and the rude assaults of ridicule. We may trace, even to its palmiest days, that tendency to present itself in extravagant contrast to the dictates of sober sense which ultimately made it the butt of popular ridicule. The splendour of the institution under Frederick was so attractive, that a crowd of imitators sprung up, deficient in the inward calling, the true enthusiasm necessary to sustain the knight-errant at his proper degree of dignity. Hence we find the original profession of high devotion to honourable ladies lapsing into license, and the vocation of the chivalrous minstrel degenerating in the hands of mechanical composers of monotonous stanzas. Indeed minstrelsy became a trade, and, like other trades, was injured by overabundant success.

"The decline of morals aroused some minds to express their censures freely on clergy and laity in satirical and didactic poems; and among these the best of minstrel-reformers was Walter, whose verses are full of sound proverbs on the affairs of public and private life. The didactic tendency which he gave to the lays of the Minnesingers appeared afterward in the 'Walsche Gäst,' a system of lay morals. By degrees it descended to the lower classes. Poetry turned away from courtly to popular audiences; and the conventional morality of the Minnesingers was changed for a popular didactic and satiric style, often coarse enough. Hans Rosenplut, in 1460, was one of the most popular poets of this class; and was followed by Michael Beheim, whose style was very rude. As the knightly school of poetry had left out of its consideration, as unworthy of celebration, the lives and doings of *the people*, these could not be expected to remain satisfied with a strain of poetry which never appealed to their feelings. They revenged themselves for this neglect by producing a poetry of their own, in the shape of satirical fables, on the hypocrisies and mummeries of courtly life. In the fourteenth century this style of poetry, if we may so cheaply employ the name, prevailed over the decaying school of chivalry. Thus a false and conventional refinement lapsed into the tone of vulgar satire. So every covering thrown over the surface of society, unaccompanied by a true general improvement of the minds and dispositions of the people, is sure to be torn away by some rude outbreak of the real popular character."

Of German poetry, or rather versification, in the fourteenth and fifteenth centuries, we can hardly speak, except in a style which to English readers may look like caricature. Surely the Muses never had so great a number of unworthy worshippers as during these times in Germany! Never, elsewhere, were such a number of hopeless subjects simultaneously afflicted with the *cacoëthes scribendi*. Versification was now, indeed, the favourite popular amusement. The ropemakers, the smiths, barbers, bakers, potters, weavers, butchers, coopers, wheelwrights, and tailors, all had their songs, celebrating their several occupations. There is something very good, though sometimes comical, in the spirit of these homely productions. We should well like to see such a fashion revived, but in a better style, so that life and its interests might be once more linked with song. By-the-by, we have heard some very prosaic persons condemn all notions of spreading such influences as poetry and music among the people, calling them "dreamy," "Utopian," and "fantastic;" yet we find that such "dreamy notions" were facts, realities, and so long ago as in the fifteenth century. 'Tis true we cannot say much for the quality of the poetry then current; but it was a poetry for the people; it had a living interest; it was a moving power in

society; and we must leave the reader to consider if such a poetry has not more import than a great part of the printed verse of modern times, which fills the pages of neat foolscap octavo volumes, and, escaping the notice of the public, falls into the hands of some "stale, flat, and unprofitable" critic, to be manufactured into a stinging article. We must say something more of the curious productions of the fifteenth century; but, as we have already noticed, our statements here are so much in danger of seeming like exaggerations, that we shall prudently take shelter under a quotation from a German literary historian and critic, Gervinus, whose authority on this point will not be disputed:—"If we would understand the coarse and low style in which poetry was written in these times, we must remember with what a strange medley of topics versification was connected in the fifteenth and also in the sixteenth century. There was, in fact, hardly any class or calling in society which did not meddle with poetry [so-called], and the lowest and most vulgar topics were now thought worthy of illustration in verse. The doctors gave their *regimina sanitatis* and their rules of diet, &c. in Latin and German verses; astrology and physiognomy were explained in rhymes; artists described their paintings and carvings in rhyme; topography and histories of towns were given in verse; the pious man had his book of prayers and confessions done into rhyme, and the hypochondriac carried about with him his little book of rules of eating and drinking, with prescriptions of physic, all neatly done up in verse. The peasant had his rules for foretelling the weather put into verse to assist his memory, and verses for the same purpose were written on all the sciences. One Jacob Mennel gave an analysis of the game of chess in rhyme; Hans Folz wrote a poem on 'Crockery,' describing carefully the important uses of jugs, mugs, basins, plates, spoons, and pewter-dishes; the same writer also gave essays in rhyme on the use of 'Warm Baths,' and the 'Rise of the Roman Empire;' one Jacob Kobel wrote a poem (?) on 'Good Behaviour at Meals;' Martin Agricola gave in rhyme a treatise on 'Instrumental Music;' the military art was put into rhyme; fencing-masters explained in verses the use of the sword; falconers made stanzas on the proper mode of cramming and training young birds; farriers prescribed in common metre; confectioners extolled in rhymes their own pie-crust; and lastly, one named Schaller wrote a whole 'Natural History' in rhyme!"

Said we not truly that a fair account of the poetry (!) of these times must read like a caricature? Yet the above paragraph is simply a fair statement of facts, of which abundant evidences have been preserved. Nay, we have more than all this to tell: the art of rhyming was not left in these times to individual cultivation; it was not a solitary occupation pursued in the lonely garret, but, like other handicrafts, had its guilds and unions, and was taught like shoemaking. In fact, joint-stock companies were formed to produce rhymes! But now we will put away the tone of ridicule; for really there was something very good in these said companies, or, to call them by their proper name, Singing and Versifying Clubs. They afforded some intellectual recreation to the people in times when it was greatly needed; and even we in England, in the nineteenth century, when we consider what are the prevailing popular amusements of our own day, must confess that we do not find ourselves in a condition to laugh fairly at these honest German citizens and handworkers of the fifteenth century, who united themselves to serve the Muses as well as they could—who met together, when their daily tasks were done, and forgot all their toil and care while the evening hours were devoted to the recitation and singing of verses. The example is so pleasing that our readers will perhaps like to see some of its details. Improbable as it may appear to an English reader, it is a fact that versification was the favourite amusement of many of the respectable citizens and handworkers; and meetings for the composition and recitation of verse were established and well attended in Mayence, Ulm, Nuremberg, and other places. Indeed, the "Singing School" (or *Sängerzunft*) at Nuremberg was maintained until the year 1770; while the ancient club of the same kind at Ulm has been formally dissolved even in our own times, or in the year 1839. The tone of these societies was generally, but not exclusively, religious; while their influence in affording a moral and intellectual recreation in the place of the coarse physical pleasures of the times was undoubtedly very commendable.

We will endeavour to give a slight sketch of the manners of the times in connection with one of these singing schools. At Ulm the weavers united to form a singing school. Let us imagine one of these good men preparing for the meeting a copy of verses. All day, while he is employed in his loom, he beguiles the hours of labour by conning over his verses on some scriptural topic; and now and then, perhaps, he sings over the melody which he has composed to fit his stanzas. In this he flatters himself that the *merker* (or umpire) will not find any four consecutive notes borrowed from any melody hitherto known in the school: such originality is demanded by the rules of the *Sängerzunft*. But now the time of work is over: the weaver puts aside his shuttle, covers up the good cloth, leaves the loom, and repairs (not to the "Jolly Sailor," or the noted "Cordial Gin Establishment") but to the house of some good brother singer, to converse on the topics which will be brought forward at the next meeting on Sunday evening. And now the Sunday comes. In the church a board is suspended (something like the board with the number of the psalm to be sung in English churches) announcing that "the singing-school will meet in the evening, when verses and sacred melodies on several topics will be recited and sung." Sometimes the meeting is held in the parish church at the close of the afternoon service. In other cases, the members and their friends assemble in the town-hall. Here we find the makers of verses and the composers of sacred melodies, with their friends and pupils, and a considerable audience formed of respectable citizens with their wives. All the proceedings are conducted with great order and solemnity. In the most prominent seat we find the chief officer of the society, named the *Gemerk*, and beside him sit three or four other solemn and official persons, for whose respective offices we can hardly find suitable English names: among them, however, is the Merker, whom we may represent as the umpire. The society has also its "properties." In that large oaken chest beside the Merker are deposited chains of gold and silver, with suspended jewels, which have been worn by successful candidates for metrical honours. And now the solemn president, or Gemerk (who is, in fact, a good honest weaver of broadcloth,) opens the ponderous folio Bible which lies on the desk before him, and opens at the same time

the proceedings of the meeting by beginning to read the passages which have been selected for versification. Various copies of verses are now recited and sung; faults are noticed by the Merker; sometimes (in a tune, for instance) a plagiarism is suspected, and on this perhaps some little discussion arises; but this is soon put to rest by an appeal to a heavy and strongly-clasped volume containing the notation of tunes which have gained prizes or honours. Here is discovered the exact sequence of notes on which the present candidate has founded his melody, either by accidental coincidence or by unconscious memory. Of course he withdraws his tune, determined to be more careful another time, and to trust in nothing less than strict originality. At last, after several recitations and criticisms, one is declared to be the victorious candidate. Now the Merker opens the great oaken chest, takes out a chaplet, which he places on the head of the victor, and puts round his neck a silver chain, from which a jewel is suspended. These articles still remain the property of the Zunft, or club; but the master-singer is allowed to wear them publicly on great occasions. Such a coronation was of course a source of triumph for the wife, the family, and all the relatives of the victor. Glorious with these decorations, he now secretly determines that he will go and recite his verses at the next meeting in the neighbouring town, and vanquish all the versifying shoemakers there. We may add that, at the close of a meeting the best verses were carefully copied in a large volume, which was strictly preserved as the common property of the Zunft. In this way many productions of the master-singers have been left to our time.

"Such," says Dr. Vilmar, "were the recreations on Sunday evenings and saints' days of our honest working forefathers in the olden time; and those who, like myself, have sprung from the working-classes, may now look back upon those quiet and innocent pastimes without being ashamed of their ancestors." We have dwelt rather long upon this pleasing picture of olden times, because we think it carries a good and wholesome moral for our own times. Of course we do not think of any thing like reviving such institutions as those old singing and versifying schools; but it is encouraging for all who would endeavour to spread any intellectual recreations among the people, to reflect that they are not aiming at an object which is imaginary and unattainable, but at one which has been a reality, and may be so again.

Apart from any of the schools of versification just described, this period was remarkable for the simple but often pathetic lyrics or secular songs which arose, as if spontaneously, among the people. Some of these have been preserved to our day: no writer's name is affixed to them; all we know of their origin is, that they sprung from the people in a time when all the feelings of the heart and the most affecting events of life seemed naturally to find expression in songs. Many of them were linked to melodies so well loved by the people, that Luther or his friends found it expedient to set their new hymns to the old song-tunes. As a specimen of their simplicity, we translate an old "farewell" song.

Many stars are in the sky:
Many sheep together lie
   In the quiet meadow;

Many birds about us fly,
And as many times I'll sigh,
   "Fare you well, my treasure!"

433

Shall we, after long dull years,
Many sorrows, many fears,
Meet again, my treasure?

Every morn, while you're away,
Soon as I awake I'll say,
"Oh return, my treasure!"

At the close of every day,
Ere I shut my eyes I'll pray,
Heaven preserve my treasure!

If it must be so, when lying
On my deathbed, I'll, when dying,
Think of thee, my treasure!

We must not leave the fifteenth century without some notice of the low and coarse *satires* which formed, indeed, the most prominent features in the versification of these times. The favourite objects of these satires were the clergy and the aristocracy; and the popularity gained by the most wretched productions can only be explained on the supposition that such satires truly indicated the state of popular feeling, and were received as indirect but effectual organs of the democratic principles which were now rapidly spreading. We can hardly give any quotations from these singular remains of old times, though they might furnish rich materials for "curiosities of literature." In one, Parson Amis, a beneficed clergyman, is represented as gaining his livelihood by a series of scandalous impositions on public credulity. Parson Kalenberg is no better: on one occasion he finds all the good ale in his cellar turned sour, and instantly devises a plan for selling it at a good price to his parishioners. He announces that on a certain day he will take a flight from the top of the steeple. Of course the peasantry collect in great numbers to witness the feat: it is a sultry summer afternoon; and as the parson keeps the spectators long waiting while he is preparing to fly, they are glad to refresh themselves even with sour ale, and pay for it the extortionate price demanded. In another popular tale, a parish priest is represented as so fatuous that he could not remember the days in a week. To remedy this defect he adopts a curious expedient: every day he "makes a birch-broom," and by placing the six brooms in a row, and sedulously counting them, he knows when Sunday comes, and prepares for reading mass. But some wag, aware of the priest's stratagem, steals the broom that should mark Saturday, and, consequently, on Sunday morning the poor priest is found making another broom instead of going to church. These are very mild and comparatively harmless specimens of the satires current in this period. The most pointed and severe are exactly those which, for obvious reasons, we cannot quote. We have seen nothing in Dean Swift more truculent than some of the stories which might be selected from the popular books of this period. The knight had been the hero of romances in the preceding times, and the common people—the boors, as they were called—were hardly mentioned in aristocratic poetry. But now the people, having acquired the art of versification, employed it to be revenged upon their superiors. The favourite hero of the most popular tales was now generally represented as a boor, an illiterate peasant, a professed fool, but with a strong taint of the rogue in his character—one who, by the mere force of his native wit, could refute all the clergy, answer the queries of the most learned doctor or lawyer, and reduce a bishop to silence. The coming times of insurrection and revolution were thus foreshadowed in popular literature; and we may safely assert that the very spirit which afterward found an outlet in the terrible "Peasants' War" may be distinctly recognised in the familiar and comic versification of the fifteenth century. For what were the marks of the "*Volks-bücher*" (the "People's Books,") of this time? Satire, wild and coarse, expressing a contempt of all authority, ridicule of the pretensions of the scholastic or educated class, and mockery of every thing represented as high and sacred. We may go so far as to say, that any reflective reader, after a fair perusal of such a series of satires, might venture to assert, even if we suppose him to be quite ignorant of the historical facts of the case, that some great revolution, political or religious, must have followed such a popular literature. Here is surely a good comment on the old text about making ballads for the people, and also a warning for those who neglect to employ the proper means of diffusing good information and intellectual recreation—who refuse, indeed, to give to a wholesome and improving literature a fair chance in its contest with the low and vile productions of the press which are the disgrace of our times. Thus speaks the fifteenth century in Germany to the nineteenth in England.

We must now leave this interesting part of our topic, and hasten to notice the progress of German poetry in the times of Luther. Of poetry, in the higher or more exclusive sense of the word, we have still little to say. Luther holds a place in the annals of poetical literature on account of the hymns he wrote in connection with the movement of the Reformation. His bold and stirring version of the psalm—"Ein' feste Burg ist unser Gott:"—

"A safe stronghold our God is still,
A trusty shield and weapon!"

is well known, but cannot be fairly translated. This may, indeed, be said of many other popular hymns written by Luther and his friends. Their merit does not consist merely in the sentiments they convey, but rather in the union of style and purport; in the force, directness, and euphony of language: and also in the music of their rhymes, for which we could find no equivalents in English. To attempt to translate such hymns would only prove that we did not truly understand their character. A German must be the best judge of their merits, and therefore we quote the following description from Dr. Vilmar's "Lectures on German Poetry:"— "It must be especially noticed that these hymns, like our secular popular songs, were not composed to be *read*, but to be *sung*; and so closely is their melody inwoven with their meaning, that if we would judge them fairly, we must have their spirit, their metre, and their music given at once, as when they are sung by the congregation. They were indeed the sacred popular songs of the Lutheran times, and were founded in many instances on the secular melodies dear to the people from old remembrance. Thus we account for their rapid and marvellous effect in spreading the Lutheran faith. A hymn in these times was scarcely composed before its echoes were heard in every street. The people crowded around the itinerant singer (who now, in accordance with the spirit of the times, sang Luther's hymns instead of ballads,) and as soon as they had heard a new hymn sung once, they would heartily take up the last verse as a chorus. Thus these sacred melodies found their way into every church and every private house; yea, and whole towns were won over to the new faith, as by a single blow, by the sound of a hymn. Such lyrics as those of Luther

434

—'Rejoice my Brother Christians all!' and 'From depths of wo to thee I call!' or that by Paul Speratus, 'Salvation now has come for all!' or that by Nicolaus Decius, 'To God on high be thanks and praise!'—flew, as on the wings of the wind, from one side of Germany to another: they were not read merely, but, in the strongest sense of the words, were learned by heart; and so deeply printed in the memories and affections of the people, that their impression remains in the present day."

We now turn to the secular poetry of the Lutheran times, and here we find Hans Sach, a rhyming shoemaker, busily engaged in writing a voluminous series of familiar tales and fables in verse. Sachs has been too much despised. His name was once covered-with ridicule, on account of the homely characteristics of his writings ; but Goethe and other critics have restored to the honest rhymer the honour due to him in connection with the national literature of Germany. Though we can discover nothing like poetry in its highest meaning in his verses, he wrote with remarkable facility, could tell a story well, had a rich fund of genial, unaffected humour, and often conveyed a deep and good moral under the disguise of a grotesque narrative. Indeed, the incidents in many of his stories are so grotesque, that, although we should like to give some specimen of his verse, we have turned over many pages of his tales, vainly endeavouring to find one which would be relished by a modern taste. There is an apparent irreverence in many of them which, in Luther's times, was regarded as not inconsistent with piety. Hans sometimes directed his homely and good-humoured satire against the soldiery. In one tale, for instance, he tells us that the Prince of Darkness had despatched a demon to bring away some half dozen of the foot-soldiers, who were notorious for their profane conversation; but the demon himself was so terrified by their talk, and gave to his master such a description of their mode of life, that it was resolved they should be excluded even from Pandemonium. In another tale on the same subject, St. Peter, the gatekeeper of Paradise, exercising charity rather than good judgment, admits a few of these "land-soldiers" (lands-knechten) into the abode of happiness, where they soon prove the truth of the old saying, that a change of place does not insure a change of mind. Unable to enjoy any of the pleasures of the place, they soon collected their pence, and began their old amusement of gambling, which ended as usually in a violent quarrel. After some difficulty, St. Peter contrives to eject these unpleasant guests. Such were the stories with which Hans Sachs filled so many pages. His verses may be regarded as giving a summary of the characteristics of many familiar and humorous versifiers before his times; while in ease and fluency of style, combined with not inconsiderable power of invention, he surpassed them all.

Leaving the times of Luther and Hans Sachs, we must pass very briefly over a period in national literature marked by the tame, cold, and artificial character of its so-called poetry. Style and language were now the almost exclusive objects regarded by German writers in verse. Martin Opitz (1597—1639) was the most celebrated versifier of his times, and with the aid of several compeers, contributed something toward the refinement of the native tongue, but left little or nothing worthy of notice for its poetical merits. Paul Fleming and Paul Gerhard, the writers of devotional hymns which still hold a place in German psalmody, are the two chief exceptions to the prevailing rule of dulness in the poetical literature of the seventeenth century.

The former part of the eighteenth century produced a crowd of inferior poets or versifiers, of whom we can give no particular notices. In many respects they were superior to Opitz and his followers, but as poets they were soon lost in the superior lustre of Goethe and Schiller. Perhaps the most noticeable feature in their poems was their didactic purport. Among the writers of moral fables in verse, Christian Gellert may be distinguished on account of the surprising celebrity which his fables once enjoyed. These fables being simply the results and maxims of common sense, given in a clear, familiar, and pleasing style, were suited for a large audience; but this fact alone can hardly account for all the favour bestowed upon them. To explain it we must refer to the high popular esteem in which the personal character of Gellert was held during his lifetime, and long afterward. He was admired and revered as a moral teacher by men of every station. The king's physician was sent to attend this writer when dying; and his death produced in Germany a general mourning, such as has seldom or never attended the fate of any other literary man. The tale of the poor countryman who took to the house of Gellert a cartload of firewood as a grateful acknowledgment of the enjoyment he had found in reading the "Fables," is a fair instance of the admiration with which even the lower classes regarded the amiable moralist. In all the higher qualities of poetry, the didactic versification of Gellert was totally wanting. This judgment is equally applicable to the fables written by Hagedorn, Lichtwer, and others in this period.

Among those inferior poets (the followers of Bodmer, Gottsched, and Gellert) Friedrich Klopstock (1724—1803) arose; and when, inspired by recollections of Milton's great work, he produced in 1748 the first three cantos of the "Messiah," all Germany believed that at last a great epic poet had appeared. As, when we would understand the effect of a light in painting, we must consider the shade with which it forms a contrast; so, to explain the admiration of Klopstock's poem, we must fairly estimate the contemporaneous minor poetry. Above this it arose as a cedar over shrubs and brambles. It was indeed a great poem when compared with the productions of Opitz, Gottsched, Gellert, and a crowd of other versifiers. We can scarcely imagine that any future poet, however great, can enjoy such enthusiastic praises as were lavished on Klopstock; for the estimation of the poet was in a great measure the result of the circumstances amid which he came forth. A critic says of Klopstock: "He was like the morning star, hardly foretold by the faintest dawn, but arising almost suddenly out of darkness." And he adds, very truly, "It must again be deep, dark night in the world of poetry before any other star can by its appearance awaken the enthusiasm which hailed the 'Messiah!'" Apart from these favourable circumstances, the qualities which recommended Klopstock's epic and other poems—especially the odes—were warmth and depth of feeling, a flowing and sometimes eloquent style, with considerable power of description. But, taken as a whole, the "Messiah" must be regarded as heavy, prolix, and unworthy of a place among epic poems, on account of its poverty of action and progress. It has now fallen to that rank in literature where lie the works occasionally named, but seldom or never read. The fame of Klopstock is traditional, telling what the poet *was* for his contemporaries, rather than what he *is* for modern readers. Yet his name must ever hold a distinguished place in the history of his country's literature, and will always be associated with remembrance of his amiable character and happy life; for Klopstock was one who found in literature, especially in poetry, something better than fame—happiness.

The next important epoch in the annals of German poetry is marked by the names of Lessing, Herder, Goethe, and Schiller. These four writers, unlike in other respects, may be here associated, as their united influence produced a great change in the character of poetical literature. Lessing, an able critic, prepared a path for genius by sweeping aside old pedantries; Herder enlarged the views of his contemporaries by his translations of "Popular Ballads;" and Goethe, with Schiller, began to cultivate the new field of poetry now opened for them. These latter names have such a prominence in German literature, that we must not attempt to discuss their merits within the limits of this Paper. Their contemporaries are more easily described. Among these were many weak sentimental writers, whose names are now remembered rather on account of their connection with a great era in national literature than on account of their individual merits. It is curious that in Germany, during the latter half of the eighteenth century, or from 1767 to the time of the French Revolution, something which we may style an intellectual epidemic of a sentimental and romantic character pervaded the literary world, and produced as its symptoms a mass of wild and crude poetry and romances. The dissatisfaction, restlessness, and longing for novelty which in France was manifested in political theories, was in Germany chiefly confined to literature; and its results here were rather absurd than alarming. Goethe and Schiller suffered for a time under the prevailing disease: in the former it found a vent in the "Sorrows of Werter;" in the latter it produced a crude drama—"The Robbers." But these, being strong men, shook off the malady, which in others assumed the form of a chronic complaint.

"What is the position of Goethe as a poet?" is a question more easily asked than answered. Goethe, compared with many other German writers, is as clear as noonday; but surrounded as his works are now with endless criticisms and commentaries of the misty style, their light seems struggling through a fog. On no writer, ancient or modern, has such a vast amount of weak, mystical admiration, and vague, cloudy criticism been expended. His name is well known by English readers; yet not one in five hundred would be able to reply, in a clear and concise style, to the question, Why is the name of Goethe so prominent in German literature? Is it because he wrote "Faust?" Nay; for the best critics say that this poem displays only a part of the writer's character and genius. Is it on account of his lyrics and other short poems? These are very good in their kind, but surely not sufficient to make a European reputation. We need not ask, Did his greatness consist in his dramatic powers? for his "Tasso," "Egmont," and "Natural Daughter," when regarded as dramas, are very deficient. Or was he a great artist in the construction of his novels? No; it must be confessed by every one who is not a blind admirer that, when seen in an artistic point of view, the "Wilhelm Meister" and the other novel are very imperfect. Then why is Goethe so widely celebrated? Or why have his character and his works called forth voluminous comments equal in number to those upon Shakspeare? Who can answer this question as clearly and concisely as we could reply to a query about any celebrated English author? For instance, if asked for the characteristics of such poets as Pope, Cowper, and Crabbe, how easily we refer to the pointed wit and happy language of the first, the pleasant didactic verse of the second, and the graphic details of human character by the third! But as soon as we ask for an explanation of Goethe's greatness, we are lost amid clouds of German mysticism; and, to mend the matter, some English and American authors increase the confusion by trying to write like Germans, and only producing what honest Sir Hugh Evans would have called "affectations." We believe indeed that affectation, especially what we may call "the affectation of profundity," has contributed greatly to the confused heap of verbiage about Goethe; and, to explain how this has been done, one instance may be given. The most mysterious of all Goethe's writings is the second part of "Faust," which was the latest of the writer's poetical productions. At first sight, to any English reader, it would appear to be an extremely fantastic production, as it is full of the talk of such personages as the Sirens, the Oreads, Proteus, Nereus, and Mephistopheles. On this work, which has an allegorical character, the most confused and mystical criticisms have been written. Some have regarded it as a most profoundly-significant poem: others have honestly confessed that they do not see much in it beyond good versification. To give instances: one English writer says—"The second part of 'Faust' is remarkable only as a specimen of varied and harmonious versification, of which a considerable part was written when the poet was more than eighty years old." On this a writer in an English review, supposed to be conversant with German literature, expresses a very contemptuous opinion of such a shallow judgment pronounced on such a profound work. Emerson, the American writer and lecturer, speaks of the same work in the following terms:—"The Helena, or the second part of 'Faust,' is a philosophy of literature set in poetry; the work of one who found himself the master of histories, mythologies, philosophies, sciences, and national literatures in the encyclopædical manner of modern erudition." "This reflective and critical wisdom makes the poem more truly the flower of this time." "The wonder of the book is its intelligence," &c. Now, as a curiosity in literature, let the reader contrast all this mystical admiration of a very cloudy book with the following clear and fair statement by an able critic—a German—and one of the most sincere and enthusiastic of all Goethe's admirers:—Dr. Vilmar says—"The allegory in this second part of 'Faust' is so imperfect, that it affords not in many parts a proper veil for the figures intended to be covered by it. Already many passages in this second part have become riddles, for the hopeless solution of which we may vainly strive until we lose our temper! Others may indeed be very easily guessed; but not without the vexation of *finding, under a great array of symbols, nothing more than a small, insignificant, and trivial result!* So we may conclude, that in the course of some fifty years *the whole of this second part will be almost entirely destitute of meaning, and consequently of interest.*"

Is there not something very curious here? The accomplished and sound German critic, with an enthusiastic admiration of Goethe (having also a German's peculiar patience in solving riddles and explaining mysteries,) still gives the above very unfavourable judgment of a book in which the English reviewer sees true profundity; while the American lecturer, with a *clairvoyance* almost peculiar to himself, sees through the work at once, makes no complaint of its mystery, but finds in it "critical wisdom" and "the results of eighty years of observation." Such writing is, as Charles Lamb said jocosely of the Germans, "very profound indeed!" We are tempted to explain the puzzle by an anecdote. On one occasion we heard an eloquent lecture on one of Goethe's works; but some of the praise bestowed did not seem to us fairly applicable to the book. So we carried the said book to the lecturer; and, when we expressed our dissent from some of his statements, he, in a very good-humoured style, confessed that he had never read through the work in question!

The preceding remarks will not be understood to imply any depreciation of Goethe as an author. We have been speaking of his critics and commentators, and not of himself. It is obvious, after the specimens of contradictory views given above, that some considerable space would be required for a fair analysis of Goethe's character. At present, we may, however, notice that the interest excited by his works in Germany is not to be explained simply by reference to his poetical works. The catalogue of his writings might show that he must not be regarded solely as a poet. He wrote, besides his lyrical or occasional poems and his dramas, novels, memoirs, criticisms on literature and art, autobiography, essays on natural history and physical science, and a multitude of letters. Throughout all these multifarious writings we may trace the influence of a peculiar, individual, refined, and yet practical philosophy, which is implied rather than distinctly or formally inculcated; and it is partly this philosophy, as we think, which has attracted so much attention, and called forth so many comments. For ourselves, we readily confess that Goethe is more interesting as a practical philosopher than as a poet.

No such obscurity attends the characteristics of Schiller. His poetical works may be divided into two chief sections—the ballads and the dramas. In the heroic ballads, "the Cranes of Ibycus," the "Fight with the Dragon," and others, we find noble purport united with graphic narration. In other poems we see a tendency to abstract thought, which is injurious to a poet. In his dramas, which contain powerful scenes and fine sentimental passages, we often find the didactic purport brought forward in too direct a style. We are inclined to agree with A. W. Schlegel when he questions the "reality" of Schiller's dramatic characters—to these the poet often gave either an ideal virtue or an unredeemed propensity to vice; thus making them impersonations rather than men. But our limits will not admit a full description of Schiller as a poet and a dramatist.

We have purposely omitted, in its chronological order, the name of Christoph Martin Wieland, an elder contemporary of Goethe, and one of the most prolific poetical writers of the eighteenth century; but we may now pay some attention to this writer, who affords us a very remarkable instance

of that uncertainty of some reputations in German literature to which we have alluded in the beginning of this Paper. Wieland was a man most widely celebrated in his day (1733–1813,) though he is now virtually forgotten. He wrote numerous romances and poems, which were loudly applauded, and are now seldom or never read. Yet such is the influence of a traditional reputation, that it might now seem presumptuous to some English readers if we said that Wieland was hardly worthy of the name of a poet, or that his writings, taken altogether, are almost worthless. Yet we will venture to say, that in our opinion he was an artificial maker of verses rather than a true-born poet, and that we cannot even see sufficient reason for all that has been said in commendation of his prose style. To confirm this judgment, it may be well to quote the remarks of an able German critic, Dr. Vilmar—the strongest part of his censure of Wieland's writings we leave untranslated.—"Wieland," says Dr. Vilmar, "was the man of his day, especially for the higher classes of society; for people infected by the fine and sweet poison of French literature, people to whom thought was tedious, and all enthusiasm was ridiculous. To such readers Wieland introduced a suitable German literature; and it is almost solely by this interest in the materials or subjects of his books that we can now comprehend how he could have been so lauded and celebrated during his life. After his death he was soon forgotten. Of the materials of his works, modern French levity in a masquerade dress, or the most insipid philosophy of the day, given *à-la*-Shaftesbury or *à-là*-Voltaire, as we find it in 'Agathon,' or 'Peregrinus Proteus,' or 'Aristippus'—what can we call them but mummeries, destitute of both moral meaning and artistic taste? But what must be said of such contents as we find in the 'Nadine,' 'in Diana' and Endymion,' in the 'New Amadis,' or the truly abominable 'Kombabus;' not to mention so many other pieces in the same vein, regarding which pieces Wieland was quite pleased with himself, because he had been able to say in plain German so many things which, as people had believed, could be fitly expressed only in French—these are matters in which none save a most degraded mind could have found pleasure, and such as could not have found readers except in a very dissolute state of society. Yea, and even in his better subjects, say rather in the only good subject (excepting the 'Abderites') on which he ever wrote—I mean in his poem of 'Oberon'—how deficient is the style—how arbitrary, artificial, and fantastical, and, at the same time, how flat and dull!"

Such is the severe censure passed upon a poetical writer who was once numbered among the great men of his age. And if such a judgment is pronounced on Wieland by a very fair critic, we may venture to say that many other names in the literature of this period are now remembered merely on account of the celebrity which they once enjoyed, and not on account of their intrinsic merits. With this remark we may pass over a crowd of names which, in German works of literary history, are found around the more significant names of Goethe and Schiller. In comparison with these writers, all the other versifiers of their period must be regarded as, at best, poetical writers of mediocrity.

We can only mention, in the most cursory style, the names of a few poets among the contemporaries and followers of Goethe and Schiller. Voss deserves to be remembered rather as an able translator of Homer and

Virgil than as a poet. Schubart will be remembered for his singular history rather than on account of his poems. This writer was a very unfortunate and ill-regulated man. After he had published some frivolous satires, he was seized in the most despotic manner by the Duke of Würtemberg, and imprisoned for ten years in the fortress of Asperg. His poems are curious instances of that taste for the horrible, which had its day in Germany, and is still found among the lowest classes of society. His ballads, decorated with such lines as, "See you the blood-stain on the wall?" or, "Ha! here's one bone, and here's another!" were once read with thrilling interest. Matthison and Gaudenz were both descriptive poets and writers of pleasing sentimental verses. Hölderlin and Schulze resembled each other in the melody of their language: the latter affords a remarkable instance of misdirected talent. After losing, by early death, the young lady whom he loved, he devoted his genius to celebrate her name, "Cecilia," in a poem of twenty cantos! Platen was one of the most polished and correct of poetical writers; but his poems want life and interest. A similar opinion may be expressed with regard to Rückert, who has written a great number of poems. He is a fine master of versification, and has put many good sentiments in sweet metres; but is deficient in dramatic power and narrative interest. Chamisso was by birth a Frenchman, but gained a place in German literature by his tale of "Peter Schlemihl" and several poems, which show a partiality for gloomy topics. Uhland holds a very high place among the modern poets, chiefly on account of his popular and national ballads. Schwab in some respects resembles Uhland as a writer of ballads. The name of Theodor Körner is well known. After writing several poems and dramatic pieces of considerable promise, he joined a troop of volunteers to defend his country, and fell in a skirmish with an ambuscade. His character, and the circumstances of his death, have doubtless contributed some part of the interest attending his poems. Since the days of Schiller, poetical writers have been numerous; but we are not able to trace any sure progress in poetry. Individuality, power, and originality are wanting in a great number of productions. For every one original poet we have a crowd of imitators. This indeed is the case everywhere; but, as it appears to us, the names of such imitators are soon forgotten in England, while in Germany they are preserved too carefully in literary memoirs. It would surely improve several German works of literary history, if many insignificant names were thrown aside and forgotten. An author, of whom we can mention no one clear and strong characteristic or original trait, can hardly be worthy of remembrance. We pass over, therefore, many followers or imitators of Lessing, Wieland, and Goethe, and many others who have written poems which we cannot clearly characterize. It must be confessed that the reading public of Germany have been far too indulgent toward indifferent and imitative versifiers. Next to Goethe and Schiller, who are, in a sense of which an English reader hardly comprehends the force, the *great* poets of Germany, we would class, not the writers of long and ambitious poems, but the authors of songs and ballads which are among the most genuine and pleasing productions of German literature. Excepting the works of her two leading poets, of which we may speak in another Paper, Germany has produced little that can be called great in poetry. It is hardly necessary

to state that there never was a German Shakspeare; and for names having equal significance with such as Milton, Dryden, Pope, Cowper, Burns, Crabbe, Wordsworth, or Byron, we may look in vain through the roll of German poets. Pleasing and popular songs and romantic ballads are the best features of the poetical literature of our neighbours. In didactic purport, in mastery of real life, in vigorous narrative, stern satire, or, briefly, in strength or variety of character, it is immeasurably inferior to our English poetry.

We may now look at poetry in another way, by dividing it into several classes; and, in accordance with our belief concerning its origin, we must give the first place to lyrical productions, sacred and secular. In hymns, full of devotional feeling and powerful expression, Germany is rich; but, as we have said, these lyrics will not bear translation; for to represent them truly, meaning, metre, rhyme, and melody must be kept united: to alter their form is to destroy their character. Luther was the leader of German hymnology, and was worthily followed by such hymn-writers as Flemming and Gerhard. By other composers of sacred lyrics, a mystical and sentimental style was introduced, which was carried to its highest degree in the hymns of the "Brüdergemeinde," or United Brethren.

In secular songs—not merely so-called lyrics, but songs that may be *sung*—Germany has been rich ever since the times of the Minnesingers. Here we have songs celebrating the changes of nature, especially the revival of the year—full of fresh interest, such as nature alone can inspire. The first notes of the nightingale, the opening of the rose, the unfolding of the glossy green foliage in the woods; these were the darling topics of the old minstrels, and are still the themes of poetry. Here is monotony; but it is one of which the healthy mind never tires. We might endeavour to translate a specimen of these songs; for instance, an old lyric by Walter von der Vogelweide—

"Fresh flowers are springing through the grass,
    And laughing at the sun;"

or a song by Philip Harsdörffer—

"The frosty old winter has hurried away,
    The hillocks of snow
Have melted beneath the warm breathing of May,
    And the sweet flowers blow;"

or that by Philip von Zesen—

"Awake, happy thoughts! be forgotten all sorrow!
    For winter is passing away!"

But it would not be easy to preserve both the spirit and the form of such songs; and we like them too well to hurt them. The same observation may be applied to a great number of popular lyrics, such as may be found in that true German volume, to which we have no counterpart in English, "Fincke's Household Treasury of Popular Songs;" including "Student Songs," "Workmen's Songs," "Soldiers' Songs," "Lyrics for Children," and a host of others which we cannot specify. Of one of the Bacchanalian songs, the famous "Rhine-Wine Lied," we give two or three verses; but this, we think, could not be fairly translated entirely:—

438

RHINE-WINE SONG.

Deck with green leaves the bright o'erflowing goblet,
  And drain the cup of bliss!
In all the lands of Europe, jovial comrades,
  You'll find no wine like this!

The Rhine! the Rhine! 'tis there our grapes are growing;
  Upon its banks the vine
Spreads out her purple clusters, richly glowing;
  Be blessings on the Rhine!

Drink and sing gladly while the cup is shining,
  "Be blessing on the Rhine!"
And if you know where some sick man is pining,
  Go: give to him this wine!

Next to songs we may rank odes, elegies, and sonnets; but these we regard as generally cold and artificial. The sonnets written by Goethe and Platen are among the best of their kind, and Goethe's elegies, "Alexis and Dora" and "Euphrosyne," are full of poetic beauty. But passing thus briefly over this section, we find a more fruitful field in Narrative Poetry. This includes a wide range of topics and modes of treatment—fables, legends, ballads, romances, and epics. Of German epic poems we will say little; for, as we have already confessed, the notion of a long, long poem covering, with verses all in one metre, some five or six hundred octavo pages, appears to us unreasonable, even after the great works of Homer, Virgil, and Milton; and the German epics by Klopstock, Bodmer, Zacharia, Wieland, Sonnenberg, and Krug von Nidda, have only confirmed our opinion. These are certainly "great works," when measured as we measure cloth; but in truth, nature, and genial inspiration, they may be inferior to many short poems in our next section—Romances and Ballads. These form one of the most interesting departments of German poetry. Between the romance and the ballad we can find hardly any distinction except in the shorter form of the romance. Both give poetical narratives, interspersed with sentiment; and have for their topics either events of history, or legendary lore (sometimes supernatural,) or private anecdotes, or even facts of common life. Herder may be regarded as the introducer of a new style in this department by his "Popular Ballads of many Nations." Bürger, having gained an acquaintance with the true, popular tone of English and Scottish ballads, imitated it very successfully in several metrical tales. The success of Bürger was chiefly due to his spirited and fluent versification, which sometimes reminds us of the melody of Burns; a far greater poet in other respects. In the topics of his poems, and their mode of treatment, Bürger is often low, coarse, and trivial. Goethe and Schiller wrote ballads which may be described in another Paper: at present, we can only notice that the latter gave to the heroic or historical ballad its highest character, as we see in his "Fight with the Dragon," and other similar pieces. To notice here all the names of writers who have contributed to modern poetical literature in the form of ballads and romances would be impossible; for in this fertile department writers are very numerous, and many good productions are from names of little celebrity. The name of Bürger reminds us of that long series of goblin legends to which so many ballads have been devoted. Bürger's story of "Leonora," who is carried away by her spectre-lover to the charnel-house, is recommended by a vivid style of narrative and force of versification, and may represent a large class of such legends which have been received with favour in Germany. At the close of some such legend of the "Erl-King," or the "Goblin of the Harz Mountains," an English reader is disposed to ask: "But what does it all mean?" or, "What is the purport?" while the contented German simply enjoys the supernatural imagery without troubling himself about its human interest. There is here a very strong distinction between the tastes of the two nations. We may even say that some favourite pieces of this kind would be condemned by an English taste as weak and meaningless.

We may now give translations of a few poems culled from a large collection, but it should be premised, that our choice does not always imply that the poem has the highest degree of merit: general interest, facility of translation, and other circumstances, partly direct our selection. Many very popular ballads are founded on old legends familiar as household words in German memories, but which would fail to exercise their peculiar charm on English readers. Others are purely imaginary. To these we prefer tales having some human interest, such as we find in the following noble ballad of "Hans Euler." The writer, J. G. Seidl, is a native of Vienna, where he lived, some two or three years ago, as keeper of the Cabinet of Coins and Antiquities:—

HANS EULER.

Ha! listen, Martha! heard you not that knocking at the door?
Open and call the pilgrim in, that he may share our store:
Ha! 'tis a soldier. Welcome, sir! partake our homely fare;
Our wine and bread are good: thank God! we have enough to spare!"

"I want no food; I want no wine!" the stranger sternly said;
"Hans Euler, I have come to pay my duty to the dead:
I had a well-loved brother once, a brother whom you slew:
The threat I utter'd when he fell, I come to prove it true!"

Said Euler then, "Your brother fell in fair and open fight,
And when I struck, my arm was raised to guard my country's right;
But if you must revenge his death—this is no place for strife—
Walk out with me. Farewell awhile, my true and loving wife!"

So saying, Euler took his sword, and o'er the hilly road,
Which ended on a rocky mount, he onward boldly strode.
Without a word the stranger follow'd Euler on the way;
And now the night was vanishing before the break of day.

And as they walk'd on silently, the sun was rising higher,
Till all the mountain-ridges green were touch'd with golden fire;
Soon as they reach'd the chosen place, the night-mist o'er them curl'd,
And there, spread out below them, lay the glorious Alpine world;

With hamlets in the valleys, flocks and herds upon the hills,
Green hollows, rocky chasms deep, bright waterfalls and rills;
And, deeply felt, although unseen, the true pervading soul,
The spirit of old Switzerland was breathing from the whole.

The stranger stood and sternly gazed—his sword was in his hand—
While Euler pointed down upon his well-loved Fatherland:
" It is for *that* I've fought," said he; " for that dear land I've bled,
And, when he would have hurt that land, I smote thy brother dead.

" And now that death must be revenged, and this must be the place."
But here the stranger dropt his sword, and look'd in Euler's face:
Said he, " I do forgive thee—it was done for *Fatherland*—
And now, if thou canst pardon me, brave Euler, here's my hand!"

This, though it may be injured in our translation, seems to us a very favourable specimen of the romantic ballad, and far preferable to others telling of strange sprites rising from waters, or dwelling in the forests, or of the " nymph of the glacier falling in love with the Alpine shepherd-boy." There is a national taste, founded on local traditions and associations, which give a charm to many legends. Some of the legends of Germany are suited to this local or national taste; while others, like the short ballad which follows, have a true universal interest.

The tale of " Count Eberhard" of Würtemberg, who boasted that he could safely fall asleep in his own forests in a time when other nobles lived in enmity with their dependants, has been versified, if we remember well, by several hands. The following graphic version is by Zimmermann:—

COUNT EBERHAR.

Four counts together sat to dine,
    And when the feast was done,
Each, pushing round the rosy wine,
    To praise his land begun.

The Margrave talk'd of healthful springs,
    Another praised his vines;
Bohemia spoke of precious things
    In many darksome mines.

Count Eberhard sat silent there—
    " Now, Würtemberg, begin !
There must be something good and fair,
    Your pleasant country in !"

" In healthful springs and purple wine,"
    Count Eberhard replied ;
" In costly gems and gold to shine,
    I cannot match your pride.

" But you shall hear a simple tale :—
    One night I lost my way
Within a wood, along a vale,
    And down to sleep I lay.

" And there I dream'd that I was dead,
    And funeral lamps were shining
With solemn lustre round my head,
    Within a vault reclining.

" And men and women stood beside
    My cold, sepulchral bed ;
And, shedding many tears, they cried,
    ' Count Eberhard is dead !'

" A tear upon my face fell down,
    And, waking with a start,
I found my head was resting on
    A Würtembergian heart !

" A woodman, 'mid the forest-shade,
    Had found me in my rest,
Had lifted up my head, and laid
    It softly on his breast !"

The princes sat, and wond'ring heard,
    Then said, as closed the story,
" Long live the good Count Eberhard—
    His people's love his glory !"

If we have omitted to notice at length the ballads of Uhland, it is not because we are insensible to their merits. Several of them have been fairly translated into English ; and as the faithful version of such poems is certainly no easy task, we will not attempt to mend what has been well done. It will be better to introduce a few pieces by writers less celebrated than Uhland. A few years ago we heard loud praise and severe censure bestowed on a young poet, Ferdinand Freiligrath, who since then has lived in London as correspondent of a foreign mercantile house. On the same day we read in an English review the praise of Freiligrath, as one of the greatest modern poets; and in a German review a bitter article, deriding the sudden reputation of the new poet, and representing him as little more than a writer of pompous and affected phraseology. Guessing that the truth might lie somewhere between these extremes, we read the poems in question, and were pleased to find that, among many poems merely descriptive of foreign scenery, and marked by a tone of exaggeration, there were others, such as the lines on " German Emigrants," the " Pictured Bible," and the poem quoted below, which evinced true poetical genius. As a favourable specimen of Freiligrath's style, we quote the

DEATH OF THE EMIGRANT LEADER.

" In the fog the sails are dripping,
    Mist lies thickly o'er the bay.
On the masts suspend the lanterns—
    Sea and sky are leaden-gray.
Deadly weather ! sickness breathing—
    Come to prayers with cover'd head,
Women, come and bring your children—
    In the cabin see the dead."

And the German peasant-people,
    With the Boston seamen, go
Down the ladder, bow their heads
    In the cabin small and low:
There the pilgrims, new homes seeking,
    Sailing o'er the western sea,
Find, in burial-garments lying,
    The leader of their company.

He had built of German firs
    The raft which all their chattels bore
Along the Neckar to the Rhine,
    And down the Rhine to the sea-shore.
The old man, with a heavy heart,
    Torn loose from his paternal ground,
Had said to them, " We must depart—
    Another country must be found:

" In the west, our day is breaking—
    Westward lies our morning-red—
Let us raise our log-huts yonder
    Where freedom lives within a shed.
Let us sow our sweat-drops yonder
    Where they will not idly sleep—
Yonder let us turn the clods
    Where he who ploughs may dare to reap !

"To the old, unbroken forest,
  Let us all our households bear,
Plant them mid the wide savannas—
  I will be your patriarch there.
From our land, like those old Shepherds,
  Famed in Bible-story, going,
Let our guiding, fiery pillar,
  Be the light for ever glowing.

"In that constant light confiding,
  I will lead you to your rest:
Happy, for my children seeing
  New homes rising in the West.
Children, 'tis for you I travel—
  (Home would give these limbs a grave)
'Tis for you I bind my girdle,
  And nerve my heart to cross the wave.

"Up! away! your Goshen leaving,
  Like the men of olden day."
Ah, he only saw, like Moses,
  Cannan's pastures far away!
On the sea the old man died—
  He and all his wishes rest:
Nor success nor disappointment
  More shall move his quiet breast!

Now the men without a leader
  Come to give him to the deep:
Children hide themselves in terror,
  While their mothers come to weep.
And the men, with earnest faces,
  Gaze upon the foreign shore,
Where the patriarch, old and saintly,
  Guides their pilgrimage no more.

"In the fog the sails are dripping,
  Sleeps the bay in misty gloom.
Breathe a prayer—the ropes are slipping—
  Give him to his watery tomb."
Tears are flowing, waves are plashing,
  Sea-birds scream above the dead.
For fifty years he ploughed the ground;
  But 'neath the billows rests his head!

As a specimen of Freiligrath's more melodious versification, we give the "Pictured Bible," a remembrance of childhood. The last verse appears to us to be full of genuine pathos:—

THE PICTURED BIBLE.

Friend of my earlier days,
  Thou old, brown, folio tome,
Oft open'd with amaze
  Within my childhood's home;
Thy many-pictured pages,
  Beheld with great surprise,
Would lure me from my playmates
  To Oriental skies.

Of foreign zones the portals
  Thy magic keys unfolding—
In thee, as in a mirror,
  The eastern lands beholding,
I saw before me spreading
  A world of new delight—
Palms, deserts, camels, shepherds,
  And tents of snowy white.

I found in thee, for friends,
  The wise and valiant men
Of Israel, whose heroic deeds
  Are writ with holy pen;
And dark-brown Jewish maidens
  With festive dance and song,
Or fairly dress'd for bridal,
  Thy pictur'd leaves among.

The old life patriarchal
  Did beautifully shine
With angels hovering over
  The good old men divine.
Their long, long pilgrimages
  I traced through all the way,
While on the stool before me
  Thy pages open lay.

I feel as if thy covers
  Were open'd for me now;
Again to see thy wonders,
  I bend my eager brow;
Again behold thy pictures,
  With rapt and earnest gaze,
In fresh and shining colours,
  As in my early days.

The borders of grotesque,
  With figures strange and wild,
I see their subtle tracery,
  Admiring as a child.
The flowers and branches cunningly
  Round every picture twin'd,
In every curious leaf and bloom
  Some meaning for the mind!

And my mother, as she taught me,
  When questioning, I came,
Tells every picture's story,
  Gives every place its name,
Fills with old songs and sayings
  My memory all the while—
My father sits beside us
  And listens with a smile.

Oh childhood! lost for ever!
  Gone like a vision by—
The pictur'd Bible's splendour,
  The young, believing eye
The father and the mother,
  The still, contented mind,
The love and joy of childhood—
  All, all are left behind!

The following simple but pathetic little romance, by a poet named Reichenau, has an interest like that of the "Emigrant-Leader." The style of the original is so melodious that it might well be set to music as a glee for four voices:—

THE BANISHED LITHUANIANS

Son. Why, oh my father, must you break
  From the green ash this sturdy stake?
Father. 'Tis to prop my worn limbs on our long, long way—
  We must leave our dear land at the break of day!

Daughter. And, mother, why must you put away
  My cap and frock and boddice gay?
Mother. My daughter, here we no more must stay—
  We must leave our dear home in the morning gray!

S. In yon new land, are the meadows green?
  Are the trout in the clear, swift rivers seen?
F. My boy, you must rove in the fields no more,
  Nor throw out your line from the pebbled shore.

D. In yon new land, are the flax-fields blue?
  Will the roses shine in the morning dew?
M. Such joys, oh my daughter, no more must be ours;
  We must say farewell to the fields and flowers!

S. Then, father, how long sadly must we roam?
  Ah, when shall we once more come to our home?
D. And, mother, when may we return and see
  Our flax-field and garden, so dear to me?

441

All. When backward the river Niemen flows—
When on the salt sea blooms the rose—
When fruit on the barren rocks we find—
Or, when our rulers are just and kind!

The above simple verses confirm the opinion given by a German critic, that the only way in which the poet can serve the people is by seizing on the poetical features of real life. Young poets recently have written directly on social and political topics, but have generally fallen into mere declamation, and degraded the character of poetry, which, when true, is always sure to be useful, though indirectly. Burns's familiar tale of the "Twa Dogs" has perhaps done more to awaken kindly feelings toward the poor than any essay or sermon written formally for that purpose.

The above have been given as specimens of the ballad having connection with the interests of real life. We must pass over very briefly a number of romances founded on supernatural legends. Some of the ballads of Ludwig Uhland, one of the best modern poets, have this character. The water-nymph, the eel-king, the wood-nymph, Lorelei, and many other creatures of German fiction, play their parts in these romances. But, as a superior specimen of the imaginative ballad, we may select one by Joseph Matzerath, a poet of whom we only know that a short time ago he was living at Cologne. These verses, though vague, present to us a fine ideal; and the scenery, though slightly touched, is grand:—

THE KING OF THE SEVEN HILLS.

In ancient times, beside the Rhine, a king sat on his throne,
And all his people called him "good"—no other name is known.

Seven hills and seven old castles mark'd the land beneath his sway.
His children all were beautiful and cheerful as the day.

Oft, clad in simple garments, he travell'd through the land,
And to the poorest subject there he gave a friendly hand.

Now when this good old king believed his latest hour was nigh,
He bade his servants bear him to a neighbouring mountain high:

Below he saw the pleasant fields in cloudless sunlight shine,
While through the valleys, brightly green, flow'd peacefully the Rhine;

And pastures, gayly deck'd with flowers, extended far away;
While round them stood the mighty hills in darkly-blue array;

And on the hills along the Rhine seven noble castles frown,
Stern guardians! on their charge below for ever looking down.

Long gazed the king upon that land; his eyes with tears o'erflow—
He cries, "My own loved country! I must bless thee ere I go!—

"Oh fairest of all rivers! my own beloved Rhine!
How beauteous are the pastures all that on thy margin shine.

"To leave thee, oh my land! wakes my bosom's latest sigh,
Let me spend my breath in blessing thee, and so, contented, die.

"My good and loving people all! my land! farewell for ever!
May sorrow and oppression come within your borders never!

"May people, land, and river all, in sure protection lie
For ever 'neath the guardianship of the Almighty's eye."

Soon as the blessing was pronounced, the good old king was dead,
And the halo of the setting sun shone all around his head.

That king was always called "the good"—no other name is known;
But his blessing still is resting on the land he called his own.

Other ballads are rather sentimental than narrative, and give us traits of individual character and feeling. As a brief specimen of this class, the following verses by Robert Reinick, who is a painter as well as a poet, may be given:—

THE RETURN.

When one returns, with hopeful tread,
From travel to his place of birth,
And finds his dearest maiden dead—
That is the greatest wo on earth!

One bright and early Sabbath-day,
I came into my native place;
Long had I carried, far away,
The memory of one lovely face.

I stepp'd into the church to see
The spot where first that face I saw;
The organ's solemn harmony
Pour'd thrilling tones of love and awe.

"And here," I whisper'd, "kneels in prayer
That maiden, and for me she prays;"
I moved with silent footstep there,
And hardly dared around to gaze.

Then suddenly (I did not know
Why seem'd the church so sad and dim)
The choir began, with voices low,
To sing an old funereal hymn.

Amid the mourners on I press'd,
And to the burial-chancel came:
There stood the bier, with roses dress'd,
And on the coffin was *her name!*

In the following short poem by Franz Gaudy, who died in 1840, the vein of sentiment is truly German:—

MUSIC FOR THE DYING.

In the darkly curtain'd chamber,
The lamp's flame glimmers low,
And throws a trembling lustre
On the old man's pallid brow.

His children stand together
In silence round his bed,
And strive to dry their tears,
But more will still be shed.

They press each other's hand,
Their anguish to conceal;
No human words can tell
How sorrowful they feel!

But hark! some blithe companions
Come, singing, down the street:
The tones come nearer, nearer,
In concord full and sweet.

The old man lifts his eyelids;
His soul is deeply stirr'd—
He listens to the music,
And catches every word.

"My son's songs they are singing!"
Says he, as life's strings sever;
Then down he lays his head,
And shuts his eyes for ever.

We should be pleased to find among these ballads a greater number descriptive of national life and manners; but in this style of writing many German poets are remarkably deficient. Platen, for instance, who was one

442

of the greatest masters of poetical diction, devoted nearly all his poems to foreign topics. His best productions are his odes and sonnets, which are very chaste and beautiful in style. From his miscellaneous verses we may cull the following ballad on an incident in Oriental history:—

HARMOSAN.

The throne of the Sassanides was shatter'd on the ground,
The Moslem hand thy hoard of wealth, O Ctesiphon, had found,
When Omar to the Oxus came, through many a bloody day,
And Jesdegerd, the Persian king, among the corpses lay.

And as the Arabian caliph to count the spoil began,
Before him came a satrap bound—his name was Harmosan:
The last was he to quit the field, where many fell in vain,
Or yield his sword; but now his hands were fasten'd with a chain.

Then Omar darkly frown'd on him, and thus the victor said:—
"Know you how crimson is the hand that faithful blood hath shed?"
"My doom awaits your pleasure now—the power is on your side—
A victor's word is always right!"—so Harmosan replied.

"I have but one request to make, whatever fate be mine—
For these three days I have not drunk—bring me a cup of wine!"
Then Omar nodded, and his slaves brought presently the cup,
But, fearing fraud, suspiciously the captive held it up.

"Why drink you not? the Mussulman will ne'er deceive a guest:
You shall not die till you have drunk that wine—'Tis of the best."
The Persian seized the cup at once, and cast a smile around,
Then dash'd the goblet down—the wine ran streaming o'er the ground.

As Omar's chieftains saw the trick, they drew with savage frown,
Out from their sheaths their scimitars to cut the Persian down;
But Omar cried—"So let him live! Faithful, put up the sword!
If aught on earth is holy still, it is a hero's word!"

Many of the short poems classed among romances and ballads are only remarkable for the melody and force of language with which they relate some tale or anecdote. Such is the character of the following lines by Leitner, telling the well-known story of our King Canute:—

KING CANUTE.

On the strand at Southampton, King Canute sat down,
Clad in purple array, and with sceptre and crown—
And the waves are loudly roaring.

At the nod of his brow his vassals all bow,
And he looks in his pride, o'er the foaming tide,
Where the waves were loudly roaring.

Said he, "On my throne, I am ruler alone
Over all the dry ground, far, far, all around"—
(And the waves are loudly roaring.)

"And now, swelling sea! I will rule over thee;
I will master thy waves—they shall serve me as slaves,
Though blustering now so loudly!"

But a wave, with a roar, threw itself on the shore,
And cast its salt spray o'er the monarch's array,
And curled round his footstool proudly.

Then Canute laid down his sceptre and crown;
For the voice of the tide had astounded his pride,
While the billows were round him roaring;

And he said, "What is man! Let all worship be paid
To Him who the sea and the dry land made,
And who ruleth the billows roaring!"

It might be supposed that a people so famous for their metaphysical speculations would make even poetry itself a vehicle for abstract thought; but this is not the case with the Germans. They have no contemplative poet like our lately-deceased Wordsworth; nor have they received with any marked favour, didactic poetry, like that of Young and Cowper. With some few exceptions, their didactic verse may be described as very poor. Among the exceptions we may mention the poems of Leopold Schefer, who may be styled the poet of German philosophy, as his verses give, in bold and often very eloquent language, the results of Schelling and Hegel's systems. Interspersed among such verses we find many ethical lessons, which are made poetical by the imagery used to illustrate them. The following pieces may serve as specimens of his style:—

A LESSON FROM A FOUNTAIN.

"What one can never do for me again,
That I'll not do for him. To none I owe
What he ne'er did for me, and ne'er can do."
And thus will you live justly, well, and nobly?
Then first of all, grant not your child a grave;
For sure your child can never bury you!
Follow no friend to his last resting-place;
For he can never rise to follow you!
Give no poor wanderer a crust of bread,
Lest he should never meet you and return it!
Clothe not the poor till he can so clothe you!
And bind not up your house-dog's broken limb:
He'll ne'er return that self-same benefit;
The hound can only bark and keep your door,
The beggar only says, "May God reward you?"
But I say—Whatsoever thing you do,
None other can do that for you again,
Either that same thing you may never need,
Or, if you need it, it may not be found.
Humanity will always be around you;
Hear, then, my counsel—hear the word divine;
To every man give that which most he needs,
Do that which he can never do for you!
Thus live you like the spring that gives you water,
And like the grape that sheds for you its blood,
And like the rose that perfume sheds for you,
And like the bread that satisfies your need.
*   *   *   *

443

THANKSGIVING FOR SORROWS.

To care for others, that they may not suffer
What we have suffer'd, is divine well-doing—
The noblest vote of thanks for all our sorrows!
And daily thus the good man giveth thanks
To God, and also to humanity,
Which hourly is in need of aid and guidance.
And who has not known misery? Dear soul!
Who would not thank God for his sorrows all,
When in their working they become so sweet!
Good for ourselves and for humanity!
'Tis thus the roots of the aloe-tree are bitter,
But cast upon the glowing coals, how sweet,
How lasting and diffusive is their fragrance!
Yea, I have seen a lame and halting child
Prop up most tenderly a broken plant;
And a poor mother, whose own child was burnt,
Snatch from the flame the children of another.
So, generous man, return thou constant thanks
For all thy griefs to God and to mankind,
And ending grief will make unending joy!
Or, if it end not, it will be pure blessing
While in the trying furnace, thou dost good.
And if from wo released, and happy, spread,
Thy happiness all round thee. So doth God.
Suffering or happy, man, be always thankful

Of recent poetical productions it would not be easy to speak with perfect fairness. As some interval of space is required, that we may see and judge well the proportions of the town in which we dwell, so an interval of time seems necessary to form a fair judgment of the works of our contemporaries. As an instance of this—how much better can we now estimate Wordsworth than in the time when he was regarded, even by the acute and excellent Francis Jeffrey, as a writer of mere puerile verses! The most remarkable feature in recent German poetry is, perhaps, its tendency to meddle with political and social questions. We allude to the poems of Hoffman von Fallersleben and the war-lyrics of Herwegh. Hoffmann is a satirist of considerable humour, but has not improved his poetry by devoting it to politics—the "King of Prussia," the "Zollverein," "the constitution," and "German unity," not forgetting that equally dreamy affair, the "German fleet:" these may be good things to fill newspapers, but are very dry and dreary topics for poetry. Herwegh is a very terrible poet. For every evil he has one remedy—the sword; and he seems to have forgotten that this nostrum has been tried frequently, but generally with such bad effect as to make wise men ask for another mode of treatment. "It is now the time for hate!" cries Herwegh—meaning, we suppose, for party rancour, as if that time had not lasted long enough. In another lyric he exclaims—

"Tear the crosses from the earth,
And turn them into swords!"

On this a very cool critic observes, that "it would be a mere waste of time, as iron crosses are very rare in Germany, while iron in other shapes is plentiful enough." Another recent poet, Geibel, one who is not smitten with the war-mania, addresses to Herwegh a poetical remonstrance, from which we translate one verse:—

TO GEORGE HERWEGH.

Like Peter, then, "put up thy sword,"
And close at once your martial rhymes;
Or look at Paris now and learn,
Freedom is not the child of crimes!
With earnest minds and patient labour
The world's *true* battle must be fought
Better than musket, pike, and sabre,
The spirit's power—the power of thought!

The name of Geibel affords an instance of the uncertainty of a great part of contemporary criticism. We have read several of Geibel's poems, and have found in them no signs of great creative genius, but melody of language and poetical taste; yet an able German critic gives the following contemptuous estimate of this young poet, who happens to enjoy a small pension from the King of Prussia:—"The task of appreciating Herr Geibel's value as a poet is very easy, as he is annually credited by the state to the extent of 300 dollars. This, at the rate of three and a half per cent., makes the nominal capital value of Herr G. not less than 8571 dollars, 12 gröschen, and 10¾ pfennige—a very high estimate of a young poet in these times!" Surely Jeremy Bentham himself could not have desired a more utilitarian style of poetical criticism than this! We append a translation of one of Emanuel Geibel's poems:—

SPRING'S REVELATION.

Come to the forests, sceptics, leave your poring,
List to its thousand voices, all combining;
See its live columns, twined with roses, soaring,
See its bright roof, green boughs with boughs entwining.

Like incense, perfumes from all flowers abounding,
Like golden tapers see the sunbeams quiver;
And "jubilate" to the heavens are sounding
Voices from birds, green boughs, and flowing river.

And heaven itself, in love, is lowly bowing
To fold the earth, its bride, in dalliance new;
All creatures thrill, with love's fire inly glowing,
Your hearts, however cold, must tremble too!

Now say you "Nay, 'tis all a hollow show,
A mere machine, and nothing more we trace;"
Now say "'Tis nought" to all love's overflow,
And from your lips dash off the cup of grace

In vain—you cannot—if you did the wrong,
Creation's voice would hush your wretched *nay*;
Unheard amid the thousand-voiced song
Of all glad creatures loudly uttering—*yea!*

444

The preceding remarks on Herwegh, and other recent writers of political verses, by no means imply that poetry must be confined to imagination, and must have no relation to the interests of real life. We would rather urge that a poetry of true living interest is wanting in our day; but it must treat the questions of practical life in a truly poetical, and not a mere declamatory style. With this condition we would welcome the lowliest verses of true human interest rather than more ambitious poems of a purely imaginative cast. No poetry can long delight which is altogether alien to our real life. The poet may transcend our real life, he may exalt it by imagination, but he must not leave it behind him. And in our day, when the life-breath of an elevating philanthropic poetry ought to be infused throughout our social institutions, pervading the dwellings of the poor, and sanctifying the low by bringing it into communion with the lofty; when men are waiting to know themselves that they may fulfil their mission upon earth; when they feel

"How small of all the ills which hearts endure,
That part which kings or laws can cause or cure;"

when we peculiarly need a sincere union between our literature and our life; when we want books that we may take to ourselves as bosom-friends —books that we may not only read, but believe and love; at such a time, the poet who would treat us with another epic about Prince Arthur, or any similar composition, would be very much like the comforters of Job, who attempted to cure his sorrows by studied orations, very sublime, but very unseasonable.

It is a common opinion among literary men in Germany, that the present age is marked with a decline of poetry; and some speak even of its extinction. Gervinus, a well-known critic, advises all his poetical young friends to shun verses, and devote themselves to practical life. We do not see clearly why poetry and real life should be separated. It is true that the age for long poems, for reading verses by the thousand, seems to have passed away, and the present day, vexed with its political and social questions, is certainly not favourable to that studious and exclusive devotion to poetry which we have seen in other times; but let us reform the world as we will, external changes or amended realities will never make us independent of imaginative pleasures. After all that is done for us abroad, we shall be poor and barren unless we can say with the writer of the fine old song—

"My mind to me a kingdom is!"

But it would be idle to discuss such a question as the extinction of poetry: it will take place in that time, perhaps, when, as Jean Paul prophesies, all men (and of course all women) will be authors, and newspapers will be edited at the North Pole. In short, so far as poetry is an essential part of our mental nature, it will endure. Many artificial kinds will vanish, long epics made to measure, and other heavy pieces of verse, containing some nine parts of dry mechanism for every one of inspiration, will probably pass away and be forgotten; but the true song, the romantic ballad, the vividly-told story in verse, will continue to charm the future gene-

rations; sorrows and joys, hopes and memories, will demand poetic utterance; nature will claim her tribute of praise; and poets will doubtless hail the flowers of spring when the grandchildren of the present age will have passed away. So says Count Auersperg, a modern Austrian poet, whose verses on this topic form here a suitable conclusion:—

THE LAST POET.

"When will be poets weary,
And throw their harps away?
When will be sung and ended
The oft-repeated lay?"

* * *

As long as the sun's chariot
Rolls in the heavenly blue,
As long as human faces
Are gladden'd with the view;

Long as the sky's loud thunder
Is echoed from the hill,
And, touch'd with dread and wonder,
A human heart can thrill;

And while, through melting tempest,
The rainbow spans the air,
And gladden'd human bosoms
Can hail the token fair;

And long as night the ether
With stars and planets sows,
And man can read the meaning
That in golden letters glows:

As long as shines the moon
Upon our nightly rest,
And the forest waves its branches
Above the weary breast;

As long as blooms the spring
And while the roses blow,
While smiles can dimple cheeks,
And eyes with joy o'erflow;

And while the cypress dark,
O'er the grave its head can shake,
And while an eye can weep,
And while a heart can break;

So long on earth shall live
True poesy divine,
And make our earthly life
In heavenly colours shine.

And singing, all alone,
The last of living men,
Upon earth's garden green,
Shall be a poet then.

God holds his fair creation
In his hand, a blooming rose,
He smiles on it with pleasure,
And in his smile it glows:

But when the giant-flower
For ever dies away,
And earth and sun its blossoms,
Like blooms of spring decay;

Then ask the poet—then—
If you live to see the day—
"When will be sung and ended
The oft-repeated lay?"

32

445

81. NEW QUARTERLY REVIEW, 1 (1852), 326–329. M/H No. 4874.

RETROSPECT OF GERMAN LITERATURE FOR THE QUARTER.

WITH every allowance for the peculiar position of German authors and publishers, it must be said that the present state of their literature is a disgrace to all parties concerned—to authors, publishers, and readers. From 4,000 to 5,000 volumes have been thrown on the bookseller's shelves during the last quarter—of these but very few deserve any notice, and these few ought to be mentioned rather as things to be avoided than otherwise. The great mass call neither for praise nor for blame, they are simply contemptible; and, thanks to the prudence of our foreign booksellers, they have not found their way to this country, nor are they ever likely to cross the channel. We have consequently been spared the pain of printing an index librorum prohibitorum by common sense. But in many instances we have been compelled to warn the readers of German books, lest a trap of words on the title-page, the name of a standard author, or the eulogies of the German critical journals, should induce them to waste their time and their substance on unreadable matter.

These remarks apply chiefly to belles lettres, and to that wilderness of pamphlets, theological, political, social, and generally controversial, which the presses of Leipsig, Vienna, Stuttgard, Berlin, and of many smaller towns, have spawned forth. In their scientific works the Germans are, as usual, profound, solid, conscientious, and indigestible. But their novels and dramas, their controversial writings, their attempts at historical composition by a host of petty historians, their books on books which have been written on books, their hole-and-corner literature which embraces all subjects with equal presumption and ignorance—these seem to progress from bad to worse, nor is there any saying to what depths of wretchedness they are likely to descend.

This, however, is their own affair, not ours. We are concerned only in so far as our national literature is in danger of being affected by German practices. The Germans themselves are in the habit of boasting that all nations of Europe must ultimately accept their civilisation, and that the German "mind" will reign supreme over all lands. God forbid that it ever should come to that! We will give the Germans all the honour that is due to them, but there is no denying it that they are crude in politics, crude in their social state, and crude in literature. They boast of Lessing, but they forget that he was their first critic, and, up to the present day, he has been the last. The German mind has not, within the last fifty years, been able to produce another critic! And Lessing's mind, too, sprang from English literature, as plainly appears from almost every page of his writings. But it would seem that the modern Germans, like the Roman Catholics, believe in a superabundance of grace. Lessing's prodigious industry is, according to them, a sufficient reason for not studying the works which he studied. Because he wrote with discrimination and elegance, they think themselves justified to write without either. When they are told that their literature wants critics, they meet the rebuke with a "Look at Lessing!" If their writers are charged with ignorance they become eloquent on the subjects of Lessing's wonderful erudition; and when you tell them that they want energy, elegance, and propriety of diction, they will assure you that Lessing possesses these qualities in an eminent degree. It is the same with their two great poets—Göthe and Schiller. Because their literature has produced half a score or so of men who were eminent in their generation, the present generation of Germans believe that they derive eminence from the past, and that they are justified in producing bad works and plenty of them—"for a literature which can boast of such men must always command respect." In our opinion it commands nothing of the kind.

Another reason of the downward tendency of German literature is to be found in the degradation of the literary profession. That profession, as such, is not even acknowledged by the laws of a nation which claims to be the most intelligent and civilised among the nations of the continent. It is a fact that, in Germany, professional writers are classed with vagabonds and street beggars, and treated accordingly. They are expelled from the towns and compelled to drag on their precarious and dreary existence in small villages and various out-of-the-way places. They are ill-treated by every one, and ill-paid by their employers. Society at large shuns them as dangerous persons, who might possibly beg, borrow, or steal, since they follow no "solid" profession, and since they have not, what the Germans emphatically call, "a sure bread"—ein sicheres brod.

Göthe, whose most thoughtless pronunciamentos our Teutonic cousins regard as oracles, has encouraged the notion that literature belongs not to the necessities, but to the luxuries of civilised life. Great stress is laid on the fact that on some occasions he declared that a man ought to have a trade which kept him, and that for his daily bread he ought not to rely on literature or art. In other words there ought to be none but amateur writers and artists. Literature ought not to be man's career, but his hobby. It ought not to satisfy his necessities or gratify his ambition, but merely his vanity. For once the Germans have been docile disciples of the errors of a great man; they renounce literature for the purposes of an honest ambition, and make it an arena for the gratification of a contemptible vice. Hence their professional writers are by no means numerous, but the number of their amateur writers is legion. The printing and publishing mania pervades all classes. From the university professor to the masters of village schools, from the Minister of Justice to the lowest clerk of a country police court, from the banker to the linendraper's shopboy, they write and publish books and pamphlets, or produce squibs and contributions to the poet's corner of the numerous choralblätter. Indeed, a man does not consider himself a full man unless his name has appeared in print. And even those who abstain, have at least the proud conviction that they could enlighten the world on many things if they would only stoop to publish their lucubrations. But humble as they are they cannot condescend to do any such thing. No! not they. And on the strength of this resignation they consider literature as yearning for them, while they, coyly and chastely, stand aloof and defy temptation.

The consequences of such a state of things must be apparent to every impartial observer. Everybody's business is no man's business. All those titled and untitled writers of Germany, all those professors and schoolmasters, officers and physicians, clergymen, clerks, and shopmen, who make German literature, have no higher aim than the gratification of their vanity. Literature in that country has no other reward. The public expects it as a free gift—and books and pamphlets are flung at its feet as an alms from the rich man to the pauper. No one of these writers has anything to expect from the public—no one of them feels any respect for the multitude whom he addresses. The spectacle thus presented is at once pitiable and ludicrous. Each writer is inspired—at least, he considers himself so. He addresses a wretched, brutish, and ignorant mob, which he despises, while he yearns for its applause. And while he writes, every tenth man of that mob is writing as well, and every tenth man classes him among the mob, and asks for his applause in return for contempt. If these things be well considered—(and they are worthy of consideration just now, when we are told that the Germans ought to be our models)—if, we say, these things be considered, it is a matter of wonder not that German literature is bad, but that it is not infinitely worse.

The Germans themselves, though they praise their own literature, show a just and judicious preference for works translated from our publications. Our novels, in particular, though abused by their critics, are freely translated and extensively sold. Dickens, Marryat, James, Lever, Thackeray, and Bulwer indemnify them for the sterility of their native writers. Bleak House is being published in half-a-dozen translations, and the original English text is, moreover, reprinted by Mr. Tauchnitz, of Leipzig, who for many years past has supplied the Continent with the best and cheapest reprints of all new works of our literature. Kingsley's "Yeast," Layard's and Vann's "Nineveh," Mrs. Norton's "Stuart of Dunleath," selections from the *Household Words*, Reid's "Riflerangers," and Warburton's "Darien" have all been translated within the last quarter. Two fresh translations have been added to those that existed already of Macaulay's History. The popularity which this work enjoys in Germany may perhaps be taken as an indication that the "German mind" tends to better objects than those which of late years absorbed its attention. At all events, there is a change. It is a fact that some years ago the translation of Macaulay's Essays and History was pooh-poohed by some of the most enterprising publishers of Germany. The increasing demand for the works of our greatest living historians, and the ready sale of the translations of almost every good novel which is published in England, show, at all events, that the productions of the native press, however numerous, leave a void in the public mind, and that, however ardent may be the admiration of the Germans for their own literature, they must needs travel abroad in quest of practical instruction and rational amusement.

One grand and meritorious work, or rather the commencement of such a work, has seen the light in the course of the last three months. The Brothers Grimm have at length issued the first part of

their great "Dictionary of the German Language" from the days of Luther to the end of Göthe's career. The want of such a book has long been painfully felt. Few of the chief European languages are without such a record of the various words, their meaning and application. The Germans, who were most in want of such a work, have wanted it longest, and even now we take note of a promise rather than of a performance. For the two illustrious scholars, who, according to the opinion of the Germans themselves, are alone capable of executing the great work they have undertaken, have already reached the limits which the Psalmist ascribes to the life of man; and though it is devoutly to be hoped that they will survive the completion of the German Dictionary, the most sanguine must allow that their labours are exposed to more than usual danger of interruption by disease or death. Under these circumstances, it creates a painful feeling to read the remonstrances which the authors have been compelled to address to their countrymen immediately after the publication of the first number. The execution of the work has for many years been delayed in the hope of obtaining the active assistance and co-operation of men eminent for their knowledge of the German idiom in all parts of the country. This hope has been disappointed. No suggestions were made, no contributions sent to the authors, even by their own personal friends, who either believed not in the execution of the work, or took a greater interest in promoting their own labours. But scarcely was the publication of the first letter completed, when those who hitherto had observed an obstinate silence came forward with their suggestions and corrections. The Brothers Grimm protest against this mode of proceeding. The part that is published *is* published— it is in the hands of many thousand subscribers, and cannot be recalled. To inform the authors now of errors which they cannot possibly correct, after turning a deaf ear to their previous prayers for assistance, is wanton cruelty, if not worse. Hence they implore their generous countrymen to withhold their criticism as to the past, and to give them the benefit of their assistance towards the perfection of the unpublished parts of the German Dictionary.

Another satisfactory contribution to the annals of German science has been given by Professor Wolf, and dedicated to Jacob Grimm, under the title of "Beiträge zur Deutschen Mythologie." It contains the results of the studies of many years compressed within the compass of a small octavo volume, in which the connection between the traditions of pagan Germany and the saints' stories of Roman Catholic Germany is established with an astonishing erudition and a critical acumen which surmounts all obstacles, while its soundness arms it, as in mail of

proof, against the objections of those whom the matter may concern.

A work of a very different kind has been published by Professor Schubert, of Munich, who, envious of Humboldt's glory, comes forward with a book which we cannot better characterise than by calling it an orthodox "Cosmos." His "World Building, the Earth, and the Ages of Man on the Earth," gives evidence of much labour in collecting and arranging the results of the labours of others, and making them subservient to the one great object of all his writings—namely, the reconciliation of abstract science with orthodox belief. His work will be a valuable acquisition to many who objected to read "Cosmos," whilst its popular language and didactic form make it important for those who derived but little benefit from the perusal of Humboldt's work, because their acquaintance with the subject was not sufficiently intimate to allow of their following him through his technical terminology.

A little book which can be of no interest whatever to the general public, while it is of the highest importance to the modern historian, has been compiled by Dr. Koner, of the University Library of Berlin, and published by Herr Nicolai, of the same place. It is a collection of all historical essays, documents, and papers which have within the last fifty years been published in the German magazines and other periodicals. The subjects are ranged under the heads of the various countries and provinces. A student need but turn up the name of any country or province to obtain a full account of the periodical literature on the subject, including the names of the magazines, the titles of the articles, and the numbers of the volumes and pages at which they may be found.

The revolution of 1848 continues to occupy still the attention of the German historians, who from time to time publish special histories of those countries and parts of countries which at some period or other of the convulsion engaged the interest of the public at large. As this quarter's instalment, we have the "History of the Duchies of Schleswig and Holstein," written by Waitz, and published by Dietrich, of Göttingen; and "Der Verfassungskampf in Kurhessen" ("The Constitutional Contest in Electoral Hesse"), by Dr. Gräfe, and published by Costenoble and Remmelmann, of Leipzig. So much has been said and written about the unfortunate Schleswig question, that we think ourselves entitled to the gratitude of our readers for confining our remarks to the statement that Professor Waitz takes the *German* view of the question, and that his History is one of the numerous heavy pamphlets which the Germans have for some years past been hurling at Denmark. The Hessian contest is a less .

hackneyed subject. The spirit, the devotion, and the legality of the popular party, contrasting with the cynic shamelessness of the court, might be worked up into a powerful historical picture, and one which would have an interest for readers of all classes. Dr. Gräfe, however, has scarcely been just to his subject. His book, abounding in dates and documentary evidence, will be of some value to writers of greater ability who may come after him.

A very meritorious work, of which, however, four parts only have as yet been issued, is a "History of German Literature," by H. Kurz, who gives copious extracts from the works of the best writers, while the publisher (Teubner, of Leipzig) illustrates the work with a vast number of clever and in many instances curious woodcuts. The whole is to be finished in twenty-five parts. From the specimens before us, we should say that this work is likely to be one of the best of its kind.

It is, however, but literature on literature, and our greatest grievances against the modern Germans consists in their indolent idolatry of the past. The last few months have brought many ponderous additions to this class of books. Professor Düntzer, who lived on Göthe all his days, has published an account of the ladies amongst whom the poet passed his youth, under the title, "Frauenbilder aus Göthe's Jugendzeit;" while another writer, Lehman, devotes a volume to Göthe's intrigues and love-songs.* Professor Düntzer is valuable in his way; his statistics of Göthe are always sound, and his reading is extensive. Lehman writes with more candour and less admiration than Düntzer; indeed, he is an artist, while Düntzer is a mere mechanic and purveyor of raw material. When we add that Göthe's correspondence with Knebel has at length been published in two large volumes, and that a small book containing Göthe's opinions,* extracted from his correspondence and reported conversations, has been given to the world, we have mentioned the chief additions to the Göthe literature which have been published since March.

In the department of travels, &c., there is only one book worth noticing, and this one is not exactly German. It is a translation of Steene Bille's "Report of the Voyage of the Galathea corvette round the World," in two volumes, with a variety of illustrations and several maps. The work is very creditable to all parties concerned, but the credit belongs to Denmark and not to Germany.

Another German book by a non-German author, is Szavardy's "Paris," a humorous and ably-written account of Parisian life, doings, and manners. Herr Szavardy is a Hungarian, who for many years has been a resident in the French capital. His work, though written in a different style, is quite as good in its way as Dr. Schlesinger's "London," of which the second volume has not as yet been published.

There is also a "History of Antiquity," by Professor Dunker, a sound and well-digested work; there are two volumes on "Gastrosophy," by Baron Vaerst, who, unless we are mistaken, is the author of the "Cavalier-Perspective," and the "Cancan of a German Nobleman," two anonymous works which excited some attention during the last fifteen years. Herr von Irechtritz, a heavy, pragmatical novelist, has commenced a story of the times of the Reformation, two volumes of which have appeared. Those who read them are not likely to wish for more. These works, and the books which are more fully characterised below, contain all that is necessary to mention, either for praise or blame, among the publications up to Midsummer 1852.

---

* "Lehman, Göthe's Liebe und Liebesgedichte." Berlin.

* "Göthe in Briefen und Gesprächen." Berlin: Vereinshandlung.

GERMAN SHAKSPEARIANA.

THAT the interest which our German relations have long taken in Shakspeare is still alive, various recent publications, now before us, sufficiently prove. The liberal study of our great Poet in Germany, which has made him known there as well perhaps as he can be in any foreign nation, must always be mentioned here with due acknowledgment. There is, however, some disposition on the part of our neighbours to mistake the nature of property in their view of the acquisition: and it will not be out of place to notice here, in order to rebut, a plea which has been advanced, on the strength of their Shakspeare criticism, by certain German commentators:—to the effect, that our chief dramatist, essentially a stranger in his own country, has found his first real home among Teutonic admirers. This position may be held in a certain sense; but that sense, it must be added, is a partial and very limited one. It is true that the philosophy of criticism, which has never flourished here, is a science born in Germany; and has been so applied by some of her finest intellects to our Shakspeare, as to produce an æsthetic anatomy of his genius more exquisite and complete than anything of a similar kind that can be shown in England;—where, with some rare exceptions—Coleridge, Hazlitt, and Lamb among the first—the interpretation of our elder drama has been chiefly engrossed by antiquarian or verbal commentators. Tested by their labours alone, it might indeed be said that the allegiance to Shakspeare has been manifested in a larger sense by our German friends. The fact, rightly considered, illustrates the known difference between the two nations in mental tendencies;—which lead to reflection in the one, and to action in the other. Our love is not, like theirs, prone to self-inspection,—makes no scientific study of its emotions, and so cuts but a poor figure on paper: and it may be natural that men of the closet should from hence assume the non-existence of perceptions which they can only recognize in a metaphysical dress. But they err in taking as the measure of the influence or the understanding of a poet the degree to which these are developed in critical essays. This process has a specific, but also a merely relative worth in all cases,—above all, when the place of a great dramatist in the heart of a nation is in question. Scientific consciousness is everywhere by its nature a remote province; and is, moreover, rather florid than fruitful. But without underrating the merit of those who shine in it, we may observe that their light wholly proceeds from reflection, and as such can only illuminate or warm a limited circle: those beneath it, it either does not reach, or at best it involves them in hazy sentiment and vaporous conceit, prolific of high-sounding phrases, but barren of genial intelligence. Our learned cousins are apt to believe that the popular effect of their lucubrations corresponds with the ideas which they ventilate in studies and lecture-rooms. On the one hand, they mistake the aim for the result of their own philosophic cultivation: on the other, they are unjust to ours; because it is of a less ostensible kind, less conscious, and devoid of systematic utterance. So, they claim Shakspeare as the conquest of Germany, seeing how finely he has been dissected by a few of her superior minds; while they begrudge him to us, being unable to perceive the roots which he has struck into the whole heart of England,—whose affections are more deep than demonstrative. They see nothing on paper to inform them how his genius has become incorporated with our intellectual and moral being; and they conclude that all we possess in him is represented by the editors and minute verbal critics whose performances they can import and censure. These, however, are but "ministers of the outer court," to a worship the spirit of which is something more than can be conveyed in an æsthetic lecture. It is a national service of the heart; an appreciation and unaffected enjoyment, neither learned nor critical indeed, but thoroughly sincere,—a homage, in short, such as a great poet desires and deserves from his own country and time:—an essential sympathy, none the less genuine, and indeed genial, in its instinctive truth, because it is silent, and never dreams of the necessity of drawing itself out into philosophic tissues. For spinning these fine fabrics the German may fairly claim the prize. But it is a delusion on his part to imagine that in them a national poet ever clothes himself among any people whatever; and may therefore be claimed as the property of those by whom the "woven wind" is most artistically prepared for him.

We may describe, as a rather ordinary specimen of this kind of manufacture, the first work on our list:—

Dramaturgic Studies, by Dr. Ludwig Eckart, (Aarau, Sauerländer; London, Thimm), an octavo of 198 pages, the reprint of a course of lectures on the single play of Hamlet. A dissertation on so wide a scale promises a minute exegesis, critical and material,—which will be found here, with *sententiæ variorum*, parallels, and other illustrations. To these, as might also be expected from a comment far more ample than the piece commented upon, are applied a series of anatomical studies of the meaning both of the poet and of his *dramatis personæ*,—the total result being a discourse more tedious than profitable. For intelligent hearers no master of his subject needs so many words to unlock the secrets of genius,—so far as words can open them. Goethe's fine exposition of this very play is contained in a few paragraphs, which say all that is requisite to impress a striking view of it in the completest manner. Schlegel, who had moreover to break new ground when he first lectured on Shakspeare, took his well-known and able survey of the entire poet in hardly less space than is occupied here by one of his dramas. A multitude of words, as the proverb might have told Dr. Eckart, is apt to darken counsel.

In *Shakspeare's Venus and Adonis*, translated by Ferdinand Freiligrath (Düsseldorf, Schiller), the German poet,—whom we are glad to see re-ascending to daylight from the political Gehenna,—has done a better service to his countrymen. He takes a Shakspeare text, and instead of lecturing, closely and ably translates it in the original metre;—thus supplying one of the remaining blanks in the German copies of our author:—the other he promises to fill up by translating his 'Lucrece' at a future period.

Leaving the æsthetic department, we descend to the thorny ground of textual controversy; where it appears that the notes of the Collier Folio have raised among German critics nearly as much stir as they have excited in ours. Of the publications concerning them, it will suffice to name the authors, with the briefest possible notice of their views; after stating, in the first place, the value of foreign advice on this subject,—to which, and to the debates that it has occasioned at home, due attention has been paid by the *Athenæum*. The notices already published have shown, first, the nature of Mr. Collier's MS. authority; secondly, the nature of the grounds on which it must be accepted or denied. As to the first head, no question is raised upon facts, so far as they are known, and have been published by the editor. It is admitted, that they do not establish a positive authority in the anonymous corrector; so that, in the main, leaving bye points of discussion, the case for or against his alterations must, as the issue now lies, at least, be disposed of under the second head; and this by the weight of presumptive and internal evidence. Now, this species of proof, in matters of diction, verbal sense, and rhythm, is subject to differences of opinion, and admits of no magisterial decision, even among natives. It is emphatically of a kind which no foreigner, how profound soever may have been his studies of English in general, and of Shakspeare's in particular, is competent to weigh or to pronounce upon. For, while it is devoid of infallible certainty, whatever approach to virtual conviction it may produce, will depend in all cases where doubt is justifiable, upon a peculiar train of perceptions, conversant with the nicer shades of idiom, metre, and meaning, —upon delicacies of complexion and form, in short, the sense of which is by no means unerring in any, and is inevitably defective in all to whom English is not a mother-tongue. This is not one of the instances in which a bystander "sees the most of the play." Where the issue depends on matter of positive documentary fact, a learned and intelligent alien may perhaps be a sufficient arbiter,—especially when the passions of native disputants have grown heated in the contest; but when it is involved in presumptions resting on the subtlest qualities of language, he cannot come even within effectual sight of the argument. The verdict in this instance—in the absence of any certain discovery hereafter—must, so far as any sentence can be final in such a trial at all, be declared by the majority of a competent native jury; and it is, once for all, by the intrinsic law of the case, forbidden that foreigners should serve upon it. To assert this, is simply to put the issue where it is fixed by nature, under conditions requiring certain special qualities that acumen or study alone will not impart. The critical mind of Germany will, on reflection, perceive that there is no offence in this statement. Every faculty has its bounds, and all perception depends on opportunity for its developement. To seize and define on paper a man's features in clear daylight, a stranger, with an artist's eye, may be as apt as his oldest friend; but to distinguish him in the dusk by the sound of his footstep, you must have been born of the same family, and brought up with him from childhood.

After this, it only remains to say that *Dr. Leo*, of Berlin (Berlin, Asher; London, Nutt), edits and translates all Mr. Collier's published Notes, —adding a preface and running commentary of his own; in which he approves of most of the alterations; and where he refuses them, states his dissent in a sensible and temperate manner, — displaying a creditable knowledge of his subject; — and that *Dr. Delius*, of Bonn (Bonn, König),—an "old student of Shakspeare," author of a small tract recently published on 'The English Theatre in Shakspeare's Time,'— who has now in the press an edition of the Poet with the original English text and German notes,—comes forth in a very fierce mood to "appraise" Mr. Collier's anonymous corrector,—and contemptuously declares him a mere blundering interpolator, whose emendations, with the exception of eighteen only, are either perverse or frivolous. As the debate on our side of the Channel has not always been conducted in the mildest style, we shall not "cast the first stone" at the angry Professor on this ebullition of his; a certain pity, indeed, may be felt for an editor who, having a Shakspeare of his own on the eve of publication, is naturally dismayed by the revelation of "various readings" which cannot be introduced into the forthcoming text. It is also fair to say, that the Doctor, in his discussion of the grounds for and against the Collier notes, evinces an extensive and accurate knowledge of the various early editions, including the old quartos,—and that his objections are framed with more than ordinary dialectical skill.

As these are probably but the first drops of a shower of controversy which the Collier Folio seems likely to draw down upon us from Germany, it is a mere act of prudent self-defence to take at the outset the position to be maintained hereafter on this subject,—viz., that in the settlement of the question, which must be decided, if at all, in England, no foreign discussion can have any conclusive effect whatever.

450

ART. III. —(1.) *Der fabelhafte Geschichte von Hug Schapler.* Printed 1514.

(2.) *Die Sage vom ewigen Jude.* Printed 1602.

(3.) *Die Schöne Melusina. Aus dem französchen.* 1535.

(4.) *Schimpf und Ernst.* Von JOHANN PAULI.

(5.) *Till Eulenspiegel.* Printed 1495.

(6.) *Der Gestiefelte Kater.* Von LUDWIG TIECK. 1797.

(7.) *Genofeva und Octavian.* Dramen von LUDWIG TIECK.

(8.) *Liebesgeschichte der schönen Magelone und des Grafen Peter von Provence.* Bearbeitet von LUDWIG TIECK.

(9.) *Faust: eine Tragödie.* Von GOETHE.

(10.) *Die Deutschen Volksbücher.* Von J. GÖRRES. 1807.

(11.) *Buch der schönsten Geschichten und Sagen. Für Alt und Jung wieder erzählt von Gustav Schwab.* Dritter Auflage. 1847.

WHY there should ever have been any prose in Germany after the halcyon days of chivalry, of the courtly and minne-poetry, is a question best solved by looking briefly at the character of that poetry. If we oblige the chronological reader with a definite date, and take the twelfth century, with the early part of the thirteenth as its era, we find its productions consisting chiefly in epic or narrative poems, embracing every variety of legend, and displaying equal diversity in the mode of treatment.

The different character and acquirements of each poet are clearly traceable. No one could attribute the poem of *Tristan* and *Isolt* to the author of *Parzival,* nor Lamprecht's *Alexander* to Walther von der Vogelweide. In Gottfried's *Tristan* there is no wearisome entanglement of tournaments and adventures, no crowd of mushroom knights intruding themselves into every conceivable corner of the story without exciting our smallest interest; there is little to distract the attention from the hero and heroine of the old Celtic legend. We have the history of their love in graceful and passionate language, with fresh, pleasant images, and feel it to be the very soul of the gay life-loving poet infused into the tale of other days. As a thorough man of the world, ever eager after the pleasures it affords, Gottfried von Strasburg presents a most striking contrast to his great contemporary Wolfram, whom he somewhat compassionately designates an 'inventor of strange wild tales.' Wolfram also put a new life into the old Celtic and Asiatic legends; but it was a life more lofty, more vigorous; his grave contemplative mind found a spring of action deeper than the feelings, a standard of the evil and the good, higher than the selfish one of present pain or pleasure, and a nobility and vigour of soul rising from a well-fought battle against the enticements of present gratification, which then, as now, seduced many weak and many accounted strong. It is with the hand of a master that Gottfried represents the terrible force of passion in Tristan, the all-absorbing, self-forgetting love of Isolt—beneath the clear limpid style, bearing you along with such unconscious grace, that you feel the strength and magic of rare genius. And with no inferior skill does Wolfram draw his busy pictures of the day, and rouse your interest for hero and for heroine, but his great power lies in the masterly presentation and working out of thought, rather than of feeling. Throughout his poem of *Parzival,* we are often suddenly surprised by thoughts of great depth and beauty, dropped by the way, and apart from the one great idea of the poem, which indeed almost places it above comparison with any contemporary work. It is rather a puzzling question what Gottfried would have made of *Parzival,* and Wolfram have made of *Tristan.* The school of Gottfried in course of time exchanged their luxurious and secular character for a didactic one, and chose sacred legends as their subjects; the imitators of Wolfram directed their labours to historic poems.

One more of these narrative poems, which we may just notice, is the *Irec* and *Iwein* of Hartmann von der Aue, belonging to the same Celtic cycle of tradition. The *Irec* was a youthful production, containing a very plain unvarnished heap of adventures; the *Iwein* was composed ten years later, at least before the year 1204, and here again it is the individuality of the poet, discernible in the mode of description, in the lively dialogue, and the grave warning, which arrests our attention, and charms us beyond the story itself. This subjectivity of the poet, at once so characteristic of this period, and so fatal to its poetry, is yet more striking in such productions as Lamprecht's *Alexander,* and the *Trojan War,* or the *Eneas* of Conrad von Wurzburg. The former of these poems dates about the year 1170, and relates to a legend often remodelled, as by Ulrich von Eschenbach, Rudolph von Ems, and others. It is throughout the poet who speaks, who fights the marvellous battles, and finds, or rather loses, his way into enchanted forests. He does not realize for himself, or for his readers, the age and country of his hero, but appears to put himself in his place; and with great truth and feeling shows us what would have happened to, Clerc Lambert had he been Alexander the Great! The same remarks will apply to all the productions of the same period, even to the *Eneas* of Heinrich von Veldekin, though he of course was a man of far higher talent, and one whom the Germans are proud to rank as the father of their early poetry.

As poetry of this sort became less and less favoured in the courts, the poets, having no other masters to please, naturally pleased themselves. But in thus writing after their own taste, they fell into an artificial contemplative style, abounding in quotations and learned allusions. All poets belonging to a later date than 1240 or 1250, begin to complain of the want of sympathy in the nobles, the absence of all poetic spirit and appreciation of their works, so that some fell into a bitter misanthropical mood, while others, wrapping themselves with sublime dignity in their own self-respect, and what then passed for impenetrable learning, still wrote for those who would read them, and for—themselves. By this time, too, the famous minne-poetry, with its many votaries, had fairly run itself out. Everybody copied everybody. Walther von der Vogelweide, Reimar von Zweter, Wolfram, and Ulrich von Lichtenstein, were plagiarized without mercy. The case with their ideas was just as Jean Paul declares it ever will be in Germany—that no author can light a new torch, and hold it out to the world till he throws away the end in weariness, but all the lesser ones fall upon it and run about for years with the fragments of light. The chivalry of Germany died away: the knights became robbers, who cared nothing for the poets, and the poets became philosophical, learned, in a word, unreadable. The narrators were not careful to select the best material for their labours, and, further, became so increasingly wedded to their national failing of subjectivity, that it is no wonder they should have gradually dwindled away; while the minne-singer was, from an equally dire necessity, driven out of his last resource of borrowed plumes, and thus the German nation, poetically speaking, was in a fair way of being reduced to a very satisfactory state of subjective imbecility.

In the fourteenth century, a change, equally marked, came over the political condition of Germany. The nations which had been united against their common enemy, the Saracen, discovered that, in default of better occupation, they must fight against one another; so they set to work in good earnest—England and Scotland, England and France, Denmark and Sweden, France and Aragon, Aragon and Castile, besides the perplexing differences in Austria, Bohemia, and Poland. All the effects of such dissensions were felt to their fullest extent in Germany, not as touching the state only, but also the church, and the progress of the people. Such poems as we have above alluded to, were now almost ignored. Wolfram, indeed, was read a little, early in the fifteenth century, but with far less pleasure than the old

didactic poem of *Freidank*. The people had no taste, and probably no time for revelling, as the nobles had done, in the pleasant images, or the interminable paragraphs of the courtly poets; they required something short, pithy, and instructive, as well as amusing. The stories of the old heroes, before the days of chivalry, were the subjects with which they felt most ready sympathy, and we find numbers of them now re-written in prose. At the same time, also, religious prose legends were introduced, in great numbers and short secular tales, with jests and anecdotes. After the invention of printing, in 1430, these were very widely circulated. Barren and cheerless as was the aspect of the fourteenth century in Germany, the humbler classes still retained the healthy germs of a vigorous and manly poetry, very different from the minne-lays which had preceded it. A *Volkslied*, popular as the old Hildebrand, Niebelungen, and Roland songs, but having less of the martial, more of the impassioned caste about it. These circumstances made what the Germans call the second classic era in their history of the poetry possible. And to this we owe that era, as it appeared in the eighteenth century.

But these prose stories, at the end of the fifteenth and throughout great part of the sixteenth centuries, were then the only popular literature. The art epics, with their learning and elaboration, had lorded it so long over the poetry of the people, that when these unfortunate authors, like the owl, twisted their own necks in studying the reflection of themselves, the popular feeling rejoiced in their downfall, and consigned them to oblivion with somewhat spiteful haste. There was, however, no poetry to put in its place, save the same heroic songs which the nation had sung in its childhood. Now that it was nearing manhood, it gave to these the maturer form of prose. But when we speak of these *Volksbücher* as popular literature, it must not be supposed that they were exactly to the sixteenth century what three-volume novels have been to the nineteenth. In our day, it is a rare thing to meet with a philosopher at all times so abstruse, or a geologist imprisoned beneath so many scientific strata, that he has never, since his youth, been fascinated by any fiction—never opened with pleasure, and closed with something like regret, a volume of Bulwer or of Thackeray. In proportion to the enlightenment of that age, the rude, healthy charm of the *Volksbücher* might have entitled them to a similar welcome in their day. But this remark we cannot make without considerable trepidation. It is treasonable enough so to provoke the shades of certain educated Germans of the sixteenth century. They seem even now crowding in over our threshold, and disappearing in indignant and misty confusion, like the soap-bubbles over the edge of a boy's pipe, till one more zealous and less evanescent than the rest, solemnly compassionating our ignorance, deigns to tell us how learning, in their day, knew better what was due to its own dignity, and carefully kept aloof from the masses; how their magnificent classical attainments, their unwearied studies, which so gloriously resulted in writing Latin, and in ignoring their native tongue, raised them above any fellow-feeling for the common German herd, and that we do them unparalleled injustice to imagine the *Volksbücher*, things hawked about the country and sold at fairs, could ever have influenced the sixteenth century otherwise than mere play-bills or advertisements may influence our own. Granted, Master Scholar, that was, assuredly, about the level to which you and your fellow-shades would fain have reduced them, and, moreover, wherein you were not altogether unsuccessful. Nevertheless, in support of our opinion, we have the fact, that certain individuals, dignified (no doubt by a degenerate century) with the name of scholars, as one Goethe, and others named Tieck, Grimm, and Musæus, have bestowed no small labour on the collecting, and on the recomposition of these contemptible productions—so that the greater number are now well known as tales or dramas, and are prized alike by the scholar and the schoolboy. You must take this fact, good reader, as our plea for calling your attention to matters so childish as those which now lie before us.

The influence diffused by the commercial prosperity of the German free cities, had, in the sixteenth century, already effected much towards the amalgamation of hostile classes. The intercourse of trade brought man and man into closer contact, and served to rub off many obnoxious angles; while the new necessity for frequent journeys, stimulating a spirit of enterprise, could not fail to diffuse intelligence, and widen the range of sympathy. Still, the prevailing spirit was so much one of trade and manual industry, that the only trace of literary interest or cultivation is to be found in that dreary mechanism of the meister-singers, which they innocently called poetry. Business and travelling were then, as with us, the great occupations of life. Sober people would go, with perhaps less than six weeks' preparation, all the way from Nürnberg to see their cousins at Munich, or their grandmother at Cologne. Wealthy citizens sent their sons on a tour through the Belgian cities, or to one of the flourishing Hanse towns to bring home a rich wife. In this century, also, appeared the first symptoms of that rage for watering places, which must now have reached its climax, since we verily believe no German dies comfortably who has not in happier days been cured, or is not now professionally killed, in Carlsbad, Gräfrad, or Teplitz. Now, at such places, how could these good people have amused themselves? It must, indeed, have been a pursuit of health under difficulties. Possibly some of the men would be meistersingers, and cheat the rude weather and idle hour by making scrupulously unpoetical verses. A Strasburger might at intervals read some of Hans Sachs, and Brandt's *Ship of Fools*, or Thomas Murner's last pamphlet against Luther, while one can readily fancy a family party under the trees, compensating for the bitterness of the waters, by a chapter of the *Four Sons of Aymon*, or a young lady setting aside the distaff to resume the sorrows of *Griseldis*. But from all such popular advancement, as was thus indicated, the learned, *par excellence*, kept fitting distance; mounting their frail stilts of classic learning, they walked to and fro above the crowd, superciliously overlooking those busy lesser wheels whose ceaseless and united action urges on the great machine of social life.

Many of our readers will already know as household tales, the histories of *Fortunatus*, of *Horned Siegfrid, Doctor Faustus, Griseldis, Genoveva*, and perhaps some others, none of which therefore need further mention here. Among those which have been, and still continue to be, the most popular in Germany, is, *Duke Ernst*, a legend which existed unwritten in 1180, and in the sixteenth century received the prevailing prose form. It bears closer resemblance to the ancient heroic tradition than any which have not their origin in that remote period, and is also remarkable for its eccentric geography, and for the introduction of the Oriental wonders reported by the Crusaders, the splendour of which is fully detailed. We are here able to give only a short outline of a very long story, and can scarcely expect to do any justice to its pictorial merits. The interest is personal rather than historical, as will be found to be the case in all popular tradition. The adventures of individuals claim more ready and cordial interest than the general events of history. Many readers who might be said (more expressively than elegantly) to devour the story of Duke Ernst, would be utterly apathetic in relation to the historic events which affected whole nations. It is his personality which excites their interest, and his history which gives them their only ideas of an entire historic period. How many instances might be enumerated wherein such traditional or historic heroes have thus given character and colouring to whole centuries. It is natural for the heart and the imagination to be attracted more by men than by events. Hence, with few exceptions, it is the philosopher, and the man of culture alone, who can so far generalize as to follow out with interest all the complex causes and results of historical transactions. The peasant or the artisan has more relish for the toils and perils of Robert

453

Bruce, Robin Hood, and a score of heroes besides. This association of material of all sorts round one centre, will partly account for the extraordinary mixture found in most popular tales, and which the reader will not fail to criticise in the tales following. In the two stories to which we shall restrict our selection, there is the fantastic half truth, half fable of the Oriental poet, mixed up with the superstition of mediæval catholicism, the gloomy presages of the astrologer, and the fatalism of the Mahommedan, all linked with our own Christian teaching of patience under injury, of manly faith, and rectitude triumphing over evil. The restless chivalry of the West is sometimes lulled into luxurious siesta, and imagination hovers in a region undefined and undefinable; time, space, the probable and the improbable, are all forgotten, the reader's neat little craft of common sense goes to the bottom, and he is cast ashore on what seems to him the lonely island of the impossible.

With the assistance of Gustave Schwab's version, we shall now give the substance of one of these stories, begging the reader to forget utterly, for the next few pages, that he has anything to do with a grave reviewer of the nineteenth century, and to imagine rather that it is some simple-minded, credulous German of three or four centuries ago that is about to speak.

'The Emperor Otto the Red, after the death of his young wife, Ottogeba, followed the advice of his councillors, and sent an embassage to the Duchess of Bavaria, demanding her hand in marriage. Since the death of her husband, this virtuous princess had led a quiet life, employing herself in the education of her son, Ernst, and had refused all solicitations to marry again. She was therefore greatly distressed on hearing the emperor's message, and could only think of the dissensions which would arise between him and her son the duke. But Ernst, on the contrary, urged the matter upon her, saying, 'Dearest mother, I beseech you, 'let no fear on my account prevent your union with this mighty 'prince. With the help of God, who is our head ruler, I will 'render good service to my earthly emperor in fortune or mis- 'fortune, will always show him obedience, and will surround him 'and his with my arms, that I may always enjoy his favour.' So the wedding took place, with great state and splendour, in the town of Mainz, and for a time all things went on smoothly at the court.

'Now, there was a certain Count Heinrich, a treacherous and pitiless man, who could not bear to see the friendly terms on which the emperor and the empress stood with their son. Although the young duke was greatly respected by all, and had bravely defended his step-father's lands on more than one occasion, yet the false count goes to the emperor and represents to him how diligently his son is seeking out an opportunity to put an end to his life, and to obtain possession of the whole kingdom. At first the emperor does not believe him. But Heinrich goes on to show how he has heard it from two or three, and that the danger is very great. 'Oh, my dear Heinrich,' says the emperor, in great distress, 'I beseech you, give me good counsel. If it be as you 'say, how am I to send my son out of the country before he can 'accomplish his design ?'—'I would advise my imperial master,' said he,'that while your son rides to Regensberg, you send, secretly, 'without the knowledge of the empress, a part of your army, 'which shall drive him out of the land.' So the troops were sent, and, after great difficulty, took the town of Bamberg. The inhabitants then sent word to their good duke at Regensberg of what had befallen them. Ernst went with bitter tears to his friend, Count Wetzel, wondering what base calumnies had reached the ears of his father, that he should cause so much bloodshed in his land, and be so eager for his destruction. He then assembled his four thousand men, and went out to meet Count Heinrich, who escaped from the battle with only a few followers. This defeat only added to the rage of the emperor, and he went out with fresh troops, taking town after town, and desolating the whole land. Duke Ernst then sent a messenger to his father, assuring him of his loyalty, and begging him to spare his dominions. After hearing this, the emperor paced up and down the room in great wrath, and the empress perceiving that it concerned her son, begged that his conduct might be examined thoroughly, and that he might not be condemned without a hearing. The emperor was inexorable, and the empress went to her room in great sorrow. While upon her knees praying for the deliverance of her son, and wondering whence the evil had sprung, she heard a voice, as it were from heaven, saying to her, 'The Count Heinrich is at the root of these things.' In great amazement, she sent for the messenger, and instructed him to tell Ernst how matters stood at the court, and that all his misfortunes were owing to Count Heinrich. Upon this news, Ernst took a bold resolution, and, with his friend, Wetzel, went to Spires, where the emperor had assembled all the princes. Leaving their horses with the servants, they went up into the palace, and found the emperor sitting alone with the count. Duke Ernst then drew his sword, and exclaiming, 'Thou false 'and treacherous count, wherefore didst thou thus foully slander 'me ?' plunged it furiously into his enemy. The emperor, terrified at his son's violence, sprang down some four feet into a chapel, and remained there trembling till the murderers had time to escape. They went in great haste to the Duke of Saxony; of him Duke Ernst obtained a sufficient number of troops to conduct him in safety to Regensberg. The duke assembled the citizens, and told them all that had happened, and how his father being so much stronger than he, all further resistance was in vain; he therefore counselled them to render true allegiance to the emperor, but told them he must take his treasures, and turn his back upon his people. And their hearts were very heavy when they saw their good duke ride away. Forty knights accompanied him on a journey to the Holy Sepulchre; and his mother sent him secretly one hundred silver marks, which he divided among them. So they took the nearest road into Hungary, and were well received by the king, who sent men with them to guide them safely through the forests. At Constantinople, they were most graciously entertained, and remained for three weeks at the court. By that time a large and beautiful ship came in, which the king ordered to be well manned and well stocked with provisions. For six weeks they sailed with fair wind; but one night a storm arose, and the ship was in great danger, and the other twelve ships which were with the duke all went to pieces. At last the sailors were unable to find out where they were, and their stock of provisions was nearly ended. In the midst of these difficulties, they reached an unknown coast. Here they landed, and Duke Ernst and his knights mounted and rode towards a town, which they saw in the distance. It was beautifully built, with a thick, high wall, huge towers, and surrounded by a broad moat. After riding about it at a distance, they resolved to return to the ship, and having eaten and drank what little they had, put on their armour, and the duke gave Count Wetzel the standard with the motto, ' God's word standeth for ever.'

' Now the inhabitants of this country were called Agrippines. The king had just set out with his followers to waylay an Indian princess, who was passing through his land on her way to the foreign prince whom she was to marry. After long deliberation, and with some fear, the duke entered the town; they met no one in all the streets, and at length they dismounted before a beautiful castle. In the hall they found a table spread with delicious fare, as though for a wedding feast; so they all sat down, and ate and drank as much as they liked, and sent for those who were on board the ship also to come and refresh themselves. The next day they came again to the palace, and ate and drank, and walked from one beautiful room to another, till they found a chamber in which stood two splendid bedsteads

of pure gold, and the coverings of cloth of gold; in the middle of the room was a table covered with a magnificent cloth, on which a delicate repast was laid out. Next to this was a small saloon, and a garden with a beautiful fountain leaping from silver pipes into two golden troughs. So Duke Ernst and his friend Wetzel bathed in the fountain, and then laid themselves down to sleep in the golden beds. After they had rested, they went once more round, admiring the wonders of the palace, when Count Wetzel suddenly espied a large army advancing towards them; the duke then proposed they should hide themselves, and see what these people did. The people entered the town in great state, but Ernst and his friend were not a little amazed to see that one and all of them had the neck and bill of a crane. The king now took his seat at the table, with the beautiful princess, whom he had carried off, sitting beside him; he often turned round his bill towards her that she might kiss him, but the good maiden was full of sorrow, and turned aside her head, wishing she were in a forest with wild beasts, rather than with such fearful-looking creatures. Meanwhile, the two gentlemen behind the door whispered to one another, and noticed the distress of the lady, and Duke Ernst vowed that he would risk his life to save her. But they were much afraid the people should discover the ship, and the knights they had left there, and the knights in the ship were equally anxious for their duke and his friend. When the long meal was at last finished, the people all went away drunk, and cackling like geese; the king retired into a beautiful room laden with golden ornaments, and sent two servants to fetch the princess. Duke Ernst and Count Wetzel sprang from their hiding-place as she was led by, and struck off the head of one servant, the other rushed into the presence of the king, exclaiming that the Indians were there to carry away their princess. The king sprang up with a loud cackle, and ran his bill into the maiden's side, so that she fell to the ground. This so enraged the duke, that he ran the king through with his sword; he then raised the princess, but she had only breath to say a few words of gratitude. When they saw that she was dead, they had only their own safety to care for, and fought their way bravely to the gates of the town. But these were closed, and the enemy was fast overpowering them. Now it chanced that the gentlemen in the ship had set out to see if they could anywhere see the duke; they heard the noise in the town, and with their battle-axes at last broke the gates, and saved him and his friend, together with the body of the princess. But they had no sooner safely set sail, than the Agrippines set sail also, and showered poisoned arrows after them like snow. Fortunately, the duke had on board a sort of catapult, with which he sent three or four ships to the bottom; and the others seeing they could get no good, went back to the town and buried their king.

'On the fifth day, after fair wind, the captain of the ship saw a dark mountain rise in the distance, and at the sight broke out into fearful lamentations. No power could save the ship; for greater strength, it had been studded over with huge iron nails, and the magnetic power of the mountain now drew them out, and the ship fell, and floated piecemeal on the water.'

Then our story goes on to show how these adventurous knights escaped by the marvellous help of ox-hides and huge vultures; how they made their way through the stream of a terrible mountain pass; how this brought them into a country peopled by Cyclops, having their one eye in the centre of their forehead; how the duke and his followers did much wise and valiant service for the king of the Cyclops, against a people called Sciapodes, who had but one foot, that foot, however, being of such structure and dimensions, as to fit them for great achievements on land or water; also against a people who had ears long enough to serve them for mantles; and against giants, whom none before were ever known to conquer; and then the story proceeds.

'Now that there was no more assistance to be rendered to the King of the Cyclops, the duke one day said to his friend, 'Dear ' Wetzel, I once heard, that in India, there are very little men ' indeed, who are constantly at war with the crane-people. I ' should much like to see them. Will you go with me; and I ' will then take some more soldiers?' The count was very willing; and, taking abundance of provision, they set sail for India. The good people were very much alarmed at the sight of such great warriors, but were right glad when they heard they were come to bring peace, and not war. The duke won for them an easy victory, and only took as reward two of the dwarfs; and returned to the king of the Cyclops, who had given him five large towns and castles. One day, as he was walking on the sea-shore, a ship came into the harbour from India, driven by the wind; and they told the duke how their king, who favoured the Christians, was, on this account, at war with the sultan of Babylon, who desolated the land with fire and sword. Duke Ernst then went home, and told the count about it; and they agreed to sail the next day with the captain. Orders were given to provision the ship, the strange people the duke had collected were put on board, and all left before the king heard anything of it.'

We cannot follow the duke through all his victorious adventures in the regions of the Sultan of Babylon, and of the King of the Moors, but will rejoin him at Jerusalem.

'When he had been there half a-year, two pilgrims came who knew him, and who went away and told the Emperor Otto all about the marvellous people whom his son had brought from strange countries. The emperor was very much astonished, and gave them handsome presents. Then he went to the empress, and said, 'Dear wife; I will tell you something wonderful. Your ' son Ernst is in Jerusalem, and has grown quite grey.' The empress was amazed and delighted at these words. 'Truly, sire, ' the grey hairs which he has, have come from no small sorrow. He ' has suffered much injury in his lifetime!'

From Jerusalem the duke went to Rome: and when he had seen all the town, he said, one day, to Wetzel, 'My dearest ' friend; let us turn towards our fatherland. You know how ' many dangers we have encountered, and, with God's help, over- ' come; but my greatest misery seems still to be, that my father ' will not lessen his anger toward me, although I am innocent. ' Therefore I beg you, dear friend, tell me what I had better do.' The count then advised the duke to go to Nuremberg, where the emperor was to hold a diet; and who knows, said he, how Providence may not help us by that time. No sooner said than done. They secretly entered the town of Nuremberg; and soon after them came the emperor, and all his court. On Christmas Day, the empress and her ladies all went to the church; this the duke saw, and mixing among the people, came up to his mother with the greeting, 'Give me an alms, for Christ's sake, and for ' the sake of your son Ernst!' The empress replied, 'Alas, my ' friend, I have not seen my son for very long. Would God he ' were alive, you should then have alms enough!' Then said the duke, quickly, 'Madam, give me the alms, and I will go ' hence again, for I am in disgrace with my father, and cannot ' come into favour again!' The empress said, 'You are then ' my son Ernst?' He replied, 'Mother, I am your son; there- ' fore help me to find favour again.' The empress then told him to come the following day to the church; and when the Bishop of Bamberg read the Gospel, he and his friend Wetzel should throw themselves at the emperor's feet, and beg his forgiveness. Their example should be followed by all the court; and she hoped it would not be in vain. So the duke followed her advice; and when the service was ended, he threw his cloak over his face, and bowing before the emperor said, 'Most ' gracious lord and emperor, I beseech your majesty to forgive 'a sinner, who has long erred, but who yet is innocent of the 'chief charge against him.' The emperor replied, that the pardon must depend upon the nature of the crime. Then the empress and all the court rose, and besought him, on this holy and joyful day, to pardon the offender. The emperor, at last, consented; but said he would see who the man was. The duke then threw back his mantle; and when he saw his father's cheek redden with anger, he made a sign to his friend Wetzel, for it had been agreed that he should stab the duke rather than allow him to become the emperor's prisoner. But the emperor, seeing the whole court thus intercede for his son, said, 'And where, 'then, is thy friend, Count Wetzel?' The count then gladly approached, and received the kiss of reconciliation from the emperor. So every one went home well pleased; and the duke heard how basely the Count Heinrich had slandered him, and then told his innocence of all the charges; and how he had always been true and loyal in his heart. Then the emperor heard, in great amazement, how he had met with so many wonders, and had so many escapes; and he said to Duke Ernst, 'My dear son, because you have been so much tried and 'wronged, I promise, before these gentlemen, that you shall have 'all your lands again, and many towns beside.' So the duke rode with his friend into his own land, and received the joyful homage of his people; and he reigned there very long in peace. And the emperor went to the Diet, at Spires, and held a great feast, because his son was come back. The duke's mother also, ordered many workmen to Salza, and there built a splendid minster, in which she was afterwards buried.'

We need not mention the point of this story that will remind our readers of the tale of 'Sinbad the Sailor.' It is doubtless one of the many traveller's tales brought from the East, either by the Crusaders, or by the learned men who, some years later, not unfrequently took one or two voyages into foreign parts before giving themselves to labour for life. Accounts of such travels were read with great eagerness in the sixteenth century, and were especially congenial to its youthful enterprising spirit. The wonders of *Duke Ernst*, and other romances, would doubtless pass unquestioned, among the wild poetic versions of real discoveries, to which multitudes everywhere gave delighted credence. Many years of travel, and of newly-opened commerce, passed away, before the stories of Russian steppes, with their salt lakes, boiling springs, and ghostlike birch-woods, then for the first time heard of, were to be received as more authentic than other tales of haunted wells and desert islands. Sailors have ever been super-stitious, and travellers, in times past, hardly less so. Distant lands, in the middle ages, and long after, were all the lands of fable.

The story of the *Four Sons of Aymon* springs from the old Charlemagne tradition-cycle, and is full of exciting incident. Its length precludes us from doing more than name it. A translation has, we believe, lately appeared in the *Traveller's Library*, by William Hazlitt. As a sample of those *Volksbücher*, of a less martial character, we will just sketch an outline of the universal favourite, the *Fair Melusina*—which was translated from the French by Düring von Ringoltingen, and printed about 1535.

'Once upon a time, there lived at Poictiers, in France, a count, named Emmerich, who was a great astrologer; he had also very large estates, and spent much of his time in hunting. In the neighbouring forest lived another count, who was his cousin, but who was very poor, and had a great many children. Count Emmerich had a great respect for his cousin, and was anxious to assist him in bringing up his family as became their noble rank. He, therefore, gave a large banquet, to which he invited the Count von der Forste and his sons. As they were going away, he begged his cousin to leave his youngest son Raymond behind, that he might educate him as his own child; the manly form and engaging dispositions of the youth had so won his heart, that he should be quite unhappy if his request were not granted. So Raymond was left behind, and conducted himself so well as to gain the affections of all in his new home. One day the count, attended by Raymond and a large company of gentlemen, went out into the forest to hunt a wild boar. The animal led them a long chase, and killed many dogs; the count, with the faithful Raymond at his side, still pursued, until the moon rose, and they found themselves alone in a green glade. Raymond then proposed they should return, and endeavour to reach the nearest peasant's house; they, therefore, rode slowly on through the tangled underwood till they came upon the road to Poictiers. The count then looked up at the stars, and after studying them in grave silence, turned with a deep sigh to Raymond. 'Come here my son, I will show you a 'great phenomenon, such an aspect of the heavens as is rarely 'seen!' Raymond begged to be further instructed in the matter. 'I see,' continued the count, 'that in this hour some one will 'kill his master, and will thus become a mighty powerful lord, 'greater than all his ancestors!' Raymond listened in silence; meantime, they came upon a fire which had been lighted by the other gentlemen of the party, so they dismounted, and sat down by the fire. They were no sooner seated than they heard a loud crashing in the branches behind, and had scarcely time to seize their weapons before a wild boar was upon them, foaming and tearing up the ground with rage. Raymond begged the count to save himself in a tree; this proposal offended him greatly, and seizing his spear he rushed furiously at the boar, but the stroke was too weak, the animal pushed it aside, and with one spring brought his enemy to the ground. Raymond now drew his spear in great haste to finish the boar and save his master, but in the heat of his zeal he drove the spear through the boar deep in the body of the count; he instantly withdrew it, but too late, count Emmerich lay dead, covered with blood.

'In the greatest distress Raymond now fled from the place, he knew not whither. His eyes were blinded with tears, and he sent forth the most bitter lamentations and complaints against the destiny which had not only deprived him of his best friend, but had made him the instrument of his death. Wrapped in these gloomy thoughts he came to a well, beside which stood three beautiful maidens, and would have passed by without seeing them, but the youngest stepped forward and addressed him. Struck with the marvellous beauty of her countenance, he sprang to the ground, and besought her to forgive his unknightly conduct in passing without a greeting; he pleaded his deep and sudden grief which had almost deprived him of his senses. He then told her all that had befallen him; and the mysterious maiden gave him much kind and affectionate counsel, with many happy prophecies of the future, so that Raymond's anxious face wore a pleasanter air, and the roses of hope succeeded the paleness of despair. He promised to devote his whole life to her, and to be directed by her counsel as the shadow is by the sun. Raymond further agreed to her condition, that if she became his wife, he should on every Saturday leave her entirely to herself, should make no effort to see her, nor allow any other person to do so; at the same time she promised on that day to go nowhere, but to remain quietly in her own apartments. The beautiful Melusina, seeing Raymond readily make so great a promise, fearing he undertook more than he would be able to perform, said to him: 'You appear certainly to render cheerful 'obedience to my will, but I see you promise more than you 'intend to perform; let me tell you, however, that should you 'ever thus break your faith, at your door alone must lie all the 'misery that will arise from it—for not only must you then 'lose me inevitably and for ever, but misfortune will follow you, 'and your children's children.' After much more talk, they

at length took an affectionate farewell, Raymond promising in all things to follow the advice of Melusina, who was so beautiful and so wise, he could not tell whether she was a mortal or a spirit.

'At the castle, Raymond found all in distress and confusion at the absence of the good count, but as so many gentlemen who had been with him knew nothing of where he had gone, no one suspected Raymond of knowing more than he appeared to do. Presently two of the servants returned, bringing the body with them, which they had found in the wood, beside the boar; and a very solemn funeral took place, at which none wept more sincerely than the affectionate Raymond. All the estates now came into the possession of Count Emmerich's son, Bertram, and many nobles and gentlemen assembled to receive their lands from the new lord. Raymond, following the plan he had agreed upon with the fair Melusina, also presented his request, that for his past services, he might be allowed to have a piece of land near the well, if it were only such a piece as a deer-skin would cover. Raymond received the grant in due form, with parchment and seal. Immediately afterwards he met a man carrying a deer-skin, this he bought, and had it cut into the narrowest strips; he then set out, with proper men, to take possession of his land. One end of the skin he fastened to the well, and measured round it as far as the strip-line would reach. It was found to include a rich piece of land, watered by a broad stream; and all the men were astonished at the cunning of young Raymond, especially his cousin Bertram, who laughed heartily, and was greatly pleased when he heard it. The next time Raymond met his betrothed at the well, he received great praise for his discreet conduct. 'Follow me,' said she, 'and let us thank Heaven that it thus prospers our undertakings.' She then led him to a retired chapel in the forest, which Raymond was amazed to find filled with people, knights, ladies, citizens, and priests who conducted the service. Wondering if he were among men or spirits, he asked his bride whence all these people came in that solitary place, and who they were. Melusina then told him they were her subjects, and turning to them, enjoined upon them, thenceafter, the most implicit obedience to Raymond as their lord and master. This they all solemnly vowed.

'The court of Count Bertram soon after received another visit from Raymond, and they wondered what should have brought him there again. Raymond readily obtained an audience of his cousin, and began thus:—'Most gracious cousin, be not angry 'that I have so soon and unexpectedly presented myself at your 'court again, but I have something to tell you, which so nearly 'concerns me, that I do not think I should leave you in ignorance 'I have won a beautiful bride, and am come here to beg, most 'respectfully, that you and your mother will honour us with 'your presence at our wedding, which will take place at the Well. 'If, therefore, I and my betrothed may hope for such honour 'early on the coming Monday, we shall esteem it a peculiar hap-'piness, ever to be remembered with gratitude.' Bertram then inquired, with great curiosity, who the lady might be? 'She is 'a noble, rich, and powerful lady,' replied Raymond, 'but of her 'descent I am still ignorant, and shall remain so until after the 'ceremony.' At this communication Bertram was much astonished, and still more amused; however, he politely accepted the invitation, saying, his desire to see this goddess would make the time appear very long.

'At length the wished-for day arrived, and the Count Bertram set out with a very numerous suite, who passed many jokes by the way, wondering whether the whole might not prove to be some magical deception, since the place of meeting bore a very suspicious character. When they reached a rocky height commanding the plain in which Raymond's well lay, they were astonished to see it covered over with beautiful tents of all sizes, scattered picturesquely among the trees, and beside the stream; there were also numbers of people, apparently strangers, walking to and fro on the grass. This led them still more to believe the whole was the work of enchantment. Their thoughts, however, were now interrupted by the approach of a company of sixty knights and noblemen, all in the most magnificent attire; these conducted the gentlemen into a superb tent, and a company of noble ladies received the Countess and her attendants in the name of the bride. The company then assembled in the chapel, and were ranged in a circle round an altar of the richest workmanship. The dress of the bride sparkled with gold, pearls, and precious stones. After the mass had been performed with the most exquisite music, Raymond and Melusina were led to the altar to receive the blessing, and the bride was then conducted by the Count of Poictiers to the tent; here golden vessels were offered to the guests, and water poured upon their hands; seats were then taken at the table. After the first course, Raymond and some of his knights arose from the table and waited upon the guests. The repast was followed by a tournament, from which Raymond carried off the prize, which was a precious ornament, set in diamonds. In the evening the bridal pair were led, with a procession of music and torches, to their tent, which was of thick silk and stripes of gold, all embroidered with birds and lilies. The music of flutes and soft voices continued all night without the tent, but Melusina reminded her husband of his promise, and warned him of certain ruin if he should break it.'

It will be readily seen how much there is in these descriptions resembling the chivalric romances, more especially those of France. And apt as we are to regard such details as tedious, and to exclaim against the frequent repetition of such adventures as becoming monotonous rather than exciting, we have to bear in mind that fiction has an end to accomplish, no less than history or philosophy. From the fragments of its fiction we look for indications of an epoch in its domestic and social conditions, in its tendency and general characteristics, as shown in paths branching off from the high road of the historian —mosaic bits, which, from their very littleness, go to form what proves both harmonious and instructive. History gathers its bearded sheaves of ripe events, leaving a lesser harvest for a merry band of gleaners, who store it with laughter and song, and send it forth again, as their contribution to the general happiness.

But our philosophy must not be allowed to prevent us following the course of our story. Well, the course, in substance, is this—the wedding feast lasts fifteen days. Raymond then occupies himself in building a strong castle with many lofty towers. Melusina, in process of time, becomes the mother of ten sons. These sons differ much from each other, one, for example, having one eye, another three, and their characters are not less varied. The brothers do many striking things, each after his nature. At length a friend provokes the curiosity of Raymond about the cause of his wife's mysterious seclusion every Saturday; after much conflict, the count resolves to secure, unobserved, a sight of what passed in the secret apartment of Melusina on that day. To his amazement he sees his beautiful wife engaged in magic ceremonies, become half-fish and half-woman, and much beside. As might be supposed, this dissolves the enchantment; the mysterious wife mysteriously disappears; Raymond becomes disconsolate, makes a pilgrimage to the Holy Land, and dies at a good old age, seeing most of his sons rise to wealth and honour; and Melusina, too, having foretold the fortunes of her house before her departure, still loves her husband, Raymond, and before his decease, returns to apprise those near him of his approaching end.

Now, to enter into the spirit of such a specimen from the comparative childhood of literature, and to understand the condition of mind to which it was addressed, this story must of course be regarded with something like that unquestioning faith with which it was once received—at least, by the young and uncritical. Supernatural ladies of this beneficent order are by no means uncommon in early Teutonic literature. The charm of such illusions depends on our being able to believe as Raymond for a while believed—but in our case, as in his, all will be dispelled, if we begin to be too curious and grow sceptical.

Let us now leave these graver histories for those of a lighter description. We shall find these to be still more the immediate production of the existing social relations. Society, at that period, was made up of contrast, and gained in life and vigour from the constant friction of opposing elements. Mixed with the ungoverned love of mirth, the reckless self-indulgence, of a people, as it were, sowing their wild oats, are the signs of an approaching manhood, in grave questionings and anxious disputations. Martin Luther, with his lion heart, and ready speech, ever valiant for the highest truth; and Hans Sachs, with his shrewd wit and laughter-loving eye, pouring forth comedy and satire, are contemporaries especially characteristic of their age. And it is in such extremes that true satire must have its rise. Side by side in the soul of the satirist are *L'Allegro* and *Penseroso*. Take away the one or the other, and the power and beauty of the character are gone. If we mistake not, it is the humorist Hood who says—

> 'There is no music in the life
> That sounds to idiot laughter only;
> There is no note of mirth,
> But hath its chord in melancholy.'

The genius which speaks to us in the inspiration of the loftiest tragedy and tenderest pathos, is often that which gives itself vent in the gayest humour, the keenest repartees. The rainbow of true wit must be formed of sunshine and of cloud. Mirth saves the sadness of reality from settling into gloom, gravity points and plumes the merry arrow, that it may not go forth idly and without an aim. It is so with nations as with individuals; and hence comes the conflict and fusion we meet with in the sixteenth century, producing along with the gravest writings, the greatest German satirists, and sending forth a stream of popular farce and humour, which provided occasion for laughter to succeeding generations. At this time, moreover, the remorseless *régime* of ceremony and etiquette, which had so long frozen the higher classes, and rigidly excluded the lower from any better intercourse than with their own, was gradually breaking up. Ideas concerning the rights of the governing and the governed underwent a change. People began to see what they had long only

indistinctly felt, and the separation of classes and the excesses of the clergy were declared to be evils, and assailed as such. For many a day, the only representative of freedom had been the court fool, who, revelling in his licence of equality, made a most refreshing use of it, satirising rich and poor, but invariably levelling his hardest hits at the highest heads—careless though the effect as it came upon his back consisted of something weightier than a witticism. The satirical tendency of the period saw in these pranks and follies of the fools no insignificant weapon, and led to the collection and arrangement of them round some mythic personage, as Burkhardt Waldis, Till Eulenspiegel, or the Friar Amis of the thirteenth century.

We have already seen how the heroic tradition, in a prose form, became once more welcome in its old home among the people. In the same manner, though in a different spirit, the old brute tradition was now also revived. In its first appearance, this tradition was a development, or manifestation rather, of the forest life and tastes of the early Germans. Their daily familiar association with the habits and instincts of the animal creation, taught them to attribute to it a half-human character, which is the spirit of the brute tradition. And when this social intercourse was interrupted, as by beasts of prey, their superstition would clothe such rude disturbers with supernatural terrors. Hence it is we hear of were-wolves, and other marvels. The famous brute epic of *Reynard the Fox*, which had been brought back again out of the Netherlands, assumed, however, in the eyes of this generation, an entirely new character. It was looked on and enjoyed as a bold, elaborate satire upon kings, courts, and priests; and to the prevailing quarrels between the clergy and the laity it owed many a new edition. In imitation of this work rose fables, and numberless stories of animals; the latter, however, failing to realize the mystic half-human element, which should be their special beauty. Where such heroes are represented as definite animals, or definite men, (though still called by animal names,) their hold on the imagination is greatly lessened. Master Reynard is more than a mere fox, and yet too much of a fox to be a man; the charm thus becomes complete, and is irresistible.

From the *Volksbücher* of this humorous caste we are somewhat at a loss to select a specimen. That which will perhaps admit of being indicated in the least space, is the *Lalenbuch*, or *The Citizens of Schilda*. The inhabitants of this town were so widely celebrated for their wisdom, that they received embassies from the most distant kings and statesmen, summoning them to give their advice upon important questions. This celebrity proved, after a time, somewhat inconvenient, inasmuch as it often happened that the women were left at home alone to plough, sow, and reap. But, as we shall see, their wisdom was not for other people's use only. After mature deliberation, they resolved to lay aside this superfluous possession. From the day of that determination each was to emulate his fellow in stupidity. At first, this was rather a difficult matter; but soon, as the magistrate said, 'they were clever enough to take to it quite naturally.' One of the first improvements which they now undertook in their town was the erection of a new town-hall. It rose to a great height, with three walls forming a triangle; but notwithstanding the beauty of the design, it was discovered, on the first day of assembly, that they were unable to see anything in the interior. They, therefore, with great promptitude, ran and fetched large sacks, held them open in the sunshine, then hastily closing the mouths, rushed into the hall, concluding that this manœuvre would be followed by a full blaze of sunshine. Great was their dismay at finding themselves still in the dark; and they gladly followed the advice of a traveller, who told them to take off the roof from the building. This they did; and fortunately had a dry summer.

The citizens of Schilda also built a new mill, and for this purpose had hewn a stone from a quarry at the top of the hill. This they carried down to the mill; but then they remembered how, in felling the wood for the town-hall, one tree had rolled down by itself. 'Are we come to be real fools,' quoth the magistrate, in a great rage; 'we might have let the stone 'roll down, and have spared all this trouble.' So, with great difficulty, they carried it up again to the quarry. 'Oh!' exclaimed one of the men; 'how shall we know where the stone 'rolls to?' 'That is easily settled,' replied the magistrate; 'some 'one must put his head into the hole, and go down with it.' So the stone and the man went down the hill-side into the millpond. When the rest reached the bottom of the hill, and saw neither man nor stone, they suspected foul play; and said the man must have gone off with the millstone. They therefore sent word to all the neighbouring villages, ' that if a man were 'seen walking with a millstone round his neck, he should be 'taken, and should suffer the extremity of the law as a common 'thief.' But the poor fellow lay at the bottom of the pond, and had drunk too much water to be able to make his defence. Not long after this, there was a report of war; and the people were greatly concerned for the safety of the bell in the town-hall. They at length agreed that the sea would be the safest place to put it in. So they went out in a ship, and dropped the bell slowly down, making a notch in the ship's side, that they might know the precise spot. When the war was over, they set sail again to recover their treasure; but though the notch was still in the ship, they never found their bell. The stupidity of the Schil-

bürger had long ceased to be assumed; and their melancholy end was such as might be anticipated from their consistent life. It happened thus:—In the town of Schilda there were no cats; and barns and houses were overrun with mice. One day, a traveller passed with a cat under his arm. An innkeeper asked what it was. 'A mouse-dog,' replied the stranger; and it forthwith commenced considerable execution among the mice. So the stranger kindly settled with the good citizens, that they should have the cat for a hundred gulden. They carried it into the castle, where the corn was, and then remembered they had not inquired what the animal ate. A man was dispatched after the stranger; who, however, fearing they repented the bargain, took to his heels. 'What does it eat?' shouted the man, at a great distance. ' Wie man's beut' (what you please) replied he, hastily. But the peasant understood him, ' Vieh und Leut' (men and cattle), and ran home in great consternation. From this it was clear that when the mice were eaten, the cattle and themselves would be the next victims; but no one dared to touch the creature. So they thought it would be a lesser evil to lose their corn, and promptly set fire to the castle, in order to destroy the cat. But the cat jumped out of the window into another house; this they bought, and burned likewise; but the creature walked quietly on to the roof, and began washing her face. This solemn elevation of the paw was construed into a menace of mortal revenge. One brave man commenced an attack with a long spear; but puss calmly ran down it. This climax so horrified the beholders, that they simultaneously fled; and the village was burned all but one house. With their wives and children the Schilbürger wandered into the forest; and having lost their all, sought other homes in countries far and near. So that, even in our day, there is no town in which some of the race of the Schilbürgers may not be found.

And as we have all met with Schilbürgers in our time, so we have all heard of one Whittington, who also chanced to find a cat a very marketable commodity.

Our patient reader, now, doubtless, looks to us for some information respecting the early authors of the stories, the characteristics of which we have submitted, with our best fidelity, to his judicious criticism. But laudable as this spirit of inquiry may be in the abstract, there are occasions on which we cannot profess to admire it, if it be expected of us that we should preserve even the ghost of a conscience. In the present instance, we consider it annoying, intrusive, malicious. Our only reply is, that a few were composed and penned by a Thuringian princess, in the fifteenth century; and it is possible, that the literary dilettante, Niclas von Wyle, may have had something to do with some others of them; but this is scarcely probable, since he was far too busy in translating Italian, and running after literary ladies. Our information, therefore, on this point, becomes ' beautifully less' as we attempt to gather it up, and resolves itself into a statement of our own utter ignorance, with this consoling reservation, however, that we cannot refer the baffled inquirer to a more enlightened authority than ourselves. It is sufficient for us, humble persons as we are, that, in common with such obscure authors as the said Goethe and Tieck before mentioned, we have found it pleasant, and something more, to place ourselves amidst the times when such fictions could be invented, and amidst the wonder-loving circles among whom they could be narrated, believed, and enjoyed.

The Poetry of Germany : consisting of Selections from upwards of Seventy of the most Celebrated Poets. Translated into English Verse, with the Original Text on the opposite page, by Alfred Baskerville. Leipzig, Mayer; London, Williams & Norgate.

In compiling this neat little volume, which contains selections from upwards of seventy of the most celebrated lyric poets of Germany, the author has effected a double purpose. On the left-hand pages, he gives the German original throughout; on the opposite side his own translations. The book, therefore, will serve either as a good " Poetry-book," for those who do not wander beyond the precincts of their own tongue; or as a fair German Anthology, for those who would commence their acquaintance with a foreign literature by roving lightly through a garden of sweets, instead of dwelling on one particular flower till its treasures are exhausted. Moreover, the English translation, though metrical, is so very close, that the student may derive from it valuable assistance throughout.

In making his translations, Mr. Baskerville has laid down the principle of adhering to the original metres; almost the only licence he allows himself being the substitution of rhymeless terminations to the first and third lines of ballad verses where rhymes are employed in the German. There is no doubt that, unless we adopt the modern French plan of completely sacrificing form to substance, and giving prose versions of even lyric poets, the principle of following the original metre is a sound one. The translator who acts upon it falls instinctively into the habit of making every one of his lines as like as possible to the corresponding line set down by his author; and thus an almost material obstacle is raised against licentious aberration. Every little bit of the work being rendered with regard to closeness, and inevitable superabundance being immediately balanced by extra condensation, fidelity in the whole structure follows with greater certainty,—if we assume competence in the translator. But, if the other course be pursued—if a different measure from that of the original is chosen—the great motive for correctness at every step is taken away, and the instalments of licentiousness are likely to amount to a formidable sum when the work is complete. In the translation of German poetry especially, there can be no excuse for deviation; since the metrical sentiment of the Germans and the English is precisely the same. In the case of French verse an exception may be made; for it is sufficiently shown by the tragedies written in rhymed Alexandrines that the effect of this metre upon the Gallic ear must be totally different from that produced upon the untrained Englishman. The history of the German stage strongly illustrates the relation of the three nations with regard to metres. Deriving their culture, in the first instance, from the French, the earlier German poets wrote their plays in Alexandrines. In this metre, Goethe composed his juvenile works, ' Die Laune des Verliebten' and ' Die Mitschuldigen'; but no sooner did another metre become familiar, than all thought of Alexandrines was banished for ever, and the English blank verse became as completely naturalized on the stage of Weimar as on that of London. Indeed, a German play written in Alexandrines would now look as much a curiosity as ' Gammer Gurton's Needle.'

Mr. Baskerville is most likely to meet opposition to his metrical principle when he carries it out in the case of those antique metres which have become tolerably familiar in Germany, while they have never been adopted in England, save by poetical athletes, who have wished to show off *tours de force* in every variety. On this subject he speaks very sensibly, in a note to his preface, *à propos* of Sir E. B. Lytton's remark, that the English language has no musical analogy to the ancient hexameter and pentameter.—

" We must [says Mr. Baskerville] confess that we do not agree with this opinion. In proof of his assertion, he gives the following celebrated distich of Schiller, as translated by Coleridge :—
In the hexameter rises the fountain's silvery column,
In the pentameter aye falling in melody back.
In our humble opinion he must have an unmusical ear who can discover no music in these lines, which, we think, prove that the English language is equally capable of this metre with the German. It is true, we have had no Schiller, or Goethe, to familiarize our ear with it, though, in later times, Longfellow has done much towards it. Not that we would advocate its frequent introduction into our language, or, indeed, into any other modern language. Germany's great poets have clothed sublime thoughts in hexameter verse, but they have not succeeded in rendering it popular, in the true sense of the word. What German schoolboy, when he has to learn a piece of poetry, chooses one in hexameters? And how many millions know the long ballads of Schiller, Bürger and others by heart? Perhaps the best reason for not making too frequent a use of them is given by Schlegel :
Hexameter zu machen,
Die weder hinken noch krachen,
Das sind nicht Jedermanns Sachen.
Diffident of our own powers, we have ventured to give in this metre only one short elegy of Goethe."

These remarks exactly hit the truth. The question is not whether hexameters and pentameters are to be frequently introduced into our language, or whether they are to be employed in translations of the ancient poets. Before we admit that Voss's plan of translating Homer is the correct one, we must settle the point, that accent in the German tongue performs the same function as quantity in the Greek. Thus much, however, is certain, that the Englishman, if he pleases so to do, has just as much right to substitute accent for quantity as the German; and even if he does not consider himself justified in following Homer, he may surely, without scruple, arrange his accented syllables after the fashion of Goethe or Schiller,—the metrical principle of whose language does not differ from that of his own. As Mr. Baskerville rightly observes, the Germans have never succeeded in rendering the hexameter popular; and there can be no reason why a translator should be more popular than his original. His only business is to follow his author; and, if his author has made a mistake in the adoption of antique metres, he may let the Germans and the manes of the Greeks fight out that matter between them, without troubling himself to rectify the blunder.

The Elegy to which Mr. Baskerville refers is Goethe's first " from Rome,"—and his version runs as follows :—

Speak, ye ruins, to me, O speak, ye sumptuous mansions!
Streets, O speak but a word! Genius, wakest thou not?
All is endowed with a soul within thy reverend precincts,
Rome, the Eternal; and yet silent is all unto me.
Who in mine ear will whisper, where I may, at her lattice,
Greet the beauteous form destined to quicken my soul?
Can I divine not the path, to which I shall ever and ever
Moments so precious devote, going from her to and fro?
Still I gaze on churches, palaces, ruins, and pillars,
As a deliberate man duly each moment employs.
But it soon will be past; then will there be but one temple,
Thine, O Love, whose bright gate will to the worshipper ope.
Thou, O Rome, 'tis true, art a world, yet be but Love absent,
Then were the world not the world, Rome then no longer were Rome.

The above is not very smooth, and altogether, as far as versification is concerned, we like Mr. Baskerville's theory better than his practice. No writer, for instance, is easier to follow than Heine, who counts accents in lieu of syllables, after this fashion :—

Mein Kind, wir waren Kinder,
Zwei Kinder, klein und froh;

> Wir krochen in's Hühnerhäuschen
> Und steckten uns unter das Stroh.

Mr. Baskerville's version of this charming little song,—so typical of Heine's melancholy sportiveness,—is in the best spirit, so far as translation is concerned, but the verse has not the flippant fluency of the original.—

> My child, when we were children,
> Two children little and gay,
> We crept into the hen-roost,
> And hid behind the hay.
>
> We crowed as doth the cock,
> When people passed that road,
> Cried, " Cock-a-doodle-doo!"
> They thought the cock had crowed.
>
> The chests that lay in the court
> We papered and made so clean,
> And dwelt together therein,
> We thought them fit for a queen.
>
> Oft came our neighbour's old cat
> With us an hour to spend,
> We made her curtseys and bows,
> And compliments without end.
>
> And kindly after her health
> We asked her whene'er she came ;
> To many an ancient tabby
> We since have said the same.
>
> We often sat and spoke
> Just like grave, wise old men,
> Complaining, when we were young,
> How all had been better then :
>
> That love, and faith, and truth,
> Were lost in worldly care,
> That coffee was now so dear,
> And money become so rare.
>
> Long past are childhood's sports,
> And onwards all hath whirled,
> Fidelity, love, and faith,
> And money, the times, and the world.

—Why not say in the third verse, " And dwelt therein together"? What ponderosity is given to the fourth verse by the termination " old cat," —which we are almost obliged to pronounce " oldcat" in one word, till we begin to reflect that the author disregards Heine's plan of ending the first and third lines with an unaccented syllable, and then rectify the first reading by treating " neighbour's old" as a heavy dactyl.

These and the like are but trifling blemishes in a really good book, and our objections are in a great measure anticipated by our author, who cites, by way of preparatory defence, Lord Mahon's words—" I would rather bear a faulty rhyme than lose a noble thought." The application of this principle demands, indeed, a special inquiry in each individual case as to whether the noble thought could or could not be preserved without recourse to the faulty rhyme or rhythm.

Mr. Baskerville's collection contains specimens of German lyrical poetry from the time of Hagedorn to the present day,—that is to say, it extends from the birth of the modern Teutonic muse amid fables and such like prettinesses to, her death amid violent politicians, whose Tyrtæan strains smacked of anything but the genuine Hippocrene. An arrangement of the poets into schools has not been attempted ; they have merely been arranged according to priority of birth,—a statement of the births and deaths being given in the alphabetical index. Why he has not adopted the usual classification, Mr. Baskerville does not explain ; nor can we surmise why he omitted to follow the plan of preceding collectors, when the work of arrangement is already done to his hands. Grouping may be, and perhaps always is, defective, for there are generally a number of equivocal wights perched upon boundary lines ;—but, nevertheless, a division of German poets, accordingly as they are " Præ-Goethian," or songsters of the (Karl-) Augustan age, or " Romantiker," or "patriots of the war-time," or decidedly modern, is certainly better than no grouping at all.

The selection of poems, so that they may be typical of their several authors, is altogether fairly made. Goethe and Schiller are repre-

sented by the most orthodox specimens, and the modern poets occupy a due share of the volume,—so that the reader who has fairly gone through the book will be in no state of ignorance as to the lyrical peculiarities of Chamisso, of Heine, of Freiligrath, and the various luminaries who sparkled about them.

In some cases, however, oversights have been made. Novalis is shown in only one poem— ' Bergmannsleben '—whereas certainly the 'Lob des Weins ' should have been introduced, as an additional specimen of that remarkable genius. Rückert's Oriental tendency, as revealed in his gorgeous ' Ghazuls,' has no sign here, unless we accept for a sign the " parable" of the Syrian and his camel, which was previously sung by the old Dutch poet Jacob Cats, and which, though its subject is Eastern, is totally devoid of that arabesque luxuriance which is often so characteristic of Rückert. The melancholy side of poor Lenau,—who is almost regarded as a psychological study by his admirers,—is not exhibited at all, though the following pœm on ' Spring ' is a good specimen of another of his peculiarities, his love of audacious formations.—

> Lo ! Spring advances, lovely boy,
> To whom no heart is mute,
> He comes with tripping step of joy,
> And smiles his sweet salute.
>
> His wanton gambols to display
> He merrily prepares,
> Which he of old was wont to play
> With Winter's hoary hairs.
>
> He frees the little brooklets all,
> What though old Winter scolds,
> Who bound them in his icy thrall,
> And close imprisoned holds.
>
> Already dance the waves away,
> And gossip 'neath the trees,
> They laugh to scorn the tyrant grey
> And his annulled decrees.
>
> It glads the youth to see them play
> And prattle through the field,
> And from each other snatch away
> His image just revealed.
>
> His mother earth smiles on her boy,
> Who wakes her sleeping charms ;
> With raptures of a mother's joy
> She clasps him in her arms.
>
> Her bosom's beauties to disclose
> The youth, with wanton grace,
> Draws forth the violet and rose
> From out their hiding-place.
>
> And his attendant zephyr train
> O'er hill and dale he sends,
> " Ye winds, say I am come again
> To greet my ancient friends !"
>
> He drags o'er many a chasm dark
> With love's soft chain our hearts,
> His singing rocket, too, the lark,
> Into the air he darts.

Seume, on the other hand, though chiefly celebrated as a prose writer, fares remarkably well,—and the version of his tale of ' The Indian' may be declared one of the best executed in the collection, if we concede the point that " fire" is a dissyllable.—

> A Canadian, whose untutored breeding
> Knew not Europe's o'er-refined politeness,
> In whose bosom beat a heart uncultured,
> As to him by God it had been given,
> Brought the quarry he, with haft and sinew,
> Far in Quebeck's icy-mantled forest,
> In the chase had slaughtered to the market.
> When, without all arts of cunning discourse,
> He the rock's wing'd habitant had bartered
> For a trifle, taking what was offered,
> Joyful, with the humble gain, he hastened
> Homewards to his forest-hidden comrades,
> To the arms of his brown-featured consort.
>
> But still distant from his humble cabin,
> Overtook him, 'neath the vault of heaven,
> Suddenly a dread and fearful tempest ;
> From his drooping locks of raven blackness
> Downwards poured the stream upon his girdle,
> And the coarse, rough hair-cloth of his garment
> Cleaved unto his body's meagre members.
> Shudd'ring, quaking in the chilly torrent,
> Sped with hasty step the doughty savage
> Towards a house that from afar invited.
> " Let me, Sir, until the storm assuages,
> " 'Neath your roof enjoy a friendly shelter !"—
> Speaking to the mannered, well-bred owner.
> Thus did he beseech with heartfelt gesture,
> " Wilt thou hence, thou misshaped, hated monster?
> " Hence ! begone ! thou and thy thievish visage !"
> Cried the planter with fierce anger's accents,
> Seizing the stout oaken staff beside him.

> Sad and mournful, strode the honest Huron
> Forth from this inhospitable threshold,
> Through the storm and rain, till evening's shadows
> Oped to him his peaceful wigwam dwelling,
> And his dark-skinned spouse's fond embraces.
> Wet and weary, couching by the fire,
> With his naked little ones around him,
> He related of the busy cities,
> Of the warriors who hurl their thunder,
> Of the fearful tempest that o'ertook him,
> And the cruel treatment of the pale face.
> On his knees they hung with soft caresses,
> Clinging to his neck with infant fondness,
> Dried the long and dripping raven tresses,
> Eagerly the hunter's pouch examined,
> Till at length they found the promised treasure.
>
> Ere long time elapsed, our planter, hunting,
> Lost his path, and wandered in the forest.
> Over bush and brake, o'er stream and valley,
> Many a mountain steep with toil ascending,
> Hoping thus the pathway to discover
> Which into this wilderness had led him.
> But in vain he gazed, in vain he shouted ;
> Nought he heard, except the hollow echo
> Roll along the black rock's lofty ridges.
> Anxiously he toil'd till midnight's hour,
> When beneath the mountain height before him
> He beheld a light, that feebly glimmered.
> Fear and pleasure in his bosom throbbing,
> Softly he approached with rising courage.
> " Who is there ?" with fear awaking accents,
> Cried a voice, deep in the hollow cavern,
> And a man stepped from the lowly dwelling.
> " Friend, I've lost my pathway in the forest,"
> Cried with soothing voice the trembling planter ;
> " Let me here repose my weary members
> " For this night ; (thanks I to thee will render,)
> " And to-morrow guide me to the city."
>
> " Enter, Enter !" answered the unknown one,
> " Warm thyself, still glow the fire's embers ;"
> And he led him to a couch of rushes,
> Strode then gloomily into the corner,
> Takes the remnants of his evening supper,
> Lobster, fresh-cured ham of bear, and salmon
> To regale his midnight-guest a-hungered.
> With the keenness of a hunter feasted,
> As though at a convent's festive table,
> Gaily near his host the European.
> Steadfastly and gravely gazed the Huron
> On his guest, and scanned the stranger's features,
> Who with deep-cut trench the ham divided,
> And with rapture quaffed the mead of honey,
> From a shelly goblet deep and spacious,
> Which his host to cheer the meal had proffered.
> Yielding moss beneath a spreading bear-skin
> Was the planter's couch, where he in slumber
> Rested till the sun was high in heaven.
>
> Like the desert region's wildest war-chief,
> Fearful stood with quiver, bow, and arrow,
> Now the Huron at the stranger's pillow,
> Woke him, and the European, starting,
> Stretched his hand to grasp his faithful rifle ;
> But a bowl to him the savage tendered,
> Brimming o'er with morning's draught so grateful.
> When he with a smile the meal had proffered,
> Winding through the wilderness, he led him
> Over bush and brake, o'er stream and valley
> Through the thicket to the city's pathway.
> With politeness thanked the European ;
> Darkly frowning stood the silent Huron,
> Fixed his steadfast eye upon the planter,
> With a firm and earnest voice thus speaking,
> " Have we not before beheld each other ?"
> As by lightning struck the hunter started,
> In his host that man now recognizing,
> Whom some weeks before himself had driven
> From his threshold, while the storm was raging,
> And confused he stammered forth excuses.
> " See, ye cunning, clever, pale-faced strangers,
> " We savages know more of human feeling !"
> With these words he struck into the forest.

This rhymeless trochaic measure, which we had recently occasion to notice, in the case of a living poet, Paul Heyse [*Athen.* No. 1403] is so smooth and flowing, and so well adapted to the purpose of easy narrative, that we somewhat wonder it has not been adopted in this country. Perhaps an objection may be found in its monotony.

We have not scrupled to point out what we have deemed slight blemishes in Mr. Baskerville's book ; but we would conclude by recommending it both as a readable collection of poems and as a useful introduction to German poetical literature.

Art. III.—(1.) *Geschichte der Deutschen National Literatur im neunzehnten Jahrhundert.* Von Julian Schmidt. 2 Bände. Leipzig. 1853.

(2.) *Uriel Acosta.* Drama. Von Karl Gutzkow.

(3.) *Neues Leben. Eine Erzählung.* Von Berthold Auerbach.

(4.) *Studien.* Von Adelbert Stifter. 6 Bände.

(5.) *Ruhe ist die erste Bürgerpflicht, oder vor fünfzig Jahren Vaterländischer Roman.* Von W. Alexis. Berlin: 1852.

It was with a feeling of extreme satisfaction that we closed the two volumes which are placed at the head of this article. A satisfaction, be it observed, arising not from the fact of the history being ended, but from the conclusion at which we had arrived respecting Mr. Schmidt as having successfully accomplished a laborious task. A book must be very readable when, as in the present case, one turns over the eleven hundredth page with a feeling of regret that it should be the last. All honour to the labours of Gervinus, in his eight ponderous volumes; but honour also to the persevering reader of the same. Such an achievement is only to be realized, or at least enjoyed, by restricting his demands upon our time to small quantities, and to these at considerable intervals. It does not then so naturally appear to us to be the production of a being of some profoundly learned species, whose only link of connexion with our imbecile world, is such as must exist between the critic and his victim.

Respecting the personality of Mr. Schmidt we confess our ignorance, at the same time being, however, very firmly persuaded of his humanity. We feel instinctively assured of his possessing sympathies in common with other mortals, which expand themselves at festive seasons, gala days, and about Christmas trees; and that he rejoices in a larger acquaintance and means of observation than fell to the lot of the German professor of happy memory, who was never known to speak with any one but the printer's devil and an antiquated violin. We are, moreover, persuaded of another fact, which we would not hastily advance concerning many German scholars, namely, that Mr. Schmidt undoubtedly once was young. In all the humane and scientific sports which ever have been, and ever will be, the joy of rising generations, our philosopher must surely have excelled his liveliest companions. That faculty of keen analysis, which he now turns to such literary service, must have developed itself with great advantage in the anatomy of frogs and mice, the incarceration of beetles, or in investigations into the organization of doll's heads—delights common to the genus,

boy, on either side the German Ocean. But a truce to idle speculations, which have suggested themselves not unnaturally from that genial and manly tone of Mr. Schmidt's book, which indicates a warmth and vigour of heart, reconciling us to the severity of his criticism. His censure, as well as his praise, is scientific, straightforward, and impartial; the result of high literary culture and honest love of truth. As an account of the modern literature of Germany, his work is by far the most satisfactory which has yet appeared. The Romantic and Young Germany schools are treated with greater fullness and clearness than we find in Gervinus, with less of sprightly caprice than in Menzel, and with more poetry and rhetoric than in Vilmar—as that gentleman has seen fit, in his eloquent volumes, almost to ignore the existence of these two branches of modern literature. At the same time, the work of Professor Vilmar, though not widely known in this country, has been more extensively read in Germany than almost any other.[*] Its learning is indisputable, and the treatment of the earlier periods of German literature such as to bring those very distant days vividly before the reader. His heart is, if anywhere, in that part of the book. All that is vague and distant, aristocratic and imposing, has especial charms for Professor Vilmar. He warms the shadows into life, and becomes himself poetical and eloquent. Often, indeed, his mystical enthusiasm carries him away to that adjacent German land of '*schwärmerei*,' where the most sentimental of English readers must wander in amazement among the interminable clauses; only too happy when he succeeds in finding the right ' verb at the end,' or, better still, the end of the verbs. The amount of supernumerary adjectives alone, apart from compounds and separate particles, one would almost imagine could hardly be achieved, except perhaps upon the plan of giving each page to a secretary, with injunctions to take a large dictionary, and supply each aristocratic adjective with a becoming retinue of precisely, or very nearly, the same signification. Supposing this to have been the case, we bear hearty testimony to the zealous discharge of duty on the part of the secretary.

It is not for us to pronounce respecting the reasons which disposed Professor Vilmar to notice in so cursory a manner the later poets and prose writers of Germany. Körner is despatched in a page and a half, Rückert, Platen, and Immermann in two pages. The followers of the Schlegel dramatic school in little more than one page, and so on. The last two and twenty pages might as well have been omitted, and the work, ending with Jean Paul, have made no pretensions to discuss the merits of modern

* Mr. Schmidt, however, makes no mention of the book.

writers. There is, however, one powerful reason which might fully account for the entire omission of the Young Germany school. Surely it would be too unreasonable to expect that the stilted aristocrat in politics, the transcendental mystic in religion, should stoop to chronicle the works of democrats and of free-thinkers! The fair paragraphs of the Professor about "the people," "the poetry of the people," "the latent energy of the people," are emphatically paragraphs. Worse than mere words, they are hollow cant and mockery from the man who is a right hand in the councils of the Prince of Hesse Cassel; whose intellect and energy, since 1848, have been especially directed toward the counteraction of all efforts for the elevation and emancipation of the people. It would seem that his idea of the German nation is so exalted that he sees no room for improvement. And it is, further, not surprising that Heine and Gutzkow should find no place within his aristocratic pages, since many a man, with less extended influence, and less obnoxious views, owes it in part to Professor Vilmar that his life is one of toil and exile. It is not very long since we remember expressing to an able editor and writer in North Germany, our regret that Vilmar's history admitted of no translation into English, but would require to be recast, in order to become popular among us. He replied, 'What would I not give if Vilmar were but in reality *translated* into your English territory;' a *bon mot* whose sincerity atoned for any lack of brilliancy, it being uttered in a solitary farm-house, where the speaker found a shelter in his way of escape from the satellites of Hesse Cassel, his course being to cross the Luneburg Heath to Hamburgh, and thence to London.

In this country we are better acquainted with the lively but unsystematic history of Wolfgang Menzel, with its sweeping assertions and partial criticisms, than with Vilmar. During his editorship of the *Morgenblatt*, Menzel directed, through that channel, a most remorseless cannonade against the writers of the Young Germany school. The public authorities rubbed their eyes, in lingering amazement; and, on the 10th of December, 1835, solemnly and officially declared this school of literature to be one 'whose exertions obviously tended in all branches of its 'literary development, to assail, without reverence, the Christian 'religion, to despise existing relations of society, and to under-'mine all order and morality.'

We will not in this place question the justice of such a sentence, nor the expediency of an interference in literary matters, on the part of the German *Bundestag;*—an interference which, as might be anticipated, accomplished nothing.

The gradual rise of this school was the fruit of reaction against the growing influence of the Romanticists. In all essential points this contrast is very marked. The staunch conservativism of Tieck and Novalis, as compared with the ultra-liberalism of Gutzkow and Heine, the one school extolling a religious devotion almost superstitious, the other upholding atheism or universal scepticism. The poetry of the Romanticist is nature idealised and worshipped. Doubt, with its restless, never-answered torture, inspires the passionate poetry of the young Germanists. Their unwearying complaint rings like the startled echo from every cliff and glen. Their epic heroes are each one a Faust, while their impassioned lyrics often are like

'Infants crying for the light,
And with no language but a cry.'

In the palmy days of the Romanticists, every man did what was good in his own eyes, a state of affairs which could not reasonably be expected to last. The demon of criticism arose from the slumber which had succeeded his campaign under Gottsched; rose, moreover, no longer as a drilled and subservient aid-de-camp, but as a veritable King Stork. Small authors he snapped up entirely, without change of countenance; others were delicately tortured and dissected previous to immolation; so that writers at last learned to anticipate the possible fact that their works might be judged from two opposite points of view; but which view it might be the mood of the monster to take remained an anxious question until the hour of doom arrived. Hence we find throughout the literature of that Restoration period, as it is called, that the authors have acquired and naturalised a habit of glossing over their sentiment with irony, and sentimentalising over the ridiculous. To escape the critic they would soften satire into pathos, or crystallize their very tears into a witticism. They adopt ideas and feelings as their own, to which they give no place or credence, and often stifle those convictions which they hold with most sincerity.

This state of alternating fusion and conflict resulted in that strange and transitory phenomenon of literature characterised by the Germans as *Weltschmerz*—the poetry of universal suffering. Within its ranks, lamentably numerous for the time being, were the vague half-formed characters who with sudden energy would stake their lives for some one faith or object, the next moment swear by the very opposite, and finally sink into the hopeless victims of a feverish indecision. Among these we may mention in passing the names of Platen, Immermann, Rückert, Schefer, and Carl Möricke. Respecting the latter, we may observe, for the benefit of those whom it may concern, that his novelette of *Maler Nolten* is one of the very best among modern German tales.

The pages which Mr. Schmidt devotes to the merits and demerits of the explosive squib and cracker school of Young Germany are most impartial and most wise. It is a school that, with all its bluster, never could learn anything by experience, never could reach a riper age, never could attain to completeness in anything concerning opinions, characters, or works of art. Its founders and supporters are still in all their vigour, or have just turned towards the night side of life, but the school itself has died out in the full bloom of its extravagance; and what next? Neither you nor we, most learned or inquiring reader, would care to hazard a reply. We cannot venture speculation on the ornamental sugar work of Oscar Redwitz. We shall, moreover, allow our author to speak concerning this school before we proceed to glance at the class of prose fictions which seems for the present to be superseding the ambiguous splendour of these meteoric appearances.

'It must not be supposed,' says Mr. Schmidt, 'that the tendency and style of Young Germany was anything essentially new. All that we have already said in our analysis of Tieck's novelettes may be applied, word for word, as characteristic of Young Germany, with the exception that the delicately-balanced tone of the romanticist poet was distorted into coarseness and caricature. In the same manner the influence of Jean Paul is to be traced on every page. We find the same chaotic mixture of all possible provinces of thought and emotion, of all conceivable forms of poetry and prose, and embellished, moreover, by that dialectic skill in the invention of extraordinary modes of view, which were attributed to the traditions of Hegel, and the frivolous, farcical manner of Heine. But the most singular phenomenon is the imitation of Goethe's *Geheimrath* style. The respectable old gentleman who in earlier days passed through every nobler passion with all the ardour of youth, may experience in his later years a gradual growth of disposition so resigned, that things significant have no more claim upon him than the unimportant; but with young poets, who ought in all their vigour to grapple with the life before them, such an assumption is most obviously ridiculous.' * * *

'To the above peculiarities must be added an unlimited self-appreciation, the belief in some unheard-of mission in the history of human progress, combined with an absolute helplessness respecting what new thing it is which they really have to offer to the world; combined further with a readiness to fall in with every whim or temper of the public, to catch each audible sign of public opinion, in order thus to gain such subject matter as shall easily receive the stamp of originality, conveyed in ironic touches and paradoxical conclusions. We find also everywhere assertions maintained with a confident audacity, not unfrequently accompanied by unheard-of ignorance. From the first to the last of their writings, they have failed in all attempts to despatch any question demanding accurate knowledge or logical acuteness. But on the other side they well understand how to introduce, along with the question in hand a host of observations which certainly have no more connexion with the said question than existed between the cosmogonistic learning of Ephraim Jenkinson, in the Vicar of Wakefield, and the innocent remarks to which he appended it, but which nevertheless plainly serve to show the intercourse one has with learned and gifted people. They, however, excel Jenkinson in the skill with which they conceal their ignorance behind an invulnerable breastwork of newly-coined and newly-combined words, which frequently have no proper signification, but over which one lingers, pondering whether the writer may not have perhaps intended to say something.'

'All these remarks are not intended to characterise a definite number of authors, but rather the tendency (*ton*) which has been generally prevalent in our polite literature since the days of July. In the selection of persons who should compose this Young Germany, chance has had the principal hand, and even among those writers who bear most resemblance to each other, their common object was the result of no plan. Individual vanity loosened the links even of coterie, and the *Bundestag* had scarcely branded them as disturbers of the peace, when they attacked one another with a passion which sometimes transgressed the boundary of good taste.'—Vol. ii., pp. 55—59.

The names of Börne and Heine are those which stand at the head of this school. Their labours were cotemporary, and had, in the main, the same object. With all the vigour and acuteness of Jewish intellect, they broke upon the tranquil waters of literature which had stagnated beneath the empty elegance or the confused philosophy of its too polished priesthood. The influential position to which Börne attained, is to be traced to the general spontaneous appreciation or over estimate of his talents, rather than to ambitious efforts of his own. In this respect he differs from the whole school. The bold straightforward way in which he said what he had to say upon literature and politics, produced a powerful impression, and raised him in public estimation, very far above the misty sophistry which was afloat on all sides, and gave him the most extensive influence over the youth of Germany. Börne (1817-1837) was the foundation stone of German democracy, while the influence of Heine extended itself comparatively little beyond the refined and educated circles. Respecting Heine, Mr. Schmidt speaks at some length, and we cannot but translate a few of his excellent paragraphs :—

'In order to estimate the value of the poems of Heine, we must first of all distinguish the good from the bad. It has not unfrequently happened that Heine's very worst poems have met with the greatest success, and that in speaking of Heine's style these immediately suggest themselves. It is to those songs of sensibility and universal suffering, with some humorous termination, that Heine owes his popularity.

'In the good poems the contrast to Uhland is not so great as one might at first sight imagine. It is true that in the choice of emotion and of character he exhibits much greater freedom. He has passed out of simple melody, and with practised hand harmonises the varied chords. But the songs which have most charm for the composer are more luxuriant and blooming than those of Uhland. The species, however, is the same, since the difference is not very essential which puts the Indian lotus in place of the wild pansy of the Swabian ballads, modern poets with chaotic emotions in the place of mediæval knights and shepherds, the hectic daughter of pleasure in the place of the veiled spouse of heaven.

'The first progress to be observed is in the rhythm. It is as beautiful as that of Goethe and Uhland, and there is no other poet who can be ranked beside these three. But it is also more passionately thrilling, more vigorous and prompt to seize the mastery of the soul. With Goethe the charm lies in the harmony of a beautiful soul; with Uhland in the unity of the emotion, in the modesty of the measure, and in the correctness of the form; with Heine it is the strange undulation of passion, which carries away the soul even against its will.

'The second fact is the subjectivity of the point of view selected by the poet. The material in itself is not more modern than with Goethe or Uhland; on the contrary, the best of his songs have almost exclusively to do with romantic subjects. But he knows how to rouse the feeling of contrast, and by means of perspective, of apportionment of light and shadow, of a colouring vivid though not always correct, he throws a life into his figures which has a sort of intoxicating charm. With Goethe we have only the individual emotion, with Uhland we are lost in the fanciful subject, with Heine we feel the power of contrast.　　*　　*　　*　　*

'Perhaps the most brilliant side of his talent is reality in drawing. By this we do not understand the tendency to bring all possible subjects, even the unattractive and the repulsive, into the province of poetry. That is a very ambiguous merit, and has, moreover, somewhat of artifice and constraint. The horizon of his imagination is by no means very extended. Apart from the romantic subjects which reading places at his disposal: from the nightingales, the air of spring, the sunshine and moonlight, the different love scenes, all of which cannot be said to be peculiarly novel, he has conquered no new poetic subject save the North Sea and its somewhat monotonous phenomena, the sea-gulls, the surf, the sailors. It is in the form of representation that the reality lies. With slight, scarcely perceptible strokes he brings out a life and character which the memory involuntarily retains, and which resembles nothing either in Goethe or in Uhland.

'His poetry is a chaos, in which the worlds celestial and subterranean are mingled in wild confusion. The sweetest fragrance and the desolate scent of death are combined in a narcotic atmosphere, which leads the senses away captive. In this romantic direction his principal work is, perhaps, the *Atta Troll*. The poet, wet through in hunting, lies in a restless half slumber, in a witch's kitchen, stupefied with strange odours. He hears the witch monotonously murmuring while she rubs the body of her dead son with an ointment which gives him an apparent life. On all sides are distorted bird's faces, gazing mysteriously at him, and as he for one moment really sleeps, he sees in a vision a grotesque dance of bears and ghosts.

'This is a picture of Heine's poetry generally. The inner root of this romantic irony reminds us of Schlegel, Tieck, and Novalis, but the carrying of it out bears more resemblance to the younger romanticists, Arnim, Brentano, and Hoffmann. Heine, however, gave forms of real life, where they only purposed so to do. The elements are the same, but the imagination of Heine is far more bold, vigorous, and offensive. The above mentioned scene in *Atta Troll*, and similar ones in *Romancero* are brilliant variations to the theme of the *Golden Pot.*

'Heine calls his *Atta Troll* in the dedication to Varnhagen, 'the last forest lay of romanticism.'. And this justly, since the only road left open to romanticism was to laugh at the mysteries at which it had before shuddered: a progressive step which the pedantry of Friedrich Schlegel prevented him from taking. Heine not only scared away the ghost of romanticism, but remodelled it into a humorous ideal, which stood in need only of an artistic finish. His fancy is a kaleidoscope, in which the blue flower of the romanticist and the wit of the encyclopædist, the red flag of the republic and the golden sheen of the lily, the spirit of the beautiful Herodias and the hovel of the witch, the fervour of a hollow cheeked Werther and the successes of the satiated banker, who would ask even of Lotte, 'What does it cost?' are all thrown together in most capricious combination. But it never leads to a complete figure or a continuous frame of mind. The reason of this may be found partly in his defective composition, which is an organic failing in his artistic conformation, partly also in his raillery, which, allied as it is to his dread of being convicted of genuine permanent emotion, leads him sometimes into the greatest absurdities.'—pp. 36, 37.

There is another living writer belonging to this school whose works merit longer notice than we are able to bestow. Carl Gutzkow* was born at Berlin, in 1811, and seems to have been writing ever since. With all his activity, however, he remains as uncertain, unreliable, and vain, as he was twenty years ago. 'In

* 'Maha Guru;' 'Wally die Zweiflerin;' 'Blasedow und seine Söhne;' 'Die Schul der Reichen;' 'Patkul;' 'Der Königslieutenant;' 'Antonio Perez,' &c.; 'Die Ritter vom Geist, 9 Bände.'

' his views, opinions, hopes, and wishes, he becomes every moment
' a different person; he is not only destitute of all moral purpose,
' of all objective self-sacrificing interest, but destitute also of all
' passion.' Gutzkow's literary career commenced in the critical
journals, and branched off into tales, dramas, and novels. His
drama of *Uriel Acosta*, published in 1846, created for the time
a *furore* upon the German stage, and is undoubtedly the most
successful of his dramatic efforts. There is less sentiment, less
bombast, and less striving after effect. The hero, of course, does
not know his mind particularly well, but that being a defect inherited from his author, we pass it by. The story opens where
Uriel, a Jew, is on the eve of departure from Amsterdam, to
escape threatened persecutions on the score of certain freethinking sentiments just published by him. At the same time
he is in love with a rich and gifted Jewess, whose hand, of course,
has been arbitrarily bestowed in childhood on a certain Ben
Jochai, whom she neither knows nor loves. Uriel's book is declared by the synagogue to be contrary to the doctrines of
Judaism, and on his despising the only chance of safety offered
by confessing himself a Christian, the curse of the church is pronounced against him. Judith, who knows her own mind on one
point at least, is undaunted by ecclesiastical threatenings, and
bravely takes the side of Uriel. The wealthy Manasse, Judith's
father, receives Uriel into his house, and even promises him the
hand of his daughter if he became reconciled to the synagogue.
This can only happen by a recantation, which, under the pressure
of many friends and reasons, he is at last prevailed upon to
make. Meanwhile, the crafty Ben Jochai seeks his revenge by
accomplishing the bankruptcy of Manasse, at the same time promising to bring matters straight again, if his bride be restored.
Judith resolves upon the sacrifice. The last act of this drama
opens with the wedding feast, Judith gives her hand, but has taken
poison. During the ceremony, Uriel has aimed a pistol, through
the window, at Ben Jochai, but, with truly Gutzkowian indecision, changes his mind, and delivers a very dramatic oration instead; he walks off the stage, and a shot is heard. So endeth
the piece,—the curtain falls. Stout German papas leave the
theatre yawning dangerously, saying, 'Stuff!' and hoping there is
herring-salad at home for supper; intellectual daughters murmur
long and laudatory adjectives, and, in tears, refuse the salad!
Mr. Schmidt shrugs his discriminating shoulders, and pens many
wise pages which one should read in order directly to weigh the
praise and blame conveyed in a sentence which pronounces verdict on the *best* of Gutzkow's dramas.

Büchner, Grabbe, Zedlictz, Halm, Meissner, and Laube* are also
to be found among the latest dramatic writers. The latter exceeds
others of the school in his adherence to the Heine and French models.
His most successful drama was undoubtedly the 'Karlschüler,'
in which Schiller is the hero. The Duke of Wirtemberg is represented as a most amiable gentleman, who, nevertheless, exhibits a
very sanguinary desire to cut off the poet's head on account of his
obnoxious writings. Herr Devrient acted to perfection in this
piece, aided no doubt by the felicitous conformation of his nose,
which looked like Schiller's own! Of George Büchner, Mr.
Schmidt speaks thus. 'Is it probable, that had a longer life been
' granted to Büchner, he would have worked his way to more
' manly and healthy views, to a purer poetry? We believe he
' would have done so. In spite of his youth, he excels almost all
' the poets of his school in talent as well as in depth of feeling.
' Yet it is impossible to arrive at any certainty. There is in his
' mode of thought something so prematurely finished; not only
' when he plays the sceptic, but even when he goes into raptures
' there is so little of youth about them that one can scarcely pic-
' ture what the result would be of further development. He must
' always have remained within the ranks of the reflective poets—
' poets whose thought, keen and cold, borders upon the myste-
' rious mist of madness. Hebbel gives us the completed image
' of that principle which with Büchner remained only a tendency.'
—Vol. ii., p. 220.

Among the many thankless offices which have their place upon
this ungrateful globe of ours, that of the political novelist should
certainly be ranked. What he may gain in popularity on the one
hand he is sure to lose on the other. Any favourable representation of the sentiments entertained by Mr. A. and his party, cannot fail to rouse the warmest spite in the heart of Mr. B. and his
adherents. The individual bias of each reader will give a different
colouring to all the facts and opinions, however fairly and candidly
set forth. Everybody will have some darling crotchety idea which
makes it a matter of solemn duty with him to abuse or to extol
the author. Great cause for thankfulness has he that his place is
not behind the easy chair of the impulsive reader who in indignation

* Grabbe. (1801—1836). 'Don Juan und Faust;' 'Die Hohenstauffen;'
'Napoleon,' &c.
Zedlitz. (1790). 'Der Stern von Sevilla;' 'Turturel;' 'Tolltenkränze.'
Halm (1806). 'Grisedis;' 'Der Alchymist,' &c.
Laube. (1806). 'Monaldeschi;' 'Rococo;' 'Die Karlschüler;' 'Die Bern-
steinhex,' &c.
Büchner. (1816—1837). 'Danton's Tod;' 'Leonce und Lena,' &c.
Meissner. 'Das Weib Urias;' 'Reginald Armstrong,' &c.

and warm slippers, dashes pencil marks and notes of interrogation, broad and black with ire and party spirit, at those fine and forcible passages which he had fondly hoped would disarm all criticism. Believe us, gentle reader, there is but one thing more unrelenting than the critic—it is the politician! This sort of literature will be found from various causes to abound more largely in our own country than in any other. In Germany the appearance of politics within the province of fiction has been more confined to cautious side-thrusts, or, in later days, to a rare brochure from Heine or Bruno Bauer. Since 1848, however, political novels have been greatly on the increase. Politics themselves then became of universal interest. The liberal feeling of the country has ceased to be in the hands of an extreme minority. They have acquired no great politicians, indeed, but what is better, perhaps, a wider and more philosophical view of their position and responsibilities as individuals towards their country. The tumult of 1848 disturbed thousands in the heavy sleep of ignorance; little wonder that lacking presence of mind to breast the danger and carry their point, they only groped helplessly for light until the fair occasion was passed. But the nation has already grown incalculably wiser, and the next grand drama scene will scarcely end like the Chinese tragedy—in all being very much frightened. Political life is there comparatively young, and its grim nurse absolutism takes good care that it shall not run alone too soon, or become strong and vigorous by healthy action. Still it does grow, and there are many sober men in Germany, both Constitutionalists and Republicans, who labour most earnestly in the few channels left open to them, in rousing the mind of the people generally to a spirit of inquiry and self-reliance. And these efforts, though hampered on every side, will one day show their fruit. It is not teaching that is required, but animation and action. The education of the lower orders in many parts of Germany is known to be systematic and pedantic to the last degree. A lifeless stereotyping process, beginning with the name of the reigning prince and ending in the dry confirmation lessons, which set the seal of perpetual retrogression upon the children—inasmuch as they are from that day looked upon as finished men and women.

But we must return to Mr. Gutzkow and his nine-volume novel, upon which a few words must content our readers, the more especially as it is one of those books we never could make up our mind to read through. We did one day become brave enough to go into a shop and ask for it; the shopman ominously reached down eight volumes, the conclusion was yet to follow! *Die Ritter vom Geist*, is emphatically a political novel, and at the time of its appearance it became an amusing employment to infer the politics of different individuals solely from their opinion of Mr. Gutzkow's performance. In his preface, the author states his intention of presenting a complete picture of the social and political state of Germany; its rottenness and its latent good. It appears, however, that no one party has ever been willing to recognise its own portrait. The author's plan for the regeneration of the country by means of a knighthood of intellect, savours, as Mr. Schmidt justly observes, greatly too much of Romanticist and Young Germany coterieism, and is moreover in itself utterly absurd. The characters crowded into the book are linked together by an elaborate plot, including a lawsuit. Gutzkow has no power to idealize, he states plain facts or events, and proceeds to draw from them philosophical conclusions. He is, perhaps, true to life and character as he himself sees it, but his view is not unlike that presented through an unsteady telescope. His republican aristocrats drinking beer with day-labourers, and waited on by liveried lacqueys, give no true picture of the German aristocracy; neither does the man in the dirty carter's blouse, talking socialism and drinking champagne, fitly represent a German democrat. The men of all political creeds whose judgment in such matters is of most weight, agree in condemning this lengthy undertaking, both in its plan and execution.

The last novel of Berthold Auerbach, *Neues Leben*, has a similar though less ambitious object in view. Auerbach does not take us much beyond his especial province of village life. His cordial, homely dialect, seems to bring bodily before us the bony, red-cheeked and red-skirted peasant women, and the rough figures of the men, also more curious than picturesque. Still it appears to us a grave error to put into their mouths clever, pointed speeches, which though perhaps clothed in some familiar image, can be the result only of cultivation and of a power of analogy, little natural to a peasant brought up upon catechism and sauerkraut. The main idea of the story is as follows. Eugen Count Falkenberg is the son of a German prince. His liberal sentiments expose him to the wrath of the government; and as a military officer, taking part with the insurgents in 1848, imprisonment and sentence of death are the result. He makes his escape from prison, and in passing through a forest meets with a young schoolmaster on his way to his new post in the neighbouring village. This youth has an ardent longing toward America, where his sister is married to a refugee. Eugen has with him a passport, procured with great difficulty, in order to accomplish his own further escape to America, this he exchanges for the documents of the schoolmaster. The newly-made friends part the same evening equally well-pleased with their bargain.

Eugen spends a short time in a village through which he has to pass, and there makes the acquaintance of Deeger, who is also schoolmaster. He is a manly, energetic character, to whom Eugen readily attaches himself. Here he also first meets with the beautiful and talented Baroness Stephanie. This is also a thoroughly well-drawn character, charming us with her eccentricities and sprightliness of conversation. Her republicanism has just such an air of fashionable whim as one would expect to find in a person who has learnt it all from superficial books, and her own lively imagination. She is a fair sample of the clever, amiable woman, spoiled by the false culture and Gallic affectations of a small German court. In Erlenmoos, the scene of Eugen's labours, narrow prejudice is rife on all sides. Kaidl, the former master, is a blustering demagogue, on the eve of emigration to America. With talent and energy ill-directed, the whole force of his character wasted in dreams of the 'blissful democracy' which his countrymen have allowed to slip from their grasp, he spends his latest hours in ridiculing the country with a party of peasants at the village inn. Here Eugen finds him, and, anxious to counteract the bad effects of his spiteful extravagances, gains the applause of the audience by an appropriate application of the old story of the man who could not learn what fear was.

'You know,' began Eugen, 'the history of the man who set out to learn the art of fearing, and could not succeed until a barrel of cold water and dead fishes was poured over him. In the same way a man once travelled through a country, full of confidence in the people, and tried to learn fear. He came to a race in bonds and servitude, and as they looked at him and gnashed their teeth, he said, ' I am not afraid; these will save themselves.' He came to another, and amid all their degradation, their pride was inconceivable, and he said, ' I am not afraid, these will learn wisdom.' He came to a third which was silent and despairing, and he said, 'I am not afraid, salvation may come out of despair!' At last he came to a race which mocked and scorned itself and its future, then he cried, 'Now have I learnt fear, for these are lost.'

The difficulties and discouragements of Eugen are not a few. His chief motives for selecting his present position in preference to the freedom of the other hemisphere, is a well-grounded conviction, not a sentimental *idea*, that the salvation of the country from its corroding evils must be effected by means of individual effort. To teach this directly or indirectly must be the daily and self-denying labour of the educated. In furtherance of this view he resolves to devote his life to the practical working of it in a village school. The littleness and selfishness of the peasants, the roughness and stupidity of the children, are difficulties which he over-

comes with praiseworthy endurance and skill. Dangers also threaten him from his position under a false name, as a fugitive and sentenced to death, still these have wonderfully little effect upon him, and by no means interfere with his growing attachment to the miller's daughter, the high-minded handsome Vittore. Simplicity without insipidity is so charming a rarity in real life, and so seldom well-drawn in fiction, that her portrait is most refreshing. The plot of the story is purely absurd, and the great failure of the book arises from the mistake of burdening the hero with two ruling motives, while he would have commanded treble-fold our esteem had he been simply patriotic and less theoretically filial. We have in it a specimen of the faults as well as the excellencies of Auerbach—especially his love for detail, and his fatal skill in throwing a charm around separate incidents or ideas, to the great detriment of the unity of his subject.

This last remark leads us naturally to the writings of Adelbert Stifter, who is supremely the poet of detail. Great things and little things with him appear to have no comparative relation. He is, indeed, sometimes in danger of mistaking the one for the other. Of his *Studien*, the first and fifth volume, we believe, have been translated by Mrs. Howitt, in the *Parlour Library*. These are, perhaps, the most beautiful, with the exception of the delightful story of the *Two Sisters*. Another story, also charming in its simplicity, is *My Grandfather's Portfolio*; it is, however, in our judgment, only fit to be read in the dog-days, when one enjoys any subject verging on Greenland or the North Pole. Imagine nearly two hundred pages describing with frigid pertinacity all conceivable phases of frost and thaw through which the adventurous hero drives to his scattered patients, until he is at last stopped on the borders of a forest sheeted in ice. Here the slowly advancing thaw crashes the fretted roof of ice down through the stiffened branches with loud bursts of sound, greatly surpassing those we hear when we suppose the bull to make his onset upon a china shop. The doctor prudently turns back, puts up his horses, dons his skates, and slides away home over hill and valley, with the rain laying upon him in sheets of ice as it fell. We could after that never doubt the good man's right to be a hero, even though he did not marry the heroine, which, however, he has happily sufficient etiquette to do. Stifter's writings bear resemblance to Hawthorne's *House of the Seven Gables*, though without its gloom, more than to almost any other book we know. It is the same mosaic work of small facts. Not the severe analysis of thought and emotion common to much of our modern fiction; there is, indeed, little of reflection, everything is stated baldly or poetically as the case may be. The reader may yawn involuntarily but still finds an indescribable charm which binds him to the volume. He even reaches the close triumphantly, without being reduced to merely skimming the tops of the paragraphs.

The writings of Walter Scott as they became known in Germany, had gradually effected a transition from the tale and novelette of the romanticist class, to the full and systematic novel. French and English fictions dealt also in more tangible subjects than readers were accustomed to meet with, and although possibly somewhat foreign to their own experiences, they were less so than stories of such abstract creations as might have their homes with equal probability on the planet Jupiter or on the Earth. Bulwer and George Sand have raised their legion of followers. Among all the imitators of Scott the most success ful has undoubtedly been Willibald Alexis.* It is well known that his first novel of *Walladmor* was long held to be from the pen of Scott. He is an author who accommodates himself with skill to any form of composition, and passed on from sketches into the historic novel. For a time he yielded to the prevalent Young Germany epidemic, and under its influence wrote his *Haus Düsterweg*. To call him the Walter Scott of Germany implies too high a compliment; to rank him with G. P. R. James, would be to lessen a well-earned reputation and under-value his real merit. The parallel is admissible in so far that Alexis has chosen his subjects of various date and interest —that his books have succeeded each other in rapid succession, and have met with eager purchasers and readers; here, however, it ceases. Alexis does not possess the descriptive power of Scott, and mercifully spares us the descriptive tedium of James. The characters speak and act, hence alone we infer their state of mind. His plots are either clumsy or too transparent beside those of Scott, but opaque in comparison with those of James, with whom they are so much alike, that a new novel of his comes familiarly as a Saturday repetition lesson, with a few variations of time or place. The figures of Scott (save one or two of his heroes) are artistic productions, bearing in many a curve the impress of the workman's varying fancy, of his sure and skilful hand; those of James rather resemble those products which are made by dozens after certain models, receiving certain variations of gilding or grouping according to the story for which they are destined. James plays skilfully a variety of games, but always with the same machinery, the same puppets in a different costume. The characters of Alexis are carved, not

* Wilhelm Haering, known as W. Alexis, Novels and Tales, 8 vols; 'Walladmor;' 'Cabanis;' 'Rosamonde;' 'Das Haus Düsterweg;' 'Der Roland von Berlin.'

cast. They have vigour and individuality, sometimes almost too strongly drawn to be in perfect taste. His eye for the angles and corners of his fellow-creatures reminds us, though rarely, of Thackeray. The last and greatest complete work of Alexis is one which we cannot pass by, and before proceeding to make a few extracts, we will introduce it with Mr. Schmidt's criticism, doubtless more reliable than our own, though in the main the same.

' That which most agreeably impresses us throughout his 'Repose is the citizen's first duty,' is the lively spirit of patriotism with which it is written. By this we do not mean lyrical outbreaks of patriotic attachment, which are worth little, as being often mere coquetry, but the capability of representing patriotism in definite concrete forms. W. Alexis warmly and thoroughly enters into the Prussian mind; he knows how to touch and to excite us, at the same time, without scruple, bringing sharply out the dark side of our feeling and position. Moreover, the satirical delineation of those men who then (time of Bonaparte) drew down reproach and disgrace on Prussia, is so cool and so severe, that most lively hatred only can explain it, and such hate does one good, especially in our day. That there are reasons, internal and external, why this hatred should have a boundary—who can say whether this should give us most joy or sorrow? In this point of view the book is almost perfect, apart from the fact that it is impossible fully to represent a time so near our own, with anything like artistic completeness. W. Alexis has with great discrimination selected a proportionate number of types of the Prussian mind at that time, and grouped them with great skill.'—Vol. ii. p. 338.

The story is too complicated for us to enter upon it here, and is, moreover, the least praiseworthy part of the work; isolated scenes, or dialogues characteristic of the period, and coming naturally from those who utter them, display far more the tact and skill of the author than the main incidents. There are sketches of diplomatists in various styles, the unfathomable and omnipresent, who know all the private affairs of families as well as states. The would-be honest, who are to be distrusted in proportion to their straightforwardness, and others beside, are all drawn with inimitable shrewdness. There is a young tutor who is very much ashamed of his country, as he has reason to be at that time, who writes pamphlets on the improvement of the peasantry, and altogether talks and acts like a very reasonable man, considering how badly he is served by the heroine of the tale. This same Adelheid Alltag is drifted somewhat in shuttlecock fashion from one unnatural or absurd position to another in so extraordinary a manner that we are quite at a loss to understand what she does with all the mental endowments (apart from common sense) with which we are evidently intended to believe her gifted. It is a mistake that we never get at her real character so as to feel that interest which is due to every heroine. Louis Bovillard is a clever and natural compound of the patriot and the scapegrace, with a strong infusion of Young Germany enthusiasm and incoherence. His father, one of the agreeable diplomatists above referred to, leans toward the French aggressors, and would restore the peace of Germany upon any terms, however disgraceful. As a specimen of dialogue, we select, at random, a scene where Louis Bovillard becoming, by an accident upon the road, possessed of despatches of great importance, and gaining no admittance at so late an hour to the presence of the Prussian ministers, rushes with the portfolio to his father. Entering the house by a back staircase, he stands unannounced before the privy councillor. The misdeeds of the son, his debts and imprisonment, had long separated them, and the respectable old gentleman might reasonably be pardoned some slight surprise, therefore, at this intrusion :—

' The father recovered his self-possession. If the first sight had alarmed him, if he ran behind the table upon which the bottles rolled, if he did try to ring the bell, still the undefined impression passed as quickly as it arose. This son did not come with a pistol in his breast, was not fleeing from pursuers, had not forced his way to claim his purse or protection. However wildly his eye rolled, however disordered his hair and dress, Louis did not come as a prodigal son, who has eaten the husks, and in penitence will kiss the ground at his father's feet. He remained standing upright at the door; moreover, a prodigal son carries no portfolio.

' ' Father, forget for one moment the son to whom you have forbidden this threshold. See only the son of his country. His country's honour, may be its existence, is concerned.'

' He then related in short, broken sentences, what we already know.

' ' And what has that to do with you?'

' Louis drew a step nearer: ' You do not—you cannot mean that. Your eye too kindled; I saw it. Forget that your son is witness to this emotion, which is no disgrace. Hear me—you must——'

' The privy-councillor became excited, and was unable quite to conceal it.

' ' Though you will not be my son, you know this, that I am not the minister, and the despatches do not belong to me.'

' Louis had taken a step nearer and seized his father's arm, fixing upon him a look against which the privy-councillor was not proof: ' If a child falls into the water, the mother springs in after it, though she cannot swim. It is a natural impulse: she cannot live without the child, and will perish with it. With such loss we have to do; our country is dying on the Danube. The soil of our own dear country is torn by the hoofs of our enemies, like some valley overrun by the sudden mountain torrent. Our own blood, our very brothers go to recruit his army. The Bavarian follows like the jackal after the lion; Baden has long been scented. At this moment tidings have come that Wurtemberg has also joined. He carries away the small, the greater, and the greatest—he carries all before him. We alone thought ourselves better, too great for that, and we wrote the name of Friedrich upon our borders in letters a yard long. There it was our reckoning failed. A mere tradition, a shield of vapour, a mist wreath. His sappers have hewn down our boundary line, his cannons roll over it, his horsemen clear it. The black and white pales lie in the ditches, the eagle is trampled upon. If we are to take all this quietly, there is no longer any Prussian landmark, no longer any Prussia.'

' ' Should the fact be clearly proved, Prussia will demand satisfaction on account of the boundary line. Of that one may rest quite assured.'

' ' And the great emperor,' interrupted Louis, ' will give, oh, certainly, a brilliant satisfaction, if we keep quiet, and do not trouble ourselves about what does not concern us. At his own cost he will have new landmarks put up. It will be quite a pleasure to him to fix our limits. * * * * The Austrian army is already surrounded by Swabia, Franconia, and the Alps, already held in an iron grasp by a power against which courage is in vain, without further assistance. Yes, at Nordlingen or Ulm it is perhaps at this moment decided, and we—we look on and sleep.'

' The privy-councillor had entirely recovered himself. ' You know I dislike rhapsodies; most of all in state matters.'

' He took a chair and passed a handkerchief across his forehead. ' Who will deny that our position is critical. It is very embarrassing. I will speak gravely with you, because, from your excitement, I see that you are in earnest. I am not sorry; for who knows what may come to make all earnestness needful. We have allowed ourselves to be deceived; it is even possible that we did not decide at the right time, that we were not soon enough in finding true allies. It is still worse, that if we would do so now, no one would trust us. Yes, I believe, in his heart, Napoleon hates us more than any of his enemies. So matters stand, my son; yes, so they stand. And because they are thus, we dare not now act differently. When the destiny of Europe hangs on the edge of a knife, shall we lose our self-possession, and by taking up arms lose the very point at issue? We should perish with it.'

' ' 'Twould be at least a manly end——'

' ' One which gives all for lost! It is not yet so bad. But we are in a position where one cannot be too cautious, when every step, every word, look, and breath must be carefully weighed. Our policy is, and can and dare not be otherwise, than watching and waiting how the dice fall, are falling, without.'

' ' That is your policy, father?'

' ' The policy of all reasonable people. Look about you, and hear the voices in Berlin ——'

' ' Which your wise friends have demoralized. The hearts of merchant and clerk do indeed tremble at every breath of fire; it might kindle this stagnant air. Self is their country; the customers who will stay away to-morrow if the trumpet of war sounds, are their brethren. But the provinces—the country—judges differently. Even here ——'

' ' There are agitators like you, fanatics, patriots; and among them, unfortunately, some are very high and dangerous; they would stake the destiny of the state upon a card. The blood of thousands is nothing to them; the welfare and domestic peace of millions, the long future of destruction and desolation which must be over the land, is as nothing if sacrificed to the idol of honour. War is to them a chivalrous pastime, and to fight, win laurels, and return as conquerors ——'

' ' Enough, father,' said Louis Bovillard, taking the portfolio from the table. ' You will not. These despatches shall rest, like the king's minister, until—to-morrow, when it is too late.'

' ' Stay! What is too late? I have forgotten all between us, and speak as to an equal. This courier brings nothing new. Understand me, that we saw all that has occurred, weeks ago. It could not happen otherwise. We have for eight days hourly expected it, and have, therefore, not been idle. Unfortunately the wise proposal failed, that the state, yielding what it could not alter, should grant a passage through the country to all hostile powers. We had laid other schemes. Before the expedient could be tried, the mischief was done. * * * * Our honour, however, will yet remain untouched, if Bernadotte's invasion be declared by Bonaparte to be a misunderstanding. * * * * But if the agitators get the better of us, at this juncture, all is lost; and if a cabinet council be held, in the alarm of the night who knows but some half sleeper may not throw a torch upon the gunpowder.'

' ' Have you more to say, father?'

' ' That is your heart's wish, and I will forgive it—you and the young men and patriotic ladies who know nothing of our position, and think we can do everything we wish.'

' ' If the conqueror already with anxiety sees us marching behind him!'

' ' He will turn round, think you, when we show our teeth?' The privy-councillor looked about him as though fearing listeners. With suppressed voice he said,—' We are not prepared; there you have the truth, which we dare not utter. The debts of the Rhine campaign are not yet covered; the movement towards the Vistula has eaten a new hole in the treasury. We have no money, and no subsidies to reckon upon, as we have no credit with England. The state of our bank is so bad that Herr von Stein urges us to circulate paper money. But who will accept payment in that?'

' ' But, father, the millions which our army yearly ——'

' ' All go to keep up the externals of the army of Friedrich. All is polished and fresh painted, but the wood is hollow and rotten. The sentry-boxes shine and sparkle, but the magazines stagnate. Our fortresses are decayed, our generals grey-headed, our artillery mouldering away, a few only of our troops stand fire, our discipline is old; and yonder stands an enemy quick as the wind, with a genius for making soldiers out of any stuff he finds, balls out of paving-stones, stores in abundance out of a country where we should starve; an enemy, I tell you, who knows all our weak points, which is more than we do ourselves, and that's the worst of it. We rock ourselves in our pride; we cry, like children passing through a dark room, to raise our courage; we totter like a sleep-walker on the house-top, who hears his name called and falls headlong down. We know that, we few, who are abused and calumniated, and therefore it is our policy to avoid war at any price.'

' ' At any?' cried the son; ' the price of your own reputation—the honour of the name your fathers bore? Remember it does not belong to you alone. It is not a matter of indifference to me, if they point their finger of scorn at my father; if one day, in history, his name will appear among those ——'

' ' Louis,' broke in the councillor, ' I could forgive you much to-day.'

' ' Not if I remained indifferent to my father's disgrace. At the risk of your last anger, I will, I must speak! Do you know the public opinion? It is a thing which does not so easily die away, nor allow itself to be talked down in jests or merry-making. In solitary hours, when you wake at night, the ticking clock, the worm in the wood, the wind beating against the window—do you not then hear aloud what is whispered about you and your friends? No; it is spoken, cried in the market-place, that you are traitors to your country. And more, you are believed to have been won over to the enemy—bribed. For Napoleon's gold, this traitor clique gave to the king such advice as would bring destruction upon their fatherland.'

' ' I know our enemies.'

' ' You know them; that is well. Despise the venomous tongues; that is what I wish. But not by silently shrugging your shoulders, and folding your hands. The time for that has gone by. You can only despise them by open, transparent action. Here is an opportunity for promptitude. What the courier brought is no secret; to-morrow every man will know it, and know also that he found closed doors, that the ministers slept, or would be asleep. Lieutenant Schmilinski, a rough, honest soldier, blunt and outspoken, his very words fire and flame; he already knows that his despatches are in your hands, that it rests with you to assemble the ministers. Should you not do this, the reproaches which will cover them, first fall upon your head.'

' ' And this you have done?'

' ' I have, and with readiness.'

' ' Louis, to bring your father into a position which ——'

' ' Gives him an opportunity of washing off the stain. I am glad, I am proud of it. To the minister, then. Do you wish the coachman to put to? Shall I accompany you? Anything you wish; I am ready for all. Only do not delay another minute ——'

' ' And after all that I have confided to you—to you only ——'

' ' I will see my father clear from the accusation as well as the guilt.' He seized the councillor's hand:—' Disinherit me; but, for my sake, do this. I swear it, I do not believe what suspicion speaks of you or of others, but I am thirsting, longing, for proofs, for one conclusive deed, that what I believe and wish, may become conviction; that I may show a clear forehead, and looking any man in the face who dare reproach my father, may punish him as a liar deserves.'

' The councillor strode up and down in an excitement which could not be concealed. Then he suddenly rang the bell, seized the portfolio, and pressed the hand of Louis: ' Call the courier; we will drive to the count.' '—Vol. ii. pp. 326—336.

The intelligence and vigour of many conversations relating to the existing difficulties of Prussia are full of interest to those who have any wish to make themselves better acquainted with that period. To the class of English readers who may prefer works of which you digest three volumes in a day we could scarcely recommend the book, save as a narcotic. It is far too good for them.

The rich literature of travel which has of late years sprung up in Germany, is a matter on which we would fain have said more than a few words. Tempting names rise up before us as we think of it, but they are so numerous and excellent that we must speak of them only in general terms. It is a track of literature followed largely, perhaps, from that imitative spirit which disposes a German to copy an English garden whenever he can—but it has also a deeper root. The conviction of the internal rottenness in the social and political relations of the country, has long been deepening and spreading among their thinking as well as unthinking men. Repeated disappointments concerning all amendment have given a weariness, at times a hopelessness, to their thoughts upon such matters. And the casual observer of their literature cannot fail to mark the eagerness with which of late years they have turned their thoughts and dreams to some distant land or hemisphere where they picture a paradise, with no crying social evils to face you at every turn, where your hands are not so tied but that you could redress them if they did exist, and where every second man is not a soldier or policeman. It is like the wistful glance of the caged lark toward the free air and summer sky. Many have broken loose to test the lightness of the air, the reality of the sunshine, and these write books which fill the soul with longing for the fair green distance and its dewy shadowings, which carry us through the glades of American forests, over the grand calm rivers, and through flaming prairies. That instinctive yearning of the human heart toward the distant and the unknown as promising happiness, is thus fed and strengthened, and will grow in proportion to the extent of that mental disease which turns, whether in sorrow or in scorn, from the cribbed and dull life at home, and wanders seeking, hoping, desiring almost anything that

shall be different, in the hope of its being better.* Among the many names in this department of authorship, that best known in this country is Charles Sealsfield. Half novelist, half traveller, his sketches are full of life and talent, carrying you breathless through hairbreadth escapes, and fascinating your eye with clear, bold, pictures. Though strongly Anglicised, there remains throughout his writings indubitable proofs of his German origin. It is strange that of his personal history nothing seems to be known beyond the fact that a writer bearing such a name is now resident in Switzerland.

Before closing these remarks we feel somewhat bound to plead guilty to any charge of arbitrary selection that may be brought against us. We have to all intents and purposes ignored the sentimentally devout Herr von Redwitz, although his last poem of *Amaranth* has journeyed through fifteen editions, and is to build, with its symbolical title and other excellencies, a new school of poets for happy Germany. Döring, with his exciting *Pilgrimage of the Flagellants*, and a dozen novels beside, has rustled his unbound leaves in vain. Nor have we been tempted by the *Rosicrucians* of Breier; an author whose books come out as fast as daisies in spring, and are written in a spirited Parisian style without reflections. They may be safely read under a headache, which says much for a German novel. Hackländer, and the Swiss Auerbach, Jeremias Gotthelf, proved almost irresistible, but we leave them for another day, when our readers have an idle hour, and may perhaps be interested in a second gossip.

* The railway entries from Hull to Liverpool would show that some thousands of men of the class above described pass, year by year, along that line in their way to America, and other regions. Few of these will turn book-makers, but all are of the class of the dissatisfied and the restless, coveting some outlet for their energy.

GERMAN EPICS AND ENGLISH HEXAMETERS.

HERE are three poems—two of which have been, for the last half-century, the admiration of Germany; and the third, as far as we can judge from translation, seeming to us to have a rightful claim to be admired—presented to the English public. We are not sure that their chance of attention may not be increased by the fact that they are written in what is called hexameter verse. At the time that the "Luise" of Voss first appeared in Germany, the metre, though often adopted, could not be said to be naturalised in German literature; it, however, has made its way, and some popular poems have been written in it. In English the experiment has also been made, with less perfect success.

To discuss the subject of metre would be beside our present purpose. We may, however, state, that we see no reason to think that verses, equally pleasing to the ear, may not be framed on the principle of introducing dactyles into rank and file, instead of iambics. In English, it is less easy to do so than in German, as we have lost the inflected forms both of nouns and verbs; but to frame the line in English is no very difficult accomplishment. In so framing it, accent, not quantity, must be chiefly attended to, though we think the latter cannot be safely neglected. When Southey made the words "westernmost Withsop" the concluding dactyle and spondee of one of his lines, he, no doubt, regarded the first syllable of his dactyle as equivalent to a long syllable, because on it the accent fell; the second, notwithstanding its cluster of consonants, he would say was short, as being unaccented, and in the same way would deal with the last, disregarding the fact of its secondary accent, which, in combination with the position of the vowel before two consonants (the last circumstance sufficient in itself to make the syllable long in Latin or Greek), does something to interfere with the dactylic movement. The line may be constructed on the principle of accent alone, and be a line of verse; but to be a line of musical verse, quantity must also be regarded.

Whether, however, the movement of the line be dactylic or iambic, is a matter of comparative unimportance. The question which the writer of English hexameters has to ask himself is one wholly different; it is this, whether a succession of lines, in each of which there are six beats—no matter whether the lines, like the closing Alexandrine of the Spenserian stanza, consist of six iambics, each of two syllables, or, like the dactylic hexameter, of an uncertain number of syllables still measured by six feet— can be produced so as not to be displeasing to the ear. Our objection is not to the dactylic hexameter, as such, but to a succession of lines of six feet. Let any one make the attempt to string a number of iambic Alexandrines together, without interposing lines less fatiguing to the breath of the reader, and thus enable himself to judge of the effect. If the dactylic hexameter is more tolerable in such an experiment, the cause, perhaps, will be found to consist in this, that the dactyle and spondee, with which each line closes, are the only parts of the line that approach metre, and thus the four first feet—which we cannot well distinguish from interposed prose—give some relief. The length of the line is the objection. In the Spenserian or iambic hexameter, it breaks into two lines, equally divided. In the dactylic hexameter, the two last feet are so distinctly separated from the rest, to give it this advantage. While we think, then, that there is nothing absolutely to prevent the construction of such verses in English, we think that the effect of even two such lines in English would be unhappy, and to increase the number would be to increase the discord. The particular objection which we have stated, in no way applies to imitations of the classical elegiac metre—the combination of hexameter and pentameter. In Greek and Latin poetry, the inconvenience which we have mentioned, of the latter part of the verse being too distinctly marked, was felt, and the attention of the poet was directed to the arrangement of the four first

feet, and the position of the cæsura, the great object of which was to produce something of harmony in what was felt to be the part of the verse most requiring every artificial support which could be given. We transcribe from the only treatise on Latin Prosody which happens to be at the moment within our reach:—"Il faut bien comprendre l'intention de la césure. Ou la demande, parce que l'oreille exige un enchainement entre les premiers pieds d'un vers; si cet enchainement existe, elle est satisfaite, quoique cependant les régles générales ne soient pas rigoureusement respectées."

But we are passing into a discussion, which we had better postpone till at least we have made our readers acquainted with the books which suggest it.

Mr. Cochrane has, within the last year, published four volumes of verse. One is composed of original poems; another is a translation of Voss's "Luise;" a third is, "Herman and Dorothea," from Goethe; and a fourth is, "Hannah and her Chickens," from the German of Eberhard.

The original poems are, for the most part, of the class which, in the early days of Southey and Coleridge, those poets used to classify as, "Moods of my own mind." There is no very distinct subject—the fancies suggested to an amiable man by accidental circumstances are pleasingly expressed— and the poem is published, because calculated to give pleasure, always of a pure, and often of a very high kind.

We do not know whether we should, if this volume were published alone, make any effort to call attention to it. To describe a volume of modern poetry, making no peculiar claims, where the writer has the good taste not to deviate from established models, and where his chief distinction is to have expressed feelings shared by every one at his fire-side, more happily than one man in a thousand could have done, would, in our day, be of

little use. "In a community of bakers, every one," says Johnson, "must eat his own bread." In a nation of authors, men must consent, not to the hard penance of reading their own works—Dante never imagined anything so bad for his condemned spirits—but to knowing that they will be little read by others. Even the compulsion of a reviewer's office cannot make him open a new volume of poems. Why the fact is so, we cannot explain, but so is the fact.

We ourselves are not altogether an exception. We do sometimes, however, open a volume of modern poetry, and we have our reward. In this case of Mr. Cochrane's it so happens, that we read his volume with little thought that we should ever make it, even in part, the subject of a review; but as we undertake to speak of his translations, it is fit that we should first state something of his original works; for except a man be a poet we feel little inclined to encourage him as a translator of poetry. In proof, however, that Mr. Cochrane may be welcomed in that character, we may mention that we have read his volume of original poems* with much pleasure, and have among his sonnets found several of exceeding beauty.

The volume is divided into four parts. The first, sonnets illustrative of the seasons and nature; a second series of sonnets is suggested by recollections of a tour on the Continent; a third consists of poems cast in the same form, but which do not relate to any common subject; the fourth and last division of the volume is given to miscellaneous poems.

When we read the volume first, we marked with pencil many of these poems, that we might read them again; and such of them as we have read more than once appeared to us, on every reperusal, more beautiful. We shall enable our readers to judge, by giving from each of the three first divisions of the book a single poem:—

"SUMMER MORNING.

"EYE never looked upon a scene more fair,
Save in a dream, or in the Golden Age:
The mountain tops as on an embassage
To Heaven appear (like priests who may repair
Unblamed to the high altar) in the air

* "Sonnets and Miscellaneous Poems." By James Cochrane. Edinburgh: Johnstone and Hunter. 1853.

At home, the empyrean air! The trees
In leafy stoles, wooing in vain the breeze
That sleeps, stand breathless as a soul at prayer.
The lake too sleeps from shore to island knoll,
Where all these beauties clear redoubled lie;
Yea, Heaven and earth are blended into one,
For deep within the water rests the sky!
Gazing on such a scene o'erwhelms the soul:
It thinks, and must be sad: this sin hath done."

"MOUNT BLANC.

" But chiefly thee, O sovran Blanc! I greet,
Lifting thy head far up to dwell apart;
Who seest Hyperion's coursers, ere they start,
Arching their necks and pawing with their feet;
And latest seest his lessening wheels retreat:
Who with the streamers from the poles that dart,
And with the stars o' nights, familiar art,
Holding with them, as friends, communion sweet:
The clouds who seizest in the empyrean blue,
To robe thyself withal in their white folds,
Hurling them forth to pay thee homage due
As brooks, yea rivers, in thy piney wolds:
Whose vast snow fields, by Cynthia's light surveyed,
Seem Cynthia's self upon the earth low laid."

" OCEAN.

" I LOVE to stand upon the billowy shore,
What time the tumbling waves with sparkling crest
Come rolling in, and hear the distant roar
Of Ocean as he rocks himself to rest;
For then I hear a voice that speaks of yore,
That opens Memory's cells with gentle sway,
And his far voice is a symphony
My thoughts to bound, or, wandering, to restore.
His voice is awful, when from land to land
Their monstrous heads the foaming billows rear,
Like Alp o'er Alp—appear and disappear;
Or break with deafening thunder on the strand:
But these lulled tones are like the curfew's peal,
They pain, yet please me, hurt me, and yet heal."

These extracts are sufficient for our present purpose. The two first lose something by being separated from the series of which they form a part. The whole series may be regarded as one poem, and each particular sonnet a stanza, or little more. The key-note is to be looked for beyond itself; and of many such stanzas all that can be said, all that can be desired is, that they assist the progress of the poem, without disturbing the general vein of sentiment. Take Wordsworth's series of sonnets on the River Duddon; some are of singular beauty, some of no other beauty than their appropriateness for the place which they occupy gives—mere indications of Place—but without which the plan of the work would be often unintelligible, or, if intelligible, exhibit the defect of imperfect execution. In the same way his series of ecclesiastical sonnets. Points of Time must be indicated; but whole centuries may pass without presenting, in the poet's way of viewing his subject, such topics as he may wish to bring prominently forward, or as he finds harmonising with his theme; and in such circumstances it is unreasonable to expect more than such a selection of incidents as may enable him to come to what he wishes to exhibit in fuller detail, without the appearance of abruptness. We remember that, in one of the editions of Shakspeare's poems, which we knew in our boyhood—(Dublin, Ewing)—several of his sonnets were so printed as to appear parts of one poem. We know not on what authority this was done; but we believe that in Mr. Browne's modern edition something of the same kind of arrangement is adopted. In these cases it is only an editor's commentary; and, if a theory is to be sustained, is a thing to be regarded with distrust, except some distinction of type guards the reader from confusing the editor's arrangement with what is properly the author's work. Poems may, with a little dexterity, be so re-arranged as to exhibit anything but what the author intended. Our impression however is, that many of the sonnets of Shakspeare are portions—stanzas—of larger poems, and that, regarded in this way, the beauty of particular passages is more fully brought out. We however think, that by such criticism it is idle to expect the discovery of the incidents of his life; and that the expectation of this which seems to have led to the minute examination of every phrase, arises in a false conception of what poetry is, and ever must be. Shakspeare was not bound, any more than the humblest ballad-singer, to swear to the truth of a song. The truth of nature, of feeling, of sentiment, we have a right to expect, but to read such poems for the verification of facts—with a view to establish scandals against Queen Elizabeth, or to impeach the character of some innkeeper's wife—is, we think, to read them amiss.

Modern writers were fond of following the example set them by Wordsworth, and which he adopted from the Italians. Among the poems of the late Sir Aubrey de Vere, is more than one series of sonnets, in this way illustrating a single subject, each part wrought out in separate detail. There is one of twenty-two such stanzas on the Lord's Prayer, parts of which are exceedingly affecting, and many passages of which are conceived in winged words, which we can well imagine sustaining the contemplative spirit in its efforts to realise a better world. These poems might, we think, be usefully detached from the volume of which they form a part, and printed separately. The "Shadow of the Pyramid," by Robert Ferguson,* is another poem in which this form is adopted; a visit to Egypt suggests the poem, in which the fates of the country, from earliest antiquity to our own days, are shadowed out. We do not think Mr. Ferguson has taken entire advantage of the form in which his poem is cast, as the advantage of that form is, that while each sonnet must be regarded as a part of the entire, it has also an individual life of its own; and if separated from the rest, has its own unity and distinct meaning. It is best, when considered in subordination to the whole; but it is not a part of the whole in the sense in which a limb is part of the body. Mr. Ferguson's sonnets run too much into each other; each successive one assumes that you are familiar with that which precedes, and we have some difficulty in finding one which we can detach from the series.

" THE NILE.

" How sweet the breath! how calm the voice of night!
How soothingly her gentle fingers sweep
O'er the worn brow in zephyrs soft and light,
And charm with magic touch the soul to sleep!
Oh! then to wake! and feel how full and deep
The pulse of Nile throbs round thee, and to hear
No voice but his, low breathing on the ear;
Then in a thought of Him who still doth keep
His watch o'er earth, a moment's space upon
Yon sky to gaze, and in that moment see
The gleaming dart of the unsleeping One,
Flash through the sky against his enemy;†
And then to muse till, melting into dreams,
The murmur of the Nile some friend's loved accents seems.

But Mr. Cochrane and his own poem have led us away from our proper subjects—the poems which he has translated; and first, of the " Luise " of Voss, as being the first of these domestic narrative poems, and that out of which the others may be said to have grown.

---

* "Shadow of the Pyramid." By Robert Ferguson. 1847.
† The Moslems believe that a falling star is the dart of the Almighty thrown at an evil spirit.—*Author's Note.*

The "Luise" of Voss has been for more than half a century before the German public, and has continued to have some popularity. Of Voss himself let us state the facts of his life, or rather such part of them as we can give in a sentence. He was born at Lommerdorff, and sent to Penzlin, in the Duchy of Mecklenburgh; there he remained till his fourteenth year, where he was well-grounded in Latin, and had taught himself some Greek and Hebrew. His father was a farmer, but by the seven years' war reduced to entire destitution. The son made his way to New Brandenburg, where he was admitted into the free school. This gave him food and shelter, but no provision was made for clothing the young student. He gave lessons to school-fellows less destitute than himself, and was thus enabled to dress himself. A book-club was got up, and a sort of gymnasium for debate and mutual instruction. Klopstock's works were among the books, and Voss began the fabrication of German Hexameters. He continued to live on, partly as private tutor, and partly in the sort of charity which at that time, in Germany, it was not felt humiliating, in one who was called a "poor scholar," to receive; and in 1772 we find him at Gotlinger, attending Heyne's lectures. He was admitted, through Heyne's exertions, to a Philological Seminary, intended to prepare young persons as schoolmasters for the Hanoverian territory. This gave him food, and hopes for the future.

The strange wild boy was not as deferential to Heyne as the professor expected, and had perhaps a right to expect. Voss declaimed against some propositions advanced in Heyne's lectures, and "attacked his opinions, in great part with the very arguments Heyne was accustomed to produce, and to refute in his own lectures." This was too bad. Heyne and his friends complained. Voss, in his turn, got offended —begged and borrowed four gold Frederics (Heyne's fee), and sent them in payment, somewhat insolently, for the lectures which he had been gratuitously attending. Voss was removed from the Philological Seminary, and had to look for his bread elsewhere. After some task-work for the booksellers, we find him, in 1778, married, and in comparative comfort. About this time he published his first translation of the Odyssey.

In 1793, he printed a new edition of it so altered as to be, in truth, a different work. The first is said to be greatly better than the second; but on such a subject, particularly in the case of translation, we should have strong doubts. In the case of Cowper's Homer, where the changes in the second edition of his Odyssey are very considerable, Southey and Cary, the latter capable of forming some opinion on the subject, have each reprinted, in their respective editions of Cowper's works, his Homer from the first edition. Of Voss's Odyssey we happen to have the edition printed in 1821, whether from his first or second edition we do not know. After his quarrel with Heyne, there appears to have been a period of dissoluteness in the life of Voss, but it may have been little more than the permitted license of a German student. He and a number of friends contributed to periodical publications—were paid for what they wrote—and the proceeds were expended in social entertainments, of which wild and improbable stories were told. Whatever were his irregularities, he soon passed into the decencies of domestic life. For the last twenty years of his life he resided at Heidelberg.

We have read parts of the Odyssey in his translation; but, to our ear, his hexameters are not very skilfully framed, and the tone of the entire is altogether un-Homeric. There is, through all the domestic scenes in the original, a playfulness of tone which we do not think any translator has caught; which, though by no means unlike the tone of Cowper's original poetry, Cowper is the furthest of all Homer's translators from preserving—and which, though in speaking of a German translation, we do so distrusting our own judgment, we think Voss has altogether lost. The best account of the humorous parts of the Odyssey is given by Colonel Muir, and we have read the Odyssey with infinitely more pleasure since we met with Colonel Muir's book.

Of "Luise" (Louisa) there are several editions; and from a sentence in one of Mr. Cochrane's prefaces, it would appear that there are differences of opinion as to the best. Ours is of Vienna, 1816, and, it would appear, differs a good deal from that which Mr. Cochrane has used. The poem was first printed in 1781, and the

adoption of the hexameter appears to have been suggested by his translation of the Odyssey, in which he adopted that metre. Voss, we should say, in all his translations — and he was for ever translating — regarding form as of the essence of any work, as no doubt it is, thought the best mode of reproducing its effect was to imitate, as closely as he could, its form, and thus without much reference to the powers or the proprieties of the language into which he was translating, sought to echo the sound as well as the thoughts of the ancient poets. He is said to have made the effort not alone to translate Homer into hexameters, but to give dactyle for dactyle, spondee for spondee, and, in the passages we have examined, the attempt seems to have been made, but abandoned as impracticable. But, then, what dactyles and spondees are the German!

We transcribe a few lines, opening the book at random. The first lines of Voss's "Eleventh Book of the Odyssey" are:—

"Aber nachdem wir zur schiffe gelangteen, und zu dem meere
Zogen zuerst wir das schiff hinab in die heilige salzflut :
Stellten dann mast und segel hinein in das dunkele meerschif," &c.

Before reading the corresponding lines from Homer, endeavour to scan the German lines. Having ascertained each three syllables which Voss calls a dactyle, and each two which he calls a spondee, ask yourself, on what principle, either of accent or quantity, he proceeds—what is to determine a syllable to be long, or whatever other name is to designate the first syllable of a dactyle, and to distinguish it from the two last? We believe that in the lines we have quoted, he intended the flow of the verse to be the same as is found in the original:—

Αυτὰρ ἐπεί ῥ' ἐπὶ νῆα κατήλθομεν, ἠδὲ θάλασσαν,
Νῆα μὲν ἀρ' πάμπρωτον ἐρύσσαμεν εἰς ἅλα δῖαν
Εν δ' ἱστὸν τιθέμεσθα καὶ ἱστία νηΐ μελαίνη.

To our ear, read the German as we may, do what we can to humour the tune, it would appear as if it had a foot or two more than we find in a Greek hexameter — or, rather, as Southey himself somewhere says, as if it was measured, not by the foot, but by the yard. We wish that the dactylic hexameter were naturalised in our language, if it were only to escape these discussions on the form of poems, of which we should rather discuss the substance.

The story of "Luise" is a short and simple one. The scene is laid in the village of Greénau. The most important of the fixed residents are the pastor and his wife, with their daughter, Luise. A dowager countess inhabits the neighbouring Hall; her family are a daughter, Louisa's friend—a son, about to be sent to the University, and a young Lutheran minister, Walter, the son's tutor, for whom the countess has

obtained an appointment as pastor to some neighbouring congregation—his engagement with her son being at an end.

Walter is the hero of the story. He has fallen in love with Louisa, and from the first, we know him as accepted by her parents in the character of her future husband. There seems no probability that she will not be as well pleased with the arrangement as they can be.

Louisa's eighteenth birth-day has come, and Walter is invited to pass it with them. The poem is divided into three idyls: the first is entitled "The Repast in the Forest."

It would appear that the birth-day guests are received at the parsonage house, and after an early meal, there is some discussion how the day is to be passed; Louisa is the heroine of the day, and has to determine it. Her mother asks here—

"Shall we away to the forest, Louisa, or wouldst thou rather,
Seeing the sun is so bright, in the cool honeysuckle-deck'd arbour—
Down by the streamlet, thy birth-day hold? But why art thou blushing?"

"Not in the arbour, mamma, for the scent of the pale honeysuckle,
Mingled with green of the meadow and lilac, at evening is heavy;
And moreover, the midges in myriads come from the waters;
Sweetly the bright sun shines, and the skirts of the forest are pleasant."

To the forest, then, they go. In the opening of the poem we have the fowl feeding from Louisa's hand, and glimpses of her character are seen through conversations with her mother. A boat has to be borrowed for the day's excursion; every one is equally desirous to gratify Louisa. The answer to the application for the boat is—

"Boat, and whatever I can lend you, are all at the lady's disposal!"

Charles is Walter's pupil, and has all the playfulness of a boy. We have Louisa described in the following passage, surely very gracefully written:—

"Spoke thus kindly the steward, and handed the key. But the maiden,
Charles now urging them on, took hold of the arm of her lover,
Leading delighted the way to the foam-fringed sluice of the corn-mill,
Down in the valley. On this side and that, at the feet of the maiden
Lightly her white frock flapped, tucked neatly with rose-coloured loopstrings.
Rich silk gauze, scarce hiding her bosom, enveloped her shoulders,
Fastened in front with a brooch in the form of a rose; and a straw hat,
Decked with a corn-flower, shaded her countenance smiling and friendly.
Under the bonnet, her ringlets of dark hair streamed on her shoulders,
Carelessly tied in their glossy profusion with rose-coloured ribbons.
White, from the band of her brown kid glove, shone sweetly her right hand,
Holding a fan, which she sometimes used in the heat to refresh her;
And as the left on the arm of the youth confidingly rested,
Softly he held in his hand the beloved girl's delicate fingers.
Gushings of rapture he felt at his heart: thick breathing and speechless
Pressed he her small hand, trembling himself as he played with her fingers.

"Thus both wandered slow through the grass, thick studded with wild flowers,
Lively with grasshoppers chirping around, while something within them
Kept them from speaking, or raising their eyelids to look at each other."

A walk on the hill is happily described. The scenery is admirably brought out, and everywhere the narrative is bright with incident. The mountain strawberries, and the seat of the lovers under the hazels, while their young companion is preparing a basket of rushes—

"Scarce had he finished, when off to the low swamp scampered the stripling,
Leaving the lovers alone, who, with hearts fast beating, and timid,
Sat down under the shade of the nut-trees, close by each other,
Talking of common affairs to conceal their inward emotion.
Ere long, back with a well-formed basket of rushes the workman
Bounded, delighted to hear his performance applauded as skilful.
All then set to, plucking, and vieing the one with the other;
Laying the strawberries down in the basket, and bragging of large ones;
Tasting at times, and presenting each other with some of the choicest.
Soon with delicious berries the basket was filled to the edges,
Sending around from the cov'ring of leaves most exquisite fragrance.
Lifting the basket, the boy on his arm then laid it, and went on."

As they descend the hill they meet

"The old weaver of seventy winters,"

a figure that wanders among the hills like Wordsworth's leech-gatherer. The old man is singing a hymn; he receives from Walter a birth-day present, and some cheerful conversation follows. Another trait of Louisa's character is most naturally brought out—

"Thanks, sir; quaffed shall a glass be to-day to the health of the lady,
And to yourself, and to her who, *kind as an angel from heaven,*
Visits our homes."

They part, but we must give Mr. Cochrane's words, which are surpassingly beautiful—

"Parted the friends; but the old man gazed long after the lovers,
Inwardly moved, *while the tears on his light gray eye-lashes trembled.*"

We regret that we have not the opportunity of seeing the edition of the original from which Mr. Cochrane quotes. In ours the whole scene of the interview is somewhat different from Cochrane's, each being, in some respects, better than the other. In this passage we have—

"Aber der Alte
Segnete beiden nach und es bebte die thrän', an der Wimpern."

different from either Mr. Cochrane's or ours.

Coffee is prepared by the mother, and when it is ready, Louisa has to produce her good things.

Quickly Louisa uplifted the lid of the basket and took out cups of earthen ware, and a pewter basin of sugar—

They have now got to the foot of the hill, and find the old people landing from the boat.

We have the arrangements for the repast, a substantial one, if we can believe Mr. Taylor, who some fifty years ago translated parts of the poem from a copy which seems to have been

"But when all had been emptied, the butter, the rolls, and the cold ham,
Strawberries, radishes, milk, and the cowslip wine for the pastor,
Archly Louisa observed, Mamma has forgotten the tea spoons!
They laughed, also the father; the good old lady she laughed too—
Echo laughed, and the mountains repeated the wandering laughter.
Walter presently ran to the birch-tree beside them and cut off
Short, smooth sticks with his clasp knife, offering skewers for stirrers."

—*Taylor's Translation.*

We should be glad to see the edition from which Taylor translated, and to ascertain whether it contained the line which we have underlined in italics. The line, whether Taylor's own, or Voss's, seems to have suggested the passage in Wordsworth's poem of "Joanna's Rock," in which the sound of the lady's laughter is described as echoed by the surrounding mountains. There is nothing corresponding with it, or likely to suggest it, in our copy of the original, or, it would appear, in Mr. Cochrane's.

There is a passage in which, when the old pastor is refreshed with the contents of Louisa's basket, he begins to speculate on a future life. It is not a very happy one in the original, and we wish that Mr Cochrane had regarded it as within the privilege of a translator to have omitted altogether. Homer, "the lovely," is mentioned in the passage, probably a misprint for "Homer the loving." "Homer dem liebendem" is in our copy. The return of the party home in the evening is admirable:—

"Faint in the West now evening glowed: stept forth in the twilight
One star after another, and twinkled aloft in the heavens,
As by the gnarled old oaks on the margin the hurrying shallop
Grounded, which Hans made fast by the painter, according to orders.
Sweetly the fragrance arose from the meadow; but quickly they hastened
On through the mown grass, wisely avoiding the swathes that were dewy.
Carefully walking, Louisa, her gown tucked up by the border,
Showing her snow-white stockings and petticoats dim in the gloaming.
Then by the mouth of the bog where lonely the beetles were humming,
Close by the wall of the village, with thorns overrun, and with briers,
On they proceeded, the grasshoppers chirping around them, and glowworms
Shining with pale light. Now through the wicker-work gate of the village
Leisurely went they, saluting the folks in the front of their houses,
Neighbourly met to advise with each other, and gossip and tattle.
Hans now handed the key to the steward's industrious servant,
Who at the court's wide entrance the clear-ringing scythe on the anvil
Busy was hammering, fresh green clover to cut on the morrow.
Hooted the owl in the belfry, and eve-like quiet the clock clicked,
As with a wag of his tail by the dog they were welcomed."

In the second idyl we have a visit from the countess and her party. They are removing from their country residence, and come for the purpose of having the wedding take place before they go. This part of the poem does not seem to us in any way equal to the first; and in the edition from which Mr.

Cochrane quotes, would appear to have been very injudiciously extended. In ours it is but half the length of the first, and yet it is too long. The third idyl is, in Mr. Cochrane's edition, divided into two parts, the marriage and the marriage festivities. Ours gives it the name of the "Brautabend," and though very much longer than the first, is undivided. It would appear that the author was fond of touching and re-touching a favourite picture. There would be no object in our transcribing more of the poem. It will be read with pleasure of the same kind that Longfellow's "Evangeline" has given. It is not improbable that it would have been impossible to translate it with the same effect in any other metre than that which Mr. Cochrane has adopted, and which he has often rendered not unpleasing. The poem is, however, somewhat tedious, and we think that without varying its peculiar character — without omitting one trait of manners, or even one expression of feeling — it might have been easily abridged into a more effective poem. In a passage of it, translated by Mr. Taylor, he says he omitted "some lines which appeared trifling or superfluous;" adding, however, that he gave a "faithful notion of the spirit of the piece, which may," he says, "be compared with the works of the Flemish painters, in which a housewife, surrounded with kitchen-furniture, forms the main object, and in which all the minute articles for domestic use are as elaborately painted as the human individuals." In Mr. Austin's "Characteristics of Goethe" is a translation of a review by Goethe, of Voss's works, from which, had we room for it, we should wish to make extracts. It is written with the generosity which distinguishes Goethe's writing whenever he wrote of true men — the praise being somewhat higher than those less capable of appreciating what Voss had done for the literature and the language of Germany would concede.

Mr. Cochrane's books have imposed a more severe duty on us than we had proposed, and yet we cannot fully discuss some subjects, which, in examining them, it is not easy altogether to avoid. The general principles of translation, and the question whether fidelity to the form, as well as to the meaning and purpose of the work

translated can scarcely be avoided—nor the further question whether, even admitting the desirableness of such fidelity in most cases, we should think of exacting it when it would lead to the introduction of a metre unfamiliar to our literature? The possibility of producing, in our language, effects similar to those produced by that metre in other languages, is one which almost forces itself upon us, and yet is one which cannot be incidentally discussed, as it would involve an inquiry into the elementary principles of metre, and the peculiar circumstances which so fixed our language at a period when it was still in growth and pliant, and, when, no doubt, it could be easily moulded into whatever would most suit the purposes of our early poets, as to be singularly unfavourable to the purposes of those who would now force it into accordance with the system of the ancient languages. Its inflexions are gone—its pronunciation is compressed in such a manner as to crush its syllables together. The loss of inflexions has forced upon us a number of prepositions, and small unaccented words which must be very much in the way of a writer who adopts a system of metre depending on accent, not on quantity. From this and from other causes, we too are constantly obliged to use the article where it would not appear in other languages; and this, too, cannot but have an effect on metre. Where there are inflexions, and where the latter part of the word is inflected, you have the weaker syllables annexed to the original word—the root—giving the poet ready-made dactyles or trochees. The current of the language is with him when he writes in metres requiring such feet, and he is not, as in modern English, striving against the stream; and words which, in Chaucer's time, were in our poetry lengthened out so as to exhibit a dissyllabic terminations, ending in *ion*, &c.; and which, even so late as Dryden's day, were still, perhaps, reluctantly obedient to the convenience of the poet, are now, by economical people, kept within the narrowest limits. We have lost, for the most part, the marks which, in other languages kindred with ours, still express the degrees of comparison. A modern poet would be regarded as guilty of some affectation, if, like Spenser, he spoke of his "beautifullest" bride;

and though "eth," as the sign of present tense, is not absolutely driven out of good society, we think it can be scarcely said now to exist: "ed," in its uncontracted form, as the sign of the past tense, is gone. All this is hard on the hexametrist; and it is harder on the man who would employ an unusual metre in translation than on an original writer; for the translator undertakes to express thoughts in a language already formed and existing, and over which he can assume no privileges. An original writer may indulge in caprices of whatever kind. What he wishes to say, we endeavour, if he be in any true sense an original writer, to understand. We allow him a power over language which no translator can claim.

In translating "Herman and Dorothea," Mr. Cochrane has undertaken a more ambitious task than in the "Luise." Voss's is a pleasing idyl, descriptive of the manners of a class—descriptive of local scenery — true, no doubt, to the actual facts of German life, in a particular district of Germany, but making no higher claim. It is a poem, as being thrown into a poetical form; but it most probably, even in Germany, would not be given as high a place as a successful translation of Bloomfield's "Farmer's Boy" would have a right to demand. Bloomfield's "Richard and Kate," or Hector M'Neil's "Waes of War," would indicate to those who have read those poems, which were once very popular, the height to which Luise rises. "Herman and Dorothea," though often mentioned with it, and though, it would almost seem, suggested by it, is Goethe's most perfect narrative poem; and, if we except his "Iphigenie," perhaps the most perfect of all his poems. We regret that Mr. Cochrane has diminished the chance of the poem being popular, or even known in England, by not translating it into blank verse, rather than hexameters. There can be no doubt that in our language the natural flow is iambic — that in which, except violently forced from it, the current would move. Freedom of expression and propriety of language is sacrificed to produce an injurious effect. In poetry, everything depends on a writer being able to carry with him the *unconscious* sympathies of his reader; and here, at every line he is

roused into distinct consciousness. We are almost provoked into passing over any mention of Goethe's most beautiful poem, in spite of our admiration of it, so little possible is it to speak of it as it ought to be spoken of, if we are at the same time to be afflicted with the necessity of agitating these contested questions of metre.

The story is the simplest than can be conceived. The landlord of a village inn has an only son, who, he intends, shall succeed him in his business, and who, he is anxious, shall marry a person who may add to their means. The revolutionary war has driven from their homes a number of helpless fugitives, to afford assistance to whom Herman his son is sent. He is struck with the appearance and the conduct of a young woman, whom, after some resistance from his father, he marries.

The characters in the poem are taken from what would seem the humblest ranks of life — the village innkeeper, the apothecary, and, not socially classed above them, the village pastor. Yet in these Goethe finds the elements of all that we call society, and has executed a poem which, in many respects, stands higher than any other which we could name, and which brings to our mind the freshness and the power of — shall we say it? — and yet it is impossible not to say it — of the Odyssey itself. Through the Odyssey, however, there is a vein of humour with which we can more easily sympathise than with any similar element in Goethe's work. What is felt to be mirthful, and is intended to excite feelings that express themselves in gay laughter with the Germans, is not unlikely, even without passing through the process of translation, to be thought dull enough by an Englishman; and what John Bull esteems as dull, is not likely to be regarded as lively by his Irish and Scotch neighbours. We must be pardoned, then, if we cannot see all that we are told to look for in the splenetic remarks of the apothecary, and if the pastor's discourse falls heavy upon us. In the original, some of the dialogues are, we think, rather tedious, and the translator has not regarded it as among his privileges to abridge them. Where Goethe has most succeeded, is in the descriptive passages, and in the skill with which he has interwoven a dramatic story with the public incidents of the period in which it is placed. The social position of the characters of his story gives him the great advantage of being able to picture the individuals in a way which would be altogether impossible had his heroes been princes, or leaders of armies, or bishops, or any of those existences which, though called persons, are, in truth, corporations, and represent large aggregates of men—bodies of conventional thought—anything rather than the direct and instant power of the single mind. The epic poem must, almost from its nature, belong to an early period of society. As armies now consist of paid soldiers and man has become a mere machine, are a very different thing from what we suppose the bodies of men brought together by such an impulse as animated the nations whom Homer assembles; and if individual portraiture, and the exhibition of man's proper nature be the poet's object, he will, probably, select his heroes from spheres of life that are, or seem, removed from the powers that rule the modern world.

Goethe's poem opens with Herman going to the assistance of the sufferers. He is shown driving the wagon, in which are packed wine, and food, and clothes. His mother's earnest care in providing these is exhibited. Suppose a higher class of life — imagine the exercise of similar benevolence — the whole would be done by sending a money-order — the detailed picturing would be impossible. We do not say that the movements of the higher classes do not afford subjects for the poet — perhaps, even higher ones — but, then, they are such as pass into pure abstraction — are not direct pictures of actual occurrences.

The highest order of poetry will, in many respects, be identical with pure science. In true poetry it always is so, as far as the poet is concerned; but what we mean is, that in his representations to others — in his communications with his hearers — narrative must cease to be his mode of manifestation. To be distinctively a poet, he must still deal with the world of the senses; and if the religion of his coun-

try be such as it was among the nations of Greece and Rome, he will probably use the popular mythology as a language in which to communicate thoughts far beyond any which the popular mind had before received from it. In a Christian country, allegory would, in the same circumstances, most probably be adopted. Even among the ancients, the use of machinery in epic poetry seems to have arisen from a desire to assert a unity of purpose which the actions of men did not furnish, and to this can be traced, almost with certainty, the use of allegory by Dante, by Spenser, and, in more modern days, by Goethe. The first part of Faust, where he has to represent only the individual mind, is without any allegory;* the second, where society and its modifications are presented, is wholly allegorical.

In a volume which we brought before the notice of our readers a good many years ago, and which we believe has done more to aid in reconciling classes to each other, than any other book of our time—we speak of "THE CLAIMS OF LABOUR" — the writer dwells upon the tendency of modern society to separate men more from each other. The poor and rich no longer meet as they did of old. Is it through a consciousness of not being what the men of old time were, of individual power being less, that there is a shrinking and an isolation at the heart of man — that each insists on rights which he will not suffer to be examined — that we have no enjoyments in common — nothing in which man speaks to man in the feeling of their common equality — of their one nature? We do not believe that the village differs essentially from the city in this; but if there be a difference in this respect, it would be, that probably in the village each man, knowing every other, and all being less influenced by the changes of artificial life, which go on more slowly among them than in larger communities, the poet may find it more in his power to show the direct dealings of man with man. The village inn-keeper would not seem an inconvenient character for his purpose.

He must know every one — he must be the great man giving employment to numbers in every line of life — he must have intercourse with all of every rank — the customs of the Continent making such persons who reside for any time at his house members of his family, living at the same table with him, will raise his position above what, with our habits, we would at first assign to it; and we can well imagine that in the domestic epic, such man might be, with less inconvenience to the poet, made the hero of a poem, than a person embarrassing him with conventional claims of any kind. In the same way it may be said of the apothecary and of the pastor, that their education and their intercourse with all classes of men, gives the poet such advantage in selecting them for the characters of his romance, or idyl, or epic—the name by which the Germans love to designate this poem—as Wordsworth had when he made a pedlar the hero of his great work. Conventional feeling is for a moment disturbed, but the advantage gained is well worth the sacrifice.

We are unable to give an analysis of the poem. The parts of the work are so woven into each other that, under any circumstances, passages are not easily separable from the context; and though we perhaps might attempt it, were the English translation in any other metre than the hexameter, we do not think we could do so usefully, when a double discussion should be carried on, one relating to the subject of the poem, and the other to the structure of the peculiar form of verse. We can only say to our readers, that if they *study* the poem, they will probably receive as great a pleasure as it is in the power of narrative poetry to give, and that the more they think over it the more beautiful will it appear. Without, however, actual study, such as any great work of the human mind requires, we think they will, if they merely look over it, feel only a sense of disappointment.

These hexameters are queer things, and we sometimes think that we must be making some strange mistake in our modes of reading them. The first great difficulty in framing such, in such languages as form their systems of

metre on accent not on quantity, is this, that of every two syllables coming together, one is accented—it has either what is called a primary or a secondary accent. If an accented syllable be, as we are told, equivalent to what is called a long one in the Latin or Greek, then, unless the secondary accent be disregarded entirely, it will be impossible to form a dactyle at all; the foot substituted for a dactyle will consist not of a long syllable followed by two short, but by a long syllable, then a short, then a long. Such, we believe, is the real nature of the difficulty, over which we do not expect future English writers of poetry to triumph. If they do, it must be by attending to the length of sounds, and not to accent alone, as is the present practice, in obedience to a theory, that accent is to be exclusively considered, which theory we think demonstrably wrong. The English hexameter metre, if the secondary accent is to be regarded at all, consists, when analysed, of feet essentially different from what the ancients called dactyles and spondees—a matter, no doubt, of but little moment, if musical effect is produced; but against the chance of the metre ever satisfying the ear, is its having been tried and found wanting by the Elizabethan poets. Considerations which embarrassed Sidney, and which made Spenser regard the fabrication of hexameters in English as nearly impracticable, were felt as nothing by Stanhurst; and we believe that in some libraries a translation of Virgil, executed by him in this measure, is still to be found. We have never been able to get sight of a copy, but from extracts, not unfrequently printed, it seems a curiosity worth looking at. Southey thinks it ought, from its oddity, to be reprinted. In Todd's Life of Spenser, we find some extracts from a correspondence between him and Gabriel Harvey, in which the poet tells his friend some of the inconveniences of the metre. In such a word as "*carpenter*, the middle syllable being used short in speech, when it should be read long in verse, seemeth like a lame gosling that draweth one leg after her; and *heaven* being used short as one syllable, when it is in verse stretched out with a diastole, is like a lame dog that holds up one leg."*

---

* "I do not believe that in the first conception of Faust, any allegories of any kind were before the poet's mind; I have not, therefore, perplexed myself or my readers with those which have been suggested."—*Anster's Faustus,* xxvi.

* Letter from Spenser to Gabriel Harvey, "Todd's Spenser," vol. i. 35.

As far, however, as we can under-stand the passage, which is very in-accurately printed, his notion is that hexameters may be framed on the principle of accent — that the object may, however hopeless it seems at first, "be won by custom, and rough words subdued with use." We do not think it accurate to say that the failures of the Elizabethan poets to establish the hexameter in our language, arose from their endeavouring to construct their verses on the principle of quantity, not accent. They constructed them on the principle of accent, but they did not disregard quantity, which cannot safely be disregarded by any writer of verse, no matter what form of metre he may

"Night came down, as the tide still rose, swept on by the south wind!"

is stated to be inharmonious. We do not know whether the line is Mr. Cochrane's or not; we should suppose not. We have not seen the review of which he complains, and can-not judge by what Mr. Cochrane says of the case as between him and the reviewer, as the harmony of a line would depend on its position in a pa-

"'Night came down, as the tide still rose,
Swept on by the south wind!'

and it would grace any of the Percy ballads, but written in one line, it scares our critic as a six-footed monster, and makes his hair stand on end." This passage makes us think that we read these hexameters with some dif-ferent cadence from Mr. Cochrane, for surely the line is read with a wholly different emphasis and accentuation when we read it as a hexameter, from that which we use when read as two ballad lines.

In Schiller's correspondence with Humboldt, we find Humboldt express-ing his gratification that, in translating Virgil, Schiller adopted stanzas of the ordinary iambic flow, instead of hexa-meters. In the correspondence with Körner there are similar passages in which great doubt is expressed as to the suitableness of the hexameter to the German language. Mr. Coch-rane has said, no doubt inadver-tently, that Schiller has written "his own most beautiful poem in this mea-sure." This is a mistake. As far as we know, Schiller has written no poem in hexameters. The "WALK" is in hexameter and pentameter — a

adopt. If the reader takes the trouble of examining Sidney's verses, even those selected by Southey (with whom the mistake originated), in the appendix to his "Vision of Judgment," he will, we think, feel satisfied that accent, not quantity, was the principle on which his lines were framed. The mistake arose from the discussions on the sub-ject, which were confined to the only part of the question which was in dis-pute—namely, whether *quantity* should be regarded at all. Hence Spenser's case of the word "*carpenter*," &c. In the preface to one of Mr. Cochrane's books, he complains of a review of his hexameters, in which he says that the line

ragraph or a stanza, and could not ever be determined except with re-ference to a something with which it either was or was not in harmony. Mr. Cochrane says—"Now, leaving out of view the question of hexameters, we would appeal to any lover of poetry whether the line is not a beautiful one. Divided into two lines thus—

metre essentially different—as, if there be anything in what we have said in a former part of this paper, we have proved. That a single line of six feet, whether the movement be iambic or dactylic, may be musical, is perfectly consistent with the proposition that many such lines cannot exist in se-quence without fatiguing the ear. The converse of this proposition is what Mr. Cochrane has to prove; and it does not give him much help to be able to show that Schiller never writes a line of six feet without immediately following it by one of different length, and differently constructed. Neither in theory nor in practice did Schiller give any encouragement to the home-made hexameter. The question of metre is, however, one which we can-not now discuss. We will only say, that absolutely nothing is determined by exhibiting the flow of single lines without considering them in their com-bination with others. Take Gray's "Bard;" the opening lines are—

"Ruin seize thee, ruthless king,
Confusion on thy banners wait."

Suppose Mr. Cochrane, or any one

else, to tell us that, had Gray writ-ten—

"Ruin seize thee, ruthless monarch,"

it would have been a musical line. He would have said, what we should never think of contradicting; but such line could not be read in connexion with that which follows. The two would be absolute discord; and such discord to us, at least, do the sequences in Southey's hexameters — for we think rather of his than of those of any living man—often, we do not say always, but often, most often, make.

We fear that our readers may be led to think that we do not feel the great beauty of many passages in Mr. Cochrane's translations, which, in spite of what we think a false theory of ver-sification, are often quite admirable. We have read his "Louisa," and "Herman and Dorothea," together with the originals; and this justifies us in the conviction that the poem of

Eberhard, which he translates, and of which we have not seen the original, is faithful to its author. We should not be surprised if it give more plea-sure to the reader than either of the other poems. We ourselves are in-clined to place it below "Herman and Dorothea," and above "Louisa." Still it must always be remembered that "Louisa" was the first of the class. As far as Mr. Cochrane is con-cerned, the order of his translations was, "Herman and Dorothea," then "Louisa," and, last of all, "Hannah and her Chickens." His own hand has acquired, with each successive effort, more skill; and in "Hannah" his hex-ameters have almost the flow of Long-fellow's, whose "Evangeline" would, if anything could, reconcile us to the me-tre.

Eberhard's poem opens with the following passage, which will give a favourable idea of Mr. Cochrane's manner:—

"Under the Schlossberg's* wing lies safely protected the village,
Like the sequestered flock, stretched out by the tent of the shepherd,
Covered with flowers, and a vine to the thatch roof sending its tendrils,
Stands by the road side yonder a cottage of modest appearance.
There, as the shadows of evening were falling apace, in the room sat
Martha, the minister's widow, the trustful, though sunk in misfortune;
Hannah, the minister's orphan, the pious and dutiful maiden:
Both with industrious fingers engaged with the distaff and spindle;
Both with a sorrowful look upon bygone days deep musing:
When, on the linden-o'er-shadowed, retired road suddenly rolled past
Glittering carriages, posting along with caparisoned horses,
Gentlefolks sitting within, sires, young men, matrons, and maidens;
All to the castle proceeding with faces that beamed with enjoyment."

It is Hannah's early friend returned from a visit to Rome. Hannah anti-cipates nothing but delight in the re-newal of their intimacy. Her mother has fears and misgivings. Hannah's feelings, however, have not deceived her. Her friend is delighted when they have again met at the castle, for Antoinette is "the lady of the land." Hannah soon observes that among the party is a young man, whom she had not at first seen, but whom she soon learns to be engaged to Antoinette. Death and distress have been in Han-nah's household since she and her friend have last met—her father and her bro-ther have died; and "she has had other

trials." These other trials are the subject of the second canto of the poem which is called the "Confession." In a conver-sation with her mother, we learn that Gotthold, the young clergyman of the parish, has been attracted by Hannah's beauty and goodness; that Laura, the daughter of a person who seems to be agent or father to Antoinette's estate, has some design on his heart, and does what she can to undermine Hannah. The opportunity of doing Hannah se-rious mischief in Gotthold's mind soon arises, and is not lost by her malicious rival. We find Hannah thus telling the story to her mother:—

"Well, as you know, on my father's beloved grave flowers I had planted,
Where all fragrant they flourished, and garden besides I may truly
Say I had none, and to me 'twas the holiest spot in the wide world.
Thinking alone of the dead, there, far from the noise of the village,

* Castle Hill.

Used I to water the flowers with affection, and linger beside them,
Grieving and praying by turns—none seeing me, fondly believing.
Keeping my eyes on the ground, and without ever thinking of looking
Over the hedge, by the well known wide-spread elders I sauntered,
Now much grown, which the minister's garden divides from the churchyard.
Once, however, enticed by the fragrant odours they breathed forth,
Towards the hedge, half dreaming, I went to the gap at the corner,
Where as a child full often I skipped light-hearted and merry:
Joyously warbled the larks, and the dawn shone brilliant and rosy;
Lovely the garden appeared in its spring dress, smiling so sweetly.
Like to the way-worn man who refreshes himself at the fountain,
Gazing I stood 'mong the flowers, and never was weary of gazing;
Something enchanting there was which lured me on in the garden,
And I, entranced with delight, skipped happy and gay, as in childhood.
Bushes saluting, and trees, as acquaintances old and remembered:
But the delightfulest far of the whole was the shadowy arbour,
Planted around long since by myself with admired honey-suckles.
Gladly, methought, the familiar, beloved arch kindly embraced me;
That the unoccupied seats, where oft I had sat in my childhood,
Asked me to sit; and the whispering leaves seemed to my fancy
Voices of father, and mother, and brother, that went to my bosom,
Telling of bygone days, no more to return in their freshness:
Thus, forgetting alike whence coming and whitherward going,
Longer and longer I mused, deep, deep in a reverie sinking.

"Soon I was roused from my vision by footsteps plainly approaching:
Flying was out of the question; so, hoping the steps would perhaps turn
Sidewards up the ascent, thus happily avoiding the arbour,
Breathless, I stood still, hiding myself in the shadiest corner:
But I was wrong in my hopes; ere long, with a book in his hand, there
Looking me straight in the face, stood, fixed in astonishment, Gotthold.
Scarcely a word could I utter on finding myself thus taken;
Soon to my rescue, however, he came, with a kindly expression,
So that I quickly again felt easy, composure regaining.
Every word was delightful he spoke, but I could not but sometimes
Blush when I thought what might, after all, be the meaning intended.
Afterwards, further he led me, to show how everything yonder,
Which we ourselves had arranged, stood still there, just as we left them:
Even the violets which I had planted myself on the border,
Every one he minutely could tell, and the circle had fenced round,
Just, as he said, that if ever I came to revisit the garden—
Which he had long wished—all my select ones still might attract me.
While I was giving him thanks for his trouble, he quickly my hand seized,
Lifted it silently up to his closed lips, pressing it gently.
Not long silent he stood, but with eloquence greater than ever
Warmly he spoke; the industrious hand that supported the mother
Praising and praising the pious remembrance I showed for my father,
By my affectionate care of the flowers which grew on his lone grave.
Also he praised me as good, and of every happiness worthy;
Said that from this day forth, still dearer than ever the garden
Would be to him, as already the churchyard was from my visits;
Said—I forget what further he said—forget it entirely.
One thing only I know, that it pleased me at once, and bewildered,
And though wishing to fly, like one chained fast, I entranced stood.
Easy it was not to stir, but with heart all beating I hastened
Over the churchyard, never, for once, of the dear grave thinking;
Here to my chamber I flew, and in tears gave vent to my feelings—
Meant to inform you of all, but before this never had courage."

The story would be too long to tell how Laura continues to give circumstances of suspicion a colouring against Hannah. She is seen in Gotthold's garden, and Laura represents her as trampling, in spite, on a bed of carnations—Laura's gift to the young pastor. Gotthold writes to Hannah, but sends the letter by Laura. It is never delivered, and he misunderstands, as it is impossible he should not, the fact of receiving no answer. In this state things are when the castle party are rives.

The next canto is entitled, "New Griefs." The incident which gives it its name is the loss of their fowl; the "slide of the hencoop" has been left open, and the polecat has killed all. The canto, however, is not confined to griefs. Hannah and her mother visit at the castle. We are introduced to the party there, all of whom are favourably disposed to Hannah and her mother. On the whole, this canto is of happy omen.

The fourth canto carries on the story. The mother is anxious for an explanation with Gotthold, to which Hannah sees insuperable objections. The canto is called "Resignation."

The fifth, entitled, "The Nest," tells us that one of the hens has escaped. Hannah has found her nest. A visit from Antoinette concludes this canto. The conversation is confined to the incident of the discovery of the nest, but readers experienced in romance will infer something from the closing lines:—

"Antoinette stood earnestly looking, as if there were something
Troubling her heart; but the cheerful demeanour of Martha and Hannah
Pleased her so much, that she soon joined both in their laughing and joking.

"Dark clouds, threatening rain, now lowered as evening descended.
Quickly she farewell took, at the door-step saying on leaving:
'Hannah, I've something important to say, and at present was only
Passing the house, but will certainly come back early to-morrow.'"

The visit in the fifth canto is explained by the sixth, entitled, "Trust." Laura had told at the castle, with every exaggeration of malice, how Hannah had trampled the pastor's flowers. Her account is disbelieved by Antoinette and her mother; and Antoinette determines to make out the truth, which has occasioned her visit. Gotthold is now at the castle, and learns the opinions of its inmates as to both Laura and Hannah.

In the next canto we are told of Antoinette's bridegroom being suddenly summoned to see his mother, supposed to be dying, and that Antoinette and her mother are to follow on the next day. On their way they pay a hurried visit to Hannah; inquire about Gotthold's letter, and find it had never been delivered. Time, however, flows on, and no more is heard on the subject. The following passage is, we think, very pleasing:—

"Day after day passed quietly on, when both to the castle
Kindly to dinner were asked one day by the courteous baron,
There, in her absence, to hold the beloved old baroness' birthday.
Hannah, o'erjoyed, blushed sweetly: the pleasure of meeting the pastor
Vividly rose to her view, and of asking himself at the castle
Something regarding the long-lost letter, and telling him frankly,
That she the coldness she lately had shown much felt, and deserved not.
Deeper and deeper she blushed, for already a long conversation,
Sunk in a dream, with the pastor she mentally held on the subject,
More confidential by far than that in the blossoming garden!
Soon in the magical glass of the soul rose sweetly his picture,
Angry at first, then reconciled quite, and so speaking and life-like,
That she was startled before it, and waved it away with upraised hands!
Quickly the young girl's hopes now changed into fears, and she trembled,
Full of anxiety, wishing to speak of the letter and garden:
Fearing, however, it would not accord with her vow, which obliged her
Antoinette's much longed-for arrival with patience to wait for."

Our readers, we hope, have not forgotten the nest. On the very day of the party the young chickens come into life, and Hannah relinquishes the party sooner than leave them to chance. Her mother goes alone.

The party does not proceed cheerfully. Hannah's mother has to endure some impertinence from Laura. Gotthold speaks to her kindly, and inquires affectionately, it would seem, for Hannah; nay, surprises her, by his knowing the outgoings of their little household, which he has learned from Antoinette. All this would seem to show a continuing interest in Hannah. While, however, they are conversing, Laura carries him off to the piano to join her in a song. Martha returns home discontented.

The dying lady recovers, and Antoinette and party return. Antoinette's

482

wedding day is fixed, and Hannah is happy thinking to prepare the bride's wreath of myrtle. Laura continues to interpose difficulties. First, there are delays; next, it is found that she has herself prepared the bridal wreath, and has given orders—her father being in authority over gardeners and all other servants of the place — that no one shall be given one sprig of myrtle. Hannah is heart-broken at her disappointment:—

> " 'Only,' she sadly complained, 'once only the garland of myrtle
> Sweetly the maid's brow circles in life! just once, at her bridal!
> But 'tis not granted to me to adorn dear Antoinette's, though
> Me she would chose for the rite, and for none would I sooner perform it!
> What can I give dear Antoinette now? What for the brideseve?
> Long uncomplaining I've suffered, and none, no, none have I envied,
> Whom kind heaven a happier lot than my own has accorded:
> Now first feel I alas! stern Poverty's hateful restrictions!' "

She remembers the nest of chickens, and determines that this shall be her gift.

The close of the poem is exceedingly beautiful. Gotthold visits the cottage. Among the misfortunes of Hannah's family, one was the destruction of most of their little property by fire. Antoinette has furnished the cottage with a new piano, and Hannah was engaged in playing the music of the great German masters:—

> " Praying awhile she remained; then turned, and with quivering fingers
> Struck the piano, with lips all trembling, the name of her dear friend
> Often repeating the while, with a joyous and grateful expression.

> " Martha exclaimed now: 'See, from the ashes the Phœnix arises,
> Much more lovely, in truth, than before when consumed by the fierce flames!'

> " Whereupon Hannah replied: 'Oh! had but my father beloved
> Lived to behold my delight!' But her voice here failed her entirely,
> Till she relief to her warm heart found in a mournfully sweet strain
> Brought from the chords, which seemed from her own pure bosom to gush forth.
> Full and harmonious sounded the notes, still rising in fervour;
> Sorrow in them seemed telling her tale, and appealing to heaven!
> Silently listening, Martha and Gotthold stood low breathing,
> Till in a grand, loud, choral response she exultingly ended.
> Whereupon Martha exclaimed: ' That ever to him was the sweetest
> Air in the hymn-book; oft on his death-bed, even, he hummed it.'
> Then, quite softly, and hardly herself well knowing it, sung she
> Sweetly the beautiful, well-known stanzas of Luther's admired hymn.
> Soon, with her eyes tear-filled, and her countenance looking to heaven,
> Like a Cecilia, Hannah began, too, singing in melting,
> Exquisite accents—her tender, devout heart thrilling with rapture!
> But, overpowered with her feelings, she dared not attempt, though she wished it,
> Singing the words of the airs which her dear old father had relished.
> Stopt were piano and voice, and aside now Hannah in tears turned—
> Like a bedewed flow'r, showing its closed cup drooping at evening,
> Stood she with countenance lovely, and tear-filled eyes on the ground cast."

This is the hour for Gotthold's declaration of love:—

> " 'Hannah,' in tones of alarm, said Gotthold, 'tell, dost thou love me?'
> Whereupon Martha, with gentle exertion, herself from her child tore,
> Answering thus in her stead: 'Oh! do not the heart misinterpret,
> Welcome and much-loved son, which long has unconsciously loved you!'

> " 'Me long loved!' he exclaimed, in a rapturous accent; and Hannah
> Bashfully breathed out, 'Yes,' in a whisper that scarcely her lips passed:
> But, in the ears of her lover, it seemed like the music of bright spheres.
> Fondly his arms he extended his own sweet bride to encircle,
> Who, with a heart overflowing with love, sunk down on his bosom."

This, surely, is very beautiful. We wish we could have expressed our admiration of the poetry without saying one word of Mr. Cochrane's adoption of this peculiar metre. It is one of the worst effects of the introduction of any great change of the kind, that we cannot but direct our attention to the form, and thus risk losing something of the substance. It would appear, however, that the metre gains ground. Mr. Cochrane says, that two translations of Homer — one in 1846, another in 1852—have appeared in it. We have not happened to see either. Mr. Cochrane's own works in this metre are the best, or among the best, specimens of it which we have seen. Our impression, however, is, that it will be impossible for it permanently to take any root in the language.

While we are writing, a volume has reached us, which we may as well mention, though it is neither to be classed with German epics nor English hexameters. It is a translation of the Iliad of Homer, by Mr. Barter, into Spenserian stanzas. The translation professes to be more literal than any former one. The spelling of the Greek names is restored. Ulysses is Odysseus, Jove is Zeus, Juno is Here. The epithets are carefully translated. Achilles is always " Swift-foot;" Agamemnon, in a less familiar combination, is " Broad-rule;" Apollo is " Silver-bow." The epithets are not inconvenient when a Spenserian stanza is to be eked out; but we can scarce conceive any metre less suited to such parts of the poem as have to deal with rapid and animated action. Many passages of the volume before us are executed with felicity, and we do not quarrel with such unimportant points as the preservation of epithets so familiar as, in truth, to be part of a name. A serious fault, however, is the constant omission of the English article. Take as an instance, and we open the book at random;—

> " Menœtius brave son strake
> Just as he turned, Arèilycus wight
> On thigh with keen-edged spear, and brass he thrust through quite.
> Brake bone the spear. To ground he fell on 's face.
> . . . . .
> Phylides did Amphiclus rushing *eye*,
> And forehand with him, smite at end of thigh.
> Man's muscles there be thickest. Spear point sheer.
> Thro' tendons cut, and darkness clouds his *eye*.
> Of Nestor's sons, Antelochus with spear
> Atymnius smote. Thro' flank did brazen lance career."

It may be a prejudice, but we prefer Pope.

87. FRASER'S MAGAZINE, 49 (1854), 81-88. M/H No. 4991.

YOUNG GERMANY.

YOUNG Germany has at length come to the end of its strange, reckless career, and now welters on that death-bed from which we expect not to see it rise again, but as a ghost, mayhap, whom any healthy cock will scare. Latterly, in one shape or another, many recantations, confessions, and divers ceremonies incident to approaching dissolution, have issued from it; not unprofitable things to study. The scattered members of this crude association have done well, as they were on the point of being extinguished, to ease their consciences by a public renunciation of what errors seemed uppermost. Their single short-lived season of riot and extravagance, and this sad, inevitable sequel, written in such colours of contrast, teach a lesson that will not be forgotten. Indeed, if their hope was for fame, no act better than the last will preserve their histories. Thus, many a noble tree whose ambition was to have led the van upon the seas, and be

'The mast of some great ammiral,'

becomes fixed along a penitential shore, the object of universal observation—but a landmark!

We believed willingly they were in earnest, these o'er-ripe philosophers and raw *burschen*, before desire had seized their spirits to be shriven, thoroughly cleansed and purified. That was sufficient proof they had not been parading under a mask; but we required it not. Their aspect was far too comical at all times for men acting a part. A lover will make himself ridiculous to his mistress, while the gentleman who is playing her lover, assumes easy postures, trips off fluent pleasantries, and is altogether delightful, admirable, loveable. They were too much in earnest throughout, and Fortune, a capricious dame, made choice of the affable gentleman divested of those disagreeable angularities, even as the ladies of this nether sphere would have chosen. So abandoned, they did as is customary with the rejected lover, proceeded straightway to the water's edge, plunged, and made back shorewards with precipitation. But the shock was too great, and induced

a sickness of which, alas! ignominiously, they now lie stretched out to full undertaker's measure, beset with priests, possets, old women comforters, and some few howling maniac virgins. It could end in no other way. How, and in what they were to succeed, had Fortune dealt less rigorously with them, themselves knew not; but that they had an impulse, and that they were in earnest. Very much in earnest they undoubtedly were, and charged with a sufficiently powerful impulse. So have many been among us, who dubbed themselves genius, and thought to take the world by storm; and whose end was not different. What mischief do not these new cant phrases cause? They seem peculiar to eras of unbelief. Sects that deny the fountain source of inspiration, proclaim themselves inspired; and men professing atheistic doctrines, plead in extension for shameful failures and vicious faults, impulse and earnestness. What sort of virtue is earnestness by itself? There are earnest fools, and earnest villains, earnest rapscallions — all earnest, and proportionately dangerous for that same quality. It is really no other than a wishy-washy diluted expression for faith. Yet do but ask these earnest and impulsive gentlemen if indeed they have faith, and they will tell you they deal not in such intangible substances. Taking them at their word, however, they meant what they said, as far as meaning was possible, and they were earnest. They wanted change; they wanted revolution; they wanted things fresh and French; they wanted things new and inexplicable; they wanted schnaps. All these dainties they wanted, and made known their wants, concealing nought. Moreover, that they might have greater range, they coined novel phrases, and imported new Gallicisms; and by the eagerness with which they were adopted, we are to suppose the bold push of the Teutonic intellect into more real and positive realms required them. Yet this borrowing from beyond the Rhine is in itself enough to make us judge

harshly of them. Nothing could more surely prove their miserable poverty and lack of honest patriotism. Those philosophers who pretend to read the histories of nations in their languages, would agree with us that such a symptom is damning. Especially with the grand German tongue, which is to others of modern days as the organ to the rest of the orchestra, and so vital in its roots that its productive power is absolutely without limits, such innovations are sacrilege. In vain shall George Herwegh sing his 'Rhine shall still be German,' and call for chorus, while his countrymen and co-enthusiasts are guilty of these indecencies. 'And were it but for its wine,' Oh, George Herwegh! That refrain is well to hear, but there are many German throats who chant the stave and toss off the bumper which accompanies it, and are not choked by the lie that lingers in the passage. Be it how it may, the left bank is already half compromised, half bartered; whether by traitors or fools cannot be said, but the fact is so, and it will require a strong national revulsion and regeneration to prove that the Rhine is altogether, and will remain, German on both banks. Our personal experience *jenseits des Rheines*, and in the lucubrations of Cölner and Düsseldörfer poets, and prose rhapsodists, allows us not to augur hopefully for the fulfilment of Herr Herwegh's assertion, though all Pomerania shout, 'Yea, it shall be!' and prepare to maintain it against hazards, as they would manfully, were it only a question of blows. Garrisons of Pomeranians may do much, but the evil is a political one, and threatens to undermine mere strategy and skill in fortification. Stronger than the most formidable Rhenish fortress, is the 'code Napoleon' along the left bank, and more sapping of the old loyal, reverential German heart than the efforts of any drilled martial body could have been, are the doctrines of Young Germany.

When Wordsworth asked in his indignant sonnet,

Young England! what has then become of Old?

he made a just distinction between the two. Old England had not de-

parted (may she never!) and the claim of the junior for precedence was felt to be an impertinence. What may be termed the white-waistcoat era was of short duration with us. It had no growth in the soil, and took life solely from an outer impulse. Some handled it as a novelty; some adopted its badges for the same reason; but as it found none to enlist permanently in its ranks, and had no principles to instil, it wore away as a matter of course, and disappeared without commotion, dying as it had lived, *sans* experience, greenly. Young Germany, on the contrary, was the legitimate offspring of Old, and as its direct descendant and survivor, was entitled to more consideration, and could demand it. Goethe's dramatic onslaughts upon old beliefs and systems, and the serene impassibility with which the prose philosophers propounded new and startling theories, kept secret in their day the revolution that was working. Calm as oracles, they were content to labour on with time in their task of renovating the German mind. Time, however, who keeps his breath longer than the wariest of mortals in this great race, triumphed over them, and they passed, leaving the tangled threads of their deliberate toil in other hands less patient of results. Then in an instant the mask dropped. Then did venerated edifices crumble into dust.

Temples, domes, towers, pinnacles,

of the ancient faith fell, or shrank from the mockery of worship. Then were the treasures of the old Teutonic inspirations scattered to the winds. Then did respected 'isms' meet with rude buffets. Everywhere disorder, indicating a deranged state of the heart and the head.

As for the Muse, it was difficult to think what had come to her. Her rhymeless and immetrical ravings, and dulcet nonsense, Ophelia-like, were regarded with affectionate commiseration as typical of her peculiar condition, at first, but later revelations effectually banished this belief. She was this time less innocently connected with the Hamlet of the drama; wallowing, after his fashion, in speculative extremes of all sorts.

She soared to unimaginable altitudes—

Dim in the intense inane,

and grovelled in base pits of degradation ; argued for the sanctity of her vocation, and pandered it to perpetual obscenity ; prayed exquisite prayers, and rapt out swinging blasphemies. Beer, too, she drank ; and, as Dr. Johnson would say, the Muse that drinks beer, sings beer. The presence of stale malt, whether Bäyerisch or other, is exceeding perceptible about some of her subjects, and her treatment of them ; perceptible in a certain blustering Teutonicism, well enough when not wedded to verse, but offensive on her lips. She failed not to pledge Germania in her choicest vintages, nevertheless, and when warm on, and by, the theme, invoked its excellence with zeal and vigor enough; but elsewhere, with few exceptions, he is not that daughter of Mnemosyne we have been accustomed to know and love ; not that Muse who

Gives fame faster than time wastes life,
Preventing so his scythe and crooked knife;

but a personage whose benefactions are more fleeting ; something between a trull, a fishwife, and a fine lady of the French regency ; only natural when libidinous ; only fluent when reduced to invective; superb, refined, and admirable only when artificial.

There have been many who regarded the movement of Young Germany as good, or of good omen, or as a sign of health in the nation. Physicians will sometimes congratulate their patients on certain developments of disease, and these are straightway cherished as messengers of the returning favour of Hygea. Symptoms of healthy action are mistaken for signs of health rather than the struggle of nature to throw off what has been obstructing her. So Young Germany was but the turbulent eruption of a drugged and diseased system, ready to swallow any amount of nostrums infallible—only too willing to believe the monstrous growth a token of its satisfactory condition. The doctrines of Goethe and the knot of contemporaneous thinkers, lesser lights, but high planets in the German

heavens, which surrounded that refulgent orb, acted like fire-water on the unfledged youth springing up to supply their place. Scarce restrained in his presence, there were few considerations to withhold them after he had gone. The guiding hand of Mephistopheles was no longer there to control and assist them to sin by inches, so down the black gulf went this national Faust at one wild leap, pitching madly from crag to crag, and sending up weird sounds in the descent, whether of lamentation or insane glee, none knew. It has learnt the *facilis descensus* at a great cost, and if it ever climbs up again to its old sovereignty, the foundation will not be on lyrestones, as Herr v. Redwitz fondly counts ; his Amaranth, the new darling of the penitent German public, being the first of them.

Such a fermentation of the whole people, from the period of Goethe's death to the revolution of forty-eight, was surely never seen ! Professor and student, soldier and citizen, *herren und damen*, king and ministers ; for Frederick William, who coquettes with every sentiment, was certain not to let pass one pretending to hold in its shell the revivification and rejuveniscence of his country. The 'noble poetical nature,' and 'extraordinary depth of feeling' which Niebuhr ascribed to his pupil and favourite when Crown Prince in 1813, has been sadly frittered away since, what with one painted harlotry and another:

This new and gorgeous garment, majesty,
Sits not so easy on him.

Sadly has he survived,

To mock the expectation of the world,
To frustrate prophecies, and to raze out
Rotten opinion. . . .

After some little courtly dalliance with this novel love, the king, as usual with him, took fright, and called in his old counsellors to consult about measures of repudiation, preliminary to persecution. We believe he, too, was in earnest while the fit was on him. His pension to Freiligrath and interview with Herwegh did not answer well, however ; neither poet would compromise his opinions, or clothe them so as to suit the squeamishness of Royalty, though report, always ma-

licious to Herwegh, did say that the Republican Lion was somewhat abashed in the face of the Royal one, and roared 'like any nightingale' in that celebrated encounter. The 'divinity that doth hedge a king,' is after all a blind divinity, doing only the work of chain-armour. The king came out of it for a while, having really a noble nature, though a weak one, and a poetical tendency to look on the seemings of things ; but feeling himself shorn, naked, and unsafe, and becoming alarmed, he retired in haste, wrapt himself threefold in his Brandenburgian Ermine, and has remained ever since a firm and active, yet scarcely trusted ally of his associate crowned heads. He was not altogether to blame in this. All one can say of him is, that he is not a great man ; and if it requires greatness in a plebeian to rise up and attempt to reform his country, the demand is tenfold imperative when a king sets his hand to that wheel. Centuries are wanted to produce Alfreds, and Peters, and even those illustrious names might have been extinguished from the page of history, if, instead of having to emancipate a people from slavery and barbarism, they had been called to correct a nation run to seed and debauched by foul doctrines and filthy excesses. This mission his Majesty of Prussia conceived himself peculiarly fitted to fulfil, and we must honour the ambition that prompted him to so difficult and dangerous a business, though we cannot less than condemn the lack of penetration and self-knowledge by which he was so miserably betrayed, and to his subjects, ruined. For a person less equal to the task was not to be found throughout his kingdom, and in the end his indecision, fickleness, and fear of consequences, threw him on the protection of his brother, the Prince of Prussia, of whose sterling qualities, soldierly resolve, blunt readiness, shrewd perception of men and motives, and somewhat harder nature, had he possessed a larger portion, he would have been a happier man, and a better and more respected king.

But let us admit that it was likely to mislead an imaginative ardent

mind, this dream of a united, reinspirited, progressive Germany ; a Germany issuing from the realm of abstractions—casting its old mystical hieroglyphic skin and coming forth fresh and legible in exulting strength and beauty — a Germany with a fleet ! In some such sort, while the Prince was trying the temper of his steel and the condition of his ordnance, did the king idealise the movement, thinking it his duty as king and man to head it, he and the chosen few about him at that time. It was the vision of mystics exposing themselves most when they conceive they are impersonating opposites.

We put Germany with a fleet as the climax, for they were not to be confined to Terra Firma, already in a manner alien to it perchance, but yearned to traverse the seas in person, to have sight of Proteus,

And hear old Triton blow his wreathed horn.

Proteus was at home for them. To this passion add a desire for undiscovered lands strong as that of Columbus, when the weight of yet fabulous America hung over him. The world might have gained by this, probably, had so exalted a desire been matched with the smallest knowledge of the chart. As it was it becomes a curious speculation to think whither would this German fleet have sailed ; where finally would it have got a haven when once afloat and in blue water ! It was scarce fitted for any contest with the elements. Denying first the existence of that

Sweet little cherub which sits up aloft,

there was not much comfort for it in mid ocean, as Poor Jack would have forewarned it. One sees it beating about from tack to tack in search of its dream-realm ; rocked sleepily as in a new babyhood on the fathomless abysses ; the world before it in a perpetual offing, holding steady way for her sweating gold pits, arctic passages, and southern savannahs. Even in such a condition was the mental state of Germany at that time in its insatiate craving for something undefined, palpable, distant, not to be attained : out of its depth ; out of its element ; unable to evade the revolving circle ; too proud to make use of a pilot! Better to have gone down altogether, thought some. But the stomach of young Germany, if ever sufficiently strengthened for such a proceeding, was already deranged beyond its wont by the overboisterous cradling of the elements, and was prepared for no such desperate self-sacrifice. So, as might have been expected, an ignominious retreat was beaten. Stern foremost these elected leaders of the nineteenth century backed, unwitting of polestar and magnet, for what land would receive them ; ending by drifting among the breakers of the twelfth century ; a rather alarming retrogression. There now they lie stranded, listening to the lyre of Herr v. Redwitz ; himself, according to himself, another hermit sent specially to convert his countrymen into Crusaders against the Infidel.

Of course this ultra-Teutonic reaction took no one by surprise. That so much patriotic bluster, topheavy enthusiasm, inspired cosmopolitanism, scoffing unbelief, and frenzy of freedom, should finish in the old abhorrence of 'Welshland,' adoration of the pure German type, and subserviency to the ever-recruiting cowl, was to be supposed. Extremes are first cousins.

What Germany has gained by the change is another matter. Not much, we fancy ; yet in being restored, after so much piecemeal agitation, to form and national feeling, it has always advanced something, and Herr v. Redwitz can lay that unction, with his fifteenth edition of *Amaranth*, on his shaven crown. If this new phase be not, as at times we are inclined to suspect, another indication of that delicate dilettanteism for which his compatriots are remarkable, then, indeed, the case is worse.

Lessing's great service to the preceding age, Herr v. Redwitz, a smaller personage cut down, it may be, to the level of his time, has performed for this, in arresting the recurring Gallic tendency of the nation. We will by no means underrate this service, albeit we measure the man not high. This Gallic tendency is our chief charge against Young Germany. We remember not that

it has ever, despite its 'hatred to the Frank,' and 'Rhine shall still be German,' made a movement purely German in its aids and origin. George Herwegh, marching at the head of his republicans out of France to revolutionize his country, and Heinrich Heine, inditing stuff rebellious to God and man, with his usual interlarding of Gallicisms, from his Parisian retreat, present the same picture. The scoffing poet and martial singer, from different verges of feeling, unite in this grievous disgrace. Any one reading the songs of Herwegh will catch at once the fervour of the man, his thorough heartiness and faith in what he says without reserve, though some scandalizing neighbour should whisper at his shoulder that, when it did come to the fact of battle so violently invoked, he flung down his arms and was content to shelter himself in his flight even under his wife's petticoat. We vouch not for this fact, but so is it rumoured. Herwegh's patriotic songs, war songs, and all in which he sets himself to excite his countrymen, are stirring enough, windbags as many of them are, puffed out with exclamations of *Freiheit, Vaterland,* beer, Rhine wine, blood, brandy, and bombast ; not forgetting that frequent dramatic character in metrical German, *Der Teufel,* to whom the poet, or his antagonist, are to precipitate themselves headlong, and who appears to take a strong personal interest in the preservation intact of the Rhenish provinces, and the general affairs of the Gothic race. To a foreigner unacquainted with the gallant temper of these German youths, it would appear, judging from such songs, that it was rather a tough business to call them out, even though the Frank were marching to take possession of the 'natural boundary of his nation,' as M. Victor Hugo has it. But Herwegh's day is over, and since that highly connubial episode in his career already alluded to, and for which, as we have said, rumour is answerable, we have heard nothing more of him. Thus one representative of Young Germany may be considered to have been extinguished by a petticoat ; a circumstance not unknown

to the days of chivalry, and surely no reproach, for where the petticoat reaps so much honour, the gentleman must be allowed to escape ignominy.

It was wanting to complete Young Germany's overthrow that the infidel, *blasé,* cynic party which was its other darker offshoot, should acknowledge its sins, and surrender to the Eternal at discretion. Of this party, Heinrich Heine was the head, and not insignificant voice ; and in the note or pendant to the poems in *Romanzero,* we find ample admission of error, mixed with a certain manliness of tone that keeps up our respect for him. *Romanzero,* published in 1851, is, with the exception of *Les Dieux en Exil,* published in the present year, his last work. The latter, written in French prose, certainly startled us, for when *Romanzero* appeared, he had been three years stretched by a paralytic stroke in sickness and apprehension of death — physically dead to all sensation, and hopeless of recovery. The mind of the man, always lively, energetic, fresh for the conflict, seems, however, to have kindled into even greater clearness and force under this awful infliction. His constant flashing satire, exquisite lyric faculty, wonderful humour, and subtle genius are revived with tenfold vigour, and glow with unquenchable brilliancy, and he is yet more than a match for them who may have the ill-fortune to come across him. Thierry, the historian, is the only other instance we remember of so proud a triumph of the mental over the animal nature.

Heine is a true poet, and might have been a great one, if he had cared to be a better man. But his spirit was not to the measure of his power, and we see him, consequently, flinging huge hands about him, like a rebellious Titan, heaving mountains, destroying much, but building up nothing high, solid, and enduring. His poetry, as we have said, is full of Gallic phrases, and not unfrequently founded on French subjects, which, having an eye more open to what is before him and about him than most of his countrymen, was to be expected. His predilections are as anti-English as those of the most ferocious *sabreur*

in the French army, and being *aus Düsseldorf* as fervid in favour of Gaul. Heine has for many years inhabited Paris, for his doings in which city report has not flattered him. There, now, he lies, within hearing of the roar of life, dictating from what he calls his 'mattressgrave,' poems more than ever full of passion, sarcasm, and sweetness ; not prophetic of the other shore, looming grey with its thronging ghosts beyond black Lethe, as one would anticipate, but treble-charged with every motive and spring of the great drama from which he is irrevocably severed. Doubtless it is a rare pleasure to him so to disappoint people, and had he strength to chuckle over this excellent joke, would do so with all his might. Yet that he is not insensible to his state the following confession will testify. These are his words :—

Do I still exist? So sadly has my body fallen away, that scarce anything but the voice remains, and my bed reminds me of the sounding tomb of the Enchanter Merlin in the forest of Brécéliande, in Brittany, under mighty oaks whose tops blaze up toward the heavens like green flames. Alas ! for these trees and the fresh breezes that pervade them do I envy thee, friend Merlin ! for here, above my mattressgrave in Paris, no green leaf whispers, nothing late and early do I hear but the rattle of carriages, the wrangling of men and women, the din of hammers, and the jingling of pianos. A grave without peace, death without the privileges of the dead, who have not to expend money, and are not required to write either letters or books ! truly a melancholy position ! The measure of my coffin has long since been taken, also everything is prepared for the 'Necrologic,' but I die so slowly that this delay is as weary a thing for myself as for my friends. But, patience ! all must have an end. One morning, you will find the show closed in which the puppet of my imagination has so often diverted you. . . . . Lying upon one's death-bed, one becomes more and more open to conscience, and would make peace with God and the world. I admit that I have clawed and bitten many, and that I was no lamb. Yet trust me, those lauded lambs of gentleness would be less holy if they possessed the fangs and the claws of tigers. I may flatter myself that it is but seldom I have availed myself of such inbred weapons. Since I have felt the need of God's

486

mercy, I have given an amnesty to all my enemies, and many fine poems directed against very high and very ignoble people were therefore not admitted to the present collection (*Romanzero*.) Poems that only by half hints offended against God (*den lieben Gott*), I have eagerly given over to the flames. Better that the verses burn than their author!

Better that the verses burn than their author! Does he mean this? Is he absolutely propitiating hellfire at last? Or is it but another malicious trap for those tormentors who have been so long seeking to convert him? It is well to take him at his word, and let him have the laugh, if there be one meditated. Yet burning of verses is a grave matter, and looks not like trickery, as all who are acquainted with the kind *nascitur non fit*, whose labour it is to import rhymes from Parnassus, will know.

He continues :—

Yes! as with the creature so with the Creator. I have made my peace, to the great scandal of my enlightened friends, (the citizens of Young Germany,) who reproach me with this relapse into the old superstition, as they choose to denominate my return home into the bosom of my God. Others, in their intolerance, use even more bitter expressions. The convocated High Clergy of atheism has pronounced its anathema upon me, and there are certain fanatic priests of unbelief who would willingly fasten me upon the rack, in order to induce me to confess my heresies. Fortunately they have no other instrument of torture to inflict upon me, than their writings. But, without being put to the torture, I will confess everything. Yes! I have, indeed, returned to God, like the prodigal son, after long tending of swine. What was the affliction that drove me to him? It may be a less petty cause than mere human affliction and misery. The yearning of Heaven came upon me, and urged me forth, through forests and ambushed passes, over the giddiest mountain ways of logical bewilderment. On my course I discovered the God of the pantheists, but he could not help me. This poor visionary being has interwoven and incorporated itself with the world, and become so imprisoned in it, that it can do nothing but gape at you powerlessly, and without purpose. To have a will one must also have an individuality, and, in order to manifest that will, one must have free elbow-room.

When you require a God, one that can assist you—for that, in the main, is the principal matter—you must accept, also, his identity and oneness, his superhumanity and his holy attributes of infallibility, all-goodness, and all-comprehending wisdom, &c., &c. The immortality of the soul, our deathlessness after death, will be then immediately conceded to us in the bargain, in like manner as the beautiful marrow-bones which the butcher, when he is content with his purchaser, flings gratuitously into his basket.

Such a beautiful marrow-bone is called, in the language of the French kitchen, *la réjouissance*, and with it most excellent broth may be made, which, for a poor fainting invalid, is very strengthening and grateful. That I did not decline such a *réjouissance*, and that it worked, in no small degree, to the comfort of my mind, every feeling man will allow to be reasonable.

I have spoken of the God of the Pantheists, but I cannot forbear remarking, that at bottom he is no God at all, as indeed the Pantheists themselves are properly nothing but Atheists under a mask.

The same fifteen years comedy which, here in France, the constitutional royalists, principally Republicans at heart, played with the throne, was enacted towards God by the greater part of Germany during the period of the Restoration. After the revolution of July the mask was dropped on the yon as on the hither side of the Rhine. Since then, especially after the fall of Louis Philippe, the best monarch who ever wore the constitutional crown of thorns, it has been accepted in France that only two forms of government could stand the probation of reason and experience, —absolute royalty and the Republic: that one of the twain must be chosen, and that everything intermediate was mere make-shift—false, impossible, and altogether disastrous. In the same fashion it came to be regarded in Germany that we must make choice between religion and philosophy—between the clear text dogma of belief, and the last result of thought,—between the absolute God of the Bible and Atheism.

As regards myself, I cannot flatter myself of having made any remarkable political advances. I continued to persist in the same democratic principles to which I paid allegiance in my first youth, and for which, since then, I have ever more ardently burned. In theology, on the contrary, I must accuse myself of having retrograded, as above stated, by my return to the old superstition—to full trust in the personality of God. Now

this cannot be glozed over as many a well-meaning and enlightened friend endeavoured to do. But I must positively deny the report, that this falling back of mine has led me to embrace any sect, or to enter into the bosom of the church at all. No; my religious convictions and views have remained unfettered by any churchism : no bell-pealing has flattered me away; no altar-candles blinded me. I have dallied with no symbols, and not quite renounced my reason. I have forsworn nothing, not even my old Pagan gods, from whom, indeed, I have turned away, but the parting was one of love and friendship.

And then he relates how, in May, 1848, on the last day that he was able to go out, he crawled wearily to the Louvre, and there, at the feet of the Goddess of Beauty, lay long and wept vehemently, so that a stone might have taken pity on him, and so on ; all of which we are willing to accept as a poetical fact, for its own sake, whether true or not.

In his farewell to the reader, he hopes we shall meet in a better world, where he intends to write us better books, trusting that Swedenborg has not spoken false to him in promising to that effect. He then touches with humorous earnestness on the Swedenborgian doctrine of entire personality after death, even to the carrying on of whatever business occupied us in life.

But (adds Heine) sillily as these tales may sound, they are intrinsically as remarkable as deep-thoughted. The great Scandinavian Seër comprehended the oneness and indivisibility of our existence, as also he knew and recognised most justly the inalienable individuality of men. Life's continuation beyond death is with him no ideal mumming stronghold, where we put on the new man and new jackets : men and costume are with him unchanged. In the other world of Swedenborg, the poor Greenlanders will also feel comfortable, who once, as the Danish missionaries sought to convert them, desired to know whether there were seals in the Christian heaven ; and answered, on the negative reply, that the Christian heaven would not do

for the Greenlanders, who could never exist without seals.

How the soul struggles against the thought of our personal cessation, everlasting extinction ! The *horror vacui*, ascribed to Nature, is infinitely more intuitive in the human spirit. But be comforted, dear reader ; there is a life after death, and in the other world we also shall find our seals again.

That
    Eternal form shall still divide
    The eternal soul from all beside ;

is truer faith than that we finally
            shall fall
    Remerging in the general soul :

and we are glad to meet Heine upon that ground at least. But we are puzzled as to what description of religious belief he falls back upon, whether the faith of his fathers (for he branches from the Israelites), or other. It seems, after all, little better than a Young German compromise with some very obfuscated glimmer of higher things seen at the last gasp. He is careful to tell us that he has 'not quite renounced his reason,' and that his confused and monstrous transacherontic realm of life-after-death, serves to make his utter darkness visible to us. In the Swedenborgian kingdom to come, however, he will write better books, and explain all this, if, indeed, we have any right to demand explanations from a humorist. He will there give a new polish to the old joke, while all young Germans, fierce-bearded and burly in Parisian habiliments, roll and lurch round him, like varnished bears, intoxicated with the cachinnation he best loves to provoke.

To the Swedenborgian heaven let them depart then, for here among us, and on their fathers' earth, is place for them no more. The penny whistle of Herr von Redwitz, and that solemn piper himself, are not yet translated thither to torment them in the assemblage of motley who have 'not quite renounced' their reason.'

LONDON, SATURDAY, AUGUST 19, 1854.

REVIEWS.

Germany, from 1760 to 1814; or, Sketches of German Life, from the Decay of the Empire to the Expulsion of the French. By Mrs. Austin. Longman and Co.

THE greater part of Mrs. Austin's volume having already appeared in the form of contributions to periodical literature, we might refrain from giving any detailed criticism of its contents. But we feel called upon to offer some remarks, the more so as we notice that contemporary journals have spoken of it with unqualified and indiscriminate praise. The materials out of which the work is composed are three articles published in the 'Edinburgh Review,' in the years 1842, 1844, and 1847; part of an article in the 'British and Foreign Review,' in 1841, on the life of Steffens; and a fourth article, now first printed, intended as a sequel to the third in the 'Edinburgh Review.' To give a connected and consecutive form to matter so miscellaneous, and collected at various times, could not prove an easy task, and it is in this that Mrs. Austin has chiefly proved unsuccessful. She has compiled, with great industry, a volume of miscellanies, connected with Germany and its affairs during the latter part of the eighteenth and the beginning of the nineteenth century; but her work scarcely deserves to be ranked as a systematic history of the War of Liberation, which she somewhat ambitiously proposes as her subject. Assiduous study of German literature, especially of personal memoirs and autobiographies not generally known, and long residence in the country, while traditionary notices of the period were still abundant, have been the principal qualifications of the author. Certainly, few English writers could have done equal justice to the subject, or presented sketches marked on the whole by greater accuracy and truth. The criticism of German readers is sought to be disarmed by the confession that many errors will doubtless be observed by them, but for these indulgence is craved, in the absence of wilful perversions. How far Mrs. Austin may claim the benefits of this indulgence must depend on the spirit in which she receives the corrections of errors that may be pointed out. Some of these are of a serious kind, and tend to throw discredit on her general accuracy as a narrator of history. The most extraordinary blunder relates to Count Hardenberg, the Chancellor of Prussia, of whom Mrs. Austin gives a strangely contradictory account, apparently from confusing the Chancellor with another Count Hardenberg, a distant relative, who deserves all the opprobrium unwittingly heaped on the minister. The following passage contains the incongruous sketch of Hardenberg's character:

"The King and Queen, who had long known Hardenberg's mind and heart, joyfully received him as Chancellor of State from the hands of their implacable enemy; and the Emperor, in the view and belief that he should obtain larger contributions through Hardenberg's financial dexterity, placed at the head of Prussia perhaps the only man capable of organizing her for a successful resistance to his tyranny. Many might have been found able to temporize, but hardly one with such constancy and invincible faith in the future greatness of Prussia.

"Stein would have shown great vigour and determination, but he would not have had the patience to bide his time; to curb the burning hatred, and hold in check the growing force, of Prussia, till the decisive moment;—the immortal merit of Hardenberg. How could a man of Stein's iron truth have succeeded for years in utterly deceiving the French government?

"By adapting himself to his French masters with wonderful discretion on the one side, while on the other he held in check the fermenting internal elements, Hardenberg saved the country from a premature explosion, which would probably have precipitated her into the abyss.

"Hardenberg's recall took place in June, 1810. Divided as opinions are with respect to the character of this remarkable man, they seem to be nearly unanimous as to his peculiar fitness for the time and the circumstances in which he lived, and for the sort of Brutus part he had to play. 'At the time,' says Hormayr, 'when the French police in Vienna was most suspicious, vigilant, and inexorable, and when every agent of England had been obliged to flee, Count Hardenberg, the chief mediator with Münster and the British ministry, contrived for a series of years to elude their Argus eyes. An affected insignificance and a stupid indifference to political affairs, and to all that did not concern his purse; a cynical and *blasé* air; a ludicrous avarice and an eager talk about funds and exchange, concealed the acute mind, the true German spirit, and the implacable hatred of France.'"

The Count Hardenberg here truly described by Hormayr, was a most contemptible character, who if not a paid spy of the English and French governments, was generally reputed to be so. To describe the illustrious Chancellor Hardenberg, by mistake or not, as a spy, rogue, and miser, must both give offence to all Germans, and damage Mrs. Austin's book in their opinion. We must request Mrs. Austin at once frankly and plainly to acknowledge her mistake. If she does not, her book will be perpetually cited as an instance of the ignorance or arrogance of English writers when discussing German politics. This may be avoided by her at once correcting and explaining her error herself. Already a most severe judgment on her work has been passed by Ernst Moritz Arndt, the octogenarian Professor at Bonn, whose own share in public affairs during the War of Liberation was so conspicuous and honourable. He was the author, among many other patriotic pieces, of the German national song, 'Was ist des Deutschen Vaterland?' His name is venerated throughout Germany for the wonderful energy displayed by him during the wars against Napoleon, and for the spirit-stirring writings by which he sustained the enthusiasm of his countrymen. He lived in terms of intimacy with most of the leading men of the times which Mrs. Austin has undertaken to describe. Of Count, afterwards Prince Hardenberg, the Prussian Chancellor of State, he says, in a notice of Mrs. Austin's book in the 'Kölnische Zeitung,' that he was a man in every way of noble character and dignified conduct; whereas, the other Count Hardenberg, Professor Arndt tells us, on the authority of Counsellor of State Von Stägeman, and of General Grollman, was the tool and agent of Münster and of Talleyrand, who availed themselves of his instrumentality when any plot was carrying on against Prussian and Russian interests. That this man should be mistaken for the high-minded and honourable Chancellor, a perfect model of the old German nobleman of the best class, and a truly patriotic and able statesman, is a most unfortunate error, which we have dwelt upon in order to impress on the author the propriety of herself acknowledging it. At the same time we must protest against the rudeness and unfairness of Professor Arndt's general comments on her book. He commences with the remark that "English women are more in the habit, or rather are more audacious than German women, to intrude on a domain which, by its nature, seems reserved for men, the domain of history-writing. At home they have tried it sometimes not without success, but in foreign countries never." After explaining why English writers generally, and English bluestockings especially, cannot enter fully into the understanding of foreign habits, usages, and histories, Professor Arndt does Mrs. Austin the justice to say that she is not a bluestocking (using the English phrase) of the common sort, and praises her for her diligence in studying German life and literature, and for displaying a friendly tone of feeling higher than is generally exhibited by English travellers and authors. But her work is at the best described as a medley of ill-assorted gleanings from all manner of publications and memoirs, without any deep insight into German life and character, or sufficient knowledge of former periods of German history. We venture to suggest to Professor Arndt that any Englishman or Englishwomen, of ordinary intelligence and observation, may, from the knowledge of English political and social life, understand many things not discoverable by the visionary theories and subtle philosophy in which his countrymen are too apt to indulge. In spite of what the Professor says about the absence of fundamental principles in Mrs. Austin's statements, we think that in the following passages she very plainly and forcibly indicates some of the true causes of the failure of German politicians and patriots in attaining the good government and social welfare which they long to see their countrymen possess, and which England and the United States, under widely diverse political conditions, more fully enjoy. Here, for instance, is the real explanation of the imperfect results of all the efforts and sacrifices of the men with whom Professor Arndt was associated in his younger days:—

"I know that it may be objected that the splendid display of patriotism herein exhibited led to a very incomplete result, and that the remarkable constellation of men who had rescued their country, were incapable of giving to it a government such as its heroic sacrifices had deserved. There cannot be a more instructive proof that courage and honesty, united to the highest intellectual power and culture, do not suffice to qualify men for political action. The Germans had been too long confined to the domain of speculation, which is beset by no obstacles, and circumscribed by no limits, to be fit for the combined action in which a man finds himself hedged in on every side by limitations, and compelled to innumerable concessions; and in which that object so mortifying to human pride, some qualified and possible good, is all that can be attained.

"Even now the Genial is too much the national idol; and a more dangerous presiding deity of statesmen can hardly be imagined. To its worshippers perseverance in a definite course is 'Starrheit' (rigidity), and a concentration of the views on certain fixed and practicable objects, narrowness. The mixture of violence and feebleness, of boundless pretensions and pitiable short-comings, to which 1848 gave birth, showed but too clearly that the propensity to blind imitation, and the utter disdain of the Possible, which characterized Germany formerly, were not yet extinct. Change of habits, especially habits of thought, is a slow operation; but the manly spirits and high intelligences of Germany will assuredly in time devote themselves to the practical service of their country, and secure to her a government worthy of men who freed themselves from a foreign yoke."

A still more important element in national progress is the diffusion of personal morality and religion. With all the abuses and evils of political life in England and America, there is a leaven of healthy moral influence, which has ever been the great source of our power and prosperity. Even Hume, with all his Jacobite prejudices and personal infidelity, had the candour to declare in his history, that to the Puritans in the seventeenth century England owed the preservation of her constitutional liberties; and by the same influence, in forms more suited to the spirit of the times, the true greatness of England has been maintained. Some of the best and most enlightened men of recent times in Germany have perceived that here was to be sought the real hope of their country :—

"No man," says Mrs. Austin, "was more convinced of the supreme importance of moral influences than Stein. In a letter to Hardenberg, he speaks of the awakening of public spirit as indispensable to the salvation of the country; and adds, 'It can only be awakened by the cultivation of the religious feelings, and by political institutions fitted to call into action all the energies of the nation.' Stein expresses great doubts of the energy and patriotism of the higher classes, but adds, 'The clergy will co-operate vigorously.'"

As we have said so much about Professor Arndt, our readers may like to see the way in which he is referred to by Mrs. Austin, in her account of the times in which he took most active part in political affairs. A testimony so honourable scarcely deserved to be requited by the severity with which he has criticised the work in which it appears :—

"Nobly indeed did the philosophers and scholars and poets of Germany act their part, as leaders of the minds of men, especially of youth. Who has not heard of the potent appeal made by Fichte; of the Tyrtæan songs of Körner and Arndt; of the labours of Wilhelm von Humboldt, Niebuhr, and Schleiermacher, to improve the intellectual training, and raise the intellectual character, of Prussia? The first call to arms in Breslau was uttered by Professor Steffens, from his chair in the university. Scharnhorst, the great soldier and administrator, was so much of a scholar, that the poor old Duke of Brunswick, as Müffling tells us, was never at his ease in his presence, and said he felt as if he was talking before a professor. In the train of these great names follow a host of others, less illustrious, but all deserving of honour and gratitude.

"Among them, one of the earliest and the most zealous, was Ernst Moritz Arndt. His spirited war-songs contributed to stir up the torpid energies and emasculated spirit of the German people. It is the fashion with the present race of young Germans, die Freien, as they call themselves, to undervalue the exertions and deride the sentiments of the men of that period. This proves nothing but incapacity for the feelings of reverence and gratitude, and the presumption common to ignorant and untried men.

"We by no means go along with Arndt, or those whose opinions he represents, in his exaggerated and exclusive patriotism, or in his undiscriminating depreciation of the French. But at the time at which he wrote and acted, there was one thing needful, and that was, to get rid of the foreign yoke. There are moments in which the most intense and inveterate one-sidedness is a virtue. The question then was not, to appreciate the French, but to drive them out of the country; and this could never have been done without an appeal to all the passions which they had set in array against themselves. What therefore is now, in time of peace, a defect, was then a merit;—the only merit applicable to oppressed, degraded, enfeebled Germany. It was the moment for loud

cries and hard knocks,—not for calm examination or equitable judgments."

On Mrs. Austin's historical narrative we do not intend to offer any remarks, but for various reasons we cannot forbear from quoting from the latter part of her volume the account of a tragical episode, which, comparatively unimportant in itself, was pregnant with great moral consequences in rousing the resistance to the French domination :—

"Palm, a Nürnberg bookseller, a man of quiet and pious life, was arrested for selling or having in his possession a pamphlet entitled 'Germany in its deepest Degradation.' The mode of his arrest was peculiarly odious. He had escaped to Erlangen, but his anxiety for his family brought him back to Nürnberg, and he remained concealed in his own house. One day a poor boy came to the shop with a list of subscriptions for a soldier's widow, and begged to speak to Palm himself. Palm unsuspectingly admitted him, and gave him some money. Hardly was he gone, when two French gendarmes forced their way into his chamber, and took him before the General. It was in vain that the guiltless man affirmed, and offered to prove, that he had received the pamphlet in a bale or package of which he knew not the contents, and that not a single copy had been sold in his shop; he was sent by Berthier before a military commission; and, 'whereas nothing is more urgent than to check the progress of doctrines by which the rights of nations, the due reverence for crowned heads, and all order and subordination would be overthrown,' he was condemned and shot the following day at Branau. The death of this innocent man excited at the time the strongest feeling of pity, indignation, and disgust throughout Europe; among other marks of which was the subscription raised in England for his widow and children.

"We have touched on an event with which most of our readers are doubtless familiar, chiefly, we confess, that we may introduce them to a picture of obscure virtue and genuine charity, in the contemplation of which the heart, sickened by cruelty, and depressed by the triumphs of bold bad men, finds refreshment and repose. Palm, a Lutheran, was shot at Branau, where there was at the time no minister of that confession. There is extant a letter to his wife, from one of two Catholic priests who administered the last comforts of religion to him, which is one of the most beautiful and unstudied expressions of true Christian charity that we know of. We would fain insert the whole outpouring of simple, artless, tender sympathy, but space fails us.

"The following passage is worthy of everlasting remembrance.

"'In spite of the difference of our religious creed, of which he instantly and frankly informed me, our message (i. e. whether our presence and exhortations in this awful moment would be consolatory to him? and otherwise that we would on no account trouble him,) was most welcome to him, and he gave a ready ear to our expressions of general charity and faith; for, in obedience to perfect tolerance and brotherly love, we would not in the slightest degree disturb the persuasions he had entertained from youth up, or the creed he had piously obeyed. He requested me to tell you his two favourite hymns, namely, 'Alles ist an Gottes Segen,' and 'Gott Lob, nun ist es wieder Morgen,' (which he repeatedly pronounced with the greatest devotion) that you might teach them to your children, and commend them to them for their whole lives; and to assure you that they had given him the greatest comfort and peace all his life, but especially in his last hours on the 20th of August.

"'He also expressed a desire to receive the Lord's Supper after the forms of his own faith, which however could not be fulfilled, for the want of a minister of his own confession. But we tranquilized him fully on this head, by the assurance that our Lord and Saviour is of a certainty with those that seek him and follow after him in life and in death; as was especially the case with him.

"'So, amidst friendly converse, the last minutes

of his life imperceptibly drew nigh. He commended you and his children to the especial care of the Most High, and prayed that he would be a Father to the fatherless; concerning which also we strove to set his mind at rest.'

"These true ministers of Christ not only went to the French authorities and implored a respite of two or three days, but, when that was denied, accompanied the victim to the scene of his death, though with anguish and suffering which seriously affected the health of the writer. The letter, which is long, ends thus:—

"'Dearest Madam, were we not divided by so wide a space, and did my duties permit me so long a journey, I should certainly have the happiness of administering comfort and peace to you in this bitterest sorrow: we should have so much to speak of.'

"The name of this faithful servant of Christ was Thomas Pöschl, secular priest in Salzburg. While the names of the murderers of the guiltless—Ney, Bernadotte, Davoust,—enjoy a sort of immortality, that of this admirable man is unknown or forgotten. Let at least one respectful hand commend it to the love and veneration of mankind! Not however without feeling how little human respect can act as motive or reward to such virtues as his; not without a humiliating sense of the contrast such charity presents to the odious and unchristian brawls with which England continually re-echoes.

"Palm died with heroic constancy. At the last moment pardon was offered him, if he would reveal the name of the author of the pamphlet, but he steadily refused. His death, which was intended to strike terror into Germany, was one of the sparks which kindled the great fire of national vengeance; and afforded another proof of the blindness to consequences with which Heaven visits human pride and ambition."

In an Appendix, Mrs. Austin gives a variety of extracts from works illustrating the narrative of the War of Liberation. The volume presents, in compact and accessible form, much scattered information, which a student of history could only have otherwise obtained by long and laborious research; and though German critics may find some passages to object to, we commend the book, as containing truthful and genial sketches of a country and a race for which English readers must always feel the warmest sympathies.

The Poetry of Germany. Consisting of Selections of upwards of Seventy of the most Celebrated Poets. Translated into English Verse by Alfred Baskerville. Leipzig : Mayer. London : Williams and Norgate.

MR. BASKERVILLE's German poetical anthology contains specimens of the works of the most distinguished authors ; from very remote times down to our own days. Among the contemporary poets the list includes the names of Ernst Moritz Arndt, Count Auersperg, better known as Anastasius Grün, Karl Beck, Ferdinand Freiligrath, Heinrich Heine, Gottfried Kinkel, Wolfgang Müller, Ludwig Uhland, and others less known in England. Of Klopstock, Goëthe, Schiller, a number of the finest pieces are given. It is difficult to choose extracts from a collection so voluminous and varied, more than five hundred poems being contained in the work. Of the translator's capabilities and skill our readers will best be able to judge from some piece with the original of which they are familiar. We give his version of Arndt's Der Deutschen Vaterland :—

" Where is the German's fatherland?
Is't Swabia ? Is't the Prussian's land ?
Is't where the grape glows on the Rhine ?
Where sea-gulls skim the Baltic's brine ?
Oh no ! more great, more grand
Must be the German's fatherland !

" Where is the German's fatherland ?
Bavaria, or the Styrian's land ?
Is't where the Marser's cattle graze ?
Is it the Mark where forges blaze ?
O no ! more great, more grand
Must be the German's fatherland !

" Where is the German's fatherland ?
Westphalia ? Pomerania's strand ?
Is't where the sand wafts on the shore ?
Is't where the Danube's surges roar ?
O no ! more great, more grand
Must be the German's fatherland !

" Where is the German's fatherland ?
Say how is named that mighty land !
Is't Tyrol ! Where the Switzers dwell ?
The land and people please me well.
O no ! more great, more grand
Must be the German's fatherland.

" Where is the German's fatherland?
Say how is named that mighty land !
Ah ! Austria surely it must be,
In honours rich and victory.
O no ! more great, more grand
Must be the German's fatherland !

" Where is the German's fatherland ?
Say how is named that mighty land !
Is it the gem which princely guile
Tore from the German crown erewhile ?
O no ! more great, more grand
Must be the German's fatherland !

" Where is the German's fatherland ?
Name me at length that mighty land !
' Where'er resounds the German tongue,
' Where'er its hymns to God are sung.'
Be this the land,
Brave German, this thy fatherland !

" There is the German's fatherland,
Where oaths are sworn but by the hand,
Where faith and truth beam in the eyes,
And in the heart affection lies.
Be this the land,
Brave German, this thy fatherland !

" There is the German's fatherland,
Where wrath the Southron's guile doth brand,
Where all are foes whose deeds offend,
Where every noble soul's a friend.
Be this the land,
All Germany shall be the land !

" All Germany that land shall be,
Watch o'er it, God, and grant that we,
With German hearts, in deed and thought,
May love it truly as we ought.
Be this the land,
All Germany shall be the land !"

It is hardly fair to Mr. Baskerville, as a poet, to select this piece, but we do so rather to show his style as a translator. The book will be prized by the public more for containing a varied and judicious selection of German poetry, than for any display of ingenuity or art in the English versions. It is sufficient to say that the spirit of the original is generally retained without any great departure from the literal reading. The translator acts well upon the quoted words of Lord Mahon. " I would rather have a faulty rhyme than lose a noble thought." The book is very neatly printed. The original text is given on the opposite pages to the English translation. To English students of the German language the work will be useful, as well as acceptable to the lovers of German literature. Some of the passages of Schiller's Song of the Bell have not been excelled in any former version, and in other poems where comparisons are suggested with labours in the same literary field, Mr. Baskerville maintains an honourable distinction.

MRS. AUSTIN'S SKETCHES OF GERMAN LIFE.

Germany from 1760 to 1814; or, Sketches of German Life, from the Decay of the Empire to the Expulsion of the French. By Mrs. Austin. Longmans.

THERE is something peculiarly attractive in a "pleasant" book. We do not mean a witty, or a lively, or an exciting, or an imaginative, or a profound book, but something akin to all these; a book, in short, which is like the conversation of a wise, cheerful, and well-informed friend. Unfortunately, there are few books of this kind, as there are few persons whose private conversation comes even near to the ideal standard; and we are proportionately the more gratified when we light upon some new volume with fair claims to the charms we desire.

If Mrs. Austin's readers are at all of our opinion, they will hasten to enrol her *Germany from 1760 to 1814* in the list of these welcome visitors. It is pre-eminently a *pleasant* book. She is a kind-hearted, wise, liberal, and mature-minded woman; who has read many books, with a special devotion to one particular subject, but always striving to use books for the purpose of knowing more of *man*. She possesses more breadth of view than is common with women, however brilliant their liveliness or keen their power of observation. She can sympathise with the past without scorning the present; and she can value the present without being deceived by its cant. Her style is strong and vigorous, without loss of that airy delicacy which is so agreeable in the best female writers, and which it is so difficult for a man to acquire; and she possesses the rare art of mingling the entertaining and the instructive without pedantry and without affectation. We do not pretend to say there is nothing in her book from which we dissent, or that she is entirely free from the delusions of the school of which she is an ornament. Still, she has given us one of the most entertaining, informing, and sensible books we have for a long time met with.

In substance, some considerable portion of it has before appeared in the *Edinburgh* and *British and Foreign* Reviews. The whole, however, is now moulded into a continuous sketch of the life and manners of German society, during that momentous half-century when the old world of modern Europe was rapidly merging into the world of this present day; preserving, however, the shape of a review of the several autobiographical memoirs from which the authoress draws her materials. A large amount of her matter, accordingly, consists of extracts from the books she criticises. The result,

however, is by no means a mere piece of patchwork; the whole being woven together with considerable discrimination and skill, and the quotations serving the purpose of illustrations of Mrs. Austin's own reflections on the life and manners of the period before her.

A more interesting subject for observation and thought can scarcely be named. To those who would live wisely and profitably in their own generation, neither the enemy nor the slave of the age in which their lot is cast, few things are more needful than a knowledge of what their immediate forefathers really *were*, and of the characteristic merits and defects of the age that is gone, as compared with those of the day to which we ourselves belong. We have no book, however high its pretensions, which furnishes more valuable materials towards forming a just estimate of this present wildly-excited and moving time, in contrast with the era of routine to which it has succeeded, than these sketches of German life. That in some respects we have gained immeasurably on our grandfathers and great-grandfathers, is, we think, undeniable. The slightest acquaintance with the prevailing literary, courtly, and domestic history of the last century, is sufficient to show that the *morals* of Europe are improved to an extraordinary degree. Doubtless a considerable portion of this improvement is superficial, and some of it is altogether hollow and hypocritical. But where there is hypocrisy in one man, there is virtue in another; for where all are vile it is not worth while to play the hypocrite. Decency, also, is not necessarily purity, nor is honour necessarily integrity; sometimes they are, indeed, the substitutes with which the self-deceiver cheats his own degraded conscience into a conviction of its immaculate excellence. Yet, with every allowance on the score of deception, prudery, and priggishness, we are convinced that the entire tone of English and continental society is far freer from positive vice and grossness than it was a hundred years ago. We are also larger in our ideas, less narrow in our sympathies, less brutal and harsh in our exactions, less suspicious of every thing that is not familiar and our own.

The drawbacks to the true progress of human life consist in the substitution of restlessness for repose, vehemence for strength, shallowness for depth, and a commonplace uniformity for varied individuality. The prose of life has swallowed up its poetry. We are knocked against one another so unceasingly, that with the edges, points, and roughnesses of character, its distinction, varieties, and too much of its bloom and beauty, are beaten away. Our thoughts and feelings are like a stream that has been diverted from its natural course over rocks and through woods and meadows, to the dull, monotonous course of a canal. It may have become more commercially useful, more tranquil in its surface, and more equable in its flow, but the glancing sparkle, the foaming cascade, the deep rushing torrent, the glory of the woodland and the sweetness of the plain, are passed away. The profit may be greater, but it is questionable whether the enjoyment be not often less.

In the first division of her book Mrs. Austin sketches the peculiar ties of German domestic life, as it existed before the American and French revolutions had thrown all Europe into fermentation, and ultimately into war. It was one of those times which, though not distinctly recognised as periods of transition, are yet the precursors of transitional periods,—when old things are not only old, but are beginning to decay; when the abuses to which every variety of human society is liable, are hastening to tell injuriously on all its members, and induce that sense of evil which is the precursor of change. Probably, in the middle of the last century there was no part of civilised Europe in which "old-world ways" had remained so intact as in Germany; where national customs were held in such veneration, and national character displayed itself in so many and so strongly-marked varieties. The anecdotes which Mrs. Austin quotes from the memoirs of Madame Schopenhauer and Madame Pichler bring out into strong light this mingling of the venerable, the decaying, and the picturesque. The old monarchical and feudal system survived almost in its integrity, and with its abuses retained not a few of its unquestionable blessings, both to the governors and the governed. The "Ecclesiastical States," such as Cologne, Mrs. Austin singles out as special instances of a mild and patriarchal rule, and as preserving in its full significancy the old saying, ". It is good living under the Crozier.'

"German life, as we have seen it, was inextricably bound up with the existence and character of the Germanic Empire. Danzig or Nürnberg could have been no other than free imperial cities; Gotha or Weimar than the capitals of small principalities. The Ecclesiastical States, again, had a character of their own,—and one, we may add, on which it is allowable to look back with a sort of regret, as models of mild, pacific government. Towns, insignificant as to size, wealth, and population, had a moral and intellectual importance, to which the provincial cities of France or England presented no parallel."

A touching anecdote, which Mrs. Austin tells from her own experience, confirms this view of the affection that was felt both for the more worthy specimens of the nobles and for the clergy:

"I was walking with the late Countess T —— H —— near her magnificent castle in Bohemia, when we met a peasant-woman. The Countess spoke to her with her usual kindness, and passed on. Perceiving that the woman stopped, I looked round, and saw her hastily kissing the hem of Countess T——'s dress. The noble and excellent lady looked half-embarrassed that an Englishwoman should witness what might seem to her an act of degrading servility; and said something of its being 'a foolish custom.'. To me, who knew her, and the ceaseless beneficence of which the people around her were the objects, no homage could appear excessive; and I was not disposed to quarrel with the form. The misfortune is, that such demonstrations are degraded by being paid to mere power.

"In my walks in and about Carlsbad with the late venerable and pious Ladislas Pyrker, Archbishop of Erlau, I frequently saw men and women come softly behind him and kiss the skirts of his coat with the most fervent reverence, often with murmured blessings. This never surprised me. All the holiness, purity, benignity, meekness, and patience of the religion he professed and exemplified, were legibly written on his pale and suffering face. The poor people also knew the works of enlightened charity and piety to which he devoted his time, his thoughts, and his princely revenues.

"I must add, that I never happened to see the same homage offered to any of the princes and potentates who resorted to Carlsbad. Pyrker's dignities, as Magnate of Hungary and Prince of the Church, were lost and forgotten in his Christian perfections."

The civic government of the towns presented sometimes a striking contrast to the freedom enjoyed under the ecclesiastical magnates. Madame Schopenhauer herself was a Dantziger when Dantzig was free; and when young, with her republican independence, she possessed a full share of republican pride and arrogance. On a visit to Pyrmont, the earliest established of the German baths, she saw the young reigning Duke of Mecklenburgh-Schwerin take out a flower-girl to dance in the public walks at Pyrmont. "What," exclaimed she, "would the Dantzigers say, if their reigning Bürgermeister (mayor) were to demean himself so in public ?"

In those days, the patriarchal relationships of primitive times were still something more than a mere exaction of outward forms of deference, such as they remained among ourselves long after their substance had passed away:

"Not more than a quarter of a century ago," says Madame Schopenhauer, "there existed in every principal family of that city a family tribunal (Familiengericht), to which every member was amenable, and over which the head of the family presided. When a young girl, I accompanied my mother on a visit to the city of her fathers, and was taken to be introduced to this awful assembly. We went in full dress, and found the old man of eighty seated in the *Grossvaterstuhl*[*] at the top of the room, and the other members arranged in a semicircle on either side, according to age and precedence. I was presented by my mother, and welcomed as one of themselves, though a stranger. I made my obeisance, and we took our seats. Shortly after, two very young men of the family were called up by the patriarch, and, in presence of the whole company, severely reprimanded for some misdemeanour—I think it was getting into debt. They stood perfectly abashed, and pale as death. Their parents sat by, scarcely less so, but not daring to interpose a word in their behalf. The rebuke ended, they were dismissed."

There was little popular literature known among a people like this. When Richardson's novels appeared in England their fame soon spread into Germany, where they produced a vast impression, giving birth to the whole brood of morbid sentimental romances which was long the bane of German imaginative authorship.

The relations between masters and servants were naturally as little like as possible to those which now prevail. We must quote a few sentences of Mrs. Austin's remarks on this change, both on account of the rarity of such good sense in writers of the "liberal" school, and for the happiness with which she has expressed one of the characteristic and most pernicious feelings of this present time. The italics are Mrs. Austin's:

" The inquiry into the causes which unite or disunite the various classes of society, always one of the most interesting in the world, has now assumed a fearful importance. On the satisfactory solution of it rests the sole chance of stability to the social fabric. It is evident that the bonds are most relaxed, and yet are felt to be most galling, in the most advanced countries: and that impatience of all restraint and of all superiority, so far from increasing in the ratio of the severity of the restraint or the degree of the superiority, is precisely inverted. The sentiment of *belonging to another human being*, in any sense, or from any cause, seems to be becoming more and more intolerable, and personal independence to be esteemed the most indispensable of all possessions. This sentiment lies at the root of a vast proportion of modern literature. Whether it be in favour of human happiness or not, is a great and weighty question."

Returning to Dantzig and Madame Schopenhauer, we find many pretty pictures of a little world, whose enjoyments would be pains to a generation nurtured like ours:

"The main streets of Danzig," she says, " are much wider than those in any other old town. Two or even three carriages might

* Grandfather's chair,—Easy-chairs were unknown. The only sort of arm-chair was called *Grossvaterstuhl*, and was exclusively reserved for the dignity and the feebleness of age. Even now this name is commonly applied to easy-chairs, which are lamentably rare in Germany.

pass abreast between the houses, and yet leave room for a commodious footpath; yet the actual room for passage is so small, that the most experienced coachman can hardly avoid collision, and the foot-passengers have enough to do to escape with whole limbs. The flights of steps before all the houses, of which those in Hamburg or Lubeck are but the shadow of a shade, are the cause of this strange appearance. I know not how to convey an idea of these singular *propylæa*, which give to the northern city something of a southern character, and in which, during my childhood, a great part of the household business was carried on, with an openness incredible now, almost as publicly as in the street. They are not balconies; I might almost call them spacious terraces, paved with large stones, and extending along the front of the house, with broad easy steps to the street, from which they are separated by a stone parapet. These terraces are divided from each other by a wall four or five feet high. The most capricious of all rulers, fashion, has taken so many despised things under her protection, under the name of *rococo*,—may it please her to watch over the Danzig steps! She will hardly find a more *grandiose* piece of *rococo*. And what an incomparable play-place! So safe, so convenient! close under the eye of the sewing or knitting mother, yet secure from scoldings for making a noise."

Some of Madame Schopenhauer's most curious information is that which refers to the Lutheran ecclesiastics of her native city. A favourable though singular specimen of the class officiated for some time as her tutor, and a remarkable spirit of amiable toleration seems to have pervaded her early home.

In the following extract, not the least novel feature (to us at least, to whom the notion of paying for going to confession is sufficiently amusing) is the history of the penitential proceedings of the Schopenhauer family. We fancy both the rigour of academic discipline and the fees for absolution have disappeared together from Germany, now that it has substituted the speculations of Strauss for the dogmatism of Luther:

"The dress of the candidates for holy orders was entirely black, with the exception of the bands which marked their calling. A *calotte* of black velvet about the size of a dollar, on the crown of a curled and powdered periwig, also a badge of sanctity, and a narrow cloak, half covering the back and reaching to the ground, which the wearer was bound to gather up in graceful folds when he walked along the streets,—such was the dress enjoined by the dreaded head of our church, the very reverend Dr. Heller. These young divines must have trusted to the inward glow of faith for a defence against the cold, which often reached twenty degrees of Réaumur; for great coat or fur-mantle were not to be thought of. Woe to the unhappy candidate who was caught beyond the bounds of his own four walls, in any other habit than the one prescribed! All hope of a living was lost to him for ever; for Dr. Heller regarded such an offence as equal to the most abominable heresy. Not only the candidates but the officiating preachers, and even their wives and daughters, were forbidden to go to plays, concerts, or any other public amusements. The utmost they dared venture on was a modest game of ombre, and that only among friends, and under the strictest seal of secresy.

"We have already spoken of the intolerable yoke of a burgher aristocracy—of the *hauteur*, far exceeding that of kings and princes, which rendered the downfall of the patricians of Nürnberg a triumph to their subject fellow-citizens. There, indeed, the constitution of the city was oligarchical; but it is curious to see how the same temper manifested itself in a city where perfect equality was assumed as the basis of society; and how pride, civility, and worldliness went hand in hand with pharisaical rigour.

"'This aristocratical spirit,' says Madame Schopenhauer, 'bordered on the ludicrous. At every public, and especially at every religious ceremony, at marriages and christenings, and even at the Holy Supper, before God's altar, it broke forth in a flagrant manner, and gave occasion to the most disgraceful scenes, especially among women.

"'On no account could I have been confirmed in public with the other children of the town—this was esteemed proper only for the lower *bourgeoisie*; nor could the minister be invited to perform the ceremony in my father's house, in the presence of my family and intimate friends. This was the practice in the Reformed (*i.e.* Calvinistic) Church, and in our Lutheran city we strove to keep our Lutheran usages unaltered. So willed the still dark spirit of that time; there was not the least conception of the light which has since broken in upon us, and cleared and tranquillised all minds.

"'Among other remains of former days which were obstinately adhered to, I may mention the custom of private confession, which was very like that of the Catholic Church. Nobody who had not confessed could be admitted to the Lord's Supper. The fees derived from this source formed a considerable part of the income of favourite preachers; for every one was at liberty to choose his confessor, without reference to the parish he inhabited. This was not much calculated to promote brotherly love among the clergy.

"'With lively emotions of piety I followed my parents on Whit-Sunday into the *Graumünchen* church, which was decorated, according to custom, with flowers and fresh May. I was led by my mother, who was equally moved, through the church to the confession-room, commonly called the Comfort-room (*Trostkammer*). A crowd of people of the lower classes were waiting before the door. Many, it was evident, had waited longer than they could well afford, till as many as could find room could be admitted; when they were confessed, admonished, and absolved in a mass, and paid the indispensable confession-fee (*Beichtgroschen*). On our arrival, however, they were doomed to a new disappointment: they were sent back, and only we three admitted. Our spiritual guide sat enthroned in

a comfortable easy-chair in full canonicals. Kneeling before him, we made our confession. My father had condensed his into a few brief expressive words; my mother had chosen a verse of a spiritual song; and I, a very short one out of Gellert's Odes. The whole was despatched in a few minutes; we then seated ourselves opposite to his reverence, heard an admonition, and were absolved. After a little conversation about wind and weather, the last news, and, above all, polite inquiries about our health respectively, which my father, out of pity for the poor people waiting, cut short, we returned.'

"Revolted by the indecent precedence given to wealth and station, wearied by the admonition, and somewhat scandalised by the sight of a bottle of wine and glass in the room devoted to ghostly comfort, a lasting shock was given to our heroine's piety 'by the appearance of the ducats which her father secretly, but not unseen, slipped on the table near the reverend divine, and the sidelong glance with which the latter ascertained whether the usual number had received an addition of one, in consequence of her presence, together with the unctuous smile with which he nodded his thanks to her parents.'"

In the midst of this Protestantism there lingered relics of the old faith, not only tolerated, but evidently retaining some vestiges of its ancient hold on the veneration and affections of the people:

"In spite of the rigid Lutheranism of Danzig, liberty of conscience was complete. The Roman Catholic religion was not only tolerated, but the monastic orders lived as unmolested in their convents as in a Catholic country. There was also an ecclesiastic of that Church, whose presence and functions in a Protestant city presented a singular and unexplained anomaly. He bore the title of the Pope's Official, and was in fact a sort of Nuncio. Not only were Protestants who married within the forbidden degrees obliged to get a dispensation from Rome, but the official had the power of performing the ceremony of marriage for Catholics or Protestants, without the consent of parents—without license or witnesses—in a little chapel attached to his house; and a marriage so contracted was as valid as any other. This strange privilege remained unimpaired down to the time of the occupation of Danzig. The official lived in the greatest retirement, and was hardly ever seen. Madame Schopenhauer says she never knew any body who was acquainted with him, and that a sort of mystery hung over his whole existence.

"The following scene is picturesque and touching :—

"'Every Christmas-day, three of the Brothers of the Order of Mercy, in the black garb of their order, bowing humbly, entered the dining-room, just as we were assembled for dinner. They brought a quaintly-formed silver plate, on which were a few coloured wafers stamped with a crucifix; and a box filled with snuff, which they prepared from herbs in their convent, and sold for the benefit of the poor.

"'My father rose from table, and advanced a few steps to meet them. We children each received a wafer; he took a pinch of snuff out of the box, and laid some money on the plate; the monks bowed again and retired, as they had entered, in silence.

"'The whole transaction, during which not a word was spoken, made, probably for that reason, a solemn and at the same time melancholy impression upon me. I was almost ready to cry. I knew that these venerable men lived lives of the greatest privation, received into their convent the sick of whatever faith, even Jews, and carefully nursed them. Adam, who was himself a Catholic, and had been cured by the good fathers in a severe illness, always told us about them after their visit.'"

The Christmas tree, now growing so common in England, of course held a prominent place in the household pleasures of those simpler days. Mrs. Austin quotes an account of the calm course of domestic life of a quiet German city, from another of the autobiographical writers on whose narrations she has founded her book. No doubt such pictures as these must be accepted with a certain degree of modification. There were other sides to the picture, less pure and less respectable. Old age, also, so invariably forgets the discomforts and evils of the days when the world was opening in all its imagined beauty upon the young heart, that we can never accept its histories without remembering that it does not tell the *whole* truth; because youth never *knows* the whole truth, and therefore cannot record it when it has itself grown into old age:

"The life of the middle classes," says Jacob, "was then very simple. My father's income was precarious, and we grew up under restraints which would now appear melancholy and oppressive to children of our class. But the amusements to which the children of the present day are accustomed, were unknown to those of a former; and they missed not what they did not know. Spacious buildings, which kept asunder the members of a family, were rare; and those who had them used them only on rare occasions. Parents and children were generally together in one room; the children worked and played under the eyes of their parents, and a great part of education consisted in this companionship. Filial obedience, the source and foundation of all domestic and civil virtues, was a matter of course; and parents were the better for the constraint which the presence of their children imposed on their words and actions. The respect which parents (with few exceptions) inspired, spared them much admonition, teaching, and preaching;—the cheap but feeble substitutes for practical education. So, at least, was it in our house. Company was hardly thought of; at the utmost, families assembled after afternoon service on Sundays; the women to discuss the sermon, the men to talk of business or news, or, if they had nothing to say, to play backgammon. Family festivals were rare. On New-Year's day and birth-days, relations wished each other joy: the boys generally in a Latin or German speech, got by heart. Presents were

not thought of. Those for children were reserved for Christmas Eve, when the tree, with its sweetmeats and angels and wax-lights, gave an appearance of festal splendour to things which were in fact mere necessaries. Bethlehem, with its manger and crib, was indispensable; and this sacred spot was surrounded with a blooming landscape, gardens, and ponds, which my father had for weeks employed his evening hours in decorating with his own hands. He thought his labour richly rewarded on the long-expected evening, by our delight and admiration. The narrative of St. Luke, which it had not at that time occurred to any body to regard as a myth, was always read. The joyous recollection of this pious festival caused me and my brothers to retain the same custom with our children. With this exception, our winter pleasures were confined to a not very spacious court-yard, exchanged in summer for a little garden within the walls, which my father hired. We took no walks. Only once a year, when the harvest was ripe, our parents took us out to spend an evening in the fields."

Mrs. Austin's remarks on these quiet times need no qualification. Every body who has had to do with children knows their truth, though few are wise enough to draw from them the conclusion, that excess of novelty and variety destroys rather than heightens the enjoyments of the young. It is when the heart and head are *blasé*, that this endless change is craved. May God preserve the generation of children now under our teaching from the misery that must result from an excess of stimulants of any kind!

"In all Madame Pichler's personages of the middle class, we find the contentment, with the uniform and inflexible recurrence of the same amusements, which characterises children. Children in a natural state prefer an old book, a story which they have heard a hundred times, to any thing unaccustomed. The narrator who thinks to please them by various readings and new *fioriture*, finds himself completely mistaken. At the smallest departure from the authentic version, he is called to order, and brought back to the established form of the history, every deviation from which is a disappointment. So it was with the amusements of our ancestors. Each holiday had its appropriate and *obligé* diversion, its peculiar dish or confection, its fixed form of salutation. To alter these was to invert the order of nature. Surprises were unwelcome: people liked to know exactly what was coming,—what they had to see, to feel, to say, and even to eat."

Before parting with Madame Schopenhauer we must quote one more passage, as an illustration of the extravagances of pride too common among the republican people of the free cities of Germany; a pride which might have become a respectable and genuine patriotism, had it not been as intensely aristocratic and contemptuous towards all who were below the ruling class as if it were lodged in a royal or imperial bosom. In "free" Dantzig, the most wealthy and respectable of the artisan class could not give a wedding-feast without the presence of a municipal officer in full dress, with a sword by his side, to count the guests and see that they did not exceed the number prescribed by the laws of the city, and to ascertain that the bride wore no forbidden ornaments, such as real pearls. Before Madame Schopenhauer was married, Dantzig had fallen into the hands of Frederick of Prussia, and soon after their marriage her husband went to Berlin and requested an interview with the Prussian king :

"It was immediately granted, and Frederic, struck by his frank, upright character, and his knowledge of commercial affairs, pressed him to settle in his dominions, and offered him every possible privilege and protection. M. Schopenhauer was beginning to feel the resistless influence which Frederic exercised on all around him, when the king, pointing to a heap of papers in the corner, said *Voilà les calamités de la ville de Danzig.* These few words broke the spell for ever; and though Frederic afterwards repeated his offers, the sturdy patriot never would accept the smallest obligation from him. At length, seeing that all hope of the deliverance of his native city from a foreign yoke was at an end, he determined to quit it for ever, and to seek a freer home. In this determination his young wife fully concurred, and they set out on a tour of observation through the Netherlands, France, and England. The free citizen was well matched. They stopped a short time at Pyrmont,—then, except Carlsbad, the only one of those German baths whose names have become legion;—and here the republican bride, together with a sister Hanseate from Hamburg, had a glorious opportunity of showing their disdain of courts and sovereigns. The then reigning Duchess of Brunswick very good-naturedly asked to have these young ladies presented to her. They professed their ignorance of court etiquette, but were told they had only to make an inclination, as if to kiss the hand or the garment of the Duchess. This was too much. 'We, free-born women, subject of no prince, kiss the hand of another woman, neither our mother nor our grandmother? The very thought made my republican blood boil, and, supported by my Hamburg friend, I declined the proffered honour.' "

From the free towns and domestic life of German citizens Mrs. Austin takes us to the German courts of the latter portion of the last century, when the holy Roman empire was on the verge of dissolution, through the decay of its system and the impetuous onslaught of French ideas and French conquerors. As her story advances nearer to our own times, she enters more fully into the influence of public events upon private life, and illustrates the miseries that war brings, not only in its train, but to all who are remotely influenced by it.

Some of her anecdotes are striking proofs of the ruin which official stupidity and conceited pedantry bring upon a people who are living solely upon the past, when they come into conflict with such a race as the revolutionary armies of France. She has many stories which show the wretched incapacity which prevailed among the nobles of Germany, and account for the prostration of the national power before the arms of Napoleon. There is nothing of this kind in the following sketch of a Servian noble; but we may gather from it the small progress in civilisation of no inconsiderable portion of the subjects of Austria :

" ' At four in the morning,' says the Ritter von Lang, from whom Mrs. Austin quotes, ' the old lord called up his lieges with a speaking-trumpet :—*Domine Pater! surgas! Domine Provisor! Domine Cancellista Frumentarie! surgas!* He did not desist till he saw through the windows the glimmering of their newly-lighted candles, or till he was greeted in return by the morning salutation—*Salve, Domine perillustris!* In half an hour they were all assembled round him to receive their orders for the day.

" ' The castle stood in the midst of a swamp, where nothing vegetable was to be found but rushes and Indian corn; and nothing animal, but herds of swine and wolves. To keep off the latter, every evening as soon as it was dark a great fire was lighted in the castle-court, by which five-and-twenty Pandours kept watch all night. As a precaution against bands of robbers from the Turkish frontier, all the doors were strongly barred, and arms loaded every night.

" ' The Slavonian peasant seemed to me little better than half swine, half wolf. He works little, and drinks and sleeps away most of his time. When he has nothing in the house to eat, he goes to the swamp, catches a pig, kills it, and roasts it whole. Every one who enters the house cuts off what he likes, and this goes on till it is quite putrid.'

" At length our author quitted these barbarous regions, in company with several other travellers. ' We were,' said he, ' all crowded into a carriage together, the *Dominus spectabilis*, the *Domini perillustres*, myself—*Dominus clarissimus*,—and several *Domini humanissimi*. Arrived at the place where they were to stop, the drivers and Pandours who escorted us dragged all the luggage out of the carriage, kissed our coats, knelt down to ask us for a trinkgeld, and, as soon as they had got it, set off back again.'

" This was the state of things in 1790. In 1842 we happened to travel with a Mecklenburger who had lived some years in Agram, the capital of Croatia, and was returning to Mecklenburg with his Hungarian wife. We lament to say, that his description of the peasantry of that country was little more consolatory than this. He said it was no uncommon thing to see a peasant bring his whole crop into the town, sell it, take the money to a public-house, and never move from the spot till he had drunk out the whole produce of his harvest."

In the archives belonging to the Hardenberg family, the same Ritter von Lang discovered a document containing the rules established for the conduct of the Petty Court of Hardenberg about a hundred years before, which showed what were the notions of the feudal lords of the seventeenth century on the noble science of government. It is worth quoting as it stands :

"The 'Rules for House and Court,' according to which his Excellency the Lord Statthalter commands his people to conduct themselves, given the 10th March, 1666, begin by declaring to his servants that they are all rude, unpolished, stupid, and inattentive fellows ; to whom he is now, with fatherly care, going to give the following rules for the government of their lives and manners ; at the same time telling them that he shall take care to make them remember any departure therefrom. Thus, for example, he who can give no account of the sermon shall eat his dinner like a dog, lying on the ground ; whoever swears, shall kneel for an hour on the sharp edge of a plank. Whoever neglects to take the Lord's Supper when it is notified to him, shall ride upon an ass loaded with heavy weights, or receive a flogging, as circumstances may be.

"Domestic thieves are promised the gallows. Whoever peeps into a letter, even if it lies open, shall have the bastinado three days running, and be sent out of the house as infamous.

"Before the Statthalter rises, the clothes must be brushed clean, and laid in good order on the table ; shoes and boots cleaned, and set under the bench ; fresh water and a towel must be in readiness. His Excellency must be most delicately (subtilstermassen) dressed, and what he lays aside be carefully put by.

"The meals are to be served in good order, without spilling, and the dishes to be taken away with a bow. If any one nibbles at things, and puts his fingers or his mouth into the dishes, he shall be made to eat scalding food to cure him of his greediness. Every one is bound, when called upon, to step forward, making a reverence, and to say grace with a clear and audible voice. He who stutters or hesitates shall receive six fillips on the nose (spanische Nasenstüber). If any man waits at table with dirty hands, he shall do as if he were washing them, while one pours water over them, and another dries them with two sharp rods till they bleed. In like manner, he who waits uncombed, shall be well curried in the stable with the curry-comb.

"The tablecloth is to be spread at one cast ; every plate to have a napkin, and the salt-cellars to be filled with clean salt. At the proper time candles are to be brought, and to be constantly snuffed, every time beginning at the place where the highest guest sits. Lastly, the tablecloth is to be removed in a mannerly way (manierlich) ; and the servants are to retire with a reverence, under pain of six fillips on the nose.

"Whoever mixes in the conversation, or grins at what is said, shall be made to blow till he is tired ; whoever laughs loud, shall have four raps over the fingers. Whoever fills a glass too full, and then sups it out with his own mouth, shall have twenty lashes with a whip. He who hands a dirty glass, may have his choice between four boxes on the ear or six fillips on the nose. After dinner a basin of water and a clean towel is to be handed (with a bow) to every guest.

"As it is a scandalous and insufferable thing for servants to be long at meals, those who are more than a quarter of an hour at dinner shall have it taken away from them. He who will not eat what is set before him shall fast twenty-four hours. If the Statthalter orders a servant to do any thing, and he neglects it, and bids another to do it instead, he shall receive four boxes on the ear from him whom he so ordered ; who, in return, shall have six.

"If any man waits in dirty or torn clothes, he shall run the gauntlet. If two go to blows, they shall fight out their quarrel with staves, in the presence of the house-steward ; and he who spares the other shall have a flogging.

"If any one goes out without leave, or murmurs against his lord, he may expect to be flogged, put in chains, or tied to a post, according to circumstances."

It is curious also to remark the effects of Frederick the Great's influence on the Prussian army, after his living influence had passed away. It produced an intolerable arrogance, and issued in the indisputed reign of pipe-clay and pigtails. One old captain wore a pigtail which required seventy or eighty ells of ribbon to tie it up, and trailed on the ground, so that he was obliged to tuck it into his coat-pocket on parade.

At length came the battle of Jena. Certainly the absurdities of real life surpass all caricatures. In the closing sentence of the following extract the very bathos of military martinetship is surely attained :

"As the confused rout came in by the same gate through which they had marched forth, the people gathered in knots, looking on with alarm and still incredulous wonder. 'These are the first fugitives,' I heard people say : 'they are never in order ; have patience, the regular regiment will come soon.' But noon came,—afternoon came,—evening drew on, and the pell-mell had not ceased ; the disorderly mob which had been an army still filled the streets. At length came some troops in marching order, as exceptions to the miserable rule ; covered were now the banners which had floated so proudly in the breeze. Most of them marched in silence,— once only the music sounded, loud and clear, like the laughter of despair. It was the trumpeters of a cuirassier regiment ;—their regiment was not behind them,—they were quite alone, and blew the Dessauer march, just as if all were in the best possible order. They looked well too, and were mounted on high-fed horses. Indeed, generally speaking the men did not look jaded, nor hungry, nor worn ; and the contrast between their personal good condition with the general destruction, exhibited in the strongest light the depth of the calamity. In the evening every body knew that a Prussian army no longer existed. A helpless grief sat on men's faces. But even then, the indescribable spirit which characterised that period was not extinguished. I heard a man say to his neighbour, 'That may be as it will ; things have gone badly, no doubt, but we have lost with honour ; for I heard just now that the Prussians did not once lose the step through the whole battle.'"

We conclude with an anecdote, betokening a spirit in the German people as unlike as possible to the formal stupidity of their army, as it was in those terrible days :

"After the battle of Austerlitz, the Emperor Francis, a fugitive, mounted on a sorry jade, attended by one aide-de-camp, defeated and almost dethroned, was about to make his inglorious entry into his capital : he was met by the citizens, who had of their own accord dragged out the state carriage, and now seated him in it, and drew him, as if in triumph, to his palace. 'Why, what would you have done if your Emperor had been victorious ?' asked a stranger. 'Oh ! then we should not have needed to do any thing,' was the answer."

497

Shakspeare's Midsummer Night's Dream—[Ein Sommernachtstraum]. (Leipzig, Keil; London, Nutt.)—Herr C. Abel having achieved a success with the 'Winter's Tale,' [*Athen.* 1401], comes forward with another creditable specimen of Shaksperian translation. To make way for himself, he would elbow out Augustus Schlegel, whom, in a little Appendix, he charges with divers inaccuracies. In Act I. scene 1, where *Theseus* says, "The old moon wanes!" the erring Schlegel says, "nimmt ab," when he ought to have known that "wane" does not denote a growing less, but a decline in strength and beauty. How nobly therefore rises Herr Abel's line from the mist of error:

> Gar träge will der alte mir verschwinden.

In the very same speech, where *Theseus* says:

> —— Four happy days bring in
> Another moon:

Schlegel should not have adopted such a matter-of-course version of "happy days" as "frohe Tage." No; he should have recollected that "happy" also meant "rapid," and then he would have attained the felicity of Herr C. Abel, who triumphantly sets down "rasche Tage." We fear a jury of Englishmen would find Schlegel right and Abel wrong in these matters. At all events, the censure of the old translator by the new one is the very perfection of "hole-picking."

GERMAN STORY-BOOKS.

WE plead guilty to a very childlike love of story-books. We do not refer merely to the genuine works of artistic genius which all educated imaginative people may be supposed to enjoy; nor even to the orthodox three-volume novel, so largely patronised and so eagerly devoured by the devotees of the circulating library. Our taste is far more comprehensive. It descends so low as to embrace that primitive literature which, in England at least, is chiefly confined to the nursery. At the risk of incurring the contempt of many estimable people for whose opinions we entertain a sincere reverence, we may as well at once confess—and we do so unblushingly—that although the days of our childhood are over and gone, we are by no means insensible to the charms of Cinderella; that we have a great liking for the Marquis of Carrabas; that we remember the strange delight with which we read of Jack and the wonderful bean-stalk which seemed to touch the skies; and that we still feel a kind of shuddering interest in the dreadful doings of Mr Peter Berner. Above all, with what trembling anxiety we sympathise with poor Agnes in her fruitless endeavours to remove the crimson stains from the golden key! 'Madam, the key, this instant! Ha! these blood-flecks! The murder is out; you have been in the forbidden chamber!' Peter Berner, you know, reader, is the real name of that sanguinary gentleman we are accustomed to call Bluebeard; and Agnes was the Christian appellative of his wife number eight.

Fairy-legend and ghost-story, tales of witches and wizards, of ogres and genii, of 'red spirits and white, black spirits and gray,' of 'giants so tall and of dwarfs so small,' nothing comes amiss to us. We admire the commencement of the old-fashioned stories, so abrupt, straightforward, and business-like, dashing boldly into the subject without a word of preface : 'Once upon a time.' We experience a feeling of intense satisfaction when we read at last of hero and heroine, and of all good people concerned, 'Now they lived happily to the end of their days.'

Ah! as we write at this sweet, still, sunset hour, our thoughts are filled with 'sunny memories' of many a tale of knight and ladye fair, and castle proud, and noble chargers, and lances glittering in the sun, and banners streaming on the wind, and of dark, lonely woods, full of mysterious enchantments, where even the very birds sing evermore, 'songs like legends strange to hear.' If we wish for a perfect feast of legendary lore, we must turn to Germany, 'land of mystic philosophy and dreams.' Many learned Germans have taken a deep interest in this department of their literature. The brothers Grimm have given us a large collection of the popular *Mährchen*; so, also, have Musäus and others. Several celebrated writers, too, have rewritten some of the more striking and beautiful. Among these new versions, Ludwig Tieck's are perhaps the most noteworthy. We shall recur to them again by and by. In looking over the *Kinder* and *Hausmährchen*, we find many old acquaintances, such as *Tom Thumb* (*Däumchen*), *Bluebeard*, *Little Red Riding Hood* (*Rothkäppchen*), and *Puss in Boots* (*Der gestiefelte Kater*). But, indeed, this is no wonder, as all these stories had most probably one common origin. The Germans possess, besides, a series of tales of great antiquity, and which are altogether higher in character and full of a rude chivalry and poetry. To this class belong the *Horned Siegfried*, the *Wonderful History of the Beautiful Melusina*, the *Emperor Octavianus*, *Fortunatus*, the *Holy Genoveva*, the *Fair Magelona*, *Heymon's Four Children*, *Roland's Three Squires*, *Tristan and Isolde*, the *Schildburgers*, the *Chronicle of the Three Sisters*, and the *History of Griseldis and the Markgraf Walter*. The heroine of the last story is no other than the 'patient Grizel,' whose long-suffering virtues were celebrated by Chaucer.

The good, simple-hearted peasantry of the German *Vaterland* contrive to while away the long winter evenings with strange romantic narratives like these, which constitute, in fact, the people's literature. Herein they find a fountain of inexhaustible entertainment, from whence they imbibe lofty notions of chivalry and honour and glory, and lessons of patient endurance and religious trust under manifold trials. The *Volksmährchen* form the wonder-land, ever bright, and beautiful, and grand, into which the popular mind escapes from the dull and dusty paths of a toil-worn existence. There is enough of prose in real life; by all means, let us mingle therewith as much of poetry as we possibly can.

We remember well our first investment in the purchase of German books. We did not lay the foundation of our Teutonic library with an edition of Schiller, or Goethe, or Richter. No ponderous tome of history, philosophy, or science, attracted our juvenile sympathies. We selected a modest blue-covered brochure, more on account of its pretty title than for any other reason. It was the story of the *Holy Genoveva*. 'That,' says a village maiden, in Dr Justin Kerner's *Reiseschatten*—'that, next to the Bible, is the greatest love of a book.' Our copy was printed from very blunt type, on thick whity-brown paper. It bore the title of— *Genovera ; one of the most beautiful and touching Stories of the Olden Time, newly related for all Good People, and more especially for Mothers and Children ; by Christopher Schmid*, the canon of Augsburg, whose admirable tales for the young are so widely known and appreciated. As a frontispiece, the book contained a picture, rough in execution, but withal sweet and simple in expression, representing Genoveva on her knees in the desert, with her little son in her arms. The legend of St Genevieve is but another page from the 'records of woman,' exemplifying a brightness and purity of character that shines with untarnished lustre alike through 'evil and through good report;' a patience that 'endureth all things;' and a life, in fine, baptised in the furnace of affliction, and so rendered 'perfect through suffering.' With great simplicity, and with an earnest depth of religious feeling, Schmid tells us how the noble lady Genoveva was wrongfully accused by a false and wicked man ; how she went forth into a desert place, accompanied by two ruffians who had strict orders to take her life; how she prevailed upon them to leave her in the wilderness by the solemn promise to avoid evermore the haunts of humankind; and how, for long long years, she lived in the woods and wilds with her little son, the child of grief, whom she had named so appropriately Schmerzenreich, 'rich in sorrows.' Truth and justice, however, triumphed in the end. Genoveva's innocence was fully established; her retreat was discovered; and, amid the rejoicings of a sympathising people, she was conducted once more to her castle-halls, and there, with her husband, Count Siegfried, she 'lived happily for the rest of her days.'

The poet Tieck has dramatised this story under the title of the *Life and Death of the Holy Genoveva*. Without entering upon a complete analysis of the drama, it would be difficult to give an adequate idea of the charm with which it is invested. Exquisite tenderness, great simplicity, and a fervent but subdued enthusiasm, are its distinguishing characteristics. The spirit of the 'wondrous middle age' clings around every line. At one time, during its perusal, we seem to hear the bell that calls to prayer; at another, the clang of knightly armour. Now we are introduced to the hurry and excitement of a camp glowing with life and energy, and echoing with martial music; and anon, like some sad eremite, we penetrate the depths of the lonely wilderness, with the spirit-haunted gloom of its midnights, and the enchanted silence of its noons.

The stories of the *Emperor Octavianus* and of *Fortunatus* have also been dramatised by the same author. The former bears some slight resemblance to the history of Genoveva. It has more incident, and less repose ; and, though possessing much of interest, it scarcely pleases us so well. The age of chivalry has had no worthier champion than Ludwig Tieck. His spirit was steeped in the richest hues of romance, and no one was ever better fitted than he to recall

The days when giants were rife,
   With their towers and painted halls,
And heroes, each with a charmèd life,
   Rode up to their castle-walls,
And knocked with a loud and dreadful clang,
Till the roof, and the gates, and the wild woods rang.

When the good and the fair, as the wizard-wand stirred,
   Were bound in a dreamy spell;
When at each sweet word that maidens spoke
   Diamonds and roses fell;

When gentle and bright ones with golden hair
Were wooed by princes in green,
And knights, with invisible caps to wear,
Could see, and yet never be seen.

Will you hear the love-story of the beautiful Mage-lona and Count Peter of Provence? 'Once upon a time' there reigned in fair Provence a count who had an only son, a youth of exceeding beauty, and well skilled in all knightly accomplishments. It came to pass that the young Count Peter lost the joyous buoyancy of spirit natural to his age. He grew very silent and reserved. Some people thought he must be in love; but it was not so. It seemed to him that he heard distant voices calling him from the depths of the lonely woods. He wished to follow their guidance; but fear held him back, though his dreams ever beckoned him on. A tourney was held at the court of Provence; Count Peter was ever the victor. A foreign minstrel was among the strangers gathered to this festival. 'Sir Knight,' said he to our hero, 'if you take my advice, you will stay here no longer, but rather go forth into the world, and see fresh faces and other lands.' Then the minstrel took his lute, and sang—oh, so sweetly!—of the fresh, bright joys of a life of adventure—of fair countries, and their strange customs—of beautiful maidens—of noble combats, of love, and of laurelled glory. Count Peter's vague, restless thought soon assumed a definite form; he hesitated no longer, but resolved, like other gallant knights, to bid adieu to his father's halls, and to wander wherever fate might lead him in search of adventures.

Alone he rode forth, with the joy returning to his heart, and the bright sun shining overhead. An object-less life is always dull and dreary; but Peter's whole being now glowed with lofty chivalry, so he went forward, singing, most likely,

A Dieu mon ame,
Ma vie au roi;
Mon cœur aux dames,
L'honneur pour moi.

After several days' journey, he reached the beautiful city of Naples. He had heard much of the fair Magelona, daughter of the king of Naples, and his curiosity with regard to her was greatly excited. At a tournament, Peter beheld the lady of his dreams, and determined to win her love or die. He hymned her praise in songs tender and sweet as those the minne-singers used to sing, and he loved her with the devotion of the old heroic days. We will not linger over the courtship; suffice it to say, our hero induced the beautiful Magelona to consent to an elopement. At the appointed hour, the knight stood by the garden-gate with three horses—one for himself, one for the lady, and one laden with provisions for the journey. Thus they rode out into the lonely night, while through the thick greenery a soft breeze murmured, like the voice of a tender farewell. When the morning dawned, there was a strange uproar at the court of Naples. As Count Peter was nowhere to be found, the king guessed that he was the companion of his daughter's flight. A strict search was instituted, but in vain.

Let us follow the course of the fugitives. They chose a road through woods by the sea-shore, being the most unfrequented part of the country. The forest-boughs waved sadly in the night air, making a strange melancholy music. Nevertheless, Magelona was calm and joyous, for her beloved was by her side. Towards morning, a thick mist overspread the landscape; but soon the glorious sun shone out, and all nature flushed into beauty. The lady becoming somewhat weary by noon, our travellers alighted from their steeds in a charming shady spot. The count spread his mantle on the fresh fragrant grass, and while Magelona reposed thereon, he kept watch. Presently he observed a number of beautiful birds fluttering amid the neighbouring trees. They did not seem in the least shy, but hopped about hither and thither, and advanced quite close to him. All at once he remarked in their midst an ugly black raven, and he thought within himself that the unsightly bird was like to a rough and low-born clown in a company of gentle and gallant knights. Just then, it seemed to him as if Magelona breathed with difficulty: he unloosed her mantle, and in so doing he perceived upon her breast something wrapped in a piece of tinsel. Curious to know what it might be, he detached and unfolded it. The envelope contained three costly rings that Peter had presented to his love. He was affected to find them so faithfully preserved, and, refolding the packet, he laid it beside him on the grass. Suddenly the raven pounced upon the treasure, and flew off with it, attracted, doubtless, by the glittering tinsel. The count was quite frightened, thinking Magelona would be so grieved on the discovery of her loss. He disposed his mantle round her still more carefully, and went further into the wood, to see if he could recover the rings. The bird flew before him: Peter threw stones, hoping to kill him, or at least force him to drop his prize. None of the stones touched him: he still flew onwards, and Peter still followed. At last, both pursuer and pursued reached the sea-shore. The raven perched upon a steep cliff; the count threw more stones at him, and finally caused him to drop the rings and fly off with a great cry. Peter plainly saw the treasure floating on the surface of the water. He wandered on the shore, in order to find something in the shape of a boat, whereby he might reach it. At length he discovered an old skiff, left on the beach by some fishermen. With the bough of a tree for an oar, he pushed out towards the shining tinsel. Suddenly a great wind arose; the waves heaved, and the little boat, rocking from side to side, was nearly overturned. Peter exerted all his strength: but, nevertheless, he was carried further and further into the sea. He looked back, and could scarcely distinguish the floating treasure: soon it vanished altogether, and the land lay far away in the distance. Peter thought on his fair Magelona, whom he had left sleeping in the lonely wood, and his heart was full of anguish and despair. He cried aloud in his utter desolation; the wild echoes flung back his voice of wo, and the mighty ocean responded with a melancholy roar. Eventide came on: the land was far, far away. 'Ah! dearest Magelona,' exclaimed our hero, 'by what strange fate are we separated! An evil hand has drawn me from thy side into the desert sea, and thou art alone and without help. O thou daughter of kings! was it for this I enticed thee from thy princely home?'

Thus mourned Count Peter of Provence. He aban-doned hope, and gave himself up for lost. Presently the moon rose, and filled the world with its silvery splendours. All was still, except the sighing murmur of the wave and the unearthly voices of some strange sea-birds that were fluttering around; the stars shone out in solemn beauty, and the cloud-wreathed dome of heaven was mirrored in the bosom of the deep. Peter threw himself in the bottom of the boat, and floated on at the mercy of the billows. Overcome by sorrow and fatigue, he was soon fast asleep.

Let us return to Magelona. When she awoke, she was surprised to find that her lover was nowhere in sight. She waited patiently awhile, thinking he would return; then she wandered about, calling him loudly by name. Having gained a lofty point of view, she looked as far as possible into the distance, hoping to discover some traces of the truant. On one side, she could see nothing but woods, and no village or dwelling-house far as the eye could reach; and on the other, the wild sad sea. 'O thou unfaithful knight!' she cried, 'why hast thou thus left thine innocent love? Hast thou stolen me from my parents only to leave to pine in this desert?' While Magelona was wandering distracted in the woods, she descried the trees yet fastened to the trees as Peter had left him. 'Forgive me, my beloved,' she exclaimed; 'now I know thou art guiltless, and hast not intentionally deserted me.' Soon the night closed in; and after many hours of anxious thoughts and fantastic dreams, Magelona gazed once more on the dark woods, and on the far-away sea, the voice of whose heaving waters she could just distinguish. In due time, the morning dawned. How different from the preceding one, when hope danced before her like a bright glad butterfly, and all the flowers of the forest smiled as they met her gaze! Magelona resolved that she would not return to her father's house, as she feared the angry reproaches of her friends. She would rather seek for some quiet humble dwelling, where she might live in peace, secure from the intrusions of the world, and devoted to thoughts of her lost love. She therefore tied up her golden hair, and endeavoured to alter her dress, that she might not be recognised; and thus she journeyed on through many villages and towns. At length, after a long period of wandering, she discovered a pretty secluded meadow, in which stood a little cottage inwreathed with roses. On one side lay a wood. The breeze was musical with the tinkling bells of the pasturing kine. Magelona thought she should like to dwell in this peaceful region. The cottage was inhabited by an old shepherd and his wife. She asked for their protection, which was gladly accorded, although she did not relate her real history. She took up her abode with these good people, and very kind and helpful they found her. Sometimes shipwrecked mariners came to the cottage for assistance; and at such periods, there was no one so thoughtful and ready of heart and hand as Magelona.

Let us now return to poor Peter. It was high noon when he awoke from his troubled rest; the waves were glittering in the golden glory of the sun. Our hero felt new courage rise within his breast. A large ship bore down upon him: it was manned by Moors. They took him prisoner, and greatly rejoiced over their prize, for the count was really a handsome, noble-looking fellow: they intended to make a present of him to the sultan. On landing, he was conducted to his master, who was highly delighted with him, and made him overseer of a beautiful garden: here he often strolled, and sang to his guitar the praises of his lost Magelona. Two years passed away thus; and had it not been for one sad memory, Peter might have been very happy, for he was a great favourite with the sultan, and was beloved, moreover, by his beautiful daughter Sulima. The longing to regain his native land took possession of him so powerfully at one time, that he even resolved to fly with Sulima, as he thought it most likely that Magelona was dead. Accordingly, a rendezvous was appointed: the voice of a lute and singing was to be the fair infidel's signal. Peter soon, however. abandoned this idea as false and treacherous. The same evening, he wandered on the sea-shore; a little boat was moored close by; he unloosed it, entered it, and directed his course out into the open sea. It was one of the most beautiful nights of summer; the stars looked down with a tender light, as if endowed with human sympathies; the sea was smooth and clear as a mirror. Peter rowed on courageously, but all at once he heard the voice of a lute and singing, that sounded from the garden: his heart smote him. for the sweet tones reminded him of his weakness and indecision. Still he went forward. The spirit of love breathed on every side; the waves murmured musically, like a song in a foreign tongue, that falls on the ear with vague, mysterious sweetness, although we know not its meaning. Count Peter suffered the boat to take its own course; and when the morning dawned, the land seemed only like a streak of blue cloud in the distance. Soon he lost sight of it altogether, and found himself, like Coleridge's Ancient Mariner,

> Alone, alone, all, all alone,
> Alone on a wide wide sea!

After some time, he descried a ship in the distance. As it approached nearer, he was rejoiced to find that it was manned by Christians, who were sailing towards France, and gladly gave him a passage. In the course of its homeward progress, the ship stopped at a little island to take in water. Our hero stepped ashore, and wandered on in a state of dreamy enchantment, in the midst of the most beautiful scenery. Weary at last, he rested beneath the shade of a broad fair tree, and fell fast asleep. A wind arose; the sailors were eager to put off to sea again; and as Peter was missing, they sailed without him. When the count awoke, he was sadly distressed for fear the vessel should have departed, and he hurried down to the shore almost frantic. On discovering the true position of affairs, he sank on the ground, tired and dispirited, and remained in an unconscious state until midnight. Some fishermen found him, seemingly half-dead; they took him in their boat, and rowed off to the mainland. When Peter recovered himself, he heard the men saying that they should convey him to an old shepherd's cottage, where he would receive the greatest care and attention. In the morning, our hero gave the fishermen a piece of gold, and they directed him to the shepherd's house. A path through a wood led him to a pretty little meadow, blooming with wild-flowers. By the door of a cottage sat a lovely maiden, who was singing a sweet and plaintive song; an innocent lamb played at her feet; Peter felt a singular attraction towards the fair songstress. She welcomed him kindly, and invited him to take rest and refreshment in the cottage: the old people also gave him a hearty greeting. Magelona (for she it was) recognised the knight at once, and all sorrow departed from her spirit, like snow before the sun of spring. She did not immediately make herself known, however. In two days, Peter had quite recovered; he sat at the door of the cottage by the side of Magelona; a sudden impulse induced him to tell his whole history to his fair companion. She hastily arose, and re-entering the house, she unloosed her golden hair, and attired herself in the costly robes she used to wear. When she returned, Peter recognised her instantly, and embraced her with tears of joy. The lovers journeyed forthwith to the court of Provence, where they were received heartily, and all 'went merry as a marriage-bell.' A large concourse of people were gathered to the bridal, and the king of Naples was well pleased with his son-in-law. On the spot once occupied by the shepherd's cottage, Peter built a beautiful summer palace, and appointed the good old shepherd as overseer. It is needless to add, that our hero lived long and happily with Magelona, his beautiful bride.

Among other unfulfilled purposes, it was our intention to have given a sketch of the *Heymon's Four Children*. a very wild and savage story, quite a contrast to the above. This. however. must be deferred until another time. As it is. we fear we have already trespassed far too long upon the time and patience of the 'gentle reader.'

NOTICES.

Specimens of the German Lyrical Poets from Klopstock to the Present Time. Translated into English Verse, with Biographical and Literary Notes. By Mary Anne Burt. Hall, Virtue, and Co.

To students of modern German literature, or to English readers who wish to have some knowledge of the productions of the best lyrical poets of that country, this will prove an acceptable volume. The plan of the work is to give specimens of the best or most characteristic odes and minor pieces of each poet, with a biographical memoir prefixed. These memoirs are extremely interesting, both as personal sketches, and from the notices of public and political events with which continental men of letters have generally been more mixed up than our English poets and authors. The selections are from Klopstock, Schiller, Goethe, Höttly, Bürger, Uhland, Heine, Mäurer, Margraaff, Prutz, Lewis I., King of Bavaria, Rückert, Freiligrath, Salis, Dingelstadt, Platen, Anastasius Grun, Zedlitz. The names of some of these are probably new to many of our readers, but there is not one who is unworthy of being known either from personal character or from the merit of his works. Of the bards still living most are in exile, waiting for better days for their fatherland, for almost all German poets are on the popular side of politics, and are haters of despotism. Some of them occupy conspicuous literary positions, not subject to political turmoils. Thus Hermann Margraaff, formerly *collaborateur* of the 'Augsburger Allgemeine Zeitung,' and subsequently associated with M. Gervinus in the 'Deutsche Zeitung,' a moderate paper, in the stormy period of 1848, 1849, keeping midway between revolutionary and reactionary forces, is now editor of the 'Blätter für Literarische Unterhaltung,' published by Brockhaus of Leipsic, one of the best critical reviews on the continent. Lists of the principal writings of each author are appended to the biographical memoirs. The English translations of the lyrics are generally faithful and spirited.

" MÜNCHHAUSEN'S TRAVELS."

(Vol. xi., p. 485. ; Vol. xii., p. 55.)

A French writer, in *La Revue Contemporaine*, has recently claimed for France the credit of having produced the original of *Baron Münchhausen's Travels*. The title of the French work — the substance of which is said to be quite the same with the Baron's drolleries, and clearly of Norman and Gascon origin — is as follows :

" La Nouvelle Fabrique des excellents traits de vérité, livre pour inciter les resveurs tristes et mélancholiques à vivre de plaisir, par Philippe D'Alcripe, Sieur de Neri en Verbos."

This work had become so scarce that no copy of the first edition could be found to print from ; and the new edition is copied from the reprint of 1732. German critics demur to this imputed parentage of their great boaster ; and in reply to the sally of the lively Frenchman, that the soil of the German mind is too heavy for the production of so light and lively a composition, they retort by saying, that although German literature at present wears a very morose and peevish aspect, it was not always so ; for that humorous literature once flourished in Germany more than in any other country of Europe ; as even an Edinburgh reviewer confessed, when he said (vol. xlvi. 1827) that " four-fifths of all the popular mythology, humour, and romance to be found in Europe in the sixteenth and seventeenth centuries, proceeded from Germany." Gervinus remarks that the pith of the Baron's adventures is to be found in a book very popular among the people, the fictitious *Travels of the Finkenritter* (Herr Polycarp von Kirlarissa), a work given to the world 200 years before *Münchhausen* saw the light. Some of the veracious Baron's stories are also to be found in Lange's *Deliciæ Academicæ* (Heilbr., 1665), under the head of *Mendacia Ridicula*. The Baron never intended, it is said, to print his comical adventures, which he was in the habit of repeating in social circles ; and was very much surprised when he knew that they had been published in England without his knowledge, by a learned but unprincipled German scholar of the name of Raspe, who had taken refuge in this country from the pursuit of justice, and was much employed in translating works from other languages.

In further support of their claims to wit and humour, the Germans refer to their *Reineke der Fuchs*, and their *Tyll Eulenspiegel* ; the latter of which has been translated into all the languages of Europe. From *Eulenspiegel*, the French have derived their own word *Espièglerie* ; and even the word *Calembourg* may be traced to the Austrian *Eulenspiegel* — the priest Wigand von Theben, surnamed the " Jester of Kahlenberg." The reason why such injustice has been done to a highly important ingredient in the character of the German people, is said by a recent writer of their own to be this : because the literary history of Germany has been almost always written by men without any perception of the humorous, and who accordingly either pass it wholly by, or else bestow upon it very slight notice, which is deprived of all freshness and life by being overlaid with the heavy lumber of university learning.

JOHN MACRAY.

Oxford.

My friend Mr. F. L. J. Thimm, in his *Literature of Germany historically developed*, 12mo., London, attributes the authorship of this work to —

" K. K. A. Münchhausen — who recited his *Abenteuer* in company to friends, who superintended their publication — born 1759, died 1836."

Mr. Thimm, however, admits that on this point he has been led into error, and will consequently omit or modify the statement in the forthcoming edition of his useful little manual. I merely, therefore, make this allusion to his work in order that those who may consult it on this point may not be led into error.

I have reason to believe that the following quotation from the *Conversations-Lexicon* will be found to contain a more correct and explicit account of the book, its authors, translators, and compilers, than is to be found elsewhere :

" Münchhausen (Hieronymus Karl. Fried. Freiherr von) aus der sogenannten Weissen Linie des Hauses, geboren 1720 auf dem väterlichen Gute Bodenwerder im Hannoverischen, gestorb. 1797, gilt für einen der grössten Lügner und Aufschneider, so dass nach ihm noch gegenwärtig alle grotesk komischen Aufschneidereien *Münch-hausiaden* genannt werden. Er fand sein Hauptvergnügen darin, seine als russischer Cavallerie-offizier in den Feldzügen gegen die Türkei, 1737-39 erlebten Abenteuer, die er bis zum wunderbaren ausschmückte, immer und immer wieder zu erzählen. Dieses absonderliche Talent hatte ihm zwar in seinem Vaterlande schon weit und breit einen Namen gemacht, doch fand sich für die Früchte desselben zuerst in England ein Sammler und Herausgeber. Die 1ste Sammlung von Münchhausen's Reisen erschien dort unter dem Titel : *Baron Münchhausen's Narrative of his marvellous Travels and Campaigns in Russia* (London, 1785). Dieses frivole Werkchen fand vielen Beifall, und wurde in 2 Jahren fünf mal, zuletzt mit zahlreichen und umfangreichen Zusätzen aufgelegt. Nach der 4ten Englischen Ausgabe erschien die 1ste deutsche Uebersetzung von Bürger, London, 1786, welche 1788 eine vermehrte und verbesserte Auflage mit Benutzung der 5ten englischen zugleich aber mit verschiedenen Zuthaten des Uebersetzers, und wahrscheinlich auch *Lichtenberg's* erhielt. Die englische Ausgabe von der H. Döring, eine neue freie Uebersetzung unter dem Titel *Münchhausen Lügenabenteuer*, 1846, erschienen liess, rührt ohne Zweifel von dem als Mineralog und Archäolog nicht unbedeutenden, seiner Zeit auch durch belletristische Productionen bekannten, sonst aber übelberüchtigten ehemaligen Kasselschen Professor und Bibliotheker R. Z. Raspe (1737-94) her, der nach London geflüchtet war, und sich hier mit Schriftstellerei in mehreren Sprachen beschäftigte.

" Einige von Münchhausen's bekanntesten Jagd und Kriegsgeschichten finden sich schon, wenn auch in etwas ander und meist roher Gestalt in weit älteren Büchern, wie in Bebel's *Facetiæ*, aus denen sie nebst einigen anderen aus Castiglione's *Cortegiano*, und Bidermann's *Utopia*, in T. P. Lange's *Deliciæ Acedemicæ*, Heilbronn, 1765, übergingen.

" Ausführliches über Münchhausen enthällt Elissen's *Einleitung* zur neuen Ausgabe d. *Abenteuer*, Goettingen, 1849." — *Conversations-Lexicon*, 10te Ausgabe.

Southey asks :

" Who is the author of *Münchhausen's Travels*, a book which every one knows because all boys read it ?

" Two of his stories are to be found in a Portuguese magazine, if so it may be called, published about four-score years ago, with this title . . *Folheto de Ambas Lisboas*. . . . . . It is not likely that the author of *Münchhausen* should have seen these *Folhetos* ; . . . But it is probable that the Portuguese and English writers both had recourse to the same store-house of fable." — *Omniana*, vol. i. p. 155.

WILLIAM BATES.

Birmingham.

MR. BREEN will find some correspondence on the authorship of this book in Vols. ii. and iii. of " N. & Q." I refer to the matter, partly for the sake of repeating a question to which no answer was given at the time of that correspondence : Who was the Englishman spoken of in the *Percy Anecdotes* as the author of *Münchhausen*, and designated by the initial " M." (see "N. & Q." Vol. iii., p. 316.).

J. C. R.

95. BLACKWOOD'S MAGAZINE, 80 (1856), 403-429. M/H No. 5127. By Andrew Wilson.

WAYSIDE SONGS.

ORIGINAL AND TRANSLATED.

"Home-keeping youth" were considered, in Shakespeare's day, to "have ever homely wits;" but at present we are so fond of going to and fro over the face of the earth, and of walking up and down upon it, that the home-keeper has become an object of wonder and even of respect. As it is the man who has *not* written a book that ought to be entered at Stationers' Hall, and largely pensioned from the Literary Fund, so it is he who has never travelled, and (rarer virtue!) has never described his travels, that ought to receive a large grant of money from the Geographical Society. The great increase of books may not tend greatly to increase human knowledge, because it dilutes the small particle of human knowledge into such huge hogsheads of supposed knowledge or folly, that the particle of knowledge is often lost for all good ends. In like manner, travel itself and books of travel may be serious obstacles to knowledge of this earth. How can geographical research be prosecuted with much enthusiasm when the explorer knows that his hardwon volume will be lost among a fleet of compilations professing to be original and spicy sketches, got up to suit the Cockney's idea of the matter?

This travel that is no travel, and description that is no description, should not be permitted, however, to raise any prejudice against the old idea of wandering as the completion of education—of the years of apprenticeship being fitly followed by the *Wanderjahre*. An American

philosopher has expressed the opinion that it is the office of a wheel, rather than of a man, to go up mountains and down valleys; but he has himself informed us that it is his practice to re-enchant himself with a beautiful scene, by looking at it—a great moment in the life of a great man—bending down with his head between his legs. Now if a man may stand with his head between his legs—a position which is humbling, and, to persons of a certain tendency, even dangerous—in order simply to enjoy nature, much more may he, for the same purpose, go up mountains and down valleys—an exercise in itself stimulating, healthful, and humanising. The fool at home is a fool in Rome, not only because he carries his folly about with him, but also because he carries his home, or his close circle of local habits and prejudices along with him. That kind of wandering which tends to remove prejudice and widen sympathy, will, most certainly, have the effect of conducting him in the direction of wisdom. Experience, according to the old proverb, teaches even fools. All trying and tutoring in the world is useful to man. The greatest benefit of travel is when it throws us into new circumstances; removes us from the beaten paths which we safely pursue without any effort of our own; and so excites independence of mind and character. To our ancestors, a couple of centuries ago, travel really signified trying, and tutoring in the world. In the *Two Gentlemen of Verona* we have a forcible illustration of this:—

"He wonder'd that your Lordship
Would suffer him to spend his youth at home;
While other men of slender reputation,
Put forth their sons to seek preferment out:
Some to the wars to try their fortune there;
Some to discover islands far away:
Some to the studious universities.
For any or for all these exercises,
He said that Proteus, your son, was meet:
And did request me to importune you

To let him spend his time no more at home,
Which would be great impeachment to his age,
In having known no travel in his youth.
ANTONIO. Nor need'st thou much importune me to that
Whereon this month I have been hammering.
I have consider'd well his loss of time;
And how he cannot be a perfect man,
Not being try'd and tutor'd in the world."

Unfortunately there are no "islands far away" to be discovered now. The "studious universities" suggest ideas of paradisiacal innocence. Even war affords so little opportunity at present for the development of individuality, that it is of small use in the way of producing that desirable character more often sought than found, "a perfect man." A modern youth has only to live: for without any effort of his own, he may float about on the labours of others, and amuse himself by trifling only with the varied efforts of man. The true ideal of life seems to have been regarded, by our forefathers, as consisting in a stormy youth and a quiet old age. Storming away life in ancient times involved "a life o' sturt and strife" more than is attainable at present, except among the glens of the Atlas, and suchlike interesting nooks of the earth; but it involved also free and pleasant connection with nature—dwelling under the greenwood tree, wild rides and forays, and long pilgrimages. What enviable fellows the Three Archers were!

"We three archers be,
Rangers that rove through the north countrie,
Lovers of ven'son and libertie,
   That value not honours or monie.

"We three good fellows be,
That never yet ran from three times three,
At quarterstaff, broadsword, or bowmanrie,
   But give us fair play for our monie.

"We three merry men be,
At a lass or a glass under greenwood tree,
Jocundly chaunting an ancient glee,
   Though we had not a penny of monie."

If the weather were always fine in these days, a lass and a glass always procurable under a greenwood tree, and ven'son in abundance, then we can easily believe that these fine fellows would not yield up their glorious privileges at the bidding of three times three; that to any monarch even each of them would answer in the words of the outlaw Murray,—

"Ere the king my fair countrie get,—
   This land that's nativest to me,
Mony o' his nobilis sall be cauld,
   Their ladyes sall be right wearie."

It may be questioned, however, how far making "nobilis cauld," and living in entire defiance of principalities and powers, be absolutely necessary to the fit development of the modern youth. In the ideal, that is to say, in his poems, spasmodic tragedies, and veracious autobiographies, he is well known to be a most formidable person; consumed by unutterable remorse; haunted by the spirits of innumerable lost females; with the weight of several very culpable homicides resting upon his head; and to have even, possibly, committed the unknown sin; but in the depressing atmosphere of the base actual, he has rather the appearance of one who requires to be encouraged, and to be reminded that a little practical extravagance in youth may be no impeachment to his age. No doubt, under the guidance of Mephistopheles, or of Lucifer, or Zernebock, or even of plain Satan, he has visited, besides enjoying small excursions among the stars, all the wonderful parts of this *globosa*, as it is profanely called by a monkish poet; but having been unaccompanied by his body in these visits, it is possible that his descriptions may be wanting in a certain human element necessary to commend them to grosser minds. Much wandering (with the body) may not have the effect of enabling him, more grandly, in imagination, to strike the stars with his sublime head; neither will it, on the other hand, directly favour superiority in any special department of human effort; but while, on the one side, it may remove him from the region of mere ideas, on the other, it will widen his sympathies with humanity, and multiply his springs of life,—thus enlarging the possibilities of his existence, and enabling him (if aught can), to be made more one with Nature, to possess a larger inheritance on earth, and to enjoy more of the life of this our star. And really, on awaking in some other star, it will be unpleasant for any of us to confess that we have seen only a few square miles of this.

> "Hath Britain all the sun that shines? Day, night,
> Are they not but in Britain? I' the world's volume
> Our Britain seems as of it. . . . Prythee, think
> There's livers out of Britain."

So said Imogen; apprehending, though a woman, that our inheritance in space is as fair as, and more real than, our inheritance in time; that it is ours to pass from clime to clime, from sea to sea, from range to range —to embrace the world as a whole, and as, in its totality, the inheritance of individual man.

> "From the mountain to the champlaign,
> By the glens and hills along,
> Comes a rustling and a trampling—
> Comes a motion as of song.
> And this undetermined roving
> Brings delight and brings good heed,
> And thy striving, be't with loving,
> And thy loving, be't indeed.
>
> "Keep not standing, fix'd and rooted,
> Briskly venture, briskly roam;
> Head and hand, where'er thou foot it,
> And stout hearts are still at home.
> In each land the sun doth visit
> We are gay, whate'er betide;
> To give room for wandering is it
> That this world was made so wide."

It is rough but stirring language, into which this, the finest of Goethe's marching songs, has been set by the translator of *Meister*, and more appropriate words can scarcely be obtained. Both its English and German versions recall many a long march on which they have been sung, many a halt from June suns in leafy woods or wayside hoastries, many a steep mountain-side, many a rich valley, and many a mountain pass, where still, let us hope, from younger lips,

> "Da erklingt es wie von Flügeln,
> Da bewegt sich's wie Gesang."

More softly we may give another poetical argument, suggested to us by a passage in *Faust*:—

> Doth not the earth lie here below?
> Doth not the vault of heaven arch o'er?
> Do not the calm eternal stars
> Beam friendly on us evermore?
>
> Weaves not the All around the soul,
> In motion strange and stranger rest?
> The mystic meaning of the Whole
> Be ours, and we are truly blest.

The only essential condition to understanding the mystic meaning is that sympathy with pure nature which enables a man, in the first place, to see objects as they really are, and then, to enjoy the life of these objects as if it were actually his own. It does not matter what it is we look at, provided only we see it as it really is. The false romanticism of vulgar fancy requires something pretentious and unnatural to gratify its taste; but to the true poet it is indifferent whether he look on the lily of the valley or on Solomon in all his glory. The song of the nightingale, as heard by the hearing ear and the understanding heart, belongs to the music of the spheres. *Homer* and the *Scottish Ballads* will always delight, because they are such clear, undistorted reflexes of the lives of Grecian and Scottish freebooters. Byron defined poetry as the creation, from "overfeeling good or ill," of an "external life beyond our fate;" but he himself came to see that this view was false, and was passing away from it in his *Don Juan*. Goethe has spoken much more accurately on the subject. True poetry, he says, announces itself thus, that, as a worldly gospel, it can by internal cheerfulness free us from the earthly burdens which press upon us. Like an airballoon it lifts us, together with the ballast which is attached to us, into higher regions, and lets the confused labyrinths of the earth lie developed before us in a bird's-eye view. It does not elevate us into a higher region in order that we may there live a life beyond our fate, but only that, looking down, we may behold the wider plain in which the contradictions of earth appear reconciled, and all life vindicates its existence. Without apprehending something of the mystic meaning—without genial sympathy with all living things, travel would indeed be painful and unprofitable, for the more seen, the more would we be disturbed and pained. If all be "vanity and vexation of spirit," the less of it we see the better. But if the world does not so appear; if all things, rightly viewed, may put gladness into our hearts, and answer the question, "who shall show us any good?" if by sympathising with the individual we can rise to a comprehension of the general, and if our apprehension of the universal increases our love of the individual, then we may wander, with ever-increasing advantage, over the broad earth, in the sun-light or moonlight, or under the friendly stars. Such a life may, from its very nature, give us to see more of the brighter side of things. We may turn away into it from many sorrows, and of many an annoyance we may sing with that "snapper up of unconsidered trifles," the pleasant rogue Autolychus,—

> "But shall I go mourn for that, my dear?
> The pale moon shines by night:
> And when I wander here and there,
> I then do most go right."

"The earth-dust of the globe," says Jean Paul, "is inspired by the breath of the great God. The world is brimming with life: every leaf on every tree is a land of spirits." The Earth is always beloved of her more honest children. To the Greeks she was the all-nourishing mother. At this day the only oath which binds the Sumatran Rejangs is one they make by laying their hands upon the earth, and desiring that she may no more yield them nourishment after their promise is broken. In this life of the earth there is a refreshing power, of the full force of which we are only conscious when in an enfeebled state —when, recovering from severe illness, we first begin to draw in the vital power of earth, and sea, and air. The following Morning Hymn is an attempt to express this consciousness.

I

My Temple is the Morning-sky,
  My Altar is the Earth,
Where spring-tide gladness wingeth high,
  And holy thoughts have birth.

II.

A thousand snowy mountain-peaks
  Their incense upwards roll,
Whose purple glories calmly float
  As from a blessed soul.
The cattle on a thousand hills
  Their gladsome bells are ringing;
While, in the vales, full-hearted birds
  Their wonder-songs are singing.
Earth gladdens, with a mother's joy,
  At childhood's flute-like voice;
And fills her lap with early flowers
  That it may more rejoice.
To sturdy manhood and to youth
  The forest monarchs nod;
And maidens' feet cast snowy light
  Upon the grassy sod.

III.

Still weakly life flows on again;
  The knapsack presses sore,
From ills to which our flesh is heir,
  And griefs which injure more.
The lower woods have changed to green
  Since last I wander'd free,
Yet little solace to my pain
  Their budding brought to me.
Men reckon'd in a stranger tongue
  What fill'd my scanty scrip,
And woodmen's carols rudely rang
  From woodman's rough-bark'd lip.
There was no aid, the while I lay
  Upon a sharp-thorn'd bed;
No voice to scare the dark-cloud shades
  Which wander'd round my head,—
The silent shades that gather'd round,
  Whose awful figures fell
On blackness, streak'd athwart the gloom
  As in a dim-lit hell.
I long'd but for that Lethal sleep
  Which laps the Elysian'd soul,
Where, in some calm translucent deep,
  No waves of sorrow roll:
Or but to hear the wild woods wave
  Their heavy boughs afar,
Or dew-tranced flowers upon a grave,
  Beneath a blood-red star.

IV.

But ever on the earth-born, thou,
  O Earth! thy freshness pourest,
New soundness to the soul most soil'd,
  And when its need is sorest.
In thee the conscious spirit may
  Its jaded powers refresh,
Plunged in thy streaming, ever germing
  Divine unconsciousness.

V.

Each step we take is over graves,
  On which we careless tread;
For ever fresh-creative power
  Glows in the quick and dead:
Not dead! the slime that greens the ditch
  Is quick: a vital force
Coheres the stone, and rolls the star
  Along its life-sprung course.
The purest flower, the proudest tree
  In rottenness are planted,
And draw their tints and fragrant life
  From what the gods have granted.
Man too, who, lonely, foremost stands
  On Being's awful height,
Between Life's many-colour'd lands
  And vasty plains of night,—
Man too, whose bold, light-beaming brows
  Their light through darkness throw,
Springs from thick slimes and all foul things
  Which writhe and seethe below;
And never, though his soul revolt,
  Shall that connection cease,
Till, having fram'd a higher king,
  The man-soul rest in peace.

VI.

Meanwhile, as soaring songsters fall,
  And great thoughts sink to earth,
And noblest things will backwards turn
  To where they had their birth,
So conscious man, when consciousness
  Droops, in its lonely flight,
Its wings of sin and righteousness,
  Falls through the golden light—
Falls back on the unconscious earth,
  Upon its twofold sphere,—
One bath'd in light, the other sunk
  In darkness and in fear:
The one, the fouler, darker swamp
  Of procreative power,
Where, life untwining, loathsome life
  Prepares creation's hour;
The other perfect, fair, life-fill'd,
  In broad-thrown light of day,
Smiling, in open, fearless glee,
  Its over-life away.

VII.

Thus the unconscious varying Earth
  Her powers and knowledge lends us ;
And so alternate, are reveal'd,
  The terrors and the splendours.

Every part of the universe has its glorious time, in so far as life may be there in the ascendant, and its perfect completeness and beauty when the culminating point is gained.

Goethe has a subtle poem in his *Zahme Xenien*, on this subject, on the balance of rest and motion, or *Nivritti* and *Pravritti* of the Buddhists.

Life from each star above is beaming—
Each star that wanders, brightly gleaming,
  Along its chosen path of light.
Deep in the earth-ball beat the Powers
Which lead us to the shining hours,
  Then backward to returning night.
And as into Infinity,
  This Life, itself repeating, flies,
The mighty dome, close-bound, we see
  In thousand firm-lock'd arches rise.
Life's joy from every star is flowing,
  From small and great, from sky and sod,
While all the thronging, all the glowing,
  Is rest, eternal rest in God.

The proper time for benefiting by travel and entering into the life of the earth is the season of youth, when we are neither exhausted as regards our emotions, nor affect to be so, when we are full of wonder, of ingenuousness, of varied sympathy, and of capability for enjoyment. He who has never wandered free over the earth in the days of his youth, is to be pitied as we pity him who has never known the delirium of youthful love. He has lost a chance which he can never have again. To him the Earth has not revealed itself in her wildest, yet divinest beauty ; the skies have not beamed on him with their sweetest smiles ; the winds have not whispered to him their rarest secrets ; the stars have not swept before him in joyful dance

through the gladdened deep. Happy he who, as Marlborough, looking up at his portrait, exclaimed, " That was a man !" can look back upon his youth and say, " That was a time !" It cannot, however, afford a satisfactory retrospect because of its enjoyment, unless that enjoyment was broken by the stern lessons of experience, and proceeded not so much from the absence of difficulties, as from difficulties overcome. There is nothing more absurd than young men feigning to be sad " from very wantonness ;" but they will undoubtedly find enough to dispirit them at times. " Cuddy," says Spenser, in his *Shepherd's Calendar*, not, that we are aware, meaning any special reflection in the address :—

"Cuddy, I wot thou kenst little good,
  So vainly to advance thy headless hood ;
For youth is a bubble blown up with breath,
  Whose wit is weakness, whose wage is death,
Whose way is wilderness, whose age penaunce,
  And stoop gallant age, the host of grievaunce."

It may safely be said that he who has nothing to be ashamed of, can have nothing to be proud of ; that he who has never fallen, has never learned to run ; that he who has never been defeated, has never learned to

conquer. And before the consciousness of victory is vouchsafed—when there is the consciousness of battle—when youth is in its " storm and stress period," wild and aimless wandering appears often to afford relief.

Through the woods storm-tost,
Darkness and tempest ;
Through wild winds raging,
Breasting the rain,
Over the plain
Where wild war's raging ;
Through fiery glow ;
'Mid hail and snow ;
In mist of mountains ;
By palm-girt fountains ;
Away, away,
No peace nor stay !

But in these lines we give only a faint echo of Goethe's

Dem Wind, dem Regen,
Dem Schnee entgegen :
In Dampf der Klüfte,
Durch Nebeldüfte :
Immer zu, immer zu,
Ohne Rast und ohne Ruh."

Still finer as a description of youth's unrest is his representation of Euphorion, in the second part of *Faust*, where that child of Power and Genius is seized by the longing to spring through all the heavens. The lightly gained pleaseth him not : of the

maidens it is the most self-willed young one that he pursues over stock and stone, whose resisting bosom he presses to his own, and whose fair opposing lips he kisses. Though rocks and bushes close him in, yet will he not be narrowed :—

Yet am I young and fresh.
Tempests are roaring there,
Billows are foaming there,
  I hear them afar,
  And rage to be near.
Hear ye not thunder from the ocean,
  Rolling its echoes high and low ?
Host upon host in billowy motion,
  Are thronging on to pain and woe ;
To yield in fiery strife their breath,
Since the command requireth death.

Elsewhere he has a beautiful verse on the value of the experience and sorrows of youth, which we may loosely paraphrase thus :—

Over mountains to the ocean,
  Ever wider o'er the deep,
Fancy waves, with mystic motion,
  Like the curtain of our sleep.
New Experience brings the Morrow,
  Though it doubt and trouble raise ;
For the food of Youth is Sorrow,
  Even tears are Songs of Praise.

Perhaps wandering is better fitted to relieve unrest and passion than it is to spirit away dejection. In one of Coleridge's finest poems, in-

deed almost the only fine poem he wrote after his twenty-sixth year, he complains—

" Ah ! lady, we receive but what we give,
  And in our life alone does Nature live."

507

There are certain moods of mind, the psychology of which is little understood, that cannot be relieved by the freshness of nature or the happiness of others. Of one of these the following may be taken as an illustration, and, at the same time, as a view of Italy from the Alps :—

Vainly, alas! I dream'd that yet,
　Amid these ancient Schweitzer hills,
This soul its burden might forget;
　Or, that the snow-born, trickling rills,
Whose footfalls through the silence break,
　Might cool my heavy brow and brain ;
Or, that the mountain-girdled lake,
　Glorious with blue, might ease my pain.

I hop'd the changing lights that played
　Like smiles upon the Splügen's side,
And pierced within the deep-sunk glade,
　Might cast a gleam *within*, to guide ;
That, dawning gladly on my sight,
　Some rosy morn might bid me live,
Some holy evening's fading light
　A gentler melancholy give.

Would that amid this cloudy war,
　I felt the madness of the fray,—
Could mount upon the storm-wind's car
　To bear me from myself away,—
Could rise with mists that upwards curl
　And break upon the mountains hoary,
Or, like that eagle, upwards hurl,
　With snow-fleck'd back—beak, talons gory.

It is no wonder some have thought
　The Infinite may dwell in Man,
Since souls may know a depth of sorrow
　Man's consciousness can never scan ;
Dark depths where thought shrinks back in awe,
　Where brooding shapes and phantoms dwell,
Where Man, flung swiftly out of time,
　Can realise the thought of hell.

O'er these dark steps my spirit broods,
　Till, roused as from ignoble sleep,
And casting off its feebler moods,
　It plunges down the cloudy steep ;
Cleaving the brown and gloomy air,
　Till feeling, action, thought and motion,
With all the rippling waves of time,
　Are lost, as in a Polar ocean.

Now, from the desolation nigh,
　Gladly my spirit floats away,
Embark'd on crimson clouds which lie
　Upon the lessening streams of day—
The trembling stream of lessening day—
　The rosy light which softly falls
O'er the snow-marbled, Alpine range,
　Betwixt the rugged, dark cloud-walls ;

Above the land whose darker hues,
　Blent with the evening light which streams
On massy lines of Apennines,
　Startle, as when fierce sorrow gleam

In passion from a woman's face,
　When, mingled with her happiness,
Dread, pity, anguish, hate, and grace,
　Troubling, increase her loveliness ;

That land where over Lombard plains,
　And over chestnut-rounded hill,
Now clouds retire and daylight wanes,
　Two mighty shapes the distance fill :—
Beauty, in robes of summer light,
　Trembling, submits with blushing grace,
As, vaster, in his garb of night,
　Death clasps her in his calm embrace.

But day and tempest flee away,
　And colder, sterner, still I view
Black cliff and snowy mount beneath
　The calm of heaven's deepening blue ;
Serene and passionless as Fate—
　The All-embracer—leave her too :
What booteth mourning? love? or hate?
　The day is falling :—*Immer zu.*

" Ever onwards " is likely to afford some relief, for the swifter we move the more forgetful are we of the tediousness and length of the way. *Reitet nur zu* was the very sensible answer of the Swiss peasant to the traveller who asked him, in a complaining humour, how far it was to Appenzell. And if we walk long enough, or ride long enough, we shall be sure to reach the traveller's bourne at last. As Friederich von Logau camped out in the German wars, he kept a case with pens and paper, besides his sword, at his side, and by the side of camp-fires wrote his innumerable versicles, which, in the after years, have cheered many a homeless wanderer ; and among these, the following, of which we give our translation, may be selected as the most appropriate to our present purpose :—

" Hoffnung ist ein fester Stab,
　Und Geduld ein Reisekleid ;
Da man mit, durch Welt und Grab,
　Wandert in die Ewigkeit."

Hope's a steady staff and stiff ;
　Patience as a cloak is given ;
Through the World and Grave therewith,
　Let us wander on to Heaven,

or elsewhither, as we may happen to be bound; for it will be observed that Friederich, with becoming modesty, by no means says, into Heaven, but only into *Ewigkeit ;* and surely whatever place we may be destined to march into, it is right to advance thither as cheerfully as possible. The sword and the camp must have been great cheerers to the German poet, for the poetic melancholy is often relieved by fitting active life. The Minnesingers and Troubadours were only sad when in love, and when Shakespeare's young men looked sad, " it was for want of money ;" but, as the world rolls, the poet's lot seems to become harder, and the poets themselves increase in bitterness, and, unquestionably, not without bitter reasons. There is no poetry more utterly sad than that of Shelley, although, as far as love and money were concerned, he was far from unfortunate. There is something pleasant in Byron's half-affected, half-real, and defiant gloom ; but Shelley seldom wrestles with grief, and much of his verse is like a woman's " wailing for her demon-lover." When he does assert himself, however, there is a frightful sincerity in his language which Byron never reached, as in these lines :—

95. continued

"To sit and curb the soul's mute rage,
Which preys upon itself alone;
To curse the life which is the cage
Of fetter'd grief that dares not groan;
Hiding from many a careless eye
Its scorned load of agony."

Somewhat similar in tone are the poems of Heine, that great German poet, the jest of whose existence was ended at Paris a few months ago. His later writings, indeed, have been unsurpassed in grim sarcasm; but his earlier poems are often exquisitely pathetic, and the pathos is not dispelled by the slight, half-conscious tinge of the ludicrous with which they are coloured. As an excellent translation of his *Buch der Lieder* has been published lately, we shall only present here our rendering of his *Bergstimme :*—

A rider through a valley pass'd,
And slowly pick'd his way.
"Ah, leads this to my loved one's arms,
Or to my grave to-day?"
The Echo answer'd, "Yea,
To your grave to-day."

Then farther rode that rider on,
His breast with gloom oppress'd,
"Ah, must I then so very soon
Fall—in the grave to rest?"
The Echo said, "'Tis best
In the grave to rest."

The rider then let fall a tear
Down from his brimming eye.
"If peace be only in the grave,
Then it is good to die."
Deep was the Echo's sigh,
"It is good to die."

Those who agree with the Echo will find an apothecary in every street, and hydrocyanic acid obtainable with a little trouble, so they need not complain of the present days in which their lot has been cast. Strange, as Bacon remarks, how many attendants we have that can overcome death!—"Revenge triumphs over death; love slighteth it; honour aspireth to it; grief flieth to it; fear pre-occupieth it." But useful as hydrocyanic acid may be as a weapon for overcoming all the ills of life, Heine himself gave the preference to jesting, and found it afford most valuable aid. When we are fully persuaded that all is vanity, there is nothing like accepting the fact and making the most of it, like the experienced and much-enduring hero of the German song *Vanitas! Vanitatum Vanitas!*—a song we shall attempt slightly to improve in translating :—

I've cast my care on nothing now:
Yuchhe!
So everything goes better now:
Yuchhe!
And who my camarade will be,
Must join in this along with me,
And then we shall agree.

The fair ones first were all my treasure:
Yuchhe!
But soon they plagued me out of measure:
Oh wae!

The false ones sought another mate,
The true ones made me quickly sate;
The best would always prate.

I placed my joy in goods and gold:
Yuchhe!
But their account was quickly told:
Oh wae!
The shiners wander'd here and there;
'Twas nought but grinding thought and care;
My pocket soon was bare.

I travell'd next by sea and land:
Yuchhe!
And wander'd from my fatherland:
Oh wae!
But little comfort could be had;
The bed had bugs, the cook was bad
Enough to set me mad.

For fame and honour much I bore;
Yuchhe!
But others ran away with more:
Oh wae!
And what myself I grudged to others,
Was grudged to me by all my brothers,
'Tis nought but thankless bothers.

I then took up the sword and shield;
Yuchhe!
To fight in many a bloody field:
Oh wae!
The castle's walls were overthrown;
I enter'd over ditch and stone,
And lost my left leg-bone.

But now my cap at nought I've hurl'd:
Yuchhe!
And so I've conquer'd all the world:
Yuchhe!
There's an end to feast and song;
But our drinking we'll prolong,
While wine is red and strong.

When men merely sip the enjoyment belonging to the various kinds of existence, they qualify themselves very prematurely for appreciating the vanity of human wishes. *Gebt mir zu thun!* is the constant wish of one German poet, the entire versicle being as follows :—

Give me TO ACT—the best,
The richest gift for Man!
The heart can never rest:
Create it must, as ere it can.

In Spenser's *Shepherd's Calendar*, Thenot says reprovingly—

"Lewdly complainest thou, lazy lad,
Of Winter's wrack for making thee sad.
Must not the world wend in his common course,
From good to bad and from bad to worse,
From worse unto that is worst of all,
And then return to his former fall?
Who will not suffer the stormy time,
Where will he live to the lusty prime?"

Self have I worn out thrice thirty years,
Some in much joy, many in many tears,
Yet never complained of cold nor heat,
Of summer's flame nor of winter's threat;
Ne never was to Fortune foeman,
But gently took that ungently came;
And ever my flock was my chief care,
Winter or summer they mought well fare."

It is he, usually, who has no flock to care for that complains of the heat of the sun, and of furious winter's rages, that becomes Fortune's foeman, or, as Dante expresses it, insists on butting against the Fates —(nelle Fata dar di cozzo.) Mr. Carlyle's recommendation that, in order to escape suffering, we should heartily do the work which lies nearest to us, is older than the days of Epictetus, and in modern times has been best and most quietly put by the great German in a few pregnant sentences :—How can man learn to know himself? Never through observation, but only through work. Seek to accomplish thy duty: so shalt thou learn what is in thee. But what is my duty? It is the demand of the Day. He has also some excellent lines on this subject, which we give in something like the familiar style of the original :—

There is but one way of rightly rounding life ;—
Sack the past, leave it with its perish'd strife.
The most of it was lost, sin and tempest toss'd ;
Leave it, be a child again, new-born by the Host.
Inquire particularly what should be done each day;
Each, if you ask of it, will readily say :—
Mind your own business, doing it right well,
Respecting that of others—that must tell :—
And, above all, nobody hate.
Work, work, work, and do not prate!

But to this gospel many serious objections may be taken. Perhaps it is not work at all. but something quite different, that men desire and require. The life of a gin-horse is not the highest ideal of existence ; and work, regarded simply as such, affords no promise of any higher. The activity of all our faculties is essential to happiness, because any faculty we possess which is not gratified, revenges itself upon us. But these faculties simply desire to be gratified, and no "gospel of work" will affect them in one way or another. In so far as a man's position and development allow of fitting exercise for them all, he will be happy ; and in so far as they are hindered in their natural exercise, he will be miserable. But out of his misery even comes good. The loss of the individual is nature's gain. And hence there are two considerations, not strictly belonging to any gospel of work, which may serve to relieve a man's pain. In the first place, he may know that the pain will reveal to him the source of the evil, and render it remediable. In the second place, he may (if he can) comfort himself with the thought that, in the great economy of nature, his individual failure will be certain to be, to a very definite extent, a guard against future failures of the same description. Let him not forget, also, that nature makes little provision for the individual, and that mental suffering springs invariably from excessive individual selfishness, an evil which nature appears to take considerable pleasure in grinding out of us. There is nothing, for instance, more painful than the feeling of remorse ; and this feeling is a most selfish one, for it is simple grief because our present state is not such as it might have been. If we will be so selfish, we must just suffer accordingly ; but if we leave the past to bury its past, and content ourselves with our poor present, nature will be kind to us, and allow us to sow future joys.

" Jog on, jog on, the footpath way,
And merrily hent the stile-a ;
A merry heart goes all the day,
Your sad tires in a mile-a."

This abnegation of the past is the more necessary, inasmuch as a man's own individuality is often not responsible for his past. Men are started into life on no conditions of their own choosing, and for long years afterwards they are guided by others. It is long before they themselves learn to know the state of their venture and the circumstances in which it is placed, and to guide it wisely as these demand. The translator of *Meister* has entirely missed, misrepresented even, the force of one of Goethe's most beautiful poems bearing on this point. It is sung by Mignon, and to give its proper meaning we translate it thus :

Who never eat with tears their bread,
Who never, through the sad, still hours,
Sat bending, weeping on their bed—
They know ye not, ye Heavenly Powers!
Ye lead us forward into life,
Ye let us weakly sin most blindly,
Then leave us to the cruel knife
Of guiltlike shame, that cuts unkindly.

It does not cut in, however, without cutting out the possibility, among other things, of suffering from it again. Once led forward into life and there left to ourselves, we may take up the staff of hope and wander lightly on. Enjoyment even, in abundance, is provided, if we only choose to pluck it boldly. What is this world made for unless it is to be used? It may plausibly be argued that the best way of establishing our fitness for another and a better world, is to show, by our life, that we appreciate and value this. It is not altogether self-apparent, though some seem to suppose it is, that a man will have a special claim to blessedness hereafter, because he has rejected happiness here, and with a sour face has fulfilled his earthly pilgrimage. Perhaps it may turn out to be better for each of us to conclude in the spirit, if not in the words of Anacreon :—

Since 'tis clear I only can
Be a weak and erring man,
And across my being's arch
Flesh and spirit quickly march,—
Since the Past can ne'er be mended,
While the Present soon is ended,—
Since the Future is as dim
As the black horizon's rim,
I shall choose upon the way
Laugh and song, and dance, and play;
Snatching gladness as I go
From the vineyard's purple glow,
From some laughing maiden's lip,
Or her velvet finger's tip;
Taking all that life can give,
While I wander, while I live.

Moving in such a spirit, the light-hearted wanderer need never, unless he chooses, be alone. Every nook and corner of the earth has companions for him, and on every path he will find a *rustawallah*, or a road-fellow, as the Indians phrase it. There are still many Highland girls whose beauty is their only dower; and dull must he be who cannot raise at least a theological disputation with Donald among the heather, or get tidings of some "man," whether a lifter of cattle or enlightener of souls

510

whose fame ought to have filled the world. Railways, by absorbing traffic, have made the highways and byways of England most delightful for the solitary pedestrian who loves to wander at will over richly wooded land, to have his cup of ale, that "dish for a king," from a blooming girl, and along with the personable host, in some quiet inn, to rally gypsies and less aristocratic campers by the wayside, or to stuff enormous gaping farmers with accounts of the marvellous. In Rhineland, among the Fichtelgebirge, on the Suabian Alp, or in Switzerland, we can always, in later summer or in autumn, connect ourselves with some band of merry knapsacked *Bürschen;* offer with them the incense of our pipes under every widespreading tree; ring our glasses with them in every beerhouse we pass: stop with them for the meeting of the *Musikverein* in every small town; sing with them incessantly about the landlady's *Töchterlein—*

Dich liebt ich immer, dich lieb' ich noch Ieut,

or the *Drei freundliche Sterne,* and break out over our red wine with Rochlitz' *Trinklied,* or with this our English version of it :—

The song of Wine is light and fine;
And drinking makes our faces shine.
Those who this wine-song scarcely know,
Shall learn it here before they go.

We talk not long, for glasses strong
Of wine inspire us soon to song.
He who can sing receives our praise,
Who can't, shall learn on drinking days.

Wine stirs the blood, gives lighter mood,
And makes our feelings mild and good;
Wine is the death of care indeed,
And lifts the soul to bolder deed.

My drinking-mate lives in no state,
And has no castle rich and great;
But gods are we, while wine is near,
And high Olympus' self is here.

Each Brother call; in Bacchus' hall
We're free and equal, one and all.
O magic drink! this noble Wine
Renews again the golden time.

In winter, again, there are innumerable sledgers; and in spring there is that strange character, the *Handwerksbursche,* to give us the history of his life and labours, to take us to his humble inn, and to introduce us to the circles of his craft. In Italy there is, every now and then, a convent, or monastery as we call it, where strangers are entertained; where the wine is better than it is to be found elsewhere; where the prior, or the librarian, will afford us abundance of gratifications, if we only allow him a little latitude on the subject of the *una sancta chiesa;* and where, if we are fortunate to light on some holyday when the bones of the founder are exposed to view, we may find the peasantry gathered, and delight ourselves with the beautiful oval faces of the girls of the higher Apennines. Once having obtained a sufficient knowledge of the language for colloquial purposes, and accepted the people as they are—two things not particularly easy of accomplishment —Italy cannot fail to afford constant recreation of the most pleasing kind. There is so much of life in the open air, so great a disposition to be amused by strangers, such excellent wines and beautiful country, and there are so many very pretty, and very simple, foolish maidens, that even a man who has been whipped out of court for some of his many virtues, may, travelling in it, be again reconciled to humanity. Even the more sensuous gratifications of Italy lose the character of sensuality. All those persons have still something to live for who have never drunk Falernian among the narrow streets of the "city disinterred," or enjoyed the sparkle of Lacrima Cristi among the blue, white-fringed, dancing waves of the Bay of Naples,—never known the ices of the Albergo Reale, or the figs of Vesuvius, or washed down bundles of plain *Maccheroni al burro* with vast quantities of Tuscan Montepulciano. Then there are all the pleasant companions, strangers like yourself, in the beautiful land: the young Germans ecstatic with artistic enthusiasm, and getting intoxicated, every now and then, without being aware of it, or even discovering the fact, on the strong wines of the south; the elderly Germans who are profoundly read in Winkelmann, and able calmly to quote Hegel's Esthetische Vorlesungen before Niobe in all her woe; the Americans who walk in large parties through the galleries of the Vatican, one of their number reading Murray's descriptions, inquiring, after the close of a paragraph, "Have you all seen the Apollo Belvidere?" and concluding, as he strokes down energetically with his pencil, "Well, let us strike off the Apollo Belvidere;" substantial Englishmen, *once,* during their Italian visit, roused to enthusiasm, like one whom we remarked stopping before the Venus di Medici, and exclaiming, in a very audible whisper, "Well, I'm ————;" and warm-hearted, intensely national Scotsmen, one of whom astonished us, on a summer evening in the Florentine Café Donin, by raising "The Campbells are coming," loud above the flow of liquid Tuscan, and getting himself in consequence turned out into the street, where he found a fiacre, and replied to the driver's "Where to, Signor?" with a singularly quiet "Al inferno." The sacred pilgrims and Indian officers, the begging monks, the Maltese couriers, the knavish Greek and Smyrniote merchants, and the solemn Moslems of the Mediterranean and the Levant, make the voyager desirous to spend ten years, like Ulysses, rather than only ten days, on these fickle seas. Every pliant Nubian of the Nile boat, and every dusky scoundrel of the Egyptian caravan, will be but too happy to make you his particular friend, and to entertain you with the history of a life worthy of a place in the Arabian Nights. Close to the mud-walled Mahratta village, where you halt in the early morning to get a cup of boiled milk and a chat, in Hindustani, with the Patell, there are the wattle tents of some wandering tribe, relations of our European gypsies; while Mogul merchants have a tent not far off, and a miscellaneous crowd of fleas, bugs, and natives are beginning to stir in the *durrhumsallah.* In the most unfrequented parts—among the deserts and barren mountains of Central Asia, we meet with the caffilah of hardy Afghans; and when the circle of kneeling camels has been made, and the watch set, and the fire lighted in the centre, we may wonder at their rapid transitions from the wild humour of their conversation to the gloomy, fierce melancholy of their favourite songs. Not having, as yet, visited Tartary, we cannot speak from personal experience of the Usbecks, but have little doubt that they, too, will be found "rather jolly," to use a phrase which we heard applied, by a young Englishman, to the inhabitants of Jerusalem! To profit by intercourse with road-fellows, however, it is necessary to be in no hurry to arrive at home. Indeed, the perfect traveller ought to have no home, in the ordinary sense, and then he always makes one of whatever place he chances to be in. "When a traveller and his horse," says Swift, in his *Tale of a Tub,* "are in heart and flight, when his purse is full and the day before him, he takes the road only where it is clean and convenient, entertains his company there as agreeably as he can, but, upon the first occasion, carries them along with him to every delightful scene in view, whether of art or of nature, or of both; and if they chance to refuse, out of stupidity or weariness, let them jog on themselves and be d—d; he'll overtake them at the next town." There should be even a spice of vagrancy, of blackguardism, in the true wanderer; and all our great travellers seem to have had, or to have, a little of this invaluable element in their composition. Individuals with green spectacles, air-cushions, potted meats, and respectabilities, may be of the excellent of the earth, and may write

Forth rushes the water
And clouds o'er the land;
But the stars, in their courses,
Both wander and stand.
As with stars, so with love,
Which in true hearts for ever
Is wandering and moving,
But yet changeth never.

That little song, which we turn into English, from *Jerry und Vätely*, sufficiently expresses the proper spirit to be cultivated. It is much to know that there are a few hearts to which yours is bound for ever; that there are gentle eyes which your fancy pictures as beaming brighter than even the stars looking down on you through the clear desert air; that tears will be shed when you are laid low; or that some manlier friend will recall you, once perhaps, in the after years, and wonder, as he looks up to the starry paths, if he shall ever meet you there. For even in the presence of Azrael, it is well not to be entirely alone. Even sorrow and sadness are better than that awful black solitude of spirit, when no light of love glides before to guide us in the dark valley. The most frightful thing ever said of any man in this: "He was alone—always alone—and gnashing his teeth in the darkness;"

Lovely eyes in loved ones gazing,
Soul and beauty meeting there,
Gladly sings the poet, praising,
All the bliss and joy they bear;
But 'tis silence bringeth fulness,
Richer trust of heart in heart;
Softly, gently! in the stillness
Only speaketh heart to heart.
When the din of war's commotion
Calls the hero to the fight,
Where the foe, on land or ocean,
Fierce he slays with godlike might.
He can bear the crowds that meet him,
Fame and all its mad caressing,
If he knows one heart will greet him
With a thankful, silent blessing.

big books on the topography of Eden and the voyages of Ulysses, but they are not travellers; they have not seen anything truly, nor can they tell us of anything new.

Still we must not say that the wanderer is to make no abiding connections.

but when this darkness is engulfed of that other darkness, what ray of light can penetrate to the human soul within? It is not good even to think of such a death. Much happier than he who thus dies, was Richardson, the late African traveller, when sick to death in the pathless desert, with no human being near but an old faithful dragoman; for even there he was not alone, since in his dying struggles, as he turned on the sand beneath the garish moon, he called incessantly on his far-distant wife. The more thorough vagrant may have the advantage in many small respects; but he must either be insensible to many things; or else furiously insane at bottom. The wanderer, also, rightly to fulfil his destiny, must have a " far-distant home" and recollections to think of and dream over in silence—in *Verschwiegenheit*,—a word which reminds us of a beautiful poem of Goethe's.

There was a Magazine article once published, in which the clause, " woman is the sharer of man's joys and happiness," was made by the misprint of a single letter, to read— "woman is the shaver of man's joys and happiness." Such a mistake, we need scarcely say, no true wanderer will ever fall into. He will conduct himself as if he were always among those Arab tribes who, when a stranger comes to them, judge of his quality, and determine on the respect which is to be paid to him, from the report of the female slave who is appointed to wait upon him; treating him as only worthy of a beggar's portion if she complain of

Happy we! united brothers,
In our circle fair and true,
Knowing what is hid from others,
That our songs are many too.
All our love and all our fulness
By no stranger's voice are praised;
Out of trusting, out of silence,
Is our sacred temple raised.

his indifference—of a common camelman's if she report of rudeness. White, and black, and brown, and yellow, will all please him as the climates change. He may wish that the little nostril of an Indian *bibi* were not deformed by a ring; or that the magnificent golden hair of the Bagdad Jewess could never be lifted off to the displayment of a little shaven skull; or that his Abyssinian slaves were of rather more slender shape; but instead of hinting at these defects he will profess to regard them as beauties. Delighted with every change, he must sing, like the German soldiers—

Nut-brown maids and bread that's white,
'Tis our lot to meet to-night;
Rosy maids and bread that's brown
Wait us in to-morrow's town.

Few women are indifferent to the admiration of the meanest of mortals, so no one need be particularly bashful if he has only a little love to give them, and can distribute it largely. "One woman," said Benedick, "is fair; yet I am well; another, virtuous; yet I am well: another is wise; yet I am well; but till all the graces be in one woman, one woman shall not come into my grace." So long as we are in this humour, and no sparkling Beatrice appears to tame the wild heart with her mocking

hand, we may give the little love, and also get a little in return, without ceasing to be "well," and without doing any serious harm to others. A sailor has a sweetheart in every port which he knows; and without exactly adopting Jack's enlarged moral views, the wanderer will easily experience much greatly to endear to him many places he may visit. Besides the plentiful Philinas, there are many sweeter souls to make night more beautiful, and to whom he may translate Philina's song:

Sing not in that strain so dulful
Of the loneliness of night;
It is given, O thou Graceful!
For a friend and for delight.

As to man is given the wife,
As the fairest half by far,
So is the night the half of life,
And its sun the lover's star.

All the day our hands are working;
Heart and soul are plagued and riven;
Secret joys are round us lurking,
But for toil the day is given.

In the eve when toil is sleeping,
　When the glimmering twilight flies,
Jests from lip to lip are leaping,
　Love is lighting up the eyes.

Then the boy, so late a stranger,
　Loving only mountain air,
Now with little gifts will linger
　Round the maiden young and fair.

Then the nightingale to loved ones
　Softly sings its dangerous lay,
Sounding only to the moved ones,
　Something like their " Ah !" and " Pray !"

Wherefore, when the day is weary,
　Then remember, sweet Delight !
Every day has joyaunce near it—
　Each has troubles, each has night.

Perhaps it will be well for him to sing rather more softly than the above song of ours can be made to flow from human lips, but, at all events, that is the strain and the hour. Eve and spring-time are associated with love in every land. "O Night ! O Night ! —O Darling ! I lie upon the sand, dying for the light of your face !" is the commencement of one Arab love-song. In the tropics, where there is no spring like ours, the voice of the bulbul and the budding of the jasmine remind the lover of his dusky fair. Even where the sands of Central Africa float, the maidens of Darfur walk, in the mild season, with their Hamitic noses raised a little higher in the air than usual. Prigging Autolychus seems to have had a similar opinion on this point, so far as we can judge from that glorious song of his—

" When daffodils begin to peer—
　With heigh ! the doxy over the dale,—
Why, then comes in the sweet o' the year ;
　For the red blood reigns in the winter's pale.

" The white sheet bleaching on the hedge,—
　With hey the sweet birds, O how they sing !
Doth set my pugging tooth on edge ;
　For a quart of ale is a dish for a king.

" The lark, that tirra-lirra chants,—
　With hey ! with hey ! the thrush and the jay,—
Are summer songs for me and my aunts,
　While we lie tumbling in the hay."

Why Autolychus chose his AUNTS, of all individuals in the world, to lie tumbling with among the hay, is susceptible of various explanations, of which let this one content us, that his tastes were peculiar. The picture of Spring and its pleasures needs to be completed only by that before the author of *Tam o' Shanter*, when he wrote—

" Now, Tam, oh Tam, had thae been queans
　A'—"

et cetera, for we had nearly forgot the age in which we live, which knoweth none of these things. So completed, we say, the picture is perfect. What a mistake it is to suppose that only modern poets have learned to devote themselves to nature ! Let us examine the second verse. Autolychus sees a sheet bleaching on a hedge, which suggests to him the pawn-broker, which suggests to him a small sum of money, which, again, reminds him of a quart of ale ; but even as he approaches the sheet with his pugging tooth on edge and felonious intent in his heart, a still deeper sympathy affects, and in the fulness of heart he breaks out into a

" Hey ! for the sweet birds, O how they sing ! "

It reminds us of a pious, converted Abyssinian whom we once heard declaring, that in his country all nature awoke, with the dawn, to praise God, and even the tiger and the snake came out of their holes, not so much to look for their breakfasts, as to join in the universal hymn. Then in the last verse, the youth, reclining with his aunts among the hay and listening to the summer songs of the thrush and the jay, presents a spectacle of the most exalted kind, and an example which young men of the present generation would do well to follow.

All the great poets have May Songs. Goethe's is very simple, and we attempt to imitate, not to translate it :—

How lordly smileth
　Nature to-day,
While Heaven lighteth
　And laughs away !

The buds are sprouting
　On every tree ;
While thousand voices
　Are singing free ;

While joy is flowing
　Beneath, above—
O Sun ! O World !
　O Life ! O Love !

O Love ! O Loving !
　Surpassing fair,
As crimson'd clouds
　In morning air,

Thou blessest richly
　The fruitful land,
Thou blessest us
　Here, hand in hand.

O Maiden ! Maiden !
　I love but thee ;
Star-bright of eye,
　Thou lovest me.

As love the larks
　Their song and flight,
Or blooming flowers
　Great Heaven's light ;

So do I love thee,
　With throbbing heart,
Who gavest me virtue,
　A nobler part ;

And joy and dancing,
　And choral song,
Moving ever
　In love along.

Perhaps that is a little in the simple style, and too devoid of the surprising and the agonistic to pass for poetry in these days. The *Früh-zeitiger Frühling* will be thought quite as childish ; but we are bound to admire, and do admire this version with which a young lady has favoured us :—

Day of delight,
And comest thou still,
Pouring gold sunshine
O'er valley and hill?

Wood-brook abundant
Whither away,
Ceaselessly flowing
By night and by day?

Freshness ethereal
Filling the sky!
Golden fish glancing
In clear water by!

Bright plumaged songsters
In groves rustling near!
Heavenly melodies
Ravish the ear.

Under the growing
Leaves soft and green,
Stealeth the wild bee
Their fresh folds between.

Quivering motion
Trembles in air:
Narcotic fragrance
Lulleth me there.

The feeling that life is pervading all things, which we experience in May, is far from being of a tumultuous nature. The freshness of the young earth, as its renewed life springs forth into myriad beauteous forms, the insects rising in conscious joy and beauty, the quadrupeds feeling their life and strength, even the moats floating in the quicker sunbeams, and the stars at night gleaming brighter in the dark blue, put gladness into our hearts, but it is gladness of a soft and chastened kind, resembling somewhat in its nature a holy joy, and leading the poet to express himself in words of beauty and thoughts of good. In our English poetry especially, how much sweetness has been drawn from the inspiration of Spring! But where all is sweet it is difficult to choose, and the singers on this subject from Chaucer to Shelley would delay us too long if we once began to choose. These lines, however, by a living poet little valued *quoad* his poetry, we must allow ourselves to quote from the *New Timon* :—

" Bright shone the stars o'er Earth's green banquet-hall.
You seemed abroad to see, to feel, to hear
The new life rushing through the Virgin Year:
The visible growth, the freshness and the balm,
The pulse of Nature throbbing through the calm,
As wakeful over every happy thing,
Watch'd, through the hush, the Earth's young mother—Spring."

And how much more conscious of the new life rushing through the Virgin Year, will he be who feels throbbing beside him the life of a virgin heart!—

Gently the mellow moonlight stream'd
O'er rustling palms and jasmine bowers,
While, hand in hand, we leant and dream'd
Away those voiceless, vanish'd hours;
Till soft and low, in silver flow,
Your rich sweet voice our silence broke,
And sung of " Time long, long ago,"
As if prophetic fears awoke.

And closer then our hands were clasp'd,
And wildly then my arm was thrown
Around your form, and warmly prest
Your heaving bosom to my own.
No word was spoken, but your song
Died on the lips by kisses prest;
While throbbing blushes thrill'd along,
Till life was love, and both were blest.

We knew that other hours were near,
Whose truths would pale the joyous light
Of loving eyes, but future fear
Fled from that dream of young delight.
O cruel Time! O waning Love!
O Fate! that sets to each our bounds,
And coldly weaves her web above
With varied touches, looks, and sounds.

It is the eyes of joy that we require to see the earth with, would we see it in all its beauty. Heine, among many others, expresses this in one of his early poems, of which the verse is peculiar :—

Ah! if thou wert mine own, love,
How lovèd thou shouldst be!
For in my breast has grown, love,
An image sweet of thee ;
And by the light thy sweet eyes shed,
My only hope of bliss is fed.

Ah! if thou wert mine own, love,
How fair the earth should be?
For not a wish I've known, love,
That centres not in thee;
And by the light thy soft eyes shed,
I through the world, entranced, am led.

Every reader of poetry, we may assume, is acquainted with Shelley's exquisite song, commencing—

"I arise from dreams of thee
In the first sweet sleep of night,
When the winds are breathing low,
And the stars are shining bright ;"

and also with Byron's—

" There be none of Beauty's daughters
With a magic like thee,
And like music on the waters
Is thy sweet voice to me ;"

or else we should quote them in full. Not greatly inferior to these is the following song, which a friend permits us to use, and which, he says, he has translated from the German,—our suspicion being that it is some fair face alone which has inspired him to sing so well—A Teutonic face, perhaps, for he is a man of truth :—

Oh, come to me when through the night
Wander the starry host;
When gleaming in the moon's clear light,
My boat lies near the coast.

The air is soft as love's first sigh,
And soft the silvery sea.
My lute swells high and in thine eye
A tender joy I see.

For loving is this midnight hour,
And loving thou and I.
No shadows on the heavens lower,
Asleep the waters lie.

And as they sleep our eyes express
What never tongue may say;
While lips to lips in kisses press
Until the dawn of day.

Oh! come to me, when through the night,
The hosts of heaven stray,
To find delight in sweet moonlight,
And float upon the bay,
In boat upon the bay,
Oh, come away! Oh! come away,
And linger to the dawning day!

While night has thus its more delightful rewards, morning also has its smiles for the wanderer who seeks it early and finds it. The gold and glory of sunrise on the ocean within the tropics, the swift but steady flow of red glowing light over the banyans and mangoes of an Indian plain, and the first gilding of snowy mountains—

"When at the break of day they stand
Like giants looking through the sky,"

are revelations of the splendours of the universe such as excite joyous worship in the soul. In northern countries one's journey never commences before morning; but in the south of Europe, and more especially in the East, we are often found, like Dante's bird on the tree-top, eagerly watching for the first streak of dawn, as we sit on the back of some slow-striding camel or cautious mule. Avoiding, as much as possible, the fiery sunlight of the day, we know exactly the hours of moonlight, and when the moon is hid or the waning smile on her face is too faint to dispel the frown on the brow of her gloomy lover, Night, we must start with the earliest rays of day, in order to accomplish the day's journey before the true tyrant of the East ascends far in his exceeding dazzling robes of light. In the North we leave the friendly shelter only when we can step out into the fresh blue morning, and we may in most glad humour arouse our companions with Shakespeare's morning song, or more fittingly, perhaps, with this our echo of it:—

Through golden eyelids now the Dawn
Peeps with her bright blue eyes,
On wooded hill and dewy lawn,
As with a glad surprise,—
As with a glad surprise to see
The gladden'd Earth and smiling Sea:
All slumber dies beneath the skies;
Up, Wanderer, arise, arise!
Up, Wanderer, arise!
Rise, rise!

These our remarks on How to Wander, and When to Wander, might be followed by an answer to Where to Wander, were not this last question easier answered if put in a negative form. Where shall we wander, but anywhere we can? The earth is not dull; and wherever we seek to know it, it will repay the labour of love. Those who eschew reading "Murray" on the decks of steamers, and hasting insanely on in railway carriages, will find but little difficulty in discovering the Promised Land. If wealth be at their disposal, then it is their own fault if they do not know the Usbecks, and, penetrating into Central Africa, behold the shows of Kilimandjaro. Those who have only the arm of the Needy, which, as a Gaelic proverb assures us, is very long, must have faith that with it they will be able to fill their wallet on the way. Only, they must have two wallets, one to give from and one to stuff into, as the Germans say; but the first needs no goods or gold, only a light spirit and capability of some kind or other. Any medical student can visit Greenland and the South Seas, without expending money. In America and India there are newspapers to be edited; and on the Continent there are tutors and translators. The Abyssinian travellers have shown how money can be dispensed with. Albert Smith has shown how a few years, or even a few hours, may bring fortunes. Happy he, indeed, who has a natal Fortunatus cap, in which, with little trouble, he can move from place to place! but happy he also who has to learn how to find wings! The first of these may suit his own tastes, being quaint and curious to his heart's content. He may bring home spoils from all climes, and reckless of critics publish his Hunter's song:—

In blue waving mists and in the deep snow,
In the wild wood and the winter night,
I heard the hunger-howl of the wolf,
I heard the cry of the owl:
Ville vou, vou, vou,
Ville vo, vo vo,
Vito hu!

In pale wearied morning, in the fiery glow,
In the dark *kin* and the jungly brake,
I heard the blood-froth'd snort of the tiger,
I heard the hiss of the snake:
Una, hrew, hrew, hrew,
Une so, so, so,
Hito so!

In pale northern lights, in the sleepless day,
On treacherous ice and on trackless snow,
I heard the hate-chok'd growl of the bear,
I heard the plunge of the seal:
Ugrou grou, grou, grou,
Ugra sa, sa, sa,
Slobo sla!

In wild gloomy forest, on the northern snow,
In the black *kin* of the black ghauts,
I heard the death-charged crack of a gun,
I heard the blood dropping slow:
Pluffo pluf, pluf, pluf,
Plito plot, plot, plot,
Ploto plo!

We have been indebted to a *Zigeunerlied*, or gipsy-song, of Goethe's for the first verse of the above singular composition, but otherwise it is original. The other happy individual, again, will—if he ever reaches home, in defiance of the beautiful Scottish song which assures us that "the weary ne'er return to their ain countrie"—bring back deeper experiences, and be able, in a humbler spirit, and with a humbler accent, to sing somewhat after this fashion:—

I scarcely hoped again to see
Auld Scotia's shores upon the lee,
When, "dwyning in a fremit land,
Had feckless made baith heart and hand,"
When little reck'd of, lonely toil,
And poverty, held fast their coil,

515

When sair forfouchten, sick I lay,
And fear'd Auld Nick was near his prey,
That Death and ugsomme fell Auld Scratchy,
Wad pounce upon me in Kurrachee—
Were puffing up the het, het wind,
Upon the sandy shores o' Sind.

I scarcely hoped again to see
The mountains o' my ain countrie,
The hoary woods and heather braes
Fair in the light of early days;
But thought perhaps I'd find a grave
Where tamarind shadows wildly wave,
Where sandy *meilans* stretch away
Beneath the burning God o' Day,
And flame-clad mountains farther stan
On borders o' Beloochistan.

I never dream'd when I should see
The mountains o' my ain countrie,
When past the liquid depths of air
The southern oceans calmly bear,
And past the tossings and alarms
And weltering of that Cape o' Storms,
That these, the mountains which I knew,
The same that o'er the waters blue
Faded, should seem to have been cast
Out of that sunny, shining past,
To stand in grey, sepulchral light,
Like mountains of a land in night
And Hades sunk, but bearing yet
A ghastly semblance—gladless met.

'Tis so. Who suffers long shall feel
No more misfortune's cruel steel;
But having found that deadly calm
Which neither seeks nor needeth balm,
Finds he has lost the power to thrill
With love and joy; that every ill
And every blessing falls unheeded
Upon the soul where Feeling ceded
Her inner throne, to flee from sorrow:—

But let that pass. Behold, to-morrow,
The hour will come for which I burn'd,
The wanderer shall have return'd.
At least the stain of Scotland's earth
Shall tell them where I had my birth.
When, from this loneliness, I go
To meet the friendlier shades below,
To claim a loftier clanship there
Than Scotia's mountains now can bear.

If he of the Fortunatus cap has the advantage on the seas, inasmuch as, in his yacht, he may linger among Grecian and Eastern isles, the other wanderer has the advantage on the ocean, in so far as the conditions of his warfare may force him to make a close acquaintanceship with the realities of seafaring life. In Central Asia and on board ships, humanity reveals itself without disguise; and is seen to have more in it of wild-beast nature than the cant of civilisation will allow. But though such is the case, it also displays itself in a free, natural, satisfactory way, and so appears beautiful after its kind. Moreover, the circumstances in which it is placed, when far out on the not always melancholy main, throw it into its proper insignificance as but a small portion of the great effort of nature. Goethe declared that he felt silenced and filled with awe when confronted with nature in the solitude of some venerable mountain;

" Waesome wail the snow-white sprites
Upon the gurlie sea,"

and the mad trembling of the affrighted deep when the red line of lightning quivers between it and the frowning sky.

Cable and shroud! the blast howls loud,
And the foam'd white blue is a cold, loose shroud.
The foot gives way, but the arm holds fast;
No lubbers are we, and the main-top's past.

Now for the cross-trees, rock'd in the wild breeze,
Narrow is the footing. Up now and seize
The slanting cable: your arm is able.
Rest on the cross-trees, swinging but stable.

Rest here for breath, since weakness is death,
And a lurch of the ship on a wave beneath,
May cast you quick, like a stone from a sling,
Down to the wave, a vanish'd thing.

So long as great events are stirring —nations falling or forming, and wars raging—the traveller will have inducements to direct his steps in special directions. The thunder on the ocean is met by the peals from tower and wall; and, doubtless, the last also have their significance and value, which we attempt to indicate in the following verses:—

Nation on Nation, Man upon Man,
Throng up from darkness, in fury and fire;
Dash into death, as they dare and they can,
Clan after clan, and son after sire.

Like the wave o'er the sea-sand, the horsemen dash on,
Plunge foaming and roaring against the dark shore;
White crests in their glory, bright armour that shone,
Leap up, for a moment, then, curling, break o'er.

Trains of artillery, rolling in thunder,
Sullen and black, crash away o'er the earth,
While the cries of the wounded, who fall and writhe under,
Are drowned by the World-spirit's fierce-mocking mirth.

Dark are the clouds, and above in their valleys,
Fight the Ghosts of the Dead, from their swift dusky cars.
Higher, the Titans and Demons and Angels,
Storm in the Infinite, tossing the stars.

Heavy accoutrements, dust, toil, and blood,
Climbing, contending, and hasting about;
Into the fire, and strait through the flood,
Slack not, but on, ever on, with a shout!

God help us! I see but the fury and battle,
The smoke and the darkness, the fire and the hosts,
The writhing of men; hear the snorting of cattle,
The groans and the curses, the shouts and the boasts.

A friend is a foe, and a foe is a friend :—
   "Death to thee, Brother!" "Now lean on this breast."
O'er mountains, through valleys, we wend and we wend,
   Till, pale on our shields, we lie down to our rest.

Still, by the battle, the daylight is clouded;
   The stars are made portents of fury afar;
Far in the cloud and the darkness is shrouded
   The one mighty captain who rules o'er the war.

Him I see not, I may wonder and doubt,
   But I see, in the fight, the white plumes of his staff,
As they gallop about, through the charge and the rout,
   Giving his orders and opening a path.

Here, for the present, enough I should know,
   That sorrow and toil are the cradles of Life,
That the Godlike springs forth from the bosom of Woe,
   And a better than Peace is the offspring of Strife!

As wanderers, Scotsmen have been famed from the first generation, as the Irish say; *Natio Scotorum,* remarked a venerable saint, *quibus consuetudo peregrinandi jam pæne in naturam conversa est.* Many a Scotsman was seen before and after the day of Sir David of the Mount,

   " With scrip on hip and pykstaff in his hand,
      As he had purposit to pass fra hame ;"

but however far they may pass, they generally return, even though it be to get only, as most unjustly befell Abyssinian Bruce, the reputation of being among the greatest liars in the country. Home, however, often fails to charm them, and they wander forth again. The unsettled habits which are formed in a life of wandering, cannot always be easily got rid of. Even in the midst of repose and plenty, the restless humour may again seize upon us, and drive us out to face the unknown. The wanderer will always be in danger of rising up and saying, like Tennyson's Ulysses,

   "I cannot rest from travel: I will drink
   Life to the lees: all times I have enjoy'd
   Greatly, have suffer'd greatly, both with those
   That loved me, and alone; on shore, and when
   Thro' scudding drifts the rainy Hyades
   Vext the dim sea: I am become a name;
   For always roaming with a hungry heart
   Much have I seen and known; cities of men,
   And manners, climates, councils, governments,
   Myself not least, but honoured of them all;
   And drunk delight of battle with my peers
   Far on the ringing plains of windy Troy.
   I am a part of all that I have met.
   .   .   .   .
   .   .   .   .   .   .   Vile it were.
   For some three suns to store and hoard myself,
   And this grey spirit yearning with desire
   To follow knowledge, like a sinking star,
   Beyond the utmost bound of human thought."

EVERY nation, like every individual, has its own peculiar office in the taskwork of the world. Of old the Hebrews were set to work out the religious sentiments ; the Greeks to develope the resources of sensuous beauty ; and the Romans to carry to their utmost outward authority and martial dominion. We English are, it is said, a practical people ; good sense is our characteristic. We are not much given to the ideal ; but anything of that kind that we evolve or appropriate we are swift to convert into the real. On the contrary, the Germans are the world's speculators, fleeing from the real the moment the ideal seems to be passing into the real. German philosophers live, move, and have their being in the air-woven clouds of their own fancies, and love a theory with as pure and intense an affection as that with which Charles Lamb loved roast pig. With this strong propension toward the theoretical, these speculators, from Kant to Hegel, have been constantly away in the upper regions of transcendentalism, stalking absolute ideas as ordinary beings stalk stags and deer. Small has been their success. The booty would not suffice to supply even Falstaff with the solids of a supper. The chief advantage of the chase has been to show men where game is not to be found, though we cannot consider of small value the discipline of mind which such exercises give. Speculation is a mental *palæstra* superior, in some respects, to any other. The activity of mind it demands and encourages ; the discursiveness it calls forth ; the wide, yet firm, grasp of ideas it gives ; the verbal discriminations it requires ; and the precision of utterance, as well as conception, to which it leads, are qualities of the highest order, and of themselves well repay years of most careful and diligent labour. Yet the world cannot live on abstractions ; human life cannot be sustained on theories, of which the chief thing that can be said is, that the second ever slays and inters the first in long and apparently endless succession. Man's wants and cravings call out for solid nutriment. Truth only can satisfy a nature which, like man's, is made for truth. But for the love of truth there would be no speculation ; and so, if speculation issues in mere forms and shadows, speculation itself will die for want of impulse. The philosophy which ends in negation must perish from inanition. This is somewhat the condition of philosophy in Germany

at the present moment. Having, within the last century, run through all the possible forms of subject and object, and issued in confounding the one with the other, mental science has, of necessity, come to a standstill, having done nothing except to show that there is nothing to do. Meanwhile the bulk of the cultivated world stand by and wonder in silence. How much has been written, they well know ; but, when they inquire about the result, they learn that nothing is certain, unless it be that nothing is certain. Will they, then, turn away their hearts from mystagogues ? O no ! A German can no more live without speculation than Sandy can do without his wee bit o' parritch. Therefore other Cassandras will be forthcoming to sing the fate of the universe in unintelligible metaphysics.

Meanwhile a process is proceeding whence much good may come. The process is one of amalgamation. Like railways—only to better effect—races, nations, clans, families, everything is at this hour undergoing amalgamation. Even Turkey is being inoculated with European blood. No wonder, then, there is an intermarriage between Germanism and Anglicanism. For our part, we pray Heaven to smile upon the nuptials. Our real would certainly be much advantaged were it to take into its essence a little of the ideal ; and as certainly German speculation would be none the worse if charged with an infusion of English good sense and practicality. The interchange is actually proceeding. As German thought is imported into England, so is English thought imported into Germany. For years the English language and literature has been a favourite, and now is almost a fashionable study in the latter country. The catalogues are constantly bringing under our notice German translations of the best new works of our English press. Macaulay, Dickens, Thackeray, and Tennyson are known on the Rhine and the Danube almost as well as they are known in their native land. In theology, however, small is the debt which Germany owes to England. They borrowed Lardner from us, and turned his labours to a good account. They also borrowed and profited by Bingham ; but little else of consequence have they imported from these shores. The public mind, however, has come into that sort of *media via* condition—the half-way house between the old notional

forms and the new misty abstractions—as to feel pleasure and find satisfaction in the spiritualism of the American Channing.* A translation of the greater part of Channing's writings has been happily executed, and conducted through the press, by two competent editors, who describe the extraordinary influence that writer has attained as resulting from this, namely, "that he inspires us with reverence for our own nature ; teaches that we were created for, and may attain to, the highest destiny ; that every human being has the germ of this within him, and it requires only his own active will to bring it to maturity. This divine germ that lies in every human soul is the great and constant theme of Channing's eloquence. Whether repressed and choked by narrow creeds, or trampled down by a brutal despotism, or chilled by want and poverty, or crushed by the slavery to which an unhappy race has been unrighteously condemned, this always finds in Channing a warm and untiring advocate. It is this which has procured, and will procure, him enthusiastic admirers wherever there are hearts sensible to human happiness and progress."

Among the more important of the recent announcements of the German publishers, we must reckon the announcement of the tenth edition of the celebrated " Conversations-Lexikon."† Scarcely had the writer placed on his shelves the last volume of the ninth edition before he received proposals for publishing the tenth. From the six volumes of the first edition, completed in 1810, to the sixteen volumes of the ninth edition, completed in 1855, the work has gone on increasing alike in bulk, in value, and in favour with the public. To calculate its diffusion is impossible, because, were we aware of the number of copies issued from the German press, we are unable to make a report of the translations in which it has appeared in the New World no less than the Old ; and still less to speak in any exact terms of the extent to which, by infiltration, its materials have passed into other compends, summaries, and dictionaries, largely affecting the great bulk of the definite and tangible literature of the world. But some notion of the spread and influence of the " Conversations-Lexikon " may be formed if we report a few facts. Of the third edition, in ten volumes, and published in the interval between 1814—1819, the first volume appeared in an impression of only 1,500 copies ; but such and so

* Dr. W. Channing's Werke. Von F. A. Schultze und A. Lydow. Berlin, Herman Schultze ; London, Nutt, 1850—5.
† Allgemeine Deutsche Real-Encyklopädia-Conversations-Lexikon, zehnte Auflage. Leipzig, Brockhaus ; London, Nutt.

immediate was the acceptance it found, that, with the second volume, the number of copies was doubled. With the fifth edition (ten volumes, 1818—1820), the work had reached something like its full form and ideal perfection. Before the last volumes were out of the press, the 12,000 copies, of which the edition consisted, were sold, so that a reprint of 10,000 copies was forthwith issued. Within a year, another reprint of 10,000 copies was called for and put forth. Of the sixth edition, the impression was 15,000: 27,000 copies were sold of the seventh edition; of the eighth, 31,000; and of the ninth, 30,000. Independent of these large issues, the publishers have put forth their matter in supplements; so that, no sooner was an edition completed, than they began to publish such additional matter as was required by the changes and the progress occasioned by the lapse of time and the march of events, in the busiest and most variable period of all history. Having for years used this admirable summary of all knowledge, we can well understand the grounds and reasons of the patronage it has received from the public. For exactness, thoroughness, compass, and compression, this Cyclopædia is not only unrivalled, but unapproached. All that the best scholarship of the most scholar-like of nations can make a summary of universal knowledge, that has it made the Leipzig " Conversations-Lexikon." Competitors for the public favour have appeared—of some the pretensions were not inconsiderable—but they have dwindled or disappeared, while the house of Brockhaus have enjoyed the, perhaps, unique satisfaction of finding their property and their usefulness exempt from the common law of decay, and, with increasing years, only growing at once more vigorous, more acceptable, and more productive. The copyright of such a work is a fortune in itself. The possession of such a work by a literary man, capable of profiting by its treasures, is as good as a library; nay, it is better than most English libraries. Our own experience is our voucher. Not only have we rarely failed to find in its capacious and overflowing pages the information we desired, but not seldom have we unexpectedly found there the information we had sought for in other cyclopædias, and even in large collections of volumes. It is equally true that the intelligence it conveys exists in a shape of a far more useful nature than that in which dictionaries usually offer their information. Not only is the knowledge minute and exact, but it is colourless; we mean, that it is free from rhetoric, free from exaggeration, free from pre-possession, aversion, prejudice,—from all likings and dislikes. The authors have practically discovered the perfec-

tion of the cyclopædic style. They write not to please, but to inform; they write not in order to be read, and, therefore, they write so as to be read; aiming to convey the greatest amount of information in the fewest possible words, they yet write with wonderful perspicuity, and prove, after a little initiation into their manner, no less interesting than instructive, at least to those who read rather for profit than pleasure. The cheapness of the work is almost as remarkable as its excellence.

Among the works of the last quarter we make mention, first, of Gruppe's "View of the Present and the Future of German Philosophy,"* a hasty production; yet, as being by a practised hand, not without value, and tending to confirm and illustrate the nothingness in which, as we have intimated, German speculation ends. In his review of the present condition of German philosophy, Gruppe begins with Schelling, and, having criticized his form of pantheism and other forms, puts forward Bacon's " Induction " as the only true and solid method, from which he thinks Locke, in a measure, departed. As a necessary preliminary to a philosophy of the future, he calls for a reform of scientific logic; and, in the course of his strictures, requires that mental science must, if it is to work to any positive and permanent result, have reality for its basis, and proceed not from the abstract to the concrete, nor from the universal to the particular; but, taking experience, and especially human consciousness, as its companion and instructor, be content to advance from the individual to the species, and from the concrete to the universal. In a word, our author holds that the business of philosophy is not to create systems, but to study and learn to know the actual system of thought, and of the relation of thought to human consciousness, and the universe already created and continually sustained by God.

We account it a healthy token that the writings and the philosophical system of Descartes are beginning to attract attention in both France and Germany. While in the former country the moral and philosophical works of the philosopher have just been put forth in a neat edition, with a valuable dissertation on their author's life and writings;† we have received from the latter a critical judgment on the characteristics, and the value of the Cartesian doctrine, which will repay a careful perusal.‡ Undertaking to set forth the philo-

* Gegenwart und Zukunft der Philosophie in Deutschland. Von O. F. Gruppe. 1855. One vol., thin 8vo. Berlin, Reimer; London, Nutt.
† Œuvres Morales et Philosophiques de Descartes, etc. Par M. A. Prevost. 1855. One vol., thin 8vo. Paris, Didot Frères; London, Nutt.
‡ Das Speculative System des René Descartes. Von Prof. J. N. Lyons. Wien, Braumüller; London, Nutt.

sopher's merits and defects, Professor Lyons exhibits as his merits the announcement of human consciousness as the only sure source of speculative thinking, the recognition of that consciousness as the way to the knowledge of God and the universe, and the distinguishing between nature and spirit as two essentially different substances, the union of which is found in man. The defects of his system our critic places in the simple exhibition of consiousness as a fact, a native or inborn faculty, apart from any attempt to trace out the genesis or formation of the faculty, and to submit its contents to a scientific (speculative) scrutiny; it being a sort of received axiom with your transcendentalists, that if man has any right to his own consciousness, he certainly has no right to recognise its disclosures, and turn them to use, until he has established his title thereto before the tribunal of speculative thought; which is pretty much the same as to say that our young friends must not think of enjoying a large slice of their " twelfth-cake " until they can explain the astronomical and social facts connected with the yet lingering observance, and further, have duly expounded the art and mystery by which so many good things are harmoniously and palatably compounded into so small and so attractive an object. The learned critic also objects that Descartes, in making God's relation to the universe one continued act of creation, destroys man's individuality and freedom, and falls into pure dualism in the broad contrast he places between nature and spirit.

THE serial publications of Germany have a peculiarity all their own. The scholarship which characterizes the higher literature does not fail to characterize the lower. Learning descends from the bulky quarto and the full bodied octavo, down to the slender periodical or the flying sheet which appears once every day or once every week, or again, once every month. The German mind cannot do without solid nutriment. The stout fare which the Englishman takes in beef and plum pudding is taken by the German in condensed summaries, or portly disquisitions, or elaborate narratives. Even if he dine on moonshine, the moonshine must be systematically constructed into "cloud-capped towers." In his literary play what a lumbering animal is the true Teuton. And so down to his daily *Feuilleton* he requires something which looks like learning, something which smells of the oil. Of course Germans, like other people, laugh and scandalize, but if true fun, if genuine humour, of all those light fairy nothings which give angel wings to this heavy lumpish life of the desk, and the warehouse, and the tribune, and German cousins seem scarcely to have the faintest idea. Some time ago we were used to see what, in order to be understood, we may call "the German Punch;" but of all dull, forced, awkward sayings, and doings, and pencillings, here was the perfection, and well are we sure that the respectable personage who bears that esteemed name in this metropolis, would, with true paternal zest, have boxed the ears soundly of each of these blunderers calling themselves his sons, had he been near when they were perpetrating their bad jokes and turning their loutish somersets. Indeed a German cannot be light any more than lead. Iron may be made to swim, but neither German smoke, nor German beer, nor German learning can be evaporated into so aerial a thing as a good pun or "a bad joke." The reason is, that the **Grammar School** and the University fasten on the student's back a load which he is never able to throw off. The German, in all his races, "carries weight." His cargo is nearly all ballast. He loves a burden as the travelling tinker loves his kit. He can no more lay down his gravity of wisdom than can the camel get rid of his hunch. And so it comes to pass that what we in old England call

"light literature" has no existence in Germany, but its place is filled by heavy things of all sorts. Let us, however, not be ungrateful. A German cannot make us laugh, but he may make us wise. Incapable of amusing, he is of all men most fitted to instruct. Proofs of his extraordinary power in this way lie around us while we write. One or two of these shall be mentioned before we pass to some formal criticisms.

A serial lies before us which seems likely to be terminated at the Greek Calends. In the year 1843 we began "to take" the Conversations-Lexikon der Bildende Kunst,* that is, "The Cyclopædia of the Fine Arts." Well pleased were we, as we still are, with the exact, minute, and comprehensive information contained in the work—nor without value did we think some of its numerous pictorial illustrations, but sore has our patience been tried by the manner in which it has "dragged its slow length along," and we think our readers will pardon our impatience, or rather pronounce our patience a miracle when we tell them that now, in this month of February, 1856, that is, thirteen years after the first number came into our hands, we have received the forty-eighth number which stops in the middle of the word House. Should this Cyclopædia not mend its pace, and should it ever be finished, it will, after this rate of progress, take six and twenty years for its completion. *C'est un peu de trop*, or in plain English, "it is too bad." In a country which showed so much favour to Hone's "Every-day Book," and has patronized similar works by the same writer and by others, it ought not to be useless to make commendatory mention of a monthly periodical specially devoted to indigenous mythology, customs, and usages.† The rather may English people study German manners and modes of thought, because in so doing they are studying themselves, and gaining power to recall and reproduce "the good old days" of their own fatherland. One of the papers contained in the last number (the first of the third volume) presents a comparative view of

"Northern, English, and German Riddles." We give a specimen in English and German, expecting that our young patrons will thank us for carrying them back to their childish play :—

ENGLISH.
Pease-porridge hot, pease-porridge cold—
Spell me that in four letters.

GERMAN.
Lirum, larum dlöffelstiel—
Schreib mir das mit drei buchstaben.

Equally excellent in its kind is "The Repertory of Engraving,"* designed specially to review copper and wood engraving historically, and to promote those arts by directing attention to superior and little known specimens. The work is produced under the co-operation of a society of artists by profession and amateur artists, and answers the purposes for which it was originated, though ease is a merit yet unattained by the German graver, whether the picture be a copy or an original. Our more learned readers, and the dignified magnates of scholarship, may not be ungrateful to these lines if, being ignorant thereof now, they purchase and make themselves familiar with the literary representative of "The German Oriental Society,"† an association which ranks among its members some of the best scholars of all civilized lands. The periodical is, for the members, a means of intercommunication and a bond of union. We scarcely need add, that it is worthy of the distinguished oriental scholars under whose auspices it comes forth, and whose varied branches of learning it no less effectually than specially promotes.

---

* Archiv für die Zeichnenden Künste. Edited by Dr. R. Naumann, Leipzig: Weigel. London: Nutt.

† Zeitschrift der Deutschen Morgenl. Gesellschaft. Leipzig: Brockhaus. London: Nutt.

---

* Published by Graul, of Leipzig; and Nutt, 270 Strand, London.
Zeitschrift für Deutsche Mythologie und Sittenkunde. Edited by Dr. W. Mannhardt, Göttingen: Dieterich. London: Nutt.

WEIMAR AND JENA.*

HERR SCHMIDT, in producing a supplemental volume to his *Geschichte der deutschen National Literatur im 19ten Jahrhundert*, was well-inspired when he thought of calling it by the attractive name of *Weimar and Jena*. Although he does not say so, the curious fact is indisputable, that German literature, unlike that of every other nation, has never found its proper *nidus* in a metropolis, but rather in these two little cities of Saxe-Weimar, which bear the same sort of relation to Berlin, Vienna, or Munich as Bath and Cheltenham bear to London. Berlin, boasting of its intellectual culture, with a magnificent university, a fine museum, a vast library, and an energetic population, is not, nor has it ever been, a great literary centre. All that can be said for its intellectual pretensions is, that much bad paper is dirtied there by muddy printer's ink, and that much dreary discussion goes on in academies, and select tea-parties, where sausage and grated ham are handed round on circles of bread and butter to shrivelled Hegelians and toothless poets. In Vienna, the people never pretended to cultivate literature. French novels and French morals occupy the leisure of that idle but agreeable race, in which the thick German blood is mingled with the more vivacious Hungarian and Italian. In Munich, indeed, struggles have been made to foster philosophy, poetry, and painting—the last with success. The present king is the Mœcenas of Germany. But all efforts to stimulate literary production have been fruitless. Nothing has ever come from these capitals, whereas the picturesque little cities lying so snugly in the charming Ilm-valley boast of having given to all Germany the literature which Europe accepts as classical; and the period of 1794-1806, which was that of the friendship between Goethe and Schiller, forms the eleven years of "the classical age." Of course there are writers belonging to other periods and other cities—Lessing, Winckelmann, Klopstock—to whom a grateful nation also awards the epithet of classical; but we are inclined to agree with Herr Schmidt in eliminating the two last from the list, though we are not inclined to do the same with the mighty Lessing, in spite of the fragmentary and polemical nature of the greater part of his works. *Nathan der Weise* and *Minna von Barnhelm* appear to us quite as worthy of the classical rank as the majority of Schiller's works.

The "classical period" Herr Schmidt styles "that in which the most eminent minds stood in intimate relation with each other, giving to their works that finish and fulness of expression which the German language admits of, and setting forth the results of German culture as a national product." It may also be named classical in another sense, being exclusively based on the study of the ancient classics. It was never meant for the people, who had their own unclassical writers—it was addressed only to the highly cultivated, and thus grew as an exotic, dying when the great gardeners died.

There is no one now who disputes the genius of Goethe and Schiller—no one insensible to the divine beauty of their works; but an unbiassed critic may perceive, on the two points we have here briefly indicated, something of the deficiency which lessens their influence, apart from all the short-comings attendant even upon genius. The points alluded to are, strictly speaking, one—namely, the want of Nationality. Poets living in insignificant cities, they had not the inspiration of a great audience in default of a great nation. Germany was not a nation, and is not yet, or it would never grow hoarse with shouting the *naïve* question, "*Where* is the German's Fatherland?" Poetry, therefore, necessarily became the voice of an individual, or of a coterie. In those terrible days when the German soil was trembling beneath the march of conquerors, the great poets tried to create a poetry which should have no object but itself—*l'art pour l'art*. And as the noblest specimens of art known to them—at least of such art as seemed to have no other object but itself—were the remains of Greece, and as the basis of all fine culture was Greek, so, by the inevitable logic of things, Goethe and Schiller aimed at restoring a Greek period. Greek art in the hands of Lessing

was used as a revolutionary weapon; but, in emancipating Germany from the yoke of France, he only left it the alternative of chaotic nonsense, irradiated by a gleam here and there, calling itself *Sturm und Drang*, and classical reaction.

We have only to look into Goethe's and Schiller's works to perceive that, in proportion as this classical element predominated, they were unsuccessful. Compare Goethe's exquisite *Hermann und Dorothea* with his tedious fragment, the *Achilleis*. Both were obviously inspired by Homer; but the former is one which we may imagine Homer himself to have written, under the same conditions—it is Homeric in *spirit*. The other is a lifeless reproduction of the Homeric *form*, at which the blind old bard would have yawned considerably. *Hermann und Dorothea* is essentially *popular*—high and low, young and old delight in it. *Achilleis* may delight a few scholars, but seduces no poetical mind to read it with patience. *Iphigenia*, again, is an almost faultless work, but its beauty does not lie in the Greek portions, which are mistakes; and *Faust*, which is intensely German, is the most popular of modern poems. So likewise with Schiller, and his unhappy attempts at classicality. Compare his *Bride of Messina* with *Wallenstein*, or his poem *Die Ideale* with his *Song of the Bell*.

We cannot pursue this vein, for it would lead us too far; but we have thought it worth indicating. The problem was—How to create a German literature? That problem still remains; for although the grand efforts of the classical period resulted in some works which will live for ever in German memories, the utterly factitious nature of the "Weimar School" was shown in the immediate collapse which ensued when Schiller died. Herr Schmidt, in the volume before us, seems perfectly sensible of the fact, although he enters into no explanations. Indeed, the defect of his book, as of almost all books of German literature, is the absence of solid information. The German critics delight in philosophizing about and about a subject, seldom condescending to plain practical details. They give you pages about the *Idee* of a work, and never think of the possibility of your not having read the work, or having forgotten it. Dates, facts, analyses, citations are disregarded—philosophy and clouds of tobacco smoke take their place. Herr Schmidt calls this a History of German Literature, and like his predecessor, Gervinus, he is a very notable companion when you happen to be familiar with the topic of which he treats; but if you know nothing on opening his book, you know not much more on closing it—which is scarcely a recommendation for a history.

We have thought it right to intimate thus much to prevent disappointment. Our readers will find the book very instructive if they bring with them some preliminary instruction, but not if they open it to learn definitely what was the course of historical development—what was the relation of one writer to another—and what, specifically, were each writer's works. Herr Schmidt is an independent, and sometimes a very clear-sighted critic. His style, for a German, is agreeable and lucid. Of course he gives neither index nor table of contents; and you have to grope your way through the whole volume in search of any particular writer or work—a process which is rendered all the more helpless, because the arrangement is not even chronological, but is thrown into three groups :—" Reawakening of Greek style;" "The German Theatre to the death of Schiller;" and " Novels and the Bourgeoisie." Picture to yourself an unhappy mortal anxious to recover a passage, or to learn something about some one of the many names which, from Lessing to Kotzebue, swell out the catalogue of German authors, and having no other clue than is to be gathered by three such headings as these! The defect to which we allude is by no means peculiar to Herr Schmidt—it is an almost universal defect in German literature. A long and sad experience tells us that the Germans are the very worst as they are the most prolific, of book-makers. In parting from *Weimar und Jena*, however, we wish the reader to understand that, if he desires a work of the Gervinus class, he will find this an excellent one.

* *Weimar und Jena in den Jahren* 1794-1806. Von Julian Schmidt. London: D. Nutt.

LITERARY LIFE OF HAMBURG.*

PEOPLE are so accustomed to think of Hamburg as a seat of trade and commerce that they may feel rather incredulous when they meet with a work professing to give an account of its literary life. Moreover, M. Feodor Wehl himself informs us that, in Hamburg itself, it is generally assumed that the city never obtained any eminence in a literary point of view. But he assures his readers that, if they will take the trouble to examine into the matter, they will find that after the Thirty Years' War Hamburg exercised an extraordinary influence over the literature of Germany; and, that we may fully understand the position the city held during the eighteenth century, he gives us a short sketch of the various phases through which it has passed anterior to that period. From its earliest history, it was characterised by the independent spirit of its burghers, and by the prudence and self-control they manifested on many critical occasions; and to the transmission of these qualities from generation to generation it in great measure owes its present pre-eminence. The moderation of the citizens was never more strikingly shown than at the time of the Reformation, which was more easily and quietly established in Hamburg than in any other city in Europe. During the Thirty Years' War, it maintained its independence, and by its spirited conduct won the respect of all parties. One of the writers of that time compares Hamburg to the land of Goshen—a sanctuary where no evil could enter, a city richly blessed by God, a beautiful pleasure-garden in an earthly paradise. The place became the resort of celebrated men of all countries, and, after the termination of the war, occupied the same position in the literary world that Strasburg and Nuremberg had done at an earlier period. Although actively engaged in commerce, the citizens found their chief enjoyment in the "feast of reason and the flow of soul" provided by the accomplished men whom they gathered round their hospitable tables. They also cultivated a taste for the fine arts, and, by the middle of the eighteenth century, the city had won a reputation as regards literature, science, and art, which for a long time remained undiminished in lustre. From a German work published anonymously in the year 1794, we give the following sketch of Hamburg as it was during the period to which we have alluded:—

In Hamburg you will find the best class of houses distinguished by an extreme amount of luxury; you will find elegant equipages, numerous servants, handsomely furnished apartments, palatial country-houses, and hospitable tables, which would not disgrace even a prince or a king. In the society of its wealthiest citizens you may spend days and weeks, and not pass an hour which is not devoted to some amusement or other. The expenditure of the Hamburgians is chiefly shown in eating and drinking, and no where else in Germany, with the exception, perhaps, of Vienna, is it carried to the same extent. You have scarcely left the tea and coffee table in the morning, when a very elegant breakfast awaits you, with an abundance of excellent wines, and English, Dutch, or Swiss cheeses; if you are partial to tea drinking, as almost all the Hamburgians are to a very great degree, you will find it ready for you again about twelve or one o'clock. At three o'clock luncheon is prepared; at four dinner is served. Then, after coffee, a small collation of ham, cold meat, &c., is set upon the table, and remains there until nine or ten o'clock, when you betake yourself to a luxurious supper, with the accompaniment of the most recherché foreign wines.

So much for the material life of Hamburg in the eighteenth century. As for its intellectual life and tendencies, these, as M. Wehl shows, were most strikingly developed in the direction of the drama. In fact, Hamburg may be styled the cradle of the German theatre. How decided the taste of the people must have been for the stage is seen from the fact that, notwithstanding the thunders which were launched against the theatre by the most popular among the Protestant preachers, it still remained a favourite place of resort. In 1678, the Hamburg Opera House was opened with the representation of the opera of *Adam and Eve* — the music by the Kapelmeister Theil—the poetry, which was very original in character, and

* *Hamburgs Litteratur Leben, im achtzehnten Jahrhundert.* Von Feodor Wehl. Leipzig. 1856.

treated sacred things with over-much familiarity, by a poet of the name of Richter. To this opera succeeded another of the same class, entitled *La Gerusalemme Liberata*, and under the direction of Matheson two hundred new operas were given between the years 1678 and 1728. This sounds scarcely credible, until we learn that it was partly owing to the fertile brain of the Kapelmeister Reinhard Keiser, who, during his residence in Hamburg, composed somewhere about 116 operas, while Kapelmeister Telemann composed thirty-five operas and no less than 600 overtures. Handel, Hasse, and Bach also exercised no small influence over the fortunes of the Opera House, and, if the libretti and the plots had been equal to the music, the operatic entertainments at Hamburg would have merited no small degree of approbation. After the death of Schott, who had been one of the most energetic directors of the theatre, it fell into various hands, but, owing to unskilful management, gradually lost the favour of the public. In 1728, the regular drama rose from its ruins, and it is to the history of its progress that the greater part of M. Wehl's book is devoted. We will, however, pass over his account of the different actors who illustrated the Hamburg stage, the opposition which the directors of the theatre had to contend with from violent Protestant preachers, and the efforts which many distinguished men made to improve and purify the plays, and raise the character of the actors. We prefer noticing a very interesting account of Lessing, which M. Wehl gives *apropos* of his connexion with the theatre, during the three years of his residence at Hamburg.

Those who knew Lessing at that time describe him as being a little above the middle height, though, on account of the slightness of his figure, he seemed shorter than he really was. In manner he was natural and open, courteous and dignified. In his dress, he was exquisitely neat, and even elegant—in his domestic affairs, he delighted not only in having everything in the most exact order, but also in a certain degree of luxury. Wine he took freely, especially Rhine wine, but he was not an epicure. He never complained of anything that was set before him at table; and we are assured that when, occasionally, an ill-dressed dish would make its appearance, he never found fault with his wife either by word or look. He was most polite and kindly in his intercourse with others, and never allowed himself to use harsh words even towards those with whom he was on the most familiar terms. Generally he rose early, refreshed by sound and unbroken sleep. His knock at the door must have had something remarkable and peculiar in it, since it was at once recognised by his friends. His favourite passion was card-playing, in which he displayed so much eagerness and excitement that frequently large drops of perspiration would stand on his forehead. Generally he was unlucky, although he showed no small amount of skill. He was fond of playing with ladies. Frequently he engaged Madame Büsch and Madame Kuorre in a game at ombre, and, when he was attacked about it, would remark with a smile—"Tous les gens de l'esprit aiment le jeu à la folie." A man of quite antique mould, he was accustomed to keep himself ever ready to face and overcome the worst trials that might happen, without, however, being insensible to the effort which it cost him. Thus, in 1778, when his wife died in childbed, the tone of the letter in which he acquaints a friend with his loss is rather composed and cold than tender in expression:—"My wife is dead," he writes, "and now I have made acquaintance with even this description of trial. I rejoice that many more such experiences cannot happen to me, and am resigned." Yet how difficult it had been for him to attain this composure may be seen in the following sentences, where he exclaims:—"If you had only known my wife! But people say it is egotism to praise one's wife. Well, then, I will say no more of her. But if you had only known her! You will never again see me as Mendelssohn has seen me, at peace and satisfied within my four walls. If, with the half of my remaining life, I could have purchased the happiness of spending the other half with her, how gladly I would have done it. But that could not be, and I must again learn to go on my way alone. I have not deserved such happiness."

In common with many of his fellow-countrymen who had adopted letters as a profession, Lessing was often exposed to the hardships of poverty. But, inspired by the love of independence which filled his breast, he was ashamed of letting those among whom he resided at Hamburg have any idea of his circumstances, and therefore he often affected to play the spendthrift that his poverty might not be suspected. "He who has health and will work," he writes to his parents, "has nothing to fear; but to fear sickness, and such like occurrences, which may prevent one from working, shows but little faith in Providence. I have more trust, and I possess friends."

Whilst Lessing was at Hamburg, his chief intercourse was with the family of Reimarus; and with his sister, Elizabeth Reimarus, a highly-cultivated and most amiable woman, he contracted a friendship which lasted all his life. Reimarus's eldest daughter, who was not less distinguished for personal charms and elegance of manner than for talent and sweetness of character, married the celebrated merchant, George Sieveking, the author of a remarkable work on Bills of Exchange. The following description of a wealthy, influential, and intelligent Hamburg merchant of those days, quoted by M. Wehl, will not be uninteresting to our readers:—

George Sieveking (says Bottiger) is a little, thick-set man, but full of activity and energy, having as much command of French as of his mother-tongue; never put out for a moment, or giving way to absence of mind. Notwithstanding the unceasing whirl of business in which he is engaged, he is, without any exception, one of the most able and upright men in Hamburg, and what he is he has made himself.

The energy of such a man as Sieveking (continues Bottiger) perfectly bewilders great students and bookworms such as we are. He often receives more than forty letters in a single hour, and frequently writes as many daily, and in different languages. Yet, notwithstanding, he has leisure left to run over all the most interesting newspapers, journals, and pamphlets belonging to foreign countries, and sent him from all quarters of the globe; to have long conferences with his fellow-merchants; to look over all his books and ledgers; to go about the city to pay necessary visits, and to make up for lost time caused by a hundred interruptions. That there is a certain mechanical mode of doing all this, the result of daily habit, I can readily believe, but it is only an able man who can accomplish it. Moreover, not a single new production touching on the fine arts ever escapes his notice, and he is the oracle of book-loving women, whose studies he takes much pleasure in directing. The question may, however, be asked, with such a monstrous amount of energy, does he enjoy life like other men? Judging by my own observations, I should say not.

"My husband," said Madame Sieveking to me, "scarcely ever comes more than once a week, during the most beautiful season of the year, to our country-house; on mail days he hardly ever dines, but remains seated at his desk till ten o'clock at night." Sunday may therefore be supposed to be the only day of relaxation in which he can enjoy the society of his wife and family. Quite a mistake. All the strangers who, during the week, have brought him letters of introduction, or who have business relations with his house, regularly receive a card of invitation for Sunday. Towards two o'clock in the afternoon coaches and pedestrians flock towards his dwelling from all quarters. The drawing-room and garden fill with guests who are not acquainted with, or introduced to one another, and frequently they are unknown to the lady of the house. I have dined there two Sundays. The first time there were eighty, the second time seventy covers, laid in two large dinner rooms, and yet there were numerous additional guests. To strangers the variety must be an interesting spectacle. For instance, both times the last scion of the house of Gonzaga—a prince without possessions, but very intelligent, and imbued with democratic principles—was present. There were also two Dutch ladies, blazing with jewels, whilst the lady of the house was clad, the first time, in a quiet silk dress, and the second time in a simple muslin, despising, with proud humility, all borrowed splendour. An Englishman from Liverpool sat next a Republican from Bordeaux; near him a Mademoiselle Ferand, who had emigrated with Dumouriez; and beside her, engaged in pleasant discourse, Barthélemy, an agent of the Republic. Farther off was a Swedish consul, just returned from Morocco, in conversation with a couple of English Jews from St. Domingo, and an American from New Jersey. The banker, Kastner, from Leipsic—how obscured was this Sirius of the Leipsic firmament here!—was unfortunately placed opposite our good friend Büsch, who, when he understood that he had a Leipsic magnate vis à vis, with true Hamburg simplicity told him how uncourteously he had been treated by the Privy Councillor Muller, who, though he had met with much kindness from him when he was staying at Hamburg, received him very coldly when he called upon him in a shabby coat, as he was passing through Leipsic. My fortunate star, on the first occasion, gave me the excellent Rickard for my neighbour; on the other side of me was a musty old emigrant, from whom I could not get a word. This varied crowd afforded me much amusement, because it introduced me into quite a new world. But what pleasure could the host and hostess find in it? After dinner, we took coffee in the drawing-room, and an emigrant displayed his skill on the harpsichord, but still there was no sign of the company dispersing. It was only towards evening, when the closing of the city gates obliged them to take their departure, that the guests withdrew. Even then Sieveking hastened back again to the city, after refreshing himself with a little food, and his good wife could therefore only enjoy her husband's company for a few moments. As to domestic happiness, it is a thing not to be thought of here in Hamburg. Men gain money in order to spend it. They show hospitality and courteous attention to strangers, and are perhaps tyrants to their own wives, capricious and peevish towards them, while outwardly they are all smoothness and amiability.

But as to the society in the circle of the Reimarus family, of which Madame Sieveking was a member, "nothing," says Pottiger, "can be more delightful and full of enjoyment. In the evening, father Reimarus, attired in a dressing-gown, and furnished with a pipe, sits sometimes with his family, sometimes in the next room preparing drugs, while through the open door he listens to the conversation, and every now and then lets fall a word of approval or dissent. The mother, meantime, sits by the smoking urn, with the excellent Eliza on one side of her, and the two unmarried daughters of the doctor on the other, one of whom, Tinchen Reimarus, is a very intelligent and yet modest young girl." After giving the details of a conversation he had had with her about Goethe, he goes on to say—"Another time the good Reimarus waxed very warm on the long continuance of priest-craft and 'Glaubensdespotism,'" and apropos to the subject, mentioned that he had once been very much against the publication of his father's writings, because he did not think the time ripe for them. "But Lessing," he remarked, "had always opposed him in this. 'Troubled waters,' said Reimarus to Lessing, 'ought never to be shaken until they are purified.' 'But,' replied Lessing, 'if the troubled water be not first shaken, it never can become pure.'"

For many interesting particulars connected with the family of Reimarus and other friends and associates of Lessing, as well as for a further account of the literary spirit and tendencies of Hamburg, we must now refer our readers to M. Wehl's little volume. It is not only a creditable performance in itself, but is valuable on account of its placing the city of Hamburg before us in a different light from that in which we have most of us been accustomed to view the great commercial emporium of North Germany.

Torquato Tasso: a Drama, from the German of Goethe, and Other Poems, Translated and Original. By M. A. H. (Longman & Co.)
The German Lyrist; or, Metrical Versions from the Principal German Lyric Poets. By W. N. (Cambridge, Macmillan & Co.)
Lenora: a Ballad, newly translated from the German of Bürger, by Albert Smith. (Printed for private circulation.)

METRICAL translations from the German are certainly on the increase in this country, and, considering what German translators (some of them men of the highest standing in their own literature) have done towards the advancement of English poetry among their compatriots, we cannot but give a hearty welcome to the fact. We are decidedly, in this respect, under great and many obligations to the Germans, and every able and well-directed attempt on our side to lay them under similar obligations may be greeted as pleasing and satisfactory. Mutual appreciation and goodwill cannot but be promoted by these international efforts. They are the stepping-stones to what Goethe, with a prophetic glance of his grasping intellect, foresaw and foreshadowed as the "Weltliteratur" of the future.

Here we have three attempts of the kind,—all of them meritorious and praiseworthy. The new translation of Goethe's 'Tasso,' by M. A. H. calls, of course, for a comparison with the excellent version of that drama by Miss Swanwick,—and we do not hesitate to say that it fully stands the test of that comparison. It is quite as faithful,—follows the original in many passages even more closely,—and, though less fluent and melodious in point of language, is yet by no means wanting in those charms of form and diction which, in a translation of this drama, are so essential. A short specimen, showing the original and the two translations in juxtaposition, will suffice to corroborate our assertion.—

Original.

O edler Mann! Du stehest fest und still,
Ich scheine nur die sturmbewegte Welle.
Allein bedenk', und überhebe nicht
Dich deiner Kraft! die mächtige Natur,
Die diesen Felsen gründete, hat auch
Der Welle die Beweglichkeit gegeben.
Sie sendet ihren Sturm, die Welle flieht
Und schwankt und schwillt und beugt sich schäumend über.
In dieser Woge spiegelte so schön
Die Sonne sich, es ruhten die Gestirne
An dieser Brust, die zärtlich sich bewegte.
Verschwunden ist der Glanz, entflohn die Ruhe.—
Ich kenne mich in der Gefahr nicht mehr,
Und schäme mich nicht mehr es zu bekennen.
Zerbrochen ist das Steuer, und es kracht
Das Schiff an allen Seiten. Berstend reisst
Der Boden unter meinen Füssen auf!
Ich fasse dich mit beiden Armen an!
So klammert sich der Schiffer endlich noch
Am Felsen fest, an dem er scheitern sollte.

Miss Swanwick.	*M. A. H.*
Oh, noble friend, thou standest firm and calm,	Oh, noble man! thou standest firm and still,
While I am like the tempest-driven wave.	And I, the while, seem as the storm-stirred wave;
But be not boastful of thy strength. Reflect!	Yet, yet bethink thee, let not thine own strength
Nature, whose mighty power hath fix'd the rock,	Exalt thee over much. That mighty nature,
Gives to the wave its instability.	Which fixed this rock's foundations, also gave
She sends her storm, the passive wave is driven,	The wave alike its mutability.
And rolls, and swells, and falls in billowy foam.	She sendeth forth her storms—the billows flee
Yet in this very wave the glorious sun	And roll, and swell—and, foaming, bow their crests.
Mirrors his splendour, and the quiet stars	How fairly did the sun upon those waters
Upon its heaving bosom gently rest.	Mirror himself! How slept the silent stars
Dimm'd is the splendour, vanish'd is the calm!—	Upon this breast, that heaved so tenderly!

In danger's hour I know myself no longer.	Now vanished is the brightness—flown the peace!
Nor am I now ashamed of the confession.	I, in this peril, know myself no more,
The helm is broken, and on ev'ry side	And shame myself no more in the confession.
The reeling vessel splits. The riven planks,	The rudder's shivered, and the vessel splits
Bursting asunder, yawn beneath my feet!	On every side. The deck is rent, and yawns
Thus with my outstretch'd arms I cling to thee!	Beneath my feet! Thee grasp I with mine arms!
So doth the shipwreck'd mariner at last	So clings, at last, the shipwrecked mariner
Cling to the rock whereon his vessel struck.	Fast to the rock on which he should have perished.

Misinterpretations and mistakes are of rare occurrence. Yet there are some. Thus, for instance, it is erroneous to render—

Da mir der Stab gebrochen ist,

by

Since shivéred is my staff,

—a version which would imply, in a moral sense, that the staff upon which Tasso leaned was broken, whereas the simile refers to the ancient custom of the judge breaking a wand over the head of the condemned criminal. Miss Swanwick's translation—

Since my doom is seal'd,

gives exactly the meaning of the original. Again, the line—

Unsittlich wie du bist, hältst du dich gut?

does not mean, as our translator has it—

Unmannered as thou art—wilt make excuse?

The words "Sitte," "sittlich," "unsittlich," like so many other German expressions, (take, for instance, "Gemüth," "gemüthlich," &c.) are most difficult for an English translator. We think that, in the case before us, "unsittlich" should not be rendered by so severe an epithet as "immoral,"—but it is, at all events, something worse than "unmannered." The meaning conveyed by the line is simply this—Weak and self-willed as thou art, dost thou think thyself faultless? Miss Swanwick's translation of the line—

Rude as thou art, dost think thyself of worth?

partly misses the mark.

If little blemishes like these be extinguished in a later edition, the translation, we do not scruple to pronounce, will take its stand worthily at the side of that of Miss Swanwick. In the mean time, we gladly welcome the author in the ranks of our metrical, and we rather say, our poetical, translators. He (or she?—the workmanship of the book, and its appendix of original poems, seem to betray a female hand,) evidently possesses a most happy turn for this branch of literary labour. The extracts from Schiller, Körner, Uhland, Kosegarten (not Rosegarten, as the name is invariably misprinted), Matthisson, Adelheid von Stolterfoth, and others, are faithful and poetical reproductions. What, perhaps, we might object to in the translation of these lyrics is, that, here and there, they do not strictly preserve the metre of the originals. Metre and melody in lyrics are but too often the dust on the butterfly's wing: take it away, and the charm vanishes. Here is the first stanza of a beautiful Ballad by Uhland :—

Wer entwandelt durch den Garten
Bei der Sterne bleichem Schein?
Hat er Süsses zu erwarten?
Wird die Nacht ihm selig seyn?
Ach! der Harfner ist 's, er sinkt
Nieder an des Thurmes Fusse,
Wo es spät herunterblinkt,
Und beginnt zum Saitengrusse.

Mark, how much of the charm of this exquisite verse depends on its structure. The alternation of its double and single rhymes, with the additional feature that in the first half of the verse the double rhyme precedes the single, while in the latter half the double is preceded by the single rhyme, makes its trochees fall upon our ear with a softness and gracefulness utterly lost in the single-rhymed iambic translation:—

Who mid the flow'rs is wand'ring late,
In the pale starlight dim?
Do hope and love his coming wait?
Will the night be bless'd for him?
No, 't is the minstrel's foot that breaks
Upon the silent hour,—
And now a mournful lay he wakes
Beneath that lofty tower.

There is, likewise, a considerable contrast between the sweetly-simple 'Reimpaare' of Uhland's Lied, 'Auf der Ueberfahrt':—

Ueber diesen Strom, vor Jahren,
Bin ich einmal schon gefahren.
Hier die Burg im Abendschimmer,
Drüben rauscht das Wehr, wie immer,—

and the alternating rhymes of the translation:—

This self-same stream, long years ago,
I mind me I was ferried o'er;
Here stands the fort in sunset glow,
The weir is rushing as of yore.

Things like these ought not to be neglected by such of our translators of foreign poetry as wish to convey to us not only the sense, but also, as much as can be done, the music and the harmony of their originals. The Germans, generally, are more conscientious in this respect than is the case with us. They take more pains, —they do not so much shrink from the difficulties of their tasks,—they set to work in a more artist-like manner.

These are hints which we should also like to throw out for the benefit of W. N., or, as the lettered back of 'The German Lyrist' gives us his full name, Mr. W. Nind,—though they can hardly be meant to apply to an artist so accomplished as Mr. Albert Smith. Mr. Nind's translations rank with those of M. A. H. They are spirited and elegant, though not always quite what an ear accustomed to the originals might desire. They comprise specimens of Klopstock, Schiller, Goethe, Bürger, De La Motte-Fouqué, Körner, Uhland, Schenkendorf, Freiligrath, and Geibel,—thus embracing (though by no means fully representing) the period from the revival of German poetry in the last century down to the present time. Among the specimens given of Bürger, we meet with a version of the ballad of 'Lenora,' which, although decidedly clever, is yet outdone by Mr. Albert Smith's new translation of that often-translated masterpiece of German ballad-poetry. Mr. Smith, indeed, has contrived to present us with the closest and ablest of the many translations of 'Lenora' which the literature of our country may boast of, from Sir Walter Scott's 'William and Helen' down to Mr. Nind's latest attempt,—a result which, to our belief and in confirmation of our above remarks, is principally attained by the translator carefully adhering to the metre of the original, and by his thus preserving all the impressiveness of its restlessly onward rushing numbers.

101. SATURDAY REVIEW, 5 (1857), 208-209. M/H No. 5254.

HISTORY OF GERMAN LITERATURE.*

A HISTORY of German literature was never more needed than at the present day. A few names of great poets and thinkers are current among us, but they are little more than names. How they came in orderly succession, moulded by the influences of the generation before them, and transmitting a life of their own to others, is what few, except students, know or care to learn. Hence the partialities of the public are not always wisely directed, and their censure is indiscriminate. The most feeble productions of Schiller abound everywhere, and even Tieck is a common favourite in England; while older writers, such as Voss and Lessing, or Novalis and Uhland in our own century, are comparatively unknown. So, again, by a singular perversion of ideas, German philosophy is denounced as rationalistic, and German style as misty—as if the extravagant use of the reasoning faculties had, somehow, a tendency to obscure the style. In fact, however, there is some excuse for our ignorance. During the whole of the sixteenth century, the best minds of Luther's fatherland were frittered away in theological discussions. The desolating wars that followed, took away another hundred years of progress. Klopstock, and Frederick of Prussia, reconstructed German national life in literature and politics; but, partly from the accident of geographical position, and partly because the commonwealth of letters in France and England could not understand a rival, it was not till the French Revolution had poured its armies across the Rhine that Madame de Stael announced the discovery of a new world of thought, or Scott began to translate and imitate Goethe. We are now, in science and art, the daily debtors of the nation we once christianized. Hard-handed workers ourselves in trade and politics, we abandon, not without some contempt, the research after abstract truth to a quiet, speculative race, as the Romans went to market in Athens for rhetoricians and sophists. It is as well, therefore, to know the worth of our teachers. Taylor's book on German literature is already obsolete, and is chiefly curious for the singular rhapsody in which he extols Kotzebue as the rival of Shakspeare. Mundt's little handbook, which has had a partial success from the nature of the subject it dealt with, is inaccurate, badly written, and critically valueless. It is scarcely wonderful, therefore, that the longer and more elaborate work of Herr Schmidt should have passed through three editions in as many years. But it has other merits of its own. The style is easy and clear—the divisions are natural. Where the author has examined for himself, he shows a patient care that inspires confidence—where he treats of matters out of his own line, he prefers quoting from others to a shallow originality. His biographies are often good, and illustrate his literary criticisms. He is, on the whole, candid and just, though perhaps, like most North Germans, a little "doctrinaire." His perceptions are not subtle, nor his judgment broad—he never rises beyond a certain level; but he has written a straightforward, sensible book on a subject that required special knowledge and research.

The period with which the history before us opens is that in which the freedom of German thought was triumphantly asserted against conventional models. The first half of the eighteenth century had witnessed the uncontested triumph of "Philisterei"—a neutral word, the precise meaning of which can scarcely be rendered by any English equivalent, for it implies the presence of orthodoxy and respectability, and the absence of imagination and reason. *Philisterei* had grown up under the influence of petty courts, a pedantic bureaucracy, and churches which derived their inspiration from the police. The main feature of its philosophical thought was an attempt to explain away the supernatural element in religion. Kuinoel and Rosenmüller are popular instances of leaders in this school, from which Strauss is not very distantly derived. Naturally, an analogous tone in literature was preserved by the imitation of French authors, and the language was copiously infiltrated with French words. Winckelmann, Wieland, Lessing, and Herder led the way in their several departments to a larger and more genial criticism, and wider sympathies with classical and foreign literature. Kant and Fichte appealed from a pragmatical common sense to an intuitive reason, and a religion which had its source in the soul. But critics and metaphysicians have little influence on a public which scarcely reads them. The change from the old world to the new was therefore effected chiefly by Goethe and Schiller. Readers of the *Dichtung und Wahrheit* will remember the rapture with which Goethe studied Shakspeare, and how the cold, scientific egotist numbered amongst his experiences the pietism of a "schöne Seele," and the morbid waywardness of his own Werther. He was, in fact, what the nation at large were becoming. Wearied of system-mongers and systems, in which "letters gave place to letters," the new generation flung itself into wider channels of life—talked sentiment with Rousseau, till it should talk philanthropy with French Jacobins—took refuge in classical antiquity from Nicolai and the Berlin journals, or sought out a truer nature with Forster and Humboldt. Herr Schmidt very happily identifies three of Goethe's greatest works with corresponding phases of thought. In *Goetz von Berlichingen*, we have the restoration of that vigorous national life which was now entombed with the old empire, or slumbered in the future of the battle of nations. Werther is the sentimentalism of the *salons*—painfully conscious of its own absurdity, and withal, like other sentimentalisms of the day, a little tragic in the issue. *Faust* represents the struggles of an idealist against the systems and practical life that surround him—trying to work out for himself a new happiness and a love that shall be blessed while it is not innocent. Actual life is stronger than the thought and will of the philosopher, and he only succeeds when he abandons the pursuit of abstract beauty, and sinks to the level of household experience and the obscure nobleness of common duties. The aspirations for a higher life, and the despair of success, belong alike to the generation which saw the French Revolution rise and wane. Schiller's nature had even less of hope. Pure and visionary, he had sought to strengthen the womanly tenderness of his feelings by dramatic efforts like the *Robbers*, or philosophical labours under Humboldt. The triumph of brute force and Imperialism over all that was grand and beautiful came upon him with a shock which he could not recover. "Freedom," he said, "is only in the world of dreams; the beautiful lives only in song." But enough was vital in his own, to expel for ever from the German stage the sentimental pruriency of Kotzebue.

From these leaders was derived the Romantic school, though Goethe looked upon his offspring with critical indifference, and Schiller with absolute loathing. Herr Schmidt has very happily indicated the nature of this movement, which has nowhere been more misunderstood than in England. It was not in any sense a restoration of faith, or even a yearning after the fold of a visible Church. Tendencies of this sort are very natural to the practical minds of English clergymen; and they caught at the analogies of a party which certainly furnished more than one convert to Catholicism. The problem in Germany was in the first place literary and intellectual. Men inoculated by Goethe with a love of universality which wanted in them the ballast of scientific culture, fell back on the art and ideas of the Middle Ages for that form and colouring which they missed in their own times. They were mostly little more than a set of petty notabilities, moving in narrow circles, filling the pages of albums, and exciting the indignation of veteran literati by the quiet impudence with which they disregarded traditional standards of excellence. Such men were the two Schlegels, who have unhappily been accepted in England as types of German thought, and on whose authority it has passed current that Molière is not an artist, and that Calderon was purer and greater than Shakspeare. The poet of the school was Tieck, who is sportively graceful in childish pieces, such as *Little Red Riding Hood*, and out of his depth when he ventures in other waters. But the movement had one great man in its ranks—Novalis—whose strange fate and beautiful spirit have given immortal interest to his words, and almost to his friends. A dreamer by constitution and mind, he seemed to pass his life on the brink of happy presages which were never realized. In the quiet strength of love he grew to spiritual insight and purity—sickness enlarged his range of sympathy—and what might have been morbid in his religious feelings was sublimed into rational devotion by the severe pursuit of science. Like Pico of Mirandola, he cherished the notion of a philosophical faith, in which all the creeds of the human heart should be blended, and all their discrepancies reconciled. Hence he did justice to Catholicism for that breadth of logical inconsistency

---

* Geschichte der Deutschen Literatur im neun.ehnten Jahrhundert. Von Julian Schmidt. London: D. Nutt.

and harmonious practice which have grown up in it with the nations and centuries that belonged to it. And he thought the Protestantism of his own times insufficient and formal. Yet those who examine him closely will see that he really desired something in which both should be fused. Little "hymns to the Virgin" are not to be more rigidly construed than the *Bride of Corinth*, or the *Gods of Greece*—from which it might, with equal justice, be inferred that Goethe and Schiller were Pagans. With the death of Novalis, the real strength of his followers passed away. Stolberg had already gone over to Rome; Frederic Schlegel followed him; and Tieck was looked upon as a bird of passage, who only waited a season to cross the Alps. Men did injustice to the insincerity of his convictions. But a cry was raised against Crypto-Catholicism. Voss gave tone to the bitter contempt of the learned world against those who went back into slavery—August Schlegel was compelled to excuse himself—Tieck drew back—and the movement died out quietly in Fouqué's and Chamisso's novels.

In fact, the nation which saw French troopers stable their horses in Berlin and Vienna was weary of universal culture and its preachers. In the day of humiliation it awoke to the consciousness of its real life. The French censorship which had proscribed Madame de Staël's *Germany*, saw nothing to correct in the labours of the Brothers Grimm, who were yet teaching the people that they had a history. Fichte renounced the notion of "world-citizenship," and proclaimed in his speeches to the German nation that the world of thought was their especial heritage, and that the grandest idea of all was the love of Fatherland. Those who have studied transcendental philosophy will understand why it was not till the thirteenth lecture had appeared that the French censor perceived the patriot's drift. W. von Humboldt and Niebuhr are among the scholars who owed the best memories of their lives and a practical education to the war of freedom. But the common cause had enlisted even stranger partisans than these. Görres, afterwards the florid rhetorician of the Ultramontane school, and Gentz, who died in the service of Austrian absolutism, wrote fiercely and openly against the Conqueror to whom kings and Goethe truckled. When at last the war was renewed, the splendid lyrics of Arndt and Körner rung out. That most enduring of all those productions which has become the German national hymn, is especially valuable as showing the direction in which the struggle against foreign arms was to end. Indeed, much of the literature of this time was as short-lived as the circumstances that called it out. But the people, who had retrieved at Leipzig what their fatherly governments had endangered at Jena and Austerlitz, began to look upon themselves as the best depositories of liberty. Uhland's poems express the hopes and longings of this time, and its bitter disappointments. In their clearness and thoughtful sweetness lies a charm which belongs to the character of a man whose sufferings were not, like those of Goethe, "evolved from his self-consciousness." The school of freedom of course ended with the last ineffectual struggles of the nations whom their kings had flattered and betrayed. Wild assemblies of enthusiastic students, secret clubs, and the fanatical murder of Kotzebue, contended vainly with standing armies, the police, and a herd of literary renegades who were headed by Frederic Schlegel and paid by Metternich.

It is melancholy to turn from that heroic idealism which imagined the *Tugend-bund* to the flippant unbelief of Young Germany. The national name was never more misapplied than to a party whose leader was the adopted child of Paris. Side by side with the ghastly cheerfulness of men who were "learning to be lively," and thought their religion the best joke at hand, went the philosophical radicalism which probed all systems, and rejected all as worthless. Hegelianism, in its many phases, is the metaphysical counterpart of Heine's poetry. The most hopeful symptom of the last thirty years has been the growth of an historical school. Ranke, Dahlmann, and Raumer have at least represented one department of letters worthily; but the time for a proper estimate of men who live so near ourselves, has scarcely yet arrived. For this reason, perhaps, the last volume of Herr Schmidt's labours is the least satisfactory. Moreover, with a praiseworthy reticence, he has forborne to give more than the barest biographical notices. But if his work, from the nature of the subject, can be little more than a handbook for living authors, there is quite enough in the earlier pages to entitle it to the praise of having redeemed the promise of its title. It is such a history of German literature as beginner and veteran student may alike be glad to consult.

PERTHES THE PUBLISHER, AND LITERARY GERMANY.*

THERE was a talk, some fifteen or twenty years ago, that the genius of old 'Faterland' was exhausted. Men, while admitting the splendid achievements of the elder Germans—of the Kants, Fichtes, Goethes, Schillers, and Richters—were in the habit of saying, 'But that people are doing little or nothing now.' Some spoke as if Goethe were at once the Alpha and the Omega of German literature and poesy. Such talk was partly founded on ignorance, partly on that principle in the human mind which leads men to depreciate the present and to exalt the past, and partly on sympathy with the sceptical spirit which had so strongly characterised the elder German authors. Of late years, more justice has been done in this country to the later fruits of the German mind; fruits which, if inferior to the first products of the tree in brilliancy of hue and piquancy of taste, are much superior in the qualities of solid nourishment and healthful influences.

Yet, ere introducing to our readers the great German publisher, whose shop formed the nucleus of the fine cluster of the later school—of Niebuhrs, Neanders, Krummachers, and Tholucks—we are tempted to look back for a little with deep interest and admiration to the more splendid, although more uncertain and dangerous, lustre of the constellation which preceded it. Certainly, in the history of letters, seldom, if ever, was such a distinguished group assembled as met at Weimar. Brilliant the days of Augustus, when Virgil and Horace met and embraced each other under the shadow of Mæcenas; when Livy and Sallust

* Memoirs of Frederick Perthes. From the German of Clement Theodore Perthes. Edinburgh: Constable.

were contending for the smiles of Clio; and when the wondrous Cicero, philosopher, orator, moral writer, epistolist, litterateur, and the more wondrous Cæsar, soldier, statesman, splendid roué, orator, and historian, had newly left the stage: brilliant the days of Queen Elizabeth, when Shakspere and Jonson drank and punned at the Mermaiden; when Burleigh nodded in the council, his nod, like Jove's,

'The stamp of fate—the fiat of a god;'

when Raleigh strode the deck, like Apollo embarked in the car of Neptune; when Bacon sat on the woolsack, his brows heavy-laden with wisdom, and his heart overflowing with serpentine wiles; and when Spenser poured his most melting, mellifluous, and unearthly strains, and had flowers and poems thrown into his premature grave: brilliant the days of Queen Anne, when Pope, Gay, and Arbuthnot mingled their streams of wit, and when Swift infused his gall, and turned them into Marah-waters of bitterness; when each morning the 'Spectators' were shed abroad on the world, like soft and snowy blossoms from a tree in May: when Addison was seated in his coffee-house senate, with Budgell as his shadow, Phillips as his echo, Tickell as his weaker *alias*, and Steele as his (never empty) *butt*: brilliant the days of George III., when, in London, Burke and Johnson talked far above singing; and Goldsmith gaped for wonderment, or got pale in envy; and Boswell hurried away to record the conversation in his journal; and Garrick caught some new oddity in Johnson's manner to help him in his next imitation of the sage; and Reynolds, through snuff-watering eyes, watched the

faces of the disputants—their words half heard—for a pictorial purpose; and Beauclerk surveyed the whole company with the coolest and civilest of sneers; and when, in Scotland, Robertson and Blair were bowing to each other their gentle contradictions and soft impeachments across the table; and David Hume was playing his rubber of whist, his ideas and impressions forgotten; and Robert Burns was interposing his sturdy sense, rough wit, and round oaths in the intervals of Dugald Stewart's delicate discriminations, and Alison's fine-spun theories: brilliant the days of George IV., or rather, of the 'Prince Regent,' when, at the 'Round Table,' or under the 'Lion's Mouth' of the 'London Magazine,' Hazlitt snarled and stormed; Leigh Hunt fluttered about like a bird, bustling with kindness, and overflowing with *bonhommie* and animal spirits; Shelley screamed out his insane sincerities; Lamb stuttered, punned, and hiccuped; and John Scott contributed his Norland sense and Aberdonian accent to the medley; and when with us Wilson poured forth his unpremeditated strains of farce and tragedy, of poetry and fun; Lockhart snapped at every subject, like a hungry and angry dog; Hogg ejaculated coarse confusions of thought and language—a chaos which another and greater mind was to fuse into form, and to round into harmony; MacGinn sang, swore, and quaffed; and De Quincey wound along through all the uproar his own quiet, deep current of philosophical and poetic imaginings, tinged with that soft shade which overlies all his better converse as well as writing, and reminds you of his own favourite words,

'The grace of forest-charms decay'd,
And pastoral melancholy:'

but more brilliant, perhaps, still than any since the Augustan or Elizabethan age, the assemblage of fine spirits, such as Goethe, Schiller, Novalis, Herder, and a host more, which met in or near Weimar, and have made that region not only classical but enchanted ground. The reason of the superiority of this assemblage, perhaps, lies here: it was a cluster of wizards—of creators, of men of original genius. In many of the brilliant groups we have rapidly pictured, there was much more of talent than of genius. But in Weimar there was a reunion of several of the very first minds of that or any age; and on the whole they contrived to

live in tolerable harmony; and their light shines on us thick and crudded as that of the Pleiades.

We are far from being idolaters of Goethe. We consider the excessive worship of him by Carlyle and Lewis as, the first, a mental, and in the second, a moral, derangement. Goethe, as a man, we not only dislike, but loathe. He had all the faults supposed to be incident to the genial temperament, without the genial temperament itself. Byron even was respectable compared to him. Byron was the slave of passion; Goethe sinned on system. Byron was the creature of impulse; Goethe came calm, if not cold, to the perpetration of seduction, and to the patronage of suicide. Byron never seduced a female; Goethe many. Byron drank to drown remorse, and to stir up despondency on the edge of despair and madness; Goethe to intensify pleasure and to nourish pride. Sin soured Byron; it agreed with Goethe's constitution, and he continued healthy, and almost happy with it. Sin was driving Byron lately toward Christianity; it drove Goethe to a belief in an immoral and lifeless God. Byron shrank, withered, and died on the poisons he had imbibed; Goethe fattened, flourished, and became an octogenarian on their strength. Byron sinned like an erring man; Goethe like a Pagan god, whose wickednesses seem all the more intolerable that they are done with a high hand, from a celestial vantage ground, and without any human result of remorse. Both became satirical; but, while the satire of Byron, in its very bitterness as well as fire, proves that the iron has entered into his soul, that of Goethe is cool, sardonic, and seems to mock, not only the objects of its scorn, but that scorn itself. The one, at its worst, is the smile of a Satan, a being of hot heart, disappointed ambition, and awful regrets; the other we may liken to that of Ahrimanes himself, the fabled aboriginal evil god, who may sneer at, but can hardly be angry at, the evil he has himself made, and which has always seemed to him good.

With these views of Goethe's character we, of course, warmly admire his genius. He united qualities seemingly the most incompatible: Horatian elegance with almost Shaksperian imagination, unbounded command over the regions of the ethereal, with the coolest intellect and stores of worldly wisdom worthy

Lord Bacon. 'No writer,' Emerson said once, 'has less nonsense in his works than Goethe.' No writer at all events has turned his nonsense to better account, or handled his filth with a more delicate touch. Some of his looser writings remind you of

'Garden gods, and not so decent either;'

but they are formed with all the elegance of Canova's sculpture. The story of the 'Elective Affinities' is one of intertangled abomination, almost incredible; the characters resemble a knot of foul toads, but few indecorous expressions occur. Many of the scenes are exquisitely beautiful; sentiment of a pure and lofty kind alternates with essential *smut;* and close to the fire-springs of guilty passion lie masses of clear, icy, but true and deep reflection. The 'Sorrows of Werter' seems to us a wondrously trashy production, and, were it appearing now, would be classed with inferior French novels. It would now fail in producing a single suicide. Altogether, Goethe's works give us the impression of extreme coldness; and not of the cheerful, bracing cold of snow, but of the deadly cold of the grave, if not rather of that cold which Milton has ventured to represent in the very heart of Pandemonium, where 'frozen Alps' nod to 'fiery,' and where alike fire and frost are everlasting. Intellect and imagination, without heart, principle, or geniality, although with considerable power of simulating sympathy with all three, were, in spite of Lewis, the true constituents of Goethe's genius; and Walsingham, in Sterling's 'Onyx-Ring,' is his perfect likeness.

Schiller was a man of a different order. Perfected through suffering, hardened by endurance, into a mere mass (intellectually) of muscle, brawn, and bone; an earnest struggler; a man of high Roman nature—with a warm heart, but a Pagan creed—Schiller might seem at first sight still more remote from men, and disconnected from general sympathy, than Goethe. But, amidst all his muscular strength, there were weaknesses and foibles in his constitution, and beneath all his iron hardihood there were softenings of humanity which have endeared him to the world. Aspiring, like Goethe, to be only an artist, he did not cease, like him, to be a man. His humanity was originally so abundant, that it survived his early and souring struggles, his long devotion to a somewhat paganised

philosophy, and a high but cold ideal of art, and was beating in his heart to the last. His final words were, 'Many things are now becoming plain and clear to me.' Curious question, what were these things? What light on the dread knots which had long perplexed him, and for which his prose essays show that he had found only a sorry solution, was darted by the radiance he saw rising through the dark valley and shadow of Death? His experience is not at all peculiar. Who has not seen a strange smile shining on the face of the departing, as if they saw some unearthly splendour or celestial shape dawning on their eyes, or as if they heard the first bells of that city which hath no need of the sun? And who has not noticed that wondrous calm which, often succeeding the most violent anguish, settles down on the dying man, and seems the rest prepared for the people of God arrived before the time? And what utterances come often from dying persons—eloquence from lips that had been dull before—wisdom from the foolish—genius from the clown—the most glowing sentiments of virtue from the depraved! And how do the good sometimes then surpass themselves; and the departing mother, rising from her couch, and blessing or counselling her children, seems absolutely inspired, and rolls out her words with supernatural force, fluency, and beauty, and the silence that succeeds seems that of a shrine newly deserted by the god!' 'Oh, just, subtle, wise, and mighty Death!' said Raleigh; but he referred to the revelations which follow; whereas the words may be as appropriately applied to those which precede it. There are sometimes 'chariots of fire and horses of fire' seen on this as well as on that side of the Black River. Not long ago, a person whom we knew, and who had been long ill, starting from a brief trance, told his attendant that he had seen, and continued to see, the gates of heaven opening to receive him. It was singular that while this person, a few days after, was committed to the dust, a lark rose directly over the grave, and poured down a strain of thrilling harmony till the funeral was over, when the sound ceased as suddenly as it had begun.

There are often apparent, but seldom any real, disparities between a man's character and his genius. As a man's imagination is, so is he. As a man's works are, so is his life. The strong.

manly work proclaims the strong man. The effeminate writing stamps the cultivated weakling. The impure conceptions of the book come from the foul fancy of the writer. The satire shows the spirit to be either permanently or temporarily soured. The man halting between two opinions, or two ideals, or two plans of life in his conduct, halts as much in his works. Milton, the semi-seraph, wrote the semi-seraphic epic; Butler and Swift, the unhappy and disappointed, wrote caricatures and libels; Thomson, the lazy lover of nature, wrote languid but beautiful love-letters to her, and these are his 'Seasons;' you see Byron's personal defect crippling or convulsing portions of his poems. Christopher North's uncertain position between the serious and the ludicrous, and his veering political, literary, and religious opinions, are visible in his 'Noctes.' And so, if we have accurately described Schiller's character, we need not describe his genius. He was just his own 'Diver' 'lean and strong,'—fearing no danger and no toil in his search after the Beautiful and the True; nay, loving to seek them in the very depths of the Maëlström, and if perishing in the plunge, perishing with the eye of love and the breathless hush of admiration attesting the profound sympathy with which the attempt was regarded. How different the conduct of those dainty bardlings, who (Scottice) *tape* their talents, who brood over their eggs for years, and at length produce their young with a portentous cackle, which only more loudly proclaims that they were but *earocks'* eggs after all! how different this from the earnest although mistaken enthusiasm of a Schiller or a Shelley, all whose poems are sobs, and the voice of whose wrestling genius often reminds you of the poet's

'Solitary shriek, the bubbling cry,
    Of some strong swimmer in his agony!'

All hail to another true-hearted child of Germany and genius, honest, fearless, strong, and simple-minded Jean Paul! From Perthes' memoir, we gather that he was rather dull and tedious in conversation, but so, too, he often was in writing. Endowed with many faculties—with fancy, imagination, language, learning, strong philosophic tendencies and gifts, humour, too, and wit of a certain kind—he seems either to have wanted naturally, or to have lost, his proper proportion of animal spirits. The Frenchman

was quite omitted in his composition. Hence he became too much dependent on artificial stimulus to put his vast mind in motion; and hence his vivacity has often a laboured and fantastic air. But let the great soul within him be once fairly roused, by visions of nature, or by memories of early love, or by anticipations of the future life, and no one can so blend pathos with sublimity, beauty of description with depth of feeling, as Jean Paul. What a picture in his 'Fruit Flower, and Thorn Pieces' that of spring! Read in the depth of winter, it brings into the room the smell of roses and the flutter of flowers. As a white substance spread without before your window gives you, even in summer, the feeling, and almost the chill, of snow, so Jean Paul's descriptions warm you with the breath and cheer you with the joy of spring. His night scenes, too, always take you out with him under the canopy, where he is sure to show you a moon waning in the east, large stars burning by thousands in the zenith, some strange clouds, like angel wings, stretching athwart the heavens and a few

'Meteors of the storm,
To plough the deep night with their fiery forms.'

Night, indeed, was his element, and had suggested to him imaginations profounder, more genial, more hopeful, if not grander or more original, than the 'Night Thoughts' of Young. And of his 'Dream in a Churchyard' we need not speak. It were enough itself to make his name immortal—enough, itself, shall we say? to demonstrate a God and a future life. The soul capable of such a vision *must* be from God, and *can* never die. It is a proof also that Jean Paul's *forte* lay in the terribly sublime. He, perhaps, loved the humorous better, but the love was not fully reciprocated. His fun seems in general sadly forced work, and you yawn instead of laugh. It has never at least been naturalised amongst us in Britain; and, compared to that of Sterne, it seems vulgar—to that of Addison, Goldsmith, and Washington Irving, overdone and outrageous—and to that of Christopher North, tedious and unmeaning. Indeed it is in extracts chiefly that 'Richter' is likely to survive out of his own country.

But we must tear ourselves away from the Dii Majorum Gentium of Germany, after repeating a previous remark, that none of these three, nor of their contemporaries, such as Herder, Novalis, Kant, &c. seem to have had any belief in Christianity as a special revelation from God, or as a special remedy for an abnormal and imported disease in human nature. It is difficult to define their different shades of opinion, but all worshipped nature as God's only and ultimate revelation, although Goethe worshipped nature principally as beauty—Schiller partly as this, and partly as benevolence, saying, with Shelley, 'Love is God,' and in one of his poems *toasting* 'the Good Spirit'—Kant as inexorable law—Richter as the envelope of a higher life—and Novalis as coming to a climax in man, according to him, the true 'Schekinah.' Let us now turn to Perthes, whom we regard, apart from his many other admirable qualities, as an index and exponent of the reaction which has taken place in Germany in favour of a modified orthodoxy.

As to Perthes' intellectual qualities, they stood deservedly very high. If hardly himself a man of genius, he had a vivid sympathy, as well with the eccentricities and weaknesses, as with the powers of the men of imaginative gifts. He saw little of the splendid group above described, but he intensely appreciated them, and his opinion of Goethe seems very nearly what has been just expressed. His powers were those of acute discrimination, a degree of strong common sense and practical sagacity not common in a German, and a keen interest and just appreciation of all the varieties and forms of his country's literature. To a sound judgment, and large liberal taste, he added the proper degree of enthusiasm. Such are the principal qualities which we would desiderate in a publisher. That he should be an author, or a philosopher, or a poet himself, is less desirable. We have known some specimens of the poetical publisher, but they did not serve to improve our conception of the class. The *poetical* was far from being the *ideal* publisher. Conceive the ludicrous aspect of an intense-looking personage, with blue eyes, yellow hair, and large lips, selling a boy a halfpenny worth of paper across the counter, with an air of huge disdain, and then hurrying away to the back-shop to indite an ode to Glencoe, or an imitation of Wilson's 'Noctes!' or a little dapper, round man, with a strong Yorkshire accent, whom calling on to settle an account you cannot find, because he is 'doing' a few sonnets, wherewith to

eclipse, if possible, his *own* Keats, and to astonish his *own* Sergeant Talfourd. We very much fear that the poetical bookseller who pens a stanza when he should be examining his ledger, is a pretty considerable particular prig, and we never intend to publish with such an one. Perthes was of a very different order. A man of highly cultivated mind, an enthusiast, and a sage, he was not actuated by any vain ambitions. He knew, and he kept his own place. He was not the mere slave of a 'Reader;' he did not gather helpless opinions about books out of the discordant clang of coteries, or the cross-firing of reviews, he read and judged for himself, and he felt that, had he become a regular author, it were equivalent to a judge leaving the bench and taking his place to be tried at the bar. His aim was not merely to estimate the literary merit of books, but to infuse a high cosmopolitan and Christian spirit into the whole business of publishing, and to make of it at once an ideal and a moral thing. Oh! for a whole Paternoster Row of such publishers as Perthes!

The intellectual qualities of this remarkable man were subordinate to his moral. He was a thoroughly earnest, true, affectionate, brave, and noble being; genial, too, and with just the due dash (latterly) of the animal in his composition. Coleridge never drew a juster distinction than that between a good and a *goody* man. As a clever acquaintance, in one of his published lectures, professes himself 'entirely unable' to understand the difference indicated by Coleridge, we shall try to make it apparent. A good man, then, we take to be a man whose goodness is unpretentious, and who wears it as a humble although comely garment, not as a flaunting, scarlet robe, who feels it, too, to be a robe *lent* him by another; a goody man is proud of his small virtues and decorums, thinks them *(as they are!)* his own, and seems to ask at every one he meets, 'Don't you know me, Mr So-and-so, the celebrated goody man?' The good man has his faults and errors, and does not seek to disguise them, feeling that the acknowledgment of an error is a pledge of sustained effort to get rid of it—nay, is that effort begun; the goody man has reached a sort of stunted perfection: the sun of his virtue is so small that its spots are hardly visible, and the faults he has he dexterously hides under loud-sounding profes-

sions, and a great outcry against the same as they occur in the lives of others. A good man is largely charitable to others, while often sternly condemnatory of himself; a goody man has no approbation or charity to spare, except for himself, for other goody men, and for those rich and great persons who, if not goody men themselves, have a respect for such as are. A good man has nothing particular to distinguish him in his dress, manners, or mode of speech; a goody man, wishing to be observed in every step of his way to heaven, elongates his countenance, and solemnises his style of talk, till it seems the echo of the earth of the grave dropping in a charnel-house. The good man sometimes does imprudent, or says daring things, which make the world stare, and make the goody man lift up his eyes and whisper, 'I always thought men were mistaken in him; he has now shown himself in his true colours.' The good man, when he hears of some glaring transgression, sighs, and says, 'What a pity!' the goody man gives a sham sigh, too, as he cries, 'What a scandal! what a burning shame.' The good man is not always *thoroughly* orthodox in his creed, but sometimes 'wears his rue with a difference;' the goody man is not always orthodox either, and then he thinks that his proprieties and respectabilities will make up for any amount of heterodoxy. He has peculiar tastes and sentiments; he prefers Addison's character to Steele's, and Swift's to both. If an infidel, he prefers Combe and Hume to Rousseau and Shelley. If a believer, he thinks Calvin far superior to Luther, shudders at the death of Archbishop Sharpe, while detesting Claverhouse, and shakes his head whenever you talk to him of Edward Irving. Out of good men have come martyrs, poets of the true breed, anti-slavery agitators, not to speak of apostles and prophets; out of goody men have come noble chairmen of Bible societies, organisers of soup-kitchens, aldermen, lord provosts, presidents of the United States, and doctors of divinity all the world over.

Perthes did *not* belong to this class. It is indeed refreshing to compare his manly form of religion, where you find virtue without austerity and without ostentation, purity without purism, and orthodoxy without cant, with that which prevails not only among goody men, and among Spurgeon-going multitudes, but among many truly excellent, but par-

tially enlightened Christians. You see his religion not labelled on his brow, inscribed on his broad phylacteries, beating in his heart, living in his beautifying his domestic life, energising his political and publishing labours, shedding a certain gentle colouring over all the movements of his intellect and imagination.

His domestic life was, as all the world knows, signally happy. Caroline Claudius Perthes is a name ranking with those of the noblest female characters in biography. Possessed of a vigorous mind and varied accomplishments, she was none the less, but all the more, a devoted wife and every inch a woman. She differed from her husband, but only as the tender tenor differs from the deep bass; and while in many things opposite, she thoroughly appreciated and warmly loved his character. She answered in all points the best definition of a good wife: she was a *leaning prop* to her husband. Beautiful the invisible tie uniting the pair, and between his restless energy and public spirit, and her meekness of wisdom, providence, and domestic virtues, constituting a unity in variety such as the married life has seldom presented. Such kindred spirits to Perthes as Arnold and Foster were, like him, most equally yoked, but we have always thought that Foster's lady was too much a duplicate of himself—too learned, and lofty, and gloomy; ever doing well to be angry because her husband was so. The two in their insulation, inaccessibility, and gloom, remind you of two peaks in the Glencoe ridge withdrawn into their own aerial hermitage, cut off by chasms and streams of snow, as well as by elevation, from the lower world, looking at each other with love, at the sun with admiration, but on the valleys and the men below with contempt, and often wrapped in mists and cloudy thunders. In his second marriage, too, Perthes was eminently fortunate.

The energy of Perthes was amazing. The quantity of work of various kinds which he went through indicated at once great versatility, great perseverance, a most buoyant spirit, and a temperament infinitely restless. Conducting a very complicated business, he carried on, too, a varied correspondence; and his letters were not mere business notes, but deep thoughtful outcomes of his mind on a thousand topics of the day, besides reading extensively, and taking a bold and frequent part in public affairs. His shop and himself formed together the centre of almost all that was intellectually, and politically, and spiritually active in Germany. In the course of his career he came in contact with most of the celebrated German authors—with Schleiermacher, that profound Christian Platonist, who, first of modern thinkers, tried to form not a scholastic but an ideal philosophy out of Christianity—with Niebuhr, the all-accomplished, the bloodhound of history, following the faintest marks, and feeling the dimmest scents of truth; wise, also, almost above the wisdom of man in political sagacity and foresight; although disappointed with society, soured at life, and saying, like David, 'All men are liars—Stendel, with his great grammatical and historical powers—Olshausen, with his versatile and teeming imagination—Krummacher, with his ingenious fancies—Tholuck, with his profound critical learning—and greatest of all, morally, Neander, that 'Hebrew of the Hebrews,' uniting much of the acuteness and learning of Paul with the glowing love and personal passion for Christ which distinguished John; more truly far, what Emerson calls 'Swedenborg,' 'the last Father of the Church.' With these, and many others of the same Christian type, Perthes mingled souls, and interchanged sympathies, as well as published many of their works. Yet he was on terms of goodwill, too, if not of friendship, with some of the Rationalistic and Pantheistic School; and many in this country will think that he has spoken too tenderly of Hegel and Strauss.

We regret we have not room to dilate on the views which these volumes open up of the literary life and bookselling *practique* of Germany:—to accompany Perthes on his frequent tours; to describe his shiftings of scene in the chequered course of his professional life; or to glance at his connection with the fluctuating and complex politics of 'Faterland.' Indeed, we do *not* regret having little time to speak of the subject mentioned in this last clause, since the only tedious parts of the volumes are those recounting the marches and countermarches—the diplomatic doubles—the endless reactions and re-reactions, and all the other three-piled confusions which make up the recent political history of the Continent; yet nothing, perhaps, in all Perthes' story serves

to show his powers in a more favourable light than the clearness of vision with which he seems to have seen through all those petty complications, and the strong, steady step with which he pursued his own path through the mazes of political intrigue and popular commotion; through and above all these he moved like a beneficent genius.

His religious career remains to be considered, and opens up by far the most interesting passages in his history. He was naturally a man of strong, sensuous passions, and in the struggle with these he depended for a season solely on what he calls rational will. To this extent, at least, he was then a rationalist, and his motto might have been, 'Every man the architect of his own eternity,' and that too by purely intellectual tools. In this he was encouraged by his admiration of the character and writings of Schiller, whose god was art, and whose worship was self-culture. His connection with Jacobi introduced him to higher views, and he began to 'listen to the voice of God speaking to, and in, feeling.' Latterly he met with some men in Holstein and Münster who seemed to be in harmony with themselves, and he discovered the cause of this to lie in the supremacy of love. From the admission of this he passed to the recognition of Divine love as incarnate in Jesus Christ, and as outpoured in the form of grace through the Holy Spirit. He then, and unalterably, took his 'stand on the revealed Word of God, as the only word, the only law which is *above* us, holding the essence of Christianity to lie in "strength and unity through love," all given by the grace of God, and received by love.' Such views he reached after many struggles and wanderings, and retained to the last. He cared comparatively little for the dogmas of creeds, founding his faith far more on love than on logic. His religion was a cheerful habit, worn all the week, not a mere Sunday suit of sables. His confidence in the final triumph of true Christianity never faltered for a moment, and this unlimited trust gave him a great advantage in contemplating the endless oscillations of German theology. He stood calm on an eminence which he had reached by effort and toil, and saw, not with the eye of unquiet sympathy, nor with the exaggerative eye of fear, but with a still, hopeful glance, those billowy movements of the German mind which De Quincey has

compared to the restless sand-clouds of the desert, and which might be more fitly perhaps likened to those changeful and capricious pomps of varied colour —those clouds of purple pursuing gold, and gold melted down in fire, and fire fading into dull grey—which appear in a summer evening sky, leading their tumultuous dance around the steadfast, though sinking sun. We are not qualified to give more than an imperfect outline of the German theological mind. In Perthes' early days scepticism was almost universal, taking various forms in various minds. In Fichte, it assumed a stern and stoical shape, amounting almost to sublimity, and animating those eloquent closing chapters of the 'Destination of Man,' which remind you of the beautiful shapes of snow-covered trees, or the flowers into which everlasting frost sometimes wreaths itself. In Goethe it was allied first with sentimentalism and unmanly despair at the era of the 'Sorrows of Werter,' and afterwards with the calm prosecution of self-culture, as the 'Be all, and the End all' of man. In Schiller it began with a fierce Queen Mablike recalcitration against the evils of society, and subsided latterly into a warmer and more energetic pursuit than Goethe's of a similar ideal. In Jean Paul it veered and fluctuated—he, according to Perthes, longed for truth and a settled creed, and yet spoke of the Redeemer as a mere product of the human imagination. Latterly, the influence of Schleiermacher—the labours of Neander—the revival of mysticism—the sorrow and misery produced by the French domination—and the felt inadequacy of Rationalism or Pantheism to satisfy the human heart, to appease the conscience, or truly to elevate the life, led to a strong, but strongly-resisted, reaction in favour of Christianity. Perthes describes himself as brought to religion by a feeling of his own sinfulness, and of his need of supernatural help and Divine forgiveness; Pantheism, denying the existence, of course deadens the sense, of sin; Rationalism dilutes the idea of its guilt, proposes no adequate punishment for it, and scouts the thought of atonement. But Perthes felt from his own struggles that sin was a dire reality; not a mere pardonable result of bodily temperament, but a deep-seated sore in the soul—that its most dangerous and inveterate shape was,

not sensualism, but pride—the 'condemnation of the devil;' and that nothing but Divine power exerted through the love and death of Christ could gain triumph for any man over his spiritual adversaries.

He was resting on this conviction, and doing all in his power to extend it to others, when a remarkable event took place in the history of German literature. This was the publication in 1835 of Strauss's 'Life of Jesus.' Several infidel publications have at different times formed eras in the history of thought. Such was Voltaire's 'Philosophical Dictionary,' Gibbon's 'Decline and Fall,' Paine's 'Age of Reason,' and Godwin's 'Political Justice.' But none of these produced a tithe of the impression in England or in France which the 'Leben Jesu' produced in Germany. It fell like a thunderbolt amidst conflicting armies, and both suffered from the shock. On the one hand, the old school of Rationalism was smitten to the ground; on the other, the scientific theology of Schleiermacher and his followers received a heavy blow and great discouragement. Perthes alone continued calm, and predicted the consequences which have actually followed. He foresaw the complete discomfiture of the rationalistic forces. He foresaw the flood of replies which were to appear on the side of orthodoxy; and that these were not to prove entirely satisfactory. He foresaw that the ultimate effect, nevertheless, of the Straussian criticism was to do good to the Christian cause, and to 'show that the only alternative is between Pantheism and the Christian faith, and that this was to be the turning-point for many individuals, perhaps for the whole generation.' He asserted strongly, that 'Christian philosophy can show only the untruth of objections, not the truth of Christianity itself, and that historical science and criticism can show only the groundlessness of objections against the sacred narrative, not the truth of the narrative in general, and much less the actuality of particular events.' 'Whoever would make the saving truths of revelation his own, or lead others to them, must start from facts coming under his own immediate knowledge. The depravity of all mankind, our double nature, wrestling, weakness and death, in every individual, and the ardent longing of the whole man for deliverance from such evils—these are facts, and they form a basis for faith in the salvation revealed in Scripture.' In other words, as the great necessity of a revelation lies in the inner nature of man, there, too, is hitherto the strongest evidence for its credibility. Perthes knowing Germany well, predicted that the Straussian sand-pillar would soon pass away, probably in ten years; and the prediction has, we understand, been fulfilled. There is now little belief in Strauss's theory, whatever respect may be still entertained for his ingenuity, learning, and intellectual powers. New forms of infidelity are arising in Germany, to have their brief day like his, and disappear; and Christianity we hear is assuming in many quarters the millennarian form, and on the whole on the increase.

Perthes was sometimes suspected of undue tenderness for Catholicism; but to this he, like Burke, in a kindred case, was led by an aversion to rationalism; thinking that a bad form of Christianity was better than no revealed religion at all. We are not exactly of this mind, and deem it an unsolved problem which of the two abominable things is the more destructive. Sometimes an ill prepared medicine is worse than a poison. The solution of such a question may probably depend on how different temperaments are effected by differing degrees and varieties of evil. Probably Popery acts more injuriously than rationalism on the clear cold intellectualist; and rationalism more injuriously than Popery on the mind of imagination. Probably it had been better for such men as Schiller, Shelley, and Byron, had they been Roman Catholics instead of sceptics. Certainly it were better that many of the Jesuits should be open instead of secret scoffers. Perhaps, too, there are states of society and eras in history when the one is more pernicious than the other, and vice versa. But the question is complicated, and always refers to a choice of evils; while we are ready to point to enlightened Protestant Christianity as what we deem a more excellent way than either Rationalism, or its alias Pantheism, or Popery, and to predict the approaching doom of all three.

Perthes, while strongly, though sanctifiedly, sensuous to the end; while keenly alive to all the innocent pleasures of this life, contemptuous of every shape of anchoritism; and while an ardent admirer of the beautiful and the sublime in nature, was, at the same time, justly indignant at the doctrines of the rationalists about the sufficiency of the material universe, and at their attempts to evolve the secrets of Divine mercy and wisdom by means of chemistry, physics, and botany. His language on this subject is very strong. He quotes with approbation Lalandes' saying, 'I looked into infinite space, but I saw no God.' He adds, 'Nature never could have given us a personal God—only the Son has revealed the Father; and had not the Son revealed God, we must have denied him.' Hear again his awful words —awful in themselves, and because his character and Christianity invest them almost with angelic authority:—' Throughout the animal world I see a process of mutual destruction, and the natural fate of man is misery and sorrow. Children are ever dying of the poison distilled from parental sins; youth is wasted in vain endeavours; the prime of life is tortured with monotony; and old age bewails a scheme of life, or many schemes of life, not fulfilled. There is no doubt a well-spring of life in man; but nature will not allow it to become clear. No one has portrayed the terrors of nature, and the cruelty of its decrees, so as to show that whoever would worship the God of nature must even fall down and worship the devil. The goodness of nature is a dream.' This is the secret of Paul's language when he represents nature 'groaning and travailing in pain, and waiting for the manifestation of the sons of God.'

These words may seem too bold; and yet they start thrilling suggestions, which are beginning to take root in some Christian minds, although they have found distinct shape as yet in none, and are as yet chiefly valuable as a reaction and protest against the contemptible cant of our nature worshippers, who ignore that fearful shade which rests on the universe, or would transfer it to Christianity; and who prate about 'the Divine meanings' of nature, and its intrinsic divinity. Nature proves a great mind, but neither an infinite mind nor a being absolutely good; it leaves both these questions unsettled, or to be settled only by the turn of a die of metaphysical speculation, or in accordance with the testimony of temperament; so true it is that 'No man hath seen God at any time; the only begotten Son, who is in the bosom of the Father, he hath declared him.' That the devil made the material universe, we do not believe; but, in some inscrutable way, he and his agents have interwoven evil with it, with every part of it with which man at least comes in contact, so inextricably, that nothing less than a supernatural force can separate the bad from the good. This we believe to be a deduction from the whole spirit and doctrine of revelation. He is the 'God of this world,' the 'Prince of the power of the air,' and the 'whole world lieth in the Wicked One.' And it is impossible, we think, for any man with a heart to contemplate many of the fearful phenomena in the natural and providential worlds, without revolting at the thought that they all proceed from a God. This is not unduly to limit the omnipotence of God. That, in effect, although not in theory, is limited by the resistance of man's wicked will already. We only show this resistance extended into regions where many think that only one mind is working and (horrible blasphemy!) complacently creating conditions and circumstances which render iniquity, injustice, and undeserved suffering inevitable, and, on the showing of nature-worshippers, everlasting.

Along with tendencies towards such speculations, rather than such speculations matured in his mind, Perthes united the most cheerful, simple, and practical piety. 'Not to love God,' he says, 'is sin; and to love him constitutes deliverance from sin.' A sentiment like this, while suggesting humility, suggested also a desire to be away from a world where there was so much tending to cloud the character, and cast doubts on the love, of God. But here we note a remarkable difference between his desire for death and that of Foster. Foster was anxious to be delivered from the earth shadows principally because they clouded himself; Perthes because they clouded God. Yet Perthes' trust in God was far more instinctive and profound than Foster's, and was so partly because he had views as to God's utter disconnection with the evil and misery of the universe, which Foster had little conception of. The last cry of Foster was essentially that of Goethe, 'Light, more light;' that of Perthes was for more 'Love and humility.' Foster's cry meant, 'Give me more light, else I cannot expect to have more love hereafter than I have here.' Perthes' meant, 'I shall take more light gladly, but I expect it to come hereafter, as it has come to me here, through the channel of love and lowliness. The one was the cry of a man who had learned to love God through light; the other, who had seen God through the atmosphere of love. The wish of Foster was more that of a baffled but hopeful man of genius; the wish of Perthes was more that of a yearning child looking toward the wall of his nursery, warmed by the radiance of the unseen sun, and eagerly expecting more heat and light when his father shall throw open the casement.

Nothing can be lovelier or more impressive than the death-bed of Perthes. A late excellent divine did not gain his ardent wish to die slowly, and 'know all about death.' Perthes, if he had ever had such a desire, was gratified in it. He tasted the cup slowly. He saw the enemy so long and so near that he ceased to fear him, and lay in serene state, expecting the conclusive blow. We have heard of, but never seen,

'The bed
Of sin delirious with its dread.'

We have seen the spirit in pain, eager to be away, writhing out of its earthly tenement, and stretching up the hand impatiently toward the coming glory. But there was no impatient haste about Perthes. He lay, even in anguish, calmly confronting and studying the great fact of death, knowing that it was the first and the last opportunity he had of seeing it, just as one passing through a rugged chasm of rocks and gloom darts his eye the more eagerly at it, that scenes of a very different kind—of beauty and summer flowers—are near, and already looming before his imagination. His expressions were full of faith, hope, submission, and love. For instance, he said, 'Thanks be to God, my faith is firm, and holds in death, as in life. For his dear Son's sake, God is merciful to me a sinner.' His dreams, which had been distressing, became delightful. He often prayed, and repeated hymns aloud. 'When he folded his cold hands, and prayed from his inmost soul,' writes his daughter, 'we, too, were constrained to fold our hands and pray; it was all so sublime, so blessed, we felt as though our Lord Jesus Christ were with us in the room. His last audible words were, "My Redeemer—Lord—forgiveness." It had now grown dark. When lights were brought in, a great change was visible in his features; every trace of pain was gone, his eyes shone, his whole aspect was, as it were, transfigured, so that those around him could only think of his bliss, not of their own sorrow. He drew one long, last breath; like a lightning flash, an expression of agony passed over his face, and then his triumph was complete. Immediately after death, a look of peace and joy settled on his face.' Thus passed away the meek, yet strong and elastic, spirit of one whom we may call, *par excellence, the* Christian Publisher.

We shall close with a few general remarks, written before we read Perthes, but containing, we are proud to say, some remarkable coincidences with his views.

Many and dark are the dangers which at present encompass Christianity. And yet there are several considerations which tend to alleviate somewhat the gloom. We are not to confound the battlements of Christianity with Christianity itself. These are often in reality the objects of assault, and while we are trembling for the foundations, the external buttresses alone may be in danger. Church establishments, for instance, are, in our judgment, only battlements, and not Christianity. Popery is another old and crazy battlement; its splendour just the ghastly lustre which shone in ancient houses infected with leprosy; it is not Christianity, and the sooner it falls the better. Even our creeds, excellent and, in the main, true as they are; even our ecclesiastical organisations, powerful as they still seem; even our pulpits, great as is the good they still do; even the office of the Ministry, honoured, and deservedly honoured, as it still is, are not identical with Christianity. Christianity is independent of them; and though they were all ignored to-morrow, she would remain intact—her doctrines, her facts, her text-book, her spirit, her blessed hope, would still survive, for they belong to the Imperishable, the Infinite, and the Divine.

Let us remember the recuperative and elastic vigour of Christianity. It is the child of the tempest, the nursling of the storm. What jeopardies it has surmounted already! It survived the fierce reaction of Paganism against it, produced by the genius and energy of Julian the Apostate. It survived the long nightmare of Popery; at the era of the Reformation, the vigour of Christianity returned, it threw off the accursed load,

and breathed free again. Two hundred years later it encountered the crude science and materialistic philosophy which had been collecting their sweltered venom during the whole eighteenth century, and which at last, through the mouth of the French Revolution, vomited it out, mingled with fire and blood, upon the nations. This tremendous assault, too, Christianity repelled, and came out from the struggle crying, 'Some of the artificial ornaments and needless props, which men had lent me, I have dropped; but I have lost nothing of my true virtue, vigour, or glory.' And if any one tells us that it is now for the first time to lose its elasticity, to be shorn, like Samson, of its giant locks, to become weak as other systems; nay, as some of its adversaries tell us, to be reduced to the mere serf of science, and to grind in the dungeon instead of ruling in the house—we reply, No! Sooner than submit to such a destiny, it shall rather, like Samson, bring down the pillars of the house, and let 'Darkness be the burier of the dead.' '*Heaven and earth*,' said its Founder, '*may pass away, but my words* cannot pass away.'

Let us rather rejoice in the present severe sifting of the character, claims, and evidences of Christianity, satisfied that it must issue in good. Let us ever distinguish between things and mere circumstances or words. Christianity is one thing, be it said again, and churches are another. Christianity is one thing, and creeds are another. Christianity is one thing, and even the best of its schemes and the strongest of its external defences are another. And the time may be come when God in his providence is to strike all these crutches, one after the other, away; to stamp age and decrepitude upon them all; to strip, as it were, our religion to its native power and simplicity, and not till it be thus stripped shall it be able, like a strong athlete, to gain the race; and not till it be reduced to its primeval elements will God probably aid the Christian faith in the same extraordinary way in which he aided it at first. We say, fearlessly, let the sifting go on. Things may require to be worse ere they are better. Let intellectual men continue to flock away, as, alas! they are flocking away, from our churches. Let philosophers in their secret conclaves take the untruth of Christianity for granted; let politicians treat it simply as an earthly fact and a matter of mere policy; let

misled and unhappy men of genius rave at it as an 'old Jew-lamp that has gone out;' let even friendly critics of the evidences find them only problematical: all this might have been expected, all this had been foretold, all this is rather to be desired, all this never touches the real merits of the Christian case, nor affects the verdict which man's heart and conscience have long ago returned in favour of real Christianity; all this, even while thinning our professed ranks, ought to intensify the zeal, hope, and activity of those that remain; and all this may bring on a crisis, when men in their misery and darkness, sick of mere science and philosophy, shall return to Christianity again, and say to a Saviour whom they had rejected, but who was still waiting at the wayside, with the lamp unquenched in his hand, 'Lord, to whom can we go but unto thee? Thou only hast the words of everlasting life.'

A friend of Perthes writes him, and he homologates the following sentences:— 'It is well to study and systematise our faith; but it is incapable of demonstration by any theology. Science in theology is no match for Straussism. The *church will stand* for all that, *but theology will fall*.' Perthes himself says, 'It was through the consciousness of sin, in the forms of sensuality and pride, that I came to recognise my need of redemption, and the truth of God's revelation in Christ. Whoever disdains this way will wander through speculation and mystic symbolism to Pantheism, if he be intellectual. You say the church has need of science. I doubt if any one was ever led through science to faith till his very bones and marrow quivered under this question, "O wretched man that thou art! who shall deliver thee from the body of this death?"'

We close this article by strongly recommending these volumes to every one that sympathises with the history of the German mind; to all who admire characters where high intellect is surmounted and sanctified by a still loftier moral nature; and to all who delight to study the life and the death of a meek and humble disciple of Jesus Christ.

POETS AND POETRY OF GERMANY.*

THESE volumes will be found highly serviceable as a succinct review of the poetical literature of Germany from the earliest times. Mme. de Pontès has evidently bestowed pains on her work, and endeavoured to make it as complete as her plan will allow. In her Preface she explicitly disavows any pretensions to give "a complete history of the poets and poetry of Germany;" but she is conscious of a right to claim—and her claim she modestly enforces—a long and intimate acquaintance with the literature of that land, and the credit of a conscientious study of the texts themselves. She is conversant, indeed, with the expositions of critics in this department, French and English as well as German; and makes frequent reference to such fellow-labourers as Villemain, and Guizot, and Magnin, and Philarète Chasles, and Aug. Thierry; Carlyle, and Hallam, and Bulwer Lytton, and Lewes; the Schlegels, and Grimm, and Villmar, and Prutz, and Gervinus, and Menzel, and Franz Horn, and Getzler, and Hildbrand. But these she makes use of as aids only, and not as substitutes for independent personal research. She is careful to cite "secondary sources" whenever they are consulted. Her method is, like that of Villemain in his celebrated Cours, to connect literary investigations by an historical thread, hoping by this means to throw "a certain interest over a subject often dry and tedious in itself, and yet of great importance in the annals of the human mind." She also enters somewhat freely into the domains of legendary lore, because legend and tradition play so important a part in Teutonic annals. After tracing the analogy between the mythology of the North and that of the East, and discussing the identity of that of Germany and Scandinavia—thence proceeding to note the translation of the Bible by Ulphilas, and giving a brief historical résumé of the state of the Vaterland from the fourth to the ninth century, —Mme. de Pontès enters with some detail into the subject-matter and manifold merits of the Niebelungen-lied, that series of lays, about the origin or genesis of which the learned are as much at loggerheads, as they are about the personality of Homer, and the unity of the Iliad. With the Iliad, indeed, enthusiastic Germans are ready to compare the Niebelungen at all points—a comparison scouted by our authoress as "simply absurd," though she is free to express her doubt if any of Homer's heroes, even Hector himself—(of Achilles she speaks as disrespectfully as Horace did)—inspires one with such mingled pity and admiration as the gallant Siegfried, so generous, so single-hearted, and so ill-starred in his doom. The nun Hroswitha, a young nursing mother to the young drama of the tenth century, has her place of honour in these pages. And then, over barren ground enough, and waste, wide-spreading moorland, we come upon the Minnesingers, and catch a far-borne strain of Walter von der Vogelweide, at once vigorous and graceful, tender and energetic. Due notice is taken of the "Tristan and Ysolde" of Godfried von Strasburg, which "attracts the reader by the charm of its images, and the interest attached to the actors, despite its enormous length and its very questionable morality." Then we come to the Alexander-lied and the Roland-lied and their congeners—followed by the decline of romantic poetry, for with the extinction of the Hohenstaufen dynasty, the golden age of chivalric verse may be said to have passed away. Commerce threatens to stifle song. But when things are looking at the worst, up rise the Meistersängers, whose "institution" lasted throughout the calamities of the Thirty Years' War,—nay, was formally closed not twenty years since. Mme. de Pontès bestows a chapter on the rise and progress of the drama, and gives the mediæval devil his due. Reynard the Fox she shows up in his proper colours. And anon we find ourselves in Reformation times, and are treated to an ample review of the life, adventures, and poetry of Ulrich von Hutten—though we do not see that Dr. Strauss's recent biography has been put under contribution, which surely, and with profit, it might. Then ensues the dismal era of the Peasant War. Hans Sachs, however, pipes on, profusely enough —and has it all to himself. With a collation of the legends of Dr. Faust, the authoress concludes the First Part of this work, the romance and poetry of the Middle Ages.

Her Second Part opens with a description of the slow and gradual revival of Poetry, after the paralysing effects of the Thirty Years' War. But it is rather with poetasters than poets that we have to do: Martin Opitz, whose whole career was "one continued series of triumphs"— some say, of truckling and time-serving (which may possibly come to the same thing); Paul Fleming, of the same school, but on a higher bench in it,—hymns of his still being sung in the churches of Germany, and still thought worthy of praise for their warmth, feeling, and sweetness of versification; Andreas Gryphius, who also wrote popular hymns, and composed historical tragedies of a bombastic sort, and comedies in which the comic element seems to have been left out, or has evaporated with time—for they are two centuries old. The eighteenth century brings us to Gottsched—once the dictator in effect of German literature, and whom even Frederick the Great permitted to spout verses in his royal hearing. His antagonist, Bodmer of Zurich, is sure of respectful consideration and interest in England, if only for his sympathy with our classics, and the zeal with which he made them known, and tried to make them dear, to that rather stolid and prosaic generation. Kestner, the once pungent epigrammatist (but then epigrams again are not warranted to keep); smooth, stiff, "studied" Professor Ramler (among German poets there seem no end of Professors), actually honoured of yore as the German Horace (Horace is lively as ever, after eighteen centuries; Ramler, after one, is dead as a door-nail); the sprightly Hagedorn, who imitated La Fontaine; Haller, a pattern of propriety, but no poet at all; cheery, chirping old Father Gleim, who passionately espoused the cause of Fritz against Maria Theresa, but to whose urgent pleadings for the "protection" of literature three Prussian kings in succession were as indifferent as, we suppose, Mr. Buckle himself could wish; mild, sweet-tempered Gellert, rich in good works, among which we can scarcely account his poems the best; and Gessner, whose Idyls were for a while the rage in France—to whom the Duchess of Choiseul sent invitations, and Denis Diderot paid compliments;—of all these, and others, Mme. de Pontès discourses in terms that equal their deserts. Klopstock stands out imposingly at the entrance of Vol. II.,—a poet of whom Menzel has said, that, regarded at a distance and as a whole, he "stands forth in bold relief," but melts away in thin vapour if we approach him too nearly. His admirers institute comparisons between him and Homer, Dante, and Milton—comparisons which are judiciously disposed of in the present work, and shown to be naught. Lessing is placed in striking contrast with him, "inferior in all poetical attributes, but immeasurably superior in variety of powers, vigour of intellect, and sound critical acumen." The biographical sketch of this largely gifted critic, of whom Gervinus is bold to affirm that he knew man, and life in all its varied forms, better even than Goethe himself,—is one of the most interesting and carefully compiled, in the collection before us, though we are far from thinking it the happiest in a critical point of view. In the case of Wieland, Mme. de Pontès finds it amusing enough, as she naturally may—yet with pity intermixed—to compare the works of his youth, breathing religious aspirations that border on the fanatical,—when he was the guest of Bodmer, as Klopstock had been before him, in that fine old gentleman's charming retreat beside the Lake of Zurich,—with those of his later life,

* Poets and Poetry of Germany. Biographical and Critical Notices. By Madame L. Davésiés de Pontès, Translator of "Egmont," "The Niebelungen Treasure," &c. In Two Vols. London: Chapman and Hall. 1858.

when a reaction had set in, and a sensual epicureanism, with plenty of French polish, was the philosophy of the sometime pietist, Christopher Martin Wieland. In his "Agathon" she censures the "cold material philosophy fatal to every pure and lofty impulse," and the licence of the descriptions, "which even the nature of his subject cannot justify." She noway shares in Goethe's admiration for his "Musarion"—the theme of which "possesses no very absorbing interest, and the moral is anything but commendable." The following is a brief specimen of her translated extracts from this admired poem—too brief, perhaps, to answer the purpose, but all we can make room for: it has at least the advantage of being its own interpreter:

> Yes, false and fleeting as the wind, are all
> Friendship's fond vows, and love's deceitful smile.
> Soon as the golden showers no longer fall,
> Cold is the heart that lures us with its wile.
> Soon as the goblet's dry, in vain we call
> On our Patroclus! Yes; that metal vile
> Is stronger still than virtue, wit, or beauty.
> That gone—the swarm goes too, and Laïs talks of duty.

Herder, like Lessing, was both poet and critic, but perhaps in inverse proportion—or rather, there was a stronger infusion of the poetical element in his critical faculty, than in that of Lessing. In opposition to depreciating allusions to Herder, personally, by Goethe's English biographer, Mme. de Pontès contrasts the former—poor, dependent on his own exertions, yet as soon as prudence permitted, at the very moment when his brightening fortunes might have assured him a more suitable alliance, wedding a portionless girl, and giving up all the enjoyments of life, and welcoming all its trials, to provide for the wants of a numerous family—with Goethe, "breaking one after the other the most solemn engagements, sacrificing the peace and happiness of the innocent girls, whose hearts he had taken such pains to win, rather than renounce one luxury, than run the risk of committing an infidelity to his genius." But she does not attempt to deny that a certain restless irritability was inherent in Herder's nature, that it increased with his years, and alienated many of his best friends. "Like Lessing, though from very different causes, he was seldom contented." As for his verses, in them he was far less of a poet than when he wrote prose. Perhaps, indeed, it is against rule to give him a chapter, especially so long a one, in a book on German Poets: but, says Jean Paul in his "Æsthetics," if Herder was not a poet, as he often declared, he was something better; he was himself a poem, wherein the good, the true, and the beautiful were inseparably blended.

Schubart is the next on the list—a profligate whose early career might qualify him to be bracketed with Edgar Allan Poe. A very full account is given of the troubles he brought on his family and himself—of his long and cruel imprisonments, and the terrible mental sufferings he endured. Seldom has solitary confinement been described in gloomier colours than by him, into whose soul its bitterness entered like a mortal venom, as it is. But it made a sadder and a wiser man of him, unless to become a pious mystic be what Carlyle calls "unwisdom." Affectionate apologists have sought to exculpate his memory from many of the charges to which he himself pleads guilty, by ascribing his self-accusations to the workings

of a morbidly excited fancy, tormented by solitude, and by the books of mystic devotion with which alone he was permitted to beguile the weary hours. Be this as it may, "one thing is certain; despite all his faults and follies, Schubart had many and ardent friends, and his wife, who so deeply suffered from his excesses, never ceased to adore him." Of his poetical talent, his present biographer allows that he had neither sustained elevation of thought nor strong creative powers, that he is always unequal, sometimes coarse and repulsive; but his imagination, she adds, is fervent and glowing, his verses so harmonious that the greater part have been set to music, his descriptions of nature true and beautiful, and in many of his lays she finds bursts of enthusiasm, with gushes of tenderness and pathos beyond the strain of art.

We come next to J. H. Voss, whose unflagging industry, untiring perseverance, and steadfast will, make him a signal contrast to that restless, impulsive "ne'er do weel," Schubart. Voss was a sort of Southey in his home life; rich in household affections, but allowing neither "domestic endearments nor social pleasures to interfere with the routine" of his studious hours. As a "poet," his original and translated verses show him to have had little of the vision and the faculty divine. Mme. de Pontès does justice, however, to his "Luise," the touching naïveté of some of its descriptions making amends for its often tediously minute details. Her version of one extract from it, not being rendered in hexameters, entirely alters the character of the idyl—the best translation of it with which we are acquainted, appeared in *Fraser's Magazine* some ten years ago, and was really charming as far as it went. The hexameters, deservedly for once, were part and parcel of the charm. But both on principle and in practice, the dislike Mme. de Pontès has for hexameters is ladylike and complete.

Frederick Stolberg is praised for his ballads, which had a warmth, feeling, sweetness, and simplicity, that made them lastingly popular; Hölty, for his passionate love of Nature in all her forms, and the melody with which he gave it expression; Bürger for his fervour of imagination, and often solemn pathos, though his compositions are not unfrequently coarse and vulgar; Tieck follows, on the score of his vaguely-tinted lyrics, now and then marked by a "spirituality and earnestness which have a peculiar charm;" then Novalis, whose sacred poems, in their "beautiful and unadorned simplicity and deep fervour," offer a singular contrast to his other works; and besides these we have La Motte Fouqué, and short-lived Schulze, and melancholy-mad Hölderlin, and Chamisso, and Matthison, picturesque in "still-life," and gentle Salis, and patriotic Körner. A chapter is devoted to the dramatic successors of Lessing—to Kotzebue, Iffland, Müllner, and Werner—and another to the modern Romanticists, Henry von Kleist, Raupach, and Grillparzer. Goethe and Schiller have no place in this collection, for there is no room for them. Many a minor star, too, is omitted. Should these volumes, however, "meet with any degree of favour," we are promised a supplementary one, which, together with sketches from the lives of Goethe and Schiller, will comprehend those of the modern school, Uhland, Rückert, Freiligrath, and others. We can hardly be wrong in bidding Mme. de Pontès hasten on her work, assured of the fulfilment of the one condition to its appearance.

GERMAN LITERATURE.

1. *Poets and Poetry of Germany; Biographical and Critical Notices.* By MADAME L. DAVESIES DE PONTÈS. 2 vols. London: Chapman & Hall, 1858.

2. *History of German Literature; based on the German Work of Vilmar.* By the Rev. F. METCALFE, M.A. London: Longmans, 1858.

3. *The German Classics, from the Fourth to the Nineteenth Century; a German Reading-Book, containing Extracts arranged Chronologically; with Biographical Notices, Translations, and Notes.* By MAX MÜLLER, M.A., Ph.D. London: Longmans, 1858.

OF all the debts which the present generation owes to Mr. Carlyle, his promotion of the study of German literature is perhaps the one whose value the generality of men would be the least disposed to question. Whatever may be the worth of his political and ethical speculations, and however injurious may be the influence which the peculiarities of his style have exercised upon many of his contemporaries, there are, doubtless, numerous persons to whom, but for his writings, Goethe and Schiller, Lessing and Richter, would have remained unknown or disregarded. He has thrown all his energy into the task of justifying his sincere admiration, and has introduced the English public, so neglectful of all foreign excellence which is not strenuously forced on its attention, to a world of beauty and sublimity, in a great degree alien to their previous habits of thought and feeling, yet sufficiently related to them in its fundamental characteristics, to testify to its common origin with our own, and to awake the sympathies of all whom insular prejudice has not restricted to the narrow limits of a purely national literature.

But those who have accepted Mr. Carlyle's guidance to this new and unfamiliar region, have in many instances failed to follow the clue with which he supplied them. They have held on, so to speak, to his skirts, and have pursued the vein of discovery no further than the specimens he had pointed out to lure them onwards. He has brought them his report of the fruitful land; but they have eaten of the grapes of Joshua, without pressing on to the vineyards of Eshcol. They have confined their acquaintance with German literature to its later and more important productions, which, however well worthy of attention in themselves as completed works—as exercises on certain themes, never before so well expressed—cannot be fully appreciated without some reference to that which preceded them, and of which they were the produce and development. It is interesting to read *Wallenstein*, or *Hermann and Dorothea*, even when they are regarded entirely apart from any relation to previous attempts by less finished artists—it is far more interesting to observe how ruder experiments prepared the way for them; on the one hand, by forming a basis on which future writers might work;

on the other, by educating the minds of their audience for the appreciation of something better. To read the isolated poems, is like having a nosegay of cut blossoms; to study them in their relative position, is like watching the growth of a plant, which, after putting forth leaf after leaf, as apparently unsuccessful trials, at length fulfils the law of its being, by the production of the perfect flower.

The three books before us are calculated not only to supply the wants of those who demand a guide through the dense Black Forest of German literature, but also probably to awaken a desire of exploring its recesses in those who have never yet thought of penetrating the region at all. Each has great merit, but we should not be disposed to recommend either exclusively, because neither alone affords a perfectly complete description of the subject from all points of view. Each, however, is admirably well adapted to supply the deficiencies of the other; and together they would furnish quite as much information as the great majority of readers wish for, or have time to acquire, on any matter which they do not intend to make an object of special and exclusive study. The work of Mr. Metcalfe is an abridgment of the much more elaborate history by Vilmar, and the expression " based upon " hardly expresses enough of the obligation under which the English writer has lain to his German authority. Mr. Metcalfe has followed the order, method, and divisions of Vilmar, and, so far as we can perceive, has also adhered to his views in every particular. He is probably right in thinking that an exact translation of his author would have been found unreadable by the English public; and as all who have followed the Fellow of Lincoln in his adaptations of *Gallus* and *Charicles*, and his excursions into the happy Hyperborean hunting-grounds which he has lately patronized, will be aware that, whatever may be his faults, dulness, tediousness, and obscurity are not to be reckoned among them. His book is certainly readable enough in gene-

ral, though the very compressed nature of his information reduces it occasionally to little more than a catalogue of names and dates; but, though far short of perfection in style, he is not without freedom and power in those portions where he has had an inspiriting subject to deal with.

Mr. Metcalfe's—or rather Vilmar's—plan, though comprehensive enough, does not profess to be exhaustive, but confines itself to those works alone which seem most faithfully to reflect the national characteristics of Germany. Its details will be best understood by the following extract from the preface :—

Vilmar divides his history into three periods :—
I. The Oldest Period.
II. The Old Period.
III. The New Period.

The First of these Periods he makes to commence at the middle of the fourth century, and go down to the year 1150. During this period occurred the struggle between Heathenism and Christianity.

The Second Period reaches from 1150 to 1624. During this period we see German Nationalism amalgamated with Christianity into one harmonious whole.

This Period is classed by the author under the following subdivisions :—

1. The Period of Preparation, 1150—1190.

2. The Classical Period, or Period of National Epic and the Minnesingers, 1190—1300, when German literature reached its zenith.

3. The Period of the decay and decadence of Poetry, 1300—1517 (about); the period when the Reformation may be said to have commenced.

4. The Period of the struggle between the new ideas and the old notions, when foreign culture was ousting national culture, 1517—1624.

The New Period begins in 1624, when German Christian elements were now thoroughly interpenetrated and amalgamated with foreign elements.

To this Period he also assigns a threefold subdivision :—

1. The Period when the foreign domineered over the domestic; the age of learned poetry, 1624—1720, i. e., from Opitz to the first appearance of Bodmer.

2. The preparation of a new state of independence, 1720—1760.

3. The Second Classical Period, beginning with Klopstock, and ending 22nd March 1832, the day of Goethe's death.

The reading-book arranged by Professor Müller is an excellent companion for either of the other works. It has grown, he tells us, out of his Oxford lectures, in which he has been in the habit of furnishing to his class specimens of the writers mentioned by him, from the earliest times to the present century. It begins with Ulphilas, who translated the gospels between A.D. 360 and 380 ; and the subsequent extracts carry us on through the various changes of the language till it assumed its present flexible form. To the poems which are written in the obsolete dialects, a translation in modern German is appended in parallel columns; and nothing is wanting, in the way of introductions and short biographical notices, which can promote the convenience of the reader. The book is printed in the ordinary English, not in the German character—a practice which appears to be gaining ground, though we have as yet hardly been able to accustom ourselves to the look of it.

The work of Madame de Pontès is, in many respects, a great contrast to that of Mr. Metcalfe. The latter confines himself almost entirely to the literary and critical view of his subject, touching either slightly or not at all on the lives of his authors—the former has evidently expended much trouble on the biographical part of her task; and even those who care little about the literature, will nevertheless find a good deal of interest in her lively and graceful narrative of the successes and reverses, the social and domestic history, of so many remarkable men. Both the merits and defects of the book are such as we should expect from the sex of the writer. There is a copious selection of personal adventure and detail, a full account of all the love-affairs of the German poets which can any how be ascertained, and a genial appreciation of their labours, without any thing in the least degree partaking of a " gushing " character. At the same time, the book is somewhat deficient in those qualities of order and arrangement which are necessary to constitute a thoroughly good book of reference, as well as one agreeable to read. The table of contents is meagre, the various schools are not discriminated with sufficient prominence, and the want of an index is severely felt. Madame de Pontès would certainly have produced a more complete and serviceable book if she had added a few dates in the margin, or elsewhere, to let us know from time to time what century we are dealing with. Following, apparently, the arrangement of Vilmar, she describes the Nibelungen series of Sagas under the head of the ninth century, because in their primitive form they undoubtedly belonged to that period. But it was in the twelfth century that they were committed to writing in the shape in which they have descended to us, and therefore formed part of the literature of that age; yet in the chapter which follows we find nothing to show this, except a statement that chronological order has been disregarded. In the beginning of Chap. IV. Vol. I., we are told that the Nibelungen Lay " far surpasses any other poetical production of the same period." But, as we have seen, it was not a " production " of that period at all, in the sense in which it can be said to " surpass " others. We might as well say that the poems of Homer surpassed others belonging to the period of the Trojan war. If we cannot tell what the original form of the Nibelungen was, we surely cannot tell whether it surpassed others or not. What " period," too, the authoress refers to, is only to be gathered from a comparison of two or three other passages in the preceding chapter. However, we have no similar instance of confusion to report in the remainder of the book, though the absence of continuous dates is certainly a serious defect.

Both Mr. Metcalfe's and Madame de Pontès's volumes are remarkable for their copious and exact notices of the early German poetry. In this respect they are much superior to any other account of the subject we possess. How meagre was our information on these matters up to the period of Menzel and the Schlegels, may be seen from a glance at " Berington's Literary History of the Middle Ages," a work which has had a standard reputation, and was long regarded as an exhaustive authority on all the subjects of which it treated. Yet there the subject of German poetry is hardly noticed at all, and there is no mention of the Sagas or of the Minnesingers, who flourished at a later period.

Madame de Pontès commences her work by an interesting chapter, in which she points out the analogy between Northern, Eastern, and Classical mythology—their derivation from the East, and such resemblances as may be perceived between Thor and Hercules, Balder and Apollo, Loki and Siva, Wayland Smith, Vulcan, and Dædalus, Hertha and Ceres; and proceeds to show the identity of the mythology of the Edda with that of Germany. In both are found gnomes, dwarfs, and cobbolds (or spirits who do household work for the sake of a little food, a sort of useful Penates), as well as elves, who, however, are not identical with the elves of Chaucer and Shakspeare.

The first great monument of the ancient German language is the Edda; the second is the translation of the Scriptures by Ulphilas, Bishop of the Visigoths, A.D. 380; for four hundred years after which date no trace of literature can be discovered. Fighting was going on at all times and seasons, and the monks took care to destroy every thing which had any tendency to perpetuate Paganism. The ravages of Alaric, Attila, and Genseric succeeded, and every vestige of learning and literature not then swept away, perished in the Lombard conquest.

That through these ages of darkness, rapine, and barbarism, Germany preserved any traces of literature or poetry, can only be accounted for by her strong nationality, and the repugnance she had always shown to the adoption of the language of her former conquerors. The cities that studded the banks of the Rhine and the Danube, the names of which betray even now their Roman origin, were little more than military colonies, infusing into the subject population hardly any tincture of civil accomplishment. After the Bible of Ulphilas, the two most ancient relics of the German language are the " Weisbrunnen Gebet " and the " Hildebrand Lied." These are written in Low German and in alliterative verse, the substitute till the ninth century for rhyme. The latter is a specimen of the traditions out of which was woven the " Nibelungen Lay," the Iliad of German heroic poetry. There are two other relics of ancient Teutonic song; but one of these, " Walter of Aquitaine," is written in Latin—the other, " Beowulf," in Anglo-Saxon; so that they can hardly be classed as belonging to German poetry, especially as the former is also claimed by France, Spain, and Italy.

It had long been supposed that the ancient heroic poetry was the creation of a regular school of bards. Mr. Metcalfe points out that there never was any such school; but that there were strolling minstrels who, like Homer, went about and embodied popular traditions, being merely the channel of that which already existed.

These poems fall into three classes, according as the poem describes the exploits of a set of heroes, of one principal hero, or adventures supplementary to both. The " Nibelungen " would be an example of the former; of the latter is the " Gudrune," a legend not so well known, but nearly as beautiful, containing 4700 verses, and describing the capture and ultimate rescue of the fair maiden from whom it is named. They are also arranged by Vilmar in six series or sets, 1. Lower Rhenish, relating to Siegfried; 2. Burgundian, relating to Chrimhild and her family; 3. East-Gothic, relating to Dietrich or Theodoric of Verona; 4. belonging to Etzel or Attila, king of the Huns; 5. North German, of which the scene is laid in Friesland ("Gudrune" belongs to this series); 6. Lombardic, the most modern of all, and relating to king Ortnit of the Lago di Garda, and his son. The cycle of Theodoric, which is full of adventures of giants and captive princesses, as constitute our regular idea of romance, contains a poem, the "Rosengarten," from which, possibly, Tennyson may have derived some hints for that part of his "Princess" where the tournament is described.

The epoch to which these poems in their primitive form belonged, was succeeded by that of Charlemagne, who ordered the German language to be taught in all the schools of the empire, and a collection to be made of the old heroic Lays.

The most important relic of this period is the "Ludwigs Lied," composed by Herschell to celebrate the victory won by Lewis over the Normans at Saulcourt. To this class of poems arose an antagonist in Christianity, to which the half-heathen mythology, with its demigods, heroes, transformations, incantations, and the like, was wholly repugnant. Lewis the Pious would not even read the collection of songs which his father had brought together; and these heroic ballads fell gradually into disuse, and only survived among the lower classes. They were replaced by a class of sacred poems, of which the Harmonies of the Gospels, in an epic and in a more modern form, are the most remarkable specimens. The one composed by Otfrid in the ninth century, is noticeable as marking the period at which alliteration was disused and rhyme adopted.

During the tenth and eleventh centuries, German poetry may be said to have been in a state of transition. The legend of Duke Ernest mingles the half-historical tone of the earlier Lays with the romantic colouring of the ages of chivalry; and it is here that we first meet with the comic element of romantic song, in the adventure of dwarfs and giants, like those which are found in Ariosto. The author of Duke Ernest was evidently acquainted with the *Odyssey*, and with some of the old geographical authors. In the "Ortnit Lied" we meet with eggs that turn into dragons; and a story which, unlike most romances, "ends ill," the hero being devoured by the said dragons in a truly awful manner.

At this point we quit what has been termed "National Poetry," and pass on to the "Art Epic." Here new and far different influences become perceptible in German poetry. Christianity had succeeded in thoroughly penetrating the spirit of the people, and the Church had become all in all. On this condition of the national mind supervened the Crusades, and the spirit which prompted those expeditions is poetically expressed in the Lays of the twelfth and thirteenth centuries, dealing with subjects like those with which our own romances of the Round Table have made us familiar. The Art Epics—says Mr. Metcalfe (p. 107)—

though inferior to the great national epics in simplicity and grandeur, are often conspicuous for noble ideas and beauty of diction. The first group is devoted to the French Sagas of Charlemagne. Of these our attention will be confined to the "Rolands Lied," and "Wilhelm von Oranse." The second group comprehends the saga of "Der Heilige Gral" (connected with that of Artus); the "Parcival" by Wolfram von Eschenbach, "Titurel," and "Lohengrin." In the third group we have the Celtic tradition of King Artus and the knights of his round table; "Tristan and Isolt," by Gottfried of Strasburg; "Erec and Iwein," by Hartman von der Aue; "Wigalois," by Wernt of Grafenberg, with a mass of other poems. The fourth group consists of elaborations of antique poems and sagas; such, for instance, as the story of the Trojan war, which appeared in a multiplicity of shapes; that of "Æneas," after Virgil, by Heinrich von Veldekin, the father of Middle High-German poetry; and of "Alexander the Great." In the fifth group we have the legends of saints; then the chronicles and historic poems; and, lastly, the smaller tales.

The first three groups, viz., the "Legend of Charlemagne," of the "Gral," and "King Artus," are generally classed under the head of Romantic poetry, although, strictly speaking, this appellation belongs only to the "Charlemagne."

The Sagas about Charlemagne are almost exclusively represented, as far as Germany is concerned, by the "Rolands Lied," which describes Charlemagne as the mighty champion of Christendom against the Moors, and the fatal fight at Roncesvalles, followed by the Emperor's signal vengeance against his Paynim foes. But the most conspicuous, and to English readers the most interesting, series of legends are those relating to the "Quest of the Sangreal," from their connection with our own King Arthur. Madame de Pontès seems to derive the word Sangreal from "sang-real," as if = the "real blood" of Christ; but the more usual meaning of the expression is "saint graal," or sacred vessel, in which had been contained the wine used at the Last Supper, and for the reception of which Joseph of Arimathea built a castle in Britain. Another version states that the host was brought down from heaven every Friday by a white dove, and placed in a precious emerald vase in the custody of guardians, who are apparently identified with the

Templars, then first instituted. The vase itself is said to have afterwards come into the possession of the Genoese, and was conveyed to Paris in 1798. The legend itself was introduced into German poetry by Wolfram von Eschenbach.

In the sequel to one of these stories, we find an anticipation of the printing variety of the electric telegraph :—

In her anguish, she bethinks her of the renowned King Arthur and his paladins, and seizing a golden bell, which has the magic property of being heard at the distance of thousands of miles, she rings it with such force that the sound reaches the court of the sovereign, while, at the same moment, an inscription suddenly starts up on the table at which he is seated, informing him of the lady's distress.—*Pontès*, i. 241.

But the most charming, though not the most moral, of this cycle of legends, is the "Tristan and Ysolde," known to many of our readers by Mr. Matthew Arnold's exquisite version, and originally composed by Godfried von Strasburg, but continued by two other authors. Another of these legends goes wildly off into the adventures of Alexander the Great, in whose story were gathered up all the experiences, both in fact and imagination, which the Crusaders had acquired in the East. The heterogeneous nature of the materials may be estimated from the fact, that it contains (*inter alia*) a duel with Porus, a letter to Aristotle, and the following pretty adventure :—

Alexander comes with his forces into a dark wood, the lofty trees of which intertwine their branches so as to exclude the sun's rays. Fresh limpid rivulets run from the wood down into the valley. Sweet songs of birds sound through the foliage, and are re-echoed from the wooded shade. The ground is covered with an incalculable multitude of unopened flowers of marvellous size. The blossoms, which look like great globes, are tinted with rose-colour and snow-white; suddenly they open, and from each perfumed chalice issues a maiden of wondrous beauty. The thousand little lovely creatures then raise a melodious strain, vying with the song of the birds; and thus they float, singing and dancing in the cool shade of the forest. The children of the green shade and noiseless solitude are pink and white, like the flowers whence they spring. But the sun's scorching ray falls upon them, they fade and die; like the flowers which May calls into life, and Autumn to death.—*Metcalfe*, p. 146.

Madame de Pontès (i. 264) furnishes an elegant translation of the same poem, from which we give an extract :—

Now would ye learn whence came the maids
Thus sporting 'neath the forest shades?,
So soon as winter's icy sway
To summer's rosy touch gives way,
When all is fresh and bright and fair,
And lovely blossoms every where
Begin to deck the world anew;
Then up spring flowers of fairy hue,
Of gorgeous crimson, snowy white,
Glowing with pure and dazzling light!
 *   *   *   *

537

Round as a ball, these summer posies;
And, when the flower its leaves uncloses,
To wondering eyes is then reveal'd,
A living maid therein conceal'd
In all her charms, scarce twelve years old.
I tell you, as to me 'twas told;
I saw them in their beauty rare,
So gentle, maidenly, and fair!
Never in women have I seen
A fairer face, a softer mien:
Then, they were innocently gay,
And, so enchanting was their lay,
That never yet has human ear
Heard accents such as they breathed here:
Yet, strange to tell, these beauteous maids
Can live but in the greenwood shades!
If once the sun's unclouded ray
Should strike them, wither'd they would lay.
Three months with these fair beings we pass'd;
Why could not bliss so heavenly last?

In pursuing the history of German literature, we must by no means omit one class of poems which is quite peculiar to Germany, and the quaint humorousness of which is thoroughly redolent of the German mind. This is the *Thier-saga* or "Beast-epic," expressing the passions and characters of animals in a connected story, and taking its origin probably from the old hunting stories, mixed up with a sort of animal mythology. The species is best known to us by the story of "Reynard the Fox;" but that poem is not a true specimen of the class, which originally had nothing didactic or satiric about it, but was as sincere and straightforward in its meaning as the heroic legends themselves.

The root of this Saga lies in the harmless natural simplicity of a primeval people. We see described the delight which the rude child of nature takes in the animals—in their slim forms, their gleaming eyes, their fierceness, nimbleness, and cunning. Such Sagas, illustrative of the ways and doings of the beasts, would naturally have their origin in an age when the ideas of the shepherd and the hunter occupied a great portion of the intellectual horizon of the people; when the herdsman saw in the ravenous bear one who was his equal, and more than his equal, in force and adroitness, the champion of the woods and wilds; when the hunter, in his lonely ramble through the depths of the forest, beheld in the hoary wolf and red fox, as they stole along, hunters like himself—mates, so to say, and companions, and whom he therefore addressed as such. But there was another reason why herdsman and hunter wished to be on a good footing with these denizens of the solitudes. It was not so much the physical violence of these beasts that they dreaded, as the invisible demon within them: that demon which glared out so terribly from the eyes of the wolf, and exercised such a supernatural power. So that these animals came to be looked on as an incorporation of the dark powers of nature. Hence it was that the herdsman would call the wolf by any name but its own. The wolf was gold-foot, the fox blue-foot. In Hessia the wolf was called Hölzing, i. e., the creature of the wood, while in other parts of Germany his name was disguised under *wul* or *wulch*, instead of plain wolf.—*Metcalfe*, p. 184.

It is curious to observe that, in the hierarchy of the forest, the *bear* was originally king.

After the Saga had been transplanted to France and restored again to Germany, the lion dispossessed him. The epic name of the he-wolf was Isengrim (iron-grim, or sharp-biting); of the she-wolf Hersuintha (swift to fight); of the fox, Reginhart (the prudent counsellor—hence our *Reynard*); of the bear, Bruno (brown, whence *Bruin*); of the cock—Chanteclêr, or Cantard, betraying the French influence; of the ass, Baldewin (jolly, *pococurante*—whence the Fr. *baudet*). After circulating in the mouths of the people for many centuries, this kind of poetry was first committed to writing in Latin in South Flanders at the end of the eleventh century. Satirical allusions soon began to appear in it; but it was not until the end of the fifteenth century that it became strongly tinctured with this spirit. The sixteenth century, which had a sharply satirical bent, took it for granted that it was a "mirror of court life," and this opinion has been commonly, but erroneously, received. The animal-*fable* is a distinct species of composition altogether.

In the twelfth century a new influence is perceptible in German literature. The minstrels of Provence had been attracted to the court of the Suabian emperors, after Frederick Barbarossa had been crowned in 1133. The wild epic grandeur of the northern Lays was exchanged for the artificial harmonies and delicate structure of the southern poetry. The Provençal Minnesingers reflected the impulse produced by the Crusades; but their German imitators, less martial in spirit than their models, expressed not national, but individual feelings—the sympathy of the mind with nature, the tenderness of womanly affection, and the devotedness of manly love. Vilmar remarks that the Minne-poetry, in its presumption of unalterable attachment on both sides, its modesty and reserve, and the generally high ideal which it conceived of love, is essentially different from the productions of the Troubadours, which are full of all the vagaries of vehement and reckless desire, and reflect the vicissitudes of ardent passion, such as its southern origin might lead us to expect. The age of the Hohenstaufen dynasty was the one in which the Minne-poetry chiefly flourished. As Madame de Pontès remarks—

The period of this dynasty forms, on the whole, the most brilliant in German annals. It is, in fact, the culminating epoch of the history of the middle ages, the moment in which the inhabitants of the north, while still retaining much of the fierce energies and hardy valour of their ancestors, became softened by the influence of a purer and loftier enthusiasm, and, losing the grossness and barbarism which had hitherto characterised them, adopted the tone of more favoured climes. This poetry, indeed, was such as might have been expected from the age to which it belonged—an age in which romance and reality were so closely en-

twined as to form the web and woof of life; when the warrior, his sword yet wet with the blood of the vanquished, went forth, harp in hand, to pour out his lay before his lady's bower, or in the tournay (the mimicry of noble war) to maintain the supremacy of her charms; when kings themselves did not disdain to practise " the gaie science," and the same hand that held the sceptre or wielded the battle-axe, delighted in striking the lute, the sole art, as we have already observed, held worthy a warrior and a knight.—*Pontès*, i. 204.

One of the most celebrated and spirited of the Minnesingers was Walter von der Vogelweide, born 1167, and died at Würtzburg in Bavaria:—

Here stands a tree, beneath whose shade he loved to wander harp in hand, amid whose branches nightingales were wont, it is said, to assemble, to listen to the sweet strains with which he would enliven his solitary rambles. In acknowledgment, perhaps, of these tokens of admiration, the poet bequeathed a legacy to the feathered warblers, ordering holes to be pierced in the stone that covered his remains, in which crumbs were to be daily strewed for their repast. For many years this bequest was punctually executed, and the nightingales evinced their gratitude by pouring forth their melody upon the tomb of their benefactor.—*Pontès*, i. 207.

Another celebrated Minnesinger—a truly characteristic specimen—albeit rather a caricature—of the class, is Ulrich Von Lichtenstein, who having heard, as a child, that it was "the correct thing" to be the faithful servant of some fair and noble lady, began betimes to carry out the lesson, by instituting his courtship of a princess at twelve years old. He was so unfortunate as to have *three* lips, a defect which he cured by getting one of them cut off. As this sacrifice did not mollify the object of his adoration, he mortified the flesh a little more. Having nearly lost a finger in maintaining the supremacy of his lady's charms in a tournament, so that it hung by a bit of skin, he cut it entirely off, and sent it to her in a green velvet box. The lady, on her marriage, wishing to get rid of her lover, had him thrown out of a window; but this treatment not proving sufficient to cool his ardour, she resorted to other means, which, from their extreme indignity, he has refused to hand down to posterity, but which at any rate proved efficacious. All this time the amorous gentleman was possessed of a wife and family of his own, and he relates his adventures at the ripe age of fifty-five.

The following is a specimen of his Lays, the grace and *naïveté* of which, however, is partly attributable to the translatress:—

Know ye the lady whom I seek,
  Have you seen her in dell or bower?
She is dainte, soft, and meek;
Blue her een, and red her cheek,
  And in her hand she holds a flower.

That flower it is the lily white,
  The emblem of her soul so pure;
Her hair is not with gems bedight,

538

Her girdle is not drawn too tight;
She never seeketh to allure.

I know her well;
As bees draw forth all hidden sweets,
E'en so she draws, with marvellous spell,
The closest secrets that do dwell
Within the hearts of those she meets.

She is sole mistress of my heart;
She rules it as the moon the tide,
She can bid all my griefs depart;
She can soothe my bosom's smart,
And much more beside.—*Pontès*, i. 218.

In the fourteenth century romantic poetry began to decline. The growth of towns and of commercial ideas was essentially unfavourable to it; and the scientific discoveries which marked that and the succeeding century, fostered a wholly adverse spirit. The invention of printing changed the poet's audience from those whom he knew and respected, to a heterogeneous multitude called the public, with whom he could have but little sympathy. Printing also became the handmaid of learning, and learning devoted itself to the resuscitation of the classics, in thorough opposition to whatever was national and vernacular. New versions appeared of some of the second-rate heroic epics; but, by the beginning of the fifteenth century, all their grace and spirit had evaporated. The subjects of these poems were not taken from the old Sagas, but from recent historical occurrences. Next came a "glut" of elaborate and heavy allegories, serious didactic narratives, droll quaint stories, none of which have sufficient vitality or power of expression to make them at all readable at the present day. Lyrical poetry, however, still continued to be cultivated. The old race of courtly Minnesingers had died out, and the art had fallen into the hands of the burgher class (Meistersingers), who formed associations for the purpose of mutually reciting their compositions, but whose strength lay rather in rhyme, and in the artificial arrangement of strophes with a view to singing, than in poetic merit, properly so called:—

The metrical system (Strophenbau) was tripartite, like that of the old Minnesingers. Sometimes there were as many as one hundred rhymes in a strophe. All sorts of odd names were applied to it. There was the blue and the red (Ton) mode, and the yellow violet mode; the red nut-blossom mode; the striped saffron-flower mode; the warm winter mode; the yellow lion-skin mode; the short ape mode, and the fat badger mode. At the end of the seventeenth century there were no less than two hundred and twenty-two different kinds of tunes or sing-strophes in full vogue.—*Metcalfe*, 237.

These guilds of the Meistersingers lasted till the end of the seventeenth century, and some specimens of them were actually extant as late as 1839, when they formally dissolved themselves, and handed over their "properties" to the Liederkranz at Ulm.

At the same period flourished the "Volks Lieder," or national songs, springing no one knows whence, but concerned with themes which reflected popular feeling, both on politics and on domestic matters. The great mass of these pieces are love poems, abrupt and unpolished, but not rude or vulgar; many others are festive and full of jovial hilarity, all simple and true to nature, and dealing with subjects of tolerably general interest. To this period also belong some didactic poets of no great merit or value.

The fourteenth and fifteenth centuries bring us to the rise of the drama, which, as among the Greeks, took its origin from religious worship. Here Christian was substituted for Gothic supernatural agency:—

On the anniversary of the Passion, the Gospel history of our Saviour's sufferings and death was declaimed by several persons, each of whom represented those who were present at the scene, as the Apostles, Herod, Pilate, the High Priest, &c., whilst the Priest spoke the words of our Saviour. This used to be done from the twelfth to the seventeenth century in Roman Catholic and Evangelical Churches. The speakers soon began to wear costume; and, at the same time, the speaking no doubt became acting. The language used was principally Latin; the place, the church. The text of the Gospels was not strictly adhered to. It was abbreviated and versified; and interpolations made in it from the ecclesiastical traditions. The clergy arranged the text; indeed, they superintended the whole affair. Even at an early period, hymns and bits of recitative in German were interspersed. The Lament of Mary under the Cross was, perhaps, the first part that was thus Germanized. So, then, the drama of Germany was in its commencement religious, and of course tragic. But, in the fourteenth century, with this tragic element a comic one was likewise combined. This part was sustained partly by the covetous Judas, partly by the merchant, who sells spices to the women on their way to the tomb of the Saviour, and who appears in the exact character and costume of a travelling quacksalver, or cheap jack of the day. The Church, impatient of this profanation of ecclesiastical and holy things, issued numerous decretals on the subject. Several of these, dating from the thirteenth and fourteenth century, drawn up by bishops and provincial synods, still survive. In them all acting in churches, and unseemly dresses and jokes, are strictly forbidden. The representation was consequently removed from the church to the open air, and assumed a more popular shape. Latin made way for German verse; and the Church seems rather to have favoured these representations, so long as they were under the management of the clergy and temporal authorities. Indeed, such plays of the "Passion" and "Resurrection" continued to be acted in some places till late in the eighteenth century. And in Southern Bavaria they have been revived of late, not without success.—*Metcalfe*, 251.

The editor tells us that the allusion here is to Ober-Ammergau, a secluded spot in the Bavarian Tyrol; and probably this is the place referred to in the Baroness Tautphœus's novel of *Quits*, where, as our readers may recollect, the performance of a religious mystery is described with much appreciation and sympathy.

In these miracle-plays the most amusing and often the most important personage was the devil, who is treated with what would no doubt seem to us shocking familiarity, had we not been inured to the comic view of that personage by legends and stories descending to us from those very times. To the clerical wits of the thirteenth century, Satan seems to have appeared much in the light of an Arabian genie, who could occasionally do a good deal of harm, but who might be induced to enter a jar or a crack in a tree, and there be locked up by his more cunning mortal adversary, and was on the whole quite as liable to have a tin kettle tied to his tail as any other sad dog of the day. Unfortunately a similar irreverence was extended to other supernatural personages; and the drama thus found itself, in its very origin, in that antagonism to the Church which has too often prevailed in subsequent periods.

We must pass over the prose of this period —chroniclers and mystic theologians—to the sixteenth century, of which, in a popular sense, Hans Sachs, the cobbler and poet of Nuremburg, is one of the principal figures. He produced altogether five quarto volumes, upon all kinds of subjects, serious and jocose—sacred and profane—stories, fables, and domestic scenes. An extract (which, by the way, is redolent of the spirit to which we have alluded in the preceding paragraph), will give some notion of his kind of humour:—

But it is not in domestic scenes only that he excels. The peculiarities of artisan life are likewise inimitably described. The tailor throws great pieces of cloth to the mouse, and is horrified in a dream to see the Devil with a huge flag made of all the odds and ends of cloth which he (the tailor) had ever "sent to the mouse" (*i. e.*, purloined as his perquisite:) Upon this he vows by all that is most sacred he will never throw any thing to the mouse again. For a long time he keeps his vow, till at last he gets a piece of gold brocade to make up. The other journeymen tailors remind him of the flag; upon which he observes he does not think there is any gold brocade in the flag; and forthwith flies a great piece after the mouse. At last the tailor dies, and St. Peter, out of compassion, permits him to sit behind the stove in heaven. One day, peeping out of his corner down upon the earth below, he sees a woman stealing a piece of cloth, and hurls the Almighty's footstool at her, which makes her humpbacked for life. Presently his escapade is discovered, and the Lord says to him, "Oh, tailor, tailor! suppose I had thrown my footstool at you every time you stole the folk's cloth and threw it after the mouse. Why, your house would not have had a tile left on it by this time, and you would have been on crutches, with your back bent and legs crooked. How dare you throw, then, you vulgar fellow?"—*Metcalfe*, 271.

In the space we have at command, it would be obviously impossible to pursue this analysis through the remaining epochs of German literature in any satisfactory manner. We

have been induced to devote the greater part
of this article to the older poetry, because it
is that which is least known among us, and
also because Vilmar's work is considered the
best account of it that has yet appeared. The
first portion of the "new period" (1624 to
1720), during which the national element of
German literature was completely in abeyance,
and nothing was popular but classical pedantry
or French sentiment, would present little to
detain an English reader. Its redeeming
feature was the evangelical poetry, consisting
of hymns which show genuine faith and feeling,
and sometimes even rise to sublimity. More
interesting, however, in a literary point of
view, are the romances, because, though in-
sufferably dull, they at least reflect the ideas
or manners of the time. Thus many of them
were borrowed from French sources, and are
full of courtly ceremonies and Louis Quatorze
notions; others were political, others geographical (!) (precursors, perhaps, of "Co-
rinne"); others seem to be inspired by a sort of
reactionary spirit, and celebrate the "return
to Nature," "abhorrence of conventionality,"
and the like, which subsequently found their
fullest expression in the works of Rousseau.
Thus, in the beginning of the eighteenth century, there appeared a number of "Robinson-
ades," or imitations of Robinson Crusoe :—

This work appeared in a German translation in 1721,
and elicited in Germany, as well as throughout Europe,
the greatest admiration and a countless host of imitators. Between 1722 and 1755 more than forty Robinsons appeared in Germany, and were read with frantic
eagerness. There were the German Robinson, the
Italian Robinson, the clerical ditto; the Saxon, the
Silesian, the Franconian Robinson; two Westphalian
Robinsons at once; the moral, the medicinal, the
invisible Robinson; and even the Bohemian Robinson.
Then there was the European Robinsonetta, "Miss
Robinson, or the cunning young maid;" "Robunse,
with her daughter, Robinschen," and so forth.—Metcalfe, 359.

To these succeeded the "Aventuriers,"
containing marvellous stories of mariners—
something like Lucian's *Veræ Historiæ*, or
Maryatt's *Pasha of Many Tales*. To the
Robinsonian succeeded the Sentimental Romances; and

after these, in the stormy times preceding the Revolution, the Romances of Knight-errantry and
Robbers. Next came the Family Romances, an apt
exponent of the political impotence of Germany, when
she was by necessity thrown back upon domestic subjects only. And last came the Historical Romance,
still in vogue. From the above remarks the truth of
the previous assertion will appear—that for two centuries the different phases of Romance have faithfully
reflected the manners of the day.—Metcalfe, 361.

To the second portion of the "New Period"
belongs Gottsched (1730), who, in spite of his bad
taste and formality, was the parent of a healthier
state of matters, by showing the value of systematic rules in poetry, and by awakening a taste
for the older German literature. He fancied,
however, that reason and not imagination was
the supreme power in poetry, and was thus
successfully opposed by Bodmer, who set up
Milton as a model for German writers. Several
writers of various degrees of merit, in verse and
prose, followed in the track of one or other of
these authors; but the influence of all was
swept away by the appearance of Klopstock,
who inaugurated a new epoch in the poetry of
his country. Here we touch upon ground more
generally known, and therefore refrain from
describing his critical or literary position, or
that of his successors, who, by translation or
recent exposition, have become tolerably familiar to our own public. The lives, and especially the domestic circumstances, of Klopstock,
Lessing, Wieland, Herder, Schubarth, Voss, and
Bürger, are interestingly described by Madame
de Pontès, and her pages will supply the details
which Mr. Metcalfe, from the nature of Vilmar's
plan, has not been able to give. Madame de
Pontès is copious—as might be expected from a
lady—on the love-affairs of her heroes. Those
whom we have mentioned were, in one sense,
exceedingly fortunate in this respect; for, although they experienced the usual share of early
disappointments, they almost all were in the
end successful in obtaining the affections of cultivated and charming women, though in some
cases poverty deferred their unions; while in
others their own waywardness destroyed their
prospects of happiness altogether. The history
of Klopstock's marriage is thoroughly German.
After a first attachment, in which the poet was
victimized for two years by a coquette, he was
shown by a friend a letter containing some just
and forcible criticism on his *Messiah*. Eagerly
inquiring the author (we may be sure the criticism was favourable), he was told that it was
the production of a young lady (Meta Moller),
and gladly accepted the offer of an introduction
to her. Furnished with a letter, he soon called,
and found the fair critic with her sister sorting
the household linen. This being put out of
sight, the poet was let in, and a long and interesting conversation ensued, followed by many
others, in which Klopstock poured the tale of
his amatory woes into no unsympathizing ear.
A correspondence was arranged, which German
etiquette does not, it would appear, forbid between young friends of opposite sexes; and before
long the author of the Messiah laid himself and
his laurels at the feet of his Meta, who on her
side, as we learn from her letters to Richardson,
already loved him with entire affection. They
were married in two years; but their happiness,
though perfect while it lasted, was of short
duration, for Madame Klopstock died in childbed four years afterwards.

The lives of Lessing, Wieland, Herder, and
Schubarth, though full of interest, must here
be passed over. From the life of Voss we
choose an extract, which strikingly illustrates
one peculiarity of German literary life. English poetry is difficult to classify; and, though
every great writer has his imitators, we have
but few instances of a knot of brother authors
setting to work in combination to pursue a particular line of composition. Coleridge and
Wordsworth form the only "school" we can at
present call to mind, and that did not last long;
some of the truest and most damaging, though
not hostile, criticism on the bard of Rydal was
written by his poetic partner. But German
literary history is full of schools, sets, and
brotherhoods, each with its organ of criticism,
and its Pierian celebrations. In 1770, for instance, there was formed the "Hainbund"
(Oak-union) by a circle of poets who venerated
Klopstock, and used to "meet every Saturday
at each others' houses to read their own productions and those of more established fame."
They had a somewhat exaggerated love of romance and nature, some particulars of which
literally warrant the satire of the Antijacobin—

You should have been here (writes Voss) on the
12th of September. The two Müllers, Hoelty, Hahn,
and I, went in the evening to a village in the neighbourhood. The weather was most lovely, the moon
full: we gave ourselves up completely to the enjoyments of nature, drank some milk in a peasant's
cottage, and then hastened to the open meadows.
Here we found a little oak wood, and at the same moment *it occurred to us all to swear the holy oath of
friendship* under the shadow of these sacred trees.
We crowned our hats with ivy, laid them beneath the
spreading branches of the oaks, and, clasping each
other's hands, danced round the massive trunk. We
called on the moon and stars to witness our union, and
swore eternal friendship. We pledged ourselves to
repeat this ceremony in a still more solemn manner
on the first occasion. I was chosen by lot as the head
of the "Bund."—*Pontès*, ii. 242.

In subsequent letters some other reunions
are described :—

Every Saturday we meet at four o'clock. Klopstock's odes and Ramler's poems lie on the table,
bound in octavo in black and gold. As soon as we
are all assembled, some one reads an ode; we decide
on its beauties and on the merits of the reader.

* * * *

Klopstock's birthday we celebrated nobly. A
long table was spread and adorned with flowers.
At the head stood an arm-chair, on which were laid
his collected works. Under the chair lay Wieland's
"Idris," torn in pieces, which we used to light our
pipes. Boie, who does not smoke, was compelled to
stamp on the "Idris." Afterwards, we drank Klopstock's health in sparkling Rhine-wine, and then the
memory of Luther, &c. We toasted freedom, hat
on head, Germany, poetry, and virtue, and you may

imagine how at last we burnt Wieland's picture, and finished the entertainment.—*Pontès*, ii. 243.

Perhaps the two most interesting biographies in Madame de Pontès's second volume are those of Voss (the translator of Homer), and Bürger (author of *Leonore*), the former from its picture of virtuous poverty, endured with steady perseverance and uncomplaining resolution, and resulting in a happy, useful, and honourable career; the other, for the very opposite of these qualities, and for the romantic tinge which often accompanies the indulgence of misplaced or unlawful affection. In the life of Voss we find a repetition of some of the characteristics noticed in the courtship of Klopstock. Voss's friend, Boie, had a charming sister, "full of poetical enthusiasm," and with her Voss kept up a correspondence. It was at first confined to literary subjects; but gradually—although the poet had never seen his correspondent—grew warmer in its character, and finally "paved the way for a lifelong attachment." Bürger was dissipated and reckless all his life, and, after marrying a girl below his own rank, fell in love with and seduced her sister, who formed part of their household. The decline of his wife's health was hastened by the spectacle of their attachment, and shortly after her death their marriage took place. His second wife, however, died only a year afterwards, and for five years he continued deeply miserable, but leading a tolerably blameless life. But a young Suabian lady, beautiful, romantic, and witty, and an enthusiastic admirer of his poetry, had conceived an ardent passion for him immediately on hearing the news of his second wife's death. This was for some time a secret, till one day

a Suabian newspaper, called "The Examiner," happened to fall beneath his eye, and, to his amazement, he beheld a copy of verses addressed to himself, commencing thus:—

> "O Bürger, Bürger! noble man,
> Who pours forth lays as no one can
> Save thee, replete with fire
> And passion, lend me, to impart
> The thoughts that fill my glowing heart,
> Thy poet's lyre."

The verses continued in the same strain, and thus concluded:—

> "For if a thousand suitors came
> Laden with gold—to press their flame,
> And Bürger too were there,
> I'd give him modestly my hand,
> And gladly change my fatherland
> For thee! no matter where.
> "Then if again inclined to woo,
> Seek thee a Suabian maiden true,
> And choose me, I implore;
> With German soul and Suabian truth,
> And all the generous warmth of youth,
> I'll love thee evermore!"—*Pontès*, ii. 354.

Bürger was first amused, then flattered, then interested, and at last wrote to the editor to discover his unknown admirer. That functionary,

less discreet than the conductors of our *London Journal* or *Family Herald*, sent him the lady's portrait. Bürger was smitten by its charms, but, honourably enough, wrote her a letter, telling her that his character was of a bad sort, that he had been twice married, was twice her age, and had three children. She only said, "Come!" They were married, but the union did not turn out well. After quarrelling with him a good deal, she ultimately proved unfaithful, was separated, and was at last reduced to gain her livelihood by singing his ballads.

For the rest of the modern poets we must refer to Madame de Pontès's own volumes. We will conclude by giving a specimen of her powers of translation, of which she has made frequent use throughout her work, and generally with considerable success. The following is from *Chamisso*, and we believe our readers will thank us for presenting it to them:—

THE THREE SISTERS.

We are three sisters worn with grief and tears,
Grown grey with sorrows rather than with years,
Well versed in love, dejected and deprest.
Each deems that her's has been the hardest part;
Approach; the poet knows the human heart,
Be it thy task to set the strife at rest.

First learn my grief, how fearful and how deep,
Starting, I woke from childhood's rosy sleep,
The bud burst forth! a secret thrill came o'er me,
The breath of love drew forth each hue so bright;
A hero raised me to his own proud height,
And life and all its charms lay spread before me.

Already with the bridal myrtle crown'd,
For him in whom my very being was bound,
I watch'd, with mingled fear and rapture glowing;
The marriage-torches cast their ruddy glare;
They brought me in his corpse and laid it there,
From seven deep wounds his crimson heart's-blood flowing.

The nameless horror of that awful night—
That is the image stamp'd upon my sight;
Waking or sleeping, I behold it still.
I cannot live! to death I now belong,
And yet I cannot die! Oh God! how long
Must all these tortures last that will not kill?

The second took the word with trembling tone:
Oh, not of shame! of blood the form alone
That sleeping still or waking meets her view;
My heart too open'd to that breath divine,
Anguish and rapture—they have both been mine;
For me the cup of love has mantled too.

The glory vanish'd from the loved one's head;
I saw him selfish, mean, his brightness fled,

And yet, alas! I loved him—him alone!
He went; if shame still chain him to her side,
Or raving madness drive him far and wide,
I know not; but the grief is all my own.

She ceased; the third then sadly took the word:
Thou pausest, now their sorrows thou hast heard,
Doubtful how to decide betwixt the twain.
Have they not lived and loved? our common doom,
Though sorrow shroud them both in grief and gloom,
And bid them to the dregs her chalice drain.

In one brief sentence all my sorrows dwell,
Till thou hast heard it, pause! consider well
Ere yet the final judgment thou assign,
And learn my better right, too clearly proved.
Four words suffice me:—I was never loved!
The palm of grief thou wilt allow is mine.

In conclusion, we warmly recommend both these works to all who wish to form an acquaintance with German literature. Mr. Metcalfe's might well have been longer; an octavo volume would not have been too much to devote to so extensive a subject, and the cursory manner in which he has been compelled to treat some subjects might thus have been avoided. The *Epistolæ Obscurorum Virorum*, for instance—a remarkable work—is only just noticed. The book bears marks of haste, and, since such large abridgments and alterations have been made, the style might have received more attention. At present, in spite of the Oxonian's "violent measures" (see *Pref.*), it oscillates, like most German styles, between philosophic (not to say pedantic) technicality, and the most homely and colloquial idiom. Should the work reach a second edition, its usefulness would be much increased by an analytical table of contents, with the proper dates to each name. As they at present stand, it is not easy to obtain a synoptical view. However, the book is a good one, and full of sound and discriminating criticism. That of Madame de Pontès is more diffuse, but there is nothing shallow about it. Her taste is correct, her tone is thoroughly healthy, and she is not, like so many biographers and some critics, carried off her feet by the excitement of her subject. Whether she would do well to continue her work, and include Schiller and Goethe, is another question. Our own opinion is, that the public knows quite as much about these writers as it wishes to know; and Mr. Carlyle and Mr. Lewes may as well be left in possession of the field.

105. SPECTATOR, 31 (1858), 525-526. M/H No. 5333.

MADAME DE PONTÈS' POETS AND POETRY OF GERMANY.*

THE object of Madame L. Davésiés de Pontès' volumes is to give a history of German poetry from the oldest poems that have been preserved, down to the productions of this generation, the lives of the authors, when known, being combined with a critically descriptive notice of their works. Some matter of a more general character. is occasionally introduced. A comparison between Eastern and Greek and Northern mythology opens the work, and in its course is presented a view of Charlemagne and his era—of the influence of the Crusades, and a discussion of other historical causes of excitement in the national mind, down to the great literary revival of the last century.

Thoroughly to carry out such an undertaking as the authoress proposes to herself would be difficult. It requires great critical acumen and poetical power, a self-denial which is rare, to write not only the history of the poetry of another nation but also to attempt by translation to convey an adequate idea of the styles and genius of authors. Madame de Pontès brings good will but scarcely a sufficient genius to the latter branch of her undertaking. In her translations of what are called " specimens" of national poetry we may find variety of subject and feeling, possibly of manner; but there is very slight gradation of merit. As regards inherent capability, all the poets seem to be upon a par. Madame de Pontès has fulfilled the most difficult part of a translator's task, the exhibition of the peculiarities of her originals. In the hands of a judicious translator the sentiments of course are safe: she also does in some degree vary style and metre; but the poetical spirit is too level and uniform. We hear of writers with the vigorous or " etherial" quality which constitutes the essence of poetry ; and of others who rather verge upon the prosaic ; but they all show very nearly alike in the specimens presented to the reader.

In other respects the task is well executed. To a great extent, a book of this kind must be a compilation. The lives and writings of contemporary and distinguished modern authors may be thoroughly mastered ; but the secondary verse-writers of the modern period beginning with the time of le Grand Monarque, and the elder writers in Latin and old German, sometimes difficult to understand, and in tedious stories of knight-errantry almost impossible to read, will be perused in their entirety by very few except archæological editors. There is, however, nothing of the " jogtrot" or heavy character of compilation about the *Poets and Poetry of Germany*. Madame de Pontès has succeeded in producing a spirited and readable survey of the poetical literature of Germany, with specimens of the most remarkable poems and the lives of the writers. It may be recommended to the general reader not only for its information but its interest.

This poetical literature may be broadly divided into three classes ; the ancient, the mediæval, and the modern, each admitting of various subdivisions. For though the modern may properly begin with the latter part of the seventeenth century, there were verse-writers in vogue during the first half, and a new school began in the middle or about the end of the last century with Schiller and Goethe. Whether the most ancient Teutonic poems were altogether indigenous may be doubted ; Scandinavia seeming to have valid claims to be their originator. Beyond all doubt this old school possesses greater force and raciness, however rugged, than those which followed rather than succeeded. Combined with this force and raciness are a lofty sense of honour born of the old Norse blood, and a real delicacy of feeling towards woman, mingled with much that is unsophisticated or something more, as the administering corporal chastisement to a wife. The claims to epical importance which enthusiastic Germans put forward for some of the early cyclical poems, and especially *The Nibelungenlied*, have no real foundation. There is no unity of action or even of story; the marvellous runs into the impossible, the homely into the gross, and there is not only a want of art but of the sustained power necessary for an heroic poem.†

* *Poets and Poetry of Germany*. Biographical and Critical Notices. By Madame L. Davésiés de Pontès,. Translator of " Egmont," " Korner's Life and Works," &c. In two volumes. Published by Chapman and Hall.
† There is a notice of Mr. Lettsan's translation of *The Nibelungenlied* in the *Spectator* for 1850, page 447.

With poems of the first class the indigenous or national character of German poetry in a measure terminates, except so far as it may be distinguished by the individual character of the writer. The subjects were no longer of the North or the nation. The " gay and gallant troubadour" set themes of love to the Germans ; tales of King Arthur, adventures of knight errantry, mingled of course with the black arts, became the fashion, as they were indeed throughout Europe. The original authorship of some of these poems is a matter of dispute, it being doubtful whether they were French or German. The authorship of a particular poem is of little importance in the question of nationality. Ideas, groundwork, character, incident—all that constitutes form as well as life, were foreign or common to literary Europe. The most original productions were the satires directed against abuses, especially among the religious orders. These, however, were not peculiar to Germany, and were rather scholarly than national ; though those of the Germans might be the most numerous and the best. A similar remark applies to the mysteries and dramas, which were also European. There is an exception to these observations in the institution of the Meistersängers ; clubs as we should call them of the humbler classes, who met to sing the songs of those among them whom the gods had made versifiers. It was only in a land given to song that an order like this could have struck root and flourished.

" These simple and untaught efforts of rude and humble minds among the lower orders, have frequently been the subject of contemptuous pleasantry. True, they are generally dry and uninteresting, and the rhymes in which they are composed often little better than doggrel ; but we must not forget that, by their means, poetry hitherto confined to one order alone, now first began to develop itself among other classes of society and to assume an independence of thought and variety of form to which it had hitherto been a stranger.

" How the institution of the Meistersängers first arose, we cannot exactly discover. By some authors they have been attributed to Frauenlob, but of this there is no satisfactory proof. All that is certain is that they flourished in their full glory in the middle of the fifteenth century, and that, towards the end of the sixteenth, the history of their origin had sunk into oblivion. The towns of southern Germany, Mainz, Augsburg, Nürnberg, and Ulm were their chosen resorts. In some, the association was composed of a single set of workmen, all belonging to the same trade, none else being admitted, while in others, it was formed of all the restless joyous spirits who had any love of verse or taste for music. When the business of the week was over and Sunday had arrived with its quiet and repose, the members of the humble society would assemble in the schoolroom, festively ornamented for the occasion, and there, surrounded by attentive and admiring listeners, commence the grand business of the evening. The member who had most distinguished himself in the previous occasions by skill, either in verse or music, and the best singer were called forward and crowned by the president with a wreath of flowers ; an ornament was then hung round their neck, and each member hastened to produce any contribution he had made since the last meeting. These, if approved, were carefully written down in a large book in text hand ; the assembly then joined in chorus, and when the favourite psalms or hymns had been sung, the honest burghers and their wives and daughters, who seem generally to have been present on the occasion, separated and returned to their homes."

There seems nothing to prevent the existence of such a body in Germany now ; for though the people may have grown more critical, their poets must have become better instructed ; if instruction does much more for a poet than enable him to imitate. However, the order has passed away, though it survived to the present generation, and then departed in due form.

" It was in the middle of the fifteenth century that the Meistersängers really flourished ; but the institution continued, though languishing, till the end of the seventeenth, amid all the calamities of the thirty years' war ; nay, at Ulm, it survived even the changes which the French revolution effected throughout Europe, and Villmar assures us that, as late as 1830, twelve old singmeisters yet remained who, after being driven from one asylum to another, sang their ancient melodies from memory in the little hostelry where the workmen, in the evening, met to drink and jest together. In 1839, four only were yet living, and on the 21st October, these veterans assembled with great solemnity, declared the Meistergesang for ever closed, and presented their songs, hymns, books, and pictures, to a more modern musical institution, the 'Liederkränze' of Ulm, with the wish that, even as the Meistersängers had, for centuries, invited the pious fathers of the church to hear their lays, even so the banner of the 'Liederkränze' might wave for centuries, and their strains charm the latest posterity."

We have formerly indicated our opinion that the substantial framework of most historical works of imagination, is rather due to traditional influences than to the writer; that it is the thought which mainly belongs to his invention. Lord Lindsay and others conceive that the early notions of monsters—"hydrus and gorgons, and chimeras dire," with the griffins and dragons of a later day, originated in antediluvian traditions, or in the actual existence in the primeval state of the earth, of gigantic reptiles long extinct. Homer not only derived his story but his characters, manners, and probably his incidents, from tradition; Shakspere borrowed his plots; and Mr. Wright has proved that the Vision of Dante, at least as regards the Inferno, existed in several forms before he turned it to poetical use, and doubtless in its origin was a real dream of some literary monk. Goethe's Faust we all know was founded on a story which had become familiar if not popular in Europe. Madame De Pontès' account of the different German plays upon the subject, show that the modern poet was indebted to more than general story. Dramas, however, they can hardly be called, being often intended for puppets. Unless translation and condensation have done a good deal for one of the older puppet plays, it had power as well as playwright's art.

"Among the Faust dramas, as they were called, which were represented on this mimic stage, one apparently the most popular, has been preserved to us. It thus commences:

"FAUST ALONE IN HIS STUDY.

"So far have I brought it with learning and might,
That everywhere I am laughed at outright;
All books and all learning I've made my own,
And yet cannot find the philosopher's stone.
Jurisprudence and medicine I know by heart;
There's no help save in the wizard's art;
Theology too is useless quite.
Who'll pay me for many a sleepless night!
I've not a single coat to my back,
And creditors too are upon my track.
With hell I must bind myself in my need,
All nature's secret depths to read.

"He then summons the evil spirits to his presence; when they appear, he inquires whether they are men or women; they reply: 'we have no sex.' To his further questions as to what form lies hid beneath their grey covering, they answer: 'we have no form of our own, but, according to thy pleasure, we will assume any in which thou desirest to see us clad; we shall always reflect thine own thoughts.' After the pact has been signed by which he forfeits his soul, on condition that all things, in heaven and earth shall be made known to him, Faust inquires about the construction of the celestial and infernal regions, and having obtained the desired information, observes that it must be too cold in the one, and too hot in the other; and that, after all, earth must be the most agreeable place to dwell in. The dæmons then present him with a magic ring, through the power of which, he suddenly beholds himself transformed into a blooming youth, his threadbare garments changed to the richest knightly attire, and the loveliest and noblest of dames and damsels only too proud to accept his homage."

There is a bitter satire in the following scene from another play—

"There is another puppet-show of which Faust is likewise the hero, but where the dæmon is called, not Mephistopheles, but Asteroth. The piece commences by Faust's declaration that he is so poor as to be always obliged to go on foot; that nor even a milkmaid will kiss him, and that he would gladly sell himself to the Devil, to get a horse and a lovely princess. The Devil appears accordingly; first in the shape of sundry animals, of a swine, an ox, and a monkey. But Faust scornfully tells him he must look more terrible than that, if he expects to frighten him. He then enters as a roaring lion, then as a hissing serpent, but in vain; at last he presents himself in a human form of the fairest proportions and wrapped in a gorgeous scarlet mantle. In reply to Faust's expression of astonishment, he reminds him that there is nothing at once more hideous and more terrible in creation than man; that he unites in himself all the vices of the brute creation; that he is filthy as the swine, brutal as the ox, ridiculous as the ape, violent as the lion, venomous as the serpent."

The history of Modern Poetry, for about the last century and a half, beginning with the once celebrated Klopstock, is not so interesting as the previous part of the work. It is less an historical survey of German poetry than a series of separate lives of poets; and the occasional efforts to connect them with a continuous view fall somewhat short. The authors as well as their writings are better known to the public through books, biographical notices, or articles in periodicals, than are those of the earlier periods. Some poets perhaps are selected less for their literary position than because their career was striking, and ample biographical materials were at hand. These "lives," however, were necessary to complete the subject, and they form a useful poetical repertory. Goethe and Schiller are omitted; probably from their weight of character rendering it impracticable to deal with them in the space at the writer's disposal.

German poetry has been the subject of this notice; but besides the lives of the poets and a consideration of historical events which influence a nation's mind, matters have been introduced into the work, to indicate the opinions, prejudices, or superstitions of the time. Here is a summary of the witchcraft persecutions increasing in Germany as in other other places on the Reformation. Luther himself maintained the existence of witches and the right to punish them. It is a more shocking picture than was afforded by any other country.

"In his eyes, witches were not human beings. They were the Devil personified and, as such, excited no compassion in his mind.

"At first the potentates spiritual and temporal hesitated to sanction these fearful practices; but, as two thirds of the possessions of the hapless victims were forfeited to church and state, their scruples were quickly silenced. The rest was assigned to the informers, the hangmen, &c., an arrangement which called forth whole swarms of this hateful brood. In a single village, containing two hundred souls, the executioner earned, in three months, no less a sum than one hundred and sixty thalers or about twenty-six pounds sterling by the burning of flags alone, and it is tolerably certain that at least one half of the accusations were the result of mere cupidity. Rich and poor, young and old, were alike subject to this deadly suspicion. Every earthly misfortune was attributed to sorcery, and those who doubted its existence were the first victims. If the wretched beings refused to confess, they were subjected to the most fearful tortures. By the law, indeed, these were limited to a quarter of an hour at a time; but they were often continued, with little intermission, for days together, till the miserable creatures, maddened by agony, confessed everything that was asked of them and more to boot. Some few, nevertheless, found in their sense of outraged innocence, an almost superhuman fortitude. A maiden of Ulm, of good family, endured the rack nine times, and still persisted in her declaration of innocence. After a long imprisonment, she was at length released to die soon after, the victim of the fearful sufferings she had undergone. Those who revoked their confession were invariably burnt alive; the rest occasionally obtained the commutation of their sentence to strangling ere the flames reached them. In one small town in Bavaria, forty-eight women were burnt in the year 1582. In the bishopric of Bamberg, out of a population of one hundred thousand souls, two hundred and twenty-five women were consigned to the flames between 1627 and 1630. In short, in the course of the century during which this fearful persecution was at its height in Germany, from 1580 to 1680, it is calculated that above a hundred thousand individuals, nine tenths of whom were women, were its victims. To the honour of humanity be it said, some voices were raised against this bloodthirsty insanity; but they were drowned in the general clamour. In every part of Germany, Protestant or Catholic, the same atrocities were committed. At length, in the year 1631, the noble-hearted Count Frederick Stein, himself a member of the order of Jesuits, an order which had been among the most violent denouncers of sorcery, ventured to step boldly forward and declare that, among the many whom he had accompanied to the scaffold, there was not one whom he could confidently declare guilty. 'Treat me so,' he added, 'treat in this manner the judges or the heads of the church, subject us to the same tortures, and see if you will not discover sorcerers in us all.'"

We are not in general desirous of remarking on small matters of a formal or technical kind; but the confusion in chronology of the printer or the writer of this book, is really something extraordinary. Wieland for instance is rightly said to have been born in 1733; by 1778 he is represented to have "reached his seventieth year," and a passage about his translation of Cicero's Letters would make him eighty in 1809. Klopstock was born in 1724; in 1802 he is reported as "sixty-seven years of age," and, not to weary by details, Herder dies in 1893!

We have here a fifth edition of Æser's famous Letters on Art,[13] addressed to a young lady, and they well deserve to be better known in England, more especially by the ladies, for whose advantage they were particularly written. The work has been enlarged, and in some respects improved, by the present editor, Herr Grube, and consists of sixty-one letters on the principal objects to be obtained by a study of the Fine Arts. There are excellent portraits in steel of Kaulbach, Beethoven, and Rauch, coryphæi in three provinces of art; and the two national poets of Germany, Goethe and Schiller, are well represented in lithograph. We may remark *en passant*, that there is an evident tendency to exalt the fine frontal development of Goethe, already commencing, such as produced the imposing caricatures of Shakspeare and Napoleon, with which we are all familiar.

For the sake of our lady readers, if we have any, we may briefly define Æsthetics—a Greek word, of German invention, naturalized in England—as the sense of the beautiful in art, from that instinctive perception which recognises the harmony of a tune, or the justness of proportion in a building, to that highest form of perception generally allied with intellect, which feels all that the greatest poets can impart even in their noblest creations—unattainable, as we constantly see, by any amount of cultivation, if the instinctive faculty is wanting. It may even apply to the sense of religious purity, beauty, and worth, and is so used by Schiller, who says, "Das Christenthum in seiner reinen Form ist Darstel-

[13] "Aesthetische Briefe, ein Weihgeschenk für Frauen und Jungfrauen." Leipsic: Nutt. 1857.

lung schöner Sittlichkeit oder Menschwerdung des Heiligen, und in diesem Sinne die höchste Aesthetische Religion." (Christianity in its Pure Form is an Exhibition of a beautiful Morality, or of the Incarnation of the Holy, and in this Sense is the highest Æsthetic Religion.)

The purpose of the letters is to guide the female student in her choice of subjects, and to present her with the purest and best examples in each style of art, in whatever direction her preference may lie.

The sixteenth letter (the previous are devoted to general preliminary considerations) treats of architecture, more particularly of its highest development, as seen in the remains of antique Greece, and the Temple of Theseus at Athens is figured in illustration; while the magnificent fane at Denderah, with its endless rows of sculptured columns, is added as a specimen of the barbaric splendour of Oriental architecture. The author enlarges on the æsthetic effect of our grand old Gothic buildings in producing an involuntary feeling of reverence, and remarks that a Gothic cathedral is in itself a sermon; "ein Gotischer Dom ist schon an sich eine Christliche Predigt."

In the nineteenth and two following letters, ancient and modern sculpture are considered, and the Vatican Apollo, with the matchless group of the Laocoön, are indicated; the latter figured as the highest attainments in this branch of art. Painting and music are treated in the letters which follow; Oriental poetry (of which there is a long and curious example taken from Dr. Holtzmann's translations of Indian poetry, entitled "King Usinara's Compassion," and is a kind of moral dialogue between the king and a hawk, from whose destructive claws the king had rescued a dove which had flown into his bosom for protection); the epic, dramatic, and lyrical productions of ancient Greece; and the modern poetry of Italy. Shakespeare, supreme in Germany as in England, has a letter to himself (the 48th); then German poetry; Goethe, Schiller, Uhland, its chief worthies, are analysed. The theatre, and even dancing and landscape gardening, are not neglected; and the last letter closes with a consideration of the influence exerted on the character by the sedulous cultivation of an æsthetic taste.

We shall conclude our notice of this excellent work by quoting therefrom a parallel between Goethe and Schiller, not because of any novelty, for both poets are duly appreciated in England, but because they are types of classes: Goethe of that small one, few in numbers, but eternal in renown, who express the noblest and wisest poetry in the actions and sufferings of their human creations—whom we recognise as invented in harmony with the invariable laws of our nature; the other, far more numerous, of which Schiller may perhaps rank as the chief, who have sought to express in language the thoughts and feelings of themselves or of others, without the power to place them before us in those embodied creations of the highest genius, which alone would seem to justify the use of that word whose equivalent is maker.

"Goethe," says Hinrichs (Schiller's "Dichtungen," &c.), "felt a lively interest in all we call na-

ture, for the visible and actual. His element of action was matter. His fixed purpose was, as Schiller said, to receive laws from the objective, and to deduce from nature her own principle. Form and substance were to him the expression of a universal idea. He did not lose himself in reveries about Nature, but examined her creations. His gift of intuition (or tendency to regard the actual) was employed with striking effect in natural history, from which he banished the clouds of reflection without observation. His theory of colours, and the metamorphosis of plants, are an eternal monument of his genius for interpreting nature. Physical science, chemistry, mineralogy and geology, physiology and comparative anatomy, occupied him incessantly. He sought to know the details of the great operations of nature; and Schiller saw with astonishment how that in his researches he ascended step by step from the simplest organizations to the most complex. 'Like Nature' herself, he was calm and tranquil in his operations and sure and fortunate in all that he undertook. In art, he had more leaning to perception than to sensation; and while music attracted him but little, he loved architecture, sculpture, and painting, and even drew landscapes after nature. He was a man complete in all parts, and demanded a definite outline and form in an object, however beautiful.

"Quite otherwise was Schiller, who, although he had studied medicine, evinced little susceptibility for the contemplation, or study of nature. According to his friend Streicher, the external world had no existence for him when he was occupied in composition; he was 'as if by a convulsion' withdrawn into himself. During his numerous wanderings in the mountains, with Streicher for a companion, the latter was obliged to draw his attention to the finest prospects, so completely was he absorbed in his own reflections. He was attracted not by nature, but by the microcosm within. His element was the subjective; on this account he was more especially occupied with history and philosophy."

Madame de Pontès' instructive and entertaining volumes are a welcome contribution to literary biography, interspersed with critical remarks on the merits of German Poets and Poetry.[12] The greater part of the first volume is devoted to the antiquities of the subject—to the origin of those wild northern lays, which arose in the dark and troubled times, when Paganism and Christianity were yet in conflict throughout Northern Europe, and when the social condition, like that in which the heroic poetry of Ancient Greece was cradled, was more favourable to the inspiration and reception of strains that appeal rather to faith and to the imagination than to reason,—a condition additionally fostered by that universal geographical ignorance which made all countries not included

[12] "Poets and Poetry of Germany. Biographical and Critical Notices." In 2 vols. By Madame L. Davesies de Pontès. London: Chapman & Hall. 1858.

in Central and Southern Europe to be regarded as the abiding-places of the supernatural.

An utter confusion of dates and of historic truth prevailed in all that group of epic ballads and lays, of which the Nibelungen Lied is the noblest exemplar; a medley of Pagan and Christian exploits and titles, strung on a thread of truth, not always easily traced. The Emperor Theodoric of Verona, as Dietrich of Berne, and Attila as Etzel King of Hungary, are the principal centres around which lesser lights revolve in this wild constellation of Facts and Fictions. The Rosengarten was the last of these epic creations, and numbers among its characters most of those which figure in the well-known Nibelungen song. A passion for roses seems to have prevailed among the inhabitants of Germany during the earliest centuries of the Christian era; and Chriemhilde's garden, in addition to her own beauty, was considered cause sufficient that noble knights without number should risk life and limb for a sight of these floral treasures, which were jealously guarded by twelve redoubted champions, whose adventures and exploits are recorded in the ballad.

There is a sketch, slight indeed, (for the materials, though more numerous than might have been expected, are not always precise and clear) of the gentle and accomplished nun Hroswitha, who entered, towards the middle of the tenth century, the ancient convent of Gandersheim, founded in 859 by a Count of Saxony. She composed in her retirement, not only a female martyrology, but some dramatic pieces, which, with the permission of her ecclesiastical superior, were performed rudely enough, no doubt, by the inmates of the convent.

A fair amount of illustration is accorded to the German Minne-singers, though the romance of gallantry sooner degenerated into licence in Germany than in France, and the yoke of beauty was never, perhaps, as gracefully worn. Nothing, indeed, can be less in accordance with modern notions of the ideal troubadour than Ulrich von Lichenstein, a noble minnesinger, who has an autobiography which closes about the year 1255, and which for minuteness of confession almost rivals Rousseau's. The valour of these noble and knightly romancers does not seem to have been accompanied by corresponding literary ability, so that their productions became so remarkable for prolixity and dulness, that by degrees they had few readers among the male sex, and counted their chief admirers in the matrons and damsels condemned to the monotonous existence of moated fortalices.

The drama gradually arose as men demanded more pungent mental pabulum; but as the church then contained almost all who were capable by attainments of literary efforts, and had the power to suppress whatever was opposed to her teaching, so religious themes were chiefly chosen, as they were selected for illustration by the great painters of Italy; and thus names sacred by tradition and custom are handled with a freedom that sounds profanely in ears accustomed to the decorous forbearance of modern times; yet nothing like profanity was intended in these bizarre efforts of early Teutonic playwrights.

The devil figures in these dramas divested of

nearly all that is either terrible or impious, as if his supernatural power and propensity to do mischief had been counteracted by the theological vaccination he has been made to undergo by the efforts of the church. A century later, and the spirit of satire arose, as the groundless pretensions of temporal and ecclesiastical authorities came to be canvassed, as we see in the Narrenschiff (Ship of Fools), Reynard the Fox, Eulenspiegel, the Curate of Calembourg, and the book of the Schildburgers; most of them dull enough to us, whom feasting has made fastidious, but much more highly relished by contemporaries, who felt their spiritual wants unsatisfied by legends of saints and martyrologies alike questionable.

Ulrich von Hutten, equally ready with pen and sword, the friend of Franz von Sickingen, champion of the oppressed German peasantry, whose free and noble spirit hoped from the Lutheran revolt something better than the substitution of one intolerable form of bigotry for another, is noticed at a length which his active and gallant career, rather than his poetical merits, would warrant. He lived in times scarcely worthy of him, and already in his own mind the revolution had occurred which Luther's coarse and vehement character soon after effected for the numbers who had long been disgusted by the absolute pretensions of the Romish hierarchy. The asylum from persecution denied him in Switzerland by the timidity of Erasmus, was granted by Zuinglius, and he died at the age of thirty-five in the little island of Ufernow, in the lake of Zurich, August 31st, 1523.

One of the strangest features of the times that followed the Protestant revolution, was the fanatical popular belief in witches, and their consequent cruel persecution, to which no one more heartily assented than Luther himself. It was perhaps a distortion of the newly-awakened principle of faith in a higher agency than the Pope, and a demonstration against the presumed agency of the devil on earth. Women, young and old, were peculiarly liable to this cruel suspicion; and youth and beauty, whose witcheries have survived this persecution, were no protection against the stupid superstition. Between 1580 and 1680 it is supposed that a hundred thousand persons, the great majority being women, were burnt or tortured to death for the imputed crime of sorcery. Protestants and Catholics were equally guilty of this cruelty; but a Jesuit, the Count von Stein, is recorded as the first who dared publicly to raise his voice against a continuance of this persecution. This was in 1631, but it was not till 1794 that the last execution for witchcraft took place on the Continent.

It was scarcely till the commencement of the eighteenth century that modern German poetry began to assert itself, and Opitz and Gottsched were but feeble harbingers of the luminaries of Weimar. Bodmar, whose critical abilities were of more service to German literature than his poetical—Ramneler excelling in graceful erotics —Haller, once popular as a poet, but much more justly celebrated as a physiologist and physician —the gentle, pious, and benevolent Gleim, who lived to see the national poetry under Goethe and Schiller almost rivalling the muse of England,—were all born at the commencement of the eighteenth century. An undue space is devoted to Kleist (primus), whose death at the battle of Kunnersdorf has endeared him as a patriot to his Prussian fellow-countrymen, and secured a vitality to his reputation denied to his verses. He was a gallant man, but it speaks ill for his genius that he seems rather to have desired the long-withheld approbation of a military pedant like Frederic II. than any higher guerdon. Prussia may if she pleases revere the memory of the most successful of her monarchs, —but was there anything great in his life or in his actions but his victories? Klopstock, whose poetry has now found its level, is noticed at a length rather due to his former influence than to his present reputation, while scarcely justice is rendered to Lessing, the greatest critic since Aristotle. The melancholy incidents of Bürger's career, whose name is so familiar through the "Wild Huntsman" and "Leonora," while the details of his life are so little known to English readers, are sensibly given, and the criticisms, whether ethical or æsthetical, are worthy of the maturity of a masculine intellect. Wieland and Herder are familiar names; and Schubart's troubled life, wherein we find the petty tyranny of a petty German prince destroying the fortunes of a man whose shoe's latchet he was unworthy to unloose, had been previously detailed by Mr. Carlyle in a book sold even at railway stations. The Schlegels, Chamisso (the naturalist poet), Voss, Arndt, Werner, the second Kleist, Novalis, find their due place and fair appreciation in Madame de Pontés' book, which may be advantageously consulted by that great majority which will never form an independent judgment from the writings of the authors.

The living do not fall within the design of this work, so that Uhland, Freiligrath, and many others, are unnoticed; nor is there anything but an allusion to the great names of Goethe and of Schiller. Yet we must record our protest against a criticism which Madame de Pontés only repeats, on the tendency of Goethe's writings, which have been accused as deficient in moral aim, if not in morality. Goethe's history shows that the object uniformly proposed in his writings was Truth, whether moral or scientific. The lofty intellectual eminence he occupied forbade all narrowness of view, and scarcely permitted the possibility of deception by those Idols of the Cave, the worshipped errors of mankind. It was on this account that he was indifferent to the stirring politics of the day, with which he has been reproached, from a conviction that, while his interference would have availed much less than that of some thick-headed Prussian or Austrian marshal, the most explosive events exert little influence on the destinies of mankind. He had the courage to question the truth of Newton's theory of colours, and with better grounds he wrote his "Metamorphosis of Plants," and confirmed Oken's great idea of the essential identity of the expanded bones of the skull, with those of the spinal column. In his great literary efforts he does not load vice with hysterical epithets of censure, nor does he make virtue invariably triumphant on earth, in deference to the prejudices of his readers. But he followed Truth and Nature as he saw them

and read them in history. In Egmont, for example, we have a high-hearted patriot; and in the gentle, noble, impassioned Clara, who lived in the life of Egmont, sacrificed to the cold-blooded, treacherous tyranny of Alva, we see despotism and bigotry suffocating truth, patriotism, and noble affection. It is all historically true, and reproduced before us without epithet or any false interposition of "poetical justice;" yet what can be stronger than the feelings of hatred and abhorrence which are excited by the agents of evil, though triumphant? In "Faust," the incidents are exactly such, so far as the human actors are concerned, as produce those domestic tragedies, scarcely known beyond the actors, which possibly will endure till the extinction of the species. Margaret has every inducement to err, and falls as only a girl of warm and generous feelings can fall; and, after the sad and bitter sufferings that expiated the crimes into which she was almost unwittingly betrayed, was saved at last by refusing any longer to hearken to temptation, even in her extremest need.

We do not admire German novels, and see little to amuse even in the "Wahlverwandtschaft," which has been so fiercely assailed by a shallow Scotch critic; yet Goethe merely sketched what we know by the records of our consistorial courts to be always in existence around us, and sought to show how human weakness may be betrayed into uncontemplated crime. Ignoring sin is not the way to cure it, any more than to refrain from piercing an ulcer which is destroying the constitution, though not apparent on the surface. For the rest, his "Life" shows that he was capable of the truest and most ostentatious benevolence, though he did not regulate his opinions by a formula.

Mr. Lewis[13] can defend himself, and we leave him to try conclusions, if he cares to do so, with a German Quixote, who has zealously couched his lance to assail a modern windmill. The biographer of Goethe is accused by Heinrich Siegfried of having most unjustifiably treated the character of Bettina Brentano (now Madame von Arnim) in the "Life and Works." Possibly in his zeal for his hero, Mr. Lewes may have been a little hasty as regarded the lady, especially when he declares that Goethe's correspondence with her was a fiction of her own invention; yet the tone adopted by Herr Siegfried hardly entitles him to a reply, apart from the merits of the case, and he professes to have addressed Mr. Lewes without the cognizance of the person immediately interested.

The German Classics from the Fourth to the Nineteenth Century: a German Reading-Book. By Max Müller, M.A. (Longman & Co.)

History of German Literature. By the Rev. Fred. Metcalfe, M.A. (Same publishers.)

Prof. Max Müller has reposed from his more recondite Oriental studies to produce a common German Anthology, embracing the period from Hagedorn downwards, with a little bit of Heine at the end by way of seasoning. Even the tolerably wide word, "Classics," is not comprehensive enough for the largeness of his grasp, which at once takes in Ulfilas and Jean Paul. The extracts of which his book is composed were originally collected for the purpose of illustrating a series of lectures on the history of the German language and literature, delivered at Oxford by him in his Taylorian capacity, and this original purpose is clearly apparent in the arrangement of the materials. So little is the volume suited to those who wish to "learn German," that a tolerable knowledge of the modern tongue is assumed by the Professor, and although the historical preface is written in English, the short biographies by which each author is selected are in German throughout. But to those more ambitious English students who, not content with a little Schiller and less Goethe, wish to trace the progress of the German language from the very beginning, as revealed in the works of the principal authors, and at the same time shrink from the bulky epics and copious Minnelieder of the Middle Ages, this collection will be most acceptable.

"Old High-German," observes Prof. Müller, "is as difficult a language to a German as Anglo-Saxon is to an Englishman ; and the Middle High-German of the *Nibelungen*, of *Wolfram* and *Walther*, nay, even of *Eckhart* and *Tauler*, is more remote from the language of Goethe than Chaucer is from Tennyson."

And with this fact deeply impressed on his mind he has taken great pains to bridge over for his countrymen by adoption, the chasm that separates the past from the present. The extracts from the fourth to the fourteenth century inclusive, beginning with the "Lord's Prayer" of the Gothic Ulfilas, and comprehending *inter alia* specimens from the epic and lyric poetry of the chivalric age, are accompanied throughout by translations into Modern German, with an exception in the case of the Hymns of the Church, with which the original Latin is given.

When the student has reached the fifteenth century, and makes acquaintance with the later *Minnesänger*, the *Meister-sänger*, and the satirical and religious poets who precede and illustrate the Reformation, he is no longer allowed such a stable crutch as a translation, but must content himself with a lighter staff, composed of marginal notes, which he may use till the end of the sixteenth century. Martin Opitz, whom fifty readers know as a landmark in literary history for every one that has read a distich from his pen, ushers in the period, that continues till the close of the eighteenth century,—Jean Paul Richter being the most modern author from whom extracts are taken. At the beginning of this period notes become scanty and long before the close they cease altogether.

The Rev. F. Metcalfe's 'History of German Literature,' based on Vilmar's work, is intended as a companion to Prof. Müller's extracts, to which it forms a sort of first volume,—bringing the record down to a still more recent date, so as to comprise not only the romantic poets of the Schlegel school, but even Heinrich Heine. Perhaps it is to be regretted that Mr. Metcalfe did not confine himself within the limits set by Prof. Müller, for while he gives a most instructive history of the old period, rendered doubly valuable by literary notes, his account of the latest writers is necessarily brief, and the remarks which he nevertheless permits himself to make have a somewhat dogmatical appearance. Few, for instance, who have read the poems of Lenau will agree with the opinion that "his lyrics owe their reputation more to the interest of the moment than to any intrinsic merit"; and possibly the brevity with which Mr. Metcalfe asserts that "posterity will judge of Heine as they judged of Bürger, that he was endowed with excellent points, nay, with almost a creative genius, which was ruined for want of moderation," will lead many to infer a closer affinity between two very diverse minds than is really intended by the historian. However, even the least satisfactory part of the book will be extremely useful as a sort of *catalogue raisonné*.

Art. III.—Weimar and its Celebrities.

1. *Geschichte des Hauses von Sachsen.* Von Dr. Eduard Vehse. Hamburg. 1848.

2. *Briefe an Seine Schwester Henrietta.* Von Karl Ludwig v. Knebel. Leipzig. 1857.

3. *Weimar der Musen Hof.* Leipzig. 1843.

4. *Göthe und die lustige Zeit zu Weimar.* Von Aug. Diezmann. Leipzig. 1857.

There is no country which presents so many difficulties to the national historian as Germany; none in which the principle of centralization was so long and so completely excluded, and in which it still exists in so imperfect a degree. The Roman Germanic empire was in its very essence opposed to that principle. It was the secular representation of the universality of the Church. Divided into above two hundred little States, which are completely independent of the other, being connected by no link save one common tongue, Germany, despite her poets' continual invocation of the "Fatherland," has never had any real existence as a nation. Indeed, until the present century, the patriotic attachments and sympathies of her sons had always been confined to the particular spot which gave them birth. Whether in the Middle Ages, after the Reformation, or during the Thirty Years' War, we find the same civil feuds and divisions. The Germans were Guelphs and Ghibellines, Saxons or Thuringians, Bavarians or Swabians. The triumphs of Frederick the Great, the most popular of German heroes, were the triumphs of one German over the other, the humiliation of the House of Hapsburg by that of Brandenburg. It was not till the galling yoke of Napoleon, by pressing with equal weight upon the whole empire, roused one universal thrill of shame and indignation, that for the first time, and for a brief space only, the Germans became indeed one nation. The peril over, the victory achieved, they relapsed once more into their former condition, and in this they still remain. This was strikingly exemplified in the revolution of 1848, when the mutual jealousies between the various States, large and small, prevented the realization of their long-cherished project of forming a "united Germany."

Under these circumstances, a national history must be admitted to be a most difficult undertaking. It is only within the last fifty years that it has been attempted, and even now, despite the high merits and popularity of Wenzel, Haüser, and some others, with but partial success. On the other hand, the number of provincial and dynastic historians is particularly large. Justes, Moeser, Spittler, Schlosser, &c., have treated successively with more or less talent the origin and history of the little principalities to which they severally belong. Dr. Vehse has followed in their footsteps. His "History of the Prussian Court and People," which appeared in 1851, though very verbose and somewhat wearisome, still attracted sufficient attention to induce the author to follow it up by others of the Courts of Austria, Bavaria, Saxony, &c. It is the last of these which has just reached a second edition, to which we now invite the reader's attention, deriving as it does a peculiar attraction from the individuals of whom it treats,—the eccentric John Frederic Carl Auguste, the friend and patron of Goethe, his mother Amelia, the noble and high-minded Duchess Louise, who forced even the conqueror and oppressor of her native land to respect and admiration, and, above all, Goethe himself, and his contemporaries Wieland, Herder, and Schiller. The other volumes prefixed to this article also throw some new light on the habits, manners, and history of the Court of Weimar. We shall therefore freely avail ourselves of them while sketching, as we now propose to do, some of the more salient features and incidents of that Court.

Weimar, indeed, is but a little spot on the map of Europe; but in the history of the empire to which it belongs, and, above all, in the history of the human mind, it occupies a far more conspicuous place than the proud capitals of Austria and Prussia. Its most brilliant days were at the close of the eighteenth and beginning of the nineteenth century. This was the golden age of German philosophy and literature, and almost all the celebrated men of the epoch seem to have met in the capital of Carl Auguste's dominions. The German rulers had never evinced much inclination to favour the development of literary genius in their own land. They either despised it as unworthy their attention, or dreaded it as inimical to their authority. It was to a foreign monarch that Klopstock was indebted for his pension, and all his worldly advantages. Schubert languished for ten long years in the prisons of Hohen-Asberg, without one neighbouring sovereign interesting himself in his behalf, and was at length indebted for his freedom to the intercession of an English prince. Burger, poor and neglected, applied in vain to the greatest of German kings in his distress. Lessing owed nothing to any earthly potentate. Thus unaided and unprotected, German poetry had slowly but successfully emerged from obscurity, and worked out its way to the light. As yet, indeed, it had achieved no signal triumph; no mighty master of song, no Homer, no Dante, Milton, or Shakspeare had shone forth with dazzling splendour to form the wonder of succeeding ages. Even the "Messiah" of Klopstock, hailed as it had been with rapturous applause, could not claim a place beside the glorious monuments of human genius of which Greece, Italy, and England may be so justly proud. But enough had been achieved to give hope and promise of brighter days. It was at this moment that a woman-regent of a little principality, numbering scarcely thirty thousand inhabitants, and hitherto almost unknown and unnoticed, stepped forward as the good genius of her country's muse, and for ever associated her name with that of its most gifted sons. While Goethe, Schiller, Wieland, and Herder are remembered, Amelia of Weimar will not be forgotten in the literary annals of the land those great names adorn.

The founder of the present reigning House of Weimar (the younger branch of the Saxon line, the "Ernestonians," called after the first of their race) was the Duke William, born in 1598. He was one of eleven brothers, among whom was that Bernard, so famous in the Thirty Years' War, and the unfortunate John Frederic, whose strange and tragic story still lives in the recollection of his countrymen. Like his brother, John Frederic offered his sword to the Protestant cause; but the singularity of his character, and the dark reports already attached to his name, made him rather shunned than sought by his companions in arms. It was rumoured that he had devoted himself to forbidden studies, and the faith in witchcraft and demonology was at that time so universally diffused, that the tale found easy credence. Far from seeking to destroy this impression, John Frederic did his best to confirm it. Shutting himself up in his hereditary castle, he devoted his days and nights to the study of Paracelsus, Cornelius Agrippa, and other necromantic writers, in the hope of discovering the awful secrets of magic; his name became a bye-word, and nothing but his rank and position saved him from the fate of a sorcerer. In the year 1625 he entered the service of King Christian of Denmark, then at the head of the Protestant cause, in whose ranks his younger brother, the famous Bernard, had already enlisted. But a dispute with a Danish officer, in which his violent and unjustifiable conduct excited general indignation, soon brought about his dismissal. Burning with rage, he abandoned the Protestant cause and faith, and joined the Imperial army, where he was well received. Ere long, however, he was compelled to fly in consequence of a duel in which he ran his adversary through the body, and falling into the hands of the enraged Protestants, was thrown into a dungeon and loaded with fetters, as at once a renegade, a traitor, a maniac, and magician—attributes, one alone of which would have sufficed to render him an object of universal horror and detestation. The Court of Weimar claiming him, he was given up to it on condition of his being kept in close custody—a condition rigorously fulfilled. Caged like a wild beast, conscious that he was the object of general hatred and terror, the mind of the wretched captive, already deeply shaken, completely gave way, till, in a fit of despair or insanity, he declared he had entered into a pact with the devil, had signed it with his blood, and hourly expected his deliverance by the Prince of Darkness. What passed on a certain awful night in the captive's chamber has never been revealed to human ear; but the next morning the wretched man was found dead on the floor, bathed in blood. The report was industriously spread that the foul fiend, enraged by his disclosure of their secret intercourse, had destroyed the wretched prisoner, as he had destroyed Faust, and so many others who had pledged their eternal weal, and that in the dead of night unearthly howlings had rent the air, and that the very walls had trembled as though shaken by an earthquake. But the immediate reception of the guards, who had watched the captive, into the Duke's service, the lavish bestowal of presents on the captains and officers, and the absence of all investigation, seem to point to a more probable, though scarcely less horrid, solution of the gloomy tale. However this may be, the popular belief, as usual in Germany, inclined to the supernatural version of the story. The building which had been the scene of the tragedy was shut up, and such was the terror with which it was regarded, that an inhabitant of Weimar would have gone miles out of his way rather than pass it after sunset. At length, in 1817, it was pulled down, and its place supplied by modern houses, to which is attached no such fearful mystery. This crime of fratricide, if indeed it was committed by the Duke of Weimar, is strangely in contrast with his general character—that of an honest, open-hearted man. He reigned peacefully for twenty

years; his successor was so deeply engrossed by theological pursuits, that he found little time for the duties of government; holding religious conferences, and examining his hearers on the state of their consciences, instead of attending to public affairs. His grandson, Ernest Augustus, was one of the most singular characters of the day, and occupies some amusing pages in the memoirs of the Margravine of Baireuth, who met him at her father-in-law's court in 1732. He was carried off by a fever when his son, the father of Carle Auguste, had attained his eleventh year; and that prince likewise dying at the age of one-and-twenty, his widow, Amelia, became Dowager Duchess of Weimar.

Amelia of Brunswick was born the 14th of October, 1742. The Court of Brunswick was at that period the most highly cultivated in Germany, and the princess enjoyed the advantages of a careful and solid education. Her youth, however, was far from happy. Her father stern, cold, and haughty, regarded his children, especially his daughters, as mere household appendages, to be disposed of as best suited his personal convenience and his political interests. The strict etiquette on which he insisted, not only deprived the young girl of all the delights of intimate friendship with those of her own age, but exercised a chilling influence even over the heart of her royal mother, and introduced itself like a dark spectre between parent and child. In 1756 she was given in marriage to the Duke of Weimar. It was a union in which the heart had little share. "I was married as princesses generally are," she said; nevertheless, she could not but rejoice at her deliverance from the harsh treatment to which she had been subjected under the parental roof, and which, it appears, went even to the length of blows. Her gentle sweetness gained the confidence and affection of her not very congenial spouse, so as to render her married life at least supportable, if not happy. In 1757 she became the mother of Carl Auguste. A year later her husband died, leaving her *enciente* with her second son, Constantine. By the Duke's will, Amelia's father was appointed Regent and guardian of mother and children; but at the expiration of a twelvemonth, the fair widow was declared of age by the Emperor, and invested with the sole regency of her little realm.

Her position was a difficult one for a young, lovely, and inexperienced woman; but the zeal and earnestness with which

she applied herself to her new duties went far to supply the place of the knowledge of affairs and practical wisdom in which she was necessarily deficient. The following document, found among her papers after her decease, will give some idea of her thoughts at this momentous epoch of her existence, and proves that it was not only in the family of Frederic William of Prussia that princesses were subject to corporeal chastisement:—

"MY THOUGHTS.

"From childhood my lot has been nothing but self-sacrifice. Never was education so little fitted as mine to form one destined to rule others. Those who directed it themselves needed direction; she to whose guidance I was entrusted was the sport of every passion, subject to innumerable wayward caprices, of which I became the unresisting victim. Unloved by my parents, ever kept in the background, I was regarded as the outcast of the family. The sensitive feelings I had received from nature made me keenly alive to this cruel treatment; it often drove me to despair; I became silent, reserved, concentrated, and thus gained a certain firmness, which gradually degenerated into obstinacy. I suffered myself to be reproached, insulted, *beaten*, without uttering a word, and still as far as possible persisted in my own course. At length in my sixteenth year I was married. In my seventeenth I became a mother. It was the first unmingled joy I had ever known. It seemed to me as though a host of new and varied feelings had sprung into life with my child. My heart became lighter, my ideas clearer; I gained more confidence in myself. In my eighteenth year arrived the greatest epoch in my life. I became a mother for the second time, a widow, and Regent of the Duchy. The sudden changes which one after another had taken place in my existence, created such a tumult in my mind, that for some time I could scarcely realize what had occurred. A rush of ideas and feelings, all undeveloped, and no friend to whom I could open my heart! I felt my own incapacity, and yet I was compelled to find everything in my own resources. Never have I prayed with truer or deeper devotion than at that moment. I believe I might have become the greatest of saints. When the first storm was over, and I could look within and around with more calmness, my feelings were, I confess, those of awakened vanity. To be Regent! so young! to rule and command! It could not be otherwise. But a secret voice whispered, Beware! I heard it, and my better reason triumphed. Truth and self-love struggled for the mastery; truth prevailed. Then came war. My brothers and nearest relations were crowned with laurels. Nothing was heard but the name of Brunswick. It was sung alike by friend and foe. This roused my ambition. I, too, longed for praise. Day and night I studied to render myself mistress of my new duties. Then I felt how absolutely I needed a friend in whom I could place my entire confidence. There were many who courted my favours; some by flattery, others by a show of disinterestedness. I seemed to accept all, in the hope that among them I should find the pearl of great price. At length I did find it, and it filled me with the same joy which others experience at the discovery of a treasure. If a prince, and the individual he selects as a confidant, are both noble-minded, the sincerest affection may exist between them; and thus the question is decided, whether or no princes can have friends."

These extracts prove how deeply the young Duchess felt the responsibility of her new position. She soon displayed talents for government which, in a wider sphere of action, might have given her a name in history. The state of the little Duchy was lamentable; the treasury was empty, agriculture was neglected, and the people were discontented. With the aid of her faithful ministers she succeeded in restoring something like order to the exhausted finances, established schools and charitable asylums, and left untried no means of promoting the general prosperity. Disgusted by the wearisome etiquette of which her youth had been a victim, she banished all that was not absolutely indispensable to the due maintenance of her dignity; while in her love of literature she succeeded in drawing round her a galaxy of genius which recalled the Court of Ferrara in the days of Alfonso. The first who answered her call was Herder. After spending some years at Bückeburg, one of the innumerable little principalities into which Germany was then divided, he accepted her proposal to settle at Weimar as chaplain and superintendent of the schools she had established there.

Few men have possessed greater virtues, or faculties more lofty and varied than Herder. Like Lessing, he may be regarded as one of the pioneers of the German intellect. But his temper was too uncertain, his sensibility too morbidly keen, to permit him to live on very good terms with those around him. He was perpetually imagining some offence where none was intended, and lending every word and action an import of which their authors probably had never even dreamt. He reminds us of an instrument of exquisite tone, in which, by some fault of mechanism, a slight but oft-recurring jar mars the delicious harmony. Perhaps his frequent attacks of ill health, his position, which never exactly suited his taste or his temperament, may in some degree account for the fits of irritability and hypochondria which at times darkened his noble nature. These defects, however, did not prevent him from being generally loved

and admired both as a writer and a man. A poet, in the highest sense of the word, perhaps he was not, for in the creative faculty he was deficient; but no man had a deeper sense of the beautiful, or keener powers of analysis and criticism. Indeed, whatever the defects of his works, they are forgotten amid their many beauties. In every line we trace a pure, noble, lofty spirit, the love of God and man; a mind equally removed from incredulity and bigotry. "He was inspired," says Edgar Quinet, one of his warmest admirers, "by something nobler than love of fame, by a sincere and constant desire to promote the best and highest interests of humanity."

Wieland played a more conspicuous part than Herder at the little Court of Weimar. When he first made his appearance, he was at the very zenith of his popularity, the pride and darling of his countrymen. His "Oberon," indeed, on which his celebrity principally if not entirely rests, the only one of his numerous productions which still maintains its place among the classic works of Germany, was not yet composed, but his poem of "Musarion," in which Goethe delighted, and the classic romance, the "Agathon," now almost forgotten, sufficed to raise him to the very pinnacle of literary fame. The latter, indeed, had called forth the unmingled praises of the severe Lessing, who, in his "Dramaturgie," declared it, without contradiction, "the most remarkable work of its era." Carl Auguste was then in his sixteenth year. The high and varied endowments, and the private virtues of Wieland, decided the Duchess on selecting him as the preceptor of the young prince. The appointment, indeed, was not unopposed, for spotless as was Wieland's life, his works were by no means equally immaculate; and it was but too easy to point out passages, both in the "Agathon" and "Musarion," strangely at variance with that sound and lofty morality which ought to form the basis of every education, more especially that of one born to rule the destinies of his fellow-men. But the Duchess, who, despite her unsullied purity, was somewhat tainted by the philosophy of the day, and who held the delusive though plausible theory, that no license of tone, or warmth of colouring, could injure any really healthful and high-toned mind, cast these objections to the wind. We have Wieland's well-known honour as guarantee that he never betrayed the sacred trust reposed in him. But there were not wanting many who

attributed that tendency to licentious habits—which was the only stain upon Carl Auguste's many virtues—if not to the instructions of his tutor, at least to the perusal of his works, the evil effects of which even his example could not suffice to neutralize. The emolument offered to Wieland was so small as to appear almost ludicrous in our eyes. He was to receive 1000 gulden, or 90l. per annum, for three years, to be followed by the magnificent pension of 300 gulden, or 23l. per annum for life. But in this world everything is comparative. The 90l. went further in Germany in the eighteenth century than 300l. would in England at the present day.

The tastes of the inhabitants were simple. The price of all the necessaries of life was comparatively small.* Schiller, some years later, declared that he could live charmingly at Jena for 300 florins, or 60l. per annum, with wife and children; that he had a servant who, when necessary, could perform the part of a secretary, for 18s. per quarter, and a carriage and horses for 60l. per annum. Thus Wieland's salary, with what he gained by his literary labours, was sufficient for his wants and those of an increasing family. The close intimacy between the Duchess Amelia and her son's tutor was broken only by death. Nor could even the more brilliant glory of a Goethe or a Schiller eclipse his in the estimation of this devoted friend.

In 1776 the Duchess resigned the reins of government to Carl Auguste, then eighteen years of age, and set out for Italy, that land which had ever been the darling dream of her existence.

"My son," were her last words on quitting her little capital, "I confide to your hands the happiness of your subjects; be it your care as it has been mine." In many respects Carl Auguste was no ordinary man. Frederick the Great, who saw him at the Court of Brunswick in 1771, when he was but fourteen, declared he had never beheld a youth who at an early age justified such lofty hopes; and in 1775, the prince-primate Dalberg, writing to Görres, observes, "he unites an excellent understanding to all the frankness and true heartiness of his age; he has a princely soul such as I have never yet seen. Taught both by precept and example to place little value upon empty pomp and splendour, he carries his dislike to all

---

* Beef was 4 kreutzers, (a penny farthing) per pound; wood 6 gulden, or 11s. a load; (it is now 28 gulden); and everything in proportion.

courtly forms and ceremonials to an even exaggerated degree." How early and how well Carl Auguste had learnt to value genius, is evident from the discourse he addressed to his Council in his nineteenth year, in which he expressed his intention of inviting Goethe to his Court. " The judgment of the world," observes the young prince, "may perhaps censure me for placing Dr. Goethe in my most important university, without his having passed the grades of professor, chancellor, &c. The world judges according to its own prejudices; but I do not act like others for the sake of fame, or the approbation of the world, but to justify myself before God and my own conscience."

Occasionally the thoughtlessness and reckless love of pleasure, which in his earlier years contrasted so strangely with the Duke's loftier qualities of head and heart, may have led him astray; but his nature was essentially generous and noble; his ear ever open to the cry of the suffering and distressed, his hand ever ready, so far as his means allowed, to aid them. In 1774 the Duke left Weimar to celebrate his union with the Princess Louise. On his way through Frankfort, Goethe, already celebrated as the author of " Götz von Berlichingen " and " Werter," was introduced to him. Fascinated by the charm of his genius, by the grace and gaiety of his manner, the Duke invited him to visit his Court; and Goethe only too happy to escape from Frankfort, and from the vicinity of the fair Lili—that bright being he had, at least as he imagined, once so passionately loved, but whom he had, as usual, discovered was not a meet partner for his glorious destinies—at once accepted the proposition.

It was arranged that the Duke's chamberlain, Herr von Kalb, who having lingered behind at Strasburg to execute some commissions for his master, was to arrive at Frankfort on a certain day, should call for the new guest. But days and weeks passed on, and no Von Kalb made his appearance. Goethe's father was a burgher of the old school, and thoroughly disliking kings and princes, had always been exceedingly averse to the project. He now insisted that the whole affair was a hoax, and urged his son to wait no longer, but to set off at once on his long-proposed journey to Italy, and Goethe at length consented. In the journal he now commenced, which, however, was carried on only for a very brief period, we find certain expressions which induce the belief that his resolutions to break off his

marriage with Lili were aided by a dawning inclination for another, Augusta Stolberg, sister to the two counts of that name. " How shall I call thee," he writes, " thou whom I cherish as a spring blossom in my heart ? Thou shalt bear the name of fairest flower. How shall I take leave of thee? Comfort—for it is time—the full time. A few days, and already—Oh, farewell! Am I, then, only in the world to involve myself eternally in involuntary guilt ?"

The meaning of these last words is not very apparent, unless it be that Goethe's feelings toward Augusta were of a warmer nature than has generally been supposed. The correspondence is altogether of the most romantic cast; and many of the letters, written long before Goethe's engagement with Lili was broken off, sound not a little strange from a man passionately attached and already affianced to another. " My dearest," he writes, in one of the earliest of these epistles, " I will give you no name, for what are the names of friend, sister, beloved, bride, or even a word which would comprehend all these, in comparison with my feelings ? I can write no more." To this he added his silhouette, entreating she would send him her's in return; the receipt of it seems to have filled him with delight. " How completely is my belief in physiognomy confirmed," he writes; " that pure thoughtful eye, that sweet firm nose, those dear lips. Thanks, my love, thanks. Oh! that I could repose in your heart, rest in your eyes." It is true that Goethe had never seen Augusta, and that her rank as Countess rendered a union with her in those days almost impossible; so strict was the line of demarcation between the nobles and burghers, that even Goethe's already brilliant fame would not have enabled him to surmount the barrier. Nor, perhaps, did the idea ever take a tangible form; but it seems pretty certain that this half-ideal, half-romantic passion for one whom imagination invested with every conceivable perfection, tended somewhat to cool his affection for the gay openhearted young creature, who, while loving him with truth and tenderness, was too much accustomed to homage to hang upon his every word and look as Fredricka had done, and Augusta seemed inclined to do.*

Goethe proceeded to Heidelburg, and from thence was about to depart to Italy

---

* Mr. Lewes does not appear to attach any importance to this correspondence, and scarcely notices it; but it will be found published *in extenso.*

when the long-expected messenger from Weimar arrived, and he set off post-haste for the little capital of which he was henceforth to be the brightest ornament. His appearance was the signal for fêtes and rejoicings, and he himself seems to have given free vent to the spirit of youthful gaiety and love of pleasure which at this time possessed him.

The author of the " Musen Hof," who is nevertheless one of his warmest admirers, declares that his *immediate* influence over the young Duke was not peculiarly beneficial, as he led him into dissipations prejudicial alike to his health and domestic happiness, and certainly the letters of his contemporaries, — of Bottiger, Berteuch, Knebel, nay of Madame von Stein herself —seem to have corroborated this assertion. " Goethe," says the latter, " causes a terrible commotion here; all our happiness has disappeared. A ruler dissatisfied with himself and every one about him, risking his life constantly in mad follies, with little health to sustain him, a mother annoyed and vexed, a wife discontented, &c." It is evident that the strange mode of existence in which the Duke and Goethe indulged, and the infelicity of the royal pair which seems to have been the result, must have attracted general attention, since it reached the ears of Klopstock, and induced the aged poet to address a letter to Goethe on the subject, which, like most advice of a similar nature, served only to displease all parties.

We will not enter further into this much-vexed question. At all events, Goethe soon grew weary of a mode of life so little in accordance with the higher aspirations of the poet's soul. He gradually retired more and more from the noisy pleasures of the court, spending a considerable portion of his time in the quiet retirement of his garden pavilion. A new and all-engrossing passion had likewise its share in withdrawing him from pursuits unworthy of his nobler nature. He loved, not indeed for the first, second, or third time, as his annals attest, but with a warmth, a tenderness, and above all, a constancy, which neither the fair, innocent, and trusting Fredricka, nor the bright and graceful Lili, had been able to inspire. And yet the woman to whom was reserved the triumph of fettering for ten long years the heart of one of the most gifted and most inconstant of mortals was no longer in the early bloom of womanhood; she had attained her 33rd year, and Goethe was but 28. Beautiful in the strict sense of the word she had never been, but there was a mingled grace, sweetness, and dignity in her glance and demeanour which exercised a singular fascination on all around her. Goethe, the young, the gallant, the admired of all admirers, was at once enthralled by her spell. "I can only explain," he writes to Wieland, "the power she exercises over me by the theory of the transmigration of souls. Yes! we were formerly man and wife. Now, I can find no name for us, for the past, the future." Unluckily, Charlotte von Stein was already the wife of another, the mother of six children. That she returned the passion of her adorer cannot be doubted; but, if we are to believe the assurance of her son, in his preface to Goethe's letters to his mother, and the testimony of many of her contemporaries, among others, that of Schiller—she never transgressed the strictest bounds of virtue. She had been indoctrinated with the questionable morality of the eighteenth century, and was married while yet a girl to a man infinitely her inferior in all mental endowments, and for whom she had little sympathy or affection. She was thrown, by her position as lady of honour to the Dowager Duchess, into the constant society of the young and brilliant genius—already the day-star of his age and country. Proud in conscious virtue, it is perhaps not to be wondered at that she could not prevail on herself to break an intercourse so replete with every charm of intellect and fancy, to refuse an homage so flattering alike to her heart and her vanity, if she permitted herself to be the Laura of this new Petrarch:—

"Indeed," observes Frederick von Stein, "if this correspondence proves that emotions even dangerous in their warmth were not far distant from this intercourse, it also serves to place in a still stronger light the virtue and prudence of the woman who, while keeping her young, gifted, and ardent lover within the limits of the strictest reserve, still contrived to reconcile him to her severity, by sincere sympathy in all his trials, both mental and material, by fully comprehending his glorious vocation, and by soothing him with the most sincere and lasting friendship."

More than one German author, especially Adolphe Stahr, in his well-known work "Weimar and Jena," has actually censured Madame von Stein in no measured terms for refusing to accede to Goethe's entreaties that she would obtain a divorce from her husband, the father of her children, against whom she had no just cause of complaint, and become his wife,—that is, when he found it impossible to induce her to listen to a suit of any other description. Upon this refusal is thrown the whole responsibility of the poet's subsequent *liaison* with Christina Vulpius These authors seem never even to imagine that there may be some slight fault on Goethe's side; that if Madame von Stein was blameable in admitting him to an intimacy endangering her peace of mind, if not her conjugal fidelity, he was not perfectly justifiable in seeking with all the eloquence of genius to win the heart of a woman already bound by the most sacred ties to another. But Nemesis was not forgetful. The connexion which in a moment of ennui and weariness Goethe formed with Christina Vulpius—a connexion which he had not the courage or cruelty to break, and which he ultimately confirmed by marriage—embittered his latter years, and could not but exercise an unfavourable influence on his whole nature. Would not Fredricka or Lili have been a more genial companion than Christina Vulpius for that great poet of whom his native land is so justly proud? Who could have dreamt of such a bride for the beautiful gifted Apollo, as Adolphe Stahr calls him, when he first set foot in the dominions of Carl Auguste!

Weimar, consecrated to all lovers of poetry, scarcely deserved the name of a town when Goethe first lived there. Schiller, in a letter to Körner, calls it "something between a town and a hamlet." Goethe laughingly observed one day to his friend Zetter, when the latter spoke of building a theatre for the people, "How is it possible to talk of the people of Weimar in this little residence, where there are ten thousand poets and five hundred inhabitants?"

The park did not then exist. A few trees alone waved on the spot now so beautifully diversified with verdant wood and grassy lawn. On the Curplatz, now covered with stately houses, stood nothing save the straw-thatched huts of the Weimar peasants; one thing only have we to regret in the changes which have gradually transformed an insignificant village into a stately city. On the esplanade, which as late as 1770 was the favourite promenade of the good inhabitants, stands a dwelling so humble as scarcely to attract attention among the more conspicuous buildings around. It is the house of Schiller. Here, in this modest retreat, did the author of "Wallenstein" spend the latter years of his existence. He purchased it at the high price, as he called it, of 4000 gulden, 360*l.* He entered it on the 29th of April, full of delight at possessing one spot on earth he could call his own. A heavy domestic calamity soon came to damp this joy. Within a few days he received a letter informing him of the death of his mother, that mother to whom he was so devotedly attached. The blow was a heavy one. Amid every change of place and scene, domestic joys and sorrows, amid fame, homage, toil and suffering, his heart had ever clung with inexpressible fondness to the home of his childhood, and above all to the parent who had watched over his infant years.

"Would," he writes to his sister, "that I had been able to aid you in tending our beloved mother during her last illness. Oh, dear sister, now our parents are sunk to rest, the most holy bond which united us is torn asunder. It makes me unspeakably sad, and I feel desolate though surrounded by the loved and loving. Yet I have *you* too, my sister, to whom I can fly in joy and sorrow. Oh! let us now, there are but three of us remaining in the paternal house, cling close to each other. Never forget you have a loving brother. I remember vividly the days of our youth, when we were all in all to each other. Life has divided our destiny; but confidence and affection may at least remain unalterable."

It is scarcely possible to enter without a feeling of deep emotion that humble dwelling, where so many glorious works of genius were brought forth, where one of the purest and noblest spirits that ever breathed on earth passed away. Three years only was Schiller permitted to inhabit this lowly but pleasant abode, so modest that even Goethe's house, though not particularly splendid, looks like a palace in comparison. The middle story, in which the family resided, is let; only the room which Schiller himself inhabited is shown to the visitor, the town having at length purchased the house. In the centre stands the table on which he was in the habit of writing, that very table which, as he informs his friend Körner, "cost two carolines," a heavy sum for his narrow finances at that period. It is of the very commonest wood, and so low as perfectly to explain his unfortunate habit of bending over it when composing. One drawer was always filled with half-rotten apples, the smell of which was peculiarly agreeable to the poet. The walls are covered with green paper; the furniture is of light mahogany, covered with leather. A little guitar, a few bad-coloured prints of Palermo, the bed in which Schiller breathed his last, a portrait taken from his bust, and a second painted after death—these complete the picture. When Schiller resided at this cottage it had nothing but green trees around and upland shades before it.

Improvements, however, so far as the duke's finances allowed, went on rapidly under the supervision of the almost ubiquitous Goethe. The park owes its origin to a tragic incident which occurred about the beginning of 1780—the suicide of a young and blooming girl, Christel von Lasberg, who in despair at the infidelity of her lover, destroyed herself on a spot Goethe was compelled to pass on his way to and from the ducal castle. This affected him painfully, the more so as his "Werter" was found in her pocket, though it appeared that this was but an accidental coincidence. At first he resolved on erecting a monument to her memory, but abandoned this project, "because," as he said, "one could neither pray nor love there." But the gloom of the spot, overhung by dark pine trees, and peopled by such terrible recollections, became intolerable to Goethe, and he determined to try and lend it a more cheerful aspect. To this end he had some of the trees cut down, the rocks planted with shrubs and flowers; this suggested the idea of further changes, which at length resulted in that beautiful park which is now the principal ornament of Weimar.

"The duke and Goethe," says Wieland to Merck, June 3rd, 1778, "came back yesterday afternoon from their trip to Leipsig, Dessau, and Berlin. In the evening I went with my wife and both my eldest girls to see the exercise grounds opposite Goethe's garden, and arranged according to his own plans; thence I proceeded to the so-named ' Star ' to show my wife the new *Poemata*, which has been made by the duke, after Goethe's designs, and is laid out with wonderful skill, to represent a wild, solitary, yet not completely sequestered assemblage of rocks, where Goethe and the duke often dine together with some goddess or half goddess. We met both with the fair Corinna Schröder, who with her exquisite attic elegance, her lovely form, her simple yet inexpressively-graceful attire, looks like the very nymph of this sequestered spot."

The words "in the society of some goddess," let us into something of the secret origin of the Weimar scandal. There was other pleasures, however, of a less objectionable character:—

"Last Saturday," writes Wieland to Merck, August 21st, 1779, "we drove to Goethe's, who had invited the Duchess Amelia to spend the evening with him in his garden, to regale her with all the poems he had composed during her

absence. We dined in a charming solitary spot. When we rose from table, and the doors were thrown open, we beheld before us a scene which resembled a realization of a poet's dream. The whole banks of the Ilm where illuminated quite in the taste of Rembrandt, a wonderous enchanting mixture of light and shadow, which produced an effect beyond all description. The duchess was delighted, so were we all. As we descended the little steps of the hermitage, and wandered along the banks of the Ilm, amid the rocks and bushes which unite this spot with the Star, the whole vision changed into a number of small pictures, ' au Rembrandt,' which one could have looked on for ever. The carnival time," he continues, "has brought with it its usual gaieties, and we have done our best to make the ordinary court malady, ' ennui,' as brilliant as possible."

The limited finances of the little court somewhat interfered with these courtly amusements. Carl Auguste often found himself in difficulties, which neither his own skill, nor that of his counsellors, could suffice to remove. When tormented by some of these petty annoyances, or fatigued with the cares of state, he would retire to a little country-house, where, dismissing all his train, he would remain alone.

"It is just ten o'clock," he writes to Knebel; "I am sitting at the window, and writing to you. The day has been exquisitely beautiful, and this my first evening of liberty I have enjoyed to the utmost. I feel so far removed from the affairs of earth, so completely in a better, a higher sphere. Man is not destined to be the miserable ' phlister' of this every-day life. Never do we feel so noble, so elevated, as when we behold the sun sink to rest, and the stars rise, and know that all this is created for its *own* sake alone, not for that of man, and yet we enjoy it as though it were all made for us. I will bathe with the evening star, and draw in new life. Till then farewell. I come from my bath. The water was cold, night already lay upon its bosom. It seems as though I had plunged into the cold night itself when I took the first dip, all was so calm, so holy. Over the distant hills rose the full moon. All was silent, and the intense stillness made me hear, or fancy I heard purer sounds than those which really reached the ear."

The individual to whom this letter is addressed enjoyed, next to Goethe, the confidence and affection of the duke. Knebel, better known as the friend and companion of poets and princes than by any celebrity of his own, was one of those peculiarly constituted natures which seem destined to act rather in calling forth the powers of others, than in displaying their own. These perhaps are, on the whole, the happiest. Free from those feverish

impulses, that burning thirst for fame which so often torment more highly gifted spirits, they can enjoy to the full the productions of genius without envy or regret. They, too, are poets; but they are content to find poetry in life and nature, in the summer flowers, in the murmur of the fountain, in the whispering of the breeze, instead of attempting to give it form and shape in verse. They compose, but only for the amusement of a leisure hour, yet no men have had more influence on the great minds of their age. Most rare and valuable are such spirits, sufficiently gifted to appreciate the lofty endowments of genius, to sympathize in all its varied moods and sublime aspirations, and yet content to play the humble part of confidant and admirer. Such a man was Knebel. His literary works, though not absolutely devoid of merit, have been long since forgotten, but the ascendancy he exerted over the intellect of the great men of his country and his time has associated his name lastingly with theirs.

Descended from a Flemish family, he was born at Wallenstein, in Ottingen, 1744. One of his ancestors having paid the penalty of his religious opinions by a cruel death under Philip II., the family had fled from the land of their birth, and taken refuge in Germany. Stern, harsh, and unbending, Knebel's father was feared rather than loved by his son, and the youth always attributed his timidity in after-life to the severity exercised towards him in childhood. His delicate and somewhat fastidious tastes seemed continually in the way. At the university they rendered the rude habits of his companions insupportable. When he entered the service of Frederick the Great, he found the want of education and literary taste among his brother officers still more intolerable. He felt like an automaton, deprived of all individuality of action; and despite the royal notice, with which he was occasionally honoured, he grew sad and dispirited.

Knebel spent ten years in the Prussian service—ten long and weary years as he calls them. In 1772 he obtained his discharge with a small pension, and a letter of introduction to the young Duchess of Weimar from the Crown Prince, in whose regiment he had served. By her he was graciously received, while by Wieland, who had already resided at Weimar, as tutor to the young duke, he was warmly welcomed. In 1773 he was himself appointed professor of mathematics to Carl Auguste and his brother. Shortly afterwards he accompanied the princes on a visit to some of the courts of Germany, and afterwards to Paris. Knebel was delighted with the novelty of all he beheld, and especially with the grace of French manners. "They may say what they like," he wrote to Wieland, "the French are an agreeable and amiable people; nowhere else does one find so much urbanity." "I saw a good deal of Diderot," he adds in a subsequent letter. He expressed his amazement that Mendelssohn was not admitted to the Royal Academy of Berlin. Though royalty still seemed to reign supreme, the revolutionary spirit was already abroad. "Many young men of distinguished talent," says Knebel in his letters, "repeated to me continually that henceforward all must be equal—nobles, peers, burghers, and peasant, and *such like trash*." He was not keen-sighted enough to discern through the bright and glowing atmosphere that surrounded him—the dark clouds, big with the mighty changes, already slowly looming on the verge of the horizon, so soon to cover all with its gloomy folds, and to burst in thunder over Europe.

Next to Goethe and Knebel, the most intimate friend of Carl Auguste was his chamberlain, Frederick von Einsedel. Born 1750, he commenced his court career as page; he was then promoted to the rank of chamberlain to the Dowager Duchess Amelia; in 1770 he was named privy councillor. Himself gay, joyous, and light-hearted, he had while page played prank upon prank, which had already become proverbial in the court chronicles of Weimar. In after-life his gladsome temperament, his frank and open manners, and generous nature, secured him the lasting favour of his royal master. His very failings served as subjects of amusement rather than anger. His constitutional laziness varied by fits of feverish activity, and his strange absence of mind, during which he might be *robbed* of hat, gloves, or watch, without his ever perceiving it, diverted the ennui to which, despite the presence of a Goethe, or a Herder and a Wieland, this little court seems to have been peculiarly subject. Einsedel, however, must have had merits of a higher order than mere harmlessness and good-humour, or he would scarcely have been admitted to the intimate friendship of Herder and Schiller. "He is an excellent, unaffected man," writes the latter to Körner, in 1803, and far from devoid of talent. Einsedel's private life, however, was anything but immaculate, and some of his adventures might serve as a curious illustration of the times and the atmosphere in which he lived. He had become desperately enamoured of a Madame von Werthein, who, yielding to her passion, abandoned home, husband, friends, and country, to follow her seducer. Not completely dead, however, to the shame of thus publicly violating all her holiest duties, she had recourse to one of the most extraordinary stratagems ever devised by a romantic female head. She took advantage of the fainting fits to which she was occasionally subject, to feign death. With the connivance of her attendants, she contrived to steal out of the house unperceived, while a doll was buried in her stead. She then proceeded with her lover to Africa, where he proposed exploring certain gold mines by which he expected to make his fortune. The affair turned out a complete failure, and Einsedel returned poorer than he went, with his fair and frail companion. Great was the amazement and indignation of husband and friends on beholding the resuscitation of her they believed long since buried in the vaults of her ancestors. But in German courts in the eighteenth century such affairs were not regarded as involving any very great amount of moral turpitude. The Court of Weimar indeed was virtue itself, compared with those of Dresden, of Wurtenberg, and Hanover; but even *here* "excess of love" was held as sufficient excuse for every sin. There was a strange mixture of the maudlin and the licentious. French immorality grafted on German sentimentality. A separation was obtained, and Madame W. became the wife of her lover. Einsedel lived to the age of seventy-eight, and died in 1828.

In 1796 Weimar received a new visitor in the author of "Hesperus." The mingled naïveté and singularity of his demeanour, his animated and poetic language, full of thoughts and images at once tender and ironical—for he spoke as he wrote—his enthusiastic belief in the progress of humanity, charmed Herder to such a degree, that he wrote to Jacobi—"Heaven has given me in Jean Paul a treasure which I dare not hope I merit. He is all intellect, all soul, a melodious sound from the mighty golden harp of humanity, that harp of which so many chords are snapped or broken." By Goethe he was more coldly received:—

"It was with apprehension, almost with terror," he writes to his friend Otto, "that I entered the abode of Goethe. Every one depicted him as cold and indifferent to all earthly things.

Madame von Kalb had told me that he no longer admired anything, not even his own works. Every word, she said, is an icicle, especially to strangers, whom he is with difficulty persuaded to admit to his presence. His house struck me. It was the only one in Weimar built in the Italian style; from the very staircase it is a museum of statues and pictures. The god at length appeared; he was cold; he expressed himself in monosyllables only, and without the slightest emphasis. Tell him, said Knebel, that the French have just entered Rome. 'Hein,' replied the god. His person is bony, his physiognomy full of fire, his look a sun. At length our conversation on the arts, and on the opinions of the public, perhaps also the champagne animated him, and then at length I felt I was with Goethe! His language is not flowery and brilliant like that of Herder; it is incisive, calm, and resolute. He concluded by reading, or rather performing, one of his unpublished poems, a composition truly sublime. Thanks to this, the flames of his heart pierced their crust of ice, and he pressed the hand of the enthusiast Jean Paul. How shall I describe his mode of reading? It was like the distant roar of thunder mingled with the soft dripping of a summer shower. No! there is no one in the world like Goethe! We must be friends."

This desire was not destined to be fulfilled. The author of "Quintus Fixlein" was too diametrically opposed, not only as a writer but as an individual, to the poet of "Faust" or "Tasso" to allow of any real or lasting intimacy.

One of the most eccentric and most troublesome personages of the little Court of Weimar was Constantine, the Duke's brother. He possessed neither the intellectual endowments nor the generous nature of Carl Auguste. Knebel, who was appointed his tutor in 1782, had in vain endeavoured to inspire him with loftier tastes. An unfortunate *liaison* with a beautiful girl, Carolina von S——, produced so much scandal, that the Duke sent him from Weimar, on his travels to Italy, accompanied by the Councillor Albrecht von ——, a talented and excellent man, but apparently not a very amusing companion. Constantine soon grew weary of so grave a Mentor. Arrived at Paris, he plunged, despite his companion's admonitions, into all the dissipations of that brilliant capital, and ere long fell into the snare of a clever actress, Mademoiselle Darsaincourt, whose wit, intrigue, and beauty completely enthralled him. Yielding to her counsel, he got rid of the perpetual presence of his guardian, by assigning him, under some pretext, a place in another carriage, while his mistress took hers beside him. He then set off, not for Italy, but to London.

Poor Albrecht, from a sense of duty, followed him, but finding his admonitions utterly useless, returned in despair to Weimar. In vain did Carl Auguste recal his brother; he disregarded his commands. Of his life in London little is recorded, but it is probable that it was not of a very reputable nature. At length, in 1803, his resources failing, he set out for Germany. Somewhat embarrassed how to dispose of his companion, he despatched her beforehand. Carl Auguste, however, would not permit her to set foot in his dominions, and she was forced to return to France, despite the entreaties and remonstrances of her despairing lover.

"This last catastrophe," writes Carl Auguste to Knebel, January 5th, 1784, "has been of service to Constantine, apparently at least. The society here endeavoured to prove its adherence to me by openly blaming his conduct, and shunning his company, so that he was left to almost complete solitude. This decided condemnation was very painful to him, and made him feel how essential is a certain degree of exterior decency at least to procure a reception in good society, and that even his rank could not protect him from contempt and neglect. He has now adopted an appearance of respectability, fulfils more exactly the ordinary duties of life, and performs his part well enough to be regarded as an educated member of society. I am seeking to obtain his admission into the Saxon service."

Constantine died in 1803.

Amid this circle of genius, wit, fancy, and gallantry, sometimes verging on libertinism, stood the Duchess Louise, like one of those pure, calm, beautiful, though somewhat stiff and stately figures of Holbein or Vandyke, among the loose and lovely groups of a Rubens or a Lily. Endowed with every grace of mind and person, seemingly formed to enjoy and bestow felicity, united to one of the most charming and noble-minded princes of the age, Louise was still unhappy and alone. The circumstances which led to this sense of isolation were trifling in themselves; yet in such a position as that of the young duchess, they sufficed to darken all her prospects of domestic bliss. Educated with the utmost severity, accustomed to the observance of the most rigid etiquette and the strictest reserve, Louise found herself suddenly transplanted into an atmosphere diametrically opposite to that in which her whole existence had hitherto been passed. We have seen how completely, both in private and public life, the Duchess Amelia and her son had thrown aside those wearisome observances

which in other German Courts were still held as necessary appendages to royalty, and which the young Louise had learned to regard with almost superstitious reverence. At Weimar, on the contrary, all was simplicity, gaiety, equality, and fraternity. In their desire to do away with the useless encumbrances imposed by their rank, the duke and duchess had in fact unconsciously gone a little too far, and infringed something of that strict decorum which is one of the best safeguards of royalty.

Louise was surprised, pained, even shocked. Her high and perhaps exaggerated sense of what was due alike to the bride and the princess, was perpetually wounded. The charms of intellectual intercourse with such men as Goethe, Herder, Wieland, and Schiller, the gay good humour of her thoughtless but really noble-minded consort, the grace and sweetness of her mother-in-law, would have reconciled most women to the sacrifice of some of their early prejudices. But Louise, with all her lofty qualities, was wanting in that flexibility of character which could alone have secured her felicity under existing circumstances, and though she never by word or deed expressed her feelings, her pallid cheek, her saddened mien, her cold, reserved manner, too plainly showed what passed within. If Carl Auguste had passionately loved his young wife, all might have been well. But Louise's was a nature so utterly antagonistic to his own, that he never fully understood her, or at least not till too late. Her timidity and reserve prevented her expressing her sentiments, while her daily increasing silence and coldness chilled her husband, and led him to believe he was utterly indifferent to her. Nay, he conceived an equally erroneous opinion of her intellect as of her heart. "She is incomprehensible," he wrote to his friend Knebel; "before her marriage she lived quite alone in the world, without ever finding a being who answered her expectations of what friends ought to be, without exercising a single talent which would have softened her nature. She runs the risk of becoming completely isolated, and losing all that grace and amiability which form the principal charm of her sex." These words speak volumes. They explain the clouds which from day to day grew darker over the domestic horizon of the royal pair. Louise felt that her husband neither understood nor appreciated her as she was conscious she deserved to be appreciated. Wounded alike in her affections and her pride, too

timid to remonstrate, too haughty to complain, she withdrew more and more from his society, till at length, though living together, the two consorts became almost strangers to each other. "The young Duchess," observes Knebel, "shone like a darkened star in a hazy atmosphere. The first meeting did not produce very favourable impressions on either side, and she certainly had in part reason to complain of the want of 'convenances' in her court. She endured much with infinite patience, and maintained her dignity with unvarying consistency. The characters of the two princesses, which did not quite agree, gave rise to much disunion. That this exercised a painful influence on those who surrounded them may easily be supposed. Nevertheless the prudence of their 'entourage,' the moderation of the duchess, and the desire of her mother-in-law to love and be loved, prevented any violent outbreak." Even the powerful bonds of parental love did not suffice to draw the royal pair closer together. For many years, indeed, the duke had cherished another passion; he loved a beautiful and gifted actress, Caroline Jägernau. With a virtue and self-denial rare in her class and time, she had long repelled his entreaties though her heart pleaded his cause. Louise was no stranger to this attachment; it scarcely sought concealment. It had often rent her heart and embittered her existence, but she knew the passionate temperament of her husband; she felt that Caroline, with whose gentle and generous character she was well acquainted, might save him from worse seduction.

Affection, womanly pride, religious principle, all opposed such a compromise of her own paramount claims and duty. But, as with Burger's Dora,[*] Louise's devoted tenderness overcame every other consideration. She not only did nothing to prevent or oppose the *liaison;* she wrote the fair actress to entreat her to listen to the duke's suit. However we may wonder at such a course, we are bound to render justice to the unselfish motives which inspired it. Louise did not, like Caroline of England, give her lord a mistress in order to rule him more easily, or less ostensibly, through her influence. It was to save him from worse courses, to confer on him a happiness she felt she had not been able to bestow. Caroline yielded, yet not without a struggle. She was

---

[*] See "Poets and Poetry of Germany." By Madame de Pontés. Vol. II., p. 337.

elevated to the dignity of Madame von Hagendorf, and presented with a superb estate in Saxony. Her influence over Carl Auguste was boundless, and ended only with his life. It is to her credit that she never abused her position, and that she always preserved a most perfect fidelity to her royal lover. She was a blonde, with light hair, and features and complexion of surpassing beauty. The duchess treated her happier rival with the delicacy and kindness natural to her own pure and noble soul, both before and after the death of the duke. How Carl Auguste's mother regarded this *liaison*, we are not informed. Between herself and her daughter-in-law there was too little congeniality of taste or character to admit of intimacy or confidence, yet that Amelia fully appreciated the lofty virtues of her son's wife can scarcely be denied. On her return from Italy the dowager duchess resided at the Belvidere, or her jointure house some little distance from Weimar, where, in the society of the gifted men she had drawn to her son's court, and the enjoyment of innocent and intellectual pleasures, she passed the remainder of her days. Her health, which had latterly shown many symptoms of decay, sank completely beneath the terrible incidents of 1806—the death of her brother, the Duke of Brunswick—the ruin of her ancestral house, and the danger which impended over the land of her adoption. She died in 1807.

But the events which overwhelmed the sensitive nature of the dowager duchess only called into action the noble qualities of her daughter-in-law. When Weimar was threatened by the victorious army of the Conqueror—when all deserted a town which seemed doomed to destruction, the Duchess Louise remained firm and unshaken at the post which she believed Providence assigned her.

Her lord, on whom Napoleon had vowed vengeance, had been forced by prudence to fly. Her children, in her maternal tenderness, she had sent to a place of safety, her troops were scattered, her friends trembling and defenceless, but still Louise, Duchess of Weimar, remained firm and unshrinking in that town, which every instant might become a prey to the flames—in that palace which was so soon to receive the presence of the imperious victor, among the people of whom she had always been the friend and protector, and of whom she was now the guardian angel. "When," says Falk in his personal reminiscences of Goethe,

"the people learnt that the Grand Duchess was still in the Castle, their joy knew no bounds. When they met, they threw themselves in each other's arms exclaiming, 'The Grand Duchess is here.'"

Nor were they mistaken in the sense of safety with which her presence inspired them. The duchess received the Conqueror (who had previously announced his intention of passing the night of the 15th of October at the Castle) at the head of the grand staircase. Pale, but calm and dignified, she awaited the approach of the terrible emperor, on whom the fate of her people depended. Napoleon turned towards her with an angry mien, "Qui êtes-vous, Madame?" "The Duchess of Weimar, sire," was the answer. "Je vous plains," replied Napoleon, abruptly; "I must crush your husband." Then turning rudely away, "Qu'on me fasse dîner dans mes apartements," he exclaimed, and left the duchess without addressing her another word. But Louise would not suffer herself to be discouraged. The following morning she requested another interview,—it was granted.

Night had brought counsel. The Conqueror, though still haughty and imperious, condescended at least to lend an ear to her remonstrance and appeal. Unmoved by his darkening brow and impatient gestures, she defended with all the eloquence of a noble nature the conduct of the duke in adhering to the Prussian cause, as commanded alike by honour and necessity. She painted in vivid colours the personal friendship which bound him to Frederic William, the marks of affectionate interest he had received from that monarch, and inquired with generous indignation whether "it was in the hour of peril and misfortune that he could desert his friend and ally?" She pictured the fearful condition of the land —the stain that would for ever rest upon the fame of the Victor if the city were, as he threatened, abandoned to pillage. Struck and impressed despite himself, Napoleon relented so far as not only to give strict orders that the town should be respected, but to rescind his repeated declaration that the duke should never again set foot on his native soil. True, the conditions appended to this concession were rigorous enough. Carl Auguste was to quit the Prussian camp within twenty-four hours. In vain the anxious wife endeavoured to obtain some delay. Here Napoleon was inflexible; and Louise, finding her efforts useless, retired to take

instant measures to inform her lord of what had occurred. She despatched messengers in all directions, for the exact spot where he was to be found was not known.

Next morning Napoleon returned the visit, accompanied by all his principal officers. Desirous, it would seem, of effacing all recollection of his former harshness, he expressed the deepest regret for the excesses committed by his soldiery, lamenting the cruel necessity of war, and declaring *that it had been forced upon him*. "Croyez-moi, madame, il y a une Providence qui dirige tout, et dont je ne suis que l'instrument," he repeated. On descending to his apartment, he exclaimed, "Voilà une femme à qui nos deux cents canons n'ont pas pu faire peur."

Perhaps political considerations induced Napoleon to prolong the term originally fixed for the duke's return to Weimar, and to admit some modification of the severe conditions he had imposed. No entreaties or remonstrances, however, could obtain any reduction of the contribution of 200,000,000 francs, a fearful burthen on a country already so terribly impoverished. All that the duchess could do to alleviate the sufferings of the people she did. Her private purse was drained to aid their necessities, and it is even said that she disposed of many of her jewels for the same purpose. This noble conduct found its reward in the adoration of her people, in the increasing regard of her lord, in the admiration of Europe. "She is the true model of a woman," writes Madame de Staël, "formed by nature for the very highest position. Equally devoid of pretension or weakness, she awakens at the same time, and in an equal degree, both confidence and veneration. The heroic soul of the olden days of chivalry still animates her without in the slightest degree diminishing the gentleness of her sex."

Though in the latter years of their union a sincere if not ardent friendship had succeeded the coldness of early life, Louise was not destined to be beside her husband at the hour of his death. He had undertaken a journey to Berlin to visit his granddaughter, the Princess Marie, who had lately married the Prince of Prussia. On his return he was suddenly seized with illness, and died at Graditz, near Torgau, 14th June, 1828, at the age of seventy. Alexander Humboldt had been his constant companion during the latter days of his life, and with him he conversed hours together, on all those subjects in which he had even felt so lively an interest.

"In Potsdam," says this gifted man, in a letter to Chancellor Müller, "I spent many hours alone with the Grand Duke on the sofa. He drank and slept alternately, drank again, rose to write to his consort, then again sank to sleep. He was cheerful, but very much exhausted. During the interval he pressed me with the most difficult questions on physics, astronomy, meteorology, and geology, on the transparency of a comet, the atmosphere of the moon, the influence of the spots on the sun, on the temperature, &c. In the midst of our conversation he would fall asleep, and was often uneasy. When he awoke, he would quickly and kindly entreat forgiveness for his want of attention. 'You see, Humboldt, it is all over with me.' All at once he would commence a desultory conversation on religion. He complained of the increase of fanaticism, the close connexion of this religious tendency with political absolutism, and the oppression of all the free movements of the intellect. 'Besides, they are false and treacherous,' he exclaimed, 'all they try for is to render themselves agreeable to princes, to receive stars and ribbons. They sneaked in with their poetical love of the middle ages.' Soon, however, his indignation appeased itself; he began to speak of all the consolation he had found in the Christian faith. 'That is a truly philanthropic doctrine,' he observed, 'but from the very commencement it has been deformed.'"

It was on occasion of this letter of Humboldt that Goethe pronounced his well-known eulogium on Carl Auguste:—

"The duke was a born nobleman; he had taste and interest for everything good and great. He was but eighteen when I came to Weimar; but even then the bud and blossom showed what the tree would become. He soon chose me for his friend, and evinced the sincerest sympathy in everything I did. My being nearly ten years older than himself was favourable to our intimacy. He would sit whole evenings beside me in deep conversation on nature, art, or anything else that was worth his attention. Often did we converse thus till nearly midnight, and it not unfrequently happened that we fell asleep beside each other on the sofa. Fifty years did we continue this intercourse. There are many princes capable of speaking admirably on subjects of interest; but they have not the real love of them in their hearts, it is only superficial. And it is no wonder, when we remember all the distractions and dissipations attending a court life to which a young prince is peculiarly exposed. He must notice everything, and know a bit of this and a bit of the other; but in this way nothing can take deep root in the mind, and it requires a really powerful nature not to turn to mere empty smoke in such an atmosphere. The Grand Duke was a man, in the full sense of the term. He was animated by the noblest benevolence, the purest philanthropy, and from his whole soul desired to do the best he could. His first thought was always his people's happiness; his own was the very last.

"His hand was ever open, and ready to aid noble individuals, and noble aims. There was much that was divine in his nature. He would fain have showered happiness on all mankind.

"He was by nature taciturn; but the action followed close upon the words. He loved simplicity, and was an enemy to all coddling and effeminacy. He never drove out except in a drosky, which really hardly kept together, wrapt in an old grey mantle and a military cap. He loved travelling, but not so much to amuse himself as everywhere to keep his eyes and ears open, and observe everything good and useful, that he might introduce it into his own country. Agriculture and manufactures owe him no common debt of gratitude. He did not seek to win the favour of his people by fine words; but the people loved him, because they knew his heart beat for them."

Carl Auguste was buried, by his own desire, in the same vault in which Schiller already reposed, and where Goethe himself was one day to sleep beside him.

Three more volumes on German poetry[7] attest, if any further attestation were required, the untiring industry of German compilers. The laborious undertaking of Wolfgang Menzel is a

[7] "Deutsche Dichtung, von der ältesten bis auf die neueste Zeit." Von Wolfgang Menzel. 1859. Nutt. 3 vols.

Biographie Universelle of German poets, as well as a dictionary of criticism on their varied literary merits, but is intended for reference, rather than deliberate perusal. The first book of the first volume records all that is known of the history of the lay of Sigfried, of the Nibelungen song, of the Heldenbuch, and generally of the early heroic lays. The second book recounts the various popular tales handed down traditionally among the people, and the origin of which is scarcely traceable; the third is devoted to a history of the religious poetry of the middle ages, and the fourth to the chivalresque poetry of the same era, as distinguished from the tales of giants and fairies current among the peasantry. The second volume, divided into four books, gives an account of the popular burgher lays as distinguished somewhat arbitrarily from those of the peasantry and nobility; also of the productions of the poetic licence which broke out with the religious revolution against the Papacy; of the early dawn or *renaissance* of modern German poetry, characterized as it was by the predominance of a vicious partiality for the French model, before Germany had acquired a classical poetry of its own.

The third volume, also divided into four books, traces the German muse through her modern phases, from the period of natural or unaffected poetry, when French influence had waned, and English and Swiss models were adopted; the era of Storm and Impulse (*Sturm und Drang*) which replaced this, and of which convulsive period Schiller's *Robbers* is the most respectable and least ridiculous example; and lastly, the time when romantic poetry had its "school" of admirers, to the latest and most recent productions of Teutonic inspiration. All this divided and subdivided, a little hypercritically it may be, with the usual minuteness and labour of German literary historians. As a work of reference it is very useful, alike for its facts and its criticisms.

Mr. Bohn could scarcely have added a better volume to his series than this translation of Schlegel's "Literary History,"[8] which now appears, for the first time entire, in an English garb. The range of information displayed is very remarkable, and as much for its soundness as its extent; for he had read, and generally with correct critical appreciation, the principal productions of the magnates of English, French, and Italian letters. He had been one of the earliest labourers in the field of Oriental research, and was well versed in the best literature of Greece and Rome. But it is as much for its suggestive spirit, as for its details or its criticism, that this volume of lectures is valuable. More than any other book with which we are acquainted, it is calculated to awaken a spirit of inquiry and reflection. A German who like Frederick Schlegel, amidst the general scepticism of his times, seems to have entertained religious opinions of peculiar earnestness; who in poetry had a decided preference for Klopstock among the poets of his own land, and for Tasso among Italians; who was prone to ascribe to systems

[8] "Schlegel's History of Literature." Translated into English. London: Bohn. 1859.

of what is called "Philosophy" a far more important influence on general opinions than they really possess, seemed scarcely fitted to handle so difficult and varied a theme in a robust, vigorous, and impartial spirit. But he combined great love of his subject with much learning, and an earnest desire to be just, and conveyed his thoughts in a peculiarly attractive style, better preserved, we may remark, in some portions of this translation than in others. On subjects purely literary, his judgment is usually correct and clear; it is only in the more speculative regions of imagination and of faith, that we find it sometimes difficult to follow him with confidence.

How justly he could estimate an English writer, is shown in his remarks on Hume's History.

"The great standards of historical composition which England produced during the eighteenth century are among the most important features of *belles lettres*. In this species of literature they have surpassed all other nations, if only in leading the way, and as historic models for foreign imitation. Unless I am mistaken, Hume ranks with the foremost in this department. But however great a safeguard scepticism may be in the process of historic investigation of facts, in which it can hardly be carried to excess; yet if the effects of doubting be to attack, to shake—nay, utterly to demolish—the great bulwark of moral and religious principle, it little becomes the historian of a powerful nation, who aims at exercising permanent and extensive influence. Narrow principles, views not perfectly correct, are in such a case much better and more productive than a deadening want of sentiment, feeling, and love. A tendency to oppose prevalent opinions, a leaning to paradox, are all that remain to invest history, when framed after this manner, with any degree of interest. Now, such a tendency to opposition is unmistakeable in Hume. In his time the republican spirit of the Whigs biassed English literature almost as completely as it does now, and with equally doubtful influence on the country's welfare. How salutary then soever it may have seemed to him to abandon the prevalent Anglican severity of party, and attaching himself to the opposition, to tinge a most important part of the national annals with evident predilection for the unfortunate house of Stuart, and sympathy with Tory principles, he can only be regarded as an eminent party historian, the first in his peculiar method and view, not the truly great author of a performance at once national in genius and in spirit."

The justice of these remarks can only be questioned by partial admirers (if any such there are) of a man who, less than any other eminent historian, wrote with an honest recognition of that admirable maxim of Cicero, "Prima historiæ lex est, ne quid falsi dicere audeat, ne quid veri non audeat."

A Review of the Literary History of Germany, from the earliest Period to the beginning of the Nineteenth Century. By Gustav Solling, of the Royal Military Academy, Woolwich, and the Charter House, London. (Williams and Norgate.)

In this small work we have one of the best digests of the Literary History of Germany that we remember to have seen. The learned author begins his account at about 100 B.C. He tells us that, according to the Grecian and Roman writers who have treated of this period, as also according to modern philological researches which fully bear out their assertions, the German language was that of an ancient and powerful race, divided into different tribes, which at a very remote age emigrated from the northern part of Asia, and spread over and settled in the northern and central parts of Europe. The word "deutsch," he says, derives from the Gothic "*thiuda*," "*diot*," "*diet*," which signifies "belonging to the people." The Germanians, or men of arms, were a mighty tribe living on the banks of the Rhine and the Danube, and "formidably known for their prowess and warlike virtues even to the Romans."

"In proportion as the Teutonic races spread over the provinces of Western Europe, the Romanic language, a mixture of Roman and German, was created and spoken in Spain, Italy, France, and the Britannic Empire, whilst the German retained its primitive character in those parts situated between the Elbe and Rhine, the Alps and Germanic Ocean."

Already in the primitive age began the distinction of dialects among the Teutonic tribes; the High-German ("oberdeutsch") being spoken in the south, and the Low-German ("niederdeutsch") in the north of Germany. The former, the distinguishing characteristic of which is what Mr. Solling calls the "full and broad pronunciation of the consonants," prevails still in the Tyrol, in Austria, Bavaria, Suabia, and Switzerland; the latter, which is more soft and more free from harshness, along the Lower Rhine, in Westphalia, Hanover, Lower Saxony, Holstein, Mecklenburg, Brandenburg, &c. There is also a medium between these principal dialects, forming the Middle-German, obtaining in Silesia, Lusatia, Saxony Proper, the Hartz mountains, and Hesse.

The most ancient literature of the Germans consisted chiefly, of course, in national songs, some festive, some warlike, some commemorative of fallen heroes. These were transmitted from generation to generation by tradition; the knowledge of written characters, called "Runen," having at that time spread but very imperfectly among the people. Of these there are still remains extant in the Icelandic *Edda*; for the Scandinavian races, Swedes, Danes, Norwegians, and Icelanders, are all of German blood, and were early acquainted with the principles of poetry.

Time thus rolled on, until the appearance of Ulfilas,—a bishop of the Moeso-Goths, now Wallachians,—who flourished from A.D 360—380. To those who are curious to see the state of the German language at that time, it will be interesting to compare the Moeso-Gothic version of the Lord's Prayer as given by Ulfilas, with the High-German version of Luther twelve hundred years later:

"Ulfilas.

"Atta unsar thu in himinam, weihnai namo thein. Quimai thiudinassus theins. wairthai wilja theins. swe in himina jah ana airthai. Hlaif unsarana thana sinteinan gif uns himmadago. Jah aflet uns thatei skulans sijaima. swaswe jah weis afletam thaim skulam unsaraim. Jah ni þriggais uns in fraistubnjai. ak lausei uns af þhamma ubilin. unte theina ist thiudangardi. jah maths. ja wultus in aiwins. Amen.

"Luther.

"Unser Vater in dem Himmel! Dein Name werde geheiliget. Dein Reich komme. Dein Wille geschehe auf Erden, wie im Himmel. Unser tägliches Brod gieb uns heute. Und vergieb uns unsere Schulden, wie wir unsern Schuldigern vergeben. Und führe uns nicht in Versuchung, sondern erlöse uns von dem Uebel. Denn Dein ist das Reich, und die Kraft, und die Herrlichkeit, in Ewigkeit. Amen."

This first age in the history of the literature of Germany our author closes at the year A.D. 708. But though we have but small records of it remaining to us, we must remember that it was during this very period, that the history and the language of our own country became identified with those of the Teutonic inhabitants of Northern Germany. Six several times were our shores successfully invaded, once by the Jutes, three times by the Saxons, and twice by the Angles, and nearly the whole of what is now called England became subject to their sway; and so entirely did the language of the invaders supersede that of the natives, that with the sole exception of Wales, there is no part of the kingdom south of the Tweed in which any vestige of it remains.

The second period of his history, which our author calls the Franconian period, he makes to extend from Charlemagne to the Suabian Emperors, that is, from A.D. 768—1137, during which time the German language, "owing to the lively interest bestowed upon it by the great Charles, improved considerably." The most important writings which have come down to us from this age are in the ancient High-German. This was the age of Alcuin and Eginhard the historian; and Mr. Solling gives us a brief sketch of the "Hildbrandslied,"—which, it appears, also exists in a somewhat altered form in the Scandinavian "Sagas,"—and a copy of the commencement of the "Wessobrunner Gebet," which, as well as the former, dates from the eighth century.

The next era will extend from the ascension of the throne by Henry III., the first of the Hohenstaufen, A.D. 1137, to the founding of the first German Universities, A.D. 1348. This age, the age of the Minnesängers, will appear to be the most prolific, as well as the most poetical and romantic. It was in itself a stirring period, the events of which were calculated in no small degree to develope and to sustain the mental life of the nation:

"Chivalry with its romantic aspirations, the glorious age of the Crusades with its lofty enthusiasm and noble deeds, the stirring example of the minstrels of the south of France, the 'Troubadours,' whose cultivated minds and more refined manners could not but exercise the most beneficial, the most refining influence on our more uncouth northern bards; the increasing prosperity of the nation, the result of the cultivation of the soil and the spread of commerce, all these combined influences developed the mental progress of an age, which we call with pride 'das Blüthenalter' of our early literature."

It was the age of Germany's great epic, "The Lay of the Nibelungen," in which are centred the various traditions of the heroic age, and which, according to Lachmann, must have appeared about A.D. 1210. It is curious how very little this wonderful poem is known in England. And yet, "all writers have agreed respecting its intrinsic literary merit; the author, who is unknown, has shown throughout the most cultivated and refined mind; and we look upon it with national pride, as being one of our greatest treasures of antiquity." Mr. Solling gives us a condensation of the events of the Nibelungenlied, as also of "Gudrun," which occupies so prominent a place in the history of ancient German literature, that competent judges have even called it "die Nebensonne," looking upon it, as it were, as a reflection of the great epic.

Next comes the fourth, the prosaic period, the age of the "Meistergesängers;" the age of Luther, whom our author calls "at once the reformer of religion and the regenerator of the language of his country, who, by the translation of the Bible into German, erected a literary monument which will last as long as the name of German literature shall be appreciated by his grateful countrymen." It was during this period that Hans Sachs, the far-famed cobbler of Nuremberg, flourished, and "Reinecke Fuchs," by Baumann, and "Das Narrenschiff," by Brandt, and other satirical writings made their appearance. The origin of the "Meistergesang" was not likely to be productive of very poetical results. It seems to have been as follows: — in several towns a corporate body of the citizens was formed, representing the various trades and handicrafts, who met after the day's work at their club for the purpose of practising the noble art of rhyming. On Sundays the singing-club met, in order to comment upon the merits of the different songs composed during the week; and prizes were awarded to the writers of those which were pronounced to be the best. Doubtless, as our author says, this was conducive enough to "the cause of morality and temperance;" "virtue, contentment, and concord are reflected" in the productions of this period; but neither the system nor the result appears to be very highly poetical. But co-existent with the fettered school of the Meistergesang, and diametrically opposed to it in its very nature, was the free, unadorned, vigorous expression of the true sentiments of the people in the Volkslied. Simplicity of style, and truthful delineation of character, are the peculiar features of the Volkslieder, and constitute their chief merit; and very many of the songs, first sung between two and three hundred years ago, are still as widely known, and as popular as ever, wherever the German language is spoken.

During the fifth period, which occupies the end of the sixteenth and the whole of the seventeenth centuries, poetry remained, comparatively speaking, dormant in Germany. The argumentative warfare upon church-matters was carried on chiefly in Latin, and the national language was therefore but little cultivated throughout this period. Martin Luther and Ulrich von Hutten, in their oratorical and didactic style, addressed, indeed, the masses in the vernacular, and so, as our author says, "kindled a sense (desire) for free discussions, conducive to civil and religious liberty."

The sixth period, "the time of Germany's intellectual degradation," is hardly marked out by our author with sufficient distinctness. The Thirty Years' War, from 1618 to 1648, had doubtless done much to spread a gloom over "Germany's literary horizon;" and in fact, from Mr. Solling's account, the language of Germany gradually ceased to a great extent to be purely German; it became fashionable, he says, "to mix foreign words with our own, and even to alienize our grammatical construction." "It was no longer *distingué* to speak one's own language." Bodmer, indeed, appeared at this period, and Godsched; but much as they both did for the literature of their country, the former was chiefly a student of the English classics, while Godsched,—or rather, if, as we believe, we use his more usual appellation, Gottsched,—seems to have been more especially an admirer of the French. It was not until the time of Klopstock, that the clouds began to break. Klopstock, the German Homer, as Menzel calls him, became the great reformer of the long-neglected language of his country. By his *Messiah*, and still more by his *Odes*, he exercised, beyond all gainsaying, a most beneficial influence upon the literature of the eighteenth century; or, to quote the words of Mr. Solling,

"He was as it were the literary sun, reappearing at last to develop by its benign rays those poetical germs, which during so long a winter had remained dormant in the German soil, and which were now to spring up and produce so splendid a harvest."

Then, too, came Gleim, and Kleist, and the still more renowned Lessing; and the Göttinger-club, which numbered among its members Voss, and Hölty, and Bürger, and Hahn, and the Counts Stolberg, and did so much for the regeneration of German poetry and German feeling, and paved the way for the seventh and last, and, as our author terms it, "the golden age" of the literature of his country,—the age of Herder, Goethe, and Schiller,—the age which, amongst the countless host of poets, historians, philosophers, and others, who have shed an undying lustre upon their land, and, "by shaking off the hereditary dust of centuries, have delivered the mind from the bondage in which it was kept, and enabled it to soar heavenwards, and roam at pleasure in the regions of the infinite,"—has produced him whom his native country and the world still mourn, "Alexander von Humboldt, the immortal writer of *Kosmos*."

But though Mr. Solling takes the opportunity of paying a graceful tribute to one, of whom, though so lately taken from us, his country had already reason to be proud, and whose genius was already shining in all its brightness, before this century had well begun to run its course, yet it does not enter into the scope of the work of which we are speaking to examine at all into the effect produced upon German language and literature by any writer of quite so late a date: and this essay, at least that part of it which refers more especially to the history of German literature, closes accordingly with a well-drawn parallel between those two great figures, which occupy so prominent a position in "the Walhalla of the German nation," Goethe and Schiller, "of whom it has been said that they were like two brothers occupying the same throne."

Of their writings Mr. Solling purposes to speak at greater length in a second volume, which will not, we trust, be long in making its appearance. Meanwhile, we can cordially recommend the present part of the work to the perusal of our readers. It is a small book, but it contains much information well put together, and of a highly interesting and instructive character.

GERMAN IDEALOGY.

BY CYRUS REDDING.

THE German imagination, fertile and active, revels amidst the shadowy and obscure. Its images are undefined, like the phantom in the Book of Job, the form of which could not be discerned. It works best in a misty atmosphere. Its wild theories, and extensive dealings with unsubstantialities, render it unsatisfactory to those who are not satisfied to take everything for granted. When, amid the dimness of metaphysics, people envelop themselves in thick darkness as they proceed, yet gropingly persevere, however self-satisfied they may be, the world will not sympathise with them. This activity of the mental constitution with a natural inactivity of the body, most probably owed its origin to instructed minds being, under a system of petty despotisms, prevented from reflecting upon topics in relation to which action is barred. Words which do not prompt to deeds obnoxious to themselves or their minions, cannot alarm arbitrary rulers. As a substitute for free action, therefore, mental speculation is permitted, the only thing which great or little despotisms cannot prevent. There is nothing more interesting to the German than meditation—meditation upon all kinds of speculative theories—and then to report progress. The result may be inconclusive, but the meditation is as attractive as when the abstract subject first came upon his fancy.

Admirable for perseverance, patient, learned, particularly in languages, the German stamp is still observable. In dramatic writing, for example, the characters are often strained and out of nature, whether designed for good or evil, to be admired or hated. The authors do not appear content with the mere delineation of men and things as they are, under the infinite variety of character the world displays. They aim to create novelties that are to outvie existing nature. The characters thus created must contribute to unfold some philosophical notion, or exhibit traits unseen before. If sentiment be the point, the doctrine of necessity, or fatalism, may be upheld. Thought is displayed rather than action, nature being secondary to the mental mystery on which all hinges, a mystery never clearly revealed. No matter if it run counter to sound philosophy, savour of materialism, tend to clothe existing things in strange habiliments, border upon injustice, or set experimental knowledge at defiance, the favourite idea must be wove so fine in texture, that the thread used cannot aid as a clue to bring out of the labyrinth those who venture into it.

We read German speculative works as we take up a puzzle; all ideas of what we are about becoming confused, we are lost in a chaos of imaginings when we suppose ourselves near the dénoûment. The Germans think deeply, but they do no more. Their thoughts are upon their dreams, shapeless clouds above them, often vapoury enough of hue, frequently rich in colour, but evanescent, passing tracklessly away, and leaving behind no worthy impress. Theorising, busy, speculative, their bearing is still marked with inertness and ponderosity. Of their material

they make good use, and excel in clearing away impediments in metaphysical difficulties. They launch their dogmas, undismayed by their novelty, upon the great ocean of opinion, for they have uniformly a persuasion that proof metaphysical must be victorious against the world's experience—a happy confidence which ever tempts the German to perseverance.

The Teutonic character is serious and heavy, and marks its literature. In their sedate, staid habit the German and Turk bear a considerable resemblance to each other. But the last may be roused to extraordinary activity, to throw the djereed or make a display of ceremony, while at at other times he sits on the shore of the blue Bosphorus, in the blissful negation of his sensual dreams. The German, with his everlasting pipe, in place of dreaming of Paradise and the Houri, stimulated with opium, sits amid the smoke of tobacco and resolves grave doubts, and analyses moonshine. Now defending his ideal subtleties among his friends, or silently, in ceaseless activity of mind, diving deeper into the "sea without shore" of his own imaginings, striving to embody them into a visible image, and only encouraged to fresh trials by non-success. Latitudinarian in thought, bold in speculation, indomitable in perseverance, but ever inconclusive. Hence, German ideas in literature, while much spoken about, have made comparatively little impression in other countries. Hence, too, out of Germany come mesmerism and all the other "isms" that pass for nine-day wonders.

That order of social existence can be but secondary, where every individual following his own will refuses to avail himself of the experience of others. Thus he who cultivates his own ideas, unguided by preceding opinion or external fact, can only follow a flickering light serving to make the darkness visible. This obscurity seems to stimulate the pursuit of the German. That state which brings hopelessness to others, animates his spirit to persevere after the discovery, to himself, of what is never discoverable to others.

The late efforts to obtain free institutions in Germany were undertaken in perfect harmony with the character of the people. Constitutions were sketched and promulgated by idealists, and changes were proposed before they could possibly have been worked out, or the means created to alter effectually the old state of things. In the midst of the short-lived struggle between the new and the old, abstract truths were hunted out for adoption in place of practical tendencies towards them. In lieu of securing the power first, they begged the question of its possession, and acted as if reverse institutions to those existing had only to be invoked like Eastern genii to appear in fulness of strength. In the mean while their opponents, who kept to existing realities, triumphed. Things lapsed into their former state. The German returned to his pipe and reveries again, and the pristine power ruled as before. If "the bare imagination of a feast" never satiated appetite, as little did ideal constitutions ever confer popular liberty. Human existence, though of short duration, is not a thing of air, and requires that its appliances should partake of its own substantiality. As in literature and art, so in political affairs, the Germans must shorten their reveries, learn to act, and place their shoulders actively to the wheel. Their philosophical notions and the nature of their governments have long been vehemently opposed to each other. Thought being free, they made much of it; action being curbed, prostrate obedience to the ruling power became a part of the social system and a matter of easiness, while the mode of thinking and reasoning belied that obedience. Thus was engendered a species of hypocrisy, political, not religious, it is true, but sufficiently inconsistent to uproot society in any other country. "Our rulers may take the 'real,' give us the realm of the ideal," was the essence of Germanism before the last feeble outbreak, and things seem already lapsed again into their old state. They no longer talk of emancipation from their petty tyrannies. The will is shackled, freedom of action is banned, but metaphysics are free, and philosophy may investigate, and out-of-the-way novelties may be broached and defended, and poetry may dream and tell its dreams, and Germans may continue to read, to meditate, and to express as much as they can, which is only half of what they have in their heads. On the ruling power or its agents literature and literary men produce no effect, being secluded more than they are elsewhere. They may have some influence in uniting public feeling where the union rarely goes beyond the common sentiment. Those who fulfil the duties of the public administrations are governed by the rules of diplomacy, and do not trouble themselves about principles. Expediency is their moral law : they steer by policy, and leave justice to her blindness. Germanic in slowness of action and in pertinacity, they do not travel out of the beaten track, it being their rulers' notion, as it is in many other countries, that what has been and is should alone have permanency. Their stolidity cannot tolerate men of letters who advance an opponent principle, and men of letters are in most instances too complacent to do so where they live near their petty courts, which are so happily constituted for stifling freedom. They will in private society discourse freely, for the authorities know that in Germany "to talk " is, as to mischief in general, a neuter verb.

But this is travelling somewhat out of the record. The literary men of Germany are less universal than any others. It was not until a recent period that even in insulated examples their literati could be said to intermingle. Their writings were the communicants of their knowledge of each other, and the similarity in the mode of their speculations or views was the bond of sympathy. In some of the states they were wholly secluded, and spoke only through their works; in very rare cases, as in Saxony and Weimar, the courts and social state were for a time more favourable to literature. Those courts, from being more refined, and from the reigning sovereigns possessing some sense of the value of the arts to the people, as well as knowing the external attention it drew upon themselves and their territories, found their patronage good policy.

A line of demarcation must be drawn between the works of the Germans that are attached to imagination and those which are the product of learning or connected with science. The latter rank deservedly high, the character of the people being adapted to plodding, persevering, patient labour. The universities possess some of the first men of the day as professors. They follow specific objects, and are peculiarly happy in conveying knowledge. There is reason to doubt whether the education bestowed in their universities is as useful as it is well taught—whether it is practical enough. There is a sufficient enthusiasm for any acquirement, but its application is the point of moment. Theory is uppermost, but youth cannot pass through life weaving cobwebs. It must be versed in the application of its knowledge. To educate the young as if all were to be philosophers, or metaphysicians, or critics, is a gross error with which the German system is too deeply marked. In all things the German teachers have the virtue of granting claims to notice and to distinction on the ground of merit alone. This is in opposition to the reigning principle in most other European states, where the merit rewarded is an assumption graduated from social position, favour, intrigue, or interest. This honest principle in the Germans shows a tendency wherever it exists towards what is right.

There are many accusations made in this country that German literature has not had justice done it. There is always a party ready to complain in similar cases in default of something more easy to do. It is impossible English literature can gain by any further insight into the German of a speculative character. For elaborate works of science and those which relate to language, wherever laborious attention is directed to investigate fact, there is no superior school, none more informing and useful to the inquirer. The matter is different in relation to German metaphysicians and idealists. These are a peculiar race, who puzzle at best rather than inform. Their habits of thinking are dissimilar from those of other nations, their means being their end, if not avowedly at least practically. It is otherwise in works of a character merely "learned," as civilised nations understand the term. None have gone deeper, or done better service to the study of the ancient languages than the Germans, nor have any given the results of investigation more disinterestedly, or with a more earnest regard to the truth. The perseverance of the German character tells here. Demonstration has with them no regard to consequences, because its truth is above them. In England, unpalatable truths are suppressed by writers because they may offend the ignorant or bigoted, whose fatuity is more dreaded than the truth is loved. It was long before the facts of geology were admitted to prevail here over prejudices that vanished before careful inquiry by those who were only moved by a regard for what was veracious. Obliquitous minds still remain proof against the evidence of the senses. The demonstrations of arithmetic will not convince some understandings. There are few or no such imperfect minds among the educated of Germany, but rather a tendency to err in the opposite direction. In learned researches some of the qualities that in philosophy and metaphysics lead into obscurity and bewilderment, become advantageous dealing with facts. The German philologists have not been estimated as highly as they merit: strong must be the love of the science where the recompense in praise is so small, the world at large having no comprehension of it, so that, like virtue, it must be loved for its own sake, that science which must be followed in solitude and silence, day by day, year by year, with a glimmering light, just exhibiting the shallow track of the footsteps of dead nations through successive ages, by scanty roots, scattered derivations, simulars of idiom and affinities of dialect, to trace out a primitive language through arid and wearisome paths, here the German is pre-eminent. He marshals his facts, reverses the mode of the idealists by using them as guides, reasoning from in place of towards them, and, collecting the harvest of his toils, gives it out for the universal benefit, like a generous cosmopolitan.

The imaginative writers of Germany fix nothing, each running wild his own way, and each striving to set up a fresh novelty. No law of taste, no rule, no sense of critical propriety governs a literature that began with criticism, in a mode different from all other countries, where there is generally a beginning, a middle, and an end. Obscurity often terminates the labour lucidly begun, from following out the idea, until, as hunters would say, "the scent is lost." To be out of the common natural course is deemed an advantage—what can be expected in such a case save inconclusiveness? But Germans are content to peruse mysteries, and to leave them so, as well satisfied as if they were solved, from their argument being conducted "too curiously." Yet cannot the inquiry be resisted as to what that pursuit avails which, not bringing refinement or utility, leaves the amusement or instruction of all but those who are disciples of the doctrine wholly unsatisfied. The German lives in a balloon, and expatiates on what his fancy whispers may be in the air higher up above him. It may be anything fancy chooses, and so much the more in his way. He cannot dwell on what is earthy and tangible, and plain beneath him. He loves wild wanderings, " des égarements," and while wishing to become a pioneer of the human mind, he endeavours to become so by following new roads, moving under systems without a regulating law, and by making excursions into infinity itself, from whence he returns no wiser than he went. He doubts all things, peruses all things, and still leaves all in obscurity. His hope is a waking sleep, abounding in semi-formed visions, which produce a greater effect upon his mind than nature itself in action. He only differs from Sancho Panza, when in his sleep he cried out, "I dream," in that honest Sancho slept, while the German is wide awake in the midst of his demons, his phantoms, his omens, his oracles of destiny, his doctrine of fatalism—in short, his preference of all but the natural course of things, the result of cause and effect. Nature dresses too simply to be his mistress. He subsists upon ideas without reference to their application, and hence they are either *couleur de rose* or colossal, whether of earth or super-mundane.

The two periods of German literature, if the crude productions before the middle of the last century may be so denominated, are not alike. The German ideal school is the later, and wholly of modern origin. The old poem of the thirteenth or fourteenth century, called the " Niebelungen," adheres to nature, to character, in the natural mode of description, to kindness and simplicity, in the same way as the earlier poems of most countries have sung of " peace, war, and faithful love." It remained for later times to displace action with phantasm, and, with the utmost latitude of thought, to reconcile servile political obedience; to unchain the eagle, but to prevent its soaring by enveloping the noble bird in the twilight that delights the owl, though his plumes are expanded, and his piercing eyes ever looking for an unshackled flight.

The literature of France, which preceded the German in that country among well-educated persons, was always sufficiently clear. If Frederick the Great of Prussia disdained to use his native tongue in his writings, upon its rejection the Germans might have borrowed a hint or two from it with advantage; above all, its abhorrence of the no meaning which " puzzles more than sense." On changing the adoption of a foreign tongue for their own, though they had produced no writer worthy of their nation at that time except Wieland, they would have done well not to run from one extreme to the other. In excluding foreign literature, they seemed not to have been content with its banishment, they would fain obliterate its traces, and in so doing endeavoured to stamp their originality by rejecting for their own that which was common to every other. Yet the early German writers, towards the middle and close of the last century, were not so much distinguished by their talents as their capacity of profound thought, and their aptitude for transferring their ideas; in fact, for a sort of universality in treating different subjects, and for their ingenious combinations.

They who are not affected with that species of German mania which has been observable at times in this country, feel a dissatisfaction in reading some of their best authors. They rise from them as from a meal which has not satisfied the appetite. They are too obscure, or unsubstantial, or lax in moral feeling. We ask ourselves to what does all this lead, when we read " Faust," for example, so lauded by Germans and the devotees to German literature in this country, who seem to imbibe the same taste for inconclusiveness which the Germans themselves display. We obtain only something metaphysical, the attempted elucidation of some dark ingenious theory at the end, unprofitable and often dissonant with our own religious sensations. A curiosity, not and never to be satisfied, to prompt all, the gratification of which is to be sought for in the internal man, in the constitution of mind, of which nothing is known, and much is in consequence begged. A mystery to man is set up, the elucidation of which, seen by others to be impossible, only whets the German appetite to attempt. His zeal redoubles, only to be doubly perplexed, and the perplexity prolongs his efforts indefinitely. Just so to refine without end, to follow idle abstractions, to construct theories in art in order to set going something inexplicable about the balance of love and beauty, of the ideal and real, are a long and earnest pursuit. In following out the " æsthetic," their own term, they will plunge into a troubled sea of metaphysics, wading, swimming, diving into profundity, till they can never more find dry land with their feet. They abandon circumstance and accident as of no account; all must be spiritual, all, like the universe, must be formed out of nothing, all must be explained from within. The mind is the source and outlet of all. Spirit must vindicate itself over what is material. Not the good Bishop Berkeley himself was more sensible of the possibility of the impossible. All is innate and from the mind. The existing is secondary. The union of both the how and wherefore is another favourite problem, that, like the squirrel's cage, still goes round, and the motive power remains no further advanced. The attempt to rule an unmastered abstraction is truly German, and of the modern school. Frederick Schlegel had an inkling this way. Schiller, with his delightful genius, left poetry to fish in the same turbid pool sometimes, but the hook was never burdened with the expected inhabitant of the waters. Nothing is realised, but the hope lingers still, and lures to the disappointment that only "spurs the sides of the intent" anew.

But the Germans began their later literature with criticisms, while in England it is observed that bad and incompetent authors become reviewers. It is possible that the same cause operates in both cases—incipient knowledge in the one case, and conscious deficiency of ability in the other. The practice, however, has been continued in Germany, where more critics publish than original writers, just as in Paris there are said to be more doctors than patients. Perhaps there is more assumptive vanity in being a German critic, possessing, too, a power in the public view by sitting in judgment upon others, rather than in being judged. The critic may lay down the principles he could not carry out, and get an illegitimate credit for being able to do it. After all, the German plan is but an inversion of the custom observed elsewhere. Literature followed in the wake of criticism, and its rules were laid down too late to restrain discursive fancies. Every one set up his own literary standard according to his individual impressions. Genius ran wild, and that which was unsubstantial or erratic took an embodied form in the eyes of enthusiasts, and led to a style of literature unreined and wild in all but German eyes. The impression of the moment ruled. Authors ran into extravagances accordingly, the object being to astonish, not to convince, to amuse, not instruct, except in doctrines that are themselves unfixed, keeping the human mind in doubt, and making man dissatisfied with his station, while substituting nothing, however problematical, in its place. Reason becomes subservient to imagination, under the exclusive reign of which Germans may be as fully satisfied as with demonstration, though the rest of the great family of mankind will not. The latter must have some end or aim. The Germans are content with the retracting figures of the phantasmagoria if they can follow them to the remotest point where form ceases, and even then keep up the pursuit. It is nothing that they are led into difficulty and darkness amid the strange and marvellous. They must astonish under any category of style, manner, or creed that will answer the purpose. They will entangle clear truths in metaphysical quags rather than adopt them in their simplicity. This will account for the many extraordinary scenes introduced into their works which sensation repels, and shows why nature is not their sole guide. All that comes into the sensorium accustomed to combine as well as invent extravagances, even beyond the range of the probable and possible, may be found in German writers. All is legitimate that is new, profound, or obscure. This may be discovered in works translated into the vernacular tongue by those who are attached in a certain degree to the same system here, but who cannot render their own admiration for the incomprehensible as current as they desire, though they do not spare praise for the purpose. The rule of morality is no check upon a German, nor contrariety to nature a bar to the introduction of a dramatic scene so constituted. In Mülner we find a father challenging a son to fight a duel to avenge the murder of another of his children, under the unfounded pretence of its being illustrative of Spanish character, but really because it was new on the stage, and out of the beaten road. Nor was the incident badly received by the public, which in England or France would have been hissed

off. Improbable situations, or such as are scarcely within the verge of possibility, are favourite resorts of German writers. Abstract notions and recondite and abstruse doctrines are placed in the mouths of dramatic characters, or in those which figure in romances, the fruits of the author's reveries, and not the words which a Shakspeare would have made them use. It is true that in such cases the characters are often rather the depositaries and vehicles of the author's ideas than actors in the great social family of man, as he is. The fidelity and morality of the sentiments are in the same way frequently secondary matters, though primary elsewhere when good taste governs. The doctrine laid down by Lessing they did not adhere to. They sought a freer system, but there is a great difference between freedom and licentiousness.

German literature is of the romantic school. By the term "romantic," distinguished from the "classic," they do not, as in England is commonly done, comprehend that marked as ancient and modern literature, or that which receives or rejects the rules of the old critics, as in the example of the drama of Shakspeare, who paid no regard to the rules of Aristotle. They apply the term classical to ancient literature, and that of romantic to chivalry, with its traditions, of which last they make their own literature the heir. Some have contended for the terms "Pagan" and "Christian" in place of "classic" and "romantic." The discussions on this subject have far outdone those that arose from Perrault's parallel between the "Ancients and Moderns." The mode of treating similar subjects in ancient and modern times—in poetry, for example—would not in many cases out of Germany be particularly marked. In the Greek mythology, for example, there are verses that might have been the productions of either era in England, France, or the south of Europe, because they belong to subjects common to all nations and ages; in other words, to our common nature, which is ever the same.

The poetry of Germany is a fertile field of research, and is in many points original in style. It is varied, rich, full of agreeable images, but it is often fanciful and discursive; nor is it at times free from metaphysics and philosophy, from mental vagary and dissatisfied reason. But this is too copious a subject to enter upon here.

In their novels and romances the same tendencies may be remarked as have been before mentioned; peculiarities, mannerisms, or what, considered nationally and applied to their literature in other departments, may be called Germanisms. The variety under these heads is very great. Love tales, sorcery, chivalry, the natural and supernatural, the feelings of dissatisfaction with life, the sentimental, and much not measured by moral considerations, are to be found in this category. The "Wilhelm Meister" of Goethe is well known in this country, and is one of a class of works not directed to the noblest purposes. The beauty of the descriptions, the verisimilitude of the painting, the delineation of feelings under the most improbable circumstances, the characters worked out of an immoral origin, natural feelings forcibly described in place of conventional habits, or the latter violated in an absurd manner; a heroine born, bred, reared in a fashion rather emulative of peculiarity than any other object, and acting in an accordant manner, under the guidance of a vigorous fancy uncontrolled by any moral check, and out of all a character worked discordantly with the course of existent being, now simple and childlike, now profound and imaginative ; in short, a mysterious medley of character, wiser than one of her age would be, and ignorant of her own history.

Ardent love and an unhappy life, its pains and hopes, and most evanescent impressions, are detailed with wonderful ability ; but all is secondary to the mind which created them, not for the sake of the magical picture thus drawn, but to exhibit certain traits, and particular sentiments not always consonant with nature, which were more easily effected in this mode than in any other. The observation of some writers on the workings of the human heart has been profound, and their power of vivid description has been lavishly used to show that all human impulses are in the end indifferent. In the German school, genius wastes its treasures to render mankind a disservice, to make it hopeless of progress, and to inculcate indifference about the value of life, which, abounding in moral maladies, are to be cured by ourselves, if not, we become their victims. There are virtues and passions, one of which counteracts another, according to some; others deny this, and the public is to judge between them. If the scepticism thus developed were well founded, and proof were brought to bear in its favour, it would be better, and more humane, to soften than exacerbate the consciousness of the calamity. We are alluding here to no religion beyond that from the light of nature. Materialism is a cold, cheerless doctrine, to which, notwithstanding, it would be our duty to give way, were it a substantial truth. But all that reason and experience exhibit in examining the question is decidedly opposed to it. The light of nature, and the consciousness of being and action, cannot be overturned by mere idealogy. If religion were, indeed, a chimera, and that poetry of our existence were a nonentity; if reason might be passed by, and the concentrated evidence of our senses, and the plainest associations they generate in unison with incontrovertible truth, according to the clearest human judgment and the *consensus gentium*,— if these may go for nothing upon the question, then it would be better to resign nature's instincts at once, to abandon the consolatory character of those principles which enable us to meet the calamities of life with fortitude, not to avoid the abuse of prosperity should it be our good lot to share it, to look with chill indifference upon the chapter of human existence, and to make life miserable with hopelessness. We are now enabled to cultivate a few flowers in the path of existence, not to trample them underfoot, nor cancel the enjoyments proffered ; and they are by no means few, if we understand how to avail ourselves of them aright, in place of endeavouring to establish for a fact a demoralising uncertainty. Such an aim is a misuse of talent, and an error unworthy of genius.